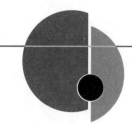

SIXTH EDITION

# Psychological Testing

## History, Principles, and Applications

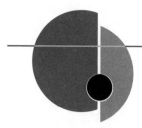

**SIXTH EDITION**

# Psychological Testing

## History, Principles, and Applications

**Robert J. Gregory**

*Wheaton College, Wheaton, Illinois*

**Allyn & Bacon**

Boston   Columbus   Indianapolis   New York   San Francisco   Upper Saddle River   Amsterdam
Cape Town   Dubai   London   Madrid   Milan   Munich   Paris   Montreal   Toronto   Delhi
Mexico City   Sao Paulo   Sydney   Hong Kong   Seoul   Singapore   Taipei   Tokyo

**Editor-in-Chief:** Jessica Mosher
**Executive Editor:** Susan Hartman
**Associate Editor:** Kara Kikel
**Marketing Manager:** Nicole Kunzmann
**Marketing Assistant:** Amanda Olweck
**Production Manager:** Meghan DeMaio
**Editorial Production and Composition Service:** Jogender Taneja/Aptara®, Inc.
**Cover Designer:** Bruce Kenselaar
**Creative Director:** Jayne Conte
**Printer/Binder:** Edwards Brothers
**Cover Printer:** Lehigh-Phoenix Color

Library of Congress Cataloging-in-Publication Data

Gregory, Robert J.
  Psychological testing: history, principles, and applications / Robert J. Gregory. — 6th ed.
    p. cm.
  ISBN-13: 978-0-205-78214-7
  ISBN-10: 0-205-78214-0
  1. Psychological tests.   2. Psychological tests—History.   I. Title.
  BF176.G74 2011
  150.28'7—dc22

                                                    2010021204

10 9 8 7 6 5 4 3 2 1   EB   14 13 12 11 10

**Allyn & Bacon**
is an imprint of

www.pearsonhighered.com

ISBN-13: 978-0-205-78214-7
ISBN-10:   0-205-78214-0

# Brief Contents

# Contents

## 3    Norms and Reliability    67

**4** Validity and Test Development 109

 **5** Theories and Individual Tests of Intelligence and Achievement 151

## Group Tests and Controversies in Ability Testing    214

## Testing Special Populations    273

# 8 Origins of Personality Testing    314

# 9 Assessment of Normality and Human Strengths    373

# 10 Neuropsychological Assessment and Screening    414

# 11 Industrial, Occupational, and Forensic Assessment    467

## 12 Legal Issues and the Future of Testing    530

# Preface

Psychological testing began as a timid enterprise in the scholarly laboratories of nineteenth-century European psychologists. From this inauspicious birth, the practice of testing proliferated throughout the industrialized world at an ever accelerating pace. As the reader will discover within the pages of this book, psychological testing now impacts virtually every corner of modern life, from education to vocation to remediation.

## ● PURPOSE OF THE BOOK

The sixth edition of this book is based on the same assumptions as earlier versions. Its ambitious purpose is to provide the reader with knowledge about the characteristics, objectives, and wide-ranging effects of the consequential enterprise, psychological testing. In pursuit of this goal, I have incorporated certain well-worn traditions but proceeded into some new directions as well. For example, in the category of customary traditions, the book embraces the usual topics of norms, standardization, reliability, validity, and test construction. Furthermore, in the standard manner, I have assembled and critiqued a diverse compendium of tests and measures in such traditional areas as intellectual, achievement, industrial-organizational, vocational, and personality testing.

### Special Features

In addition to the traditional topics previously listed, I have emphasized certain issues, themes, and concepts that are, in my opinion, essential for an in-depth understanding of psychological testing. For example, the second chapter of the book examines the history of psychological testing. The placement of this chapter underscores my view that the history of psychological testing is of substantial relevance to present-day practices. Put simply, a mature comprehension of modern testing can be obtained only by delving into its heritage. Of course, students of psychology typically shun historical matters because these topics are often presented in a dull, dry, and pedantic manner, devoid of relevance to the present. However, I hope the skeptical reader will approach my history chapter with an open mind—I have worked hard to make it interesting and relevant.

Psychological testing represents a contract between two persons. One person—the examiner—usually occupies a position of power over the other person—the examinee. For this reason, the examiner needs to approach testing with utmost sensitivity to the needs and rights of the examinee. To emphasize this crucial point, I have devoted the first topic to the subtleties of the testing process, including such issues as establishing rapport and watching for untoward environmental influences upon test results. The second topic in the book also emphasizes the contractual nature of assessment by reviewing professional issues and ethical standards in testing.

Another topic emphasized in this book is neuropsychological assessment, a burgeoning subfield of clinical psychology that is now a well-established specialty in its own right. Neuropsychological assessment is definitely a growth area and now constitutes one of the major contemporary applications of psychological testing. I have devoted an entire chapter to this important subject. So that the reader can better appreciate the scope and purpose of neuropsychological assessment, I begin the chapter with a succinct review of neurological principles before discussing specific instruments.

Tangentially, this review introduces important concepts in neuropsychological assessment such as the relationship between localized brain dysfunction and specific behavioral symptoms. Nonetheless, readers who need to skip the section on neurological underpinnings of behavior may do so with minimal loss—the section on neuropsychological tests and procedures is comprehensible in its own right.

New to this edition is a chapter on assessment of normality and human strengths. This includes a lengthy topic on positive psychological assessment, such as the testing of creativity, emotional intelligence, optimism, gratitude, and humor. I hope this concentration on life-affirming concepts will provide some balance to the field of assessment which, for too long, has emphasized pathology.

This is more than a book about tests and their reliabilities and validities. I also explore numerous value-laden issues bearing on the wisdom of testing. Psychological tests are controversial precisely because the consequences of testing can be harmful, certainly to individuals and perhaps to the entire social fabric as well. I have not ducked the controversies surrounding the use of psychological tests. Separate topics explore genetic and environmental contributions to intelligence, origins of race differences in IQ, test bias and extravalidity concerns, cheating on group achievement tests, courtroom testimony, and ethical issues in psychological testing.

### Note on Case Exhibits

This edition continues the use of case histories and brief vignettes that feature testing concepts and illustrate the occasionally abusive application of psychological tests. These examples are "boxed" and referred to as Case Exhibits. Most are based on my personal experience rather than scholarly undertakings. All of these case histories are real. The episodes in question really happened—I know because I have direct knowledge of the veracity of each anecdote. These points bear emphasis because the reader will likely find some of the vignettes to be utterly fantastical and almost beyond belief.

Of course, to guarantee the privacy of persons and institutions, I have altered certain unessential details while maintaining the basic thrust of the original events.

### ● CHANGES FROM THE FIFTH EDITION

In this revision, my goals were threefold. First, I wanted to add the latest findings about established tests. For this purpose, I have made use of about 300 new scholarly references, and "retired" an almost equal number of outdated citations. Second, I wanted to incorporate worthwhile topics overlooked in previous editions. A prominent example in this category is the assessment of creativity, which receives extended coverage in the book. And, third, I sought to include coverage of innovations and advances in testing. One example of this is inclusion of the Neuropsychological Assessment Battery, a new and promising test battery unparalleled in its thoroughness. I was also aware that several tests have been revised since the last edition went to press, including the WAIS-IV, DAS-II, and MBTI, to name just a few. For these instruments, I have described the newest editions and included relevant research.

More specifically, the improvement and enhancements in the current edition include the following:

1. Chapter 2 on the History of Psychological Testing includes two additions: a brief section on the origins of rating scales and a short summary of the contributions of Leta Hollingworth to IQ testing in giftedness.
2. Topic 4A, Basic Concepts of Validity, now concludes with brief reference to the overlooked concept of test utility: Does use of tests yield better patient outcomes or more efficient delivery of services?
3. Updates on the WAIS-IV are included in Topic 5B: Individual Tests of Intelligence and Achievement.
4. The section on Learning Disabilities in Topic 5B: Individual Tests of Intelligence and

Achievement includes new material on RTI (Response to Intervention), which is rapidly becoming the preferred conceptual approach.

5. The coverage of the Cognitive Abilities Test (CogAT) in Topic 6A: Group Tests of Ability and Related Concepts has been increased, including a presentation of sample questions.

6. In Topic 6B: Test Bias and Other Controversies, new examples of the impact on IQ of test bias, environmental deprivation, race differences, age differences, and generational shifts, have been added.

7. The coverage of the Bayley-III has been significantly expanded in Topic 7A: Infant and Preschool Assessment.

8. Updates on the DAS-II and the DIAL-III are included in Topic 7A: Infant and Preschool Assessment.

9. The coverage of mental retardation (in Topic 7B: Testing Persons with Disabilities) has been revamped to reflect the important shift in terminology to the preferred concept of *intellectual disability*.

10. In Topic 8A, Theories of Personality and Projective Techniques, my prior skepticism about the Rorschach has been softened in light of the blue ribbon panel report from the Society for Personality Assessment (which concluded that the inkblot test has validity on a par with other accepted tests like the MMPI-2).

11. Substantial new material on the MBTI and CPI, two instruments widely used in "normal" assessment, has been added to Topic 9A: Assessment within the Normal Spectrum.

12. Topic 9B: Positive Psychological Assessment is entirely new and includes extended coverage on the assessment of creativity (e.g., Torrance Tests of Creative Thinking), emotional intelligence (e.g., the Mayer-Salovey-Caruso Emotional Intelligence Test), optimism, gratitude, and sense of humor.

13. Topic 10B: Neuropsychological Tests, Batteries, and Screening Tools, includes updating of references on most instruments and addition of the Neuropsychological Assessment Battery, a promising approach that is both comprehensive and modular.

14. A new section on personality tests such as the NEO-PI-R as a useful basis for employee selection has been added to Topic 11A: Industrial and Organizational Assessment.

15. In Topic 11B: Forensic Applications of Assessment, the section on malingering has been expanded to include the Test of Memory Malingering (TOMM) and the use of the MMPI-2 validity scales in the detection of malingering.

16. A brief section on cognitive disability and the death penalty has been added to Topic 12A: Psychological Testing and the Law.

17. In addition to updating several topics and tests, Topic 12B: Computerized Assessment and the Future of Testing, now includes a closing section on "Testing and the Next Big Questions in Psychology."

Of course, minor but essential changes have been made throughout the entire book to capture the latest developments in testing. For example, I have searched the literature to include the most recent studies bearing on the validity of well-established instruments.

## ● OUTLINE OF THE BOOK

### Topical Organization

To accommodate the widest possible audience, I have incorporated an outline that partitions the gargantuan field of psychological testing—its history, principles, and applications—into 24 small, manageable, modular topics. I worked hard to organize the 24 topics into natural pairings. Thus, the reader will notice that the book is also organized as an ordered series of 12 chapters of 2 topics each. The chapter format helps identify pairs of topics that are more or less contiguous and also reduces the need for redundant preambles to each topic.

The most fundamental and indivisible unit of the book is the topic. Each topic stands on its own. In each topic, the reader encounters a manageable number of concepts and reviews a modest number of tests. To the student, the advantage of topical organization is that the individual topics are small enough to read at a single sitting. To the instructor, the advantage of topical organization is that subjects deemed of lesser importance can be easily excised from the reading list. Naturally, I would prefer that every student read every topic, but I am a realist too. Often, a foreshortened textbook is necessary for practical reasons such as the length of the school term. In those instances, the instructor will find it easy to fashion a subset of topics to meet the curricular needs of almost any course in psychological testing.

The 12 chapters break down into five broad areas, as follows:

**Nature, History, and Consequences of Testing**

Chapter 1: Applications and Consequences of Psychological Testing

Topic 1A: The Nature and Uses of Psychological Testing

Topic 1B: Ethical and Social Implications of Testing

Chapter 2: The History of Psychological Testing

Topic 2A: The Origins of Psychological Testing

Topic 2B: Early Testing in the United States

**Foundations of Testing**

Chapter 3: Norms and Reliability

Topic 3A: Norms and Test Standardization

Topic 3B: Concepts of Reliability

Chapter 4: Validity and Test Development

Topic 4A: Basic Concepts of Validity

Topic 4B: Test Construction

**Ability Testing and Controversies**

Chapter 5: Theories and Individual Tests of Intelligence and Achievement

Topic 5A: Theories of Intelligence and Factor Analysis

Topic 5B: Individual Tests of Intelligence and Achievement

Chapter 6: Group Tests and Controversies in Ability Testing

Topic 6A: Group Tests of Ability and Related Concepts

Topic 6B: Test Bias and Other Controversies

Chapter 7: Testing Special Populations

Topic 7A: Infant and Preschool Assessment

Topic 7B: Testing Persons with Disabilities

**Assessment of Personality and Related Constructs**

Chapter 8: Origins of Personality Testing

Topic 8A: Theories of Personality and Projective Techniques

Topic 8B: Self-Report and Behavioral Assessment of Psychopathology

Chapter 9: Assessment of Normality and Human Strengths

Topic 9A: Assessment within the Normal Spectrum

Topic 9B: Positive Psychological Assessment

**Specialized Applications, Legal Issues, and the Future of Testing**

Chapter 10: Neuropsychological Assessment and Screening

Topic 10A: A Primer of Neurobiological Concepts

Topic 10B: Neuropsychological Tests, Batteries, and Screening Tools

Chapter 11: Industrial, Occupational, and Forensic Assessment

Topic 11A: Industrial and Organizational Assessment

Topic 11B: Forensic Applications of Assessment

Chapter 12: Legal Issues and the Future of Testing

Topic 12A: Psychological Testing and the Law

Topic 12B: Computerized Assessment and the Future of Testing

The book also features an extensive glossary, appendices for locating tests and publishers, and a table for converting percentile ranks to standard and standardized-score equivalents. In addition, an important feature is Appendix A, Major Landmarks in the History of Psychological Testing. To meet personal needs, readers and course instructors will pick and choose from these topics as they please.

## Supplements

Pearson Education is pleased to offer the following supplements to qualified adopters.

**Instructor's Manual and Test Bank (0205718388)** The instructor's manual is a wonderful tool for classroom preparation and management. Corresponding to the topics from the text, each of the manual's 24 topics contains classroom discussion questions, extramural assignments, classroom demonstrations, and essay questions. In addition, the test bank portion provides instructors with more than 1,000 readymade multiple choice questions.

**PowerPoint Presentation (0205003567)** Prepared by Errol Yudko (University of Hawaii at Hilo), the PowerPoint Presentation is an exciting interactive tool for use in the classroom. Each chapter pairs key concepts with images from the textbook to reinforce student learning.

## ● ACKNOWLEDGMENTS

I want to express my gratitude to several persons for helping the sixth edition become a reality. The following individuals reviewed the previous edition and provided numerous valuable suggestions:

Wendy Folger, Central Michigan University

Philip Moberg, Northern Kentucky University

Herman Huber, College of St. Elizabeth

Zandra Gratz, Kean University

Ken Linfield, Spalding University

Darrell Rudmann, Shawnee State University

William Rogers, Grand Valley State University

Mark Runco, University of Georgia, Athens

William Struthers, Wheaton College

A number of people at Allyn and Bacon played pivotal roles along the way, providing encouragement and tactical advice in the various phases of revision. These individuals include Susan Hartman, who provided overall editorial guidance and arranged for excellent reviews; Stephen Frail, who was involved in the early stages of revision; and Mary Lombard, who managed the many details of manuscript submission and preparation. In addition, I want to thank Somdotta Mukherjee (Copy Editor), Rajshri Walia (Art Coordinator), Jogender Taneja (Project Manager), and the team involved in the final phase of development of this book.

Dozens of psychologists and educators permitted me to reproduce tables, figures, and artwork from their research and scholarship. Rather than gathering these names in an obscure appendix that few readers would view, I have cited the contributors in the context of their tables and figures.

In addition, these individuals helped with earlier editions and their guidance has carried forward to the current version:

George M. Alliger, University of Albany

Linda J. Allred, East Carolina University

Kay Bathurst, California State University, Fullerton

Fred Brown, Iowa State University

Michael L. Chase, Quincy University

Milton J. Dehn, University of Wisconsin–La Crosse

Timothy S. Hartshorne, Central Michigan University

Herbert W. Helm, Jr., Andrews University

Ted Jaeger, Westminster College

Richard Kimball, Worcester State College

Haig J. Kojian

Phyllis M. Ladrigan, Nazareth College

Terry G. Newell, California State University, Fresno

Walter L. Porter, Harding University

Linda Krug Porzelius, SUNY, Brockport

Robert W. Read, Northeastern University

Robert A. Reeves, Augusta State University

James R. Sorensen, Northeastern University

Billy Van Jones, Abilene Christian University

Thanks are due to the many publishers who granted permission for reproduction of materials.

Administrators and colleagues at Wheaton College (Illinois) helped with the book by providing excellent resources and a supportive atmosphere. My graduate assistant, David Tubman, deserves special thanks for finding relevant references quickly.

Finally, special thanks to Mary, Sara, and Anne, who continue to support my preoccupation with textbook writing. For at least a few years, I promise not to mention "the book" when my loved ones ask me how things are going.

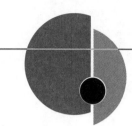

SIXTH EDITION

# Psychological Testing

## History, Principles, and Applications

# Chapter 1

# Applications and Consequences of Psychological Testing

## TOPIC 1A

## The Nature and Uses of Psychological Testing

If you ask average citizens "What do you know about psychological tests?" they might mention something about intelligence tests, inkblots, and true-false inventories such as the widely familiar MMPI. Most likely, their understanding of tests will focus on quantifying intelligence and detecting personality problems, as this is the common view of how tests are used in our society. Certainly, there is more than a grain of truth to this common view: Measures of personality and intelligence are still the essential mainstays of psychological testing. However, modern test developers have produced many other kinds of tests for diverse and imaginative purposes that even the early pioneers of testing

1

could not have anticipated. The purpose of this chapter is to discuss the varied applications of psychological testing and also to review the ethical and social consequences of this enterprise.

The chapter begins with a panoramic survey of psychological tests and their often surprising applications. In Topic 1A, The Nature and Uses of Psychological Testing, we summarize the different types and varied applications of modern tests. We also introduce the reader to a host of factors that can influence the soundness of testing such as adherence to standardized procedures, establishment of rapport, and the motivation of the examinee to deceive. In Topic 1B, Ethical and Social Implications of Testing, we further develop the theme that testing is a consequential endeavor. In this topic, we survey professional guidelines that impact testing and review the influence of cultural background on test results.

## ● THE CONSEQUENCES OF TESTING

From birth to old age, we encounter tests at almost every turning point in life. The baby's first test conducted immediately after birth is the Apgar test, a quick, multivariate assessment of heart rate, respiration, muscle tone, reflex irritability, and color. The total Apgar score (0 to 10) helps determine the need for any immediate medical attention. Later, a toddler who previously received a low Apgar score might be a candidate for developmental disability assessment. The preschool child may take school-readiness tests. Once a school career begins, each student endures hundreds, perhaps thousands, of academic tests before graduation—not to mention possible tests for learning disability, giftedness, vocational interest, and college admission. After graduation, adults may face tests for job entry, driver's license, security clearance, personality function, marital compatibility, developmental disability, brain dysfunction—the list is nearly endless. Some persons even encounter one final indignity in the frailness of their later years: a test to determine their competency to manage financial affairs.

Tests are used in almost every nation on earth for counseling, selection, and placement. Testing occurs in settings as diverse as schools, civil service, industry, medical clinics, and counseling centers. Most persons have taken dozens of tests and thought nothing of it. Yet, by the time the typical individual reaches retirement age, it is likely that psychological test results will have helped to shape his or her destiny. The deflection of the life course by psychological test results might be subtle, such as when a prospective mathematician qualifies for an accelerated calculus course based on tenth-grade achievement scores. More commonly, psychological test results alter individual destiny in profound ways. Whether a person is admitted to one college and not another, offered one job but refused a second, diagnosed as depressed or not—all such determinations rest, at least in part, on the meaning of test results as interpreted by persons in authority. Put simply, psychological test results change lives. For this reason it is prudent—indeed, almost mandatory—that students of psychology learn about the contemporary uses and occasional abuses of testing. In Case Exhibit 1.1, the life-altering aftermath of psychological testing is illustrated by means of several true case history examples.

The idea of a test is thus a pervasive element of our culture, a feature we take for granted. However, the layperson's notion of a test does not necessarily coincide with the more restrictive view held by psychometricians. A **psychometrician** is a specialist in psychology or education who develops and evaluates psychological tests. Because of widespread misunderstandings about the nature of tests, it is fitting that we begin this topic with a fundamental question, one that defines the scope of the entire book: What is a test?

## ● DEFINITION OF A TEST

A **test** is a standardized procedure for sampling behavior and describing it with categories or scores. In addition, most tests have norms or standards by which the results can be used to predict other, more important behaviors. We

## True-Life Vignettes of Testing

The influence of psychological testing is best illustrated by example. Consider these brief vignettes:

- A shy, withdrawn 7-year-old girl is administered an IQ test by a school psychologist. Her score is phenomenally higher than the teacher expected. The student is admitted to a gifted and talented program where she blossoms into a self-confident and gregarious scholar.
- Three children in a family living near a lead smelter are exposed to the toxic effects of lead dust and suffer neurological damage. Based in part on psychological test results that demonstrate impaired intelligence and shortened attention span in the children, the family receives an $8 million settlement from the company that owns the smelter.
- A candidate for a position as police officer is administered a personality inventory as part of the selection process. The test indicates that the candidate tends to act before thinking and resists supervision from authority figures. Even though he has excellent training and impresses the interviewers, the candidate does not receive a job offer.
- A student, unsure of what career to pursue, takes a vocational interest inventory. The test indicates that she would like the work of a pharmacist. She signs up for a prepharmacy curriculum but finds the classes to be both difficult and boring. After three years, she abandons pharmacy for a major in dance, frustrated that she still faces three more years of college to earn a degree.

These cases demonstrate that test results impact individual lives and the collective social fabric in powerful and far reaching ways. In the first story about the hidden talent of a 7-year-old girl, cognitive test results changed her life trajectory for the better. In the second case involving the tragic saga of children exposed to lead poisoning, the test data helped redress a social injustice. In the third situation—the impulsive candidate for police officer—personality test results likely served the public interest by tipping the balance against a questionable applicant. But test results do not always provide a positive conclusion. In the last case mentioned above, a young student wasted time and money following the seemingly flawed guidance of a well-known vocational inventory.

elaborate these characteristics in the sections that follow, but first it is instructive to portray the scope of the definition. Included in this view are traditional tests such as personality questionnaires and intelligence tests, but the definition also subsumes diverse procedures that the reader might not recognize as tests. For example, all of the following could be tests according to the defi-

nition used in this book: a checklist for rating the social skills of a youth with mental retardation; a nontimed measure of mastery in adding pairs of three-digit numbers; microcomputer appraisals of reaction time; and even situational tests such as observing an individual working on a group task with two "helpers" who are obstructive and uncooperative.

In sum, tests are enormously varied in their formats and applications. Nonetheless, most tests possess these defining features:

- Standardized procedure
- Behavior sample
- Scores or categories
- Norms or standards
- Prediction of nontest behavior

In the sections that follow, we examine each of these characteristics in more detail. The portrait that we draw pertains especially to norm-referenced tests—tests that use a well-defined population of persons for their interpretive framework. However, the defining characteristics of a test differ slightly for the special case of criterion-referenced tests—tests that measure what a person can do rather than comparing results to the performance levels of others. For this reason, we provide a separate discussion of criterion-referenced tests.

**Standardized procedure** is an essential feature of any psychological test. A test is considered to be *standardized* if the procedures for administering it are uniform from one examiner and setting to another. Of course, standardization depends to some extent on the competence of the examiner. Even the best test can be rendered useless by a careless, poorly trained, or ill-informed tester, as the reader will discover later in this topic. However, most examiners are competent. Standardization, therefore, rests largely on the directions for administration found in the instructional manual that typically accompanies a test.

The formulation of directions is an essential step in the standardization of a test. In order to guarantee uniform administration procedures, the test developer must provide comparable stimulus materials to all testers, specify with considerable precision the oral instructions for each item or subtest, and advise the examiner how to handle a wide range of queries from the examinee.

To illustrate these points, consider the number of different ways a test developer might approach the assessment of *digit span*—the maximum number of orally presented digits a subject can recall

from memory. An unstandardized test of digit span might merely suggest that the examiner orally present increasingly long series of numbers until the subject fails. The number of digits in the longest series recalled would then be the subject's digit span. Most readers can discern that such a loosely defined test will lack uniformity from one examiner to another. If the tester is free to improvise any series of digits, what is to prevent him or her from presenting, with the familiar inflection of a television announcer, "1-800-325-3535"? Such a series would be far easier to recall than a more random set, such as, "7-2-8-1-9-4-6-3-7-4-2." The speed of presentation would also crucially affect the uniformity of a digit span test. For purposes of standardization, it is essential that every examiner present each series at a constant rate, for example, one digit per second. Finally, the examiner needs to know how to react to unexpected responses such as a subject asking, "Could you repeat that again?" For obvious reasons, the usual advice is "No."

A psychological test is also a limited sample of behavior. Neither the subject nor the examiner has sufficient time for truly comprehensive testing, even when the test is targeted to a well-defined and finite behavior domain. Thus, practical constraints dictate that a test is only a sample of behavior. Yet, the sample of behavior is of interest only insofar as it permits the examiner to make inferences about the total domain of relevant behaviors. For example, the purpose of a vocabulary test is to determine the examinee's entire word stock by requesting definitions of a very small but carefully selected sample of words. Whether the subject can define the particular 35 words from a vocabulary subtest (e.g., on the Wechsler Adult Intelligence Scale-IV, or the WAIS-IV) is of little direct consequence. But the indirect meaning of such results is of great import because it signals the examinee's general knowledge of vocabulary.

An interesting point—and one little understood by the lay public—is that the test items need not resemble the behaviors that the test is attempting to predict. The essential characteristic of a good test is that it permits the examiner to predict other behaviors—not that it mirrors the to-be-predicted behaviors. If answering "true" to the question "I drink a lot of water" happens to help predict depression, then this seemingly unrelated question is a useful index of depression. Thus, the reader will note that successful prediction is an empirical question answered by appropriate research. While most tests do sample directly from the domain of behaviors they hope to predict, this is not a psychometric requirement.

A psychological test must also permit the derivation of scores or categories. Thorndike (1918) expressed the essential axiom of testing in his famous assertion, "Whatever exists at all exists in some amount." McCall (1939) went a step further, declaring, "Anything that exists in amount can be measured." Testing strives to be a form of measurement akin to procedures in the physical sciences whereby numbers represent abstract dimensions such as weight or temperature. Every test furnishes one or more scores or provides evidence that a person belongs to one category and not another. In short, psychological testing sums up performance in numbers or classifications.

The implicit assumption of the psychometric viewpoint is that tests measure individual differences in traits or characteristics that exist in some vague sense of the word. In most cases, all people are assumed to possess the trait or characteristic being measured, albeit in different amounts. The purpose of the testing is to estimate the amount of the trait or quality possessed by an individual.

In this context, two cautions are worth mentioning. First, every test score will always reflect some degree of measurement error. The imprecision of testing is simply unavoidable: Tests must rely on an external sample of behavior to estimate an unobservable and, therefore, inferred characteristic. Psychometricians often express this fundamental point with an equation:

$$X = T + e$$

where $X$ is the observed score, $T$ is the true score, and $e$ is a positive or negative error component. The best that a test developer can do is make $e$ very small. It can never be completely eliminated, nor

can its exact impact be known in the individual case. We discuss the concept of measurement error in Topic 3B, Concepts of Reliability.

The second caution is that test consumers must be wary of reifying the characteristic being measured. Test results do not represent a *thing* with physical reality. Typically, they portray an abstraction that has been shown to be useful in predicting nontest behaviors. For example, in discussing a person's IQ, psychologists are referring to an abstraction that has no direct, material existence but that is, nonetheless, useful in predicting school achievement and other outcomes.

A psychological test must also possess norms or standards. An examinee's test score is usually interpreted by comparing it with the scores obtained by others on the same test. For this purpose, test developers typically provide **norms**—a summary of test results for a large and representative group of subjects (Petersen, Kolen, & Hoover, 1989). The norm group is referred to as the standardization sample.

The selection and testing of the **standardization sample** is crucial to the usefulness of a test. This group must be representative of the population for whom the test is intended or else it is not possible to determine an examinee's relative standing. In the extreme case when norms are not provided, the examiner can make no use of the test results at all. An exception to this point occurs in the case of criterion-referenced tests, discussed later.

Norms not only establish an average performance but also serve to indicate the frequency with which different high and low scores are obtained. Thus, norms allow the tester to determine the degree to which a score deviates from expectations. Such information can be very important in predicting the nontest behavior of the examinee. Norms are of such overriding importance in test interpretation that we consider them at length in a separate section later in this text.

Finally, tests are not ends in themselves. In general, the ultimate purpose of a test is to predict additional behaviors, other than those directly sampled by the test. Thus, the tester may have more interest in the nontest behaviors predicted by the test than in the test responses per se. Perhaps a concrete example will clarify this point. Suppose an examiner administers an inkblot test to a patient in a psychiatric hospital. Assume that the patient responds to one inkblot by describing it as "eyes peering out." Based on established norms, the examiner might then predict that the subject will be highly suspicious and a poor risk for individual psychotherapy. The purpose of the testing is to arrive at this and similar predictions—not to determine whether the subject perceives eyes staring out from the blots.

The ability of a test to predict nontest behavior is determined by an extensive body of validational research, most of which is conducted after the test is released. But there are no guarantees in the world of psychometric research. It is not unusual for a test developer to publish a promising test, only to read years later that other researchers find it deficient. There is a lesson here for test consumers: The fact that a test exists and purports to measure a certain characteristic is no guarantee of truth in advertising. A test may have a fancy title, precise instructions, elaborate norms, attractive packaging, and preliminary findings—but if in the dispassionate study of independent researchers the test fails to predict appropriate nontest behaviors, then it is useless.

## ● FURTHER DISTINCTIONS IN TESTING

The chief features of a test previously outlined apply especially to norm-referenced tests, which constitute the vast majority of tests in use. In a **norm-referenced test**, the performance of each examinee is interpreted in reference to a relevant standardization sample (Petersen, Kolen, & Hoover, 1989). However, these features are less relevant in the special case of criterion-referenced tests, since these instruments suspend the need for comparing the individual examinee with a reference group. In a **criterion-referenced test,** the objective is to determine where the examinee stands with respect to very tightly defined educational objectives (Berk, 1984). For example, one

part of an arithmetic test for 10-year-olds might measure the accuracy level in adding pairs of two-digit numbers. In an untimed test of 20 such problems, accuracy should be nearly perfect. For this kind of test, it really does not matter how the individual examinee compares to others of the same age. What matters is whether the examinee meets an appropriate, specified criterion—for example, 95 percent accuracy. Because there is no comparison to the normative performance of others, this kind of measurement tool is aptly designated a criterion-referenced test. The important distinction here is that, unlike norm-referenced tests, criterion-referenced tests can be meaningfully interpreted without reference to norms. We discuss criterion-referenced tests in more detail in Topic 3A, Norms and Test Standardization.

Another important distinction is between testing and assessment, which are often considered equivalent. However, they do not mean exactly the same thing. *Assessment* is a more comprehensive term, referring to the entire process of compiling information about a person and using it to make inferences about characteristics and to predict behavior. **Assessment** can be defined as appraising or estimating the magnitude of one or more attributes in a person. The assessment of human characteristics involves observations, interviews, checklists, inventories, projectives, and other psychological tests. In sum, tests represent only one source of information used in the assessment process. In assessment, the examiner must compare and combine data from different sources. This is an inherently subjective process that requires the examiner to sort out conflicting information and make predictions based on a complex gestalt of data.

The term *assessment* was invented during World War II (WWII) to describe a program to select men for secret service assignment in the Office of Strategic Services (OSS Assessment Staff, 1948). The OSS staff of psychologists and psychiatrists amassed a colossal amount of information on candidates during four grueling days of written tests, interviews, and personality tests. In addition, the assessment process included a variety of real-life situational tests based on the realization that there was a difference between know-how and can-do:

> We made the candidates actually attempt the tasks with their muscles or spoken words, rather than merely indicate on paper how the tasks could be done. We were prompted to introduce realistic tests of ability by such findings as this: that men who earn a high score in Mechanical Comprehension, a paper-and-pencil test, may be below average when it comes to solving mechanical problems with their hands. (OSS Assessment Staff, 1948)

The situational tests included group tasks of transporting equipment across a raging brook and scaling a 10-foot-high wall, as well as individual scrutiny of the ability to survive a realistic interrogation and to command two uncooperative subordinates in a construction task.

On the basis of the behavioral observations and test results, the OSS staff rated the candidates on dozens of specific traits in such broad categories as leadership, social relations, emotional stability, effective intelligence, and physical ability. These ratings served as the basis for selecting OSS personnel.

## ● TYPES OF TESTS

Tests can be broadly grouped into two camps: group tests versus individual tests. **Group tests** are largely pencil-and-paper measures suitable to the testing of large groups of persons at the same time. **Individual tests** are instruments that by their design and purpose must be administered one on one. An important advantage of individual tests is that the examiner can gauge the level of motivation of the subject and assess the relevance of other factors (e.g., impulsiveness or anxiety) on the test results.

For convenience, we will sort tests into the eight categories depicted in Table 1.1. Each of the categories contains norm-referenced, criterion-referenced, individual, and group tests. The reader will note that any typology of tests is a purely arbitrary determination. For example, we could argue for yet another dichotomy: tests that seek to measure maximum performance (e.g., an intelligence test) versus tests that seek to gauge a typical response (e.g., a personality inventory).

In a narrow sense, there are hundreds—perhaps thousands—of different kinds of tests, each measuring a slightly different aspect of the individual.

---

**● TABLE 1.1    The Main Types of Psychological Tests**

**Intelligence Tests:**  Measure an individual's ability in relatively global areas such as verbal comprehension, perceptual organization, or reasoning and thereby help determine potential for scholastic work or certain occupations.

**Aptitude Tests:**  Measure the capability for a relatively specific task or type of skill; aptitude tests are, in effect, a narrow form of ability testing.

**Achievement Tests:**  Measure a person's degree of learning, success, or accomplishment in a subject or task.

**Creativity Tests:**  Assess novel, original thinking and the capacity to find unusual or unexpected solutions, especially for vaguely defined problems.

**Personality Tests:**  Measure the traits, qualities, or behaviors that determine a person's individuality; such tests include checklists, inventories, and projective techniques.

**Interest Inventories:**  Measure an individual's preference for certain activities or topics and thereby help determine occupational choice.

**Behavioral Procedures:**  Objectively describe and count the frequency of a behavior, identifying the antecedents and consequences of the behavior.

**Neuropsychological Tests:**  Measure cognitive, sensory, perceptual, and motor performance to determine the extent, locus, and behavioral consequences of brain damage.

---

For example, even two tests of intelligence might be arguably different types of measures. One test might reveal the assumption that intelligence is a biological construct best measured through brain waves, whereas another might be rooted in the traditional view that intelligence is exhibited in the capacity to learn acculturated skills such as vocabulary. Lumping both measures under the category of *intelligence tests* is certainly an oversimplification, but nonetheless a useful starting point.

**Intelligence tests** were originally designed to sample a broad assortment of skills in order to estimate the individual's general intellectual level. The Binet-Simon scales were successful, in part, because they incorporated heterogeneous tasks, including word definitions, memory for designs, comprehension questions, and spatial visualization tasks. The group intelligence tests that blossomed with such profusion during and after WWII also tested diverse abilities—witness the Army Alpha with its eight different sections measuring practical judgment, information, arithmetic, and reasoning, among other skills.

Modern intelligence tests also emulate this historically established pattern by sampling a wide variety of proficiencies deemed important in our culture. In general, the term *intelligence test* refers to a test that yields an overall summary score based on results from a heterogeneous sample of items. Of course, such a test might also provide a profile of subtest scores as well, but it is the overall score that generally attracts the most attention.

**Aptitude tests** measure one or more clearly defined and relatively homogeneous segments of ability. Such tests come in two varieties: single aptitude tests and multiple aptitude test batteries. A single aptitude test appraises, obviously, only one ability, whereas a multiple aptitude test battery provides a profile of scores for a number of aptitudes.

Aptitude tests are often used to predict success in an occupation, training course, or educational endeavor. For example, the Seashore Measures of Musical Talents (Seashore, 1938), a series of tests covering pitch, loudness, rhythm, time, timbre, and tonal memory, can be used to identify children with potential talent in music. Specialized aptitude tests also exist for the assessment of clerical skills, mechanical abilities, manual dexterity, and artistic ability.

The most common use of aptitude tests is to determine college admissions. Most every college student is familiar with the SAT (Scholastic Assessment Test, previously called the Scholastic Aptitude Test) of the College Entrance Examination Board. This test contains a Verbal section stressing word knowledge and reading comprehension; a Mathematics section stressing algebra, geometry, and insightful reasoning; and a Writing section. In effect, colleges that require certain minimum scores on the SAT for admission are using the test to predict academic success.

**Achievement tests** measure a person's degree of learning, success, or accomplishment in a subject matter. The implicit assumption of most achievement tests is that the schools have taught the subject matter directly. The purpose of the test is then to determine how much of the material the subject has absorbed or mastered. Achievement tests commonly have several subtests, such as reading, mathematics, language, science, and social studies.

The distinction between aptitude and achievement tests is more a matter of use than content (Gregory, 1994a). In fact, any test can be an aptitude test to the extent that it helps predict future performance. Likewise, any test can be an achievement test insofar as it reflects how much the subject has learned. In practice, then, the distinction between these two kinds of instruments is determined by their respective uses. On occasion, one instrument may serve both purposes, acting as an aptitude test to forecast future performance and an achievement test to monitor past learning.

**Creativity tests** assess a subject's ability to produce new ideas, insights, or artistic creations that are accepted as being of social, aesthetic, or scientific value. Thus, measures of **creativity** emphasize novelty and originality in the solution of fuzzy problems or the production of artistic works. A creative response to one problem is illustrated in Figure 1.1.

Tests of creativity have a checkered history. In the 1960s, they were touted as a useful alternative

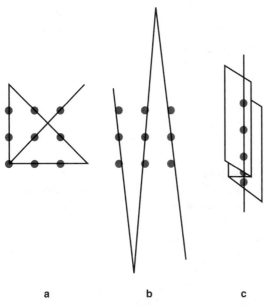

a                    b                    c

Note: Without lifting the pencil, draw through all the dots with as few straight lines as possible. The usual solution is shown in *a*. Creative solutions are depicted in *b* and *c*.

● **FIGURE 1.1**  Solutions to the Nine-Dot Problem as Examples of Creativity

to intelligence tests and used widely in U.S. school systems. Educators were especially impressed that creativity tests required divergent thinking—putting forth a variety of answers to a complex or fuzzy problem—as opposed to convergent thinking—finding the single correct solution to a well-defined problem. For example, a creativity test might ask the examinee to imagine all the things that would happen if clouds had strings trailing from them down to the ground. Students who could come up with a large number of consequences were assumed to be more creative than their less-imaginative colleagues. However, some psychometricians are skeptical, concluding that creativity is just another label for applied intelligence.

**Personality tests** measure the traits, qualities, or behaviors that determine a person's individuality; this information helps predict future behavior. These tests come in several different varieties, in-

cluding checklists, inventories, and projective techniques such as sentence completions and inkblots (Table 1.2).

**Interest inventories** measure an individual's preference for certain activities or topics and thereby help determine occupational choice. These tests are based on the explicit assumption that interest patterns determine and, therefore, also predict job satisfaction. For example, if the examinee has the same interests as successful and satisfied accountants, it is thought likely that he or she would enjoy the work of an accountant. The assumption that interest patterns predict job

● **TABLE 1.2**    **Examples of Personality Test Items**

*(a) An Adjective Checklist*

Check those words which describe you:

| | |
|---|---|
| ( ) relaxed | ( ) assertive |
| ( ) thoughtful | ( ) curious |
| ( ) cheerful | ( ) even-tempered |
| ( ) impatient | ( ) skeptical |
| ( ) morose | ( ) impulsive |
| ( ) optimistic | ( ) anxious |

*(b) A True-False Inventory*

Circle true or false as each statement applies to you:
T  F  I like sports magazines.
T  F  Most people would lie to get a job.
T  F  I like big parties where there is lots of noisy fun.
T  F  Strange thoughts possess me for hours at a time.
T  F  I often regret the missed opportunities in my life.
T  F  Sometimes I feel anxious for no reason at all.
T  F  I like everyone I have met.
T  F  Falling asleep is seldom a problem for me.

*(c) A Sentence Completion Projective Test*

Complete each sentence with the first thought that comes to you:
I feel bored when
What I need most is
I like people who
My mother was

satisfaction is largely born out by empirical studies, as we will review in a later chapter.

Many kinds of **behavioral procedures** are available for assessing the antecedents and consequences of behavior, including checklists, rating scales, interviews, and structured observations. These methods share a common assumption that behavior is best understood in terms of clearly defined characteristics such as frequency, duration, antecedents, and consequences. Behavioral procedures tend to be highly pragmatic in that they are usually interwoven with treatment approaches.

**Neuropsychological tests** are used in the assessment of persons with known or suspected brain dysfunction. *Neuropsychology* is the study of brain–behavior relationships. Over the years, neuropsychologists have discovered that certain tests and procedures are highly sensitive to the effects of brain damage. Neuropsychologists use these specialized tests and procedures to make inferences about the locus, extent, and consequences of brain damage. A full neuropsychological assessment typically requires three to eight hours of one-on-one testing with an extensive battery of measures. Examiners must undergo comprehensive advanced training in order to make sense out of the resulting mass of test data.

● **USES OF TESTING**

By far the most common use of psychological tests is to make decisions about persons. For example, educational institutions frequently use tests to determine placement levels for students, and universities ascertain who should be admitted, in part, on the basis of test scores. State, federal, and local civil service systems also rely heavily on tests for purposes of personnel selection.

Even the individual practitioner exploits tests, in the main, for decision making. Examples include the consulting psychologist who uses a personality test to determine that a police department hire one candidate and not another, and the neuropsychologist who employs tests to conclude that a client has suffered brain damage.

But simple decision making is not the only function of psychological testing. It is convenient to distinguish five uses of tests:

- Classification
- Diagnosis and treatment planning
- Self-knowledge
- Program evaluation
- Research

These applications frequently overlap and, on occasion, are difficult to distinguish one from another. For example, a test that helps determine a psychiatric diagnosis might also provide a form of self-knowledge. Let us examine these applications in more detail.

The term **classification** encompasses a variety of procedures that share a common purpose: assigning a person to one category rather than another. Of course, the assignment to categories is not an end in itself but the basis for differential treatment of some kind. Thus, classification can have important effects such as granting or restricting access to a specific college or determining whether a person is hired for a particular job. There are many variant forms of classification, each emphasizing a particular purpose in assigning persons to categories. We will distinguish placement, screening, certification, and selection.

**Placement** is the sorting of persons into different programs appropriate to their needs or skills. For example, universities often use a mathematics placement exam to determine whether students should enroll in calculus, algebra, or remedial courses.

**Screening** refers to quick and simple tests or procedures to identify persons who might have special characteristics or needs. Ordinarily, psychometricians acknowledge that screening tests will result in many misclassifications. Examiners are, therefore, advised to do follow-up testing with additional instruments before making important decisions on the basis of screening tests. For example, to identify children with highly exceptional talent in spatial thinking, a psychologist might administer a 10-minute paper-and-pencil test to every child in a school system. Students who scored in the top 10 percent might then be singled out for more comprehensive testing.

**Certification** and selection both have a pass/fail quality. Passing a certification exam confers privileges. Examples include the right to practice psychology or to drive a car. Thus, certification typically implies that a person has at least a minimum proficiency in some discipline or activity. Selection is similar to certification in that it confers privileges such as the opportunity to attend a university or to gain employment.

Another use of psychological tests is for diagnosis and treatment planning. **Diagnosis** consists of two intertwined tasks: determining the nature and source of a person's abnormal behavior, and classifying the behavior pattern within an accepted diagnostic system. Diagnosis is usually a precursor to remediation or treatment of personal distress or impaired performance.

Psychological tests often play an important role in diagnosis and treatment planning. For example, intelligence tests are absolutely essential in the diagnosis of mental retardation. Personality tests are helpful in diagnosing the nature and extent of emotional disturbance. In fact, some tests such as the MMPI were devised for the explicit purpose of increasing the efficiency of psychiatric diagnosis.

Diagnosis should be more than mere classification, more than the assignment of a label. A proper diagnosis conveys information—about strengths, weaknesses, etiology, and best choices for remediation/treatment. Knowing that a child has received a diagnosis of **learning disability** is largely useless. But knowing in addition that the same child is well below average in reading comprehension, is highly distractible, and needs help with basic phonics can provide an indispensable basis for treatment planning.

Psychological tests also can supply a potent source of self-knowledge. In some cases, the feedback a person receives from psychological tests can change a career path or otherwise alter a person's life course. Of course, not every instance of psychological testing provides self-knowledge. Perhaps in

the majority of cases the client already knows what the test results divulge. A high-functioning college student is seldom surprised to find that his IQ is in the superior range. An architect is not perplexed to hear that she has excellent spatial reasoning skills. A student with meager reading capacity is usually not startled to receive a diagnosis of "learning disability."

Another use for psychological tests is the systematic evaluation of educational and social programs. We have more to say about the evaluation of educational programs when we discuss achievement tests in a later chapter. We focus here on the use of tests in the evaluation of social programs. Social programs are designed to provide services that improve social conditions and community life. For example, Project Head Start is a federally funded program that supports nationwide pre-school teaching projects for underprivileged children (McKey and others, 1985). Launched in 1965 as a precedent-setting attempt to provide child development programs to low-income families, Head Start has provided educational enrichment and health services to millions of at-risk preschool children.

But exactly what impact does the multibillion-dollar Head Start program have on early childhood development? Congress wanted to know if the program improved scholastic performance and reduced school failure among the enrollees. But the centers vary by sponsoring agencies, staff characteristics, coverage, content, and objectives, so the effects of Head Start are not easy to ascertain. Psychological tests provide an objective basis for answering these questions that is far superior to anecdotal or impressionistic reporting. In general, Head Start children show immediate gains in IQ, school readiness, and academic achievement, but these gains dissipate in the ensuing years (Figure 1.2).

So far we have discussed the practical application of psychological tests to everyday problems such as job selection, diagnosis, or program evaluation. In each of these instances, testing serves an immediate, pragmatic purpose: helping the tester make decisions about persons or programs. But tests also play a major role in both the applied and

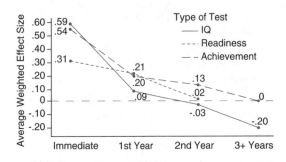

● **FIGURE 1.2** Longitudinal Test Results from the Head Start Project

*Source:* From McKey, R. H., and others. (1985). *The impact of Head Start on children, families and communities.* Washington, DC: U.S. Government Printing Office. In the public domain.

theoretical branches of behavioral research. As an example of testing in applied research, consider the problem faced by neuropsychologists who wish to investigate the hypothesis that low-level lead absorption causes behavioral deficits in children. The only feasible way to explore this supposition is by testing normal and lead-burdened children with a battery of psychological tests. Needleman and associates (1979) used an array of traditional and innovative tests to conclude that low-level lead absorption causes decrements in IQ, impairments in reaction time, and escalations of undesirable classroom behaviors. Their conclusions inspired a tumultuous and bitter exchange of opinions that we will not review here (Needleman et al., 1990). However, the passions inspired by this study epitomize an instructive point: Academicians and public policymakers respect psychological tests. Why else would they engage in lengthy, acrimonious debates about the validity of testing-based research findings?

● **FACTORS INFLUENCING THE SOUNDNESS OF TESTING**

Psychological testing is a dynamic process influenced by many factors. Although examiners strive to ensure that test results accurately reflect the traits or capacities being assessed, many extraneous factors can sway the outcome of psychological testing. In this section, we review the potentially crucial impact of several sources of influence: the manner of administration, the characteristics of the tester, the context of the testing, the motivation and experience of the examinee, and the method of scoring.

The sensitivity of the testing process to extraneous influences is obvious in cases where the examiner is cold, hurried, or incompetent. However, invalid test results do not originate only from obvious sources such as blatantly nonstandard administration, hostile tester, noisy testing room, or fearful examinee. In addition, there are numerous, subtle ways in which method, examiner, context, or motivation can alter test results. We provide a comprehensive survey of these extraneous influences in the remainder of this topic.

● **STANDARDIZED PROCEDURES IN TEST ADMINISTRATION**

The interpretation of a psychological test is most reliable when the measurements are obtained under the standardized conditions outlined in the publisher's test manual. Nonstandard testing procedures can alter the meaning of the test results, rendering them invalid and, therefore, misleading. Standardized procedures are so important that they are listed as an essential criterion for valid testing in the *Standards for Educational and Psychological Testing* (1999), a reference manual published jointly by the American Psychological Association and other groups:

> In typical applications, test administrators should follow carefully the standardized procedures for administration and scoring specified by the test publisher. Specifications regarding instructions to test takers, time limits, the form of item presentation or response, and test materials or equipment should be strictly observed. Exceptions should be made only on the basis of carefully considered professional judgment, primarily in clinical applications. (AERA, APA, NCME, 1999)

Suppose the instructions to the vocabulary section of a children's intelligence test specify that the examiner should ask, "What does *sofa* mean, what is a sofa?" If a subject were to reply, "I've never heard that word," an inexperienced tester might be tempted to respond, "You know, a couch—what is a couch?" This may strike the reader as a harmless form of fair play, a simple rephrasing of the original question. Yet, by straying from standardized procedures, the examiner has really given a different test. The point in asking for a definition of *sofa* (and not *couch*) is precisely that *sofa* is harder to define and, therefore, a better index of high-level vocabulary skills.

Even though standardized testing procedures are normally essential, there are instances in which flexibility in procedures is desirable or even necessary. As suggested in the APA *Standards,* such deviations should be reasoned and deliberate. An analogy to the spirit of the law versus the letter of the law is relevant here. An overly zealous examiner might capture the letter of the law, so to speak, by adhering literally and strictly to testing procedures outlined in the publisher's manual. But is this really what most test publishers intend? Is it even how the test was actually administered to the normative sample? Most likely publishers would prefer that examiners capture the spirit of the law even if, on occasion, it is necessary to adjust testing procedures slightly.

The need to adjust standardized procedures for testing is especially apparent when examining persons with certain kinds of disabilities. A subject with a speech impediment might be allowed to write down the answers to orally presented questions or to use gesture and pantomime in response to some items. For example, a test question might ask, "What shape is a ball?" The question is designed to probe the subject's knowledge of common shapes, not to examine whether the examinee can verbalize "round." The written response *round* and the gestured response (a circular motion of the index finger) are equally correct, too.

Minor adjustments in procedures that heed the spirit in which a test was developed occur on a regular basis and are no cause for alarm. These minor adjustments do not invalidate the established norms—

on the contrary, the appropriate adaptation of procedures is necessary so that the norms remain valid. After all, the testers who collected data from the standardization sample did not act like heartless robots when posing questions to subjects. Examiners who wish to obtain valid results must likewise exercise a reasoned flexibility in testing procedures.

However, considerable clinical experience is needed to determine whether an adjustment in procedure is minor or so substantial that existing norms no longer apply. This is why psychological examiners normally receive extensive supervised experience before they are allowed to administer and interpret individual tests of ability or personality.

In certain cases an examiner will knowingly depart from standard procedures to a substantial degree; this practice precludes the use of available test norms. In these instances, the test is used to help formulate clinical judgments rather than to determine a quantitative index. For example, when examining aphasic patients, it may be desirable to ignore time limits entirely and accept roundabout answers. The examiner might not even calculate a score. In these rare cases, the test becomes, in effect, an adjunct to the clinical interview. Of course, when the examiner does not adhere to standardized procedures, this should be stated explicitly in the written report.

## ● DESIRABLE PROCEDURES OF TEST ADMINISTRATION

A small treatise could be written on desirable procedures of test administration, but we will have to settle for a brief listing of the most essential points. For more details, the interested reader can consult Sattler (2001) on the individual testing of children and Clemans (1971) on group testing. We discuss individual testing first, then briefly list some important points about desirable procedures in group testing.

An essential component of individual testing is that examiners must be intimately familiar with the materials and directions before administration begins. Largely this involves extensive rehearsal and anticipation of unusual circumstances and the appropriate response. A well-prepared examiner has memorized key elements of verbal instructions and is ready to handle the unexpected.

The uninitiated student of assessment often assumes that examination procedures are so simple and straightforward that a quick once-through reading of the manual will suffice as preparation for testing. Although some individual tests are exceedingly rudimentary and uncomplicated, many of them have complexities of administration that, unheeded, can cause the examinee to fail items unnecessarily. For example, Choi and Proctor (1994) found that 25 of 27 graduate students made serious errors in the administration of the Stanford-Binet: Fourth Edition, even though the sessions were videotaped and the students knew their testing skills were being evaluated. Appropriate attention to the details of administration is essential for valid results.

The necessity for intimate familiarity with testing procedures is well illustrated by the Block Design subtest of the WAIS-IV (Wechsler, 2008). The materials for the subtest include nine blocks (cubes) colored red on two sides, white on two sides, and red/white on two sides. The examinee's task is to use the blocks to construct patterns depicted on cards. For the initial designs, four blocks are needed, while for more difficult designs, all nine blocks are provided (Figure 1.3).

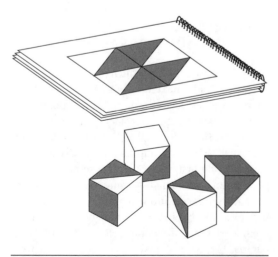

● **FIGURE 1.3**    Materials Similar to WAIS-IV Block Design Subtest

Bright examinees have no difficulty comprehending this task and the exact instructions do not influence their performance appreciably. However, persons whose intelligence is average or below average need the elaborate demonstrations and corrections that are specified in the WAIS-IV manual (Wechsler, 2008). In particular, the examiner demonstrates the first two designs and responds to the examinee's success or failure on these according to a complex flow of reaction and counterreaction, as outlined in *three pages* of instructions. Woe to the tester who has not rehearsed this subtest and anticipated the proper response to examinees who falter on the first two designs.

### Sensitivity to Disabilities

Another important ingredient of valid test administration is sensitivity to disabilities in the examinee. Impairments in hearing, vision, speech, or motor control may seriously distort test results. If the examiner does not recognize the physical disability responsible for the poor test performance, a subject may be branded as intellectually or emotionally impaired when, in fact, the essential problem is a sensory or motor disability.

Vernon and Brown (1964) reported the tragic case of a young girl who was relegated to a hospital for the mentally retarded as a consequence of the tester's insensitivity to physical disability. The examiner failed to notice that the child was deaf and concluded that her Stanford-Binet IQ of 29 was valid. She remained in the hospital for five years, but was released after she scored an IQ of 113 on a performance-based intelligence test! After dismissal from the hospital, she entered a school for the deaf and made good progress.

Persons with disabilities may require specialized tests for valid assessment. The reader will encounter a lengthy discussion of available tests for exceptional examinees in Chapter 7, Testing Special Populations. In this section, we concentrate on the vexing issues raised when standardized tests for normal populations are used with mildly or moderately disabled subjects. We include separate discussions of the testing process for examinees with a hearing, vision, speech, or motor control problem.

However, the reader needs to know that many exceptional examinees have multiple disabilities.

Valid testing of a subject with a hearing impairment requires first of all that the examiner detect the existence of the disability! This is often more difficult than it seems. Many persons with mild hearing loss learn to compensate for this disability by pretending to understand what others say and waiting for further conversational cues to help clarify faintly perceived words or phrases. As a result, other persons—including psychologists—may not perceive that an individual with mild hearing loss has any disability at all.

Failure to notice a hearing loss is particularly a problem with young examinees, who are usually poor informants about their disabilities. Young children are also prone to fluctuating hearing losses due to the periodic accumulation of fluid in the middle ear during intervals of mild illness (Vernon & Alles, 1986). A child with a fluctuating hearing loss may have normal hearing in the morning, but perceive conversational speech as a whisper just a few hours later.

Indications of possible hearing difficulty include lack of normal response to sound, inattentiveness, difficulty in following oral instructions, intent observation of the speaker's lips, and poor articulation (Sattler, 1988). In all cases in which hearing impairment is suspected, referral for an audiological examination is crucial. If a serious hearing problem is confirmed, then the examiner should consider using one of the specialized tests discussed in Chapter 7, Testing Special Populations. In persons with a mild hearing loss, it is essential for the examiner to face the subject squarely, speak loudly, and repeat instructions slowly. It is also important to find a quiet room for testing. Ideally, a testing room will have curtains and textured wall surfaces to minimize the distracting effects of background noises.

In contrast to those with hearing loss, subjects with visual disabilities generally attend well to verbally presented test materials. The examinee with visual impairment introduces a different kind of challenge to the examiner: detecting that a visual impairment exists, and then ensuring that the subject can see the test materials well.

Detecting visual impairment is a straightforward matter with adult subjects—in most cases, a mature examinee will freely volunteer information about visual impairment, especially if asked. However, children are poor informants about their visual capacities, so testers need to know the signs and symptoms of possible visual impairment in a young examinee. Common sense is a good starting point: Children who squint, blink excessively, or lose their place when reading may have a vision problem. Holding books or testing materials up close is another suspicious sign. Blurred or double vision may signify visual problems, as may headaches or nausea after reading. In general, it is so common for children to require corrective lenses that examiners should be on the lookout for a vision problem in any young subject who does not wear glasses and has not had a recent vision exam.

Depending on the degree of visual impairment, examiners need to make corresponding adjustments in testing. If the child's vision is of no practical use, special instruments with appropriate norms must be used. For example, the Perkins-Binet is available for testing children who are blind. These tests are discussed in Topic 7B, Testing Persons with Disabilities. For obvious reasons, only the verbal portions of tests should be administered to sighted children with an uncorrected visual problem.

Speech impairments present another problem for diagnosticians. The verbal responses of subjects with speech impairment are difficult to decipher. Owing to the failed comprehension of the examiner, subjects may receive less credit than is due. Sattler (1988) relates the lamentable case of Daniel Hoffman, a youngster with speech impairment who spent his entire youth in classes for those with mental retardation because his Stanford-Binet IQ was 74. In actuality, his intelligence was within the normal range, as revealed by other performance-based tests. In another tragic miscarriage of assessment, a patient in England was mistakenly confined to a ward for those with severe retardation because cerebral palsy rendered his speech incomprehensible. The patient was wheelchair-bound and had almost no motor control, so his performance on nonverbal tests was also grossly impaired.

The staff assumed he was severely retarded, so the patient remained on the back ward for decades. However, he befriended a fellow resident who could comprehend the patient's gutteral rendition of the alphabet. The friend was severely retarded but could nonetheless recognize keys on a typewriter. With laborious letter-by-letter effort, the patient with incapacitating cerebral palsy wrote and published an autobiography, using his friend with mental disability as a conduit to the real world.

Even if their disability is mild, persons with cerebral palsy or other motor impairments may be penalized by timed performance tests. When testing a person with a mild motor disability, examiners may wish to omit timed performance subtests or to discount these results if they are consistently lower than scores from untimed subtests. If a subject has an obvious motor disability—such as a difficulty in manipulating the pieces of a puzzle—then standard instruments administered in the normal manner are largely inappropriate. A number of alternative instruments have been developed expressly for examinees with cerebral palsy and other motor impairments, and standard tests have been cleverly adapted and renormed (Topic 7B, Testing Persons with Disabilities).

## Desirable Procedures of Group Testing

Psychologists and educators commonly assume that almost any adult can accurately administer group tests, so long as he or she has the requisite manual. Administering a group test would appear to be a simple and straightforward procedure of passing out forms and pencils, reading instructions, keeping time, and collecting the materials.

In reality, conducting a group test requires as much finesse as administering an individual test, a point recognized years ago by Traxler (1951). There are numerous ways in which careless administration and scoring can impair group test results, causing bias for the entire group or affecting only certain individuals. We outline only the more important inadequacies and errors in the following paragraphs, referring the reader to

Traxler (1951) and Clemans (1971) for a more complete discussion.

Undoubtedly the greatest single source of error in group test administration is incorrect timing of tests that require a time limit. Examiners must allot sufficient time for the entire testing process: setup, reading instructions out loud, and the actual test taking by examinees. Allotting sufficient time requires foresightful scheduling. For example, in many school settings, children must proceed to the next class at a designated time, regardless of ongoing activities. Inexperienced examiners might be tempted to cut short the designated time limit for a test so that the school schedule can be maintained. Of course, reduced time on a test renders the norms completely invalid and likely lowers the score for most subjects in the group.

Allowing too much time for a test can be an equally egregious error. For example, consider the impact of receiving extra time on the Miller Analogies Test (MAT), a high-level reasoning test once required by many universities for graduate school application. Since the MAT is a speeded test that requires quick analogical thinking, extra time would allow most examinees to solve several extra problems. This kind of testing error would likely lower the validity of the MAT results as a predictor of graduate school performance.

A second source of error in group test administration is lack of clarity in the directions to the examinees. Examiners must read the instructions slowly in a clear, loud voice that commands the attention of the subjects. Instructions must not be paraphrased. Where allowed by the manual, examiners must stop and clarify points with individual examinees who are confused.

Noise is another factor that must be controlled in group testing. It has been known for some time that noise causes a decrease in performance, especially for tasks of high complexity (e.g., Boggs & Simon, 1968). Surprisingly, there is little research on the effects of noise on psychological tests. However, it seems almost certain that loud noise, especially if intermittent and unpredictable, will cause test scores to decline substantially. Elementary schoolchildren should not be expected to perform well while a construction worker jackhammers a cement wall in the next room. In fairness to the examinees, there are times when the test administrator should reschedule the test.

Another source of error in the administration of a group test is failure to explain when and if examinees should guess. Perhaps more frequently than any other question, examiners are asked, "Is there a penalty if I guess wrong?" In most instances, test developers anticipate this issue and provide explicit guidance to subjects as to the advantages and/or pitfalls of guessing. Examiners should not give supplementary advice on guessing—this would constitute a serious deviation from standardized procedure.

Most test developers incorporate a **correction for guessing** based on established principles of probability. Consider a multiple-choice test that has four alternatives per item. On those items that the subject makes a wild, uneducated guess, the odds on being correct are 1 out of 4, while the odds on being wrong are 3 out of 4. Thus, for every three wrong guesses, there will be one correct guess that reflects luck rather than knowledge. Suppose a young girl answers correctly on 35 questions from a 50-item test but answers erroneously on 9 questions. In all she has answered 44 questions, leaving 6 blank. The fact that she selected the wrong alternative on 9 questions suggests that she also gained 3 correct answers due to luck rather than knowledge. Remember, on wild guesses we expect there to be, on average, 3 wrong answers for every correct answer, so for 9 wrong guesses we would expect 3 correct guesses on other questions. The subject's corrected score—the one actually reported and compared to existing norms—would then be 32; that is, 35 minus 3. In other words, she probably knew 32 answers but by guessing on 12 others she boosted her score another 3 points.

The scoring correction outlined in the preceding paragraph pertains only to wild, uneducated guesses. The effect of such a correction is to eliminate the advantage otherwise bestowed on unabashed risk takers. However, not all guesses are wild and uneducated. In some instances, an examinee can eliminate one or two of the alternatives, thereby increasing the odds of a correct guess among the remaining choices. In this situation, it may be wise for the examinee to guess.

Whether an educated guess is really to the advantage of the examinee depends partly on the diabolical skill of the item writer. Traxler (1951) notes:

> In effect, the item writer attempts to make each wrong response so plausible that every examinee who does not possess the desired skill or ability will select a wrong response. In other words, the item writer's aim is to make all or nearly all considered guesses wrong guesses.

A skilled item writer can fashion questions so that the correct alternative is completely counterintuitive and the wrong alternatives are persuasively appealing. For these items, an educated guess is almost always wrong.

Nonetheless, many test developers now advise subjects to make educated guesses but warn against wild guesses. For example, a recent edition of the test preparation manual *Taking the SAT* advises:

> Because of the way the test is scored, haphazard or random guessing for questions you know nothing about is unlikely to change your score. When you know that one or more choices can be eliminated, guessing from among the remaining choices should be to your advantage.

Whether or not a group test uses a scoring correction, the important point to emphasize in this context is that the administrator should follow standardized procedure and never offer supplementary advice about guessing. In group testing, deviations from the instructions manual are simply unacceptable.

## ● INFLUENCE OF THE EXAMINER

### The Importance of Rapport

Test publishers urge examiners to establish **rapport**— a comfortable, warm atmosphere that serves to motivate examinees and elicit cooperation. Initiating a cordial testing milieu is a crucial aspect of valid testing. A tester who fails to establish rapport may cause a subject to react with anxiety, passive-aggressive noncooperation, or open hostility. Failure to establish rapport distorts test findings: Ability is underestimated and personality is misjudged.

Rapport is especially important in individual testing and particularly so when evaluating children. Wechsler (1974) has noted that establishing rapport places great demands on the clinical skills of the tester:

> To put the child at ease in his surroundings, the examiner might engage him in some informal conversation before getting down to the more serious business of giving the test. Talking to him about his hobbies or interests is often a good way of breaking the ice, although it may be better to encourage a shy child to talk about something concrete in the environment—a picture on the wall, an animal in his classroom, or a book or toy (not a test material) in the examining room. In general, this introductory period need not take more than 5 to 10 minutes, although the testing should not start until the child seems relaxed enough to give his maximum effort.

Testers may differ in their abilities to establish rapport. Cold testers will likely obtain less cooperation from their subjects, resulting in reduced performance on ability tests or distorted, defensive results on personality tests. Overly solicitous testers may err in the opposite direction, giving subtle (and occasionally blatant) cues to correct answers. Both extremes should be avoided.

### Examiner Sex, Experience, and Race

A wide body of research has sought to determine whether certain characteristics of the examiner cause examinee scores to be raised or lowered on ability tests. For example, does it matter whether the examiner is male or female? Experienced or novice? Same or different race from the examinee? We will contain the urge to review these studies—with a few exceptions—for one simple reason: The results are contradictory and, therefore, inconclusive. Most studies find that sex, experience, and race of the examiner make little, if any, difference.

Furthermore, the few studies that report a large effect in one direction (e.g., female examiners elicit higher IQ scores) are contradicted by other studies showing the opposite trend. The interested reader can consult Sattler (1988) for a discussion and extensive listing of references.

Yet, it would be unwise to conclude that sex, experience, or race of the examiner never affect test scores. In isolated instances, a particular examiner characteristic might very well have a large effect on examinee test scores. For example, Terrell, Terrell, and Taylor (1981) ingeniously demonstrated that the race of the examiner interacts potently with the trust level of African American examinees in IQ testing. These researchers identified African American college students with high and low levels of mistrust of whites; half of each group was then administered the WAIS by a white examiner, the other half by an African American examiner. The high-mistrust group with an African American examiner scored significantly higher than the high-mistrust group with a white examiner (average IQs of 96 versus 86, respectively). In addition, the low-mistrust group with a white examiner scored slightly higher than the low-mistrust group with an African American examiner (average IQs of 97 versus 92, respectively). In sum, the authors concluded that mistrustful African Americans do poorly when tested by white examiners. Data bearing on this type of racial effect are meager, and there is certainly room for additional research.

### ● BACKGROUND AND MOTIVATION OF THE EXAMINEE

Examinees differ not only in the characteristics that examiners desire to assess but also in other extraneous ways that might confound the test results. For example, a bright subject might perform poorly on a speeded ability test because of test anxiety; a sane murderer might seek to appear mentally ill on a personality inventory to avoid prosecution; a student of average ability might undergo coaching to perform better on an aptitude test. Some subjects utterly lack motivation and don't care if they do well on psychological tests. In all of these instances, the test results may be inaccurate because of the filtering and distorting effects of certain examinee characteristics such as anxiety, malingering, coaching, or cultural background.

## Test Anxiety

**Test anxiety** refers to those phenomenological, physiological, and behavioral responses that accompany concern about possible failure on a test. There is no doubt that subjects experience different levels of test anxiety ranging from a carefree outlook to incapacitating dread at the prospect of being tested.

Several true-false questionnaires have been developed to assess individual differences in test anxiety (e.g., Sarason, 1980). Following, we list characteristic items and their direction of keying (*T* for True, *F* for False):

- (T) When taking an important examination, I sweat a great deal.
- (T) I freeze up when I take intelligence tests or school exams.
- (F) I really don't understand why some people get so upset about tests.
- (T) I dread courses in which the instructor likes to give "pop" quizzes.

An extensive body of research has confirmed the commonsense notion that test anxiety is negatively correlated with school achievement, aptitude test scores, and measures of intelligence (Naveh-Benjamin, McKeachie, & Lin, 1987). However, the interpretation of these correlational findings is not straightforward. One possibility is that students develop test anxiety because of a history of performing poorly on tests. That is, the decrements in performance may precede and cause the test anxiety. In support of this viewpoint, Paulman and Kennelly (1984) found that—independent of their anxiety—many test-anxious students also display ineffective test taking in academic settings. Such students would do poorly on tests whether or not they were anxious. Moreover, Naveh-Benjamin et al. (1987) determined that a large proportion of

test-anxious college students have poor study habits that predispose them to poor test performance. The test anxiety of these subjects is partly a by-product of lifelong frustration over mediocre test results.

Other lines of research indicate that test anxiety has a directly detrimental effect on test performance. That is, test anxiety is likely both cause and effect in the equation linking it with poor test performance. Consider the seminal study on this topic by Sarason (1961), who tested high- and low-anxious subjects under neutral or anxiety-inducing instructions. The subjects were college students required to memorize two-syllable words low in meaningfulness—a difficult task. Half of the subjects performed under neutral instructions—they were simply told to memorize the lists. The remaining subjects were told to memorize the lists and told that the task was an intelligence test. They were urged to perform as well as possible. The two groups did not differ significantly in performance when the instructions were neutral and nonthreatening. However, when the instructions aroused anxiety, performance levels for the high-anxious subjects dropped markedly, leaving them at a huge disadvantage compared to low-anxious subjects. This indicates that test-anxious subjects show significant decrements in performance when they perceive the situation as a test. In contrast, low-anxious subjects are relatively unaffected by such a simple redefinition of the context.

Tests with narrow time limits pose a special problem to persons with high levels of test anxiety. Time pressure seems to exacerbate the degree of personal threat, causing significant reductions in the performance of test-anxious persons. Siegman (1956) demonstrated this point many years ago by comparing performance levels of high- and low-anxious medical/psychiatric patients on timed and untimed subtests from the WAIS. The WAIS consists of eleven subtests, including six subtests for which the examiner uses a stopwatch to enforce strict time limits, and five subtests for which the subject has unlimited time to respond. Interestingly, the high- and low-anxious subjects were of equal overall ability on the WAIS. However, each group excelled on different kinds of subtests in predictable directions. In particular, the low-anxious subjects surpassed the high-anxious subjects on timed subtests, whereas the reverse pattern was observed on untimed subtests (Figure 1.4).

## Motivation to Deceive

Test results also may be inaccurate if the examinee has reasons to perform in an inadequate or unrepresentative manner. Overt faking of test results is rare, but it does happen. A small fraction of persons seeking benefits from rehabilitation or social agencies will consciously fake bad on personality and ability tests. The topic of malingering (faking bad for personal gain) is discussed in a later chapter.

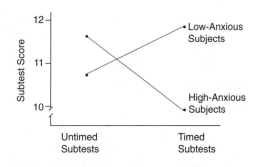

● **FIGURE 1.4**    Influence of Timing and Anxiety Level on WAIS Subtest Results

*Source:* Based on data from Siegman, A. W. (1956). The effect of manifest anxiety on a concept formation task, a nondirected learning task, and on timed and untimed intelligence tests. *Journal of Consulting Psychology, 20,* 176–178.

## ● SUMMARY

1. A test can be defined as a standardized procedure for sampling behavior and describing it with categories or scores. In addition, most tests have norms or standards by which the results can be used to predict other, more important behaviors.

2. Tests always constitute a sample of behavior, never the totality of that which the examiner seeks to measure. For this reason, test results always incorporate some degree of measurement error.

3. In a norm-referenced test, the examinee's test score is interpreted in relation to scores obtained by others on the same test. In a criterion-referenced test, the emphasis is on what the examinee can do with respect to very tightly defined educational criteria.

4. Assessment is the process of compiling information about a person and using it to make inferences about characteristics and to predict behavior. Assessment incorporates testing but is more comprehensive and may include observations, interviews, and other sources of information.

5. Group tests are pencil-and-paper measures suitable to testing large groups of persons at one time. Individual tests are designed for one-

on-one administration; the examiner can thereby observe motivation and other characteristics of the examinee.

6. An arbitrary but useful classification of psychological tests is as follows: intelligence, aptitude, achievement, creativity, personality, interest, behavioral, and neuropsychological. The characteristics of these tests are outlined in Table 1.1.

7. Five uses of tests may be distinguished: classification, diagnosis and treatment planning, self-knowledge, program evaluation, and research.

8. Classification can be further broken down into placement, the sorting of persons into appropriate programs; screening, quick identification of persons with special characteristics or needs; and certification (e.g., for a driver's license) and selection (e.g., for college).

9. Standardized testing procedures are essential to valid testing. The use of nonstandard procedures may alter the meaning of the test results, rendering them invalid and misleading.

10. Flexibility in testing procedures is nonetheless appropriate when it is reasoned and deliberate. In determining whether a flexible shift in testing

procedures is acceptable, the examiner should surmise how the test was most likely administered to the normative sample.

11. In individual testing, it is desirable for the examiner to become highly familiar with the test materials. Tests need to be rehearsed so that the examiner can anticipate the appropriate responses to the numerous contingencies of testing.

12. Another important ingredient of valid testing is sensitivity to disabilities in the examinee. When disabilities go unrecognized, serious errors of test interpretation may occur; for example, a deaf examinee may be misdiagnosed as having a mental disability.

13. In the administration of group tests, examiners must adhere strictly to oral instructions and defined time limits. In addition, the physical conditions of testing must be appropriate, such as proper lighting and minimal noise.

14. Especially in the administration of individual tests, examiners are urged to establish rapport. In testing, rapport is a comfortable, warm atmosphere that serves to motivate examinees and elicit cooperation.

15. Contrary to popular expectation, most studies find that the sex, experience, and race of the examiner have little effect on psychological test results. Nonetheless, there may be specialized cases in which examiner–examinee interactions produce a detrimental effect on test scores.

16. Test anxiety refers to those phenomenological, physiological, and behavioral responses that accompany concern about possible failure on a test. Test anxiety has been shown to correlate negatively with school achievement, aptitude test scores, measures of intelligence, and performance on timed tests.

## ● KEY TERMS AND CONCEPTS

psychometrician   p. 2

test   p. 2

standardized procedure   p. 4

norms   p. 5

standardization sample   p. 5

norm-referenced test   p. 6

criterion-referenced test   p. 6

assessment   p. 6

group tests   p. 7

individual tests   p. 7

intelligence tests   p. 8

aptitude tests   p. 8

achievement tests   p. 8

creativity tests   p. 8

creativity   p. 8

personality tests   p. 9

interest inventories   p. 9

behavioral procedures   p. 10

neuropsychological tests   p. 10

classification   p. 10

placement   p. 10

screening   p. 10

certification   p. 11

diagnosis   p. 11

learning disability   p. 11

correction for guessing   p. 17

rapport   p. 17

test anxiety   p. 19

# Ethical and Social Implications of Testing

The general theme of this book is that psychological testing is a beneficial influence in modern society. When used ethically and responsibly, testing provides a basis for arriving at sensible inferences about individuals and groups. After all, the intention of the enterprise is to promote proper guidance, effective treatment, accurate evaluation, and fair decision making—whether in one-on-one clinic testing or institutional group testing. Who could possibly complain about these goals?

Thankfully, tests generally are applied in an ethical and responsible manner by psychologists, educators, administrators, and others. But there are exceptions. Almost everyone has heard the horrific anecdotes: the minority grade schooler casually labeled as having mental retardation on the basis of a single IQ score; the college student implausibly diagnosed as schizophrenic from a projective test; the job applicant wrongfully screened from employment based on an irrelevant measure; the aspiring teacher given unfair advantage when a competency test is mysteriously leaked beforehand; or the minority child penalized in testing because English is not her first language. Exceptions such as these illustrate the need for ethical and professional standards in testing.

A major purpose of this topic is to introduce the reader to the ethical and professional standards that inform the practice of psychological testing. We also pursue the related theme of special considerations in the testing of cultural and linguistic minorities. The two topics share substantial overlap: When an examinee is not from the majority Anglo-American culture (predominantly Caucasian, English-speaking, individualistic, future-oriented), ethical and professional concerns in testing rise to the forefront.

Finally, we examine a troubling and under-reported implication of widespread testing, namely, to the extent that society uses test results to make important decisions, the motivation for stakeholders to cheat is intensified. As a result, cheating has emerged as a dark, unintended consequence of high-stakes testing, especially in the school systems of our nation.

## ● THE RATIONALE FOR PROFESSIONAL TESTING STANDARDS

Testing is generally applied in a responsible manner, but as previously noted, there are exceptions. On rare occasions, testing is irresponsible by design rather than by accident. Consider, with shuddering amazement, the advertisement for Mind Prober featured in a pop psychology magazine:

> Read Any Good Minds Lately? With the Mind Prober you can. In just minutes you can have a scientifically accurate personality profile of anyone. This new expert systems software lets you discover the things most people are afraid to tell you. The strengths, weaknesses, sexual interests and more. (Eyde & Primhoff, 1992)

In this case the irresponsibility is so blatant that discussion of ethical and professional guidelines is almost superfluous.

However, testing practices do not always present in sharply contrasting shades, responsible or irresponsible. The real challenge of competent assessment is to determine the boundaries of ethical and professional practice. As usual, it is the borderline cases that provide pause for thought. The reader is encouraged to read the quandaries of testing described in Case Exhibit 1.2 and form an opinion about each. These examples are based on firsthand reports to the author. At the close of this chapter, we will return to these problematic vignettes.

The dilemmas of psychological testing do not always have simple, obvious answers. Even thoughtful and experienced psychologists may disagree as to what is ethical or professional in a given instance. Nonetheless, the scope of ethical and professional practice is not a matter of individual taste or personal judgment. Responsible test use is defined by written guidelines published by professional associations such as the American Psychological Association, the American Counseling Association, the National Association of School Psychologists, and other groups. Whether they know it or not, all practitioners owe allegiance to these guidelines, which we review in the following sections.

In general, the evolution of professional and ethical standards has been almost uniformly restrictive, providing an ever-narrowing demarcation of where, when, and how psychological tests may be used. Partly in response to the modern climate of litigation, organizations concerned with psychological testing have published guidelines that collectively define the ethical and professional standards relevant to the practice of assessment.

These standards also pertain to corporations and individuals who publish tests. We begin with a survey of guidelines for test publishers before examining the responsibilities of test users. The chapter closes with a review of special concerns in the testing of cultural and linguistic minorities.

## ● RESPONSIBILITIES OF TEST PUBLISHERS

The responsibilities of publishers pertain to the publication, marketing, and distribution of their tests. In particular, it is expected that publishers will release tests of high quality, market their product in a responsible manner, and restrict distribution of tests only to persons with proper qualifications. We consider each of these points in turn.

### Publication and Marketing Issues

Regarding the publication of new or revised instruments, the most important guideline is to guard against premature release of a test. Testing is a noble enterprise but it is also big business driven by the profit motive, which provides an inherent pressure toward early release of new or revised materials. Perhaps this is why the American Psychological Association and other organizations have published standards that relate to test publication (AERA/APA/NCME, 1999). These standards pertain especially to the technical manuals and user guides that typically accompany a test. These sources must be sufficiently complete so that a qualified user or reviewer can evaluate the appropriateness and technical adequacy of the test. This means that manuals and guides will report detailed statistics on reliability analyses, validity studies, normative samples, and other technical aspects.

**Case Exhibit**
**1.2**

## Ethical and Professional Quandaries in Testing

1. A consulting psychologist agrees to perform preemployment screening for psychopathology in police officer candidates. At the beginning of each consultation, the psychologist asks the candidate to read and sign a detailed consent form that openly and honestly describes the evaluation process. However, the consent form explains that specific feedback about the test results will not be provided to job candidates. Question: Is it ethical for the psychologist to deny such feedback to the candidates?

2. A competent counselor who has received extensive training in the interpretation of the MMPI continues to use this instrument even though it has been superceded by the MMPI-2. His rationale is simply that there is a huge body of research on the MMPI and he feels secure about the meaning of elevated MMPI test profiles, whereas he knows very little about the MMPI-2. He intends to switch over to the MMPI-2 at some undetermined future date, but finds no compelling reason to do so immediately. Question: Is the counselor's refusal to use the MMPI-2 a breach of professional standards?

3. A consulting psychologist is asked to evaluate a 9-year-old boy of Puerto Rican descent for possible learning disability. The child's primary language is Spanish and his secondary language is English. The psychologist intends to use the Wechsler Intelligence Scale for Children-IV (WISC-IV) and other tests. Because he knows almost no Spanish, the psychologist asks the child's after-school babysitter to act as translator when this is required to communicate test directions, specific questions, or the child's responses. Question: Is it an appropriate practice to use a translator when administering an individual test such as the WISC-IV?

4. In the midst of taking a test battery for learning disability, a distraught 20-year-old female college student confides a terrifying secret to the psychologist. The client has just discovered that her 25-year-old brother, who died three months ago, was most likely a pedophile. She shows the psychologist photographs of naked children posing in the brother's bedroom. To complicate matters, the brother lived with his mother—who is still unaware of his well-concealed sexual deviancy. Question: Is the psychologist obligated to report this case to law enforcement?

Marketing tests in a responsible manner refers not only to advertising (which should be accurate and dignified) but also to the way in which information is portrayed in manuals and guides. In particular, test authors should strive for a balanced presentation of their instruments and refrain from a one-sided presentation of information. For example, if some preliminary studies reflect poorly on a test, these should be given fair weight in the manual alongside positive findings. Likewise, if a potential misuse or inappropriate use of a test can be anticipated, the test author needs to discuss this matter as well.

## Competence of Test Purchasers

Test publishers recognize the broad responsibility that only qualified users should be able to purchase their products. By way of brief review, the reasons for restricted access include the potential for harm if tests fall into the wrong hands (e.g., an undergraduate psychology major administers the MMPI-2 to his friends and then makes frightful pronouncements about the results) and the obvious fact that many tests are no longer valid if potential examinees have previewed them (e.g., a teacher memorizes the correct answers to a certification exam).

These examples illustrate that access to psychological tests needs to be limited. But limited to whom? The answer, it turns out, depends on the complexity of the specific test under consideration. Guidelines proposed many years ago by the American Psychological Association (APA) are still relevant today, even though they are not enforced by all publishers. The APA proposed that tests fall into three levels of complexity (Levels A, B, and C) that require different degrees of expertise from the examiner.

*Level A:* These instruments are straightforward paper-and-pencil measures that can be administered, scored, and interpreted with minimal training. With the aid of a manual, these tests can be used by responsible nonpsychologists such as business executives or educational administrators. This category includes vocational proficiency and group educational achievement tests.

*Level B:* These tests require knowledge of test construction and training in statistics and psychology. These products are available to persons who have completed an advanced-level course in testing from an accredited college or university, or equivalent training under the supervision of a qualified psychologist. This category includes aptitude tests and personality inventories applicable to normal populations.

*Level C:* These tests require substantial understanding of testing and supporting topics. Supervised experience is essential for the proper administration, scoring, and interpretation of these instruments. Typically, Level C tests are available only to persons with a minimum of a master's degree in psychology or an allied field. These instruments include individual tests of intelligence, projective personality tests, and neuropsychological test batteries (American Psychological Association, 1953).

In general, test publishers try to screen out inappropriate requests by requiring that purchasers have the necessary credentials. For example, the Psychological Corporation, one of the major suppliers of test materials in the United States, requires prospective customers to fill out a registration form detailing their training and experience with tests. Buyers who do not hold an advanced degree in psychology must list details of courses in the administration and interpretation of tests and in statistics. References are required, too.

Most test publishers also specify that individuals or groups who provide testing and counseling by mail are not allowed to purchase materials. On a related note, ethical standards now discourage practitioners from giving "take-home" tests to clients. Until recent years, this has been an occasional practice with lengthy personality tests such as the MMPI. The ethics committee endorsed the following point:

> Nonmonitored administration of the MMPI generally does not represent sound testing practice and may result in invalid assessment for a variety of reasons (e.g., influence from other people or completion of the test while intoxicated).

In general, users are advised to refrain from giving take-home tests and publishers are counseled to deny access to practitioners or groups who promote this practice.

Even though publishers attempt to filter out unqualified purchasers, there may still be instances in which sensitive tests are sold to unscrupulous individuals. Oles and Davis (1977) discovered that graduate students in psychology could purchase the WISC-R, MMPI, TAT, Stanford-Binet, and 16PF if they typed their orders on college stationery, placed the letters *Ph.D.* after their names, enclosed payment, and used a post office box return address. Although illicit test orders are few in number, they do occur.

### ● RESPONSIBILITIES OF TEST USERS

The psychological assessment of personality, interests, brain functioning, aptitude, or intelligence is a sensitive professional action that should be completed with utmost concern for the well-being of the examinee, his or her family, employers, and the wider network of social institutions that might be affected by the results of that particular clinical assessment (Matarazzo, 1990). Over the years, the profession of psychology has proposed, clarified, and sharpened a series of thorough and thoughtful standards to provide guidance for the individual practitioner. Professional organizations publish formal ethical principles that bear upon test use, including the American Psychological Association (APA, 1992a), the American Association for Counseling and Development (AACD, 1988), the American Speech-Language-Hearing Association (ASHA, 1991), and the National Association of School Psychologists (NASP, 1992).

In addition to ethical principles, several testing organizations have published practice guidelines to help define the scope of responsible test use. Sources of test use guidelines include teaching groups (AFT, NCME, NEA, 1990), the American Psychological Association (APA, 1992b), the Educational Testing Service (ETS, 1989), the Joint Committee on Testing Practices (JCTP, 1988), the Society for Industrial and Organizational Psychology (SIOP, 1987), and professional alliances (AERA, APA, NCME, 1999). Finally, we should mention that the principles of responsible test use have been distilled in an illuminating casebook published jointly by several testing groups (Eyde, Robertson, Krug, and others, 1993).

The dozens of guidelines relevant to testing are quite specific, for example:

> Standard 5.9: When test score information is released to students, parents, legal representatives,

teachers, clients, or the media, those responsible for testing programs should provide appropriate interpretations. The interpretations should describe in simple language what the test covers, what scores mean, the precision of the scores, common misinterpretations of test scores, and how scores will be used.

Because of their specificity, a detailed analysis of relevant ethical and professional standards is beyond the scope of this text. What follows is a summary of the general provisions that pertain to the responsible practice of psychological testing and clinical psychological assessment.

These principles apply to psychologists, students of psychology, and others who work under the supervision of a psychologist. We restrict our discussion to those principles that are directly pertinent to the practice of psychological testing. Proper adherence to these principles would eliminate most—but not all—legal challenges to testing.

### Best Interests of the Client

Several ethical principles recognize that all psychological services, including assessment, are provided within the context of a professional relationship. Psychologists are, therefore, enjoined to accept the responsibility implicit in this relationship. In general, the practitioner is guided by one overriding question: What is in the best interests of the client? The functional implication of this guideline is that assessment should serve a constructive purpose for the individual examinee. If it does not, the practitioner is probably violating one or more specific ethical principles. For example, Standard 11.15 in the *Standards* manual (AERA, APA, NCME, 1999) warns testers to avoid actions that have unintended negative consequences. Allowing a client to attach unsupported surplus meanings to test results would not be in the best interests of the client and would, therefore, constitute an unethical testing practice. In fact, with certain worry-prone and self-doubting clients, a psychologist may choose not to use an appropriate test, since these clients are almost certain to engage in self-destructive misinterpretation of virtually any test findings.

## Confidentiality and the Duty to Warn

Practitioners have a primary obligation to safeguard the confidentiality of information, including test results, that they obtain from clients in the course of consultations (Principle 5; APA, 1992a). Such information can be ethically released to others only after the client or a legal representative gives unambiguous consent, usually in written form. The only exceptions to confidentiality involve those unusual circumstances in which the withholding of information would present a clear danger to the client or other persons. For example, most states have passed laws that mandate that health care practitioners must report all cases of suspected abuse in children and vulnerable elderly persons. In most states, a psychologist who learns in the course of testing that the client has physically or sexually abused a child is obligated to report that information to law enforcement.

Psychologists also have a **duty to warn** that stems from the 1976 decision in the *Tarasoff* case (Wrightsman, Nietzel, Fortune, & Greene, 2002). Tanya Tarasoff was a young college student in California who was murdered by Prosenjit Poddar, a student from India. What makes the case relevant to the practice of psychology is that Poddar had made death threats regarding Tarasoff to his campus-based therapist. Although the therapist warned the police that Poddar had made death threats, he did not warn Tarasoff. Two months later, Poddar stabbed Tarasoff to death at her home. The parents of Tanya Tarasoff sued, and the California Supreme Court later agreed that therapists have a duty to use "reasonable care" to protect potential victims from their clients. Although the Tarasoff ruling has been modified by legislation in many states, the thrust of the case still stands: Clinicians must communicate any serious threat to the potential victim, law enforcement agencies, or both.

Finally, the clinician should consider the client's welfare in deciding whether to release information, especially when the client is a minor who is unable to give voluntary, informed consent. When appropriate, practitioners are advised to inform their clients of the legal limits of confidentiality.

## Expertise of the Test User

A number of principles acknowledge that the test user must accept ultimate responsibility for the proper application of tests. From a practical standpoint, this means that the test user must be well trained in assessment and measurement theory. The user must possess the expertise needed to evaluate psychological tests for proper standardization, reliability, validity, interpretive accuracy, and other psychometric characteristics. This guideline has special significance in areas such as job screening, special education, testing of persons with disabilities, or other situations in which potential impact is strong.

Psychologists who are poorly trained in their chosen instruments can make serious errors of test interpretation that harm examinees. Furthermore, inept test usage may expose the examiner to professional sanctions and civil lawsuits. A common error observed among inexperienced test users is the overzealous, pathologized interpretation of personality test results (Case Exhibit 1.3).

The expertise of the psychologist is particularly relevant when test scoring and interpretation services are used. The Ethical Principles of the American Psychological Association leave no room for doubt:

> Psychologists retain appropriate responsibility for the appropriate application, interpretation, and use of assessment instruments, whether they score and interpret such tests themselves or use automated or other services. (APA, 1992a)

The reader is referred to Topic 12B, Computerized Assessment and the Future of Testing, for further discussion of this point.

## Informed Consent

Before testing commences, the test user needs to obtain informed consent from test takers or their legal representatives. Exceptions to informed consent can

---

**Case Exhibit**

**1.3**

### Overzealous Interpretation of the MMPI

An inexperienced consulting psychologist routinely used the MMPI for pre-employment screening of law enforcement candidates. One candidate subsequently filed a lawsuit, alleging that she had been harmed by the psychologist's report. The plaintiff, a young woman with extensive training and background in law enforcement, was denied a position as police officer because of a supposedly "defensive" MMPI profile. Her profile was entirely within normal limits, although she did obtain a *T* score of 72 on the K scale. The K scale is usually considered a good index of defensive test-taking attitudes, especially for mental health evaluations with clinic or hospital referrals. By way of quick review, MMPI *T* scores of approximately 50 are average, whereas elevations of 70 or higher are considered noteworthy. The consulting psychologist noticed the candidate's elevated score on the K scale, surmised hastily that the candidate was unduly defensive, and cautioned the police chief not to hire her.

What the psychologist did not know is that elevated K-scale scores are extremely common among law enforcement job applicants. For example, Hiatt and Hargrave (1988) found that about 25 percent of a sample of peace officers produced MMPI profiles with K scales at or above a *T* score of 70. In fact, successful police officers tend to have higher K-scale scores than "problem" peace officers! In this case the test user did not possess sufficient expertise to use the MMPI for job screening. His ignorance on this point constituted a breach of professional ethics. Incidentally, the case was settled out of court for a substantial sum of money, showing that trespasses of responsible test use can have serious legal consequences.

---

be made in certain instances, for example, legally mandated statewide testing programs, school-based group testing, and when consent is clearly implied (e.g., college admissions testing). The principle of **informed consent** is so important that the *Standards* manual devotes a separate standard to it:

> Informed consent implies that the test takers or representatives are made aware, in language that they can understand, of the reasons for testing, the type of tests to be used, the intended use and the range of material consequences of the intended use. If written, video, or audio records are made of the testing session, or other records are kept, test takers are entitled to know what testing information will be released and to whom. (AERA et al., 1999)

Even young children or test takers with limited intelligence deserve an explanation of the reasons for assessment. For example, the examiner might explain, "I'm going to ask you some questions and have you work on some puzzles so I can see what you can do and find out what things you need more help with."

From a legal standpoint, the three elements of informed consent include disclosure, competency, and voluntariness (Melton, Petrila, Poythress, & Slobogin, 1998). The heart of disclosure is that the client receive sufficient information (e.g., about risks, benefits, release of reports) to make a thoughtful decision about continued participation in the testing. Competency refers to the mental capacity of the examinee to provide consent. In general, there is a presumption of competency unless the examinee is a child, very elderly, or has mental disabilities (e.g., has mental retardation). In these cases, a guardian will need to provide legal consent. Finally, the standard of voluntariness implies that the choice to undergo an assessment battery is given freely and not based on subtle coercion (e.g., inmates are promised release time if they participate in research testing). In most cases, the examiner uses a written informed consent form such as that found in Figure 1.5.

---

Informed Consent for Psychological Assessment

This is an agreement between [Client's Name] and Dr. [Practitioner's Name], a licensed psychologist in the state of Illinois. You are encouraged to ask questions at any time about my training and background, and about the process of testing.

1. General Information: The purpose of this assessment is to provide you (and possibly others) with information about your psychological functioning that could prove helpful. The assessment will involve a brief interview and psychological testing. The entire process will take about three to four hours.

2. Specific Procedures: In addition to interview, the following tests will be administered: [List of tests and brief descriptions], e.g.
   MMPI-2, a 567-item true-false inventory of psychological functioning.
   WAIS-IV, a general test of adult intelligence in varied areas.

3. Test Report: The relevant information from the interview and the test results will be summarized in a written report. The results and the report will be reviewed with you in approximately one week. I will keep a copy of this report in a locked file for at least seven years.

4. Confidentiality: The report will not be released to any other source unless you sign a formal request. A few (remote) exceptions to the confidentiality guideline include situations of potential harm to self or others, abuse of children or elderly, or a court order to release the test results.

5. Cost: An hourly rate of $____ is used in determining the total fee. I will bill your insurance company, but you are responsible for the cost. The estimated total cost for your assessment is $____.

6. Side Effects: While most people find these tests and procedures to be interesting, some people experience anxiety when tested. Yet, it is unlikely that you will experience any long-term adverse effects from this assessment. You are encouraged to talk about the experience as we proceed.

7. Refusal of Assessment: Most people find the process of psychological assessment to be beneficial. However, you are not required to undergo this assessment. You can withdraw consent and discontinue at any time. On request, I will discuss referral options with you.

_____          _____
Client's Signature                              Date

---

● **FIGURE 1.5**   Abbreviated Example of Informed Consent for Psychological Assessment

Note: This form is illustrative only. Practitioners should consult legal counsel in regard to the details of an informed consent form.

## Obsolete Tests and the Standard of Care

Standard of care is a loose concept that often arises in the professional or legal review of specific health practices, including psychological testing. The prevailing **standard of care** is one that is "usual, customary or reasonable" (Rinas & Clyne-Jackson, 1988). To cite an extreme example, in medicine the standard of care for a fever might include the administration of aspirin—but would not include the antiquated practice of bleeding the patient.

Practitioners of psychological testing must be wary of obsolete tests, because their use might violate the prevailing standard of care. A case in point is the MMPI versus the MMPI-2. Even though the MMPI-2 is a relatively conservative revision of the highly esteemed MMPI, the improvements in norming and scale construction are substantial. The MMPI-2 is now the standard of care in MMPI-based assessment of psychopathology. Practitioners who continue to rely on the original MMPI could be liable for malpractice suits, especially if the test interpretation resulted in misleading interpretive statements or an incorrect diagnosis.

Another concern relevant to the standard of care is reliance on test results that are outdated for the current purpose. After all, individual characteristics and traits show valid change over time. A student who meets the criteria for learning disability (LD) in the fourth grade might show large gains in academic achievement, such that the LD diagnosis is no longer accurate in the fifth grade. Personality test results are especially prone to quixotic change. A short-term personal crisis might cause an MMPI-2 profile to look like a range of mountains. A week later, the test profile could be completely normal. It is difficult to provide comprehensive guidelines as to the "shelf life" of psychological test results. For example, GRE test scores that are years old still might be validly predictive of performance in graduate school, whereas Beck Depression Inventory test results from yesterday could mislead a therapist as to the current level of depression. Practitioners must evaluate the need for retesting on an individual basis.

## Responsible Report Writing

Except for group testing, the practice of psychological testing invariably culminates in a written report that constitutes a semipermanent record of test findings and examiner recommendations. Effective report writing is an important skill because of the potential lasting impact of the written document. It is beyond the scope of this text to illuminate the qualities of effective report writing, although we can refer the reader to a few sources (Gregory, 1999; Tallent, 1993).

Responsible reports typically use simple and direct writing that steers clear of jargon and technical terms. The proper goal of a report is to provide helpful perspectives on the client, not to impress the referral source that the examiner is a learned person! When Tallent (1993) surveyed more than one thousand health practitioners who made referrals for testing, one respondent declared his disdain toward psychologists who "reflect their needs to shine as a psychoanalytic beacon in revealing the dark, deep secrets they have observed." On a related note, effective reports stay within the bounds of expertise of the examiner. For example:

> It is never appropriate for a psychologist to recommend that a client undergo a specific medical procedure (such as a CT scan for an apparent brain tumor) or receive a particular drug (such as Prozac for depression). Even when the need for a special procedure seems obvious (e.g., the symptoms strongly attest to the rapid onset of a brain disease), the best way to meet the needs of the client is to recommend immediate consultation with the appropriate medical profession (e.g., neurology or psychiatry). (Gregory, 1999)

Additional advice on effective report writing can be found in Ownby (1991) and Sattler (2001).

## Communication of Test Results

Individuals who take psychological tests anticipate that the results will be shared with them. Yet practitioners often do not include one-to-one feedback as part of the assessment. A major reason for reluctance is a lack of training in how to provide feedback, especially when the test results appear to be negative. For example, how does a clinician tell a college student that her IQ is 93 when most students in that milieu score 115 or higher?

Providing effective and constructive feedback to clients about their test results is a challenging skill to learn. Pope (1992) emphasizes the responsibility of the clinician to determine that the client has understood adequately and accurately the information that the clinician was attempting to convey. Furthermore, it is the responsibility of the clinician to check for adverse reactions:

> Is the client exceptionally depressed by the findings? Is the client inferring from findings suggesting a learning disorder that the client—as the client has always suspected—is "stupid"? Using scrupulous care to conduct this assessment of the client's understanding of and reactions to the feedback is no less important than using adequate care in administering standardized psychological tests; test administration and feedback are equally important, fundamental aspects of the assessment process. (p. 271)

Proper and effective feedback involves give-and-take dialogue in which the clinician ascertains how the client has perceived the information and seeks to correct potentially harmful interpretations.

Destructive feedback often arises when the clinician fails to challenge a client's incorrect perceptions about the meaning of test results. Consider IQ tests in particular—a case in which many persons deify test scores and consider them an index of personal worth. Prior to providing test results, a clinician is advised to investigate the client's understanding of what IQ scores mean. After all, IQ is a limited slice of intellectual functioning: It does not evaluate drive or character of any kind, it is accurate only to about ±5 points, it may change over time, and it does not assess many important attributes such as creativity, social intelligence, musical ability, or athletic skill. But a client may have an unrealistic perspective about IQ and, hence, might jump to erroneous conclusions when hearing that her score is "only" 93. The careful practitioner will elicit the client's views and challenge them when

needed before proceeding. Further thoughts on feedback can be found in Pope (1992).

Going beyond the general pronouncement to avoid harm when providing test feedback, Finn and Tonsager (1997) present the intriguing view that information about test results should be directly and immediately therapeutic to individuals experiencing psychological problems. In other words, they propose that psychological assessment is a form of short-term intervention, not just a basis for gathering information that is *later* used for therapeutic purposes. In one study (Finn & Tonsager, 1992), they examined the effects of a brief psychological assessment on clients at a university counseling center. Thirty-two students took part in an initial interview, completed the MMPI-2, and then received a one-hour feedback session conducted according to a method developed by Finn (1996). A comparison group of 29 students was interviewed and received an equal amount of supportive, nondirective psychotherapy instead of the test feedback. The clients in the MMPI-2 assessment group showed a greater decline in symptomatic distress and a greater increase in self-esteem, immediately following their feedback session and also two weeks later, than the clients in the comparison group. The feedback group also felt more hopeful about their problems after the brief assessment. These findings illustrate the importance of providing thoughtful and constructive test feedback instead of rushing through a perfunctory review of the results.

## Consideration of Individual Differences

Knowledge of and respect for individual differences is highlighted by all professional organizations that deal with psychological testing. The American Psychological Association lists this as one of six guiding principles:

> Principle D: Respect for People's Rights and Dignity . . . Psychologists are aware of cultural, individual, and role differences, including those due to age, gender, race, ethnicity, national origin, religion, sexual orientation, disability, language, and socioeconomic status. Psychologists try to eliminate the

effect on their work of biases based on those factors, and they do not knowingly participate in or condone unfair discriminatory practices. (APA, 1992a)

The relevance of this principle to psychological testing is that practitioners are expected to know when a test or interpretation may not be applicable because of factors such as age, gender, race, ethnicity, national origin, religion, sexual orientation, disability, language, and socioeconomic status. We can illustrate this point with a case study reported in Eyde et al. (1993). A psychologist evaluated a 75-year-old man at the request of his wife, who had noticed memory problems. The psychologist administered a mental status examination and a prominent intelligence test. Performance on the mental status examination was normal, but standard scores on the intelligence test revealed a large discrepancy between verbal subtests and subtests measuring spatial ability and processing speed. The psychologist interpreted this pattern as indicating a deterioration of intellectual functioning in the husband. Unfortunately, this interpretation was based on faulty use of non-age-corrected standard scores. Also, the psychologist did not assess for depression, which is known to cause visuospatial performance to drop sharply (Wolff & Gregory, 1992). In fact, a series of further evaluations revealed that the husband was a perfectly healthy 75-year-old man. The psychologist failed to consider the relevance of the gentleman's age and emotional status when interpreting the intelligence test. This was a costly oversight that caused the client and his wife substantial unnecessary worry.

## ● TESTING OF CULTURAL AND LINGUISTIC MINORITIES

### Background and Historical Notes

Persons of ethnic minority descent (non-European origin) currently constitute about a third of the U.S. population, and it is estimated that they will comprise more than 50 percent within several decades. Yet the enterprise of testing is based almost entirely on the efforts of white psychologists who bring an Anglo-American viewpoint to their work. The suitability of existing tests for the evaluation of diverse populations cannot be taken for granted. The assessment of ethnic minority individuals raises important questions, especially when test results translate to placement decisions or other sensitive outcomes, as is commonly the case within educational institutions.

Unfortunately, the early pioneers in the testing movement largely ignored the impact of cultural background on test results. For example, in the 1920s Henry Goddard concluded that the intelligence of the average immigrant was alarmingly low, "perhaps of moron grade." Yet he downplayed the likelihood that language and cultural differences could explain the low test scores of immigrants. Goddard's role in the history of testing is discussed in the next chapter.

Perhaps as a rebound against these early methods, beginning in the 1930s psychologists displayed an increased sensitivity to cultural variables in the practice of testing. A shining example in this regard was Stanley Porteus, who undertook a wide-ranging investigation of the temperament and intelligence of Australian aboriginal peoples. Porteus (1931) used many traditional instruments (block designs, mazes, digit span), but to his credit he also devised an ecologically valid measure of intelligence for this group, namely, footprint recognition. Whereas the aboriginal examinees performed poorly on the Eurocentric tests, their ability to recognize photographed footprints was on a par with other racial groups studied. Even so, Porteus displayed an acute awareness that his procedures *still* might have handicapped the aboriginals:

> The photograph of a footprint is not the same as the footprint itself, and quite probably a number of cues that are made use of by the aboriginal tracker are absent from a photograph. The varying depths of parts of the foot impression are not visible in the photograph, and the individual peculiarities other than general shape and size of the footprint may not be brought out clearly. Hence we must expect that the aboriginal subjects would be under some disadvantage in matching these photographs of

footprints, as against recognition of the footprints themselves. (pp. 399–400)

In a similar vein, DuBois (1939) found that Pueblo Indian children displayed superior ability on his specially devised horse drawing test of mental ability, whereas they performed less well on the mainstream Goodenough (1926) Draw-A-Man test. From these early studies onward, psychologists have maintained a keen interest in the impact of language and culture on the meaning of test results.

## The Impact of Cultural Background on Test Results

Practitioners need to appreciate that the cultural background of examinees will impact the entire process of assessment. For this reason, Sattler (1988) advises assessment psychologists to approach their task from a pluralistic standpoint:

> Cultural groups may vary with respect to cultural values (stemming in part from cultural shock, discontinuity, or conflict); language and nuances in language style; views of life and death; roles of family members; problem-solving strategies; attitudes toward education, mental health, and mental illness; and stage of acculturation (the group may follow traditional values, accept the dominant group's values, or be at some point between the two). You should adopt a frame of reference that will enable you to understand how particular behaviors make sense within each culture. (p. 505)

For example, it is often noted that Native Americans display a distinctive conception of time, emphasizing *present-time* as opposed to the *future-time* orientation that is so powerfully formative in white, middle-class America (Panigua, 1994). A possible implication of this cultural difference is that time limits might not mean the same thing for a Native American child as for a child from the mainstream culture. Perhaps the minority child will disregard the subtest instructions and work at a careful, measured pace rather than seeking quick solutions. Of course, this child would then obtain a misleadingly low score on that measure.

While acknowledging the impact of cultural differences on testing, it is also important to avoid stereotypical overgeneralization. Culture is not monolithic. Every person is unique. Some Native Americans will exhibit a distinctive orientation to time but perhaps most will not. The challenge for the practitioner is to observe the clinical details of performance and to identify the culture-based nuances of behavior that help determine the test results.

An ingenious study by Moore (1986) powerfully illustrates the relevance of cultural background for understanding the test performance of ethnic minority examinees. She compared not only the intelligence test scores but also *the qualitative manner* of responding to test demands in two groups of adopted African American children. One group of 23 children had been transracially adopted into middle-class white families. The other group of 23 children had been intraracially adopted into middle-class African American families. All children were adopted prior to age 2 and the backgrounds of the adoptive families were similar in terms of education and social class. Thus, group difference in test scores and test behaviors could be attributed mainly to differences in cultural background arising from the fact that one group was adopted into African American families, the other adopted into white families. Testing and observations were completed by two female African American examiners who were "blind" to the purposes of the study. Tested at 7 to 10 years of age, the transracially adopted children scored an average IQ of 117 on the WISC compared to an average IQ of 104 for the traditionally adopted children. These IQ results were not remarkable, insofar as Scarr and Weinberg reported similar findings years before.

The surprising and informative outcome of the study was that the two groups of children showed very different *qualitative* behaviors during testing. As a group, the children with lower IQ scores (those adopted by African American families) were less likely to spontaneously elaborate on their work responses and more likely simply to refuse to respond when presented with a test demand. Moore (1986) offers the following interpretations:

> Children's tendency to spontaneously elaborate on their work responses may be a very important index of their level of involvement in task performance, strategies for problem solving, level of motivation to generate a correct response, and level of adjustment to the standardized test situation. . . . Although the terminal not-work response is treated as an incorrect response, it does not actually provide any empirical documentation of what the child does or does not know or of what the child can and cannot do. The only information available is that the child did not respond to the demand. (p. 322)

The essential lesson of this study is that culturally based differences in response style may function to conceal the underlying competence of some examinees. Cautious interpretation of test results is always advisable, but this is especially important for examinees from culturally or linguistically diverse backgrounds.

The influence of cultural factors is not limited to the test performance of children but extends to adults as well. Terrell, Terrell, and Taylor (1981) investigated the effects of racial trust/mistrust on the intelligence test scores of African American college students. They identified African American students with high and low levels of mistrust of whites. Using a 2 × 2 design, half of each group was then administered an individual intelligence test by a white examiner, the other half by an African American examiner. As predicted, the analysis of variance revealed no differences for the main effects of race of examiner (white versus African American) or level of mistrust (high versus low) (Figure 1.6). But a substantial interaction was revealed; namely, the high-mistrust group with an African American examiner scored much better than the high-mistrust group with a white examiner (average IQs of 96 versus 86, respectively). Put simply, cultural mistrust among African Americans was associated with significantly lower IQ scores, but *only* when the examiner was white.

Further illustrating cultural influences, Steele (1997) has proposed a theory that societal stereotypes about groups influence the immediate intellectual performance and also the long-term identity development of individual group members. He has applied this theory both to women—when stereotypes affect their achievement in math and sciences—and to African Americans—when stereotypes apparently depress their performance on standardized tests. Here we discuss his research on stereotype threat with African American college students (Steele & Aronson, 1995).

The idea of stereotype threat is essentially a sophisticated version of a self-fulfilling prophecy. The researchers define **stereotype threat** as the threat of confirming, as self-characteristic, a negative stereotype about one's group. For example, based on published data and media coverage about race and IQ scores, African Americans are stereotyped as possessing less intellectual ability than others. As a consequence, whenever they encounter tests of intelligence or academic achievement, individuals from this group may perceive a risk that they will confirm the stereotype. In the short run, stereotype threat is hypothesized to depress test performance through heightened anxiety and other mechanisms. In the long run, it may have the further impact of pressuring African American students to "protectively disidentify" with achievement in school and related intellectual domains.

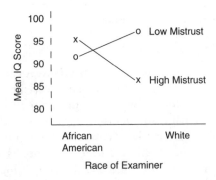

● **FIGURE 1.6** Mean IQ Scores of African American Students as a Function of Race of Examiner and Cultural Mistrust

*Source:* Based on data in Terrell, F., Terrell, S., & Taylor, J. (1981). Effects of race of examiner and cultural mistrust on the WAIS performance of Black students. *Journal of Consulting and Clinical Psychology, 49,* 750–751.

Steele and Aronson (1995) conducted a series of four studies to evaluate the hypothesis of stereotype threat. All the investigations supported the hypothesis. We focus here on the first study, in which African American and white college students were given a 30-minute test composed of challenging items from the verbal Graduate Record Examination. Students from both racial groups were randomly assigned to one of three test conditions: stereotype-threat, in which the test was described as diagnostic of individual verbal ability; control, in which the test was described as a research tool only; and control-challenge, in which the test was described as a research tool only but participants were exhorted to "take this challenge seriously." Scores on the verbal test were adjusted (covariate analysis) on the basis of prior achievement scores so as to eliminate the effects of preexisting differences between groups.

Race differences were small and nonsignificant in the control and control-challenge conditions, whereas African Americans scored much lower than whites in the stereotype-threat condition (Figure 1.7). In other studies, Steele and Aronson

(1995) investigated the mechanism of mediation by which stereotype threat caused African Americans to score lower on standardized tests. The details are beyond the scope of this text, but the overall conclusion is not:

> Our best assessment is that stereotype threat caused an inefficiency of processing much like that caused by other evaluative pressures. Stereotype-threatened participants spent more time doing fewer items more inaccurately—probably as a result of alternating their attention between trying to answer the items and trying to assess the self-significance of their frustration. (Steele & Aronson, 1995, p. 809)

In sum, the authors propose a social-psychological perspective on the meaning of lower test scores in African Americans and perhaps other stereotype-threatened groups as well. Their viewpoint emphasizes that test results do not reside within individuals. Test scores occur within a complex social-psychological field that is potentially influenced by national history, predicaments of race, and many other subtle factors.

## ● UNINTENDED EFFECTS OF HIGH-STAKES TESTING

The prevailing view in the general public is that cheating rarely or never occurs in nationally administered testing programs. We tend to think that the risks are too high and the opportunities too limited for cheaters to prevail. Therefore, we rest assured that test fraud must be a rare event. Unfortunately, this view is probably naive. After all, a growing number of people must pass a test to gain college entry, get a job, or obtain a promotion. Furthermore, school officials increasingly are evaluated on the basis of average test scores in their district. Precisely because the stakes are so high, unscrupulous individuals will try to beat the system.

Widespread cheating in public school systems is sporadically reported in many large cities across the United States. In most cases, the cheating is motivated by the desire of teachers and principals to further their own careers by creating the

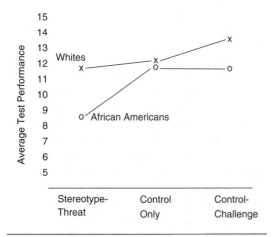

● **FIGURE 1.7** Average Verbal Items Correct for Whites and African Americans under Three Conditions

*Source:* Based on data in Steele, C. M., & Aronson, J. (1995). Stereotype threat and the intellectual test performance of African Americans. *Journal of Personality and Social Psychology, 69,* 797–811.

illusion of educational excellence. For example, in 1999, dozens of teachers and two principals in the New York City public school system were charged with helping students cheat on the standardized reading and math tests used to rank schools and determine whether students move on to the next grade (*New York Times,* December 12, 1999). The cheating scheme was described as "one of the largest in the recent history of American public schools." In 2000, an entire eighth-grade class in a Chicago elementary school was required to retake the Iowa Tests of Basic Skills because a school administrator allegedly filled in incomplete tests and changed incorrect answers to correct ones (*Chicago Tribune,* June 2, 2000). Officials were tipped off to the fraud because the test scores were simply too good to be true—the *average* score for the class was two years above their standing. In 2005, the *Dallas Morning News* reported strong evidence of "organized, educator-led cheating" in dozens of schools on the statewide achievement test and found suspicious scores in *hundreds* more (www.dallasnews.com, March 21, 2005). Disturbingly, one assessment expert noted, "You're catching the dumb cheaters. The smart cheaters you're not going to be able to detect." We only read about the cases of cheating that are detected. The number of undetected cases is simply unknown, although probably larger than the public would like to believe.

An especially flagrant instance of cheating on national tests was uncovered in Louisiana in 1997. This case involved wholesale circulation of the Educational Testing Service (ETS) exam administered to teachers who want to be school principals. As reported in the *New York Times* (September 28, 1997), copies of the 145-item test, along with correct answers, had circulated among teachers throughout southern Louisiana, most likely for several years. In a state ranked at or near the bottom on nearly every educational index, it appears that many potentially unqualified persons cheated their way into running the schools. ETS handled this case quietly by asking more than 200 teachers to retake the test so as to "confirm" their initial scores. Unfortunately, the Louisiana case was not an isolated instance. In another case, ETS

allegedly failed to monitor its handling of the federal government's test for immigrants who want to become citizens, with the likely result that test supervisors accepted bribes. English-proficiency tests for foreign students also were vulnerable to cheating. In 1994, ETS canceled the scores of 30,000 students from China after discovering a ring that was selling the examinations abroad. Cizek (1999) catalogues literally dozens of ingenious ways that students have developed for cheating on tests: writing information on the floor, in tissues, on the back of a bottled water label; using an ultraviolet pen to write information on "blank" paper; and using a video transmitter (e.g., hidden in an eyeglass case) to send pictures of the test to an outside accomplice who then coaches the student by means of an audio receiver (e.g., hidden in the ear).

Stories about miniature transmitters are not fanciful. Consider the following story reported from a monolithic culture where test results literally make or break a child's future. In China, 10 million 18-year-olds take a two day exam each year that determines whether they will be allowed to attend public universities. Success or failure drastically impacts their lives and those of their families who might depend on their future income. In 2009, eight parents were jailed for up to three years after it was determined that they were transmitting stolen test answers to their children through miniature earpieces. The subterfuge was discovered when police detected unusual radio signals near the school (www.guardian.co.uk, April 3, 2009).

Recently, efforts to circumvent exam security have become even more brazen, with some test preparation companies encouraging students to *steal* copies of college entrance exams such as the Scholastic Assessment Tests (SAT) (*Los Angeles Times,* October 12, 2005). Fortunately, the publisher of the SAT was granted a restraining order in federal court, prohibiting individuals or companies from soliciting stolen copies of the test. Even so, this episode illustrates once again that high-stakes testing has had a corrupting influence on the testing process.

Dishonest and inappropriate practices by school officials are implicated in the recent inflation of scores on nationally normed group tests of achievement. By definition, for a norm-referenced test, 50 percent of the examinees should score above the 50th percentile, 50 percent below. If the same test is used in a large sample of typical and representative school systems, average scores for the school systems should be split evenly—about half above the nationally normed 50th percentile, half below.

According to a survey reported in the news media (Foster, 1990), virtually all states of the union claim that average achievement scores for their school systems exceed the 50th percentile. The resulting overly optimistic picture of student achievement is labeled the **Lake Wobegon Effect**, in reference to humorist Garrison Keillor's mythical Minnesota town where "all the children are above average."

How does inflation of achievement test scores arise? According to Cannell (1988), the major cause is educational administrators who are desperate to demonstrate the excellence of their school systems. Precisely because our society attaches so much importance to achievement test results, some educators apparently help students cheat on standardized tests. The alleged cheating includes the following:

- Teachers and principals coach students on test answers.
- Examiners give more than the allotted time to take tests.
- Administrators alter answer sheets.
- Teachers teach directly to the specific test items.
- Teachers make copies of the tests to give to their students.

In sum, the importance that our society attaches to achievement test scores has caused a number of unappealing side effects that undermine the very foundations of nationally normed group-testing programs.

Moore (1994) reports on a special case in educational testing, namely, the districtwide consequences of court-ordered achievement testing. He surveyed 79 teachers from third- through fifth-grade level in a midwestern town in which the court

required the use of a standardized test to determine the effectiveness of a desegregation effort. The test in question, the Iowa Tests of Basic Skills (ITBS), is a well-respected group achievement test that requires strict adherence to instructions and time limits for obtaining valid results. Yet the teachers found little value in the testing program, complaining that its benefits did not offset the time and costs involved. As a consequence of their devaluing the effort, nonstandard testing was practically the rule rather than the exception. The teachers engaged in several nonstandard practices, most of which tended to inflate the test scores. Inappropriate testing practices included praising students who answered a question correctly during the test (67 percent), using last year's test questions for practice (44 percent), recoding a student's answer sheet because he or she just "miscoded" the answer (26 percent), giving students as much time as they needed (24 percent), giving students items that were directly off the test (24 percent), and giving hints or clues during the test (23 percent). In general, Moore (1994) notes that teachers modified their instructional efforts and curriculum in anticipation of having their students take the test. More than 90 percent of the teachers added test-related lessons to the curriculum, and more than 70 percent eliminated topics so that they could spend more time on test-related skills.

What this study demonstrates is that mandated educational testing can have the unanticipated consequence of polluting the validity of a worthy test—especially when crucial stakeholders have no voice in the process.

Further, in teaching to the tests, educators may emphasize bits and pieces of factual knowledge rather than imparting a general ability to think clearly and solve problems. In conclusion, it appears that an excessive emphasis on nationally normed achievement tests for selection and evaluation promotes inappropriate behavior, including outright fraud and cheating on the part of students and school officials. Just how widespread is the problem? Although we live with the optimistic assumption that fraud in nationally normed testing programs is rare, the disturbing truth is that we really don't know how often this occurs.

## ● REPRISE: RESPONSIBLE TEST USE

We return now to the real-life quandaries of testing mentioned at the beginning of the topic. The reader will recall that the first quandary had to do with whether a consulting psychologist responsibly could refuse to provide feedback to police officer candidates referred for preemployment screening. Surprisingly, the answer to this query is "Yes." Under normal circumstances, a practitioner must explain assessment results to the client. But there are exceptions, as explained by Principle 9.10 of the APA Ethical Code:

> Psychologists take reasonable steps to ensure that explanations of results are given to the individual or designated representative unless the nature of the relationship precludes provision of an explanation of results (such as in some organizational consulting, preemployment or security screenings, and forensic evaluations), and this fact has been clearly explained to the person being assessed in advance.

The second quandary concerned a counselor who continued to use the MMPI even though the MMPI-2 has been available for several years. Is the counselor's refusal to use the MMPI-2 a breach of professional standards? The answer to this query is probably "Yes." The MMPI-2 is well validated and constitutes a significant improvement upon the MMPI. As mentioned previously, the MMPI-2 is now the standard of care in MMPI-based assessment of psychopathology. The counselor who continued to rely on the original MMPI could be liable for malpractice suits, especially if his test interpretations resulted in misleading interpretive statements or a false diagnosis.

The third predicament involved the use of a neighborhood friend as translator in the administration of the WISC-IV to a 9-year-old boy whose first language was Spanish. This is usually a mistake as it sacrifices strict control of the testing material. The examiner was not bilingual and, therefore, he would have no way of knowing whether the translator was remaining faithful to the original text or was possibly supplying additional cues. In an ideal world, the proper procedure would be to enlist a Spanish-speaking examiner who would use a test formally translated and also standardized with Hispanic examinees. For example, the Escala de Inteligencia Wechsler Para Ninos-Revisada de Puerto Rico (EIWN-R PR) would be a good choice.

The final quandary concerned the client who informed a psychologist that her recently deceased brother was most likely a pedophile. Is the psychologist obligated to report this case to law enforcement? The answer to this query is probably "Yes," but it may depend on the jurisdiction of the psychologist and the wording of the relevant statutes. In fact, the psychologist did report the case to authorities with unexpected consequences. Police obtained a search warrant, went to the home of the client's mother (where the brother had lived), and ransacked the brother's bedroom. The mother was traumatized by the unexpected visit from the police and blamed the fiasco on her daughter. A bitter estrangement followed, and the client then sued the psychologist for violation of confidentiality!

## ● SUMMARY

1. As is true of all professional activities of psychologists, testing is guided by ethical and professional standards. Responsible test use is defined by written guidelines published by professional associations such as the American Psychological Association and other groups.

2. Test publishers also follow professional guidelines, including the expectation that they will release tests of high quality, market their products in a responsible manner, and restrict distribution of tests only to persons with proper qualifications.

3. Although there are exceptions, testing is generally guided by one overriding question: What is in the best interests of the client? The functional implication of this guideline is that assessment should serve a constructive purpose for the individual examinee.

4. Psychologists have a primary obligation to safeguard the confidentiality of information, including test results, that they obtain from clients in the course of consultations. Exceptions include those unusual circumstances in which the withholding of information would present a clear danger to the client or other persons.

5. Psychologists have a duty to warn that stems from the 1976 decision in the *Tarasoff* case. Clinicians must communicate any serious threat to a potential victim, law enforcement agencies, or both.

6. The ultimate responsibility for the proper application of tests always rests with the test user. From a practical standpoint, this means that the test user must be well trained in assessment and measurement theory.

7. The professional standard on informed consent provides that test takers must be informed of the reasons for testing, the types of tests to be used, the possible consequences of the testing, and what testing information will be released and to whom.

8. The prevailing standard of care is one that is usual, customary, or reasonable. Meeting the standard of care means that psychologists should refrain from using outdated tests, especially when a new edition is available.

9. Other guidelines for the responsible use of tests include thoughtful and effective report writing, as well as a reflective and sensitive delivery of feedback to examinees in which their misconceptions are carefully dispelled.

10. Another expectation is that assessment will be guided by a knowledge of, and respect for, individual differences. For example, practitioners should know about the effects of age, gender, race, ethnicity, and other background variables on test results.

11. Cultural factors that may influence test results include the *qualitative* manner of approaching a test, racial trust/mistrust, and stereotype threat, which is the threat of confirming, as self-characteristic, a negative stereotype about one's group.

12. Linguistic barriers also may inhibit test performance of minority individuals. Bilingual persons and individuals whose first language is not English may encounter subtle problems on tests developed for use in the dominant culture.

13. A lack of sophistication about the nature of tests is another factor encountered by some minority individuals. Linguistic barriers and a lack of sophistication about testing are strong arguments in favor of using a *multidisciplinary* approach to assessment (e.g., psychology, speech, reading specialists).

14. The prevalence of cheating on nationally administered achievement tests is unknown. However, many reports have surfaced in recent years, including the alteration of answer sheets by school officials, wholesale circulation of some licensing examinations, and inappropriate testing practices by individual teachers (e.g., giving extra time to finish tests).

## ● KEY TERMS AND CONCEPTS

duty to warn   p. 27

informed consent   p. 28

standard of care   p. 30

stereotype threat   p. 34

Lake Wobegon Effect   p. 37

# Chapter 2

# The History of Psychological Testing

## The Origins of Psychological Testing

The history of psychological testing is a fascinating story and has abundant relevance to present-day practices. After all, contemporary tests did not spring from a vacuum; they evolved slowly from a host of precursors introduced over the last one hundred years. Accordingly, Chapter 2 features a review of the historical roots of present-day psychological tests. In Topic 2A, The Origins of Psychological Testing, we focus largely on the efforts of European psychologists to measure intelligence during the late nineteenth century and pre–World War I era. These early intelligence tests

and their successors often exerted powerful effects on the examinees who took them, so the first topic also documents the historical impact of psychological test results. Topic 2B, Early Testing in the United States, catalogues the profusion of tests developed by American psychologists in the first half of the twentieth century.

Psychological testing in its modern form originated little more than one hundred years ago in laboratory studies of sensory discrimination, motor skills, and reaction time. The British genius Francis Galton (1822–1911) invented the first battery of tests, a peculiar assortment of sensory and motor measures, which we review in the following. The American psychologist James McKeen Cattell (1860–1944) studied with Galton and then, in 1890, proclaimed the modern testing agenda in his classic paper entitled "Mental Tests and Measurements." He was tentative and modest when describing the purposes and applications of his instruments:

> Psychology cannot attain the certainty and exactness of the physical sciences, unless it rests on a foundation of experiment and measurement. A step in this direction could be made by applying a series of mental tests and measurements to a large number of individuals. The results would be of considerable scientific value in discovering the constancy of mental processes, their interdependence, and their variation under different circumstances. Individuals, besides, would find their tests interesting, and, perhaps, useful in regard to training, mode of life or indication of disease. The scientific and practical value of such tests would be much increased should a uniform system be adopted, so that determinations made at different times and places could be compared and combined. (Cattell, 1890)

Cattell's conjecture that "perhaps" tests would be useful in "training, mode of life or indication of disease" must certainly rank as one of the prophetic understatements of all time. Anyone reared in the Western world knows that psychological testing has emerged from its timid beginnings to become a big business and a cultural institution that permeates modern society.

As we shall see, the importance of testing is evident from historical review. Students of psychology generally regard historical issues as dull, dry, and pedantic, and sometimes these prejudices are well deserved. After all, many textbooks fail to explain the relevance of historical matters and provide only vague sketches of early developments in mental testing. As a result, students of psychology often conclude incorrectly that historical issues are boring and irrelevant.

In reality, the history of psychological testing is a captivating story that has substantial relevance to present-day practices. In later chapters, we examine the principles of psychological testing, investigate

applications in specific fields (e.g., personality, intelligence, neuro-psychology), and reflect on the social and legal consequences of testing. However, the reader will find these topics more comprehensible when viewed in historical context. So, for now, we begin at the beginning by reviewing rudimentary forms of testing that existed over four thousand years ago in imperial China.

## ● RUDIMENTARY FORMS OF TESTING IN CHINA IN 2200 B.C.

Although the widespread use of psychological testing is largely a phenomenon of the twentieth century, historians note that rudimentary forms of testing date back to at least 2200 B.C. when the Chinese emperor had his officials examined every third year to determine their fitness for office (Bowman, 1989; Chaffee, 1985; Franke, 1963; Teng, 1942–43). Such testing was modified and refined over the centuries until written exams were introduced in the Han dynasty (202 B.C.–A.D. 200). Five topics were tested: civil law, military affairs, agriculture, revenue, and geography.

The Chinese examination system took its final form about 1370 when proficiency in the Confucian classics was emphasized. In the preliminary examination, candidates were required to spend a day and a night in a small isolated booth, composing essays on assigned topics and writing a poem. The 1 to 7 percent who passed moved up to the district examinations, which required three separate sessions of three days and three nights.

The district examinations were obviously grueling and rigorous, but this was not the final level. The 1 to 10 percent who passed were allowed the privilege of going to Peking for the final round of examinations. Perhaps 3 percent of this final group passed and became mandarins, eligible for public office.

Although the Chinese developed the external trappings of a comprehensive civil service examination program, the similarities between their traditions and current testing practices are, in the main, superficial. Not only were their testing practices unnecessarily grueling, but the Chinese also failed to validate their selection procedures. Nonetheless, it does appear that the examination program incorporated relevant selection criteria. For example, in the written exams beauty of penmanship was weighted very heavily. Given the highly stylistic features of Chinese written forms, good penmanship was no doubt essential for clear, exact communication. Thus, penmanship was probably a relevant predictor of suitability for civil service employment. In response to widespread discontent, the examination system was abolished by royal decree in 1906 (Franke, 1963).

## ● PHYSIOGNOMY, PHRENOLOGY, AND THE PSYCHOGRAPH

**Physiognomy** is based on the notion that we can judge the inner character of people from their outward appearance, especially the face. Albeit misguided and now largely discredited, physiognomy represents an early form of psychological testing. Hence, we provide a primer on the topic, including its more recent cousin, phrenology.

Interest in physiognomy can be dated to the fourth century, when the Greek philosopher Aristotle (384–322 B.C.) published a short treatise based on the premise that the soul and the body "sympathize" with each other. Essentially, Aristotle argued that changes in a person's soul (inner character) could impact the appearance of the body, and vice versa. The relationship between the two allowed the astute observer to infer personality characteristics from individual appearance. Aristotle catalogued a vast array of traits that could be discerned from features of hair, forehead, eyebrows, eyes, nose, lips, and so on. Here are some examples:

> Hair that hangs down without curling, if it be of a fair complexion, thin, and soft withal, signifies a man to be naturally fainthearted, and of a weak body but of a quiet and harmless disposition. Hair that is big, and thick, and short withal, denotes a man to be of a strong constitution, secure, and deceitful, and for the most part unquiet, and vain, lusting after beauty, and more foolish than wise,

> though fortune may favor him. (Aristotle, *Of Physiognomy,* www.exclassics.com/arist/arist63.htm)

Many other classical Latin authors wrote about physiognomy, including Juvenal, Suetonius, and Pliny the Elder. But it was not until centuries later that physiognomy began to flourish when a Swiss theologian penned a popular best-seller on the topic.

Johann Lavater (1741–1801) published his *Essays on Physiognomy* in Germany in the late eighteenth century. English and French translations followed shortly and sales exploded in Western Europe and the United States. Eventually, more than 150 editions of the text were published (Graham, 1961). Lavater's book contained hundreds of meticulous drawings depicting his principles of physiognomy by which character could be judged from details of facial appearance. Lukasik (2004) describes the allure of this approach:

> Since Lavaterian physiognomy read moral character from unalterable and involuntary facial features, it created a visual system for discerning a person's permanent moral character despite his or her social masks. Readers of the 1817 *Pocket Lavater,* for instance, learned how to look at the features of various white male faces in order to discriminate "the physiognomy of . . . a man of business" from that of "a rogue." (p. 1)

Physiognomy remained popular for centuries and laid the foundation for the more specialized form of quackery known as **phrenology**—reading "bumps" on the head.

The founding of **phrenology** is usually attributed to the German physician Franz Joseph Gall (1758–1828). His "science" actually was based on a veneer of plausibility. In his major work, *The Anatomy and Physiology of the Nervous System in General, and of the Brain in Particular* (1810), Gall argued that the brain is the organ of sentiments and faculties and that these capacities are localized. Furthermore, he reasoned, to the extent that a specific faculty was well developed, the corresponding component of the brain would be enlarged. In turn, because the skull conforms to the shape of the brain, a cranial "bump" would signify an enlargement of the underlying faculty. These plausible (but incorrect) assumptions allowed Gall and his followers to decide if an individual was amorous, secretive, hopeful, combative, benevolent, self-confident, happy, imitative—in all, dozens of traits were discerned from cranial bumps.

Johann Spurzheim (1776–1832), a disciple of Gall, popularized phrenology and disseminated it to the United States and Great Britain, where it became enormously popular. In fact, a few entrepreneurs developed automated devices to measure the bumps with precision. In 1931, after decades of tinkering, Henry C. Lavery, a self-proclaimed genius and ardent believer in phrenology, spent a small fortune developing his machine known as the Psychograph (McCoy, 2000). It consisted of hundreds of moving parts assembled in a large helmet-like device fitted over the examinee's head. Each of 32 mental faculties was rated 1 through 5 ("deficient" to "very superior") based on the way that probes made contact with the head. A belt-driven motor stamped out statements for each of the 32 faculties, providing one of the first automated personality descriptions. Initially, the Psychograph was a spectacular success, and its promoters earned small fortunes. But by the mid-1930s public skepticism held sway, and the company that manufactured the instrument went out of business (McCoy, 2000).

## ● THE BRASS INSTRUMENTS ERA OF TESTING

Experimental psychology flourished in the late 1800s in continental Europe and Great Britain. For the first time in history, psychologists departed from the wholly subjective and introspective methods that had been so fruitlessly pursued in the preceding centuries. Human abilities were instead tested in laboratories. Researchers used objective procedures that were capable of replication. Gone were the days when rival laboratories would have raging arguments about "imageless thought," one group saying it existed, another group saying that such a mental event was impossible.

Even though the new emphasis on objective methods and measurable quantities was a vast improvement over the largely sterile mentalism that preceded it, the new experimental psychology was itself a dead end, at least as far as psychological testing was concerned. The problem was that the early experimental psychologists mistook simple sensory processes for intelligence. They used assorted brass instruments to measure sensory thresholds and reaction times, thinking that such abilities were at the heart of intelligence. Hence, this period is sometimes referred to as the Brass Instruments era of psychological testing.

In spite of the false start made by early experimentalists, at least they provided psychology with an appropriate methodology. Such pioneers as Wundt, Galton, Cattell, and Clark Wissler showed that it was possible to expose the mind to scientific scrutiny and measurement. This was a fateful change in the axiomatic assumptions of psychology, a change that has stayed with us to the current day.

Most sources credit Wilhelm Wundt (1832–1920) with founding the first psychological laboratory in 1879 in Leipzig, Germany. It is less well recognized that he was measuring mental processes years before, at least as early as 1862, when he experimented with his thought meter (Diamond, 1980). This device was a calibrated pendulum with needles sticking off from each side. The pendulum would swing back and forth, striking bells with the needles. The observer's task was to take note of the position of the pendulum when the bells sounded. Of course, Wundt could adjust the needles beforehand and thereby know the precise position of the pendulum when each bell was struck. Wundt thought that the difference between the observed pendulum position and the actual position would provide a means of determining the swiftness of thought of the observer.

Wundt's analysis was relevant to a longstanding problem in astronomy. The problem was that two or more astronomers simultaneously using the same telescope (with multiple eyepieces) would report different crossing times as the stars moved across a grid line on the telescope. Even in Wundt's time, it was a well-known event in the history of science that Kinnebrook, an assistant at the Royal Observatory in England, had been dismissed in

1796 because his stellar crossing times were nearly a full second too slow (Boring, 1950). Wundt's analysis offered another explanation that did not assume incompetence on the part of anyone. Put simply, Wundt believed that the speed of thought might differ from one person to the next:

> For each person there must be a certain speed of thinking, which he can never exceed with his given mental constitution. But just as one steam engine can go faster than another, so this speed of thought will probably not be the same in all persons. (Wundt, 1862, as translated in Rieber, 1980)

This analysis of telescope reporting times seems simplistic by present-day standards and overlooks the possible contribution of such factors as attention, motivation, and self-correcting feedback from prior trials. On the positive side, this was at least an empirical analysis that sought to explain individual differences instead of trying to explain them away. And that is the relevance to current practices in psychological testing. However crudely, Wundt measured mental processes and begrudgingly acknowledged individual differences. This emphasis on individual differences was rare for Wundt. He is more renowned for proposing common laws of thought for the average adult mind.

## Galton and the First Battery of Mental Tests

Sir Francis Galton (1822–1911) pioneered the new experimental psychology in nineteenth-century Great Britain. Galton was obsessed with measurement, and his intellectual career seems to have been dominated by a belief that virtually anything was measurable. His attempts to measure intellect by means of reaction time and sensory discrimination tasks are well known. Yet, to appreciate his wide-ranging interests, the reader should be apprised that Galton also devised techniques for measuring beauty, personality, the boringness of lectures, and the efficacy of prayer, to name but a few of the endeavors that his biographer has catalogued in elaborate detail (Pearson 1914, 1924, 1930ab).

Galton was a genius who was more interested in the problems of human evolution than in psychology per se (Boring, 1950). His two most influential works were *Hereditary Genius* (1869), an empirical analysis purporting to prove that genetic factors were overwhelmingly important for the attainment of eminence, and *Inquiries into Human Faculty and Its Development* (1883), a disparate series of essays that emphasized individual differences in mental faculties.

Boring (1950) regards *Inquiries* as the beginning of the mental test movement and the advent of the scientific psychology of individual differences. The book is a curious mixture of empirical research and speculative essays on topics as diverse as "just perceptible differences" in lifted weight and diminished fertility among inbred animals. There is, nonetheless, a common theme uniting these diverse essays; Galton demonstrates time and again that individual differences not only exist but also are objectively measurable.

Galton borrowed the time-consuming psychophysical procedures practiced by Wundt and others on the European continent and adapted them to a series of simple and quick sensorimotor measures. Thus, he continued the tradition of brass instruments mental testing but with an important difference: his procedures were much more amenable to the timely collection of data from hundreds if not thousands of subjects. Because of his efforts in devising practicable measures of individual differences, historians of psychological testing usually regard Galton as the father of mental testing (Goodenough, 1949; Boring, 1950).

To further his study of individual differences, Galton set up a psychometric laboratory in London at the International Health Exhibition in 1884. It was later transferred to the London Museum, where it was maintained for six years. Various anthropometric and psychometric measures were arranged on a long table at one side of a narrow room. Subjects were admitted at one end for threepence and given successive tests as they moved down the table. At least 17,000 individuals were tested during the 1880s and 1890s. About 7,500 of the individual data records have survived to the present day (Johnson et al., 1985).

The tests and measures involved both the physical and behavioral domains. Physical characteristics assessed were height, weight, head length, head breadth, arm span, length of middle finger, and length of lower arm, among others. The behavioral tests included strength of hand squeeze determined by dynamometer, vital capacity of the lungs measured by spirometer, visual acuity, highest audible tone, speed of blow, and reaction time (RT) to both visual and auditory stimuli.

Ultimately, Galton's simplistic attempts to gauge intellect with measures of reaction time and sensory discrimination proved fruitless. Nonetheless, he did provide a tremendous impetus to the testing movement by demonstrating that objective tests could be devised and that meaningful scores could be obtained through standardized procedures.

## Cattell Imports Brass Instruments to the United States

James McKeen Cattell (1860–1944) studied the new experimental psychology with both Wundt and Galton before settling at Columbia University where, for 26 years, he was the undisputed dean of American psychology. With Wundt, he did a series of painstakingly elaborate RT studies (1880–1882), measuring with great precision the fractions of a second presumably required for different mental reactions. He also noted, almost in passing, that he and another colleague had small but consistent differences in RT. Cattell proposed to Wundt that such individual differences ought to be studied systematically. Although Wundt acknowledged individual differences, he was philosophically more inclined to study general features of the mind, and he offered no support for Cattell's proposal (Fancher, 1985).

But Cattell received enthusiastic support for his study of individual differences from Galton, who had just opened his psychometric laboratory in London. After corresponding with Galton for a few years, Cattell arranged for a two-year fellowship at Cambridge so that he could continue the study of individual differences. Cattell opened his own research laboratory and developed a series of tests that were mainly extensions and additions to Galton's battery.

Cattell (1890) invented the term *mental test* in his famous paper entitled "Mental Tests and Measurements." This paper described his research program, detailing 10 mental tests he proposed for use with the general public. These tests were clearly a reworking and embellishment of the Galtonian tradition:

Strength of hand squeeze as measured by dynamometer

Rate of hand movement through a distance of 50 centimeters

Two-point threshold for touch—minimum distance at which two points are still perceived as separate

Degree of pressure needed to cause pain—rubber tip pressed against the forehead

Weight differentiation—discern the relative weights of identical-looking boxes varying by one gram from 100 to 110 grams

Reaction time for sound—using a device similar to Galton's

Time for naming colors

Bisection of a 50-centimeter line

Judgment of 10 seconds of time

Number of letters repeated on one hearing

Strength of hand squeeze seems a curious addition to a battery of mental tests, a point that Cattell (1890) addressed directly in his paper. He was of the opinion that it was impossible to separate bodily energy from mental energy. Thus, in Cattell's view, an ostensibly physiological measure such as dynamometer pressure was an index of one's mental power as well. Clearly, the physiological and sensory bias of the entire test battery reflects its strongly Galtonian heritage (Fancher, 1985).

In 1891, Cattell accepted a position at Columbia University, at that time the largest university in the United States. His subsequent influence on American psychology was far in excess of his individual scientific output and was expressed in large part through his numerous and influential students (Boring, 1950). Among his many famous doctoral students and the years of their degrees were E. L. Thorndike (1898) who made monumental contributions to learning theory and educational psychology; R. S. Woodworth (1899) who was to author the very popular and influential *Experimental Psychology* (1938); and E. K. Strong (1911) whose Vocational Interest Blank—since revised—is still in wide use. But among Cattell's students, it was probably Clark Wissler (1901) who had the greatest influence on the early history of psychological testing.

Wissler obtained both mental test scores and academic grades from more than 300 students at Columbia University and Barnard College. His goal was to demonstrate that the test results could predict academic performance. With our early twenty-first-century perspective on research and testing, it seems amazing that the early experimentalists waited so long to do such basic validational research. Wissler's (1901) results showed virtually no tendency for the mental test scores to correlate with academic achievement. For example, class standing correlated .16 with memory for number lists, −.08 with dynamometer strength, .02 with color naming, and −.02 with reaction time. The highest correlation (.16) was statistically significant because of the large sample size. However, so humble a correlation carries with it very little predictive utility.[1]

Also damaging to the brass instruments testing movement was the very modest correlations between the mental tests themselves. For example, color naming and hand movement speed correlated only .19, while RT and color naming correlated −.15. Several physical measures such as head size (a holdover measure from the Galton era) were, not surprisingly, also uncorrelated with the various sensory and RT measures.

With the publication of Wissler's (1901) discouraging results, experimental psychologists largely abandoned the use of RT and sensory discrimination as measures of intelligence. This turning away from the brass instruments approach was a desirable development in the history of psychological testing. The way was thereby paved for immediate acceptance of Alfred Binet's more sensible and useful measures of higher mental processes.

A common reaction among psychologists in the early 1900s was to begrudgingly conclude that Galton had been wrong in attempting to infer complex abilities from simple ones. Goodenough (1949) has likened Galton's approach to "inferring the nature of genius from the nature of stupidity or the qualities of water from those of the hydrogen and oxygen of which it is composed." The academic psychologists apparently agreed with her, and American attempts to develop intelligence tests virtually ceased at the turn of the twentieth century. For his own part, Wissler was apparently so discouraged by his results that he immediately switched to anthropology, where he became a strong environmentalist in explaining differences between ethnic groups.

The void created by the abandonment of the Galtonian tradition did not last for long. In Europe, Alfred Binet was on the verge of a major breakthrough in intelligence testing. Binet introduced his scale of intelligence in 1905, and shortly thereafter H. H. Goddard imported it to the United States, where it was applied in a manner that Gould (1981) has described as "the dismantling of Binet's intentions in America." Whether early twentieth-century American psychologists subverted Binet's intentions is an important question that we review in the next topic. First we turn to a more general topic, the rise of rating scales in the history of psychology.

## ● RATING SCALES AND THEIR ORIGINS

Rating scales are widely used in psychology as a means of quantifying subjective psychological variables of many kinds. An example of a simple rating scale might be the eleven-point scale used by doctors when they ask patients in the emergency room "On a

---

1. We discuss the correlation coefficient in more detail in Topic 3B, Concepts of Reliability. By way of quick preview, correlations can range from −1.0 to +1.0. Values near zero indicate a weak, negligible linear relationship between the two variables. For example, correlations between −.20 and +.20 are generally of minimal value for purposes of individual prediction. Note also that negative correlations indicate an inverse relationship.

scale from 0 to 10, where 0 is no pain at all, and 10 is the worst pain you have ever felt, how bad is your pain right now?" Albeit crude, this is a form of psychological measurement. Psychometricians have developed a rich literature on the qualities and applications of rating scales of this type (Guilford, 1954; Nunnally, 1967; Nunnally & Bernstein, 1994).

Historians of psychology used to think that numerical rating scales originated in the "brass instruments" era of Francis Galton (McReynolds & Ludwig, 1987). However, it now appears that a crude form of rating scale can be traced to Galen, the second century Greco-Roman physician. Galen believed in the prevailing humor theory of health and disease, in which the harmony or disharmony among four bodily fluids or "humors" determined one's health. The four humors were yellow bile, black bile, phlegm, and blood. The humorology of the time also featured the dichotomies of hot–cold and wet–dry as elements of health or illness. With respect to the hot-cold dimension, Galen recognized the need for something more sophisticated than a simple dichotomy:

> This standard, or neutral value, he suggested should be the temperature, as reflected in direct sense–perception, of a mixture of equal quantities of boiling water and ice (Taylor, 1942). Further, Galen proposed a convention of four degrees of heat and four degrees of cold, on either side of that standard, that could be induced in patients by various drugs (McReynolds & Ludwig, 1987, p. 281).

Although he did not say so explicitly, Galen was in effect proposing a nine-point rating scale consisting of four points above and four points below a neutral point. Whether the successive increases of heat or cold were equal in the hot-cold scale— what we would now refer to as the underlying scale of measurement—was an issue left to others, including the ninth-century Islamic philosopher, Al-kindi (Taylor, 1942). Al-kindi was an Arab polymath considered by many the father of Islamic philosophy. He questioned whether the successive degrees of heat and cold could be equal but did not propose a means for answering the inquiry. Al-kindi made important contributions in many fields, including astronomy, chemistry, and medicine (www.muslimphilosophy.com/kindi).

According to McReynolds and Ludwig (1984), the first person to devise and apply rating scales for psychological variables was Christian Thomasius (1655–1728). Thomasius was a German jurist and philosopher whose career spanned numerous fields of inquiry. He developed a theory of personality that posited four major dimensions—sensuousness, acquisitiveness, social ambition, and rational love. He employed judges to assess individuals on all four inclinations on a 12-point scale (5, 10, 15, 20, all the way up to 60). In 1692, he published numerical data—including reliability data—on five individuals as rated by himself and other judges. This was a landmark accomplishment: "This work appears to constitute the first systematic collection and analysis of quantitative empirical data in the entire history of psychology" (McReynolds & Ludwig, 1984, p. 282).

Ratings scale slowly caught on in the years after their first serious use by Thomasius. Among those applying these new devices were phrenologists, including the renowned practitioner Orson Fowler. Phrenology is described in an earlier section of this chapter. Fowler depicted the application of seven-point rating scales in his *Practical Phrenology* (1851). The bulges in different areas of the skull were rated as 1, VERY SMALL; 2, SMALL; 3, MODERATE; 4, AVERAGE; 5, FULL; 6, LARGE; 7, VERY LARGE. From these ratings, the relative strengths of specific moral and intellectual qualities were presumed to be quantified.[2]

The use of ratings scale may have provided Fowler's practice of phrenology a facade of respectability. Even so, this did not prevent his arrest in 1886 for practicing medicine without a license (New York Times, January 17, 1886). According to the *Times* article:

> The phrenologist denies that he practices medicine and asserts that he has violated no law, that he is simply a phrenologist, and does not give remedies

---

2. The common idiom "You should have your head examined" probably alludes to the (now discredited) practice of phrenology (Ammer, 2003).

to persons who apply to him to have their craniums examined. There was quite a crowd of patrons in the Professor's anteroom at the hotel when the detective served the warrant. Prof. Fowler was held to await action by the Grand Jury, and released on his own recognizance.

Phrenology, which surrounded itself with the trappings of science, including models of the head and brain, authoritative pronouncements, and, yes, even ratings scales, phrenology which flourished into the early 1900s, eventually faded into disrepute.

## ● CHANGING CONCEPTIONS OF MENTAL RETARDATION IN THE 1800s

Many great inventions have been developed in response to the practical needs created by changes in societal values. Such is the case with intelligence tests. To be specific, the first such tests were developed by Binet in the early 1900s to help identify children in the Paris school system who were unlikely to profit from ordinary instruction. Prior to this time, there was little interest in the educational needs of children with mental retardation. A new humanism toward those with mental retardation thus created the practical problem—identifying those with special needs—that Binet's tests were to solve.

The Western world of the late 1800s was just emerging from centuries of indifference and hostility toward the psychiatrically and mentally impaired. Medical practitioners were just beginning to acknowledge a distinction between individuals with emotional disablties and mental retardation. For centuries, all such social outcasts were given similar treatment. In the Middle Ages, they were occasionally "diagnosed" as witches and put to death by burning. Later on, they were alternately ignored, persecuted, or tortured. In his comprehensive history of psychotherapy and psychoanalysis, Bromberg (1959) has an especially graphic chapter on the various forms of maltreatment toward those with mental and emotional disabilities, from which only one example will be provided here. In 1698, a prominent physician wrote a gruesome book,

*Flagellum Salutis,* in which beatings were advocated as treatment "in melancholia; in frenzy; in paralysis; in epilepsy; in facial expression of feeble-minded" (Bromberg, 1959).

By the early 1800s, saner minds began to prevail. Medical practitioners realized that some of those with psychiatric impairment had reversible illnesses that did not necessarily imply diminished intellect, whereas other exceptional persons, those with mental retardation, showed a greater developmental continuity and invariably had impaired intellect. In addition, a newfound humanism began to influence social practices toward individuals with psychological and mental disabilities. With this humanism there arose a greater interest in the diagnosis and remediation of mental retardation. At the forefront of these developments were two French physicians, J. E. D. Esquirol and O. E. Seguin, each of whom revolutionized thinking about those with mental retardation, thereby helping to create the necessity for Binet's tests.

### Esquirol and Diagnosis in Mental Retardation

Around the beginning of the nineteenth century, many physicians had begun to perceive the difference between mental retardation (then called *idiocy*) and mental illness (often referred to as *dementia*). J. E. D. Esquirol (1772–1840) was the first to formalize the difference in writing. His diagnostic breakthrough was noting that mental retardation was a lifelong developmental phenomenon whereas mental illness usually had a more abrupt onset in adulthood. He thought that mental retardation was incurable, whereas mental illness might show improvement (Esquirol, 1845/1838).

Esquirol placed great emphasis on language skills in the diagnosis of mental retardation. This may offer a partial explanation as to why Binet's later tests and the modern-day descendents from them are so heavily loaded on linguistic abilities. After all, the original use of the Binet scales was, in the main, to identify children with mental retardation who would not likely profit from ordinary schooling.

Esquirol also proposed the first classification system in mental retardation and it should be no surprise that language skills were the main diagnostic criteria. He recognized three levels of mental retardation: (1) those using short phrases, (2) those using only monosyllables, and (3) those with cries only, no speech. Apparently, Esquirol did not recognize what we would now call *mild mental retardation,* instead providing criteria for the equivalents of the modern-day classifications of moderate, severe, and profound mental retardation.

## Seguin and Education of Individuals with Mental Retardation

Perhaps more than any other pioneer in the field of mental retardation, O. Edouard Seguin (1812–1880) helped establish a new humanism toward those with mental retardation in the late 1800s. He had been a student of Esquirol and had also studied with J. M. G. Itard (1774–1838), who is well known for his five-year attempt to train the Wild Boy of Aveyron, a feral child who had lived in the woods for his first 11 or 12 years (Itard, 1932/1801).

Seguin borrowed from techniques used by Itard and devoted his life to developing educational programs for persons with mental retardation. As early as 1838, he had established an experimental class for such individuals. His treatment efforts earned him international acclaim and he eventually came to the United States to continue his work. In 1866, he published *Idiocy, and Its Treatment by the Physiological Method,* the first major textbook on the treatment of mental retardation. This book advocated a surprisingly modern approach to education of individuals with mental retardation and even touched on what would now be called *behavior modification.*

Such was the social and historical background that allowed intelligence tests to flourish. We turn now to the invention of the modern-day intelligence test by Alfred Binet. We begin with a discussion of the early influences that shaped his famous test.

## ● INFLUENCE OF BINET'S EARLY RESEARCH ON HIS TEST

As most every student of psychology knows, Alfred Binet (1857–1911) invented the first modern intelligence test in 1905. What is less well known, but equally important for those who seek an understanding of his contributions to modern psychology, is that Binet was a prolific researcher and author long before he turned his attentions to intelligence testing. The character of his early research had a material bearing on the subsequent form of his well-known intelligence test. For those who seek a full understanding of his pathbreaking influence, brief mention of Binet's early career is mandatory. For more details the reader can consult Fancher (1985), Goodenough (1949), Gould (1981), and Wolf (1973).

Binet began his career in medicine but was forced to drop out because of a complete emotional breakdown. He switched to psychology, where he studied the two-point threshold and dabbled in the associationist psychology of John Stuart Mill (1806–1873). Later, he selected an apprenticeship with the neurologist J. M. Charcot (1825–1893) at the famous Salpetriere Hospital. Thus, for a brief time Binet's professional path paralleled that of Sigmund Freud, who also studied hysteria under Charcot. At the Salpetriere Hospital, Binet coauthored (with C. Fere) four studies supposedly demonstrating that reversing the polarity of a magnet could induce complete mood changes (e.g., from happy to sad) or transfer of hysterical paralysis (e.g., from left to right side) in a single hypnotized subject. In response to public criticism from other psychologists, Binet later published a recantation of his findings. This was a painful episode for Binet, and it sent his career into a temporary detour. Nonetheless, he learned two things through his embarrassment. First, he never again used sloppy experimental procedures that allowed for unintentional suggestion to influence his results. Second, he became skeptical of the zeitgeist (spirit of the times) in experimental psychology. Both of these lessons were applied when he later developed his intelligence scales.

In 1891, Binet went to work at the Sorbonne as an unpaid assistant and began a series of studies and publications that were to define his new "individual psychology" and ultimately to culminate in his intelligence tests. Binet was an ardent experimentalist, often using his two daughters to try out existing and new tests of intelligence. Binet's experiments with his children greatly influenced his views on proper testing procedures:

> The experimenter is obliged, to a point, to adjust his method to the subject he is addressing. There are certain rules to follow when one experiments on a child, just as there are certain rules for adults, for hysterics, and for the insane. These rules are not written down anywhere; each one learns them for himself and is repaid in great measure. By making an error and later accounting for the cause, one learns not to make the mistake a second time. In regard to children, it is necessary to be suspicious of two principal causes of error: suggestion and failure of attention. This is not the time to speak on the first point. As for the second, failure of attention, it is so important that it is always necessary to suspect it when one obtains a negative result. One must then suspend the experiments and take them up at a more favorable moment, restarting them 10 times, 20 times, with great patience. Children, in fact, are often little disposed to pay attention to experiments which are not entertaining, and it is useless to hope that one can make them more attentive by threatening them with punishment. By particular tricks, however, one can sometimes give the experiment a certain appeal. (Binet, 1895, quoted in Pollack, 1971)

It is interesting to contrast modern-day testing practices—which go so far as to specify the exact wording the examiner should use—with Binet's advice to exercise nearly endless patience and use entertaining tricks when testing children.

## ● BINET AND TESTING FOR HIGHER MENTAL PROCESSES

In 1896, Binet and his Sorbonne assistant, Victor Henri, published a pivotal review of German and American work on individual differences. In this historically important paper, they argued that intelligence could be better measured by means of the higher psychological processes rather than the elementary sensory processes such as reaction time. After several false starts, Binet and Simon eventually settled on the straightforward format of their 1905 scales, discussed subsequently.

The character of the 1905 scale owed much to a prior test developed by Dr. Blin (1902) and his pupil, M. Damaye. They had attempted to improve the diagnosis of mental retardation by using a battery of assessments in 20 areas such as spoken language; knowledge of parts of the body; obedience to simple commands; naming common objects; and ability to read, write, and do simple arithmetic. Binet criticized the scale for being too subjective, for having items reflecting formal education, and for using a yes or no format on many questions (DuBois, 1970). But he was much impressed with the idea of using a battery of tests, a feature that he adopted in his 1905 scales.

In 1904, the Minister of Public Instruction in Paris appointed a commission to decide on the educational measures that should be undertaken with those children who could not profit from regular instruction. The commission concluded that medical and educational examinations should be used to identify those children who could not learn by the ordinary methods. Furthermore, it was determined that these children should be removed from their regular classes and given special instruction suitable to their more limited intellectual prowess. This was the beginning of the special education classroom.

It was evident that a means of selecting children for such special placement was needed, and Binet and his colleague Simon were called on to develop a practical tool for just this purpose. Thus arose the first formal scale for assessing the intelligence of children.

The 30 tests on the 1905 scale ranged from utterly simple sensory tests to quite complex verbal abstractions. Thus, the scale was appropriate for assessing the entire gamut of intelligence—from severe mental retardation to high levels of giftedness. The entire scale is outlined in Table 2.1.

## ● TABLE 2.1  The 1905 Binet-Simon Scale

1. Follows a moving object with the eyes.
2. Grasps a small object which is touched.
3. Grasps a small object which is seen.
4. Recognizes the difference between a square of chocolate and a square of wood.
5. Finds and eats a square of chocolate wrapped in paper.
6. Executes simple commands and imitates simple gestures.
7. Points to familiar named objects, e.g., "Show me the cup."
8. Points to objects represented in pictures, e.g., "Put your finger on the window."
9. Names objects in pictures, e.g., "What is this?" [examiner points to a picture of a sign].
10. Compares two lines of markedly unequal length.
11. Repeats three spoken digits.
12. Compares two weights.
13. Shows susceptibility to suggestion.
14. Defines common words by function.
15. Repeats a sentence of 15 words.
16. Tells how two common objects are different, e.g., "paper and cardboard."
17. Names from memory as many as possible of 13 objects displayed on a board for 30 seconds. [This test was later dropped because it permitted too many possibilities for distraction.]
18. Reproduces from memory two designs shown for 10 seconds.
19. Repeats a longer series of digits than in item 11 to test immediate memory.
20. Tells how two common objects are alike, e.g., "butterfly and flea."
21. Compares two lines of slightly unequal length.
22. Compares five blocks to put them in order of weight.
23. Indicates which of the previous five weights the examiner has removed.
24. Produces rhymes, e.g., "What rhymes with 'school'?"
25. A word completion test based on those proposed by Ebbinghaus.
26. Puts three nouns, e.g., "Paris, river, fortune" (or three verbs) in a sentence.
27. Responds to 25 abstract (comprehension) questions, e.g., "When a person has offended you, and comes to offer his apologies, what should you do?"
28. Reverses the hands of a clock.
29. After paper folding and cutting, draws the form of the resulting holes.
30. Defines abstract words by designating the difference between, e.g., "boredom and weariness."

*Source:* Based on translations in Jenkins and Paterson (1961) and Jensen (1980).

Except for the very simplest tests, which were designed for the classification of very low-grade *idiots* (an unfortunate diagnostic term that has since been dropped), the tests were heavily weighted toward verbal skills, reflecting Binet's departure from the Galtonian tradition.

An interesting point that is often overlooked by contemporary students of psychology is that

Binet and Simon did not offer a precise method for arriving at a total score on their 1905 scale. It is well to remember that their purpose was classification, not measurement, and that their motivation was entirely humanitarian, namely, to identify those children who needed special educational placement. By contemporary standards, it is difficult to accept the fuzziness inherent in such an approach, but that may reflect a modern penchant for quantification more than a weakness in the 1905 scale. In fact, their scale was popular among educators in Paris. And, even with the absence of precise quantification, the approach was successful in selecting candidates for special classes.

## ● THE REVISED SCALES AND THE ADVENT OF IQ

In 1908, Binet and Simon published a revision of the 1905 scale. In the earlier scale, more than half the items had been designed for the very retarded, yet the major diagnostic decisions involved older children and those with borderline intellect. To remedy this imbalance, most of the very simple items were dropped and new items were added at the higher end of the scale. The 1908 scale had 58 problems or tests, almost double the number from 1905. Several new tests were added, many of which are still used today: reconstructing scrambled sentences, copying a diamond, and executing a sequence of three commands. Some of the items were absurdities that the children had to detect and explain. One such item was amusing to French children: "The body of an unfortunate girl was found, cut into 18 pieces. It is thought that she killed herself." However, this item was very upsetting to some American subjects, demonstrating the importance of cultural factors in intelligence (Fancher, 1985).

The major innovation of the 1908 scale was the introduction of the concept of mental level. The tests had been standardized on about 300 normal children between the ages of 3 and 13 years. This allowed Binet and Simon to order the tests according to the age level at which they were typically passed. Whichever items were passed by 80 to 90 percent of the 3-year-olds were placed in the 3-year level, and similarly on up to age 13. Binet and Simon also devised a rough scoring system whereby a basal age was first determined from the age level at which not more than one test was failed. For each five tests that were passed at levels above the basal, a full year of mental level was granted. Insofar as partial years of mental level were not credited and the various

age levels had anywhere from three to eight tests, the method left much to be desired.

In 1911, a third revision of the Binet-Simon scales appeared. Each age level now had exactly five tests. The scale was also extended into the adult range. And with some reluctance, Binet introduced new scoring methods that allowed for one-fifth of a year for each subtest passed beyond the basal level. In his writings, Binet emphasized strongly that the child's exact mental level should not be taken too seriously as an absolute measure of intelligence.

Nonetheless, the idea of deriving a mental level was a monumental development that was to influence the character of intelligence testing throughout the twentieth century. Within months, what Binet called mental level was being translated as mental age. And testers everywhere, including Binet himself, were comparing a child's mental age with the child's chronological age. Thus, a 9-year-old who was functioning at the mental level (or mental age) of a 6-year-old was retarded by three years. Very shortly, Stern (1912) pointed out that being retarded by three years had different meanings at different ages. A 5-year-old functioning at the 2-year-old level was more impaired than a 13-year-old functioning at the 10-year-old level. Stern suggested that an intelligence quotient computed from the mental age divided by the chronological age would give a better measure of the relative functioning of a subject compared to his or her same-aged peers.

In 1916, Terman and his associates at Stanford revised the Binet-Simon scales, producing the Stanford-Binet, a successful test that is discussed in a later chapter. Terman suggested multiplying the intelligence quotient by 100 to remove fractions; he was also the first person to use the abbreviation *IQ*. Thus was born one of the most popular and controversial concepts in the history of psychology. Binet died in 1911 before the IQ swept American testing, so we will never know what he would have thought of this new development based on his scales. However, Simon, his collaborator, later called the concept of IQ a "betrayal" of their scale's original objectives (Fancher, 1985, p. 104), and we can assume from Binet's humanistic concern that he might have held a similar opinion.

# ● SUMMARY

1. For better or for worse, psychological test results possess the power to alter lives. A review of historical trends is crucial if we desire to comprehend the contemporary influence of psychological tests.

2. Rudimentary forms of testing date back to 2200 B.C. in China. The Chinese emperors used grueling written exams to select officials for civil service.

3. In the mid- to late 1800s, several physicians and psychiatrists developed standardized procedures to reveal the nature and extent of symptoms in the mentally ill and brain injured. For example, in 1885, Hubert von Grashey developed the precursor to the memory drum to test the visual recognition skill of brain-injured patients.

4. Modern psychological testing owes its inception to the era of brass instruments psychology that flourished in Europe during the late 1800s. By testing sensory thresholds and reaction times, pioneer test developers such as Sir Francis Galton demonstrated that it was possible to measure the mind in an objective and replicable manner.

5. Wilhelm Wundt founded the first psychological laboratory in 1879 in Leipzig, Germany. Included among his earlier investigations was his 1862 attempt to measure the speed of thought with the thought meter, a calibrated pendulum with needles sticking off from each side.

6. The first reference to mental tests occurred in 1890 in a classic paper by James McKeen Cattell, an American psychologist who had studied with Galton. Cattell imported the brass instruments approach to the United States.

7. One of Cattell's students, Clark Wissler, showed that reaction time and sensory discrimination measures did not correlate with college grades, thereby redirecting the mental-testing movement away from brass instruments.

8. In the late 1800s, a newfound humanism toward the mentally retarded, reflected in the diagnostic and remedial work of French physicians Esquirol and Seguin, helped create the necessity for early intelligence tests.

9. Alfred Binet, who was to invent the first true intelligence test, began his career by studying hysterical paralysis with the French neurologist Charcot. Binet's claim that magnetism could cure hysteria was, to his pained embarrassment, disproved. Shortly thereafter, he switched interests and conducted sensory-perceptual studies, using his children as subjects.

10. In 1905, Binet and Simon developed the first useful intelligence test in Paris, France. Their simple 30-item measure of mainly higher mental functions helped identify schoolchildren who could not profit from regular instruction. Curiously, there was no method for scoring the test.

11. In 1908, Binet and Simon published a revised 58-item scale that incorporated the concept of mental level. In 1911, a third revision of the Binet-Simon scales appeared. Each age level now had exactly five tests; the scale extended into the adult range.

12. In 1912, Stern proposed dividing the mental age by the chronological age to obtain an intelligence quotient. In 1916, Terman suggested multiplying the intelligence quotient by 100 to remove fractions. Thus was born the concept of IQ.

# ● KEY TERMS AND CONCEPTS

physiognomy   p. 42

phrenology   p. 42

# Early Testing in the United States

The Binet-Simon scales helped solve a practical social quandary, namely, how to identify children who needed special schooling. With this successful application of a mental test, psychologists realized that their inventions could have pragmatic significance for many different segments of society. Almost immediately, psychologists in the United States adopted a utilitarian focus. Intelligence testing was embraced by many as a reliable and objective response to perceived social problems such as the identification of immigrants with mental retardation and the quick, accurate classification of Army recruits (Boake, 2002).

Whether these early tests really solved social dilemmas—or merely exacerbated them—is a fiercely debated issue reviewed in the following sections. One thing is certain: The profusion of tests developed early in the twentieth century helped shape the character of contemporary tests. A review of these historical trends will aid in the comprehension of the nature of modern tests and a better appreciation of the social issues raised by them.

## ● EARLY USES AND ABUSES OF TESTS IN THE UNITED STATES

### First Translation of the Binet-Simon Scale

In 1906, Henry H. Goddard was hired by the Vineland Training School in New Jersey to do research on the classification and education of "feebleminded" children. He soon realized that a diagnostic instrument would be required and was, therefore, pleased to read of the 1908 Binet-Simon scale. He quickly set about translating the scale, making minor changes so that it would be applicable to American children (Goddard, 1910a).

Goddard (1910b) tested 378 residents of the Vineland facility and categorized them by diagnosis and mental age. He classified 73 residents as *idiots* because their mental age was 2 years or lower; 205 residents were termed *imbeciles* with mental age of 3 to 7 years; and 100 residents were deemed *feebleminded* with mental age of 8 to 12 years. It is instructive to note that originally neutral and descriptive terms for portraying levels of mental retardation—idiot, imbecile, and feebleminded—have made their way into the everyday lexicon of pejorative labels. In fact, Goddard made his own contribution by coining the diagnostic term *moron* (from the Greek *moronia,* meaning "foolish").

Goddard (1911) also tested 1,547 normal children with his translation of the Binet-Simon scales. He considered children whose mental age was four or more years behind their chronological age to be feebleminded—these constituted 3 percent of his sample. Considering that all of these children were found outside of institutions for the retarded, 3 percent is rather an alarming rate of mental deficiency. Goddard (1911) was of the opinion that these children should be segregated so that they would be prevented from "contaminating society." These early studies piqued Goddard's curiosity about "feebleminded" citizenry and the societal burdens they imposed. He also gained a reputation as one of the leading experts on the use of intelligence tests to identify persons with impaired intellect. His talents were soon in heavy demand.

### The Binet-Simon and Immigration

In 1910, Goddard was invited to Ellis Island by the commissioner of immigration to help make the examination of immigrants more accurate. A dark and foreboding folklore had grown up around mental deficiency and immigration in the early 1900s:

> It was believed that the feebleminded were degenerate beings responsible for many if not most social problems; that they reproduced at an alarming rate and menaced the nation's overall biological fitness; and that their numbers were being incremented by undesirable "new" immigrants from southern and eastern European countries who had largely supplanted the "old" immigrants from northern and western Europe. (Gelb, 1986)

Initially, Goddard was unconcerned about the supposed threat of feeblemindedness posed by the immigrants. He wrote that adequate statistics did not exist and that the prevalent opinions about undue percentages of mentally defective immigrants were "grossly overestimated" (Goddard,

1912). However, with repeated visits to Ellis Island, Goddard became convinced that the rates of feeblemindedness were much higher than estimated by the physicians who staffed the immigration service. Within a year, he reversed his opinions entirely and called for congressional funding so that Ellis Island could be staffed with experts trained in the use of intelligence tests. In the following decade, Goddard became an apostle for the use of intelligence tests to identify feebleminded immigrants. Although he wrote that the rates of mentally deficient immigrants were "alarming," he did not join the popular call for immigration restriction (Gelb, 1986).

The story of Goddard and his concern for the "menace of feeblemindedness," as Gould (1981) has satirically put it, is often ignored or downplayed in books on psychological testing. The majority of textbooks on testing do not mention or refer to Goddard at all. The few books that do mention him usually state that Goddard "used the tests in institutions for the retarded," which is surely an understatement. In his influential *History of Psychological Testing,* DuBois (1970) has a portrait of Goddard but devotes less than one line of text to him.

The fact is that Goddard was one of the most influential American psychologists of the early 1900s. Any thoughtful person must, therefore, wonder why so many contemporary authors have ignored or slighted the person who first translated and applied Binet's tests in the United States. We will attempt an answer here, based in part on Goddard's original writing, but also relying on Gould's (1981) critique of Goddard's voluminous writings on mental deficiency and intelligence testing. We refer to Gelb's (1986) more sympathetic portrayal of Goddard as well.

Perhaps Goddard has been ignored in the textbooks because he was a strict hereditarian who conceived of intelligence in simpleminded Mendelian terms. No doubt his call for colonization of "morons" so as to restrict their breeding has won him contemporary disfavor as well. And his insistence that much undesirable behavior—crime, alcoholism, prostitution—was due to inherited mental deficiency also does not sit well with the modern environmentalist position.

However, the most likely reason that modern authors have ignored Goddard is that he exemplified a large number of early prominent psychologists who engaged in the blatant misuse of intelligence testing. In his efforts to demonstrate that high rates of immigrants with mental retardation were entering the United States each day, Goddard sent his assistants to Ellis Island to administer his English translation of the Binet-Simon tests to newly arrived immigrants. The tests were administered through a translator, not long after the immigrants walked ashore. We can guess that many of the immigrants were frightened, confused, and disoriented. Thus, a test devised in French, then translated to English was, in turn, retranslated back to Yiddish, Hungarian, Italian, or Russian; administered to bewildered farmers and laborers who had just endured an Atlantic crossing; and interpreted according to the original French norms.

What did Goddard find and what did he make of his results? In small samples of immigrants (22 to 50), his assistants found 83 percent of the Jews, 80 percent of the Hungarians, 79 percent of the Italians, and 87 percent of the Russians to be feebleminded, that is, below age 12 on the Binet-Simon scales (Goddard, 1917). His interpretation of these findings is, by turns, skeptically cautious and then provocatively alarmist. In one place he claims that his study "makes no determination of the actual percentage, even of these groups, who are feebleminded." Yet, later in the report he states that his figures would only need to be revised by "a relatively small amount" in order to find the actual percentages of feeblemindedness among immigrant groups. Furthermore, he concludes that the intelligence of the average immigrant is low, "perhaps of moron grade," but then goes on to cite environmental deprivation as the primary culprit. Simultaneously, Goddard appears to favor deportation for low IQ immigrants but also provides the humanitarian perspective that we might be able to use "moron laborers" if only "we are wise enough to train them properly."

There is much, much more to the Goddard era of early intelligence testing, and the interested reader is urged to consult Gould (1981) and Gelb (1986). The most important point that we wish to stress here is that—like many other early psychologists—Goddard's scholarly views were influenced by the social ideologies of his time. Finally, Goddard was a complex scholar who refined and contradicted his professional opinions on numerous occasions. One ironic example: After the damage was done and his writings had helped restrict immigration, Goddard (1928) recanted, concluding that feeblemindedness was not incurable and that the feebleminded did not need to be segregated in institutions.

The Goddard chapter in the history of testing serves as a reminder that even well-meaning persons operating within generally accepted social norms can misuse psychological tests. We need be ever mindful that disinterested "science" can be harnessed to the goals of a pernicious social ideology.

## Testing for Giftedness: Leta Stetter Hollingworth

One of the earliest uses of IQ tests like the Stanford-Binet was testing for giftedness. A pioneer in this application was Leta Stetter Hollingworth (1886–1939) who spent her short career (she died of cancer at the age of 53) focusing on the psychology of genius. In one study, Hollingworth (1928) demonstrated that children of high genius (Stanford-Binet IQs hovering around 165) showed significantly greater school achievement than those of mere ordinary genius (IQs clustering around 146). In another study, she dispelled the belief, common at the time, that gifted children should not be moved ahead in school because they would lag behind older children in penmanship and other motor skills (Hollingworth & Monahan, 1926). In yet another study, she found that highly gifted adolescents were judged by total strangers to be significantly better looking than matched controls of the same age (Hollingworth, 1935).

Hollingworth was a prolific researcher who advanced the science of IQ testing. Being an idealist, she was ahead of her time. She proposed a revolving fund from which gifted children could draw for their development, with the moral (but not legal) obligation to pay the money back in twenty years. She surmised that such a fund would grow exponentially over the decades and benefit the nation in unforeseeable ways (H. Hollingworth, 1943). Unfortunately, this remarkable plan never came to fruition.

Hollingworth also was a feminist who attributed gender differences in eminence and achievement to social and cultural impacts:

> It is undesirable to seek for the cause of sex differences in eminence in ultimate and obscure affective and intellectual differences until we have exhausted as a cause the known, obvious, and inescapable fact that women bear and rear the children, and that this has had as an inevitable sequel the occupation of housekeeping, a field where eminence is not possible.
>
> As a corollary it may be added that . . . It is desirable, for both the enrichment of society and the peace of individuals, that women may find a way to vary from their mode as men do, and yet procreate. Such a course is at present hindered by individual prejudice, poverty, and the enactment of legal measures. But public expectation will slowly change, as the conditions that generated that expectation have already changed, and in another century the solution to this problem will have been found. (Hollingworth, 1914, p. 529)

It is now a century, more or less, since Hollingworth's proclamation. Gender differences in eminence and achievement still exist, but they have been greatly reduced.

### The Stanford-Binet:
### The Early Mainstay of IQ

Although it was Goddard who first translated the Binet scales in the United States, it was Stanford professor Lewis M. Terman (1857–1956) who popularized IQ testing with his revision of the Binet scales in 1916. The new Stanford-Binet, as it was called, was a substantial revision, not just an extension, of the earlier Binet scales. Among the many changes that led to the unquestioned prestige of the Stanford-Binet was the use of the now familiar IQ for expressing test results. The number of items was increased to 90, and the new scale was suitable for those with mental retardation, children, and both normal and "superior" adults. In addition, the Stanford-Binet had clear and well-organized instructions for administration and scoring. Great care had been taken in securing a representative sample of subjects for use in the standardization of the test. As Goodenough (1949) notes: "The publication of the Stanford Revision marked the end of the initial period of experimentation and uncertainty. Once and for all, intelligence testing had been put on a firm basis."

The Stanford-Binet was the standard of intelligence testing for decades. New tests were always validated in terms of their correlations with this measure. It continued its preeminence through revisions in 1937 and 1960, by which time the Wechsler scales (Wechsler, 1949, 1955) had begun to compete with it. The latest revision of the Stanford-Binet was completed in 2003. This test and the Wechsler scales are discussed in detail in a later chapter. It is worth mentioning here that the Wechsler scales became a quite popular alternative to the Stanford-Binet mainly because they provided more than just an IQ score. In addition to Full Scale IQ, the Wechsler scales provided 10 to 12 subtest scores and a Verbal and Performance IQ. By contrast, the earlier versions of the Stanford-Binet supplied only a single overall summary score, the global IQ.

### ● GROUP TESTS AND THE CLASSIFICATION OF WWI ARMY RECRUITS

Given the American penchant for efficiency, it was only natural that researchers would seek group mental tests to supplement the relatively time-consuming individual intelligence tests imported from France. Among the first to develop group tests was Pyle (1913), who published schoolchildren norms for a battery consisting of such well-worn measures as memory span, digit-symbol substitution, and oral word association (quickly writing down words in response to a stimulus word). Pintner (1917) revised and expanded Pyle's battery, adding to it a timed cancellation test in which the child crossed out the letter *a* wherever it appeared in a body of text.

But group tests were slow to catch on, partly because the early versions still had to be scored laboriously by hand. The idea of a completely objective test with a simple scoring key was inconsistent with tests such as logical memory for which the judgment of the examiner was required in scoring. Most amazing of all—at least to anyone who has spent any time as a student in American schools—the multiple-choice question was not yet in general use.

The slow pace of developments in group testing picked up dramatically as the United States entered World War I in 1917. It was then that Robert M. Yerkes, a well-known psychology professor at Harvard, convinced the U.S. government and the Army that all of its 1.75 million recruits should be given intelligence tests for purposes of classification and assignment (Yerkes, 1919). Immediately upon being commissioned into the Army as a colonel, Yerkes assembled a Committee on the Examination of Recruits, which met at the Vineland school in New Jersey to develop the new group tests for the assessment of Army recruits. Yerkes chaired the committee; other famous members included Goddard and Terman.

Two group tests emerged from this collaboration: the Army Alpha and the Army Beta. It would be difficult to overestimate the influence of the Alpha and Beta on subsequent intelligence tests. The format and content of these tests inspired developments in group and individual testing for decades to come. We discuss these tests in some detail so that the reader can appreciate their influence on modern intelligence tests.

## The Army Alpha and Beta Examinations

The Alpha was based on the then unpublished work of Otis (1918) and consisted of eight verbally loaded tests for average and high-functioning recruits. The eight tests were (1) following oral directions, (2) arithmetical reasoning, (3) practical judgment, (4) synonym–antonym pairs, (5) disarranged sentences, (6) number series completion, (7) analogies, and (8) information. Figure 2.1 lists some typical items from the Army Alpha examination.

The Army Beta was a nonverbal group test designed for use with illiterates and recruits whose first language was not English. It consisted of various visual-perceptual and motor tests such as tracing a path through mazes and visualizing the correct number of blocks depicted in a three-dimensional drawing. Figure 2.2 depicts the blackboard demonstrations for all eight parts of the Beta examination.

In order to accommodate illiterate subjects and recent immigrants who did not comprehend English, Yerkes instructed the examiners to use largely pictorial and gestural methods for explaining the tests to the prospective Army recruits. The examiner and an assistant stood atop a platform at the front of the class and engaged in pantomime to explain each of the eight tests.

The Army testing was intended to help segregate and eliminate the mentally incompetent, to classify men according to their mental ability, and to assist in the placement of competent men in responsible positions (Yerkes, 1921). However, it is not really clear whether the Army made much use of the masses of data supplied by Yerkes and his eager assistants. A careful reading of his memoirs reveals that Yerkes did little more than produce favorable testimonials from high-ranking officers. In the main, his memoirs say that the Army could have saved millions of dollars and increased its efficiency if the testing data had been used.

To some extent, the mountains of test data had little practical impact on the efficiency of the Army because of the resistance of the military mind

FOLLOWING ORAL DIRECTIONS

Mark a cross in the first and also the third circle:

○          ○          ○          ○          ○

ARITHMETICAL REASONING

Solve each problem:
How many men are 5 men and 10 men?                    Answer (   )
If 3 1/2 tons of coal cost $21, what will 5 1/2 tons cost?      Answer (   )

PRACTICAL JUDGMENT

Why are high mountains covered with snow? Because
　　☐ they are near the clouds
　　☐ the sun shines seldom on them
　　☐ the air is cold there

SYNONYM–ANTONYM PAIRS

Are these words the same or opposite?
largess—donation                          same? or opposite?
accumulate—dissipate                      same? or opposite?

DISARRANGED SENTENCES

Can these words be rearranged to form a sentence?
envy bad malice traits are and                    true? or false?

NUMBER SERIES COMPLETION

Complete the series:   3   6   8   16   18   36   ...   ...

ANALOGIES

Which choice completes the analogy?
tears—sorrow :: laughter—              joy   smile   girls   grin
granary—wheat :: library—       desk   books   paper   librarian

INFORMATION

Choose the best alternative:
The pancreas is in the            abdomen   head   shoulder   neck
The Battle of Gettysburg was fought in      1863   1813   1778   1812

Note: Examinees received verbal instructions for each subtest.

● **FIGURE 2.1**　Sample Items from the Army Alpha Examination

*Source:* Reprinted from Yerkes, R. M. (Ed.). (1921). *Psychological examining in the United States Army. Memoirs the National Academy of Sciences, Volume 15.* With permission from the National Academy of Sciences, Washington, DC.

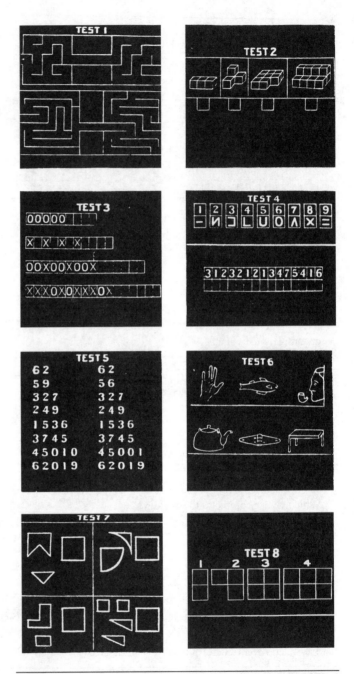

● **FIGURE 2.2** The Blackboard Demonstrations for All Eight Parts of the Beta Examination

*Source:* Reprinted from Yerkes, R. M. (Ed.). (1921). *Psychological examining in the United States Army. Memoirs of the National Academy of Sciences, Volume 15.* With permission from the National Academy of Sciences, Washington, DC.

to scientific innovation. However, it is also true that the Army brass had good reason to doubt the validity of the test results. For example, an internal memorandum described the use of pantomime in the instructions to the nonverbal Beta examination:

> For the sake of making results from the various camps comparable, the examiners were ordered to follow a certain detailed and specific series of ballet antics, which had not only the merit of being perfectly incomprehensible and unrelated to mental testing, but also lent a highly confusing and distracting mystical atmosphere to the whole performance, effectually preventing all approach to the attitude in which a subject should be while having his soul tested. (cited in Samelson, 1977)

In addition, the testing conditions left much to be desired, with wave upon wave of recruits ushered in one door, tested, and virtually shoved out the other side. Tens of thousands of recruits received a literal zero for many subtests, not because they were retarded but because they couldn't fathom the instructions to these enigmatic new instruments. Many recruits fell asleep while the testers gave esoteric and mysterious pantomime instructions.

On the positive side, the Army testing provided psychologists with a tremendous amount of experience in the psychometrics of test construction. Thousands of correlation coefficients were computed, including the prominent use of multiple correlations in the analysis of test data. Test construction graduated from an art to a science in a few short years.

## ● EARLY EDUCATIONAL TESTING

For good or for ill, Yerkes's grand scheme for testing Army recruits helped to usher in the era of group tests. After WWI, inquiries rushed in from industry, public schools, and colleges about the potential applications of these straightforward tests that almost anyone could administer and score (Yerkes, 1921). The psychologists who had worked with Yerkes soon left the service and carried with them to industry and education their newfound notion of paper-and-pencil tests of intelligence.

The Army Alpha and Beta were also released for general use. These tests quickly became the prototypes for a large family of group tests and influenced the character of intelligence tests, college entrance examinations, scholastic achievement tests, and aptitude tests. To cite just one specific consequence of the Army testing, the National Research Council, a government organization of scientists, devised the National Intelligence Test, which was eventually given to 7 million children in the United States during the 1920s. Thus, such well-known tests as the Wechsler scales, the Scholastic Aptitude Tests, and the Graduate Record Exam actually have roots that reach back to Yerkes, Otis, and the mass testing of Army recruits during WWI.

The College Entrance Examination Board (CEEB) was established at the turn of the twentieth century to help avoid duplication in the testing of applicants to U.S. colleges. The early exams had been of the short answer essay format, but this was to change quickly when C. C. Brigham, a disciple of Yerkes, became CEEB secretary after WWI. In 1925, the College Board decided to construct a scholastic aptitude test for use in college admissions (Goslin, 1963). The new tests reflected the now familiar objective format of unscrambling sentences, completing analogies, and filling in the next number in a sequence. Machine scoring was introduced in the 1930s, making objective group tests even more efficient than before. These tests then evolved into the present College Board tests, in particular, the Scholastic Aptitude Tests, now known as the Scholastic Assessment Tests.

The functions of the CEEB were later subsumed under the nonprofit Educational Testing Service (ETS). The ETS directed the development, standardization, and validation of such well-known tests as the Graduate Record Examination, the Law School Admissions Test, and the Peace Corps Entrance Tests.

Meanwhile, Terman and his associates at Stanford were busy developing standardized achievement tests. The Stanford Achievement Test (SAchT) was first published in 1923; a modern version of it is still in wide use today. From the very beginning, the SAchT incorporated such modern psychometric principles as norming the subtests so that within-subject variability could be assessed and selecting a very large and representative standardization sample.

## ● THE DEVELOPMENT OF APTITUDE TESTS

Aptitude tests measure more specific and delimited abilities than intelligence tests. Traditionally, intelligence tests assess a more global construct such as general intelligence, although there are exceptions to this trend that will be discussed later. By contrast, a single aptitude test will measure just one ability domain, and a multiple aptitude test battery will provide scores in several distinctive ability areas.

The development of aptitude tests lagged behind that of intelligence tests for two reasons, one statistical, the other social. The statistical problem was that a new technique, factor analysis, was often needed to discern which aptitudes were primary and, therefore, distinct from each other. Research on this question had been started quite early by Spearman (1904) but was not refined until the 1930s (Spearman, 1927; Kelley, 1928; Thurstone, 1938). This new family of techniques, factor analysis, allowed Thurstone to conclude that there were specific factors of primary mental ability such as verbal comprehension, word fluency, number facility, spatial ability, associative memory, perceptual speed, and general reasoning (Thurstone, 1938; Thurstone & Thurstone, 1941). More will be said about this in the later chapters on intelligence and ability testing. The important point here is that Thurstone and his followers thought that global measures of intelligence did not, so to speak, "cut nature at its joints." As a result, it was felt that such measures as the Stanford-Binet were not as useful as multiple aptitude test batteries in determining a person's intellectual strengths and weaknesses.

The second reason for the slow growth of aptitude batteries was the absence of a practical application for such refined instruments. It was not until WWII that a pressing need arose to select candidates who were highly qualified for very difficult and specialized tasks. The job requirements of pilots, flight engineers, and navigators were very specific and demanding. A general estimate of intellectual ability, such as provided by the group intelligence tests used in WWI, was not sufficient to choose good candidates for flight school. The armed forces solved this problem by developing a specialized aptitude battery of 20 tests that was administered to men who passed preliminary screening tests. These measures proved invaluable in selecting pilots, navigators, and bombadiers, as reflected in the much lower washout rates of men selected by test battery instead of the old methods (Goslin, 1963). Such tests are still used widely in the armed services.

## ● PERSONALITY AND VOCATIONAL TESTING AFTER WWI

Although such rudimentary assessment methods as the free association technique had been used before the turn of the twentieth century by Galton, Kraepelin, and others, it was not until WWI that personality tests emerged in a form resembling their contemporary appearance. As has happened so often in the history of testing, it was once again a practical need that served as the impetus for this new development. Modern personality testing began when Woodworth attempted to develop an instrument for detecting Army recruits who were susceptible to psychoneurosis. Virtually all the modern personality inventories, schedules, and questionnaires owe a debt to Woodworth's Personal Data Sheet (1919).

The Personal Data Sheet consisted of 116 questions that the subject was to answer by underlining *Yes* or *No*. The questions were exclusively of the "face obvious" variety and, for the most part, involved fairly serious symptomatology. Representative items included:

- Do ideas run through your head so that you cannot sleep?
- Were you considered a bad boy?
- Are you bothered by a feeling that things are not real?
- Do you have a strong desire to commit suicide?

Readers familiar with the Minnesota Multiphasic Personality Inventory (MMPI) must surely recognize the debt that this more recent inventory has to Woodworth's instrument.

The next major development was an inventory of neurosis, the Thurstone Personality Schedule (Thurstone & Thurstone, 1930). After first culling hundreds of items answerable in the yes-no-? manner from Woodworth's inventory and other sources, Thurstone rationally keyed items in terms of how the neurotic would typically answer them. Reflecting Thurstone's penchant for statistical finesse, this inventory was one of the first to use the method of internal consistency whereby each prospective item was correlated with the total score on the tentatively identified scale to determine whether it belonged on the scale.

From the Thurstone test sprang the Bernreuter Personality Inventory (Bernreuter, 1931). It was a little more refined than its Thurstone predecessor, measuring four personality dimensions: neurotic tendency, self-sufficiency, introversion-extroversion, and dominance-submission. A major innovation in test construction was that a single test item could contribute to more than one scale.

Any chronology of self-report inventories must surely include the Minnesota Multiphasic Personality Inventory, or MMPI (Hathaway & McKinley, 1940). This test and its revision, the MMPI-2, are discussed in detail later. It will suffice for now to point out that the scales of the MMPI were constructed by the method that Woodworth pioneered, contrasting the responses of normal and psychiatrically disturbed subjects. In addition,

the MMPI introduced the use of validity scales to determine fake bad, fake good, and random response patterns.

## ● THE ORIGINS OF PROJECTIVE TESTING

The projective approach originated with the word association method pioneered by Francis Galton in the late 1800s. Galton gave himself four seconds to come up with as many associations as possible to a stimulus word and then categorized his associations as parrotlike, image-mediated, or histrionic representations. This latter category convinced him that mental operations "sunk wholly below the level of consciousness" were at play. Some historians have even speculated that Freud's application of free association as a therapeutic tool in psychoanalysis sprang from Galton's paper published in *Brain* in 1879 (Forrest, 1974).

Galton's work was continued in Germany by Wundt and Kraepelin and finally brought to fruition by Jung (1910). Jung's test consisted of 100 stimulus words. For each word, the subject was to reply as quickly as possible with the first word coming to mind. Kent and Rosanoff (1910) gave the association method a distinctively American flavor by tabulating the reactions of 1,000 normal subjects to a list of 100 stimulus words. These tables were designed to provide a basis for comparing the reactions of normal and "insane" subjects.

While the Americans were pursuing the empirical approach to objective personality testing, a young Swiss psychiatrist, Hermann Rorschach (1884–1922), was developing a completely different vehicle for studying personality. Rorschach was strongly influenced by Jungian and psychoanalytic thinking, so it was natural that his new approach focused on the tendency of patients to reveal their innermost conflicts unconsciously when responding to ambiguous stimuli. The Rorschach and other projective tests discussed subsequently were predicated on the projective hypothesis: When responding to ambiguous or unstructured stimuli, we inadvertently disclose our innermost needs, fantasies, and conflicts.

Rorschach was convinced that people revealed important personality dimensions in their responses to inkblots. He spent years developing just the right set of 10 inkblots and systematically analyzed the responses of personal friends and different patient groups (Rorschach, 1921). Unfortunately, he died only a year after his monograph was published, and it was up to others to complete his work. Developments in the Rorschach are reviewed later in the text.

Whereas Rorschach's test was originally developed to reveal the innermost workings of the abnormal subject, the TAT, or Thematic Apperception Test (Morgan & Murray, 1935), was developed as an instrument to study normal personality. Of course, both have since been expanded for testing with the entire continuum of human behavior.

The TAT consists of a series of pictures that largely depict one or more persons engaged in an ambiguous interaction. The subject is shown one picture at a time and told to make up a story about it. He or she is instructed to be as dramatic as possible, to discuss thoughts and feelings, and to describe the past, present, and future of what is depicted in the picture.

Murray (1938) believed that underlying personality needs, such as the need for achievement, would be revealed by the contents of the stories. Although numerous scoring systems were developed, clinicians in the main have relied on an impressionistic analysis to make sense of TAT protocols. Modern applications of the TAT are discussed in a later chapter.

The sentence completion technique was also begun during this era with the work of Payne (1928). There have been numerous extensions and variations on the technique, which consists of giving subjects a stem such as "I am bored when ———," and asking them to complete the sentence. Some modern applications are discussed later, but it can be mentioned now that the problem of scoring and interpretation, which vexed early

sentence completion test developers, is still with us today.

An entirely new approach to projective testing was taken by Goodenough (1926), who tried to determine not just intellectual level but also the interests and personality traits of children by analyzing their drawings. Buck's (1948) test, the House-Tree-Person, was a little more standardized and structured and required the subject to draw a house, a tree, and a person. Machover's (1949) *Personality Projection in the Drawing of the Human Figure* was the logical extension of the earlier work. Figure drawing as a projective approach to understanding personality is still used today, and a later chapter discusses modern developments in this practice.

Meanwhile, projective testing in Europe was dominated by the Szondi Test, a wacky instrument based on wholly faulty premises. Lipot Szondi was a Hungarian-born Swiss psychiatrist who believed that major psychiatric disorders were caused by recessive genes. His test consisted of 48 photographs of psychiatric patients divided into six sets of the following eight types: homosexual, epileptic, sadistic, hysteric, catatonic, paranoiac, manic, and depressive (Deri, 1949). From each set of eight pictures, the subject was instructed to select the two pictures he or she liked best and the two disliked most. A person who consistently preferred one kind of picture in the six sets was presumed to have some recessive genes that made him or her have sympathy for the pictured person. Thus, projective preferences were presumed to reveal recessive genes predisposing the individual to specific psychiatric disturbances.

Deri (1949) imported the test to the United States and changed the rationale. She did not argue for a recessive genetic explanation of picture choice but explained such preferences on the basis of unconscious identification with the characteristics of the photographed patients. This was a more palatable theoretical basis for the test than the dubious genetic theories of Szondi. Nonetheless, empirical research cast doubt on the validity of the Szondi Test, and it shortly faded into oblivion.

## ● THE DEVELOPMENT
   ## OF INTEREST INVENTORIES

While the clinicians were developing measures for analyzing personality and unconscious conflicts, other psychologists were devising measures for guidance and counseling of the masses of more normal persons. Chief among such measures was the interest inventory, which has roots going back to Thorndike's (1912) study of developmental trends in the interests of 100 college students. In 1919–1920, Yoakum developed a pool of 1,000 items relating to interests from childhood through early maturity (DuBois, 1970). Many of these items were incorporated in the Carnegie Interest Inventory. Cowdery (1926–1927) improved and refined previous work on the Carnegie instrument by increasing the number of items, comparing responses of three criterion groups (doctors, engineers, and lawyers) with control groups of nonprofessionals, and developing a weighting formula for items. He was also the first psychometrician to realize the importance of cross validation. He tested his new scales on additional groups of doctors, engineers, and lawyers to ensure that the discriminations found in the original studies were reliable group differences rather than capitalizations on error variance.

Edward K. Strong (1884–1963) revised Cowdery's test and devoted 36 years to the development of empirical keys for the modified instrument

known as the Strong Vocational Interest Blank (SVIB). Persons taking the test could be scored on separate keys for several dozen occupations, providing a series of scores of immeasurable value in vocational guidance. The SVIB became one of the most widely used tests of all time (Strong, 1927). Its modern version, the Strong Interest Inventory, is still widely used by guidance counselors.

For decades the only serious competitor to the SVIB was the Kuder Preference Record (Kuder, 1934). The Kuder differed from the Strong by forcing choices within triads of items. The Kuder was an ipsative test; that is, it compared the relative strength of interests within the individual, rather than comparing his or her responses to various professional groups. More recent revisions of the Kuder Preference Record include the Kuder General Interest Survey and the Kuder Occupational Interest Survey (Kuder, 1966; Kuder & Diamond, 1979).

## ● SUMMARY OF MAJOR LANDMARKS
   ## IN THE HISTORY OF TESTING

We conclude our historical survey of psychological testing with a brief tabular summary of landmark events—including a chronology of post-1950 developments—in Appendix A at the end of the book.

## ● SUMMARY

**1.** In 1910, Henry Goddard translated the 1908 Binet-Simon scale. In 1911, he tested more than a thousand schoolchildren with the test, relying on the original French norms. He was disturbed to find that 3 percent of the sample was "feebleminded" and recommended segregation from society for these children.

**2.** Nonverbal intelligence tests were invented in the early 1900s to facilitate testing of non-English-speaking immigrants. For example, Knox published a wooden puzzle test in 1914 and also used the now familiar digit-symbol substitution test.

**3.** In 1916, Lewis Terman released the Stanford-Binet, a revision of the Binet scales. This well-designed and carefully normed test placed intelligence testing on a firm footing once and for all.

**4.** During WWI, Robert Yerkes headed a team of psychologists that produced the Army Alpha, a verbally loaded group test for average and superior recruits, and the Army Beta, a nonverbal group test for illiterates and non-English-speaking recruits.

**5.** Early testing pioneers such as C. C. Brigham used results of individual and group intelligence tests to substantiate ethnic differences in intelligence and thereby justify immigration restrictions. Later, some of these testing pioneers disavowed their prior views.

6. Educational testing fell under the purview of the College Entrance Examination Board (CEEB), founded at the turn of the twentieth century. In 1947, the CEEB was replaced by the Educational Testing Service (ETS), which supervised the release of such well-known tests as the Scholastic Aptitude Tests and the Graduate Record Exam.

7. The advent of multiple aptitude test batteries was made possible with the development of factor analysis by L. L. Thurstone and others. Later, the improvement of these test batteries was spurred on by the practical need for selecting WWII recruits for highly specialized positions.

8. Personality testing began with Woodworth's Personal Data Sheet, a simple yes-no checklist of symptoms used to screen WWI recruits for

psychoneurosis. Many later inventories, including the popular Minnesota Multiphasic Personality Inventory, borrowed content from the Personal Data Sheet.

9. Projective testing began with the word association technique pioneered by Francis Galton and brought to fruition by C. G. Jung in 1910. Hermann Rorschach published his famous inkblot test in 1921.

10. The Thematic Apperception Test (TAT), a picture storytelling test introduced in 1935 by Morgan and Murray, was based on the projective hypothesis: When responding to ambiguous or unstructured stimuli, examinees inadvertently disclose their innermost needs, fantasies, and conflicts.

11. The assessment of vocational interest began with Yoakum's Carnegie Interest Inventory developed in 1919–1920. After several revisions and extensions, this instrument emerged as E. K. Strong's Vocational Interest Blank.

# Chapter 3

# Norms and Reliability

This chapter concerns two basic concepts needed to facilitate the examiner's interpretation of test scores: norms and reliability. In most cases, scores on psychological tests are interpreted by reference to norms that are based on the distribution of scores obtained by a representative sample of examinees. In Topic 3A, Norms and Test Standardization, we review the process of standardizing a test against an appropriate norm group so that test users can make sense out of individual test scores. Since the utility of a test score is also determined by the consistency or repeatability of test results, we introduce the essentials of reliability theory and measurement in Topic 3B, Concepts of Reliability. The next chapter flows logically from

the material presented here and investigates the complex issues of validity—does a test measure what it is supposed to measure? First, we begin with the more straightforward issues of establishing a comparative frame of reference (norms) and determining the consistency or repeatability of test results (reliability).

The initial outcome of testing is typically a raw score such as the total number of personality statements endorsed in a particular direction or the total number of problems solved correctly, perhaps with bonus points added in for quick solutions. In most cases, the initial score is useless by itself. For test results to be meaningful, examiners must be able to convert the initial score to some form of derived score based on comparison to a standardization or norm group. The vast majority of tests are interpreted by comparing individual results to a norm group performance; criterion-referenced tests are an exception, discussed subsequently.

A **norm group** consists of a sample of examinees who are representative of the population for whom the test is intended. Consider a word knowledge test designed for use with prospective first-year college students. In this case, the performance of a large, heterogeneous, nationwide sampling of such persons might be collected for purposes of standardization. The essential objective of test standardization is to determine the distribution of raw scores in the norm group so that the test developer can publish derived scores known as norms. Norms come in many varieties, for example, percentile ranks, age equivalents, grade equivalents, or standard scores, as discussed in the following. In general, norms indicate an examinee's standing on the test relative to the performance of other persons of the same age, grade, sex, and so on.

To be effective, norms must be obtained with great care and constructed according to well-known precepts discussed in the following. Furthermore, norms may become outmoded in just a few years, so periodic renorming of tests should be the rule, not the exception. We approach the topic of norms indirectly, first providing the reader with a discussion of raw scores and then reviewing statistical concepts essential to an understanding of norms.

## ● RAW SCORES

The most basic level of information provided by a psychological test is the **raw score**. For example, in personality testing, the raw score is often the number of questions answered in the keyed direction for a specific scale. In ability testing, the raw score commonly consists of the number of problems answered correctly, often with bonus points added for quick performance. Thus, the initial outcome of testing is almost always a numerical tally such as

17 out of 44 items answered in the keyed direction on a depression scale, or 29 of 55 raw score points earned on the block design subscale of an intelligence test.

However, it should be obvious to the reader that raw scores, in isolation, are absolutely meaningless. For example, what use is it to know that a subject correctly solved 12 of 20 abstract reasoning questions? What does it mean that an examinee responded in the keyed direction to 19 out of 33 true-false questions from a psychological-mindedness scale?

It is difficult to even think about such questions without resorting to comparisons of one variety or another. We want to know how others have done on these tests, whether the observed scores are high or low in comparison to a representative group of subjects. In the case of ability tests, we are curious whether the questions were easy or hard, especially in relation to the age of the subject.

In fact, it seems almost a truism that a raw score becomes meaningful mainly in relation to norms, an independently established frame of reference derived from a standardization sample. We have much to say about the derivation and use of norms later in this unit. For now it will suffice to know that norms are empirically established by administering a test to a large and representative sample of persons. An examinee's score is then compared to the distribution of scores obtained by the standardization sample. In this manner, we determine from the norms whether an obtained score is low, average, or high.

The vast majority of psychological tests are interpreted by consulting norms; as noted, these instruments are called *norm-referenced tests*. However, the reader is reminded that other kinds of instruments do exist. In particular, criterion-referenced tests help determine whether a person can accomplish an objectively defined criterion such as adding pairs of two-digit numbers with 97 percent accuracy. In the case of criterion-referenced tests, norms are not essential. We elaborate on criterion-referenced tests at the end of this topic.

There are many different kinds of norms, but they share one characteristic: Each incorporates a statistical summary of a large body of scores. Thus, in order to understand norms, the reader needs to master elementary descriptive statistics. We take a modest digression here to review essential statistical concepts.

# ● ESSENTIAL STATISTICAL CONCEPTS

Suppose for the moment that we have access to a high-level vocabulary test appropriate for testing the verbal skills of college professors and other professional persons (Gregory & Gernert, 1990). The test is a multiple-choice quiz of 30 difficult words such as *welkin, halcyon,* and *mellifluous.* A curious professor takes the test and chooses the correct alternative for 17 of the 30 words. She asks how her score compares to others of similar academic standing. How might we respond to her question?

One manner of answering the query would be to give her a list of the raw scores from the preliminary standardization sample of 100 representative professors at her university (Table 3.1). However, even with this relatively small norm sample (thousands of subjects is more typical), the list of test scores is an overpowering display.

When confronted with a collection of quantitative data, the natural human tendency is to summarize, condense, and organize it into meaningful patterns. For example, in assessing the meaning of the curious professor's vocabulary score, the reader might calculate the average score for the entire sample, or tally the relative position of the professor's score (17 correct) among the 100 data points found in Table 3.1. We review these and other approaches to organizing and summarizing quantitative data in the following sections.

## Frequency Distributions

A very simple and useful way of summarizing data is to tabulate a frequency distribution (Table 3.2). A **frequency distribution** is prepared by specifying a small number of usually equal-sized class intervals and then tallying how many scores fall within each interval. The sums of the frequencies for all intervals will equal $N$, the total number of scores in the sample. There is no hard and fast rule for determining the size of the intervals. Obviously, the size of the intervals depends on the number of intervals desired. It is common for frequency distributions to include between 5 and 15 class intervals. In the case of Table 3.2, there are 9 class intervals of 3 scores each. The table indicates that one professor scored 4, 5, or 6, eight professors scored 7, 8, or 9, and so on.

● TABLE 3.1   **Raw Scores of 100 Professors on a 30-Item Vocabulary Test**

| | | | | | | | | | |
|---|---|---|---|---|---|---|---|---|---|
| 6, | 10, | 16, | 16, | 17, | 14, | 19, | 14, | 16, | 15 |
| 17, | 17, | 19, | 20, | 20, | 22, | 17, | 24, | 14, | 25 |
| 13, | 20, | 11, | 20, | 21, | 11, | 20, | 16, | 18, | 12 |
| 13, | 7, | 20, | 27, | 21, | 7, | 15, | 18, | 18, | 25 |
| 20, | 27, | 28, | 13, | 21, | 17, | 12, | 18, | 12, | 15 |
| 9, | 24, | 25, | 9, | 17, | 17, | 9, | 19, | 24, | 15 |
| 20, | 21, | 22, | 12, | 21, | 12, | 19, | 19, | 23, | 16 |
| 8, | 12, | 12, | 17, | 13, | 19, | 13, | 11, | 16, | 16 |
| 7, | 19, | 14, | 17, | 19, | 14, | 18, | 15, | 15, | 15 |
| 14, | 14, | 17, | 18, | 18, | 22, | 11, | 15, | 13, | 9 |

*Source:* Based on data from Gregory, R. J., & Gernert, C. H. (1990). *Age trends for fluid and crystallized intelligence in an able subpopulation.* Unpublished manuscript.

● TABLE 3.2   **Frequency Distribution of Scores of 100 Professors on a Vocabulary Test**

| Class Interval | Frequency |
|---|---|
| 4–6 | 1 |
| 7–9 | 8 |
| 10–12 | 12 |
| 13–15 | 21 |
| 16–18 | 24 |
| 19–21 | 21 |
| 22–24 | 7 |
| 25–27 | 5 |
| 28–30 | 1 |
| | $N = 100$ |

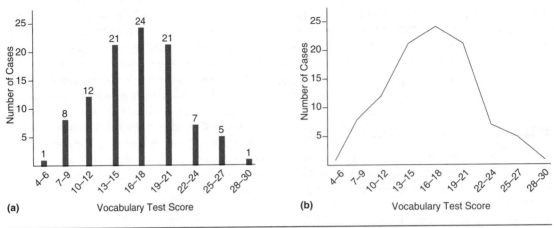

● **FIGURE 3.1** (a) A Histogram Representing Vocabulary Test Scores for 100 Professors. (b) A Frequency Polygon of Vocabulary Test Scores for 100 Professors

A **histogram** provides a graphic representation of the same information contained in the frequency distribution (Figure 3.1a). The horizontal axis portrays the scores grouped into class intervals, whereas the vertical axis depicts the number of scores falling within each class interval. In a histogram, the height of a column indicates the number of scores occurring within that interval. A **frequency polygon** is similar to a histogram, except that the frequency of the class intervals is represented by single points rather than columns. The single points are then joined by straight lines (Figure 3.1b).

The graphs shown in Figure 3.1 constitute visual summaries of the 100 raw score data points from the sample of professors. In addition to visual summaries of data, it is also possible to produce numerical summaries by computing statistical indices of central tendency and dispersion.

## Measures of Central Tendency

Can we designate a single, representative score for the 100 vocabulary scores in our sample? The mean (*M*), or arithmetic average, is one such measure of central tendency. We compute the **mean** by adding all the scores up and dividing by *N*, the number of scores. Another useful index of central tendency is the **median,** the middlemost score when all the scores have been ranked. If the number of scores is

even, the median is the average of the middlemost two scores. In either case, the median is the point that bisects the distribution so that half of the cases fall above it, half below. Finally, the **mode** is simply the most frequently occurring score. If two scores tie for highest frequency of occurrence, the distribution is said to be bimodal.

The mean of the scores listed in Table 3.1 is 16.8; the median and mode are both 17. In this instance, the three measures of central tendency are in very good agreement. However, this is not always so. The mean is sensitive to extreme values and can be misleading if a distribution has a few scores that are unusually high or low. Consider an extreme case in which nine persons earn $10,000 and a tenth person earns $910,000. The mean income for this group is $100,000, yet this income level is not typical of anyone in the group. The median income of $10,000 is much more representative. Of course, this is an extreme example, but it illustrates a general point: If a distribution of scores is skewed (that is, asymmetrical), the median is a better index of central tendency than the mean.

## Measures of Variability

Two or more distributions of test scores may have the same mean, yet differ greatly in the extent of dispersion of the scores about the mean (Figure 3.2).

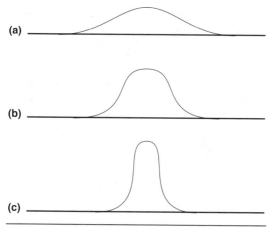

**(a)**

**(b)**

**(c)**

● **FIGURE 3.2**    Three Distributions with Identical Means but Different Variability

To describe the degree of dispersion, we need a statistical index that expresses the variability of scores in the distribution.

The most commonly used statistical index of variability in a group of scores is the **standard deviation,** designated as *s* or abbreviated as SD. From a conceptual standpoint, the reader needs to know that the standard deviation reflects the degree of dispersion in a group of scores. If the scores are tightly packed around a central value, the standard deviation is small. In fact, in the extreme case in which all the scores are identical, the standard deviation is exactly zero. As a group of scores becomes more spread out, the standard deviation becomes larger. For example, in Figure 3.2, distribution *a* would have the largest standard deviation, distribution *c* the smallest.

The standard deviation, or *s,* is simply the square root of the variance, designated as $s^2$. The formula for the **variance** is

$$s^2 = \frac{\Sigma(X - \overline{X})^2}{(N - 1)}$$

where $\Sigma$ designates "the sum of," *X* stands for each individual score, $\overline{X}$ is the mean of the scores, and *N* is the total number of scores. As the name suggests, the variance is a measure of variability. However,

psychologists usually prefer to report the standard deviation, which is computed by taking the square root of the variance. Of course, the variance and the standard deviation convey interchangeable information—one can be computed from the other by squaring (the standard deviation to obtain the variance) or taking the square root (of the variance to obtain the standard deviation). The standard deviation is nonetheless the preferred measure of variance in psychological testing because of its direct relevance to the normal distribution, as discussed in the next section.

## The Normal Distribution

The frequency polygon depicted in Figure 3.1b is highly irregular in shape, a typical finding with real-world data based on small sample sizes. What would happen to the shape of the frequency polygon if we increased the size of the normative sample and also increased the number of class intervals by reducing their size? Possibly, as we added new subjects to our sample, the distribution of scores would more and more closely resemble a symmetrical, mathematically defined, bell-shaped curve called the **normal distribution** (Figure 3.3).

Psychologists prefer a normal distribution of test scores, even though many other distributions are theoretically possible. For example, a rectangular distribution of test scores—an equal number of outcomes in each class interval—is within the realm of possibility. Indeed, many laypersons might even prefer a rectangular distribution of test scores on

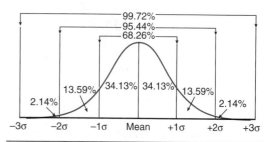

● **FIGURE 3.3**    The Normal Curve and the Percentage of Cases within Certain Intervals

the egalitarian premise that individual differences are thereby less pronounced. For example, a higher proportion of persons would score in the superior range if psychological tests conformed to a rectangular rather than normal distribution of scores.

Why, then, do psychologists prefer a normal distribution of test scores, even to the point of selecting test items that help produce this kind of distribution in the standardization sample? There are several reasons, including statistical considerations and empirical findings. We digress briefly here to explain the psychometric fascination with normal distributions.

One reason that psychologists prefer normal distributions is that the normal curve has useful mathematical features that form the basis for several kinds of statistical investigation. For example, suppose we wished to determine whether the average IQs for two groups of subjects were significantly different. An inferential statistic such as the *t*-test for a difference between means would be appropriate. However, many inferential statistics are based on the assumption that the underlying population of scores is normally distributed, or nearly so. Thus, in order to facilitate the use of inferential statistics, psychologists prefer that test scores in the general population follow a normal or near-normal distribution.

Another basis for preferring the normal distribution is its mathematical precision. Since the normal distribution is precisely defined in mathematical terms, it is possible to compute the area underneath different regions of the curve with great accuracy. Thus, a useful property of normal distributions is that the percentage of cases falling within a certain range or beyond a certain value is precisely known. For example, in a normal distribution, a mere 2.14 percent of the scores will exceed the mean by two standard deviations or more (Figure 3.3). In like manner, we can determine that the vast bulk of scores—more than 68 percent—fall within one standard deviation of the mean in either direction.

A third basis for preferring a normal distribution of test scores is that the normal curve often arises spontaneously in nature. In fact, early investigators were so impressed with the ubiquity of the normal distribution that they virtually deified the

normal curve as a law of nature. For example, Galton (1888) wrote:

> It is the supreme law of Unreason. Whenever a large sample of chaotic elements are taken in hand and marshalled in the order of their magnitude, an unsuspected and most beautiful form of regularity proves to have been latent all along.

Certainly there is no "law of nature" regarding the form that frequency distributions must take. Nonetheless, it is true that many important human characteristics—both physical and mental—produce a close approximation to the normal curve when measurements for large and heterogeneous samples are graphed. For example, a near-normal distribution curve is a well-known finding for physical characteristics such as birthweight, height, and brain weight (Jensen, 1980).

An approximately normal distribution is also found with numerous mental tests, even for tests constructed entirely without reference to the normal curve. To illustrate this point, we refer to early tests devised before the current psychometric fixation upon the normal distribution. Wechsler (1944) chose items for the original Wechsler-Bellevue Intelligence Scale largely on the basis of variety of item types, paying no heed to the resulting distribution of scores. In fact, he considered the belief that mental measures must distribute themselves according to the normal curve to be "mistaken." Yet, when he graphed the distribution of Full Scale IQs on his test, the predictably near-normal distribution emerged (Figure 3.4). Lindvall (1967) found the same thing when plotting data from the 1923 Pintner Ability Test. We see, then, that even in the absence of psychometric tinkering, the distribution of mental test scores in standardization samples typically approximates a normal curve.

### Skewness

**Skewness** refers to the symmetry or asymmetry of a frequency distribution. If test scores are piled up at the low end of the scale, the distribution is said to be positively skewed. In the opposite case, when test scores are piled up at the high end of the scale,

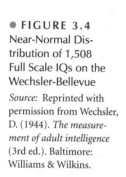

● **FIGURE 3.4**
Near-Normal Distribution of 1,508 Full Scale IQs on the Wechsler-Bellevue

*Source:* Reprinted with permission from Wechsler, D. (1944). *The measurement of adult intelligence* (3rd ed.). Baltimore: Williams & Wilkins.

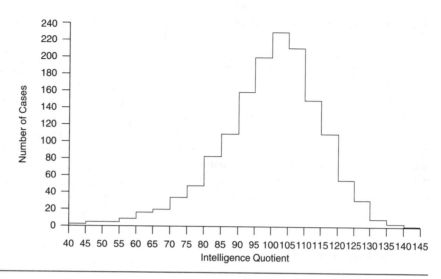

the distribution is said to be negatively skewed (Figure 3.5).

In psychological testing, skewed distributions usually signify that the test developer has included

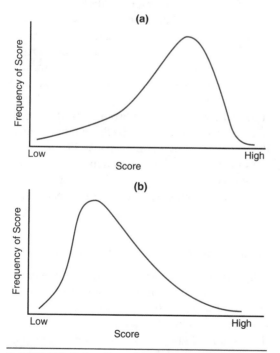

● **FIGURE 3.5** Skewed Distribution Curves: (a) Negative Skew; (b) Positive Skew

too few easy items or too few hard items. For example, when scores in the standardization sample are massed at the low end (positive skew), the test probably contains too few easy items to make effective discriminations at this end of the scale. In this case, examinees who obtain zero or near-zero scores might actually differ with respect to the dimension measured. However, the test is unable to elicit these differences, since most of the items are too hard for these examinees. Of course, the opposite pattern holds as well. If scores are massed at the high end (negative skew), the test probably contains too few hard items to make effective discriminations at this end of the scale.

When initial research indicates that an instrument produces skewed results in the standardization sample, test developers typically revamp the test at the item level. The most straightforward solution is to add items or modify existing items so that the test has more easy items (to reduce positive skew) or more hard items (to reduce negative skew). If it is too late to revise the instrument, the test developer can use a statistical transformation to help produce a more normal distribution of scores (see the following). However, the preferred strategy is to revise the test so that skewness is minimal or nonexistent.

## ● RAW SCORE TRANSFORMATIONS

Making sense out of test results is largely a matter of transforming the raw scores into more interpretable and useful forms of information. In the preceding discussion of normal distributions, we hinted at transformations by showing how knowledge of the mean and standard deviation of such distributions can help us determine the relative standing of an individual score. In this section we continue this theme in a more direct manner by introducing the formal requirements for several kinds of raw score transformations.

### Percentiles and Percentile Ranks

A **percentile** expresses the percentage of persons in the standardization sample who scored below a specific raw score. For example, on the vocabulary test depicted in Table 3.2, 94 percent of the sample fell below a raw score of 25. Thus, a raw score of 25 would correspond to a percentile of 94, denoted as $P_{94}$. Note that higher percentiles indicate higher scores. In the extreme case, an examinee who obtained a raw score that exceeded every score in the standardization sample would receive a percentile of 100, or $P_{100}$.

The reader is warned not to confuse percentiles with percent correct. Remember that a percentile indicates only how an examinee compares to the standardization sample and does not convey the percentage of questions answered correctly. Conceivably, on a difficult test, a raw score of 50 percent correct might translate to a percentile of 90, 95, or even 100. Conversely, on an easy test, a raw score of 95 percent correct might translate to a percentile of 5, 10, or 20.

Percentiles can also be viewed as ranks in a group of 100 representative subjects, with 1 being the lowest rank and 100 the highest. Note that percentile ranks are the complete reverse of usual ranking procedures. A percentile rank (PR) of 1 is at the bottom of the sample, while a PR of 99 is near the top.

A percentile of 50 ($P_{50}$) corresponds to the median or middlemost raw score. A percentile of 25

($P_{25}$) is often denoted as Q1 or the first quartile because one-quarter of the scores fall below this point. In like manner, a percentile of 75 ($P_{75}$) is referred to as Q3 or the third quartile because three-quarters of the scores fall below this point.

Percentiles are easy to compute and intuitively appealing to laypersons and professionals alike. It is not surprising, then, that percentiles are the most common type of raw score transformation encountered in psychological testing. Almost any kind of test result can be reported as a percentile, even when other transformations are the primary goal of testing. For example, intelligence tests are used to obtain IQ scores—a kind of transformation discussed subsequently—but also yield percentile scores, too. Thus, an IQ of 130 corresponds to a percentile of 98, meaning that the score is not only well above average but, more precisely, also exceeds 98 percent of the standardization sample.

Percentile scores do have one major drawback: They distort the underlying measurement scale, especially at the extremes. A specific example will serve to clarify this point. Consider a hypothetical instance in which four persons obtain the following percentiles on a test: 50, 59, 90, and 99. (Remember that we are speaking here of percentiles, not percent correct.) The first two persons differ by 9 percentile points (50 versus 59) and so do the last two persons (90 versus 99). The untrained observer might assume, falsely, that the first two persons differed in underlying raw score points by the same amount as the last two persons. An inspection of Figure 3.6 reveals the fallacy of this assumption. The difference in underlying raw score points between percentiles of 90 and 99 is far greater than between percentiles of 50 and 59.

### Standard Scores

Although percentiles are the most popular type of transformed score, standard scores exemplify the most desirable psychometric properties. A standard score uses the standard deviation of the total distribution of raw scores as the fundamental unit of measurement. The **standard score** expresses the distance from the mean in standard deviation

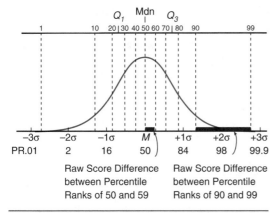

Raw Score Difference between Percentile Ranks of 50 and 59

Raw Score Difference between Percentile Ranks of 90 and 99

● **FIGURE 3.6**    Percentile Ranks in a Normal Distribution

units. For example, a raw score that is exactly one standard deviation above the mean converts to a standard score of +1.00. A raw score that is exactly one-half a standard deviation below the mean converts to a standard score of −0.50. Thus, a standard score not only expresses the magnitude of deviation from the mean, but the direction of departure (positive or negative) as well.

Computation of an examinee's standard score (also called a *z* score) is simple: Subtract the mean of the normative group from the examinee's raw score and then divide this difference by the standard deviation of the normative group. Table 3.3 illustrates the computation of *z* scores for three subjects of widely varying ability on a hypothetical test.

Standard scores possess the desirable psychometric property of retaining the relative magnitudes of distances between successive values found in the original raw scores. This is because the distribution of standard scores has exactly the same shape as the distribution of raw scores. As a consequence, the use of standard scores does not distort the underlying measurement scale. This fidelity of the transformed measurement scale is a major advantage of standard scores over percentiles and percentile ranks. As previously noted, percentile scores are very distorting, especially at the extremes.

A specific example will serve to illustrate the nondistorting feature of standard scores. Consider four raw scores of 55, 60, 70, and 80 on a test with mean of 50 and standard deviation of 10. The first two scores differ by 5 raw score points, while the last two scores differ by 10 raw score points—twice the difference of the first pair. When the raw scores are converted to standard scores, the results are +0.50, +1.00, +2.00, and +3.00, respectively. The reader will notice that the first two scores differ by 0.50 standard scores, while the last two scores differ by 1.00 standard scores—twice the difference of the first pair. Thus, standard scores always retain the relative magnitude of differences found in the original raw scores.

Standard score distributions possess important mathematical properties that do not exist in the raw score distributions. When each of the raw scores in a distribution is transformed to a standard score, the resulting collection of standard scores always has a mean of zero and a variance of 1.00. Because the standard deviation is the square root of the variance, the standard deviation of standard scores ($\sqrt{1.00}$) is necessarily 1.00 as well.

One reason for transforming raw scores into standard scores is to depict results on different tests according to a common scale. If two distributions of test scores possess the same form, we can make direct comparisons on raw scores by transforming

● **TABLE 3.3    Computation of Standard Scores on a Hypothetical Test**

For the normative sample: $M = 50, \text{SD} = 8$

$$\text{Standard Score} = z = \frac{X - M}{SD}$$

Person A: raw score of 35 (below average)

$$z = \frac{35 - 50}{8} = -1.88$$

Person B: raw score of 50 (exactly average)

$$z = \frac{50 - 50}{8} = 0.00$$

Person C: raw score of 70 (above average)

$$z = \frac{70 - 50}{8} = +2.50$$

them to standard scores. Suppose, for example, that a first-year college student earned 125 raw score points on a spatial thinking test for which the normative sample averaged 100 points (with SD of 15 points). Suppose, in addition, he earned 110 raw score points on a vocabulary test for which the normative sample averaged 90 points (with SD of 20 points). In which skill area does he show greater aptitude, spatial thinking or vocabulary?

If the normative samples for both tests produced test score distributions of the same form, we can compare spatial thinking and vocabulary scores by converting each to standard scores. The spatial thinking standard score for our student is $(125 - 100)/15$ or $+1.67$, whereas his vocabulary standard score is $(110 - 90)/20$ or $+1.00$. Relative to the normative samples, the student has greater aptitude for spatial thinking than vocabulary.

But a word of caution is appropriate when comparing standard scores from different distributions. If the distributions do not have the same form, standard score comparisons can be very misleading. We illustrate this point with Figure 3.7, which depicts two distributions: one markedly skewed with average score of 30 (SD of 10) and another normally distributed with average score of

60 (SD of 8). A raw score of 40 on the first test and a raw score of 68 on the second test both translate to identical standard scores of $+1.00$. Yet, a standard score of 1.00 on the first test exceeds 92 percent of the normative sample, while the equivalent standard score on the second test exceeds only 84 percent of the normative sample. When two distributions of test scores do not possess the same form, equivalent standard scores do not signify comparable positions within the respective normative samples.

## T Scores and Other Standardized Scores

Many psychologists and educators appreciate the psychometric properties of standard scores but regard the decimal fractions and positive/negative signs (e.g., $z = -2.32$) as unnecessary distractions. In response to these concerns, test specialists have devised a number of variations on standard scores that are collectively referred to as *standardized scores*.

From a conceptual standpoint, standardized scores are identical to standard scores. Both kinds of scores contain exactly the same information. The shape of the distribution of scores is not affected, and a plot of the relationship between standard and

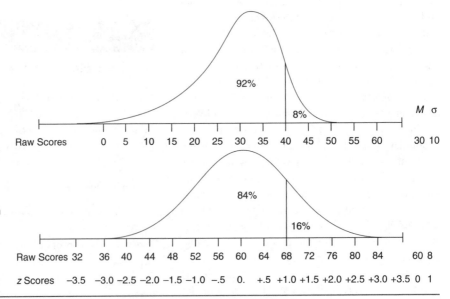

● FIGURE 3.7
Relationships between
Raw Scores, z Scores,
and Relative Standing
for Two Distributions
of Markedly Different
Form

standardized scores is always a straight line. However, standardized scores are always expressed as positive whole numbers (no decimal fractions or negative signs), so many test users prefer to depict test results in this form.

Standardized scores eliminate fractions and negative signs by producing values other than zero for the mean and 1.00 for the standard deviation of the transformed scores. The mean of the transformed scores can be set at any convenient value, such as 100 or 500, and the standard deviation at, say, 15 or 100. The important point about standardized scores is that we can transform any distribution to a preferred scale with predetermined mean and standard deviation.

One popular kind of standardized score is the *T* score, which has a mean of 50 and a standard deviation of 10. *T* score scales are especially common with personality tests. For example, on the MMPI, each clinical scale (e.g., Depression, Paranoia) is converted to a common metric for which 50 is the average score and 10 is the standard deviation for the normative sample.

To transform raw scores to *T* scores, we use the following formula:

$$T = \frac{10(X - M)}{\text{SD}} + 50$$

The term $(X - M)/\text{SD}$ is, of course, equivalent to *z*, so we can rewrite the formula for *T* as a simple transformation of *z*:

$$T = 10z + 50$$

For any distribution of raw scores, the corresponding *T* scores will have an average of 50. In addition, for most distributions the vast majority of *T* scores will fall between values of 20 and 80, that is, within three standard deviations of the mean. Of course, *T* scores outside this range are entirely possible and perhaps even likely in special populations. In clinical settings it is not unusual to observe very high *T* scores—even as high as 90—on personality inventories such as the MMPI.

Standardized scores can be tailored to produce any mean and standard deviation. However, to eliminate negative standardized scores, the preselected mean should be at least five times as large as the standard deviation. In practice, test developers rely upon a few preferred values for means and standard deviations of standardized scores, as outlined in Table 3.4.

## Normalizing Standard Scores

As previously noted, psychologists and educators prefer to deal with normal distributions because the statistical properties of the normal curve are well known and standard scores from these distributions can be directly compared. Perhaps the reader has wondered what recourse is available to test developers who find that their tests produce an asymmetrical distribution of scores in the normative sample. Fortunately, distributions of scores that are skewed or otherwise nonnormal can be transformed or normalized to fit a normal curve. Although test specialists have devised several methods for transmuting a

| ● TABLE 3.4 Means and Standard Deviations of Common Standardized Scores | | | |
|---|---|---|---|
| Type of Measure | Specific Examples | Mean | Standard Deviation |
| Full Scale IQ | WAIS-IV | 100 | 15 |
| IQ Test Subscales | Vocabulary, Block Design | 10 | 3 |
| Personality Test Scales | MMPI-2 Depression, Paranoia | 50 | 10 |
| Aptitude Tests | Graduate Record Exam, Scholastic Assessment Tests | 500 | 100 |

nonnormal distribution into a normal one, we will discuss only the most popular approach—the conversion of percentiles to normalized standard scores. Oddly enough, it is easier to explain this approach if we first describe the reverse process: conversion of standard scores to percentiles.

We have noted that a normal distribution of raw scores has, by definition, a distinct, mathematically defined shape (Figure 3.3). In addition, we have pointed out that transforming a group of raw scores to standard scores leaves the original form of a distribution unchanged. Thus, if a collection of raw scores is normally distributed, the resulting standard scores will obey the normal curve, too.

We also know that the mathematical properties of the normal distribution are precisely calculable. Without going into the details of computation, it should be obvious that we can determine the percentage of cases falling below any particular standard score. For example, in Figure 3.6, a standard score of $-2.00$ (designated as $-2\sigma$) exceeds 2.14 percent of the cases. Thus, a standard score of $-2.00$ corresponds to a percentile of 2.14. In like manner, any conceivable standard score can be expressed in terms of its corresponding percentile. Appendix D lists percentiles for standard scores and several other transformed scores.

Producing a **normalized standard score** is accomplished by working in the other direction. Namely, we use the percentile for each raw score to determine its corresponding standard score. If we do this for each and every case in a nonnormal distribution, the resulting distribution of standard scores will be normally distributed. Notice that in such a normalized standard score distribution, the standard scores are not calculated directly from the usual computational formula but are determined indirectly by first computing the percentile and then ascertaining the equivalent standard score.

The conversion of percentiles to normalized standard scores might seem an ideal solution to the problem of unruly test data. However, there is a potentially serious drawback: Normalized standard scores are a nonlinear transformation of the raw scores. Thus, mathematical relationships established with the raw scores may not hold true for the normalized standard scores. In a markedly skewed distribution, it is even possible that a raw score that is significantly below the mean might conceivably have a normalized standard score that is above the mean.

In practice, normalized standard scores are used sparingly. Such transformations are appropriate only when the normative sample is large and representative and the raw score distribution is only mildly nonnormal. Incidentally, the most likely cause of these nonnormal score distributions is inappropriate difficulty level in the test items, such as too many difficult or easy items.

There is a catch-22 here, in that mildly nonnormal distributions are not changed much when they are normalized, so little is gained in the process. Ironically, normalized standard scores produce the greatest change with markedly nonnormal distributions. However, when the raw score distribution is markedly nonnormal, test developers are better advised to go back to the drawing board and adjust the difficulty level of test items so as to produce a normal distribution, rather than succumb to the partial statistical fix of normalized standard scores.

### Stanines, Stens, and C Scale

Finally, we give brief mention to three raw score transformations that are mainly of historical interest. The stanine (standard nine) scale was developed by the United States Air Force during World War II. In a **stanine scale,** all raw scores are converted to a single-digit system of scores ranging from 1 to 9. The mean of stanine scores is always 5, and the standard deviation is approximately 2. The transformation from raw scores to stanines is simple: The scores are ranked from lowest to highest, and the bottom 4 percent of scores convert to a stanine of 1, the next 7 percent convert to a stanine of 2, and so on (see Table 3.5). The main advantage of stanines is that they are restricted to single-digit numbers. This was a considerable asset in the premodern computer era in which data was keypunched on Hollerith cards that had to be physically carried and stored on shelves. Because a stanine could be keypunched in a single column,

| ● TABLE 3.5 | Distribution Percentages for Use in Stanine Conversion | | | | | | | | |
|---|---|---|---|---|---|---|---|---|---|
| Percentage | 4 | 7 | 12 | 17 | 20 | 17 | 12 | 7 | 4 |
| Stanine | 1 | 2 | 3 | 4 | 5 | 6 | 7 | 8 | 9 |

far fewer cards were required than if the original raw scores were entered.

Statisticians have proposed several variations on the stanine theme. Canfield (1951) proposed the 10-unit **sten scale,** with 5 units above and 5 units below the mean. Guilford and Fruchter (1978) proposed the **C scale** consisting of 11 units. Although stanines are still in widespread use, variants such as the sten and C scale never roused much interest among test developers.

### A Summary of Statistically Based Norms

We have alluded several times to the ease with which standard scores, *T* scores, stanines, and percentiles can be transformed into each other, especially if the underlying distribution of raw scores is normally distributed. In fact, the exact form in which scores are reported is largely a matter of convention and personal preference. For example, a WAIS-III IQ of 115 could also be reported as a standard score of +1.00, or a *T* score of 60, or a percentile rank of 84. All of these results convey exactly the same information.[1] Figure 3.8 summarizes the relationships that exist between the most commonly used statistically based norms.

This ends the brief introduction to the many techniques by which test data from a normative sample can be statistically summarized and transformed. We should never lose sight of the overriding purpose of these statistical transmutations, namely, to help the test user make sense out of one individual's score in relation to an appropriate comparison group.

But what is an appropriate comparison group? What characteristics should we require in our norm group subjects? How should we go about choosing these subjects? How many subjects do we need? These are important questions that influence the relevance of test results just as much as proper item selection and standardized testing procedure. In the remainder of this topic, we examine the procedures involved in selecting a norm group.

### ● SELECTING A NORM GROUP

When choosing a norm group, test developers strive to obtain a representative cross section of the population for whom the test is designed (Petersen, Kolen, & Hoover, 1989). In theory, obtaining a representative norm group is straightforward and simple. Consider a scholastic achievement test designed for sixth graders in the United States. The relevant population is all sixth graders coast to coast and in Alaska and Hawaii. A representative cross section of these potential subjects could be obtained by computerized random sampling of 10,000 or so of the millions of eligible children. Each child would have an equal chance of being chosen to take the test; that is, the selection strategy would be simple **random sampling.** The results for such a sample would comprise an ideal source of normative data. With a large random sample, it is almost certain that the diversities of ethnic background, social class, geographic location, urban versus rural setting, and so on would be proportionately represented in the sample.

In the real world, obtaining norm samples is never as simple and definitive as the hypothetical case previously outlined. Researchers do not have a

---

1. A WAIS-III IQ of 115 also can be expressed as a stanine of 7. However, it is worth noting that some information is lost when scores are reported as stanines. Note that IQs in the range of 111 to 119 *all* convert to a stanine of 7. Thus, if we are told only that an individual has achieved at the 7th stanine on an intelligence test, we do not know the exact IQ equivalent.

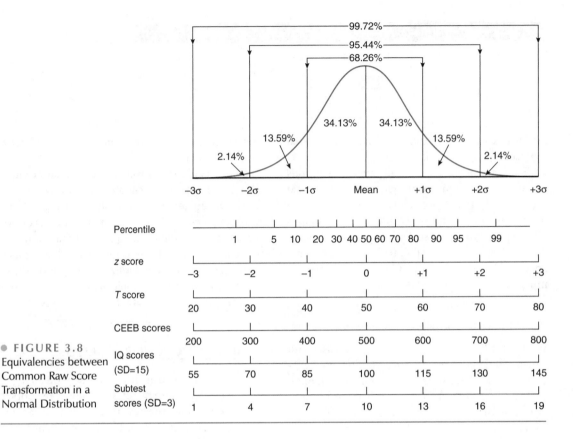

● FIGURE 3.8
Equivalencies between
Common Raw Score
Transformation in a
Normal Distribution

complete list of every sixth grader in the nation, and even if they did, test developers could not compel every randomly selected child to participate in the standardization of a test. Questions of cost arise, too. Psychometricians must be paid to administer the tests to the norm group. Test developers may opt for a few hundred representative subjects instead of a larger number.

To help ensure that smaller norm groups are truly representative of the population for which the test was designed, test developers employ **stratified random sampling.** This approach consists of stratifying, or classifying, the target population on important background variables (e.g., age, sex, race, social class, educational level) and then selecting an appropriate percentage of persons at random from each stratum. For example, if 12 percent of the relevant population is African American,

then the test developer chooses subjects randomly but with the constraint that 12 percent of the norm group is also African American.

In practice, very few test developers fully emulate either random sampling or stratified random sampling in the process of selecting the norm group. What is more typical is a good faith effort to pick a diverse and representative sample from strong and weak schools, minority and white neighborhoods, large and small cities, and northern, eastern, central, and southern communities. If this sample then embodies about the same percentage of minorities, city dwellers, and upper- and lower-class families as the national census, then the test developer feels secure that the norm group is representative.

There is an important lesson in the uncertainties, compromises, and pragmatics of norm group selection; namely, psychological test norms are not absolute, universal, or timeless. They are relative to one historical era and the particular normative population from which they were derived. We will illustrate the ephemeral nature of normative statistics in a later section when we show how a major IQ test normed at a national average of 100 in 1974 yielded a national average of 107 in 1988. Even norms that are selected with great care and based on large samples can become obsolete in a decade—sometimes less.

## Age and Grade Norms

As we grow older, we change in measurable ways, for better or worse. This is obviously true in childhood, when intellectual skills improve visibly from one month to the next. In adulthood, personal change is slower but still discernible. We expect, for example, that adults will show a more mature level of vocabulary with each passing decade (Gregory & Gernert, 1990).

An **age norm** depicts the level of test performance for each separate age group in the normative sample. The purpose of age norms is to facilitate same-aged comparisons. With age norms, the performance of an examinee is interpreted in relation to standardization subjects of the same age. The age span for a normative age group can vary from a month to a decade or more, depending on the degree to which test performance is age-dependent. For characteristics that change quickly with age—such as intellectual abilities in childhood—test developers might report separate test norms for narrowly defined age brackets, such as four-month intervals. This allows the examiner, for example, to compare test results of a child who is 5 years and 2 months old (age 5-2) to the normative sample of children ranging from age 5-0 to age 5-4. By contrast, adult characteristics change more slowly and it might be sufficient to report normative data by 5- or 10-year age intervals.

Grade norms are conceptually similar to age norms. A **grade norm** depicts the level of test performance for each separate grade in the normative sample. Grade norms are rarely used with ability tests. However, these norms are especially useful in

school settings when reporting the achievement levels of schoolchildren. Since academic achievement in many content areas is heavily dependent on grade-based curricular exposure, comparing a student against a normative sample from the same grade is more appropriate than using an age-based comparison.

## Local and Subgroup Norms

With many applications, local or subgroup norms are needed to suit the specific purpose of a test. **Local norms** are derived from representative local examinees, as opposed to a national sample. Likewise, **subgroup norms** consist of the scores obtained from an identified subgroup (African Americans, Hispanics, females), as opposed to a diversified national sample. As an example of local norms in action, the admissions officer of a junior college that attracts mainly local residents might prefer to consult statewide norms rather than national norms on a scholastic achievement test.

As a general rule, whenever an identifiable subgroup performs appreciably better or worse on a test than the more broadly defined standardization sample, it may be helpful to construct supplementary subgroup norms. The subgroups can be formed with respect to sex, ethnic background, geographical region, urban versus rural environment, socioeconomic level, and many other factors.

Whether local or subgroup norms are beneficial depends on the purpose of testing. For example, ethnic norms for standardized intelligence tests may be superior to nationally based norms in predicting competence within the child's non-school environment. However, ethnic norms may not predict how well a child will succeed in mainstream public school instructional programs (Mercer & Lewis, 1978). Thus, local and subgroup norms must be used cautiously.

## Expectancy Tables

One practical form that norms may take is an expectancy table. An **expectancy table** portrays the established relationship between test scores and expected outcome on a relevant task (Harmon, 1989). Expectancy tables are especially useful with predictor tests used to forecast well-defined criteria. For example, an expectancy table could depict the relationship between scores on a scholastic aptitude test (predictor) and subsequent college grade point average (criterion).

Expectancy tables are always based on the previous predictor and criterion results for large samples of examinees. The practical value of tabulating normative information in this manner is that new examinees receive a probabilistic preview of how well they are likely to do on the criterion. For example, high school examinees who take a scholastic aptitude test can be told the statistical odds of achieving a particular college grade point average.

Based on 7,835 previous examinees who subsequently attended a major university, the expectancy table in Table 3.6 provides the probability of achieving certain first-year college grades as a function of score on the American College Testing (ACT) examination. The ACT test is typically given to high school seniors who have expressed an interest in attending college. The first column of the table shows ACT test scores, divided into 10 class intervals. The second column gives the number of students whose scores fell into each interval. The remaining entries in each row show the percentage of students within each test-score interval who subsequently received college grade points within a designated range. For example, of the 117 students who scored 31 to 33 points on the ACT, only 2 percent received a first-year college grade point average below 1.50, while 64 percent earned superlative grades of 3.50 up to a perfect A or 4.00. At the other extreme, of the 102 students who scored below 10 points on the ACT, fully 80 percent (60 percent plus 20 percent) received first-year college grades below a C average of 2.00.

Of course, expectancy tables do not foreordain how new examinees will do on the criterion. In an individual case, it is conceivable that a low–ACT scoring student might beat the odds and earn a 4.00 college grade point average. More commonly, though, new examinees discover that expectancy tables provide a broadly accurate preview of criterion performance.

But there are some exceptional instances in which expectancy tables can become inaccurate. An

● TABLE 3.6  Expectancy Table Showing Relation between ACT Composite Scores and First-Year College Grades for 7,835 Students at a Major State University

| ACT Test Score | Number of Cases | Grade Point Average (4.00 Scale) | | | | | |
|---|---|---|---|---|---|---|---|
| | | 0.00–1.49 | 1.50–1.99 | 2.00–2.49 | 2.50–2.99 | 3.00–3.49 | 3.50–4.00 |
| 34–36 | 3 | 0 | 0 | 33 | 0 | 0 | 67 |
| 31–33 | 117 | 2 | 2 | 4 | 9 | 19 | 64 |
| 28–30 | 646 | 10 | 6 | 10 | 17 | 23 | 35 |
| 25–27 | 1,458 | 12 | 10 | 16 | 19 | 24 | 19 |
| 22–24 | 1,676 | 17 | 10 | 22 | 20 | 20 | 11 |
| 19–21 | 1,638 | 23 | 14 | 25 | 18 | 16 | 4 |
| 16–18 | 1,173 | 31 | 17 | 24 | 15 | 11 | 3 |
| 13–15 | 690 | 38 | 18 | 25 | 12 | 6 | 1 |
| 10–12 | 332 | 54 | 16 | 20 | 6 | 3 | 1 |
| below 10 | 102 | 60 | 20 | 13 | 8 | 0 | 0 |

Note: Some rows total to more than 100 percent because of rounding errors.

*Source:* Courtesy of Archie George, Management Information Services, University of Idaho.

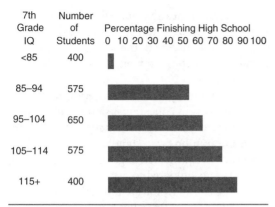

| 7th Grade IQ | Number of Students | Percentage Finishing High School |
|---|---|---|
| <85 | 400 | |
| 85–94 | 575 | |
| 95–104 | 650 | |
| 105–114 | 575 | |
| 115+ | 400 | |

● **FIGURE 3.9**  Expectancy of High School Graduation as a Function of Seventh-Grade IQ

*Source:*  Based on data from Dillon, H. J. (1949). *Early school leavers: A major educational problem.* New York: National Child Labor Committee. Cited in Matarazzo (1972).

expectancy table is always based on the previous performance of a large and representative sample of examinees whose test performances and criterion outcomes reflected existing social conditions and institutional policies. If conditions or policies change, an expectancy table can become obsolete and misleading. Consider the expectancy table in Figure 3.9, which depicts the likelihood of finishing high school as a function of seventh-grade IQ (Dillon, 1949, cited in Matarazzo, 1972, p. 283). Notice that in the 1940s only 4 percent of seventh-grade students with IQs below 85 went on to finish high school. However, social policies and school environments have changed since the 1940s. There is currently a strong emphasis on special services for students with disabilities, with the aim of retention and eventual graduation. As a result, the expectancy table in Figure 3.9 surely would be pessimistically erroneous if applied to contemporary seventh-grade students with low IQs.

● **CRITERION-REFERENCED TESTS**

We close this unit with a brief mention of an alternative to norm-referenced tests, namely, criterion-referenced tests. These two kinds of tests differ

in their intended purposes, the manner in which content is chosen, and the process of interpreting results (Berk, 1984; Bond, 1996; Frechtling, 1989; Popham, 1978).

The purpose of a norm-referenced test is to classify examinees, from low to high, across a continuum of ability or achievement. Thus, a norm-referenced test uses a representative sample of individuals—the norm group or standardization sample—as its interpretive framework. Examiners might want to classify individuals in this way for purposes of selection to a specialized curriculum or placement in remedial or gifted programs. In a classroom setting, a teacher might use a norm-referenced test to assign students to different reading levels or math instructional groups (Bond, 1996).

Whereas norm-referenced tests are used to rank students along a continuum in comparison to one another, criterion-referenced tests are used to compare examinees' accomplishments to a pre-defined performance standard. For example, consider a hypothetical school system in which fourth graders are expected to master the addition of pairs of two-digit numbers (e.g., 23 + 19 = 42). Perhaps the performance standard is set at 80 percent accuracy when doing ten such addition problems in a 15-minute time period. Results for a specific fourth grader are then descriptively stated as a particular percentage (e.g., 70 percent). While it is possible to compare this result to the predetermined *standard,* no comparison is made to other *students.* In fact, it is entirely possible (and even desirable) for all students to exceed the standard.

Criterion-referenced tests represent a fundamental shift in perspective. The focus is on what the test taker can do rather than on comparisons to the performance levels of others. Thus, criterion-referenced tests identify an examinee's relative mastery (or nonmastery) of specific, predetermined competencies. These kinds of tests are increasingly popular in educational systems, where they are used to evaluate how well students have mastered the academic skills expected at each grade level. This information, in turn, provides a basis for intervention with students who are lagging behind. In addition, system-wide results of criterion-referenced tests can be used to evaluate the curriculum and to determine how well individual schools are teaching the curriculum.

A major difference between norm-referenced tests and criterion-referenced tests is the manner in which test content is chosen. In a norm-referenced test, items are chosen so that they provide maximal discrimination among respondents along the dimension being measured. Within this framework, well-defined psychometric principles are used to identify ideal items according to difficulty level, correlation with the total score, and other properties. In contrast, with a criterion-referenced test, the content is selected on the basis of its relevance in the curriculum. This involves the judgment and consensus of educators and other stakeholders in the educational enterprise. In Table 3.7, we have summarized and compared some distinctive characteristics of criterion-referenced and norm-referenced tests.

Criterion-referenced tests are best suited to the testing of basic academic skills (e.g., reading level, computation skill) in educational settings. However, these kinds of instruments are largely inappropriate for testing higher-level abilities because it is difficult to formulate specific objectives for such content domains. Consider a particular case: How could we develop a criterion-referenced test for expert computer programming? It would be difficult to propose specific behaviors that all expert computer programmers would possess

and, therefore, nearly impossible to construct a criterion-referenced test for this high-level skill. Berk (1984) discusses the technical problems in the construction and evaluation of criterion-referenced tests.

A common application of criterion-referenced tests (CRTs) is in educational settings where they are used to determine whether students have met the minimum or basic standards in curriculum areas such as algebra, reading, or science. As noted, students are compared to a standard, not to one another. CRTs allow for the possibility that everyone might pass. At first glance, they might appear to be more equitable than norm-referenced tests which feature comparisons among students. However, as noted by FairTest, the National Center for Open and Fair Testing (www.fairtest.org), whether CRTs are really fair depends upon how the cut-off scores are determined:

> On a standardized CRT (one taken by students in many schools), the passing or "cut-off" score is usually set by a committee of experts, while in a classroom the teacher sets the passing score. In both cases, deciding the passing score is subjective, not objective. Sometimes cut scores have been set in a way that maximizes the number of low-income or minority students who fail the test. A small change in the cut score would not change the meaning of the test but would greatly increase minority pass rates. (www.fairtest.org)

● **TABLE 3.7   Distinctive Characteristics of Criterion-Referenced and Norm-Referenced Tests**

| Dimension | Criterion-Referenced Tests | Norm-Referenced Tests |
|---|---|---|
| Purpose | Compare examinees' performance to a standard | Compare examinees' performance to one another |
| Item Content | Narrow domain of skills with real-world relevance | Broad domain of skills with indirect relevance |
| Item Selection | Most items of similar difficulty level | Items vary widely in difficulty level |
| Interpretation of Scores | Scores usually expressed as a percentage, with passing level predetermined | Scores usually expressed as a standard score, percentile, or grade equivalent |

Another concern is the degree to which the test matches the curriculum. Many state tests are developed by a committee of experts who have only general ideas about what students might be taught. The tests that emerge from the committee might not match the curricula for specific school systems. Thus, they might include areas that some students have not studied.

## ● S U M M A R Y

1. A norm group consists of a sample of examinees who are representative of the population for whom the test is intended. A frequency distribution is useful in portraying the distribution of test scores within certain score intervals for a norm group. A histogram is a graphic representation of a frequency distribution.

2. Measures of central tendency for collections of scores include the mean or arithmetic average; the median or middlemost of the ranked scores; and the mode, which is the most frequently occurring score.

3. Measures of variability for a group of scores include the variance and its square root, the standard deviation, which is the preferred measure in psychological testing. These indices help gauge the dispersion of scores by incorporating the sums of squared deviations from the mean score in their formulas.

4. The distribution of test scores for large groups of heterogeneous examinees often resembles the normal distribution, a symmetrical, mathematically defined, bell-shaped curve. Psychologists prefer to deal with normally distributed test scores because the statistical characteristics of the normal distribution are well known.

5. A skewed distribution is one in which the scores pile up at the low end (positive skew) or the high end (negative skew). On psychological tests, the most common cause of positive skew is too few easy items, whereas the most common cause of negative skew is too few hard items.

6. A percentile expresses the percentage of persons in the standardization sample who scored below a specific raw score. Percentiles vary from 0 to 100. It is important to distinguish percentile (a relative measure) from percent correct (an absolute measure).

7. A standard score expresses an examinee's raw score in terms of its distance from the mean in standard deviation units. The formula for a standard score is $z = (X - M)/\text{SD}$. A $T$ score is a standardized score with mean of 50 and standard deviation of 10. The formula for a $T$ score is

$$T = 10(X - M)/\text{SD} + 50$$

8. The most common approach to selecting a norm group is through stratified random sampling. In this procedure, the target population is stratified or classified on important background variables (e.g., age, sex, race, social class, educational level) and then an appropriate percentage of persons is chosen at random within each stratum.

9. For many tests, it is important to provide separate age and grade norms. Age norms are necessary for characteristics that change quickly with developing age—for example, intellectual abilities in childhood. Grade norms are commonly used in school settings when reporting the achievement levels of schoolchildren.

10. Local and subgroup norms may be valuable if an identifiable subgroup performs appreciably better or worse on a test than the more broadly defined standardization sample.

11. An expectancy table—one form of test standardization—portrays the established relationship between test scores and expected outcome on a relevant task. For example, an expectancy table might depict the relationship between scores on a scholastic aptitude test and subsequent college grade point average.

**12.** A criterion-referenced test compares an examinee's test accomplishments to a well-defined content domain. These tests help identify an examinee's mastery or nonmastery of specific behaviors. For example, results of a criterion-referenced test might specify that the examinee can add two 3-digit numbers correctly 100 percent of the time.

## ● KEY TERMS AND CONCEPTS

norm group   p. 68

raw score   p. 68

frequency distribution   p. 69

histogram   p. 70

frequency polygon   p. 70

mean   p. 70

median   p. 70

mode   p. 70

standard deviation   p. 71

variance   p. 71

normal distribution   p. 71

skewness   p. 72

percentile   p. 74

standard score   p. 74

*T* score   p. 77

normalized standard score   p. 78

stanine scale   p. 78

sten scale   p. 79

C scale   p. 79

random sampling   p. 79

stratified random sampling   p. 80

age norm   p. 81

grade norm   p. 81

local norms   p. 81

subgroup norms   p. 81

expectancy table   p. 81

# Concepts of Reliability

eliability refers to the attribute of consistency in measurement. However, reliability is seldom an all-or-none matter; more commonly it is a question of degree. Very few measures of physical or psychological characteristics are completely consistent, even from one moment to the next. For example, a person who steps on a scale twice in quick succession might register a weight of 145½ pounds the first time and 145¾ pounds the second. The same individual might take two presumably equivalent forms of an IQ test and score 114 on one and 119 on the other. Two successive measures of speed of response—pressing a key quickly whenever the letter *X* appears on a microcomputer screen—might produce a reaction time of 223 milliseconds on the first trial and 341 milliseconds on the next. We see in these examples a pattern of consistency—the pairs of measurements are not completely random—but different amounts of inconsistency are evident, too. In the short run, measures of weight are highly consistent, intellectual test scores are moderately stable, but simple reaction time is somewhat erratic.

The concept of **reliability** is best viewed as a continuum ranging from minimal consistency of measurement (e.g., simple reaction time) to near-perfect repeatability of results (e.g., weight). Most psychological tests fall somewhere in between these two extremes. With regard to tests, an acceptable degree of reliability is more than an academic matter. After all, it would be foolish and unethical to base important decisions on test results that are not repeatable.

Psychometricians have devised several statistical methods for estimating the degree of reliability of measurements, and we will explore the computation of such reliability coefficients in some detail. But first we examine a more fundamental issue to help clarify the meaning of reliability: What are the sources of consistency and inconsistency in psychological test results?

## ● CLASSICAL TEST THEORY AND THE SOURCES OF MEASUREMENT ERROR

The theory of measurement introduced here has been called the classical test theory because it was developed from simple assumptions made by test theorists since the inception of testing. This approach is also called the *theory of true and error scores,* for reasons explained below. Charles Spearman (1904) laid down the foundation for the theory which was subsequently extended and revised by contemporary psychologists (Feldt & Brennan, 1989; Lord & Novick, 1968; Kline, 1986). We should mention that a rival model does exist and is slowly supplanting classical test theory as a basis for test development. Item response theory, or latent trait theory (Embretson & Hershberger, 1999), is an appealing alternative to classical test theory. We close this chapter with a brief review of item response theory. However, classical test theory was the basis for test development throughout most of the twentieth century. Accordingly, we begin our coverage with this model.

The basic starting point of the **classical theory of measurement** is the idea that test scores result from the influence of two factors:

1. Factors that contribute to consistency. These consist entirely of the stable attributes of the individual, which the examiner is trying to measure.
2. Factors that contribute to inconsistency. These include characteristics of the individual, test, or situation that have nothing to do with the attribute being measured, but that nonetheless affect test scores.

It should be clear to the reader that the first factor is desirable because it represents the true amount of the attribute in question, while the second factor represents the unavoidable nuisance of error factors that contribute to inaccuracies of measurement. We can express this conceptual breakdown as a simple equation:

$$X = T + e$$

where $X$ is the obtained score, $T$ is the **true score,** and $e$ represents errors of measurement.

Errors in measurement, thus, represent discrepancies between the obtained scores and the corresponding true scores:

$$e = X - T$$

Notice in the preceding equations that errors of measurement $e$ can be either positive or negative. If $e$ is positive, the obtained score $X$ will be higher than the true score $T$. Conversely, if $e$ is negative, the obtained score will be lower than the true score. Although it is impossible to eliminate all **measurement error,** test developers do strive to minimize this psychometric nuisance through careful attention to the sources of measurement error outlined in the following section.

Finally, it is important to stress that the true score is never known. As the reader will discover, we can obtain a probability that the true score resides within a certain interval and we can also derive a best estimate of the true score. However, we can never know the value of a true score with certainty.

## ● SOURCES OF MEASUREMENT ERROR

As indicated by the formula $X = T + e$, measurement error $e$ is everything other than the true score that makes up the obtained test score. Errors of measurement can arise from innumerable sources (Feldt & Brennan, 1989). Stanley (1971) provides an unusually thorough list. We will outline only the most important and likely contributions here: item selection, test administration, test scoring, and systematic errors of measurement.

## Item Selection

One source of measurement error is the instrument itself. A test developer must settle on a finite number of items from a potentially infinite pool of test questions. Which questions should be included? How should they be worded? Item selection is crucial to the accuracy of measurement.

Although psychometricians strive to obtain representative test items, the particular set of questions chosen for a test might not be equally fair to all persons. A hypothetical and deliberately extreme example will serve to illustrate this point: Even a well-prepared student might flunk a classroom test that emphasized the obscure footnotes in the textbook. By contrast, an ill-prepared but curious student who studied only the footnotes might do very well on such an exam. The scores for both persons would reflect massive amounts of measurement error. Remember in this context that the true score is what the student really knows. For the conscientious student, the obtained score would be far lower than the true score because of a hefty dose of negative measurement error. For the serendipitous second student, the obtained score would be far higher than the true score, owing to the positive measurement error.

Of course, in a well-designed test the measurement error from item sampling will be minimal. However, a test is always a sample and never the totality of a person's knowledge or behavior. As a result, item selection is always a source of measurement error in psychological testing. The best a psychometrician can do is minimize this unwanted nuisance by attending carefully to issues of test construction. We discuss technical aspects of item selection in Topic 4B, Test Construction.

## Test Administration

Although examiners usually provide an optimal and standardized testing environment, numerous sources of measurement error may nonetheless arise from the circumstances of administration. Examples of general environmental conditions that may exert an untoward influence on the accuracy of measurement include uncomfortable room temperature, dim lighting, and excessive noise. In some cases it is not possible to anticipate the qualities of the testing situation that will contribute to measurement error. Consider this example: An otherwise lackluster undergraduate correctly answers a not very challenging information item, namely, "Who wrote *Canterbury Tales*?" When queried later whether he had read any Chaucer, the student replies, "No, but you've got that book right behind you on your bookshelf."

Momentary fluctuations in anxiety, motivation, attention, and fatigue level of the test taker may also introduce sources of measurement error. For example, an examinee who did not sleep well the night before might lack concentration and, therefore, misread questions. A student distracted by temporary emotional distress might inadvertently respond in the wrong columns of the answer sheet. The classic nightmare in this regard is the test taker who skips a question—let us say, question number 19—but forgets to leave the corresponding part of the answer sheet blank. As a result, all the subsequent answers are off by one, with the response to question 20 entered on the answer sheet as item 19, and so on.

The examiner, too, may contribute to measurement error in the process of test administration. In an orally administered test, an unconscious nod of the head by the tester might convey that the examinee is on the right track, thereby guiding the test taker to the correct response. Conversely, a terse and abrupt examiner may intimidate a test taker who would otherwise volunteer a correct answer.

## Test Scoring

Whenever a psychological test uses a format other than machine-scored multiple-choice items, some degree of judgment is required to assign points to answers. Fortunately, most tests have well-defined criteria for answers to each question. These guidelines help minimize the impact of subjective judgment in scoring (Gregory, 1987). However, subjectivity of scoring as a source of measurement error can be a serious problem in the evaluation of projective tests or essay questions. With regard to projective tests, Nunnally (1978) points out that the projective tester might undergo an evolutionary change in scoring criteria over time, coming to regard a particular type of response as more and more pathological with each encounter.

### Systematic Measurement Error

The sources of inaccuracy previously discussed are collectively referred to as *unsystematic measurement error,* meaning that their effects are unpredictable and inconsistent. However, there is another type of measurement error that constitutes a veritable ghost in the psychometric machine. A **systematic measurement error** arises when, unknown to the test developer, a test consistently measures something other than the trait for which it was intended. Suppose, for example, that a scale to measure social introversion also inadvertently taps anxiety in a consistent fashion. In this case, the equation depicting the relationship between observed scores, true scores, and sources of measurement error would be

$$X = T + e_s + e_u$$

where $X$ is the obtained score, $T$ is the true score, $e_s$ is the systematic error due to the anxiety subcomponent, and $e_u$ is the collective effect of the unsystematic measurement errors previously outlined.

Because by definition their presence is initially undetected, systematic measurement errors may constitute a significant problem in the development of psychological tests. However, if psychometricians use proper test development procedures discussed in Topic 4B, Test Construction, the impact of systematic measurement errors can be greatly minimized. Nonetheless, systematic measurement errors serve as a reminder that it is very difficult, if not impossible, to truly assess a trait in pure isolation from other traits.

### ● MEASUREMENT ERROR AND RELIABILITY

Perhaps at this point the reader is wondering what measurement error has to do with reliability. The most obvious connection is that measurement error reduces the reliability or repeatability of psychological test results. In fact, we will show here that reliability bears a precise statistical relationship to measurement error. Reliability and measurement error are really just different ways of expressing the same concern: How consistent is a psychological test? The interdependence of these two concepts will become clear if we provide a further sketch of the classical theory of measurement.

A crucial assumption of classical theory is that unsystematic measurement errors act as random influences. This does not mean that the sources of measurement error are completely mysterious and unfathomable in every individual case. We might suspect for one person that her score on digit span reflected a slight negative measurement error caused by the auditory interference of someone coughing in the hallway during the presentation of the fifth item. Likewise, we could conjecture that another person received the benefit of positive measurement error by glimpsing in the mirror behind the examiner to see the correct answer to the ninth item on an information test. Thus, measurement error is not necessarily a mysterious event in every individual case.

However, when we examine the test scores of groups of persons, the causes of measurement error are incredibly complex and varied. In this context, unsystematic measurement errors behave like random variables. The classical theory accepts this essential randomness of measurement error as an axiomatic assumption.

Because they are random events, unsystematic measurement errors are equally likely to be positive or negative and will, therefore, average out to zero across a large group of subjects. Thus, a second assumption is that the mean error of measurement is zero. Classical theory also assumes that measurement errors are not correlated with true scores. This makes intuitive sense: If the error scores were related to another score, it would suggest that they were systematic rather than random, which would violate the essential assumption of classical theory. Finally, it is also assumed that measurement errors are not correlated with errors on other tests.

We can summarize the main features of classical theory as follows (Gulliksen, 1950, chap. 2):

1. Measurement errors are random.
2. Mean error of measurement = 0.
3. True scores and errors are uncorrelated: $r_{Te} = 0$.
4. Errors on different tests are uncorrelated: $r_{12} = 0$.

Starting from these assumptions, it is possible to develop a number of important implications for reliability and measurement. (The points that follow are based on the optimistic assumption that systematic measurement errors are minimal or nonexistent for the instrument in question.) For example, we know that any test administered to a large group of persons will show a variability of obtained scores that can be expressed statistically as a variance, that is, $\sigma^2$. The value of classical theory is that it permits us to partition the variance of obtained scores into two separate sources. Specifically, it can be shown that the variance of obtained scores is simply the variance of true scores plus the variance of errors of measurement:

$$\sigma_X^2 = \sigma_T^2 + \sigma_e^2$$

We will refer the interested reader to Gulliksen (1950, chap. 3) for the computational details.

The preceding formula demonstrates that test scores vary as the result of two factors: variability in true scores, and variability due to measurement error. The obvious implication of this relationship is that errors of measurement contribute to inconsistency of obtained test scores; results will not remain stable if the test is administered again.

## ● THE RELIABILITY COEFFICIENT

We are finally in a position to delineate the precise relationship between reliability and measurement error. By now the reader should have discerned that reliability expresses the relative influence of true and error scores on obtained test scores. In more precise mathematical terms, the **reliability coefficient** ($r_{XX}$) is the ratio of true score variance to the total variance of test scores. That is:

$$r_{XX} = \frac{\sigma_T^2}{\sigma_X^2}$$

or equivalently:

$$r_{XX} = \frac{\sigma_T^2}{\sigma_T^2 + \sigma_e^2}$$

Note that the range of potential values for $r_{XX}$ can be derived from analysis of the preceding formula. Consider what happens when the variance due to measurement error ($\sigma_e^2$) is very small, close to zero. In that event, the reliability coefficient ($r_{XX}$) approaches a value of ($\sigma_T^2/\sigma_T^2$) or 1.0. At the opposite extreme, where the variance due to measurement error is very large, the value of the reliability coefficient becomes smaller, approaching a theoretical limit of 0.0. In sum, a completely unreliable test (large measurement error) will yield a reliability coefficient close to 0.0, while a completely reliable test (no measurement error) will produce a reliability coefficient of 1.0. Thus, the possible range of the reliability coefficient is between 0.0 and 1.0. In practice, all tests produce reliability coefficients somewhere in between, but the closer the value of $r_{XX}$ to 1.0, the better.

In a literal sense, $r_{XX}$ indicates the proportion of variance in obtained test scores that is accounted for by the variability in true scores. However, the formula for the reliability coefficient $r_{XX}$ indicates an additional interpretation of it as well. The reader will recall that obtained scores are symbolized by $X$s. In like manner, the subscripts in the symbol for the reliability coefficient signify that $r_{XX}$ is an index of the potential or actual consistency of obtained scores. Thus, tests that capture minimal amounts of measurement error produce consistent and reliable scores; their reliability coefficients are near 1.0. Conversely, tests that reflect large amounts of measurement error produce inconsistent and unreliable scores; their reliability coefficients are closer to 0.0.

Up to this point, the discussion of reliability has been conceptual rather than practical. We have pointed out that reliability refers to consistency of measurement; that reliability is diminished to the extent that errors of measurement dominate the obtained score; and that one statistical index of reliability, the reliability coefficient, can vary between 0.0 and 1.0. But how is a statistical measure of reliability computed? We approach this topic indirectly, first reviewing an essential statistical tool, the correlation coefficient. The reader will discover that the correlation coefficient, a numerical index of the degree of linear relationship between two sets of scores, is an excellent tool for appraising the consistency or repeatability of test scores. We provide a short refresher on the meaning of correlation before proceeding to a summary of methods for estimating reliability.

## ● THE CORRELATION COEFFICIENT

In its most common application, a **correlation coefficient** (*r*) expresses the degree of linear relationship between two sets of scores obtained from the same persons. Correlation coefficients can take on values ranging from −1.00 to +1.00. A correlation coefficient of +1.00 signifies a perfect linear relationship between the two sets of scores. In particular, when two measures have a correlation of +1.00, the rank ordering of subjects is identical for both sets of scores. Furthermore, when arrayed on a scatterplot (Figure 3.10a), the individual data points (each representing a pair of scores from a single subject) conform to a perfectly straight line with an upward slope. A correlation coefficient of −1.00 signifies an equally strong relationship but with inverse correspondence: the highest score on one variable corresponding to the lowest score on the other, and vice versa. In this case, the individual data points conform to a perfectly straight line with a downward slope (Figure 3.10b). Correlations of +1.00 or −1.00 are extremely rare in psychological research and usually signify a trivial finding. For example, if on two occasions in quick succession we counted the number of letters in the last name of 100 students, these two sets of "scores" would show a correlation of +1.00.

Negative correlations usually result from the manner in which one of the two variables was scored. For example, scores on the Category Test (Reitan & Wolfson, 1993) are reported as errors, whereas results on the Raven Progressive Matrices (Raven, Court, & Raven, 1983, 1986) are reported

as number of items correct. Persons who obtain a high score on the Category Test (many errors) will most likely obtain a low score on the Progressive Matrices test (few correct). Thus, we would expect a substantial negative correlation for scores on these two tests.

Consider the scatterplot in Figure 3.10c, which might depict the hypothetical heights and weights of a group of persons. As the reader can see, height and weight are strongly but not perfectly related to one another. Tall persons tend to weigh more, short persons less, but there are some exceptions. If we were to compute the correlation coefficient between height and weight—a simple statistical task outlined in the following—we would obtain a value of about +.80, indicating a strong, positive relationship between these measures.

When two variables have no relationship, the scatterplot takes on an undefined bloblike shape and the correlation coefficient is close to 0.00 (Figure 3.10d). For example, in a sample of adults, the correlation between reaction time and weight would most likely be very close to zero.

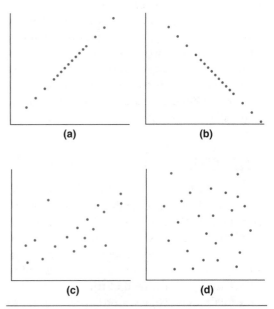

● FIGURE 3.10   Scatterplots Depicting Different Degrees of Correlation

Finally, it is important to understand that the correlation coefficient is independent of the mean. For example, a correlation of $+1.00$ can be found between two administrations of the same test even when there are significant mean differences between pretest and posttest. In sum, perfect correlation does not imply identical pre- and posttest scores for each examinee. However, perfect correlation does imply perfectly ordered ranking from pretest to posttest, as discussed previously.

## ● THE CORRELATION COEFFICIENT AS A RELIABILITY COEFFICIENT

One use of the correlation coefficient is to gauge the consistency of psychological test scores. If test results are highly consistent, then the scores of persons taking the test on two occasions will be strongly correlated, perhaps even approaching the theoretical upper limit of $+1.00$. In this context, the correlation coefficient is also a reliability coefficient. Even though the computation of the Pearson $r$ makes no reference to the theory of true and error scores, the correlation coefficient does, nonetheless, reflect the proportion of variance in obtained test scores accounted for by the variability in true scores. Thus, in some contexts a correlation coefficient is a reliability coefficient.

This discussion introduces one method for estimating the reliability of a test: Administer the instrument twice to the same group of persons and compute the correlation between the two sets of scores. The test-retest approach is very common in the evaluation of reliability, but several other strategies exist as well. As we review the following methods for estimating reliability, the reader may be temporarily bewildered by the apparent diversity of approaches. In fact, the different methods fall into two broad groups; namely, temporal stability approaches, which directly measure the consistency of test scores, and internal consistency approaches, which rely upon a single test administration to gauge reliability. Keep in mind that one common theme binds all the eclectic methods together: Reliability is always an attempt to gauge the likely accuracy or repeatability of test scores.

## ● RELIABILITY AS TEMPORAL STABILITY

### Test-Retest Reliability

The most straightforward method for determining the reliability of test scores is to administer the identical test twice to the same group of heterogeneous and representative subjects. If the test is perfectly reliable, each person's second score will be completely predictable from his or her first score. On many kinds of tests, particularly ability and achievement tests, we might expect subjects generally to score somewhat higher the second time because of practice, maturation, schooling, or other intervening effects that take place between pretest and posttest. However, so long as the second score is strongly correlated with the first score, the existence of practice, maturation, or treatment effects does not cast doubt on the **test-retest reliability** of a psychological test.

An example of a reliability coefficient computed as a test-retest correlation coefficient is depicted in Figure 3.11. In this case, 60 subjects were administered the Finger Tapping Test (FTT) on two occasions separated by a week (Morrison, Gregory, & Paul, 1979). The FTT, one component of the Halstead-Reitan neuropsychological test

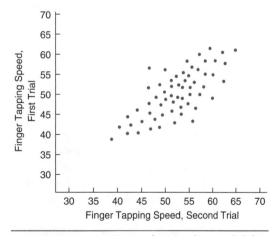

● **FIGURE 3.11** Scatterplot Revealing a Reliability Coefficient of .80

*Source:* Based on data from Morrison, M. W., Gregory, R. J., & Paul, J. J. (1979). Reliability of the Finger Tapping Test and a note on sex differences. *Perceptual and Motor Skills, 48,* 139–142.

battery (Reitan & Wolfson, 1993), is a relatively pure measure of motor speed. Using a standardized mechanical counting apparatus, the subject is instructed to tap with the index finger as fast as possible for 10 seconds. This procedure is continued until five trials in a row reveal consistent results. The procedure is repeated for the nondominant hand. The score for each hand is the average of the five consecutive trials.

The correlation between scores from repeated administrations of this test works out to be about .80. This is at the low end of acceptability for reliability coefficients, which usually fall in the .80s or .90s. We discuss standards of reliability in more detail subsequently.

### Alternate-Forms Reliability

In some cases test developers produce two forms of the same test. These alternate forms are independently constructed to meet the same specifications, often on an item-by-item basis. Thus, alternate forms of a test incorporate similar content and cover the same range and level of difficulty in items. Alternate forms of a test possess similar statistical and normative properties. For example, when administered in counterbalanced fashion to the same group of subjects, the means and standard deviations of alternate forms are typically quite comparable.

Estimates of **alternate-forms reliability** are derived by administering both forms to the same group and correlating the two sets of scores. This approach has much in common with test-retest methods—both strategies involve two test administrations to the same subjects with an intervening time interval. For both approaches, we would expect that intervening changes in motivation and individual differences in amount of improvement would produce fluctuations in test scores and thereby reduce reliability estimates somewhat. Thus, test-retest and alternate-forms reliability estimates share considerable conceptual similarity.

However, there is one fundamental difference between these two approaches. The alternate-forms methodology introduces item-sampling differences as an additional source of error variance.

That is, some test takers may do better or worse on one form of a test because of the particular items sampled. Even though the two forms may be equally difficult on average, some subjects may find one form quite a bit harder (or easier) than the other because supposedly parallel items are not equally familiar to every person. Notice that item-sampling differences are not a source of error variance in the test-retest approach because identical items are used in both administrations.

Alternate forms of a test are also quite expensive—nearly doubling the cost of publishing a test and putting it on the market. Because of the increased cost and also the psychometric difficulties of producing truly parallel forms, fewer and fewer tests are being released in this format.

### ● RELIABILITY AS INTERNAL CONSISTENCY

We turn now to some intriguing ways of estimating the reliability of an individual test without developing alternate forms and without administering the test twice to the same examinees (Feldt & Brennan, 1989). The first approach correlates the results from one-half of the test with the other half and is appropriately termed split-half reliability. The second approach examines the internal consistency of individual test items. In this method, the psychometrician seeks to determine whether the test items tend to show a consistent interrelatedness. Finally, insofar as some tests are less than perfectly reliable because of differences among scorers, we also take up the related topic of inter-scorer reliability.

### Split-Half Reliability

We obtain an estimate of **split-half reliability** by correlating the pairs of scores obtained from equivalent halves of a test administered only once to a representative sample of examinees. The logic of split-half reliability is straightforward: If scores on two half tests from a *single* test administration show a strong correlation, then scores on two whole tests from two *separate* test administrations (the traditional approach to evaluating reliability) also should reveal a strong correlation.

Psychometricians typically view the split-half method as supplementary to the gold standard approach, which is the test-retest method. For example, in the standardization of the WAIS-IV, the reliability of most scales was established by the test-retest approach *and* the split-half approach. These two estimates of reliability are generally similar, although split-half approaches often yield higher estimates of reliability.

One justification for the split-half approach is that logistical problems or excessive cost may render it impractical to obtain a second set of test scores from the same examinees. In this case, a split-half estimate of reliability is the only thing available, and it is certainly better than no estimate at all. Another justification for the split-half approach is that the test-retest method is potentially misleading in certain cases. For example, some ability tests are prone to large but inconsistent practice effects—such as when examinees learn concepts from feedback given as part of the standardized testing procedure. When practice effects are large and variable, the rank order of scores from a second administration will at best sustain only a modest association to the rank order of scores from the first administration. For these kinds of instruments, test-retest reliability coefficients could be misleadingly low. Finally, test-retest approaches also will yield misleadingly low estimates of reliability if the trait being measured is known to fluctuate rapidly (e.g., certain measures of mood).

The major challenge with split-half reliability is dividing the test into two nearly equivalent halves. For most tests—especially those with the items ranked according to difficulty level—the first half is easier than the second half. We would not expect examinees to obtain equivalent scores on these two portions, so this approach to splitting a test rarely is used. The most common method for obtaining split halves is to compare scores on the odd items versus the even items of the test. This procedure works particularly well when the items are arranged in approximate order of difficulty.

In addition to calculating a Pearson *r* between scores on the two equivalent halves of the test, the computation of a coefficient of split-half reliability entails an additional step: adjusting the half-test reliability using the Spearman-Brown formula.

### The Spearman-Brown Formula

Notice that the split-half method gives us an estimate of reliability for an instrument half as long as the full test. Although there are some exceptions, a shorter test generally is less reliable than a longer test. This is especially true if, in comparison to the shorter test, the longer test embodies equivalentcontent and similar item difficulty. Thus, the Pearson *r* between two halves of a test will usually underestimate the reliability of the full instrument. We need a method for deriving the reliability of the whole test based on the half-test correlation coefficient.

The **Spearman-Brown formula** provides the appropriate adjustment:

$$r_{SB} = \frac{2r_{hh}}{1 + r_{hh}}$$

In this formula, $r_{SB}$ is the estimated reliability of the full test computed by the Spearman-Brown method, while $r_{hh}$ is the half-test reliability. Table 3.8 shows conceivable half-test correlations alongside the corresponding Spearman-Brown reliability coefficients for the whole test. For example, using the Spearman-Brown formula, we could

● TABLE 3.8    **Comparison of Split-Half Reliabilities and Corresponding Spearman-Brown Reliabilities**

| Split-Half Reliability | Spearman-Brown Reliability |
|---|---|
| .5 | .67 |
| .6 | .75 |
| .7 | .82 |
| .8 | .89 |
| .9 | .95 |

determine that a half-test reliability of .70 is equivalent to an estimated full-test reliability of .82.

## Critique of the Split-Half Approach

Although the split-half approach is widely used, nonetheless it has been criticized for its lack of precision:

> Instead of giving a single coefficient for the test, the procedure gives different coefficients depending on which items are grouped when the test is split into two parts. If one split may give a higher coefficient than another, one can have little faith in whatever result is obtained from a single split. (Cronbach, 1951)

Why rely on a single split? Why not take a more typical value such as the mean of the split-half coefficients resulting from all possible splittings of a test? Cronbach (1951) advocated just such an approach when proposing a general formula for estimating the reliability of a psychological test.

## Coefficient Alpha

As proposed by Cronbach (1951) and subsequently elaborated by others (Novick & Lewis, 1967; Kaiser & Michael, 1975), **coefficient alpha** may be thought of as the mean of all possible split-half coefficients, corrected by the Spearman-Brown formula. The formula for coefficient alpha is

$$r_\alpha = \left(\frac{N}{N-1}\right)\left(1 - \frac{\Sigma \sigma_j^2}{\sigma^2}\right)$$

where $r_\alpha$ is the coefficient alpha, $N$ is the number of items, $\sigma_j^2$ is the variance of one item, $\Sigma \sigma_j^2$ is the sum of variances of all items, and $\sigma^2$ is the variance of the total test scores. As with all reliability estimates, coefficient alpha can vary between 0.00 and 1.00.

Coefficient alpha is an index of the internal consistency of the items, that is, their tendency to correlate positively with one another. Insofar as a test or scale with high internal consistency will also tend to show stability of scores in a test-retest approach, coefficient alpha is therefore a useful estimate of reliability.

Traditionally, coefficient alpha has been thought of as an index of unidimensionality, that is, the degree to which a test or scale measures a single factor. Recent analyses by Schmitt (1996) serve to dispel this misconception. Certainly coefficient alpha is an index of the interrelatedness of the individual items, but this is not synonymous with the unidimensionality of what the test or scale measures. In fact, it is possible for a scale to measure two or more distinct factors and yet still possess a very strong coefficient alpha. Schmitt (1996) gives the example of a six-item test in which the first three items correlate .8 one with another, the last three items also correlate .8 one with another, whereas correlations across the two three-item sets are only .3 (Table 3.9). Even though this is irrefutably a strong two-factor test, the value for coefficient alpha works out to be .86! For this kind of test, coefficient alpha probably will overestimate test-retest reliability. This is why psychometricians look to test-retest approaches as essential to the evaluation of reliability. Certainly the split-half approach in general and coefficient alpha in particular are valuable approaches to reliability, but they cannot replace the common sense of the test-retest approach: When the same test is administered twice to a representative sample of examinees, do they obtain the same relative placement of scores?

● TABLE 3.9    A Six-Item Test with Two Factors and Strong Coefficient Alpha

| Variable | 1 | 2 | 3 | 4 | 5 | 6 |
|---|---|---|---|---|---|---|
| 1 | — | | | | | |
| 2 | .8 | — | | | | |
| 3 | .8 | .8 | — | | | |
| 4 | .3 | .3 | .3 | — | | |
| 5 | .3 | .3 | .3 | .8 | — | |
| 6 | .3 | .3 | .3 | .8 | .8 | — |

Note:  Coefficient alpha = .86

*Source:*  Reprinted with permission from Schmitt, N. (1996). Uses and abuses of coefficient alpha. *Psychological Assessment, 8,* 350–353.

## The Kuder–Richardson Estimate of Reliability

Cronbach (1951) has shown that coefficient alpha is the general application of a more specific formula developed earlier by Kuder and Richardson (1937). Their formula is generally referred to as **Kuder–Richardson formula 20** or, simply, **KR-20**, in reference to the fact that it was the twentieth in a lengthy series of derivations. The KR-20 formula is relevant to the special case in which each test item is scored 0 or 1 (e.g., wrong or right). The formula is

$$\text{KR-20} = \left(\frac{N}{N-1}\right)\left(1 - \frac{\Sigma pq}{\sigma^2}\right)$$

where

$N$ = the number of items on the test,
$\sigma^2$ = the variance of scores on the total test,
$p$ = the proportion of examinees getting each item correct,
$q$ = the proportion of examinees getting each item wrong.

Coefficient alpha extends the Kuder–Richardson method to types of tests with items that are not scored as 0 or 1. For example, coefficient alpha could be used with an attitude scale in which examinees indicate on each item whether they strongly agree, agree, disagree, or strongly disagree.

## Interscorer Reliability

Some tests leave a great deal of judgment to the examiner in the assignment of scores. Certainly, projective tests fall into this category, as do tests of moral development and creativity. Insofar as the scorer can be a major factor in the reliability of these instruments, a report of interscorer reliability is imperative. Computing **interscorer reliability** is a very straightforward procedure. A sample of tests is independently scored by two or more examiners and scores for pairs of examiners are then correlated. Test manuals typically report the training and experience required of examiners and then list representative interscorer correlation coefficients.

Interscorer reliability supplements other reliability estimates but does not replace them. It would still be appropriate to assess the test-retest or other type of reliability in a subjectively scored test. We provide a quick summary of methods for estimating reliability in Table 3.10.

## Which Type of Reliability Is Appropriate?

As noted, even when a test has only a single form, there are still numerous methods available for assessing reliability: test-retest, split-half, coefficient alpha, and interscorer methods. For tests that

---

### ● TABLE 3.10   Brief Synopsis of Methods for Estimating Reliability

| Method | No. Forms | No. Sessions | Sources of Error Variance |
|---|---|---|---|
| Test-Retest | 1 | 2 | Changes over time |
| Alternate-Forms (immediate) | 2 | 1 | Item sampling |
| Alternate-Forms (delayed) | 2 | 2 | Item sampling<br>Changes over time |
| Split-Half | 1 | 1 | Item sampling<br>Nature of split |
| Coefficient Alpha | 1 | 1 | Item sampling<br>Test heterogeneity |
| Interscorer | 1 | 1 | Scorer differences |

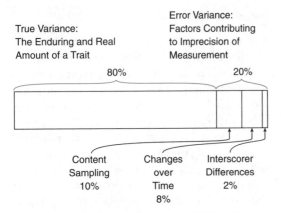

Note: The results are similar to what might be found if alternative forms of an individual intelligence test were administered to the same person by different examiners.

● **FIGURE 3.12** Sources of Variance in a Hypothetical Test

possess two forms, we can add a fifth method: alternate-forms reliability. Which method is best? When should we use one method but not another? To answer these questions, we need to know the nature and purpose of the individual test in question.

For tests designed to be administered to individuals more than once, it would be reasonable to expect that the test demonstrate reliability across time—in this case, test-retest reliability is appropriate. For tests that purport to possess factorial purity, coefficient alpha would be essential. In contrast, factorially complex tests such as measures of general intelligence would not fare well by measures of internal consistency. Thus, coefficient alpha is not an appropriate index of reliability for all tests but applies only to measures that are designed to assess a single factor. Split-half methods work well for instruments that have items carefully ordered according to difficulty level. Of course, interscorer reliability is appropriate for any test that involves subjectivity of scoring.

It is common for test manuals to report multiple sources of information about reliability. For example, the WAIS-IV Manual (Wechsler, 2008)

reports split-half reliabilities for most subtests and also provides test-retest coefficients for all subtests and IQ scores. The manual also cites information akin to alternate-forms reliability—it reports the correlations between the WAIS-IV and its predecessor, the WAIS-III.

In order to analyze the error variance into its component parts, a number of reliability coefficients will need to be computed. Although it is difficult to arrive at precise data in the real world, on a theoretical basis we can partition the variability of scores into true and error components as depicted in Figure 3.12.

## ● ITEM RESPONSE THEORY

The classical test theory summarized previously dominated test development for most of the twentieth century. However, beginning slowly in the 1960s and continuing to the present time, psychometricians have favored an alternative model of test theory known as **item response theory** (IRT) or **latent trait theory** (Embretson, 1996; Lord & Novick, 1968; Rasch, 1960). IRT is more than a theory; it is also a collection of mathematical models and statistical tools with widespread uses. The applications of IRT include analyzing items and scales, developing homogeneous psychological measures, measuring individuals on psychological constructs (e.g., depression, intelligence, leadership), and administering psychological tests by computer. The foundational elements of IRT include item response functions (IRFs), information functions, and the assumption of invariance (Reise, Ainsworth, & Haviland, 2005).

### Item Response Functions

An **item response function** (IRF), also known as an item characteristic curve (ICC), is a mathematical equation that describes the relation between the amount of a latent trait an individual possesses and the probability that he or she will give a designated response to a test item designed to measure that construct. In the case of ability measures, the designated response is the correct answer, whereas in other situations (e.g., the measurement of personality constructs such as leadership), the designated response would be the one indicating the presence of the trait being assessed. For the sake of simplicity, we will refer to the designated response as the "correct" response in the discussion that follows.

Each respondent is assumed to have a certain amount of the latent trait being measured, whether this is verbal proficiency, spatial memory, or leadership ability. In turn, the latent trait is assumed to influence directly the examinee's responses to the items on the test, which has been carefully designed to measure the trait in question. The mathematical models and statistical tools of IRT are designed to establish the IRF for each item on the test. Collectively, the IRFs can be used for many purposes, including the refinement of the instrument, the calculation of reliability, and the estimation of examinee trait levels. For example, test developers commonly use IRFs to eliminate items that don't function optimally in a psychometric sense.

Each test item has its own IRF. The IRFs for four dichotomously scored items are plotted in Figure 3.13. The trait level is depicted on the abscissa, with standard scores ranging from $-3$ to $+3$. An average amount of the trait in question would be indicated by a score of 0. Actually, for mathematical reasons, the scores in an IRF can range hypothetically from $-\infty$ to $+\infty$, but in actual practice, scores rarely escape the bounds of $-3$ to $+3$. The ordinate depicts the probability of a correct response on a scale from 0 to 1.

Upon careful reflection, the IRF provides a wealth of information about each item. For example, it can be used to determine the difficulty level of test items. In the IRT approach, difficulty level is gauged differently than in classical test theory. According to classical test theory, the difficulty level of an item is equivalent to the proportion of examinees in a standardization sample who pass the item. In contrast, according to IRT, difficulty is indexed by how much of the trait is needed to

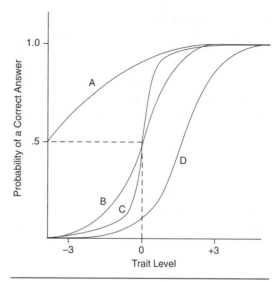

● **FIGURE 3.13**    Item Response Functions for Four Test Items

answer the item correctly. For the items shown in Figure 3.13, item A has the lowest difficulty level—it is passed by almost everyone, even examinees possessing only a small amount of the trait in question. In contrast, item D has the highest difficulty level—only those with high amounts of the trait typically answer correctly. Although not immediately obvious, items B and C are equal in difficulty level—for example, individuals with an average trait level (a score of 0) have a 50 percent chance of answering these items correctly.

Another quality evident in the IRF is the item discrimination parameter, which is a gauge of how well the item differentiates among individuals at a specific level of the trait in question. Consider items B and C in Figure 3.13. Although they are equally difficult overall—both answered correctly by 50 percent of the examinees—item C with its steeper curve possesses better discrimination, meaning that it is better able to differentiate among individuals at this level of the trait.

The appealing advantage of the IRT approach to measurement is that the probability of a respondent answering a particular question correctly can be expressed as a precise mathematical equation. Although it is beyond the scope of our presentation to go into the derivation, seeing an IRT equation might help the reader appreciate the sophistication of this approach. We denote the item difficulty as *b* and the amount of the trait that an examinee possesses as $\theta$. Then the relevant equation looks like this:

$$p(\theta) = 1/(1 + e^{-(\theta - b)})$$

where $p(\theta)$ is the probability of a respondent with trait level $\theta$ correctly responding to an item of difficulty *b*. When the parameters are filled in and this equation is plotted, the outcome is an IRF for each test item, similar to those shown in Figure 3.13. The symbol *e* in the equation refers to the base for natural logarithms, which has a constant value of 2.71828. The parameter $\theta$ refers to the examinee trait level measured on a standard scale, which typically varies from −3 to +3. This particular formula was developed by the Danish mathematician Georg Rasch (1960); hence, in his honor this IRT application is also known as a **Rasch Model.** This is a simple and elegant application of IRT—more complex models have also been developed (Embretson & Reise, 2000).

### Information Functions

In general terms, information is that which reduces uncertainty. In psychological measurement, information represents the capacity of a test item to differentiate among people (Reise, Ainsworth, & Haviland, 2005). On most scales, certain items are intended to differentiate among individuals low on the trait being measured, whereas other items are designed for discrimination at higher trait levels. Consider items A and D from Figure 3.13. Item A is useful only for testing individuals low on the relevant trait—at higher levels, everyone answers correctly, and no information is gained. It would be pointless to administer this item to individuals at the higher end of the trait spectrum because it is certain they will answer correctly. Conversely, item D is useful only for individuals with high trait levels—at lower trait levels, it is certain that everyone

fails the item and, likewise, no information is gained.

Another way of stating this is to say that a test item typically provides a different level of information at each level of the trait in question. For example, item A provides a lot of information at low trait levels but none at high levels, whereas item D shows the reverse pattern—no information at low trait levels but more information at high levels. Using a simple mathematical conversion, an **item information function** can be derived from the IRF for each item. This function portrays graphically the relationship between the trait level of examinees and the information provided by the test item. The information functions for items A and D are displayed in Figure 3.14.

The beauty of IRT is that the item information functions from different scale items can be *added together* to derive the scale information function:

> Because information is directly related to measurement precision (more information equals more precise measurement), the scale information function estimates how well a measure functions as a whole in different trait ranges. The fact that item information functions can be added together is the foundation for scale construction with IRT. (Reise, Ainsworth, & Haviland, 2005, p. 96)

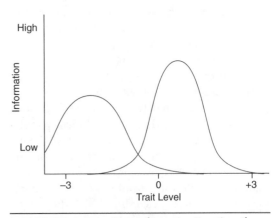

● **FIGURE 3.14** Item Information Functions for Two Test Items

The scale information function is analogous to test reliability as elucidated in classical test theory with two important differences. First, in IRT the precision of measurement can vary, depending on where an individual falls in the trait range, whereas in classical test theory a single reliability (precision of measurement) is typically calculated for the entire test. Second, in IRT a different collection of test items might be used for each examinee to obtain a predetermined precision of measurement, whereas in classical test theory a single set of items is typically administered to all examinees.

### Invariance in IRT

Invariance is a challenging concept to understand because it is contrary to the traditional lore of testing, which posits that test scores are meaningful only in a relative sense—in relation to fixed scales administered to large standardization samples. Certainly, it is true within IRT that huge databases are needed to make sense of individual test results. Yet, within IRT the manner in which we estimate the trait level (i.e., acquire a score) is fundamentally different from traditional approaches such as classical test theory.

Within the IRT framework, invariance refers to two separate but related ideas (Reise, Ainsworth, & Haviland, 2005). First, invariance means that an examinee's position on a latent-trait continuum (his or her score) can be estimated from the responses to any set of test items with known IRFs. In other words, as long as the IRFs for a particular set of test items have been previously calculated, a trait level can be estimated for an examinee who has answered those items. In fact, the particular items used might differ from one examinee to another, and the number of items administered might even differ. But as long as the IRFs of the particular items are known, the methods of IRT provide an estimate of the trait level (i.e., a test score). Preferably, of course, items with appropriate difficulty levels corresponding to the trait level of the examinee will be administered. Typically, this is accomplished by using computer programs that flexibly select test items based on the prior responses of the examinee.

The second meaning of invariance is that the IRFs do not depend on the characteristics of a particular population. In other words, the IRF for each item is presumed to exist in some abstract, independent, and enduring manner, waiting to be discovered by the psychometrician. The results for different samples might help fine-tune different parts of the IRF, but the outcome always should fall on the same curve. This means, as well, that the scale of the trait exists independently of any set of items and independently of any particular population. Reise, Ainsworth, and Haviland (2005) describe the advantages of item-parameter invariance as follows:

> For example, in large-scale educational assessment, item-parameter invariance facilitates the linking of scales from different measures (i.e., placing scores on a single, common scale), across students in different grade levels (e.g., third through sixth grade in the same school) and within a grade level (e.g., fourth graders in different schools). Similarly, using IRT methods to compare individuals who have responded to different measures is relevant to cross-cultural and developmental researchers. . . . (p. 98)

Although IRT analyses typically require large samples—several hundred or thousands of respondents—the necessary software is straightforward and commonly available. Given its advantages, IRT approaches to test development likely will become increasingly prominent in the years ahead.

## ● THE NEW RULES OF MEASUREMENT

When fully explicated, IRT leads to what Embretson (1996) has called "the new rules of measurement." By this she means that several conclusions from classical testing theory do not hold true within the framework of IRT. For example, within classical testing theory, the standard error of measurement is assumed to be a constant that applies to all examinee scores regardless of the ability level of a particular respondent. However, within IRT the standard error of measurement becomes substantially larger at both extremes of ability. In other words, the IRT model concludes that test scores are more reliable for individuals of average ability and increasingly less reliable for those with very high or very low ability.

Another difference pertains to the relationship between test length and reliability. In classical test theory, it is almost an axiom that longer tests are more reliable than shorter tests. For example, this follows from the Spearman-Brown formula discussed earlier in the chapter. However, when IRT models are used, shorter tests can be more reliable than longer tests. This is especially true when there is a good match between the difficulty level of the specific items administered and the proficiency level of the examinee. A good fit between these two parameters allows for a precise (reliable) estimate of ability using a relatively smaller number of test items.

In general, tests developed within an IRT model are better suited to computerized adaptive testing, in which a computer program is used not only to administer test items but also to select them in a flexible manner based on each examinee's ongoing responses to prior items. Computerized adaptive testing is discussed in more detail in Topic 12B, Computerized Assessment and the Future of Testing.

## ● SPECIAL CIRCUMSTANCES IN THE ESTIMATION OF RELIABILITY

Traditional approaches to estimating reliability may be misleading or inappropriate for some applications. Some of the more problematic situations involve unstable characteristics, speed tests, restriction of range, and criterion-referenced tests.

### Unstable Characteristics

Some characteristics are presumed to be ever changing in reaction to situational or physiological variables. Emotional reactivity as measured by electrodermal or galvanic skin response is a good example. Such a measure fluctuates quickly in reaction to loud noises, underlying thought processes, and stressful environmental events. Even just talking to another person can arouse a strong electrodermal response. Because the true amount of emotional reactivity changes so quickly, test and retest must be nearly instantaneous in order to provide an accurate index of reliability for unstable characteristics such as an electrodermal measure of emotional reactivity.

### Speed and Power Tests

A speed test typically contains items of uniform and generally simple levels of difficulty. If time permitted, most subjects should be able to complete most or all of the items on such a test. However, as the name suggests, a speeded test has a restrictive time limit that guarantees few subjects complete the entire test. Since the items attempted tend to be correct, an examinee's score on a speeded test largely reflects speed of performance.

Speed tests are often contrasted with power tests. A power test allows enough time for test takers to attempt all items but is constructed so that no test taker is able to obtain a perfect score. Most tests contain a mixture of speed and power components.

The most important point to stress about the reliability of speed tests is that the traditional split-half approach (comparing odd and even items) will yield a spuriously high reliability coefficient. Consider one test taker who completes 60 of 90 items on a speed test. Most likely, the odd-even approach would show 30 odd items correct and 30 even items correct. With similar data from other subjects, the correlation between scores on odd and even items necessarily would approach +1.00. The reliability of a speed test should be based on the test-retest method or split-half reliability from two, separately timed half tests. In the latter instance, the Spearman-Brown correction is needed.

### Restriction of Range

Test-retest reliability will be spuriously low if it is based on a sample of homogeneous subjects for whom there is a **restriction of range** on the characteristic being measured. For example, it would be inappropriate to estimate the reliability of an intelligence test by administering it twice to a sample of college students. This point is illustrated by the hypothetical but realistic scatterplot shown in Figure 3.15, where the reader can see a strong test-retest correlation for the entire range of diverse subjects, but a weak correlation for brighter subjects viewed in isolation.

### Reliability of Criterion-Referenced Tests

The reader will recall from the first topic of this chapter that criterion-referenced tests evaluate performance in terms of mastery rather than assessing a continuum of achievement. Test items are designed to identify specific skills that need remediation; therefore, items tend to be of the "pass/fail" variety.

The structure of criterion-referenced tests is such that the variability of scores among examinees is typically quite minimal. In fact, if test results are used for training purposes and everyone continues training until all test skills are mastered, variability in test scores becomes nonexistent. Under these conditions, traditional approaches to the assessment of reliability are simply inappropriate.

With many criterion-referenced tests, results must be almost perfectly accurate to be useful. For example, any classification error is serious if the purpose of a test is to determine a subject's ability to drive a manual transmission, or stick shift, automobile. The key issue here is not whether test and retest scores are close to one another, but whether the classification ("can do/can't do") is the same in both instances. What we really want to know is the percentage of persons for whom the same decision is reached on both occasions—the closer to 100 percent, the better. This is but one illustration of the need for specialized techniques in the evaluation of non-normative tests. Berk (1984) and Feldt and Brennan (1989) discuss approaches to the reliability of criterion-referenced tests.

## ● THE INTERPRETATION OF RELIABILITY COEFFICIENTS

The reader should now be well versed in the different approaches to reliability and should possess at least a conceptual idea of how reliability coefficients are computed. In addition, we have discussed the distinctive testing conditions that dictate the use of one kind of reliability method as opposed to others. No doubt, the reader has noticed that we have yet to discuss one crucial question: What is an acceptable level of reliability?

Many authors suggest that reliability should be at least .90 if not .95 for decisions about individuals (e.g., Nunnally & Bernstein, 1994). However, there is really no hard and fast answer to this question. We offer the loose guidelines suggested by Guilford and Fruchter (1978):

> There has been some consensus that to be a very accurate measure of individual differences in some characteristic, the reliability should be above .90. The truth is, however, that many standard tests with reliabilities as low as .70 prove to be very useful. And tests with reliabilities lower than that can be useful in research.

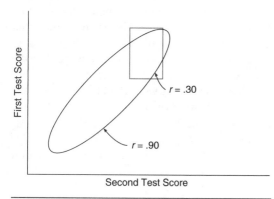

● **FIGURE 3.15** Sampling a Restricted Range of Subjects Causes Test-Retest Reliability to Be Spuriously Low

On a more practical level, acceptable standards of reliability hinge on the amount of measurement error the user can tolerate in the proposed application of a test. Fortunately, reliability and measurement error are mutually interdependent concepts. Thus, if the test user can specify an acceptable level of measurement error, then it is also possible to determine the minimum standards of reliability required for that specific application of a test. We pursue this topic further by introducing a new concept: standard error of measurement.

## ● RELIABILITY AND THE STANDARD ERROR OF MEASUREMENT

To introduce the concept of standard error of measurement we begin with a thought experiment. Suppose we could administer thousands of equivalent IQ tests to one individual. Suppose further that each test session was a fresh and new experience for our cooperative subject; in this hypothetical experiment, practice and boredom would have no effect on later test scores. Nonetheless, because of the kinds of random errors discussed in this chapter, the scores of our hapless subject would not be identical across test sessions. Our examinee might score a little worse on one test because he stayed up late the night before; the score on another test might be better because the items were idiosyncratically easy for him. Even though such error factors are random and unpredictable, it follows from the classical theory of measurement that the obtained scores would fall into a normal distribution with a precise mean and standard deviation. Let us say that the mean of the hypothetical IQ scores for our subject worked out to be 110, with a standard deviation of 2.5.

In fact, the mean of this distribution of hypothetical scores would be the estimated true score for our examinee. Our best estimate, then, is that our subject has a true IQ of 110. Furthermore, the standard deviation of the distribution of obtained scores would be the **standard error of measurement** (SEM). Note that while the true score on a test likely differs from one person to the next, the SEM is regarded as constant, an inherent property of the test. If we repeated this hypothetical experiment with another subject, the estimated true score would probably differ, but the SEM should work out to be a similar value.[2]

As its name suggests, the SEM is an index of measurement error that pertains to the test in question. In the hypothetical case in which SEM = 0, there would be no measurement error at all. A subject's obtained score would then also be his or her true score. However, this outcome is simply impossible in real-world testing. Every test exhibits some degree of measurement error. The larger the SEM, the greater the typical measurement error. However, the accuracy or inaccuracy of any individual score is always a probabilistic matter and never a known quantity.

As noted, the SEM can be thought of as the standard deviation of an examinee's hypothetical obtained scores on a large number of equivalent tests, under the assumption that practice and boredom effects are ruled out. Like any standard deviation of a normal distribution, the SEM has well-known statistical uses. For example, 68 percent of the obtained scores will fall within one SEM of the mean, just as 68 percent of the cases in a normal curve fall within one SD of the mean.

The reader will recall from earlier in this chapter that about 95 percent of the cases in a normal distribution fall within two SDs of the mean. For this reason, if our examinee were to take one more IQ test, we could predict with 95 percent odds that the obtained score would be within two SEMs of the estimated true IQ of 110. Knowing that the SEM is 2.5, we would therefore predict that the obtained IQ score would be 110 ± 5; that is, the true score would very likely (95 percent odds) fall between 105 and 115.

Unfortunately, in the real world we do not have access to true scores and we most certainly cannot

---

2. This would hold true for subjects of similar age. The SEM may differ from one age group to the next—see Wechsler (2008) for an illustration with the WAIS-IV.

obtain multiple IQs from large numbers of equivalent tests; nor for that matter do we have direct knowledge of the SEM. All we typically possess is a reliability coefficient (e.g., a test-retest correlation from normative studies) plus one obtained score from a single test administration. How can we possibly use this information to determine the likely accuracy of our obtained score?

## Computing the Standard Error of Measurement

We have noted several times in this chapter that reliability and measurement error are intertwined concepts, with low reliability signifying high measurement error, and vice versa. It should not surprise the reader, then, that the SEM can be computed indirectly from the reliability coefficient. The formula is

$$SEM = SD\sqrt{1 - r}$$

where SD is the standard deviation of the test scores and $r$ is the reliability coefficient, both derived from a normative sample or other large and representative group of subjects.

We can use WAIS-R Full Scale IQ to illustrate the computation of the SEM. The SD of WAIS-R scores is known to be about 15, and the reliability coefficient is .97 (Wechsler, 1981). The SEM for Full Scale IQ is, therefore,

$$SEM = 15\sqrt{1 - .97}$$

which works out to be about 2.5.

## The SEM and Individual Test Scores

Let us consider carefully what the SEM tells us about individual test results, once again using WAIS-R IQs to illustrate a general point. What we would really like to know is the likely accuracy of IQ. Let us say we have an individual examinee who obtains a score of 90, and let us assume that the test was administered in competent fashion. Nonetheless, is the obtained IQ score likely to be accurate?

In order to answer this question, we need to rephrase it. In the jargon of classical test theory, questions of accuracy really involve comparisons between obtained scores and true scores. Specifically, when we inquire whether an IQ score is accurate, we are really asking: How close is the obtained score to the true score?

The answer to this question may seem perturbing at first glance. It turns out that, in the individual case, we can never know precisely how close the obtained score is to the true score! The best we can do is provide a probabilistic statement based on our knowledge that the hypothetical obtained scores for a single examinee would be normally distributed with a standard deviation equal to the SEM. Based on this premise, we know that the obtained score is accurate to within plus or minus 2 SEMs in 95 percent of the cases. In other words, Full Scale IQ is 95 percent certain to be accurate within ±5 IQ points. This range of plus or minus 5 IQ points corresponds to the 95 percent **confidence interval** for WAIS-R Full Scale IQ, because we can be 95 percent confident that the true score is contained within it.

Testers would do well to report test scores in terms of a confidence interval because this practice would help place scores in proper perspective (Sattler, 1988). An examinee who obtains an IQ of 90 should be described as follows: "Mr. Doe obtained a Full Scale IQ of 90 which is accurate to ±5 points with 95 percent confidence." This wording helps forewarn others that test scores always incorporate some degree of measurement error.

## The SEM and Differences between Scores

Testers are often expected to surmise whether an examinee has scored significantly higher in one ability area than another. For example, it is usually germane to report whether an examinee is stronger at verbal or performance tasks or to say that no real difference exists in these two skill areas. The issue is not entirely academic. An examinee who has a relative superiority in performance intelligence might be counseled to pursue practical, hands-on careers. In contrast, a strength in verbal intelligence might result in a recommendation to pursue academic interests. How is an examiner to determine whether one test score is significantly better than another?

Keep in mind that every test score incorporates measurement error. It is therefore possible for an examinee to obtain a verbal score higher than his or her performance score when the underlying true scores—if only we could know them—would reveal no difference or even the opposite pattern! (See Figure 3.16.) The important lesson here is that when each of two obtained scores reflects measurement error, the difference between these scores is quite volatile and must not be overinterpreted.

The **standard error of the difference** between two scores is a statistical measure that can help a test user determine whether a difference between scores is significant. The standard error of the difference between two scores can be computed from the SEMs of the individual tests by the following formula:

$$SE_{diff} = \sqrt{(SEM_1)^2 + (SEM_2)^2}$$

where $SE_{diff}$ is the standard error of the difference and $SEM_1$ and $SEM_2$ are the respective standard errors of measurement.

It is assumed that the two scores are on the same scale or have been converted to the same scale. That is, the tests must have the same overall mean and standard deviation in the normative sample. By substituting $SD\sqrt{1 - r_{11}}$ for $SEM_1$ and $SD\sqrt{1 - r_{22}}$ for $SEM_2$, we arrive at

$$SE_{diff} = SD\sqrt{2 - r_{11} - r_{22}}$$

We return to our original question to illustrate the computation and use of $SE_{diff}$. How is an examiner to determine whether one test score is significantly better than another? In particular, suppose an examinee obtains Verbal IQ 112 and Performance IQ 105 on the WAIS-R. Is 7 IQ points a significant difference?

We know from the WAIS-R Manual (Wechsler, 1981) that Verbal and Performance IQ each have standard deviations of approximately 15; and their respective reliabilities are .97 and .93. The standard error of the difference between these two scores can be found from

$$SE_{diff} = 15\sqrt{2 - .97 - .93} = 4.74$$

Recall from the discussion of normal distributions that 5 percent of the cases occur in the tails, beyond $\pm1.96$ standard deviations. Thus, differences that are approximately twice as large as $SE_{diff}$ (that is, $1.96 \times 4.74$) can be considered significant in the sense that they will occur by chance only 5 percent of the time. We may conclude, then, that differences of about 9 points or more between Verbal and Performance IQ likely reflect real differences in scores rather than chance contributions from errors of measurement. Thus, more likely than not, a difference of merely 7 IQ points does not signify a bona fide, significant difference between verbal and performance intelligence.

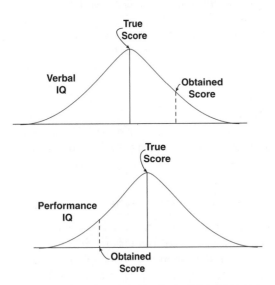

Note: In this hypothetical case the obtained Verbal IQ is higher than the obtained Performance IQ, whereas the underlying true scores show the opposite pattern.

● **FIGURE 3.16**   Obtained Scores Reflect Measurement Error and May Obscure the Relationship between True Scores

## ● S U M M A R Y

**1.** In psychological testing, reliability refers to the attribute of consistency of measurement. Few behavioral measurements are perfectly reliable—some degree of inconsistency is almost always present from one measurement to the next. Reliability should be viewed as a continuum.

**2.** According to the classical theory of true and error scores, any test score reflects the influence of two factors: factors that contribute to consistency, namely, the stable attributes that the examiner seeks to measure; and factors that contribute to inconsistency, which include subject, test, and situational variables.

**3.** The fundamental equation of classical measurement theory is

$$X = T + e$$

where $X$ is the obtained score, $T$ is the true score, and $e$ represents errors of measurement.

**4.** Measurement error can arise during item selection, test administration, and test scoring. Systematic errors may also contribute to measurement error. An example of measurement error caused by item selection: In the process of item selection, the test developer may pick items that are not equally fair to all persons.

**5.** Systematic errors of measurement may arise when, unknown to the test developer, a test consistently measures something other than the trait for which it was intended. For example, a test designed to measure social introversion might inadvertently measure anxiety in a consistent manner.

**6.** The basic assumptions of classical measurement theory are (1) measurement errors are random, (2) the mean error of measurement is zero, (3) true scores and error scores are uncorrelated, and (4) errors on different tests are uncorrelated. It follows from these assumptions that the variance of obtained scores is simply the variance of true scores plus the variance of errors of measurement.

**7.** Reliability expresses the relative influence of true and error scores on obtained test scores. The reliability coefficient is the ratio of true score variance to the total variance of test scores (true score variance plus error score variance). The value of the reliability coefficient can vary between 0.0 and 1.0.

**8.** The Pearson product-moment correlation coefficient can be used to gauge the consistency of psychological test scores. This form of reliability is referred to as test-retest reliability. Alternate-forms reliability is computed by correlating scores on two equivalent forms, administered in counterbalanced fashion to a large group of heterogeneous subjects.

**9.** Internal consistency approaches to reliability include split-half reliability, in which scores on half tests are correlated with each other, and coefficient alpha, which can be thought of as the mean of all possible split-half coefficients.

**10.** For tests that require examiner judgment for assignment of scores, interscorer reliability is needed. Computing interscorer reliability is straightforward: A sample of tests is independently scored by two or more examiners and scores for pairs of examiners are then correlated.

**11.** Item response theory (IRT) has been replacing classical test theory as the preferred model for test development. IRT posits a single dimension of skill or underlying trait on which all of the test items rely and hypothesizes that each respondent has a certain amount of the latent trait being measured. This allows for precise formulas linking the probability of a correct response to item difficulty and the respondent's level of the latent trait.

**12.** Traditional approaches to estimating reliability may be misleading or inappropriate for these applications: when the characteristic measured is highly volatile or unstable; for speeded tests with simple item difficulty; when the subjects are highly homogeneous for the characteristic being measured.

**13.** For many criterion-referenced tests, the results must be almost perfectly reliable to be useful. Since criterion-referenced tests often have a "can do/can't do" quality, repeatability of classification is one method of assessing the reliability of criterion-referenced tests.

14. Reliability is inversely related to the standard error of measurement (SEM). The SEM determines the confidence interval that surrounds every examinee's score. For example, the 95 percent confidence interval is ±2 SEMs from the examinee's obtained score.

## KEY TERMS AND CONCEPTS

reliability   p. 87

classical theory of measurement   p. 88

true score   p. 88

measurement error   p. 88

systematic measurement error   p. 90

reliability coefficient   p. 91

correlation coefficient   p. 92

test-retest reliability   p. 93

alternate-forms reliability   p. 94

split-half reliability   p. 94

Spearman-Brown formula   p. 94

coefficient alpha   p. 96

Kuder–Richardson formula 20   p. 97

interscorer reliability   p. 97

item response theory   p. 98

latent trait theory   p. 98

item response function   p. 98

Rasch Model   p. 100

item information function   p. 100

speed test   p. 102

power test   p. 102

restriction of range   p. 102

standard error of measurement   p. 104

confidence interval   p. 105

standard error of the difference   p. 106

# Chapter 4

# Validity and Test Development

## TOPIC 4A

## Basic Concepts of Validity

**A**s most every student of psychology knows, the merit of a psychological test is determined first by its reliability but then ultimately by its validity. In the preceding chapter we pointed out that reliability can be appraised by many seemingly diverse methods ranging from the conceptually straightforward test-retest approach to the theoretically more complex methodologies of internal consistency. Yet, regardless of the method used, the assessment of reliability invariably boils down to a simple summary statistic, the reliability coefficient. In this chapter, the more difficult and complex issue

of validity—what a test score means—is investigated. The concept of validity is still evolving and, therefore, stirs up a great deal more controversy than its staid and established cousin, reliability (AERA, APA, & NCME, 1999). In Topic 4A, Basic Concepts of Validity, we introduce essential concepts of validity, including the standard tripartite division into content, criterion-related, and construct validity. We also discuss extravalidity concerns, which include side effects and unintended consequences of testing. Extravalidity concerns have fostered a wider definition of test validity that extends beyond the technical notions of content, criteria, and constructs. In Topic 4B, Test Construction, we stress that validity must be built into the test from the outset rather than being limited to the final stages of test development.

Put simply, the validity of a test is the extent to which it measures what it claims to measure. Psychometricians have long acknowledged that validity is the most fundamental and important characteristic of a test. After all, validity defines the *meaning* of test scores. Reliability is important, too, but only insofar as it constrains validity. To the extent that a test is unreliable, it cannot be valid. We can express this point from an alternative perspective: Reliability is a necessary but not a sufficient precursor of validity.

Test developers have a responsibility to demonstrate that new instruments fulfill the purposes for which they are designed. However, unlike test reliability, test validity is not a simple issue that is easily resolved on the basis of a few rudimentary studies. Test validation is a developmental process that begins with test construction and continues indefinitely:

> After a test is released for operational use, the interpretive meaning of its scores may continue to be sharpened, refined, and enriched through the gradual accumulation of clinical observations and through special research projects. . . . Test validity is a living thing; it is not dead and embalmed when the test is released. (Anastasi, 1986)

Test validity hinges upon the accumulation of research findings. In the sections that follow, we examine the kinds of evidence sought in the validation of a psychological test.

## ● VALIDITY: A DEFINITION

We begin with a definition of **validity**, paraphrased from the influential *Standards for Educational and Psychological Testing* (AERA, APA, & NCME, 1999):

> A test is valid to the extent that inferences made from it are appropriate, meaningful, and useful.

Notice that a test score per se is meaningless until the examiner draws inferences from it based on the test manual or other research findings. For example, knowing that an examinee has obtained a slightly elevated score on the MMPI-2 Depression scale is not particularly helpful. This result becomes valuable only when the examiner infers behavioral characteristics from it. Based on existing research, the examiner might conclude, "The elevated Depression score suggests that the examinee has little energy and has a pessimistic outlook on life." The MMPI-2 Depression scale possesses psychometric validity to the extent that such inferences are appropriate, meaningful, and useful.

Unfortunately, it is seldom possible to summarize the validity of a test in terms of a single, tidy statistic. Determining whether inferences are appropriate, meaningful, and useful typically requires numerous studies of the relationships between test performance and other independently observed behaviors. Validity reflects an evolutionary, research-based judgment of how adequately a test measures the attribute it was designed to measure. Consequently, the validity of tests is not easily captured by neat statistical summaries but is instead characterized on a continuum ranging from *weak* to *acceptable* to *strong*.

Traditionally, the different ways of accumulating validity evidence have been grouped into three categories:

- Content validity
- Criterion-related validity
- Construct validity

We will expand on this tripartite view of validity shortly, but first a few cautions. The use of these convenient labels does not imply that there are distinct types of validity or that a specific validation procedure is best for one test use and not another:

> An ideal validation includes several types of evidence, which span all three of the traditional categories. Other things being equal, more sources of evidence are better than fewer. However, the quality of the evidence is of primary importance,

and a single line of solid evidence is preferable to numerous lines of evidence of questionable quality. Professional judgment should guide the decisions regarding the forms of evidence that are most necessary and feasible in light of the intended uses of the test and any likely alternatives to testing. (AERA, APA, & NCME, 1985)

We may summarize these points by stressing that validity is a unitary concept determined by the extent to which a test measures what it purports to measure. The inferences drawn from a valid test are appropriate, meaningful, and useful. In this light, it should be apparent that virtually any empirical study that relates test scores to other findings is a potential source of validity information (Anastasi, 1986; Messick, 1995).

## ● CONTENT VALIDITY

**Content validity** is determined by the degree to which the questions, tasks, or items on a test are representative of the universe of behavior the test was designed to sample. In theory, content validity is really nothing more than a sampling issue (Bausell, 1986). The items of a test can be visualized as a sample drawn from a larger population of potential items that define what the researcher really wishes to measure. If the sample (specific items on the test) is representative of the population (all possible items), then the test possesses content validity.

Content validity is a useful concept when a great deal is known about the variable that the researcher wishes to measure. With achievement tests in particular, it is often possible to specify the relevant universe of behaviors in advance. For example, when developing an achievement test of spelling, a researcher could identify nearly all possible words that third graders should know. The content validity of a third-grade spelling achievement test would be assured, in part, if words of varying difficulty level were randomly sampled from this preexisting list.

However, test developers must take care to specify the relevant universe of responses as well.

All too often, a multiple-choice format is taken for granted:

> If the constructor thinks about his aims with an open mind he will often decide that the task should call for a response constructed by the student—written open-end responses or, if inhibitions are to be minimized, oral responses. Nor are the directions to the subject and the social setting of the test to be neglected in defining the task. (Cronbach, 1971)

In reference to spelling achievement, it cannot be assumed that a multiple-choice test will measure the same spelling skills as an oral test or a frequency count of misspellings in written compositions. Thus, when evaluating content validity, response specification is also an integral part of defining the relevant universe of behaviors.

Content validity is more difficult to assure when the test measures an ill-defined trait. How could a test developer possibly hope to specify the universe of potential items for a measure of anxiety? In these cases in which the measured trait is less tangible, no test developer in his or her right mind would try to construct the literal universe of potential test items. Instead, what usually passes for content validity is the considered opinion of expert judges. In effect, the test developer asserts that "a panel of experts reviewed the domain specification carefully and judged the following test questions to possess content validity." Figure 4.1 reproduces a sample judge's item rating form for determining the content validity of test questions.

### Quantification of Content Validity

Martuza (1977) and others have discussed statistical methods for determining the overall content validity of a test from the judgments of experts. These methods tend to be very specialized and have not been widely accepted. Nonetheless, their approaches can serve as a model for a commonsense viewpoint on interrater agreement as a basis for content validity.

When two expert judges evaluate individual items of a test on the four-point scale proposed in Figure 4.1, the ratings of each judge on each item

● **FIGURE 4.1**
Sample Judges Item-Rating Form for Determining Content Validity
*Source:* Based on Martuza (1977), Hambleton (1984), Bausell (1986).

Reviewer: _____ Date: _____

Please read carefully through the domain specification for this test. Next, please indicate how well you feel each item reflects the domain specification. Judge a test item solely on the basis of match between its content and the content defined by the domain specification. Please use the four-point rating scale shown below:

| 1 | 2 | 3 | 4 |
|---|---|---|---|
| *not relevant* | *somewhat relevant* | *quite relevant* | *very relevant* |

can be dichotomized into weak relevance (ratings of 1 or 2) versus strong relevance (ratings of 3 or 4). For each item, then, the conjoint ratings of the two judges can be entered into the two-by-two agreement table depicted in Figure 4.2. For example, if both judges believed an item was quite relevant (strong relevance), it would be placed in cell D. If the first judge believed an item was very relevant (strong relevance) but the second judge deemed it be only slightly relevant (weak relevance), the item would be placed in cell B.

Notice that cell D is the only cell that reflects valid agreement between judges. The other cells involve disagreement (cells B and C) or agreement that an item doesn't belong on the test (cell A). We have reproduced hypothetical results for a 100-item test in Figure 4.3. A coefficient of content validity can be derived from the following formula:

$$\text{content validity} = \frac{D}{(A + B + C + D)}$$

For example, on our 100-item test both judges concurred that 87 items were strongly relevant (cell D), so the coefficient of content validity would be $87/(4 + 4 + 5 + 87)$ or .87. If more than two judges are used, this computational procedure could be completed with all possible pair-wise combinations of judges, and the average coefficient reported. An important note: A coefficient of content validity is just one piece of evidence in the

EXPERT JUDGE #1

| | Weak Relevance (item rated 1 or 2) | Strong Relevance (item rated 3 or 4) |
|---|---|---|
| **EXPERT JUDGE #2** Weak Relevance (item rated 1 or 2) | A | B |
| Strong Relevance (item rated 3 or 4) | C | D |

● **FIGURE 4.2**  Interrater Agreement Model for Content Validity

EXPERT JUDGE #1

| | Weak Relevance (item rated 1 or 2) | Strong Relevance (item rated 3 or 4) |
|---|---|---|
| **EXPERT JUDGE #2** Weak Relevance (item rated 1 or 2) | 4 items | 5 items |
| Strong Relevance (item rated 3 or 4) | 4 items | 87 items |

● **FIGURE 4.3**  Hypothetical Example of Agreement Model of Content Validity for a 100-Item Test evaluation of a test. Such a coefficient does not by itself establish the validity of a test.

The commonsense approach to content validity advocated here serves well as a flagging mechanism to help cull out existing items that are deemed inappropriate by expert raters. However, it cannot identify nonexistent items that should be added to a test to help make the pool of questions more representative of the intended domain. A test could possess a robust coefficient of content validity and still fall short in subtle ways. Quantification of content validity is no substitute for careful selection of items.

### Face Validity

We digress briefly here to mention face validity, which is not really a form of validity at all. Nonetheless, the concept is encountered in testing and, therefore, needs brief explanation. A test has **face validity** if it looks valid to test users, examiners, and especially the examinees. Face validity is really a matter of social acceptability and not a technical form of validity in the same category as content, criterion-related, or construct validity (Nevo, 1985). From a public relations standpoint, it is crucial that tests possess face validity—otherwise those who take the tests may be dissatisfied and doubt the value of psychological testing. However, face validity should not be confused with objective validity, which is determined by the relationship of test scores to other sources of information. In fact, a test could possess extremely strong face validity—the items might look highly relevant to what is presumably measured by the instrument—yet produce totally meaningless scores with no predictive utility whatever.

### ● CRITERION-RELATED VALIDITY

**Criterion-related validity** is demonstrated when a test is shown to be effective in estimating an examinee's performance on some outcome measure. In this context, the variable of primary interest is the outcome measure, called a *criterion*. The test score

is useful only insofar as it provides a basis for accurate prediction of the criterion. For example, a college entrance exam that is reasonably accurate in predicting the subsequent grade point average of examinees would possess criterion-related validity.

Two different approaches to validity evidence are subsumed under the heading of criterion-related validity. In **concurrent validity,** the criterion measures are obtained at approximately the same time as the test scores. For example, the current psychiatric diagnosis of patients would be an appropriate criterion measure to provide validation evidence for a paper-and-pencil psychodiagnostic test. In **predictive validity,** the criterion measures are obtained in the future, usually months or years after the test scores are obtained, as with the college grades predicted from an entrance exam. Each of these two approaches is best suited to different testing situations, discussed in the following sections. However, before we review the nature of concurrent and predictive validity, let us examine a more fundamental question: What are the characteristics of a good criterion?

### Characteristics of a Good Criterion

As noted, a *criterion* is any outcome measure against which a test is validated. In practical terms, a criterion can be most anything. Some examples will help to illustrate the diversity of potential criteria. A simulator-based driver skill test might be validated against a criterion of "number of traffic citations received in the last 12 months." A scale measuring social readjustment might be validated against a criterion of "number of days spent in a psychiatric hospital in the last three years." A test of sales potential might be validated against a criterion of "dollar amount of goods sold in the preceding year." The choice of criteria is circumscribed, in part, by the ingenuity of the test developer. However, criteria must be more than just imaginative; they must also be reliable, appropriate, and free of contamination from the test itself.

The criterion must itself be reliable if it is to be a useful index of what the test measures. If you recall the meaning of reliability—consistency of scores—the need for a reliable criterion measure is intuitively obvious. After all, unreliable means unpredictable. An unreliable criterion will be inherently unpredictable, regardless of the merits of the test.

Consider the case in which scores on a college entrance exam (the test) are used to predict subsequent grade point average (the criterion). The validity of the entrance exam could be studied by computing the correlation ($r_{xy}$) between entrance exam scores and grade point averages for a representative sample of students. For purposes of a validity study, it would be ideal if the students were granted open or unscreened enrollment so as to prevent a restriction of range on the criterion variable. In any case, the resulting correlation coefficient is called a *validity coefficient*.[1]

The theoretical upper limit of the validity coefficient is constrained by the reliability of both the test and the criterion:

$$r_{xy} = \sqrt{(r_{xx})(r_{yy})}$$

The validity coefficient is always less than or equal to the square root of the test reliability multiplied by the criterion reliability. In other words, to the extent that the reliability of either the test or the criterion (or both) is low, the validity coefficient is also diminished. Returning to our example of an entrance exam used to predict college grade point average, we must conclude that the validity coefficient for such a test will always fall far short of +1.00, owing in part to the unreliability of college grades and also in part to the unreliability of the test itself.

A criterion measure must also be appropriate for the test under investigation. The *Standards for Educational and Psychological Testing* sourcebook (AERA, APA, & NCME, 1985) incorporates this important point as a separate standard:

> All criterion measures should be described accurately, and the rationale for choosing them as relevant criteria should be made explicit.

For example, in the case of interest tests, it is sometimes unclear whether the criterion measure should indicate satisfaction, success, or continuance in the activities under question. The choice between these subtle variants in the criterion must be made carefully, based on an analysis of what the interest test purports to measure.

A criterion must also be free of contamination from the test itself. Lehman (1978) has illustrated this point in a criterion-related validity study of a life change measure. The Schedule of Recent Events, or the SRE (Holmes & Rahe, 1967) is a widely used instrument that provides a quantitative index of the accumulation of stressful life events (e.g., divorce, job promotion, traffic tickets). Scores on the SRE correlate modestly with such criterion measures as physical illness and psychological disturbance. However, many seemingly appropriate criterion measures incorporate items that are similar or identical to SRE items. For example, screening tests of psychiatric symptoms often check for changes in eating, sleeping, or social activities. Unfortunately, the SRE incorporates questions that check for the following:

Change in eating habits

Change in sleeping habits

Change in social activities

If the screening test contains the same items as the SRE, then the correlation between these two measures will be artificially inflated. This potential source of error in test validation is referred to as *criterion contamination*, since the criterion is "contaminated" by its artificial commonality with the test.

Criterion contamination is also possible when the criterion consists of ratings from experts. If the experts also possess knowledge of the examinees' test scores, this information may (consciously or unconsciously) influence their ratings. When validating a test against a criterion of expert ratings, the test scores must be held in strictest confidence until the ratings have been collected.

Now that the reader knows the general characteristics of a good criterion, we will review the

---

1. We have purposefully refrained from referring to such a statistic as *the* validity coefficient. Remember that validity is a unitary concept determined by multiple sources of information that may include the correlation between test and criterion.

application of this knowledge in the analysis of concurrent and predictive validity.

## Concurrent Validity

In a concurrent validation study, test scores and criterion information are obtained simultaneously. Concurrent evidence of test validity is usually desirable for achievement tests, tests used for licensing or certification, and diagnostic clinical tests. An evaluation of concurrent validity indicates the extent to which test scores accurately estimate an individual's present position on the relevant criterion. For example, an arithmetic achievement test would possess concurrent validity if its scores could be used to predict, with reasonable accuracy, the current standing of students in a mathematics course. A personality inventory would possess concurrent validity if diagnostic classifications derived from it roughly matched the opinions of psychiatrists or clinical psychologists.

A test with demonstrated concurrent validity provides a shortcut for obtaining information that might otherwise require the extended investment of professional time. For example, the case assignment procedure in a mental health clinic can be expedited if a test with demonstrated concurrent validity is used for initial screening decisions. In this manner, severely disturbed patients requiring immediate clinical workup and intensive treatment can be quickly identified by paper-and-pencil test. Of course, tests are not intended to replace mental health specialists, but they can save time in the initial phases of diagnosis.

Correlations between a new test and existing tests are often cited as evidence of concurrent validity. This has a catch-22 quality to it—old tests validating a new test—but is nonetheless appropriate if two conditions are met. First, the criterion (existing) tests must have been validated through correlations with appropriate nontest behavioral data. In other words, the network of interlocking relationships must touch ground with real-world behavior at some point. Second, the instrument being validated must measure the same construct as the criterion tests. Thus, it is entirely appropriate

that developers of a new intelligence test report correlations between it and established mainstays such as the Stanford-Binet and Wechsler scales.

## Predictive Validity

In a predictive validation study, test scores are used to estimate outcome measures obtained at a later date. Predictive validity is particularly relevant for entrance examinations and employment tests. Such tests share a common function—determining who is likely to succeed at a future endeavor. A relevant criterion for a college entrance exam would be first-year-student grade point average, while an employment test might be validated against supervisor ratings after six months on the job. In the ideal situation, such tests are validated during periods of open enrollment (or open hiring) so that a full range of results is possible on the outcome measures. In this manner, future use of the test as a selection device for excluding low-scoring applicants will rest on a solid foundation of validational data.

When tests are used for purposes of prediction, it is necessary to develop a regression equation. A **regression equation** describes the best-fitting straight line for estimating the criterion from the test. We will not discuss the statistical approach to fitting the straight line, except to mention that it minimizes the sum of the squared deviations from the line (Ghiselli, Campbell, & Zedeck, 1981). For current purposes, it is more important to understand the nature and function of regression equations.

Ghiselli and associates (1981) provide a simple example of regression in the service of prediction, summarized here. Suppose we are trying to predict success on a job $Y$ (evaluated by the supervisor on a 7-point scale ranging from poor to excellent performance) from scores on a preemployment test $X$ (with scores that range from a low of 0 to a high of 100). The regression equation

$$Y = .07X + .2$$

might describe the best-fitting straight line and therefore produce the most accurate predictions. For an individual who scored 55 on the test, the predicted performance level would be 4.05; that is,

.07(55) + .2. A test score of 33 yields a predicted performance level of 2.51, that is, .07(33) + .2. Additional predictions are made likewise.

## Validity Coefficient and the Standard Error of the Estimate

The relationship between test scores and criterion measures can be expressed in several different ways. Perhaps the most popular approach is to compute the correlation between test and criterion ($r_{xy}$). In this context, the resulting correlation is known as a **validity coefficient.** The higher the validity coefficient $r_{xy}$, the more accurate is the test in predicting the criterion. In the hypothetical case where $r_{xy}$ is 1.00, the test would possess perfect validity and allow for flawless prediction. Of course, no such test exists, and validity coefficients are more commonly in the low- to midrange of correlations and rarely exceed .80. But how high should a validity coefficient be? There is no general answer to this question. However, we can approach the question indirectly by investigating the relationship between the validity coefficient and the corresponding error of estimate.

The **standard error of estimate** ($SE_{est}$) is the margin of error to be expected in the predicted criterion score. The error of estimate is derived from the following formula:

$$SE_{est} = SD_y \sqrt{1 - r_{xy}^2}$$

In this formula, $r_{xy}^2$ is the square of the validity coefficient and $SD_y$ is the standard deviation of the criterion scores. Perhaps the reader has noticed the similarities between this index and the standard error of measurement (SEM). In fact, both indices help gauge margins of error. The SEM indicates the margin of measurement error caused by unreliability of the test, whereas $SE_{est}$ indicates the margin of prediction error caused by the imperfect validity of the test.

The $SE_{est}$ helps answer the fundamental question: "How accurately can criterion performance be predicted from test scores?" (AERA, APA, & NCME, 1985). Consider the common practice of attempting to predict college grade point average from high school scores on a scholastic aptitude test. For a specific aptitude test, suppose we determine that the $SE_{est}$ for predicted grade point average is .2 (on the usual 0.0 to 4.0 grade point scale). What does this mean for the examinee whose college grade point is predicted to be 3.1? As is the case with all standard deviations, the standard error of the estimate can be used to bracket predicted outcomes in a probabilistic sense. Assuming that the frequency distribution of grades is normal, we know that the chances are about 68 in 100 that the examinee's predicted grade point will fall between 2.9 and 3.3 (plus or minus one $SE_{est}$). In like manner, we know that the chances are about 95 in 100 that the examinee's predicted grade point will fall between 2.7 and 3.5 (plus or minus two $SE_{est}$).

What is an acceptable standard of predictive accuracy? There is no simple answer to this question. As the reader will discern from the discussion that follows, standards of predictive accuracy are, in part, value judgments. To explain why this is so, we need to introduce the basic elements of decision theory (Taylor & Russell, 1939; Cronbach & Gleser, 1965).

## Decision Theory Applied to Psychological Tests

Proponents of **decision theory** stress that the purpose of psychological testing is not measurement per se but measurement in the service of decision making. The personnel manager wishes to know whom to hire; the admissions officer must choose whom to admit; the parole board desires to know which felons are good risks for early release; and the psychiatrist needs to determine which patients require hospitalization.

The link between testing and decision making is nowhere more obvious than in the context of predictive validation studies. Many of these studies use test results to determine who will likely succeed or fail on the criterion task so that, in the future, examinees with poor scores on the predictor test can be screened from admission, employment, or other privilege. This is the rationale by which admissions officers or employers require applicants to obtain a certain minimum score on an appropriate entrance or employment exam—previous studies of predictive validity can be cited to show that candidates scoring below a certain cutoff face steep odds in their educational or employment pursuits.

Psychological tests frequently play a major role in these kinds of institutional decision making. In a typical institutional decision, a committee—or sometimes a single person—makes a large number of comparable decisions based on a cutoff score on one or more selection tests. In order to present the key concepts of decision theory, let us oversimplify somewhat and assume that only a single test is involved.

Even though most tests produce a range of scores along a continuum, it is usually possible to identify a cutoff or pass/fail score that divides the sample into those predicted to succeed versus those predicted to fail on the criterion of interest. Let us assume that persons predicted to succeed are also selected for hiring or admission. In this case, the proportion of persons in the "predicted-to-succeed" group is referred to as the *selection ratio*. The selection ratio can vary from 0 to 1.0, depending on the proportion of persons who are considered good bets to succeed on the criterion measure.

If the results of a selection test allow for the simple dichotomy of "predicted to succeed" versus "predicted to fail," then the subsequent outcome on the criterion measure likewise can be split into two categories, namely, "did succeed" and "did fail." From this perspective, every study of predictive validity produces a two-by-two matrix, as portrayed in Figure 4.4.

Certain combinations of predicted and actual outcomes are more likely than others. If a test has good predictive validity, then most persons predicted to succeed will succeed and most persons predicted to fail will fail. These are examples of correct predictions and serve to bolster the validity of a selection instrument. Outcomes in these two cells are referred to as *hits* because the test has made a correct prediction.

But no selection test is a perfect predictor, so two other types of outcomes are also possible. Some persons predicted to succeed will, in fact, fail.

PERFORMANCE ON CRITERION MEASURE

|  |  | Did Succeed | Did Fail |
|---|---|---|---|
| PREDICTION OF SELECTION TEST | Will Succeed | Correct Prediction (hit) | False Positive (miss) |
|  | Will Fail | False Negative (miss) | Correct Prediction (hit) |

● **FIGURE 4.4** Possible Outcomes When a Selection Test Is Used to Predict Performance on a Criterion Measure

These cases are referred to as **false positives.** And some persons predicted to fail would, if given the chance, succeed. These cases are referred to as **false negatives.** False positives and false negatives are collectively known as misses, because in both cases the test has made an inaccurate prediction. Finally, the hit rate is the proportion of cases in which the test accurately predicts success or failure, that is, hit rate = (hits)/(hits + misses).

False positives and false negatives are unavoidable in the real-world use of selection tests. The only way to eliminate such selection errors would be to develop a perfect test, an instrument which has a validity coefficient of +1.00, signifying a perfect correlation with the criterion measure. A perfect test is theoretically possible, but none has yet been observed on this planet. Nonetheless, it is still important to develop selection tests with very high predictive validity, so as to minimize decision errors.

Proponents of decision theory make two fundamental assumptions about the use of selection tests:

1. The value of various outcomes to the institution can be expressed in terms of a common utility scale. One such scale—but by no means the only one—is profit and loss. For example, when using an interest inventory to select salespersons, a corporation can anticipate profit from applicants correctly identified as

successful but will lose money when, inevitably, some of those selected do not sell enough even to support their own salary (false positives). The cost of the selection procedure must also be factored in to the utility scale as well.

2. In institutional selection decisions, the most generally useful strategy is one that maximizes the average gain on the utility scale (or minimizes average loss) over many similar decisions. For example, which selection ratio produces the largest average gain on the utility scale? Maximization is, thus, the fundamental decision principle.

The application of decision theory is much more complicated than illustrated here, mainly because of the difficulty of finding a common utility scale for different outcomes. Consider the plight of the admissions officer at any large university. If the selection ratio is quite strict, then most of the admitted students will also succeed. But some students not admitted might have succeeded, too, and their financial support to the university (tuition, fees) is, therefore, lost. However, if the selection ratio is too lenient, then the percentage of false positives (students admitted who subsequently fail) skyrockets. How is the cost of a false positive to be calculated? The financial cost can be estimated—for example, advisers dedicate a certain number of hours at a known pay rate counseling these students. But no single utility scale can encompass the other diverse consequences such as the need for additional remedial services (which require money), the increase in faculty cynicism (an issue of morale), and the dashed hopes of misled students (whose heartbreak affects public perception of the university and may even influence future state funding!). Clearly, the neat statistical notions of decision theory oversimplify the complex influences that determine utility in the real world.

Nonetheless, in large institutional settings where a common utility scale can be identified, principles of decision theory can be applied to selection problems with thought-provoking results. For example, Schmidt, Hunter, McKenzie, and Muldrow (1979) analyzed the potential impact of using the Programmer Aptitude Test (PAT, Hughes & McNamara, 1959) in the selection of computer programmers by the federal government. They based their analysis on the following facts and assumptions:

1. PAT scores and measures of later on-the-job programming performance correlate quite substantially; the validity coefficient of the PAT is .76 (fact).
2. The government hires 600 new programmers each year (fact).
3. The cost of testing is about $10 per examinee (fact).
4. Programmers stay on the job for about nine years and receive pay raises according to a known pay scale (fact).
5. The yearly productivity in dollars of low-performing, average, and superior programmers can be accurately estimated by supervisors (assumption).

Based on these facts and assumptions, Schmidt et al. (1979) then compared the hypothetical use of the PAT against other selection procedures of lesser validity. Since the usefulness of a test is partly determined by the percentage of applicants who are selected for employment, the researchers also looked at the impact of different selection ratios on overall productivity. In each case, they estimated the yearly increase in dollar-amount productivity from using the PAT instead of an alternative and less efficacious procedure. In general, the use of the PAT was estimated to increase productivity by tens of millions of dollars. The specific estimated increase depended on the selection ratio and the validity coefficient of hypothetical alternative procedures. For example, if 80 percent of the applicants were hired (selection ratio of .80), using the PAT would increase the productivity of the federal government by at least $5.6 million (if the alternative procedure had a validity coefficient of .50) and possibly as much as $16.5 million (if the alternative procedure had no validity at all). If the selection ratio were quite small, the use of the PAT for selection boosted productivity even more—possibly as much as nearly $100 million. Schmidt et al. (1979) concluded that "the impact of valid selection procedures on work-force productivity is considerably greater than most personnel psychologists have believed."

## ● CONSTRUCT VALIDITY

The final type of validity discussed in this unit is construct validity, and it is undoubtedly the most difficult and elusive of the bunch. A **construct** is a theoretical, intangible quality or trait in which individuals differ (Messick, 1995). Examples of constructs include leadership ability, overcontrolled hostility, depression, and intelligence. Notice in each of these examples that constructs are inferred from behavior but are more than the behavior itself. In general, constructs are theorized to have some form of independent existence and to exert broad but to some extent predictable influences on human behavior. A test designed to measure a construct must estimate the existence of an inferred, underlying characteristic (e.g., leadership ability) based on a limited sample of behavior. Construct validity refers to the appropriateness of these inferences about the underlying construct.

All psychological constructs possess two characteristics in common:

1. There is no single external referent sufficient to validate the existence of the construct; that is, the construct cannot be operationally defined (Cronbach & Meehl, 1955).
2. Nonetheless, a network of interlocking suppositions can be derived from existing theory about the construct (AERA, APA, & NCME, 1985).

We will illustrate these points by reference to the construct of psychopathy (Cleckley, 1976), a personality constellation characterized by antisocial behavior (lying, stealing, and occasionally violence), a lack of guilt and shame, and impulsivity.[2]

---

2. The construct of psychopathy is very similar to what is now designated as antisocial personality disorder (American Psychiatric Association, 1994).

Psychopathy is surely a construct, in that there is no single behavioral characteristic or outcome sufficient to determine who is strongly psychopathic and who is not. On average we might expect psychopaths to be frequently incarcerated, but so are many common criminals. Furthermore, many successful psychopaths somehow avoid apprehension altogether (Cleckley, 1976). Psychopathy cannot be gauged only by scrapes with the law.

Nonetheless, a network of interlocking suppositions can be derived from existing theory about psychopathy. The fundamental problem in psychopathy is presumed to be a deficiency in the ability to feel emotional arousal—whether empathy, guilt, fear of punishment, or anxiety under stress (Cleckley, 1976). A number of predictions follow from this appraisal. For example, psychopaths should lie convincingly, have a greater tolerance for physical pain, show less autonomic arousal in the resting state, and get into trouble because of their lack of behavioral inhibition. Thus, to validate a measure of psychopathy, we would need to check out a number of different expectations based on our theory of psychopathy.

**Construct validity** pertains to psychological tests that claim to measure complex, multifaceted, and theory-bound psychological attributes such as psychopathy, intelligence, leadership ability, and the like. The crucial point to understand about construct validity is that "no criterion or universe of content is accepted as entirely adequate to define the quality to be measured" (Cronbach & Meehl, 1955). Thus, the demonstration of construct validity always rests on a program of research using diverse procedures outlined in the following sections. To evaluate the construct validity of a test, we must amass a variety of evidence from numerous sources.

Many psychometric theorists regard construct validity as the unifying concept for all types of validity evidence (Cronbach, 1988; Messick, 1995). According to this viewpoint, individual studies of content, concurrent, and predictive validity are regarded merely as supportive evidence in the cumulative quest for construct validation.

## ● APPROACHES TO CONSTRUCT VALIDITY

How does a test developer determine whether a new instrument possesses construct validity? As previously hinted, no single procedure will suffice for this difficult task. Evidence of construct validity can be found in practically any empirical study that examines test scores from appropriate groups of subjects. Most studies of construct validity fall into one of the following categories:

- Analysis to determine whether the test items or subtests are homogeneous and therefore measure a single construct
- Study of developmental changes to determine whether they are consistent with the theory of the construct
- Research to ascertain whether group differences on test scores are theory-consistent
- Analysis to determine whether intervention effects on test scores are theory-consistent
- Correlation of the test with other related and unrelated tests and measures
- Factor analysis of test scores in relation to other sources of information
- Analysis to determine whether test scores allow for the correct classification of examinees

We examine these sources of construct validity evidence in more detail in the following.

### Test Homogeneity

If a test measures a single construct, then its component items (or subtests) likely will be homogeneous (also referred to as *internally consistent*). In most cases, homogeneity is built into the test during the development process discussed in more detail in the next unit. The aim of test development is to select items that form a **homogeneous scale.** The most commonly used method for achieving this goal is to correlate each potential item with the total score and select items that show high correlations with the total score. A related procedure is to correlate subtests with the total score in the early phases of test development. In this manner, wayward scales that do not correlate to some minimum degree with the total test score can be revised before the instrument is released for general use.

Homogeneity is an important first step in certifying the construct validity of a new test, but standing alone it is weak evidence. Kline (1986) has pointed out the circularity of the procedure:

> If all our items in the item pool were wide of the mark and did not measure what we hoped, they would be selecting items by the criterion of their correlation with the total score, which can never work. It is to be noted that the same argument applies to the factoring of the item pool. A general factor of poor items is still possible. This objection is sound and has to be refuted empirically. Having found by item analysis a set of homogeneous items, we must still present evidence concerning their validity. Thus to construct a homogeneous test is not sufficient, validity studies must be carried out.

In addition to demonstrating the homogeneity of items, a test developer must provide multiple other sources of construct validity, discussed subsequently.

### Appropriate Developmental Changes

Many constructs can be assumed to show regular age-graded changes from early childhood into mature adulthood and perhaps beyond. Consider the construct of vocabulary knowledge as an example. It has been known since the inception of intelligence tests at the turn of the century that knowledge of vocabulary increases exponentially from early childhood into late childhood. More recent research demonstrates that vocabulary continues to grow, albeit at a slower pace, into old age (Gregory & Gernert, 1990). For any new test of vocabulary, then, an important piece of construct validity evidence would be that older subjects score better than younger subjects, assuming that education and health factors are held constant.

Of course, not all constructs lend themselves to predictions about developmental changes. For example, it is not clear whether a scale measuring "assertiveness" should show a pattern of increasing, decreasing, or stable scores with advancing age.

| ● TABLE 4.1 Mean Scores on the Social Interest Scale for Selected Groups | | |
|---|---|---|
| Group | N | Mean Score |
| Ursuline sisters | 6 | 13.3 |
| Adult church members | 147 | 11.2 |
| Charity volunteers | 9 | 10.8 |
| High school students nominated for high social interest | 23 | 10.2 |
| University students nominated for high social interest | 21 | 9.5 |
| University employees | 327 | 8.9 |
| University students | 1,784 | 8.2 |
| University students nominated for low social interest | 35 | 7.4 |
| Professional models | 54 | 7.1 |
| High school students nominated for low social interest | 22 | 6.9 |
| Adult atheists and agnostics | 30 | 6.7 |
| Convicted felons | 30 | 6.4 |

*Source:* Adapted with permission from Crandall, J. (1981). *Theory and measurement of social interest: Empirical tests of Alfred Adler's concept.* New York: Columbia University Press.

Developmental changes would be irrelevant to the construct validity of such a scale. We should also mention that appropriate developmental changes are but one piece in the construct validity puzzle. This approach does not provide information about how the construct relates to other constructs.

## Theory-Consistent Group Differences

One way to bolster the validity of a new instrument is to show that, on average, persons with different backgrounds and characteristics obtain theory-consistent scores on the test. Specifically, persons thought to be high on the construct measured by the test should obtain high scores, whereas persons with presumably low amounts of the construct should obtain low scores.

Crandall (1981) developed a social interest scale that illustrates the use of theory-consistent group differences in the process of construct validation. Borrowing from Alfred Adler, Crandall (1984) defined *social interest* as an "interest in and concern for others." To measure this construct, he devised a brief and simple instrument consisting of 15 forced-choice items. For each item, one of the two alternatives includes a trait closely related to the Adlerian concept of social interest (e.g.,

helpful), whereas the other choice consists of an equally attractive but nonsocial trait (e.g., quick-witted). The subject is instructed to "choose the trait which you value more highly." Each of the 15 items is scored 1 if the social interest trait is picked, 0 otherwise; thus, total scores on the Social Interest Scale (SIS) can range from 0 to 15.

Table 4.1 presents average scores on the SIS for 13 well-defined groups of subjects. The reader will notice that individuals likely to be high in social interest (e.g., nuns) obtain the highest average scores on the SIS, whereas the lowest scores are earned by presumably self-centered persons (e.g., models) and those who are outright antisocial (felons). These findings are theory-consistent and support the construct validity of this interesting instrument.

## Theory-Consistent Intervention Effects

Another approach to construct validation is to show that test scores change in appropriate direction and amount in reaction to planned or unplanned interventions. For example, the scores of elderly persons on a spatial orientation test battery should increase after these subjects receive cognitive training specifically designed to enhance their spatial orientation abilities. More precisely, if the test battery possesses construct validity, we can predict that spatial orientation scores should show a greater increase from pretest to posttest than found on unrelated abilities not targeted for special training (e.g., inductive reasoning, perceptual speed, numerical reasoning, or verbal reasoning). Willis and Schaie (1986) found just such a pattern of test results in a cognitive training study with elderly subjects, supporting the construct validity of their spatial orientation measure.

## Convergent and Discriminant Validation

**Convergent validity** is demonstrated when a test correlates highly with other variables or tests with which it shares an overlap of constructs. For example, two tests designed to measure different types of intelligence should, nonetheless, share enough of the general factor in intelligence to produce a hefty correlation (say, .5 or above) when jointly administered to a heterogeneous sample of subjects. In fact, any new test of intelligence that did not correlate at least modestly with existing measures would be highly suspect, on the grounds that it did not possess convergent validity.

**Discriminant validity** is demonstrated when a test does not correlate with variables or tests from

which it should differ. For example, social interest and intelligence are theoretically unrelated, and tests of these two constructs should correlate negligibly, if at all.

In a classic paper often quoted but seldom emulated, Campbell and Fiske (1959) proposed a systematic experimental design for simultaneously confirming the convergent and discriminant validities of a psychological test. Their design is called the *multitrait-multimethod matrix,* and it calls for the assessment of two or more traits by two or more methods. Table 4.2 provides a hypothetical example of this approach. In this example, three traits (*A, B,* and *C*) are measured by three methods (1, 2, and 3). For example, traits *A, B,* and *C* might be social interest, creativity, and dominance. Methods 1, 2, and 3 might be self-report inventory, peer ratings, and projective test. Thus, $A_1$ would represent a self-report inventory of social interest, $B_2$ a peer rating of creativity, $C_3$ a dominance measure derived from projective test, and so on.

Notice in this example that nine tests are studied (three traits are each measured by three methods). When each of these tests is administered twice to the same group of subjects and scores on all pairs of tests are correlated, the result is a **multitrait-multimethod matrix** (Table 4.2). This

| TABLE 4.2 Hypothetical Multitrait-Multimethod Matrix | | | Self-Report | | | Peer Rating | | | Projective Test | | |
|---|---|---|---|---|---|---|---|---|---|---|---|
| Traits | | | $A_1$ | $B_1$ | $C_1$ | $A_2$ | $B_2$ | $C_2$ | $A_3$ | $B_3$ | $C_3$ |
| Self-Report | Social interest | $A_1$ | (88) | | | | | | | | |
| | Creativity | $B_1$ | 52 | (89) | | | | | | | |
| | Dominance | $C_1$ | 31 | 36 | (79) | | | | | | |
| Peer Rating | Social interest | $A_2$ | 57 | 21 | 69 | (92) | | | | | |
| | Creativity | $B_2$ | 22 | 59 | 10 | 68 | (88) | | | | |
| | Dominance | $C_2$ | 11 | 12 | 48 | 58 | 59 | (85) | | | |
| Projective Test | Social interest | $A_3$ | 56 | 22 | 11 | 68 | 42 | 33 | (94) | | |
| | Creativity | $B_3$ | 23 | 58 | 13 | 43 | 66 | 34 | 68 | (92) | |
| | Dominance | $C_3$ | 11 | 11 | 43 | 34 | 32 | 69 | 60 | 60 | (86) |

Note: Letters *A, B,* and *C* refer to traits; (social interest, creativity, dominance); subscripts 1, 2, and 3 refer to methods of measurement (self-report, peer rating, projective test). The matrix consists of correlation coefficients (decimals omitted). See text.

matrix is a rich source of data on reliability, convergent validity, and discriminant validity.

For example, the correlations along the main diagonal (in parentheses) are reliability coefficients for each test. The higher these values, the better, and preferably we like to see values in the .80s or .90s here. The correlations along the three shorter diagonals (in boldface) supply evidence of convergent validity—the same trait measured by different methods. These correlations should be strong and positive, as shown here. Notice that the table also includes correlations between different traits measured by the same method (in solid triangles) and different traits measured by different methods (in dotted triangles). These correlations should be the lowest of all in the matrix, insofar as they supply evidence of discriminant validity.

The Campbell and Fiske (1959) methodology is an important contribution to our understanding of the test validation process. However, the full implementation of this procedure typically requires too monumental a commitment from researchers. It is more common for test developers to collect convergent and discriminant validity data in bits and pieces, rather than producing an entire matrix of intercorrelations. Meier (1984) provides one of the few real-world implementations of the multitrait-multimethod matrix in an examination of the validity of the "burnout" construct.

## Factor Analysis

Factor analysis is a specialized statistical technique that is particularly useful for investigating construct validity. We discuss factor analysis in substantial detail in Topic 5A, Intelligence Tests and Factor Analysis; here, we provide a quick preview so that the reader can appreciate the role of factor analysis in the study of construct validity. The purpose of **factor analysis** is to identify the minimum number of determiners (factors) required to account for the intercorrelations among a battery of tests. The goal in factor analysis is to find a smaller set of dimensions, called *factors*, that can

account for the observed array of intercorrelations among individual tests. A typical approach in factor analysis is to administer a battery of tests to several hundred subjects and then calculate a correlation matrix from the scores on all possible pairs of tests. For example, if 15 tests have been administered to a sample of psychiatric and neurological patients, the first step in factor analysis is to compute the correlations between scores on the 105 possible pairs of tests.[3] Although it may be feasible to see certain clusterings of tests that measure common traits, it is more typical that the mass of data found in a correlation matrix is simply too complex for the unaided human eye to analyze effectively. Fortunately, the computer-implemented procedures of factor analysis search this pattern of intercorrelations, identify a small number of factors, and then produce a table of factor loadings. A **factor loading** is actually a correlation between an individual test and a single factor. Thus, factor loadings can vary between −1.0 and +1.0. The final outcome of a factor analysis is a table depicting the correlation of each test with each factor.

A table of factor loadings helps describe the factorial composition of a test and thereby provides information relevant to construct validity. We will illustrate this point with factor analytic data from a hypothetical study of the Category Test. The Category Test is a relatively complex concept formation test designed to be different from traditional psychometric measures of intelligence and superior to them at detecting neurological disorders (Reitan & Wolfson, 1993). If the Category Test does, indeed, measure something different from traditional tests of intelligence, then it should load strongly on one or more factors not represented by the subtests of the WAIS-IV. Such a finding would strengthen the construct validity of the Category Test by distinguishing it from traditional measures of intelligence.

---

3. The general formula for the number of pairings among $N$ tests is $N(N − 1)/2$. Thus, if 15 tests are administered, there will be $15 \times 14/2$ or 105 possible pairings of individual tests.

● **TABLE 4.3** **Factor Loadings for the Category Test, Finger Tapping Test, and WAIS Subtests**

| Test | \multicolumn{4}{c}{Factor Loading} |
|------|------|------|------|------|
| | *I* | *II* | *III* | *IV* |
| Information | .88 | .15 | .07 | .07 |
| Comprehension | .83 | −.03 | .06 | −.09 |
| Arithmetic | .43 | .26 | .67 | −.12 |
| Similarities | .78 | .30 | .17 | .02 |
| Digit Span | .23 | .08 | .83 | .12 |
| Vocabulary | .92 | .07 | .06 | .01 |
| Coding | .25 | .31 | .21 | .61 |
| Visual Puzzles | .64 | .50 | −.24 | −.01 |
| Block Design | .39 | .74 | .06 | .20 |
| Matrix Reasoning | .29 | .73 | .00 | .31 |
| Category Test | .19 | .82 | .11 | −.18 |
| Finger Tapping Test | .07 | −.08 | .18 | .76 |

*Source:* Modeled on Lansdell and Donnelly (1977).

Suppose we administered the 10 subtests of the Wechsler Adult Intelligence Scale-IV, the Category Test, and the Finger Tapping Test to hundreds of psychiatric and neurological patients. The test scores could be factor analyzed, producing the factor loadings shown in Table 4.3. Notice that the verbal subtests from the WAIS have the highest loadings on factor I, which is surely a factor of verbal comprehension. The Category Test has a minimal loading on this factor, indicating that verbal abilities are not particularly important for good performance on this test. Factor II has its strongest loadings on Block Design (.74) and Matrix Reasoning (.73) and is typically labeled a perceptual organization factor.[4] Unfortunately, the

Category Test has a substantial loading (.82) on this factor and this factor alone. At least for this hypothetical study, it appears that the Category Test is merely an alternative measure of perceptual organizational skills and not a new and different test, as many of its users might like to claim. Incidentally, factor III seems to measure working memory, and factor IV appears to be a pure measure of motor speed.

## Classification Accuracy

Many tests are used for screening purposes to identify examinees who meet (or don't meet) certain diagnostic criteria. For these instruments, accurate classification is an essential index of validity. As a basis for illustrating this approach to validation, we consider the Mini-Mental State Examination (MMSE), a short screening test of cognitive functioning. The MMSE consists of a number of simple questions (e.g., What day is this?) and easy tasks (e.g., remembering three words). The test yields a score from 0 (no items correct) to 30 (all items correct). Although used for many purposes, a major application of the MMSE is to identify elderly individuals who might be experiencing dementia. *Dementia* is a general term that refers to significant cognitive decline and memory loss caused by a disease process such as Alzheimer's disease or the accumulation of small strokes. Both the MMSE and various forms of dementia are described in more detail in Chapter 10, Neuropsychological Assessment and Screening.

The MMSE is one of the most widely researched screening tests in existence. Much is known about its measurement qualities, such as the accuracy of the tool in detecting individuals with dementia. In exploring its utility, researchers have paid special attention to two psychometric features that bear upon validity: sensitivity and specificity. **Sensitivity** has to do with accurate identification of patients who have a syndrome— in this case, dementia. **Specificity** has to do with accurate identification of normal patients. These

---

4. Notice that humans provide the label for a factor based on an analysis of the tests that load most strongly on it. Two investigators might conceivably use different names for the same factor—for example, referring to factor II as either *perceptual organization* or *visuospatial analysis*.

ideas are clarified later. Understanding these concepts is pertinent to the validity of every screening test used in mental health and medicine. Thus, we provide modest coverage here, using the MMSE as an exemplar of a more general principle. Our discussion loosely follows the presentation found in Gregory (1999).

The concepts of sensitivity and specificity are chiefly helpful in dichotomous diagnostic situations in which individuals are presumed either to manifest a syndrome or not. For example, in medicine a patient either has prostate cancer or he does not. In this case, the criterion of truth, against which a screening test is measured, would be a tissue biopsy. Similarly, in research studies on the sensitivity and specificity of the MMSE, patients are known from independent, comprehensive medical and psychological workups either to meet the criteria for dementia or not. This is the "gold standard" against which the screening instrument is validated. The rationale for the screening test is pragmatic: It is unrealistic to refer every patient with suspected dementia for comprehensive evaluations that would include, for example, many hours of professional time (psychologist, neurologist, geriatric specialist, etc.) and expensive brain scans. The purpose of the MMSE—or any screening test—is to determine the need for additional assessment.

Screening tests typically provide a cutoff score used to identify possible cases of the syndrome in question. With the MMSE, a common cutting score is 23/24 out of the 30 points possible. Thus, a score of 23 points and below indicates the likelihood of dementia, whereas 24 points and above is considered normal. In this context, the sensitivity of the MMSE is the percentage of patients known to have dementia who score 23 points or lower. For example, if 100 patients are known from independent, comprehensive evaluations to exhibit dementia, and 79 of them score 23 or below, then the sensitivity of the test is 79 percent. The specificity of the MMSE is the other side of the coin, the percentage of patients known to be normal who score 24 points or

higher. For example, if 83 of 100 normal patients score 24 points or higher, then the specificity of the test is 83 percent.

In general, the validity of a screening test is bolstered to the extent that it possesses both high sensitivity and high specificity. There are no exact cutoffs, but for many purposes a test will need sensitivity and specificity that exceed 80 or 90 percent in order to justify its use. As we will see later, the standards for sensitivity and specificity are unique to each situation and depend on the costs—both financial and otherwise—of different kinds of errors in classification.

An ideal screening test, of course, would yield 100 percent sensitivity and 100 percent specificity. No such test exists in the real world. The reality of assessment is that the examiner must choose a cutoff score that provides a balance between sensitivity and specificity. What makes this problematic is that sensitivity and specificity are inversely related. Choosing a cutoff score that increases sensitivity invariably will reduce specificity, and vice versa. The inverse relationship between sensitivity and specificity is not only an empirical fact, but it is also a logical necessity—if one improves, the other must decline—no exceptions are possible. Consider the data in Table 4.4, a display of findings on sensitivity and specificity of the MMSE (Tombaugh et al., 1996). Notice how sensitivity and specificity vary as a function of the age and education level of the patients. Notice also that sensitivity and specificity typify an inverse relationship in every case.

Practitioners need to select a cutoff score that produces a livable balance between sensitivity and specificity. But exactly where is that point of equilibrium? In the case of the MMSE, the answer depends not just on the age and education of the client but also on the relative advantages and drawbacks of correct or incorrect decisions. Robust levels of sensitivity and specificity provide corroborating evidence of test validity, and test developers should strive to achieve the highest possible levels of both.

| | **TABLE 4.4**   Sensitivity and Specificity of the MMSE as a Function of Age and Education | | | |

| | Education | | | |
| MMSE Cutoff Score | 0–8 Years | | 9+ Years | |
| | Sensitivity | Specificity | Sensitivity | Specificity |
| --- | --- | --- | --- | --- |
| Age 65–79 | | | | |
| 26/27 | 100 | 24 | 96 | 59 |
| 15/26 | 100 | 38 | 93 | 71 |
| 24/25 | 100 | 52 | 91 | 79 |
| 23/24 | 100 | 64 | 82 | 86 |
| 22/23 | 100 | 74 | 68 | 91 |
| 21/22 | 89 | 81 | 59 | 94 |
| 20/21 | 83 | 84 | 52 | 95 |
| 19/20 | 67 | 90 | 46 | 96 |
| 18/19 | 33 | 95 | 36 | 96 |
| 17/18 | 28 | 95 | 27 | 98 |
| 16/17 | 24 | 96 | 25 | 99 |
| Age 80–89 | | | | |
| 26/27 | 100 | 10 | 100 | 43 |
| 25/26 | 100 | 17 | 100 | 63 |
| 24/25 | 98 | 34 | 97 | 70 |
| 23/24 | 93 | 42 | 95 | 82 |
| 22/23 | 88 | 51 | 82 | 89 |
| 21/22 | 70 | 65 | 69 | 94 |
| 20/21 | 63 | 77 | 44 | 96 |
| 19/20 | 50 | 86 | 39 | 97 |
| 18/19 | 48 | 92 | 36 | 98 |
| 17/18 | 45 | 95 | 28 | 98 |
| 16/17 | 35 | 96 | 26 | 100 |

Note:  All results are given in percentages.

*Source:*  Reprinted with permission from Tombaugh, T., McDowell, I., Kristjansson, B., & Hubley, A. (1996). Mini-Mental Stage Examination (MMSE) and the Modified MMSE (3MS): A psychometric comparison and normative data. *Psychological Assessment, 8,* 48–59.

## ● EXTRAVALIDITY CONCERNS AND THE WIDENING SCOPE OF TEST VALIDITY

We begin this section with a review of **extravalidity concerns,** which include side effects and unintended consequences of testing. By acknowledging the importance of the extravalidity domain, psychologists confirm that the decision to use a test involves social, legal, and political considerations that extend far beyond the traditional questions of technical validity. In a related development, we will also review how the interest in extravalidity concerns has spurred several theorists to broaden the concept of test validity. As the reader will discover, value implications and social consequences are now encompassed within the widening scope of test validity.

Even if a test is valid, unbiased, and fair, the decision to use it may be governed by additional considerations. Cole and Moss (1998) outline the following factors:

- What is the purpose for which the test is used?
- To what extent are the purposes accomplished by the actions taken?
- What are the possible side effects or unintended consequences of using the test?
- What possible alternatives to the test might serve the same purpose?

We survey only the most prominent extravalidity concerns here and show how they have served to widen the scope of test validity.

## Unintended Side Effects of Testing

The intended outcome of using a psychological test is not necessarily the only consequence. Various side effects also are possible, indeed, they are probable. The examiner must determine whether the benefits of giving the test outweigh the costs of the potential side effects. Furthermore, by anticipating unintended side effects, the examiner might be able to deflect or diminish them.

Cole and Moss (1998) cite the example of using psychological tests to determine eligibility for special education. Although the intended outcome is to help students learn, the process of identifying students eligible for special education may produce numerous negative side effects:

- The identified children may feel unusual or dumb.
- Other children may call the children names.
- Teachers may view these children as unworthy of attention.
- The process may produce classes segregated by race or social class.

A consideration of side effects should influence an examiner's decision to use a particular test for a specified purpose. The examiner might appropriately choose not to use a test for a worthy purpose if the likely costs from side effects outweigh the expected benefits.

Consider the common practice in years past of using the Minnesota Multiphasic Personality Inventory (MMPI) to help screen candidates for peace officer positions such as police officer or sheriff's deputy. Although the MMPI was originally designed as an aid in psychiatric diagnosis, subsequent research indicated that it is also useful in the identification of persons unsuited to a career in law enforcement (Hiatt & Hargrave, 1988). In particular, peace officers who produce MMPI profiles with mild elevations (e.g., $T$ score 65 to 69) on Scales F (Frequency), Masculinity-Femininity, Paranoia, and Hypomania tend to be involved in serious disciplinary actions; peace officers who produce more "defensive" MMPI profiles with fewer clinical scale elevations tend not to be involved in such actions. Thus, the test possessed modest validity for the worthy purpose of screening law enforcement candidates. But no test, not even the highly respected MMPI, is perfectly valid. Some good applicants will be passed over because their MMPI results are marginal. Perhaps their Paranoia Scale is at a $T$ score of 66, or the Hypomania Scale is at a $T$ score of 68. On the MMPI, a $T$ score of 70 is often considered the upper limit of the "normal" range.

One unintended side effect of using the MMPI for evaluation of peace officer applicants is that job candidates who are unsuccessful with one agency may be tagged with a pathological label such as psychopathic, schizophrenic, or paranoid. The label may arise in spite of the best efforts of the consulting psychologist, who may never have used any pejorative terms in the assessment report on the candidate. Typically, the label is conceived when administrators at the referring department look at the MMPI profile and see that the candidate obtained his or her highest score on a scale with a horrendous title such as Psychopathic Deviate, Schizophrenia, Hypochondriasis, or Paranoia. Unfortunately, the law enforcement community can be a very closed fraternity. Police chiefs and sheriffs commonly exchange verbal reports about their job applicants, so a pejorative label may follow the candidate from one setting to another, permanently barring the applicant from entry into the law enforcement profession. The repercussions are not only unfair to the candidate, but they also raise the specter of lawsuits against the agency and the consulting psychologist. All things considered, the consulting psychologist may find it preferable to use a technically less valid test for the same purpose, particularly if the alternative instrument does not produce these unintended side effects.

The renewed sensitivity to extravalidity issues has caused several test theorists to widen their definition of test validity. We review these recent developments in the following section, cautioning the reader that a final consensus about the nature of test validity is yet to emerge.

## The Widening Scope of Test Validity

By now the reader is familiar with the narrow, traditionalist perspective on test use, which states that a test is valid if it measures "what it purports to measure." The implicit implication of this perspective is that technical validity is the most essential basis for recommending test use. After all, valid tests provide accurate information about examinees—and what could be wrong with that?

Recently, several psychometric theoreticians have introduced a wider, functionalist definition of validity that asserts that a test is valid if it serves the purpose for which it is used (Cronbach, 1988; Messick, 1995). For example, a reading achievement test might be used to identify students for assignment to a remedial section. According to the functionalist perspective, the test would be valid—and its use, therefore, appropriate—if the students selected for remediation actually received some academic benefit from this application of the test.

The functionalist perspective explicitly recognizes that the test validator has an obligation to determine whether a practice has constructive consequences for individuals and institutions and especially to guard against adverse outcomes (Messick, 1980). Test validity, then, is an overall evaluative judgment of the adequacy and appropriateness of inferences *and actions* that flow from test scores.

Messick (1980, 1995) argues that the new, wider conception of validity rests on four bases. These are (1) traditional evidence of construct validity, for example, appropriate convergent and discriminant validity, (2) an analysis of the value implications of the test interpretation, (3) evidence for the usefulness of test interpretations in particular applications, and (4) an appraisal of the potential and actual social consequences, including side effects, from test use. A valid test is one that answers well to all four facets of test validity.

This wider conception of test validity is admittedly controversial, and some theorists prefer the traditional view that consequences and values are important but nonetheless separate from the technical issues of test validity. Everyone can agree on one point: Psychological measurement is not a neutral endeavor, it is an applied science that occurs in a social and political context.

## Utility: The Last Horizon of Test Validity

Finally, we introduce the concept of test utility, which is widely neglected in the research literature on psychological testing (Hunsley & Bailey, 1999). As noted by Wood, Garb, and Nezworski (2007), **test utility** can be summed up by the question "Does use of this test result in better patient outcomes or more efficient delivery of services?" For example, we might envision an experiment in which individual psychotherapy clients were randomly assigned to two groups. One group is tested with the Beck Depression Inventory-2 (Beck, Steer, & Brown, 1996) and the results provided to their therapists, while the other group is not tested but instead proceeds directly for treatment. If the tested group showed more improvement or required fewer sessions to achieve the same level of improvement, we would conclude that utility has been demonstrated for the test.

Unfortunately, there is very little research on the utility of psychological tests, and the research that does exist is indirect. For example, Finn and

Tonsager (1992) have shown that a highly structured method for giving feedback on personality test findings to college students awaiting psychotherapy has initial therapeutic effects in its own right. However, this does not answer the question whether the ultimate client outcome is better as a result of the test usage. For some tests such as the Rorschach inkblot technique, discussed later in the text, the question of utility is especially pertinent because of the time required by a psychologist to administer, score, interpret, and document the results. The total time easily can run to many hours. It is lamentable that the utility of this instrument and many other tests has not been systematically investigated.

## ● SUMMARY

1. The validity of a test is the degree to which it measures what it claims to measure. A test is valid to the extent that inferences made from it are appropriate, meaningful, and useful. Reliability is a necessary but not a sufficient precursor to validity.

2. Traditionally, the different ways of accumulating validity evidence have been grouped into three categories: content validity, criterion-related validity, and construct validity. However, validity is a unitary concept and any empirical study may bear upon the validity of a test.

3. Content validity is determined by the degree to which the questions, tasks, or items on a test are representative of the universe of behavior the test was designed to sample. Content validity is easy to assure for well-defined traits such as spelling ability, but more difficult to specify for inexplicit traits such as anxiety.

4. A test has face validity if it looks valid to test users, examiners, and especially the examinees. Face validity is important for social acceptability of a test but is irrelevant for psychometric purposes.

5. Criterion-related validity is demonstrated when a test is effective in predicting performance on an appropriate outcome measure. Criterion-related validity subsumes concurrent validity, in which the criterion measures are obtained at approximately the same time as the predictor test scores, and predictive validity, in which the criterion measures are obtained in the future.

6. When tests are used for purposes of prediction, it is necessary to develop a regression equation. A regression equation describes the best-fitting straight line (one that minimizes the sum of the squared deviations from the line) for estimating the criterion from the test. For example, the equation $Y = .07X + .2$ might be used to predict job ratings from an employment test.

7. The correlation between test and criterion ($r_{xy}$) is known as a validity coefficient. The higher the correlation, the more accurate is the test in estimating the criterion.

8. The standard error of estimate ($SE_{est}$) is the margin of error to be expected in the predicted criterion score. The error of estimate is derived from the following formula:

$$SE_{est} = SD_y\sqrt{1 - r_{xy}^2}$$

where $r_{xy}$ is the validity coefficient.

9. Proponents of decision theory stress that a test must aid in accurate decision making. The accurate prediction of success versus failure on an outcome measure is essential. Tests should avoid two kinds of errors: false positives, in which subjects are predicted to succeed but fail, and false negatives, in which subjects are predicted to fail but succeed.

10. Decision theory assumes that the costs of accurate and inaccurate predictions can be measured on a common utility scale such as profit/loss. A fundamental assumption of decision theory is maximization: In institutional selection decisions, the most appropriate test-use strategy is one that maximizes the average gain or minimizes the average loss.

11. A construct is a theoretical, intangible quality or trait in which individuals differ. Construct

validity pertains to psychological tests that claim to measure complex, multifaceted, and theory-bound psychological attributes such as leadership ability, overcontrolled hostility, and intelligence.

12. Studies of construct validity generally fall into one of these categories: analysis of item homogeneity, assessment of developmental and group changes on the test, analysis of intervention effects, correlation and factor analysis of test scores in relation to other sources of information, and evaluation of classification accuracy. In each case, the crucial question is whether the results are consistent with the underlying theory of the construct that is measured.

13. Extravalidity concerns include the side effects and unintended consequences of testing. For example, a valid assessment for special education placement may nonetheless cause identified children to feel unusual or dumb. A consideration of side effects should influence an examiner's decision to use a particular test for a specific purpose.

14. The new, wider, functionalist perspective on test validity asserts that a test is valid if it serves the purposes for which it is used. For example, the validity of a reading achievement test might be linked to successful remediation of the reading-impaired students identified by the test.

## ● KEY TERMS AND CONCEPTS

validity   p. 110

content validity   p. 111

face validity   p. 113

criterion-related validity   p. 113

concurrent validity   p. 113

predictive validity   p. 113

regression equation   p. 115

validity coefficient   p. 116

standard error of estimate   p. 116

decision theory   p. 116

false positives   p. 117

false negatives   p. 117

construct   p. 119

construct validity   p. 119

homogeneous scale   p. 120

convergent validity   p. 122

discriminant validity   p. 122

multitrait-multimethod matrix   p. 122

factor analysis   p. 123

factor loading   p. 123

sensitivity   p. 124

specificity   p. 124

extravalidity concerns   p. 126

test utility   p. 128

# Test Construction

Creating a new test involves both science and art. A test developer must choose strategies and materials and then make day-to-day research decisions that will affect the quality of his or her emerging instrument. The purpose of this section is to discuss the process by which psychometricians create valid tests. Although we will discuss many separate topics, they are united by a common theme: Valid tests do not just materialize on the scene in full maturity—they emerge slowly from an evolutionary, developmental process that builds in validity from the very beginning. We will emphasize the basics of test development here; readers who desire a more advanced presentation should consult Kline (1986), McDonald (1999), and Bernstein and Nunnally (1994).

Test construction consists of six intertwined stages:

| | |
|---|---|
| Defining the test | Testing the items |
| Selecting a scaling method | Revising the test |
| Constructing the items | Publishing the test |

By way of preview, we can summarize these steps as follows: defining the test consists of delimiting its scope and purpose, which must be known before the developer can proceed to test construction. Selecting a scaling method is a process of setting the rules by which numbers are assigned to test results. Constructing the items is as much art as science, and it is here that the creativity of the test developer may be required. Once a preliminary version of the test is available, the developer usually administers it to a modest-sized sample of subjects in order to collect initial data about test item characteristics. Testing the items entails a variety of statistical procedures referred to collectively as item analysis. The purpose of item analysis is to determine which items should be retained, which revised, and which thrown out. Based on item analysis and other sources of information, the test is then revised. If the revisions are substantial, new items and additional pretesting with new subjects may be required. Thus, test construction involves a feedback loop whereby second, third, and fourth drafts of an instrument might be produced (Figure 4.5). Publishing the test is the final step. In addition to releasing the test materials, the developer must produce a user-friendly test manual. Let us examine each of these steps in more detail.

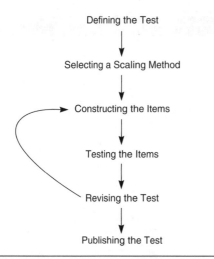

Defining the Test

↓

Selecting a Scaling Method

↓

Constructing the Items

↓

Testing the Items

↓

Revising the Test

↓

Publishing the Test

● **FIGURE 4.5** The Test Construction Process

1. Measure intelligence from a strong theoretical and research basis
2. Separate acquired factual knowledge from the ability to solve unfamiliar problems
3. Yield scores that translate to educational intervention
4. Include novel tasks
5. Be easy to administer and objective to score
6. Be sensitive to the diverse needs of preschool, minority group, and exceptional children (Kaufman & Kaufman, 1983)

As the reader will discover in a later topic, the K-ABC represents an interesting departure from traditional intelligence tests. For now, the important point is that the developers of this recent instrument explained its purpose explicitly and proposed a fresh focus for measuring intelligence, long before they started constructing test items.

## ● DEFINING THE TEST

In order to construct a new test, the developer must have a clear idea of what the test is to measure and how it is to differ from existing instruments. Insofar as psychological testing is now entering its second one hundred years, and insofar as thousands of tests have already been published, the burden of proof clearly rests on the test developer to show that a proposed instrument is different from, and better than, existing measures.

Consider the daunting task faced by a test developer who proposes yet another measure of general intelligence. With dozens of such instruments already in existence, how could a new test possibly make a useful contribution to the field? The answer is that contemporary research continually adds to our understanding of intelligence and impels us to seek new and more useful ways to measure this multifaceted construct.

Kaufman and Kaufman (1983) provide a good model of the test definition process. In proposing the Kaufman Assessment Battery for Children (K-ABC), a new test of general intelligence in children, the authors listed six primary goals that define the purpose of the test and distinguish it from existing measures:

## ● SELECTING A SCALING METHOD

The immediate purpose of psychological testing is to assign numbers to responses on a test so that the examinee can be judged to have more or less of the characteristic measured. The rules by which numbers are assigned to responses define the scaling method. Test developers select a scaling method that is optimally suited to the manner in which they have conceptualized the trait(s) measured by their test. No single scaling method is uniformly better than the others. For some traits, ordinal ranking of expert judges might be the best measurement approach; for other traits, complex scaling of self-report data might yield the most valid measurements.

There are so many distinctive scaling methods available to psychometricians that we will be satisfied to provide only a representative sample here. Readers who wish a more thorough and detailed review should consult Gulliksen (1950), Nunnally (1978), or Kline (1986). However, before reviewing selecting scaling methods, we need to introduce a related concept, levels of measurement, so that the reader can better appreciate the differences between scaling methods.

## Levels of Measurement

According to Stevens (1946), all numbers derived from measurement instruments of any kind can be placed into one of four hierarchical categories: nominal, ordinal, interval, or ratio. Each category defines a level of measurement; the order listed is from least to most informative.

In a **nominal scale,** the numbers serve only as category names. For example, when collecting data for a demographic study, a researcher might code males as "1" and females as "2." Notice that the numbers are arbitrary and do not designate "more" or "less" of anything. In nominal scales the numbers are just a simplified form of naming.

An **ordinal scale** constitutes a form of ordering or ranking. If college professors were asked to rank order four cars as to which they would prefer to own, the preferred order might be "1" Cadillac, "2" Chevrolet, "3" Volkswagen, "4" Hyundai. Notice here that the numbers are not interchangeable. A ranking of "1" is "more" than a ranking of "2," and so on. The "more" refers to the order of preference. However, ordinal scales fail to provide information about the relative strength of rankings. In this hypothetical example, we do not know whether college professors strongly prefer Cadillacs over Chevrolets or just marginally so.

An **interval scale** provides information about ranking, but also supplies a metric for gauging the differences between rankings. To construct an interval scale, we might ask our college professors to rate on a scale from 1 to 100 how much they would like to own the four cars previously listed. Suppose the average ratings work out as follows: Cadillac, 90; Chevrolet, 70; Volkswagen, 60; Hyundai, 50. From this information we could infer that the preference for a Cadillac is much stronger than for a Chevrolet, which, in turn, is mildly stronger than the preference for a Volkswagen. More important, we can also make the assumption that the intervals between the points on this scale are approximately the same: The difference between professors' preference for a Chevrolet and Volkswagen (10 points) is about the same as that between a Volkswagen and a Hyundai (also 10 points). In short, interval scales are based on

|         | *Characteristics* | | | |
|---------|---------|---------|---------|---------|
| *Level* | *Allows for Categoriz-ing* | *Allows for Ranking* | *Uses Equal Intervals* | *Possesses Real Zero Point* |
| Nominal | × | | | |
| Ordinal | × | × | | |
| Interval | × | × | × | |
| Ratio | × | × | × | × |

● **FIGURE 4.6**   Essential Characteristics of Four Levels of Measurement

the assumption of equal-sized units or intervals for the underlying scale.

A **ratio scale** has all the characteristics of an interval scale but also possesses a conceptually meaningful zero point in which there is a total absence of the characteristic being measured. The essential characteristics of the four levels of measurement are summarized in Figure 4.6.

Ratio scales are rare in psychological measurement. Consider whether there is any meaningful sense in which a person can be thought to have zero intelligence. Not really. The same is true for most constructs in psychology: Meaningful zero points just do not exist. However, a few physical measures used by psychologists qualify as ratio scales. For example, height and weight qualify, and perhaps some physiological measures such as electrodermal response qualify, too. But by and large the best a psychologist can hope for is interval-level measurement.

Levels of measurement are relevant to test construction because the more powerful and useful parametric statistical procedures (e.g., Pearson $r$, analysis of variance, multiple regression) should be used only for scores derived from measures that meet the criteria of interval or ratio scales. For scales that are only nominal or ordinal, less-powerful nonparametric statistical procedures (e.g., chi-square, rank order correlation, median tests) must be employed. In practice, most major psychological testing instruments (especially intelligence tests and personality scales) are assumed to employ approximately interval-level measurement even though, strictly speaking, it is very difficult to demonstrate absolute equality of intervals for such instruments (Bausell, 1986). Now that the reader is familiar with levels of measurement, we introduce a representative sample of scaling methods, noting in advance that different scaling methods yield different levels of measurement.

## ● REPRESENTATIVE SCALING METHODS

### Expert Rankings

Suppose we wanted to measure the depth of coma in patients who had suffered a recent head injury that rendered them unconscious. A depth of coma scale could be very important in predicting the course of improvement, because it is well known that a lengthy period of unconsciousness offers a poor prognosis for ultimate recovery. In addition, rehabilitation personnel have a practical need to know whether a patient is deeply comatose or in a partially communicative state of twilight consciousness.

One approach to scaling the depth of coma would be to rely on the behavioral **rankings of experts.** For example, we could ask a panel of neurologists to list patient behaviors associated with different levels of consciousness. After the experts had submitted a large list of diagnostic behaviors, the test developers—preferably experts on head injuries—could rank the indicator behaviors along a continuum of consciousness ranging from deep coma to basic orientation. Using precisely this approach, Teasdale and Jennett (1974) produced the Glasgow Coma Scale. Instruments similar to this scale are widely used in hospitals for the assessment of traumatic brain injury (Figure 4.7).

The Glasgow Coma Scale is scored by observing the patient and assigning the highest level of functioning on each of three subscales. On each subscale, it is assumed that the patient displays all levels of behavior below the rated level. Thus, from a psychometric standpoint, this scale consists of three subscales (eyes, verbal response, and motor response) each yielding an ordinal ranking of behavior.

In addition to the rankings, it is possible to compute a single overall score that is something more than an ordinal scale, although probably less than true interval-level measurement. If numbers

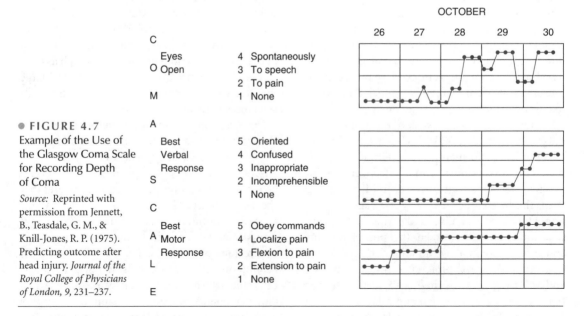

● **FIGURE 4.7**
Example of the Use of the Glasgow Coma Scale for Recording Depth of Coma

*Source:* Reprinted with permission from Jennett, B., Teasdale, G. M., & Knill-Jones, R. P. (1975). Predicting outcome after head injury. *Journal of the Royal College of Physicians of London, 9,* 231–237.

are attached to the rankings (e.g., for eyes open a coding of "none" = 1, "to pain" = 2, and so on), then the numbers for the rated level for each subscale can be added, yielding a maximum possible score of 14. The total score on the Glasgow Coma Scale predicts later recovery with a very high degree of accuracy (Jennett, Teasdale, & Knill-Jones, 1975). We see, then, that quite plain psychological tests derived from the very simplest scaling methods can, nonetheless, provide valid and useful information.

## Method of Equal-Appearing Intervals

Early in the twentieth century, L. L. Thurstone (1929) proposed a method for constructing interval-level scales from attitude statements. His **method of equal-appearing intervals** is still used today, marking him as one of the giants of psychometric theory. The actual methodology of constructing equal-appearing intervals is somewhat complex and statistically laden, but the underlying logic is easy to explain (Ghiselli, Campbell, & Zedeck, 1981). To illustrate the method, we summarize the steps involved in constructing a scale of attitudes toward church membership:

1. Collect as many true-false statements as possible reflecting a variety of positive and negative attitudes toward the church. Two extreme examples might be:

   "I feel that church services give me inspiration and help me to live up to my best during the following week."

   "I think that churches seek to impose a lot of worn-out dogmas and medieval superstitions."

   Of course, many moderate items would be collected as well.

2. Next, have 10 or so known experts or judges rate these statements to determine the degree of favorability/unfavorability toward the attitude. The judges should be qualified for the task at hand; ministers might be used for a church membership attitude scale. Usually, each judge is requested to sort each statement into 1 of 11 categories that range from "extremely favorable" to "extremely unfavorable." Judges are told to disregard their own biases and to regard the 11 categories as equidistant.

3. After the judges have completed the evaluation process, the mean favorability rating (from 1 to 11) and standard deviation for each item is determined. For example, 10 judges may have given an average favorability rating of 9.2 to the first item previously noted; but ratings would likely differ from one judge to another, as reflected in a standard deviation of 1.1 for this item.

4. Because the standard deviation of an item favorability rating reflects ambiguity, items with large standard deviations are therefore dropped. Usually, about 20 to 30 items are chosen such that the statements cover the range of the dimension (favorable to unfavorable). It is assumed that the differences between items on the final scale fulfill the properties of an interval scale.

5. Persons who take the attitude scale are asked to mark all the statements with which they agree. Their score is determined by averaging the scale values of those items endorsed.

Ghiselli et al. (1981) note that the preceding scaling method merely produces the attitude scale. Reliability and validity analyses of the scale are still needed to determine its appropriateness and usefulness.

A study by Russo (1994) illustrates a modern application of the Thurstone method. She used a Thurstone scaling approach to evaluate 216 items from three prominent self-report depression inventories. The judges included 527 undergraduates and 37 clinical faculty members at a medical school. The 216 items were randomized and rated with respect to depressive severity from 1 representing no depression to 11 representing extreme depression. She discovered that all three self-report inventories lacked items and response options typical of mild depression. The distribution of the 216 items was bimodal with many items bunched near the bottom (no depression) and many items bunched near the middle (moderate depression).

A characteristic finding for one set of items from a prominent depression scale was as follows:

| Rated Depression | Original Scoring | Item Content |
|---|---|---|
| 1.0 | 1 | I never feel downhearted or sad. |
| 3.4 | 2 | I sometimes feel downhearted or sad. |
| 4.1 | 3 | I feel downhearted or sad a good part of the time. |
| 4.4 | 4 | I feel downhearted or sad most of the time. |

The reader will notice that the original scoring on these items deviates substantially from the depression ratings provided by the panel of students and clinical faculty. It is also evident that the actual scale values are discontinuous, jumping from 1.0 to 3.4 and higher. A similar pattern was observed for many items on all three inventories, leading Russo (1994) to conclude:

> The present results suggest that if the original scoring is used for the three scales examined here, then the distinctions between well-being and absence of depression as well as between moderate and severe will be difficult to make. Such imprecision will make it difficult to assess the efficacy of treatments for depression, because a lack thereof must be a function of added measurement error due to ordinal measures. Such error could also wreak havoc in longitudinal studies, especially in those in which memory is involved.

We see in this example that Thurstone's approach to item scaling has powerful applications in test development. Based on these findings, researchers are now in a position to develop improved self-report scales that assess the full range of symptomatology in depression.

## Method of Absolute Scaling

Thurstone (1925) also developed the **method of absolute scaling,** a procedure for obtaining a measure of absolute item difficulty based on results for different age groups of test takers. The methodology for determining individual item difficulty on an absolute scale is quite complex, although the underlying rationale is not too difficult to understand. Essentially, a set of common test items is administered to two or more age groups. The relative difficulty of these items between any two age groups serves as the basis for making a series of interlocking comparisons for all items and all age groups. One age group serves as the anchor group. Item difficulty is measured in common units such as standard deviation units of ability for the anchor group. The method of absolute scaling is widely used in group achievement and aptitude testing (Donlon, 1984).

Thurstone (1925) illustrated the method of absolute scaling with data from the testing of 3,000 schoolchildren on the 65 questions from the original Binet test. Using the mean of Binet test intelligence of 3½-year-old children as the zero point and the standard deviation of their intelligence as the unit of measurement, he constructed a scale that ranged from $-2$ to $+10$ and then located each of the 65 questions on that scale. Thurstone (1925) found that the scale "brings out rather strikingly the fact that the questions are unduly bunched at certain ranges [of difficulty] and rather scarce at other ranges." A modern test developer would use this kind of analysis as a basis for dropping redundant test items (redundant in the sense that they measure at the same difficulty level) and adding other items that test the higher (and lower) ranges of difficulty.

## Likert Scales

Likert (1932) proposed a simple and straightforward method for scaling attitudes that is widely used today. A **Likert scale** presents the examinee with five responses ordered on an agree/disagree or approve/disapprove continuum. For example, one item on a scale to assess attitudes toward church membership might read:

Church services give me inspiration and help me to live up to my best during the following week.

Do you:

| | | | | | | | | | |
|---|---|---|---|---|---|---|---|---|---|
| Strongly Agree | | Agree | | Undecided | | Disagree | | Strongly Disagree | |

Depending on the wording of an individual item, an extreme answer of "strongly agree" or "strongly disagree" will indicate the most favorable response on the underlying attitude measured by the questionnaire. Likert (1932) assigned a score of 5 to this extreme response, 1 to the opposite extreme, and 2, 3, and 4 to intermediate replies. The total scale score is obtained by adding the scores from individual items. For this reason, a Likert scale is also referred to as a *summative scale.*

## Guttman Scales

On a **Guttman scale,** respondents who endorse one statement also agree with milder statements pertinent to the same underlying continuum (Guttman, 1947). Thus, if the examiner knows an examinee's most extreme endorsement on the continuum, it is possible to reconstruct the intermediate responses as well. Guttman scales are produced by selecting items that fall into an ordered sequence of examinee endorsement. A perfect Guttman scale is seldom achieved because of errors of measurement, but is nonetheless a fitting goal for certain types of tests.

Although the Guttman approach was originally devised to determine whether a set of attitude statements is unidimensional, the technique has been used in many different kinds of tests. For example, Beck used Guttman-type scaling to produce the individual items of the Beck Depression Inventory (BDI, Beck, Steer, & Garbin, 1988). Items from the BDI resemble the following:

( ) I occasionally feel sad or blue.
( ) I often feel sad or blue.
( ) I feel sad or blue most of the time.
( ) I always feel sad and I can't stand it.

Clients are asked to "check the statement from each group that you feel is most true about you." A client who endorses an extreme alternative (e.g., "I always feel sad and I can't stand it") almost certainly agrees with the milder statements as well.

## Method of Empirical Keying

The reader may have noticed that most of the scaling methods discussed in the preceding section rely

upon the authoritative judgment of experts in the selection and ordering of items. It is also possible to construct measurement scales based entirely on empirical considerations devoid of theory or expert judgment. In the **method of empirical keying,** test items are selected for a scale based entirely on how well they contrast a criterion group from a normative sample. For example, a Depression scale could be derived from a pool of true-false personality inventory questions in the following manner:

1. A carefully selected and homogeneous group of persons experiencing major depression is gathered to answer the pool of true-false questions.
2. For each item, the endorsement frequency of the depression group is compared to the endorsement frequency of the normative sample.
3. Items which show a large difference in endorsement frequency between the depression and normative samples are selected for the Depression scale, keyed in the direction favored by depression subjects (true or false, as appropriate).
4. Raw score on the Depression scale is then simply the number of items answered in the keyed direction.

The method of empirical keying can produce some interesting surprises. A common finding is that some items selected for a scale may show no obvious relationship to the construct measured. For example, an item such as "I drink a lot of water" (keyed true) might end up on a Depression scale. The momentary rationale for including this item is simply that it works. Of course, the challenge posed to researchers is to determine why the item works. However, from the practical standpoint of empirical scale construction, theoretical considerations are of secondary importance. We discuss the method of empirical keying further in Topic 8B, Self-Report and Behavioral Assessment of Psychopathology.

## Rational Scale Construction (Internal Consistency)

The rational approach to scale construction is a popular method for the development of self-report personality inventories. The name *rational* is somewhat of a misnomer, insofar as certain statistical methods are essential to this approach. Also, the name implies that other approaches are nonrational or irrational, which is untrue. The heart of the **method of rational scaling** is that all scale items correlate positively with each other and also with the total score for the scale. An alternative and more appropriate name for this approach is internal consistency, which emphasizes what is actually done. Gough and Bradley (1992) explain how the rational approach earned its descriptive title:

> The idea of rationality enters the scene in that the central theme or unifying dimension around which the items cluster is one that was conceptually articulated beforehand by the developer of the measure and from which the scoring of each item is determined in a logical and understandable way.

We will follow their presentation to illustrate the features of the rational approach.

Suppose a test developer desires to develop a new self-report scale for leadership potential. Based on a review of relevant literature, the researcher might conclude that leadership potential is characterized by self-confidence, resilience under pressure, high intelligence, persuasiveness, assertiveness, and the ability to sense what others are thinking and feeling. These notions suggest that the following true-false items might be useful in the assessment of leadership potential (Gough & Bradley, 1992):

- I generally feel sure of myself and self-confident. (T)
- When others disagree with me, I usually just keep quiet or else give in. (F)
- I believe that I am distinctly above average in intellectual ability. (T)
- I often feel that I have a poor understanding of how other people will react to things. (F)
- My friends would probably describe me as a strong, forceful person. (T)

The *T* and *F* after each statement indicate the rationally keyed direction for leadership potential.

Of course, additional items with similar intentions also would be proposed. The test developer might begin with 100 items that appear—on a rational basis—to assess leadership potential. These preliminary items would be administered to a large sample of individuals similar to the target population for whom the scale is intended. For instance, if the scale is designed to identify college students with leadership potential, then it should be administered to a cross section of several hundred college students. For scale development, very large samples are desirable. In this hypothetical case, let us assume that we obtain results for 500 college students.

The next step in rational scale construction is to correlate scores on each of the preliminary items with the total score on the test for the 500 subjects in the tryout sample. Because scores on the items are dichotomous (1 is arbitrarily assigned to an answer corresponding to the scoring key, 0 to the alternative), a biserial correlation coefficient $r_{bis}$ is needed. Once the correlations are obtained, the researcher scans the list in search of weak correlations and reversals (negative correlations). These items are discarded because they do not contribute to the measurement of leadership potential. Up to half of the initial items might be discarded. If a large proportion of items is initially discarded, the researcher might recalculate the item-total correlations based upon the reduced item pool to verify the homogeneity of the remaining items. The items that survive this iterative procedure constitute the leadership potential scale. The reader should keep in mind that the rational approach to scale construction merely produces a homogeneous scale thought to measure a specified construct. Additional studies with new subject samples would be needed to determine the reliability and validity of the new scale.

## ● CONSTRUCTING THE ITEMS

Constructing test items is a painful and laborious procedure that taxes the creativity of test developers. The item writer is confronted with a profusion of initial questions:

- Should item content be homogeneous or varied?
- What range of difficulty should the items cover?
- How many initial items should be constructed?

- Which cognitive processes and item domains should be tapped?
- What kind of test item should be used?

We will address the first three questions briefly before turning to a more detailed discussion of the last two topics, which are commonly referred to under the rubrics of table of specifications and item formats.

### Initial Questions in Test Construction

The first question pertains to the homogeneity versus heterogeneity of test item content. In large measure, whether item content is homogeneous or varied is dictated by the manner in which the test developer has defined the new instrument. Consider a culture-reduced test of general intelligence. Such an instrument might incorporate varied items, so long as the questions do not presume specific schooling. The test developer might seek to incorporate novel problems equally unfamiliar to all examinees. On the other hand, with a theory-based test of spatial thinking, subscales with homogeneous item content would be required.

The range of item difficulty must be sufficient to allow for meaningful differentiation of examinees at both extremes. The most useful tests, then, are those that include a graded series of very easy items passed by almost everyone as well as a group of incrementally more difficult items passed by virtually no one. A ceiling effect is observed when significant numbers of examinees obtain perfect or near-perfect scores. The problem with a ceiling effect is that distinctions between high-scoring examinees are not possible, even though these examinees might differ substantially on the underlying trait measured by the test. A floor effect is observed when significant numbers of examinees obtain scores at or near the bottom of the scale. For example, the WAIS-R possessed a serious floor effect in that it failed to discriminate between moderate, severe, and profound levels of mental retardation—all persons with significant developmental disabilities would fail to answer virtually every question.

Test developers expect that some initial items will prove to make ineffectual contributions to the overall measurement goal of their instrument. For this reason, it is common practice to construct a first draft that contains excess items, perhaps double the number of questions desired on the final draft. For example, the 550-item MMPI originally consisted of more than 1,000 true-false personality statements (Hathaway & McKinley, 1940).

### Table of Specifications

Professional developers of achievement and ability tests often use one or more item-writing schemes to help ensure that their instrument taps a desired mixture of cognitive processes and content domains. For example, a very simple item-writing scheme might designate that an achievement test on the Civil War should consist of 10 multiple-choice items and 10 fill-in-the-blank questions, half of each on factual matters (e.g., dates, major battles) and the other half on conceptual issues (e.g., differing views on slavery).

Before development of a test begins, item writers usually receive a table of specifications. A **table of specifications** enumerates the information and cognitive tasks on which examinees are to be assessed. Perhaps the most common specification table is the content-by-process matrix, which lists the exact number of items in relevant content areas and details the precise composite of items that must exemplify different cognitive processes (Millman & Greene, 1989).

Consider a science achievement test suitable for high school students. Such a test must cover many different content areas and should require a mixture of cognitive processes ranging from simple recall to inferential reasoning. By providing a table of specifications prior to the item-writing stage, the test developer can guarantee that the resulting instrument contains a proper balance of topical coverage and taps a desired range of cognitive skills. A hypothetical but realistic table of specifications is portrayed in Table 4.5.

### Item Formats

When it comes to the method by which psychological attributes are to be assessed, the test developer

● **TABLE 4.5 Example of a Content-by-Process Table of Specifications for a Hypothetical 100-Item Science Achievement Test**

| Content Area | Process | | |
| --- | --- | --- | --- |
| | Factual Knowledge[a] | Information Competence[b] | Inferential Reasoning[c] |
| Astronomy | 8 | 3 | 3 |
| Botany | 6 | 7 | 2 |
| Chemistry | 10 | 5 | 4 |
| Geology | 10 | 5 | 2 |
| Physics | 8 | 5 | 6 |
| Zoology | 8 | 5 | 3 |
| Totals | 50 | 30 | 20 |

[a]Factual Knowledge: Items can be answered based on simple recognition of basic facts.

[b]Information Competence: Items require usage of information provided in written text.

[c]Inferential Reasoning: Items can be answered by making deductions or drawing conclusions.

is confronted with dozens of choices. Indeed, it would be easy to write an entire chapter on this topic alone. For reviews of item formats, the interested reader should consult Bausell (1986), Jensen (1980), and Wesman (1971). In this section, we will quickly survey the advantages and pitfalls of the more common varieties of test items.

For group-administered tests of intellect or achievement, the technique of choice is the multiple-choice question. For example, an item on an American history achievement test might include this combination of stem and options:

The president of the United States during the Civil War was

a. Washington
b. Lincoln
c. Hamilton
d. Wilson

Proponents of multiple-choice methodology argue that properly constructed items can measure conceptual as well as factual knowledge. Multiple-choice tests also permit quick and objective machine scoring. Furthermore, the fairness of multiple-choice

questions can be proved (or occasionally disproved!) with very simple item analysis procedures discussed subsequently. The major shortcomings of multiple-choice questions are, first, the difficulty of writing good distractor options and, second, the possibility that the presence of the response may cue a half-knowledgeable respondent to the correct answer. Guidelines for writing good multiple-choice items are listed in Table 4.6.

Matching questions are popular in classroom testing, but suffer serious psychometric shortcomings. An example of a matching question:

Using the letters on the left, match the name to the accomplishment:

A. Binet    _____ translated a major intelligence test

B. Woodworth    _____ no correlation between grades and mental tests

C. Cattell    _____ developed true/false personality inventory

D. McKinley    _____ battery of sensorimotor tests

E. Wissler    _____ developed first useful intelligence test

F. Goddard    _____ screening test for emotional disturbance

The most serious problem with matching questions is that responses are not independent—missing one match usually compels the examinee to miss

● **TABLE 4.6 Guidelines for Writing Multiple-Choice Items**

Choose words that have precise meanings.
Avoid complex or awkward word arrangements.
Include all information needed for response selection.
Put as much of the question as possible in the stem.
Do not take stems verbatim from textbooks.
Use options of equal length and parallel phrasing.
Use "none of the above" and "all of the above" rarely.
Minimize the use of negatives such as *not*.
Avoid the use of nonfunctional words.
Avoid unessential specificity in the stem.
Avoid unnecessary clues to the correct response.
Submit items to others for editorial scrutiny.

another. Another problem is that the options in a matching question must be very closely related or the question will be too easy.

For individually administered tests, the procedure of choice is the short-answer objective item. Indeed, the simplest and most straightforward types of questions often possess the best reliability and validity. A case in point is the Vocabulary subtest from the WAIS-IV, which consists merely of asking the examinee to define words. This subtest has very high reliability (.96) and is often considered the single best measure of overall intelligence on the test.

Personality tests often use true-false questions because they are easy for subjects to understand. Most people find it simple to answer true or false to items such as:

T    F
——— ———    I like sports magazines.

Critics of this approach have pointed out that answers to such questions may reflect social desirability rather than personality traits (Edwards, 1961). An alternative format designed to counteract this problem is the **forced-choice methodology** in which the examinee must choose between two equally desirable (or undesirable) options:

Which would you rather do:
——— Mop a gallon of syrup from the floor.
——— Volunteer for a half day at a nursing home.

Although the forced-choice approach has many desirable psychometric properties, personality test developers have not rushed to embrace this interesting methodology.

## ● TESTING THE ITEMS

Psychometricians expect that numerous test items from the original tryout pool will be discarded or revised as test development proceeds. For this reason, test developers initially produce many, many excess items, perhaps double the number of items they intend to use. So, how is the final sample of test questions selected from the initial item pool?

Test developers use item analysis, a family of statistical procedures, to identify the best items. In general, the purpose of item analysis is to determine which items should be retained, which revised, and which thrown out. In conducting a thorough item analysis, the test developer might make use of item-difficulty index, item-reliability index, item-validity index, item-characteristic curve, and an index of item discrimination. We turn now to a brief review of these statistical approaches to item analysis. Readers who wish an in-depth discussion and critique of these topics should consult Hambleton (1989) and Nunnally (1978).

### Item-Difficulty Index

The *item difficulty* for a single test item is defined as the proportion of examinees in a large tryout sample who get that item correct. For any individual item $i$, the index of item difficulty is $p_i$, which varies from 0.0 to 1.0. An item with difficulty of .2 is more difficult than an item with difficulty of .7, because fewer examinees answered it correctly.

The **item-difficulty index** is a useful tool for identifying items that should be altered or discarded. Suppose an item has a difficulty index near 0.0, meaning that nearly everyone has answered it incorrectly. Unfortunately, this item is psychometrically unproductive because it does not provide information about differences between examinees. For most applications, the item should be rewritten or thrown out. The same can be said for an item with a difficulty index near 1.0, where virtually all subjects provide a correct answer.

What is the optimal level of item difficulty? Generally, item difficulties that hover around .5, ranging between .3 and .7, maximize the information the test provides about differences between examinees. However, this rule of thumb is subject to one important qualification and one very significant exception.

For true-false or multiple-choice items, the optimal level of item difficulty needs to be adjusted for the effects of guessing. For a true-false test, a difficulty level of .5 can result when examinees merely guess. Thus, the optimal item difficulty for such items would be .75 (halfway between .5 and 1.0). In general, the optimal level of item difficulty can be computed from the formula $(1.0 + g)/2$, where $g$ is the chance success level. Thus, for a four-option multiple-choice item, the chance success level is .25, and the optimal level of item difficulty would be $(1.0 + .25)/2$, or about .63.

If a test is to be used for selection of an extreme group by means of a cutting score, it may be desirable to select items with difficulty levels outside the .3 to .7 range. For example, a test used to select graduate students for a university that admits only a select few of its many applicants should contain many very difficult items. A test used to designate children for a remedial-education program should contain many extremely easy items. In both cases, there will be useful discrimination among examinees near the cutting score—a very high score for the graduate admissions and a very low score for students eligible for remediation—but little discrimination among the remaining examinees.

## Item-Reliability Index

A test developer may desire an instrument with a high level of internal consistency in which the items are reasonably homogeneous. A simple way to determine whether an individual item "hangs together" with the remaining test items is to correlate scores on that item with scores on the total test. However, individual items are typically right or wrong (often scored 1 or 0), whereas total scores constitute a continuous variable. In order to correlate these two different kinds of scores it is necessary to use a special type of statistic called the *point-biserial correlation coefficient.* The computational formula for this correlation coefficient is equivalent to the Pearson $r$ discussed earlier, and the point-biserial coefficient conveys much the same kind of information regarding the relationship between two variables (one of which happens to be dichotomous and scored 0 or 1). In general, the higher the point-biserial correlation $r_{iT}$ between an individual item and the total score, the more useful is the item from the standpoint of internal consistency.

The usefulness of an individual dichotomous test item is also determined by the extent to which scores on it are distributed between the two outcomes of 0 and 1. Although it sounds incongruous, it is possible to compute the standard deviation for dichotomous items; as with a continuously scored variable, the standard deviation of a dichotomous item indicates the extent of dispersion of the scores. If an individual item has a standard deviation of zero, everyone is obtaining the same score (all right or all wrong). The more closely the item approaches a 50–50 split of right and wrong scores, the greater is its standard deviation. In general, the greater the standard deviation of an item, the more useful is the item to the overall scale. Although we will not provide the derivation, it can be shown that the item-score standard deviation $s_i$ for a dichotomously scored item can be computed from

$$s_i = \sqrt{p_i(1 - p_i)}$$

We may summarize the discussion up to this point as follows: The potential value of a dichotomously scored test item depends jointly on its internal consistency as indexed by the correlation with the total score ($r_{iT}$) and also its variability as indexed by the standard deviation ($s_i$). If we compute the product of these two indices, we obtain $s_i r_{iT}$, which is the **item-reliability index.** Consider the characteristics of an item that possesses a relatively large item-reliability index. Such an item must exhibit strong internal consistency and produce a good dispersion of scores between its two alternatives. The value of this index in test construction is simply this: By computing the item-reliability index for every item in the preliminary test, we can eliminate the "outlier" items that have the lowest value on this index. Such items would possess poor internal consistency or weak dispersion of scores and therefore not contribute to the goals of measurement.

## Item-Validity Index

For many applications, it is important that a test possess the highest possible concurrent or predictive validity. In these cases, one overriding question governs test construction: How well does each preliminary test item contribute to accurate prediction of the criterion? The **item-validity index** is a useful tool in the psychometrician's quest to identify predictively useful test items. By computing the item-validity index for every item in the preliminary test, the test developer can identify ineffectual items, eliminate or rewrite them, and produce a revised instrument with greater practical utility.

The first step in figuring an item-validity index is to compute the point-biserial correlation between the item score and the score on the criterion variable. In general, the higher the point-biserial correlation $r_{iC}$ between scores on an individual item and the criterion score, the more useful is the item from the standpoint of predictive validity. As previously noted, the utility of an item also depends upon its standard deviation $s_i$. Thus, the item-validity index consists of the product of the standard deviation and the point-biserial correlation: $s_i r_{iC}$.

## Item-Characteristic Curves

Also known as an item response function, an **item-characteristic curve** (ICC) is a graphical display of the relationship between the probability of a correct response and the examinee's position on the underlying trait measured by the test. However, we do not have direct access to underlying traits, so observed test scores must be used to estimate trait quantities.

A separate ICC is graphed for each item, based upon a plot of the total test scores on the horizontal axis versus the proportion of examinees passing the item on the vertical axis (Figure 4.8). An ICC is actually a mathematical idealization of the relationship between the probability of a correct response and the amount of the trait possessed by test respondents. Different ICC models use different mathematical functions based on initial assumptions. The simplest ICC model is the Rasch Model, based upon the item-response theory of the Danish mathematician Georg Rasch (1966). The Rasch Model is the simplest model because it makes just two assumptions: (1) test items are unidimensional and measure one common trait, and (2) test items vary on a continuum of difficulty level.

In general, a good item has a positive ICC slope. If the ability to solve a particular item is normally distributed, the ICC will resemble a **normal ogive** (curve $a$ in Figure 4.8). The normal ogive is simply the normal distribution graphed in cumulative form.

The desired shape of the ICC depends on the purpose of the test. Psychometric purists would prefer that test item ICCs approximate the normal ogive, because this curve is convenient for making mathematical deductions about the underlying trait (Lord & Novick, 1968). However, for selection decisions based on cutoff scores, a step function is preferred. For example, when combined with other similar items, the item that produced curve $b$ in Figure 4.8 would be the best for selecting examinees with high levels of the measured trait.

ICCs are especially useful for identifying items that perform differently for subgroups of examinees (Allen & Yen, 1979). For example, a test developer may discover that an item performs differently for men and women. A sex-biased question involving football facts comes to mind here. For men, the ICC for this item might have the desired positive slope, whereas for women the ICC might be quite flat (such as curve $c$ in Figure 4.8). Items with ICCs that differ among subgroups of examinees can be revised or eliminated.

The underlying theory of ICC is also known as *item response theory* and *latent trait theory*. The usefulness of this approach has been questioned by Nunnally (1978), who points out that

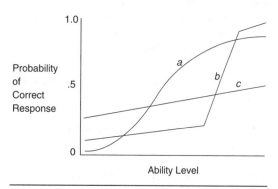

● **FIGURE 4.8**    Some Sample Item-Characteristic Curves

the assumption of test unidimensionality (implied in the ICC curve, which plots percentage passing against the unidimensional horizontal axis of trait value) is violated when many psychological tests are considered. If there were no serious technical and practical problems involved, "one wonders why ICC theory was not adopted long ago for the actual construction and scoring of tests" (Nunnally, 1978).

The merits of the ICC approach are still debated. ICC theory seems particularly appropriate for certain forms of computerized adaptive testing (CAT) in which each test taker responds to an individualized and unique set of items that are then scored on an underlying uniform scale (Weiss, 1983). The CAT approach to assessment would not be possible in the absence of an ICC approach to measurement. CAT is discussed in Topic 12B, Computerized Assessment and the Future of Testing. Readers who wish a more detailed discussion of ICC and other latent trait models should consult Hambleton (1989) and Embretson and Reise (2000).

### Item-Discrimination Index

It should be clear from the discussion of ICCs that an effective test item is one that discriminates between high scorers and low scorers on the entire test. An ideal test item is one that most of the high scorers pass and most of the low scorers fail (see curve *a* in Figure 4.8). Simple visual inspection of the ICC provides a coarse basis for gauging the discriminability of a test item: If the slope of the curve is positive and the curve is preferably ogive-shaped, the item is doing a good job of separating high and low scorers. But visual inspection is not a completely objective procedure; what is needed is a statistical tool that summarizes the discrimination power of individual test items.

An **item-discrimination index** is a statistical index of how efficiently an item discriminates between persons who obtain high and low scores on the entire test. There are many indices of item discrimination, including such indirect measures as $r_{iT}$, the point-biserial correlation between scores on an individual item and the total test score.

However, we will restrict our discussion here to a direct measure, the item-discrimination index, symbolized by the lowercase, italicized letter *d*. On an item-by-item basis, this index compares the performance of subjects in the upper and lower regions of total test score. The upper and lower ranges are generally defined as the upper- and lower-scoring 10 percent to 33 percent of the sample. If the total test scores are normally distributed, the optimal comparison is the highest-scoring 27 percent versus the lowest-scoring 27 percent of the examinees. If the distribution of total test scores is flatter than the normal curve, the optimal percentage is larger, approaching 33 percent. For most applications, any percentage between 25 and 33 will yield similar estimates of *d* (Allen & Yen, 1979).

The item-discrimination index for a test item is calculated from the formula:

$$d = (U - L)/N$$

where *U* is the number of examinees in the upper range who answered the item correctly, *L* is the number of examinees in the lower range who answered the item correctly, and *N* is the total number of examinees in the upper or lower range.

Let us illustrate the computation and use of *d* with a hypothetical example. Suppose that a test developer has constructed the preliminary version of a multiple-choice achievement test and has administered the exam to a tryout sample of 400 high school students. After computing total scores for each subject, the test developer then identifies the high-scoring 25 percent and low-scoring 25 percent of the sample. Since there are 100 students in each group (25 percent of 400), *N* in the preceding formula will be 100. Next, for each item, the developer determines the number of students in the upper range and the lower range who answered it correctly. To compute *d* for each item is a simple matter of plugging these values into the formula $(U - L)/N$. For example, suppose on the first item that 49 students in the upper range answered it correctly, whereas 23 students in the lower range answered it correctly. For this item, *d* is equal to $(49 - 23)/100$ or .26.

| ● TABLE 4.7 | | Item-Discrimination Indices for Six Hypothetical Items | | |
|---|---|---|---|---|
| *Item* | *U* | *L* | *(U − L)/N* | *Comment* |
| 1 | 49 | 23 | .26 | Very good item with high difficulty |
| 2 | 79 | 19 | .60 | Excellent item but rarely achieved |
| 3 | 52 | 52 | .00 | Poor item that should be revised |
| 4 | 100 | 0 | 1.00 | Ideal item but never achieved |
| 5 | 20 | 80 | −.60 | Terrible item that should be eliminated |
| 6 | 0 | 100 | −1.00 | Theoretically worst possible item |

It is evident from the formula for $d$ that this index can vary from −1.0 to +1.0. Notice, too, that a negative value for $d$ is a warning signal that a test item needs revision or replacement. After all, such an outcome indicates that more of the low-scoring subjects answered the item correctly than did the high-scoring subjects. If $d$ is zero, exactly equal numbers of low- and high-scoring subjects answered the item correctly; since the item is not discriminating between low- and high-scoring subjects at all, it should be revised or eliminated. A positive value for $d$ is preferred, and the closer to +1.0 the better. Table 4.7 illustrates item-discrimination indices for six items from the hypothetical test proposed here.

A test developer can supplement the item-discrimination approach by inspecting the number of examinees in the upper- and lower-scoring groups who choose each of the incorrect alternatives. If a multiple-choice item is well written, the incorrect alternatives should be equally attractive to subjects who do not know the correct answer. Of course, we expect that high-scoring examinees will choose the correct alternative more often than low-scoring examinees—that is the purpose in computing item-discrimination indices. But, in addition, a good item should show proportional dispersion of incorrect choices for both high- and low-scoring subjects.

Assume that we investigate the choices of 100 high-scoring and 100 low-scoring subjects on a hypothetical multiple-choice test. Correct choices are indicated by an asterisk (*). Item 1 demonstrates the desired pattern of answers, with incorrect choices about equally dispersed

| | **Alternatives** | | | | |
|---|---|---|---|---|---|
| Item 1 | *a* | *b* | *c\** | *d* | *e* |
| High Scorers | 5 | 6 | 80 | 5 | 4 |
| Low Scorers | 15 | 14 | 40 | 16 | 15 |

On item 2, we notice that no examinees picked alternative $d$. This alternative should be replaced with a more appealing distractor:

| Item 2 | *a* | *b\** | *c* | *d* | *e* |
|---|---|---|---|---|---|
| High Scorers | 5 | 75 | 10 | 0 | 10 |
| Low Scorers | 21 | 34 | 20 | 0 | 25 |

Item 3 is probably a poor item in spite of the fact that it discriminates effectively between high- and low-scoring subjects. The obvious problem is that high-scoring examinees prefer alternative $a$ to the correct alternative, $d$:

| Item 3 | *a* | *b* | *c* | *d\** | *e* |
|---|---|---|---|---|---|
| High Scorers | 43 | 6 | 5 | 37 | 9 |
| Low Scorers | 20 | 19 | 22 | 10 | 29 |

Perhaps by rewriting alternative $a$, this item could be rescued. In any case, the main point here is that test developers should pry into every corner of every test item by every means possible, including visual inspection of the pattern of answers.

### Reprise: The Best Items

From all the methods of item analysis previously portrayed, which ones should the test developer use to identify the best items for a test? The answer to this question is neither simple nor straightforward. After all, the choice of "best" items depends on the objectives of the test developer. For example, a theoretically inclined research psychologist might desire a measurement instrument with the highest possible internal consistency; item-reliability indices are crucial to this goal. A practically minded college administrator might wish for an instrument with the highest possible criterion validity; item-validity indices would be useful for this purpose. A remediation-oriented mental retardation specialist might desire an intelligence test with minimal floor effect; item-difficulty indices would be helpful in this regard. In sum, there is no single preferred method for item selection ideally suited to every context of assessment and test development.

## ● REVISING THE TEST

The purpose of item analysis, discussed previously, is to identify unproductive items in the preliminary test so that they can be revised, eliminated, or replaced. Very few tests emerge from this process unscathed. It is common in the evolutionary process of test development that many items are dropped, others refined, and new items added. The initial repercussion is that a new and slightly different test emerges. This revised test likely contains more discriminating items with higher reliability and greater predictive accuracy—but these improvements are known to be true only for the first tryout sample.

The next step in test development is to collect new data from a second tryout sample. Of course, these examinees should be similar to those for whom the test is ultimately intended. The purpose of collecting additional test data is to repeat the item analysis procedures anew. If further changes are of the minor fine-tuning variety, the test developer may decide the test is satisfactory and ready for cross-validational study, discussed in the following section. If major changes are needed, it is desirable to collect data from a third and even perhaps a fourth tryout sample. But at some point, psychometric tinkering must end; the developer must propose a finalized instrument and proceed to the next step, cross validation.

## Cross Validation

When a tryout sample is used to ascertain that a test possesses criterion-related validity, the evidence is quite preliminary and tentative. It is prudent practice in test development to seek fresh and independent confirmation of test validity before proceeding to publication. The term **cross validation** refers to the practice of using the original regression equation in a new sample to determine whether the test predicts the criterion as well as it did in the original sample. Ghiselli, Campbell, and Zedeck (1981) outline the rationale for cross validation:

> Whether items are chosen on the basis of empirical keying or whether they are corrected or weighted, the obtained results should, unless additional data are collected, be viewed as specific to the sample used for the statistical analyses. This is necessary because the obtained results have likely capitalized on chance factors operating in that group and therefore are applicable only to the sample studied.

## Validity Shrinkage

A common discovery in cross-validation research is that a test predicts the relevant criterion less accurately with the new sample of examinees than with the original tryout sample. The term **validity shrinkage** is applied to this phenomenon. For example, a biographically based predictor of sales potential might perform quite well for the sample of subjects used to develop the instrument but demonstrate less validity when applied to a new group of examinees. Mitchell and Klimoski (1986) studied validity shrinkage of an instrument designed to foretell which students will succeed in real estate, as measured by the real-world criterion of obtaining a real estate license two years later. In one analysis based on the sample used to derive the test, the biographically based predictor test correlated .6 with the criterion. But when this same test was tried out on a new sample of real estate students, the correlation with the criterion was lower, about .4, demonstrating typical validity shrinkage.

Validity shrinkage is an inevitable part of test development and underscores the need for cross validation. In most cases, shrinkage is slight and the instrument withstands the challenge of cross validation. However, shrinkage of test validity can be a major problem when derivation and cross-validation samples are small, the number of potential test items is large, and items are chosen on a purely empirical basis without theoretical rationale.

A classic paper by Cureton (1950) demonstrates a worst-case scenario: using a very small sample to select empirically keyed items from a large item pool, then validating the test on the same sample. The criterion in his study was grade point average, artificially dichotomized into grades of B or better and grades below B. His "test" items consisted of 85 tags, numbered on one side. For each of 29 students, the tags were shaken in a container and dropped on the table. All tags that fell with numbers up were recorded as indicating the presence of that "item" for the student. Next, Cureton conducted an item analysis, using the dichotomized grades as the criterion. Based on this analysis, 24 items were found to be maximally predictive of students' grades. Nine items occurred more often among students with the higher grades, and these items were weighted $+1$. Fifteen items occurred more often among students with the lower grades, and these items were weighted $-1$. The score on this test (facetiously named the "B-Projective Psychokinesis Test") consisted of the sum of these 24 item weights.

In spite of the nonsensical nature of his test, Cureton (1950) found that test scores correlated .82 with grades. Of course, the strength of this correlation was due entirely to capitalization upon chance. If we were to conduct a series of cross-validation studies using new samples of students, the correlation between the B-Projective Psychokinesis Test and grades would likely hover right around zero, because this test is completely devoid of predictive validity. There is an important lesson here that applies to serious tests as well: Demonstrate validity through cross validation, do not assume it based merely on the solemn intentions of a new instrument.

## Feedback from Examinees

In test revision, feedback from examinees is a potentially valuable source of information that is normally overlooked by test developers. We can illustrate this approach with research by Nevo (1992). He developed the Examinee Feedback Questionnaire (EFeQ) to study the Inter-University Psychometric Entrance Examination, a major requirement for admission to the six universities in Israel. The Inter-University entrance exam is a group test consisting of five multiple-choice subtests: General Knowledge, Figural Reasoning, Comprehension, Mathematical Reasoning, and English. The EFeQ was designed as an anonymous posttest administered immediately after the Inter-University entrance exam.

The EFeQ is a short and simple questionnaire designed to elicit candid opinions from examinees as to these features of the test-examiner-respondent matrix:

- Behavior of examiners
- Testing conditions
- Clarity of exam instructions
- Convenience in using the answer sheet
- Perceived suitability of the test
- Perceived cultural fairness of the test
- Perceived sufficiency of time
- Perceived difficulty of the test
- Emotional response to the test
- Level of guessing
- Cheating by the examinee or others

The final question on the EFeQ is an open-ended essay: "We are interested in any remarks or suggestions you might have for improving the exam." Some examples of feedback questions in the EFeQ tradition are provided in Figure 4.9.

Nevo (1992) determined that the EFeQ questionnaire possesses modest reliability, with a test-retest reliability of about .70. Regardless of the psychometric properties of his scale, the tradition of asking examinees for feedback about tests has proved invaluable. The Inter-University entrance exam was modified in numerous ways in response to feedback: The answer sheet format was modified in ways suggested by examinees; the time limit was increased for specific tests reported to be too speeded; certain items perceived as culturally biased or unfair were deleted. In addition, security measures were revised and tightened in order to

What is your opinion of the amount of time alloted for each test? Mark each box with a number from 1 to 5 according to these ratings:

| 5 | 4 | 3 | 2 | 1 |
|---|---|---|---|---|
| Way too much time | Too much time | Adequate time | Too little time | Way too little time |

☐ General Knowledge
☐ Figural Reasoning
☐ Comprehension
☐ Mathematical Reasoning
☐ English

Did you or others cheat on this exam? Please check the boxes that apply. You can check more than one box.

☐ Yes—I obtained a copy of the test.
☐ Yes—one of the testers illegally helped me.
☐ Yes—one of the examinees helped me during the test.
☐ Yes—I helped one of the other examinees.
☐ Yes—I used hidden notes during the test.
☐ Yes—I saw another person cheating.
☐ No—I did not cheat in any way.
☐ No—I did not see anyone else cheating.

● **FIGURE 4.9**
Examples of Examinee Feedback Questionnaire Items

*Source:* Based on Nevo, B. (1992). Examinee feedback: Practical guidelines. In M. Zeidner & R. Most (Eds.), *Psychological testing: An inside view.* Palo Alto, CA: Consulting Psychologists Press.

minimize cheating, which was much more prevalent than examiners had anticipated. Nevo (1992) also cites a hidden advantage to feedback questionnaires: They convey the message that someone cares enough to listen, which reduces postexamination stress. Examinee feedback questionnaires should become a routine practice in group standardized testing.

## ● PUBLISHING THE TEST

The test construction process does not end with the collection of cross-validation data. The test developer also must oversee the production of the testing materials, publish a technical manual, and produce a user's manual. A number of relevant guidelines can be offered for each of these final steps, as outlined in the following sections. Finally, we close this chapter with a provocative comment on the conservatism of modern test publishers.

## Production of Testing Materials

Testing materials must be user friendly if they are to receive wide acceptance by psychologists and educators. Thus, a first guideline for test production is that the physical packaging of test materials must allow for quick and smooth administration. Consider the challenge posed by some performance tests, in which the examiner must wrestle with pencil, clipboard, test form, stopwatch, test manual, item shield, item box, and a disassembled cardboard object, all the while maintaining conversation with the examinee. If it is possible for the test developer to simplify the duties of the examiner while leaving examinee task demands unchanged, the resulting instrument will have much greater acceptability to potential users. For example, if the administration instructions can be summarized on the test form, the examiner can put the test manual aside while setting out the task for the examinee. Another welcome addition to psychological test packaging is the stand-up ring binder that shows the test question on the side facing the examinee and provides instructions for administration on the reverse side facing the examiner.

## Technical Manual and User's Manual

Technical data about a new instrument are usually summarized with appropriate references in a **technical manual.** Here, the prospective user can find information about item analyses, scale reliabilities, cross-validation studies, and the like. In some cases, this information is incorporated in the **user's manual,** which gives instructions for administration and also provides guidelines for test interpretation.

Test manuals should communicate information to many different groups ranging in background and training from measurement specialist to classroom teacher. Test manuals serve many purposes, as outlined in the *Standards for Educational and Psychological Testing* (AERA, APA, & NCME, 1985, 1999). The influential *Standards* manual suggests that test manuals accomplish the following goals:

- Describe the rationale and recommended uses for the test
- Provide specific cautions against anticipated misuses of a test
- Cite representative studies regarding general and specific test uses
- Identify special qualifications needed to administer and interpret the test
- Provide revisions, ammendations, and supplements as needed
- Use promotional material that is accurate and research based
- Cite quantitative relationships between test scores and criteria

- Report on the degree to which alternative modes of response (e.g., booklet versus an answer sheet) are interchangeable
- Provide appropriate interpretive aids to the test taker
- Furnish evidence of the validity of any automated test interpretations

Finally, test manuals should provide the essential data on reliability and validity rather than referring the user to other sources—an unfortunate practice encountered in some test manuals.

## Testing Is Big Business

By now the reader should appreciate the intimidating task faced by anyone who sets out to develop and publish a new test. Aside from the gargantuan proportions of the endeavor, test development is extraordinarily expensive, which means that publishers are inherently conservative about introducing new tests. Jensen (1980) provides the following provocative view on this topic:

> To produce a new general intelligence test that would be a really significant improvement over existing instruments would be a multimillion-dollar project requiring a large staff of test construction experts working for several years. Today we possess the necessary psychometric technology for producing considerably better tests than are now in popular use. The principal hindrances are copyright laws, vested interests of test publishers in the established tests in which they have already made enormous investments, and the market economy for tests. Significant improvement of tests is not an attractive commercial venture initially and would probably have to depend on large-scale and long-term subsidies from government agencies and private foundations.

## ●SUMMARY

1. Test construction consists of six intertwined stages: defining the test, selecting a scaling method, constructing the items, testing the items, revising the test, and publishing the test.

2. Test developers need to select a scaling method that is optimally suited to the manner in

which they have conceptualized the trait(s) measured by the test. The notion of levels of measurement is highly relevant in this context.

3. Four levels of measurement are recognized: Nominal scales constitute mere naming or categorizing; ordinal scales allow for ranking;

interval scales possess equal intervals; ratio scales incorporate all the previous characteristics and also introduce an absolute zero point.

4. Dozens of scaling methods exist. Representative examples include the method of absolute scaling, in which item difficulty is located on an axis or baseline and measured in standard deviation units of an anchor group; Likert scales, which present items with five responses ordered on an agree/disagree continuum; and the rational scaling approach, in which rationally derived items are correlated with total test scores.

5. Constructing test items is a laborious and time-consuming procedure. Test developers should seek to avoid ceiling and floor effects. In a ceiling effect, significant numbers of examinees obtain perfect or near-perfect scores. In a floor effect, significant numbers of examinees obtain scores at or near the bottom of the scale.

6. A table of specifications enumerates the information and cognitive tasks on which examinees are to be assessed. With achievement and ability tests, item writers usually work from a table of specifications to ensure that the emerging instrument taps the desired mixture of cognitive processes and item contents.

7. Test items can be written in many different formats, including multiple-choice, open-ended response, true-false, and forced-choice formats. Matching questions, popular in classroom testing, are psychometrically questionable since the choices are not independent of one another.

8. The purpose of item analysis is to determine which initial items should be retained, which revised, and which thrown out. Many statistical procedures are available for item analysis, including item-difficulty index, item-reliability index, item-validity index, item-characteristic curve, and item-discrimination index.

9. The term *cross validation* refers to the practice of revalidating a test on a new sample of examinees. *Validity shrinkage* refers to the common phenomenon wherein a test predicts the relevant criterion less accurately with a new sample than with the original tryout sample.

10. Tests must be user friendly if they are to receive wide acceptance by psychologists and educators. For example, stand-up ring binders that show instructions on one side and display the test stimuli on the other side are especially desirable. Test users also welcome a thorough technical manual that summarizes technical data and validation research.

## ● KEY TERMS AND CONCEPTS

nominal scale   p. 133

ordinal scale   p. 133

interval scale   p. 133

ratio scale   p. 133

rankings of experts   p. 134

method of equal-appearing intervals   p. 135

method of absolute scaling   p. 136

Likert scale   p. 136

Guttman scale   p. 137

method of empirical keying   p. 137

method of rational scaling   p. 138

Table of specifications   p. 139

forced-choice methodology   p. 141

item-difficulty index   p. 141

item-reliability index   p. 142

item-validity index   p. 143

item-characteristic curve   p. 143

normal ogive   p. 143

item-discrimination index   p. 144

cross validation   p. 146

validity shrinkage   p. 146

technical manual   p. 149

user's manual   p. 149

# Chapter 5

# Theories and Individual Tests of Intelligence and Achievement

## TOPIC 5A

## Theories of Intelligence and Factor Analysis

This chapter opens an extended discussion of intelligence and achievement testing, a topic so important and immense that we devote the next two chapters to it as well. In order to understand contemporary cognitive testing, the reader will need to assimilate certain definitions, theories, and mainstream assessment practices. The goal of Topic 5A, Theories of Intelligence and Factor Analysis, is to investigate the various meanings given to the term *intelligence* and to discuss how definitions and theories have influenced the structure and content of intelligence tests. An important justification for this topic is that an understanding of theories of intelligence is crucial for establishing the construct validity of IQ measures. Furthermore, because the statistical tools of factor analysis are so vital to many theories of intelligence, we provide a primer of the topic here. In Topic 5B, Individual Tests of Intelligence and Achievement, we summarize a number of noteworthy approaches to individual assessment and focus on one important application, the evaluation of learning disabilities. We begin with a foundational question: How is intelligence defined?

Intelligence is one of the most highly researched topics in psychology. Thousands of research articles are published each year on the nature and measurement of intelligence. New journals such as *Intelligence* and *The Journal of Psychoeducational Assessment* have flourished in response to the scholarly interest in this topic. Despite this burgeoning research literature, the definition of intelligence remains elusive, wrapped in controversy and mystery. In fact, the discussion that follows will illustrate a major paradox of modern testing: Psychometricians are better at measuring intelligence than conceptualizing it!

Even though defining intelligence has proved to be a frustrating endeavor, there is much to be gained by reviewing historical and contemporary efforts to clarify its meaning. After all, intelligence tests did not materialize out of thin air. Most tests are grounded in a specific theory of intelligence and most test developers offer a definition of the construct as a starting point for their endeavors. For these reasons, we can better understand and evaluate the multifaceted character of contemporary tests if we first review prominent definitions and theories of intelligence.

## ● DEFINITIONS OF INTELLIGENCE

Before we discuss definitions of intelligence, we need to clarify the nature of definition itself. Sternberg (1986) makes a distinction between operational and "real" definitions that is important in this context. An **operational definition** defines a concept in terms of the way it is measured. Boring (1923) carried this viewpoint to its extreme when he defined intelligence as "what the tests test."

Believe it or not, this was a serious proposal, designed largely to short-circuit rampant and divisive disagreements about the definition of intelligence.

Operational definitions of intelligence suffer from two dangerous shortcomings (Sternberg, 1986). First, they are circular. Intelligence tests were invented to measure intelligence, not to define it. The test designers never intended for their instruments to define intelligence. Second, operational definitions block further progress in understanding the nature of intelligence, because they foreclose discussion on the adequacy of theories of intelligence.

This second problem—the potentially stultifying effects of relying on operational definitions of intelligence—casts doubt on the common practice of affirming the concurrent validity of new tests by correlating them with old tests. If established tests serve as the principal criterion against which new tests are assessed, then the new tests will be viewed as valid only to the extent that they correlate with the old ones. Such a conservative practice drastically curtails innovation. The operational definition of intelligence does not allow for the possibility that new tests or conceptions of intelligence may be superior to the existing ones.

We must conclude, then, that operational definitions of intelligence leave much to be desired. In contrast, a **real definition** is one that seeks to tell us the true nature of the thing being defined (Robinson, 1950; Sternberg, 1986). Perhaps the most common way—but by no means the only way—of producing real definitions of intelligence is to ask experts in the field to define it.

### Expert Definitions of Intelligence

Intelligence has been given many real definitions by prominent researchers in the field. Following, we list several examples, paraphrased slightly for editorial consistency. The reader will note that many of these definitions appeared in an early but still influential symposium, "Intelligence and Its Measurement," published in the *Journal of Educational Psychology* (Thorndike, 1921). Other definitions stem from a modern update of this early symposium, *What Is Intelligence?*, edited by Sternberg and

Detterman (1986). Intelligence has been defined as the following:

Spearman (1904, 1923): a general ability that involves mainly the eduction of relations and correlates.

Binet and Simon (1905): the ability to judge well, to understand well, to reason well.

Terman (1916): the capacity to form concepts and to grasp their significance.

Pintner (1921): the ability of the individual to adapt adequately to relatively new situations in life.

Thorndike (1921): the power of good responses from the point of view of truth or fact.

Thurstone (1921): the capacity to inhibit instinctive adjustments, flexibly imagine different responses, and realize modified instinctive adjustments into overt behavior.

Wechsler (1939): The aggregate or global capacity of the individual to act purposefully, to think rationally, and to deal effectively with the environment.

Humphreys (1971): the entire repertoire of acquired skills, knowledge, learning sets, and generalization tendencies considered intellectual in nature that are available at any one period of time.

Piaget (1972): a generic term to indicate the superior forms of organization or equilibrium of cognitive structuring used for adaptation to the physical and social environment.

Sternberg (1985a, 1986): the mental capacity to automatize information processing and to emit contextually appropriate behavior in response to novelty; intelligence also includes metacomponents, performance components, and knowledge-acquisition components (discussed later).

Eysenck (1986): error-free transmission of information through the cortex.

Gardner (1986): the ability or skill to solve problems or to fashion products that are valued within one or more cultural settings.

Ceci (1994): multiple innate abilities that serve as a range of possibilities; these abilities develop (or fail to develop, or develop and later atrophy) depending upon motivation and exposure to relevant educational experiences.

Sattler (2001): intelligent behavior reflects the survival skills of the species, beyond those associated with basic physiological processes.

The preceding list of definitions is representative although definitely not exhaustive. For one thing, the list is exclusively Western and omits several cross-cultural conceptions of intelligence. Eastern conceptions of intelligence, for example, emphasize benevolence, humility, freedom from conventional standards of judgment, and doing what is right as essential to intelligence. Many African conceptions of intelligence place heavy emphasis on social aspects of intelligence such as maintaining harmonious and stable intergroup relations (Sternberg & Kaufman, 1998). The reader can consult Bracken and Fagan (1990), Sternberg (1994), and Sternberg and Detterman (1986) for additional ideas. Certainly, this sampling of views is sufficient to demonstrate that there appear to be as many definitions of intelligence as there are experts willing to define it!

In spite of this diversity of viewpoints, two themes recur again and again in expert definitions of intelligence. Broadly speaking, the experts tend to agree that intelligence is (1) the capacity to learn from experience, and (2) the capacity to adapt to one's environment. That learning and adaptation are both crucial to intelligence stands out with poignancy in certain cases of mental disability in which persons fail to possess one or the other capacity in sufficient degree (Case Exhibit 5.1).

How well do intelligence tests capture the experts' view that intelligence consists of learning from experience and adaptation to the environment? The reader should keep this question in mind as we proceed to review major intelligence tests in the topics that follow. Certainly, there is cause for concern: Very few contemporary intelligence tests appear to require the examinee to learn something new or to adapt to a new situation as part and

| Case Exhibit 5.1 | Learning and Adaptation as Core Functions of Intelligence |
|---|---|

Persons with mental disability often demonstrate the importance of experiential learning and environmental adaptation as key ingredients of intelligence. Consider the case history of a 61-year-old newspaper vendor with moderate mental retardation well known to local mental health specialists. He was an interesting if not eccentric gentleman who stored canned goods in his freezer and cursed at welfare workers who stopped by to see how he was doing. In spite of his need for financial support from a state agency, he was fiercely independent and managed his own household with minimal supervision from case workers. Thus, in some respects he maintained a tenuous adaptation to his environment. To earn much-needed extra income, he sold a local 25-cent newspaper from a streetside newsstand. He recognized that a quarter was proper payment and had learned to give three quarters in change for a dollar bill. He refused all other forms of payment, an arrangement that his customers could accept. But one day the price of the newspaper was increased to 35 cents, and the newspaper vendor was forced to deal with nickels and dimes as well as quarters and dollar bills. The amount of learning required by this slight shift in environmental demands exceeded his intellectual abilities, and, sadly, he was soon out of business. His failed efforts highlight the essential ingredients of intelligence: learning from experience and adaptation to the environment.

parcel of the examination process. At best, prominent modern tests provide indirect measures of the capacities to learn and adapt. How well they capture these dimensions is an empirical question that must be demonstrated through validational research.

## Layperson and Expert Conceptions of Intelligence

Another approach to understanding a construct is to study its popular meaning. This method is more scientific than it may appear. Words have a common meaning to the extent that they help provide an effective portrayal of everyday transactions. If laypersons can agree on its meaning, a construct such as intelligence is in some sense "real" and, therefore, potentially useful. Thus, asking persons on the street, "What does intelligence mean to you?" has much to recommend it.

Sternberg, Conway, Ketron, and Bernstein (1981) conducted a series of studies to investigate conceptions of intelligence held by American adults. In the first study, people in a train station, entering a supermarket, and studying in a college library were asked to list behaviors characteristic of different kinds of intelligence. In a second study—the only one discussed here—both laypersons and experts (mainly academic psychologists) rated the importance of these behaviors to their concept of an "ideally intelligent" person.

The behaviors central to expert and lay conceptions of intelligence turned out to be very similar, although not identical. In order of importance, experts saw verbal intelligence, problem-solving ability, and practical intelligence as crucial to intelligence. Laypersons regarded practical problem-solving ability, verbal ability, and social competence to be the key ingredients in intelligence. Of course, opinions were not unanimous; these conceptions represent the consensus view of each group. The components of intelligence and representative descriptors are shown in Table 5.1.

In their conception of intelligence, experts place more emphasis on verbal ability than problem solving, whereas laypersons reverse these priorities. Nonetheless, experts and laypersons alike consider verbal ability and problem solving to be essential aspects of intelligence. As the reader will see, most intelligence tests also accent these two competencies. Prototypical examples would be vocabulary (verbal ability) and block design (problem solving) from the Wechsler scales, discussed later. We see then that everyday conceptions of intelligence are, in part, mirrored quite faithfully by the content of modern intelligence tests.

Some disagreement between experts and laypersons is also evident. Experts consider practical intelligence (sizing up situations, determining how to achieve goals, awareness and interest in the world) an essential constituent of intelligence, whereas laypersons identify social competence (accepting others for what they are, admitting mistakes, punctuality, and interest in the world) as a third component. Yet, these two nominations do share one property in common: Contemporary tests generally make no attempt to measure either practical intelligence or social competence. Partly, this reflects the psychometric difficulties encountered in devising test items relevant to these content areas. However, the more influential reason intelligence tests do not measure practical intelligence or social competence is inertia: Test developers have

---

**● TABLE 5.1   Factors and Sample Items Underlying Conceptions of Intelligence for Laypersons and Experts**

| *Laypersons* | *Experts* |
|---|---|
| *Practical Problem-Solving Ability* | *Verbal Intelligence* |
| Reasons logically and well | Displays a good vocabulary |
| Identifies connections among ideas | Reads with high comprehension |
| Sees all aspects of a problem | Displays curiosity |
| Keeps an open mind | Is intellectually curious |
| *Verbal Ability* | *Problem-Solving Ability* |
| Speaks clearly and articulately | Able to apply knowledge to problems at hand |
| Is verbally fluent | Makes good decisions |
| Converses well | Poses problems in an optimal way |
| Is knowledgeable about a particular field of knowledge | Displays common sense |
| *Social Competence* | *Practical Intelligence* |
| Accepts others for what they are | Sizes up situations well |
| Admits mistakes | Determines how to achieve goals |
| Displays interest in the world at large | Displays awareness to world |
| Is on time for appointments | Displays interest in the world at large |

Note:  For each factor, only the four items with the highest loading are listed here. Factor names were provided by the researchers.

*Source:*  Reprinted with permission from Sternberg, R. J., Conway, B. E., Ketron, J. L., & Bernstein, M. (1981). People's conceptions of intelligence. *Journal of Personality and Social Psychology, 41,* 37–55.

blindly accepted historically incomplete conceptions of intelligence. Until recently, the development of intelligence testing has been a conservative affair, little changed since the days of Binet and the Army Alpha and Beta tests for World War I recruits. There are some signs that testing practices may soon evolve, however, with the development of innovative instruments. For example, Sternberg and colleagues have proposed innovative tests based on his model of intelligence. Another interesting instrument based on a new model of intelligence is the Everyday Problem Solving Inventory (Cornelius & Caspi, 1987). In this test, examinees must indicate their typical response to everyday problems such as failing to bring money, checkbook, or credit card when taking a friend to lunch.

Many theorists in the field of intelligence have relied on factor analysis for the derivation or validation of their theories. In fact, it is not an overstatement to say that perhaps the majority of the theories in this area have been impacted by the statistical tools of factor analysis, which provide ways to portion intelligence into its subcomponents. One of the most compelling theories of intelligence, the Cattell-Horn-Carroll theory reviewed later, would not exist without factor analysis. Thus, before summarizing theories, we provide a brief review of this essential statistical tool.

## ● A PRIMER OF FACTOR ANALYSIS

Broadly speaking, there are two forms of factor analysis: confirmatory and exploratory. In confirmatory factor analysis, the purpose is to confirm that test scores and variables fit a certain pattern predicted by a theory. For example, if the theory underlying a certain intelligence test prescribed that the subtests belong to three factors (e.g., verbal, performance, and attention factors), then a confirmatory factor analysis could be undertaken to evaluate the accuracy of this prediction. Confirmatory factor analysis is essential to the validation of many ability tests.

The central purpose of exploratory **factor analysis** is to summarize the interrelationships among a large number of variables in a concise and accurate manner as an aid in conceptualization (Gorsuch, 1983). For instance, factor analysis may help a researcher discover that a battery of 20 tests represents only four underlying variables, called **factors.** The smaller set of derived factors can be used to represent the essential constructs that underlie the complete group of variables.

Perhaps a simple analogy will clarify the nature of factors and their relationship to the variables or tests from which they are derived. Consider the track-and-field decathlon, a mixture of 10 diverse events including sprints, hurdles, pole vault, shot put, and distance races, among others. In conceptualizing the capability of the individual decathlete, we do not think exclusively in terms of the participant's skill in specific events. Instead, we think in terms of more basic attributes such as speed, strength, coordination, and endurance, each of which is reflected to a different extent in the individual events. For example, the pole vault requires speed and coordination, while hurdle events demand coordination and endurance. These inferred attributes are analogous to the underlying factors of factor analysis. Just as the results from the 10 events of a decathlon may boil down to a small number of underlying factors (e.g., speed, strength, coordination, and endurance), so too may the results from a battery of 10 or 20 ability tests reflect the operation of a small number of basic cognitive attributes (e.g., verbal skill, visualization, calculation, and attention, to cite a hypothetical list). This example illustrates the goal of factor analysis: to help produce a parsimonious description of large, complex data sets.

We will illustrate the essential concepts of factor analysis by pursuing a classic example concerned with the number and kind of factors that best describe student abilities. Holzinger and Swineford (1939) gave 24 ability-related psychological tests to 145 junior high school students from Forest Park, Illinois. The factor analysis described later was based on methods outlined in Kinnear and Gray (1997).

It should be intuitively obvious to the reader that any large battery of ability tests will reflect

## TABLE 5.2 The 24 Ability Tests Used by Holzinger and Swineford (1939)

| | |
|---|---|
| 1. Visual Perception | 13. Straight and Curved Capitals |
| 2. Cubes | 14. Word Recognition |
| 3. Paper Form Board | 15. Number Recognition |
| 4. Flags | 16. Figure Recognition |
| 5. General Information | 17. Object-Number |
| 6. Paragraph Comprehension | 18. Number-Figure |
| 7. Sentence Completion | 19. Figure-Word |
| 8. Word Classification | 20. Deduction |
| 9. Word Meaning | 21. Numerical Puzzles |
| 10. Add Digits | 22. Problem Reasoning |
| 11. Code (Perceptual Speed) | 23. Series Completion |
| 12. Count Groups of Dots | 24. Arithmetic Problems |

a smaller number of basic, underlying abilities (factors). Consider the 24 tests depicted in Table 5.2. Surely some of these tests measure common underlying abilities. For example, we would expect Sentence Completion, Word Classification, and Word Meaning (variables 7, 8, and 9) to assess a factor of general language ability of some kind. In like manner, other groups of tests seem likely to measure common underlying abilities. But how many abilities or factors? And what is the nature of these underlying abilities? Factor analysis is the ideal tool for answering these questions. We follow the factor analysis of the Holzinger and Swineford (1939) data from beginning to end.

### The Correlation Matrix

The beginning point for every factor analysis is the **correlation matrix,** a complete table of intercorrelations among all the variables.[1] The correlations between the 24 ability variables discussed here can be found in Table 5.3. The reader will notice that

variables 7, 8, and 9 do, indeed, intercorrelate quite strongly (correlations of .62, .69, and .53), as we suspected earlier. This pattern of intercorrelations is presumptive evidence that these variables measure something in common; that is, it appears that these tests reflect a common underlying factor. However, this kind of intuitive factor analysis based on a visual inspection of the correlation matrix is hopelessly limited; there are just too many intercorrelations for the viewer to discern the underlying patterns for all the variables. Here is where factor analysis can be helpful. Although we cannot elucidate the mechanics of the procedure, factor analysis relies on modern high-speed computers to search the correlation matrix according to objective statistical rules and determine the smallest number of factors needed to account for the observed pattern of intercorrelations. The analysis also produces the factor matrix, a table showing the extent to which each test loads on (correlates with) each of the derived factors, as discussed in the following section.

### The Factor Matrix and Factor Loadings

The **factor matrix** consists of a table of correlations called factor loadings. The factor loadings (which can take on values from −1.00 to +1.00) indicate the weighting of each variable on each

---

1. In this example, the variables are tests that produce more or less continuous scores. But the variables in a factor analysis can take other forms, so long as they can be expressed as continuous scores. For example, all of the following could be variables in a factor analysis: height, weight, income, social class, and rating-scale results.

● **TABLE 5.3    The Correlation Matrix for 24 Ability Variables**

|    | 1 | 2 | 3 | 4 | 5 | 6 | 7 | 8 | 9 | 10 | 11 | 12 | 13 | 14 | 15 | 16 | 17 | 18 | 19 | 20 | 21 | 22 | 23 |
|----|---|---|---|---|---|---|---|---|---|----|----|----|----|----|----|----|----|----|----|----|----|----|----|
| 2  | 32 |    |    |    |    |    |    |    |    |    |    |    |    |    |    |    |    |    |    |    |    |    |    |
| 3  | 40 | 32 |    |    |    |    |    |    |    |    |    |    |    |    |    |    |    |    |    |    |    |    |    |
| 4  | 47 | 23 | 31 |    |    |    |    |    |    |    |    |    |    |    |    |    |    |    |    |    |    |    |    |
| 5  | 32 | 29 | 25 | 23 |    |    |    |    |    |    |    |    |    |    |    |    |    |    |    |    |    |    |    |
| 6  | 34 | 23 | 27 | 33 | 62 |    |    |    |    |    |    |    |    |    |    |    |    |    |    |    |    |    |    |
| 7  | 30 | 16 | 22 | 34 | 66 | 72 |    |    |    |    |    |    |    |    |    |    |    |    |    |    |    |    |    |
| 8  | 33 | 17 | 38 | 39 | 58 | 53 | 62 |    |    |    |    |    |    |    |    |    |    |    |    |    |    |    |    |
| 9  | 33 | 20 | 18 | 33 | 72 | 71 | 69 | 53 |    |    |    |    |    |    |    |    |    |    |    |    |    |    |    |
| 10 | 12 | 06 | 08 | 10 | 31 | 20 | 25 | 29 | 17 |    |    |    |    |    |    |    |    |    |    |    |    |    |    |
| 11 | 31 | 15 | 09 | 11 | 34 | 35 | 23 | 30 | 28 | 48 |    |    |    |    |    |    |    |    |    |    |    |    |    |
| 12 | 31 | 15 | 14 | 16 | 22 | 10 | 18 | 27 | 11 | 59 | 43 |    |    |    |    |    |    |    |    |    |    |    |    |
| 13 | 49 | 24 | 32 | 33 | 34 | 31 | 35 | 40 | 28 | 41 | 54 | 51 |    |    |    |    |    |    |    |    |    |    |    |
| 14 | 13 | 10 | 18 | 07 | 28 | 29 | 24 | 25 | 26 | 17 | 35 | 13 | 20 |    |    |    |    |    |    |    |    |    |    |
| 15 | 24 | 13 | 07 | 13 | 23 | 25 | 17 | 18 | 25 | 15 | 24 | 17 | 14 | 37 |    |    |    |    |    |    |    |    |    |
| 16 | 41 | 27 | 26 | 32 | 19 | 29 | 18 | 30 | 24 | 12 | 31 | 12 | 28 | 41 | 33 |    |    |    |    |    |    |    |    |
| 17 | 18 | 01 | 18 | 19 | 21 | 27 | 23 | 26 | 27 | 29 | 36 | 28 | 19 | 34 | 35 | 32 |    |    |    |    |    |    |    |
| 18 | 37 | 26 | 21 | 25 | 26 | 17 | 16 | 25 | 21 | 32 | 35 | 35 | 32 | 21 | 33 | 34 | 45 |    |    |    |    |    |    |
| 19 | 27 | 11 | 31 | 14 | 19 | 25 | 23 | 27 | 27 | 19 | 29 | 11 | 26 | 21 | 19 | 26 | 32 | 36 |    |    |    |    |    |
| 20 | 37 | 29 | 30 | 34 | 40 | 44 | 45 | 43 | 45 | 17 | 20 | 25 | 24 | 30 | 27 | 39 | 26 | 30 | 17 |    |    |    |    |
| 21 | 37 | 31 | 17 | 35 | 32 | 26 | 31 | 36 | 27 | 41 | 40 | 36 | 43 | 18 | 23 | 35 | 17 | 36 | 33 | 41 |    |    |    |
| 22 | 41 | 23 | 25 | 38 | 44 | 39 | 40 | 36 | 48 | 16 | 30 | 19 | 28 | 24 | 25 | 28 | 27 | 32 | 34 | 46 | 37 |    |    |
| 23 | 47 | 35 | 38 | 34 | 44 | 43 | 41 | 50 | 50 | 26 | 25 | 35 | 38 | 24 | 26 | 36 | 29 | 27 | 30 | 51 | 45 | 50 |    |
| 24 | 28 | 21 | 20 | 25 | 42 | 43 | 44 | 39 | 42 | 53 | 41 | 41 | 36 | 30 | 17 | 26 | 33 | 41 | 37 | 37 | 45 | 38 | 43 |

Note: Decimals omitted.

*Source:* Reprinted with permission from Holzinger, K., & Harman, H. (1941). *Factor analysis: A synthesis of factorial methods.* Chicago: University of Chicago Press. Copyright © 1941 The University of Chicago Press.

factor. For example, the factor matrix in Table 5.4 shows that five factors (labeled I, II, III, IV, and V) were derived from the analysis. Note that the first variable, Series Completion, has a strong positive loading of .71 on factor I, indicating that this test is a reasonably good index of factor I. Note also that Series Completion has a modest negative loading of −.11 on factor II, indicating that, to a slight extent, it measures the opposite of this factor; that is, high scores on Series Completion tend to signify low scores on factor II, and vice versa.

The factors may seem quite mysterious, but in reality they are conceptually quite simple. A factor is nothing more than a weighted linear sum of the variables; that is, each factor is a precise statistical combination of the tests used in the analysis. In a sense, a factor is produced by "adding in" carefully determined portions of some tests and perhaps "subtracting out" fractions of other tests. What makes the factors special is the elegant analytical methods used to derive them. Several different methods exist. These methods differ in subtle ways beyond the scope of this text; the reader can gather a sense of the differences by examining names of procedures: principal components factors, principal axis factors, method of unweighted least squares, maximum-likelihood method, image factoring, and alpha factoring (Tabachnick & Fidell, 1989). Most of the methods yield highly similar results.

| ● TABLE 5.4   The Principal-Axes Factor Analysis for 24 Variables | | | | | |
|---|---|---|---|---|---|
| | Factors | | | | |
| | I | II | III | IV | V |
| 23. Series Completion | .71 | −.11 | .14 | .11 | .07 |
| 8. Word Classification | .70 | −.24 | −.15 | −.11 | −.13 |
| 5. General Information | .70 | −.32 | −.34 | −.04 | .08 |
| 9. Word Meaning | .69 | −.45 | −.29 | .08 | .00 |
| 6. Paragraph Comprehension | .69 | −.42 | −.26 | .08 | −.01 |
| 7. Sentence Completion | .68 | −.42 | −.36 | −.05 | −.05 |
| 24. Arithmetic Problems | .67 | .20 | −.23 | −.04 | −.11 |
| 20. Deduction | .64 | −.19 | .13 | .06 | .28 |
| 22. Problem Reasoning | .64 | −.15 | .11 | .05 | −.04 |
| 21. Numerical Puzzles | .62 | .24 | .10 | −.21 | .16 |
| 13. Straight and Curved Capitals | .62 | .28 | .02 | −.36 | −.07 |
| 1. Visual Perception | .62 | −.01 | .42 | −.21 | −.01 |
| 11. Code (Perceptual Speed) | .57 | .44 | −.20 | .04 | .01 |
| 18. Number-Figure | .55 | .39 | .20 | .15 | −.11 |
| 16. Figure Recognition | .53 | .08 | .40 | .31 | .19 |
| 4. Flags | .51 | −.18 | .32 | −.23 | −.02 |
| 17. Object-Number | .49 | .27 | −.03 | .47 | −.24 |
| 2. Cubes | .40 | −.08 | .39 | −.23 | .34 |
| 12. Count Groups of Dots | .48 | .55 | −.14 | −.33 | .11 |
| 10. Add Digits | .47 | .55 | −.45 | −.19 | .07 |
| 3. Paper Form Board | .44 | −.19 | .48 | −.12 | −.36 |
| 14. Word Recognition | .45 | .09 | −.03 | .55 | .16 |
| 15. Number Recognition | .42 | .14 | .10 | .52 | .31 |
| 19. Figure-Word | .47 | .14 | .13 | .20 | −.61 |

The factor loadings depicted in Table 5.4 are nothing more than correlation coefficients between variables and factors. These correlations can be interpreted as showing the weight or loading of each factor on each variable. For example, variable 9, the test of Word Meaning, has a very strong loading (.69) on factor I, modest negative loadings (−.45 and −.29) on factors II and III, and negligible loadings (.08 and .00) on factors IV and V.

## Geometric Representation of Factor Loadings

It is customary to represent the first two or three factors as reference axes in two- or three-dimensional space.[2] Within this framework the factor loadings for each variable can be plotted for examination. In our example, five factors were discovered, too many for simple visualization. Nonetheless, we can illustrate the value of geometric representation by oversimplifying somewhat and depicting just the first two factors (Figure 5.1). In this graph, each of the 24 tests has been plotted against the two factors that correspond to axes I and II. The reader will notice that the factor loadings on the first factor (I) are uniformly positive, whereas the factor loadings on the

2. Technically, it is possible to represent all the factors as reference axes in $n$-dimensional space, where $n$ is the number of factors. However, when working with more than two or three reference axes, visual representation is no longer feasible.

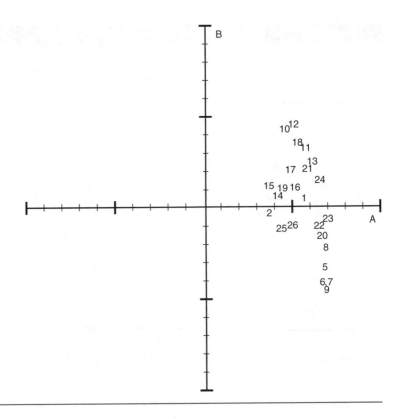

**FIGURE 5.1**
Geometric Representation of the
First Two Factors from 24 Ability
Tests

second factor (II) consist of a mixture of positive and negative.

### The Rotated Factor Matrix

An important point in this context is that the position of the reference axes is arbitrary. There is nothing to prevent the researcher from rotating the axes so that they produce a more sensible fit with the factor loadings. For example, the reader will notice in Figure 5.1 that tests 6, 7, and 9 (all language tests) cluster together. It would certainly clarify the interpretation of factor I if it were to be redirected near the center of this cluster (Figure 5.2). This manipulation would also bring factor II alongside interpretable tests 10, 11, and 12 (all number tests).

Although rotation can be conducted manually by visual inspection, it is more typical for researchers to rely on one or more objective statistical criteria to produce the final rotated factor matrix.

Thurstone's (1947) criteria of positive manifold and simple structure are commonly applied. In a **rotation to positive manifold**, the computer program seeks to eliminate as many of the negative factor loadings as possible. Negative factor loadings make little sense in ability testing, because they imply that high scores on a factor are correlated with poor test performance. In a **rotation to simple structure**, the computer program seeks to simplify the factor loadings so that each test has significant loadings on as few factors as possible. The goal of both criteria is to produce a rotated factor matrix that is as straightforward and unambiguous as possible.

The rotated factor matrix for this problem is shown in Table 5.5. The particular method of rotation used here is called varimax rotation. Varimax should not be used if the theoretical expectation suggests that a general factor may occur. Should we expect a general factor in the analysis of ability tests? The answer is as much a matter of faith as of

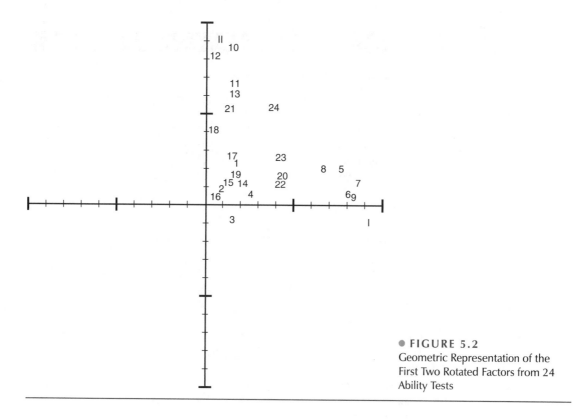

● **FIGURE 5.2**
Geometric Representation of the First Two Rotated Factors from 24 Ability Tests

science. One researcher may conclude that a general factor is likely and, therefore, pursue a different type of rotation. A second researcher may be comfortable with a Thurstonian viewpoint and seek multiple ability factors using a varimax rotation. We will explore this issue in more detail later, but it is worth pointing out here that a researcher encounters many choice points in the process of conducting a factor analysis. It is not surprising, then, that different researchers may reach different conclusions from factor analysis, even when they are analyzing the same data set.

## The Interpretation of Factors

Table 5.5 indicates that five factors underlie the intercorrelations of the 24 ability tests. But what shall we call these factors? The reader may find the answer to this question disquieting, because at this juncture we leave the realm of cold, objective statistics and enter the arena of judgment, insight,

and presumption. In order to interpret or name a factor, the researcher must make a reasoned judgment about the common processes and abilities shared by the tests with strong loadings on that factor. For example, in Table 5.5 it appears that factor I is verbal ability, because the variables with high loadings stress verbal skill (e.g., Sentence Completion loads .86, Word Meaning loads .84, and Paragraph Comprehension loads .81). The variables with low loadings also help sharpen the meaning of factor I. For example, factor I is not related to numerical skill (Numerical Puzzles loads .18) or spatial skill (Paper Form Board loads .16). Using a similar form of inference, it appears that factor II is mainly numerical ability (Add Digits loads .85, Count Groups of Dots loads .80). Factor III is less certain but appears to be a visual-perceptual capacity, and factor IV appears to be a measure of recognition. We would need to analyze the single test on factor V (Figure-Word) to surmise the meaning of this factor.

● **TABLE 5.5** **The Rotated Varimax Factor Matrix for 24 Ability Variables**

| | | | *Factors* | | |
|---|---|---|---|---|---|
| | *I* | *II* | *III* | *IV* | *V* |
| 7. Sentence Completion | **.86** | .15 | .13 | .03 | .07 |
| 9. Word Meaning | **.84** | .06 | .15 | .18 | .08 |
| 6. Paragraph Comprehension | **.81** | .07 | .16 | .18 | .10 |
| 5. General Information | **.79** | .22 | .16 | .12 | −.02 |
| 8. Word Classification | **.65** | .22 | .28 | .03 | .21 |
| 22. Problem Reasoning | **.43** | .12 | .38 | .23 | .22 |
| 10. Add Digits | .18 | **.85** | −.10 | .09 | −.01 |
| 12. Count Groups of Dots | .02 | **.80** | .20 | .03 | .00 |
| 11. Code (Perceptual Speed) | .18 | **.64** | .05 | .30 | .17 |
| 13. Straight and Curved Capitals | .19 | **.60** | .40 | −.05 | .18 |
| 24. Arithmetic Problems | .41 | **.54** | .12 | .16 | .24 |
| 21. Numerical Puzzles | .18 | **.52** | .45 | .16 | .02 |
| 18. Number-Figure | .00 | **.40** | .28 | .38 | .36 |
| 1. Visual Perception | .17 | .21 | **.69** | .10 | .20 |
| 2. Cubes | .09 | .09 | **.65** | .12 | −.18 |
| 4. Flags | .26 | .07 | **.60** | −.01 | .15 |
| 3. Paper Form Board | .16 | −.09 | **.57** | −.05 | .49 |
| 23. Series Completion | .42 | .24 | **.52** | .18 | .11 |
| 20. Deduction | .43 | .11 | **.47** | .35 | −.07 |
| 15. Number Recognition | .11 | .09 | .12 | **.74** | −.02 |
| 14. Word Recognition | .23 | .10 | .00 | **.69** | .10 |
| 16. Figure Recognition | .07 | .07 | .46 | **.59** | .14 |
| 17. Object-Number | .15 | .25 | −.06 | **.52** | .49 |
| 19. Figure-Word | .16 | .16 | .11 | .14 | **.77** |

Note: Boldfaced entries signify subtests loading strongly on each factor.

These results illustrate a major use of factor analysis, namely, the identification of a small number of marker tests from a large test battery. Rather than using a cumbersome battery of 24 tests, a researcher could gain nearly the same information by carefully selecting several tests with strong loadings on the five factors. For example, the first factor is well represented by test 7, Sentence Completion (.86) and test 9, Word Meaning (.84); the second factor is reflected in test 10, Add Digits (.85), while the third factor is best illustrated by test 1, Visual Perception (.69). The fourth factor is captured by test 15, Number Recognition (.74) and Word

Recognition (.69). Of course, the last factor loads well on only test 19, Figure-Word (.77).

## Issues in Factor Analysis

Unfortunately, factor analysis is frequently misunderstood and often misused. Some researchers appear to use factor analysis as a kind of divining rod, hoping to find gold hidden underneath tons of dirt. But there is nothing magical about the technique. No amount of statistical analysis can rescue data based on trivial, irrelevant, or haphazard measures. If there is no gold to be found, then none will be found; factor analysis is not alchemy. Factor analysis will yield meaningful results only when the research was meaningful to begin with.

An important point is that a particular kind of factor can emerge from factor analysis only if the tests and measures contain that factor in the first place. For example, a short-term memory factor cannot possibly emerge from a battery of ability tests if none of the tests requires short-term memory. In general, the quality of the output depends upon the quality of the input. We can restate this point as the acronym GIGO, or "garbage in, garbage out."

Sample size is crucial to a stable factor analysis. Comrey (1973) offers the following rough guide:

| Sample Size | Rating |
| --- | --- |
| 50 | Very poor |
| 100 | Poor |
| 200 | Fair |
| 300 | Good |
| 500 | Very good |
| 1,000 | Excellent |

In general, it is comforting to have at least five subjects for each test or variable (Tabachnick & Fidell, 1989).

Finally, we cannot overemphasize the extent to which factor analysis is guided by subjective choices and theoretical prejudices. A crucial question in this regard is the choice between orthogonal axes and oblique axes. With **orthogonal axes,** the factors are at right angles to one another, which means that they are uncorrelated (Figures 5.1 and 5.2 both depict orthogonal axes). In many cases the clusters of factor loadings are situated such that oblique axes provide a better fit. With **oblique axes,** the factors are correlated among themselves. Some researchers contend that oblique axes should always be used, whereas others take a more experimental approach. Tabachnick and Fidell (1989) recommend an exploratory strategy based on repeated factor analyses. Their approach is unabashedly opportunistic:

> During the next few runs, researchers experiment with different numbers of factors, different extraction techniques, and both orthogonal and oblique rotations. Some number of factors with some combination of extraction and rotation produces

the solution with the greatest scientific utility, consistency, and meaning; this is the solution that is interpreted.

With oblique rotations it is also possible to factor analyze the factors themselves. Such a procedure may yield one or more second-order factors. Second-order factors can provide support for the hierarchical organization of traits and may offer a rapprochement between ability theorists who posit a single general factor (e.g., Spearman) and those who promote several group factors (e.g., Thurstone). Perhaps both camps are correct, with the group factors sitting underneath the second-order general factor.

We turn now to a review of major theories of intelligence. A reminder: The justification for reviewing theories is to illustrate how they have influenced the structure and content of intelligence tests. In addition, the construct validity of IQ tests depends on the extent to which they embody specific theories of intelligence, so a review of theories is pertinent to test validation as well.

## ● GALTON AND SENSORY KEENNESS

The first theories of intelligence were derived in the Brass Instruments era of psychology at the turn of the twentieth century. The reader will recall from Topic 2A that Sir Francis Galton and his disciple J. McKeen Cattell thought that intelligence was underwritten by keen sensory abilities. This incomplete and misleading assumption was based on a plausible premise:

> The only information that reaches us concerning outward events appears to pass through the avenues of our senses; and the more perceptive the senses are of difference, the larger is the field upon which our judgment and intelligence can act. (Galton, 1883)

The sensory keenness theory of intelligence promoted by Galton and Cattell proved to be largely a psychometric dead end. However, we do see vestiges of this approach in modern chronometric analyses of intelligence such as the Reaction Time–Movement Time (RT-MT) apparatus, an

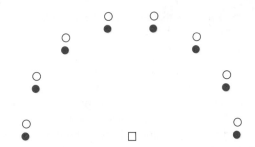

Note: The square box □ indicates the starting point; the open circles O indicate the signal lights; the dark circles ● indicate the push buttons.

● **FIGURE 5.3**    Schematic Diagram of a Reaction Time—Movement Time Apparatus

experimental method favored by Jensen (1980) for the culture-reduced study of intelligence (Figure 5.3). In RT-MT studies, the subject is instructed to place the index finger of the preferred hand on the home button; then an auditory warning signal is sounded, followed (in 1 to 4 seconds) by one of the eight green lights going on, which the subject must turn off as quickly as possible by touching the microswitch button directly below it. RT is the time the subject takes to remove his or her finger from the home button after a green light goes on. MT is the interval between removing the finger from the home button and touching the button that turns off the green light. Jensen (1980) reported that indices of RT and MT correlated as high as .50 with traditional psychometric tests of intelligence.[3] P. A. Vernon has also reported substantial relationships—as high as .70 for multiple correlations—between speed-of-processing RT-type measures and traditional measures of intelligence (Vernon, 1994). These findings suggest that speed-of-processing measures such as RT might be a useful addition to standardized intelligence test batteries. In general, test developers have resisted the implications of this line of research.

---

3. Actually, the raw correlation coefficient is negative because *faster* reaction times (*lower* numerical scores) are associated with *higher* intelligence scores.

● **SPEARMAN AND THE *g* FACTOR**

Based on extensive study of the patterns of correlations between various tests of intellectual and sensory ability, Charles Spearman (1904, 1923, 1927) proposed that intelligence consisted of two kinds of factors: a single **general factor** *g* and numerous **specific factors** $s_1$, $s_2$, $s_3$, and so on. As a necessary adjunct to his theory, Spearman helped invent factor analysis to aid his investigation of the nature of intelligence. Spearman used this statistical technique to discern the number of separate underlying factors that must exist to account for the observed correlations between a large number of tests.

In Spearman's view, an examinee's performance on any homogeneous test or subtest of intellectual ability was determined mainly by two influences: *g*, the pervasive general factor, and *s*, a factor specific to that test or subtest. (An error factor *e* could also sway scores, but Spearman sought to minimize this influence by using highly reliable instruments.) Because the specific factor *s* was different for each intellectual test or subtest and was usually less influential than *g* in determining performance level, Spearman expressed less interest in studying it. He concentrated mainly on defining the nature of *g*, which he likened to an "energy" or "power" that serves in common the whole cortex. In contrast, Spearman considered *s*, the specific factor, to have a physiological substrate localized in the group of neurons serving the particular kind of mental operation demanded by a test or subtest. Spearman (1923) wrote, "These neural groups would thus function as alternative 'engines' into which the common supply of 'energy' could be alternatively distributed."

Spearman reasoned that some tests were heavily loaded with the *g* factor, whereas other tests—especially purely sensory measures—were representative mainly of a specific factor. Two tests each heavily loaded with *g* should correlate quite strongly. In contrast, psychological tests not saturated with *g* should show minimal correlation with one another. Much of Spearman's research was aimed at demonstrating the truth of these basic propositions derived from his theory. We have

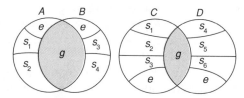

Note: Tests *A* and *B* correlate strongly, whereas *C* and *D* correlate weakly. See text.

● **FIGURE 5.4** Spearman's Two-Factor Theory of Intelligence

illustrated these points graphically in Figure 5.4. In this figure, each circle represents an intelligence test, and the degree of overlap between circles indicates the strength of correlation. Notice that tests A and B, each heavily loaded on *g*, correlate quite strongly. Tests C and D have weak loadings on *g* and subsequently do not correlate well.

Spearman (1923) believed that individual differences in *g* were most directly reflected in the ability to use three principles of cognition: apprehension of experience, eduction of relations, and eduction of correlations. Incidentally, the little-used term *eduction* refers to the process of figuring things out. These three principles can be explained by examining how we solve analogies of the form *A:B::C:*? that is, *A* is to *B* as *C* is to? A simple example might be HAMMER:NAIL::SCREWDRIVER:? To solve this analogy, we must first perceive and understand each term based on past experience; that is, we must have apprehension of experience. If we have no idea what a hammer, nail, and screwdriver are, there is little chance we can complete the analogy correctly. Next, we must infer the relation between the first two analogy terms, in this case, HAMMER and NAIL. Using a somewhat stilted phrase, Spearman referred to the ability to infer the relation between two concepts as eduction of relations. The final step, eduction of correlates, refers to the ability to apply the inferred principle to the new domain, in this case, applying the rule inferred to produce the correct response, namely, SCREW-DRIVER:SCREW.

Although Spearman's physiological speculations have been largely dismissed, the idea of a general factor has been a central topic in research on intelligence and is still very much alive today (Jensen, 1979). The correctness of the *g* factor viewpoint is more than an academic issue. If it is true that a single, pervasive general factor is the essential wellspring of intelligence, then psychometric efforts to produce factorially pure subtests (e.g., measuring verbal comprehension, perceptual organization, short-term memory, and so on) are largely misguided. To the extent that Spearman is correct, test developers should forgo subtest derivation and concentrate on producing a test that best captures the general factor.

The most difficult issue faced by Spearman's two-factor theory is the existence of group factors. As early as 1906, Spearman and his contemporaries noted that relatively dissimilar tests could have correlations higher than the values predicted from their respective *g* loadings (Brody & Brody, 1976). This finding raised the possibility that a group of diverse measures might share in common a unitary ability other than *g*. For example, several tests might share a common unitary memorization factor that was halfway between the *g* factor and the various *s* factors unique to each test. Of course, the existence of group factors is incompatible with Spearman's meticulous two-factor theory.

● **THURSTONE AND THE PRIMARY MENTAL ABILITIES**

Thurstone (1931) developed factor-analysis procedures capable of searching correlation matrices for the existence of group factors. His methods permitted a researcher to discover empirically the number of factors present in a matrix and to define each factor in terms of the tests that loaded on it. In his analysis of how scores on different kinds of intellectual tests correlated with each other, Thurstone concluded that several broad group factors—and not a single general factor—could best explain empirical results. At various points in his research career, he proposed approximately a dozen different factors. Only seven of these factors have been frequently corroborated (Thurstone, 1938; Thurstone

& Thurstone, 1941) and they have been designated **primary mental abilities** (PMAs). They are as follows:

- Verbal Comprehension: The best measure is vocabulary, but this ability is also involved in reading comprehension and verbal analogies.
- Word Fluency: Measured by such tests as anagrams or quickly naming words in a given category (e.g., foods beginning with the letter *S*).
- Number: Virtually synonymous with the speed and accuracy of simple arithmetic computation.
- Space: Such as the ability to visualize how a three-dimensional object would appear if it was rotated or partially disassembled.
- Associative Memory: Skill at rote memory tasks such as learning to associate pairs of unrelated items.
- Perceptual Speed: Involved in simple clerical tasks such as checking for similarities and differences in visual details.
- Inductive Reasoning: The best measures of this factor involve finding a rule, as in a number series completion test.

Thurstone (1938) published the Primary Mental Abilities Test consisting of separate subtests, each designed to measure one PMA. However, he later acknowledged that his primary mental abilities correlated moderately with each other, proving the existence of one or more second-order factors. Ultimately, Thurstone acknowledged the existence of *g* as a higher-order factor. By this time, Spearman had admitted the existence of group factors representing special abilities, and it became apparent that the differences between Spearman and Thurstone were largely a matter of emphasis (Brody & Brody, 1976). Spearman continued to believe that *g* was the major determinant of correlations between test scores and assigned a minor role to group factors. Thurstone reversed these priorities.

P. E. Vernon (1950) provided a rapprochement between these two viewpoints by proposing a hierarchical group factor theory. In his view, *g* was the single factor at the top of a hierarchy that included two major group factors labeled verbal-educational (V:ed) and practical-mechanical-spatial-physical

(k:m). Underneath these two major group factors were several minor group factors resembling the PMAs of Thurstone; specific factors occupied the bottom of the hierarchy.

Thurstone's analysis of PMAs continues to influence test development even today. Schaie (1985) has revised and modified the Primary Mental Abilities Test and used these measures in an enormously influential longitudinal study of adult intelligence. If intelligence were mainly a matter of *g*, then the group factors should change at about the same rate with aging. In support of the group factor approach to intellectual testing, Schaie (1985) reports that some PMAs show little age-related decrement (Verbal Comprehension, Word Fluency, Inductive Reasoning), whereas other PMAs decline more rapidly in old age (Space, Number). Thus, there may be practical real-world reasons for reporting group factors and not condensing all of intelligence into a single general factor.

## ● CATTELL-HORN-CARROLL (CHC) THEORY

Raymond Cattell (1941, 1971) proposed an influential theory of the structure of intelligence that has been revised and extended by John Horn (1968, 1994) and John Carroll (1993). Based on the reanalysis of 461 data sets from hundreds of independent studies published by other researchers, Carroll's contributions to the theory are especially vital. The ensuing theory, known as Cattell-Horn-Carroll (CHC) theory, is a taxonomic tour de force that synthesizes the findings from almost a century of factor-analytic research on intelligence. Many psychometricians consider CHC theory to possess the strongest empirical foundation of any theory of intelligence and also to provide the most far-reaching implications for psychological testing (McGrew, 1997). Although the "big picture" of CHC theory is well established, researchers continue to refine the details. Under the direction of Kevin McGrew, the Institute for Applied Psychometrics manages an informative website dedicated

| Stratum III | Stratum II | | Stratum I |
|---|---|---|---|
| | Fluid Intelligence/Reasoning | (Gf) | 5 narrow abilities |
| | Crystallized Intelligence/Knowledge | (Gc) | 10 narrow abilities |
| | Domain-Specific Knowledge | (Gkn) | 7 narrow abilities |
| General Intelligence, g | Visual-Spatial Abilities | (Gv) | 11 narrow abilities |
| | Auditory Processing | (Ga) | 13 narrow abilities |
| | Broad Retrieval [Memory] | (Gr) | 13 narrow abilities |
| | Cognitive Processing Speed | (Gs) | 7 narrow abilities |
| | Decision/Reaction Time or Speed | (Gt) | 5 narrow abilities |

● **FIGURE 5.5**
Outline of the CHC Three-Stratum Theory of Cognitive Abilities

*Source:* Based on Carroll, J. B. (1993). *Cognitive abilities: A survey of factor analytic studies.* New York: Cambridge University Press, and table 3 from www.iapsych.com.

to the advancement of CHC theory and applications (www.iapsych.com).

According to CHC theory, intelligence consists of pervasive, broad, and narrow abilities that are hierarchically organized (Figure 5.5). At the highest and most pervasive level known as Stratum III, a single general factor known as little g oversees all cognitive activities. Stratum II capacities, which reside beneath general intelligence, include several prominent and well-established abilities. In Figure 5.5, we have depicted eight abilities originally identified by Carroll (1993), but other researchers have proposed a slightly larger list that includes additional tentative entries such as psychomotor, olfactory, and kinesthetic abilities. The precise name given to each broad factor differs slightly from one theorist to another, as well as the scale abbreviations. Even so, there is strong consensus for the essential list. These broad factors include "basic constitutional and longstanding characteristics of individuals that can govern or influence a great variety of behaviors in a given domain" (Carroll, 1993, p. 634). The narrow abilities at Stratum I include approximately 70 abilities identified by Carroll (1993) in his comprehensive review of factor-analytic studies of intelligence. As might be expected, the list of narrow abilities is continually revised and expanded with ongoing research. These narrow abilities "represent greater specializations of abilities, often in quite specific ways that reflect the effects of experience and learning, or the adoption of

particular strategies of performance" (Carroll, 1993, p. 634).

## Definitions of CHC Broad Ability Factors

As noted, the broad factors of CHC are more firmly established than the narrow abilities, which continue to undergo revision and extension. We provide brief definitions of the broad factors, based on Carroll (1993), McGrew (1997), and www.iapsych.com.

- Fluid Intelligence/Reasoning (Gf): Fluid intelligence encompasses high-level reasoning and is used for novel tasks that cannot be performed automatically. The mental operations of **fluid intelligence** may involve drawing inferences, forming concepts, generating and testing hypotheses, understanding implications, inductive reasoning, and deductive reasoning. The classic example of fluid intelligence is found in matrix reasoning tasks such as Raven's Progressive Matrices (Raven, 2000).

  The abilities that make up fluid intelligence are largely nonverbal and not heavily dependent on exposure to a specific culture. For these reasons, Cattell (1940) believed that measures of fluid intelligence were culture-free. Based on this assumption, he devised the Culture Fair Intelligence Test (CFIT) in an attempt to eliminate cultural bias in testing. Of course, calling a test culture fair does not make it necessarily so. In fact, the goal of a completely culture-free intelligence test has proved elusive. We discuss the CFIT in more detail in Topic 6A, Group Tests of Ability and Related Concepts.

Crystallized Intelligence/Knowledge (*Gc*): This form of intelligence is typically defined as an individual's breadth and depth of acquired cultural knowledge—knowledge of the language, information, and concepts of a person's culture. The quintessential example is the extent of vocabulary that an individual understands. But **crystallized intelligence** also includes the application of verbal and cultural knowledge (e.g., oral production, verbal fluency, and communication ability). Because crystallized intelligence arises when fluid intelligence is applied to cultural products, we would expect these two kinds of cognitive ability to possess a strong correlation. In fact, it is commonly found that measures of crystallized and fluid intelligence possess a healthy relationship ($r = .5$).

- Domain-Specific Knowledge (*Gkn*): Domain-specific knowledge represents a person's acquired knowledge in one or more specialized domains that do not represent the typical experiences of individuals in the culture. This might include, for example, knowledge of biology, skill in lipreading, or knowledge of how to use computers.
- Visual-Spatial Abilities (*Gv*): This ability has to do with imagining, retaining, and transforming mental representations of visual images. For example, visual-spatial ability involves the capacity to predict how a shape will appear when it is rotated, or to identify quickly a known object from a vague, incomplete picture, or to find an object hidden in a picture. This capacity includes visual memory.
- Auditory Processing (*Ga*): This is the ability to perceive accurately auditory information, which involves the capacity to analyze, comprehend, and synthesize patterns or groups of sounds. Auditory processing involves the ability to discriminate speech sounds and to judge and discriminate tonal patterns in music. A key characteristic of *Ga* abilities is the cognitive talent needed to control the perception of

auditory information (i.e., to filter signal from noise).

- Broad Retrieval [Memory] (*Gr*): Broad retrieval includes the ability to consolidate and store new information in long-term memory and then to retrieve the information later through association. Included in broad retrieval are such narrow abilities as associative memory (e.g., when provided the first part, recalling the second part of a previously learned but unrelated pair of items), ideational fluency (e.g., ability to call up ideas), and naming facility (e.g., rapidly providing the names of familiar faces). Some researchers further divide the broad memory factor into additional subtypes. In addition, some theorists propose a separate broad factor for short-term memory (*Gsm*), the ability to retain awareness of events that have occurred in the last minute or less (Horn & Masunaga, 2000).
- Cognitive Processing Speed (*Gs*): This ability refers to the speed of executing overlearned or automatized cognitive processes, especially when high levels of attention and focused concentration are required. For example, the ability to perform simple arithmetic calculations with lightning speed would indicate a high level of *Gs* ability.
- Decision/Reaction Time or Speed (*Gt*): This is the ability to make decisions quickly in response to simple stimuli, typically measured by reaction time. For example, the capacity to quickly press the space bar whenever the letter *X* appears on a computer screen would involve the use of *Gt* ability.

## Utility of CHC Theory

CHC theory is unusual in its detail, which permits robust theory testing. A number of lines of evidence support its validity. For example, the structure of intelligence as posited by CHC theory has been shown to be invariant across a number of key variables, including age, ethnicity, and gender (Bickley, Keith, & Wolfe, 1995; Keith, 1999; Carroll, 1993). In empirical studies, the broad CHC abilities also reveal theory-confirming relationships with numerous academic and occupational variables (McGrew & Flanagan, 1998). In one study, for example, measures of CHC broad and narrow cognitive abilities were selectively and appropriately related to mathematics achievement in a representative sample of children and adolescents (Floyd, Evans, & McGrew, 2003). In general, practitioners praise the CHC approach to partitioning intelligence because the broad and narrow abilities are empirically verified and possess meaningful real-world implications (Fiorello & Primerano, 2005).

## ● GUILFORD AND THE STRUCTURE-OF-INTELLECT MODEL

After World War II, J. P. Guilford (1967, 1985) continued the search for the factors of intelligence that had been initiated by Thurstone. Guilford soon concluded that the number of discernible mental abilities was far in excess of the seven proposed by Thurstone. For one thing, Thurstone had ignored the category of creative thinking entirely, an unwarranted oversight in Guilford's view. Guilford also found that if innovative types of tests were included in the large batteries of tests he administered his subjects, then the pattern of correlations between these tests indicated the existence of literally dozens of new factors of intellect. Furthermore, Guilford noticed that some of these new factors had recurring similarities with respect to the kinds of mental processes involved, the kinds of information featured, or the form that the items of information took. As a result of these recurring similarities in the newly discovered factors of intellect, he became convinced that these multitudinous factors could be grouped along a small number of main dimensions. Guilford (1967) proposed an elegant structure-of-intellect (SOI) model to summarize his findings. Visually conceived, Guilford's SOI model classifies intellectual abilities along three dimensions called operations, contents, and products.

By *operations,* Guilford has in mind the kind of intellectual operation required by the test. Most test items emphasize just one of the operations listed here:

| | |
|---|---|
| Cognition | Discovering, knowing, or comprehending |
| Memory | Committing items of information to memory, such as a series of numbers |
| Divergent production | Retrieving from memory items of a specific class, such as naming objects that are both hard and edible |
| Convergent production | Retrieving from memory a correct item, such as a crossword puzzle word |
| Evaluation | Determining how well a certain item of information satisfies specific logical requirements |

*Contents* refers to the nature of the materials or information presented to the examinee. The five content categories are as follows:

| | |
|---|---|
| Visual | Images presented to the eyes |
| Auditory | Sounds presented to the ears |
| Symbolic | Such as mathematical symbols that stand for something |
| Semantic | Meanings, usually of word symbols |
| Behavioral | The ability to comprehend the mental state and behavior of other persons |

The third dimension in Guilford's model, *products,* refers to the different kinds of mental structures that the brain must produce to derive a correct answer. The six kinds of products are as follows:

| | |
|---|---|
| Unit | A single entity having a unique combination of properties or attributes |
| Class | What it is that similar units have in common, such as a set of triangles or high-pitched tones |
| Relation | An observed connection between two items, such as two tones an octave apart |

| System | Three or more items forming a recognizable whole, such as a melody or a plan for a sequence of actions |
|---|---|
| Transformation | A change in an item of information, such as a correction of a misspelling |
| Implication | What an individual item implies, such as to expect thunder following lightning |

In total, then, Guilford (1985) identified five types of operations, five types of content, and six types of products, for a total of $5 \times 5 \times 6$ or 150 factors of intellect. Each combination of an operation (e.g., memory), a content (e.g., symbolic), and a product (e.g., units) represents a different factor of intellect. Guilford claims to have verified over 100 of these factors in his research.

The SOI model is often lauded on the grounds that it captures the complexities of intelligence. However, this is also a potential Achilles' heel for the theory. Consider one factor of intellect, memory for symbolic units. A test that requires the examinee to recall a series of *spoken* digits (e.g., Digit Span on the WAIS-III) might capture this factor of intellect quite well. But so might a *visual* digit span test and perhaps even an analogous test with *tactile* presentation of symbols, such as vibrating rods applied to the skin. Perhaps we need a separate cube for hearing, vision, and touch; such an expanded model would incorporate 450 factors of intellect, surely an unwieldy number.

Although it seems doubtful that intelligence could involve such a large number of unique abilities, Guilford's atomistic view of intellect nonetheless has caused test developers to rethink and widen their understanding of intelligence. Prior to Guilford's contributions, most tests of intelligence required mainly convergent production—the construction of a single correct answer to a stimulus situation. Guilford raised the intriguing possibility that **divergent production**—the creation of numerous appropriate responses to a single stimulus situation—is also an essential element of intelligent

behavior. Thus, a question such as "List as many consequences as possible if clouds had strings hanging down from them" (divergent production) might assess an aspect of intelligence not measured by traditional tests.

## ● THEORY OF SIMULTANEOUS AND SUCCESSIVE PROCESSING

Some modern conceptions of intelligence owe a debt to the neuropsychological investigations of the Russian psychologist Aleksandr Luria (1902–1977). Luria (1966) relied primarily on individual case studies and clinical observations of brain-injured soldiers to arrive at a general theory of cognitive processing. The heart of his theory is as follows:

> Analysis shows that there is strong evidence for distinguishing two basic forms of integrative activity of the cerebral cortex by which different aspects of the outside world may be reflected. . . . The first of these forms is the integration of the individual stimuli arriving in the brain into simultaneous, and primarily spatial groups, and the second is the integration of individual stimuli arriving consecutively in the brain into temporally organized, successive series. (Luria, 1966)

Since this approach focuses upon the mechanics by which information is processed, it is often called an information-processing theory.

**Simultaneous processing** of information is characterized by the execution of several different mental operations simultaneously. Forms of thinking and perception that require spatial analysis, such as drawing a cube, require simultaneous information processing. In drawing, the examinee must simultaneously apprehend the overall shape and guide hand and fingers in the execution of the shape. A sequential approach to drawing a cube (if one were even possible) would be horrifically complex. In effect, the examinee would have to draw individual lines of highly specific lengths and angular orientations, and just hope that everything would line up. In the absence of a simultaneous mental gestalt to guide the drawing, a distorted production is almost guaranteed. Luria discovered that simultaneous processing is associated with the occipital and parietal lobes in the back of the brain.

**Successive processing** of information is needed for mental activities in which a proper sequence of operations must be followed. This is in sharp contrast to simultaneous processing (such as drawing), for which sequence is unimportant. Successive processing is needed in remembering a series of digits, repeating a string of words (e.g., *shoe, ball, egg*), and imitating a series of hand movements (fist, palm, fist, fist, palm). Luria localized successive processing to the temporal lobe and the frontal regions adjacent to it.

Most forms of information processing require an interplay of simultaneous and successive mechanisms. Das (1994) cites the example of reading an unfamiliar word such as *taciturn*:

> The single letters are to be recognized, and that involves simultaneous coding. The reader matches the visual shape of the letter with a mental dictionary and comes up with a name for it. The letter sequences, then, have to be formed (successive coding) and blended together as a syllable (simultaneous). Then the string of syllables has to be made into a word (successive), the word is recognized (simultaneous), and a pronunciation program is then assembled (successive), leading to oral reading (successive and simultaneous).

Das admits that this may be a simplified view of what occurs when a reader is confronted with a word. The essential point is that higher-level information processing relies upon an interplay of specific, anatomically localizable forms of information processing.

The challenge of a simultaneous-successive approach to the assessment of intelligence is to design tasks that tap relatively pure forms of each approach to information processing. Tests that use this strategy are the Kaufman Assessment Battery for Children (K-ABC), discussed in the next topic, and the Das-Naglieri Cognitive Assessment System (Das & Naglieri, 1993). The Das-Naglieri battery includes successive tasks that involve rapid articulation (such as, "Say *can, ball, hot* as fast as you can

10 times") and simultaneous measures of both verbal and nonverbal tasks. The battery also assesses planning and attention, which leads to the acronym PASS (planning, attention, simultaneous, successive) (Das, Naglieri, & Kirby, 1994).

## ● INFORMATION-PROCESSING THEORIES OF INTELLIGENCE

Information-processing conceptions of intelligence propose models of how individuals mentally represent and process information. Borrowing from Campione and Brown (1978), Borkowski (1985) has put forward a comprehensive theory that bears a loose analogy to the functioning of a computer. The **architectural system** (hardware) refers to biologically based properties necessary for information processing, such as memory span and speed of encoding/decoding information. Properties of the architectural system include capacity (e.g., number of slots in short-term memory, capacity of long-term memory), durability (rate of information loss), and efficiency of operation (e.g., rate of memory search). The architectural system is considered to be relatively "hardwired" and impervious to change by the environment.

In addition to the structural component of intelligence, there are various functional components (software). The **executive system,** which refers to environmentally learned components that steer problem solving, provides overall guidance to the functional components. Elements of the executive system include the knowledge base (retrieval of knowledge from long-term memory), schemes (rules of thinking), control processes (rules and strategies such as self-checking and rehearsal), and metacognition (self-awareness of one's own thought processes). Metacognition is the process of thinking about thinking. Flavell (1976), who pioneered research on this topic, explained it as follows:

> Metacognition refers to one's knowledge concerning one's own cognitive processes or anything related to them, e.g., the learning-relevant properties of information or data. For example, I am engaging in

metacognition if I notice that I am having more trouble learning A than B; if it strikes me that I should double check C before accepting it as fact. (p. 232)

The information-processing approach to intelligence has generated a large body of research, especially on the concept of metacognition. A consistent finding in this literature is that individuals who use metacognitive strategies perform at much higher levels than those who do not (Montague & Bos, 1990). For example, in a study of 32 Israeli kindergarten children who were taught metacognition related to mathematics, metacognitive skills explained more of the variance in mathematics performance than general ability (Mevarech, 1995). Metacognition is essential to intelligence and is one of the primary influences on student learning (Wang, Haertel, & Walberg, 1990).

## ● GARDNER AND THE THEORY OF MULTIPLE INTELLIGENCES

Howard Gardner (1983, 1993) has proposed a theory of multiple intelligences based loosely on the study of brain–behavior relationships. He argues for the existence of several relatively independent human intelligences, although he admits that the exact nature, extent, and number of the intelligences have not yet been definitively established. Gardner (1983) outlines the criteria for an autonomous intelligence as follows:

- Potential isolation by brain damage—the faculty can be destroyed, or spared in isolation, by brain injury.
- Existence of exceptional individuals such as savants—the faculty is uniquely spared in the midst of general intellectual mediocrity.
- Identifiable core operations—the faculty relies upon one or more basic information-processing operations.
- Distinctive developmental history—the faculty possesses an identifiable developmental history, perhaps including critical periods and milestones.

- Evolutionary plausibility—admittedly speculative, a faculty should have evolutionary antecedents shared with other organisms (e.g., primate social organization).
- Support from experimental psychology—the faculty emerges in laboratory studies in cognitive psychology.
- Support from psychometric findings—the faculty reveals itself in measurement studies and is susceptible to psychometric measurement.
- Susceptibility to symbol encoding—the faculty can be communicated via symbols including (but not limited to) language, picturing, and mathematics.

Based on these criteria, Gardner (1983, 1993) proposes that the following seven natural intelligences have been substantially confirmed. The seven intelligences are linguistic, logical-mathematical, spatial, musical, bodily-kinesthetic, interpersonal, and intrapersonal. Three of these seven types of intelligence are well known—linguistic (i.e., verbal) intelligence, logical-mathematical intelligence, spatial intelligence—and numerous formal tests have been devised to measure them, so we will not discuss them further here. The other four variations of intelligence are somewhat novel and, therefore, require more detailed presentation.

Bodily-kinesthetic intelligence includes the types of skills used by athletes, dancers, mime artists, typists, or "primitive" hunters. Although Western cultures are generally loath to consider the body as a form of intelligence, this is not the case in much of the rest of the world, nor was it true in our evolutionary history. Indeed, persons who could skillfully avoid predators, climb trees, hunt animals, and prepare tools were more likely to survive and pass on their genes to succeeding generations.

The personal intelligences include the capacity to have access to one's own feeling life (intrapersonal) as well as the ability to notice and make distinctions about the moods, temperaments, motivations, and intentions of others (interpersonal). Thus, personal intelligence encompasses both an intrapersonal and an interpersonal version. The former is found in great novelists who can write introspectively about their feelings, while the latter is often seen in religious and political leaders (e.g., Mahatma Ghandi or Lyndon Johnson) who can fathom the intentions and desires of others and use this information to influence them and form useful alliances.

Musical intelligence is perhaps the least understood of Gardner's intelligences. Persons with good musical intelligence easily learn to perform an instrument or to write their own compositions. Although knowledge of the structural aspects of melody, rhythm, and timbre is important to musical intelligence, Gardner notes that many experts place the affective or feeling aspects of music at its core. He believes that when the neurological underpinnings of music are finally unraveled, we will have "an explanation of how emotional and motivational factors are intertwined with purely perceptual ones" (Gardner, 1983).

The savant phenomenon provides strong support for the existence of separate intelligences, including musical intelligence.[4] A **savant** is a mentally deficient individual who has a highly developed talent in a single area such as art, rapid calculation, memory, or music. An example is the extraordinary case of Leslie Lemke, who was born blind and with mental retardation and cerebral palsy. He was not supposed to live. His adoptive mother had to coax him to suck milk from a bottle. Later, she strapped him to her back to help him learn to walk. In spite of his severe disabilities, Leslie became enamored of the piano and showed incredible precocity at picking out melodies on it. Within a few years, at the age of 18, he could listen to a piece of classical piano music a single time and then play it back flawlessly (Patton, Payne, & Beirne-Smith, 1986). The reader can find additional savant case studies in Miller (1989) and Treffert (1989).

Recently, Gardner (1998) has added three tentative candidates to his list of intelligences. These are naturalistic, spiritual, and existential intelligences. Naturalistic intelligence is the kind shown by people who are able to discern patterns in nature. Charles Darwin would be a prime example of such a person. Gardner believes that the evidence for this kind of intelligence is relatively strong. In contrast, spiritual intelligence (a concern with cosmic and spiritual issues in one's development) and existential intelligence (a concern with ultimate issues, including the meaning of life) are less well proved as independent intelligences. In general, the theory of multiple intelligence is compelling in its simplicity, but there is little empirical investigation of its validity.

## ● STERNBERG AND THE TRIARCHIC THEORY OF INTELLIGENCE

Sternberg (1985b, 1986, 1996) takes a much wider view on the nature of intelligence than most previous theorists. In addition to proposing that certain mental mechanisms are required for intelligent behavior, he also emphasizes that intelligence involves adaptation to the real-world environment. His theory emphasizes what he calls successful intelligence or "the ability to adapt to, shape, and select environments to accomplish one's goals and those of one's society and culture" (Sternberg & Kaufman, 1998, p. 494).

Sternberg's theory is called *triarchic* (ruled by three) because it deals with three aspects of intelligence: componential intelligence, experiential intelligence, and contextual intelligence. Each of these types of intelligence has two or more subcomponents. The entire theory is outlined in Table 5.6.

**Componential intelligence,** also known as analytical intelligence, consists of the internal mental mechanisms that are responsible for intelligent behavior. The components of intelligence serve three different functions. *Metacomponents* are the executive processes that direct the activities of all the other components of intelligence. They are responsible for determining the nature of an intellectual problem, selecting a strategy for solving it, and making sure that the task is completed. The

---

4. Historically, savants have also been called *idiot savants,* which refers, literally, to a person who is both profoundly retarded and yet "wise" at the same time. For obvious reasons, the prefix has been dropped.

---

● **TABLE 5.6   An Outline of Sternberg's Triarchic Theory of Intelligence**

**Componential (Analytical) Intelligence**
   Metacomponents or executive processes (e.g., planning)
   Performance components (e.g., syllogistic reasoning)
   Knowledge-acquisition components (e.g., ability to acquire vocabulary words)

**Experiential (Creative) Intelligence**
   Ability to deal with novelty
   Ability to automatize information processing

**Contextual (Practical) Intelligence**
   Adaptation to real-world environment
   Selection of a suitable environment
   Shaping of the environment

---

*Source:* Summarized from Sternberg, R. J. (1986). *Intelligence applied: Understanding and increasing your intellectual skills.* San Diego, CA: Harcourt Brace Jovanovich.

---

metacomponents receive constant feedback as to how things are going in problem solving. Persons who are strong on the metacomponential aspect of intelligence are very good at allocating their intellectual resources.

In a problem-solving study using novel forms of analogies, Sternberg (1981) found that higher intelligence is associated with spending relatively more time on global or higher-order planning, and relatively less time on local or lower-order planning. For example, consider this analogy problem:

Man: Skin:: (Dog, Tree):(Bark, Cat)

The examinee must choose the two correct terms on the right that will complete the analogy. (The correct choices are Tree and Bark). Using reaction time measures for a series of such novel or nonentrenched problems, Sternberg (1981) found that persons of higher intelligence spend more time in global planning—forming a macrostrategy that applies to this and similar problems—than did persons of lower intelligence. Thus, a crucial aspect of intelligence is knowing when to step back and allocate intellectual effort instead of obtusely attacking a difficult problem.

*Performance* components are the well-entrenched mental processes that might be used to perform a task or solve a problem. These aspects of intelligence are the ones that are probably measured the best by existing intelligence tests. Examples of performance components include short-term memory and syllogistic reasoning.

*Knowledge-acquisition* components are the processes used in learning. Sternberg has emphasized that in order to understand what makes some people more skilled than others, we must understand their increased capacity to acquire those skills in the first place. A case in point is vocabulary knowledge, which is learned mainly in context rather than through direct instruction. More-intelligent persons are better able to use surrounding contexts to figure out what a word means; that is, they have greater knowledge-acquisition skills. Their increased vocabulary results, in large measure, from their increased ability to "soak up" the meanings of words they see and hear in their environment. Thus, vocabulary is an excellent measure of intelligence because it reflects people's ability to acquire information in context.

The second aspect of Sternberg's theory involves experiential intelligence. According to the theory, a person with good **experiential intelligence** is able to deal effectively with novel tasks. Experiential intelligence is also known as creative intelligence. This aspect of his theory explains why Sternberg is so critical of most intelligence tests. For the most part, the existing tests measure things already learned by presenting tasks that the subject has already encountered. According to Sternberg, intelligence also involves the capacity to learn and think within new conceptual systems, not just to deal with tasks already encountered. A second aspect of experiential intelligence is the ability to automatize or "make routine" tasks that are encountered repeatedly. An example of automatizing that applies to most of us is reading, which is carried out largely without conscious thought. But any task or mental skill can be automatized, if it is practiced enough. Playing music is an example of an extremely high-level skill that can become automatized with enough practice.

The third aspect of Sternberg's theory involves contextual intelligence. **Contextual intelligence,** also known as practical intelligence, is defined as "mental activity involved in purposive adaptation to, shaping of, and selection of real-world environments relevant to one's life" (Sternberg, 1986, p. 33). This aspect of Sternberg's theory appears to acknowledge that human behavior has been shaped by selective pressures during our evolutionary history. Contextual intelligence has three parts: adaptation, selection, and shaping.

*Adaptation* refers to developing skills required by one's particular environment. Successful adaptation will differ from one culture to the next. In the pygmy cultures of Africa, adaptation might involve the ability to track elephants and kill them with poison-tipped spears. In the Western industrial nations, adaptation might involve presenting oneself favorably in a job interview.

*Selection* might be called niche finding. This aspect of contextual intelligence involves the ability to leave the environment we are in and to select a different environment more suitable to our talents and needs. Feldman (1982) has illustrated how selection can operate in the career choices of gifted children, thereby determining whether they are highly accomplished as adults. She followed up on the Quiz Kids who were featured in radio and television shows of the 1950s. These were extremely bright children by conventional standards, most with IQs of 140 and higher. A few became highly successful as adults. However, most of them led rather ordinary lives, devoid of the spectacular accomplishments that might have been predicted from their childhood precocity. Those who were most successful had found occupations highly suited to their abilities and interests. In sum, they had selected environmental niches that fitted them well. Sternberg would argue that the ability to select such environments is an important aspect of intelligence.

*Shaping* is another way to improve the fit between oneself and the environment, especially when selection of a new environment is not practical. In this application of contextual intelligence, we shape the environment itself so that it better fits our needs. An employee who convinces the boss to do things differently has used shaping to make the work environment more suited to his or her talents.

Sternberg (1993) has developed a research instrument based on his theory and has used the test to examine the validity of the triarchic approach. The Sternberg Triarchic Abilities Test (STAT) is unique in going beyond the typical questions that invoke analytical intelligence; the test includes creative and practical questions as well. For example, in one subtest examinees are presented with a map of an area, such as an entertainment park, and then must answer questions about navigating effectively through the area shown in the map (practical intelligence). In another subtest examinees are presented with verbal analogies preceded by incorrect, counterfactual premises (e.g., money falls off trees). Examinees must solve the analogies as though the counterfactual premises were true (creative intelligence). In factor-analytic studies of American, Finish, and Spanish samples, the triarchic model was a better fit to the data than the usual outcome of finding a single factor of general intelligence (Sternberg, Castejon, Prieto, Hautamaki, & Grigorenko, 2001).

Although Sternberg's triarchic theory is the most comprehensive and ambitious model yet proposed, not all psychometric researchers have rushed to embrace it. Detterman (1984) cautions that we should investigate the basic cognitive components of intelligence before introducing higher-order constructs that may be unnecessary. Rogoff (1984) questions whether the three subtheories (componential, experiential, contextual) are sufficiently linked. Other comments on the triarchic theory can be found in *Behavioral and Brain Sciences* (1984, pp. 287–304).

Whatever the final verdict on the triarchic theory of intelligence, Sternberg's insistence that intelligence has several components not measured by traditional tests rings true to anyone who has studied or administered these tests. He cites the case of a colleague who was asked to test a number of residents at an institution for those with mental retardation. These residents had just planned and successfully executed an escape from the security-conscious school, a feat requiring high levels of practical intelligence. Yet, when administered the Porteus Maze Test (Porteus, 1965), a standardized test reputed to involve planning ability, they could not solve even the simplest maze correctly. Sternberg (1986) has made it clear that intelligence just has too many components to be measured by any single test.

## ● SUMMARY

1. In spite of symposia and scholarly analysis, the concept of "intelligence" has eluded consensual definition. Yet, two themes recur with some frequency in expert definitions of intelligence. According to the scholars, intelligence encompasses (1) the capacity to learn from experience, and (2) the capacity to adapt to one's environment.

2. Lay and expert conceptions of intelligence are very similar. In order of importance, laypersons regard practical problem-solving ability, verbal ability, and social competence as the key ingredients; experts see verbal intelligence, problem-solving ability, and practical intelligence as crucial.

3. Factor analysis is a family of procedures employed to summarize relationships among variables that are correlated in highly complex ways. For example, factor analysis might help a researcher discover that a battery of 24 ability tests represents only four underlying variables, called factors.

4. The beginning point for every factor analysis is the correlation matrix, a complete table of intercorrelations among all the variables. The variables in a factor analysis can include results for any more-or-less continuous dimension, such as test scores, social class, and behavior ratings.

5. The factor matrix consists of a table of factor loadings showing the weighting of each variable on each factor. A factor is a weighted linear sum of the variables. The factor loading for each variable is a correlation coefficient between the factor and that variable.

6. Factors can be represented as geometric reference axes, and the loadings for each variable on each factor can be plotted within this space. This allows the researcher to visualize the location of each variable on the two or three most important factors.

7. Because the position of the reference axes is arbitrary, the researcher is free to rotate the axes so that they produce a more sensible fit with the factor loadings for the variables. A number of different methods of rotation exist (e.g., rotation to positive manifold, rotation to simple structure).

8. The naming of factors requires judgment and inference. In particular, the researcher must attempt to determine the common processes and abilities shared by the tests or variables with strong loadings on a factor. Also, tests or variables with low loadings may help sharpen the definition and naming of a factor.

9. In order for a particular kind of factor to emerge from an analysis, some of the tests and measures must contain that factor in the first place. Large samples, in excess of 200 persons, are preferred. The choice of strategies for rotation is important: Orthogonal axes assume that factors are uncorrelated; oblique axes accept that factors are correlated.

10. The first theories of intelligence, proposed in the late 1800s, emphasized sensory acuity. Sir Francis Galton and J. McKeen Cattell both believed that intelligence was underwritten by keen sensory abilities. They developed several sensory measures in unsuccessful attempts to measure intelligence.

11. In the early 1900s, Charles Spearman proposed that intelligence consisted of two kinds of factors: a single general factor $g$ and numerous specific factors $s_1$, $s_2$, $s_3$, and so on. He helped invent factor analysis to aid his investigations into the nature of intelligence.

12. L. L. Thurstone favored the view that intelligence consists of approximately seven group factors rather than a single general factor. These

factors were verbal comprehension, word fluency, number, space, associative memory, perceptual speed, and inductive reasoning. Ultimately, Thurstone acknowledged the existence of *g* as a higher-order factor.

13. Cattell-Horn-Carroll or CHC theory proposes that intelligence consists of three strata: a pervasive factor defined by general intelligence, eight or more broad factors subsumed under general intelligence, and about 70 narrow factors. The virtue of CHC theory is that it is based on careful analysis of literally hundreds of factor analyses conducted by independent researchers and synthesized by John Carroll and others.

14. J. P. Guilford proposed a structure-of-intellect (SOI) model to summarize his views on the multifaceted nature of intelligence. He classified intellectual abilities along three dimensions called operations (5 kinds), contents (5 kinds), and products (6 kinds). Thus, in all, Guilford proposed 150 different kinds of intelligence.

15. According to the theory of simultaneous and successive processing, the human brain has two distinct forms of information processing: simultaneous, in which primarily spatial groups of information are processed all at once, and successive, in which information is temporally organized in a linear series.

16. Information-processing conceptions of intelligence are based on a loose analogy with the functioning of a computer. An architectural system (hardware), which is relatively "hardwired" and impervious to change by the environment, operates in conjunction with the functional components (software), which include the executive system (environmentally learned components that steer problem solving).

17. H. Gardner has proposed a theory of multiple intelligences based loosely on the study of brain–behavior relationships. He argues for the existence of several relatively independent intelligences, including linguistic, musical, logical-mathematical, spatial, bodily-kinesthetic, and personal.

18. R. Sternberg proposes a triarchic theory of intelligence with these aspects: componential intelligence (the internal mental mechanisms that are responsible for intelligent behavior), experiential intelligence (the ability to deal effectively with novel tasks), and contextual intelligence (adaptation to, shaping of, and selection of real-world environments).

## ● KEY TERMS AND CONCEPTS

operational definition   p. 152

real definition   p. 152

factor analysis   p. 156

factors   p. 156

correlation matrix   p. 157

factor matrix   p. 157

rotation to positive manifold   p. 160

rotation to simple structure   p. 160

orthogonal axes   p. 163

oblique axes   p. 163

general factor   p. 164

specific factors   p. 164

primary mental abilities   p. 166

fluid intelligence   p. 167

crystallized intelligence   p. 168

divergent production   p. 170

simultaneous processing   p. 170

successive processing   p. 171

architectural system   p. 171

executive system   p. 171

savant   p. 173

componential intelligence   p. 173

experiential intelligence   p. 174

contextual intelligence   p. 175

# Individual Tests of Intelligence and Achievement

Individual intelligence testing is one of the major achievements of psychology since the founding of the discipline. In response to the success of the Binet-Simon scales in the early 1900s, psychologists developed and refined dozens of individual tests of intelligence patterned after this pathbreaking instrument. The explosive growth in group tests of intelligence, fostered by the enthusiastic acceptance of the Army Alpha and Beta tests during and after World War I, also provided impetus to the individual testing movement. Many contemporary individual tests of intelligence owe their lineage to Binet, Simon, and the Army testing programs.

The successful application of intelligence tests inspired educators and psychologists to look for ways to appraise the academic progress of students with school-based achievement tests. In turn, this led to the puzzling discovery that many children of normal or even superior intelligence lagged far behind in school achievement. From this discovery, the concept of learning disability gradually developed, and a whole new field of assessment was born.

The purpose of this topic is to provide an overview of noteworthy approaches to the testing of individual intelligence and achievement, and to introduce the reader to the essentials of learning disability assessment. However, an exhaustive survey of individual cognitive tests is simply beyond the scope of this or any other basic reference. New and revised tests appear practically every month, and thousands of new research findings are published every year. We have chosen to review tests that are widely used or that illustrate interesting developments in theory or method. Readers can find information on additional tests in the *Mental*

*Measurements Yearbook* series, now published every two or three years by the Buros Institute.

## ● ORIENTATION TO INDIVIDUAL INTELLIGENCE TESTS

The individual intelligence tests reviewed in this topic include the following:

Wechsler Adult Intelligence Scale-IV (WAIS-IV)

Wechsler Intelligence Scale for Children-IV (WISC-IV)

Stanford-Binet: Fifth Edition (SB5)

Detroit Tests of Learning Aptitude-4 (DTLA-4)

Kaufman Assessment Battery for Children-II (KABC-II)

Kaufman Brief Intelligence Test-2 (KBIT-2)

Collectively, these instruments probably account for 95 percent of the intellectual assessments conducted in the United States.

The Wechsler scales have dominated intelligence testing in recent years, but they are by no means the only viable choices for individual assessment. Many other instruments measure general intelligence just as well—some would say better. Consider the implications of a now familiar observation: For large, heterogeneous samples, scores on any two mainstream instruments (e.g., Wechsler, Stanford-Binet, McCarthy, Kaufman scales) typically correlate .80 to .90. Often the correlation between two mainstream instruments is nearly as high as the test-retest correlation for either instrument alone. For purposes of producing a global score, it would appear that any well-normed mainstream intelligence test will suffice.

But producing an overall score is not the only goal of assessment. In addition, the examiner usually desires to gain an understanding of the subject's intellectual functioning. For this purpose, the overall IQ is important, but there are instances in which the global score may be irrelevant or even misleading. To understand a referral's intellectual functioning, the examiner should also inspect the subtest scores in search of hypotheses that might explain the unique functioning of that individual. Of course, examiners need to undertake subtest analysis cautiously, armed with research-based findings on the nature and meaning of subtest scatter for the test in use (Gregory, 1994b).

If the examiner's goal is to understand intellectual functioning and not merely to determine an overall score, the differences between tests become quite real. Every instrument approaches the measurement of intelligence from a different perspective and yields a distinctive set of subtest scores. Furthermore, a test well suited for one referral issue might perform abysmally in another context. For example, the WAIS-IV performs admirably in the testing of mild mental retardation but contains too few simple items for the effective assessment of persons with moderate or severe developmental disability.

A central axiom of assessment is that the choice of a testing instrument should be based on knowledge of its strengths and weaknesses as they pertain to the referral question. Put simply, the skilled examiner does not blindly rely on a single test for every referral! Instead, the skilled examiner flexibly chooses one or more instruments in light of the perceived assessment needs of the examinee. Each of the tests discussed in this topic has its special merits and also its particular shortcomings. The test user must know these strong and weak facets in order to choose the instruments best suited for each unique referral.

## ● THE WECHSLER SCALES OF INTELLIGENCE

Beginning in the 1930s, David Wechsler, a psychologist at Bellevue Hospital in New York City, conceived a series of elegantly simple instruments that virtually defined intelligence testing in the mid- to late twentieth century. His influence on intelligence testing is exceeded only by the pathbreaking contributions of Binet and Simon. It is fitting that we begin the survey of individual tests with a historical summary of the Wechsler tradition, followed by a discussion of individual instruments.

## Origins of the Wechsler Tests

Wechsler began work on his first test in 1932, seeking to devise an instrument suitable for testing the diverse patients referred to the psychiatric section of Bellevue Hospital in New York (Wechsler, 1932). In describing the development of his first test, he later wrote, "Our aim was not to produce a set of brand new tests but to select, from whatever source available, such a combination of them as would meet the requirements of an effective adult scale" (Wechsler, 1939). In fact, the content of his scales was largely inspired by earlier efforts such as the Binet scales and the Army Alpha and Beta tests (Frank, 1983). Readers who peruse *Psychological Examining in the United States Army,* a volume edited by Yerkes (1921) just after World War I, might be astonished to discover that Wechsler purloined dozens of test items from this source, many of which have survived to the present day in contemporary revisions of the Wechsler tests. Wechsler was not so much a creative talent as a pragmatist who fashioned a new and useful instrument from the spare parts of earlier, discontinued attempts at intelligence testing.

The first of the Wechsler tests, named the Wechsler-Bellevue Intelligence Scales, was published in 1939. In discussing the rationale for his new test, Wechsler (1941) explained that existing instruments such as the Stanford-Binet were woefully inadequate for assessing adult intelligence. The Wechsler-Bellevue was designed to rectify several flaws noted in previous tests:

- The test items possessed no appeal for adults.
- Too many questions emphasized mere manipulation of words.
- The instructions emphasized speed at the expense of accuracy.
- The reliance on mental age was irrelevant to adult testing.

To correct these shortcomings, Wechsler designed his test specifically for adults, added performance items to balance verbal questions, reduced the emphasis upon speeded questions, and

invented a new method for obtaining the IQ. Specifically, he replaced the usual formula

$$IQ = \frac{Mental\ Age}{Chronological\ Age}$$

with a new age-relative formula

$$IQ = \frac{Attained\ or\ Actual\ Score}{Expected\ Mean\ Score\ for\ Age}$$

This new formula was based on the interesting presumption—stated in the form of an axiom—that IQ remains constant with normal aging, even though raw intellectual ability might shift or even decline. The assumption of **IQ constancy** is basic to the Wechsler scales. As Wechsler (1941) put it:

> The constancy of the I.Q. is the basic assumption of all scales where relative degrees of intelligence are defined in terms of it. It is not only basic, but absolutely necessary that I.Q.'s be independent of the age at which they are calculated, because unless the assumption holds, no permanent scheme of intelligence classification is possible.

Although Wechsler's view has been largely accepted by contemporary test developers, it is important to stress that the assumption of IQ invariance with age is really a statement of values, a philosophical choice, and not necessarily an inherent characteristic of human nature.

Wechsler also hoped to use his test as an aid in psychiatric diagnosis. In pursuit of this goal, he divided his scale into separate verbal and performance sections. This division allowed the examiner to compare an examinee's facility in using words and symbols (verbal subtests) versus the ability to manipulate objects and perceive visual patterns (performance subtests). Large differences between verbal ability ($V$) and performance ability ($P$) were thought to be of diagnostic significance. Specifically, Wechsler believed that organic brain disease, psychoses, and emotional disorders gave rise to a marked $V > P$ pattern, whereas adolescent psychopaths and persons with mild mental retardation yielded a strong $P > V$ pattern. Subsequent research demonstrated many exceptions to these simple diagnostic rules, and also helped refine the nature of these two major elements of intelligence. For example, verbal intelligence is now better known as verbal comprehension, and performance intelligence is more commonly recognized as perceptual reasoning. Nonetheless, the distinction between verbal and performance skills has proved useful for many purposes, such as studying brain-behavior relationships, and examining age effects on intelligence. Wechsler's armchair division of subtests into verbal and performance sections, even though refined and extended by others, continues to endure as a major contribution to contemporary intelligence testing (Kaufman, Lichtenberger, & McLean, 2001).

## General Features of the Wechsler Tests

Including revisions, David Wechsler and his followers have produced more than a dozen intelligence tests in a span of about 70 years. A major reason for the continued success of these instruments has been the faithful adherence to the familiar content and format first introduced in the Wechsler-Bellevue. By sticking with a single successful formula, Wechsler and company ensured that examiners could switch from Wechsler test to another with minimal retraining. This was not only good psychometrics but also shrewd marketing insofar as it guaranteed several generations of faithful test users.

The latest editions of the Wechsler intelligence tests—the WPPSI-III, WISC-IV, and WAIS-IV—possess the following common features:

- Fourteen or fifteen subtests. The multisubtest approach allows the examiner to analyze intra-individual strengths and weaknesses rather than just to compute a single global score. In addition, it is possible to combine subtest scores in theoretical meaningful ways that provide useful information on the broad factors of intelligence. As the reader will learn subsequently, the pattern of subtest and factor scores may convey useful information that is hidden in the overall level of performance.
- An empirically based breakdown into composite scores and a full scale IQ. Whereas the original

Wechsler intelligence scales provided only two composite scores—Verbal IQ and Performance IQ—the revisions have been moving toward a more sophisticated partitioning into composites confirmed from factor-analytic research. The WISC-IV and WAIS-IV now yield composite or index scores in the same four areas:

Verbal Comprehension
Perceptual Reasoning
Working Memory
Processing Speed

The WPPSI-III retains the Verbal IQ and Performance IQ breakdown but also provides for the computation of a Processing Speed composite score.

- A common metric for IQ and Index scores. The mean for IQ and Index scores is 100 and the standard deviation is 15 for all tests and all age groups. In addition, the scaled scores on each subtest have a mean of 10 and a standard deviation of approximately 3, which permits the examiner to analyze the subtest scores of the examinee for relative strengths and weaknesses.
- Common subtests for the different test versions. For example, the preschool, child, and adult Wechsler tests (WPPSI-III, WISC-IV, and WAIS-IV) all share a common core of the same nine subtests (Table 5.7). An examiner who masters the administration of a core subtest on any of the Wechsler tests (such as the Information subtest on the WAIS-IV) easily can transfer this skill within the Wechsler family of intellectual measures.

## ● THE WECHSLER SUBTESTS: DESCRIPTION AND ANALYSIS

Wechsler (1939) defined *intelligence* as "the aggregate or global capacity of the individual to act purposefully, to think rationally and to deal effectively with his environment." He also believed that we can only know intelligence by what it enables a person to do. In designing his tests, then, Wechsler selected components to represent a wide array of underlying abilities so as to estimate the global capacity of

● **TABLE 5.7   Subtest Composition of the Wechsler Intelligence Tests**

|  | WPPSI-III | WISC-IV | WAIS-IV |
|---|:---:|:---:|:---:|
| **Similarities** | × | × | × |
| **Vocabulary** | × | × | × |
| **Comprehension** | × | × | × |
| **Information** | × | × | × |
| Word Reasoning | × | × | |
| Receptive Vocabulary | × | | |
| Picture Naming | × | | |
| **Block Design** | × | × | × |
| Picture Concepts | × | × | |
| **Matrix Reasoning** | × | × | × |
| **Picture Completion** | × | × | × |
| Visual Puzzles | | | × |
| Figure Weights | | | × |
| Object Assembly | × | | |
| L-N Sequencing[a] | | × | × |
| Arithmetic | | × | × |
| Digit Span | | × | × |
| **Coding** | × | × | × |
| **Symbol Search** | × | × | × |
| Cancellation | | × | × |

[a]Letter-Number Sequencing

Note: The subtests common to all Wechsler intelligence tests are in boldface. Some subtests are optional or used as substitutions. See text for details.

intelligence. Furthermore, he asked his subjects to do things, not merely to answer questions. The Wechsler subtests are quite diverse and often rely on what Wechsler referred to as "mental productions."

We present here a description of subtests from the WISC-IV and WAIS-IV. We also analyze the abilities tapped by each subtest and offer research-based comments. The reader is referred to Topic 7A, Infant and Preschool Assessment, for a description of the two subtests unique to the WPPSI-III.

## Information

The Information subtest is found on all three Wechsler intelligence tests. Factual knowledge of persons, places, and common phenomena is tested here. Questions for children are like the following:

> "How many eyes do you have?"
> "Who invented the telephone?"
> "What causes a solar eclipse?"
> "Which is the largest planet?"

Questions for adults are similar but progress to higher levels of difficulty. Difficult questions on the adult Information subtest resemble:

> "Which is the most common element in air?"
> "What is the population of the world?"
> "How does fruit juice get converted to wine?"
> "Who wrote *Madame Bovary*?"

Information items test general knowledge normally available to most persons raised in the cultural institutions and educational systems of Western industrialized nations. Indirectly, this subtest measures learning and memory skills insofar as subjects must retain knowledge gained from formal and informal educational opportunities in order to answer the Information items.

Information is usually regarded as one of the best measures of general ability among the Wechsler subtests (Kaufman, McLean, & Reynolds, 1988). For example, the WAIS-IV manual reveals that Information typically has the second or third highest correlation with Full Scale IQ across the 13 age groups (Wechsler, Coalson, & Raiford, 2008). Information consistently loads strongly on the first factor identified in factor analyses of the WAIS-IV subtest correlations (see the following). The first factor is labeled Verbal Comprehension. However, Information tends to reflect formal education and motivation for academic achievement and may therefore yield spuriously high ability estimates for perpetual students and avid readers.

## Digit Span

Digit Span consists of two separate sections, Digits Forward and Digits Backward. In Digits Forward, the examiner reads a series of digits at one per second, then asks the subject to repeat them. If the subject answers correctly on two consecutive trials of the same length, the examiner proceeds to the next series, which is one digit longer, up to a maximum length of nine digits. For Digits Backward, a similar procedure is used, except the examinee must repeat the digits in reverse order, up to a maximum length of eight digits. For example, the examiner reads:

"6–1–3–4–2–8–5"

and the subject tries to repeat the numbers in the reverse order:

"5–8–2–4–3–1–6."

On the WAIS-IV only, the Digit Span subtest also includes a third section called Digit Sequencing. For this part, the examinee is asked to sort the series of digits into their correct order. For example, if the examiner says:

"1–7–4–9–2"

the examinee should respond:

"1–2–4–7–9."

Digit Span is a measure of immediate auditory recall for numbers. Facility with numbers, good attention, and freedom from distractibility are required. Performance on this subtest may be affected by anxiety or fatigue, and many clinicians have noted that patients hospitalized for medical or psychiatric reasons frequently perform poorly on Digit Span.

Digits Forward and Digits Backward may assess fundamentally different abilities. Digits Forward seems to require the examinee to access an auditory code in sequential fashion. In contrast, to perform Digits Backward, the examinee must form an internal visual memory trace from the orally presented numerical sequences and then visually scan from end to beginning. Digits Backward is clearly the more complex test; not surprisingly, it loads higher on general intelligence than does Digits Forward (Jensen & Osborne, 1979). Gardner (1981) argues that examiners should supplement standard reporting procedures and list separate subscores for Digit Span. He presents separate means, standard deviations, and percentile ranks on Digits Forward and Backward for children ages 5 to 15.

## Vocabulary

The Vocabulary subtest is found on all three Wechsler intelligence tests. The examinee is asked to define up to several dozen words of increasing difficulty while the examiner writes down each response verbatim. For example, on an easy item the examiner might ask, "What is a cup?" and the examinee would get partial credit for answering, "You drink with it" and full credit for answering, "It has a handle, holds liquids, and you drink from it." For adults and bright children, the advanced items on the Wechsler Vocabulary subtests can be very challenging, on a par with *tincture, obstreperous,* and *egregious.*

Vocabulary is learned largely in context from reading books and listening to others. It is a rare individual who picks up vocabulary by reading the dictionary or memorizing word lists from the "Building Your Wordpower" section of popular magazines. In the main, a person's vocabulary is a measure of sensitivity to new information and the ability to decipher meanings based on the context in which words are encountered. Precisely because the acquisition of word meaning depends on contextual inference, the Vocabulary subtest turns out to be the single best measure of overall intelligence on the Wechsler scales (Gregory, 1999). This is a surprise to many laypersons who regard vocabulary as merely synonymous with educational exposure and, therefore, a mediocre index of general intelligence. However, there is simply no denying the empirical evidence: Vocabulary has among the highest subtest correlations with Full Scale IQ on both the WISC-IV and also the WAIS-IV.

## Arithmetic

Except for the very easiest items for young people or persons who have mental retardation, the Arithmetic subtest consists of orally presented mathematics problems. The examinee must solve the problems without paper or pencil within a time limit (usually 30 to 60 seconds). The simple items stress fundamental operations of addition or subtraction, for example:

"If you have fifteen apples and give seven away, how many are left?"

The more difficult items require proper conceptualization of the problem and the application of two arithmetic operations, for example:

> "John bought a stereo that was marked down 15 percent from the original sales price of $600. How much did John pay for the stereo?"

Although the mathematical requirements of the Arithmetic items are not excessively demanding, the necessity of solving the problems mentally within a time limit makes this subtest quite challenging for most examinees. In addition to rudimentary arithmetic skills, successful performance on Arithmetic requires high levels of concentration and the ability to maintain intermediate calculations in short-term memory. In factor analyses of the WISC-IV and WAIS-IV, Arithmetic often loads on a third factor interpreted as Working Memory.

## Comprehension

Found on all three Wechsler intelligence tests, the Comprehension subtest is an eclectic collection of items that require explanation rather than mere factual knowledge. The easy questions stress common sense, whereas the more difficult questions require an understanding of social and cultural conventions. On the WAIS-IV, several of the most difficult questions require the examinee to interpret proverbs.

An easy item on Comprehension is of the form "Why do people wear clothes?" Difficult items resemble the following:

> "What does this saying mean: 'A bird in the hand is worth two in the bush.'"

> "Why are Supreme Court Judges appointed for life?"

Comprehension would appear to be, in part, a measure of "social intelligence" in that many items tap the examinee's understanding of social and cultural conventions. Sipps, Berry, and Lynch (1987) found that Comprehension scores were moderately related to measures of social intelligence on the California Psychological Inventory. Of course, a high score signifies only that the ex-aminee is knowledgeable about social and cultural conventions; choosing the right action may or may not flow from this knowledge. However, studies by Campbell and McCord (1996) and Lipsitz, Dworkin, and Erlenmeyer-Kimling (1993) provide no support for the commonly accepted clinical lore that Comprehension scores are sensitive to social functioning.

## Similarities

In this subtest, the examinee is asked questions of the type, "In what way are shirts and socks alike?" The Similarities subtest evaluates the examinee's ability to distinguish important from unimportant resemblances in objects, facts, and ideas. Indirectly, these questions assess the assimilation of the concept of likeness. The examinee must also possess the ability to judge when a likeness is important rather than trivial. For example, "shirts" and "socks" are alike in that both begin with the letter *s*, but this is not the essential similarity between these two items. The important similarity is that shirts and socks are both exemplars of a concept, namely, "clothes." As this example illustrates, Similarities can be thought of as a test of verbal concept formation and is found on all three Wechsler intelligence tests.

## Letter–Number Sequencing

The examiner orally presents a series of letters and numbers that are in random order. The examinee must reorder and repeat the list by saying the numbers in ascending order and then the letters in alphabetical order. For example, if the examiner says "R-3-B-5-Z-1-C," the examinee should respond "1-3-5-B-C-R-Z." This test measures attention, concentration, and freedom from distractibility. Together with Arithmetic and Digit Span, this subtest contributes to the Working Memory Index score on the WAIS-IV (see the following). Donders, Tulsky, and Zhu (2001) found the Letter–Number Sequencing subtest to be highly sensitive to the effects of moderate and severe traumatic brain injury.

● **FIGURE 5.6**   Picture Completion Item Similar to Those Found on the WAIS-IV

## Picture Completion

For this subtest, the examiner asks the examinee to identify the "important part" that is missing from a picture. For example, a simple item might be of this type: a picture of a table with one leg missing. The items get harder and harder; testing continues until the examinee misses several in a row. Figure 5.6 depicts an item similar to those found on the WAIS-IV. The Picture Completion subtest presupposes that the examinee has been exposed to the object or situation represented. For this reason, Picture Completion may be inappropriate for culturally disadvantaged persons.

## Picture Concepts

This subtest is found on the WPPSI-III and the WISC-IV. For each item, the child is shown a card with two or three rows of pictures and instructed to choose one picture from each row to form a group with a common characteristic. This is a recent subtest designed to measure abstract, categorical reasoning. The 28 items reflect increasingly more difficult levels of abstraction. For example, for an easy

item the commonality might be that a fruit is found in each row, whereas for a more difficult item the commonality might be that a device used for signaling (bell, flashlight, flags) is found in each row.

## Block Design

On the Block Design subtest, the examinee must reproduce two-dimensional geometric designs by proper rotation and placement of three-dimensional colored blocks. For all of the Wechsler scales, the first few Block Design items can be solved through trial and error. However, the more difficult items require the analysis of spatial relations, visual-motor coordination, and the rigid application of logic. Block Design demands much more problem-solving and reasoning ability than most of the Performance subtests in which memory and prior experience are more heavily weighted.

Block Design is a strongly speeded test. Consider the WAIS-IV version, which consists of 14 designs of increasing difficulty. To obtain a high score on this subtest, adults must not only reproduce each of the designs correctly, but they must also earn bonus points on the last six designs by completing them quickly. An examinee who solves all the designs within the time limit but who fails to garner any bonus points will test out at just slightly above average on this subtest. Block Design scores may be misleading for examinees who do not value speeded performance.

## Matrix Reasoning

Matrix Reasoning is included on all of the Wechsler intelligence tests. The subtest consists of figural reasoning problems arranged in increasing order of difficulty (Figure 5.7). Finding the correct answer requires the examinee to identify a recurring pattern or relationship between figural stimuli drawn along a straight line (simple items) or in a 3 × 3 grid (hard items) in which the last item is missing. Based on nonverbal reasoning about the patterns and relationships, the examinee must infer the missing stimulus and select it from five choices provided at the bottom of the card.

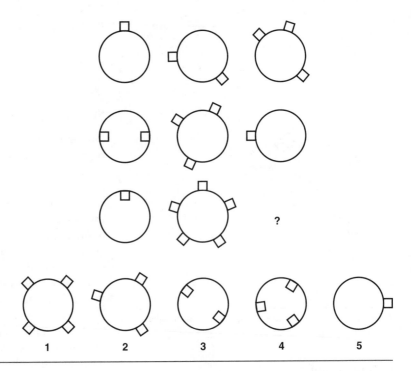

● **FIGURE 5.7**
Matrix Reasoning Item Similar to
Those Found on the WAIS-IV

1       2       3       4       5

Matrix Reasoning was designed to be a measure of fluid intelligence, which is the capacity to perform mental operations such as manipulation of abstract symbols. The items tap pattern completion, reasoning by analogy, and serial reasoning. Overall, the subtest is an excellent measure of inductive reasoning based on figural stimuli. Matrix Reasoning is not timed. Interestingly, Donders et al. (2001) report that the Matrix Reasoning subtest is relatively unaffected by moderate and severe traumatic brain injury.

### Object Assembly

This subtest is found only on the WPPSI-III. For each item, the examinee must assemble the pieces of a jigsaw puzzle to form a common object (Figure 5.8). The examiner does not identify the items, so the examinee must first discern the identity of each item from its disarranged parts. Success on this subtest requires high levels of

perceptual organization; that is, the examinee must grasp a larger pattern or gestalt based on perception of the relationships among the individual parts.

Object Assembly is one of the least reliable of the Wechsler subtests. The modest reliability of Object Assembly may reflect, in part, the small

● **FIGURE 5.8**   Object Assembly Item Similar to Those Found on the WPPSI-III

number of items as well as the role of chance factors in solving jigsaw puzzles.

## Coding

The WISC-IV version consists of two separate and distinct parts, one for examinees under age 8 (Coding A) and another for those 8 years of age and over (Coding B). In Coding A, the child must draw the correct symbol inside a series of randomly sequenced shapes. The task utilizes five shapes (star, circle, triangle, cross, and square), and each shape is assigned a unique symbol (vertical line, two horizontal lines, single horizontal line, circle, and two vertical lines, respectively). After a brief practice session, the child is told to draw the correct symbol inside 43 of the randomly sequenced shapes. However, since there is a two-minute time limit, high scores require rapid performance. The WPPSI-III includes a similar version of the Coding subtest.

Coding B on the WISC-IV and Coding on the WAIS-IV are identical in format (Figure 5.9). For both subtests, the examinee must associate one symbol with each of the digits 0 through 9 and quickly draw the appropriate symbol underneath a long series of random digits. The time limit for both versions is two minutes. Very few examinees manage to code all the stimuli in this amount of time.

Estes (1974) analyzed the Coding subtest from the standpoint of learning theory and concluded that efficient performance requires the ability to quickly produce distinctive verbal codes to represent each of the symbols in memory. For example,

in Figure 5.9, the examinee might code the symbol underneath the number 2 as an "inverted T." Verbal coding mediates quick performance by simplifying a difficult task. Efficient performance also demands immediate learning of the digit-symbol pairings so that the examinee need not look from each digit to the reference table to determine the correct response. In this regard, Coding is unique: It is the only Wechsler subtest that necessitates on-the-spot learning of an unfamiliar task.

Coding scores show a steep decrement with advancing age. In cross-sectional studies, raw scores on Coding decline by as much as 50 percent from age 20 to age 70 (Wechsler, 1981). The decrement is approximately linear and not easily explained by superficial references to motivational differences or motor slowing. Of course, cross-sectional results are not necessarily synonymous with longitudinal trends. However, the age decrement on Coding is so steep that it must indicate, in part, a real age change in the speed of basic information-processing skills. Coding is one of the most sensitive subtests to the effects of organic impairment (Donders et al., 2001; Lezak, 1995).

## Symbol Search

This is a highly speeded subtest in which the examinee looks at a target group of symbols, then quickly examines a search group of symbols, and finally marks a "YES" or "NO" box to indicate whether one or more of the symbols in the target group occurred within the search group. A Symbol Search item is depicted in Figure 5.10. This subtest would appear to be a measure of processing speed. Symbol Search is highly sensitive to the impact of traumatic brain injury (Donders et al., 2001).

| 1 | 2 | 3 | 4 | 5 | 6 | 7 | 8 | 9 |
|---|---|---|---|---|---|---|---|---|
| ╦ | ⊔ | ⊥ | = | ∨ | ⊃ | ✗ | ⊢ | ∟ |

| 6 | 2 | 5 | 9 | 1 | 3 | 2 | 6 | 4 |
|---|---|---|---|---|---|---|---|---|
|   |   |   |   |   |   |   |   |   |

● **FIGURE 5.9**  Digit Symbol Items Similar to Those Found on the WAIS-IV

Note: The examinee's task is to determine whether either shape at the left occurs among the five shapes to the right.

● **FIGURE 5.10**  Symbol Search Item Similar to Those Found on the WISC-IV

## Cancellation

On the WISC-IV, this is a timed subtest in which the child is instructed to draw a line through or "cancel" drawings of animals placed randomly among drawings of inanimate objects (e.g., umbrella, car, hydrant, lightbulb). For example, on a standard-sized sheet of paper, about 160 stimuli are pictured, including 30 animals (horse, bear, seal, fish, chicken). Cancellation consists of two trials: one with a random arrangement of visual stimuli, and one with clearly structured rows and columns of stimuli. In addition to a total subtest score, separate process scores for the random and the structured trials are available for comparison. This subtest is similar to existing cancellation tasks designed to measure processing speed, vigilance, and visual attention. It is well established that examinees with neuropsychological impairments perform poorly, especially on the random trial (e.g., Bate, Mathias, & Crawford, 2001; Geldmacher, 1996). On the WAIS-IV, Cancellation is somewhat more complex, involving *two* target stimuli consisting of geometric shapes. The examinee is told, for example, to cancel "red squares and yellow triangles" among an array of red and yellow squares and red and yellow triangles. A second trial involves stars and circles in orange and blue. This timed task (45 seconds per trial) is much more difficult than it seems.

## Visual Puzzles

Visual Puzzles is found only on the WAIS-IV. The examinee is shown a picture of a completed shape such as a rectangle, and asked to select from six smaller shapes the three that could be used to assemble the larger completed shape. Successful performance requires visual-spatial analysis and the mental rotation of shapes. According to the WAIS-IV Technical Manual, this subtest taps for "visual perception, broad visual intelligence, fluid intelligence, simultaneous processing, spatial visualization and manipulation, and the ability to anticipate relationships among parts" (Wechsler, 2008b, p. 14). The 26 items have strict time limits of 20 seconds for the initial easy items and 30 seconds for the

remaining items. Visual Puzzles is a core subtest that contributes to the Perceptual Reasoning Index of the WAIS-IV.

## Figure Weights

Figure Weights is found only on the WAIS-IV. It is a supplemental subtest that contributes to the Perceptual Reasoning Index. The examinee is shown a picture of an old-fashioned fulcrum scale that is missing weight(s) on one side. The task is to select from six options the response that would bring the scale into balance. This subtest is a measure of quantitative and analogical reasoning; inductive and deductive logic are essential for success. Easy items provide a time limit of 20 seconds, hard items allow 40 seconds.

## ● WECHSLER ADULT INTELLIGENCE SCALE-IV

The WAIS-IV is a significant revision of the WAIS-III, even though many of the previous items were retained (Wechsler, 2008). The most significant changes include the addition of two subtests, a simplified test structure, and an emphasis on index scores that provide a sharper demarcation of discrete domains of cognitive functions. In addition, the WAIS-IV abandons the familiar (but psychometrically indefensible) bifurcation of intelligence into Verbal IQ and Performance IQ, preferring instead the fourfold breakdown discussed below. In addition to traditional approaches to scoring the WAIS-IV subtests, the new edition also provides neuropsychologically relevant process scores for four of the subtests. These scores are useful mainly for advanced forms of test interpretation in the context of a comprehensive test battery. We do not discuss process scores in this section. Because of improvements in the WAIS-IV protocol forms (e.g., prominent display of discontinue rules), this test is somewhat easier to administer than its predecessor. Lichtenberger and Kaufman (2009) provide an outstanding overview of the WAIS-IV in clinical practice.

The WAIS-IV is comprised of 15 subtests, but only ten of the subtests, known as core subtests, are needed to obtain the traditional IQ score and the component index scores. The other five subtests are deemed supplemental. These are often used to provide additional clinical information; in specific instances, supplemental subtests may be used as acceptable substitutes for core subtests.

In addition to the traditional Full Scale IQ score, normed to a mean of 100 and standard deviation of 15, the WAIS-IV is scored for four index scores, each based on 2 or 3 of the 10 core subtests. These are derived from factor analysis of the subtests, which revealed four domains: Verbal Comprehension, Perceptual Reasoning, Working Memory, and Processing Speed. The index scores are also based on the familiar mean of 100 and standard deviation of 15. The breakdown of subtests for the four index scores is as follows:

**Verbal Comprehension Index**
Similarities
Vocabulary
Information

**Perceptual Reasoning Index**
Block Design
Matrix Reasoning
Visual Puzzles

**Working Memory Index**
Digit Span
Arithmetic

**Processing Speed Index**
Symbol Search
Coding

The Verbal Comprehension Index (VCI) is similar to the outdated notion (used on the WAIS-III) of Verbal IQ or VIQ. However, from a psychometric standpoint, VCI is a cleaner and more direct measure of verbal comprehension than VIQ, hence it is now the preferred index. Likewise, the Perceptual Reasoning Index (PRI) is similar to the former notion (from the WAIS-III) of Performance IQ or PIQ. Yet, as a more refined measure of perceptual reasoning, PRI is therefore the preferred index. Put simply, VCI and PRI fit the factor analytic data better. Long-held conventions tend to persist, but it is time to let the outdated notions of Verbal IQ and Performance IQ fade into oblivion.

The Working Memory Index (WMI) is comprised of subtests sensitive to attention and immediate memory (Digit Span and Arithmetic). A relatively low score on this index may signify that the examinee has an attentional or memory problem, especially with orally presented materials. The Processing Speed Index (PSI) comprises subtest that require the *highly* speeded process of visual information (Symbol Search and Coding). The PSI is sensitive to a wide variety of neurological and neuropsychological conditions (Tulsky, Zhu, & Ledbetter, 1997).

## WAIS-IV Standardization

The standardization of the WAIS-IV was undertaken with great care and based on data gathered by the U.S. Bureau of the Census in 2005. The total sample of 2,200 adults (ages 16 to 91) was carefully stratified on these variables: gender, race/ethnicity, education level, and geographic region. Census figures from 2005 were used as the target values for the stratification variables. For example, of persons in the 55- to 64-year-old range, the Census Bureau found that 3.35 percent are African Americans with high school education. In like manner, 3.00 percent of the standardization participants were African Americans with high school education.

The standardization sample was divided into 13 age bands: 16–17, 18–19, 20–24, 25–29, 30–34, 35–44, 45–54, 55–64, 65–69, 70–74, 75–79, 80–84, 85–90. Except for the four oldest age groups, each sample included 200 participants carefully stratified on the demographic variables noted earlier; the last four age groups included 100 participants each. The resulting sample bears a very close correspondence to the U.S. Census proportions. However, persons suspected of even mild cognitive impairment were excluded, so that the standardizations sample likely is healthier than its census counterparts. Specifically, several exclusionary criteria were used in the standardization sample, including: uncorrected visual or hearing impairment, current hospitalization, evidence of drug/alcohol problems, upper extremity impairment, use of certain prescription drugs such as anticonvulsants, and a variety of potentially brain-impairing conditions (e.g., head injury, stroke, epilepsy, dementia, and mood disorder). Uncooperative participants and those for whom English was a second language also were excluded. In sum, the standardization sample was restricted to cooperative, reasonably healthy, English-speaking individuals who did not manifest significant brain-impairing conditions.

Although the WAIS-IV is similar to the WAIS-III and has a substantial item overlap, the two tests do not yield analogous IQs. In counterbalanced studies comparing scores of 240 adults on the two tests, WAIS-IV IQ scores are lower by 3 points. In sum, the WAIS-IV is a harder test than the WAIS-III. There is a troubling enigma here: Why does the normative sample for the WAIS-IV appear to be smarter than the normative sample for the WAIS-III. We take up this point in more detail in Topic 6B, Test Bias and Other Controversies.

## Reliability

The reliability of the WAIS-IV is exceptionally good. Composite split-half reliabilities averaged across all age groups for the Index scores and IQ are: VCI .96, PCI .95, WMI .94, PSI .90, and Full Scale IQ .98. Further supporting the reliability of the WAIS-IV, reliability estimates for subtest scores of special groups (e.g., persons with intellectual disability, probable Alzheimer's disease, traumatic brain injury, major depression, autism) are equal to or higher than reliability estimates found in the general population (Wechsler, 2008b). This suggests that the WAIS-IV is a reliable tool not just with the general population but also with the special populations who are more likely to be the focus of assessment.

For Full Scale IQ, the standard error of measurement is 2.6 points for the youngest examinees (ages 16 and 17), but even smaller at 2.1 points for all other age groups. Consider what this means: 95 percent of the time, an examinee's *true* Full Scale IQ will be with ±4 points (2 standard errors of measure) of the obtained value. In common parlance, psychometrists would say that WAIS-IV

IQ has an 8-point band of error, that is, IQ scores are accurate within about ±4 points. In contrast to the strong reliabilities found for IQ and Index scores, the reliabilities of the 15 individual subtests are generally much weaker. The only subtests with stability coefficients in excess of .90 are Information (.90) and Vocabulary (.91). For the remaining subtests, reliability values range from the low .70s to the mid .80s. The most important implication of these weaker reliability findings is that examiners should approach subtest profile analysis with extreme caution. Subtest scores that appear discrepantly high (or low) for an individual examinee might be a consequence of the generally weak reliability of certain subtests rather than indicating true cognitive strengths or weaknesses. Some reviewers conclude that profile analysis (the identification of specific cognitive strengths and weaknesses based on analysis of peaks and valleys in the subtest scores) is not justified by the evidence.

## Validity

The developers of the WAIS-IV provide a number of different lines of evidence to support the validity of this instrument (Wechsler, 2008b). Good content validity was built in from the beginning through comprehensive literature review and consultation with experts to assure that items and subtests tap the relevant range of cognitive processes. Good criterion-related validity was demonstrated in several studies correlating the WAIS-IV with mainstream intelligence tests and other measures. For example, WAIS-IV Full Scale IQ correlates strongly with global scores on other mainstream measures: .94 with the WAIS-III, .91 with the WISC-IV (for 16-year-olds in the overlapping age group), and .88 with the Wechsler Individual Achievement Test-II. The WAIS-IV also reveals appropriate convergent and discriminant validity in the patternings of strong and weak correlations with a wide variety of other instruments, including measures of attention deficit disorder, executive functions, and memory. As a generalization, correlations are appropriately strong among similar subtests and constructs from the WAIS-IV and other tests, and appropriately weak among dissimilar subtests and constructs.

Studies with special groups also provide theory-confirming results that speak to the validity of the WAIS-IV. The multiplicity of these studies is such that we can only provide a few examples here. Specifically, when 41 young adults with diagnosed Mathematics Disorder were compared to matched controls on WAIS-IV subtests, the most substantial difference by far was found on the Arithmetic subtest, where the clinical group averaged 6.6 compared to 8.8 for the matched controls (a subtest score of 10 is average in the general population). This corroborates the sensitivity of the instrument to the elements of one specific learning disability. In like manner, when 22 individuals with a history of moderate or severe brain injury were compared to matched controls, the largest difference among the four index scores was found on the Processing Speed Index (mean of 80.5 versus mean of 97.6), whereas the smallest difference among the four index scores was found on the Verbal Comprehension Index (mean of 92.1 versus mean of 100.8). These findings are exactly what would be predicted from a wide body of research on the impact of traumatic brain injury (e.g., Lezak, Howieson, & Loring, 2004).

The construct validity of the WAIS-IV is also supported by confirmatory factor analyses of the subtest scores from the standardization sample, as detailed in the technical manual (Wechsler, 2008b). These complex analyses were designed to determine if the relations among observed subtest scores support the existence of the hypothesized factors of intelligence measured by the four index scores of VCI, PRI, WMI, and PSI. The goodness-of-fit of the four factor hierarchical model of intelligence (Full Scale IQ at the top, sitting above the four index scores, each sitting above two or three constituent subtest scores) turns out to be exceptionally strong, although difficult to summarize in visual form. A simple way to depict the strong confirmatory fit is through a 4 × 10 table that shows the correlations among the four index scores and the 10 core subtest scores (Table 5.8). Where appropriate, these correlations are corrected for overlap between the subtest scores and the index

scores. For example, Similarities is a component of VCI, so the simple correlation between these two variables is artificially inflated. The values shown in Table 5.8 are corrected for this kind of overlap. The reader will notice that with only a single exception, the subtests that compose each index score reveal their highest correlations with that index score. The only exception is the Arithmetic subtest, which is factorially more complex than other subtests, showing an almost identical relationship with VCI, PRI, and WMI.

Finally, the validity of the WAIS-IV is also buttressed by its strong overlap with the previous three editions of the test, for which there is an impressive array of validity data. For a full review of these findings the reader can consult Matarazzo (1972) and Kaufman (1990). We will present one representative and impressive study here, a correlational analysis of academic standing and intelligence scores. Conry and Plant (1965) correlated WAIS scores with high school rank (HSR) of graduates for 98 students. They also correlated WAIS Scores with grade point average (GPA) at the end of the first year of college for 335 students in a second sample. The results are portrayed in Figure 5.11. Notice that Verbal IQ bears a strong relationship

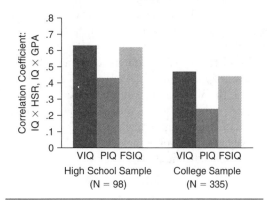

● **FIGURE 5.11** Correlations Between WAIS IQs and Academic Standing in High School and College

Note: HSR = high school rank; GPA = grade point average

*Source:* Based on data in Conry, R., & Plant, W. T. (1965). WAIS and group test predictions of an academic success criterion: High school and college. *Educational and Psychological Measurement,* 25, 493–500.

| ● TABLE 5.8   Correlations Among WAIS-IV Subtests and Index Scores | | | | |
|---|---|---|---|---|
| | *VCI* | *PRI* | *WMI* | *PSI* |
| **Verbal Comprehension Subtests** | | | | |
| Similarities | 74 | 57 | 57 | 42 |
| Vocabulary | 81 | 55 | 60 | 41 |
| Information | 63 | 54 | 56 | 37 |
| **Perceptual Reasoning Subtests** | | | | |
| Block Design | 51 | 67 | 53 | 45 |
| Matrix Reasoning | 56 | 59 | 55 | 46 |
| Visual Puzzles | 48 | 66 | 49 | 41 |
| **Working Memory Subtests** | | | | |
| Digit Span | 53 | 52 | 60 | 47 |
| Arithmetic | 63 | 59 | 60 | 44 |
| **Processing Speed Subtests** | | | | |
| Symbol Search | 38 | 47 | 43 | 65 |
| Coding | 43 | 48 | 49 | 65 |

Note: Decimals have been omitted. Where appropriate, these correlations are corrected for overlap. For example, because Similarities is a component of VCI, the simple uncorrected correlation between these two variables would be artificially inflated. The values above are corrected for any componental overlap between subtests and index scores.

*Source:* Based on data in Wechsler, D. (2008). *WAIS-IV Technical and Interpretive Manual.* San Antonio, TX: Pearson.

with academic success—just as strong as Full Scale IQ—whereas Performance IQ bears a weaker relationship to achievement levels in both samples. Conry and Plant (1965) also reported the correlations between WAIS subtest scores and the two indices of academic success. For high school students, the Vocabulary subtest score correlated $r = .65$ with high school rank, the highest overall correlation in the entire analysis. This finding speaks convincingly in favor of including vocabulary measures on intelligence tests.

## ● WECHSLER INTELLIGENCE SCALE FOR CHILDREN-IV

The Wechsler Intelligence Scale for Children (WISC) was published in 1949 as a downward extension of the original Wechsler-Bellevue. Although used widely in the next two decades, psychometricians perceived a number of flaws in the WISC: absence of nonwhites in the standardization sample, ambiguities of scoring, inappropriate items for children (e.g., reference to "cigars"), and absence of females and African Americans in the pictorial content of items. The WISC-R, WISC-III, and WISC-IV corrected these flaws.

The WISC-IV consists of 15 subtests, 10 of which are designated as core subtests used in the computation of composite scores and Full Scale IQ, and five of which are designated as supplemental:

**Core Subtests**

| | |
|---|---|
| Block Design | Vocabulary |
| Similarities | Letter–Number Sequencing |
| Digit Span | Matrix Reasoning |
| Picture Concepts | Comprehension |
| Coding | Symbol Search |

Supplemental Subtests
  Picture Completion
  Cancellation
  Information
  Arithmetic
  Word Reasoning

Although the supplemental subtests are not required for the computation of Full Scale IQ and composite scores (discussed later), careful examiners nonetheless may choose to administer them because of the important diagnostic information they often provide. For example, the Cancellation subtest is supplemental but affords important information about vigilance and visual attention; hence, many examiners use it. The Arithmetic subtest also is supplemental but often chosen by examiners because it is helpful in the assessment of auditory attention (the questions are presented orally).

Another function of the supplementary subtests is suitable substitution for a core subtest. In well-defined circumstances, an examiner may elect to give a supplemental subtest in place of a core subtest. For example, when testing a child with fine motor problems—such as might be observed in a child with cerebral palsy—an examiner would be well advised to use Cancellation in place of Coding, and Picture Completion in place of Block Design. Both of these supplementary tests (Cancellation and Picture Completion) are relatively unaffected by fine motor difficulties. In contrast, the core subtests (Coding and Block Design) would be severely impacted by fine motor difficulties and, therefore, could yield unfair assessments of cognitive functioning. Substitutions also are allowed when a core subtest accidentally is invalidated. However, an examiner may not elect to substitute a supplemental subtest merely because a child has performed poorly on a core subtest.

The standardization of the WISC-IV is first class, based on 100 boys and girls at each year of age from 6½ through 16½ (total $N = 2,200$). These cases were carefully selected and stratified on the basis of the 2000 U.S. Census with respect to gender, race/ethnicity (white, African American, Hispanic, and Asian), geographic region, and parent educa-

tional level. A desirable feature of the standardization sample is that 5.7 percent of the sample consisted of children with defined characteristics such as giftedness, learning disability, expressive language disorder, head injury, autism, and motor impairment. The purpose of adding these children was to ensure that the normative sample accurately represented the population of children attending school. The correspondence between the standardization sample and the U.S. Census data on essential stratification variables was nearly perfect (Wechsler, 2003, p. 40).

The reliability of the WISC-IV is strong and comparable to previous editions of the test. For example, the IQ and composite scores show split-half and test-retest reliabilities in the .90s, whereas the individual subtests possess somewhat lower reliability coefficients, ranging from .79 (Cancellation and Symbol Search) to .90 (Letter–Number Sequencing). Most reliabilities are in the high .80s, for example, Block Design and Similarities at .86, and Vocabulary and Matrix Reasoning at .89. Test-retest reliabilities tend to be slightly lower.

The validity of the WISC-IV rests, in part, on its overlap with the WISC-III, for which dozens of supportive studies could be cited. We do not want to overwhelm with excessive detail, so we refer the interested reader to Sattler (2001) for a good review of earlier studies. The WISC-IV manual cites an impressive array of validity studies, which we summarize here. First, we discuss correlations of WISC-IV test scores with its predecessor and with other Wechsler intelligence tests. The preliminary findings indicate strong correlations with comparable WISC-III subtests, most in the high .70s or low .80s. The correlation for Full Scale IQ is much higher, $r = .89$. Likewise, correlations with the WPPSI-III are strong for comparable subtests, and, again, exceptionally strong for Full Scale IQ, $r = .89$. A similar pattern is found with 16-year-old examinees, who can be tested legitimately with both the WISC-IV and the WAIS-III. In a sample of 198 children tested in counterbalanced order over a period of about three weeks, correlations were strong for comparable subtests and exceptionally strong for composite and Full Scale IQ scores ($r = .89$).

Overall, these are remarkable correlations, nearly as strong as the reliabilities of the respective scales would allow. An interesting finding is that WISC-IV IQs are an average of 2.5 points lower than WISC-III IQs and 3 points lower than WAIS-III IQs. This is a consistent finding in the history of individual intelligence tests; namely, newer tests almost invariably yield lower Q scores in comparison to older tests. We discuss this intriguing result, called the Flynn effect, in the next chapter.

Factor-analytic studies of the standardization sample provided additional evidence for the utility of the WISC-IV in the diagnostic assessment of children. The results of numerous factor analyses, including separate analyses for four age groups (6–7, 8–10, 11–13, 14–16) strongly confirmed a four-factor solution that was used to define the composite scores, called Index scores, for the test (Wechsler, 2003). The factors and the core subtests assigned to them were as follows:

**Verbal Comprehension Index**
  Similarities
  Vocabulary
  Comprehension

**Perceptual Reasoning Index**
  Block Design
  Picture Concepts
  Matrix Reasoning

**Working Memory Index**
  Digit Span
  Letter–Number Sequencing

**Processing Speed Index**
  Coding
  Symbol Search

The four Index scores are based on the familiar mean of 100 and standard deviation of 15. Thus, the WISC-IV provides substantial detail about the nuances of intellectual functioning—up to 15 subtest scores, four Index scores, and the Full Scale IQ. The robust findings of the four-factor solution to the WISC-IV provided the rationale for abandoning Wechsler's original two-factor division of Verbal IQ and Performance IQ. In fact,

there is no longer any method on the WISC-IV to obtain a Verbal IQ or a Performance IQ—precisely because these partitions no longer fit with the emerging consensus about the nature of intelligence.

The WISC-IV also revealed theory-confirming correlations with a variety of cognitive, ability, and achievement tests (Wechsler, 2003). In general, correlations with other measures were appropriately high for similar constructs and predictably low for dissimilar constructs—these are the prerequisites for convergent validity and discriminant validity, respectively. For example, in a sample of 550 children aged 6–16, reading achievement subtest scores from the Wechsler Individual Achievement Test-II correlated more strongly with Verbal Comprehension Index scores from the WISC-IV than with the other Index scores. Likewise, in a sample of 126 children aged 6–16, the Attention/Concentration subtest from the Children's Memory Scale (Cohen, 1997) correlated substantially ($r = .74$) with Working Memory Index scores from the WISC-IV but less robustly with the other Index scores. These and other findings indicate general support for the convergent validity of the WISC-IV Index scores. Discriminant validity was confirmed by the negligible relationships among WISC-IV Index scores and measures of emotional intelligence from the BarOn Emotional Quotient Inventory (BarOn EQI, Bar-On & Parker, 2000). For the most part, research has shown that emotional intelligence is independent of cognitive intelligence. Thus, relationships among Index scores from the WISC-IV and subtest scores from the BarOn EQI should bear out as insignificant. In fact, the correlations were negligible, in the range of .06 to .20. The only exceptions were sensible ones. For example, scores on the Adaptability subscale from the BarOn EQI correlated .34 with WISC-IV Full Scale IQ. Certainly, it is plausible that adaptability as measured by the BarOn EQI is rooted, in part, in a foundation of cognitive skills, as mirrored in IQ, thus illuminating the modest correlation between these two measures.

## ● STANFORD-BINET INTELLIGENCE SCALES: FIFTH EDITION

With a lineage that goes back to the Binet-Simon scale of 1905, the Stanford-Binet: Fifth Edition (SB5) has the oldest and perhaps the most prestigious pedigree of any individual intelligence test. In Table 5.9, we outline some important milestones in the development of the SB5 and its predecessors. Released in 2003, the SB5 is a very new test (Roid, 2002, 2003). For this reason, evaluation of this instrument is based, in part, on its resemblance in content and subtests to the SB4, for which a large body of independent research literature has been amassed.

### The SB5 Model of Intelligence

In early editions of the Stanford-Binet, the examiner obtained only a composite IQ. Although the pattern of right and wrong answers could be analyzed qualitatively, the earlier Stanford-Binet tests (prior to the fourth edition) did not provide a basis for quantitative analysis of the subcomponents of the entire scale. The fourth and fifth editions corrected this shortcoming.

The organization of the SB5 was guided by the principle that each of five factors of intelligence can be assessed in two distinct domains—nonverbal and verbal. The five factors—derived from modern cognitive theories such as Carroll (1993) and Baddeley (1986)—are fluid reasoning, knowledge, quantitative reasoning, visual-spatial processing, and working memory. When these five factors of intelligence are "crossed" with the two domains (nonverbal and verbal), the result is an instrument with ten subtests (Figure 5.12). Thus, the SB5 provides a number of different perspectives on the cognitive functioning of an examinee: ten subtest scores (mean of 10, SD of 3), three IQ scores (the familiar Full Scale IQ, Verbal IQ, and Nonverbal IQ), as well as five factor scores (Fluid Reasoning, Knowledge, Quantitative Reasoning, Visual-Spatial Processing, and Working Memory). The IQ and factor scores are normed to a mean of 100 and SD of 15.

### Routing Procedure and Tailored Testing

The SB5 maintains the historical tradition of this instrument by using a **routing procedure** to estimate the general cognitive ability of the examinee

---

● **TABLE 5.9    Milestones in the Development of the Stanford-Binet and Predecessor Tests**

| Year | Test/Authors | Comment |
|------|--------------|---------|
| 1905 | Binet and Simon | Simple 30-item test |
| 1908 | Binet and Simon | Introduced the mental age concept |
| 1911 | Binet and Simon | Expanded to include adults |
| 1916 | Stanford-Binet Terman and Merrill | Introduced the IQ concept |
| 1937 | Stanford-Binet-2 Terman and Merrill | First use of parallel forms (L and M) |
| 1960 | Stanford-Binet-3 Terman and Merrill | Modern item-analysis methods used |
| 1972 | Stanford-Binet-3 Terman and Merrill | SB-3 restandardized on 2,100 persons |
| 1986 | Stanford-Binet-4 Thorndike, Hagen, and Sattler | Complete restructuring into 15 subsets |
| 2003 | Stanford-Binet-5 Roid | Five factors of intelligence |

|  |  | DOMAINS | |
|  |  | Nonverbal | Verbal |
| --- | --- | --- | --- |
|  | Fluid Reasoning | Nonverbal Fluid Reasoning | Verbal Fluid Reasoning |
|  | Knowledge | Nonverbal Knowledge | Verbal Knowledge |
|  | Quantitative Reasoning | Nonverbal Quantitative Reasoning | Verbal Quantitative Reasoning |
| FACTORS | Visual-Spatial Reasoning | Nonverbal Visual-Spatial Processing | Verbal Visual-Spatial Processing |
|  | Working Memory | Nonverbal Working Memory | Verbal Working Memory |
|  |  | Nonverbal IQ | Verbal IQ |

● **FIGURE 5.12**
Structure of the Standford-Binet: Fifth Edition

FULL SCALE IQ

before proceeding to the remainder of the test. The purpose of the routing procedure is to identify the appropriate starting points for subsequent subtests. The routing items are both nonverbal (object series and matrices) and verbal (vocabulary). These items also provide the Abbreviated IQ, sometimes used for screening purposes. Roid (2002) describes the advantages of using a routing procedure:

> This tailored approach to assessment provides greater richness of factor measurement within a shorter, efficient test administration. The use of modern item response theory in the design of SB5 allows for greater precision of measurement due to the adaption of the test to the functional level of the examinee in an efficient time frame.

Thus, the purpose of the routing procedure is not just to reduce the number of items administered (and, therefore, save time), but to do so without loss of measurement precision. This is possible because the SB5 was constructed according to the principles of item response theory (Embretson, 1996). When a test is constructed within the framework of item response theory, item difficulty levels and other parameters are precisely calibrated during the development phase.

### Special Features of the SB5

In addition to providing a more familiar partition of intelligence into Full Scale IQ, Verbal IQ, and Nonverbal IQ, the SB5 also features a number of other improvements over its predecessor, the SB4. The test now includes extensive high-end items, designed to assess the highest level of gifted performance. Many of these items are updates from very early editions of the Stanford-Binet, when the instrument was renowned for its very high ceiling. At the other extreme, improved low-end items provide better assessment for very young children (as young as age 2) and adults with mental retardation. In addition, the items and subtests that contribute to the Nonverbal IQ do not require expressive language, which makes this part of the test ideal for assessing individuals with limited English, deafness, or communication disorders. The developers of the SB5 also screened test items for fairness based on religious as well as traditional concerns. Expert panels examined the entire test on fairness issues related to the standard variables (gender, race, ethnicity, and disability) and religious tradition (Christian, Jewish, Muslim, Hindu, and Buddhist backgrounds). This is the first time in the history of intelligence testing that religious tradition has been considered in test development. Finally, the Working Memory factor, consisting of both verbal and nonverbal subtests, shows promise in helping to assess and understand children with attention-deficit/hyperactivity disorder.

## Standardization and Psychometric Properties of the SB5

The SB5 is suitable for children age 2 through adults age 85 and older, and the standardization sample consists of 4,800 individuals stratified by gender, ethnic, regional, and educational levels in the United States, based on the year 2000 census. In part because item selection was determined by modern item response theory, the reliability of subtests, indices, and IQ scores is very strong and comparable to other mainstream individual intelligence tests. For example, the Verbal IQ, Nonverbal IQ, and Full Scale IQ each have reliabilities in the .90s, and the individual subtests are in the range of .70 to .85 (Roid, 2002).

As is typical in the release of a new test, the manual for the SB5 (Roid, 2003) reports on numerous affirming correlational studies (e.g., with the Wechsler scales, the SB4, the UNIT) that provide strong support for criterion-related validity. The validity of the test as a measure of general intelligence is also supported by its resemblance to the SB4, about which a large body of research can be cited. For example, Lamp and Krohn (2001) studied the longitudinal predictive validity of the SB4 in a sample of 89 Head Start children (39 African American and 50 white) from impoverished backgrounds who ranged in age from about 4 to 6½. These children were retested several times over an eight-year period on both the SB4 and the Metropolitan Achievement Test. The correlations between the initial SB4 score and the subsequent achievement scores were very strong (mainly in the .50s), and the test was equally good at predicting outcome for African American and white children. In another study (Atkinson, Bevc, Dickens, & Blackwell, 1992), the concurrent validity of the SB4 was tested against the Leiter International Performance Scale and the Vineland

Adaptive Behavior Scales in a sample of 24 children with developmental delays. The correlations were very robust (.78 and .70, respectively). These and many other studies strongly support the validity of the SB4 as a measure of general intelligence. As new research is reported on the SB5, it is likely that this recent edition also will prove to be highly valid and even more useful than its predecessor as a measure of intelligence.

In summary, the SB5 is a very promising new test that is especially useful at both ends of the cognitive spectrum—the very young or those with developmental delays, and very gifted persons. Based on the care with which the instrument was constructed, the test is likely to become a mainstay of individual intelligence testing in a wide variety of settings.

## ● DETROIT TESTS OF LEARNING APTITUDE-4

The Detroit Tests of Learning Aptitude-4 (DTLA-4; Hammill, 1999) is a recent revision of an instrument first published in 1935. The test is individually administered and designed for schoolchildren from 6 through 17 years of age. The DTLA-4 consists of 10 subtests that form the basis for computing 16 composites, including general intelligence, optimal level, and 14 ability areas. The subtests are largely within the Binet-Wechsler tradition, although there are a few surprises such as the inclusion of Story Construction, a measure of storytelling ability (Table 5.10).

The General Mental Ability composite is formed by combining standard scores for all 10 subtests in the battery. The Optimal Level composite is based on the highest four standard scores earned by the examinee and is thought to represent how well the examinee might perform under optimal circumstances. Each of the remaining 14 composite scores is derived from a combination of several subtests thought to measure a common attribute. For example, subtests that involve knowledge of words and their use are combined to form the Verbal Composite, whereas subtests that do not involve reading, writing, or speech

● **TABLE 5.10  Brief Description of the DTLA-4 Subtests**

| Subtest | Task |
| --- | --- |
| Word Opposites | Provide antonyms—word opposites. |
| Design Sequences | Discriminate and remember nonsensical graphic material. |
| Sentence Imitation | Repeat orally presented sentences. |
| Reversed Letters | Short-term visual memory and attention. |
| Story Construction | Create a logical story from several pictures. |
| Design Reproduction | Copy designs from memory. |
| Basic Information | Knowledge of everyday facts and information. |
| Symbolic Relations | Select from a series of designs the part that was missing from a previous design. |
| Word Sequences | Repeat a series of unrelated words. |
| Story Sequences | Organize pictorial material into meaningful sequences. |

comprise the Nonverbal Composite. Several of the composite scores are designed to represent major constructs within contemporary theories of intelligence. In addition to the General Mental Ability composite and the Optimal Level composite, the remaining 14 DTLA-4 composite scores are as follows:

| | | |
| --- | --- | --- |
| Verbal | Nonverbal | (Linguistic) |
| Attention-enhanced | Attention-reduced | (Attentional) |
| Motor-enhanced | Motor-reduced | (Motoric) |
| Fluid | Crystallized | (Horn & Cattell) |
| Simultaneous | Successive | (Das) |
| Associative | Cognitive | (Jensen) |
| Verbal | Performance | (Wechsler) |

The 16 composite scores are based on the familiar mean of 100 and standard deviation of 15. The 10 subtests are normed for a mean of 10 and standard deviation of 3.

The composites were designed to offer contrasting assessments such that a difference between scores may be of diagnostic significance. For example, an examinee who scored well on Attention-Reduced aptitude but poorly on Attention-Enhanced aptitude (in the Attentional domain) presumably experiences difficulty with immediate recall, short-term memory, or focused concentration.

The DTLA-4 was standardized on 1,350 students whose backgrounds closely matched census data for sex, race, urban/rural residence, family income, educational attainment of parents, and geographic area. The reliability of this instrument is similar to other individual tests of intelligence, with internal consistency coefficients generally exceeding .80 for the subtests and .90 for the composites, and test-retest coefficients for the subtests and the composites in the .80s and .90s. Criterion-related validity is well established through correlational studies with other mainstream instruments such as the WISC-III, K-ABC, and Woodcock-Johnson.

A concern with the DTLA-4 is that the conceptual breakdown into composites is not sufficiently supported by empirical evidence. For example, while it may be true that the Simultaneous composite does measure the simultaneous cognitive processes proposed by Das, Kirby, and Jarman (1979), there is scant empirical support to buttress this claim. Another problem with this instrument is that there are more composites than there are subtests! Inevitably, the composites will be highly intercorrelated, because each subtest occurs in several composites. In sum, DTLA-4 may be a good measure of general intelligence, but the use of composite scores for purposes of psychoeducational planning requires additional empirical study. Smith (2001) provides a thorough review of the DTLA-4.

● **KAUFMAN ASSESSMENT BATTERY FOR CHILDREN-II**

The Kaufman Assessment Battery for Children-II (KABC-II) is an individually administered test of cognitive abilities designed for children and adolescents ages 3 through 18 (Kaufman & Kaufman, 2004). This is a pioneering test with many innovative features, including the intentional goal of reducing the score differences among children from diverse ethnic and cultural groups. Yet, providing a succinct description of the instrument presents a challenge because the test (1) is grounded simultaneously in two modern theoretical models of intelligence, (2) consists of different subtests and global scales at each of three age ranges (ages 3, 4–6, and 7–18), and (3) provides for an optional nonverbal scale that also varies by age group. In this section, we will focus on the battery for children ages 7–18.

### KABC-II Overview

Whereas the first edition of the test, the K-ABC (Kaufman & Kaufman, 1983), was grounded only in Luria's neuropsychological theory of processing (Luria, 1966; Das, Kirby, & Jarman, 1979), the KABC-II operates within two theoretical models: the original Luria model, and the Cattell-Horn-Carroll (CHC) theory of broad and narrow abilities (Carroll, 1993). The scales from the KABC-II and the corresponding concepts from the Luria and CHC approach are depicted in Figure 5.13.

The authors of the KABC-II purposely refrained from any reference to *Intelligence Quotient* in scale names or scores. Instead, they prefer the term *Fluid-Crystallized Index* (FCI) as the summary score within the CHC model because it carries less historical baggage and also communicates the cognitive qualities assessed, and they prefer the term *Mental Processing Index* (MPI) as the summary score within the Luria model because it captures the notion of

*processing* that is central to this approach. There is also a third summary score, the Nonverbal Index (NVI), comprised of subtests that may be administered in pantomime and, therefore, useful in the assessment of children with hearing loss, speech or language disabilities, and limited English proficiency. As noted previously, the subtests used for the Nonverbal Index differ by age group; we do not discuss this aspect of the KABC-II in any detail. For all three global index scores, the overall mean is 100 and the standard deviation is 15.

### KABC-II Subtests, Scales, and the Two Models of Intelligence

The KABC-II consists of 18 subtests, which are described in Table 5.11. Not all subtests are necessarily used with every examinee—some are age restricted, and others are supplementary, designed to provide a broad basis for the assessment of cognitive functioning and the detection of processing deficits. Certain subtests are used for the Nonverbal Index as well. The supplementary subtests are administered at the option of the examiner. The subtests are scaled to a mean of 10 and standard deviation of 3 for all age groups.

The KABC-II concurrently embodies two models of intelligence—the approach of Luria (1966) and the CHC model (Carroll, 1993). The examiner is admonished by the test developers to select either the Luria or CHC model prior to testing the child or adolescent (Kaufman & Kaufman, 2004, p. 4). One important difference between the

| KABC-II Scale Name | CHC Term | Luria Term |
|---|---|---|
| Sequential | Short-Term Memory | Sequential Processing |
| Simultaneous | Visual Processing | Simultaneous Processing |
| Learning | Long-Term Storage and Retrieval | Learning Ability |
| Planning | Fluid Reasoning | Planning Ability |
| Knowledge | Crystallized Ability | |
| **KABC-II Global Scale:** | Fluid-Crystallized Index | Mental Processing Index |

● FIGURE 5.13
KABC-II Scales and Two Theoretical Orientations

● **TABLE 5.11**   **Brief Descriptions of the 18 Subtests from the KABC-II**

### Sequential Scale

**Number Recall:** This is the familiar digit span test in which the child repeats, in the same order, a series of digits orally presented by the examiner. A unique feature is that "10" is used instead of "7" so that all numbers are a single syllable. Core 4–18, Supplementary 3.

**Word Order:** The examiner says the names of several common objects, and the child touches their silhouettes in the same order. Core 3–18.

**Hand Movements:** The examiner displays a series of hand movements (fist, palm, or side of the hand), and the child repeats these in the correct order. Supplementary 4–18, Nonverbal 3–18.

### Simultaneous Scale

**Block Counting:** The child determines the exact number of blocks in several drawings of stacks of blocks. Some supporting blocks are hidden from view. Core 13–18, Supplementary 5–12, Nonverbal 7–18.

**Conceptual Thinking:** The child examines four or five pictures of objects and determines which one doesn't belong with the others (e.g., "not a fruit"). Core 3–16, Nonverbal 3–6.

**Face Recognition:** The child views a photograph of one or two faces exposed for a few seconds and then identifies the correct face or faces from a group photograph of several people. The group photograph embodies the correct faces in a different pose. Core 3–4, Supplementary 5, Nonverbal 3–5.

**Pattern Reasoning:** See Planning Scale for a description. Core 5–6.

**Rover:** On a checkerboard that contains both empty spaces and occupied spaces, the child moves a toy dog to reach a destination in the fewest moves possible. Core 6–18.

**Story Completion:** See Planning Scale for a description. Supplementary 6.

**Triangles:** Using identical foam triangles (blue on one side, yellow on the other), the child constructs a design to match a stimulus picture. (The first few items use simple colored shapes and designs instead.) Core 3–12, Supplementary 13–18, Nonverbal 3–18.

**Gestalt Closure:** This is a perceptual task in which the child identifies an object from a partially completed drawing. Requires the child visually to "fill in the gaps." Supplementary 3–18.

### Planning Scale

**Pattern Reasoning:** One stimulus is missing from a series of stimuli that embody a logical linear succession. Most of the stimuli are abstract, geometric shapes. The child is asked to identify the missing stimulus and select it from four to six alternatives shown below the series. Core 7–18, Nonverbal 5–18.

**Story Completion:** The child views a row of pictures that tell a story, but some of the pictures are missing. From additional pictures, the child selects and places the ones needed to complete the story properly. Core 7–18, Nonverbal 6–18.

### Learning Scale

**Atlantis:** The examiner sets the stage for this subtest by assigning nonsense names to imaginative pictures of nonexistent fish, shells, and plants. The child is then asked to point to each picture when named (from an array of pictures) as proof of learning. Core 3–18.

**Rebus:** A rebus is a simple, abstract line drawing. The examiner teaches the child a word or concept assigned to each particular rebus. Then, as a demonstration of learning, the child "reads" aloud sentences or phrases composed of the rebuses. Core 4–18.

**Atlantis Delayed:** This is a surprise retest on the original Atlantis items about 15–25 minutes later. Supplementary 5–18.

**Rebus Delayed:** This is a surprise retest on the original Rebus items about 15–25 minutes later. Supplementary 5–18.

### Knowledge Scale (CHC Model Only)

**Expressive Vocabulary:** The child says the name of a pictured object. Core 3–6, Supplementary 7–18.

**Riddles:** The examiner provides several characteristics of a concrete object (easy items) or abstract verbal concept (hard items), and the child points to the object or names the concept. Core 3–18.

**Verbal Knowledge:** From an array of six pictures, the child selects the one that depicts the meaning of a vocabulary word or the answer to a general information query. Core 7–18, Supplementary 3–6.

Notes:  After each subtest description, core, supplementary, and nonverbal designations and relevant age groups are listed. For example, "Core 13–18, Supplementary 5–12, Nonverbal 7–18" indicates a core subtest for ages 13 through 18, a supplementary subtest for ages 5 through 12, and a nonverbal subtest for ages 7 through 18.

two methods is that the CHC model contains a scale that gauges crystallized ability—the breadth and depth of knowledge assimilated from one's culture. Normally, the CHC model is the preferred choice, but there are many circumstances where it could be misleading because it contains crystallized ability. Kaufman and Kaufman (2004, p. 5) list testing situations in which the Luria model would be preferred:

- a child from a bilingual background
- a child whose nonmainstream cultural background may affect knowledge acquisition and verbal development
- a child with known or suspected language disorders, whether expressive, receptive, or mixed receptive-expressive
- a child with known or suspected autism
- a child who is deaf or hard of hearing

In contrast, the CHC approach generally is favored for evaluating children for gifted and talented programs because these settings emphasize crystallized abilities.

Briefly, the correspondence between the five KABC-II scales and the two models of intelligence is as follows:

*Sequential:* This scale assesses the kind of information processing that Luria labeled "successive" and involves mental activities in which a suitable sequence of operations must be followed to solve a problem—so-called linear thinking. Within the CHC framework, the essential cognitive demands of this scale engage short-term memory—taking in and retaining information and then using it within a few seconds.

*Simultaneous:* According to Luria, simultaneous processing of information involves the execution of several different mental operations simultaneously—so-called holistic processing. An example would be the instantaneous recognition of a human face. Within the CHC approach, this scale assesses visual processing—perceiving, remembering, manipulating, and thinking with visual images.

*Learning:* Within the Luria model, learning is a complex function that involves attention and concentration, coding and storage of information, and developing efficient strategies to learn and retain the new information. The comparable function within CHC theory is long-term storage and retrieval—storing and effectively retrieving recently or previously learned information.

*Planning:* According to Luria (1966), planning involves making decisions, monitoring goals, and generating hypotheses. This is complex behavior that involves the overall efficiency of the brain. The comparable function within CHC theory is fluid reasoning—the exercise of abstract thinking such as induction and deduction.

*Knowledge:* This scale is administered only within the CHC model and involves crystallized abilities. These are knowledge-based abilities such as vocabulary, information, and a thorough familiarity with one's culture.

## KABC-II Standardization, Reliability, and Validity

Exceptional care and quality control were used in the selection of the standardization sample, which consisted of 3,025 examinees ages 3 through 18 tested at 127 sites in 39 states and the District of Columbia. Consequently, the norm sample is closely aligned to national trends for educational level of the parents, ethnic group, geographic region, and gender. Using data from the National Center for Educational Statistics, the test developers also established that the norm sample closely resembles national trends for children with special needs such as learning disability, language impairment, attention-deficit/hyperactivity disorder, mental retardation, emotional disturbance, and gifted-talented (Kaufman & Kaufman, 2004, p. 83).

The split-half reliability of the global scales is superb: .95 to .97 for the MPI and FCI, and .90 to .92 for the NVI. Likewise, reliability of the five component scales (Sequential, Simultaneous, Learning, Planning, and Knowledge) is also outstanding, ranging from .88 to .93. Reliability of the individual subtests is more variable, ranging from a low of .69 for Hand Movements in young children to a high of .93 for Rebus in older children and adolescents. As is commonly the case, the test-retest reliability coefficients for the subtests, scales, and global scales are lower than the split-half reliability coefficients but nonetheless respectable. For example, the coefficients for MPI and FCI range from .86 to .94, depending on the age group.

Regarding validity, the test developers report a wealth of supportive evidence, including appropriate correlations with other cognitive measures, good fit with the theoretical model of the test in confirmatory factor analyses, suitable correlations with measures of academic achievement, and clinical validity studies in which test profiles for selected diagnostic groups proved affirmative. We want to focus here on one feature of the validity studies, the analysis of ethnic group differences.

One goal of the test developers was to provide an instrument that measured abilities ". . . in a way that reduces score differences between ethnic and cultural groups, providing confidence in the assessment of children and adolescents from a variety of backgrounds" (Kaufman & Kaufman, 2004, p. 1). The test authors approached this objective in a number of ways, including the decision to use teaching items at the beginning of many subtests to assure that all children understand the directions. Similarly, the instructions for subtests rely on clear examples and use simple concepts—in fact, some subtests can be administered entirely by pantomime. How well did the test authors meet their goal of developing a culture-reduced test? First, we need to point out that some degree of disparity in scores is to be expected, given that educational access and accomplishments are not equal among all ethnic and cultural groups. Thus, a fitting research strategy would be to provide a statistical correction for educational differences and then examine the average group scores to determine the impact of ethnic/cultural background. When scores are corrected for mother's educational level, the results indicate that KABC-II scores are influenced relatively little by children's

ethnic and cultural background. For example, rounding to the nearest number, the average scores on the Sequential scale were:

| African American | 100 |
| American Indian | 97 |
| Asian American | 103 |
| Hispanic | 95 |
| White | 101 |

On the Simultaneous scale, group differences also were minimal:

| African American | 93 |
| American Indian | 100 |
| Asian American | 105 |
| Hispanic | 99 |
| White | 102 |

Similar trends of reduced group differences also were found for the Learning, Planning, and Knowledge scales. The data for the three global scales—MPI, FCI, and NVI—are shown in Table 5.12. In general, these ethnic/cultural group differences on the KABC-II are smaller than found on other prominent tests of general ability such as the Wechsler scales (Kaufman & Lichtenberger, 2002).

● **TABLE 5.12    Global Scale Means on the KABC-II for Five Ethnic/Racial Groups**

| Ethnic/Racial Group | Global Scale | | |
|---|---|---|---|
| | MPI | FCI | NVI |
| African American | 95 | 95 | 93 |
| American Indian | 97 | 96 | 97 |
| Asian American | 105 | 104 | 103 |
| Hispanic | 97 | 96 | 98 |
| White | 102 | 102 | 102 |

Notes: Scores are statistically corrected for educational level of the mother and rounded to the nearest point. MPI is Mental Processing Index, FCI is Fluid-Crystallized Index, and NVI is Nonverbal Index.

Source: Kaufman, A. S., & Kaufman, N. L. (2004). *Kaufman Assessment Battery for Children,* Second Edition. Copyright © 2004 AGS Publishing. Reprinted with permission from Pearson Assessments. P.O. Box 1416, Minneapolis, MN 55440. KABC-II is a trademark of NCS Pearson Inc.

## ● KAUFMAN BRIEF INTELLIGENCE TEST-2 (KBIT-2)

The individual intelligence tests previously discussed in this and the preceding topic are excellent measures of intellectual ability, but they are not without their drawbacks. One problem is the time required to administer them. Testing sessions with the Wechsler scales, Kaufman Assessment Battery for Children, and the Stanford-Binet easily can last one hour, and two hours is not unusual if the examinee is bright and highly verbal. A second disadvantage to these mainstream tests is the amount of training required to administer them. Proper administration of most individual intelligence tests is based upon the assumption that the examiner has an advanced degree in psychology or a related field and has received extensive supervised experience with the instruments in question.

Alan Kaufman responded to the need for a brief, easily administered screening measure of intelligence by developing the Kaufman Brief Intelligence Test (K-BIT), recently released in a second edition, the KBIT-2 (Kaufman & Kaufman, 2004). The KBIT-2 consists of a Verbal or Crystallized scale that includes two types of items (Verbal Knowledge and Riddles) and a Nonverbal or Fluid Scale that consists of Matrices items (2 × 2 and 3 × 3 figural analogies).

The KBIT-2 is normed for examinees ages 4 to 90 and can be administered in approximately 20 minutes. The test yields standard scores with means of 100 and standard deviation of 15 for Verbal, Nonverbal, and combined scores. In spite of the comparability of these scoring dimensions with well-known intelligence tests, the KBIT-2 authors make it clear that their instrument is not intended as a substitute for traditional approaches (e.g., WPPSI-III, KABC-2, WISC-IV, or SB5). The KBIT-2 is mainly a screening test useful in signaling the need for more extensive assessment. The brevity of this test makes it a natural choice for research on intelligence.

The test authors suggest a number of uses for the instrument, including the following:

- Provide a quick estimate of intelligence where accuracy is not essential
- Estimate verbal versus nonverbal intelligence in children or adults
- Reevaluate intellectual status of previously tested examinees
- Screen students who may benefit from placement in gifted programs
- Screen high-risk students who may need further assessment
- Obtain a quick estimate of intelligence in adult treatment or institutional settings

The KBIT-2 manual reports highly supportive validity data from numerous correlational studies. However, the most compelling evidence for the validity of the instrument is its strong resemblance to the K-BIT, for which a substantial body of research has been published. For example, Naugle, Chelune, and Tucker (1993) compared K-BIT results and WAIS-R scores for 200 referrals to a neuropsychological assessment center.

The patient sample included persons with seizure disorders, head injuries, substance abuse, psychiatric disturbance, stroke, dementia, and other neurological conditions. The heterogeneity of the referral sample guaranteed a wide range of functional ability, a desirable feature in a validation study. Although the K-BIT scores tended to be about 5 points higher than their WAIS-R counterparts, the correlations between these two instruments were extremely high and theory-confirming. Vocabulary IQ (K-BIT) and Verbal IQ (WAIS-R) correlated .83; Matrices IQ (K-BIT) and Performance IQ (WAIS-R) correlated .77; and overall IQs from the two instruments correlated an amazing .88. In a study comparing the K-BIT and the WISC-III scores for 50 referred students, Prewett (1995) also reported strong correlations ($r = .78$ for overall scores) and also discovered that the K-BIT scores tended to be about 5 points higher than their WISC-III counterparts. In a sample of 65 children with reading disability, Chin, Ledesma, Cirino, and others (2001) also found that the K-BIT overestimated

WISC-III IQs by 1.2 to 5.0 points, on average. However, their study also showed that, in individual cases, K-BIT scores can underestimate or overestimate WISC-III scores by as much as 25 points, reaffirming that the K-BIT is not appropriate for placement and diagnostic purposes. Canivez (1995) found comparable scores between the K-BIT and the WISC-III for 137 elementary and middle school children and also reported very strong correlations between the two tests, especially for overall scores ($r = .87$). Eisenstein and Engelhart (1997) found that the K-BIT performed well in estimating IQs in adult neuropsychology referrals, but Donders (1995) recommends caution when using the test with brain-injured children. The reason for caution is that K-BIT scores show a negligible relationship with length of coma; that is, the test is not a good index of neuropsychological status in children. In spite of these cautions about its predecessor, the KBIT-2 is an outstanding screening measure of general intelligence for use in research or in those situations listed earlier in which time constraints preclude use of a longer instrument.

# ● INDIVIDUAL TESTS OF ACHIEVEMENT

Whereas intelligence tests are designed to measure the broad mental abilities of the individual, achievement tests are intended to appraise what a person has learned in school or some other course of study. Group achievement tests are paper-and-pencil measures given to dozens of students at a time. These kinds of measures are discussed in Topic 6A, Group Tests of Ability and Related Concepts. Our focus here is on *individual* achievement tests administered one-on-one and, therefore, better suited for the appraisal of learning problems.

Of course, scores on intelligence and achievement tests should bear a strong relationship to one another—brighter children likely are capable of higher achievement. In fact, as we shall see,

the notion that intelligence and achievement typically parallel one another is at the very heart of the concept of learning disability—which commonly involves a discrepancy between the two. We introduce the reader here to the makeup of individual achievement tests as a backdrop to the final topic in this chapter, the assessment of learning disabilities.

More than a dozen individually administered intelligence tests exist, but only a few are widely used in clinical and educational assessment. A number of prominent individual achievement tests are summarized in Table 5.13. Owing to limitations of space, we have selected one test, the Kaufman Test of Educational Achievement-II (KTEA-II), for more detailed presentation (Kaufman & Kaufman, 2004b). Readers who seek further information are encouraged to consult Sattler (2001, Chapter 17) or the *Mental Measurements Yearbook* series.

## Kaufman Test of Educational Achievement-II (KTEA-II)

The KTEA-II is an untimed test of educational achievement for children ages 4½ through 25. A brief, three-subtest version exists and extends the age range to 90+, but for diagnostic assessment of learning difficulties the Comprehensive Form is preferred. The core of the KTEA-II Comprehensive Form consists of eight subtests in four areas:

> **Reading**
> Letter and Word Recognition
> Reading Comprehension
>
> **Mathematics**
> Math Concepts and Applications
> Math Computation
>
> **Written Language**
> Written Expression
> Spelling
>
> **Oral Language**
> Listening Comprehension
> Oral Expression

## ● TABLE 5.13   Survey of Widely Used Individual Achievement Tests

### Diagnostic Achievement Battery-3 (DAB-3)
(Newcomer, 2001)

Suitable for ages 6 through 14, the DAB-3 consists of 14 subtests used to compute eight diagnostic composites. The composite scores include Listening, Speaking, Reading, Writing, Mathematics, Spoken Language, Written Language, and Total Achievement. More comprehensive than most achievement tests, the DAB-3 takes up to two hours to administer. The test was carefully normed on 1,534 children nationwide.

### Kaufman Test of Educational Achievement (KTEA-II)
(Kaufman & Kaufman, 2004b)

A well-normed individual test of educational achievement, a special feature of the KTEA-II is the detailed error analysis (see text). Currently, norms extend from age 4½ through age 25. A separate brief form that can be administered in 30 minutes or less is useful for screening purposes.

### Mini-Battery of Achievement (MBA)
(Woodcock, McGrew, & Werder, 1994)

Assesses four broad achievement areas—reading, writing, mathematics, and factual knowledge—for persons ages 4 through 90+. The complete battery can be administered in 30 minutes. The MBA provides a more extensive coverage of basic and applied skills than any other brief battery. For example, the reading component assesses letter-word identification, vocabulary, and comprehension.

### Peabody Individual Achievement Test-Revised-Normative Update (PIAT-R/NU)   (Markwardt, 1989)

For ages 5 through 22, this 60-minute test includes subtests of general information, reading recognition, reading comprehension, mathematics, and spelling. A new subtest, written expression, is now offered for screening written language skills. Administration of the PIAT-R/NU requires minimal training; the test can be administered by properly trained classroom teachers.

### Wechsler Individual Achievement Test-II
(WIAT-II)   (Wechsler, 2001)

The WIAT-II consists of nine subtests: oral language, listening comprehension, written expression, spelling, word reading, pseudoword decoding, reading comprehension, numerical operations, and mathematics reasoning. The test is suitable for children age 4 through adults age 89 and is empirically linked with all of the Wechsler intelligence scales. Administration to older persons can take up to 75 minutes. Selected subtests can be administered for brief screening purposes.

### Woodcock-Johnson III Tests of Achievement
(WJ III)   (Woodcock, McGrew, & Mather, 2001)

The WJ III covers individuals from 2 years of age through adulthood. The WJ III is co-normed with a separate set of cognitive measures, the WJ III Tests of Cognitive Abilities. The achievement battery is perhaps the most extensive and comprehensive of any test in this area and provides for assessment in reading, oral language, math, written language, and academic knowledge. Area scores are directly linked to federal standards of Public Law 94-142.

### Wide Range Achievement Test-4 (WRAT-4)
(Wilkinson & Robertson, 2006)

Well normed for ages 5 through 94, the WRAT-IV is widely used as a screening instrument. The subtests include: Word Reading (letter and word recognition as gauged by correct pronunciation), Sentence Comprehension (ability to comprehend ideas and information in sentences), Spelling (traditional dictated spelling test), and Math Computation (ability to perform basic mathematical computations). This brief test (15 to 25 minutes) is not suited for the identification of specific achievement deficits.

---

In addition to yielding scores on each subtest, the battery provides three composite scores (Reading, Mathematics, and Written Language) and a Total Battery Composite. For diagnostic purposes, a number of supplemental subtests designed to evaluate reading skills (e.g., Phonological Awareness) are also available. For older children, the test takes about 80 minutes to administer; for younger children about 30 minutes are needed. The KTEA-II is co-normed with the KABC-II.

Brief examples of KTEA-II-like items are shown in Table 5.14. These examples would be at

● **TABLE 5.14    Examples of Characteristic KTEA-II Items Applicable to Older Children**

**Letter and Word Recognition**

The examiner points to each word in turn and says, "What word is this?"

duodecagon        obstreperous        correlative
indolence          perspicacity

**Reading Comprehension**

The examiner says, "Do what this says."

Utter a fallacious response to the question, "How many eyes does a cyclops have?"

**Math Concepts and Applications**

The examiner says, "The Missoula Muggers played 80 ball games last year. They won 16 games. What percentage of the games did they win?"

**Mathematics Computation**

The examiner says "Now I want you to work these problems."

$$(X - 7)(X - 9) = \quad \begin{array}{r} 5\text{ lb}\quad5\text{ oz} \\ -2\text{ lb}\;14\text{ oz} \\ \hline \end{array}$$

**Written Expression**

The examiner shows a picture depicting people interacting and asks the student to write a story about the picture.

**Spelling**

The examiner explains the rules for a traditional spelling test concluding with, "I want you to write the word on this sheet."

"Paramour. One's lover is called a paramour."

**Listening Comprehension**

The examiner plays an audio CD track of a story. Then the examiner asks questions about the story designed to assess comprehension.

**Oral Expression**

The student is shown a full-color picture and then asked to tell a story about it. Due to similar format, results can be compared to Written Expression.

the upper end of the subtests, suitable for high school students. The KTEA-II utilizes entry and exit rules for each subtest to ensure that students only encounter items of appropriate difficulty. Scoring is objective and highly reliable. Raw scores

are converted to standard scores (mean of 100, SD of 15) for each subtest, the composite scores, and the Total Battery Composite.

In addition to formal scoring, the KTEA-II provides a systematic method for evaluating the qualitative nature of subtest errors. For example, on the Spelling subtest, errors can be classified according to whether they involve prefixes, suffixes, vowel digraphs (such as *ue* in *blue*) and diphthongs, consonant clusters (such as *scr* in *unscrupulous*), r-controlled patterns (such as *er* in *inferior*), and several other patterns.

Kaufman and Kaufman (2004b) stress that the error analysis provides the diagnostician with a source of information from which instructional objectives can be developed. For example, a weakness in vowel digraphs and diphthongs on the Spelling subtest translates directly to classroom objectives: practice in the spelling and reading of these elements in isolation, progressing to spelling and pronouncing words containing digraphs and diphthongs, and ending in writing and reading sentences containing words with vowel digraphs and diphthongs. The KTEA-II manual contains many useful clinical insights with educational ramifications.

The content validity of the KTEA-II appears to be very strong, but this point may vary from one school system to another. After all, individual school systems may choose to emphasize different domains of achievement. Salvia and Ysseldyke (1991) warn that users must be sensitive to the correspondence of test content with the students' curriculum. As with any achievement test, the user should verify that the content of the KTEA-II is appropriate within the curricular setting. Nonetheless, Kaufman and Kaufman (2004b) offer sufficient evidence for the validity of the test to make a case for general adequacy.

● **NATURE AND ASSESSMENT OF LEARNING DISABILITIES**

Because individual intelligence and achievement tests are foundational to the assessment of learning disabilities, we close this chapter with brief review of this topic. The learning disability (LD) field is one of the fastest-growing areas within assessment. Paradoxically, it is also one of the most controversial and perplexing domains of psychological testing. Some background is needed to understand the role of intelligence and achievement tests in the evaluation of learning disabilities. We begin by asking a seemingly simple question that turns out to have a complicated answer: What is a **learning disability**?

## The Federal Definition of Learning Disabilities

For decades the essential nature of learning disabilities has been understood in terms of a definition embedded in federal law. In 1975, Congress passed Public Law 94-142, the Education for All Handicapped Children Act. One of the provisions of this act was a definition of learning disabilities as follows:

> The term "specific learning disability" means a disorder in one or more of the basic psychological processes involved in understanding or in using language, spoken or written, which may manifest itself in imperfect ability to listen, speak, read, write, spell, or to do mathematical calculations. The term includes such conditions as perceptual handicaps, brain injury, minimal brain dysfunction, dyslexia, and developmental aphasia. The term does not include children who have learning disabilities which are primarily the result of visual, hearing, or motor handicaps, of mental retardation, or emotional disturbance, or of environmental, cultural, or economic disadvantage. (USDE, 1977, p. 65083)

The commitment to a federally mandated definition was reaffirmed in 1990 by passage of Public Law 101-476, the Individuals with Disabilities Education Act (IDEA). Slightly more than half of the states in the United States now follow this model. The remaining states mandate similar approaches.

The federal definition embodied in IDEA also stipulates an operational approach to the identification of children with learning disabilities. Specifically, candidates for an LD diagnosis must demonstrate a severe discrepancy between general ability (intelligence) and specific achievement in one or more of these seven areas:

Oral expression
Listening comprehension
Written expression
Basic reading skill
Reading comprehension
Mathematics calculation
Mathematics reasoning

The discrepancy model for the identification of LD children has functioned as a directive for school psychologists. In effect, the model mandates that psychologists should administer an individual intelligence test (general ability measure) and an individual achievement test (specific achievement measure) and then look for a discrepancy between Full Scale IQ and one or more areas of school achievement (e.g., reading, mathematics, written expression).

In practical terms, a severe discrepancy has been defined as a difference of one standard deviation or more between general intelligence and specific achievement. A common practice in identification of LD children is to compare Full Scale IQ on an individual intelligence test such as the WISC-III with specific achievement scores on an individual achievement test such as the WIAT (Wechsler Individual Achievement Test) or similar instrument that has subtests normed with a mean of 100 and a standard deviation of 15. A difference of 15 points or more between Full Scale IQ and specific achievement in any of the previously listed areas would then raise the suspicion of learning disability.

Unfortunately, the federal definition has not served its intended purposes, and, increasingly, school psychologists and other professionals look to other approaches for understanding and assessing learning disabilities in children. The fundamental problem is that many, many children who exhibit serious learning problems in school and who would benefit from services for LD simply do not meet the psychometric criteria of a severe discrepancy.

## The National Joint Committee on Learning Disabilities Definition

After a lengthy period of confusion and struggle over the definition of learning disabilities, specialists and educators began to rally around a consensus view in the early 1990s. The new definition was proposed by the National Joint Committee on Learning Disabilities (NJCLD), a group of representatives from eight national organizations with a special interest in learning disabilities. Although similar to the federal definition, the new approach contains important contrasts:

> *Learning disabilities* is a general term that refers to a heterogeneous group of disorders manifested by significant difficulties in the acquisition and use of listening, speaking, reading, writing, reasoning, or mathematical abilities. These disorders are intrinsic to the individual, presumed to be due to central nervous system dysfunction, and may occur across the life span. Problems in self-regulatory behaviors, social perception and social interaction may exist with learning disabilities but do not by themselves constitute a learning disability. Although learning disabilities may occur concomitantly with other handicapping conditions (for example, sensory impairment, mental retardation [MR], serious emotional disturbance [ED]) or with extrinsic influences (such as cultural differences, insufficient or inappropriate instruction), they are not the result of those conditions or influences. (NJCLD, 1988, p. 1)

The new definition avoids vague reference to "basic psychological processes," specifies that the disorder is intrinsic to the individual, identifies central nervous system dysfunction as the origin of LD problems, and states explicitly that learning disabilities may extend into adulthood.

Perhaps most important of all, the NJCLD approach abandons the excessive reliance upon discrepancy between ability and achievement as the hallmark of LD. Instead, the new model specifies that the necessary (but not sufficient) condition of LD is that the individual (child or adult) exhibit an intraindividual weakness in one or more of the core areas of academic functioning (listening, speaking, reading, writing, reasoning, or

**Step 1. Intraindividual Discrepancy**
The examiner identifies a significant difficulty in one or more core areas alongside relative strengths in several areas. Core Areas: Listening, Speaking, Reading, Writing, Reasoning, Math, Subject Area.

**Step 2. Discrepancy Intrinsic to the Individual**
The examiner traces the discrepancy to central nervous system dysfunction (e.g., brain injury) or links the discrepancy with information-processing problems (e.g., memory, organization, or learning efficiency).

**Step 3. Related Considerations**
The examiner evaluates the relevance of psychosocial skills, physical abilities, and sensory abilities to the learning disability.

**Step 4. Alternative Explanations**
The examiner rules out alternative explanations (e.g., environmental, cultural, or economic factors; or inappropriate or inadequate instruction).

**Step 5. LD Diagnosis**
The examiner determines that children who pass steps 1 through 4 meet the criteria for an LD diagnosis.

● **FIGURE 5.14** Operationalizing the NJCLD Definition of Learning Disability

*Source:* Based on Brinckerhoff, L., Shaw, S., & McGuire, J. (1993). *Promoting postsecondary education for students with learning disabilities: A handbook for practitioners.* Austin, TX: PRO-ED.

mathematical abilities). Shaw et al. (1995) illustrate how the NJCLD model might look in practice (Figure 5.14). In this approach, the first task is to identify one or more intraindividual weaknesses in the core areas. These are always relative to strengths in several other core areas. In other words, persons who are slow learners in all areas do not meet the criteria of LD. The second step is to trace the learning difficulties to central nervous system dysfunction, which may manifest as problems with information processing. For example, a young adult with a severe weakness in listening (as judged by her inability to learn from the traditional lecture approach to teaching) might exhibit a deficit on a test of verbal memory—confirming that an information-processing problem was at the heart of her disability. The purpose of the third step (examining psychosocial skills, physical and sensory abilities) is to specify additional problems that may need to be addressed for program-planning purposes. Finally, in the fourth step the examiner rules out non-LD explanations for the learning difficulties (since these explanations would mandate a different strategy for remediation).

## The New Face of Learning Disabilities: Response to Intervention

In 2004, Congress reauthorized the Individuals with Disabilities Education Act (IDEA), which is the ongoing legislation governing special services, including the assessment of LD, in school systems that receive federal funding. IDEA 2004 changed the law about how to identify children with specific learning disabilities by moving away from the discrepancy model that had reigned supreme since the 1970s. Instead, the new law recommended **response to intervention** (RTI) as the preferred method for identifying children with learning disabilities. In particular, IDEA 2004 says that a school "may use a process that determines if the child responds to scientific, research-based intervention as part of the evaluation procedures . . . " in its evaluation for LD.

RTI is a broader concept than LD and refers both to (1) methods for increasing the capacity of school systems to respond effectively to the diverse academic needs of students, and (2) approaches for identifying LD children who need special education services. The RTI approach specifically deemphasizes cognitive discrepancies in the diagnostic process, focusing instead on low age-based achievement levels and failure to respond to evidence-based instructional approaches (Fletcher & Vaughn, 2009; Torgerson, 2009).

The implementation of RTI is complicated and multifaceted. The process involves multiple feedback loops and decision points. Yet, proponents of

RTI view it as an improvement because it provides for early, preventive intervention in contrast to the "wait to fail" approach of the discrepancy model. Fuchs and Fuchs (2005) provide a blueprint of how RTI might be put into practice in a school system:

- Step 1: In the first weeks of the school year, students are screened to identify those "at risk" for school failure. For example, system-wide assessment scores might be used to identify students scoring below the 25th percentile in reading or math; also, at-risk students can be nominated by parents and teachers.
- Step 2a: Teachers implement evidence-based curricula/instruction, and the fidelity of implementation is documented.
- Step 2b: At-risk students are monitored for eight weeks to identify those who don't respond adequately, for example, those who score below the 16th percentile in reading or math.
- Step 3a: The nonresponders receive an addition eight weeks of supplementary instruction with evidence-based teaching approaches.
- Step 3b: Appropriate ongoing assessment is used to identify continuing nonresponders; for example, brief monitoring tools could reveal a student's failure to meet the criterion-referenced outcomes designated by the school intervention team.
- Step 4a: Continuing nonresponders receive an individualized, comprehensive evaluation that rules out mental retardation and eliminates other diagnostic possibilities such as visual disabilities or emotional disturbance.
- Step 4b: With the involvement of parents, the designation of LD is then made and special education placement is authorized.

In sum, RTI is a shift in perspective that focuses on early results and outcomes with at-risk children instead of later spending excessive time and resources on questions of discrepancy-based eligibility after children are already failing because of their LD. The hope is that the RTI perspective will catch at-risk children earlier and thereby reduce the number of children needing special education services.

## Essential Features of Learning Disabilities

Even though the definition of LD remains a point of contention, we can cite several features of these disorders that are less controversial. As the reader will discover, the features discussed in the following dictate, to some extent, the nature of testing practices in the assessment of learning disabilities. There is general agreement—with occasional dissenting votes—on the following features of learning disabilities:

1. A learning disability involves an intraindividual discrepancy in cognitive functioning. The child (or adult) with LD reveals a relative weakness in one area compared to strengths in most other areas. According to the federal definition followed within many school systems, the discrepancy is between general ability (intelligence) and specific achievement. We have described previously some of the pitfalls of this definition and prefer the NJCLD approach in which the discrepancy is not rigidly tied to a difference between IQ and achievement test scores.

2. An exclusionary clause is included in most definitions of learning disability. If the academic difficulties are primarily caused by other disabling conditions (mental retardation, emotional disturbance, visual or hearing impairment, cultural or social disadvantage), then a diagnosis of learning disability is typically ruled out. This clause is often misinterpreted. A person can be both learning disabled and impaired in other ways (e.g., have mental retardation). The important point is that the co-existing condition must not be the primary cause of the learning difficulties.

3. Learning disabilities are heterogeneous; that is, there are many different varieties. Research on the identification of subtypes is still in its infancy, but most researchers express optimism that meaningful subgroups of persons with learning disabilities can be identified. Pending further research and refinement, only two broad

categories of learning disability are recognized currently (Forster, 1994). These are as follows:

- Dyslexia or verbal learning disability
- Right hemisphere or nonverbal learning disability

The characteristics of these two major categories of LD are outlined in Table 5.15.

4. A learning disability is a developmental phenomenon that is usually evident in early childhood that may persist into adulthood. Even though remediation efforts should be based upon optimism—so as to avoid self-fulfilling prophecies—a dose of realism is needed, too. Longitudinal studies of children with severe learning disabilities suggest that marked improvement in academic achievement is the exception, not the rule, even when these subjects receive intensive educational intervention. For example, Frauenheim and Heckerl (1983) retested 11 adults diagnosed as having learning disabilities in childhood. All the participants had received special help for reading; nine had graduated from high school, and two completed the tenth grade. Full Scale IQs were typically in the low 90s, with Verbal IQ below average (mean of 85) and Performance IQ above average (mean of 104). In spite of the remedial intervention, when retested as adults on *exactly* the same achievement test (Wide Range Achievement Test), these examinees were scarcely improved from their elementary school results. These findings are corroborated by several other follow-up studies (see Kolb & Whishaw, 1990, chap. 29, for a review). Such results indicate that specialists who work with children with learning disabilities should not become fixated solely on academic concerns. Social and emotional problems—which may be more amenable to intervention—also cry out for notice.

5. Individuals with learning disabilities frequently experience social and emotional difficulties that are as pervasive and consequential as the deficits in academic achievement. These problems may persist into adolescence and

| ● TABLE 5.15   Characteristics of Two Broad Categories of Learning Disability | |
| --- | --- |
| *Dyslexia or Verbal Learning Disability* | *Right Hemisphere or Nonverbal Learning Disability* |
| **Primary Manifestation** | |
| Unexpected difficulty in learning to read or spell | Poor skills in mathematics, handwriting, or social cognition |
| **Fundamental Deficiency** | |
| Problems in phonological coding (associating sounds with letter combinations) | Problems in spatial cognition (visuospatial perception of relationships) |
| **Physiological Correlates** | |
| Subtle anomalies in the left cerebral hemisphere (revealed by brain scans and EEG studies) | Likely origin in right cerebral hemisphere dysfunction |
| **Relative Prevalence** | |
| About 90% of all LD cases | About 10% of all LD cases |
| **Ratio of boys to girls** | |
| 3:1 or 4:1 | 1:1 |

*Source:* Based on Forster, A. (1994). Learning disabilities. In R. J. Sternberg (Ed.), *Encyclopedia of human intelligence.* New York: Macmillan.

adulthood. In fact, the socioemotional sequelae often become the primary presenting complaint, which can complicate the testing process and obscure the diagnosis. For example, in a needs assessment study of 381 adults with learning disabilities, Hoffman, Sheldon, Minskoff, and others (1987) identified several crucial nonacademic areas meriting intervention by service providers. These adults self-endorsed several social and emotional problems with high frequency: feeling frustrated (40 percent), talking or acting before thinking (33 percent), being shy (31 percent), no self-confidence (28 percent), controlling emotions and temper (28 percent), and dating (27 percent). Many other problems were also endorsed, but by less than 25 percent of the sample. These findings indicate that learning disability assessments should incorporate measures of social and emotional functioning. Vaughn and Haager (1994) provide an excellent overview on

the measurement of social skills in persons with learning disability.

## Causes and Correlates of Learning Disabilities

Approximately 4 to 5 percent of all school-aged children receive a diagnosis of LD, so this is not a rare problem (Lyon, 1996). The most common form of LD is dyslexia, and boys outnumber girls by about 3:2 (Nass, 1992). In a minority of cases, the etiology is clear and can be attributed to a specific cause such as a known brain injury. Left hemisphere impairment is especially likely to result in verbal difficulties, whereas right hemisphere impairment may lead to problems with spatial thinking or other nonverbal skills. Thus, head injury or other neurological problems can be the proximate cause of a child receiving an LD diagnosis.

However, in the majority of cases the direct etiology of LD problems is unclear. A number of possibilities have been proposed and these may explain some but not all cases of LD. For example, pathological neurodevelopmental processes have been identified in some persons with severe dyslexia (Culbertson & Edmonds, 1996). Individuals with this disorder appear to have alterations in brain structures such as the planum temporale (the flat surface on the top of the temporal lobes) known to be important for language processing. Whereas in normal individuals the planum temporale is much larger in the left temporal lobe than in the right, persons with severe dyslexia do not show this pattern of asymmetry (tending toward symmetry instead). Moreover, researchers have identified microscopic cortical malformations called polymicrogyria (numerous small convolutions) that parallel these structural differences. Several postmortem studies of persons with severe dyslexia have revealed these deviations at the cellular level. Spreen (2001) provides an outstanding review of the possible neurological substrates of learning disabilities. Dyslexia also appears to show a significant genetic component for some persons such that the idea of familial dyslexia needs to be taken seriously. However, what must be emphasized is that for most individuals the etiology of LD (whether dyslexia or other forms) remains a mystery.

## Achievement Tests in LD Assessment: A Final Word

Learning disabilities manifest primarily as academic problems; that is, a child with LD is typically unable to master skills important for school success such as reading, mathematics, or written communication. Because school-based accom-

plishment is at the heart of the problem, an evaluation for LD must include relevant measures of academic achievement. Furthermore, the evaluation of school achievement—one small part of an LD assessment—must be based on an *individual* test of achievement. Even though a group achievement test might raise the suspicion of a learning disability, practitioners must rely on individual achievement tests for definitive assessment.

Individual achievement tests typically are administered one-on-one with the examiner sitting across from the respondent and posing structured questions and problems. Of course, any well-standardized achievement test will yield normative data about the functioning of a schoolchild. But the special virtue of individual achievement tests is that the examiner can observe the clinical details of deficient (or superior) performance and form hypotheses about the cognitive capacities of the examinee.

Consider the problem of poor spelling, widely observed in children and adults with verbal LD. Any good spelling achievement test will document the disability; however, little insight is gained from mere scores. What the examiner should seek to know is the qualitative nature of the problem, not just its quantitative dimensions. Individual achievement tests are invaluable in this regard. By observing the details of deficient performance, an astute examiner can form hypotheses about the origin of an achievement problem. For example, a child whose spelling is phonetically correct is at least *hearing* the words correctly, whereas a child with nonphonetic spelling might very well reveal a problem with auditory processing of speech sounds.

## ●SUMMARY

1. For purposes of estimating general intelligence, any well-normed mainstream instrument will suffice. However, for purposes of individualized assessment, examiners need to consider the particular strengths and weaknesses of potential instruments.

2. David Wechsler was a pragmatist who borrowed heavily from the Army Alpha and Beta tests in fashioning many of the subtests for the various Wechsler tests. For each of his intelligence tests, Wechsler used 10 to 15 subtests, with a mix of verbal and performance components.

3. The first Wechsler test was the Wechsler-Bellevue, published in 1939 and updated in 1946. Other tests and their dates of latest revision are Wechsler Preschool and Primary Scale of Intelligence-III (2002), Wechsler Intelligence Scale for Children-IV (2003), and Wechsler Adult Intelligence Scale-IV (2008).

4. All of the Wechsler scales use the same format: 10 to 15 subtests; a common metric for IQ, with a mean of 100 and standard deviation of 15; a common core of subtests, so that examiners can easily transfer their test-administering skill from one scale to another.

5. The Wechsler Adult Intelligence Scale-IV (WAIS-IV) is the most widely used individual test of adult intelligence. The test has excellent reliability and well-established validity.

6. Factor analysis of the Wechsler Intelligence Scale for Children-IV (WISC-IV, for children ages 6 to 16½) often yields a four-factor solution: Verbal Comprehension, Perceptual Reasoning, Working Memory, and Processing Speed.

7. The newly released Stanford-Binet: Fifth Edition (SB5) features the partition of intelligence into five factors and two domains (verbal and non-verbal), resulting in 10 subtests. The five factors, each represented by verbal and nonverbal subtests, are Fluid Reasoning, Knowledge, Quantitative Reasoning, Visual-Spatial Reasoning, and Working Memory.

8. Special features of the SB5 include extensive high-end and improved low-end items, so that the test excels at both extremes of the cognitive spectrum. The SB5 is also the first intelligence test to consider religious diversity (Christian, Jewish, Muslim, Hindu, and Buddhist backgrounds) in the evaluation of test fairness.

9. The Detroit Tests of Learning Aptitude-4 (DTLA-4) consists of 10 subtests that form the basis for computing 16 composites. The DTLA-4 is a good measure of general intelligence, but the conceptual breakdown into 14 ability areas needs empirical support.

10. The Kaufman Assessment Battery for Children-II (KABC-II) is an appealing test designed for children and adolescents ages 3 to 18. The instrument is grounded in two theories of intelligence: Luria's neuropsychological theory of processing and the Cattell-Horn-Carroll (CHC) theory of broad and narrow abilities.

11. The Kaufman Adolescent and Adult Intelligence Test (KAIT) is a brief measure of intelligence constructed broadly within the Cattell-Horn model of fluid and crystallized intelligence. Suitable for ages 11 to 85+, the core battery of the test consists of six subtests that can be administered in roughly two-thirds the time needed for most individual intelligence tests.

12. The Kaufman Brief Intelligence Test-2 (KBIT-2) is a well-normed screening test of general intelligence that consists of Vocabulary and Matrices. KBIT-2 scores show strong correlations with other mainstream measures of intelligence.

13. Individual achievement tests such as the Kaufman Test of Educational Achievement-II (KTEA-II) are designed to appraise student progress in academic areas such as reading, mathematics, written language, and oral expression. These instruments are essential to the evaluation of learning disabilities.

14. Although difficult to define, a learning disability may signify a discrepancy between general ability and specific achievement, although this is no longer considered a defining feature. Two broad forms of learning disability are recognized: dyslexia or verbal learning disability, and nonverbal learning disability.

## ● KEY TERMS AND CONCEPTS

IQ constancy   p. 180

routing procedure   p. 195

learning disability   p. 195

response to intervention   p. 209

# Chapter 6

# Group Tests and Controversies in Ability Testing

## TOPIC 6A

## Group Tests of Ability and Related Concepts

The practical success of early intelligence scales such as the 1905 Binet-Simon test motivated psychologists and educators to develop instruments that could be administered simultaneously to large numbers of examinees. Test developers were quick to realize that group tests allowed for the efficient evaluation of dozens or hundreds of examinees at the same time. As reviewed in an earlier chapter, one of the first uses of group tests was for screening and assignment of military personnel during World War I. The need to quickly test thousands of Army recruits inspired psychologists in the United States, led by Robert M. Yerkes, to make rapid advances in psychometrics and test development (Yerkes, 1921). Many new applications followed immediately—in education, industry, and other fields. In Topic 6A, Group Tests of Ability and Related Concepts, we introduce the reader to the varied applications of group tests and also review a sampling of typical instruments. In addition, we explore a key question raised by the consequential nature of these tests—can examinees boost their scores significantly by taking targeted test preparation courses? This is but one of many unexpected issues raised by the widespread use of group tests. In Topic 6B, Test Bias and Other Controversies, we continue a reflective theme by looking into test bias and other contentious issues in testing.

## ● NATURE, PROMISE, AND PITFALLS OF GROUP TESTS

Group tests serve many purposes, but the vast majority can be assigned to one of three types: ability, aptitude, or achievement tests. In the real world, the distinction among these kinds of tests often is quite fuzzy (Gregory, 1994a). These instruments differ mainly in their functions and applications, less so in actual test content. In brief, ability tests typically sample a broad assortment of proficiencies in order to estimate current intellectual level. This information might be used for screening or placement purposes, for example, to determine the need for individual testing or to establish eligibility for a gifted and talented program. In contrast, aptitude tests usually measure a few homogeneous segments of ability and are designed to predict future performance. Predictive validity is foundational to aptitude tests, and often they are used for institutional selection purposes. Finally, achievement tests assess current skill attainment in relation to the goals of school and training programs. They are designed to mirror educational objectives in reading, writing, math, and other subject areas. Although often used to identify educational attainment of students, they also function to evaluate the adequacy of school educational programs.

Whatever their application, group tests differ from individual tests in five ways:

- Multiple-choice versus open-ended format
- Objective machine scoring versus examiner scoring
- Group versus individualized administration
- Applications in screening versus remedial planning
- Huge versus merely large standardization samples

These differences allow for great speed and cost efficiency in group testing, but a price is paid for these advantages.

Although the early psychometric pioneers embraced group testing wholeheartedly, they recognized fully the nature of their Faustian bargain: Psychologists had traded the soul of the individual examinee in return for the benefits of mass testing. Whipple (1910) summed up the advantages of group testing but also pointed to the potential perils:

> Most mental tests may be administered either to individuals or to groups. Both methods have advantages and disadvantages. The group method has, of course, the particular merit of economy of time; a class of 50 or 100 children may take a test in less than a fiftieth or a hundredth of the time needed to administer the same test individually. Again, in certain comparative studies, e.g., of the effects of a week's vacation upon the mental efficiency of school children, it becomes imperative that all S's should take the tests at the same time. On the other hand, there are almost sure to be some S's in every group that, for one reason or another, fail to follow instructions or to execute the test to the best of their ability. The individual method allows E to detect these cases, and in general, by the exercise of personal supervision, to gain, as noted above, valuable information concerning S's attitude toward the test.

In sum, group testing poses two interrelated risks: (1) some examinees will score far below their true ability, owing to motivational problems or difficulty following directions; and (2) invalid scores will not be recognized as such, with undesirable consequences for these atypical examinees. There is really no simple way to entirely avoid these risks, which are part of the trade-off for the efficiency of group testing. However, it is possible to minimize the potentially negative consequences if examiners scrutinize very low scores with skepticism and recommend individual testing for these cases.

We turn now to an analysis of group tests in a variety of settings, including cognitive tests for schools and clinics, placement tests for career and military evaluation, and aptitude tests for college and postgraduate selection.

# ● GROUP TESTS OF ABILITY

## Multidimensional Aptitude Battery-II (MAB-II)

The Multidimensional Aptitude Battery-II (MAB-II; Jackson, 1998) is a recent group intelligence test designed to be a paper-and-pencil equivalent of the WAIS-R. As the reader will recall, the WAIS-R is a highly respected instrument (now replaced by the WAIS-III), in its time the most widely used of the available adult intelligence tests. Kaufman (1983) noted that the WAIS-R was "the criterion of adult intelligence, and no other instrument even comes close." However, a highly trained professional needs about 1½ hours just to administer the Wechsler adult test to a single person. Because professional time is at a premium, a complete Wechsler intelligence assessment—including administration, scoring, and report writing—easily can cost hundreds of dollars. Many examiners have long suspected that an appropriate group test, with the attendant advantages of objective scoring and computerized narrative report, could provide an equally valid and much less expensive alternative to individual testing for most persons.

The MAB-II was designed to produce subtests and factors parallel to the WAIS-R but employing a multiple-choice format capable of being computer scored. The apparent goal in designing this test was to produce an instrument that could be administered to dozens or hundreds of persons by one examiner (and perhaps a few proctors) with minimal training. In addition, the MAB-II was designed to yield IQ scores with psychometric properties similar to those found on the WAIS-R. Appropriate for examinees from ages 16 to 74, the MAB-II yields 10 subtest scores, as well as Verbal, Performance, and Full Scale IQs.

Although it consists of original test items, the MAB-II is mainly a sophisticated subtest-by-subtest

clone of the WAIS-R. The 10 subtests are listed as follows:

| Verbal | Performance |
|---|---|
| Information | Digit Symbol |
| Comprehension | Picture Completion |
| Arithmetic | Spatial |
| Similarities | Picture Arrangement |
| Vocabulary | Object Assembly |

The reader will notice that Digit Span from the WAIS-R is not included on the MAB-II. The reason for this omission is largely practical: There would be no simple way to present a Digit-Span-like subtest in paper-and-pencil format. In any case, the omission is not serious. Digit Span has the lowest correlation with overall WAIS-R IQ, and it is widely recognized that this subtest makes a minimal contribution to the measurement of general intelligence.

The only significant deviation from the WAIS-R is the replacement of Block Design with a Spatial subtest on the MAB-II. In the Spatial subtest, examinees must mentally perform spatial rotations of figures and select one of five possible rotations presented as their answer (Figure 6.1). Only mental rotations are involved (although "flipped-over" versions of the original stimulus are included as distractor items). The advanced items are very complex and demanding.

The items within each of the 10 MAB-II subtests are arranged in order of increasing difficulty, beginning with questions and problems that most adolescents and adults find quite simple and proceeding upward to items that are so difficult that very few persons get them correct. There is no penalty for guessing and examinees are encouraged to respond to every item within the time limit. Unlike the WAIS-R in which the verbal subtests are untimed power measures, every MAB-II subtest incorporates elements of both power and speed: Examinees are allowed only seven minutes to work on each subtest. Including instructions, the Verbal and Performance portions of the MAB-II each take about 50 minutes to administer.

The MAB-II is a relatively minor revision of the MAB, and the technical features of the two

**Picture Completion** — Choose the letter that begins the word describing the missing part of the picture.

| A. | L |
|----|---|
| B. | E |
| C. | B |
| D. | W |
| E. | F |

The answer is **Light**, so **A** should be marked.

**Spatial** — Choose one figure to the right of the vertical line which is the same as the figure on the left. One figure can be turned to look like the figure on the left; the others would have to be flipped over.

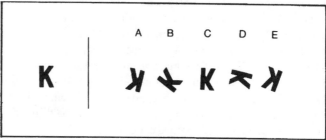

The correct answer is **A**, so **A** should be marked. The others **BCDE** would have to be flipped over.

**Object Assembly** — Choose the order, from left to right, in which these parts should be placed to form the object.

| A. | 3 | 2 | 1 |
|----|---|---|---|
| B. | 2 | 1 | 3 |
| C. | 1 | 3 | 2 |
| D. | 2 | 3 | 1 |
| E. | 3 | 1 | 2 |

The correct answer is **C-132** so **C** should be marked. Only this order would create the object **teacup**.

● **FIGURE 6.1** Demonstration Items from Three Performance Tests of the Multidimensional Aptitude Battery-II (MAB)

*Source:* Reprinted with permission from Jackson, D. N. (1984a). *Manual for the Multidimensional Aptitude Battery.* Port Huron, MI: Sigma Assessment Systems, Inc. (800) 265-1285.

versions are nearly identical. A great deal of psychometric information is available for the original version, which we report here. With regard to reliability, the results are generally quite impressive.

For example, in one study of over 500 adolescents ranging in age from 16 to 20, the internal consistency reliability of Verbal, Performance, and Full Scale IQs was in the high .90s. Test-retest data for this instrument also excel. In a study of 52 young psychiatric patients, the individual subtests showed reliabilities that ranged from .83 to .97 (median of .90) for the Verbal scale and from .87 to .94 (median of .91) for the Performance scale (Jackson, 1984). These results compare quite favorably with the psychometric standards reported for the WAIS-R.

Factor analyses of the MAB-II are broadly supportive of the construct validity of this instrument and its predecessor (Lee, Wallbrown, & Blaha, 1990). Most recently, Gignac (2006) examined the factor structure of the MAB-II using a series of confirmatory factor analyses with data on 3,121 individuals reported in Jackson (1998). The best fit to the data was provided by a nested model consisting of a first-order general factor, a first-order Verbal Intelligence factor, and a first-order Performance Intelligence factor. The one caveat of this study was that Arithmetic did not load specifically on the Verbal Intelligence factor independent of its contribution to the general factor.

Other researchers have noted the strong congruence between factor analyses of the WAIS-R (with Digit Span removed) and the MAB. Typically, separate Verbal and Performance factors emerge for both tests (Wallbrown, Carmin, & Barnett, 1988). In a large sample of inmates, Ahrens, Evans, and Barnett (1990) observed validity-confirming changes in MAB scores in relation to education level. In general, with the possible exception that Arithmetic does not contribute reliably to the Verbal factor, there is good justification for the use of separate Verbal and Performance scales on this test.

In general, the validity of this test rests upon its very strong physical and empirical resemblance to its parent test, the WAIS-R. Correlational data between MAB and WAIS-R scores are crucial in this regard. For 145 persons administered the MAB and WAIS-R in counterbalanced fashion, correlations between subtests ranged from .44 (Spatial/Block Design) to .89 (Arithmetic and Vocabulary), with a median of .78. WAIS-R and MAB IQ correlations were very healthy, namely, .92 for Verbal IQ, .79 for Performance IQ, and .91 for Full Scale IQ (Jackson, 1984a). With only a few exceptions, correlations between MAB and WAIS-R scores exceed those between the WAIS and the WAIS-R. Carless (2000) reported a similar, strong overlap between MAB scores and WAIS-R scores in a study of 85 adults for the Verbal, Performance, and Full Scale IQ scores. However, she found that 4 of the 10 MAB subtests did not correlate with the WAIS-R subscales they were designed to represent, suggesting caution in using this instrument to obtain detailed information about specific abilities.

The MAB-II shows great promise in research, career counseling, and personnel selection. In addition, this test could function as a screening instrument in clinical settings, as long as the examiner views low scores as a basis for follow-up testing with an individual intelligence test. Examiners must keep in mind that the MAB-II is a group test and, therefore, carries with it the potential for misuse in individual cases. The MAB-II should not be used in isolation for diagnostic decisions or for placement into programs such as classes for intellectually gifted persons.

### A Multilevel Battery: The Cognitive Abilities Test (CogAT)

One important function of psychological testing is to assess students' abilities that are prerequisite to traditional classroom-based learning. In designing tests for this purpose, the psychometrician must contend with the obvious and nettlesome problem that school-aged children differ hugely in their intellectual abilities. For example, a test appropriate for a sixth grader will be much too easy for a tenth grader, yet impossibly difficult for a third grader.

The answer to this dilemma is a multilevel battery, a series of overlapping tests. In a multilevel battery, each group test is designed for a specific age or grade level, but adjacent tests possess some common content. Because of the overlapping content with adjacent age or grade levels, each test possesses a suitably low floor and high ceiling for proper assessment of students at both extremes of ability. Virtually every school system in the United States uses at least one nationally normed multilevel battery.

The Cognitive Abilities Test (CogAT) is one of the best school-based test batteries in current use (Lohman & Hagen, 2001). A recent revision of the test is the CogAT Multilevel Edition, Form 6, released in 2001. Norms for 2005 also are available. We discuss this instrument in some detail.

The CogAT evolved from the Lorge-Thorndike Intelligence Tests, one of the first group tests of intelligence intended for widespread use within school systems. The CogAT is primarily a measure of scholastic ability but also incorporates a nonverbal reasoning battery with items that bear no direct relation to formal school instruction. The two primary batteries, suitable for students in kindergarten through third grade, are briefly discussed at the end of this section. Here we review the multilevel edition intended for students in third through twelfth grade.

The nine subtests of the multilevel CogAT are grouped into three areas: Verbal, quantitative, and nonverbal, each including three subtests. Representative items for the subtests of the CogAT are depicted in Figure 6.2. The tests on the Verbal Battery evaluate verbal skills and reasoning strategies (inductive and deductive) needed for effective reading and writing. The tests on the Quantitative Battery appraise quantitative skills important for mathematics and other disciplines. The Nonverbal Battery can be used to estimate cognitive level of students with limited reading skill, poor English proficiency, or inadequate educational exposure.

For each CogAT subtest, items are ordered by difficulty level in a single test booklet. However, entry and exit points differ for each of eight overlapping levels (A through H). In this manner, grade-appropriate items are provided for all examinees.

## Verbal Battery

1. *Verbal Classification*
Circle the item below that belongs with these three:

milk    butter    cheese

A. eggs       B. yogurt       C. grocery
D. bacon      E. recipe

2. *Sentence Completion*
Circle the word below that best completes this sentence:

Fish _____ in the ocean.

A. sit        B. next        C. fly
D. swim       E. climb

3. *Verbal Analogies*
Circle the word that best fits this analogy:

Right $\rightarrow$ Left : Top $\rightarrow$

A. Side       B. Out        C. Wrong
D. On         E. Bottom

## Quantitative Battery

4. *Quantitative Relations*
Circle the choice that depicts the relationship between I and II:

I. 6/2 + 1
II. 9/3 − 1

A. I is greater than II       B. I is equal to II
C. I is less than II

5. *Number Series*
Circle the number below that comes next in this series:

1   11   6   16   11   21   16

A. 31     B. 16     C. 26     D. 6     E. 11

6. *Equation Building*
Circle the choice below that could be derived from these:

1   2   4   +   −

A. −1     B. 7     C. 0     D. 1     E. −3

● **FIGURE 6.2**    Subtests and Representative Items of the Cognitive Abilities Test, Form 6

**Nonverbal Battery**

7. *Figure Classification*
Circle the item below that belongs with these three figures:

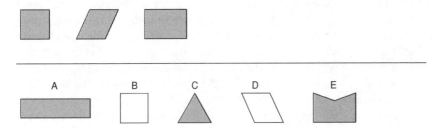

8. *Figure Analogies*
Circle the figure below that best fits with this analogy:

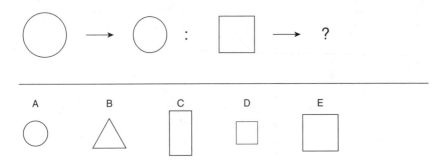

9. *Figure Analysis*
Circle the choice below that fits this paper folding and hole punching:

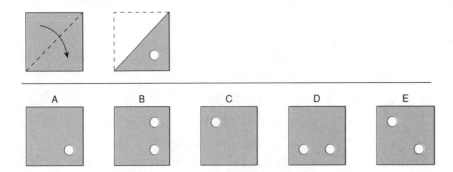

Note: These items resemble those on the CogAT 6. Correct answers: *1: B. yogurt* (the only dairy product). *2: D. swim* (fish swim in the ocean). *3: E. bottom* (the opposite of top). *4: A. I is greater than II* (4 is greater than 2). *5: C. 26* (the algorithm is add 10, subtract 5, add 10 ... ). *6: A. −1* (the only answer that fits) *7: A* (four-sided shape that is filled in). *8: D* (same shape, bigger to smaller). *9: E* (correct answer).

● **FIGURE 6.2**    *continued*

The subtests are strictly timed, with limits that vary from eight to twelve minutes. Each of the three batteries can be administered in less than an hour. However, the manual recommends three successive testing days for younger children. For older children, two batteries should be administered the first day, with a single testing period the next.

Raw scores for each battery can be transformed into an age-based normalized standard score with mean of 100 and standard deviation of 15. In addition, percentile ranks and stanines for age groups and grade level are also available. Interpolation was used to determine fall, winter, and spring grade-level norms.

The CogAT was co-normed (standardized concurrently) with two achievement tests, the Iowa Tests of Basic Skills and the Iowa Tests of Educational Development. Concurrent standardization with achievement measures is a common and desirable practice in the norming of multilevel intelligence tests. The particular virtue of joint norming is that the expected correspondence between intelligence and achievement scores is determined with great precision. As a consequence, examiners can more accurately identify underachieving students in need of remediation or further assessment for potential learning disability.

The reliability of the CogAT is exceptionally good. In previous editions, the Kuder-Richardson-20 reliability estimates for the multilevel batteries averaged .94 (Verbal), .92 (Quantitative), and .93 (Nonverbal) across all grade levels. The six-month test-retest reliabilities for alternate forms ranged from .85 to .93 (Verbal), .78 to .88 (Quantitative), and .81 to .89 (Nonverbal).

The manual provides a wealth of information on content, criterion-related, and construct validity of the CogAT; we summarize only the most pertinent points here. Correlations between the CogAT and achievement batteries are substantial. For example, the CogAT verbal battery correlates in the .70s to .80s with achievement subtests from the Iowa Tests of Basic Skills.

The CogAT batteries predict school grades reasonably well. Correlations range from the .30s to the .60s, depending on grade level, sex, and ethnic group. There does not appear to be a clear trend as to which battery is best at predicting grade point average. Correlations between the CogAT and individual intelligence tests are also substantial, typically ranging from .65 to .75. These findings speak well for the construct validity of the CogAT insofar as the Stanford-Binet is widely recognized as an excellent measure of individual intelligence.

Ansorge (1985) has questioned whether all three batteries are really necessary. He points out that correlations among the Verbal, Quantitative, and Nonverbal batteries are substantial. The median values across all grades are as follows:

| | |
|---|---|
| Verbal and Quantitative | .78 |
| Nonverbal and Quantitative | .78 |
| Verbal and Nonverbal | .72 |

Since the Quantitative battery offers little uniqueness, from a purely psychometric point of view there is no justification for including it. Nonetheless, the test authors recommend use of all batteries in hopes that differences in performance will assist teachers in remedial planning. However, the test authors do not make a strong case for doing this.

A study by Stone (1994) provides a notable justification for using the CogAT as a basis for student evaluation. He found that CogAT scores for 403 third graders provided an unbiased prediction of student achievement that was more accurate than teacher ratings. In particular, teacher ratings showed bias against caucasian and Asian American students by underpredicting their achievement scores.

### Culture Fair Intelligence Test (CFIT)

The Culture Fair Intelligence Test (Cattell, 1940; IPAT, 1973) is a nonverbal measure of fluid intelligence first conceived in the 1920s by the prominent measurement psychologist Raymond B. Cattell. The goal of the CFIT is to measure fluid intelligence—analytical and reasoning ability in abstract and novel situations—in a manner that is as "free" of cultural bias as possible. This test was originally called the Culture Free Intelligence Test.

The name was changed when it became evident that cultural influences cannot be completely extirpated from tests of intelligence.

The CFIT has undergone several revisions, emerging in its current form in 1961. The test consists of three versions: Scale 1 is for use with mentally defective adults and children ages 4 to 8; Scale 2 is for adults in the average range of intelligence and children ages 8 to 13; Scale 3 is for high-ability adults and for high school and college students. Scale 1 involves considerable interaction between tester and examinee—four of the subtests must be administered individually. Thus, in some respects Scale 1 is more of an individual intelligence test than a group test. We discuss only Scales 2 and 3 here, because they are truly group tests of intelligence. These two tests differ mainly in difficulty level.

Two equivalent forms, called Form A and Form B, are available for each scale. The test developers recommend administering both forms to each examinee to obtain what is called the full test. Each form by itself is referred to as a short test. In spite of the recommendation to use both forms as a combined test, it is very common for CFIT users to rely on a single, brief form for purposes of screening.

Each form consists of four subtests: Series, Classification, Matrices, and Conditions. All of these subtests are figural and nonverbal in nature. Of course, each subtest is preceded by several practice items. The entire test is neatly packaged in an eight-page booklet.

The CFIT is a highly speeded test. Each form of Scales 2 and 3 takes about 30 minutes to administer, but only 12.5 minutes is devoted to actual test taking. Results can, therefore, be misleading for persons who place no premium on speed of performance in problem solving. Fortunately, Scale 2 can be used as an untimed power test. However, the norms for this manner of administration are limited (IPAT, 1973).

Test-retest, alternate-forms, and internal consistency reliabilities are generally in the .70s for individual forms of Scales 2 and 3. The reliabilities of the full test are higher, generally in the mid-.80s.

These results are based on dozens of studies with thousands of subjects and indicate a respectable degree of reliability for such a short instrument (IPAT, 1973).

The validity of the CFIT as a measure of general intelligence is established beyond any reasonable skepticism. CFIT scores correlate in the mid-.80s with the general factor of intelligence and show consistently robust relationships—largely in the .70s and .80s—with other mainstream measures of intelligence (WAIS, WISC, Raven Progressive Matrices, Stanford-Binet, Otis, and General Aptitude Test Battery; see IPAT, 1973, p. 11). There is no doubt that the CFIT is a well-designed, useful, and valid test of intelligence.

But is the CFIT a **culture-fair test,** as its title proclaims? One professed goal of this instrument was to "minimize irrelevant influences of cultural learning and social climate" and thereby produce a "cleaner separation of natural ability from specific learning" (IPAT, 1973). Unfortunately, the available evidence indicates that the CFIT is no more successful than traditional measures in the pursuit of a culturally fair method for measuring intelligence. For example, Willard (1968) found that 83 culturally disadvantaged African American children scored about the same on the Stanford-Binet ($M = 68.1$) as on the CFIT ($M = 70.0$). Moreover, 14 of the children hit the CFIT "floor" and received the lowest possible CFIT IQ score of 57, whereas Stanford-Binet IQs scores were dispersed in a pattern more like a bell-shaped curve. Nenty (1986) administered the CFIT to 600 Americans, 231 Indians, and 803 Nigerians to assess the cross-cultural validity of the test and concluded that many individual test items did not retain the same relative difficulty level in the three samples. This suggests that the CFIT does not have universal validity as a measure of fluid intelligence.

The CFIT is an excellent brief, nonverbal measure of general intelligence. Even when Form A and Form B are both used to obtain what is referred to as the full test, the CFIT can be administered to large groups in less than an hour. An important caution to test users is that the laudable goal of producing a culture-fair test has not been accomplished by the CFIT. Moreover, the goal itself may be chimerical:

> Cultures differ with respect to the importance they place on competition with peers in performing tasks or solving problems, on speed or quality of performance, and on a variety of other test-related behaviors. Some cultures emphasize concrete rather than abstract problem solving, often to the extent that a problem has no meaning except in a concrete setting. The very notion of taking some artificially contrived test is nonsensical in such situations. (Koch, 1984)

It is doubtful that a truly culture-fair test is even possible. In future editions, the CFIT developers would be well advised to rename their test so that unsophisticated users do not invest this instrument with imaginary properties.

Even though the CFIT is a worthy test, it is badly in need of revision and renorming. The test is rather old-fashioned in appearance. Some of the test item drawings are so small that only persons with perfect vision can infer the figural relations depicted in the item components. Previous standardization samples have been poorly specified and would appear to be convenience samples rather than carefully selected stratified representations of the population at large.

## Raven's Progressive Matrices (RPM)

First introduced in 1938, Raven's Progressive Matrices (RPM) is a nonverbal test of inductive reasoning based on figural stimuli (Raven, Court, & Raven, 1986, 1992). This test has been very popular in basic research and is also used in some institutional settings for purposes of intellectual screening.

RPM was originally designed as a measure of Spearman's g factor (Raven, 1938). For this reason, Raven chose a special format for the test that presumably required the exercise of g. The reader is reminded that Spearman defined g as the "eduction of correlates." The term *eduction* refers to the process of figuring out relationships based on the perceived fundamental similarities between stimuli. In particular, to correctly answer items on the

RPM, examinees must identify a recurring pattern or relationship between figural stimuli organized in a $3 \times 3$ matrix. The items are arranged in order of increasing difficulty, hence the reference to progressive matrices.

Raven's test is actually a series of three different instruments. Much of the confusion about validity, factorial structure, and the like stems from the unexamined assumption that all three forms should produce equivalent findings. The reader is encouraged to abandon this unwarranted hypothesis. Even though the three forms of the RPM resemble one another, there may be subtle differences in the problem-solving strategies required by each.

The Coloured Progressive Matrices is a 36-item test designed for children from 5 to 11 years of age. Raven incorporated colors into this version of the test to help hold the attention of the young children. The Standard Progressive Matrices is normed for examinees from 6 years and up, although most of the items are so difficult that the test is best suited for adults. This test consists of 60 items grouped into 5 sets of 12 progressions. The Advanced Progressive Matrices is similar to the Standard version but has a higher ceiling. The Advanced version consists of 12 problems in Set I and 36 problems in Set II. This form is especially suitable for persons of superior intellect.

Large sample U.S. norms for the Coloured and Standard Progressive Matrices are reported in Raven and Summers (1986). Separate norms for Mexican American and African American children are included. Although there was no attempt to use a stratified random-sampling procedure, the selection of school districts was so widely varied that the American norms for children appear to be reasonably sound. Sattler (1988) summarizes the relevant norms for all versions of the RPM. Raven, Court, and Raven (1992) produced new norms for the Standard Progressive Matrices, but Gudjonsson (1995) has raised a concern that these data are compromised because the testing was not monitored.

For the Coloured Progressive Matrices, split-half reliabilities in the range of .65 to .94 are reported, with younger children producing lower values (Raven, Court, & Raven, 1986). For the Standard Progressive Matrices, a typical split-half reliability is .86, although lower values are found with younger subjects (Raven, Court, & Raven, 1983). Test-retest reliabilities for all three forms vary considerably from one sample to the next (Raven, 1965; Raven et al., 1986). For normal adults in their late teens or older, reliability coefficients of .80 to .93 are typical. However, for preteen children, reliability coefficients as low as .71 are reported. Thus, for younger subjects, RPM may not possess sufficient reliability to warrant its use for individual decision making.

Factor-analytic studies of the RPM provide little, if any, support for the original intention of the test to measure a unitary construct (Spearman's *g* factor). Studies of the Coloured Progressive Matrices reveal three orthogonal factors (e.g., Carlson & Jensen, 1980). Factor I consists largely of very difficult items and might be termed closure and abstract reasoning by analogy. Factor II is labeled pattern completion through identity and closure. Factor III consists of the easiest items and is defined as simple pattern completion (Carlson & Jensen, 1980). In sum, the very easy and the very hard items on the Coloured Progressive Matrices appear to tap different intellectual processes.

The Advanced Progressive Matrices breaks down into two factors that may have separate predictive validities (Dillon, Pohlmann, & Lohman, 1981). The first factor is composed of items in which the solution is obtained by adding or subtracting patterns (Figure 6.3a). Individuals performing well on these items may excel in rapid decision making and in situations where part–whole relationships must be perceived. The second factor is composed of items in which the solution is based on the ability to perceive the progression of a pattern (Figure 6.3b). Persons who perform well on these items may possess good mechanical ability as well as good skills for estimating projected movement and performing mental rotations. However, the skills represented by each factor are conjectural at this point and in need of independent confirmation.

A huge body of published research bears on the validity of the RPM. The early data are well summarized by Burke (1958), while later findings are compiled in the current RPM manuals (Raven & Summers, 1986; Raven, Court, & Raven, 1983, 1986, 1992). In general, validity coefficients with achievement tests range from the .30s to the .60s. As might be expected, these values are somewhat lower than found with more traditional (verbally loaded) intelligence tests. Validity coefficients with other intelligence tests range from the .50s to the .80s. Also, as might be expected, the correlations tend to be higher with performance than with verbal tests. In a massive study involving thousands of schoolchildren, Saccuzzo and Johnson (1995)

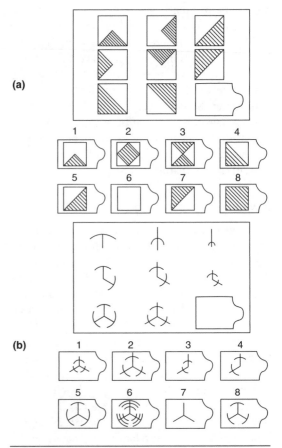

**(a)**

**(b)**

● **FIGURE 6.3**    Raven's Progressive Matrices: Typical Items

concluded that the Standard Progressive Matrices and the WISC-R showed approximately equal predictive validity and no evidence of differential validity across eight different ethnic groups. In a lengthy review, Raven (2000) discusses stability and variation in the norms for the Raven's Progressive Matrices across cultural, ethnic, and socioeconomic groups over the last 60 years. Indicative of the continuing interest in this venerable instrument, Costenbader and Ngari (2001) describe the standardization of the Coloured Progressive Matrices in Kenya.

Even though the RPM has not lived up to its original intentions of measuring Spearman's *g* factor, the test is nonetheless a useful index of nonverbal, figural reasoning. The recent updating of norms was a much-welcomed development for this well-known test, in that many American users were leary of the outdated and limited British norms. Nonetheless, adult norms for the Standard and Advanced Progressive Matrices are still quite limited.

The RPM is particularly valuable for the supplemental testing of children and adults with hearing, language, or physical disabilities. Often these examinees are difficult to assess with traditional measures that require auditory attention, verbal expression, or physical manipulation. In contrast, the RPM can be explained through pantomime, if necessary. Moreover, the only output required of the examinee is a pencil mark or gesture denoting the chosen alternative. For these reasons, the RPM is ideally suited for testing persons with limited command of the English language. In fact, the RPM is about as culturally reduced as possible: The test protocol does not contain a single word in any language. Mills and Tissot (1995) found that the Advanced Progressive Matrices identified a higher proportion of minority children as gifted than did a more traditional measure of academic aptitude (the School and College Ability Test).

## Perspective on Culture-Fair Tests

Cattell's Culture Fair Intelligence Test (CFIT) and Raven's Progressive Matrices (RPM) often are cited as examples of culture-fair tests, a concept with a long and confused history. We will attempt to clarify terms and issues here.

The first point to make is that intelligence tests are merely samples of what people know and can do. We must not reify intelligence and overvalue intelligence tests. Tests are never samples of innate intelligence or culture-free knowledge. All knowledge is based in culture and acquired over time. As Scarr (1994) notes, there is no such thing as a culture-free test.

But what about a culture-fair test, one that poses problems that are equally familiar (or unfamiliar) to all cultures? This would appear to be a more realistic possibility than a culture-free test, but even here the skeptic can raise objections. Consider the question of what a test *means,* which differs from culture to culture. In theory, a test of matrices would appear to be equally fair to most cultures. But in practice, issues of equity arise. Persons reared in Western cultures are trained in linear, convergent thinking. We know that the purpose of a test is to find the single, best answer and to do so quickly. We examine the $3 \times 3$ matrix from left to right and top to bottom, looking for the logical principles invoked in the succession of forms. Can we assume that persons reared in Nepal or New Guinea or even the remote, rural stretches of Idaho will do the same? The test may mean something different to them. Perhaps they will approach it as a measure of aesthetic progression rather than logical succession. Perhaps they will regard it as so much silliness not worthy of intense intellectual effort. To assume that a test is equally fair to all cultural groups merely because the stimuli are equally familiar (or unfamiliar) is inappropriate. We can talk about degrees of cultural fairness (or unfairness), but the notion that any test is absolutely culture-fair surely is mistaken.

## ● MULTIPLE APTITUDE TEST BATTERIES

In a multiple aptitude test battery, the examinee is tested in several separate, homogeneous aptitude areas. Typically, the development of the subtests is dictated by the findings of factor analysis. For example, Thurstone developed one of the first multiple aptitude test batteries, the Primary Mental Abilities Test, a set of seven tests chosen on the basis of factor analysis (Thurstone, 1938).

More recently, several multiple aptitude test batteries have gained favor for educational and career counseling, vocational placement, and armed services classification (Gregory, 1994a). Each year hundreds of thousands of persons are administered one of these prominent batteries: the Differential Aptitude Test (DAT), the General Aptitude Test Battery (GATB), and the Armed Services Vocational Aptitude Battery (ASVAB). These batteries either used factor analysis directly for the delineation of useful subtests or were guided in their construction by the accumulated results of other factor-analytic research. The salient characteristics of each battery are briefly reviewed in the following sections.

## The Differential Aptitude Test (DAT)

The DAT was first issued in 1947 to provide a basis for the educational and vocational guidance of students in grades seven through twelve. Subsequently, examiners have found the test useful in the vocational counseling of young adults out of school and in the selection of employees. Now in its fifth edition (1992), the test has been periodically revised and stands as one of the most popular multiple aptitude test batteries of all time (Bennett,

Seashore, & Wesman, 1982, 1984). Wang (1995) provides a succinct overview of the test.

The DAT consists of eight independent tests:

1. Verbal Reasoning (VR)
2. Numerical Reasoning (NR)
3. Abstract Reasoning (AR)
4. Perceptual Speed and Accuracy (PSA)
5. Mechanical Reasoning (MR)
6. Space Relations (SR)
7. Spelling (S)
8. Language Usage (LU)

A characteristic item from each test is shown in Figure 6.4.

The authors chose the areas for the eight tests based on experimental and experiential data rather than relying on a formal factor analysis of their own. In constructing the DAT, the authors were guided by several explicit criteria:

- Each test should be an independent test: There are situations in which only part of the battery is required or desired.
- The tests should measure power: For most vocational purposes to which test results contribute, the evaluation of power—solving difficult problems with adequate time—is of primary concern.
- The test battery should yield a profile: The eight separate scores can be converted to percentile ranks and plotted on a common profile chart.

---

VERBAL REASONING
Choose the correct pair of words to fill in the blanks.

_____ is to eye as eardrum is to _____

A. vision — sound
B. iris — hear
C. retina — ear
D. sight — cochlea
E. eyelash — earlobe

---

NUMERICAL ABILITY
Choose the correct answer.

4(−5) (−3) =
A. −60      B. 27      C. −27      D. 60      E. none of these

---

● **FIGURE 6.4** Differential Aptitude Tests and Characteristic Items

## ABSTRACT REASONING

The four figures in the row to the left make a series. Find the single choice on the right that would be next in the series.

| | | | | | | | |
|---|---|---|---|---|---|---|---|
| < | <>> | <<>> | <<>>>> | <> | <<<>> | <<<>>>> | <<<<>>>> |
| | | | | A | B | C | D |

## CLERICAL SPEED AND ACCURACY

In each test item, one of the combinations is underlined. Mark the same combination on the answer sheet.

1.  AB  Ab  AA  <u>BA</u>  Bb      2.  5m  5M  <u>M5</u>  Mm  m5

    Ab  Bb  AA  BA  AB            M5  m5  Mm  5m  5M

1.  O  O  O  O  O      2.  O  O  O  O  O

## MECHANICAL REASONING

Which lever will require more force to lift an object of the same weight? If equal, mark C.

?????? ? ??????

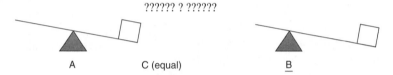

A                C (equal)                <u>B</u>

## SPACE RELATIONS

Which of the figures on the right can be made by folding the pattern at the left? The pattern always displays the outside of the figure.

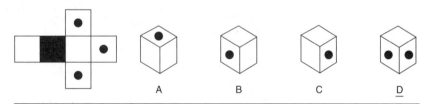

A              B              C              <u>D</u>

## SPELLING

Mark whether each word is spelled right or wrong.

1. irelevant          R          <u>W</u>
2. parsimonious       <u>R</u>          W
3. excellant          R          <u>W</u>

## LANGUAGE USAGE

Decide which part of the sentence contains an error and mark the corresponding letter on the answer sheet. Mark N (None) if there is no error.

In spite of public criticism, / the researcher studied /
    A        B
the affects of radiation / on plant growth.
  <u>C</u>       D

● **FIGURE 6.4**  *continued*

- The norms should be adequate: In the fifth edition, the norms are derived from 100,000 students for the fall standardization, 70,000 for the spring standardization.
- The test materials should be practical: With time limits of 6 to 30 minutes per test, the entire DAT can be administered in a morning or an afternoon school session.
- The tests should be easy to administer: Each test contains excellent "warm-up" examples and can be administered by persons with a minimum of special training.
- Alternate forms should be available: For purposes of retesting, the availability of alternate forms (currently forms C and D) will reduce any practice effects.

The reliability of the DAT is generally quite high, with split-half coefficients largely in the .90s and alternate-forms reliabilities ranging from .73 to .90, with a median of .83. Mechanical Reasoning is an exception, with reliabilities as low as .70 for girls. The tests show a mixed pattern of intercorrelations with each other, which is optimistically interpreted by the authors as establishing the independence of the eight tests. Actually, many of the correlations are quite high and it seems likely that the eight tests reflect a smaller number of ability factors. Certainly, the Verbal Reasoning and Numerical Reasoning tests measure a healthy general factor, with correlations around .70 in various samples.

The manual presents extensive data demonstrating that the DAT tests, especially the VR + NR combination, are good predictors of other criteria such as school grades and scores on other aptitude tests (correlations in the .60s and .70s). For this reason, the combination of VR + NR often is considered an index of scholastic aptitude. Evidence for the *differential* validity of the other tests is rather slim. Bennett, Seashore, and Wesman (1974) do present results of several follow-up studies correlating vocational entry/success with DAT profiles, but their research methods are more impressionistic than quantitative; the independent observer will find it difficult to make use of their

results. Schmitt (1995) notes that a major problem with the battery is the

> lack of discriminant validity between the eight subtests. With the exception of the Perceptual Speed and Accuracy test, all of the subscales are highly intercorrelated (.50 to .75). If one wants only a general index of the person's academic ability, this is fine; if the scores on the subtests are to be used in some diagnostic sense, this level of intercorrelation makes statements about students' relative strengths and weaknesses highly questionable.

Even so, the revised DAT is better than previous editions. One significant improvement is the elimination of apparent sex bias on the Language Usage and Mechanical Reasoning tests—a source of criticism from earlier reviews. The DAT has been translated into several languages and is widely used in Europe for vocational guidance and research applications (e.g., Nijenhuis, Evers, & Mur, 2000; Colom, Quiroga, & Juan-Espinosa, 1999).

A computerized version of the DAT has been available for several years, although its equivalence to the traditional paper and pencil format cannot be taken for granted (Alkhadher, Clarke, & Anderson, 1998). We will have more to say about computerized testing in a later section of the book. For now, it will suffice to mention that the psychometric qualities of a test may shift when the mode of administration is changed. Using counterbalanced testing in which examinees completed both versions (half taking the traditional version first, half taking the computerized version first), Alkhadher et al. (1998) found that oil refinery trainees (N = 122) scored higher on one subtest of the computerized version than on the traditional version of the DAT, namely, the Numerical Ability subtest. The researchers conjectured that the computerized version reduced test fatigue, alleviated time pressure, and also provided novelty—thus boosting test performance modestly.

### The General Aptitude Test Battery (GATB)

In the late 1930s, the U.S. Department of Labor developed aptitude tests to predict job performance in 100 specific occupations. In the 1940s, the department hired a panel of experts in measurement and industrial-organizational psychology to create a multiple aptitude test battery to assess the 100 occupations previously studied and many more. The outcome of this Herculean effort was the General Aptitude Test Battery (GATB), widely acknowledged as the premiere test battery for predicting job performance (Hunter, 1994).

The GATB was derived from a factor analysis of 59 tests administered to thousands of male trainees in vocational courses (United States Employment Service, 1970). The interpretive standards have been periodically revised and updated, so the GATB is a thoroughly modern instrument even though its content is little changed. One limitation is that the battery is available mainly to state employment offices, although nonprofit organizations, including high schools and certain colleges, can make special arrangements for its use.

The GATB is composed of eight paper-and-pencil tests and four apparatus measures. The entire battery can be administered in approximately two and a half hours and is appropriate for high school seniors and adults. The twelve tests yield a total of nine factor scores:

- *General Learning Ability* (intelligence) (G). This score is a composite of Vocabulary, Arithmetic Reasoning, and Three-Dimensional Space.
- *Verbal Aptitude* (V). Derived from a Vocabulary test that requires the examinee to indicate which two words in a set are either synonyms or antonyms.
- *Numerical Aptitude* (N). This score is a composite of both the Computation and Arithmetic Reasoning tests.
- *Spatial Aptitude* (S). Consists of the Three-Dimensional Space test, a measure of the ability to perceive two-dimensional representations of three-dimensional objects and to visualize movement in three dimensions.
- *Form Perception* (P). This score is a composite of Form Matching and Tool Matching, two tests in which the examinee must match identical drawings.

- *Clerical Perception* (Q). A proofreading test called Name Comparison, the examinee must match names under pressure of time.
- *Motor Coordination* (K). Measures the ability to quickly make specified pencil marks in the Mark Making test.
- *Finger Dexterity* (F). A composite of the Assemble and Disassemble tests, two measures of dexterity with rivets and washers.
- *Manual Dexterity* (M). A composite of Place and Turn, two tests requiring the examinee to transfer and reverse pegs in a board.

The nine factor scores on the GATB are expressed as standard scores with a mean of 100 and an SD of 20. These standard scores are anchored to the original normative sample of 4,000 workers obtained in the 1940s. Alternate-forms reliability coefficients for factor scores range from the .80s to the .90s. The GATB manual summarizes several studies of the validity of the test, primarily in terms of its correlation with relevant criterion measures. Hunter (1994) notes that GATB scores predict training success for all levels of job complexity. The average validity coefficient is a phenomenal .62.

The absolute scores are of less interest than their comparison to updated Occupational Aptitude Patterns (OAPs) for dozens of occupations. Based on test results for huge samples of applicants and employees in different occupations, counselors and employers now have access to a wealth of information about score patterns needed for success in a variety of jobs. Thus, one way of using the GATB is to compare an examinee's scores with OAPs believed necessary for proficiency in various occupations.

Hunter (1994) recommends an alternative strategy based on composite aptitudes (Figure 6.5). The nine specific factor scores combine nicely into three general factors: Cognitive, Perceptual, and Psychomotor. Hunter notes that different jobs require various contributions of the Cognitive, Perceptual, and Psychomotor aptitudes. For example, an assembly line worker in an automotive plant might need high scores on the Psychomotor and Perceptual composites, whereas the Cognitive

SPECIFIC FACTORS                                    GENERAL FACTORS

G   General Learning Ability (intelligence)
V   Verbal Aptitude                            ⎤
N   Numerical Aptitude                         ⎦── Cognitive

S   Spatial Aptitude                           ⎤
P   Form Perception                            ⎦── Perceptual
Q   Clerical Perception

● FIGURE 6.5
Specific and General Factors on the GATB

K   Motor Coordination                         ⎤
F   Finger Dexterity                           ⎦── Psychomotor
M   Manual Dexterity

score would be less important for this occupation. Hunter's research demonstrates that general factors dominate over specific factors in the prediction of job performance. Davison, Gasser, and Ding (1996) discuss additional approaches to GATB profile analysis and interpretation.

Van de Vijver and Harsveld (1994) investigated the equivalence of their computerized version of the GATB with the traditional paper-and-pencil version. Of course, only the cognitive and perceptual subtests were compared—tests of motor skills cannot be computerized. They found that the two versions were not equivalent. In particular, the computerized subtests produced faster and more inaccurate responses than the conventional subtests. Their research demonstrates once again that the equivalence of traditional and computerized versions of a test should not be assumed. This is an empirical question answerable only with careful research. Nijenhuis and van der Flier (1997) discuss a Dutch version of the GATB and its application in the study of cognitive differences between immigrants and majority group members in the Netherlands.

### The Armed Services Vocational Aptitude Battery (ASVAB)

The ASVAB is probably the most widely used aptitude test in existence. This instrument is used by the Armed Services to screen potential recruits and to assign personnel to different jobs and training programs. The ASVAB is also available in a computerized version that is rapidly supplanting the original paper-and-pencil test (Segall & Moreno, 1999). The computerized ASVAB is discussed in more detail at the end of this section. More than 2 million examinees take the ASVAB each year. The current version consists of nine subtests, four of which produce the Armed Forces Qualification Test (AFQT), the common qualifying exam for all services (Table 6.1). Alternate-forms reliability coefficients for ASVAB scores are in the mid-.80s to mid-.90s, and test-retest coefficients range from the mid-.70s to the mid-.80s (Larson, 1994). The one exception is Paragraph Comprehension with a reliability of only .50. The test is well normed on a representative sample of 12,000 persons between the ages of 16 and 23 years. The ASVAB manual reports a median validity coefficient of .60 with measures of training performance.

Decisions about ASVAB examinees are typically based on composite scores, not subtest scores. For example, an Electronics Composite is derived by combining Arithmetic Reasoning, Mathematics Knowledge, Electronics Information, and General Science. Persons scoring well on this composite might be assigned to electronics-related positions. Since the composite scores are empirically derived, new ones can be developed for placement decisions at any time. Composite scores are continually updated and revised.

| ● TABLE 6.1     The Armed Services Vocational Aptitude Battery (ASVAB) Subtests | |
| --- | --- |
| Arithmetic Reasoning* | 16-item test of arithmetic word problems based on simple calculation |
| Mathematics Knowledge* | 25-item test of algebra, geometry, fractions, decimals, and exponents |
| Word Knowledge* | 35-item test of vocabulary knowledge and synonyms |
| Paragraph Comprehension* | 15-item test of reading comprehension in short paragraphs |
| General Science | 25-item test of general knowledge in physical and biological science |
| Mechanical Comprehension | 25-item test of mechanical and physical principles |
| Electronics Information | 20-item test of electronics, radio, and electrical principles |
| Assembling Objects | 16-item test of mechanical and assembly concepts |
| Auto and Shop | 25-item test of basic knowledge of autos, shop practices, and tool usage |

*Armed Forces Qualifying Test (AFQT).

At one point, the Armed Services relied heavily on the seven composites in the following list (Murphy, 1984). The Coding Speed subtest, listed here, is no longer used. The first three constitute academic composites, whereas the remaining are occupational composites. The reader will notice that individual subtests may appear in more than one composite:

1. Academic Ability: Word Knowledge, Paragraph Comprehension, and Arithmetic Reasoning
2. Verbal: Word Knowledge, Paragraph Comprehension, and General Science
3. Math: Mathematics Knowledge and Arithmetic Reasoning
4. Mechanical and Crafts: Arithmetic Reasoning, Mechanical Comprehension, Auto and Shop Information, and Electronics Information
5. Business and Clerical: Word Knowledge, Paragraph Comprehension, Mathematics Knowledge, and Coding Speed
6. Electronics and Electrical: Arithmetic Reasoning, Mathematics Knowledge, Electronics Information, and General Science
7. Health, Social, and Technology: Word Knowledge, Paragraph Comprehension, Arithmetic Reasoning, and Mechanical Comprehension

The problem with forming composites in this manner is that they are so highly correlated with one another as to be essentially redundant. In fact, the average intercorrelation among these seven composite scores is .86 (Murphy, 1984)! Clearly, composites do not always provide differential information about specific aptitudes. Perhaps that is why recent editions of the ASVAB have steered clear of multiple, complex composites. Instead, the emphasis is on simpler composites that are composed of highly related constructs. For example, a Verbal Ability composite is derived from Word Knowledge and Paragraph Comprehension, two highly interrelated subtests. In like manner, a Math Ability composite is obtained from the combination of Arithmetic Reasoning and Mathematics Knowledge.

Some researchers have concluded that the ASVAB does not function as a multiple aptitude test battery but achieves success in predicting diverse vocational assignments because the composites invariably tap a general factor of intelligence. For example, Dunai and Porter (2001) report favorably on the ASVAB as a predictor of entry-level success of radiography students in Air Force medical training. The ASVAB may be a good test of general intelligence, but it falls short as a multiple aptitude test battery. Another concern is that the test may possess different psychometric structures for men and women. Specifically, the Electronics Information subtest is a good measure of $g$ (the general factor of intelligence) for men but not women (Ree & Carretta, 1995). The likely explanation for this is that men are about nine times more likely to enroll in high school classes in electronics and auto shop, and men, therefore, have the opportunity for their general ability to shape what they learn about electronics information, whereas women do not. Scores on this subtest will, therefore, function as a measure of achievement (what has already been learned) but not as an index of aptitude (forecasting future results).

Research on a computerized adaptive testing (CAT) version of the ASVAB has been under way since the 1980s. Computerized adaptive testing is discussed in Topic 12B, Computerized Assessment and the Future of Testing. We provide a brief overview here. In CAT, the examinee takes the test while sitting at a computer terminal. The difficulty level of the items presented on the screen is continually readjusted as a function of the examinee's ongoing performance. In general, an examinee who answers a subtest item correctly will receive a harder item, whereas an examinee who fails that item will receive an easier item. The computer uses item response theory as a basis for selecting items. Each examinee receives a unique set of test items tailored to his or her ability level.

In 1990, the CAT-ASVAB began to replace the paper-and-pencil ASVAB. Currently, more than two-thirds of all military applicants are tested with the computerized version. Larson (1994) lists the reasons for adopting the CAT-ASVAB as follows:

1. Shorten overall testing time (adaptive tests require roughly one-half the items of standard tests).
2. Increase test security by eliminating the possibility that test booklets could be stolen.
3. Increase test precision at the upper and lower ability extremes.
4. Provide a means for immediate feedback on test scores, since the computers used for testing can immediately score the tests and output the results.
5. Provide a means for flexible test start times (unlike group-administered paper-and-pencil tests, for which everyone must start and stop at the same time, computer-based testing can be tailored to the examinees' personal schedules).

Reliability and validity studies of the CAT-ASVAB provide strong support for its equivalence to the original test. In general, the computerized version of the instrument measures the same constructs as its paper-and-pencil counterpart—and does so in less time and with greater precision (Moreno & Segall, 1997). With the success of this project, the CAT-ASVAB and other tests likely will be expanded to measure new aspects of performance such as response latencies and to display unique item types such as visuospatial tests of objects in motion (Larson, 1994). The CAT-ASVAB has the potential to change the future of testing.

## ● PREDICTING COLLEGE PERFORMANCE

As most every college student knows, a major use of aptitude tests is the prediction of academic performance. In most cases, applicants to college must contend with the Scholastic Assessment Tests (SAT) or the American College Test (ACT) assessment program. Institutions may set minimum standards on the SAT or ACT tests for admission, based on the knowledge that low scores foretell college failure. In this section we will explore the technical adequacy and predictive validity of the major college aptitude tests.

### The Scholastic Assessment Tests (SAT)

Formerly known as the Scholastic Aptitude Tests, the Scholastic Assessment Tests, or SAT, is the oldest of the college admissions tests, dating back to 1926. The SAT is published by the College Board (formerly the College Entrance Examination Board), a group formed in 1899 to provide a national clearinghouse for admissions testing. As noted by historian Fuess (1950), the purpose of a nationally based admissions test was "to introduce law and order into an educational anarchy which towards the close of the nineteenth century had become exasperating, indeed almost intolerable, to schoolmasters." Over the years, the test has been extensively revised, continuously updated, and repeatedly renormed. In the early 1990s, the SAT was renamed the Scholastic Assessment Tests to emphasize changes in content and format. The

● **TABLE 6.2    Sections and Subtests of the SAT Reasoning Test**

| Section | Subtests |
|---------|----------|
| Critical Reading | Extended Reasoning |
|  | Literal Comprehension |
|  | Vocabulary in Context |
| Math | Numbers and Operations |
|  | Algebra and Functions |
|  | Geometry and Measurement |
|  | Data Analysis, Statistics, |
|  | and Probability |
| Writing | Essay |
|  | Improving Sentences |
|  | Identifying Sentence Errors |
|  | Improving Paragraphs |

new SAT assesses mastery of high school subject matter to a greater extent than its predecessor but continues to tap reasoning skills. The SAT represents state of the art for aptitude testing.

The new SAT, released in 2005, consists of the SAT Reasoning Test and the SAT Subject Tests. The SAT Reasoning Test is used for college admission decisions, whereas the optional SAT Subject Tests typically are needed for advanced college placement in fields such as Biology, Chemistry, History, Foreign Languages, and Mathematics. We restrict our discussion here to the SAT Reasoning Test. For ease of discussion, we refer to it simply as the "SAT."

The SAT consists of three sections, each containing three or four subtests (Table 6.2). The Critical Reading section involves reading individual paragraphs and then answering multiple-choice questions about the passages. The questions embody three approaches:

Vocabulary in Context—discerning the meaning of words from their context in the passage

Literal Comprehension—understanding significant information directly available in the passage

Extended Reasoning—following an argument or making inferences from the passage

Some questions in the Critical Reading section also engage a complex form of fill in the blanks. However, instead of testing for mere factual knowledge, the questions evaluate verbal comprehension. Here is a straightforward example:

Hoping to _____ the dispute, the family therapist proposed a concession that he felt would be _____ to both mother and daughter.

A. end . . . divisive
B. overcome . . . unappealing
C. protract . . . satisfactory
D. resolve . . . acceptable
E. enforce . . . useful

The correct answer is D. Of course, the SAT incorporates more difficult items of this genre.

The second part of the SAT is the Math section, consisting of three subtests. Collectively, these subtests assess basic math skills in algebra, geometry, statistics, and data analysis needed for successful navigation of college. Most of the questions are multiple-choice format, for example:

A special lottery was announced to select the student who will live in the only luxury apartment in student housing. In all, 50 juniors, 125 sophomores, and 175 freshmen applied. However, juniors were allowed to purchase 4 tickets each. What is the probability that the room will be awarded to a junior?

A. 1/5
B. 1/2
C. 2/5
D. 1/7
E. 2/7

The correct answer is C. In addition to multiple-choice questions, the Math section includes several items that require the student to generate a single correct answer and then enter it on the response sheet. For example:

What value of $x$ satisfies both equations below?

$x^2 - 4 = 0$

$|4x + 6| = 2$

The correct answer is –2. Strategies for finding a solution that might work with a multiple-choice question—trial and error, or process of elimination—are not likely to help with this style of question. Here the examinee must generate the correct answer by dint of careful analysis.

The Writing portion of the SAT now consists of a 25-minute Essay section and three multiple-choice subtests that evaluate the ability of the examinee to improve sentences, identify sentence errors, and improve paragraphs. In the Essay test, the examinee reads a short excerpt and then writes a short paper that takes a point of view. Here is an example of an excerpt and assignment:

> A sense of happiness and fulfillment, not personal gain, is the best motivation and reward for one's achievements. Expecting a reward of wealth or recognition for achieving a goal can lead to disappointment and frustration. If we want to be happy in what we do in life, we should not seek achievement for the sake of winning wealth and fame. The personal satisfaction of a job well done is its own reward.
>
> **Assignment:** Are people motivated to achieve by personal satisfaction rather than by money or fame? Plan and write an essay in which you develop your point of view on this issue. Support your position with reasoning and examples taken from your reading, studies, experience, or observations. (College Board, 2005)

The essay is evaluated by two trained readers on a 1 to 6 scale, resulting in a total score of 2 to 12 for the Essay test. Students also receive a separate score on a scale from 20 to 80 for the multiple-choice portion of the Writing section. Both these scores are combined for the overall section score for Writing. SAT scores for each of the three sections—Critical Reading, Math, and Writing—are now reported on the familiar 200- to 800-point scale, with an approximate mean of 500 and standard deviation of 100.

Great care is taken in the construction of new forms of the SAT because unfailing reliability and a high degree of parallelism are essential to the mission of this testing program. Historically, the internal consistency reliability of all sections is repeatedly in the range of .91 to .93; with only a few exceptions, test-retest correlations vary between .87 and .89. The standard error of measurement is 30 to 35 points.

The primary evidence for SAT validity is criterion-related, in this case, the ability to predict first-year college grades. Donlon (1984, chap. VIII) reports a wealth of information on this point for earlier editions; we can only summarize trends here. In 685 studies, the combined SAT Verbal and Math scores correlated .42, on average, with college first-year grade point average. Interestingly, high school record (e.g., rank or grade point average) fares better than the SAT in predicting college grades ($r = .48$). But the combination of SAT and high school record proves even more predictive; these variables correlated .55, on average, with college first-year grade point average. Of course, these findings reflect a substantial restriction of range: low SAT-scoring high school students tend not to attend college. Donlon (1984) estimated that the real correlation without restriction of range (SAT + high school record) would be in the neighborhood of .65. According to the College Board website, the combination of SAT and high school GPA continues to provide a robust correlation ($r = .62$) with freshman grades. Based on a sample of 151,316 students attending 110 colleges and universities across the U.S., these results leave no room for doubt as to the general predictive power of SAT scores (www.collegeboard.com). However, the results also show that for students whose best language is not English (e.g., children of recent immigrants), the crucial reading and writing portions of the SAT underpredict freshman grades.

## The American College Test (ACT)

The American College Test (ACT) assessment program is a recent program of testing and reporting designed for college-bound students. In addition to traditional test scores, the ACT assessment program includes a brief 90-item interest inventory (based on Holland's typology) and a student profile section (in which the student may list subjects studied, notable accomplishments, work experience, and community service). We will not discuss these ancillary measures here, except to note that they are useful in generating the Student Profile Report, which is sent to the examinee and the colleges listed on the registration folder.

Initiated in 1959, the ACT is based on the philosophy that direct tests of the skills needed in college courses provide the most efficient basis for predicting college performance. In terms of the number of students who take it, the ACT occupies second place behind the SAT as a college admissions test. The four ACT tests require knowledge of a subject area, but emphasize the use of that knowledge:

- English (75 questions, 45 minutes). The examinee is presented with several prose passages excerpted from published writings. Certain portions of the text are underlined and numbered, and possible revisions for the underlined sections are presented; in addition, "no change" is one choice. The examinee must choose the best option.
- Mathematics (60 questions, 60 minutes). Here the examinee is asked to solve the kinds of mathematics problems likely to be encountered in basic college mathematics courses. The test emphasizes concepts rather than formulas and uses a multiple-choice format.
- Reading (40 questions, 35 minutes). This subtest is designed to assess the examinee's level of reading comprehension; subscores are reported for social studies/sciences and arts/ literature reading skills.
- Science Reasoning (40 questions, 35 minutes). This test assesses the ability to read and understand material in the natural sciences. The questions are drawn from data representations, research summaries, and conflicting viewpoints.

In addition to the area scores listed previously, ACT results are also reported as an overall Composite score, which is the average of the four tests. ACT scores are reported on a standard score 36-point scale. In 2008, the average ACT Composite score of high school graduates was 21.1, with a standard deviation of about 5 points.

Critics of the ACT program have pointed to the heavy emphasis on reading comprehension that saturates all four tests. The average intercorrelation of the tests is typically around .60. These data suggest that a general achievement/ability factor pervades all four tests; results for any one test should not be overinterpreted. Fortunately, college admission officers probably place the greatest emphasis on the Composite score, which is the average of the four separate tests. The ACT test appears to measure much the same thing as the SAT; the correlation between these two tests approaches .90. It is not surprising, then, that the predictive validity of the ACT Composite score rivals the SAT combined score, with correlations in the vicinity of .40 to .50 with college first-year grade point average. The predictive validity coefficients are virtually identical for advantaged and disadvantaged students, indicating that the ACT tests are not biased.

Kifer (1985) does not question the technical adequacy of the ACT and similar testing programs but does protest the enormous symbolic power these tests have accrued. The heavy emphasis on test scores for college admissions is not a technical issue, but a social, moral, and political concern:

> Selective admissions means simply that an institution cannot or will not admit each person who completes an application. Choices of who will or will not be admitted should be, first of all, a matter of what the institution believes is desirable and may or may not include the use of prediction equations. It is just as defensible to select on talent broadly construed as it is to use test scores however high. There are talented students in many areas—leaders, organizers, doers, musicians, athletes, science award winners, opera buffs—who may have moderate or low ACT scores but whose presence on a campus would change it.

The reader may wish to review Topic 6B, Test Bias and Other Controversies, for further discussion of this point.

## ● POSTGRADUATE SELECTION TESTS

Graduate and professional programs also rely heavily on aptitude tests for admission decisions. Of course, many other factors are considered when selecting students for advanced training, but there

| GRE Scores | 0 | 6 | 12 | 18 | 24 | 30 |
| --- | --- | --- | --- | --- | --- | --- |
|    GRE-V + GRE-Q total: | | 1,000 | 1,100 | 1,200 | 1,300 | 1,400 |
| Undergraduate GPA | 0 | 5 | 10 | 15 | 20 | 25 |
| | | 3.0 | 3.2 | 3.4 | 3.6 | 3.8 |
| Psychology GPA | 0 | 1 | 2 | 3 | 4 | 5 |
| | | 3.0 | 3.2 | 3.4 | 3.6 | 3.9 |
| Background in Statistics/Experimental | 0 | 1 | 2 | 3 | 4 | 5 |
| Background in Biology/Chemistry | 0 | 1 | 2 | 3 | 4 | 5 |
| Background in Math/Computer Science | 0 | 1 | 2 | 3 | 4 | 5 |
| Research Experience | 0 | 1 | 2 | 3 | 4 | 5 |
| Positive Interpersonal Skills | 0 | 2 | 4 | 6 | 8 | 10 |
| Ethnic/Linguistic/Cultural Diversity | 0 | 2 | 4 | 6 | 8 | 10 |
| | | | | | Maximum Total: | 100 |

● FIGURE 6.6 Representative Weighting Scheme Used by Graduate Program Admission Committees in Psychology

is no denying the centrality of aptitude test results in the selection decision. For example, Figure 6.6 depicts a fairly typical quantitative weighting system used in evaluating applicants for graduate training in psychology. The reader will notice that an overall score on the Graduate Record Exam (GRE) receives the single highest weighting in the selection process. We review the GRE in the following sections, as well as admission tests used by medical schools and law schools.

## Graduate Record Exam (GRE)

The GRE is a multiple-choice and essay test widely used by graduate programs in many fields as one component in the selection of candidates for advanced training. The GRE offers subject examinations in many fields (e.g., Biology, Computer Science, History, Mathematics, Political Science, Psychology), but the heart of the test is the general test designed to measure verbal, quantitative, and analytical writing aptitudes. The verbal section (GRE-V) includes verbal items such as analogies, sentence completion, antonyms, and reading comprehension. The quantitative section (GRE-Q) consists of problems in algebra, geometry, reasoning, and the interpretation of data, graphs, and diagrams. The analytical writing section (GRE-AW) was added in October 2002 as a measure of higher-level critical thinking and analytical writing skills. It consists of two writing tasks: a 45-minute essay in which the applicant takes a position on an issue, and a 30-minute essay in which the applicant analyzes an argument. This new addition to the GRE replaced a multiple-choice test of analytical thinking that is no longer used.

The first two scores (GRE-V and GRE-Q) are reported as standard scores with an *approximate* mean of 500 and standard deviation of 100. Actually, the mean score may differ from year to year because all test results are anchored to a standard reference group of 2,095 college seniors tested in 1952 on the verbal and quantitative portions of the test. Historically, graduate programs have tended to pay attention to the combination of scores on the first two parts (GRE-V + GRE-Q), where combined scores above 1,000 would be considered above average. Recently, graduate programs have paid more attention to writing skills in their applicants, which explains the addition of the analytical writing section (GRE-AW) to the test.

Scoring of the analytical writing section is based on 6-point holistic ratings provided independently by two trained raters. If the two scores differ by more than one point on the scale, the discrepancy is adjudicated by a third GRE-AW reader. According to the GRE Board (www.gre.org), the GRE-AW test reveals smaller ethnic group differences than found in the multiple-choice sections. For example, the differences between African American and Caucasian examinees and between Hispanic and Caucasian examinees are smaller on the GRE-AW than on the GRE-V or GRE-Q. This suggests that the new test does not unduly penalize ethnic groups traditionally underrepresented in graduate programs.

The reliability of the GRE is strong, with internal consistency reliability coefficients typically around .90 for the three components. The validity of the GRE commonly has been examined in relation to the ability of the test to predict performance in graduate school. Performance has been operationalized mainly as grade point average, although faculty ratings of student aptitude also have been used. For example, based on a meta-analytic review of 22 studies with a total of 5,186 students, Morrison and Morrison (1995) concluded that GRE-V correlated .28 and GRE-Q correlated .22 with graduate grade point average. Thus, on average, GRE scores accounted for only 6.3 percent of the variance in graduate-level academic performance. In a recent study of 170 graduate students in psychology at Yale University, Sternberg and Williams (1997) also found minimal correlations between GRE scores and graduate grades. When GRE scores were correlated with faculty ratings on five variables (analytical, creative, practical, research, and teaching abilities), the correlations were even lower, for the most part hovering right around zero. The single exception was the GRE analytical thinking score, which correlated

modestly with almost all of the faculty ratings. However, this correlation was observed *only* for men (on the order of $r = .3$), whereas for women it was almost exactly zero in every case! Based on these and similar studies, the consensus would appear to be that excessive reliance on the GRE for graduate school selection may overlook a talented pool of promising graduate students.

However, other researchers are more supportive in their evaluation of the GRE, noting that the correlation of GRE scores and graduate grades is not a good index of validity because of the restriction of range problem (Kuncel, Campbell, & Ones, 1998). Specifically, applicants with low GRE scores are unlikely to be accepted for graduate training in the first place and, thus, relatively little information is available with respect to whether low scores predict poor academic performance. Put simply, the correlation of GRE scores with graduate academic performance is based *mainly* on persons with middle to high levels of GRE scores, that is, GRE-V + GRE-Q totals of 1,000 and up. As such, the correlation will be attenuated precisely because those with low GREs are not included in the sample. Another problem with validating the GRE against grades in graduate school is the unreliability of the criterion (grades). Based on the expectation that graduate students will perform at high levels, some professors may give blanket A's such that grades do not reflect real differences in student aptitudes. This would lower the correlation between the predictor (GRE scores) and the criterion (graduate grades). When these factors are accounted for, many researchers find reason to believe the GRE is still a valid tool for graduate school selection (Powers, 2004).

In a comprehensive meta-analysis of 1,753 independent groups of students, Kuncel, Hezlett, and Ones (2001) confirmed the validity of the GRE tests (Verbal, Quantitative, and Analytical) for the prediction of graduate student performance. The total sample size for their analysis was huge, including 82,659 students. The breadth of their investigation allowed them to code studies for several different forms of student accomplishment. GRE general test scores were significantly associated with the following student outcomes: first-year GPA, overall GPA, comprehensive exam scores, faculty ratings, and publication citation counts. The researchers also discovered that the GRE Psychology subject test outperformed the general test as a predictive measure of student success.

## Medical College Admission Test (MCAT)

The MCAT is required of applicants to almost all medical schools in the United States. The test is designed to assess achievement of the basic skills and concepts that are prerequisites for successful completion of medical school. There are three multiple-choice sections (Verbal Reasoning, Physical Sciences, Biological Sciences) and one essay section (Writing Sample). The Verbal Reasoning section is designed to evaluate the ability to understand and apply information and arguments presented in written form. Specifically, the test consists of several passages of about 500 to 600 words each, taken from humanities, social sciences, and natural sciences. Each passage is followed by several questions based on information included in the passage. The Physical Sciences section is designed to evaluate reasoning in general chemistry and physics. The Biological Sciences is designed to evaluate reasoning in biology and organic chemistry. These physical and biological science sections contain 10 to 11 problem sets described in about 250 words each, with several questions following.

The Writing Sample Test consists of two 30-minute essays. This test is designed to assess basic writing skills such as developing a central idea, synthesizing concepts and ideas, writing logically, and following accepted practices of grammar, syntax, and punctuation. The writing sample essays begin with a prompt, which consists of a topic statement (printed in boldface) followed by instructions for interpretation and response. The writing sample prompts resemble the following (www.aamc.org):

> **Scientists should seek to confirm theories or hypotheses rather than to refute them.**
>
> Describe a specific situation in which a scientist might seek to refute a theory or hypothesis rather than to confirm it. Discuss what you

think determines when scientists should seek to confirm theories or hypotheses and when they should seek to refute them.

The writing samples are scored on a 6-point scale by independent raters. The basis for the inclusion of writing samples in the MCAT is that physicians are expected to communicate clearly with patients, write lucid and effective medical notes, and contribute persuasively to local and national debates about health care policy.

Each of the MCAT scores (except Writing Samples) is reported on a scale from 1 to 15 (means of about 8.0 and standard deviations of about 2.5). The reliability of the test is lower than that of other aptitude tests used for selection, with internal consistency and split-half coefficients mainly in the low .80s (Gregory, 1994a). MCAT scores are mildly predictive of success in medical school, but once again the restriction of range conundrum (previously discussed in relation to the GRE) is at play. In particular, examinees with low MCAT scores who would presumably confirm the validity of the test by performing poorly in medical school are rarely admitted, which reduces the apparent validity of the test.

Julian (2005) confirmed the validity of the MCAT for predicting medical school performance by following 4,076 students who entered 14 medical schools in 1992 and 1993. Outcome variables included GPA and national medical licensing exam scores. When corrected for restriction of range, the predictive validity coefficients for MCAT scores were impressive, on the order of .6 for medical school grades, and as high as .7 for licensing exam scores. In fact, the MCAT scores were so strongly predictive of licensing exam scores that adding undergraduate GPAs into the equation did not appreciably boost the correlation. Julian (2005) concludes that MCAT scores essentially replace the need for undergraduate GPAs in medical school student selection because of their remarkable capacity to predict medical licensing exam scores.

## Law School Admission Test (LSAT)

The LSAT is a half-day standardized test required of applicants to virtually every law school in the

United States. The test is designed to measure skills considered essential for success in law school, including the reading and understanding of complex material, the organization and management of information, and the ability to reason critically and draw correct inferences. The LSAT consists of multiple-choice questions in four areas: reading comprehension, analytical reasoning, and two logical reasoning sections. An additional section is used to pretest new test items and to preequate new test forms, but this section does not contribute to the LSAT score. The score scale for the LSAT extends from a low of 120 to a high of 180. In addition to the objective portions, a 30-minute writing sample is administered at the end of the test. The section is not scored, but copies of the writing sample are sent to all law schools to which the examinee applies.

The LSAT has acceptable reliability (internal consistency coefficients in the .90s) and is regarded as a moderately valid predictor of law school grades. Yet, in one fascinating study, LSAT scores correlated more strongly with state bar test results than with law school grades (Melton, 1985). This speaks well for the validity of the test, insofar as it links LSAT scores with an important, real-world criterion.

In recent years, those responsible for law school admissions have shown interest in selection methods that go beyond the LSAT. One example is a promising project from the University of California, Berkeley, which ambitiously seeks to assess 26 traits identified as crucial to effective performance of lawyers (Chamberlin, 2009). Using focus groups and individual interviews, psychologist Sheldon Zedeck and lawyer Marjorie Shultz distilled these 26 traits, which include varied capacities like practical judgment, researching the law, writing, integrity/honesty, negotiation skills, developing relationships, stress management, fact finding, diligence, listening, and community involvement/ service. Next they developed realistic scenarios designed to evaluate one or more of these qualities. A sample question might ask the applicant to take the role of a team leader in a law firm. A verbal fight breaks out between two of the team members over the best way to proceed with the project. What should the team leader do? A number of options are listed, and the applicant is asked to rank them from best to worst. The format of the questions is varied. For other questions, the applicant might be asked to provide a short written response. Initial research with this yet-unnamed instrument indicates that it predicts success in the practice of law substantially better than the LSAT.

## ● EDUCATIONAL ACHIEVEMENT TESTS

Achievement tests permit a wide range of potential uses. Practical applications of group achievement tests include the following:

- To identify children and adults with specific achievement deficits who might need more detailed assessment for learning disabilities
- To help parents recognize the academic strengths and weaknesses of their children and thereby foster individual remedial efforts at home
- To identify classwide or schoolwide achievement deficiencies as a basis for redirection of instructional efforts
- To appraise the success of educational programs by measuring the subsequent skill attainment of students
- To group students according to similar skill level in specific academic domains
- To identify the level of instruction that is appropriate for individual students

Thus, achievement tests serve institutional goals such as monitoring schoolwide achievement levels, but also play an important role in the assessment of individual learning difficulties. As previously noted, different kinds of achievement tests are used to pursue these two fundamental applications (institutional and individual). Institutional goals are best served by group achievement test batteries, whereas individual assessment is commonly pursued with individual achievement tests (even though group tests may play a role here, too). Here we focus on group educational achievement tests.

Virtually every school system in the nation uses at least one educational achievement test, so it is not surprising that test publishers have responded to the widespread need by developing a panoply of excellent instruments.

In the following section, we describe several of the most widely used group standardized achievement tests. We limit our coverage here to three educational achievement tests, each distinctive in its own way. The Iowa Tests of Basic Skills (ITBS) is representative of the huge industry of standardized achievement testing used in virtually all school systems nationwide. The Metropolitan Achievement Test is of the same genre as the ITBS but embodies a new and powerful technique of reading assessment known as the Lexile approach and, thus, merits special attention. Finally, almost everyone has heard of the Tests of General Educational Development, known familiarly as the "GED." We would be remiss not to discuss this testing program.

### Iowa Tests of Basic Skills (ITBS)

First published in 1935, the Iowa Tests of Basic Skills (ITBS) were most recently revised and restandardized in 2001. The ITBS is a multilevel battery of achievement tests that covers grades K through 8. A companion test, the Tests of Achievement and Proficiency (TAP), covers grades 9 through 12. In order to expedite direct and accurate comparisons of achievement and ability, the ITBS and the TAP were both concurrently normed with the Cognitive Abilities Test (CogAT), a respected group test of general intellectual ability.

The ITBS is available in several levels that correspond roughly with the ages of the potential examinees: levels 5–6 (grades K–1), levels 7–8 (grades 2–3), and levels 9–14 (grades 3–8). The basic subtests for the older levels measure vocabulary, reading, language, mathematics, social studies, science, and sources of information (e.g., uses of maps and diagrams). A brief description of the subtests for grades 3–8 is provided in Table 6.3.

From the first edition onward, the ITBS has been guided by a pragmatic philosophy of educational measurement. The manual states the purpose of testing as follows:

● **TABLE 6.3    Brief Description of ITBS Subtests for Grades 3–8**

Vocabulary: A word is presented in the context of a short phrase or sentence, and students select the correct meaning from multiple-choice alternatives.

Reading Comprehension: Students read a brief passage and answer multiple-choice questions that require inference or generalization.

Spelling: Each multiple-choice item presents four words, one of which may be misspelled, and fifth option, *no mistakes.*

Capitalization: Test items require students to identify errors of under- or overcapitalization present in brief written passages.

Punctuation: Multiple-choice items require students to identify errors of punctuation involving commas, apostrophes, quotation marks, colons, and so on, or choose *no mistakes.*

Usage and Expression: In the first part, students identify errors in usage or expression; in the second part, students choose the best way to express an idea.

Math Concepts and Estimation: Questions deal with computation, algebra, geometry, measurement, and probability and statistics.

Math Problem Solving and Data Interpretation: Questions may involve multistep word problems or interpretation of tables and graphs.

Math Computation: These test items require the use of one arithmetic operation (addition, subtraction, multiplication, or division) with whole numbers, fractions, and decimals.

Social Studies: These questions involve aspects of history, geography, economics, and so on that are ordinarily covered in most school systems.

Science: These test items involve aspects of biology, ecology, space science, and physical sciences ordinarily covered in most school systems.

Maps and Diagrams: These questions evaluate the ability to use maps for a variety of purposes such as determining locations, directions, and distances.

Reference Materials: These questions measure the ability to use reference materials and library resources.

The purpose of measurement is to provide information which can be used in improving instruction. Measurement has value to the extent that it results in better decisions which directly affect pupils.

To this end, the ITBS incorporates a criterion-referenced skills analysis to supplement the usual array of norm-referenced scores. For example, one feature available from the publisher's scoring service is item-level information. This information indicates topic areas, items sampling the topic, and correct or wrong response for each item. Teachers, therefore, have access to a wealth of diagnostic-instructional information for each student. Whether this information translates to better instruction—as the test authors desire—is very difficult to quantify. As Linn (1989) notes, "We must rely mostly on logic, anecdotes, and opinions when it comes to answering such questions."

The technical properties of the ITBS are beyond reproach. Historically, internal consistency and equivalent-form reliability coefficients are mostly in the mid-.80s to low .90s. Stability coefficients for a one-year interval are almost all in the .70 to .90 range. The test is free from overt racial and gender bias, as determined by content evaluation and item bias studies. The year 2000 norms for the test were empirically developed from large, representative national probability samples.

Item content of the ITBS is judged relevant by curriculum experts and reviewers, which speaks to the content validity of the test (Lane, 1992; Linn, 1989). Although the predictive validity of the latest ITBS has not been studied extensively, evidence from prior editions is very encouraging. For example, ITBS scores correlate moderately with high school grades (*r*s around .60). The ITBS is not a perfect instrument, but it represents the best that modern test development methods can produce.

## Metropolitan Achievement Test (MAT)

The Metropolitan Achievement Test dates back to 1930 when the test was designed to meet the curriculum assessment needs of New York City. The stated purpose of the MAT is "to measure the achievement of students in the major skill and content areas of the school curriculum." The MAT is concurrently normed with the Otis-Lennon School Ability Test (OLSAT).

Now in its eighth edition, the MAT is a multi-level battery designed for grades K through 12 and was most recently normed in 2000. The areas tested by the MAT include the traditional school-related skills:

Reading
Mathematics
Language
Writing
Science
Social Studies

An attractive feature of the MAT is that student reading scores are reported as Lexile measures, a new and practical indicator of reading level. Lexile measures are likely to become a standard feature in most group achievement tests in the years ahead, so it is worth a brief detour to explain their nature and significance.

### Lexile Measures

The Lexile approach is a major new improvement in the assessment of reading skill. It was developed over a span of more than 12 years using millions of dollars in grant funds from the National Institute of Child Health and Human Development (NICHD) (www.lexile.com). The Lexile approach is based on two simple, commonsense assumptions, namely (1) reading materials can be placed on a continuum as to difficulty level (comprehensibility), and (2) readers can be ordered on a continuum as to reading ability. The Lexile framework provides a common metric for matching readers and text, which, in turn, permits parents and educators to choose appropriate reading materials for children.

The **Lexile scale** is a true interval scale. The Lexile measure for a reading selection is a specific number indicating the reading demand of the text based on the semantic difficulty (vocabulary) and syntactic complexity (sentence length). Lexile measures for reading selections typically range from 200L to 1,700L (Lexiles). The Lexile score for a student, obtained from the Reading Comprehension test of the MAT or other achievement tests, is a precise index of the student's reading ability, calibrated on the same scale as the Lexile measure for text. The value of the Lexile approach is that student comprehension can be predicted as a function of the disparity between the demands of the text and the student's ability. For example, when readers are well targeted (the difference between text and reader is close to 0 Lexiles), research indicates that reader comprehension will be about 75 percent. When the text difficulty exceeds the reader's ability by 250L, comprehension drops to about 50 percent. When the skill of the reader exceeds the demands of the text by 250L, comprehension is about 90 percent (www.lexile.com).

The Lexile approach has a number of potential benefits and applications for teachers and parents. Teachers can look up Lexile measures for specific books (the Lexile corporation has evaluated over 30,000 titles to date) as a way of building a library of titles at varying levels. Also, they can produce individualized reading lists suitable for each student. Likewise, parents can select well-matched books to read to their children. Stenner (2001) captures the allure of the Lexile approach as follows:

> One of the great strengths of the Lexile Framework is the way it encourages thought about what forecasted comprehension rate would be optimal for different instructional contexts. *Harry Potter and the Goblet of Fire* is a 910L text. Readers at 400L to 500L can nonetheless enjoy listening to this story read aloud. A 700L reader could read the text in a one-on-one tutoring context. A 900L reader will disappear for an hour or two, fully capable of self-engaging with the text, and a 1600L adult reader can become so engrossed that a two-hour plane ride flies by.

The Lexile approach is not a panacea, but it is a major improvement in the assessment of reading skill.

## Tests of General Educational Development (GED)

Another widely used achievement test battery is the Tests of General Educational Development (GED), developed by the American Council on Education and administered nationwide for high school equivalency certification (www.acenet.edu). The GED consists of multiple-choice examinations in five educational areas:

Language Arts—Writing
Language Arts—Reading
Mathematics
Science
Social Studies

The Language Arts—Writing section also contains an essay question that examinees must answer in writing. The essay question is scored independently by two trained readers according to a 6-point holistic scoring method. The readers make a judgment about the essay based on its overall effectiveness in comparison to the effectiveness of other essays.

The GED comes in numerous alternate forms. Typically, internal consistency reliabilities for the subscales are above .90. However, the interrater

---

● **TABLE 6.4  Selected Group Achievement Tests for Elementary and Secondary School Assessment**

**Iowa Tests of Educational Development (ITED)**
Designed for grades 9 through 12, the objective of this test battery is to measure the fundamental goals or generalized skills of education that are independent of the curriculum. Most of the test items require the synthesis of knowledge or a multiple-step solution.

**Tests of Achievement and Proficiency (TAP)**
This instrument is designed to provide a comprehensive appraisal of student progress toward traditional academic goals in grades 9 through 12. This test is co-normed with the ITED and the CogAT.

**Stanford Achievement Test (SAchT)**
Along with the ITBS, the SAchT is one of the leading contemporary achievement tests. Dating back more than 80 years and now in its tenth edition, it is administered to more than 15 million students every year.

**TerraNova CTBS**
For grades 1 through 12, this multi-level test combines multiple-choice questions with constructed-response items that require students to produce correct answers, not just select them from alternatives.

reliability of scoring on the writing samples is more modest, typically between .6 and .7. These findings indicate that a liberal criterion for passing this subtest is appropriate so as to reduce decision errors. Regarding validity, the GED correlates very strongly ($r = .77$) with the graduation reading test used in New York (Whitney, Malizio, & Patience, 1985). Furthermore, the standards for passing the GED are more stringent than those employed by most high schools: Currently, individuals who receive a passing score for a GED credential outperform at least 40 percent of graduating high school seniors (www.acenet.edu).

The GED emphasizes broad concepts rather than specific facts and details. In general, the purpose of the GED is to allow adults who did not graduate from high school to prove that they have obtained an equivalent level of knowledge from life experiences or independent study. Employers regard the GED as equivalent (if not superior) to earning a high school diploma. Successful performance on the GED enables individuals to apply to colleges, seek jobs, and request promotions that require a high school diploma as a prerequisite. Rogers (1992) provides an unusually thorough review of the GED.

### Additional Group Standardized Achievement Tests

In addition to the previously described batteries, a few other widely used group standardized achievement tests deserve brief listing. These instruments are depicted in Table 6.4.

## ●SUMMARY

1. Group tests differ from individual tests in five ways: multiple-choice versus open-ended format, objective machine scoring versus examiner scoring, group versus individualized assessment, applications in screening versus remedial planning, and huge versus merely large standardization samples.

2. The Multidimensional Aptitude Battery-II (MAB-II) is a multiple-choice group intelligence test designed to be a paper-and-pencil equivalent of the WAIS-R. The test-retest reliability of the instrument is excellent, and factor analyses support its construct validity. One drawback is that the instrument parallels an outdated test, the WAIS-R.

3. The Cognitive Abilities Test (CogAT) is representative of the many multilevel, school-based test batteries in current use. The nine subtests of the CogAT include a Verbal Battery, a Quantitative Battery, and a Nonverbal Battery.

4. The Culture Fair Intelligence Test (CFIT) is a nonverbal measure of fluid intelligence that attempts to minimize cultural bias. Although a good test of intelligence, the CFIT is probably as culturally bound as most traditional tests. The test needs revision and restandardization.

5. Raven's Progressive Matrices (RPM) is a nonverbal test of inductive reasoning that comes in three different versions. The RPM is useful for the supplemental testing of persons with hearing, language, or physical disabilities.

6. Culture-fair testing is an idealized abstraction that is never achieved in the real world. Even the meaning of a test may differ among cultural groups, which will affect the validity of comparisons. Some tests are more culture-fair than others, but it is not possible for any test to be equally fair to all cultural groups.

7. Used for educational and vocational guidance in the high school years, the Differential Aptitude Test (DAT) consists of eight independent tests. A lack of discriminant validity between the tests is one concern with this respected battery.

8. The General Aptitude Test Battery (GATB) consists of eight paper-and-pencil tests and four apparatus measures derived from a factor analysis of 59 tests. The test yields nine factor scores helpful in the prediction of job performance.

9. The Armed Services Vocational Aptitude Battery (ASVAB), used by the Armed Services to

screen and assign recruits, is probably the most widely used aptitude test in existence. A limitation of the ASVAB is that the composites are highly correlated with one another.

10. The prediction of academic performance in college is facilitated by such tests as the Scholastic Assessment Tests (SAT) and the American College Test (ACT) assessment program. Whereas the SAT is normed to a mean of 500 and standard deviation of 100 for three subtests, the ACT overall score is reported on a 36-point standard score scale with a mean of about 21 and standard deviation of 5.

11. Used for admission to many graduate programs, the Graduate Record Exam general test consists of three sections (Verbal, Quantitative, and Analytical Writing). The Verbal and Quantitative exams are normed to a mean of about 500 and standard deviation of 100. The Analytical Writing exam is scored holistically by trained raters on a 6-point scale.

12. Some professions have developed their own specialized entrance exams. These include the Medical College Admissions Test (MCAT), required by almost all medical schools in the United States, and the Law School Admissions Test (LSAT), mandatory for applicants to law schools.

13. The Iowa Tests of Basic Skills (ITBS) is typical of many group educational achievement tests used to monitor student progress and gauge the effectiveness of school curricula. Geared to typical school curricula, this test assesses achievement in such areas as vocabulary, reading, language, mathematics, social studies, science, and sources of information (e.g., map reading).

14. The Metropolitan Achievement Test (MAT) is a multilevel battery for grades K through 12. The MAT was one of the first achievement tests to report reading scores with the Lexile approach that allows for matching readers and text.

15. The Tests of General Educational Development (GED) are administered nationwide for high school equivalency certification. The GED consists of multiple-choice examinations in five educational areas and includes an essay question to assess writing skills.

## ● KEY TERMS AND CONCEPTS

culture-fair test   p. 222

Lexile scale   p. 241

# Test Bias and Other Controversies

An intelligence test is a neutral, inconsequential tool until someone assigns significance to the results derived from it. Once meaning is attached to a person's test score, that individual will experience many repercussions, ranging from superficial to life-changing. These repercussions will be fair or prejudiced, helpful or harmful, appropriate or misguided—depending on the meaning attached to the test score.

Unfortunately, the tendency to imbue intelligence test scores with inaccurate and unwarranted connotations is rampant. Laypersons and students of psychology commonly stray into one thicket of harmful misconceptions after another. Test results are variously overinterpreted or underinterpreted, viewed by some as a divination of personal worth but devalued by others as trivial and unfair.

The purpose of this topic is to clarify further the meaning of intelligence test scores in the light of relevant behavioral research. We begin by dispelling a number of everyday misconceptions about IQ and then pursue several empirically based issues—some would say controversies—that bear on the meaning of intelligence test scores:

- The question of test bias
- Genetic and environmental effects on intelligence
- Origins of IQ differences between African Americans and Caucasian Americans
- The fate of intelligence in middle and old age
- Generational changes in intelligence test scores

The underlying theme of this section is that intelligence test scores are best understood within the framework of modern psychological research. The reader is warned that the research issues pursued here are complex, confusing, and occasionally contradictory. However, the rewards for grappling with these topics are substantial. After all, the meaning of intelligence tests is demarcated, sharpened, and refined entirely by empirical research.

## ● THE QUESTION OF TEST BIAS

Beyond a doubt, no practice in modern psychology has been more assailed than psychological testing. Commentators reserve a special and often vehement condemnation for ability testing in particular.

In his wide-ranging response to the hundreds of criticisms aimed at mental testing, Jensen (1980) concluded that test bias is the most common rallying point for the critics. In proclaiming **test bias,** the skeptics assert in various ways that tests are culturally and sexually biased so as to discriminate unfairly against racial and ethnic minorities, women, and the poor. We cite here a sampling of verbatim criticisms (Jensen, 1980):

- Intelligence tests are sadly misnamed because they were never intended to measure intelligence and might have been more aptly called CB (cultural background) tests.
- Persons from backgrounds other than the culture in which the test was developed will always be penalized.
- There are enormous social class differences in a child's access to the experiences necessary to acquire the valid intellectual skills.
- IQ scores reported for African Americans and low socioeconomic groups in the United States reflect characteristics of the test rather than of the test takers.
- The poor performance of African American children on conventional tests is due to the biased content of the tests; that is, the test material is drawn from outside the African American culture.
- Women are not so good as men at mathematics only because women have not taken as much math in high school and college.

Are these criticisms valid? The investigation of this question turns out to be considerably more complicated than the reader might suppose. A most important point is that appearances can be deceiving. As we will explain subsequently, the fact that test items "look" or "feel" preferential to one race, sex, or social class does not constitute proof of test bias. Test bias is an objective, empirical question, not a matter of personal judgment.

Although critics may be loath to admit it, dispassionate and objective methods for investigating test bias do exist. One purpose of this section is to present these methods to the reader. However, an aseptic discussion of regression equations and statistical definitions of test bias would be incomplete, only half of the story. Conceptions of test bias are irretrievably intermingled with notions of test fairness. A full explanation of the story surrounding the test-bias controversy requires that we investigate the related issue of test fairness, too.

Differences in terminology abound in this area, so it is important to set forth certain fundamental distinctions before proceeding. Test bias is a technical concept amenable to impartial analysis. The most salient methods for the objective assessment of test bias are discussed in the following. In contrast, test fairness reflects social values and philosophies of test use, particularly when test use extends to selection for privilege or employment. Much of the passion that surrounds the test-bias controversy stems from a failure to distinguish test bias from test fairness. To avoid confusion, it is crucial to draw a sharp distinction between these two concepts. We include separate discussions of test bias and test fairness, beginning with an analysis of why test bias is such a controversial topic.

### The Test-Bias Controversy

The test-bias controversy has its origins in the observed differences in average IQ among various racial and ethnic groups. For example, African Americans score, on average, about 15 points lower than white Americans on standardized IQ tests. This difference reduces to 7 to 12 IQ points when socioeconomic disparities are taken into account. The existence of marked racial/ethnic differences in ability test scores has fanned the fires of controversy over test bias. After all, employment opportunities, admission to college, completion of a high school diploma, and assignment to special education classes are all governed, in part, by test results. Biased tests could perpetuate a legacy of racial discrimination. Test bias is deservedly a topic of intense scrutiny by both the public and the testing professions.

One possibility is that the observed IQ disparities indicate test bias rather than meaningful group differences. In fact, most laypersons and even some psychologists would regard the magnitude of race differences in IQ as prima facie evidence that intelligence tests are culturally biased. This is an appealing argument, but a large difference between defined subpopulations is not a sufficient basis for proving test bias. The proof of test bias must rest on other criteria outlined in the following section.

When do test score differences between groups signify test bias? We begin by reviewing the criteria that should be used to investigate test bias of any kind, whether for race, gender, or any other defining characteristic.

## Criteria of Test Bias and Test Fairness

The topic of test bias has received wide attention from measurement psychologists, test developers, journalists, test critics, legislators, and the courts. Cole and Moss (1998) underscore an unsettling consequence of the proliferation of views held on this topic; namely, concepts of test bias have become increasingly intricate and complex. Furthermore, the understanding of test bias is made difficult by the implicit and often emotional assumptions—held even by scholars—that may lead honest persons to view the same information in different ways.

In part, disagreements about test bias are perpetuated because adversaries in this debate fail to clarify essential terminology. Too often, terms such as *test bias* and *test fairness* are considered interchangeable and thrown about loosely without definition. We propose that test bias and test fairness commonly refer to markedly different aspects of the test-bias debate. Careful examination of both concepts will provide a basis for a more reasoned discussion of this controversial topic.

As interpreted by most authorities in this field, *test bias* refers to objective statistical indices that examine the patterning of test scores for relevant subpopulations. Although experts might disagree about nuances, on the whole there is a consensus about the statistical criteria that indicate when a test is biased. We will expand this point later, but we can provide the reader with a brief preview here: In general, a test is deemed biased if it is differentially valid for different subgroups. For example, a test would be considered biased if the scores

from appropriate subpopulations did not fall on the same regression line for a relevant criterion.

In contrast to the narrow concept of test bias, *test fairness* is a broad concept that recognizes the importance of social values in test usage. Even a test that is unbiased according to the traditional technical criteria of homogeneous regression might still be deemed unfair because of the social consequences of using it for selection decisions. The crux of the debate is this: Test bias (a statistical concept) is not necessarily the same thing as test fairness (a values concept). Ultimately, test fairness is based on social conceptions such as one's image of a just society. In the assessment of test fairness, subjective values are of overarching importance; the statistical criteria of test bias are merely ancillary. We will return to this point later when we analyze the link between social values and test fairness. But let us begin with a traditional presentation of technical criteria for test bias.

## The Technical Meaning of Test Bias: A Definition

One useful way to examine test bias is from the technical perspective of test validation. The reader will recall from an earlier chapter that a test is valid when a variety of evidence supports its utility and when inferences derived from it are appropriate, meaningful, and useful. One implication of this viewpoint is that test bias can be equated with differential validity for different groups:

> Bias is present when a test score has meanings or implications for a relevant, definable subgroup of test takers that are different from the meanings or implications for the remainder of the test takers. Thus, bias is differential validity of a given interpretation of a test score for any definable, relevant subgroup of test takers. (Cole & Moss, 1998)

Perhaps a concrete example will help clarify this definition. Suppose a simple word problem arithmetic test were used to measure youngsters' addition skills. The problems might be of the form "If you have two six-packs of pop, how many cans do you have altogether?" Suppose, however, the test is used in a group of primarily Spanish-speaking seventh graders. With these children, low scores might indicate a language barrier, not a problem with arithmetic skills. In contrast, for English-speaking children low scores would most likely indicate a deficit in arithmetic skills. In this example, the test has differential validity, predicting arithmetic deficits quite well for English-speaking children but very poorly for Spanish-speaking children. According to the technical perspective of test validation, we would conclude that the test is biased.

Although the general definition of test bias refers to differential validity, in practice the particular criteria of test bias fall under three main headings: content validity, criterion-related validity, and construct validity. We will review each of these categories, discussing relevant findings along the way. The coverage is illustrative, not exhaustive. Interested readers should consult Jensen (1980), Cole and Moss (1998), and Reynolds and Brown (1984b).

### Bias in Content Validity

Bias in content validity is probably the most common criticism of those who denounce the use of standardized tests with minorities (Helms, 1992; Hilliard, 1984; Kwate, 2001). Typically, critics rely on their own expert judgment when they expound one or more of the following criticisms of the content validity of ability tests:

1. The items ask for information that ethnic minority or disadvantaged persons have not had equal opportunity to learn.
2. The scoring of the items is improper, since the test author has arbitrarily decided on the only correct answer and ethnic minorities are inappropriately penalized for giving answers that would be correct in their own culture but not that of the test maker.
3. The wording of the questions is unfamiliar, and an ethnic minority person who may "know" the correct answer may not be able to respond because he or she does not understand the question (Reynolds, 1998).

Any of these criticisms, if accurate, would constitute bona fide evidence of test bias. However, merely stating a criticism does not comprise proof. Where these criticisms fall short is that they are seldom buttressed by empirical evidence.

Reynolds (1998) has offered a definition of **content bias** for aptitude tests that addresses the preceding points in empirically defined, testable terms:

> An item or subscale of a test is considered to be biased in content when it is demonstrated to be relatively more difficult for members of one group than another when the general ability level of the groups being compared is held constant and no reasonable theoretical rationale exists to explain group differences on the item (or subscale) in question.

This definition is useful because it proposes an empirical approach to the question of test bias.

In general, attempts to prove that expert-nominated items are culturally biased have not yielded the conclusive evidence that critics expect. McGurk (1953a, 1953b, 1975) has written extensively on this topic, and we will use his classic study to illustrate this point. For his doctoral dissertation, McGurk asked a panel of 78 judges (professors, educators, and graduate students in psychology and sociology) to classify each of 226 items from well-known standardized tests of intelligence into one of three categories: least cultural, neutral, most cultural. McGurk administered these test items to hundreds of high school students. His primary analysis involved the test results for 213 African American students and 213 white students matched for curriculum, school, length of enrollment, and socio-economic background.

McGurk (1953a, 1953b) discovered that the mean difference between African American and white students for the total hybrid test, expressed in standard deviation units, was .50. More pertinent to the topic of test bias in content validity was his comparison of scores on the 37 "most cultural" items versus the 37 "least cultural" items. For the "most cultural" items—the ones nominated by the judges as highly culturally biased—the difference was .30. For the "least cultural" items—the ones judged to be more fair to African Americans and other cultural minorities—the difference was .58. In other words, the items nominated as most cultural were relatively easier for African Americans; the items nominated as least cultural were relatively harder. This finding held true even after item difficulty was partialed out. Furthermore, the item difficulties for the two groups were almost perfectly correlated ($r = .98$ for "most cultural" and $r = .96$ for "least cultural" items). There is an important lesson here that test critics often overlook: "Expert" judges cannot identify culturally biased test items based on an analysis of item characteristics. Recent studies continue to reaffirm this conclusion (Reynolds, Lowe, & Saenz, 1999).

In general, with respect to well-known standardized tests of ability and aptitude, research has not supported the popular belief that the specific content of test items is a source of cultural bias against minorities. This conclusion does not exonerate these tests with respect to other criteria of test bias, discussed in the following sections. Furthermore, we can point out that savvy test developers should be vigilant even to the impression of bias in test content, since the appearance of unfairness can affect public attitudes about psychological tests in quite tangible ways.

## Bias in Predictive or Criterion-Related Validity

The prediction of future performance is one important use of intelligence, ability, and aptitude tests. For this application of psychological testing, predictive validity is the most crucial form of validity in relation to test bias. In general, an unbiased test will predict future performance equally well for persons from different subpopulations. For example, an unbiased scholastic aptitude test will predict future academic performance of African Americans and white Americans with near-identical accuracy.

Reynolds (1998) offers a clear, direct definition of test bias with regard to criterion-related or **predictive validity bias:**

> A test is considered biased with respect to predictive validity if the inference drawn from the test score is not made with the smallest feasible random

error or if there is constant error in an inference or prediction as a function of membership in a particular group.

This definition of test bias invokes what might be referred to as the criterion of homogeneous regression. According to this viewpoint, a test is unbiased if the results for all relevant subpopulations cluster equally well around a single regression line. In order to clarify this point, we need to introduce concepts relevant to simple regression. The discussion is modeled after Cleary, Humphreys, Kendrick, and Wesman (1975).

Suppose we are using a scholastic aptitude test to predict first-year grade point average (GPA) in college. In the case of a simple regression analysis, prediction of future performance is made from an equation of the form:

$$Y = bX + a$$

where $Y$ is the predicted college GPA, $X$ is the score on the aptitude test, and $b$ and $a$ are constants derived from a statistical analysis of test scores and grades of prior students. We will not concern ourselves with how $b$ and $a$ are derived; the reader can find this information in any elementary statistics textbook.

The values of $b$ and $a$ correspond to important aspects of the regression line—the straight line that facilitates the most accurate prediction of the criterion (college grades) from the predictor (aptitude score) (Figure 6.7). In particular, $b$ corresponds to the slope of the line, with higher values of $b$ indicating a steeper slope and more accurate prediction. The value of $a$ depicts the intercept on the vertical axis. The units of measurement for $b$ and $a$ cannot be specified in advance because they depend on the underlying scales used for $X$ and $Y$. Notice in Figure 6.7 that the regression line is the reference for predicting grades from observed aptitude score.

According to the criterion of homogeneous regression, in an unbiased test a single regression line can predict performance equally well for all relevant subpopulations, even though the means for the different groups might differ. For example,

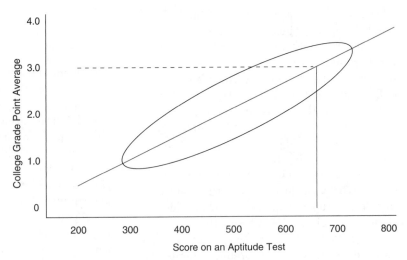

● **FIGURE 6.7**
Test Scores, Grades, and
Regression Line for a
Hypothetical Large Group
of College Students

Note: The dotted line shows how the regression line can be used to predict grade point average
from the test score for a single, new subject.

in Figure 6.8 group A performs better than group
B on both predictor and criterion. Yet, the relationship between aptitude score and grades is the same
for both groups. In this hypothetical instance, the
graph depicts the absence of bias on the aptitude
test with respect to criterion-related validity.

A more complicated situation known as intercept bias is shown in Figure 6.9. In this case, scores

for the two groups do not cluster tightly around
the single best regression line shown as a dotted
line in the graph. Separate, parallel regression lines
(and, therefore, separate regression equations)
would be needed to facilitate accurate prediction.
If a single regression line were used (the dotted
line), criterion scores for group A would be overpredicted, whereas criterion scores for group B

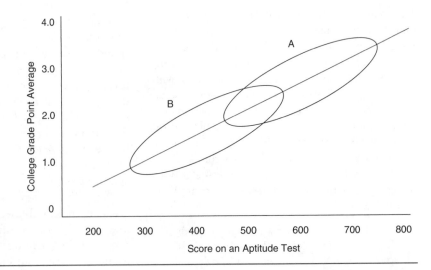

● **FIGURE 6.8**
Test Scores, Grades, and
Single Regression Line for
Two Hypothetical Large
Subpopulations of College
Students

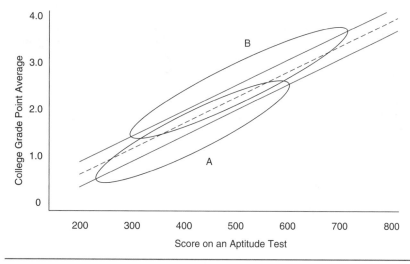

● **FIGURE 6.9**
Test Scores, Grades, and Parallel Regression Lines for Two Hypothetical Large Subpopulations of College Students

would be underpredicted. Thus, the use of a single regression line would constitute a clear instance of test bias, because the test has differential predictive validity for different subgroups.[1]

But what about using separate regression lines for each subgroup? Would this solve the problem and rescue the test from criterion-related test bias? Opinions differ on this point. Although there is no doubt that separate regression equations would maximize predictive accuracy for the combined sample, whether this practice would produce test fairness is debated. We return to this issue later, when we discuss the relevance of social values to test fairness.

The Scholastic Aptitude Test (now known as the Scholastic Assessment Test and discussed in a later chapter) has been analyzed by several researchers with regard to test bias in criterion-related validity (Cleary, Humphreys, Kendrick, & Wesman, 1975; Manning & Jackson, 1984). A consistent finding is that separate, parallel, regression lines are needed for African American and white examinees. For example, in one school the best

regression equations for African American, white, and combined students were as follows:

African American: $Y = .055 + .0024\,V + .0025M$

White: $Y = .652 + .0026V + .0011M$

Combined: $Y = .586 + .0027V + .0012M$

where $Y$ is the predicted college grade point, $V$ is the SAT Verbal score, and $M$ is the SAT Mathematics score (Cleary et al., 1975, p. 29). The effect of using the white or the combined formula is to overpredict college grades for African American subjects based on SAT results. On the traditional four-point scale ($A = 4, B = 3$, etc.), the average amount of overprediction from 17 separate studies was .20 or one-fifth of a grade point (Manning & Jackson, 1984). What these results mean is open to debate, but it seems clear, at least, that the SAT and similar entrance examinations do not underpredict college grades for minorities.

The most peculiar regression outcome, known as slope bias, is depicted in Figure 6.10. In this case, the regression lines for separate subgroups are not even parallel. Using a single regression line (the dotted line) for prediction might, therefore, result in both under- and overprediction of scores for selected subjects in both groups. Professional opinion would be unanimous in this case: This test

---

1. Contrary to widely held belief, test bias in these cases actually favors the *lower*-scoring group because its performance on the criterion is overpredicted. On occasion, then, test bias can favor minority groups.

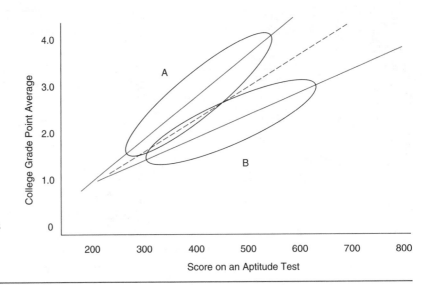

● **FIGURE 6.10**
Test Scores, Grades, and
Nonparallel Regression Lines
for Two Hypothetical Large
Subpopulations of College
Students

possesses a high degree of test bias in criterion-related validity.

## Bias in Construct Validity

The reader will recall that the construct validity of a psychological test can be documented by diverse forms of evidence, including appropriate developmental patterns in test scores, theory-consistent intervention changes in test scores, and confirmatory factor analysis. Because construct validity is such a broad concept, the definition of **bias in construct validity** requires a general statement amenable to research from a variety of viewpoints with a broad range of methods. Reynolds (1998) offers the following definition:

> Bias exists in regard to construct validity when a test is shown to measure different hypothetical traits (psychological constructs) for one group than for another; that is, differing interpretations of a common performance are shown to be appropriate as a function of ethnicity, gender, or another variable of interest, one typically but not necessarily nominal.

From a practical standpoint, two straightforward criteria for nonbias flow from this definition (Reynolds & Brown, 1984a). If a test is nonbiased,

then comparisons across relevant subpopulations should reveal a high degree of similarity for (1) the factorial structure of the test, and (2) the rank order of item difficulties within the test. Let us examine these criteria in more detail.

An essential criterion of nonbias is that the factor structure of test scores should remain invariant across relevant subpopulations. Of course, even within the same subgroup, the factor structure of a test might differ between age groups, so it is important that we restrict our comparison to same-aged persons from relevant subpopulations. For same-aged subjects, a nonbiased test will possess the same factor structure across subgroups. In particular, for a nonbiased test the number of emergent factors and the factor loadings for items or subscales will be highly similar for relevant subpopulations.

In general, when the items or subscales of prominent ability and aptitude tests are factor-analyzed separately in white and minority samples, the same factors emerge in the relevant subpopulations (Reynolds, 1982; Jensen, 1980, 1984). Although minor anomalies have been reported in a handful of studies (Scheuneman, 1987; Gutkin & Reynolds, 1981; Johnston & Bolen, 1984), research in this area is more notable for its consistent findings with respect to factorial invariance across subgroups (e.g., Geary & Whitworth, 1988).

A second criterion of nonbias in construct validity is that the rank order of item difficulties within a test should be highly similar for relevant subpopulations. Since age is a major determinant of item difficulty, this standard is usually checked separately for each age group covered by a test. The reader should note what this criterion does not specify. It does not specify that relevant subgroups must obtain equivalent passing rates for test items. What is essential is that the items that are the most difficult (or least difficult) for one subgroup should be the most difficult (or least difficult) for other relevant subpopulations.

The criterion of similar rank order of item difficulties can be tested in a very straightforward and objective manner. If the difficulty level of each item is computed by means of the $p$ value (percentage passing) for each relevant subpopulation, then it is possible to compare the relative item difficulties across same-aged subgroups. In fact, the similarity of the rank order of item difficulties for any two groups can be gauged objectively by means of a correlation coefficient ($r_{xy}$). The paired $p$ values for the test items constitute the values of $x$ and $y$ used in the computation. The closer the value of $r$ to 1.00, the more similar the rank ordering of item difficulties for the two groups.

In general, cross-group comparisons of relative item difficulties for prominent aptitude and ability tests have yielded correlations bordering on 1.00; that is, most tests show extremely similar rank orderings for item difficulties across relevant subpopulations (Jensen, 1980; Reynolds, 1982). In a representative study, Miele (1979) investigated the relative item difficulties of the WISC for African American and white subjects at each of four grade levels (preschool, first, third, and fifth grades). He found that the average cross-racial correlations (holding grade level constant) for WISC item $p$ values was .96 for males and .95 for females. These values were hardly different from the cross-sex correlations (holding grade level constant) within race, which were .98 (whites) and .97 (African Americans). As noted, these findings are not unusual.

In general, for mainstream cognitive tests, the rank order of item difficulties is nearly identical for relevant subpopulations, including minority groups. However, some exceptions have been noted. For example, Urquhart Hagie, Gallipo, and Svien (2003) report some striking examples of apparent item bias in a WISC-III study of 28 teenage children on the Lakota Sioux reservation in South Dakota. These authors computed the passing rates for the WISC-III subtest items and found dramatic deviations in the relative difficulty levels of consecutive items on a few of the subtests. For example, consider the Information subtest, which consists of 30 items ranked from very easy (nearly 100% passing rate) to very hard (less than 1% passing rate). These items evaluate the child's fund of basic information, with questions on a par with "How many legs does a cat have?" (easy) or "Which continent includes Argentina?" (medium) or "Who is the Dalai Lama?" (hard). The problem noted by Urquhart Hagie et al. (2003) on the Information subtest is that item 13 was passed at a substantially lower rate than expected. Specifically, the percentage of the sample passing items 11 through 15 did not show a smooth decline, as would be found in a nonbiased test:

| Item Number | Percent Passing |
|---|---|
| Item 11 | 81 |
| Item 12 | 61 |
| **Item 13** | **16** |
| Item 14 | 45 |
| Item 15 | 31 |

Item 13 reveals clear evidence of bias in construct validity—it is substantially more difficult than the preceding and following items. We cannot reveal the content of these copyrighted test items. However, we can say that item 13 requires the child to know about a well known Italian explorer who reputedly discovered America. Actually, which foreigners first landed on American shores is an item of dispute—but that is another issue (Menzies, 2003). What is clear in this case is that item 13 on the WISC-III Information subtest requires knowledge that is unpalatable to most Native American examinees. The explorer in question is not a revered figure in this subculture. As Gregory (2009) notes:

> We can well imagine the confusion of these indigenous people who have been on this continent for many thousands of years trying to fathom the notion that a European "discovered" their land.

In fairness, we should mention that clear examples of psychometrically confirmed test bias such as this are not common in published literature. Even so, this example serves as a reminder that ongoing investigations of test bias are still needed.

### Reprise on Test Bias

Critics who hypothesize that tests are biased against minorities assert that the test scores underestimate the ability of minority members. As we have argued in the preceding sections, the hypothesis of test bias is a scientific question that can be answered empirically through such procedures as factor analysis, regression equations, intergroup comparisons of the difficulty levels for "biased" versus "unbiased" items, and rank ordering of item difficulties. In general, ability and aptitude tests fare quite well by these criteria. In fact, there is no domain of ability or aptitude testing in which there has been cumulative evidence suggesting test bias. To the contrary, extensive reviews of the empirical studies provide overwhelming evidence disconfirming the bias hypothesis (Reynolds, 1982, 1994a; Jensen, 1980; Manning & Jackson, 1984).

We turn now to the broader concept of test fairness. How well do existing instruments meet reasonable criteria of test fairness? As the reader will learn, **test fairness** involves social values and is, therefore, an altogether more debatable—and more debated—topic than test bias.

### ● SOCIAL VALUES AND TEST FAIRNESS

Even an unbiased test might still be deemed unfair because of the social consequences of using it for selection decisions. In contrast to the narrow, objective notion of test bias, the concept of test fairness incorporates social values and philosophies of test use. We will demonstrate to the reader that, in the final analysis, the proper application of psychological tests is essentially an ethical conclusion that cannot be established on objective grounds alone.

In a classic article that deserves detailed scrutiny, Hunter and Schmidt (1976) proposed the first clear distinction between statistical definitions of test bias and social conceptions of test fairness. Although the authors reviewed the usual technical criteria of test bias with incisive precision, their article is most famous for its description of three mutually incompatible ethical positions that can and should affect test use.

Hunter and Schmidt (1976) noted that psychological tests are often used for institutional selection procedures such as employment or college admission. In this context, the application of test results must be guided by a philosophy of selection. Unfortunately, in many institutions the selection philosophy is implicit, not explicit. Nonetheless, when underlying values are made explicit, three ethical positions can be distinguished. These positions are unqualified individualism, quotas, and qualified individualism. Since these ethical stances are at the very core of public concerns about test fairness, we will review these positions in some detail.

### Unqualified Individualism

In the American tradition of free and open competition, the ethical stance of **unqualified individualism** dictates that, without exception, the best qualified candidates should be selected for employment, admission, or other privilege. Hunter and Schmidt (1976) spell out the implications of this position:

> Couched in the language of institutional selection procedures, this means that an organization should use whatever information it possesses to make a scientifically valid prediction of each individual's performance and always select those with the highest predicted performance. This position looks appealing at first glance, but embraces some implications that most persons find troublesome. In particular, if race, sex, or ethnic group membership contributed to valid

prediction of performance in a given situation over and above the contributions of test scores, then those who espouse unqualified individualism would be ethically bound to use such a predictor.

## Quotas

The ethical stance of **quotas** acknowledges that many bureaucracies and educational institutions owe their very existence to the city or state in which they function. Since they exist at the will of the people, it can be argued that these institutions are ethically bound to act in a manner that is "politically appropriate" to their location. The logical consequence of this position is quotas. For example, in a location whose population is one-third African American and two-thirds white, selection procedures should admit candidates in approximately the same ratio. A selection procedure that deviates consistently from this standard would be considered unfair.

By definition, fair share quotas are based initially upon population percentages. Within relevant subpopulations, factors that predict future performance such as test scores would then be considered. However, one consequence of quotas is that those selected do not necessarily have the highest scores on the predictor test.

## Qualified Individualism

**Qualified individualism** is a radical variant of individualism:

This position notes that America is constitutionally opposed to discrimination on the basis of race, religion, national origin, or sex. A qualified individualist interprets this as an ethical imperative to refuse to use race, sex, and so on, as a predictor even if it were in fact scientifically valid to do so. (Hunter & Schmidt, 1976)

For selection purposes, the qualified individualist would rely exclusively on tested abilities, without reference to age, sex, race, or other demographic characteristics. This seems laudable, but examine the potential consequences. Suppose a qualified individualist used SAT scores for purposes of college admission. Even though SAT scores for African

Americans and whites produce separate regression lines for the criterion of college grades, the qualified individualist would be ethically bound to use the single, less-accurate regression line derived for the entire sample of applicants. As a consequence, the future performance of African Americans would be overpredicted, which would seemingly boost the proportion of persons selected from this applicant group. With respect to selection ratios, the practical impact of qualified individualism is therefore midway between quotas and unqualified individualism.

## Reprise on Test Fairness

Which philosophy of selection is correct? The truth is, this problem is beyond the scope of rational solution. At one time or another, each of the ethical stances outlined previously has been championed by wise, respected, and thoughtful citizens. However, no consensus has emerged, and one is not likely to be found soon. The dispute reviewed here

is typical of ethical arguments—the resolution depends in part on irreconcilable values. Furthermore, even among those who agree on values there will be disagreements about the validity of certain relevant scientific theories that are not yet adequately tested. Thus, we feel that there is no way that this dispute can be objectively resolved. Each person must choose as he sees fit (and in fact we are divided). (Hunter & Schmidt, 1976)

When ethical stances clash—as they most certainly do in the application of psychological tests to selection decisions—the court system may become the final arbiter, as discussed later in this book.

## ● GENETIC AND ENVIRONMENTAL __DETERMINANTS OF INTELLIGENCE__

### Genetic Contributions to Intelligence

The nature-nurture debate regarding intelligence is a well-known and overworked controversy that we will largely sidestep here. We concur with McGue, Bouchard, Iacono, and Lykken (1993) that a substantial genetic component to intelligence has been proved by decades of adoption studies, familial research, and twin projects, even though individual studies may be faulted for particular reasons:

> When taken in aggregate, twin, family, and adoption studies of IQ provide a demonstration of the existence of genetic influences on IQ as good as can be achieved in the behavioral sciences with nonexperimental methods. Without positing the existence of genetic influences, it simply is not possible to give a credible account for the consistently greater IQ similarity among monozygotic (MZ) twins than among like-sex dizygotic (DZ) twins, the significant IQ correlations among biological relatives even when they are reared apart, and the strong association between the magnitude of the familial IQ correlation and the degree of genetic relatedness. (p. 60)

Of course, the demonstration of substantial genetic influence for a trait does not imply that heredity alone is responsible for differences between individuals—environmental factors are formative, too, as reviewed subsequently.

The genetic contribution to human characteristics such as intelligence (as measured by IQ tests) is usually measured in terms of a heritability index that can vary from 0.0 to 1.0. The **heritability index** is an estimate of how much of the total variance in a given trait is due to genetic factors. Heritability of 0.0 means that genetic factors make no contribution to the variance in a trait, whereas heritability of 1.0 means that genetic factors are exclusively responsible for the variance in a trait. Of course, for most measurable characteristics, heritability is somewhere between the two extremes. McGue et al. (1993) discuss the various methods for computing heritability based on twin and adoption studies.

It is important to stress that heritability is a population statistic that cannot be extended to explain an individual score. Furthermore, heritability for a given trait is not a constant. As Jensen (1969) notes, estimates of heritability "are specific to the population sampled, the point in time, how the measurements were made, and the particular test used to obtain the measurements." For IQ, most studies

report heritability estimates right around .50, meaning that about half of the variability in IQ scores is from genetic factors. However, for some studies, the heritability of IQ is much higher, in the .70s (Bouchard, 1994; Bouchard, Lykken, McGue, Segal, & Tellegen, 1990; Pedersen, Plomin, Nesselroade, & McClearn, 1992).

Dozens of studies could be cited to demonstrate the importance of genetic factors in the determination of intelligence as measured by IQ tests. The relevant literature on this question is almost legion. For a basic initiation to the topic, the reader can consult Bouchard (1994) and Jensen (1998).

A most fascinating demonstration of the genetic contribution to IQ is found in the Minnesota Study of Twins Reared Apart (Bouchard et al., 1990). In this ongoing study, identical twins reared apart are reunited for extensive psychometric testing. Bouchard (1994) reports that the IQs of identical twins reared apart correlate almost as highly as those of identical twins reared together, even though the twins reared apart often were exposed to different environmental conditions (in some cases, sharply contrasting environments). In sum, differences in environment appeared to cause very little divergence in the IQs of identical twin pairs reared apart. These findings strongly corroborate a genetic contribution to intelligence, with heritability estimated in the vicinity of .70.

However, we must avoid the tendency to view any corpus of research in a simplistic either/or frame of mind. Even the most diehard hereditarians acknowledge that a person's intelligence is shaped also by the quality of experience. The crucial question is: To what extent can enriched or deprived environments modify intelligence upward or downward from the genetically circumscribed potential? The reader is reminded that the genetic contribution to intelligence is indirect, most likely via the gene-coded physical structures of the brain and nervous system. Nonetheless, the brain is quite malleable in the face of environmental manipulations, which can even alter its weight and the richness of neuronal networks (Greenough, Black, & Wallace, 1987). How much can such environmental impacts sway intelligence as measured by IQ tests? We will review several studies indicating that environmental extremes help determine intellectual outcome within a range of approximately 20 IQ points, perhaps more.

## Environmental Effects: Impoverishment and Enrichment

First, we examine the effects of environmental disadvantage. Vernon (1979, chap. 9) has reviewed the early studies of severe deprivation, noting that children reared under conditions in which they received little or no human contacts can show striking improvements in IQ—as much as 30 to 50 points—when transferred to a more normal environment. Yet, we must regard this body of research with some skepticism, owing to the typically exceptional conditions under which the initial tests were administered. Can a meaningful test be administered to 7-year-old children raised almost like animals (Koluchova, 1972)?

Typical of this early research is the follow-up study by Skeels (1966) of 25 orphaned children originally diagnosed as having mental retardation (Skeels & Dye, 1939). These children were first tested at approximately 1½ years of age when living in a highly unstimulating orphanage. Thirteen of them were then transferred to another home where they received a great deal of supervised, doting attention from older girls with mental retardation. These children showed a considerable increase in IQ, whereas the 12 who remained behind decreased further in IQ. When traced at follow-up 26 years later, the 13 transferred cases were normal, self-supporting adults, or were married. The other subjects—the contrast group—were still institutionalized or in menial jobs. The enriched group showed an average increase of 32 IQ points when retested with the Stanford-Binet, whereas the contrast group fell below their original scores. Even though we are disinclined to place much credence in the original IQ scores and might, therefore, quarrel with the exact magnitude of the change, the Skeels (1966) study surely indicates that the difference between

a severely depriving early environment and a more normal one might account for perhaps 15 to 20 IQ points.

More recently, Breslau, Chilcoat, Susser, and others (2001) conducted a rigorous longitudinal study that illustrates the detrimental impact of growing up in a racially segregated and economically disadvantaged community. Using the WISC-R, they collected longitudinal IQ scores at age 6 and age 11 for large samples of urban and suburban children, some low birth weight ($\leq 2500$ grams) and some normal birth weight ($>2500$ grams). The urban samples were primarily Black, from inner city Detroit, and reared by a single mother with high school (or less) education. These children typically experienced economic deprivation, inferior education, family stress, and racial segregation. The suburban samples were primarily White, from economically advantaged communities, and reared by a married mother with college education. As the authors note, "the sampling design provided for a comparison of populations with starkly contrasting social conditions." (p. 712)

The mean IQ scores for all samples at both times of testing (age 6 and age 11) are depicted in Figure 6.11. The reader will observe that suburban samples scored higher than inner city samples, and that normal birth weight children scored higher than low birth weight children. These results are not especially remarkable—the negative impacts of low birth weight and economic disadvantage are well documented in the literature on group differences in IQ outcomes (e.g., Breslau, 1994; Ceci, 1996). What is noteworthy about the results—one might even say astonishing—is that both of the inner city samples (low birth weight and normal birth weight) apparently *lost* an average of 5 IQ points during the five years between initial testing at age 6 and follow-up testing at age 11. In contrast, the suburban samples held constant in IQ during the same time period. It is difficult to conceive a benign explanation for these findings. Apparently, growing up in the poverty, segregation, and turmoil of the inner city imposes hardships that lead to a decline in IQ scores from

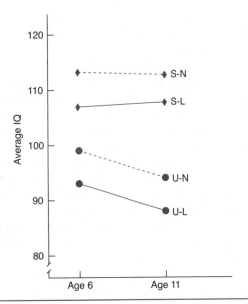

● **FIGURE 6.11** Average IQ Scores for Urban and Suburban Children at Age 6 and Age 11

S-N: Suburban Normal Birth Weight

S-L: Suburban Low Birth Weight

U-N: Urban Normal Birth Weight

U-L: Urban Low Birth Weight

*Source:* Based on data in Breslau, N., Chilcoat, H., Susser, E., and others (2001). Stability and change in children's Intelligence Quotient scores: A comparison of two socio-economically disparate communities. *American Journal of Epidemiology,* 154, 711–717.

age 6 to age 11. The authors summarize the significance of their study as follows:

> On average, the IQs of urban children declined by more than 5 points. A change of 5 points in an individual child might be judged by some as clinically nonsignificant. Nevertheless, a change of this size in a population's mean IQ, which reflects a downward shift in the distribution (rather than a change in the shape of the distribution), means that the proportion of children scoring 1 standard deviation or more below the standardized IQ mean of 100 would increase substantially. In this study, the change from age 6 to age 11 years increased the percentage of urban children scoring less than 85 on the WISC-R from 22.2 to 33.2. (Breslau et al., 2001, p. 716)

Sadly, the apparent drop of 5 points in average IQ from age 6 to age 11 found in this study may represent only part of the overall impact of environmental deprivation. The full effect over a lifetime could be substantially greater.

An earlier study by Jensen (1977) bears on the cumulative influence of long-term environmental deprivation. Using a methodologically novel approach, he tested 653 white children and 826 African American children from a small rural town in the southeastern part of Georgia. The working hypothesis of his study was that older African American children should score lower than their younger siblings, owing to the cumulative, intellect-depressing effects of their bleak, profoundly deprived environment. According to the cumulative deficit hypothesis, a consistent downward trend in IQ is a result of the cumulative effects of environmental disadvantages in factors related to mental development. In contrast, white children, who are less environmentally deprived, should not show a cumulative intellectual deficit as a linear function of age.

All children were administered the California Test of Mental Maturity (CTMM, 1963 revision), a standardized test of general intelligence, as part of a state-mandated testing program. The CTMM yielded carefully standardized deviation IQ scores (national mean of 100, standard deviation of 15) computed separately from national norms for each grade level from kindergarten through grade 12. Jensen (1977) noted that the sampled populations, particularly the African American group, were not intended to be representative of the wider U.S. population, white or African American:

> Blacks in the locality under study are probably as severely disadvantaged, educationally and economically, as can be found anywhere in the United States. If an age decrement does not exist in this group, it would seem most doubtful that it could be found in any subpopulation within our borders.

As predicted, older African American children scored lower than their younger brothers and sisters, the magnitude of the difference being directly related to the difference in age. In particular, African American children appeared to lose approximately one IQ point a year, on average,

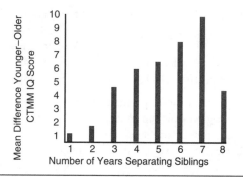

● **FIGURE 6.12**   Average Difference in CTMM IQ between Younger and Older African American Siblings as a Function of the Difference in Age

*Source:* Based on data from Jensen, A. R. (1977). Cumulative deficit in IQ of blacks in the rural south. *Developmental Psychology, 13,* 184–191.

between the ages of 6 and 16, with the cumulative loss totalling 5 to 10 IQ points. The exact amount of the loss depends on how we interpret some apparent sampling peculiarities in the data (Figure 6.12). Furthermore, if we factor in the probable IQ deficit that occurred between birth and age 5, we can surmise that the overall effect of a depriving environment is substantially more than the 5- to 10-point IQ decrement reported by Jensen (1977).

Scarr and Weinberg (1976, 1983) reversed the question probed by Jensen (1977); namely, they asked: What happens to their intelligence when African American children are adopted into the relatively enriched environment provided by economically and educationally advantaged white families? As discussed later, it is well known that African American children reared by their own families obtain IQ scores that average about 15 points below whites (Jensen, 1980). Some portion of this difference—perhaps all of it—is likely due to the many social, economic, and cultural differences between the two groups. We put that issue aside for now. Instead, we pursue a related question that bears on the malleability of IQ: What difference does it make when African American children are adopted into a more economically and educationally advantaged environment?

Scarr and Weinberg (1976, 1983) found that 130 African American and interracial children

adopted into upper-middle-class white families averaged a Full Scale IQ of 106 on the Stanford-Binet or the WISC, a full 6 points higher than the national average and some 18 to 21 points higher than typically found with African American examinees. African American children adopted early in life, before 1 year of age, fared even better, with a mean IQ of 110. We can only wonder what the IQ scores would have been if the adoptions had taken place at birth and if excellent prenatal care had been provided. This study indicates that when the early environment is optimal, IQ can be boosted by perhaps 20 points.

Limitations of space prevent us from further detailed discussion of environmental effects on IQ. It is worth noting, though, that a huge literature has emerged from early intervention and enrichment-stimulation studies of children at risk for school failure and mental retardation (e.g., Barnett & Camilli, 2002; Ramey & Ramey, 1998). In general, these studies show that intervention and enrichment can boost IQ in children at risk for school failure and mental retardation. Summarizing four decades of research, Ramey and Ramey (1998) extracted six principles from the research on early intervention for at-risk children. They refer to these as "remarkable consistencies in the major findings" on intervention studies:

1. Interventions that begin earlier (e.g., during infancy) and continue longer provide the best benefits to participating children.
2. More-intensive interventions (e.g., number of visits per week) produce larger positive effects than less-intensive interventions.
3. Direct enrichment experiences (e.g., working directly with the kids) provide greater impact than indirect experiences.
4. Programs with comprehensive services (e.g., multiple enhancements) produce greater positive changes than those with a narrow focus.
5. Some children (e.g., those with normal birthweight) show greater benefits from participation than other children.
6. Initial positive benefits diminish over time if the child's environment does not encourage positive attitudes and continued learning.

One concern about early intervention programs is their cost, which has been excessive for some of the demonstration projects. Skeptics wonder about the practicality and also the ultimate payoff of providing extensive, broad-based, continuing intervention virtually from birth onward for the millions of children at risk for developmental problems. This is a realistic concern because "relatively few early intervention programs have received long-term follow-up" (Ramey & Ramey, 1998). Critics also wonder if the programs merely teach children how to take tests without affecting their underlying intelligence very much (Jensen, 1981). Finally, there is the issue of cultural congruence. Intervention programs are mainly designed by white psychologists and then applied disproportionately to minority children. This a concern because programs need to be culturally relevant and welcomed by the consumers, otherwise the interventions are doomed to failure.

## Teratogenic Effects on Intelligence and Development

In normal prenatal development, the fetus is protected from the external environment by the placenta, a vascular organ in the uterus through which the fetus is nourished. However, some substances known as **teratogens** cross the placental barrier and cause physical deformities in the fetus. Especially if the deformities involve the brain, teratogens may produce lifelong behavioral disorders, including low IQ and mental retardation. The list of potential teratogens is almost endless and includes prescription drugs, hormones, illicit drugs, smoking, alcohol, radiation, toxic chemicals, and viral infections (Berk, 1989; Martin, 1994). We will briefly highlight the most prevalent and also the most preventable teratogen of all, alcohol.

Heavy drinking by pregnant women causes their offspring to be at very high risk for **fetal alcohol syndrome** (FAS), a specific cluster of abnormalities first described by Jones, Smith, Ulleland, and Streissguth (1973). Intelligence is markedly lower in children with FAS. When assessed in adolescence or adulthood, about half of all persons with

this disorder score in the range of mental retardation on IQ tests (Olson, 1994). Prenatal exposure to alcohol is one of the leading known causes of mental retardation in the Western world. The defining criteria of FAS include the following:

1. Prenatal and/or postnatal growth retardation—weight below the tenth percentile after correcting for gestational age
2. Central nervous system dysfunction—skull or brain malformations, mild to moderate mental retardation, neurological abnormalities, and behavior problems
3. Facial dysmorphology—widely spaced eyes, short eyelid openings, small up-turned nose, thin upper lip, and minor ear deformities (Sokol & Clarren, 1989)

The full-blown FAS previously described occurs mainly in offspring of women alcoholics—those who ingest many drinks per occasion. With lower levels of drinking, a more muted manifestation of the syndrome known as **fetal alcohol effect** may arise. A child with fetal alcohol effect typically has a normal physical appearance but exhibits demonstrably impaired attentional capacities and is slower to respond in a reaction time paradigm (Streissguth, Martin, Barr, & Sandman, 1984). Furthermore, the effect is linear-dose-related; that is, there may be no safe level of drinking during pregnancy (Streissguth, Bookstein, & Barr, 1996). For this reason, physicians now routinely advise women to abstain from alcohol during pregnancy. Nonetheless, a *conservative* estimate for the incidence of FAS (mild to severe forms) in the Western world is 1 per 1,000 live births, with most cases going undiagnosed and unrecognized (Abel, 1995). Spohr and Steinhausen (1996) provide an excellent review of research on the FAS syndrome.

## Effects of Environmental Toxins on Intelligence

Many industrial chemicals and by-products may impair the nervous system temporarily, or even cause permanent damage that affects intelligence. Examples include lead, mercury, manganese, arsenic, thallium, tetra-ethyl lead, organic mercury compounds, methyl bromide, and carbon disulphide (Lishman, 1997). Certainly, the most widely studied of these environmental toxins is lead, which we examine in modest detail here.

Sources of human lead absorption include eating of lead-pigmented paint chips by infants and toddlers; breathing of particulate lead from smelter emissions; eating of food from lead-soldered cans or lead-glazed pottery; and the drinking of water that has passed through lead pipes. Because the human body excretes lead slowly, most citizens of the industrialized world carry a lead burden substantially higher—perhaps 500 times higher—than known in pre-Roman times (Patterson, 1980).

The hazards of high-level lead exposure are acknowledged by every medical and psychological researcher who has investigated this topic. High doses of lead are irrefutably linked to cerebral palsy, seizure disorders, blindness, mental retardation, even death. The more important question pertains to "asymptomatic" lead exposure: Can a level of absorption that is insufficient to cause obvious medical symptoms nonetheless produce a decrement in intellectual abilities?

Research findings on this topic are complex and controversial. Using tooth lead from shed teeth of young children as their index of cumulative lead burden, Needleman and associates (1979) reported that "asymptomatic" lead exposure was associated with decrements in overall intelligence (about 4 IQ points) and lowered performance on verbal subtests, auditory and speech processing tests, and a reaction time measure of attention. These differences persisted at follow-up 11 years later (Needleman, Schell, Bellinger, Leviton, & Allred, 1990). Yet, using a similar study method, Smith, Delves, Lansdown, Clayton, and Graham (1983) found a nonsignificant effect from children's lead exposure when social factors such as the parents' level of education and social status were controlled.

In part, research findings on this topic are contradictory because it is difficult to disentangle the effects of lead from those of poverty, stress, poor nutrition, and other confounding variables (Kaufmann, 2001ab). Most likely, asymptomatic lead exposure has harmful effects on the nervous system that translate to reduced intelligence, impaired attention, and a host of other undesirable behavioral consequences. Even in the absence of a scientific consensus on this point, prudence dictates that we should reduce lead exposure in humans to the lowest levels possible.

## ● ORIGINS AND TRENDS IN RACIAL IQ DIFFERENCES

### Early Studies of African-American and White IQ Differences

Racial differences in IQ have been recorded since the beginnings of standardized testing. The most widely studied disparity is between African-American and White samples, where a discrepancy favoring Whites of about one standard deviation (15 points) is historically reported. We should add that the term Black is used interchangeably with African American, and that White refers to non-Hispanic White individuals. The IQ difference fluctuates from one analysis to the next—as small as 10 points in a few studies but as large as 20 points in others. For example, in the 1960 restandardization of the Stanford-Binet, the White sample ($M = 101.8$) outscored the Black sample ($M = 80.7$) by slightly more than 20 IQ points (Kennedy, Van de Riet, & White, 1963). A lesser difference was revealed on the 1981 WAIS-R where Whites ($M = 101.4$) outscored Blacks ($M = 86.9$) by 14½ points (Reynolds, Chastain, Kaufman, & McLean, 1987). In the standardization sample for the fourth edition of the Stanford-Binet (Thorndike, Hagen, & Sattler, 1986) a difference of about 17½ points (mean of 103.5 versus 86.1) was observed. For these early studies, when demographic variables such as socioeconomic status are taken into account, the size of the mean difference reduces to .5 to .7 standard deviations (7 to 10 IQ points) but does not disappear (Reynolds & Brown, 1984a). Put simply, the existence of race differences in IQ has been reported with such consistency that is it no longer the focus of serious dispute.

However, the *interpretation* of race differences in IQ is an issue of fierce ongoing debate. Why the disparity exists, what it means from a practical standpoint, and whether the gap is narrowing—all these topics engender a full range of opinions (Fagan & Holland, 2007; Rushton & Jensen, 2005). We begin our discussion with the question of origins—what are the causes of the Black-White IQ difference?

One viewpoint (discussed previously) is that the observed IQ disparity is caused, partly or wholly, by test bias. This is a popular and widely held viewpoint rarely supported by technical studies of test bias. Test bias may play a small role in race differences, but it cannot explain the persistent difference in IQ scores between Black and White Americans. Here we intend to examine a different hypothesis; namely: Is the IQ difference between Black and White Americans due, in significant part, to genetic sources?

## The Genetic Hypothesis for Race Differences in IQ

The hypothesis of a genetic basis for race differences in IQ first gained scholarly prominence in 1969 when Arthur Jensen published a provocative paper titled "How Much Can We Boost IQ and Scholastic Achievement?" (Jensen, 1969). Jensen set the tone for his paper in the opening sentence when he asserted that "compensatory education has been tried and it apparently has failed." He further contended that compensatory education programs were based on two fallacious theoretical underpinnings, namely, the "average child concept," which views children as more or less homogeneous, and the "social deprivation hypothesis," which asserts that environmental deprivation is the primary cause of lowered achievement and IQ scores. Jensen argued forcefully against both suppositions. Furthermore, leaning heavily on the literature in behavior genetics, Jensen implied that the reason whites scored higher than African Americans on IQ tests was probably related more to genetic factors than to the effects of environmental deprivation. The thrust of his paper was to suggest that, since compensatory education has

proved ineffectual, and since the evidence suggests a strong genetic component to IQ, therefore, it is appropriate to entertain a genetic explanation for the well-documented difference in favor of whites on IQ tests. He formulated the genetic hypothesis in a careful, tentative, scholarly manner:

> The fact that a reasonable hypothesis has not been rigorously proved does not mean that it should be summarily dismissed. It only means that we need more appropriate research for putting it to the test. I believe such definitive research is entirely possible but has not been done. So all we are left with are various lines of evidence, no one of which is definitive alone, but which, viewed all together, make it a not unreasonable hypothesis that genetic factors are strongly implicated in the average Negro-white intelligence difference. The preponderance of the evidence is, in my opinion, less consistent with a strictly environmental hypothesis than with a genetic hypothesis, which, of course, does not exclude the influence of environment or its interaction with genetic factors. (Jensen, 1969)

With the articulation of a genetic hypothesis for race differences in IQ, Jensen provoked an intense debate that has raged on, with periodic lulls, to the present day.

In the mid-1990s the controversy over a genetic basis for race differences in IQ was intensified once again with the publication of *The Bell Curve* by Richard Herrnstein and Charles Murray (1994). This massive tome was primarily a book about the importance of IQ as a predictor of poverty, school leaving, unemployment, illegitimacy, crime, and a host of other social pathologies. But two chapters on ethnic differences in intelligence caused an uproar among social scientists and the lay public. The authors reviewed dozens of studies and concluded that the IQ gap between African Americans and whites has changed little in this century. They also argued that test bias cannot explain the race differences. Furthermore, they noted that races differ not just in average IQ scores but also in the profile of intellectual abilities. In addition, they concluded that intelligence is only slightly malleable even in the face of intensive environmental intervention. As did Jensen, Herrnstein and Murray (1994) stated their genetic hypothesis with considerable circumspection:

> It seems highly likely to us that both genes and the environment have something to do with racial differences [in cognitive ability]. What might the mix be? We are resolutely agnostic on that issue; as far as we can determine, the evidence does not yet justify an estimate.

Although the authors declined to provide an estimate of the genetic contribution to race differences in IQ, it is clear from the tone of their pessimistic book that they believe it to be substantial. Recently, Arthur Jensen has reentered the debate on the origins of IQ differences between African Americans and white Americans and reaffirmed his earlier judgment that the disparity is "partly heritable" (Rushton & Jensen, 2005). Is this conclusion warranted by the evidence?

## Tenability of the Genetic Hypothesis

The genetic hypothesis for race IQ differences is an unpopular idea that is anathema to many laypersons and social scientists. But contempt for an idea does not constitute disproof, and superficiality is no substitute for a reasoned examination of evidence. In light of additional analysis and research, is the genetic hypothesis for IQ differences tenable? We will examine three lines of evidence here that indicate that the answer is "no."

Several critics have pointed out that the genetic hypothesis is based on the questionable assumption that evidence of IQ heritability within groups can be used to infer heritability between racial groups. Jensen (1969) expressed this premise rather explicitly, pointing to the substantial genetic component in IQ as suggestive evidence that differences in IQ between African Americans and white Americans are, in part, genetically based. Echoing earlier critics, Kaufman (1990) responds as follows:

> One cannot infer heritability between groups from studies that have provided evidence of the IQ's heritability within groups. Even if IQ is equally heritable within the black and white races separately, that does not prove that the IQ differences between the

races are genetic in origin. Scarr-Salapatek's (1971, p. 1226) simple example explains this point well: Plant two randomly drawn samples of seeds from a genetically heterogeneous population in two types of soil—good conditions versus poor conditions—and compare the heights of the fully grown plants. Within each type of soil, individual variations in the heights are genetically determined; but the average difference in height between the two samples is solely a function of environment.

Another criticism of the genetic hypothesis is that careful analysis of environmental factors provides a sufficient explanation of race differences in IQ; that is, the genetic hypothesis is simply unnecessary. This is the approach taken by Brooks-Gunn, Klebanov, and Duncan (1996) in a study of 483 African American and white low-birthweight children. What makes their study different from other similar analyses is the richness of their data. Instead of using only one or two measures of the environment (e.g., a single index of poverty level), they collected longitudinal data on income level and many other cofactors of poverty such as length of hospital stay, maternal verbal ability, home learning environment, neighborhood condition, and other components of family social class. When the children's IQs were tested at age 5 with the WPPSI, the researchers found the usual disparity between the white children (mean IQ of 103) and the African American children (mean IQ of 85). However, when poverty and its cofactors were statistically controlled, the IQ differences were almost completely eliminated. Their study suggests that previous research has underestimated the pervasive effects of poverty and its cofactors as a contribution to African American and white IQ differences.

A third criticism of the genetic hypothesis is that race as a biological entity is simply nonexistent; that is, *there are no biological races*. Fish (2002) and other proponents of this viewpoint argue that "race" is a socially constructed concept, not a biological reality:

> *Homo sapiens* has no extant subspecies: There are no biological races. Human physical appearance varies gradually around the planet, with the most geographically distant peoples generally appearing the most different from one another. The concept

of human biological races is a construction socially and historically localized to 17th and 18th-century European thought. Over time, different cultures have developed different sets (folk taxonomies) of socially defined "races." (p. 29)

Put another way, racial categories are social constructions based on superficial physical differences (especially skin color) that serve cultural-psychological objectives (e.g., reducing uncertainty about how we should respond to one another). However, racial categories do not signify meaningful biological differences. A biologist expresses the point this way: "All of humanity shares in common the vast majority of its molecular genetic variation and the adaptive traits that define us as a single species" (Templeton, 2002, p. 51). Thus, insofar as race has no biological reality, the argument that "race" differences in IQ originate from a genetic basis is not only pernicious, it is also absurd. Neisser, Boodoo, Bouchard, and others (1996) offer additional perspectives on race differences in IQ and related topics.

Before leaving the topic of race differences in IQ, we should point out that the emotion attached to this topic is largely undeserved, for two reasons. First, racial groups always show large overlaps in IQ—meaning that the peoples of the earth are much more alike than they are different. Second, as previously noted, the existing race differences in IQ certainly reflect cultural differences and environmental factors to a substantial degree. Wilson (1994) has catalogued the numerous differences in cultural background between African Americans and white Americans. In 1992, for example, 64 percent of African American parents were divorced, separated, widowed, or never married; 63 percent of African American births were to unmarried mothers; and 30 percent of African American births were to adolescents (U.S. Bureau of the Census, 1993). On average, these realities of family life for many African Americans inevitably will lead to lowered performance on intelligence tests. Lest the reader conclude that we are hereby endorsing a subtle form of Anglocentric superiority, consider Lynn's (1987) conclusion that the mean IQ of the Japanese is 107, a full 7 points higher than the average for American whites. So what?

## Recent Trends in Race Differences in IQ

An important question is whether Black-White IQ differences have remained stable over recent decades (which could support a genetic basis for the IQ disparity) or whether the gap has narrowed in response to environmental progress (which could indicate a substantial ecological source for the IQ disparity). The former conclusion (stability of the IQ difference) has been stated by Jensen and others who hypothesize, in part, a genetic basis for the discrepancy (Jensen, 1980; Jensen & Rushton, 2005).

In contrast, a recent analysis by Dickens and Flynn (2006) supports a significant narrowing of the racial IQ gap. These researchers considered comparative longitudinal data for Black and White examinees for the period 1970 to 2000 with successive editions of four carefully standardized instruments: The Stanford-Binet, the Wechsler Intelligence Scale for Children, the Wechsler Adult Intelligence Scale, and the Armed Forces Qualifying Test. Their findings are complex and statistically laden, but here is the big picture: on all four instruments, Blacks gained in IQ compared to Whites during 1970 to 2000, the average gain amounting to 4 to 7 IQ points. The authors conclude:

> The constancy of the Black-White IQ gap is a myth and therefore cannot be cited as evidence that the racial IQ gap is genetic in origin. (p. 917)

Overall, the average IQ for Black schoolchildren was estimated to be 90.5 in 2002, indicating that Black children have made large IQ gains relative to Whites since the 1960s. Dickens and Flynn (2006) conclude that further Black economic progress would produce additional gains in IQ. This conclusion provides an optimistic outlook on a contentious social issue.

## ● AGE CHANGES IN INTELLIGENCE

We turn now to another controversial topic—whether intelligence declines with age. Certainly, one of the most pervasive stereotypes about aging is that we lose intellectual ability as we grow older.

This stereotype is so pervasive that few laypersons question it. But we should question it.

In general, the empirical study of this topic provides a more optimistic conclusion than the common stereotype suggests. However, the research also reveals that age changes in intelligence are complex and multifaceted. The simple question, "Does intelligence decline with age?" turns out to have several labyrinthine answers.

We can trace the evolution of research on age-related intellectual changes as follows:

1. Early cross-sectional research with instruments such as the WAIS painted a somber picture of a slow decline in general intelligence after age 15 or 20 and a precipitously accelerated descent after age 60.

2. Just a few years later, more sophisticated studies using sequential testing with multidimensional instruments such as the Primary Mental Abilities Test suggested a more optimistic trajectory for intelligence: minimal change in most abilities until at least age 60.

3. Parallel research utilizing the fluid/crystallized distinction posited a gradual increase in crystallized intelligence virtually to the end of life, juxtaposed against a rapid decline in fluid intelligence.

4. Most recently, a few psychologists have proposed that adult intelligence is qualitatively different, akin to a new Piagetian stage that might be called postformal reasoning. This research calls into question the ecological validity of using standard instruments with older examinees.

We examine each of these research epochs in more detail in the following sections.

## Early Cross-Sectional Research

One of the earliest comprehensive studies of age trends on an individually administered intelligence test was reported by Wechsler (1944) shortly after publication of the Wechsler-Bellevue Form I. As is true of all the Wechsler tests designed for adults, raw scores on the W-B I subtests were first transformed into standard scores (referred to as scaled scores) with a mean of 10 and standard deviation of 3. Regardless of the age of the subject, these scaled scores were based on a fixed reference group of 350 subjects ages 20 to 34 included in the standardization sample. By consulting the appropriate age table, the sum of the 11 scaled scores was then used to find an examinee's IQ.

However, the sum of the scaled scores by itself is a direct index of an examinee's ability relative to the reference group. Wechsler used this index to chart the relationship between age and intelligence. His results indicated a rapid growth in general intelligence in childhood through age 15 or 20, followed by a slow decline to age 65. He was characteristically blunt in discussing his findings:

> If the fact that intellectual growth stops at about the age of fifteen has been a hard fact to accept, the indication that intelligence after attaining its maximum forthwith begins to decline just as any other physiological capacity, instead of maintaining itself at its highest level over a long period of time, has been an even more bitter pill to swallow. It has, in fact, proved so unpalatable that psychologists have generally chosen to avoid noticing it. (Wechsler, 1952)

Normative studies with subsequent Wechsler adult tests revealed exactly the same pattern. For example, results for the WAIS-IV have been computed in Figure 6.13, which shows the average uncorrected subtest scores for all age groups in the normative sample, relative to results for the highest scoring age group (25- to 29-year-olds).

Overlooked by Wechsler and many other **cross-sectional design** researchers was the influence of their methodology on their findings. It has been recognized for quite some time that cross-sectional studies often confound age effects with educational disparities or other age-group differences (see Baltes, Reese, & Nesselroade, 1977; Kausler, 1991). For example, in the normative studies of the Wechsler tests, it is invariably true that the younger standardization subjects are better educated than the older ones. In all likelihood, the lower scores of the older subjects are caused, in part, by these educational differences rather than signifying an inexorable age-related decline.

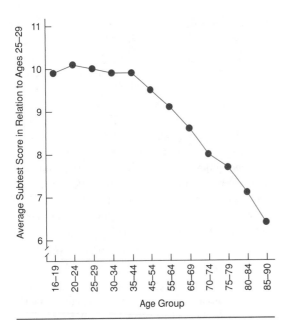

● **FIGURE 6.13** The Curve of Supposed Age-Related Decline in Average WAIS-IV Subtest Scores

*Source:* Based on data in Wechsler, D. (2008). *Manual for the Wechsler Adult Intelligence Scale—Fourth Edition.* San Antonio, TX: Pearson.

## Sequential Studies of Intelligence

To control for age-group differences, many researchers prefer a **longitudinal design** in which the same subjects are retested one or more times over periods of 5 to 10 years and, in rare cases, up to 40 years later. Because there is only one group of subjects, longitudinal designs eliminate age-group disparities (e.g., more education in the young than the old subjects) as a confounding factor. However, the longitudinal approach is not without its shortcomings. Longitudinal studies suffer from four potential pitfalls:

1. Time of measurement is the most serious problem. Major historical events such as an economic depression can warp the intellectual and psychological development of entire generations. As a result, longitudinally measured age changes may reflect the peculiarities of the time of measurement rather than any universal age effects.

2. Selective attrition—the less capable subjects may be the most likely to drop out, artificially inflating the mean scores of retested subjects.
3. Practice effects—examinees improve when they take the same test two, three, even five times.
4. Regression to the mean—especially a problem when participants are selected because of their initial extreme scores such as very low IQ scores (Hayslip & Panek, 1989).

The most efficient research method for studying age changes in ability is a **cross-sequential design** that combines cross-sectional and longitudinal methodologies (Schaie, 1977):

> In brief, the researchers begin with a cross-sectional study. Then, after a period of years, they retest these subjects, which provides longitudinal data on several cohorts—a longitudinal sequence. At the same time, they test a new group of subjects, forming a second cross-sectional study—and, together with the first cross-sectional study, a cross-sectional sequence. This whole process can be repeated over and over (every five or ten years, say) with retesting of old subjects (adding to the longitudinal data) and first-testing of new subjects (adding to the cross-sectional data). (Schaie & Willis, 1986)

In 1956, Schaie began the most comprehensive cross-sequential study ever conducted in what is referred to as the Seattle Longitudinal Study (Schaie, 1958, 1996, 2005). He administered Thurstone's test of five primary mental abilities (PMAs) and other intelligence-related measures to an initial cross-sectional sample of 500 community-dwelling adults. The PMA Test subtests include Verbal Meaning, Space, Reasoning, Number, and Word Fluency. In 1963, he retested these subjects and added a new cross-sectional cohort. Additional waves of data were collected in 1970, 1977, 1984, 1991, and 1998.

Three conclusions emerged from Schaie's cross-sequential study of adult mental abilities:

1. Each cross-sectional study indicated some degree of apparent age-related decrement in

mental abilities, postponed until after age 50 for some abilities, but beginning after age 35 for others. In particular, Number skills and Word Fluency showed an age-related decrement only after age 50, whereas Verbal Meaning, Space, and Reasoning scores appeared to decline sooner, after age 35.

2. Successive cross-sectional studies—the cross-sectional sequence—revealed significant intergenerational differences in favor of those born most recently. Even holding age constant, those born and tested most recently performed better than those born and tested at an earlier time. For example, 30-year-old examinees tested in 1977 tended to score better than 30-year-old examinees tested in 1970, who tended to score better than 30-year-old examinees tested in 1963, who, in turn, outperformed 30-year-old examinees tested in 1956. However, these cohort differences in intelligence were not uniform across the different abilities measured by the PMA Test. The pattern of rising abilities was most apparent for Verbal Meaning, Reasoning, and Space. Cohort changes for Number and Word Fluency were more complex and contradictory.

3. In contrast to the moderately pessimistic findings of the cross-sectional comparisons, the *longitudinal* comparisons showed a tendency for mean scores either to rise slightly or to remain constant until approximately age 60 or 70. The only exceptions to this trend involved highly speeded tests such as Word Fluency, in which the examinee must name words in a given category as quickly as possible, and Number, in which the examinee must complete arithmetic computations quickly and accurately.

The results of the Schaie study are even more optimistic when individual longitudinal findings are disentangled from the group averages. As previously noted, the longitudinal findings differed from one mental ability to another. Nonetheless, taking the average of the five PMAs and using the 25th percentile for 25-year-olds as his standard of

meaningful decline, Schaie has shown that no more than 25 percent of those studied had declined by age 67. From age 67 to age 74 about a third of the subjects had declined, whereas from age 74 to age 81, slightly more than 40 percent had declined (Schaie, 1980, 1996; Schaie & Willis, 1986). In sum, the vast majority of us show no meaningful decline in the skills measured by the Primary Mental Abilities Test until we are well into our seventies. Perhaps even more impressive is the fact that approximately 10 percent of the sample improved significantly when retested in their seventies and eighties. Based on his research and other longitudinal studies, Schaie arrives at this conclusion:

> If you keep your health and engage your mind with the problems and activities of the world around you, chances are good that you will experience little if any decline in intellectual performance in your lifetime. That's the promise of research in the area of adult intelligence. (Schaie & Willis, 1986)

### Age and the Fluid/Crystallized Distinction

Although we concur with the conclusions of Schaie and Willis (1986), it would be unfair to leave the impression that all authorities in this area agree. Horn and Cattell have been the most vocal skeptics, arguing for a significant age-related decrement in fluid intelligence because of its reliance upon neural integrity, which is presumed to decline with advancing age (Horn & Cattell, 1966; Horn, 1985). Cross-sectional studies certainly support this view. For example, Wang and Kaufman (1993) plotted age differences in vocabulary and matrices scores from the Kaufman Brief Intelligence Test and found little change in vocabulary (crystallized measure) but a sharp drop in matrices (fluid measure). These results held true even when the scores were adjusted for educational level. Of course, cross-sectional studies are open to rival interpretations and can, therefore, only suggest longitudinal patterns. Readers who wish to pursue this controversy should consult Hofer, Sliwinski, & Flaherty (2002) and Lindenberger and Baltes (1994).

More recently, Schaie, Caskie, Revell, and others (2005) demonstrated the same age-related patterns (negligible changes in crystallized measures, large decrements in fluid measures) in a follow-up study of older participants from the Seattle Longitudinal Study. Their participants comprised three groups: early-old (ages 60–69, $N = 180$), middle-old (ages 70–79, $N = 205$), and old-old (ages 80–95, $N = 114$). On average, the three groups were 64.2, 74.6, and 84.3 years of age, respectively. These individuals were administered a battery of 37 cognitive and neuropsychological measures assembled from well-known instruments, including the Wechsler Adult Intelligence Scale-Revised (WAIS-R, Wechsler, 1981), the Primary Mental Abilities test (PMA, Schaie, 1985), and several other tests. In Figure 6.14, we have depicted the results from four key subtests. Two of these subtests depend heavily on fluid cognitive factors (Reasoning and Spatial Thinking from the PMA), and two require significant crystallized abilities (Vocabulary and Comprehension from the WAIS-R). Scores are depicted as a percentage of the early-old group (ages 60–69) which typically earned the highest average score on all subtests. The reader will notice that raw scores on Comprehension and Vocabulary (crystallized abilities) reveal a nearly flat trend for the three age groups, whereas raw scores on Reasoning and Spatial Thinking (fluid abilities) disclose a steep decline for individuals in their 70s, 80s, and beyond.

## ● GENERATIONAL CHANGES IN IQ SCORES

What happens to the intelligence of a population from one generation to the next? For example, how does the intelligence of Americans in the year 2010 compare to the intelligence of their forebears in the early 1900s? We might expect that any differences would be small. After all, the human gene pool has remained essentially constant for centuries, perhaps millennia. Furthermore, only a small fraction of any generation is exposed do the extremes of environmental deprivation or enrichment that might stunt or boost intelligence dramatically. Common sense dictates that any generational changes in population intelligence would be minimal.

On this issue, common sense appears to be incorrect. Flynn (1984, 1987) charted the comparison data from successive editions of the Stanford-Binet and the Wechsler tests from 1932 to 1981 and found that, with only one exception, each edition established a higher standard than its predecessor. For example, when the latest edition of the WISC-R was released in the 1970s, a large sample of five- and six-year-old children was tested on both this instrument and the earlier WPPSI, released in the 1960s. The testing was counterbalanced, half of the sample taking the WPPSI first, half taking the WISC-R first. The average WPPSI IQ for these 140 children was 112.8, whereas the

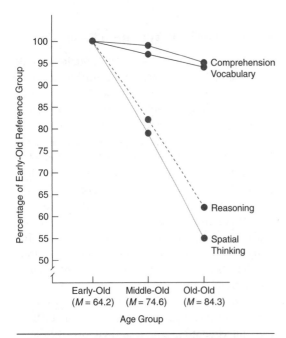

● **FIGURE 6.14** Cross-Sectional Comparison of Age Trends for Four Cognitive Subtests

*Source:* Based on data from Schaie, K. W., Caskie, G., Revell, A., & others (2005). Extending neuropsychological assessments in the Primary Mental Ability space. *Aging, Neuropsychology, and Cognition,* 12, 245–277.

● TABLE 6.5    Comparative Average IQs of Children from Successive
Editions of the Stanford-Binet and Wechsler Tests

| | Standardization Year | | Average IQ Score | | |
|---|---|---|---|---|---|
| Comparison Tests | Test 1 | Test 2 | Test 1 | Test 2 | Apparent Gain |
| SB-L & WISC | 1932 | 1948 | 107.1 | 101.6 | 5.5 |
| WB-I & WISC | 1937 | 1948 | 103.5 | 105.5 | −2.0 |
| WISC & WAIS | 1948 | 1954 | 101.8 | 99.1 | 2.7 |
| WISC & WPPSI | 1948 | 1965 | 93.6 | 90.9 | 2.7 |
| WISC & WISC-R | 1948 | 1972 | 97.2 | 88.8 | 8.4 |
| WPPSI & SB-72 | 1965 | 1972 | 93.1 | 88.7 | 4.4 |
| WPPSI & WISC-R | 1965 | 1972 | 112.8 | 108.6 | 4.2 |
| WISC-R & WAIS-R | 1972 | 1978 | 99.6 | 98.7 | 0.9 |
| WISC-R & WISC-III | 1972 | 1988 | 108.2 | 102.9 | 5.3 |
| WISC-III & WAIS-III | 1988 | 1996 | 104.6 | 103.9 | 0.7 |
| WAIS-III & WISC-IV | 1996 | 2001 | 101.6 | 98.5 | 3.1 |
| SB-IV & SB5 | 1985 | 2001 | 111.4 | 107.9 | 3.5 |
| WISC-III & SB5 | 1988 | 2001 | 105.9 | 100.9 | 5.0 |
| WISC-IV & WAIS-IV | 2001 | 2006 | 103.7 | 102.5 | 1.2 |

Note: Standardization Year refers to the year of standardization for the comparison tests. Average IQ Score refers to the average IQs of tested participants who were children ages 4 to 17, as appropriate for the tests involved. For example, the WAIS-IV and WISC-IV overlap for children 16 years of age, hence the average IQs are for 16-year-olds only.

Source: Based on data from the technical manuals for the Stanford-Binet and Wechsler tests.

same children earned an average WISC-R IQ of about 108.6. Because each new test is calibrated to a general population average of 100, this difference indicates an apparent 4-point gain in the population from the time the WPPSI was standardized (in 1965) to the time the WISC-R was standardized (in 1972). When new revisions are charted against their predecessors in the manner described here, the total apparent gain in mean IQ amounts to about 14 points in the five decades from 1932 to 1981 (Flynn, 1984).

This apparent rise in IQ over generations is known as the **Flynn effect** in honor of the psychologist who first delineated the occurrence (Flynn, 2007a). Although the Flynn effect may have slowed down in recent decades, it is still found in nearly every comparison of average IQs for successive editions of mainstream intelligence tests. We have charted several representative comparisons over the years, including data for the latest editions of the Stanford-Binet and the Wechsler tests (Table 6.5). A point of clarification: In these studies, the comparison groups typically are convenience samples. Thus, there is no expectation that the average scores should parallel the standardization mean of 100. What is of interest is not the absolute level of the IQs, rather, the *difference* between the average scores for the same group of children on each pair of tests. The reader will notice that, with only one exception, children perform better on the previous version than on the new version of the comparison tests. This trend of rising performance has been observed in many other nations using other tests as well, including Raven's Progressive Matrices and the Peabody Picture Vocabulary Test (Daley, Whaley, Sigman, Espinosa, & Neuman, 2003; Nettelbeck & Wilson, 2004).

However, IQ gains of the magnitude observed pose a serious problem of causal explanation. Flynn (1994) is skeptical that any real and meaningful intelligence of a population could vault upward so quickly. He concludes that current tests do not measure intelligence but rather a correlate with a weak causal link to intelligence:

> Psychologists should stop saying that IQ tests measure intelligence. They should say that IQ tests measure abstract problem-solving ability (APSA), a term that accurately conveys our ignorance. We know people solve problems on IQ tests; we suspect those problems are so detached, or so abstracted from reality, that they ability to solve them can diverge over time from the real-world problem-solving ability called intelligence; thus far we know little else. (Flynn, 1987)

Other explanations for the Flynn effect include better nutrition, improved prenatal care, greater educational access, and increased environmental complexity (Lynn, 2009; Sundet, Borren, & Tambs, 2008). On this last point, environmental complexity, Flynn (2007b) provides a telling illustration by way of generational changes in TV programs. He notes that early 1960s shows like *I Love Lucy* or *Dragnet* required almost no concentration to follow, whereas in the 1980s dramas like *Hill Street Blues* introduced up to 10 threads in the story line. More recently, the hit action-thriller drama *24* portrays as many as 20 characters and multiple plot lines.

The existence of the Flynn effect has sensitized psychologists to the dangers of rendering conclusions based on ever-shifting intelligence test norms. Changes in IQ over time make it imperative to restandardize tests frequently, otherwise examinees are being scored with obsolete norms and will receive inaccurate IQ scores. This is especially a problem when IQ scores are used for important decisions such as eligibility for learning disability programs, or entitlement to social security benefits. At the other extreme, issues literally of life and death can be at stake when IQ scores impact capital punishment decisions via the diagnosis of mental retardation (Kanaya, Scullin, & Ceci, 2003).

Several recent studies indicate that the Flynn effect may have abated or even reversed in the beginning of the twenty-first century. Reviewing data from more than a half-million Danish men over the period 1959 to 2004, Teasdale and Owen (2005) found that average performance on a military entry intelligence test gained slowly, peaked in the late 1990s, and has since declined slowly. Sundet, Barlaug, and Torjussen (2004) found a similar pattern with Norwegian conscripts on a test of matrix reasoning, with improved performance from the 1950s until the 1990s, followed by a reversal and decline. Using Piagetian tests of conservation of weight, volume, and quantity with seventh-grade British schoolchildren, Shayer, Ginsburg, and Coe (2007) documented a steady decline in performance from 1975 to 2003, a phenomenon they dubbed the "anti-Flynn effect."

## ● SUMMARY

1. Test bias is defined as differential validity of a given interpretation of a test score for any definable, relevant subgroup of test takers. As an example of test bias, an oral arithmetic test delivered in English might function well for English-speaking children, whereas for Hispanic children, the same test might predict arithmetic skill poorly.

2. Bias in content validity is demonstrated when an item or subscale of a test is relatively more difficult for members of one group than another after general ability level is held constant. In general, for the major standardized tests of ability and aptitude, evidence of bias in content validity is scant or nonexistent.

3. Bias in predictive or criterion-related validity is demonstrated when a test does not predict a relevant criterion equally well for persons from different subpopulations. An unbiased test possesses homogeneous regression: The results for all relevant subpopulations cluster equally well around a single regression line.

4. Bias in construct validity is demonstrated when a test is shown to measure different traits or constructs for one group than another. In comparisons across relevant subpopulations, a nonbiased test will reveal a high degree of similarity for the factorial structure of the test and the rank order of item difficulties within the test.

5. Test fairness incorporates social values and philosophies of test use. Three philosophies have been outlined: unqualified individualism (select the best person using all predictors), quotas (select by ratios), and qualified individualism (select the best person not using race, sex, etc., as predictors). Which of these philosophies is correct? This is an ethical question that is beyond objective solution.

6. The genetic contribution to human characteristics is usually measured in terms of a heritability index that can vary from 0.0 to 1.0. Heritability is an estimate of how much of the total variance in a given trait is caused by genetic factors. Heritability is relative to the population sampled and does not explain individual scores. For IQ, most estimates of heritability are around .50.

7. Evidence of a genetic contribution to intelligence is documented by the Minnesota twin studies in which identical twins separated at birth are reunited for extensive psychometric testing. Even though many twin pairs were reared in dissimilar environments, their adult IQs are remarkably similar. These findings corroborate earlier adoption studies.

8. Cross-sectional and longitudinal studies both indicate that growing up in economically deprived settings can cause IQ to drop significantly over a period of several years. Jensen (1977) came to this conclusion by comparing siblings from poor rural areas, and Breslau et al. (2001) demonstrated the same result in a longitudinal study of inner city children.

9. Scarr and Weinberg studied the effects of environmental enrichment: They found that African American children adopted into upper-middle-class white families showed above-average IQs.

10. Heavy drinking by pregnant women causes their offspring to be at very high risk for fetal alcohol syndrome, characterized by facial abnormalities, growth deficiencies, motor problems, hyperactivity, and mild to moderate mental retardation. With lower levels of drinking, offspring may show attentional impairment and other subtle problems known as fetal alcohol effect.

11. Environmental toxins also may affect intelligence. For example, children who absorb undue amounts of lead (such as by eating lead pigmented paint chips) may evidence long-term decrements in mental functioning (lowered IQ, problems with auditory and speech processing, and slowed reaction time).

12. On the average, African Americans score about 15 points lower than white Americans on standardized IQ tests. When demographic variables such as social class are accounted for, the difference reduces to 7 to 10 IQ points. Apparently, the magnitude of the difference has remained constant in the mid- to late twentieth through the early twenty-first centuries.

13. Jensen (1969) and others have proposed that whites score higher than African Americans on IQ tests partly because of genetic factors. This hypothesis is based on the questionable assumption that evidence of IQ heritability within groups can be used to infer heritability between racial groups. Research on racial admixture and IQ does not support a genetic view.

14. Longitudinal research on age and intelligence provides a more optimistic perspective than does cross-sectional research. In longitudinal studies, most abilities change little until at least age 60. Fluid abilities—largely nonverbal and culture-reduced mental efficiency—show a greater age decline than other abilities.

**15.** Flynn has charted the standardization data for each edition of the Stanford-Binet and the Wechsler scales from 1932 to the present time. Each test established a higher standard than its predecessor, with a total gain of about 14 IQ points. These apparent IQ gains pose serious problems of explanation and indicate that norms for tests may shift very rapidly.

## ● KEY TERMS AND CONCEPTS

test bias   p. 246

content bias   p. 248

predictive validity bias   p. 249

bias in construct validity   p. 252

test fairness   p. 254

unqualified individualism   p. 254

quotas   p. 255

qualified individualism   p. 255

heritability index   p. 256

teratogens   p. 260

fetal alcohol syndrome   p. 260

fetal alcohol effect   p. 260

cross-sectional design   p. 265

longitudinal design   p. 266

cross-sequential design   p. 266

# Chapter 7

# Testing Special Populations

The individual and group tests reviewed in previous chapters are suitable for persons with normal or near-normal capacities in speech, hearing, vision, movement, and general intellectual ability. However, not every examinee falls within the ordinary spectrum of physical and mental abilities. By reason of immature age, physical disability, language weakness, or diminished intellect, a large proportion of the population falls outside the reach of traditional tests and procedures.

Infants and very young children certainly require exceptional approaches to assessment because of their limited capacities for communication. In Topic 7A, Infant and Preschool Assessment, we review the nature and application of infant and early childhood assessment devices and then investigate a

fundamental question pertaining to these tests: What is the practical utility of testing children early in life? In particular, is there any predictive validity for test results obtained from infants or toddlers? If instruments for very young examinees do not predict important outcomes later in life, then using them would appear to be pointless and perhaps even misleading. We examine this quandary in some detail. Finally, we conclude the topic with a discussion of an important application of preschool testing—screening for school readiness. In Topic 7B, Testing Persons with Disabilities, we scrutinize a variety of tests needed for the assessment of individuals with special needs. These special needs cover a wide spectrum, including language, hearing, and visual impairments. Of course, persons with developmental disabilities also require special approaches to assessment, and we provide coverage of this field as well. By one estimate, as many as 7.5 million U.S. citizens manifest mental retardation, and 1 in 10 families are directly affected by this functional disability (Grossman, Richards, Anglin, & Hutson, 2000).

## ● ASSESSMENT OF INFANT ABILITY

The infant and preschool period extends from birth to roughly 6 years of age. The changes that occur during this period are obviously profound. The infant develops basic reflexes, masters developmental milestones (grasping, crawling, sitting, standing, and so forth), learns a language, and establishes the capacity for symbolic thought. For most children, the pattern and pace of development is visibly within normal limits.

However, parents and professionals trained in the assessment of infants and preschoolers occasionally encounter children whose development seems to be slow, delayed, or even overtly retarded. These children elicit a flurry of anxious questions: How delayed is this child? What are the prospects for normal functioning in school? Will this child achieve personal independence in the adult years?

At the opposite extreme are those precocious children who achieve developmental milestones months or years ahead of the normative schedule. In these cases, the proud parents have a different set of concerns: How advanced is my child? What are the strongest and weakest areas of intellectual functioning? Will this child be a gifted adult?

Infant and preschool assessment devices can help answer questions about children at both extremes of the spectrum—those who might be developmentally delayed, and those who might be intellectually gifted. Of course, these tests also provide useful information about the vast majority of children who fall in the middle of the distribution. In this topic, we review the nature and application of prominent infant and preschool measures. These tools include individual tests, developmen-

tal schedules, and rating scales. We begin with a description of several prominent instruments and then investigate the fundamental question of purpose or utility. What is the use of these measures? What is the meaning of a score on a developmental schedule or preschool intelligence test? To what extent do these procedures allow us to prognosticate adult abilities or, for that matter, help us to predict early school performance? These questions will be more meaningful if we first review the relevant instruments.

We divide the review into two parts: infant measures for children from birth to age 2½, and preschool tests for children from age 2½ to age 6. The division is somewhat arbitrary, but not entirely so. Infant tests tend to be multidimensional and to load significantly on sensory and motor development. Beginning at age 2½, standardized measures such as the Stanford-Binet: Fifth Edition, Kaufman Assessment Battery for Children-2, and Differential Ability Scales-II typically used in the assessment of preschool children. These tests load heavily on cognitive skills such as verbal comprehension and spatial thinking. Thus, infant scales and preschool tests measure somewhat different components of intellectual ability.

### Neonatal Behavioral Assessment Scale (NBAS)

The Neonatal Behavioral Assessment Scale (NBAS) is unique because of its theoretical basis, which emphasizes the need to document the contributions of the newborn to the parent–infant system. The pediatrician T. Berry Brazelton (Brazelton & Nugent, 1995) developed this instrument to identify and understand the "deviant" infant and to explore the baby's reciprocal impact on parents:

> My goal in developing the NBAS was to assess the baby's contributions to the failures that resulted, when parents were presented with a difficult or deviant infant. If we could understand the reasons behind the infant's deviant behavior, perhaps we could in turn lead parents to a better understanding of their role. This then could lead to a more optimal outcome. (Brazelton & Nugent, 1995)

The NBAS is suitable for infants up to two months of age but is most commonly administered in the first week of life. The scale assesses the infant's behavioral repertoire on 28 behavior items, each scored on a 9-point scale. Examples of the behavior items include the following:

- Response decrement to light
- Orientation to inanimate visual stimulus
- Cuddliness
- Consolability

In addition, the infant's neurological status is evaluated on 18 reflex items, each scored on a 4-point scale. Examples include the following:

- Plantar grasp
- Babinski reflex
- Rooting reflex
- Sucking reflex

Finally, seven supplementary items can be used to summarize the qualities of responsiveness of frail, high-risk infants, including these:

- Quality of alertness
- General irritability
- Examiner's emotional response to infant

Brazelton and Nugent (1995) do not provide an integrative scoring system; that is, there are no summary scores for the entire battery or its subcomponents. Instead, the "scoring" of the NBAS consists of a summary sheet with ratings on each specific item. In clinical work, the instrument is used to provide feedback to parents. Specifically, Brazelton recommends that health care professionals demonstrate the NBAS in order to sensitize parents to their baby's uniqueness and to promote a positive parent–infant relationship. Hawthorne (2009) describes the clinical application of the instrument for promoting successful caregiving strategies. Regarding clinical use of the test, Fowles (1999) compared mothers who received a demonstration of the NBAS with a matched control group and showed that the intervention group subsequently rated their infants as significantly more predictable. Thus, the NBAS was found to be useful in helping mothers anticipate their infants' responses to environmental stimuli. However,

based on a comprehensive review of published studies, Britt and Myers (1994) provide a less optimistic review of the effects of the NBAS intervention, noting inconsistent findings in areas such as parent–infant interaction, infant development, temperament, and parental attitudes and satisfaction.

For research on newborn outcomes, various investigators have developed scoring systems for the NBAS, including a popular seven-cluster scoring method proposed by Lester (1984). This method provides summary scores for identified clusters (habituation, orientation, motor performance, arousal/lability, regulation, autonomic stability, and reflexes). Using a quantitative scoring approach, researchers have linked prenatal cocaine exposure to inferior performance on the NBAS (Morrow et al., 2001; Schuler, 1999). In addition, the NBAS is also sensitive to the detrimental effects of polychlorinated biphenyls (PCBs) on babies born to women who consumed contaminated Lake Ontario fish (Stewart, Reihman, Lonky, Darvill, & Pagano, 1999). The NBAS also shows sensitivity to the impact of major depression in mothers by revealing greater arousal and less attentiveness to face/voice stimuli in their newborn babies (Hernandez-Reif, Field, Diego, & Ruddock, 2006). Further, the instrument is sensitive to changes in feeding behavior of premature infants (Medoff-Cooper & Ratcliffe, 2005). In general, these studies demonstrate the value of the NBAS in a wide variety of research endeavors with infants.

In spite of the proven utility of the NBAS as a clinical and research tool, reviewers have been somewhat skeptical about the psychometric properties of the instrument. For example, Majnemer and Mazer (1998) point to very low test-retest reliability coefficients ($r = -0.15$ to $+0.32$ for the individual items) and weak interrater agreement. One likely explanation is that in newborn infants, individual traits may fluctuate rapidly over short periods of time, which would produce an underestimate of true reliability when the NBAS is given twice over a period of days or weeks. For this reason, deviant scores from a single administration of the NBAS should not be overinterpreted.

## Bayley-III

Originally released in 1969, the Bayley test is now in its third edition (Bayley, 2006). Suitable for children 1 month to 42 months of age, this instrument is an important mainstay for the evaluation of developmental delay in infants and toddlers. Known formally as the Bayley Scales of Infant and Toddler Development-III and informally as the Bayley-III, the most recent version represents a vast extension and revision of the earlier editions. For example, the first edition of the test evaluated only the cognitive and motor capacities of infants, whereas the latest edition provides for the assessment of five domains. The domains and representative capacities tested are listed here.

- *Cognitive Scale:* 91 items involving sensory acuity, perceptual skill, attention, object permanence, exploration and manipulation, puzzle solving, color matching, and counting. The Cognitive Scale does not contain separate subtests.
- *Language Scale:* 48 items involving receptive and expressive communication. Items involve recognition of sounds, nonverbal expression, following simple directions, identifying action pictures, naming objects, and answering questions. The Language Scale yields separate scores for Expressive Communication and Receptive Communication as well as a composite Language Scale score.
- *Motor Scale:* 138 items pertaining to gross motor and fine motor skills. Items involve object manipulation, functional hand skills, postural control, dynamic movement, and motor planning. The Motor Skill yields separate scores for Gross Motor and Fine Motor as well as a composite Motor Scale score.
- *Social-Emotional:* 35 items involving interactive and purposeful use of emotions, ability to convey feelings, and connection of ideas and emotions. The Social-Emotional Scale does not contain separate subtests.
- *Adaptive Behavior Scale:* Caregivers complete items on a 4-point scale of 0 (*is not able*), 1 (*never when needed*), 2(*sometimes when needed*),

or 3 (*always when needed*); items pertain to Communication, Community Use, Health and Safety, Leisure, Self-Care, Self-Direction, Functional Pre-Academics, Home Living, Social, and Motor. This scale yields separate scaled scores for each of the ten areas listed, as well as a General Adaptive Composite (GAC).

The five major clusters listed above each yield a composite score reported as a standard score ($M = 100$, $SD = 15$). Note that the Bayley-III does not yield an overall score akin to an IQ score on a traditional test. Such a score could be misleading in light of the broad range of diverse skills now assessed in the third edition of the test. Instead, the instrument seeks to yield a profile of scores useful in infant assessment and diagnosis. To this end, all scores on the instrument (including the many subscales listed above) can be reported as scaled scores (mean = 10, SD = 3) for purposes of intra-individual comparison. This yields a useful chart that helps pinpoint areas of needed intervention. For example, the child depicted in Table 7.1, a 37-month-old boy referred for assessment, appears to present with mild intellectual disability characterized by problems

● **TABLE 7.1    Bayley-III Scaled Score Results for a 37-Month-Old Infant**

| Cog | Language | | Motor | | SE |
|---|---|---|---|---|---|
| Cog | RC | E | FM | GM | SE |
| 6 | 7 | 4 | 3 | 8 | 4 |

| | | | | *Adaptive Behavior* | | | | | |
|---|---|---|---|---|---|---|---|---|---|
| Com | CU | FA | HL | HS | LS | SC | SD | Soc | MO |
| 4 | 7 | 4 | 8 | 7 | 7 | 5 | 4 | 6 | 6 |

Cog = Cognitive, RC = Receptive Communication, EC = Expressive Communication, FM = Fine Motor, GM = Gross Motor, SE = Social-Emotional, Com = Communication, CU = Community Use, FA = Functional Pre-Academics, HL = Home Living, HS = Health and Safety, LS = Leisure, SC = Self-Care, SD = Self-Direction, Soc = Social, MO = Motor.

Note:  An average score in the general population is 10, and scores between 8 and 12 typically are considered normal. Scores of 4 or below, indicated in bold, are areas of potential concern.

with expressive communication, fine motor skills, communication, functional pre-academics, and self-direction.

The technical quality and excellent standardization of the Bayley-III mark this test as the psychometric pinnacle of its field. The normative sample of 1,700 children was stratified according to age and essential demographic variables, and the test developers also collected extensive data on children with high-incidence clinical diagnoses such as autism and intellectual disability. Internal consistency reliability of the five composite scores appears to be strong, with average reliability coefficients as high as .93 (Language) and .91 (Cognitive). Test-retest reliability over a short period (average of 6 days) is predictably lower, with coefficients ranging from .67 (Fine Motor) to .80 (Expressive Communication). Average stability coefficient across all ages for the major composites was .80, which is decent given that infants and toddlers are notoriously distractible.

Validity evidence for the Bayley-III is scant at this time, but wholly supportive. For example, confirmatory factor analysis of the subtests of the Cognitive, Language, and Motor scales supported the three-factor model across all age groups of the standardization sample, except for the youngest age group (Bayley, 2006). Concurrent validity coefficients with other instruments are strong as well. For example, The WPPSI-III Full Scale IQ scores correlated .72 to .79 with Bayley-III Cognitive composites. Correlations of the Motor and Adaptive Behavior composites with suitable instruments also were appropriately strong, on the order of .50 to .70. We agree with reviewers who assert that the Bayley-III continues to set the standard for early childhood assessment, and will maintain its status as the most frequently used measure of infant and toddler development (Albers & Grieve, 2007).

### In Brief: Additional Measures of Infant Ability

The assessment of infants is so important and yet so difficult. Infants do not ordinarily follow directions

and they may not be able to verbalize what they know. The assessment of infant abilities is an extraordinary challenge. Nonetheless, dozens of test developers have risen to the summons. Even a brief review of alternative instruments would be chapter-length. We provide a quick summary of better-known approaches in Table 7.2. Most of these instruments involve observation or the presentation of simple tasks to the examinee. For additional reviews of infant assessment, the reader is encouraged to read Nuttall, Romero, and Kalesnik (1992), Ricciuti (1994), and Salvia and Ysseldyke (1991).

### ● ASSESSMENT OF PRESCHOOL INTELLIGENCE

Preschool children exhibit wide variability in emotional maturity and responsiveness to adults. One child may warm up to the examiner and strive for optimal performance on all questions. Another child may stare mutely at the floor rather than attempt a simple block design task. For the first child, we can rest assured that the test results are an appropriate index of cognitive functioning. But for the second child, uncertainty prevails. Does the nonresponsiveness signal a lack of skill or a lack of cooperation? With preschool children, a large measure of humility is required of the examiner. Scarr (1981) has expressed this sentiment as follows:

> Whenever one measures a child's cognitive functioning, one is also measuring cooperation, attention, persistence, ability to sit still, and social responsiveness to an assessment situation.

The special danger in preschool assessment is that the examiner may infer that a low score indicates low cognitive functioning when, in truth, the child is merely unable to sit still, attend, cooperate, and so forth. Preschool assessment needs to be approached with unusual caution to avoid negative consequences of labeling and overdiagnosis of disabling conditions.

---

> ● **TABLE 7.2**    **Additional Measures of Infant Ability**
>
> **Battelle Developmental Inventory—Second Edition (BDI-2)** (Newborg, 2005). Birth to age 8; the 450 items assess Adaptive, Personal/Social, Communication, Motor, and Cognitive domains. The full battery takes 1–2 hours to administer; a screening version (100 items) is available; child-friendly materials make this an appealing instrument.
>
> **Developmental Assessment of Young Children (DAYC)** (Voress & Maddox, 1998). Birth to age 6; assessment in five domains (cognition, communication, social-emotional, physical, and adaptive) is completed through observation, interview of caregivers, and direct assessment. DAYC provides a brief assessment (20 minutes) based on outstanding normative data (1,300 children divided into 23 age groups approximating the 1996 census). The resulting five indices and global index are highly reliable (coefficients ranging from .90 to .99).
>
> **Developmental Indicators for the Assessment of Learning-3 (DIAL-3)** (Mardell-Czudnowski & Goldenberg, 1998). Ages 3 through 6; domains assessed include Motor (e.g., catching, cutting, writing), Concepts (e.g., naming, counting, sorting), and Language (e.g., nouns/verbs, problem solving, sentence length). The test-retest reliability in the high .80s is extraordinary for an instrument of this type. English and Spanish versions are available in the same kit.
>
> **Early Screening Inventory-Revised (ESI-R)** (Meisels, Wiske, & Henderson, 2008). Ages 3 to 6; a brief screening instrument that comes in two forms, the Preschool version (ESI-P), and the Kindergarten version (ESI-K). Three areas of development are sampled: Visual-Motor/Adaptive, Language and Cognition, and Gross Motor. The total score is used to classify children into one of three referral groups: "OK" (above average to minus 1 SD), "rescreen" (between minus 1 and minus 2 SDs), and "refer" (below minus 2 SDs).
>
> **Early Screening Profiles (ESP)** (Harrison, Kaufman, Kaufman, and others, 1990). Ages 2 through 6; domains assessed include Cognitive/Language, Motor, and Self-Help/Social; four Surveys (Articulation, Behavior, Health History, and Home) supplement the assessment. This instrument has strong psychometric qualities; the manual reports detailed information on seven validation studies completed independently of the standardization study. Barnett (1995) offers a skeptical review; Telzrow (1995) is more positive.

---

There are several individually administered intelligence tests suitable for preschool children. The most commonly used instruments include:

- Kaufman Assessment Battery for Children-2 (KABC-2)
- McCarthy Scales of Children's Abilities (MSCA)
- Differential Ability Scales-II (DAS-II)
- Wechsler Preschool and Primary Scale of Intelligence-III (WPPSI-III)
- Stanford-Binet Intelligence Scales for Early Childhood, Fifth Edition (Early SB5)

The KABC-2 was described in the previous chapter. We will focus here on the, the Differential Ability Scales-II, the WPPSI-III, and the Early SB5.

## Differential Ability Scales-II

The Differential Ability Scales-2 (DAS-II) is the latest edition of a highly respected test initially published in 1990 (Elliott, 1990, 2007). The test consists of three batteries: The Early Years Battery (lower-level) for ages 2-6 to 3-5, the Early Years Battery (upper-level) for ages 3-6 to 6-11, and the School-Age Battery for ages 7-0 to 17-11. We focus here on the battery used with preschool children ages 3-6 to 6-11.

The DAS-II includes 10 core subtests and 10 diagnostic subtests; however, rarely is a child administered all 20 subtests. The core subtests are the primary measures of cognitive abilities whereas the diagnostic subtests provide supplementary information about school readiness and information processing. The particular combination of subtests administered depends on the child's age, ability level, and the purposes of assessment. For preschool children age 3½ and above, a comprehensive test battery would include 6 core subtests and 7 diagnostic subtests, which are described in Table 7.3.

The core subtests are heavily saturated with the *g* factor and are used to derive three core cluster scores (Verbal, Nonverbal Reasoning, and Spatial) and an overall composite score known as General Conceptual Ability (GCA). An optional cluster score known as the Special Nonverbal Composite (SNC) can be computed from four nonverbal subtests as well. In developing the DAS and its revision, Elliott (2007) steered away from concepts of intelligence and IQ, using the more neutral designation of GCA instead. Even so, most experts in the field would consider GCA to be essentially the same as IQ.

### ● TABLE 7.3  DAS-II Subtests on the Early-Years Battery, Upper Level

| Subtest | Abilities Measured | Contribution to Composite(s) |
|---|---|---|
| **Core Subtests** | | |
| Verbal Comprehension | Receptive language, understanding of oral instructions | GCA, Verbal Ability |
| Naming Vocabulary | Expressive language, knowledge names and object | GCA, Verbal ability |
| Picture Similarities | Nonverbal reasoning, matching pictures with common themes | GCA, Nonverbal reasoning ability |
| Matrices | Abstract reasoning, deducing the missing pattern in a matrix | GCA, Nonverbal reasoning ability |
| Pattern Construction | Nonverbal, spatial visualization with colored blocks and squares | GCA, Spatial Ability |
| Copying | Design copying, fine-motor coordination, visual-spatial matching | GCA, Spatial Ability |
| **Diagnostic Subtests** | | |
| Early Number Concepts | Knowledge of numerical concepts— number, order, addition, subtraction | School Readiness |
| Matching Letter-Like Forms | Seeing spatial relationships, visually discriminating similar forms | School Readiness |
| Phonological Processing | Ability to process syllables, sounds, and phonemes, e.g., rhyming, blending | School Readiness |
| Recall of Sequential Order | Visualization and recall, e.g., order of body parts (belly, hair, toe, chin) | Working Memory |
| Recall of Digits Backward | Short-term auditory recall for sequences, mental manipulation | Working Memory |
| Speed of Information Processing | Rapid visual scanning and simple decision-making | Processing Speed |
| Rapid Naming | Naming colors and pictures as quickly as possible | Processing Speed |

Note: GCA = General Conceptual Ability. Also, a Special Nonverbal Composite (SNC) can be computed from the four nonverbal core subtests.

The diagnostic subtests measure early number concepts, phonological processing, short-term memory, and processing speed. These subtests and the diagnostic composites derived from them are used for clinical analysis only. The diagnostic subtests are less dependent on the $g$ factor and therefore do not figure in the GCA or any core composites. The diagnostic subtests contribute to three diagnostic cluster scores (School Readiness, Working Memory, and Processing Speed). These subtests provide information useful in assessing learning problems and school readiness, thereby complementing the core subtests. The DAS-II is normed to standard scores ($M = 100$, $SD = 15$) for the GCA and cluster scores, whereas the individual subtests are based on $T$ scores ($M = 50$, $SD = 10$). The DAS-II was normed on 3,480 U.S. children, with careful stratification (2002 census data) on age, gender, race/ethnicity, parental education, and geographic region.

The reliability of DAS-II scores is commendable for an instrument used at the preschool level. Typically, preschool children are easily distracted and plainly influenced by situational factors, which tends to lower the reliability of test scores. The DAS-II seems relatively immune to these influences. For preschoolers, GCA internal consistency reliability is reported to be .95. The cluster scores also show excellent reliability with values ranging from .89 to .95. Internal consistency reliability of the subtests is predictably lower, although still laudable, ranging from .81 to .91. As is often found in reliability studies, test-retest reliability figures were significantly lower, based on retesting of 369 children after a period ranging from 7 to 63 days. These coefficients ranged from .51 to .92, with most values in the .70s and .80s.

The validity of the DAS-II looks promising from several perspectives. First, the measure reveals very strong correlations with other tests of preschool cognitive functioning and achievement. For example, DAS-II GCA scores correlate strongly with mainstream intelligence tests, for example, $r = .87$ with WPPSI-III IQ, and $r = .84$ with WISC-IV IQ. Likewise strong correlations are observed with major achievement tests, for example, $r = .82$ with WIAT-II total achievement, and $r = .81$ with KTEA-II total achievement. Another line of validity evidence for the DAS-II consists of test data for twelve special groups, including children with giftedness, mental retardation, reading disorder, ADHD and learning disorder, and limited English proficiency. In general, these groups reveal theory-consistent patterning of scores, for example, those with reading disorders score relatively low on the Verbal Ability cluster, those with ADHD and learning disorder score relatively low on the School Readiness cluster, those known to be gifted earn average GCA scores of 125, and so forth.

Confirmatory factor analyses reported in the technical manual leave a confusing picture as to the underlying structure of the DAS-II. The number of factors providing the best fit to the test data differs by age group, ranging from a 2-factor solution for the youngest age group (age 2-6 to 3-5) to a 7-factor solution for children ages 6-0 to 12-11, with 5- and 6-factor models for other age groups. On the other hand, the DAS-II is not predicated on any particular model of intelligence, so the pertinence of confirmatory factor analyses is questionable.

Even though the DAS-II has been available for a few years, there is almost no published research using the test. One study found the instrument valuable in the evaluation of specific learning disability (SLD). In particular, regression equations using the cluster scores were helpful in identifying children with SLD in mathematics (Hale, Fiorello, Dumont, and others, 2008). Beran (2007) reviews the test favorably, with this understatement: "The test is complex." In fact, the summary page of the record form for hand scoring proves so difficult to follow that computer scoring is nearly mandatory. Sattler (2008) provides an especially thorough overview of the DAS-II.

## Wechsler Preschool and Primary Scale of Intelligence-III (WPPSI-III)

The WPPSI-III is very similar to its predecessors but offers updated norms, more expansive assessment of cognitive functions, and application to a wider age range—ages 2½ to 7 years and 3 months

(Wechsler, 2002). The test consists of 14 subtests that are designated as one of three types:

- *Core:* These subtests are required for the computation of the Verbal, Performance, and Full Scale IQ.
- *Supplemental:* These subtests provide additional information about cognitive abilities or can be used as replacements for inappropriate or "spoiled" subtests.
- *Optional:* These subtests provide additional information about cognitive functioning but cannot be used as replacements for core subtests.

The WPPSI-III is divided into two age ranges: ages 2-6 to 3-11, and ages 4-0 to 7-3. The battery for the younger group includes four core subtests and one supplemental subtest. In brief, this battery consists of the Receptive Vocabulary and Information subtests, from which the Verbal IQ is computed, and the Block Design and Object Assembly subtests, from which the Performance IQ is computed. The supplemental subtest Picture Naming can be substituted for Receptive Vocabulary or Information. The battery for older children is much more comprehensive and consists of seven core subtests, five supplemental subtests, and two optional subtests. Our discussion here pertains only to the battery for older children, ages 4-0 to 7-3. The structure of the WPPSI-III for this age group is shown in Table 7.4.

## Stanford-Binet Intelligence Scales for Early Childhood

Known informally as the Early SB5, the Stanford-Binet Intelligence Scales for Early Childhood (Roid, 2005) combine the subtests from the Stanford-Binet Intelligence Scales, Fifth Edition (SB5) with a new Test Observation Checklist and a software-generated Parent Report. The subtests of the SB5 were described in the previous chapter. We focus here on the Test Observation Checklist (TOC), which summarizes essential information about child test-taking behaviors—in particular, behaviors that may have a stunning impact on test scores.

The Early SB5 was developed for children ages 2 years to 7 years and 3 months. This is precisely the age range in which a child's true level of functioning can be radically underestimated due to behavior problems such as distractibility, low frustration tolerance, or noncompliance. For example, many preschool children simply stop responding when subtest items become difficult—they may look down, or look away, or offer a comment on an unrelated topic. Noncompliant behavior of this nature is common; in fact, occasional refusals are reported in 41 percent of young children (Aylward & Carson, 2005). But a refusal can mean many things. Perhaps the child really doesn't know the answer; or perhaps the child knows the answer but is bored with testing, or afraid to hazard a guess, or simply distracted. The examiner will never know for sure, but there is a good chance that the true cognitive abilities of a noncompliant child will be underestimated. The purpose of the TOC is to provide a qualitative but

**TABLE 7.4  Structure of the WPPSI-III at Ages 4-0 to 7-3**

| Area | Designation | Subtests |
|---|---|---|
| Verbal | Core | Information Vocabulary Word Reasoning |
| | Supplemental | Comprehension Similarities |
| Performance | Core | Block Design Matrix Reasoning Picture Concepts |
| | Supplemental | Picture Completion Object Assembly |
| Processing Speed | Core | Coding |
| | Supplemental | Symbol Search |
| General Language Composite | Optional | Receptive Vocabulary Picture Naming |

Note: All administered subtests contribute to the Full Scale IQ.

highly structured format for describing a wide range of behaviors, including noncompliance, known to affect test performance.

The test-taking behaviors listed on the TOC are divided into two groups: (1) Characteristics, and (2) Specific Behaviors. The former are general traits most likely found in many situations, whereas the latter are specific behaviors actually observed during the testing session. The focus of the TOC is behaviors that negatively impact test performance. Many of the characteristics and behaviors are rated on a continuum, whereas others are categorical.

The characteristics rated include (Aylward & Carson, 2005):

> Motor Skills—includes gross motor skills such as clumsiness and fine motor skills such as pencil dexterity.
>
> Activity Level—includes both excessive restlessness as well as underactivity in relation to child's age.
>
> Attention/Distractibility—refers to age-inappropriate inattention, a need for redirection.
>
> Impulsivity—indicates the examiner saw fit to intervene, slow the child down.
>
> Language—includes articulation, receptive language, and expressive language.

The specific behaviors rated include (Aylward & Carson, 2005):

> Consistency in Performance—may indicate a haphazard approach to the test.
>
> Mood—includes specific behavioral indicators such as negative mood, tantrums, or crying.
>
> Frustration Tolerance—includes aggressiveness, refusal to participate.
>
> Change in Mental Set—includes noted tendencies toward rigidity of approach or perseveration.
>
> Motivation—includes disinterest or boredom and related behaviors.
>
> Fear of Failure—is qualitatively judged through inference and can be corroborated through parental report.

> Degree of Cooperativeness/Refusals—a crucial category because numerous refusals can lead to underestimating cognitive ability.
>
> Anxiety—includes excessive fearfulness, shyness, or need for parental presence.
>
> Need for Redirection—is noted when the child cannot stay on task and constantly needs reminders.
>
> Parental Behaviors—includes items such as parental reassurance, tacit approval for misbehavior, or giving verbal cues.
>
> Representativeness of Test Behaviors—is based on brief interview with parent(s), if present during testing.

The TOC helps the examiner identify problematic behaviors that may affect the validity of the test results. But this is not the only purpose of this instrument. In addition, the documentation of these behavior problems may prove helpful in the early detection of developmental difficulties such as learning disabilities, behavior problems, attentional difficulties, borderline cognitive function, and neuropsychological deficits (Aylward & Carson, 2005).

## ● PRACTICAL UTILITY OF INFANT AND PRESCHOOL ASSESSMENT

The history of child assessment has shown time and again that, in general, test scores earned in the first year or two of life show minimal predictive validity. For example, in her review of infant intelligence testing, Goodman (1990) concludes:

> If the successful prediction of adolescent and adult intelligence from early childhood scores is one of the great accomplishments of applied psychology, then the failure to predict intelligence from infancy to early childhood ranks as one of its greatest failures.

Given this dismal record of repeated failures of predictive validity, we must ask a difficult question: What is the purpose and practical utility of infant assessment? In fact, infant tests do have an important but limited role to play. We return to that issue after a review of predictive studies.

## Predictive Validity of Infant and Preschool Tests

With heterogeneous samples of normal children, the general finding is that infant test scores correlate positively but unimpressively with childhood test scores (Goodman, 1990; McCall, 1979). A few studies are more optimistic in tone (e.g., Wilson, 1983), but most researchers agree with McCall's (1976) conclusion:

> Generally speaking, there is essentially no correlation between performance during the first six months of life with IQ score after age 5; the correlations are predominantly in the 0.20s for assessments made between 7 and 18 months of life when one is predicting IQ at 5–18 years; and it is not until 19–30 months that the infant test predicts later IQ in the range of 0.40–0.55.

McCall (1979) reconfirmed his original conclusion in a later review, finding that the correlations between infant and school-age test scores do not ex-

ceed .40 until the subjects are at least 19 months of age for the initial testing.

The findings with preschool tests are somewhat more positive in tone. The correlation between preschool test results and later IQ is typically strong, significant, and meaningful. The simplest way to investigate this question is to measure the stability of IQ results in longitudinal studies. In Table 7.5, we have summarized the age-to-age stability of children's IQ scores on the Stanford-Binet from the Fels Longitudinal Study, an early, classic follow-up investigation of children's intellectual and emotional development (Sontag, Baker, & Nelson, 1958). The lowest correlation in this table is .43, and that is between IQ tested at age 4 and again at age 12. What stands out in the table is the robustness of the link between IQ in preschool and later childhood. The older the child at initial testing, the stronger the relationship with later IQ. In fact, the results suggest that IQ becomes reasonably stable, on average, by 8 years of age.

Collectively, these findings confirm that infant tests generally have poor prognostic value, whereas preschool tests are moderately predictive of later intelligence. This brings us back to the question

| ● TABLE 7.5 | Stability of IQ from 3 to 12 Years of Age | | | | | | | | |
|---|---|---|---|---|---|---|---|---|---|
| | *Age at Retesting* | | | | | | | | |
| Age at Initial Testing | 4 | 5 | 6 | 7 | 8 | 9 | 10 | 11 | 12 |
| 3 | .83 | .72 | .73 | .64 | .60 | .63 | .54 | .51 | .46 |
| 4 | | .80 | .85 | .70 | .63 | .66 | .55 | .50 | .43 |
| 5 | | | .87 | .83 | .79 | .80 | .70 | .63 | .62 |
| 6 | | | | .83 | .79 | .81 | .72 | .67 | .67 |
| 7 | | | | | .91 | .83 | .82 | .76 | .73 |
| 8 | | | | | | .92 | .90 | .84 | .83 |
| 9 | | | | | | | .90 | .82 | .81 |
| 10 | | | | | | | | .90 | .88 |
| 11 | | | | | | | | | .90 |

*Source:* Adapted with permission from Sontag, L. W., Baker, C., & Nelson, V. (1958). Mental growth and personality development: A longitudinal study. *Monographs of the Society for Research in Child Development, 23* (Whole No. 68). Copyright © by The Society for Research in Child Development, Inc.

posed at the beginning of this section: What is the purpose and practical utility of infant assessment?

## Practical Utility of Infant Scales

The most important and sound use of infant tests is in screening for developmental disabilities. Early detection of children at risk for mental retardation is vital because it provides for early intervention and, consequently, allows for improved outcomes later in life. Although existing infant tests are poor predictors of childhood and adult intelligence, an exception to this rule is encountered for infants who obtain very low scores on the Bayley test and other screening tests. For example, infants who score two or more standard deviations below the mean on the original Bayley (1969) and the Bayley-II (Bayley, 1993), particularly on the Mental Scale, reveal a high probability of meeting the criteria for mental retardation later in childhood (Goodman, Malizia, Durieux-Smith, MacMurray, & Bernard, 1990). There is no longitudinal research with the very recent Bayley-III (Bayley, 2005), but this test likely possesses good predictive validity for low scores as well.

With at-risk children, the correlation between infant test scores and later childhood IQ is much stronger than for samples of normal children. The most consistent finding is that a very low score on an infant test—two or more standard deviations below the mean—accurately prognosticates mental retardation in childhood. For example, studies with the Denver Developmental Screening Test-Revised (since revised and published as the Denver-II) revealed a false positive rate of only 5 to 11 percent, meaning that infants and preschoolers identified as at risk for mental retardation rarely achieve normal range cognitive functioning in childhood (Frankenburg, 1985). Most studies with the Bayley test also conform to this pattern. For example, VanderVeer and Schweid (1974) found that 23 young children with mild, moderate, and severe mental retardation confirmed by the Bayley at ages 18 to 30 months continued to merit a diagnosis of mental retardation one to three years later. Although some of the children with moderate and severe

mental retardation were functioning at a higher level (mild retardation), none of the children with initial mental retardation was normal at follow-up. In an ostensibly contradictory finding, Hack, Taylor, Drotar, and others (2005) reported that very low scores on the Bayley-II for low birth weight infants tested at 20 months of age did not strongly predict low scores on the K-ABC at age 8. These findings are cautionary, but not definitive, insofar as the K-ABC is not a good criterion for mental retardation.

## Fagan Test of Infant Intelligence (FTII)

The infant tests discussed in this chapter could be described as traditional, in the sense that their methods are a natural outgrowth of the long sweep of individual intelligence tests reaching back to the early 1900s. But perhaps new approaches are needed with infants. Lewis has argued that traditional infant tests overlook early information-processing behaviors, such as recognition memory and attentiveness to the environment, that might better predict childhood cognitive function (Lewis & Sullivan, 1985). In one study, simple visual habituation to a novel stimulus (measured by the duration of fixation) assessed at 3 months of age correlated .61 with the Bayley Mental score at 24 months of age (Lewis & Brooks-Gunn, 1981). Fagan and McGrath (1981) reported similar findings. In their study, infants first observed a picture of a baby's face for a short period of time and were then shown the same picture alongside an unfamiliar picture (e.g., picture of a bald-headed man). The investigators kept careful track of which picture the infants looked at more. The logic of the procedure is simple: Staring mainly at the new picture signifies that an infant recognizes the old picture; that is, an infant with good recognition memory prefers to look at something new. Preference for novelty—as measured by visual fixation time on the new picture—thus becomes an index of early recognition memory. Years later, the investigators administered the Peabody Picture Vocabulary Test (PPVT) to gauge early childhood intelligence. Infant recognition memory scores and early child PPVT scores correlated .37 at 4 years of age and .57 at 7 years of age. Infant cognitive measures would appear to be promising predictors of childhood intelligence (Fagan & Haiken-Vasen, 1997).

Using the paradigm described previously, Fagan (1984) developed a new approach to infant assessment known as the Fagan Test of Infant Intelligence (FTII). The FTII assesses visual recognition memory using a 10-trial habituation format (Fagan & Shepherd, 1986). In each trial, a photograph of a face is shown to the infant, followed by paired presentation of the original face with either (1) a photograph of a similar but new face or (2) a photograph of the original face in a different orientation. The amount of time spent looking at the new photograph is presumed to indicate the degree to which the infant has noticed that it is different from the original picture. The examiner observes the infant's corneal reflections to determine a percent Novelty Preference, averaged across the 10 trials. The procedure shows very high interrater agreement (O'Neill, Jacobson, & Jacobson, 1994). A score of less than 53 percent for novelty preference identifies children who are at risk for later mental retardation.

Validation studies of the FTII as a predictor of childhood intelligence and as a screening tool for mental retardation are mixed in outcome. With regard to the prediction of intelligence, FTII scores obtained at 7 to 9 months of age correlated only .32 with Stanford-Binet IQ at age 3 for a sample of 200 infants (DiLalla, Thompson, Plomin, and others, 1990). In another study, overall correlations between FTII scores obtained at 7 to 9 months of age and WPPSI-R IQ at age 5 were very low, about .2, for two Norwegian samples of healthy children (Andersson, 1996). Tasbihsazan, Nettelbeck, and Kirby (2003) have identified a likely reason that FTII scores correlate weakly with later IQ; namely, the test may possess poor reliability. In particular, for healthy, not at-risk infants, the test-retest stability coefficients for percent Novelty Preference were .29 for 12 infants tested at 27 and 29 weeks, −.07 for 12 infants tested at 29 and 39 weeks, and −.17 for 13 infants tested at 39 and 52 weeks.

These stability coefficients are not just low—they are indistinguishable from zero, which raises doubts as to the soundness of the FTII instrument.

The FTII may perform better as a screening test than as a general predictor of childhood intelligence. With regard to screening infants at risk for developmental disability, Fagan, Singer, Montie, and Shepherd (1986) reported very positive findings in a study of 62 infants who experienced adverse factors such as premature birth or maternal diabetes. When evaluated at 3 years of age, eight children revealed cognitive delay (IQ ≤ 70), whereas 54 were considered normal. The FTII, previously administered between 3 and 7 months of age, correctly detected 6 of the 8 children with delay (75 percent sensitivity) and suitably identified 49 of 54 normal children (91 percent specificity). However, not all FTII screening studies of at-risk infants are positive in tone. For example, McGrath, Wypij, Rappaport, Newburger, and Bellinger (2004) used FTII scores from 1 year of age to predict low IQ at age 8 in 100 at-risk infants and found poor sensitivity of 32 percent in detecting cognitive delay (IQ ≤ 85) but fair specificity of 80 percent. Yuan (2002) published Chinese norms for the FTII and found a strong concurrent validity. Coefficient of .72 for 73 infants tested with the Bailey-II. Further research is needed before we abandon traditional infant measures in favor of the Fagan test and similar measures.

## ● SCREENING FOR SCHOOL READINESS

The purpose of **screening** is to identify at-risk children so they can be referred for more comprehensive evaluation (Kamphaus, 1993). But "at risk" for what? The general answer refers to likelihood of failure in the early elementary years of schooling. The notion of being at risk is intimately linked to the concept of developmental delay, which refers to children whose cognitive development is well below age expectations. Some children identified with this label "catch up" later in life. For these children, developmental delay is an appropriate designation. Certainly, it is a more optimistic and less stigmatizing label than mental retardation—which is often the ultimate outcome of developmental delay.

Children with low intelligence are substantially at risk for school failure, which explains why individual intelligence tests play an important role in the evaluation of preschool children. But individual intelligence tests require a substantial commitment of time (up to two hours) and must be administered by carefully trained practitioners. For practical reasons, then, individual intelligence tests are not suitable as screening instruments.

The ideal screening instrument is a short test that can be administered by teachers, school nurses, and other individuals who have received limited training in assessment. In addition, a sensible screening test is one that provides a cutoff score that is accurate in classifying children as normal or at risk. In the context of screening tests, two kinds of errors can occur. Normal children who fail the test would be referred to as false-positive cases (because they are falsely classified as positive for potential disability). At-risk children who pass the test would be referred to as false-negative cases (because they are falsely classified as negative for potential disability). The reader must keep in mind that the purpose of screening is merely to identify children in need of additional evaluation, which means that false-positive cases will receive further evaluation. Hence, a false-positive misclassification rarely leads to undesirable consequences. However, false-negative cases typically do not receive further evaluation, so this kind of misclassification is potentially more serious—because a needy child is deemed to be normal. Glascoe (1991) recommends that a useful instrument should yield a false-negative rate of less than 20 percent (meaning that 80 percent of truly at-risk children are flagged by the test) and an even lower false-positive rate of less than 10 percent (meaning that 90 percent of normal children pass the test).

Glascoe and Shapiro (2005) outline five common pitfalls of developmental and behavioral screening in infancy and early childhood:

- Waiting until the problem is observable. Some clinicians use a screening test only after the problem is manifest—a waste of time and effort.
- Ignoring screening results. Practitioners may adopt a "wait and see" outlook—early intervention is then pointlessly postponed.
- Relying on informal methods. Clinicians often employ their own informal methods—consequently, children in need of services go undetected.
- Using inappropriate tests. Some clinicians sparingly use long batteries instead of screening tests—as a result, children with disabilities are overlooked.
- Assuming services are limited or nonexistent. Practitioners often incorrectly assume that services are not available—consequently, they are reluctant to administer screening tests.

These pitfalls lead to two adverse outcomes: underdetection of developmental problems and delayed discovery of disabilities. In both cases, needy infants and children do not receive the services they need.

## Qualities of a Good Preschool Screening Instrument

What are the qualities of a good preschool screening instrument? School readiness involves a number of broad areas, including motor, language, cognitive, social, and emotional functioning. Success in early schooling requires that children function at or near age-appropriate levels in all these areas. Thus, a useful screening tool must address at least a few of these prerequisite domains. In addition to appropriate coverage, other qualities are needed in a suitable preschool screening tool as well. For example, the Minnesota Interagency Developmental Screening Task Force—a leading advocacy group in preschool screening—has published extensive standards by which it recommends and approves screening instruments (www.health.state.mn.us). The following list of criteria is modeled loosely on their recommendations:

- The primary purpose is screening rather than assessment, diagnosis, or prediction of academic success.

- Screening is provided in most or all of these areas: motor, language, cognitive, social, and emotional functioning.
- Overall test-retest reliability coefficient is a minimum of .70, preferably higher.
- Concurrent validity against a comprehensive assessment is a minimum of .70, preferably higher.
- Sensitivity and specificity of "at risk" and "not at risk" classifications, respectively, are both at least .70.
- Practicality and ease of administration are built in, with testing time of 30 minutes or less.
- Cultural, ethnic, and linguistic sensitivity is evident, i.e., the test accurately screens children from diverse cultures.
- Minimum expertise is required for administration, i.e., the test is suitable for paraprofessionals to administer.

The Interagency Task Force further notes that social-emotional domains embedded within current screening instruments do not demonstrate sufficient reliability and validity to determine if a child needs further assessment. Thus, separate instruments may be required to determine if children are "at risk" for school failure due to social-emotional difficulties.

### Instruments for Preschool Screening

As noted by Meisels and Atkins-Burnett (2005), dozens of instruments have been produced to screen for developmental delays, but only a few have withstood the test of time. In Table 7.6 we summarize a few recommended tools (Glascoe, 2005; Meisels & Atkins-Burnett, 2005). An interesting feature of these evaluations is that nearly all of them are available in multiple languages, including Spanish, French, Korean, Vietnamese,

---

### ● TABLE 7.6    A Sample of School Readiness Screening Tests

**Ages and Stages Questionnaire (Brookes Publishing Company)**  Birth to 60 months; parent report of language, cognition, personal-social, and motor skills; available in English, Spanish, French, and Korean; takes 10 to 20 minutes; clerical or paraprofessional tester.

**Brigance Screens (Curriculum Associates)**  Birth to 60 months; observation of social-emotional skills, speech-language, motor, readiness, and general knowledge; available in English, Spanish, Laotian, Vietnamese, Cambodian, and Tagalog; takes 15 to 20 minutes; consult online training module before scoring.

**Early Screening Inventory-Revised (Pearson Assessments)**  36 to 60 months; observation of visual motor/adaptive, language and cognition, and gross motor skills; available in English and Spanish; takes 15 to 20 minutes; screeners and scorers can be trained with a manual and video.

**FirstSTEP Preschool Screening Tool (Pearson Assessment)**  33 to 62 months; observation of cognitive, communication, and motor domains and classifications of: within acceptable limits, caution, or at-risk; available in English only; takes 15 to 20 minutes; screeners and scorers can be trained with a manual and video.

**Minneapolis Preschool Screening Instrument-Revised (Minneapolis Public Schools)**  36 to 60 months; 64 dichotomous items pertaining to cognitive, language, literacy, motor, and perceptual development; available in English, Spanish, Somali, Hmong; takes 12 to 15 minutes to administer, 2 to 5 minutes to score; easy to learn, suitable for paraprofessionals.

**Parents' Evaluation of Developmental Status (Ellsworth & Vandemeer Press)**  Birth to 96 months; parental response in ten areas such as cognitive, expressive language, fine motor, social-emotional; available in English, Spanish, and Vietnamese; takes 5 minutes to administer, 2 minutes to score; suitable for paraprofessionals and clinic office staff.

Laotian, Cambodian, Hmong (the language of the ethnic group from mountainous regions of southeast Asia), and Tagalog (the language of the Philippines). These tools reflect the increasing diversity of American culture and the desire to provide adequate school-based services to recent immigrants.

We limit our discussion here to just three tests: the DIAL-III (Developmental Indicators for the Assessment of Learning-III), the Denver II (a revision of the Denver Developmental Screening Test-Revised), and the HOME (Home Observation for the Measurement of the Environment). The first two tests use conventional approaches for the identification of developmental delay, whereas the third instrument, the HOME, embodies a radical departure from traditional procedures.

## DIAL-III

The Developmental Indicators for the Assessment of Learning-III is an individually administered screening procedure designed for the quick and efficient detection of developmental problems (or giftedness) in preschool children ages 3:0 through 6:11 (Mardel-Czudnowski & Goldenberg, 1998). The test kit includes materials and normative data for both English-speaking and Spanish-speaking children. The test screens the performance of children in three developmental domains: motor, concepts, and language. The instrument consists of 7 subtests in each domain, for a total of 21 subtests (Table 7.7). Items in these domains are administered directly to the child by the examiner. In addition, standardized scores are also obtained in Self-Help and Social Development by means of a parent questionnaire. Examples of test items within the three developmental domains include the following:

*Motor:* Fine-motor items include block building, cutting, copying shapes and letters, name writing, and finger touching; gross-motor items include catching, jumping, hopping, and skipping.

*Concepts:* Pointing to named body parts, naming or identifying colors, rote counting, counting blocks, positioning blocks, identifying concepts, and sorting shapes.

*Language:* Giving personal information (name, age, sex), naming objects and actions, proper articulation, and phonemic awareness (e.g., rhyming).

Scoring for some items is discrete and objective, whereas for other questions the scoring criteria in the manual leave room for subjective interpretation, which detracts from the reliability of the instrument. A total score is obtained by summing the three area scores. For each area score and also the total score, the manual provides cutoff scores for assigning the child to one of two outcome groups labeled "potential delay" and "okay." The standardization samples consisted of 1,560 children (English-speaking) and 605 children (Spanish-speaking) stratified roughly by 1994 census data for gender, race, geographic region, and parental education.

| ● TABLE 7.7 Conceptual Clustering of the DIAL-III Subtests | | |
|---|---|---|
| *Language* | *Concepts* | *Motor* |
| Articulation | Body Parts | Catching |
| Personal Information | Colors | Jump, Hop, Skip |
| Objects | Rapid Color Naming | Building |
| Actions | Counting | Thumbs/Fingers |
| Letters/Sounds | Positions | Cutting |
| Rhyming/I Spy | Concepts | Copying |
| Problem Solving | Shapes | Name Writing |

Reliability of the DIAL-III is fair, given that it is a brief test for screening purposes. Internal consistency coefficients range from .66 for Motor to .84 for Concepts, with a total scale reliability of .87. Test-retest data are similar, which is to say, not up to the suggested minimum reliability of .90 for tests used to make individual decisions (Nunnally & Bernstein, 1994). Validity of the instrument has been evaluated along the familiar lines of content, construct, and criterion-related. Content validity is judged to be high insofar as a panel of experts provided content reviews and helped eliminate inappropriate and biased items. Criterion-related validity is strong, as judged by correlations with similar instruments such as the Early Screening Profiles, Differential Abilities Scale, and Peabody Picture Vocabulary Test-IV.

A recent study favorably evaluates the construct validity of the DIAL-III through confirmatory factor analysis (Assel & Anthony, 2009). As noted, the instrument was designed to screen for developmental delays in three domains: motor abilities, conceptual knowledge, and language competence. An essential feature of the test is that separate scores are reported for each domain. These domains and the 21 subtests comprising them were rationally preconceived by the test authors. An important question is whether the 21 subtests "hang together" statistically in a manner that supports the rational grouping into the three domains provided by the test developers. In other words, do the three domains possess a latent reality, or are they merely figments of the imaginations of the test developers? Using test results for 1,560 children ages 3 to 6, Assel and Anthony (2009) found an excellent fit between the three domains traditionally reported on the DIAL-3 and three empirically derived domains found through factor analysis, which supports the construct validity of the test. However, these authors did note that Articulation subtest was a poor index of language competence, and the Catching subtest was a poor index of motor abilities. Further, the authors found that Name Writing, Rapid Color Naming, and Letters/Sounds demonstrated floor effects, that is, even the easiest items on these subtests were

failed by young, low-SES, and minority children. These findings indicate the need for adding simpler items on these subtests for future revisions of the test. The DIAL-III also comes in a Spanish version that is separately validated on a sample of 588 Spanish-speaking Head Start children (Anthony & Assel, 2007).

It is with regard to practical utility that the DIAL-III and its precursor editions have raised the greatest skepticism. The value of a screening test is best judged by the extent to which it *accurately* identifies children in need of further developmental assessment. One useful statistic is sensitivity, which is the proportion of confirmed problem cases accurately "flagged" as problem cases by a test (i.e., children with delay who are accurately classified as "potential delay"). Unfortunately, brief screening tests such as the DIAL-III do not reveal strong sensitivity when the recommended cutoff scores are used to identify children as showing "potential delay." The only way to achieve high sensitivity is to liberalize the cutoff scores, that is, classify a larger proportion of children as showing "potential delay." However, this will create problems with specificity, which is the percentage of normal children correctly identified as normal.

### Denver II

The Denver II (Frankenburg, Dodds, Archer, and others, 1990) is an updated version of the highly popular Denver Developmental Screening Test-Revised (Frankenburg, 1985; Frankenburg & Dodds, 1967). The Denver test is probably the most widely known and researched pediatric screening tool in the United States. The instrument is popular worldwide—it has been translated into 44 different languages. Suitable for infants and children ages 1 month to 6 years, the test consists of 125 items in four areas: personal-social, fine motor-adaptive, language, and gross motor. The items are a mix of parent report, direct elicitation, and observation. Each item is arranged chronologically on the test by age of the child and marked pass/fail. Testing begins at an age-appropriate level and continues until the child fails three items. Total time for evaluation is 20 minutes or less.

Unlike other screening tests, the Denver II does not produce a developmental quotient or score. Instead, results on about 30 age-appropriate items provide a score that can be interpreted as normal, questionable, or abnormal in reference to age-based norms. A category of "untestable" also is included. The standardization sample consisted of 2,096 children, all from the state of Colorado, stratified by age, race, and socioeconomic status. Reliability of the Denver II is reported to be outstanding for a brief screening test. Interrater reliability among trained raters averaged an outstanding .99. Test-retest reliability for total score over a 7- to 10-day interval averaged .90.

The Denver possesses excellent content validity insofar as the behaviors tested are recognized by authorities in child development as important markers of development. However, the test interpretation categories (normal, questionable, abnormal) were based on clinical judgment and therefore await additional study for validation. A few initial studies raise significant concerns. Glascoe and Byrne (1993) evaluated 89 children in day care settings who were 7 to 70 months of age. Based on extensive independent evaluation, 18 of these 89 children were confirmed to have developmental delays according to federal definitions of disabling conditions (e.g., language delays, mental retardation, and autism). While the Denver II functioned well in correctly identifying 15 of the 18 at-risk children, the instrument performed poorly with the normal children. In fact, 38 of the 71 normal children failed the test and were classified as questionable or abnormal. Overall, almost four in six children taking the test would be referred for additional assessment, and of the four, only one would have a true disability. The researchers recommend further validational study with recalibration and possible discarding of some test items before the test receives widespread use. Other reviewers are even more skeptical. For example, a blue-ribbon review panel of the Minnesota Interagency Developmental Screening Task Force flatly concluded that the Denver-II is not suitable for developmental

and social-emotional screening of preschool children (www.health.state.mn.us).

## HOME

The Home Observation for Measurement of the Environment (HOME), popularly known as the HOME Inventory, is probably the most widely used index of children's environment. Based on in-home observation and an interview with the primary caretaker, the instrument provides a measure of children's physical and social environments. The HOME Inventory comes in three forms: Infant and Toddler, Early Childhood, and Middle Childhood. The latest editions of the instrument, dated 1984, emerged after 15 years of methodical revision and refinement (Caldwell & Richmond, 1967; Caldwell & Bradley, 1984, 1994).

### Background and Description

Prior to the development of the HOME Inventory, the measurement of children's environments was based largely upon demographic data such as parental education, occupation, income, and location of residence. Often these indices were combined into a cumulative measure referred to as social class or socioeconomic status (SES). For example, Hollingshead and Redlich (1958) developed a continuum of social class derived from residence, occupation, and education of the head of the household. The SES score for a family whose household head worked at a clerical job, was a high school graduate, and lived in a middle-rank residential area would be computed as follows (Hollingshead & Redlich, 1958):

| Factor | Scale Value | × | Factor Weight | = | Partial Score |
|---|---|---|---|---|---|
| Residence | 3 | | 6 | | 18 |
| Occupation | 4 | | 9 | | 36 |
| Education | 4 | | 5 | | 20 |
| Index of Socioeconomic Status | | | | = | 74 |

For research purposes, social scientists may categorize families into a fivefold hierarchy of social classes (classes I through V) based on the total score. The reader will notice that the Hollingshead and Redlich measure was derived entirely from *status* indices. The unstated assumption is that these indices reflect, indirectly, meaningful environmental variation. Put bluntly, proponents of SES as an environmental measure believe that, on average, children from a higher social class will experience a richer and more nurturant environment than children from a lower social class.

In contrast to the SES approach, the HOME Inventory was developed to provide a direct *process* measure of children's environments. The guiding philosophy of this instrument is that direct assessment of children's experiences is a better index of the home environment than such indirect measures as parental occupation and education. Although it is true that social class—as embodied in occupation, education, residence—provides an oblique measure of environmental richness, the authors of the HOME Inventory would argue that direct assessment of children's experiences provides a more accurate index of variations in the home environment. Thus, assessment with the HOME involves, in part, direct observation of children's home environments to determine whether certain types of crucial interactions and experiences are present or absent. For example, during an hour-long visit, the examiner observes whether the parent spontaneously communicates with the child at least five times, determines whether the child has at least 10 children's books or story records, and assesses whether the neighborhood is aesthetically pleasing according to detailed standards, to cite just a few examples.

The purpose of the HOME Inventory is to measure the quality and quantity of stimulation and support for cognitive, social, and emotional development available to the child in the home. The scales and items of the HOME were derived from a list of environmental processes identified from existing research and theory as important for optimal childhood development (Caldwell & Bradley, 1984). These growth-promoting processes include basic need gratification; frequent contact with a relatively small number of adults; a positive emotional climate that fosters trust of self and

others; appropriate, varied, and patterned sensory input; consistency in the physical, verbal, and emotional responses of others; a minimum of social restrictions on exploratory and motor behavior; structure and order in the daily environment; provision and adult interpretation of varied cultural experiences; appropriate play materials and environment; contact with adults who value achievement; and the cumulative programming of experiences to match the child's developmental level (Caldwell & Bradley, 1984). In brief, then, the purpose of the HOME is to measure specific, designated patterns of nurturance and stimulation available to children in the home.

In order to complete the HOME Inventory, the examiner must observe the child and caregiver (usually the mother) interacting in the home environment. Ratings for a few inventory items are derived from observation of the physical environment. In addition, completion of some items is based upon self-report of the caregiver. Items are dichotomously scored, 1 for present, 0 for absent. For example, one item asks whether the child is included in grocery store shopping at least once a week. The manual for the inventory encourages a relaxed, semistructured approach to observation and interview (Caldwell & Bradley, 1984). Completion of the inventory takes about an hour.

The three forms of the HOME are Infant and Toddler (ages 0 to 3 years), Early Childhood (ages 3 to 6 years), and Middle Childhood (ages 6 to 10 years). The Infant and Toddler form consists of 45 items organized into the following six subscales:

Emotional and Verbal Responsivity of Parent
Acceptance of the Child's Behavior
Organization of the Environment
Provision of Appropriate Play Materials
Parent Involvement with Child
Variety of Stimulation

The Early Childhood version consists of 55 items organized into eight subscales, whereas the Middle Childhood version consists of 59 items organized into eight subscales. The items for the Infant and Toddler version of the HOME Inventory are listed in Table 7.8. Details on the specific items

---

**● TABLE 7.8   Subscales and Representative Items on the Infant and Toddler Version of the HOME Inventory**

---

**Instructions:** Evaluator places a check in the box for each item that is observed during the visit or that is reported to be characteristic by the parent.

Emotional and Verbal RESPONSIVITY
☐ Parent touches child with affection
☐ Parent initiates verbal exchange with child
☐ Parent's voice shows warmth toward child

ACCEPTANCE of Child's Behavior
☐ Parent does not express anger or irritation toward child
☐ Parent does not yell at or criticize child
☐ At least 5 children's books are within reach

ORGANIZATION of Environment
☐ Child is taken to the doctor as needed, once or more per year
☐ Child accompanies parent to grocery store once or more a week
☐ Child has a designated space for playing with toys

Provision of PLAY MATERIALS
☐ Toys or equipment for strenuous activity are present
☐ Child has at least one push or pull toy
☐ Parent provides toys or books to child during visit

Parental INVOLVEMENT with Child
☐ Parent is involved in child's play activities
☐ Parent talks to child while doing household chores
☐ Parent encourages new skill development in child

Opportunities for VARIETY
☐ Child interacts with at least one other adult during the week
☐ Parents eat dinner with the child almost every evening
☐ Family visits with relatives at least once a week

---

*Note:* These items resemble those on the HOME. The full instrument consists of 45 items similar to the above.

*Source:* Based on Caldwell, B. M., & Bradley, R. H. (1984). *Home Observation for Measurement of the Environment.* Little Rock: University of Arkansas at Little Rock.

---

included in the HOME can be found in Caldwell and Bradley (1984).

## Technical Features

Relevant norms for the HOME Inventory are available from several sources. For the Infant and Toddler version, Caldwell and Bradley (1984) report subscale means and standard deviations for 174 families from Little Rock, Arkansas. Compared to the general population, this sample appears to overrepresent lower-SES families. For example, 34 percent of the families were on welfare, and 29 percent were single-parent households. For the Early Childhood version, standardization data were available from 232 families in Little Rock, with lower-SES families similarly overrepresented. For the Middle Childhood version, Bradley and Rock (1985) report subscale means and standard deviations for 141 families from Little Rock. Approximately half of these families were

African American, the remainder Caucasian; boys and girls were sampled equally. These families were thought to be representative of all families rearing elementary-aged children in Little Rock, Arkansas. However, for all three versions it is clear that the standardization samples provide only local norms. These data may be useful as points of reference but should not be equated with a stratified, random, national sample.

The reliability of the HOME Inventory has been demonstrated in a variety of ways, particularly for the Infant and Toddler version, which we discuss here. The authors note that short-term test-retest studies are inappropriate, since a respondent is quite likely to remember a specific answer given to a question, which would artificially inflate test-retest correlations (Bradley & Caldwell, 1984). Methods used for the assessment of reliability included interobserver agreement, internal consistency, and long-range test-retest stability coefficients for 91 families from the standardization sample. By definition, interobserver agreement for the subscale items is reported to be 90 percent or higher, since this is the training criterion for new raters. Internal consistency estimates using Kuder–Richardson formula 20 ranged from .67 to .89 for all subscales except Variety of Stimulation, which yielded a coefficient of only .44. This rather low reliability coefficient was due to the small number of items in the subscale (five). Test-retest data were available from 91 families tested when their infant/toddler was 6, 12, and 24 months of age. The coefficients indicated a moderate to high degree of stability for the subscales, with most correlations in the .50s, .60s, and .70s. The correlation between total score for testings at 12 and 24 months of age was a highly respectable .77.

The validity of the HOME Inventory has been bolstered by research findings that show modest correlations with SES indices. Because the inventory was proposed as a more meaningful, sensitive index of environment than social class, HOME scores should be significantly but not highly related to SES indices. For the Infant and Toddler version, HOME Inventory subscale correlations with SES are mainly in the .30s and .40s, while the total score–SES correlation is .45 (Bradley, Rock, Caldwell, & Brisby, 1989). HOME scores also revealed a strong relationship with poverty status in Caucasian and minority samples (Bradley, Corwyn, Pipes McAdoo, & Garcia Coll, 2001). Furthermore, higher HOME scores predicted that children would exhibit fewer behavior problems and better preschool ability in a study of 93 single African American mothers (Jackson, Brooks-Gunn, Huang, & Glassman, 2000).

HOME scores also show strong, theory-confirming relationships with appropriate external criteria, including language and cognitive development, school failure, therapeutic intervention, and mental retardation (Caldwell & Bradley, 1984). The correlations between HOME scores and intellectual measures such as the Stanford-Binet are particularly informative. In one study of 174 families, the total score on the HOME at 12 months of age correlated a robust $r = .58$ with Stanford-Binet IQ at 36 months of age. Factor-analytic studies of the HOME also support the construct validity of this instrument (Bradley, Mundfrom, Whiteside, and others, 1994. In sum, the HOME inventory shows promise not only in research but also as a practical adjunct to intervention.

## ● SUMMARY

1. The infant and preschool period extends from birth to about age 6. An important application of infant and preschool tests is to help answer questions about developmental delay. Most infant tests (ages birth to 2½) load heavily on sensory and motor skills. Preschool tests (ages 2½ to 6) tend to tap cognitive skills to a significant degree.

2. The Gesell Developmental Schedules (GDS) gauge the developmental progress of babies from 4 weeks to 60 months of age.

3. The Neonatal Behavioral Assessment Scale (NBAS) assesses the newborn infant's behavioral repertoire on 28 behavior items (scored on a 9-point scale), 18 reflexes (scored on a 4-point scale), and 7 qualities of responsiveness. The instrument is sensitive to prenatal cocaine exposure and other neurotoxins. The NBAS is also used to sensitize parents to the uniqueness of their infants.

4. The Ordinal Scales of Psychological Development were designed as a Piagetian-based measure of intellectual development (ages 2 weeks to 2 years). The scales measure development of object permanence, means-ends, vocal and gestural imitation, operational causality, object relations in space, and schemes for relating to objects.

5. The Bayley Scales of Infant and Toddler Development-III assess mental and motor development of children from 1 month to 42 months of

age. The Bayley is very carefully standardized and highly reliable. Like other infant tests, very low scores predict an intellectually disabled outcome in later childhood, while near-normal and higher scores possess little predictive validity.

6. Designed for children ages 2 years 6 months through 17 years 11 months, the Differential Ability Scales-II consist of 10 core subtests and 10 diagnostic subtests. Initial research indicates that the DAS-II yields reliable and reasonably independent subtest scores useful in the assessment of learning disability.

7. Used with children ages 2½ to 7 years and 3 months, the Wechsler Preschool and Primary Scale of Intelligence-III (WPPSI-III) is a well-designed instrument with 14 subtests that yields Verbal, Performance, and Full Scale IQs.

8. Developed for children ages 2½ to 7 years and 3 months, the Stanford-Binet Intelligence Scales for Early Childhood (Early SB5) combines the subtests of the SB5 with a new Test Observation Checklist (TOC). The TOC summarizes valuable information about test-taking behaviors.

9. Although infant test scores correlate weakly with childhood and adult test scores, low scores on such devices as the Bayley-III and the Denver II tend to predict developmental disability later in life. Tests of recognition memory, such as the Fagan Test of Infant Intelligence, also show promise as predictors of developmental disability.

10. The Developmental Indicators for the Assessment of Learning-III (DIAL-III) is a useful instrument for preschool screening that assesses motor skills, cognitive concepts, and language skills. The Denver II, which assess development in four areas—personal-social, fine motor-adaptive, language, and gross motor—is another respected instrument of this genre.

11. The Home Observation for the Measurement of the Environment (HOME) is an index of the child's environment based on in-home observation and interview with the primary caretaker. The HOME measures the quality and quantity of stimulation and support for cognitive, social, and emotional development available to the child in the home.

## ● KEY TERMS AND CONCEPTS

screening    p. 285

# Testing Persons with Disabilities

In this topic we discuss instruments designed for exceptional and difficult consultations, such as persons with sensory/motor impairment, recent immigrants from non-English-speaking countries, and individuals with significant intellectual deficiencies. According to the U.S. Census Bureau, about 32 million Americans over the age of 5 (one in eight) have a sensory, physical, mental, or self-care disability (www.census.gov, 2000). This estimate does not include persons living in institutions. In these extraordinary circumstances—evaluating persons with sensory, motor, language, or intellectual disability—specialized tests are needed for valid assessment. However, before introducing specific instruments, we examine a background issue: How did these instruments arise?

## ● ORIGINS OF TESTS FOR SPECIAL POPULATIONS

Beginning in the 1950s, a renewed commitment to the needs and rights of physically and mentally disabled persons arose in the United States (Maloney &

Ward, 1979; Patton, Payne, & Beirne-Smith, 1986). Societal attitudes toward those with special needs shifted from outright disdain to a more supportive stance that favored new programs and initiatives on behalf of the disabled. Progress has been slow, but we are no longer surprised to see bathroom facilities with wheelchair access for persons with physical disability, large-print books for persons with visual impairments, or closed-captioned television programs for persons with hearing disabilities. Furthermore, the special needs of citizens with mental retardation are increasingly served by small community care facilities instead of massive, impersonal institutions.

In the early 1970s, the renewed concern for the needs of disabled persons was translated into federal legislation. In 1973, **Public Law 93-112** was passed, serving as a "Bill of Rights" for individuals with disabilities. This legislation outlawed discrimination on the basis of disability. Two years later, the landmark Education for All Handicapped Children Act (Public Law 94-142) was enacted. This legislation mandated that disabled schoolchildren receive appropriate assessment and educational opportunities. In particular, psychologists were directed to assess children in all areas of possible disability—mental, behavioral, and physical—and to use instruments validated for those express purposes. We turn now to a review of tests that can be used for the assessment of persons with sensory, motor, or mental disabilities.

## ● NONLANGUAGE TESTS

Nonlanguage tests require little or no written or spoken language from examiner or examinee. Thus, they are particularly suited for assessment of non-English-speaking persons, referrals with speech impairments, and examinees with weak language skills. These instruments can also be used as supplementary tests for examinees who have no disabilities.

### Leiter International Performance Scale-Revised

The Leiter International Performance Scale-Revised (LIPS-R, Roid & Miller, 1997) is a recent revision of a classic and highly praised test of nonverbal intelligence and cognitive abilities (Leiter, 1948, 1979). Leiter devised an experimental edition of the test in 1929 to assess the intelligence of those with hearing or speech impairment, those who were bilingual, or non-English-speaking examinees. The scale was field-tested with several ethnic groups in Hawaii, including children of Japanese and Chinese descent. The first edition was based on test results for American children, high school students, and WWII Army recruits. Although highly praised and widely used after its initial release, this test received strong criticism in recent years because of poor illustrations and outdated norms. The revised Leiter answers all criticisms handily, and the LIPS-R deserves wide use as a culture-reduced measure of nonverbal intelligence.

A remarkable feature of the Leiter is the complete elimination of verbal instructions. The

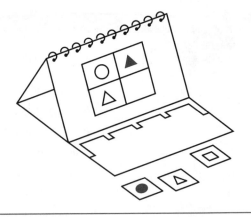

● **FIGURE 7.1** A Characteristic Item from the Leiter International Performance Scale-Revised

Leiter-R does not require a single spoken word from the examiner or the examinee. With an age range of 2 years to 20 years and 11 months, the Leiter-R is particularly suitable for children and adolescents whose English language skills are weak. This includes children with any of these features: non-English-speaking, autism, traumatic brain injury, speech impairment, hearing problems, or an impoverished environment. The test is also useful in the assessment of attentional problems, as described in the following.

Testing is performed by the child or adolescent matching small laminated cards underneath corresponding illustrations on an easel display (Figure 7.1). The test is untimed. Because the initial items are transparently obvious, most examinees catch on quickly without need of pantomime demonstration. The Leiter-R contains 20 subtests organized into two batteries: Visualization and Reasoning, and Memory and Attention. The ten subtests of the Visualization and Reasoning Battery are described in Table 7.9. Not all subtests are administered to every child. For example, the figure rotation subtest is too difficult for 2-year-olds and the immediate recognition subtest is too easy for adolescent examinees. The four Reasoning subtests include classification and design analogies. The six Visualization subtests include matching, figure-ground, paper folding, and figure rotation. The

| ● **TABLE 7.9**    **Visualization and Reasoning Subtests of the Leiter-R** |
|---|

1. Figure Ground: Identification of designs or figures embedded within a stimulus. (All ages)
2. Design Analogies: Like the matrix analogies subtests found on many cognitive tests. (Ages 6 to 20)
3. Form Completion: Ability to recognize objects from fragmented line drawings. (All ages)
4. Matching: Matching and discrimination of simple visual stimuli. (Ages 2 to 10)
5. Sequential Order: Logical progression of pictorial or figural items. (All ages)
6. Repeated Patterns: Identify the missing part of a repeated pattern of figural items. (All ages)
7. Picture Context: Using visual cues to identify a pictured object that has been removed. (Ages 2 to 5)
8. Classification: Categorization of objects or geometric designs. (Ages 2 to 5)
9. Paper Folding: Ability to mentally "fold" an item shown in unfolded two-dimensional form. (Ages 6 to 20)
10. Figure Rotation: Capacity to mentally rotate a two-or three-dimensional object. (Ages 11 to 20)

eight Memory subtests include memory span, spatial memory, associative memory, and delayed recognition memory. The two Attention subtests consist of an underlining test (e.g., marking all squares printed on a page full of geometric shapes) and a measure of divided attention (e.g., observing a moving display and simultaneously sorting cards correctly).

The Leiter-R yields a composite IQ with the familiar mean of 100 and standard deviation of 15. The test also produces subtest scaled scores with a mean of 10 and standard deviation of 3, as well as a variety of composite scores useful in clinical diagnosis. The test was normed on over 2,000 children and adolescents, from 2 to 21 years of age. Using 1993 census statistics, these subjects were carefully stratified according to race, age, gender, social class, and geographic region. Internal consistency reliability for subtests, domain scores, and IQ scores is excellent. Typical coefficient alphas are in the high .80s for subtests and the low .90s for domain scores and IQ scores. Extensive studies of item bias reveal that the items appear to function similarly in separate racial groups (white, African American, and Hispanic samples); that is, there is

no evidence of bias (defined as differential item functioning). Coupled with the fact that the test is completely nonverbal, the absence of test bias indicates that the Leiter-R is a good choice for culture-reduced testing of minority children. But the test is useful in a wide range of other situations as well. For example, Tsatsanis, Dartnall, Cicchetti, and others (2003) also recommend the Leiter-R for use in testing low-functioning children with autism.

Empirical research with the Leiter-R is scant at this time. The test has been shown to have utility in the assessment of medically fragile children (Hooper, Hatton, Baranek, Roberts, & Bailey, 2000), the assessment of low-functioning children with autism (Tsatsanis, Dartnall, Cicchetti, and others, 2003), and the evaluation of children classified as language impaired (Farrell & Phelps, 2000). In this latter study, the Leiter-R also demonstrated a validity-confirming correlation of $r = .80$ with another nonverbal measure of intelligence. Further, in testing with ethnic minorities, the Leiter-R appears to avoid the confounding of intellectual assessment with English language proficiency that is common with other tests. For example, one study of 47 Spanish-speaking and

47 English-speaking children reported average WAIS-III IQs of 94 versus 88, respectively, whereas average Leiter-R IQs were nearly identical, 98 versus 99 (Cathers-Schiffman & Thompson, 2007).

The Leiter-R is a welcome revision of an obsolete test. In the hands of a careful clinician, the test is helpful in the intellectual assessment of children with weak skills in English. Other uses for the revised test include the assessment of attention-deficit/hyperactivity disorder (comparisons of the Attention subtests with the other domains are crucial here) and the evaluation of giftedness in young children (the extremely high ceiling of the test proves invaluable for this application). Whereas reviewers warned against using the original Leiter for placement or decision-making purposes (Sattler, 1988; Salvia & Ysseldyke, 1991), the revised Leiter is a huge improvement in regards to psychometric quality and standardization excellence. Thorough reviews of the Leiter-R and other nonverbal assessment instruments are provided by McCallum, Bracken, and Wasserman (2001).

### Human Figure Drawing Tests

Most children enjoy drawing human figures and do so routinely and spontaneously. Since the early 1900s, psychologists have tried to tap into this almost instinctive behavior as a basis for measuring intellectual development. The first person to use human figure drawing (HFD) as a standardized intelligence test was Florence Goodenough (1926). Her test, known as the Draw-A-Man test, was revised by Harris (1963) and renamed the Goodenough-Harris Drawing Test. More recently, the HFD technique has been adapted by Naglieri (1988). We should also mention that human figure drawings are *widely* used as measures of emotional adjustment, but we do not discuss that application here.

The Goodenough-Harris Drawing Test is a brief, nonverbal test of intelligence that can be administered individually or in a group. Goodenough (1926) published the first edition of this test, while Harris (1963) provided important refinements in scoring and standardization, including the use of a deviation IQ. Strictly speaking, the Goodenough-Harris test doesn't fit the criteria for nonlanguage tests insofar as the examiner must convey certain instructions in English or through a translator. However, the instructions are brief and basic ("I want you to draw a picture of a man [or woman]; make the very best picture you can"). The Goodenough-Harris test is, for all practical purposes, a nonlanguage test.

The purpose of the Goodenough-Harris Drawing Test is to measure intellectual maturity, not artistic skill. Thus, the scoring guide emphasizes accuracy of observation and the development of conceptual thinking. The child receives credit for including body parts and details, as well as for providing perspective, realistic proportion, and implied freedom of movement.

The 73 scorable items are transformed to a scaled score with the familiar mean of 100 and standard deviation of 15. Of course, these norms, developed in the 1960s, are now thoroughly outdated. Even so, a large body of research confirmed that the test captured something important. For example, Frederickson (1985) reported correlations between Goodenough-Harris Drawing Test scores and WPPSI Full Scale IQ in the range of .72 to .80. In several other studies, correlations with individual IQ tests are more variable, but the majority are over .50 (Abell, Briesen, & Watz, 1996; Anastasi, 1975).

In response to criticisms of the Goodenough-Harris Drawing Test, Naglieri (1988) developed a quantitative scoring system and renormed the human figure drawing procedure. His scoring system, The Draw A Person: A Quantitative Scoring System (DAP), was normed on a sample of 2,622 individuals ages 5 through 17 years who were representative of the 1980 U.S. Census data on age, sex, race, geographic region, ethnic group, social class, and community size. The DAP yields standard scores with the familiar mean of 100 and standard deviation of 15. In a study of 61 subjects ages 6 to 16 years, the DAP correlated .51 with WISC-R IQ and produced similar overall scores, with a mean IQ of 100 versus mean DAP score of 95 (Wisniewski & Naglieri, 1989). Lassiter and

Bardos (1995) found that the DAP score underestimated IQ scores obtained from the WPPSI-R and the K-BIT in a sample of 50 kindergartners and first graders.

Reviewers praise the DAP for its clear scoring system, strong reliability, and careful standardization (Cosden, 1992). However, results of validity studies are more cautionary. Harrison and Schock (1994) note that the accumulated evidence with HFD tests indicates low to moderate predictive validity. In spite of their popularity and appeal, HFD tests do not effectively identify children with learning difficulties or developmental disabilities, and they may not be valid for use even as screening measures.

### Hiskey-Nebraska Test of Learning Aptitude

The Hiskey-Nebraska Test of Learning Aptitude (H-NTLA) is a nonlanguage performance scale for use with children ages 3 to 17 years (Hiskey, 1966). This test can be administered entirely through pantomime and requires no verbal response from the examinee. However, verbal instructions can be used with children with normal and mild hearing impairment. The H-NTLA consists of 12 subtests:

| | |
|---|---|
| Bead Patterns | Block Patterns |
| Memory for Color | Completion of Drawings |
| Picture Identification | Memory for Digits |
| Picture Association | Puzzle Blocks |
| Paper Folding | Picture Analogies |
| Visual Attention Span | Spatial Reasoning |

Raw scores on the subtests are converted into a Deviation Learning Quotient (LQ) with mean of 100 and standard deviation of 16. For a sample of 43 hearing-impaired children, the test-retest stability of the LQ scores was reported to be .79, .85, and .62 after intervals of about 1 year, 3 years, and 5 years, respectively, which is similar to data for normal children (Watson, 1983). Even so, more than one third of the sample showed a 15-point or greater change in scores over the 5-year time span, which demonstrates the importance of basing important decisions on more than a single measure.

H-NTLA scores correlate quite robustly with achievement scales for grades 2 through 12 (median $r = .49$) and also with WISC-R Performance IQ ($r = .85$). Although the LQ yields average scores that are remarkably close to WISC-R Performance IQ for samples of children with hearing impairment and those who are deaf, the H-NTLA scores are substantially more variable (Phelps & Ensor, 1986). Thus, use of the H-NTLA may increase the risk of false positive misclassification—labeling children as gifted when they are only bright or as having mental retardation when they are merely borderline.

The H-NTLA is useful with children who are deaf, have speech or language impairments or mental retardation, or those who are bilingual. An interesting feature of this test is the development of parallel norms: The H-NTLA was standardized on 1,079 children who were deaf and 1,074 normal-hearing children ages 2½ to 17½. However, the chief weakness of the instrument is the inadequacy of these norms. For example, the representativeness of the sample of those who were deaf—picked on an opportunistic basis from schools for those who are deaf—is largely unknown. Standardization of the normal-hearing sample was based on occupational level of parents according to the 1960 U.S. Census. A contemporary and more detailed restandardization of the test would be quite helpful. Qu (1997) reports favorably on the reliability and validity of the test with huge samples of Chinese deaf children.

### Test of Nonverbal Intelligence-3

The Test of Nonverbal Intelligence-3 (TONI-3) is a language-free measure of cognitive ability designed for disabled or minority populations (Brown, Sherbenou, & Johnsen, 1998). In particular, the authors recommend the test for assessing persons with aphasia, non-English speakers, those with hearing impairments, and persons who have experienced a variety of severe neurological traumas. The test instructions are pantomimed by the examiner and the examinee answers by pointing to one of six possible responses. The test consists of two equivalent forms of 50 abstract/figural problem-solving items. These items were carefully selected from an initial pool of items according to item-total correlations, appropriate difficulty level, and acceptability to potential users and technical experts. The TONI-3 items fall into several categories, including the following:

Simple matching
Analogies
Classification
Intersection
Progressions

Except for the simple-matching items, the TONI-3 items require the examinee to solve problems by identifying relationships among abstract figures. Many of the items are similar in format to those found on Raven's Progressive Matrices. The test yields two kinds of scores: percentile ranks and TONI-3 quotients (mean of 100 and standard deviation of 15).

The TONI-3 was carefully standardized on over 3,000 subjects ranging in age from 6 through 89. Sample characteristics paralleled census data for sex, race, ethnicity, urban-suburban-rural residence, grade, parental education/occupation, and geographic region. Reliability data are quite satisfactory, with internal consistency coefficients typically exceeding .90 and alternate-forms reliability in the range of .80 to .95.

Validity studies of the TONI-3 are scant, but investigation of prior editions (which are highly similar in content) is supportive of this test as a culture-reduced index of general intelligence. Nonetheless, research does not support the view that the TONI-3 is a nonverbal test, except in the trivial sense that verbal responses are not required. For example, the TONI-2 manual reports correlation coefficients in the .70s between TONI-2 scores and the Language Arts subtest of the SRA Achievement Series. In general, research studies with precursors to the TONI-3 indicate that it is a good measure of general intelligence, but they do not support the view that it is mainly a measure of *nonverbal* intelligence (Murphy, 1992). Overall, the TONI-3 is highly regarded as a brief nonlanguage screening device for

subjects with impaired language abilities (e.g., for those who are aphasic, deaf, or non-English-speaking or who have mental retardation). Barrett (2000) also recommends use of the TONI-3 with immigrants from English-speaking countries such as Jamaica. The test is more carefully standardized than most and possesses excellent reliability. A useful feature of the TONI-3 is that the untimed administration seldom exceeds 20 minutes.

## ● NONREADING AND MOTOR-REDUCED TESTS

Nonreading tests are designed for illiterate examinees who can, nonetheless, understand spoken English well enough to follow oral instructions. Nonreading tests of intelligence are well suited to young children, illiterate examinees, and persons with speech or expressive-language impairments. These tests need not be specialized or esoteric: The performance subtests of most mainstream instruments qualify as nonreading tests. For example, examiners may use the WISC-III performance subtests to estimate the intelligence of examinees with language disabilities.

However, clients with cerebral palsy or other orthopedically impairing conditions will score very poorly on nonreading tests that require manipulatory responses. Obtaining valid test results from such persons can present an enormous challenge (Case Exhibit 7.1). The motor deficits, increased tendency to fatigue, and inexactness of purposive movements common to persons with cerebral palsy will negatively affect their performance on cognitive assessment tools. Orthopedically impaired clients need tests that are both nonreading and motor reduced. In particular, tests that permit a simple pointing response are well suited to the assessment of children and adults with cerebral palsy or other motor-impairing conditions.

### Peabody Picture Vocabulary Test-IV

The Peabody Picture Vocabulary Test-IV (PPVT-4) is the best known and most widely used of the

## The Challenge of Assessment in Cerebral Palsy

The challenges inherent to special consultations are well typified by a client with cerebral palsy recently tested by a consulting psychologist. The young examinee was totally confined to a battery-powered wheelchair, except when a live-in attendant would transfer him to a bed or chair. Even a dispassionate observer would have to agree that the client didn't look very capable, sitting hunched over in his chair, unable to control his drooling, one arm arched out at an awkward angle. Yet, in spite of his disability, he had achieved a fair degree of personal independence. Using a simple joystick control device, he could guide his wheelchair to the grocery store, library, and community center where he would complete simple transactions by pointing to appropriate words and phrases in a plastic-bound spiral notebook. Because of his poor motor control, interactions with this client took quite a long time. Nonetheless, he was very efficient with short communications. Here is a typical exchange, with the client's notebook-designated responses shown in capital letters:

"I understand you have a new synthesized-voice communication box, how do you like it?" YOU ASKED TWO QUESTIONS. "You're right. I'll bet that happens a lot. Do you have a communication box?" YES. "What do you think of it?" IT'S NOT EASY. "Now that we are done testing, should I find your driver?" NO, I'LL WAIT. HE IS COMING BACK.

How intelligent is this client? What is his level of verbal comprehension? How well does he understand abstract concepts? For example, is he capable of understanding the essentials of microcomputer usage such as data entry, file storage, and directory commands? Could he learn to program a microcomputer? These are precisely the referral questions asked by a vocational rehabilitation counselor who was contemplating huge expenditures—thousands of dollars—to purchase a computer system for this disabled client.

Certainly, it would be easy to underestimate the potential of this young man with severe motor and language disabilities because—in a quite literal sense—his intelligence was hidden away, trapped inside his incapacitated body. The task of the examiner was to find the able mind inside the disabled body, a formidable challenge indeed. Using the Test of Nonverbal Intelligence and the Peabody Picture Vocabulary Test, the examiner determined that the young client possessed at least average intelligence and could likely learn the fundamentals of data processing with microcomputers.

nonreading, motor-reduced tests (Dunn & Dunn, 1998). The PPVT-4 is used to obtain a rapid measure of listening vocabulary with persons who are deaf or who have neurological or speech impairments.

Although the PPVT-4 is useful with any examinee who cannot verbalize well, the test is especially useful with examinees who also manifest motor-impairing conditions such as cerebral palsy or stroke.

The PPVT-4 comes in two parallel versions, each consisting of 4 practice plates and 228 testing plates. Each plate contains four line drawings of objects or everyday scenes. The examiner presents a plate, states the stimulus word orally, and asks the examinee to point to the one picture that best depicts the stated word. The test items are precisely ordered according to difficulty level, arranged in 19 sets of 12 items each for efficient identification of basal and ceiling levels. The entry level is determined by age, and examinees continue until they reach their ceiling level. Although the test is untimed, administration seldom exceeds 15 minutes. Raw scores are converted to age equivalents or standard scores (mean of 100, standard deviation of 15).

The PPVT-4 was standardized on a representative national sample of 3,540 individuals ranging from 2½ to 90 or more years of age. Reliability data for the new edition are exceptionally strong, with typical internal consistency coefficients of .94, alternate-forms reliabilities of .89, and test-retest correlations of .93. Concurrent validity studies are also highly supportive, demonstrating robust correlations with verbal measures. For example, the test developers report a correlation of .7 with scores on the latest edition of the Clinical Evaluation of Language Fundamentals (CELF-4).

The test developers of the PPVT-4 took great care to minimize and balance cultural influences in the test items. Independent consultants representing the perspectives of African Americans, Asians, Hispanics, Native Americans, and women reviewed the content and artwork of the test during development, and adjustments were made following these reviews. The test items demonstrate attractive artwork that is balanced for racial and gender differences, including persons with physical disabilities. However, based on research with prior editions, the evidence is mixed as to whether the Peabody is a culturally fair instrument that serves as a valid measure with minority children. For example, Washington and Craig (1999) found that 59 African American preschoolers at risk for academic failure averaged 91 on the test (SD of 11), which was seen as commensurate with their envi-

ronmental disadvantages. These authors laud the test as "culturally fair." However, Campbell, Bell, and Keith (2001) reported an average score of 82 (SD of 12) for 416 African American children of low socioeconomic status, which was 8 points lower than their overall score on the K-ABC. These researchers concluded: "Despite the attempts to reduce racial differences, the PPVT-III appears to perform similarly to prior editions of the Peabody scales. On average, the PPVT-III tends to underestimate both intellectual ability and scholastic achievement, as measured by the K-ABC, in low SES, African American children" (p. 91). Further research will be needed to clarify the utility of this test with minority children.

Several lines of evidence support the validity of the Peabody test, but only as a narrow measure of vocabulary, not as a general measure of intelligence (Altepeter & Johnson, 1989). Dunn and Dunn (1981) sought to ensure content validity by searching *Webster's New Collegiate Dictionary* for all words whose meanings could be represented by a picture. Thus, the authors had a specific content universe in mind, and the items from the Peabody appear to be a fair sampling from this domain. In addition, the authors used sophisticated item-selection techniques based on the Rasch-Wright latent-trait model to help build construct validity into the test. This model enables researchers to construct a growth curve for the latent trait being measured (hearing vocabulary) and to select items that best fit the curve. Using tryout and calibration data, the curve was drawn repeatedly on a computer. If an item did not fit the Rasch-Wright latent-trait model (too flat or too steep an item-characteristic curve) it was discarded from consideration.

Concurrent and predictive validity data for the Peabody are somewhat limited but promising. Several investigators have correlated the PPVT-R with achievement measures, where modest relationships (*r*'s from .30 to .60) are common (Naglieri, 1981; Naglieri & Pfeiffer, 1983). Correlations with reading achievement tend to be higher than with spelling and arithmetic achievement, suggesting that the PPVT-R has appropriate discriminant validity (Vance, Kitson, & Singer, 1985).

Several investigators have correlated earlier versions of the Peabody with intelligence measures, particularly the WISC-R and WAIS-R, and healthy correlations (near .70) are the rule (e.g., Naglieri & Yazzie, 1983). As might be expected, correlations tend to be higher with Verbal IQ than Performance IQ.

In a very important and ingenious study, Maxwell and Wise (1984) investigated the vocabulary loading of the Peabody in a sample of 84 inpatients from psychiatry and psychology wards. Their study utilized the PPVT, but this earlier edition is similar to the PPVT-IV, so that the conclusions are pertinent here. The researchers investigated the hypothesis that the PPVT assesses more than vocabulary in adults. In addition to the PPVT, the researchers collected data on the following: WAIS-R, Wechsler Memory Scale, name-writing speed, and years of education. Name-writing speed is simply the number of seconds required for the examinee to write his or her full name. Even though all variables had significant correlations with PPVT IQ, WAIS-R Vocabulary had by far the strongest correlation ($r = .88$). More important, when the variance accounted for by Vocabulary was removed, none of the remaining variables had any predictive relationship with the PPVT. In short, the Peabody is a good measure of vocabulary (hearing vocabulary, in particular) but could be misleading if used as a global measure of intellect.

The PPVT-4 is a recent revision, so independent research with the test is limited. One caution with the previous edition, the PPVT-III, is that standard scores may be substantially lower than Wechsler IQs, particularly with persons with mental retardation and minority examinees. In a sample of 21 adults with mild mental retardation, Prout and Schwartz (1984) found the PPVT-R standard scores (mean of 56) to be an average of 9 points lower than the WAIS-R IQ (mean of 65). Naglieri and Yazzie (1983) found a huge 26-point difference with a sample of Navajo Indian children, who averaged a standard score of 61 on the PPVT-R in contrast to WISC-R IQ of 87. On a similar note, with the PPVT-III, Bell, Lassiter, Matthews, and Hutchinson (2001) found that the instrument tended to underestimate WAIS-III IQ scores of bright college students by about 10 points.

Overall, we may conclude that the Peabody is a well-normed measure of hearing vocabulary that is useful with nonreading and motor-impaired examinees. However, the instrument is not a substitute for a general intelligence test and PPVT-4 scores may underestimate intellectual functioning in some groups (e.g., minority children, high-functioning adults).

## ● TESTING PERSONS WITH VISUAL IMPAIRMENTS

Many millions of American adults have some degree of visual impairment, including more than 1 million individuals who are **legally blind**—a term used in determining eligibility for government benefits. This term applies to individuals with central visual acuity of 20/200 or less in the better eye (with correction) or to those with significant reduction in their visual field to a diameter of 20 degrees or less (Bradley-Johnson & Ekstrom, 1998). The number of children with visual impairment is substantially smaller, with only 0.4 percent of students between the ages of 6 and 21 years receiving special education services because of a vision problem (U.S. Department of Education, 1992). In addition to special arrangements in testing, individuals with visual impairment may require unique instruments for valid assessment.

In assessing the intellectual functioning of the visually impaired, examiners have historically relied on adaptations of the Stanford-Binet. The Hayes-Binet revision for testing those with visual impairment was based on the 1916 Stanford-Binet; this instrument has since undergone several revisions. The most recent adaptation is the Perkins-Binet (Davis, 1980). The Perkins-Binet retains most of the verbal items from the Stanford-Binet but also adapts other items to a tactual mode. The Perkins-Binet possesses acceptable split-half reliability and shows high correlations with verbal scales of the WISC-R (Teare & Thompson, 1982). The developers of the Perkins-Binet have acknowledged that visual problems exist on a continuum by developing separate norms for children with usable vision (Form U) and no usable vision (Form N).

Test developers have also succeeded in modifying the Wechsler Performance scales for use with individuals with visual impairments. The Haptic Intelligence Scale for the Adult Blind (HISAB) consists of six subtests, four of which resemble the Digit Symbol, Block Design, Object Assembly, and Picture Completion tests of the WAIS Performance scale (Shurrager, 1961; Shurrager & Shurrager, 1964). The remaining two subtests consist of Bead Arithmetic, which involves the use of an abacus to solve arithmetic problems, and a Pattern Board, which requires the examinee to reproduce the pattern felt on a board that has rows of holes with pegs in them. The reliability of the HISAB is excellent and the authors provide normative data on a sample of adults with visual impairment. Most encouraging of all, HISAB scores correlate .65 with the WAIS Verbal IQ (Shurrager & Shurrager, 1964). Although the HISAB is still manufactured and sold by Stoelting Company, unfortunately, the test has never been investigated empirically. A search of PsychINFO for research with this instrument did not locate a single article.

Another interesting instrument is the Blind Learning Aptitude Test (BLAT), a tactile test for children from 6 to 16 years of age who are blind (Newland, 1971). The BLAT items are in bas-relief form, consisting of dots and lines similar to Braille. The items consist of six different types: recognition of differences, recognition of similarities, identification of progressions, identification of the missing element in a $2 \times 2$ matrix, completion of a figure, and identification of the missing element in a $3 \times 3$ matrix. Most of the items were adapted from Raven's Progressive Matrices and the Cattell Culture Fair Intelligence Test. The BLAT was standardized on 961 functionally blind children 6 to 17½ years of age, in residential and day-care settings (Newland, 1990). The sample is said to be socioeconomically and racially representative of the U.S. population. The BLAT reveals excellent reliability, with internal consistency (Kuder-Richardson) of .93, and test-retest reliability over a 7-month period of .87 and .92 (two studies). The test correlates very well with the Hayes-Binet ($r = .74$) and the WISC Verbal scale ($r = .71$). The BLAT also shows strong correlations with Braille oral reading speed and comprehension (Baker, Koenig, & Sowell, 1995). In conjunction with a verbal test, the BLAT is a promising instrument for testing the intelligence of children with visual disabilities. However, the test would profit substantially from minor revisions, updated norms, and a more thorough test manual.

Dekker (1993) has developed a promising instrument for visually impaired children: the Intelligence Test for Visually Impaired Children (ITVIC). This test includes a number of haptic subtests (those relying only on the sense of touch) which are intended to replace traditional performance subtests like Block Design that require intact vision. Boter and Hoekstra-Vrolijk (1994) provide the compelling rationale for using haptic subtests with visually impaired children:

> Although the necessity for an IQ test with haptic subtests for visually impaired children is evident in practice, the intelligence of visually impaired children is usually still measured only through the use of the verbal subtests of the WISC-R. The risk of this is that an incomplete and one-sided picture is obtained. Children with little education, with a disadvantaged background or missing a good command of the language may be underestimated. (p. 135)

Designed for children 6 to 15 years of age, the test has separate norms for partially sighted and totally blind examinees. The instrument includes five verbal subtests adapted from existing instruments such as the Wechsler scales and seven new nonverbal subtests that rely on tactile perception:

| **Verbal** | **Nonverbal/Haptic** |
| --- | --- |
| Vocabulary | Perception of Objects |
| Digit Span | Perception of Figures |
| Verbal Fluency | Block Design |
| Verbal Analogies | Rectangle Puzzles |
| Learning Names | Map and Plan Tests |
| | Exclusion of Figures |
| | Figural Analogies |

The full battery takes about three hours to administer. Currently, the test is published in Dutch, German, and English but has received limited use in the United States. This may be due, in part, to the size and weight of the test kit. The ITVIC comes in a large "hold-all" that cannot be easily carried from one location to another. Information about this specialized instrument can be found at www.bartimeus.nl.

## ● TESTING INDIVIDUALS WHO ARE DEAF OR HARD OF HEARING

More than 1 million Americans are deaf or sufficiently hard of hearing that they rely on American Sign Language (ASL) as their primary means of communication (Brauer, Braden, Pollard, & Hardy-Braz, 1998). Given the typical limited mastery of the English language of persons who are deaf and, vice versa, the typical psychologist's limited (or nonexistent) skill in ASL, the proper and valid assessment of individuals who are deaf poses a profound cross-cultural challenge.

More is involved than just picking a test developed for, and normed upon, individuals who are deaf or hard of hearing and who use sign language. One problem is that sign language "can now be characterized on a multidimensional continuum encompassing numerous styles, lexical variants, syntactic structures, dialects, and approximations to or departures from English word ordering" (Brauer et al., 1998, p. 299). Thus, a test developed in standard ASL is not equally fair to all persons who are deaf. In general, the proper and valid assessment of persons who are deaf requires that interested psychologists immerse themselves in the Deaf culture and also seek relevant educational and training experiences:

> One especially needs a thorough understanding of the implications of deafness and the use of sign language for making diagnoses for people who are deaf. Few hearing psychologists have these skills. The push is for specialized training programs in deafness and psychology, a need that has been recognized for decades. (Brauer et al., 1998, p. 303)

If a consulting psychologist does not possess these skills, then the assessment of persons who are deaf should be referred to a person or agency with the requisite talents and expertise.

The use of a sign language interpreter in the testing of persons who are deaf is a complicated and controversial matter. One concern is that the interpreter may inadvertently alter the content of the test, therefore affecting the validity of the findings. Certainly, it is unwise for parents or teachers to serve as interpreters. However, it is also true that persons who are deaf and who use sign language achieve higher IQs when the directions are signed than when they are delivered in the traditional manner (Braden, 1992). The preferred resolution is for the examiner to be fluent in sign language, so that any necessary translations stay within the bounds of standardized procedure.

For the intellectual assessment of persons who are deaf or hard of hearing, the Wechsler Performance subtests remain the tools of choice (Braden & Hannah, 1998). The impact of English language facility is minimized on these subtests, so it is thought that they provide a more accurate measure of cognitive skill than the Verbal subtests. Other tests sometimes used with persons who are deaf include Raven's Progressive Matrices (Raven, Court, & Raven, 1992) and the Hiskey-Nebraska Test of Learning Aptitude, discussed previously. The WAIS-III is now available in a formal ASL translation (demonstrated on videotape), endorsed and disseminated by the test publisher (Kostrubala & Braden, 1998).

## ● ASSESSMENT OF ADAPTIVE BEHAVIOR IN INTELLECTUAL DISABILITY

The term *intellectual disability* is the currently preferred designation for the disability historically referred to as *mental retardation*. In fact, the authoritative 130-year-old agency that has promoted the interests of affected individuals, the American Association on Mental Retardation (AAMR), recently changed its name to the

American Association on Intellectual and Developmental Disabilities (AAIDD). The next edition of its authoritative manual (AAMR, 2002), slated for release in 2011, will eliminate all references to the term *mental retardation*. The reasons for the change have to do with providing a more hopeful and optimistic outlook for persons with intellectual disability:

> The construct of intellectual disability belongs within the general construct of disability. Intellectual disability has evolved to emphasize an ecological perspective that focuses on the person-environment interaction and recognizes that the systematic application of individualized supports can enhance human functioning. (Schalock, Luckasson, Shogren, and others, 2007)

In contrast, the outdated concept of mental retardation gradually has taken on excess meanings that tend to isolate the problem within the individual rather than recognizing an ecological perspective.

The assessment of intellectual disability is a complex and multifaceted concern that rightfully deserves a chapter or book of its own. Owing to space limitations, our coverage is necessarily abridged; interested readers are referred to American Association on Mental Retardation (2002) and Jackson, Mulick, and Rojahn (2007). Here we briefly summarize the diagnostic criteria for intellectual disability and then review several intriguing assessment instruments in modest detail.

The most authoritative source for the definition of intellectual disability is the American Association on Intellectual and Developmental Disabilities. That organization defines intellectual disability as follows:

> Intellectual disability is characterized by significant limitations both in intellectual functioning and in adaptive behavior as expressed in conceptual, social, and practical adaptive skills. This disability originates before age 18 (Schalock, et al., 2007, p. 118).

The AAIDD further stipulates that significantly subaverage intellectual functioning is an IQ of 70 to 75 or below on scales with a mean of 100 and a standard deviation of 15. The agency explicitly affirms the importance of professional judgment in individual cases.

A low IQ by itself is an insufficient foundation for the diagnosis of intellectual disability. As noted, the definition also specifies a second criterion—limitations in adaptive behavior as expressed in conceptual, social, and practical adaptive skills. A diagnosis of mental retardation is warranted only when an individual displays a sufficiently low IQ and limitations in one or more of the broad areas of adaptive functioning. Furthermore, these deficits in intellect and adaptive functioning must have arisen during the developmental period—defined as between birth and the eighteenth birthday.

Intellectual disability represents a continuum from very mild to substantially disabling. For this reason, previous terminology recognized four levels of disability: mild, moderate, severe, and profound. However, current AAIDD designations represent a departure from this terminology. Instead of focusing on the shortcomings of the person, the manual introduces a hierarchy of "Intensities of Needed Supports," which redirects attention to the rehabilitation needs of the client. The four levels of needed supports are intermittent, limited, extensive, and pervasive. However, the previous terminology referring to levels of disability will likely prevail for quite some time, so we have chosen to blend the old and the new approach in Table 7.10. The reader will notice a zone of uncertainty between levels of disability, which signifies that clinical judgment about all sources of information is required in diagnosis. Furthermore, even though these levels are calibrated by IQ ranges, we remind the reader that the examinee must also show corresponding deficits in adaptive skill. Under no circumstances is an IQ test a sufficient basis for diagnosing intellectual disability.

Limitations in adaptive skill are more difficult to confirm than a low IQ. Fortunately, the AAIDD

● **TABLE 7.10    Four Levels of Intellectual Disability**

*Mild Intellectual Disability:* IQ of 50–55 to 70–75+, **Intermittent Support** required. Reasonable social and communication skills; with special education, attain sixth grade level by late teens; achieve social and vocational adequacy with special training and supervision; partial independence in living arrangements.

*Moderate Intellectual Disability:* IQ of 35–40 to 50–55, **Limited Support** required. Fair social and communication skills but little self-awareness; with extended special education, attain fourth grade level; function in a sheltered workshop but need supervision in living arrangements.

*Severe Intellectual Disability:* IQ of 20–25 to 35–40, **Extensive Support** required. Little or no communication skills; sensory and motor impairments; do not profit from academic training; trainable in basic health habits.

*Profound Intellectual Disability:* IQ below 20–25, **Pervasive Support** required. Minimal functioning; incapable of self-maintenance; need constant nursing care and supervision.

*Source:* Based on AAMR (2002) and Beirne-Smith, Ittenbach, and Patton (2002).

stipulates specific skills within the three areas of adaptive functioning, namely:

- Conceptual skills—language and literacy; money, time, and number concepts; and self-direction.
- Social skills—interpersonal skills, social responsibility, self-esteem, gullibility, naïveté (i.e., wariness), social problem solving, and the ability to follow rules/obey laws and to avoid being victimized.
- Practical skills—activities of daily living (personal care), occupational skills, healthcare, travel/transportation, schedules/routines, safety, use of money, use of the telephone (www.aamr.org).

In regard to the assessment of these limitations, the agency proposes that well-normed measures of adaptive skills are desirable, but the final determination is always a matter of clinical judgment.

The first standardized instrument for assessing adaptive behavior was the Vineland Social Maturity Scale (Doll, 1935). Somewhat simplistic and coarse-grained by modern standards, the original Vineland scale consisted of 117 discrete items arranged in a year-scale format. An informant familiar with the examinee would check off applicable items. From these results the examiner would calculate an equivalent social age, helpful in the diagnosis of mental retardation. Still a respected instrument, the Vineland has undergone several revisions and is now known as the Vineland Adaptive Behavior Scales, Second Edition (Sparrow, Cicchetti, & Balla, 2005).

Since the release of the original Vineland scale, over 100 scales of adaptive behavior have been published (Matson, 2007; Reschly, Myers, & Hartel, 2002). These instruments vary greatly in structure, intended purpose, and targeted population. Broadly speaking, we can distinguish two types of instruments designed for two different purposes. One group of mainly norm-referenced scales is used largely to assist in diagnosis and classification. Another group of mainly criterion-referenced scales is used largely to assist in training and rehabilitation. We have chosen a few representative instruments for more detailed analysis.

### Scales of Independent Behavior-Revised

The Scales of Independent Behavior-Revised (SIB-R; Bruininks, Woodcock, Weatherman, & Hill, 1996) is an ambitious, multidimensional measure of adaptive behavior that is highly useful in the assessment of intellectual disability. The instrument consists of 259 adaptive behavior items organized into 14 subscales. The scale is completed with the help of a parent, caregiver, or teacher well acquainted with the examinee's daily behaviors. For each subscale, the examiner reads a series of items and for each item records a score from 0 (never or rarely does task) to 3 (does task very well). A useful feature of the SIB-R is that examiners need a minimum of training and experience. Of course, a much higher level of competence is

---

● **TABLE 7.11** **The Subscales and Clusters of the Scales of Independent Behavior-Revised**

1. *Motor Skills*

   Gross Motor—19 large muscle skills such as sitting without support or taking part in strenuous physical activities.

   Fine Motor—19 small muscle skills such as picking up small objects or assembling small objects.

2. *Social and Communication Skills*

   Social Interaction—18 skills requiring interaction with other people such as handing toys to others or making plans with friends to attend social activities.

   Language Comprehension—18 skills involving the understanding of spoken and written language such as looking toward a speaker or reading.

   Language Expression—20 tasks involving talking such as making sounds to get attention or explaining a written contract.

3. *Personal Living Skills*

   Eating and Meal Preparation—19 skills related to eating and meal preparation, ranging from drinking from a glass to planning a meal.

   Toileting—17 skills necessary to bathroom and toilet use.

   Dressing—18 skills related to dressing, ranging from holding out arms and legs while being dressed to arranging for clothing alterations.

   Personal Self-Care—16 tasks involved in basic grooming and health maintenance, for example, washing hands and making a medical appointment.

   Domestic Skills—18 tasks needed to maintain a home, ranging from putting empty dishes in the sink to selecting appropriate housing.

4. *Community Living Skills*

   Time and Punctuality—19 tasks involving time concepts and time management such as keeping appointments.

   Money and Value—20 skills related to money concepts, such as saving money and using credit.

   Work Skills—20 skills related to prevocational and work habits, for example, indicating that an assigned task is completed.

   Home-Community Orientation—18 skills involved in getting around the home and neighborhood and traveling in the community, for example, locating a dentist.

---

required to evaluate results and make decisions about placement or treatment.

The 14 subscales of the SIB are arranged into four clusters, as outlined in Table 7.11. In turn, these four clusters constitute the Broad Independence Scale. Each subscale consists of a small number of discrete, developmentally ordered items. For example, the subscale on Eating and Meal Preparation has 19 graded items, including spearing food with a fork, eating soup with a spoon, taking appropriate-sized portions, and preparing snacks that do not

require cooking. For each subscale, items are administered until a predetermined ceiling is reached (e.g., 3 of 5 consecutive items scored 0).

Raw scores for a subtest are added to obtain a part score. The part scores for each cluster are then added to obtain the cluster score. The score for the Broad Independence Scale is derived from the four cluster scores. The subtest scores, cluster scores, and the Broad Independence score can then be converted to a variety of normative scores to permit comparison of the examinee's performance with the performance of the national norming sample. The normative scales include age scores, percentile ranks, standard scores, stanines, and normal curve equivalents.

A separate, unique part of the SIB-R also assesses maladaptive behavior by measuring the frequency and severity of problem behaviors. The Problem Behaviors Scale includes eight major categories of personal and social maladjustment that could affect adaptive behavior: Hurtful to Self, Hurtful to Others, Destructive to Property, Disruptive Behavior, Unusual or Repetitive Habits, Socially Offensive Behavior, Withdrawal or Inattentive Behavior, and Uncooperative Behavior. Examples of problem behaviors are listed, and the respondent must indicate the behaviors displayed by the examinee. In addition, the respondent describes the one most serious behavior in each category and rates it according to frequency of occurrence, severity, and typical management.

The standardization of the SIB-R was well conceived and executed. The norm group consisted of 2,182 persons sampled to reflect the 1990 census characteristics. The normative data cover persons from age 3 months to adults over age 80. An additional sample of persons with mental retardation, learning or hearing disabilities, and behavior disorders was also tested. The value of the SIB-R was further strengthened by anchoring it to the norms for the Woodcock-Johnson Psycho-Educational Battery-Revised. The SIB-R is one component of this larger test battery, but can be used on its own.

The reliability of the SIB-R is generally respectable, but somewhat variable from subscale to subscale and from one age group to another. The individual subscales tend to show split-half reliabilities in the vicinity of .80; the four clusters have median composite reliabilities around .90; the Broad Independence Scale has a very robust reliability in the high .90s (Bruininks, Woodcock, Weatherman, & Hill, 1996).

Validity data for the SIB-R are very promising. For example, the mean scores of various samples of disabled and nondisabled subjects show confirmatory relationships: SIB-R scores are lowest among those persons known to be most severely impaired in learning and adjustment. For disabled examinees, SIB-R scores correlate very strongly with intelligence scores (in the .80s), whereas with nondisabled examinees, the relationship is minimal (Bruininks et al., 1996). The SIB-R also possesses excellent convergent validity—the Broad Independence Score correlated .83 with the composite score from a similar instrument, the Vineland Adaptive Behavior Scales (Middleton, Keene, & Brown, 1990).

In sum, the SIB-R is an excellent tool for providing insights into an examinee's current level of functioning in real-life situations in the home, school, and community settings. Although this instrument does not have a precise correspondence with the areas of adaptive skill listed in the definition of intellectual disability, there is substantial similarity. For example, the following areas of adaptive skills are well covered by subscales or clusters of the SIB-R: communication, self-care, home living, social skills, community use, health and safety, and work. The SIB-R or a similar instrument ranks as a mandatory supplement to individual intelligence testing in the diagnosis and assessment of mental retardation.

## Independent Living Behavior Checklist (ILBC)

The Independent Living Behavior Checklist (ILBC) is an extensive list of 343 independent living skills classified and presented in six categories: mobility, self-care, home maintenance and safety, food, social and communication, and functional academic (Walls, Zane, & Thvedt, 1979). Unlike most of the instruments discussed so far in this text, the ILBC is completely nonnormative. The sole purpose of the ILBC is to facilitate the training of the individual examinee in the skills required for independent living. For this purpose, a collection of carefully selected criterion-referenced skills works better than a group of norm-based scores. The ILBC focuses on what the examinee can do, not on how the examinee compares to other persons. An exact age range is not specified, but the instrument appears to be suitable for persons 16 years of age through adulthood.

For each skill, the ILBC specifies a condition, a behavior, and a standard. For example, one item titled Rubber Scraper provides the following:

*Condition:* Given a bowl containing ingredients, a pan, and a rubber scraper.

*Behavior:* Client pours the ingredients into the pan and scrapes the sides of the bowl.

*Standard:* Behavior within 2 minutes; No ingredients spilled. All ingredients removed. (Walls et al., 1979, p. 93)

The reader will notice that all three components (condition, behavior, and standard) are defined with enough precision that reasonable observers would likely agree when a skill has been mastered. In fact, test-retest and interobserver agreement for ILBC skills range from .96 to a perfect 1.00.

The items within each ILBC category were carefully selected to encompass the important and relevant skills for independent living. Apparently, the authors succeeded in identifying essential skills, insofar as their instrument has a 100 percent overlap with another—initially unknown—checklist for independent living (Schwab, 1979). In addition, the ILBC items were carefully ordered from easiest to hardest. When used on a continuing basis over a several-year training period, the ILBC thus provides a checklist of skills mastered and also furnishes guidance for further rehabilitation.

### Inventory for Client and Agency Planning (ICAP)

The Inventory for Client and Agency Planning (Hill, 2005) is one of the most widely used tests in the field of developmental disabilities. This test is suitable for children and adults with mental retardation, individuals who become disabled as adults through illness or accident, and elderly persons who have slowly lost their independence and, therefore, need special assistance. The focus of the instrument is on determining the need for special services such as personal care, remedial education, vocational training, or sheltered work environment.

The test is a 16-page booklet that evaluates adaptive behavior, maladaptive behavior, and the need for assistance and supports. Amazingly, it can be completed in about 15 minutes by a parent, teacher, or caregiver who is well acquainted with the client. The scales and subscales of the ICAP are depicted in Table 7.12. Identical to the SIB-R, adaptive behaviors are rated on a scale from 0 to 3,

● **TABLE 7.12** Scales and Subscales of the Inventory for Client and Agency Planning

| Scale | Number of Items | Subscales or Domains Measured |
|---|---|---|
| Descriptive | 10 | Data on age, height, weight, legal status |
| Primary and Additional Diagnoses | 14 | All relevant medical and psychological diagnoses |
| Special Needs | 10 | Special needs in vision, hearing, mobility, health care, medications |
| Residential Supports | 2 | Residential supports now and in future |
| School/Vocational Supports | 2 | School and vocational supports now and in future |
| Other Support Services | 26 | Survey of all support services needed, now and in future |
| Social/Leisure Activities | 16 | Survey of social and leisure activities |
| Adaptive Behavior | 77 | Level of functioning in motor skills, social and communication skills, personal living skills, and community living skills |
| Maladaptive Behavior | 24 | Self-injury, stereotyped, withdrawn, offensive, uncooperative, disruptive, destructive, hurts others |

Note: The ICAP also yields a Service Score based on Adaptive Behavior and Maladaptive Behavior.

with 0 indicating never or rarely does a behavior well (even if asked), 1 indicating does the task but not well, 2 indicating does the task fairly well, and 3 indicating does the task well without being asked. The maladaptive behaviors are assessed in a more complex manner using open-ended questions and follow-up queries as to frequency, severity, and consequences of the maladaptive behaviors. This technique provides for a maladaptive behavior subscale with enhanced reliability ($r = .80$) in comparison to similar subscales from other instruments that reveal low reliability ($r = .60$). From a psychometric standpoint, the ICAP meets the highest standards.

One of the most useful and appealing aspects of the ICAP is that it provides an overall Service Score based on both adaptive and maladaptive behavior. The Service Score, which ranges from 0 to 100, indicates the likely level of attention, supervision, and training needed by the client. The lower the score, the greater the need for oversight. For example, a child with severe disabilities and many maladaptive behaviors might earn a score of 5, indicating the need for intensive supervision virtually 24 hours a day. At the other extreme, a normal young adult with no behavior problems might earn a score of 95, indicating almost complete self-sufficiency.

By intention, the Service Score was designed to predict not only the service intensity needed but also the costs associated with delivering the assistance. For this reason, state and regional users often collate their ICAP data in a computer database provided by the test publishers.

In many states in the United States, the human services departments have linked their disability services with results from the ICAP. For example, in Colorado, the ICAP is used by the Division of Services for People with Disabilities to determine eligibility and to allocate funds for individuals receiving residential services and day care services (www.cdhs.state.co.us). Resources are allocated for other reasons as well, but the ICAP is foundational to the entire system of disabilities services. Certainly, this is an example of consequential testing: The fate of an entire group of individuals is linked to the soundness of the ICAP for purposes of determining services.

## Additional Measures of Adaptive Behavior

We remind the reader that measures of adaptive behavior vary greatly. Some scales are designed mainly for diagnosis, others for remediation. Some scales are useful with persons with severe and profound mental retardation who will never be employed, others with individuals with mild mental retardation seeking vocational training. Some scales are useful exclusively with children, others with adults. These instruments are not interchangeable, and the potential user must study their strengths and limitations carefully.

The Vineland Adaptive Behavior Scales-II (VABS-II; Sparrow, Cicchetti, & Balla, 2005) is the most widely used measure of adaptive behavior in existence. The instrument is the outcome of a major revision and restandardization of the Vineland Social Maturity Scale, originally published in 1935 by Edgar A. Doll. Based on a semistructured interview with a caregiver or parent, the VABS provides an evaluation in the following domains and subdomains: Communication (receptive, expressive, written), Daily Living Skills (personal, domestic, community), Socialization (interpersonal relationships, play and leisure time, coping skills), Motor Skills (gross, fine).

The VABS-II is a widely respected instrument with good concurrent validity, including correlations in the range of .50 to .80 with the Wechsler scales and Stanford-Binet. However, some of the interview items require knowledge that the informants may not possess (e.g., whether a child says 100 recognizable words). Silverstein (1986) faults the normative data, noting discontinuous jumps in standard scores from one age group to another. Even so, the Vineland continues to be a highly popular test in clinical practice and research. A promising development in research is the increasing use of this instrument in other countries. For example, de Bildt, Kraijer, Sytema, and Minderaa (2005) report favorably on the validity of the VABS in a sample of 826 Dutch children with mental retardation, and Balboni, Pedrabissi, Molteni, and Villa (2001) established that the instrument accurately identifies mentally retarded individuals with and without communication impairment, social behavior problems, and motor disabilities.

The American Association on Intellectual and Developmental Disability (AAIDD) has developed several scales useful in the assessment of persons with cognitive limitations. We mention here just one of its products, the AAMR Adaptive Behavior Scales: Second Edition (Nihira, Leland, & Lambert, 1993). The residential and community version of this test, suitable for persons 18 to 80 years of age, is a psychometric tour de force that borders on overkill. The normative sample includes more than 4,000 persons with developmental disabilities from 43 states residing in the community or in residential settings. In addition to assessing the appropriate behavioral domains (e.g., independent functioning, domestic activity, self-direction, responsibility), a noteworthy feature of the instrument is the careful attention to maladaptive behaviors, which are evaluated in eight domains:

- Violent and antisocial behavior
- Rebellious behavior
- Eccentric and self-abusive behavior
- Untrustworthy behavior
- Withdrawal
- Stereotyped and hyperactive behavior
- Inappropriate body exposure
- Disturbed behavior

This scale has been extensively validated and clearly distinguishes persons independently classified at different adaptive behavior levels.

## ●SUMMARY

1. In the 1970s, a renewed societal concern for the needs of persons with disabilities was translated into federal legislation. Public Law 93-112 outlawed discrimination on the basis of disability. Public Law 94-142 mandated that disabled schoolchildren receive appropriate assessment and educational opportunities.

2. The Leiter International Performance Scale-Revised is an untimed measure of perceptual organization and reasoning ability. The test can be administered completely by pantomime—the examinee matches small laminated cards underneath corresponding illustrations on an easel display.

3. The Goodenough-Harris Drawing Test is a brief screening test of intelligence in which the examinee is encouraged to draw a good picture of a man. The 73 scorable items include body parts, details, perspective, proportion, and implied freedom of movement. The Draw A Person test of Naglieri (1988) is an updated version of the Drawing Test.

4. The Hiskey-Nebraska Test of Learning Aptitude is a nonlanguage performance scale for use with children ages 3 to 17 years. The test is used with children who are deaf or bilingual or those who have speech or language impairment or mental retardation. Originally normed in 1960, the test is in need of restandardization.

5. The Test of Nonverbal Intelligence-3 (TONI-3) is a language-free, multiple-choice measure of cognitive ability designed for special populations and carefully standardized for ages 5 through 85. Most items require the examinee to identify relationships among abstract figures. The TONI-3 is a good index of general—as opposed to nonverbal—intelligence.

6. The Peabody Picture Vocabulary Test-4 (PPVT-4) is suitable for obtaining a rapid measure of hearing vocabulary with persons who are deaf or disabled (e.g., from stroke or cerebral palsy). The examiner says a word and the examinee tries to select from four pictures the one that depicts the word.

7. Respected tests for subjects with visual impairment include the Perkins-Binet, an adaptation of the Stanford-Binet; the Haptic Intelligence Scale for the Adult Blind (HISAB), a modification of the Wechsler Performance subtests; and the Blind

Learning Aptitude Test (BLAT), a Braille-like measure of concept formation and abstract reasoning.

8. Testing persons who are deaf, especially those who rely upon sign language, requires specialized training and sensitivity to issues of Deaf culture. The Performance subtests of the Wechsler scales remain the tools of choice. A formal ASL translation of the WAIS-III (with videotaped demonstration) has been released by the test publisher.

9. Intellectual disability is defined by three criteria: significantly subaverage general intellectual functioning, typically defined as an IQ under 70 (or 75 in exceptional cases); limitations in adaptive skill areas; and onset prior to the eighteenth birthday.

10. The Inventory for Client and Agency Planning (ICAP) helps determine the need for special services such as personal care, remedial education, vocational training, or sheltered work environment for persons with mental retardation and other disabilities. The ICAP also helps predict the costs associated with service delivery for individual clients.

11. The Scales of Independent Behavior-R (SIB-R) is a measure of adaptive behavior that is highly useful in the assessment of mental retardation. A parent, caregiver, or teacher completes a series of 14 subscales pertaining to motor skills, social and communication skills, personal living skills, and community living skills.

## ● KEY TERMS AND CONCEPTS

Public Law 93-112   p. 295

legally blind   p. 303

# Origins of Personality Testing

## Theories of Personality and Projective Techniques

In psychological testing a fundamental distinction often is drawn between ability tests and personality tests. Defined in the broadest sense, ability tests include a plethora of instruments for measuring intelligence, achievement, and aptitude. In the preceding seven chapters we have explored the nature, construction, application, reliability, and validity of ability tests. In the next two chapters we shift the emphasis to personality tests. Personality tests seek to measure one or more of the following: personality traits, dynamic motivation, symptoms of distress, personal strengths, and attitudinal characteristics.

Theories of personality provide an underpinning for the multiplicity of instruments available in the field. For this reason, we begin this chapter with a survey of prominent personality theories. The many ways in which theorists conceptualize personality clearly have impacted the design of personality tests and assessments. This is especially evident with projective techniques such as the Rorschach inkblot method, which emanated from psychoanalytic conceptions of personality. Thus, in Topic 8A, Theories of Personality and Projective Techniques, in addition to the survey of personality theories, we have included an introduction to several instruments based on the turn-of-the-twentieth-century psychoanalytic hypothesis where responses to ambiguous stimuli reveal the innermost, unconscious mental processes of the examinee. The coverage of personality assessment continues in Topic 8B, Self-Report and Behavioral Assessment of Psychopathology, which includes a review of structured tests and procedures, including self-report inventories and behavioral assessment approaches. These time-honored topics of Chapter 8—theories of personality, projective techniques, and structured personality tests—are followed by the relatively new focus of Chapter 9—the assessment of normality and human strengths.

## ● PERSONALITY: AN OVERVIEW

Although personality is difficult to define, we can distinguish two fundamental features of this vague construct. First, each person is consistent to some extent; we have coherent traits and action patterns that arise repeatedly. Second, each person is distinctive to some extent; behavioral differences exist between individuals. Consider the reactions of three graduate students when their midterm examinations were handed back. Although all three students received nearly identical grades (solid Bs), personal reactions were quite diverse. The first student walked off sullenly and was later overheard to say that a complaint to the departmental administrator was in order. The second student was pleased, stating out loud that a B was, after all, a respectable grade. The third student was disappointed but stoical. He blamed himself for not studying harder.

How are we to understand the different reactions of these three persons, each of whom was responding to an identical stimulus? Psychologists and laypersons alike invoke the concept of **personality** to make sense out of the behavior and expressed feelings of others. The notion of personality is used to explain behavioral differences between persons (for example, why one complains and another is stoical) and to understand the behavioral consistency within each individual (for example, why the complaining student noted previously was generally sour and dissatisfied).

In addition to understanding personality, psychologists also seek to measure it. Literally hundreds of personality tests are available for this purpose; we will review historically prominent instruments and also discuss some promising new approaches. However, in order that the reader can better comprehend the diversity of instruments and approaches, we begin with a more fundamental question: How is personality best conceptualized? As the reader will discover, in order to measure personality we must first envision what it is we seek to measure. The reader will better appreciate the multiplicity of tests and procedures if we also briefly describe the personality theories that comprise the underpinnings for these instruments.

## ● PSYCHOANALYTIC THEORIES OF PERSONALITY

Psychoanalysis was the original creation of Sigmund Freud (1856–1939). While it is true that many others have revised and adapted his theories, the changes have been slight in comparison to the substantial foundations that can be traced to this singular genius of the Victorian and early-twentieth-century era. Freud was enormously prolific in his writing and theorizing. We restrict our discussion to just those aspects of psychoanalysis that have influenced psychological testing. In particular, the Rorschach, the Thematic Apperception Test, and most of the projective techniques critiqued in the next topic dictate a psychoanalytic framework for interpretation. Readers who wish a more thorough review of Freud's contributions can start with the *New Introductory Lectures on Psychoanalysis* (Freud, 1933). Reviews and interpretations of Freud's theories can be found in Stafford-Clark (1971) and Fisher and Greenberg (1984).

### Origins of Psychoanalytic Theory

Freud began his professional career as a neurologist but was soon specializing in the treatment of hysteria, an emotional disorder characterized by histrionic behavior and physical symptoms of psychic origin such as paralysis, blindness, and loss of sensation. With his colleague Joseph Breuer, Freud postulated that the root cause of hysteria was buried memories of traumatic experiences such as childhood sexual molestation. If these memories could be brought forth under hypnosis, a release of emotion called abreaction would take place and the hysterical symptoms would disappear, at least briefly (*Studies on Hysteria*, Breuer & Freud, 1893–1895).

From these early studies Freud developed a general theory of psychological functioning with the concept of the unconscious as its foundation. He believed that the unconscious was the reservoir of instinctual drives and a storehouse of thoughts and wishes that would be unacceptable to our conscious self. Thus, Freud argued that our most significant personal motivations are largely beyond conscious awareness. The concept of the unconscious was discussed in elaborate detail in his first book (*The Interpretation of Dreams*, Freud, 1900). Freud believed that dreams portray our unconscious motives in a disguised form. Even a seemingly innocuous dream might actually have a hidden sexual or aggressive meaning, if it is interpreted correctly.

Freud's concept of the unconscious penetrated the very underpinnings of psychological testing early in the twentieth century. An entire family of projective techniques emerged, including inkblot tests, word association approaches, sentence completion techniques, and storytelling (apperception) techniques (Frank, 1939, 1948). Each of these methods was predicated on the assumption that unconscious motives could be divined from an examinee's responses to ambiguous and unstructured stimuli. In fact, Rorschach (1921) likened his inkblot test to an X ray of the unconscious mind. Although he patently overstated the power of projective techniques, it is evident from Rorschach's view that the psychoanalytic conception of the unconscious had a strong influence on testing practices.

### The Structure of the Mind

Freud divided the mind into three structures: the id, the ego, and the superego. The id is the obscure and inaccessible part of our personality that Freud likened to "a chaos, a cauldron of seething excitement." Because the **id** is entirely unconscious, we must infer its characteristics indirectly by analyzing dreams and symptoms such as anxiety. From such an analysis, Freud concluded that the id is the seat of all instinctual needs such as for food, water, sexual gratification, and avoidance of pain. The id has only one purpose, to obtain immediate satisfaction for these needs in accordance with the pleasure principle. The **pleasure principle** is the impulse toward immediate satisfaction without regard for values, good or evil, or morality. The id is also incapable of logic and possesses no concept of time. The chaotic mental processes of the id are, therefore, unaltered by the passage of time, and impressions that have been pushed down into the id "are virtually immortal and are preserved for whole decades as though they had only recently occurred" (Freud, 1933).

If our personality consisted only of an id striving to gratify its instincts without regard for reality, we would soon be annihilated by outside forces. Fortunately, soon after birth part of the id develops into the **ego** or conscious self. The purpose of the ego is to mediate between the id and reality. The ego is part of the id and servant to it, but the ego "interpolates between desire and action the procrastinating factor of thought" (Freud, 1933). Thus, the ego is largely conscious and obeys the **reality principle;** it seeks realistic and safe ways of discharging the instinctual tensions that are constantly pushing forth from the id.

The ego must also contend with the **superego,** the ethical component of personality that starts to emerge in the first five years of life. The superego is roughly synonymous with conscience and comprises the societal standards of right and wrong that are conveyed to us by our parents. The superego is partly conscious, but a large part of it is unconscious; that is, we are not always aware of its existence or operation. The function of the superego is to restrict the attempts of the id and ego to obtain gratification. Its main weapon is guilt, which it uses to punish the wrongdoings of the ego and id. Thus, it is not enough for the ego to find a safe and realistic way for the gratification of id strivings. The ego must also choose a morally acceptable outlet, or it will suffer punishment from its overseer, the superego. This explains why we may feel guilty for immoral behavior such as theft even when getting caught is impossible. Another part of the superego is the ego ideal, which consists of our aims and aspirations. The ego measures itself against the ego ideal and strives to fulfill its demands for perfection. If the ego falls too far short of meeting the standards of the ego ideal, a feeling of guilt may result. We commonly interpret this feeling as a sense of inferiority (Freud, 1933).

## The Role of Defense Mechanisms

The ego certainly has a difficult task, acting as mediator and servant to three tyrants: id, superego, and external reality. It may seem to the reader that the task would be essentially impossible and that the individual would, therefore, be in a constant state of anxiety. Fortunately, the ego has a set of tools at its disposal to help carry out its work, namely, mental strategies collectively labeled **defense mechanisms.**

Defense mechanisms come in many varieties, but they all share three characteristics in common. First, their exclusive purpose is to help the ego reduce anxiety created by the conflicting demands of id, superego, and external reality. In fact, Freud felt that anxiety was a signal telling the ego to invoke one or more defense mechanisms in its own behalf. Defense mechanisms and anxiety are, therefore, complementary concepts in psychoanalytic

theory, one existing as a counterforce to the other. The second common feature of defense mechanisms is that they operate unconsciously. Thus, even though defense mechanisms are controlled by the ego, we are not aware of their operation. The third characteristic of defense mechanisms is that they distort inner or outer reality. This property is what makes them capable of reducing anxiety. By allowing the ego to view a challenge from the id, superego, or external reality in a less-threatening manner, defense mechanisms help the ego avoid crippling levels of anxiety. Of course, because they distort reality, the rigid, excessive application of defense mechanisms may create more problems than it solves.

## Assessment of Defense Mechanisms and Ego Functions

Although Freud introduced the concept of defense mechanisms, it was left to his followers to elucidate these unconscious mental strategies in more detail (Paulhus, Fridhandler, & Hayes, 1997). Vaillant (1971) developed a hierarchy of ego adaptive mechanisms based on the assumption that some defensive mechanisms are intrinsically healthier than others. In his view, defense mechanisms can be grouped into four different types. Listed in order of increasing healthiness, the types are psychotic, immature, neurotic, and mature (Table 8.1). Psychotic mechanisms such as gross denial of external reality are the least healthy because they distort reality to an extreme degree. They appear "crazy" to the beholder. Immature mechanisms such as the projection of one's own unacknowledged feelings to others are healthier than psychotic mechanisms. Nonetheless, they are easily detected by outside observers and seen as undesirable. Neurotic defense mechanisms typically alter private feelings so that they are less threatening. An example is intellectualization, a defense mechanism in which threatening matters are analyzed in bland terms that are void of feelings. For example, a physician whose mother died recently might talk at great length about the medical characteristics of her cancer, thereby easing his sense of loss. Mature

● **TABLE 8.1    Levels of Defense Mechanisms Proposed by Vaillant (1977)**

I. **Psychotic**

Delusional Projection: frank delusions about external reality, usually of a persecutory nature

Denial: denial of external reality; e.g., failing to acknowledge that one has a terminal illness

Distortion: grossly reshaping external reality to suit inner needs; e.g., wish-fulfilling delusions

II. **Immature**

Projection: attributing one's own unacknowledged feelings to others; e.g., "You're angry, not me!"

Schizoid Fantasy: use of fantasy and inner retreat for the purpose of conflict resolution and gratification

Hypochondriasis: transforming reproach toward others first into self-reproach then into complaints of physical illness

Passive-Aggressive Behavior: aggression toward others expressed indirectly and ineffectively through passivity or directed against the self

Acting Out: direct expression of an unconscious wish or impulse in order to avoid being conscious of the feeling that accompanies it

III. **Neurotic**

Intellectualization: thinking about wishes in formal, unfeeling terms, but not acting upon them

Repression: seemingly inexplicable memory lapses or failure to acknowledge information; e.g., "forgetting" a dental appointment

Displacement: directing of feelings toward something or someone other than the real object; e.g., kicking the dog when angry with the boss

Reaction Formation: unconsciously turning an impulse into its opposite; e.g., over-solicitousness to a hated coworker

Dissociation: temporary but drastic modification of one's character to avoid emotional distress; e.g., a brief devil-may-care attitude

IV. **Mature**

Altruism: vicarious but constructive and gratifying service to others; e.g., philanthropy

Humor: playful acknowledgment of ideas and feelings without discomfort and without unpleasant effects on others; does not include sarcasm

Suppression: conscious or semiconscious decision to postpone paying attention to a conscious conflict or impulse

Anticipation: realistic anticipation of or planning for future inner discomfort; e.g., realistic anticipation of surgery or separation

Sublimation: indirect expression of instinctual wishes without adverse consequences or loss of pleasure; e.g., channeling aggression into sports

*Source:* Based on Vaillant, G. (1977). *Adaptation to life: How the best and the brightest came of age.* Boston: Little, Brown.

mechanisms of defense appear to the beholder as convenient virtues. An example is certain forms of humor that do not distort reality but that can ease the burden of matters "too terrible to be borne" (Vaillant, 1977).

Considering the degree of skilled judgment required by the evaluation task, the interrater reliability of the defense mechanism ratings was—with a few exceptions—respectable. The individual defense mechanisms possessed reliabilities that ranged from .53 (Fantasy) to .96 (Projection); most reliabilities were in the .70s and .80s. Reliability of a global rating (reflecting the ratio of mature to immature ratings) was .77.

The validity of defense mechanism ratings hinges mainly on the demonstration that developmental changes and group differences are consistent with psychoanalytic theory regarding these constructs. We would expect, for example, that the Grant Study subjects would use fewer immature and more mature defense mechanisms as they grew into middle age, and this is precisely what Vaillant discovered. In addition, we would expect that persons found to be maladjusted by other criteria (e.g., frequent divorce, underachievement) would rate less favorably on defense mechanisms in comparison to adjusted persons, and this is also what Vaillant observed. In sum, the analysis of defense mechanisms is a promising approach to personality assessment. However, this approach does have two drawbacks: The examiner needs specialized training to recognize defense mechanisms, and the process of collecting relevant information from examinees is very time-consuming.

## ● TYPE THEORIES OF PERSONALITY

The earliest personality theories attempted to sort individuals into discrete categories or types. For example, the Greek physician Hippocrates (ca. 460–377 B.C.) proposed a humoral theory with four personality types (sanguine, choleric, melancholic, and phlegmatic) that was too simplistic to be useful. In the 1940s, Sheldon and Stevens (1942) proposed a type theory based on the relationship between

body build and temperament. Their approach stimulated a flurry of research and then faded into obscurity. Nonetheless, typological theories have continued to capture intermittent interest among personality researchers. We will illustrate type theories by reviewing contemporary research on coronary-prone personality types.

### Type A Coronary-Prone Behavior Pattern

Friedman and Rosenman (1974) investigated the psychological variables that put individuals at higher risk of coronary heart disease. They were the first to identify a **Type A coronary-prone behavior pattern,** which they described as "an action–emotion complex that can be observed in any person who is aggressively involved in a chronic, incessant struggle to achieve more and more in less and less time, and if required to do so, against the opposing efforts of other things or persons" (Friedman & Rosenman, 1974). At the opposite extreme is the Type B behavior pattern, characterized by an easygoing, noncompetitive, relaxed lifestyle. Of course, people vary along a continuum from "pure" Type A to "pure" Type B.

Friedman and Ulmer (1984) have listed the specific components of the full-fledged Type A behavior pattern:

- *Insecurity of status:* A hidden lack of self-esteem seems to plague many Type A persons. No matter how successful, they often compare themselves unfavorably to other superachievers.
- *Hyperaggressiveness:* A desire to dominate others and damage their self-esteem is part of the pattern. Type A persons are often indifferent to the feelings or rights of competitors.
- *Free-floating hostility:* The Type A person finds too many things to get upset about, and the anger is out of proportion to the situation.
- *Sense of time urgency (hurry sickness):* This includes two basic strategems: speeding up daily activities (one Type A used an electric shaver in each hand!), and doing two things at once such as conversing on the phone while reviewing correspondence.

Type A behavior can be diagnosed from a short interview consisting of questions about habits of working, talking, eating, reading, and thinking (Friedman, 1996). The more flagrant cases of Type A behavior can also be detected by paper-and-pencil tests (Jackson & Gray, 1987). However, the questionnaire approach is limited because it cannot reveal the facial, vocal, and psychomotor indices of hostility and time urgency that are usually evident in interview (Friedman & Ulmer, 1984).

Early studies indicated that persons who exhibited the Type A behavior pattern were at greatly increased risk of coronary disease and heart attack. In one 9-year study of more than 3,000 healthy men, persons with the Type A behavior pattern were 2½ times more likely to suffer heart attacks than those with Type B behavior pattern (Friedman & Ulmer, 1984). In fact, not one of the "pure" Type Bs—the extremely relaxed, easygoing, and noncompetitive members of the study—had suffered a heart attack. In the famous Framingham longitudinal study, Type A men ages 55 to 64 were about twice as likely at 10-year follow-up to develop coronary heart disease as Type B men (Haynes, Feinleib, & Eaker, 1983). In this study, the link between Type A behavior and heart disease was especially strong for white-collar workers.

In other studies, researchers have found only a weak relationship—or no relationship at all—between Type A behavior and coronary heart disease (e.g., Eaker & Castelli, 1988; Smedslund & Rundmo, 1999). Other researchers have found that heart disease is linked not so much with the full-blown Type A behavior pattern as it is with specific components such as being anger-prone (Dembroski, MacDougall, Williams, & Haney, 1985) or possessing time urgency (Wright, 1988). Certainly, there is a need to sort out the specific risk factors in this area of investigation. In a review of current thinking, Wielgosz and Nolan (2000) identify hostility, cynicism, and suppression of anger, as well as stress, depression, and social isolation, as significant risk factors in Type A behavior. A good review of the complex and confusing research on Type A behavior can be found in Wiebe and Smith (1997).

## ● PHENOMENOLOGICAL THEORIES OF PERSONALITY

Phenomenological theories of personality emphasize the importance of immediate, personal, subjective experience as a determinant of behavior. Some of the theoretical positions subsumed under this title have been given other labels also, such as humanistic theories, existential theories, construct theories, self-theories, and fulfillment theories (Maddi, 2000). Nonetheless, these approaches share a common focus on the person's subjective experience, personal worldview, and self-concept as the major wellsprings of behavior.

### Origins of the Phenomenological Approach

The orientation briefly reviewed in this section has numerous sources that reach back to turn-of-the-twentieth-century European philosophy and literature. Nonetheless, two persons, one a philosopher and the other a writer, stand out as seminal contributors to the modern phenomenological viewpoint. The German philosopher Edmund Husserl (1859–1938) invented a complex philosophy of phenomenology that was concerned with the description of pure mental phenomena. Husserl's approach was heavily introspective and nearly inscrutable. More approachable was the Danish writer Søren Kierkegaard (1813–1855), well known for his contributions to existentialism. Existentialism is the literary and philosophical movement concerned with the meaning of life and an individual's freedom to choose personal goals. The phenomenology of Husserl and the existentialism of Kierkegaard influenced dozens of prominent philosophers and psychologists. Vestiges of these early viewpoints are evident in virtually every contemporary phenomenological personality theory (Maddi, 2000).

### Carl Rogers, Self-Theory, and the Q-Technique

The most influential phenomenological theorist was Carl Rogers (1902–1987). His contributions to personality theory, known as self-theory, are extensive and generally well appreciated by students of psychology (Rogers, 1951, 1961, 1980). But it is also true, albeit little recognized, that Rogers helped shape a small part of psychological testing by popularizing the Q-technique.

The **Q-technique** is a procedure for studying changes in the self-concept, a key element in Rogers's self-theory. The technique was developed by Stephenson (1953) but a series of studies by Rogers and his colleagues served to popularize this measurement approach (Rogers & Dymond, 1954). Also known as a Q-sort, the Q-technique is a generalized procedure that is especially useful for studying changes in self-concept.[1] The Q-sort consists of a large number of cards, each containing a printed statement such as the following:

I am poised
I put on a false front
I make strong demands on myself
I am a submissive person
I am likeable

The examinee is asked to sort a hundred or so statements into nine piles, putting a prescribed number of cards into each, thus forcing a near-normal distribution. The instructions specify that the examinee put the cards most descriptive of him or her at one end, those least descriptive at the opposite end, and those about which he or she is indifferent or undecided around the middle of the distribution. The required distribution might look like this:

| | Least Like Me | | | | | Most Like Me | | | |
|---|---|---|---|---|---|---|---|---|---|
| Pile No. | 1 | 2 | 3 | 4 | 5 | 6 | 7 | 8 | 9 |
| No. of cards | 1 | 4 | 11 | 21 | 26 | 21 | 11 | 4 | 1 |

The nature of the items is determined by the needs of the researcher or practitioner. Rogers used a set of items devised by Butler and Haigh (Rogers

---

1. The Q-technique has additional applications as well. Marks and Seeman (1963) employed Q-sorts by therapists to describe patients with specific MMPI profiles. Bem and Funder (1978) recommend a Q-sort to derive a profile of characteristics associated with successful performance of a specific task. Persons whose self-descriptions match the derived profile can be predicted to succeed at the selected task.

& Dymond, 1954, chap. 4) to tap the self-concept. These statements were taken at random from available therapeutic protocols; their Q-sort items represented actual client statements, reworded for clarity. But a special virtue of the Q-technique is that other researchers or practitioners are free to craft their own items. For example, Marks and Seeman (1963) used a psychodynamic perspective in devising items for the therapist description of patient groups. Examples of their items include the following:

Utilizes acting out as a defense mechanism

Tends to be flippant in both word and gesture

Genotype has paranoid features

Appears to be poised, self-assured, socially at ease

Exhibits depression (manifest sad mood)

Scoring a Q-sort is usually a matter of comparing or correlating the distribution of items against an established norm. For example, well-adjusted persons might be asked to sort the items so as to derive an average pile placement number (ranging from 1 to 9) for each item. An individual examinee would be considered more- or less-adjusted according to the resemblance between his or her sortings and the average sorting for adjusted persons. We will refer the reader to Block (1961) for details.

Another way to use the Q-sort is to compare an examinee's self-sort with his or her ideal sort. Rogers used the discrepancy between these two sortings as an index of adjustment. His subjects were required to sort the items twice, according to the following instructions:

1. *Self-sort.* Sort these cards to describe yourself as you see yourself today, from those that are least like you to those that are most like you.
2. *Ideal sort.* Now sort these cards to describe your ideal person—the person you would most like within yourself to be (Rogers & Dymond, 1954).

Using the item pile numbers, Rogers then correlated the two sorts for each subject separately. Consider what these data mean: If the self-sort and the ideal sort are highly similar, the correlation of Q-sort data will approach 1.0; if the two sorts are

| ● TABLE 8.2 | Average Self-Ideal Correlations for Client and Control Groups | | |
|---|---|---|---|
| | *Precounseling* | *Postcounseling* | *Follow-Up* |
| Client Group (*N* = 25) | −.01 | .36 | .32 |
| Control Group (*N* = 16) | .58 | | .59 |

*Source:* Based on Rogers, C. R., & Dymond, R. F. (Eds.). (1954). *Psychotherapy and personality change: Co-ordinated research studies in the client-centered approach.* Chicago: University of Chicago Press.

opposite one another, the correlation will approach −1.0. Of course, most sorts will be somewhere in between but typically on the positive side. Butler and Haigh found that psychotherapy clients increased their congruence between self and ideal (Rogers & Dymond, 1954, chap. 4). Even so, adjusted control subjects possessed a greater congruence (Table 8.2).

## ● BEHAVIORAL AND SOCIAL LEARNING THEORIES

Behavioral and social learning theories have their origins in laboratory studies on operant learning and classical conditioning. A fundamental assumption of all behavioral theorists is that many of the behaviors that make up personality are learned. To understand personality, then, we must know about the learning history of the individual. Behavioral theorists also believe that the environment is of supreme importance in shaping and maintaining behavior. Behavioral inquiry, therefore, seeks to identify the specific components of the current environment that are controlling a person's behavior. The behavioral approach to personality has produced a variety of direct assessment methods, which we discuss in the next chapter.

Behavioral theorists disagree mainly on the role that cognitions play in determining behavior. *Cognitions* are inferred mental processes such as problem solving, judging, or reasoning. Radical behaviorists believe that resorting to mentalistic explanations of any kind is futile: "When what a person does is attributed to what is going on inside him, investigation is brought to an end" (Skinner, 1974). By contrast, social learning theorists make cautious reference to cognitions in explaining

what it is, specifically, that a person learns. A social learning theorist might argue that we learn expectations or rules about the environment, not just stimulus and response connections.

Modern social learning theory can be viewed as a cognitive variant of the strict behaviorism that was dominant in U.S. psychology early in the twentieth century. Social learning theorists accept the Skinnerian premise that external reinforcement is an important determinant of behavior. But they also maintain that cognitions have a critical influence on our actions as well. For example, Rotter (1972) has popularized the view that our expectations about future outcomes are the primary determinants of behavior. The probability that a person will behave self-assertively, for example, depends on his or her expectations about the likely results of self-assertiveness. If the expected outcome is valued by the person, the behavior is more likely. Of course, expectations are a function of the person's history of reinforcement, so Rotter's social learning perspective is similar to the behavioral viewpoint. But the implication of social learning theory is that behavior is the result of a belief, in particular, a belief that the behavior will result in a desired outcome. Thus, cognitions are assumed to affect actions.

Based on his social learning views, Rotter (1966) developed the Internal-External (I-E) Scale, an interesting measure of internal versus external locus of control. The construct of **locus of control** refers to the perceptions that individuals have about the source of things that happen to them. In particular, the I-E Scale seeks to assess the examinee's generalized expectancies for internal versus external control of reinforcement. The purpose of the I-E Scale is to determine the extent to which the examinee believes that reinforcement is contingent upon his or her behavior (internal locus of control) as opposed to the outside world (external locus of control). The instrument is a forced-choice self-report inventory. For each item, the examinee chooses the single statement (from a pair) with which he or she more strongly concurs. Items resemble the following:

> In general, most people get the respect they deserve.
>
> OR
>
> In reality, a person's worth often passes unrecognized.

For the preceding item, the first alternative indicates an internal locus of control, whereas the second alternative signifies an external locus of control. The balance of internal to external responses determines the overall score on the scale. The I-E Scale is a reliable and valid instrument that has stimulated a huge body of research on the nature and meaning of locus of control and related variables. Research indicates that locus of control has a strong relationship to occupational success, physical health, academic achievement, and numerous other variables. As the reader might suspect, an internal locus of control generally predicts a more positive outcome than an external locus of control. The interested reader can consult Lefcourt (1991) for further details.

Important contributions to social learning theory have also been made by Albert Bandura. In his early studies, Bandura examined the role of observational learning and vicarious reinforcement in the development of behavior (Bandura, 1965, 1971; Bandura & Walters, 1963). More recently, he has proposed that perceived self-efficacy is a central mechanism in human action (Bandura, 1982; Bandura, Taylor, Ewart, Miller, & DeBusk, 1985). **Self-efficacy** is a personal judgment of "how well one can execute courses of action required to deal with prospective situations" (Bandura, 1982). The concept of self-efficacy is useful in explaining why correct knowledge does not necessarily predict efficient action. For example, two boys may be equally convinced that a garden snake in the bathtub presents no hazard, but one will pick it up while the other runs out the door. These differences in behavior illustrate the role of self-referential

thought as a mediator between knowledge and action. The boy who ran out the door did not believe he could deal with the situation effectively. He had little perceived self-efficacy for snake handling. Bandura would argue that the primary determinant of the boy's behavior is a self-judgment about personal capabilities. Cognitions are, therefore, assumed to be a major determinant of behavior.

Bandura has developed an interesting instrument for the assessment of self-efficacy expectancies (Bandura, Taylor, Ewart, Miller, & DeBusk, 1985). For a variety of situations that might arouse anxiety, annoyance, or anger, the examinee checks whether he or she "can do" the task, and also rates the degree of confidence using a number from 10 to 100. The format of the checklist is as follows:

| 10 | 20 | 30 | 40 | 50 | 60 | 70 | 80 | 90 | 100 |
|----|----|----|----|----|----|----|----|----|-----|
| Quite Uncertain | | | Moderately Certain | | | | | Certain | |

**Can Do  Confidence**

Go to a party at which
there is no one you know.     _____     _____
Complain about poor food
at a restaurant.              _____     _____

Bandura's instrument is essentially a criterion-referenced tool for use in psychotherapy and research.

## ● TRAIT CONCEPTIONS OF PERSONALITY

A **trait** is any "relatively enduring way in which one individual differs from another" (Guilford, 1959). Psychologists developed the concept of trait from the ways people describe other people in everyday life. As language evolved, people found words to portray the consistencies and differences they encountered in their daily interactions with others. Thus, when we say one person is sociable and another is shy we are using trait names to describe consistencies within individuals and also differences between them (Goldberg, 1981a; Fiske, 1986).

Trait conceptions of personality have been enormously popular throughout the history of psychological testing, so the coverage here is necessarily selective. We will review three prominent and influential positions from the dozens of trait theories that have been proposed. These approaches differ primarily in terms of whether traits are split off into finely discriminable variants or grouped together into a small number of broad dimensions:

1. Cattell's factor-analytic viewpoint identifies 16 to 20 bipolar trait dimensions.
2. Eysenck's trait-dimensional approach coalesces dozens of traits into two overriding dimensions.
3. Goldberg and others have sought a modern synthesis of all trait approaches by proposing a five-factor model of personality.

For readers who desire a more detailed discussion of this topic, Pervin (1993) and Wiggins (1997) provide an excellent review of trait approaches to personality theory.

### Cattell's Factor-Analytic Trait Theory

Cattell (1950, 1973) refined existing methods of factor analysis to help reveal the basic traits of personality. He referred to the more obvious aspects of personality as **surface traits.** These would typically emerge in the first stages of factor analysis when individual test items were correlated with each other. For example, true-false items such as "I enjoy a good prize fight," "Getting stuck behind a slow driver really bothers me," and "It's important to let people know who is in charge" might be answered similarly by subjects, revealing a surface trait of aggressiveness.

But surface traits themselves tended to come in clusters, as revealed by Cattell's more sophisticated application of factor analysis. For Cattell, this was evidence of the existence of **source traits,** the stable and constant sources of behavior. Source traits are, therefore, less visible than surface traits but are more important in accounting for behavior.

Cattell (1950) was unrivaled in his use of factor analysis to discover how traits were organized and how they were related to each other. One approach was to have persons rate others they knew well by checking various adjectives such as *aggressive, thoughtful,* and *dominating* from a list of 171 choices. When the results from 208 subjects were subsequently factor analyzed, about 20 underlying personality factors or traits were tentatively identified. Another approach was to have thousands of persons answer questions about themselves and then factor-analyze their responses. Sixteen of the original 20 personality traits were independently confirmed by this second approach (Cattell, 1973). These 16 source traits have been incorporated into the Sixteen Personality Factor Questionnaire (16PF), a trait-based paper-and-pencil test of personality that is discussed in the next chapter.

### Eysenck's Trait-Dimensional Theory

Eysenck used factor analysis to put a modern face on the centuries old classical doctrine of the four temperaments (Eysenck & Eysenck, 1975, 1985). This theory was founded by Hippocrates and extolled by Galen, a second-century Roman physician. According to their approach, people come in four temperaments: sanguine, melancholic, choleric, and phlegmatic. A long list of traits is associated with each temperament; for example, the person with melancholic temperament is anxious, worried, serious, and thoughtful. In its original form the theory was too simplistic to be taken seriously. The genius of Eysenck was to use factor analysis of trait ratings to reveal that the four temperaments are hidden within two basic dimensions of personality: introverted–extraverted and emotionally stable–emotionally unstable (Figure 8.1). Specific traits are found in varying degrees along each dimension. The Eysenck Personality Questionnaire, which we review in the next chapter, is based on this trait-dimensional approach to personality.

### The Five-Factor Model of Personality

The five-factor model of personality has its origins in a review chapter by Goldberg (1981b). In his analysis of factor-analytic trait research, Goldberg identified several consistencies, which he referred to as the "Big Five" dimensions. Although researchers

|  | INTROVERTED | EXTRAVERTED |
|---|---|---|
| **EMOTIONALLY UNSTABLE** | **Melancholic**<br><br>Worried<br>Unhappy<br>Sober<br>Thoughtful | **Choleric**<br><br>Egocentric<br>Impulsive<br>Excitable<br>Active |
| **EMOTIONALLY STABLE** | **Phlegmatic**<br><br>Passive<br>Peaceful<br>Persistent<br>Calm | **Sanguine**<br><br>Sociable<br>Carefree<br>Hopeful<br>Contented |

● **FIGURE 8.1**
The Two-Dimensional Classification of Personality

*Source:* Based on the classical theory of temperaments and Eysenck's trait-dimensional theory of personality (Eysenck & Eysenck, 1985).

have used slightly different terms for these factors, the most common labels are

Neuroticism
Extraversion
Openness to Experience
Agreeableness
Conscientiousness

Rearranging the factors yields a simple acronym: OCEAN. The five-factor model is rapidly becoming the consensus model of personality. Support for the five-factor approach comes from several sources, including factor analysis of trait terms in language and the analysis of personality from an evolutionary perspective. Following, we discuss these perspectives.

The use of trait terms in the analysis of personality is based upon the **fundamental lexical hypothesis.** The essential point of this hypothesis is that trait terms have survived in language because they convey important information about our dealings with others:

The variety of individual differences is nearly boundless, yet most of these differences are

insignificant in people's daily interactions with others and have remained largely unnoticed. Sir Francis Galton may have been among the first scientists to recognize explicitly the fundamental lexical hypothesis—namely that the most important individual differences in human transactions will come to be encoded as single terms in some or all of the world's languages. (Goldberg, 1990)

When trait terms in English are distilled down to a reasonably distinct and nonoverlapping set of adjectives, a few hundred characteristics typically emerge (Allport, 1937). For decades, researchers have been asking individuals to rate themselves or others on these or similar traits. When these ratings are subjected to factor analysis, the "Big Five" dimensions previously listed usually appear in one guise or another. In sum, a mounting body of research indicates that the five-factor model captures a valid and useful representation of the structure of human traits.

The five-factor approach also possesses evolutionary plausibility. Specifically, the five factors of personality previously listed capture individual differences that relate to such basic evolutionary functions as survival and reproductive success

(Buss, 1997; Pervin, 1993). Goldberg (1981b) has theorized that people implicitly ask the following questions in their interactions with others:

1. Is X active and dominant or passive and submissive? (Can I bully X or will X try to bully me?)
2. Is X agreeable (warm and pleasant) or disagreeable (cold and distant)?
3. Can I count on X? (Is X responsible and conscientious or undependable and negligent?)
4. Is X crazy (unpredictable) or sane (stable)?
5. Is X smart or dumb? (How easy will it be for me to teach X?)

Directly or indirectly, each of these evaluations has a bearing on survival and reproductive success. For example, point 3 (conscientiousness) involves a trait that might ensure group survival in a hostile world. A person low on this trait (undependable) would be a poor choice for guarding the food supply. The ability to discern conscientiousness in others therefore has adaptive value. Not surprisingly, the five points previously listed correspond to the five-factor personality model.

The five-factor model of personality has inspired several personality scales and other systems for assessment (deRaad & Perugini, 2002). For example, Costa and McCrae have developed two personality tests based on the five-factor model (Costa, 1991; McCrae & Costa, 1987). The Revised NEO Personality Inventory (NEO-PI-R) contains 240 items rated on a five-point scale. In addition to the five major domains of personality, the inventory measures six specific traits (called facets) within each domain. A shortened 60-item version known as the NEO Five-Factor Inventory (NEO-FFI) also is available. Trull, Widiger, Useda, and others (1998) have published a semistructured interview for the assessment of the five-factor model of personality. These tests are discussed in the next chapter.

## Comment on the Trait Concept

All trait approaches to personality share certain problems in common. First, there is disagreement whether traits cause behavior or merely describe behavior (Fiske, 1986). It can be persuasively argued that invoking traits as causes is an empty

form of circular reasoning. For example, a person with extremely high standards might be said to possess the trait of perfectionism. But when asked to explain what is meant by perfectionism, we invariably end up referring to a pattern of extremely high standards. Thus, when we assert that someone is perfectionistic, are we really doing anything more than providing a short-hand description of their past behavior? Miller (1991) has voiced this criticism of the five-factor approach, noting that the model merely describes psychopathology but does not explain it.

A second problem with traits is their apparently low predictive validity. Mischel (1968) is credited with the first effective disparagement of the trait concept in his influential book *Personality and Assessment.* He stated that "while trait theory predicts behavioral consistency, it is behavior inconsistency that is typically observed" (Mischel, 1968). In a wide-ranging review of existing research, Mischel noted that trait scales produced validity coefficients with an upper limit of $r = .30$. He coined the term **personality coefficient** to describe these low correlations. Undoubtedly significant for large samples of subjects, correlations of $r = .30$ are of minimal value in the prediction of individual behavior.

Trait researchers responded to Mischel's attack by refining and limiting the trait concept. Researchers sought to identify subgroups of persons whose behavior could be accurately predicted on the basis of trait scores and also attempted to distinguish the kinds of situations in which behavior is largely determined by traits (e.g., Mischel, Shoda, & Mendoza-Denton, 2002; Wasylkiw & Fekken, 2002). These efforts met with modest success, raising the validity of some trait questionnaires—in some contexts with some persons—substantially beyond the ominous $r = .30$ barrier posited by Mischel (1968). But gone forever are the days of simplistic, generalized assertions such as "trait X predicts behavior Y."

## ● THE PROJECTIVE HYPOTHESIS

Frank (1939, 1948) introduced the term *projective method* to describe a category of tests for studying personality with unstructured stimuli. In a projective test the examinee encounters vague, ambiguous stimuli and responds with his or her own constructions. Disciples of projective testing are heavily vested in psychoanalytic theory and its postulation of unconscious aspects of personality. These examiners believe that unstructured, vague, ambiguous stimuli provide the ideal circumstance for revelations about inner aspects of personality. The central assumption of projective testing is that responses to the test represent projections from the innermost unconscious mental processes of the examinee. We introduce this topic with some preliminary concepts and distinctions relevant to projective testing.

The assumption that personal interpretations of ambiguous stimuli must necessarily reflect the unconscious needs, motives, and conflicts of the examinee is known as the **projective hypothesis**. Frank (1939) is generally credited with popularizing the projective hypothesis:

> When we scrutinize the actual procedures that may be called projective methods we find a wide variety of techniques and materials being employed for the same general purpose, to obtain from the subject, "what he cannot or will not say," frequently because he does not know himself and is not aware what he is revealing about himself through his projections.

The challenge of projective testing is to decipher underlying personality processes (needs, motives, and conflicts) based on the individualized, unique, subjective responses of each examinee. In the sections that follow we will examine how well projective tests have met this portentous assignment.

## A Classification of Projective Techniques

Lindzey (1959) has offered a classification of projective techniques that we will follow here. Based on the response required, he divided projectives into five categories:

- Association to inkblots or words
- Construction of stories or sequences
- Completions of sentences or stories
- Arrangement/selection of pictures or verbal choices
- Expression with drawings or play

Association techniques include the widely used Rorschach inkblot test and its psychometrically superior cousin the Holtzman Inkblot Technique, as well as word association tests. Construction techniques include the Thematic Apperception Test and the many variations upon this early instrument. Completion techniques consist mainly of sentence completion tests, discussed later. Arrangement/selection procedures such as the Szondi test (discussed in the first chapter) are currently seldom used. Finally, expression techniques such as the Draw-A-Person or House-Tree-Person test are very popular among clinicians in spite of dubious validity data.

We will review prominent techniques within each category except the antiquated arrangement/selection approaches, which are almost never used. However, the literature on major projective techniques is simply overwhelming, running to perhaps tens of thousands of articles on the Rorschach alone. We can suggest major trends in the research, but the reader will need to consult other sources for comprehensive reviews.

## ● ASSOCIATION TECHNIQUES

### The Rorschach

The Rorschach consists of 10 inkblots devised by Herman Rorschach (1884–1922) in the early 1900s. He formed the inkblots by dribbling ink on a sheet of paper and folding the paper in half, producing relatively symmetrical bilateral designs. Five of the inkblots are black or shades of gray, while five contain color; each is displayed on a white background. An inkblot of the type employed by Rorschach is shown in Figure 8.2. The Rorschach is suited to persons age 5 and up but is most commonly used with adults.

In administering the Rorschach, the examiner sits by the examinee's side to minimize body language communication. Administration consists of two phases. In the free association phase, the examiner presents the first blot and asks, "What might this be?" If the examinee asks for clarification (e.g., "Should I use the whole blot or only part of it?"),

● **FIGURE 8.2**   An Inkblot Similar to Those Found on the Rorschach

the examiner always responds in a nondirective manner ("It's up to you"). The test proceeds at a leisurely pace, so there is an implicit expectation that the examinee will give more than one response per card. However, this is not required; it is even permissible for the examinee to reject a card entirely, although this rarely happens. All 10 cards are presented in a similar manner.

Next, the examiner begins the inquiry phase. In this phase the examiner asks questions to clarify the exact blot location of each percept and to determine which aspects of the blot, such as the form or color, played a part in the creation of the response. Based on the information collected during the inquiry phase, the examiner can then code the location, determinants, form quality, and content of each response according to one or more formal scoring systems. For example, if the examinee used the entire blot for a percept, the response is coded W (whole); if the form of the blot was important in the percept, the response is further coded F (form); if human movement is depicted in the percept, the response is coded M

(movement); the use of color in a percept is coded C (color), CF (color/form), or FC (form/color), depending on whether form is totally absent, primary, or secondary to color as a determinant. The content of the percept is also coded, for example, H (human), Hd (human detail), An (anatomy), Cg (clothing), and so on (Table 8.3). Proper scoring of the Rorschach requires extensive training and supervision; we have touched on just a few basic aspects here.

Regrettably, Rorschach died before he could complete his scoring methods, so the systematization of Rorschach scoring was left to his followers. Five American psychologists produced overlapping but independent approaches to the test—Samuel Beck, Marguerite Hertz, Bruno Klopfer, Zygmunt Piotrowski, and David Rapaport (Erdberg, 1985). Predictably, the nuances of scoring vary from one scoring method to another. Fortunately, Exner and his colleagues have synthesized these earlier approaches into the Comprehensive Scoring System (Exner, 1991, 1993; Exner & Weiner, 1994). The Comprehensive Scoring System is better grounded in empirical research and clearly has supplanted all other approaches to Rorschach scoring.

Once the entire protocol has been coded, the examiner can compute a number of summary scores that form the primary basis for hypothesizing about the personality of the examinee. For example, the F+ percent is the proportion of the total responses that uses pure form as a determinant. A voluminous literature exists on the meaning of this index, but it seems safe to hypothesize that when the F+ percentage falls below 70 percent, the examiner should consider the possibility of severe psychopathology, brain impairment, or intellectual deficit in the examinee (Exner, 1993). The F+ percent is also considered to be an index of ego strength, with higher scores indicating a greater capacity to deal effectively with stress. However, support for this conjecture is mixed at best.

Frank (1990) has emphasized that formal scoring of the Rorschach is insufficient for some purposes such as the diagnosis of schizophrenia. He stresses that an analysis of the patient's thinking for

| ● TABLE 8.3    **Summary of Major Rorschach Scoring Criteria** |||
|---|---|---|

I. Location: Where on the blot was the percept located?

| W | Whole | Entire inkblot used |
|---|---|---|
| D | Common detail | Well-defined part used |
| Dd | Unusual detail | Unusual part used |
| S | Space | Percept defined by white space |

II. Determinant: What feature of the blot determined the response?

| F | Form | Shape or outline used |
|---|---|---|
| F+ | Form+ | Excellent match of percept and inkblot |
| F– | Form– | Very poor match of percept and inkblot |
| M | Movement | Movement seen or implied in percept |
| C | Color | Color helped determine the response |
| T | Texture | Shading involved in the response |

III. Content: What was the percept?

| H | Human | Percept of a whole human form |
|---|---|---|
| Hd | Human detail | Human form incomplete in any way |
| Ex | Explosion | An actual explosion |
| Xy | X-ray | X-ray of any human part; involves shading |

IV. Popular versus Original

| P | Popular | Response given by many normal persons |
|---|---|---|
| O | Original | Rare and creative response |

Note: This table represents a consensus of all the major scoring systems. The list is incomplete and illustrative only. Full scoring systems are very complex and allow for blends (e.g., FM, CF, WS-, Do). For examples, see Exner, J. E., Jr. (1993). *The Rorschach: A comprehensive system, Volume 1. Basic foundations* (3rd ed.). New York: Wiley.

the presence of highly personal, illogical, and bizarre associations to the blots is essential for psychodiagnosis. In his approach, the Rorschach is really an adjunct to the interview, and not a test per se.

Recently, Bornstein and Masling (2005) have reminded us that the Comprehensive System should not be confused with being "the Rorschach." After all, there are many other helpful and validated approaches to scoring the test. Their book, *Scoring the Rorschach: Seven Validated Systems* (2005), is a wonderful compendium of alternative scoring systems that can be used to answer specialized assessment questions. A case in point is the Rorschach Prognostic Rating Scale (RPRS; Handler & Clemence, 2005), a promising and validated system for predicting who will be successful in psychotherapy and who will not. Scoring the RPRS is complex and consists of assigning or subtracting points for various categories of clearly defined responses. For example, a positive score is

given if a response depicts a human as dancing, running, talking, or pointing, whereas a score of zero is coded if humans are seen as sleeping, lying down, sitting, or balancing. The meaningful use of color in the response also contributes to a positive score, whereas using color to depict explosions or diseases results in points being subtracted. Several categories are scored, yielding a total score that ranges from $-12$ to $+17$. The following interpretations are then assigned to different ranges of the RPRS score (Handler & Clemence, 2005, p. 54):

17 to 13:  The person is almost able to help himself. A very promising case that just needs a little help.

12 to 7:  Not quite so capable as the previous case to work out his problems himself but with some help is likely to do pretty well.

6 to 2:     Better than 50-50 chance; any treatment will be of some help.

1 to −2:    50-50 chance.

−3 to −6:   A difficult case that may be helped somewhat but is generally a poor treatment prospect.

−7 to −12:  A hopeless case.

Meyer and Handler (1997) used meta-analysis to synthesize the results of 18 validity studies of the RPRS, comprising a total sample of 752 participants. Their results translated to a 78 percent success rate in psychotherapy for clients with high scores on the RPRS, but only a 22 percent success rate for clients with low scores on the scale. The RPRS is a promising scale that should receive wider use in clinical practice.

Another useful scoring system for the Rorschach is the Thought Disorder Index (TDI), which assesses formal thought disorder (Holtzman, Levy, & Johnston, 2005). Thought disorder exists on a continuum from mild slippage to bizarre disorganization and is especially characteristic of patients with schizophrenia. Thus, the assessment of thought disorder is pivotal in the diagnosis and treatment of individuals with schizophrenia or other serious mental illness.

The following examples of thought disorder are from Holzman et al. (2005). Mild examples would include clients with peculiar language that employs stilted, inappropriate, or odd expressions. For example, in responding to the Rorschach, a patient with mild thought disorder might use expressions such as "He's organizing in his organs" or "There's a segregation between mouth and nose" or "Red is trouble, and Africa being red symbolizes that maybe the origin of man was in Africa and that's why it looks red." As thought disorder becomes more prominent, Rorschach responses reveal increasingly queer and confused qualities. The patient might describe portions of the blot as being "A foxed comic dog" or "The adhesive adjunctive extensions" or "These are the posterior pronunciations." Extreme examples of thought disorder show an incoherent quality such as "Blood, and break their neck, you

know, reject" or the invention of words, for example, "The property is more closely centulated to the trailroads."

The TDI is calculated by scoring each response for the severity level of thought disorder from none to extreme, with possible scores of 0, .25, .50, .75, and 1.0. Then the average score is computed across all responses. This number is multiplied by 100 to yield the final score on a range from 0 to 100. Thus, an overall score of 0 would mean that not one response revealed any thought disorder, whereas a score of 100 would signify that, without exception, every response was highly bizarre and disorganized.

The reliability of the TDI is reasonably good, with split-half correlations around .80 and interrater reliability coefficients of .90 and higher. Validity has been supported from a number of directions, such as huge improvements in scores when patients with schizophrenia are tested before and after comprehensive interventions including drug therapies (Holtzman et al., 2005). Mastering the TDI scoring criteria is far easier than learning the Comprehensive System. Insofar as the TDI provides valuable information about the extent of thought disorder—one of the foremost reasons that practitioners use the Rorschach—we can expect to see increased reliance on this approach to test scoring.

Space does not permit us to summarize the other validated scoring systems, but a brief listing is appropriate. These scales are derived largely from psychoanalytic theory and include an index of object relations, a measure of oral dependency, barrier and penetration indices based on body image, a measure of primary process thinking, and a scale that assesses primitive psychological defenses (Bornstein & Masling, 2005).

## Comment on the Rorschach

The Rorschach has provoked more controversy in the field of assessment than any other personality test or instrument. Opinions tend to be polarized, and both proponents and detractors cite studies and analyses to support their case. For example, critics of the test refer to a fascinating study by

Albert, Fox, and Kahn (1980) on the susceptibility of the Rorschach to faking. We remind the reader that literally thousands of Rorschach research studies have been published. In fact, a search of PsychINFO using the key title word Rorschach yielded 5,324 articles dating back to 1925 (the test was published in 1921). The majority of these studies are positive in tone. But the skeptical results reported by Albert, Fox, and Kahn (1980) are not isolated. They submitted the Rorschach protocols of 24 persons to a panel of experts, asking for psychiatric diagnoses of each examinee. The 24 Rorschach protocols consisted of results from four groups of six persons each:

- Mental hospital patients with a diagnosis of paranoid schizophrenia
- Uninformed fakers given instructions to fake the responses of a paranoid schizophrenic
- Informed fakers who listened to a detailed audiotape about paranoid schizophrenia
- Normal controls who took the test under standard instructions

The uninformed fakers, informed fakers, and normal controls were students who had passed an MMPI screening and were judged reasonably normal during interview. Each protocol was rated by six to nine judges, all fellows of the Society for Personality Assessment. The judges were told to provide a psychiatric diagnosis as well as other information not reported here. The judges were not informed as to the purpose of the study but were told to assess whether any profiles appeared to be malingered.

The informed fakers must have done an excellent job, for they were more likely to be diagnosed psychotic than the real patients themselves (72 percent versus 48 percent, respectively). The uninformed fakers were fairly convincing, too, with a 46 percent rate of diagnosed psychosis. The normal controls were diagnosed as psychotic 24 percent of the time. Granted that the diagnostic challenge in this study was immense, it is still disturbing to find that the expert judges rated 24 percent of the normal protocols as psychotic, while correctly identifying psychosis in only 48 percent

of the actual psychotic protocols. A more recent study by Netter and Viglione (1994) also concluded that the Rorschach was susceptible to the faking of psychosis.

In general, critics portray the test as possessing low reliability and a general lack of predictive validity (Carlson, Kula, & St. Laurent, 1997; Wood, Nezworski, & Stejskal, 1996; Lilienfeld, Wood, & Garb, 2000). In their meta-analytic review, Garb, Florio, and Grove (1998) concluded that the Rorschach explained a dismal 8 to 13 percent of the variance in client characteristics, as compared to the MMPI, which explained 23 to 30 percent of the variance.

Supporters of the test cite improvements in scoring offered by the Exner approach and are more optimistic in their outlook (e.g., Exner, 1995; Meyer, 1997; Ornberg & Zalewski, 1994; Piotrowski, 1996). A recent study by McGrath, Pogge, Stokes, and others (2005) found that the Rorschach could be scored with respectable reliability, even in the less controlled conditions typical of real-world testing. This was an important finding because virtually all prior studies of reliability have been conducted in research settings. In response to the ongoing controversy, the prestigious *Society for Personality Assessment* requisitioned external reviews by an independent panel of "blue ribbon" experts, who concluded that the Rorschach possesses reliability and validity similar to other accepted tests like the MMPI-2. The trustees of the society assert that the continued use of the Rorschach, therefore, is appropriate and justified (Board of Trustees for the Society for Personality Assessment, 2005).

The controversy over the Rorschach probably will subside for awhile, but it is not likely to disappear entirely. Even if the test continues to prevail because of studies supporting the reliability of scoring and the validity of inferences, there are other concerns seldom mentioned by skeptics. One liability is that learning the complex and convoluted Exner scoring system is an arduous and time consuming task that requires dozens of hours of practice and years of supervised experience. Some doctoral programs offer an entire course (or two) on the

Rorschach, and this is just the beginning of the training needed. A second problem is that administering and scoring the Rorschach requires a few hours of professional time from a licensed psychologist. This time is a precious and expensive commodity. Someone has to pay for it. These practical issues are daunting. In regard to learning the test in the first place, and devoting the time to administer and score it in the second place, many clinical training directors and practitioners (and not a few insurance companies) are asking "Is it worth it?"

## ● COMPLETION TECHNIQUES

### Sentence Completion Tests

In a sentence completion test, the respondent is presented with a series of stems consisting of the first few words of a sentence, and the task is to provide an ending. As with any projective technique, the examiner assumes that the completed sentences reflect the underlying motivations, attitudes, conflicts, and fears of the respondent. Usually, sentence completion tests can be interpreted in two different ways: subjective-intuitive analysis of the underlying motivations projected in the subject's responses, or objective analysis by means of scores assigned to each completed sentence.

An example of a sentence completion test is shown in Figure 8.3. This test is quite similar to existing instruments in that the stems are very short

and restricted to a small number of basic themes. The reader will notice that three topics reoccur in this short test (the respondent's self-concept, mother, and father). In this manner the examinee has multiple opportunities to reveal underlying motivations about each topic. Of course, most sentence completion tests are much longer—anywhere from 40 to 100 stems—and contain more themes—anywhere from 4 to 15 topics.

Dozens of sentence completion tests have been developed; most are unpublished and unstandardized instruments produced to meet a specific clinical need. Some representative sentence completion tests in current use are outlined in Table 8.4. Of these instruments, Loevinger's Washington University Sentence Completion Test is the most sophisticated and theory-bound (e.g., Weiss, Zilberg, & Genevro, 1989). However, the Rotter Incomplete Sentences Blank has the strongest empirical underpinnings and is the most widely used in clinical settings. We examine this instrument in more detail.

### Rotter Incomplete Sentences Blank

The Rotter Incomplete Sentences Blank (RISB) consists of three similar forms—high school, college, and adult—each containing 40 sentence stems written mostly in the first person (Rotter & Rafferty, 1950; Rotter, Lah, & Rafferty, 1992). Although the test can be subjectively interpreted in the usual manner through qualitative analysis of

● FIGURE 8.3
Example of a Short Sentence Completion Test

Directions: Finish these sentences to indicate how you feel.
1. My best characteristic is _____
2. My mother _____
3. My father _____
4. My greatest fear is _____
5. The best thing about my mother was _____
6. The best thing about my father was _____
7. I am proudest about _____
8. I only wish my mother had _____
9. I only wish my father had _____

● **TABLE 8.4** **Brief Outline of Representative Sentence Completion Tests**

**Sentence Completion Series**
**Psychological Assessment Resources**

The SCS consists of 50 sentence stems designed to aid the clinician in identifying underlying concerns and specific areas of client distress. A unique feature of this instrument is the publication of eight different forms, parallel in content, which allow for repeated testing.

**Forer Structured Sentence Completion Test**
**Western Psychological Services**

This instrument is available in separate forms for men, women, adolescent boys, and adolescent girls. Each form contains 100 sentence stems designed to cover attitude–value systems, evasiveness, and defense mechanisms.

**Geriatric Sentence Completion Form**
**Psychological Assessment Resources**

The GSCF is a 30-item form specifically developed for use with older adult clients. The GSCF elicits personal responses to four content domains: physical, psychological, social, and temporal orientation. The test manual includes a number of clinical case illustrations.

**Washington University Sentence Completion Test,**
**Privately published by Loevinger**

The WUSC uses separate forms for men, women, and younger male and female subjects. This test is highly theory-bound; responses are classified according to seven stages of ego development: presocial and symbiotic, impulsive, self-protective, conformist, conscientious, autonomous, integrated.

---

needs projected in the subject's responses, it is the objective and quantitative scoring of the RISB that has drawn the most attention.

In the objective scoring system each completed sentence receives an adjustment score from 0 (good adjustment) to 6 (very poor adjustment). These scores are based initially on the categorizing of each response as follows:

- *Omission*—no response or response too short to be meaningful
- *Conflict response*—indicative of hostility or un-happiness

- *Positive response*—indicative of positive or hopeful attitude
- *Neutral response*—declarative statement with neither positive nor negative affect

Examples of the last three categories include:

> I hate . . . the entire world. (conflict response)
> The best . . . is yet to come. (positive response)
> Most girls . . . are women. (neutral response)

Conflict responses are scored 4, 5, or 6, from lowest to highest degree of the conflict expressed. Positive responses are scored 2, 1, or 0, from least to most positive response. Neutral responses and omissions receive no score. The manual gives examples of each scoring category. The overall adjustment score is obtained by adding the weighted ratings in the conflict and positive categories. The adjustment score can vary from 0 to 240, with higher scores indicating greater maladjustment.

The reliability of the adjustment score is exceptionally good, even when derived by assistants with minimal psychological expertise. Typically, interscorer reliabilities are in the .90s and split-half coefficients are in the .80s (Rotter et al., 1992; Rotter, Rafferty, & Schachtitz, 1965). The validity of this index has been investigated in numerous studies using the RISB as a screening device with a "maladjustment" cutoff score. For example, a cutoff score of 135 has been found to correctly screen delinquent youths 60 percent of the time while identifying nondelinquent youths correctly 73 percent of the time (Fuller, Parmelee, & Carroll, 1982). The same cutoff identifies heavy drug users 80 to 100 percent of the time (Gardner, 1967). These and similar findings support the construct validity of the adjustment index but also indicate that classification rates are much lower than needed for individual decision making or effective screening. It also appears that the norms for the adjustment index are outdated. Lah and Rotter (1981) found that current student scores differ significantly from those obtained in the original study by Rotter and Rafferty (1950). Lah (1989) and Rotter et al. (1992) provide new normative, scoring, and validity data for the RISB.

As discussed by P. Goldberg (1965), the simplicity of the single adjustment score is both the test's strength and weakness. True, the test provides a quick and efficient method for obtaining an overall index of how respondents are functioning on a day-to-day basis. However, a single score cannot possibly capture any nuances of personality functioning. In addition, the RISB is subject to the same types of bias as other self-report measures, namely, the information will reflect mainly what the respondent wants the examiner to know.

## ● CONSTRUCTION TECHNIQUES

### The Thematic Apperception Test (TAT)

The TAT consists of 30 pictures that portray a variety of subject matters and themes in black-and-white drawings and photographs; one card is blank. Most of the cards depict one or more persons engaged in ambiguous activities. Some cards are used for adult males (M), adult females (F), boys (B), or girls (G), or some combination (e.g., BM). As a consequence, exactly 20 cards are appropriate for every examinee.

A picture similar to those on the TAT is shown in Figure 8.4. In administering the TAT, the examiner requests the examinee to make up a dramatic story for each picture, telling what led up to the current scene, what is happening at the moment, how the characters are thinking and feeling, and what the outcome will be. The examiner writes down the story verbatim for later scoring and analysis.

The TAT was developed by Henry Murray and his colleagues at the Harvard Psychological Clinic (Morgan & Murray, 1935; Murray, 1938). The test was originally designed to assess constructs such as needs and press, elements central to Murray's personality theory. According to Murray, needs organize perception, thought, and action and energize behavior in the direction of their satisfaction. Examples of needs include the needs for achievement, affiliation, and dominance. In contrast, press refers to the power of environmental events to influence a person. Alpha press is objective or "real" external forces, whereas beta press concerns the subjective or perceived components of external forces. Murray (1938, 1943) developed an elaborate TAT scoring system for measuring 36 different needs and various aspects of press, as revealed by the examinee's stories.

Almost as soon as Murray released the TAT, other clinicians began to develop alternative scoring systems (e.g., Dana, 1959; Tomkins, 1947). Literature on the administration, scoring, and interpretation of the TAT burgeoned extensively, as documented by reviews (Aiken, 1989, chap. 12; Groth-Marnat, 1997; Weiner & Kuehnle, 1998). By the 1950s, there was no single preferred mode of administration, no single preferred system of scoring, and no single preferred method of interpretation, a predicament that still endures today. Clinicians even vary the wording of the instructions and commonly select an individualized subset of TAT cards for each client. Indeed, the absence of standardized procedures is such that we should rightly regard the TAT as a method, not a test.

It is worth mentioning that Murray's instructions included a statement that the TAT was "a test

● **FIGURE 8.4**    A Picture Similar to Those on the Thematic Apperception Test

of imagination, one form of intelligence" and further stipulated:

> I am going to show you some pictures, one at a time; and your task will be to make up as dramatic a story as you can for each. Tell what has led up to the event shown in the picture, describe what is happening at the moment, what the characters are feeling and thinking; and then give the outcome. Speak your thoughts as they come to your mind. Do you understand? Since you have fifty minutes for ten pictures, you can devote about five minutes to each story. Here is the first picture. (Murray, 1943)

Currently, clinicians downplay the emphasis on imagination and intelligence when giving instructions. Surely, this omission must influence the quality of the stories produced.

Even though more than a dozen scoring systems have been proposed, interpretation of the TAT is usually based on a clinical-qualitative analysis of the story productions. A central consideration harks back to Murray's "hero" assumption. According to this viewpoint, the hero is the protagonist of the examinee's story. It is assumed that the examinee clearly identifies with this character and projects his or her own needs, strivings, and feelings onto the hero. Conversely, thoughts, feelings, or actions avoided by the hero may represent areas of conflict for the examinee. A specific example will help clarify these points. Consider the response to Card 3BM given by a depressed examinee[2]:

> Looks like . . . I can't tell if it's a girl or boy. Could be either. I guess it doesn't matter. This person just had a hard physical workout. I guess it's a her. She's just tired. No trauma happened or anything. She was sitting around a table with friends and she got real tired. She's not in a health danger or anything. These are her keys. Her friends drag her back to her room and put her to bed. She's O.K. the next day. No trauma. She's tired physically, not mentally. (Ryan, 1987)

What stands out in this response is the repetitive denial of danger or trauma. But later in the testing, the denial of trauma is no longer maintained. Read how the examinee responded to the blank card, relating a story of a young man, traumatized at school, who takes his car down to the river:

> He sees the bridge, he's really down. He remembers that he's heard stories about people jumping off and killing themselves. He could never understand why they did that. Now he understands, he jumps and dies . . . he should have waited 'cause things always get better sometime. But he didn't wait, he died. (Ryan, 1987)

Most clinicians would conclude that the examinee who produced these stories had been traumatized and was defending against self-destructive impulses. Correspondingly, the clinician would be well advised to explore these issues in psychotherapy.

The psychometric adequacy of the TAT is difficult to evaluate because of the abundance of scoring and interpretation methods. Clinicians defend the test on an anecdotal basis, pointing out remarkable and confirmatory findings such as illustrated here. However, data-minded researchers are more cautious. One problem is that formally scored TAT protocols possess very low test-retest reliability, with a reported median value of $r = .28$ (Winter & Stewart, 1977). Furthermore, an astonishing 97 percent of test users employ subjective and "personalized" procedures for interpreting the TAT; that is, only a tiny fraction of clinical practitioners rely on a standardized scoring system (Lilienfeld, Wood, & Garb, 2001). This is troubling because a consistent theme in research on projective testing is that intuitive interpretations are likely to overdiagnose psychological disturbance.

## The Picture Projective Test

The Picture Projective Test (PPT) is a long overdue attempt to construct a general-purpose instrument with improved psychometric qualities (Ritzler, Sharkey, & Chudy, 1980; Sharkey & Ritzler, 1985). The developers of the PPT note that the majority of the TAT pictures exert a

---

2. Card 3BM depicts one person—arguably male or female—kneeling or slumped over on a couch with head bowed on one arm. In the corner is a vaguely drawn object interpreted by some examinees to be a handgun or other weapon.

strong negative stimulus "pull" on storytelling. The TAT cards are cast in dark, shaded tones and most scenes portray persons in low-key or gloomy situations. It is not surprising, then, that projective responses to the TAT are strongly channeled toward negative, melancholic stories (Goldfried & Zax, 1965).

In contrast, the PPT uses a new set of pictures taken from the *Family of Man* photo essay published by the Museum of Modern Art (1955). The following criteria were used in selecting 30 pictures:

- The pictures had to show promise of eliciting meaningful projective material.
- Most but not all of the pictures had to include more than one human character.
- About half of the pictures had to depict humans showing positive affective expression (e.g., smiling, embracing, dancing).
- About half of the pictures had to depict humans in active poses, not simply standing, sitting, or lying down.

In an initial pilot study, the authors compared TAT and PPT story productions of eight undergraduates on several variables such as length of stories, emotional tone, and activity level (Ritzler, Sharkey, & Chudy, 1980). Compared to the TAT productions, the PPT stories were of comparable length but were much more positive in thematic content and emotional tone. The PPT stories were also much more active, meaning that the central character had an active, self-determined effect on the situation in the story. Furthermore, the PPT stories placed greater emphasis on interpersonal rather than intrapersonal themes. In other words, the PPT stories placed more emphasis on "healthy," adaptive aspects of personality adjustment than did the TAT productions.

The PPT developers also compared their instrument against the TAT in a diagnostic validity study (Sharkey & Ritzler, 1985). PPT and TAT story productions of 50 subjects were compared: normals, nonhospitalized depressives, hospitalized depressives, hospitalized psychotics with good premorbid histories, and hospitalized psychotics with poor premorbid histories (10 subjects in each group). Although the TAT and PPT were essentially equal in their capacity to discriminate normal from depressed subjects, the PPT was superior in differentiating psychotics from normals and depressives. On the PPT, depressives told stories with gloomier emotional tone and psychotics made more perceptual distortions, and thematic/interpretive deviations. The PPT appears to be a very promising instrument, although it is obvious that further research is needed on its psychometric qualities. One noteworthy feature is that anyone can purchase the PPT stimuli at their local bookstore. The requisite materials are found in the *Family of Man* photo collection (Museum of Modern Art, 1955).

## Children's Apperception Test

Designed as a direct extension of the TAT, the Children's Apperception Test (CAT) consists of 10 pictures and is suitable for children 3 to 10 years of age. The preferred version for younger children (CAT-A) depicts animals in unmistakably human social settings (Bellak & Bellak, 1991). The test developers used animal drawings on the assumption that young children would identify better with animals than humans. A human figure version (CAT-H) is available for older children (Bellak & Bellak, 1994). No formal scoring system exists for the CAT and no statistical information is provided on reliability or validity. Instead, the examiner prepares a diagnosis or personality description based on a synthesis of 10 variables recorded for each story: (1) main theme; (2) main hero; (3) main needs and drives of hero; (4) conception of environment (or world); (5) perception of parental, contemporary, and junior figures; (6) conflicts; (7) anxieties; (8) defenses; (9) adequacy of superego; (10) integration of ego (including originality of story and nature of outcome) (Bellak, 1992). The lack of attention to psychometric issues of scoring, reliability, and validity of the CAT is troublesome to most testing specialists.

## Other Variations on the TAT

The TAT has inspired a number of similar tests designed for children and older adults (Table 8.5). In

## ● TABLE 8.5 Thematic Apperception Tests for Specific Populations

**Adolescent Apperception Cards**

This is the only thematic apperception test designed specifically for adolescents (12- to 19-year-olds). The 11 cards represent contemporary issues relevant to adolescents; themes include loneliness, parenting styles, domestic violence, gang activity, and drug abuse (Silverton, 1993). Problems with this instrument include the negative themes depicted in the cards (which preclude positive associations) and the absence of any objective approach to scoring. Like many thematic apperception techniques, the AAC is really an idiographic clinical tool, not a test.

**Blacky Pictures**

For children ages 5 and older, the Blacky Pictures test was also based on the premise that children identify more readily with animals than humans. The 11 cartoon stimuli depict the adventures of the dog Blacky and his family (Mama, Papa, and sibling Tippy). In addition to requesting a story for each card, the examiner also presents multiple-choice questions based on stages of psychosexual development derived from psychoanalytic theory (Blum, 1950). Although the test was originally developed with adults, children enjoy taking the Blacky and are quite responsive to the pictures. Problems with this test include the absence of norms, especially for children, and poor stability of scores (LaVoie, 1987).

**Michigan Picture Test-Revised**

For older children ages 8 to 14 years, the MPT-R consists of 15 pictures and a blank card. Responses are scored for Tension Index (e.g., portrayal of personal adequacy), Direction of Force (whether the central figure acts or is acted upon), and Verb Tense (e.g., past, present, future). These three scores can be combined to yield a Maladjustment Index. Reliability and norms are adequate, although evidence of validity is unsatisfactory. A major problem with this test is that the cards portray interpersonal relationships so vividly that little is left to the child's imagination (Aiken, 1989).

**Senior Apperception Test (SAT)**

Although the 16 situations depicted on the SAT cards include some positive circumstances, the majority of pictures were designed to reflect themes of helplessness, abandonment, disability, family problems, loneliness, dependence, and low self-esteem (Bellak, 1992). Critics complain that the SAT stereotypes the elderly and therefore discourages active responding (Schaie, 1978).

addition, modifications and variations of the TAT have been developed for ethnic, racial, and linguistic minorities. One of the first was the Thompson TAT (T-TAT) in which 21 of the original TAT pictures were redrawn with African American figures (Thompson, 1949). This TAT modification incorporated certain unintended changes—for example, in facial expressions and the situations portrayed. As a result, the T-TAT should be considered a new test and not just a TAT translation suited to African American individuals (Aiken, 1989).

Another specialized TAT-like test is the TEMAS, which consists of 23 colorful drawings that depict Hispanic persons interacting in contemporary, inner-city settings (Aiken, 1989; Constantino, Malgady, & Rogler, 1988). TEMAS is Spanish for *themes* and an acronym for "tell me a story." The thematic content of TEMAS stories is scored for 18 cognitive functions, 9 personality (ego) functions, and 7 affective functions. The test can also be scored for various objective indices such as reaction time, fluency, unanswered inquiries, and stimulus transformations (e.g., a letter is transformed into a bomb). Hispanic children respond well to the TEMAS, even though they may be inarticulate in response to traditional projective tests.

The inconsistent reliability of the TEMAS is a source of concern, because reliability constrains validity. The manual reports that Cronbach's alpha for the 34 scoring functions ranged from .31 to .98 with half below .70. Test-retest reliabilities were even lower; the highest correlation was $r = .53$ and for 26 of the 34 functions the correlations were near zero! In spite of the questionable reliability of the instrument, several studies provide support for its concurrent and predictive validity. For example, in a clinical sample of 210 Puerto Rican children, TEMAS scale scores predicted independent criteria of ego development, trait anxiety, and adaptive behavior reasonably well, with correlations ranging from .27 to .51 (Malgady, Constantino, & Rogler, 1984). A steady stream of research has continued to bolster the utility of this instrument, as surveyed by Constantino & Malgady (1996). Flanagan and di Guiseppe (1999) provide a critical review of the

TEMAS; Constantino and Malgady (2000) describe recent developments with the test.

## ● EXPRESSION TECHNIQUES

### The Draw-A-Person Test

As the reader will recall from an earlier chapter, Goodenough (1926) used the Draw-A-Man task as a basis for estimating intelligence. Subsequently, psychodynamically minded psychologists adapted the procedure to the projective assessment of personality. Karen Machover (1949, 1951) was the pioneer in this new field. Her procedure became known as the Draw-A-Person Test (DAP). Her test enjoyed early popularity and is still widely used as a clinical assessment tool. Watkins, Campbell, Nieberding, and Hallmark (1995) report that projective drawings such as the DAP rank eighth in popularity among clinicians in the United States.

The DAP is administered by presenting the examinee with a blank sheet of paper and a pencil with eraser, then asking the examinee to "draw a person." When the drawing is completed the examinee usually is directed to draw another person of the sex opposite that of the first figure. Finally, the examinee is asked to "make up a story about this person as if he [or she] were a character in a novel or a play" (Machover, 1949).

Interpretation of the DAP proceeds in an entirely clinical-intuitive manner, guided by a number of tentative psychodynamically based hypotheses (Machover, 1949, 1951). For example, Machover maintained that examinees were likely to project acceptable impulses onto the same-sex figure and unacceptable impulses onto the opposite-sex figure. She also believed that the relative sizes of the male and female figures revealed clues about the sexual identification of the examinee. Several of Machover's interpretive hypotheses are listed in Table 8.6.

These interpretive premises are colorful, interesting, and plausible. However, they are based entirely on psychodynamic theory and anecdotal observations. Machover made little effort to validate the interpretations. The empirical support for her

| ● TABLE 8.6     Illustrative Interpretations of the Draw-A-Person Test | |
|---|---|
| *Sign* | *Hypothesized Interpretive Significance* |
| Disproportionately large head | Organic brain disease; previous brain surgery; preoccupation with headaches |
| Deliberate omission of facial features | Evasive about highly conflictual interpersonal relationships |
| Mouth drawn with heavy line slash | Verbally aggressive, overcritical, and sometimes sadistic personality |
| Chin changed, erased, or reinforced | Compensation for weakness, indecision, and fear of responsibility |
| Large male eyes with lashes | Homosexually inclined male, often very extraverted |
| Hair emphasis, e.g., a beard | An indication of a striving for virility |
| Graphic emphasis of the neck | Disturbed about the lack of control over impulses |
| Conspicuous treatment of index finger, thumb | Preoccupation with masturbation |
| Anatomical indications of internal organs | Found only in schizophrenic or actively manic patients |

*Source:* Based on Machover, K. (1949). *Personality projection in the drawing of the human figure.* Springfield, IL: Charles C. Thomas.

hypotheses is somewhere between meager and nonexistent (Swensen, 1968). In favor of the DAP, the overall quality of drawings does weakly predict psychological adjustment (Lewinsohn, 1965; Yama, 1990). However, judged by contemporary standards of evidence, the sweeping and cavalier assessments of personality so often derived from the DAP are embarrassing. Some reviewers have concluded that the DAP is an unworthy test that should no longer be used (Gresham, 1993; Motta, Little, & Tobin, 1993).

Rather than using the DAP to infer nuances of personality, a more appropriate application of this test is in the screening of children suspected of behavior disorder and emotional disturbance. For this purpose, Naglieri, McNeish, and Bardos (1991) developed the Draw A Person: Screening Procedure for Emotional Disturbance (DAP:SPED). In one study, diagnostic accuracy of problem children was significantly improved by application of the DAP:SPED scoring approach (Naglieri & Pfeiffer, 1992).

### The House-Tree-Person Test (H-T-P)

The H-T-P is a projective test that uses freehand drawings of a house, tree, and person (Buck, 1948, 1981). The examinee is given almost complete freedom in sketching the three objects; separate pencil and crayon drawings are requested. Although the examiner can improvise an H-T-P Test with mere blank pieces of paper, Buck (1981) recommends the use of a four-page drawing form with identification information on the first page. Pages two, three, and four are titled House, Tree, and Person. Two drawing forms are needed for each examinee, one for pencil drawings and the other for crayon drawings. Buck (1981) also provides a separate four-page form for a postdrawing interrogation phase, which consists of 60 questions designed to elicit the examinee's opinions about elements of the drawings. Many practitioners feel the postdrawing interrogation phase is not worth the extended effort. Also, the value of separate crayon drawings is questioned (Killian, 1987).

The House-Tree-Person Test has much the same familial lineage as the Draw-A-Person Test.

Like the DAP Test, the H-T-P Test was originally conceived as a measure of intelligence, complete with a quantitative scoring system to appraise an approximate level of ability (Buck, 1948). However, clinicians soon abandoned the use of the H-T-P as a measure of intelligence, and it is now used almost exclusively as a projective measure of personality.

Although we will not delve into any details here, the interpretation of the H-T-P rests on three general assumptions: the House drawing mirrors the examinee's home life and intrafamilial relationships; the Tree drawing reflects the manner in which the examinee experiences the environment; and the Person drawing echoes the examinee's interpersonal relationships. Buck (1981) provides numerous interpretive hypotheses for both quantitative and qualitative aspects of the three drawings.

The H-T-P is an alluring test that has fascinated clinicians for more than 40 years. Unfortunately, Buck (1948, 1981) has never provided any evidence to support the reliability or validity of this instrument. Indeed, he is perhaps his own worst critic. At one point in his test manual, he even asserts that validational research is not possible with the H-T-P (Buck, 1981, p. 164). Among the impediments to such research, he cites the following points:

1. No single sign itself is an infallible indication of any strength or weakness in the S.
2. No H-T-P sign has but one meaning.
3. The significance of a sign may differ markedly from one constellation to another.
4. The amount of diagnostic and prognostic data derivable from each of the points of analysis may vary greatly from S to S.
5. Colors do not have any absolute and universal meaning.
6. Nothing in the quantitative scoring system can be taken automatically at face value (Buck, 1981).

In general, attempts to validate the H-T-P as a personality measure have failed miserably (for reviews see Krugman, 1970; Killian, 1987). Thoughtful reviewers have repeatedly recommended the abandonment of the H-T-P and

**Case Exhibit 8.1**

### Projective Tests as Ancillary to the Interview

A specific example may help to clarify the role of projective techniques as ancillary to the clinical interview. During the Vietnam War, a Veteran's Administration psychologist tested a young soldier who had accidentally shot himself in the leg with a 45-caliber pistol while practicing quick draw in the jungle. Surgeons found it necessary to amputate the soldier's leg from the knee down. He was quite depressed, and everyone assumed that he suffered from grief and guilt over his great personal tragedy. He was virtually mute and nearly untestable. However, he was persuaded to complete a series of figure drawings. In one drawing he depicted himself as a helicopter gunner, spraying bullets indiscriminately into the jungle below. When questioned about this drawing, he became quite animated and confessed that he relished combat. Guided by the possible implications of the morbid drawing, the psychologist sought to learn more about the veteran's attitudes toward combat. In the course of several interviews, the veteran revealed that he particularly enjoyed firing on moving objects—animals, soldiers, civilians—it made no difference to him. Gradually, it became clear that the young veteran was an incipient war criminal who was depressed because his injury would prevent him from returning to the front lines. Needless to say, this information had quite an impact on the tenor of the psychological report.

similar figure-drawing approaches to personality assessment. But these pronouncements apparently fall on deaf ears. The popularity of the H-T-P and other projective techniques continues unabated. In the final section of this topic, we offer some reflections on the continued acceptance of projective techniques.

Many clinicians do not use projective methods as tests at all but as auxiliary approaches to the clinical interview. These practitioners use projective techniques as clinical tools to derive tentative hypotheses about the examinee. Most of these hypotheses will turn out to be false when examined more closely. However, the few that are confirmed may have important implications for the clinical management of the examinee. Furthermore, we suspect that these fruitful hypotheses might not emerge—or might emerge more slowly—if the practitioner relied entirely on the interview or used only formal tests with established reliability and validity (Case Exhibit 8.1). However, this assertion is difficult to test empirically.

## SUMMARY

1. Personality is a vague construct that we invoke to explain behavioral consistency within persons and behavioral distinctiveness between persons. In order to appreciate the nature of personality tests, it is helpful to review theories of personality.

2. Psychoanalytic theories of personality originated with the seminal work of Sigmund Freud. According to Freud's tripartite theory of mind, behavior is the dynamic outcome of the struggle between id, ego, and superego. The id is

completely unconscious, pleasure oriented, and is the seat of all instinctual needs such as for food, water, sexual gratification, and avoidance of pain.

3. Soon after birth, part of the id develops into the ego or conscious self. The ego is servant to the id but obeys the reality principle. The ego must also contend with the superego, the ethical component of personality that is modeled on parental and societal standards of right and wrong.

4. To aid in its difficult task, the ego uses defense mechanisms, which consist of a variety of unconscious cognitive strategies for warding off anxiety. Defense mechanisms such as projection (attributing one's faults to others) work because they distort reality.

5. In a longitudinal interview study, Vaillant has shown that defense mechanisms tended toward greater maturity in middle age. Also, the use of mature defense mechanisms in young adulthood predicted better adult outcome as measured by independent criteria such as marital stability, absence of drug problems, and the like.

6. Type theories attempt to sort individuals into discrete categories or types. For example, the Type A coronary-prone behavior pattern consists of insecurity of status, hyperaggressiveness, free-floating hostility, and a sense of time urgency (hurry sickness). Type A persons—especially those with anger proneness or time urgency—may be at increased risk of coronary disease and heart attack.

7. Phenomenological theories of personality emphasize the importance of immediate, personal, subjective experience as a determinant of behavior. The phenomenological viewpoint originated with the German philosopher Husserl and the Danish existential writer Kierkegaard.

8. The most influential phenomenological theorist was Carl Rogers, who believed that the self or self-concept was central to personality. Rogers invented the Q-sort to measure the self-concept and the ideal self. In a Q-sort, the examinee sorts self-referential statements in nine or so piles (least like me to most like me).

9. A fundamental assumption of all behavioral and social learning theories is that many of the behaviors that comprise personality are learned. Radical behavior theorists such as Skinner see no role for cognitions in explaining behavior. In contrast, social learning theorists such as Rotter believe that expectations (cognitions) about environmental reinforcers are the primary determinants of behavior.

10. Guilford defines a trait as any relatively enduring way in which one individual differs from another. Trait theories evolved from the ways in which people describe other people in everyday life. Mischel has pointed out a major weakness of the trait approach: Traits possess low predictive validity, seldom exceeding $r = .30$.

11. Cattell's factor-analytic trait theory refers to the more obvious aspects of personality as surface traits, such as aggressiveness. These emerge in the first stages of factor analysis. Source traits—more important and predictive of behavior than surface traits—are revealed by the clusterings of surface traits. Cattell's 16PF is based on this model.

12. The five-factor model proposes a modern synthesis of trait approaches in terms of five dimensions of personality: Neuroticism, Extraversion, Openness, Agreeableness, and Conscientiousness. Costa and McCrae have developed two inventories based on this approach (NEO-PI-R and NEO-FFI).

13. Projective tests are based on the projective hypothesis: Personal interpretations of ambiguous stimuli must necessarily reflect the unconscious needs, motives, and conflicts of the examinee. Popular projectives include the Rorschach inkblot test, the Thematic Apperception Test, sentence completion tests, and drawing tests (e.g., Draw-A-Person).

14. The Rorschach, released in 1921, consists of 10 roughly symmetrical inkblots. For each card, the examiner asks "What might this be?" In the inquiry phase, the examiner clarifies which aspects of the blot (e.g., form or color) played a part in the creation of each response.

**15.** The preferred Rorschach scoring method by Exner codes each response for location, form, human movement, the use of color, content, and other variables. Summary scores and ratios of variables provide hypotheses about personality functioning. In spite of its enduring popularity, the Rorschach is still haunted by questions about reliability and validity.

**16.** The Rotter Incomplete Sentences Blank (RISB) contains 40 sentence stems written mostly in the first person. Each completed sentence receives an adjustment score from 0 (good) to 6 (poor); the sum is the overall adjustment score. Correct classification rates (e.g., adjusted versus maladjusted) are too low for individual decision making.

**17.** The Thematic Apperception Test (TAT) consists of 30 black-and-white drawings and photographs; one card is blank. The examinee is asked to make up a dramatic story for each picture, including past, present, future, and feelings of the main characters. TAT interpretation usually rests on clinical-qualitative analysis of story productions.

**18.** Variations on the TAT include the Picture Projective Test, based on photographs from the *Family of Man* photo essay; the Thompson TAT for African Americans; the Children's Apperception Test (CAT) which utilizes drawings of animals; TEMAS, an apperception test designed for Hispanic persons; and apperception tests for elderly citizens.

**19.** In Machover's Draw-A-Person (DAP), the examinee is asked simply to "draw a person." Interpretation proceeds in a clinical-intuitive manner based on published hypotheses, for example, a redrawn chin indicates indecision. Another test in a similar vein is the House-Tree-Person (the examinee draws these) for which validity evidence is also meager.

## ● KEY TERMS AND CONCEPTS

personality   p. 315

id   p. 316

pleasure principle   p. 316

ego   p. 316

reality principle   p. 316

superego   p. 317

defense mechanisms   p. 317

Type A coronary-prone behavior pattern   p. 319

Q-technique   p. 321

locus of control   p. 322

self-efficacy   p. 323

trait   p. 323

surface traits   p. 324

source traits   p. 324

fundamental lexical hypothesis   p. 325

personality coefficient   p. 326

projective test   p. 327

# Self-Report and Behavioral Assessment of Psychopathology

Although there are many methods for the assessment of personality and related qualities, broadly speaking two approaches have dominated the field: unstructured and structured. Unstructured methods such as the Rorschach, TAT, and sentence completion blanks permit broad latitude in the responses of the examinee. These approaches dominated personality testing in the early twentieth century but then slowly faded in standing. In contrast, structured approaches such as self-report inventories and behavior rating scales gained prominence in the mid-twentieth century and have continued to expand in popularity to the present time. Whereas only a handful of unstructured techniques has ever risen to distinction, the number of structured instruments for assessment has grown almost exponentially.

In the previous topic we introduced the reader to the many varieties of unstructured tests such as inkblots, stimulus cards, and sentence completion blanks. These methods are resplendent in the richness of the hypotheses they yield; however, projective techniques largely lack the approval of psychometrically oriented clinicians. In this topic, we focus on the more structured, objective methods for personality assessment favored by measurement-minded psychologists. We review a wide variety of true-false, rating scale, and forced-choice instruments for assessing personality and other qualities. This review takes in a variety of personality tests, including the Minnesota Multiphasic Personality Inventory-2, arguably the most famous personality test ever published. We also examine contemporary approaches that rely upon structured interview, behavioral observation, and ratings.

The self-report approaches to testing discussed in the following sections are steeped in the details of psychometric methodology. These tests feature prominent references to reliability indices, criterion keying, factor analysis, construct validation, and other forms of technical craftsmanship. For this reason, the approaches discussed here often are considered objective—as contrasted with projective. However, whether they are objective in any meaningful sense is really an empirical question that must be answered on the basis of research. Perhaps it is more accurate to call these methods *structured*. They are structured in the sense that highly specific rules are followed in the administration, scoring, interpretation, and narrative reporting of results. In fact, some of the approaches are so completely structured that an examinee can answer questions presented on a computer screen and observe a computer-generated narrative report spewed forth from the printer, literally seconds later.[3]

We begin our discussion of structured assessment by reviewing several prominent personality tests. Contemporary psychometricians have relied mainly upon three tactics for personality test development: theory-bounded approaches, factor-analytic approaches, and criterion-key methods. We will organize the discussion of personality inventories around these three categories. Of course, the boundaries are somewhat artificial and many test developers use a combination of methods.

## ● THEORY-GUIDED INVENTORIES

The construction of several self-report inventories was guided closely by formal or informal theories of personality. In these cases, the test developer designed the instrument around a preexisting theory. Theory-guided inventories stand in contrast to factor-analytic approaches which often produce a retrospective theory based upon initial test findings. Theory-guided inventories also differ from the stark atheoretical empiricism found in criterion-key instruments such as the MMPI and MMPI-2. An example of a theory-guided inventory is the Personality Research Form (PRF), based on Murray's (1938) need-press theory of personality. The Jenkins

Activity Survey, designed to assess the Type A coronary-prone behavior pattern, also epitomizes a theory-guided instrument. Finally, some theory-guided inventories such as the State-Trait Anxiety Inventory (STAI) attempt to measure very specific components of personality. Following we review these tests in more detail.

### Personality Research Form

The Personality Research Form (Jackson, 1999) is a true-false inventory based loosely on Murray's (1938) theory of manifest needs. The reader will recall from an earlier discussion that Murray posited 15 needs and developed a projective test, the Thematic Apperception Test, to tap those needs. Based on factor-analytic approaches, Jackson expanded the number of needs and produced several forms for assessment. The forms differ in the number of scales and number of items per scale. In addition to parallel short tests (forms A and B), the Personality Research Form (PRF) also exists as parallel long forms (forms AA and BB). These forms, used primarily with college students, consist of 440 true-false items. The long forms yield 20 personality-scale scores and two validity scores, Infrequency and Desirability (Table 8.7). The most popular version of the PRF is form E, which consists of all 22 scales in a modified 352-item test.

In constructing the PRF form E, Jackson first formulated rigorous and theoretically based definitions of the traits to be measured, following Murray's (1938) system for personality description. Next, for each scale over 100 items were written to tape the traits underlying the hypothesized needs. After editorial review, these items were administered to large samples of college students. Item selection was based on simplicity of wording, high biserial correlations with total scale scores, low correlations with other scales (maximizing scale independence), and low correlations with the Desirability scale (minimizing social desirability bias). Convergent and discriminant validity was considered throughout. For the original long forms AA and BB, 20 items were selected for each scale, resulting in 20 × 22 or 440 items. For the

---

3. Computerized narrative reports may not be altogether a positive development. We discuss the benefits and pitfalls of computer-generated reports in the next chapter.

● TABLE 8.7 **Personality Research Form Scales**

| Scale | Interpretation of High Score |
|---|---|
| Abasement | Self-effacing, humble, blame-accepting |
| Achievement | Goal striving, competitive |
| Affiliation | Friendly, accepting, sociable |
| Aggression | Argues, combative, easily annoyed |
| Autonomy | Independent, avoids restrictions |
| Change | Avoids routine, seeks change |
| Cognitive Structure | Prefers certainty, dislikes ambiguity |
| Defendence | On guard, takes offense easily |
| Dominance | Influential, enjoys leading |
| Endurance | Persevering, hard-working |
| Exhibition | Dramatic, enjoys attention |
| Harm Avoidance | Avoids risk and excitement |
| Impulsivity | Impulsive, speaks freely |
| Nurturance | Caring, sympathetic, comforting |
| Order | Organized, dislikes confusion |
| Play | Playful, light-hearted, enjoys jokes |
| Sentience | Notices, remembers sensations |
| Social Recognition | Concern for reputation and approval |
| Succorance | Insecure, seeks reassurance |
| Understanding | Values logical thought |
| Desirability | Validity Scale: favorable presentation |
| Infrequency | Validity Scale: infrequent responses |

*Source:* Adapted from Personality Research Form Scales and Descriptions from Jackson, D. N. (1989). *Personality research form manual* (3rd ed.). Port Huron, MI: Sigma Assessment Systems, Inc., Research Psychologists Press division. (800) 265-1285.

PRF form E, about four items were dropped from each scale, yielding a 352-item test.

Unlike many other personality inventories, the PRF scales have no item overlap. As a result, the scales are unusually independent, with most inter-correlation coefficients in the vicinity of ±.30 (Gynther & Gynther, 1976). Furthermore, the rigorous scale construction procedures employed by Jackson (1970) yielded scales with good internal consistency, with a median coefficient alpha of .70. Test-retest reliabilities are exceptionally strong, ranging from .80 to .96 for a two-week interval, with a median of .91 (Jackson, 1999). Norms are based on thousands of college students from North America, and also include subgroup norms

for psychiatric inpatients and criminal offenders. A desirable feature of the PRF is its readability: The test requires only a fifth- or sixth-grade reading level (Reddon & Jackson, 1989).

The validity of the PRF rests upon a substantial body of research over many decades. A lengthy bibliography citing more than 300 articles about the test can be found at www.sigmaassessmentsystems.com. For example, correlations between self and roommate ratings on the PRF constructs are reported to range from .27 to .74, with a median of .53.

The construct validity of the PRF rests especially upon confirmatory factor analyses corroborating the grouping of the items into 20 scales (Jackson, 1970, 1984b). In addition, research indicates positive correlations with comparable scales on other inventories (Mungas, Trontel, & Weingardner, 1981). For example, Edwards and Abbott (1973) found exceptionally strong and confirmatory correlations between similar scales on the PRF and the Edwards Personality Inventory (EPI; Edwards, 1967). The EPI is a respected but little-used test consisting of 1,200(!) true-false questions. Some of the confirmatory correlations between PRF and EPI scales for 218 male and female college students are reported as follows:

Achievement (PRF) × Is a Hard Worker (EPI)   .74
Change (PRF) × Likes a Set Routine (EPI)   −.54
Nurturance (PRF) × Helps Others (EPI)   .64
Succorance (PRF) × Dependent (EPI)   .73

Because these instruments were developed independently according to different test construction philosophies, the findings bolster the validity of both tests. Several recent empirical comparisons also support the validity and utility of the PRF. For example, Goffin, Rothstein, and Johnston (2000) proved that the PRF outperformed the more widely used Sixteen Personality Factor Questionnaire (16PF, discussed later in this section) in predicting the job performance of 487 candidates for managerial positions. Vernon (2000) also reports favorably on the validity of the PRF in his review of recent studies.

## Measures of Type A Behavior

By way of quick review, Type A behavior refers to a hard-driving, aggressive behavior pattern that might be called "hurry sickness" (Friedman & Rosenman, 1974). Several questionnaire measures of Type A behavior are available for research purposes. The most recent is the Time Urgency and Perpetual Activation (TUPA) scale (Wright, McCurdy, & Rogoll, 1992). The TUPA scale is respected by researchers in behavioral medicine because of its psychometric excellence. As evidence of the utility of the instrument, scores on the TUPA mildly predict a number of physical health problems in college students, including respiratory illnesses, pain, and sensory disturbances (Wright, Nielsen, Abranato, Jackson, & Lancaster, 1995).

The best-known and most widely used instrument of this type is the Jenkins Activity Survey (JAS). The JAS is a 52-item, multiple-choice, self-report questionnaire designed to identify the Type A coronary-prone behavior pattern (Jenkins, Zyzanski, & Rosenman, 1979). Items on the JAS resemble the following:

Currently, do you consider yourself to be:

A. Definitely competitive and ambitious?
B. Probably competitive and ambitious?
C. Probably more relaxed and easygoing?
D. Definitely more relaxed and easygoing?

In addition to the composite Type A behavior score, the JAS yields three factor-analytically derived subscales: Speed and Impatience, Job Involvement, and Hard-Driving/Competitiveness. Correlations between the composite Type A scale and the three subscales are modest (.42 to .67), indicating that the factor scores may provide independent contributions to the assessment of Type A tendencies. The JAS is normed on 2,588 employed middle-class males ages 48 to 65 years. The instrument was standardized to have a mean of 0.0 and standard deviation of 10.0, with positive scores indicating Type A tendencies and negative scores indicating the opposite, Type B tendencies.

The Type A behavior pattern also consists of insecurity of status, hyperaggressiveness, free-floating hostility, and a sense of time urgency (Friedman & Ulmer, 1984). Some studies indicate that persons with this behavior pattern are at increased risk of coronary heart disease (CHD). Early identification of high-risk individuals, therefore, might have portentous implications for intervention. Prior to the JAS, a lengthy structured interview provided the only means for identifying persons with the Type A behavior pattern. The JAS was developed in an attempt to duplicate the structured interview, thereby providing a quick and economical method of screening for Type A behavior.

Unfortunately, the JAS has not fulfilled its ambitious aspirations. The test-retest reliability of the three subscales is marginal at best, with values as low as .58 for Speed and Impatience, .66 for Job Involvement, and .71 for Hard-Driving/

Competitiveness (Bishop, Hailey, & O'Rourke, 1989; Igbokwe, 1989). Furthermore, the level of agreement between the structured interview and JAS scores is only fair, not strong enough to warrant the use of this test for individual diagnosis (Yarnold & Bryant, 1988). Another problem with the JAS is that patients with CHD do not differ from general medical patients on its subscales. In comparing 40 patients with CHD and 40 patients with other medical problems, Wright (1992) found that the Speed and Impatience scale produced a significant and appropriate difference, but Hard-Driving/Competitiveness yielded a significant difference in the wrong direction—the CHD patients scored lower than the non-CHD medical patients.

## ● FACTOR-ANALYTICALLY DERIVED INVENTORIES

### Eysenck Personality Questionnaire

The Eysenck Personality Questionnaire (EPQ) was designed to measure the major dimensions of normal and abnormal personality (Eysenck & Eysenck, 1975). Based on a lifelong program of factor-analytic questionnaire research and laboratory experiments on learning and conditioning, Eysenck isolated three major dimensions of personality: Psychoticism (P), Extraversion (E), and Neuroticism (N). The EPQ consists of scales to measure these dimensions and also incorporates a Lie (L) scale to assess the validity of an examinee's responses. The EPQ contains 90 statements answered "yes" or "no" and is designed for persons aged 16 and older. A Junior EPQ containing 81 statements is suitable for children ages 7 to 15.

Items on the P scale resemble the following:

Do you often break the rules? (T)
Would you worry if you were in debt? (F)
Do you take risks just for fun? (T)

High scores on the P scale indicate aggressive and hostile traits, impulsivity, a preference for liking odd or unusual things, and empathy defects. Antisocial and schizoid patients often obtain high scores on this dimension. In contrast, low scores

on P foretell more desirable characteristics such as empathy and interpersonal sensitivity. Items on the E scale resemble the following:

Do you like to meet new people? (T)
Are you quiet when with others? (F)
Do you like lots of excitement? (T)

High scores on the E scale indicate a loud, gregarious, outgoing, fun-loving person. Low scores on the E scale indicate introverted traits such as a preference for solitude and quiet activities. Items on the N scale resemble the following:

Are you a moody person? (T)
Do you feel that life is dull? (T)
Are your feelings easily hurt? (T)

The N scale reflects a dimension of emotionality that ranges from nervous, maladjusted, and overemotional (high scores) to stable and confident (low scores).

The reliability of the EPQ is excellent. For example, the one-month test-retest correlations were .78 (P), .89 (E), .86 (N), and .84 (L). Internal consistencies were in the .70s for P and the .80s for the other three scales. The construct validity of the EPQ is also well established through dozens of studies using behavioral, emotional, learning, attentional, and therapeutic criteria (reviewed in Eysenck & Eysenck, 1985). Friedman (1987) provides a short but thorough introduction to other sources on the EPQ.

A major focus of research with the EPQ has been on the empirical correlates of **extraversion** and its polar opposite, **introversion**. Eysenck and Eysenck (1975) describe the typical extravert as follows:

> The typical extravert is sociable, likes parties, has many friends, needs to have people to talk to, and does not like reading or studying by himself. He craves excitement, takes chances, often sticks his neck out, acts on the spur of the moment, and is generally an impulsive individual.

They describe the typical introvert as follows:

> The typical introvert is a quiet, retiring sort of person, introspective, fond of books rather than people; he is reserved and distant except to intimate

friends. He tends to plan ahead, "looks before he leaps," and mistrusts the impulse of the moment.

Eysenck and his followers have linked a number of perceptual and physiological factors to the extraversion/introversion dimension. Because of space limitations, we can only list representative findings here:

- Introverts are more vigilant in watchkeeping.
- Introverts do better at signal-detection tasks.
- Introverts are less tolerant of pain but more tolerant of sensory deprivation.
- Extraverts are more easily conditioned to stimuli associated with sexual arousal.
- Extraverts have a greater need for external stimulation.

Aiken (1989) summarizes additional research on the real-world correlates of the EPQ extraversion/introversion dimension.

In general, the technical characteristics of the EPQ are very strong, certainly stronger than found in most self-report inventories. The practical utility of the instrument is supported by voluminous research literature. Nonetheless, the EPQ has never caught on among American psychologists, who seem enamored of multiphasic instruments that produce 10, 20, or 30 scores, not a simple trio of basic dimensions.

## Comrey Personality Scales

For practitioners who desire a short self-report inventory suitable for college students and other adults, the Comrey Personality Scales (Comrey, 1970, 1980) would be a good choice. As a protégé of Guilford, Comrey pursued a factor-analytic strategy in developing his 180-item test. Comrey relied exclusively upon college students in the development and standardization of his test, so the CPS is well suited to assessment of personality in this subpopulation.

A special virtue of the CPS is its brevity. Consisting of 180 statements, the test is only one-third as long as competing instruments such as the MMPI-2. The eight CPS personality scales consist of 20 items each, divided equally between positively and negatively worded statements. Another 20 items are devoted to a validity check and the assessment of social desirability response bias.

The following description of CPS scales is based upon Merenda (1985):

(V) *Validity Check.* A score of 8 is the expected raw score. Any score on the V scale which gives a $T$-score equivalent below 70 is still within the normal range, however. Higher scores are suggestive of an invalid record.

(R) *Response Bias.* High scores indicate a tendency to answer questions in a socially desirable way, making the respondent look like a "nice" person.

(T) *Trust versus Defensiveness.* High scores indicate a belief in the basic honesty, trustworthiness, and good intentions of other people.

(O) *Orderliness versus Lack of Compulsion.* High scores are characteristic of careful, meticulous, orderly, and highly organized individuals.

(C) *Social Conformity versus Rebelliousness.* Individuals with high scores accept society as it is, resent nonconformity in others, seek the approval of society, and respect the law.

(A) *Activity versus Lack of Energy.* High-scoring individuals have a great deal of energy and endurance, work hard, and strive to excel.

(S) *Emotional Stability versus Neuroticism.* High-scoring persons are free from depression, optimistic, relaxed, stable in mood, and confident.

(E) *Extraversion versus Introversion.* High-scoring individuals meet people easily, seek new friends, feel comfortable with strangers, and do not suffer from stage fright.

(M) *Masculinity versus Femininity.* High-scoring individuals tend to be rather tough-minded people who are not bothered by blood, crawling creatures, vulgarity, and who do not cry easily or show much interest in love stories.

(P) *Empathy versus Egocentrism.* High-scoring individuals describe themselves as helpful, generous, sympathetic people who are interested in devoting their lives to the service of others.

Reflecting its careful factor-analytic derivation, the CPS scales possess exceptional internal consistencies, which range from .91 to .96. These findings indicate that the CPS is most likely a reliable test, but traditional test-retest data are scant. Cross—cultural studies with the CPS are highly supportive of its validity. Brief and Comrey (1993) report that the eight-factor solution to CPS item responses is found in factor analyses with Russian, U.S., Brazilian, Israeli, Italian, and New Zealand samples. Other validational studies with the CPS are not straightforward in their interpretation. On the one hand, the correlations between CPS scale scores and personality-relevant biographical data are very small (Comrey & Backer, 1970; Comrey & Schiebel, 1983). On the other hand, extreme scores on the CPS scales are strongly associated with psychological disturbance (Comrey & Schiebel, 1985). This is particularly true for low scores on Trust versus Defensiveness, Activity versus Lack of Energy, Emotional Stability versus Neuroticism, Extraversion versus Introversion, and high scores on Orderliness versus Lack of Compulsion. Shen and Comrey (1997) describe the utility of the CPS with medical students, showing that the test is a reasonable predictor of clinical performance and personal suitability. In general, reviewers conclude that the CPS is a promising test that needs updated standardization and additional documentation on its technical qualities. Comrey (1995) summarizes validity studies of his test.

## ● CRITERION-KEYED INVENTORIES

The final self-report inventories that we will review embody a criterion-keyed test development strategy. In a criterion-keyed approach, test items are assigned to a particular scale if, and only if, they discriminate between a well-defined criterion group and a relevant control group. For example, in devising a self-report scale for depression, items endorsed by depressed persons significantly more (or less) frequently than by normal controls would be assigned to the depression scale, keyed in the appropriate direction. A similar approach might be

used to develop scales for other constructs of interest to clinicians such as schizophrenia, anxiety reaction, and the like. Notice that the test developer does not consult any theory of schizophrenia, depression, or anxiety reaction to determine which items belong on the respective scales. The essence of the criterion-keyed procedure is, so to speak, to let the items fall where they may.[4]

### Minnesota Multiphasic Personality Inventory-2 (MMPI-2)

First published in 1943, the MMPI was a 566-item true-false personality inventory designed originally as an aid in psychiatric diagnosis (Hathaway & McKinley, 1940, 1943; McKinley & Hathaway, 1940, 1944; McKinley, Hathaway, & Meehl, 1948). The test authors followed a strict empirical keying approach in the construction of the MMPI scales. The clinical scales were developed by contrasting item responses of carefully defined psychiatric patient groups (average $N$ of about 50) with item responses of 724 control subjects. The result was a remarkable test useful both in psychiatric assessment and the description of normal personality. Within a few years, the MMPI became the most widely used personality test in the United States.

At first the MMPI aged gracefully; what appeared to be minor flaws were tolerated by practitioners. But as the MMPI reached middle age, the need for rejuvenation became increasingly obvious. The most serious problem was the original control group, which consisted primarily of relatives and visitors of medical patients at the University of Minnesota Hospital. The narrow choice of control subjects, tested mainly in the 1930s, proved to be a persistent source of criticism for the MMPI. All of the control subjects were white, and most were young (average age about 35), married, and from a small town or rural area. This was a sample of

---

4. We are glossing over certain complexities here. Some items reflecting general psychopathology might discriminate *all* the contrast groups from the control group. The test developer might discard these in favor of items that are *differentially* discriminating for just one contrast group but not the others.

convenience that was significantly unrepresentative of the population at large.

The item content of the MMPI also raised concerns (Graham, 1993). Several items used archaic and obsolete terminology, referring to "drop the handkerchief" (a parlor game from the 1930s), sleeping powders (sleeping pills), and streetcars (electric-powered buses). Other items used sexist language. Examinees found some items objectionable, especially those dealing with Christian religious beliefs. These items were the source of occasional lawsuits alleging invasion of privacy. Finally, a few items dealing with bowel functions and sexual behavior were just downright offensive.

From the standpoint of measurement, a more serious problem with item content was that of omission. The MMPI item pool was not broad enough to assess many important characteristics, including suicidal tendencies, drug abuse, and treatment-related behaviors. An additional motive for MMPI revision was to extend the range of item coverage.

The MMPI-2 was released in 1989 after nearly a decade of revision and restandardization. The new, improved MMPI-2 incorporates a contemporary normative sample of 2,600 individuals who are loosely representative of the general population on major demographic variables (geographic location, race, age, occupational level, and income). Although higher educational levels are overrepresented, the MMPI-2 normative sample is still a vast improvement over the MMPI normative sample. The item pool has been significantly improved by revision of obsolete items, deletion of offensive items, and addition of new items to extend content coverage.

The MMPI-2 is a significant improvement upon the MMPI, but maintains substantial continuity with its esteemed predecessor. The test developers retained the same titles and measurement objectives for the traditional validity and clinical scales. The restandardization provides a better calibration for scale elevations, a much-needed improvement (Tellegen & Ben-Porath, 1992). Although dozens of items were rewritten, most of these revisions are cosmetic and do not affect the psychometric characteristics of the test (Ben-Porath & Butcher, 1989). In fact, when large samples of sub-

jects complete the MMPI and the MMPI-2, scores on the individual validity and clinical scales typically correlate near .99.

The MMPI-2 consists of 567 items carefully designed to assess a wide range of concerns. The examinee is asked to mark "true" or "false" for each statement as it applies to himself or herself. Most of the items are self-referential. The items encompass a wide variety of mainly pathological themes (Dahlstrom, Welsh, & Dahlstrom, 1972; Graham, 1993).

The MMPI requires a sixth-grade reading level and is completed by most persons in 1 to 1½ hours.

The original MMPI scales were developed by contrasting item responses of carefully defined psychiatric patient groups (average $N$ of about 50) with item responses of about 700 controls. The psychiatric patient groups included the following diagnostic categories: hypochondriasis, depression, hysteria, psychopathy, male homosexuality, paranoia, psychasthenia,[5] schizophrenia, and the early phase of mania (hypomania). In addition, samples of socially introverted and socially extraverted college students were used to construct a scale for social introversion. The MMPI-2 retains the basic clinical scales with only minor item deletions and revisions. Ben-Porath and Butcher (1989) investigated the characteristics of the rewritten items on the MMPI-2 and discovered that they are psychometrically equivalent to the original items.

The MMPI-2 can be scored for four validity scales, 10 standard clinical scales, and dozens of supplementary scales. In practice, clinicians place the greatest emphasis upon the validity and standard clinical scales. The supplementary scales are just that—supplementary. They provide information helpful in fine-tuning the interpretation of the traditional validity and clinical scales. MMPI-2 scale raw scores are converted to $T$ scores, with a mean of 50 and a standard deviation of 10. Scores that exceed $T$ of 65 merit special consideration. These elevated scores are statistically uncommon in the general population and may signify the

---

5. This outdated diagnostic term is quite similar to what would now be labeled obsessive-compulsive disorder.

presence of psychiatric symptomatology. We will concentrate upon the traditional scales here, beginning with a review of the four validity scales, known as Cannot Say (or ?), L, F, and K.

The Cannot Say score is simply the total number of items omitted or double-marked in completion of the answer sheet. The instructions for the test encourage examinees to mark all items, but omissions or double-marked items will occur. However, this is rare—the modal number of items omitted is zero (Tamkin & Scherer, 1957). Omission of up to 10 items appears to have little effect on the overall test results—one of the benefits of having a huge pool of statements in the MMPI-2. A very high score on this scale may indicate a reading problem, opposition to authority, defensiveness, or indecisiveness caused by depression.

The L Scale is composed of 15 items all scored in the false direction. By answering "false" to L Scale items, the examinee asserts that he or she possesses a degree of personal virtue that is rarely observed in our culture (e.g., never gets angry, likes everyone, never lies, reads every newspaper editorial, and would rather lose than win). The L Scale was designed to identify a general, deliberate, evasive test-taking attitude. A high score on the L Scale indicates that the examinee is not only defensive, but naively so. Persons with any degree of psychological sophistication can adopt a defensive test-taking attitude and still score in the normal range on the L Scale.

The F Scale consists of 60 items answered by normal subjects in the scored direction no more than 10 percent of the time. These items reflect a broad spectrum of serious maladjustment, including peculiar thoughts, apathy, and social alienation. Even though F Scale items seem to indicate psychiatric pathology, they are seldom endorsed by patients. Fewer than 50 percent of these items appear on the clinical scales. Many persons with significant psychiatric disturbance do produce elevated scores in the range of $T = 70$ or 80 on the F Scale. On the other hand, exceptionally high scores suggest additional hypotheses: insufficient reading ability, random or uncooperative responding, a motivated attempt to "fake bad" on the test, or an exaggerated "cry for help" in a distressed client.

The K Scale was designed to help detect a subtle form of defensiveness. The 30-item scale is composed, in part, of 22 items that differentiated normal profiles produced by defensive hospitalized psychiatric patients from those produced by normal controls. Additionally, eight items that improved discrimination of depressive and schizophrenic symptoms were added (McKinley, Hathaway & Meehl, 1948). An elevated score on the K Scale may indicate a defensive test-taking attitude. Normal range elevations on the K Scale suggest good ego strength—the presence of useful psychological defenses that allow the person to function well in spite of internal conflict.

The combined use of F and K may be useful in the detection of MMPI-2 profiles that have been faked or malingered. In one study, 81 percent of fake-good profiles were identified by a simple decision rule (using raw scores) of F-K $<$ −12, whereas 87 percent of fake-bad profiles were identified by a simple decision rule (using raw scores) of F-K $>$ 7 (Bagby, Rogers, Buis, & Kalemba, 1994).

Several clinical scales are "K-corrected" to improve their discriminatory power. The rationale for this practice is that elevations on K betoken an artificial reduction of scores on these clinical scales. Portions of the raw score on K are thus added to these clinical scale scores prior to computation of the $T$ scores. The K-corrected scales, discussed later, include Hypochondriasis, Psychopathic Deviate, Psychasthenia, Schizophrenia, and Hypomania. Whether K correction actually improves the MMPI-2 is debatable, but the test publishers continued the tradition from the MMPI for the sake of continuity. Separate norms for non-K-corrected scale score transformations are also available.

In addition to the validity scales, the MMPI-2 is always scored for 10 clinical scales. With the exception of Social Introversion, these clinical scales were constructed in the usual criterion-keyed manner by contrasting responses of clinical subjects and normal controls. As noted previously, Social Introversion was developed by contrasting the responses of college students high and low in social introversion. The 10 clinical scales and common interpretations of elevated scores are outlined in Table 8.8.

| ● TABLE 8.8 The 10 Clinical Scales from the Minnesota Multiphasic Personality Inventory-2 | | | |
|---|---|---|---|
| Scale No. and Abbreviation | Scale Name | K Correction | Typical Interpretation of Elevation |
| 1   Hs | Hypochondriasis | .5K | Excessive physical preoccupation |
| 2   D | Depression | | Sad feelings, hopelessness |
| 3   Hy | Hysteria | | Immaturity, use of repression, denial |
| 4   Pd | Psychopathic deviate | .4K | Authority conflict, impulsivity |
| 5   Mf | Masculinity-femininity | | Masculine interests [women], feminine interests [men] |
| 6   Pa | Paranoia | | Suspiciousness, hostility |
| 7   Pt | Psychasthenia | 1K | Anxiety and obsessive thinking |
| 8   Sc | Schizophrenia | 1K | Alienation, unusual thought processes |
| 9   Ma | Hypomania | .2K | High energy, possible agitation |
| 0   Si | Social introversion | | Shyness and introversion |

Dozens of supplementary scales can also be scored on the MMPI-2. Some of the supplementary scales are based upon rational identification of symptom clusters and subsequent scale purification by empirical means. Fifteen useful MMPI-2 Content Scales were developed in this manner (Butcher, Graham, Williams, & Ben-Porath, 1990). Many of the supplementary scales were developed by independent investigators; these scales vary widely in quality. In practice, only about 30 of the additional scales are routinely scored. Examples of the supplementary scales include Anxiety, Repression, Ego Strength, and the MacAndrew Alcoholism Scale-Revised. Anxiety (A) and Repression (R) are the first two major factors that always emerge from factor analysis of MMPI-2 responses. An interesting supplementary scale is Barron's (1953) Ego Strength (Es) Scale, which purports to predict positive response to psychotherapy. However, not all studies confirm this use of the scale (Graham, 1987). The MacAndrew

Alcoholism Scale-Revised (MAC-R; MacAndrew, 1965) is a useful index of alcohol or other substance abuse. The MAC-R is not only useful in assessment of alcoholism but is also helpful in the identification of heavy drinkers and drug-dependent individuals (Wolf, Schubert, Patterson, Grande, & Pendleton, 1990). We cannot possibly review all the useful supplementary scales here. The interested reader should consult Butcher and Williams (1992) and Graham (1993).

## MMPI-2 Interpretation

The interpretation of an MMPI-2 profile can proceed along two different paths: scale by scale or configural. In the simplest possible approach, scale by scale, the examiner determines the validity of the test, as discussed previously, by inspecting the four validity scales. If the test appears reasonably valid by these criteria, the examiner consults a relevant resource book and proceeds scale by scale to produce a series of hypotheses. For example, Lachar (1974) has distilled the meaning of various elevations on the Pa or Paranoia scale as follows:

$T = 27$–$44$ examinee may be stubborn, touchy, or difficult

$T = 45$–$59$ no undue sensitivity and adequate regard for others

$T = 60$–$69$ increasing probability of rigidity and oversensitivity

$T = 70$–$79$ rigid, touchy, projects blame and hostility

$T = 79$–$100$ frankly delusional paranoid features may be present

The configural approach to MMPI-2 interpretation is somewhat more complicated and consists of classifying the profile as belonging to one or another loosely defined code type that has been studied extensively. Code types are usually defined by a combination of elevation (two or more clinical scales elevated beyond a certain criterion) and definition (two or more clinical scales clearly standing out from the others). For example, in its full-blown manifestation, the 4–9 code type can be defined by a valid profile in which scale 4 (Psychopathic Deviate) and scale 9 (Hypomania) are the high-point elevations, both exceed $T$ of 65 (elevation), and both exceed the next highest clinical scale by at least 5 $T$-score points (definition). Here is how Graham (1993) describes persons who fit this code type:

> The most salient characteristics of 49/94 individuals is a marked disregard for social standards and values. They frequently get in trouble with the authorities because of antisocial behavior. They have a poorly developed conscience, easy morals, and fluctuating ethical values. Alcoholism, fighting, marital problems, sexual acting out, and a wide array of delinquent acts are among the difficulties in which they may be involved. This is a common code type among persons who abuse alcohol and other substances.

The most likely diagnosis for such individuals is antisocial personality disorder.

We should mention briefly that several computerized interpretation systems are available for the MMPI and the MMPI-2 (Fowler, 1985; Butcher, 1987). The Minnesota Report™ (Butcher, 1993) is the best. This system generates a very cautious and methodical 16-page report that includes discussion of profile validity, symptomatic patterns, interpersonal relations, diagnostic considerations, and treatment considerations. The Minnesota Report™ also provides a variety of figures and tables to illustrate test results.

The adequacy of computerized MMPI-2 narrative reports is generally good, but the reader should realize that computer programs are written by fallible human beings. There is a danger that computer-generated test reports will be erroneous. Furthermore, some less-reputable interpretive systems can be purchased on microcomputer diskette for a few hundred dollars. This increases the risk that computer-based test interpretations will be misused by unqualified persons. We discuss the pitfalls of computerized test interpretation in the final chapter of the book.

## Technical Properties of the MMPI-2

From the standpoint of traditional psychometric criteria, the MMPI-2 presents a mixed picture. Reliability data are generally positive, with median internal consistency coefficients (alpha) typically in the .70s and .80s, but as low as the .30s for some scales in some samples. One-week test-retest coefficients range from the high .50s to the low .90s, with a median in the .80s (Butcher, Dahlstrom, Graham, Tellegen, & Kaemmer, 1989). These are good figures considering that some attributes—such as those measured by the Depression scale—change so quickly that the test-retest methodology is of questionable suitability.

A shortcoming of the MMPI-2 is that intercorrelations among the clinical scales are extremely high. For example, in the case of scales 7 and 8, the Psychasthenia and Schizophrenia scales, the correlation is commonly in the .70s. In part, this reflects the item overlap between MMPI scales—scales 7 and 8 share 17 items in common. But it is also true that the criterion-keyed approach is not well suited to the development of independent measures. A high intercorrelation of basic scales is one price to be paid for using this test development strategy.

The validity of the MMPI-2 is difficult to summarize, owing to the sheer volume of research on this instrument and its predecessor, the MMPI. As of 1975, over 6,000 studies employing the MMPI had been completed (Dahlstrom, Welsh, & Dahlstrom, 1975). Of course, thousands of additional studies have been published since then. Graham (1993) provides a brief but excellent review of validity studies on the MMPI/MMPI-2. He notes that the average validity coefficient for MMPI studies conducted between 1970 and 1981 was a healthy .46. He also points out the confirming pattern of extratest correlates in dozens of studies of identified patient groups. Research also indicates that the MMPI-2 is highly comparable to the MMPI, for which a substantial body of validity data has been compiled (Hargrave, Hiatt, Ogard, & Karr, 1994). Finally, bias studies comparing MMPI-2 results for Caucasian and African American clients indicate that slight racial differences do exist in average profiles. However, these differences validly reflect emotional functioning; that is, the MMPI-2 is not racially biased (McNulty, Graham, Ben-Porath, & Stein, 1997). The MMPI-2 likely will maintain its status as the premiere instrument for assessment of psychopathology in adulthood for many years to come.

## Millon Clinical Multiaxial Inventory-III (MCMI-III)

The MCMI-III is a personality inventory designed for the same purposes as the MMPI-2, namely, to provide useful information for psychiatric diagnosis (Millon, 1983, 1987, 1994). The MCMI-III has two advantages over the MMPI-2. First, it is much shorter (175 true-false items) and, therefore, more palatable to clinical referrals; second, it is planned and organized to identify clinical patterns in a manner that is compatible with the *Diagnostic and Statistical Manual* (*DSM-IV*) of the American Psychiatric Association.

The MCMI-III is a highly theory-driven test, incorporating Millon's elaborate theoretical formulations on the nature of psychopathology and personality disorder (Millon, 1969, 1981, 1986; Millon & Davis, 1996). The test includes 27 scales, listed in Table 8.9. The first 11 scales measure personality styles or traits such as narcissism and antisocial tendencies; the next three assess more severe

---

● **TABLE 8.9  Scales of the Millon Clinical Multiaxial Inventory-III**

| Clinical Personality Patterns | | Clinical Syndromes | |
|---|---|---|---|
| 1 | Schizoid | A | Anxiety |
| 2A | Avoidant | H | Somatoform |
| 2B | Depressive | N | Bipolar: Manic |
| 3 | Dependent | D | Dysthymia |
| 4 | Histrionic | B | Alcohol Dependence |
| 5 | Narcissistic | R | Post-Traumatic Stress Disorder |
| 6A | Antisocial | | |
| 6B | Aggressive (Sadistic) | **Severe Syndromes** | |
| 7 | Compulsive | SS | Thought Disorder |
| 8A | Passive-Aggressive (Negativistic) | CC | Major Depression |
| 8B | Self-Defeating | PP | Delusional Disorder |
| **Severe Personality Pathology** | | **Validity (Modifying) Indices** | |
| S | Schizotypal | X | Disclosure |
| C | Borderline | Y | Desirability |
| P | Paranoid | Z | Debasement |

personality pathology (schizotypal, borderline, and paranoid disorders); the following seven scales assess clinical syndromes such as anxiety and depression; the next three scales assess severe clinical syndromes such as thought disorder; the last three scales are validity (response style) indices. Scores on these scales (Disclosure, Desirability, and Debasement) are used to adjust the other scale scores upward or downward, based on defensiveness or exaggeration of symptoms, respectively.

Scale development for the MCMI-III and its precursors was careful and methodical. We can only portray the broad outline here, in which 3,500 initial items were culled to 175 statements in three stages of test development: a theoretical-substantive stage (theory-guided item writing), an internal-structural stage (item-scale correlations), and an external-criterion stage (contrast of diagnostic groups with the reference group). A special feature of the last stage was Millon's use of general psychiatric patients instead of normal controls as the reference group. The purpose of this strategy was to enhance the capacity of MCMI scales to differentiate specific diagnostic groups from one another. Unfortunately, one side effect of this particular criterion-keyed approach was a rather substantial degree of item overlap for the clinical scales. Millon planned for and expected the item overlap but probably did not anticipate that some pairs of scales on the MCMI would share the majority of their items in common. Some of this overlap was eliminated with the further refinement of the test for the second and third editions. The revised instrument also incorporates an item-weighting procedure. In this approach, individual questions are weighted 2 or 1 to reflect their importance in discriminating the prototype for each scale. The item-weighting approach has been criticized as unnecessary and unwieldy (Streiner, Goldberg, & Miller, 1993).

The normative sample for the MCMI-III consisted of about a thousand men and women patients from across the United States. This is an unusual and controversial approach to the collection of a normative sample. More typically, population-proportionate sampling of reasonably normal

individuals is used. Millon offers the arguable justification that a patient sample is adequate for the normative sample because the base rates (in the general population) for specific personality and clinical disorders were consulted to calibrate the cutting points on the individual scales (Millon & Davis, 1996). But this approach is complex, experimental, and difficult to understand. The reliability of the individual scales is good: Internal consistency coefficients average .82 to .90, and test-retest coefficients for one week range from .81 to .87. Support for the validity of the MCMI-III is mixed (Haladyna, 1992; Piersma & Boes, 1997). Craig (1993) has assembled a series of articles that are largely supportive of the MCMI. Jankowski (2002) provides a beginner's guide to the test.

### Personality Inventory for Children-2 (PIC-2)

The PIC-2 (Lachar & Gruber, 2001) is a substantial revision of the PIC-R, a popular instrument that dates back to the late 1950s (Wirt & Broen, 1958; Wirt, Lachar, Klinedinst, & Seat, 1984). The current version, suitable for children 5 through 19 years of age, consists of 275 true-false statements that are completed by a parent or parental surrogate. The PIC-2 is one corner of a triad of instruments developed by David Lachar and colleagues to provide a comprehensive, multiview perspective on children's emotional and behavioral adjustment in the home, school, and community. The complementary instruments are the Personality Inventory for Youth (PIY), which is filled out by the child, and the Student Behavior Survey (SBS), which is filled out by the teacher. We discuss only the PIC-2 here. Items on the PIC-2 resemble the following:

> My child finds it difficult to fall asleep.
>
> My child is a finicky eater.
>
> My child has threatened to kill himself (herself).
>
> Sometimes my child swears at other adults.
>
> Our marriage has been full of turmoil.

The instrument also provides a shorter 96-item version known as the Behavioral Summary, suitable for screening and research purposes.

The test developers of the PIC-2 followed a complex multistage methodology to assign individual items to scales and subscales. The goal was to minimize content overlap between scales and subscales by examining preliminary item × subscale correlations and then retaining only those items for each specific subscale that showed high correlations. As a consequence of this test development strategy, each subscale possesses homogeneous content and the individual statements correlate substantially with one another. The resulting instrument consists of three response validity scales (Inconsistency, Dissimulation, Defensiveness) and nine adjustment scales. Each of the adjustment scales includes two or three subscales (Table 8.10).

Scale raw scores are converted to *T* scores with a mean of 50 and standard deviation of 10. Higher *T* scores indicated increased probability of psychopathology or deficit. Norms for children ages 5 through 19 years of age are based on a nationally representative sample of 2,306 parents of boys and girls in kindergarten through twelfth grade.

With the possible exception of the three validity scales (Inconsistency, Dissimulation, and Defensiveness), the PIC-2 scale and subscale names are self-explanatory. The validity scales are (1) Inconsistency, which includes 35 similar pairs of items to determine consistency of responding; (2) Dissimulation, a 35-item scale designed to identify deliberate exaggeration (fake bad) about symptoms or random responding; and (3) Defensiveness, a 24-item scale consisting of improbable virtues (e.g., "my child never has any problems") and therefore an index of naive defensiveness.

The reliability of PIC-2 scales and subscales is good, with test-retest values in the range of .82 to .92 and internal consistency coefficients in the range of .81 to .92. The test manual (Lachar & Gruber, 2001) summarizes a huge body of criterion-related validity studies such as correlations with independent ratings from clinicians. These correlations are very strong for similar behavioral dimensions (and weak for dissimilar behavioral dimensions), thus supporting the validity of individual scales and subscales. In like manner, PIC-2 subscale scores show theory-consistent relationships

| **TABLE 8.10   Adjustment Scales and Subscales of the Personality Inventory for Children-2** | |
| --- | --- |
| *Adjustment Scales* | *Subscales* |
| Cognitive Impairment | Inadequate Abilities |
| | Poor Achievement |
| | Developmental Delay |
| Impulsivity and Distractibility | Disruptive Behavior |
| | Fearlessness |
| Delinquency | Antisocial Behavior |
| | Dyscontrol |
| | Noncompliance |
| Family Dysfunction | Conflict among Members |
| | Parent Maladjustment |
| Reality Distortion | Developmental Deviation |
| | Hallucinations and Delusions |
| Somatic Concern | Psychosomatic Preoccupation |
| | Muscular Tension and Anxiety |
| Psychological Discomfort | Fear and Worry |
| | Depression |
| | Sleep Disturbance/Death Preoccupation |
| Social Withdrawal | Social Introversion |
| | Isolation |
| Social Skills Deficits | Limited Peer Status |
| | Conflict with Peers |

with the *DSM-IV* diagnostic categories of clinic-referred children. For example, 63 children independently diagnosed with Oppositional Defiant Disorder showed highly elevated scores (average *T* scores of 75 to 80) on the following PIC-2 subscales: Disruptive Behavior, Fearlessness, Dyscontrol, and Noncompliance. This is a perfect match to the major clinical features of this *DSM-IV* diagnostic category. Overall, the test developers have cited an impressive body of research that supports the reliability and validity of their instrument. Although independent studies of this test are yet to be published, it seems clear that the PIC-2 will earn wide usage in the behavioral and emotional assessment of school-aged children.

## ● BEHAVIORAL ASSESSMENT

**Behavioral assessment** concentrates on behavior itself rather than on underlying traits, hypothetical causes, or presumed dimensions of personality. The many methods of behavioral assessment offer a practical alternative to projective tests, self-report inventories, and other unwieldy techniques aimed at global personality assessment.

Typically, behavioral assessment is designed to meet the needs of therapists and their clients in a quick and uncomplicated manner. But behavioral assessment differs from traditional assessment in more than its simplicity. The basic assumptions, practical aspects, and essential goals of behavioral and traditional approaches are as different as night and day. Traditional assessment strategies tend to be complex, indirect, psychodynamic, and often extraneous to treatment. In contrast, behavioral assessment strategies tend to be simple, direct, behavior-analytic, and continuous with treatment.

Behavior therapists use a wide range of modalities to evaluate their clients, patients, and subjects. The methods of behavioral assessment include, but are not limited to, behavioral observations, self-reports, parent ratings, staff ratings, sibling ratings, judges' ratings, teacher ratings, therapist ratings, nurses' ratings, physiological assessment, biochemical assessment, biological assessment, structured interviews, semistructured interviews, and analogue tests. In their *Dictionary of Behavioral Assessment Techniques,* Hersen and Bellack (1988) list 286 behavioral tests used in widely diverse problems and disorders in children, adolescents, adults, and the geriatric population. Dozens more are referenced in a more recent compendium (Hersen & Bellack, 1998). So that the reader can appreciate the diversity of techniques available, we provide a sampling of these tests in Table 8.11.

In recent years, a new form of behavioral assessment known as ecological momentary assessment has become increasingly popular. In ecological momentary assessment, the client carries a wireless handheld device similar to a personal digital assistant and responds in real time to preplanned inquiries from the researcher. This approach is

### ● TABLE 8.11   A Sampling of Behavioral Assessment Tests and Techniques

Abnormal Involuntary Movement Scale

Agoraphobic Cognitions Questionnaire

Antidepressive Activity Questionnaire

Assertiveness Self-Statement Test

Behavior Profile Rating Scale

Behavioral Avoidance Slide Test

Behavioral Visual Acuity Test

Blood Alcohol Level

Body Sensations Questionnaire

Clinical Dementia Rating

Compulsive Activity Checklist

Daily Sleep Diary

Dieter's Inventory of Eating Temptations

Expired Air Carbon Monoxide Measurement

Fire Emergency Behavioral Situations Scale

Goal Attainment Scaling

Irrational Beliefs Inventory

McGill Pain Questionnaire

Musical Performance Anxiety Self-Statement Scale

Parent-Adolescent Interaction Coding System

Rape Aftermath Symptom Test

Self-Statement Assessment via Thought Listing

Sexual Experience Scales

Standardized Walk

Test Meals in the Assessment of Bulimia Nervosa

Type A Structured Interview

*Source:* Based on entries in Hersen, M., & Bellack, A. S. (Eds.). (1988). *Dictionary of behavioral assessment techniques.* New York: Pergamon.

designed to circumvent a number of limitations of traditional self-report techniques. We discuss ecological momentary assessment in more detail at the end of this chapter.

Behavioral assessment is often—but not always—an integral part of **behavior therapy** designed to change the duration, frequency, or intensity of a well-defined target behavior. For example, one therapy goal for a shy college student might be that she initiate a minimum of five conversations lasting two minutes or more each day. The therapist might recommend that she approach this goal incrementally, beginning with a few brief social exchanges before proceeding to lengthier conversations with strangers. In this example, behavioral assessment might take the form of self-monitoring in which the student uses a wrist-watch for timing and a diary for keeping track of conversations.

As noted, behavioral assessment often exists in service of behavior therapy. In many cases, the nature of behavioral assessment is dictated by the procedures and goals of behavior therapy. For this reason, the reader will better appreciate behavioral assessment tools if we interweave this topic with a discussion of behavior therapy methods.

Behavior therapy, also called behavior modification, is the application of the methods and findings of experimental psychology to the modification of maladaptive behavior (Plaud & Eifert, 1998). The roots of behavior therapy can be traced to Skinner's (1953) seminal book, *Science and Human Behavior,* which detailed the application of operant conditioning to the problems of human behavior. Skinner shunned any reference to private, nonobservable events such as thoughts or feelings; he emphasized the importance of identifying observable behaviors and methodically altering the environmental consequences of those behaviors.

Research by Wolpe (1958) on the systematic behavioral treatment of phobias also was influential in founding the methods of behavior therapy. Wolpe's clinical procedures were derived from his laboratory work on the conditioning and countercondi-tioning of fear in cats. Like Skinner, Wolpe deem-phasized the significance of thoughts and beliefs. He viewed fear as a learned phenomenon that could be unlearned by following a strict protocol of grad-uated exposure to the feared object or situation.

After Skinner, Bandura (1977), Mahoney and Arnkoff (1978), and Meichenbaum (1977) reintroduced cognitive factors into the ever-changing behavioral framework. For example, Bandura (1977) demonstrated that persons are perfectly capable of cognitively based learning. In particular, he showed that individuals can learn from mere observation of the response contingencies experienced by models. Since this learning occurs in the absence of personal consequences, it must be cognitively mediated. As a consequence of this paradigm shift, practically all modern-day behavior therapists concern themselves—at least to some extent—with the thoughts and beliefs of their clients. This new emphasis is reflected in a family of very popular treatment procedures known collectively as cognitive behavior therapy (McMullin, 1986).

## ● BEHAVIOR THERAPY AND BEHAVIORAL ASSESSMENT

At present, the specific techniques of behavior therapy can be classified into four overlapping categories (Johnston, 1986): exposure-based methods, cognitive behavior therapies, self-control procedures, and social skills training. Behavioral assessment is used in all of these approaches, as reviewed in the following sections. However, there are relatively few behaviorally based tools for the evaluation of social skills, so this category is not discussed. Readers who desire limited coverage of instruments for the behavioral evaluation of social skills training (including assertiveness) should consult Meier and Hope (1998).

### Exposure-Based Methods

Exposure-based methods of behavioral therapy are well suited to the treatment of phobias, which include intense and unreasonable fears (e.g., of spiders, blood, public speaking). One approach to phobic avoidance is systematic exposure of the client to the feared situation or object. Wolpe (1973) favored gradual exposure with minimal anxiety in a procedure known as systematic desen-sitization. In this therapeutic approach, the client first learns total relaxation and then proceeds from imagined exposure to actual or in vivo exposure to the feared stimulus. Another exposure-based method is flooding or implosion in which the client is immediately and totally immersed in the anxiety-inducing situation.

The therapist needs some type of behavioral assessment to gauge the continuing progress of a client undergoing an exposure-based treatment for a phobia. In the simplest possible assessment approach, known as a **behavioral avoidance test** (BAT), the therapist measures how long the client can tolerate the anxiety-inducing stimulus. Here is one classic example of a standardized BAT used to evaluate patients with agoraphobia, a disabling fear of open spaces often accompanied by panic attacks:

> The standardized Behavioral Avoidance Test (BAT) was conducted a week after intake. All anxiolytics, antidepressants, or other psychotropic medication had been taken away at least 4 days before the test. The test was administered by the first author, who was blind to the patients' diagnoses [and] not involved in the treatment. The patients were asked to walk alone as far as they could from the hospital along a mildly trafficated road that was 2 km long. The route was divided into eight intervals of equal length, and the patients rated their anxiety level on a 0–10 scale at the end of each interval. Uncompleted intervals were given a score of 10. An avoidance-anxiety score was computed by summing the anxiety scores for all intervals. (Hoffart, Friis, Strand, & Olsen, 1994)

The researchers discovered that the avoidance-anxiety score from the BAT technique was strongly related to self-reports of catastrophic thoughts (e.g., choking to death, having a heart attack, acting foolish, becoming helpless). This finding illustrates that behavioral assessment approaches often encompass a cognitive component as well. Notice, too, the direct relationship between the goal of therapy and the behavioral avoidance test. In agoraphobia, the primary treatment goal is to reduce patients' anxiety about walking alone in open spaces—which is exactly what the BAT measures.

The BAT approach is predicated on the reasonable assumption that the client's fear is the main determinant of behavior in the testing situation. Unfortunately, demand characteristics for desirable behavior may exert a strong influence on the client's behavior. The client's tolerance of the anxiety-inducing stimulus will bear some relationship to experienced fear but also has much to do with the situational context of assessment (McGlynn &

Rose, 1998). The results of BAT assessments may not generalize, and the therapist must be wary of foreclosing treatment too soon.

A **fear survey schedule** is another type of behavioral assessment useful in the identification and quantification of fears. Fear survey schedules are face valid devices that require respondents to indicate the presence and intensity of their fears in relation to various stimuli, typically on a 5- or 7-point Likert scale. Dozens of these instruments have been published, including versions by Wolpe (1973), Ollendick (1983), and Cautela (1977). Tasto, Hickson, and Rubin (1971) used factor analysis to develop a 40-item survey that yields a profile of fear scores in five categories. A generic fear survey schedule is shown in Table 8.12. Fear survey schedules are often used in research projects to screen large samples of persons in search of subjects who share a common fear. Another use of these schedules is to monitor changes in fears, including those that have been targeted for clinical intervention.

Klieger and Franklin (1993) have raised a number of cautions about the use of fear survey schedules in clinical research. These authors note that reliability data for fear surveys are almost nonexistent. A more serious problem has to do with the validity of these instruments. Using the Wolpe and Lang (1977) Fear Survey Schedule-III (FSS-III), a highly respected and widely used schedule, Klieger and Franklin (1993) found no relationship between reported fears on the FSS-III and BAT measures of the same fears. For example, subjects who reported a high fear of blood on the FSS-III were just as likely to approach a bloody white towel and touch it as were subjects who reported no fear of blood. Similar results were found for subjects who feared snakes, spiders, and fire. The researchers concluded that the FSS-III and similar instruments are a poor choice for identifying experimental groups and a poor basis for measuring the outcome of therapeutic interventions. The essential downfall seems to be that fear survey schedules possess such "obvious" validity that few researchers have bothered to evaluate the traditional psychometric characteristics of

● **TABLE 8.12    Example of a Fear Survey Schedule**

Please check the column that best describes your current response to these situations or objects.

Degree to which you would be disturbed

| | Not at All | Just a Little | Moderate Amount | Very Much | Extremely Bothered |
|---|---|---|---|---|---|
| Being in a strange place | | | | | |
| Speaking in public | | | | | |
| Walking into a party | | | | | |
| Getting an injection | | | | | |
| People watching me work | | | | | |
| Large open spaces | | | | | |
| Being fat | | | | | |
| Spider on the wall | | | | | |
| Cat in the room | | | | | |
| Reprimand from the boss | | | | | |

Note:  Most fear survey schedules consist of several dozen items.

reliability and validity. Fear survey schedules should be used with caution.

## Cognitive Behavior Therapies

The one factor common to all cognitive behavior therapies is an emphasis on changing the belief structure of the client. The three best-known variants of **cognitive behavior therapy** are Ellis's (1962) rational emotive therapy (RET), Meichenbaum's (1977) self-instructional training, and Beck's (1976) cognitive therapy. Ellis postulates that most disturbed behavior is caused by irrational beliefs, such as the widespread belief that one must have the love and approval of all significant persons at all times. Ellis attempts to alter such core irrational beliefs, primarily by logical argument and forceful exhortation. Meichenbaum's self-instructional technique consists of teaching the client to use coping self-statements to combat stressful situations. For example, a college student suffering from intense test-taking anxiety might be taught to use the following self-talk during examinations: "You have a strategy this time. . . . Take a deep breath and relax. . . . Just answer one question at a time. . . ." Beck's cognitive therapy concentrates mainly on the role of cognitive

distortions in the maintenance of depression and other emotional disturbances. Beck (1983) regards depression as primarily a cognitive disorder characterized by the negative cognitive triad: a pessimistic view of the world, a pessimistic self-concept, and a pessimistic view of the future. In therapy, he uses a gentle form of cognitive restructuring to help the client perceive his or her problems in alternative, solvable terms.

Cognitive behavior therapists need not use formal assessment tools in their clinical practice. Typically, these therapists monitor the belief structure of their clients on an informal session-to-session basis. Irrational and distorted thoughts are challenged as they arise during therapy. In the end, the client's self-report of improvement may constitute the main index of therapeutic success. Nonetheless, several straightforward measures of cognitive distortion are available. We have outlined a few prominent instruments in Table 8.13. These instruments are mainly research questionnaires suitable to the testing of group differences, but not sufficiently validated for individual assessment. Clark (1988) faults the developers of cognitive distortion questionnaires for premature release of their instruments. In particular, he notes the absence of

| ● TABLE 8.13    Questionnaire Measures of Cognitive Distortion |
| --- |

### Anxious Self-Statements Questionnaire (ASSQ)
### (Kendall & Hollon, 1989)

Examinee rates how often specific anxious thoughts occurred over the last week. Items are of the form:

> I can't stand it anymore.
> What's going to happen to me now?
> I'm not going to make it.

A psychometrically sound instrument, the ASSQ can be used to assess changes in the frequency of anxious self-talk.

### Automatic Thoughts Questionnaire (ATQ)
### (Hollon & Kendall, 1980; Kazdin, 1990)

The ATQ is a frequency measure of depression-related cognitions that assesses personal maladjustment, negative self-concept and expectations, low self-esteem, and giving up/helplessness. The 30-item ATQ correlates very well with the MMPI Depression scale and the Beck Depression Inventory (Ross, Gottfredson, Christensen, & Weaver, 1986).

### Cognitive Errors Questionnaire (CEQ)
### (Lefebvre, 1981)

The CEQ assesses the degree of maladaptive thinking in general situations and also situations related to chronic low back pain. Discrete vignettes concerning chronic back pain and general scenes are each followed by an illogical dysphoric cognition. The respondent indicates on a 5-point scale how similar the cognition is to the thought he or she would have in the same situation. For example: "You just finished spending three hours cleaning the basement. Your spouse, however, doesn't say anything about it. You think to yourself, 'S(he) must think I did a poor job.'" Smith, Follick, Ahern, and Adams (1986) found that overgeneralization was the specific CEQ cognitive error most consistently correlated with chronic low back pain disability.

### Attribution Styles Questionnaire (ASQ)
### (Seligman, Abramson, Semmel, & Von Baeyer, 1979)

The ASQ measures three attributional dimensions relevant to Seligman's learned helplessness model of depression: internal-external, stable-unstable, and global-specific. Depressed persons attribute bad outcomes to internal, stable, and global causes; they attribute good outcomes to external, unstable causes. The questionnaire consists of 12 hypothetical situations, 6 describing good outcomes, 6 describing bad outcomes (e.g., "You have been looking for a job unsuccessfully for some time"). The respondents rate each vignette on a 7-point scale for degree of internality, stability, and globality.

### Hopelessness Scale (HS)
### (Beck, 1987; Dyce, 1996)

A 20-item true/false scale, the HS is designed to quantify hopelessness, one component of the negative cognitive triad found in depressed persons. (The triad consists of negative views of self, world, and future.) The scale is sensitive to changes in the patient's state of depression. In a validational study, Beck, Riskind, Brown, and Steer (1988) found that HS scores had a negligible relationship to anxiety or general psychopathology when the influence of coexisting depression was partialed out. Thus, the HS appears to measure a specific attribute of depression rather than general psychopathology.

research on the concurrent and discriminant validity of most self-statement measures. Another problem is that existing questionnaires were designed to validate constructs in research and consequently do not work well in clinical practice.

An exceptional and well-validated measure not listed in Table 8.13 is the Beck Depression Inventory (BDI). The BDI is a short, simple, self-report questionnaire that focuses, in part, on the cognitive distortions that underlie depression (Beck & Steer, 1987; Beck, Ward, Mendelsohn, Mock, & Erbaugh, 1961). One reason for its popularity is that most patients can complete the 21 items on the BDI in 10 minutes or less. The test has been widely used: More than 1,900 articles using the BDI have been published (Conoley, 1992). A second edition of the inventory was released in 1996 (Beck, Steer, & Brown, 1996). On the BDI-II, several items were revised so as to bring the inventory into closer conformity with prevailing diagnostic criteria for depression. The 21 items are of the following form:

Check the statement from this group that you feel is most true about you:

0   I am upbeat about the future.
1   I feel slightly discouraged about the future.
2   I feel the future has little to offer for me.
3   I feel that the future is utterly hopeless.

Thirteen items cover cognitive and affective components of depression such as pessimism, guilt, crying, indecision, and self-accusations; eight items assess somatic and performance variables such as sleep problems, body image, work difficulties, and loss of interest in sex. The examinee receives a score of 0 to 3 for each item; the total raw score is the sum of the endorsements for the 21 items; the highest possible score is 63.

In a meta-analysis of BDI research studies, the internal consistency of the scale (coefficient alpha) ranged from .73 to .95, with a mean of .86 in nine psychiatric populations (Beck, Steer, & Garbin, 1988). The BDI-II possesses excellent internal consistency with a coefficient alpha of .92 (Beck, Steer, & Brown, 1996). Test-retest reliability of the BDI is modest, with a range of .60 to .83 in nonpsychiatric samples and .48 to .86 in psychiatric samples.

However, the test-retest methodology is not well suited to phenomena such as depression that are naturally unstable. Subjective depression fluctuates dramatically from week to week, day to day, even hour to hour. A lackluster value for test-retest reliability might signify valid change in the construct being measured rather than unwanted measurement error.

A variety of normative results are available, with BDI data for samples of patients with major depression, dysthymia, alcoholism, heroin addiction, and mixed problems. The manual also provides guidelines for degree of depression based upon BDI score (0 to 9, normal; 10 to 19, mild to moderate; 20 to 29, moderate to severe; 30 and above, extremely severe). These ratings are based upon clinical evaluations of patients.

The BDI has been extensively validated against other measures of depression and independent criteria of depression. For example, correlations with clinical ratings and scales of depression such as from the MMPI are typically in the range of .60 to .76 (Conoley, 1992). Sex differences are minimal, although there may be slight differences in the expression of depression between men and women (Steer, Beck, & Brown, 1989).

The only shortcoming of the BDI is its transparency. Patients who wish to hide their despair or exaggerate their depression can do so easily. However, for patients who are motivated to accurately reflect their emotional status, the BDI and BDI-II are probably unbeatable as an index of the presence and degree of depression (Stehouwer, 1987). Some practitioners ask patients to complete the BDI after each therapy session; they use the BDI much as a physician might use a thermometer.

## Self-Monitoring Procedures

A common misconception about behavior therapy is that it consists of authoritarian therapists applying powerful rewards and punishments to passive clients. Although this stereotypical model may be true for some impaired clients with limited behavioral repertoires, for the most part behavior therapy consists of humane practitioners teaching their clients methods of self-control. An emphasis upon self-monitoring is fundamental to all forms of behavior therapy. In **self-monitoring,** the client chooses the goals and actively participates in supervising, charting, and recording progress toward the end point(s) of therapy. According to this model, the therapist is relegated to the status of expert consultant.

Self-monitoring procedures are especially useful in the treatment of depression, a prevalent behavior disorder consisting of sad mood, low activity level, feelings of worthlessness, concentration problems, and physical symptoms (sleep loss, appetite disturbance, reduced interest in sex). Several self-monitoring programs for depression have been reported (Lewinsohn & Talkington, 1979; Rehm, Kornblith, O'Hara, & others, 1981). In order to illustrate the self-monitoring approach to the control of depression, we will summarize one small corner of the program advocated by Lewinsohn and his colleagues (Lewinsohn, Munoz, Youngren, & Zeiss, 1986).

Lewinsohn observed that depression goes hand in hand with a marked reduction in the experiencing of pleasant events. Depressed persons retreat from engaging in pleasant activities; the behavioral withdrawal only contributes further to their depression, inciting a continuous downward spiral. Fortunately, it is possible to replace the downward spiral with an upward one. To help reverse the downward spiral of depression, Lewinsohn and his colleagues devised the Pleasant Events Schedule (PES; MacPhillamy & Lewinsohn, 1982). The purpose of the PES is twofold. First, in the baseline assessment phase, the PES is used to self-monitor the frequency ($F$) and pleasantness ($P$) of 320 largely ordinary, everyday events. Examples of the kinds of events listed on the PES include the following:

> reading magazines
> going for a walk
> being with pets
> playing a musical instrument
> making food for charity
> listening to the radio
> reading poetry

> attending a church service
> watching a sports event
> playing catch with a friend
> working on my job

The frequency and pleasantness of these everyday events are both rated 0 to 2.[6] The mean rate of pleasant activities is then calculated from the sum of the $F \times P$ scores; that is, mean rate = $F \times P/320$. Normative findings for mean $F$, mean $P$, and mean $F \times P$ are reported in Lewinsohn, Munoz, Youngren, and Zeiss (1986) and serve as a basis for treatment planning. Participants in the Lewinsohn program also monitor their daily mood on a simple 1 (worst) to 9 (best) basis.

The second use of the PES is to self-monitor therapeutic progress. Based on the initial PES results, clients identify 100 or so potentially pleasant events and strive to increase the frequency of these events, monitoring daily mood along the way. Clients who increase the frequency of pleasant events generally show an improvement in mood and other depressive symptoms.

The PES is a highly useful tool for clinicians who wish to implement a self-monitoring approach to the assessment and treatment of depression. MacPhillamy and Lewinsohn (1982) report favorably on the technical qualities of the PES and discuss a variety of rational, factorial, and empirical subscales, which we cannot review here. The instrument has fair to good test-retest reliability (one-month correlations in the range of .69 to .86), excellent concurrent validity with trained observers,

---

6. The Frequency Scale is calibrated as follows:

0—This has *not* happened in the past 30 days.
1—This has happened a *few times* (1 to 6 times) in the past 30 days.
2—This has happened *often* (7 times or more) in the past 30 days.

The Pleasantness Scale is calibrated as follows:

0—This was *not* pleasant.
1—This was *somewhat* pleasant.
2—This was *very* pleasant.

and promising construct validity. In general, the subscales behave as one would predict on the basis of the constructs they purport to measure—we refer the reader to MacPhillamy and Lewinsohn (1982) for details.

## ● STRUCTURED INTERVIEW SCHEDULES

An important responsibility for many mental health practitioners is to determine a proper psychiatric diagnosis for their patients, within prevailing guidelines. Almost without exception, practitioners utilize the *Diagnostic and Statistical Manual of Mental Disorders,* now in its fourth edition (*DSM-IV;* APA, 2000). The latest version includes a "Text Revision" and for this reason is known technically as *DSM-IV-TR.* Here we use the less cumbersome acronym *DSM-IV. DSM-V* is scheduled for release in 2011.

Five axes are included in the *DSM-IV* classification. Axis I concerns clinical disorders such as Alcohol Use Disorder, Panic Disorder, Major Depressive Disorder, or Schizophrenia. Axis II pertains to personality disorders such as Borderline Personality Disorder, Avoidant Personality Disorder, or Dependent Personality Disorder. Axis III is employed to identify general medical conditions (e.g., hypothyroidism, heart disease) that may bear upon psychological adjustment. Axis IV is for reporting psychosocial and environmental problems (e.g., loss of friends, unemployment, litigation, no health insurance) that may impact personal functioning. Axis V consists of an anchored rating scale, the Global Assessment of Function (GAF) Scale, used to assign a summary score of functioning from 1 (e.g., immobilized, suicidal) to 100 (e.g., thriving, sought out). Of course, intermediate scores are available and clearly operationalized. For example, a GAF score of 70 indicates some mild symptoms but generally good psychological functioning.

Diagnosis is construed by some people as a form of pointless, overconfident, pigeonholing. In truth, it serves a number of indispensable functions.

As outlined by Andreasen and Black (1995), these key purposes include:

- Reducing the complexity of clinical phenomena
- Facilitating communication between clinicians
- Predicting the outcome of the disorder
- Deciding on an appropriate treatment
- Assisting in the search for etiology
- Determining the prevalence of diseases worldwide
- Making decisions about insurance coverage

Yet, for all of its advantages, there are also problems with *DSM-IV.* One problem is the sheer amount of time it can take to determine a multiaxial diagnosis. A second and related difficulty is that, although the *DSM-IV* textbook describes the diagnostic categories and alternatives with great precision, it does not specify a coherent method for arriving at the diagnosis. A third problem flows from the previous two; namely, psychiatric diagnosis is mixed in its reliability (Andreasen & Black, 1995). Interrater agreement for some diagnoses is very high (e.g., Alcohol Use Disorder) but for other diagnoses it is only moderate to low (e.g., Borderline Personality Disorder).

Several interview schedules have been developed to reduce the time needed for diagnosis and also to improve the reliability of the enterprise by standardizing the procedures. Broadly speaking, these instruments are of two types: semistructured approaches that allow for some clinician leeway in follow-up questioning, and structured approaches that mandate a completely scripted approach. Here we will describe two prominent schedules to illustrate this important form of psychological assessment.

The Schedule for Affective Disorders and Schizophrenia (SADS; Spitzer & Endicott, 1978) is a highly respected diagnostic interview for evaluating Axis I mood and psychotic disorders. The SADS is a semistructured inquiry that includes standard questions asked of all patients and optional probes used to clarify patient responses (Rogers, Jackson, & Cashel, 2004). Additional unstructured questions can be asked to augment the optional probes. Part I of the SADS methodically examines Axis I symptoms for the current episode, including the worst period and the current week, whereas Part II provides a survey of past episodes. Through a progression of questions and criteria, the interviewer solicits sufficient information to assess the severity of disturbance and also to elucidate the diagnosis. For example, one item on the SADS addresses prominent signs of depression: pessimism and hopelessness. A standard inquiry for this item might be: "Have you felt discouraged?" An affirmative answer would trigger optional probes such as "How do you see things working out?"

Rogers (2001) has reviewed the voluminous research on reliability and validity of the SADS and offers an encouraging endorsement of the instrument. For example, the consensus from over 21 studies is that the interrater reliability for specific diagnoses is typically strong, with median kappa coefficients of greater than .85. **Kappa** is the index of interrater agreement, corrected for chance (Cohen, 1960). Validity for the SADS also is robust with moderate predictive validity (e.g., results moderately predict the course and outcome of mood disorders) and strong concurrent validity (e.g., results correlate with other similar schedules). A child's version of the schedule, known as the "kiddie" SADS or K-SADS, also is available (Ambrosini, 2000).

Finally, we would be remiss not to mention a family of instruments known as SCID, the Structured Clinical Interview for *DSM-IV* (First & Gibbon, 2004). SCID comes in numerous editions and variations, including SCID-I for Axis I diagnoses, SCID-II for Axis II diagnoses, SCID-P for determining the differential diagnosis of psychotic symptoms, and SCID-NP for nonpatient settings in which a current psychiatric disorder is unlikely. All of the forms follow the same format in which the interviewer reads the SCID questions to the client in sequence, the objective being to elicit sufficient information to determine whether individual *DSM-IV* criteria are met. The interviewer has the leeway to ask for specific examples of affirmative answers. Thus, SCID is a semistructured interview. A logical flow sheet is followed to determine

the appropriate diagnosis. The SCID reveals generally good interrater agreement for *DSM-IV* diagnosis, but this is variable from one diagnosis to the other. In Table 8.14, we have summarized the average kappas from multiple studies of SCID reliability. Kappa values above .70 are considered good agreement, values from .50 to .69 are deemed fair, and values below .50 indicate poor agreement.

**TABLE 8.14   Average SCID Interrater Agreement for Psychiatric Diagnosis**

| Axis I Diagnoses | Weighted Kappa |
|---|---|
| Major Depressive Disorder | 79 |
| Dysthymic Disorder | 63 |
| Bipolar Disorder | 77 |
| Schizophrenia | 80 |
| Alcohol Dependence/Abuse | 90 |
| Other Substance Dependence/Abuse | 86 |
| Panic Disorder | 75 |
| Social Phobia | 63 |
| Obsessive Compulsive Disorder | 53 |
| Generalized Anxiety Disorder | 66 |
| Post-Traumatic Stress Disorder | 89 |
| Somatoform Disorder | 41 |
| Eating Disorder | 71 |

| Axis II Personality Disorders | |
|---|---|
| Avoidant | 64 |
| Dependent | 66 |
| Obsessive Compulsive | 56 |
| Passive-Aggressive | 67 |
| Self-Defeating | 62 |
| Depressive | 65 |
| Paranoid | 68 |
| Schizotypal | 70 |
| Schizoid | 76 |
| Histrionic | 64 |
| Narcissistic | 74 |
| Borderline | 62 |
| Antisocial | 72 |

Note: Decimals omitted.

Source: Average results for multiple studies reported on the SCID website (www.scid4.org).

## ● ASSESSMENT BY SYSTEMATIC DIRECT OBSERVATION

Although not a prominent approach with adults, systematic and direct observation is widely used in the evaluation of children, especially by psychologists who work in school systems. In fact, Wilson and Reschly (1996) determined that systematic observation is the single most commonly used assessment method among school-based practitioners, who reported an average of more than *15* student behavioral observations per month.

It is essential to distinguish systematic, direct observation from more casual approaches such as naturalistic observation. Anyone can engage in the informal and anecdotal methods that characterize naturalistic observation—and most people do so every day. These methods typically culminate in formless conclusions such as "Johnny seems to be out of his seat a lot during the school day." In contrast, systematic and direct observation is highly structured and set apart by five characteristics (Hintze, Volpe, & Shapiro, 2002; Salvia & Ysseldyke, 2001):

1. The goal of observation is to measure specific behaviors.
2. The target behaviors have been operationally defined beforehand.
3. Observations are conducted under objective, standardized procedures.
4. The times and places for observation are carefully specified.
5. Scoring is standardized and does not vary from one observer to another.

This form of assessment is appealing because of its direct link to intervention. In fact, it is common to employ observational assessment before, during, and after an intervention to determine the impact on the individual student.

Commonly, systematic and direct observation is executed by means of an objective, structured coding system. Many different styles of coding systems have been proposed; we have space here only to illustrate a few popular methods. Sattler (2002) provides an extensive review, devoting two chapters

to this topic. One straightforward approach is simple frequency counting of target behaviors. Typically, the target behaviors are undesirable behaviors such as a student leaving his or her seat, calling out, or being off task. Of course, the characteristics of these behaviors would be carefully specified in advance. Then an observer sits off to the side and unobtrusively records the frequency of each behavior within discrete time periods. The purpose of this kind of assessment is to objectify the extent of troublesome actions. This information serves as a baseline for later comparison to determine the effectiveness of any interventions. See Figure 8.5 for an example. In this hypothetical example, it is evident that the student "Sammy" is more out of control in the afternoon than the

Date:    November 10, 2005    Observer: Judy Jones
Student: Sammy Smith    Age: 8-5    Grade: 3

| Time Period | Target Behaviors | | |
|---|---|---|---|
| | Calling Out | Leaving Seat | Off Task |
| 9:00–9:15 | ××××  | ×× | ×××× |
| 9:15–9:30 | ××× | ××× | ×× |
| 9:30–9:45 | ××× | ××× | ×× |
| 9:45–10:00 | × | ×× | ×× |
| 2:00–2:15 | ××××× | ××××× | ×× |
| 2:15–2:30 | ×××××× | ×××× | ××××××× |
| 2:30–2:45 | ××××× | ××× | ××××××× |
| 2:45–3:00 | ×××× | ×××× | ××××××× |

Calling Out: Specific episodes of interrupting teacher, calling to classmates, making noise, yelling

Leaving Seat: Separate event such as standing without permission, leaving the seat, knees on seat

Off Task: Not doing assigned work (e.g., daydreaming, playing with objects, doing other work)

● **FIGURE 8.5**    Example of a Frequency Recording Sheet

morning, which may be valuable information when it comes to remediation planning.

Another approach to systematic, direct observation is to record the duration of target behaviors. Typically, target behaviors are undesirable actions such as temper tantrums, social isolation, or aggressive outbursts, but the focus of assessment also may include desirable behaviors such as staying on task during a designated reading period or vigilantly working on a homework assignment (Hintze, Volpe, & Shapiro, 2002). For some behaviors, duration may be more important than frequency. Consider out-of-seat behavior as an example. A third grader who is out of his seat in a morning for six brief episodes of a few seconds each is far, far less problematic—both to self and others—than a student who leaves his seat once for 10 minutes. See Figure 8.6 for an example of a duration recording sheet. In this hypothetical example, it is evident that "Susan" exhibits a high level of undesirable behavior. The goal of intervention might be to reduce both the frequency and the average duration of her tantrum behaviors.

| Date: November 10, 2005 | Observer: Judy Jones |
|---|---|
| Student: Susan Brown | Age: 8-5   Grade: 3 |
| Time Start:   9:00 | Time Stop:   12:00 |

| *Tantrum Behavior Separate Incidents* | *Elapsed Time in Minutes and Seconds* |
|---|---|
| 1 | 3 min  00 s |
| 2 | 2 min  30 s |
| 3 | 1 min  15 s |
| 4 | 4 min  30 s |
| 5 | 2 min  45 s |
| Total: | 14 min  00 s |
| Average Episode | 2 min  48 s |

● FIGURE 8.6  Example of a Duration Recording Sheet

In addition to the individualized forms of direct observation that we have illustrated here, dozens of published forms also are available (e.g., Sattler, 2002, chapters 4 and 5). For these instruments, the categories of observation and the operational definitions are prespecified, which saves time for the practitioner. For example, Shapiro (1996) has issued the Behavior Observation of Students in Schools (BOSS), a straightforward form that consists of six categories of classroom behavior—five designed for students and one for the teacher. The BOSS classifies behaviors as active engagement, passive engagement, off-task motor, off-task verbal, and off-task passive. Of course, these categories are thoroughly defined in operational terms. Direct instruction by the teacher also is recorded. The BOSS is rated in 15-second intervals for a 15-minute interval. The instrument also allows for the collection of behavioral norms for classmates to determine normative patterns in each category.

Although direct observations offer the utmost simplicity in format, it is important to recognize a number of threats to reliability and validity for this genre of assessment (Baer, Harrison, Fradenburg, Petersen, & Milla, 2005). Sattler (2002) has catalogued the sources of unreliability, which include personal qualities of the observer, poor design of instruments, and problems in obtaining a representative sample of behavior. For example, **observer drift** occurs when an observer becomes fatigued and less vigilant over time, thus failing to notice target behaviors when they occur. Expectations also can influence ratings such as when the observer has been told that a child is aggressive—and then records questionably aggressive acts as aggressive. The primary antidote to observer inaccuracy is careful training and cross-checking of one observer against another to demonstrate a high level of interrater agreement. With regard to poor design of instruments, the most common error is **coding complexity**, in which there are too many categories or ill-defined categories. Attention to design of rating scales and pretesting of instruments will avert this problem. Problems also can arise in the suitable sampling of behavior. For example, if a child's attentional difficulties mainly arise in the afternoon, clearly it is pointless to collect data only in the morning. Ratings should be collected throughout the day or, if this is not possible, during the most salient time periods.

## ● ANALOGUE BEHAVIORAL ASSESSMENT

The methods of analogue behavioral assessment are closely related to the methods of systematic, direct observation. The main difference has to do with the settings in which the observations occur. In systematic, direct observation, the assessment of clients takes place in a natural setting such as a classroom. In **analogue behavioral assessment,** clients are observed in a contrived but plausible setting and also are instructed to engage in relevant tasks designed to elicit behaviors of interest (Haynes, 2001). The goal is to create a state of affairs analogous to pivotal situations in real life—hence, the use of the word *analogue* in describing this form of observational assessment.

Perhaps some examples will help clarify the nature and scope of this approach. One application of analogue behavioral assessment is the evaluation of children referred for assessment of behavior or school problems (Mori & Armendariz, 2001). A specialist who works with these children could dedicate a separate room in his or her clinic to analogue behavioral assessment. The room might resemble a small classroom, complete with blackboard, a few student desks, and bookcases. The referred child would be given a realistic homework assignment and told to work on it for 30 minutes while waiting for the interview. The psychologist then observes through a one-way window and records relevant behaviors using a suitable rating scale.

Analogue behavioral assessment also can be used to evaluate parent–child interactions. For example, in evaluating a 3-year-old referred for behavior problems, the clinician might place the parent and child in a room full of toys with instructions to play for 10 minutes. The psychologist then instructs the parent to tell the child, "Okay, it's time to go. You have to pick up the toys just like you do at home." The clinician observes through a one-way window and codes both the parental management style and the nature and degree of child compliance.

In like manner, analogue behavioral assessment has been used in the assessment of adult couples, including husbands and wives seeking marital therapy (Heyman, 2001). In a standard paradigm, the clinician asks the couple to discuss two conflict areas for 5 to 7 minutes each. The clinician sits to the side observing the interactions and recording communication patterns with a standard form such as the Rapid Couples Interaction Scoring System (RCISS; Krokoff, Gottman, & Hass, 1989). The RCISS consists of 22 codes that address speaker and listener behaviors, both verbal and nonverbal, in such categories as criticism, disagreement, compromise, positive solution, questioning, humor, and smiling. Instruments of this genre typically do not reveal strong interrater agreement for specific constructs (e.g., put-downs), but the more inclusive constructs such as positive affect versus negative affect fare better and provide information that is helpful in characterizing communication patterns (Heyman, 2001). There are little or no data on the test-retest reliability of the RCISS or similar instruments, and some researchers advise caution in their use. For example, King (2001) faults the RCISS because it does not deal adequately with issues of subtext or "reading between the lines" in couples' communication. Consider this interaction between a divorced couple, Judy and David, from the movie *Always* (King, 2001):

> *Judy:* . . . Cooking is very logical. You just do it. One thing after another. You build it. It's like . . . logic.
>
> *David:* Like life, huh?
>
> *Judy:* Yeah. Simple and logical, like life.

Within the RCISS, would this episode be coded as agreement or disagreement? We cannot possibly know, unless we are familiar with the history of this couple. David's comment "Like life, huh?" could signify contempt for what he sees as Judy's simplistic approach to life. Or it could represent straightforward agreement. Interpretive difficulties abound in the coding of interpersonal interactions.

## ● ECOLOGICAL MOMENTARY ASSESSMENT

Recent advances in wireless connectivity have spawned an entirely new approach to assessment known as ecological momentary assessment (EMA). **Ecological momentary assessment** is defined as the "real-time measurement of patient experience in the real world, at the point of experience" (Shiffman, Hufford, & Paty, 2001). Consider the research problem of determining whether a new drug treatment is effective in ameliorating the severe pain of migraine headaches. Whereas previous research methods relied upon retrospective questionnaire reports of patients receiving a new drug treatment, an EMA approach instead would consist of patients reporting their instantaneous experiences on a handheld device, with responses immediately transmitted (via the same wireless technology used by cell phones) to a central computer for ultimate analysis with sophisticated software. For example, the handheld device might "beep" to signal that the patient should immediately respond (on a touch-sensitive screen) to a series of rating scales for pain, mood, fatigue, and other relevant dimensions. The entire self-rating procedure might take less than a minute. The ratings would be requested several times a day on a randomized schedule.

Because EMA responses of clients are immediate and based on a schedule determined by the researcher, several biases of human recall are avoided. For example, consider the biasing effects of saliency, in which emotionally charged events dominate recall. For instance, a very brief episode of severe migraine pain may be recalled as lasting much longer than the actual experience because of the emotional valence of the incident. Whereas a retrospective questionnaire report of this pain would be affected by the salience of the event, an EMA analysis, with periodic real-time sampling of the actual pain experiences, would provide a more accurate portrayal of the episode. Recency is another recall bias that is circumvented by EMA. The recency bias refers to the fact that people are more likely to recall recent events than remote events. Potentially, this could lead to underestimation of the therapeutic effects of a drug if retrospective recall coincided with the onset of symptoms. In contrast, with an EMA analysis, client reporting consists of periodic and instantaneous time samples; the results are relatively unaffected by the recency bias.

In general, EMA provides a more accurate and reliable approach to the assessment of patient experience than traditional approaches such as retrospective questionnaires. One advantage is that compliance cannot be faked (as when patients fill out a week's worth of daily questionnaires minutes before handing them in to the researcher). In fact, because EMA approaches are highly user friendly, researchers report an astonishing overall compliance of 93 to 99 percent averaged across many studies (Shiffman et al., 2001). EMA has been used in research into treatments for acute pain, alcoholism, arthritis, asthma, depression, eating disorders, headaches, hypertension, gastrointestinal disorders, schizophrenia, smoking, and urinary incontinence (Shiffman & Hufford, 2001; Shiffman, Hufford, Hickcox, and others, 1997; Smyth, Wonderlich, Crosby, and others, 2001). As EMA technology becomes streamlined and more affordable, we can expect this new technique to become commonplace in psychological outcome studies with human clients.

In addition to practical applications in health care research, the EMA methodology also can be used to test psychological theories, as illustrated by a recent study of emotions. Tong, Bishop, Enkelmann, and others (2005) enlisted the cooperation of 118 police officers in Singapore to wear an ambulatory blood pressure monitor during their work day. This device also beeped at random about every 30 minutes, a signal that the officer should fill out a simple 12-item questionnaire in a palmtop as soon as possible. The items, rated on 5-point scales, included topics such as:

- How pleasant is this event?
- To what extent are you getting what you expected?

- How much personal effort is needed to deal with it?
- How much control do you have over the event?

With practice, it would take less than a minute to fill out a questionnaire of this nature. Of course, the added advantage of the EMA approach is that data are collected in naturalistic settings in real time, and, therefore, not prone to biases in recall.

## ● SUMMARY

1. Theory-guided self-report inventories rely upon explicit personality theories for their development. A good example of a theory-guided inventory is Jackson's Personality Research Form (PRF), based upon Murray's need system. The 20 personality scales on the PRF possess no item overlap and show exceptional internal consistency (median of .92). PRF validity is buttressed by confirmatory factor analysis and appropriate correlations with similar scales on other instruments.

2. The Jenkins Activity Survey (JAS) is a 52-item multiple-choice questionnaire designed to identify the Type A coronary-prone behavior pattern. The three subscales include: Speed and Impatience, Job Involvement, and Hard-Driving and Competitiveness. The JAS has several limitations (e.g., unrepresentative norms, scoring complexities) and is, therefore, best suited to research.

3. The Eysenck Personality Questionnaire (EPQ) proposes three major factor-analytically derived dimensions of personality: Psychoticism, Extraversion, and Neuroticism. Scale reliabilities are quite strong and the construct validity of the instrument is supported by dozens of studies.

4. The Comrey Personality Scales embody a short self-report instrument suitable for college students. The eight CPS scales consist of 20 items

each and possess no overlap. The scales show excellent internal consistency. Extreme scores are especially predictive of psychological disturbance.

5. The MMPI-2 consists of 567 true-false questions. The test is scored for four validity scales (?, L, F, and K) that assess unanswered questions, naive defensiveness, deviant responses, and subtle defensiveness, respectively. The 10 clinical scales are Hypochondriasis, Depression, Hysteria, Psychopathic Deviate, Masculinity-Femininity, Paranoia, Psychasthenia, Schizophrenia, Hypomania, and Social Introversion.

6. The Millon Clinical Multiaxial Inventory, now in its third edition (MCMI-III) is a short test (175 true-false items) designed as an aid to psychiatric diagnosis. The 27 scales are organized into four broad categories relevant to *DSM-IV*: clinical personality patterns, severe personality pathology, clinical syndromes, and severe clinical syndromes.

7. Designed to provide clinically relevant descriptions of child behavior and family characteristics, the Personality Inventory for Children-2 (PIC-2) consists of 275 true-false statements that are completed by a parent or parental surrogate. The test is suitable for children 5 through 19 years of age and yields scores on 9 adjustment scales and 21 subscales.

**8.** Behavioral assessment concentrates on behavior itself rather than on underlying traits, hypothetical causes, or presumed dimensions of personality. Behavioral assessment is usually an integral part of behavior therapy designed to change the duration, frequency, or intensity of a well-defined target behavior.

**9.** One assessment approach useful in exposure-based methods of behavior therapy is the behavioral avoidance test (BAT), in which the therapist charts how long the client can tolerate the anxiety-inducing stimulus. Fear survey schedules, based upon self-ratings of commonly feared objects and situations, are also useful, but there are reasons to question their validity.

**10.** In contingency management, the therapist attempts to modify maladaptive behavior by identifying the reinforcing consequences and eliminating them. Conversely, adaptive behaviors can be strengthened by arranging for the delivery of rewards when these behaviors occur, such as in a token economy.

**11.** In cognitive behavior therapy, the therapist attempts to change the belief structure of the client. For example, Meichenbaum teaches clients to use coping self-statements (e.g., "You have a strategy . . . you can do it") to combat stressful situations.

**12.** An excellent index of depression—including the cognitive distortions—is the Beck Depression Inventory (BDI), which consists of 21 quartets of hierarchically ordered statements, each scored 0 to 3. The BDI is recognized as an excellent self-report index of depression and is extensively validated against external criteria.

**13.** Lewinsohn and his colleagues have published the Pleasant Events Schedule for self-monitoring the frequency and pleasantness of up to 320 largely ordinary, everyday behaviors. Depressed patients who increase their self-monitored frequency of pleasant events generally show improved mood.

**14.** Several structured interview schedules have been developed to reduce the time needed for psychiatric diagnosis and also to improve reliability. Respected instruments include the Schedule for Affective Disorders and Schizophrenia (SADS) and the Structured Clinical Interview for Diagnosis (SCID). Kappa coefficients of interrater agreement are variable but often exceed .85 for these instruments.

**15.** Assessment by systematic, direct observation often is used with children in school settings to document frequency and duration of specific behavior problems. In addition to individualized approaches, preconceived rating scales such as the Behavior Observation of Students in Schools (BOSS) also can be employed. A concern with direct observation approaches is the reactivity of measurement—the act of observation may change what the practitioner is hoping to assess.

**16.** In analogue behavioral assessment, clients are observed in a contrived but plausible setting and also are instructed to engage in relevant tasks designed to elicit behaviors of interest. For example, a couple might be asked to discuss a conflictual topic while being observed and rated on relevant dimensions with a tool such as the Rapid Couples Interaction Scoring System (RCISS).

**17.** Ecological momentary assessment is defined as real-time measurement of patient experience in the real world, at the point of experience. This is a relatively new approach to assessment that relies upon wireless interconnectivity to circumvent problems of retrospective report.

## ● KEY TERMS AND CONCEPTS

extraversion    p. 347

introversion    p. 347

behavioral assessment    p. 357

behavior therapy    p. 357

behavioral avoidance test    p. 359

fear survey schedule    p. 359

cognitive behavior therapy    p. 360

self-monitoring    p. 363

kappa    p. 365

observer drift    p. 367

coding complexity    p. 367

analogue behavioral assessment    p. 368

ecological momentary assessment    p. 369

# Chapter 9

# Assessment of Normality and Human Strengths

In the previous chapter we surveyed tests used by psychologists to evaluate clients for a range of symptoms and life difficulties. These instruments included the mainstays of the profession such as the MMPI-2, MCMI-III, Rorschach, and TAT. Such tests might be referred to as "clinical" in nature, because they are well suited to the needs of clinical practice. But what are practitioners to do if they want to evaluate someone who is reasonably normal? In other words, assessment does not always entail delving into symptoms, distress level, defense mechanisms, diagnosis, and the like. One

example might be a young executive who wants to know about "growth edges" in regard to leadership positions. Another example might be a college student who desires self-knowledge as part of vocational explorations.

Even though clinical tests such as those surveyed in the previous chapter can be employed within the normal spectrum, they do not excel in this application. In fact, the evaluation of normal personality was not the original purpose of tests such as the MMPI or the Rorschach. For example, the initial objective of the MMPI-2 was the diagnosis of psychopathology, which remains the most dominant and effective application of the instrument. Historically, the purpose of the Rorschach has been described by Frank (1939) and others as providing an "X-ray of the mind" to identify themes hidden away from ordinary observation. Currently, the most common application of the test is with clients who display complex psychological symptoms that do not fit neatly into the categories of the Diagnostic and Statistical Manual of Mental Disorders, Fourth Edition (DSM-IV).

When a practitioner wants to assess personality within the normal spectrum, tests designed expressly for that purpose typically provide a more helpful perspective than instruments developed from the standpoint of psychopathology. Instead of measuring concepts such as depression, paranoia, anxiety, narcissism, or suicide potential, the focus in these alternative instruments is on qualities pertinent to the normal range of human functioning. We are referring here to features like responsibility, social presence, intuition, locus of control, attachment style, or faith maturity. This chapter investigates an assortment of instruments suitable for assessment within the normal continuum and beyond.

Normality differs from abnormality by shades of gray rather than revealing a sharp demarcation (Offer & Sabshin, 1966). Understanding the various definitions of normality would involve a lengthy detour; we do not pursue the topic here. In their comprehensive textbook of psychiatry, Sadock and Sadock (2004) provide an excellent overview. Our goal here is to focus on useful tests and measures, including some that have been neglected because of the emphasis on psychopathology within the field of clinical psychology.

In Topic 9A, Assessment Within the Normal Spectrum, we explore the qualities of several tests and discuss their strengths and weaknesses. We feature a few widely used scales in this topic, including the venerable Myers-Briggs Type Indicator (Myers & McCaulley, 1985), one of the most widely employed personality tests of all time, and the California Psychological Inventory (Gough & Bradley, 1996), a measure with strong empirical roots.

Other forms of assessment pertinent to the normal spectrum of adult functioning also are covered in Topic 9A. We are referring here to the evaluation of spiritual, religious, and moral constructs. Also, the assessment of attitudes in the general population is introduced here. These specialized forms of assessment have received an increasing amount of attention in recent years.

In Topic 9B, Positive Psychological Assessment, we examine a number of relatively new scales that have emerged in response to a reawakening of interest in human potential, an interest that has remained largely dormant in psychology since the early 1900s (Seligman & Csikszentmihalyi, 2000). A special focus in this topic is the assessment of creativity.

## ● BROAD BAND TESTS OF NORMAL PERSONALITY

A broad band test is one that measures the full range of functioning, as opposed to limited aspects. Beginning in the 1940s, researchers sought to capture the nuances of normal personality by developing broad-band self-report instruments. The sheer variety of approaches to this task is a testament to the complexity of human functioning. An enduring question, related to the previous topic on theories of personality, is how best to conceptualize the multifaceted notion of personality. For example, is personality best construed as a limited number of types, with most people resembling one type or another with reasonable precision? Or, is personality best interpreted as several dimensions, with each unique individual revealing a specific level of each dimension? If a dimensional approach is preferred, how many dimensions are needed to describe the array of human responses: five, sixteen, twenty—or more?

There are no definitive answers to these questions, although dimensional approaches generally have prevailed over typological methods in the history of test development. Even so, useful and popular typological approaches do exist. In fact, we begin the discussion of broad-band tests with an instrument that flexibly permits both a typological and a dimensional approach to the understanding of normal personality.

## ● MYERS-BRIGGS TYPE INDICATOR (MBTI)

Originally published in 1962, the MBTI is a forced-choice, self-report inventory that attempts to classify persons according to an adaptation of Carl Jung's theory of personality types (Myers & McCaulley, 1985; Tzeng, Ware, & Chen, 1989). As discussed below, recent adaptations of the test also provide dimensional scores in addition to the well-known four-letter typological codes.

According to the publisher, the MBTI is the most widely used individual test in history, taken by approximately 2 million people a year. Proponents of the instrument deem it valuable in vocational guidance and organizational consulting. It comes in a number of versions, including Form M, a 93-item test which can be purchased by qualified psychologists in a self-scoring paper-and-pencil format, or administered on-line. Other forms such as the 126-item Form G and the 144-item Form Q are available on-line and must be authorized by a psychologist who has agreed to a licensing arrangement with the publisher, Consulting Psychologists Press (www.cpp.com).

Regardless of the version employed, the MBTI is scored on four theoretically independent polarities: Extraversion-Introversion, Sensing-iNtuition, Thinking-Feeling, and Judging-Perceiving. The test-taker is categorized on one side or the other of each polarity, which results in a four-letter code such as ENTJ (Extraversion, iNtuition, Thinking, Judging). Because there are two poles to each of the four dimensions, this allows for $2^4$ or 16 different personality types. Each of the 16 types has been studied extensively over the years.

The four polarities (E-I, S-N, T-F, J-P) do not necessarily correspond to common understandings of the anchor terms and hence require some explanation. It is also important to note that the concepts are intended to be value-neutral and merely descriptive. Thus, it is neither better nor worse to manifest Extraversion or Introversion. Likewise, Thinking and Feeling are simply different modalities and one is not better than the other, and so forth. The opposite ends of each polarity are simply different modes of being that may have a variety of implications for relationships, vocation, leadership, and personal functioning. Possessing the qualities of one polarity or the other may be advantageous (or not) in different situations.

Extraversion-Introversion is probably the easiest to describe. An extravert (E) directs energy outward to people and conversations, whereas an introvert (I) directs energy inward to his or her inner world. A note of clarification: The MBTI retains the original spelling of Extraversion, preferred by Jung, instead of using the synonymous concept of Extroversion, preferred by contemporary psychologists. Sensing-iNtuition involves two opposite ways of perceiving. Those who prefer sensing (S) rely on the immediate senses, whereas those who prefer intuition (N) rely upon "relationships and/or possibilities that have been worked out beyond the reach of the conscious mind (Myers & McCaulley, 1985)." Of course, the letter N is used to designate intuition because the letter I already is taken to label Introversion. Thinking-Feeling refers to basing conclusions on thinking (T), that is, logic and objectivity, as opposed to feeling (F), which involves a reliance on personal values and social harmony. Finally, Judging-Perceiving indicates a preference for decisiveness and closure (J) or an open-ended flexibility and spontaneity (P). Whereas in common parlance the notion of "judging" often has a negative connotation, this is not the case when the term is applied to this polarity of the MBTI.

The 16 possible four-letter types are not equally represented in the general population, and some types are more common in specific occupational groups. For example, in a sample of 231 education graduate students from a Midwestern university, the ENFP type was by far the most common ($N = 43$), followed by ENFJ ($N = 28$) in frequency. Codes beginning with the letter E (Extraversion) constituted nearly two-thirds of this sample, which highlights the importance of Extraversion in the field of education. Paraphrasing from Myers and McCaulley (1985, p. 78), the work expectations for someone who embodies the ENFP type are as follows:

- prefers to work interactively with a succession of people away from the desk
- likes to work with a succession of new problems to be solved
- prefers to provide service that is appreciated
- likes to work in changing situations that require adaptation

These qualities align well with the role expectations for people heading into the field of education.

Standardization data for the MBTI is extensive and based on large samples collected over many decades (Myers & McCaulley, 1985). One particularly useful table is a list of occupations empirically attractive to the sixteen types. For example, 18% of attorneys are INTJ in type, whereas only 2% of elementary school teachers fit this code. This is useful information for clients who take the test in search of personal or career guidance. Split-half reliabilities for the four scales are in the .80s for the combined subject pool of nearly 56,000 participants. Test-retest reliabilities for the four scales are somewhat lower and depend on the interval between tests. When the interval is short, on the order of a few weeks, results are strong, with coefficients mainly in the .70s and higher. Yet, when the interval is longer, on the order of several years, the coefficients are predictably lower, in the .40s and .50s. With regard to reliability, an important question with the MBTI is the stability of the four letter code from test to retest. The test manual reports on a dozen studies of code type stability, with retest intervals ranging from 5 weeks to 5 years (most intervals a year or two). On average, about 41 percent of examinees retained their identical code type, that is, all four letters of the code remained the same from test to retest. About 38 percent of examinees remained stable on three of the four letters, that is, one letter changed for them. About 17 percent of examinees retained two

of their four letters, but switched on the other two. And, 3 percent retained only one letter, switching on the other three. Overall, these are impressive results as to the long-term stability of the MBTI code types.

In a review of 17 studies reporting reliability coefficients, Capraro and Capraro (2002) found respectably strong reliability coefficients of .84 (E-I), .84 (S-N), .67 (T-F), and .82 (J-P). Salter, Forney, and Evans (2005) conducted an especially rigorous evaluation of MBTI reliability, looking at the stability of MBTI categories across three administrations with 231 graduate students in education. The three administrations were at the beginning of the first year, beginning of the second year, and end of the second year. Their report included extensive analyses, but of interest here is the percentage of respondents who received the same classification (e.g., Extraversion or Introversion) on all three occasions. The percentage who displayed complete consistency for each dimension was as follows:

- E-I    67%
- S-N    66%
- T-F    69%
- J-P    71%

Given the stringency of the reliability approach (agreement across three administrations), these are respectable findings.

More than 400 references citing the MBTI were found in PsychINFO from 2000 to 2009, many pertaining to the validity of the instrument. For example, in a study of 177 managers, Higgs (2001) reported a significant relationship between emotional intelligence and the dominant MBTI function of iNtuition. Emotional intelligence is monitoring emotions of self and others and using this information to guide thinking and actions (Mayer & Salovey, 1993). A positive relationship with MBTI iNtuition is strong support for the validity of this dimension.

Another recent study also provides support for the validity of the polarities assessed by the MBTI. Furnham, Moutafi, and Crump (2003) tested 900 adults with two instruments: the MBTI and the Revised NEO-Personality Inventory (NEO-PI-R, Costa & McCrae, 1992). The NEO-PI-R is a well validated measure of personality that evaluates five factors of personality known as the "big five." These factors are Neuroticism, Extraversion, Openness (to experience), Agreeableness, and Conscientiousness. As predicted by the authors, the MBTI dimensions revealed healthy and appropriate correlations with corresponding factors from the NEO-PI-R. Specifically, the following averaged concurrent validity correlations were found between the MBTI dimensions and the NEO-PI-R scales: E-I correlated .71 with Extraversion; S-N correlated -.65 with Openness; T-F correlated -.35 with Agreeableness; and, J-P correlated .46 with Conscientiousness. The negative correlations indicate an inverse relationship, that is, those categorized as S (Sensing) on the MBTI obtained low scores on Openness, whereas those categorized as N (iNtuition) obtained high scores on Openness. In like manner a T or Thinking type tended to obtain low scores on Agreeableness whereas an F or Feeling type tended to obtain high scores. All of these correlations are consistent with theoretical understandings of the MBTI and hence buttress the validity of the instrument.

As mentioned, recent versions of the MBTI yield additional information beyond the four-letter typological classification. For example, the 144-item form Q, available on-line, provides a highly detailed and sophisticated summary report that partitions each of the four polarities into five facet scores. Hence the report includes a total of 20 facet scores in addition to the four-letter code. For example, the Thinking-Feeling dimension includes bipolar facets such as Logical-Empathetic, Reasonable-Compassionate, and Tough-Tender. The dimensions and facets of this version of the MBTI are displayed in Table 9.1. The report includes not only the typological classifications (e.g., T or F) but also a rating for each bipolar facet on an 11-point continuum. This kind of nuanced dimensional information appeals to many users.

One concern about the MBTI is that the increasing cost of administering the instrument—in

● **TABLE 9.1    Dimensions and Facets of the MBTI, Form Q**

| **Extraversion (E)** | **(I) Introversion** |
|---|---|
| Initiating | Receiving |
| Expressive | Contained |
| Gregarious | Intimate |
| Active | Reflective |
| Enthusiastic | Quiet |
| **Sensing (S)** | **(N) Intuition** |
| Concrete | Abstract |
| Realistic | Imaginative |
| Practical | Conceptual |
| Experiential | Theoretical |
| Traditional | Original |
| **Thinking (T)** | **(F) Feeling** |
| Logical | Empathetic |
| Reasonable | Compassionate |
| Questioning | Accommodating |
| Critical | Accepting |
| Tough | Tender |
| **Judging (J)** | **(P) Perceiving** |
| Systematic | Casual |
| Planful | Open-Ended |
| Early Starting | Pressure-Prompted |
| Scheduled | Spontaneous |
| Methodical | Emergent |

the range of ten to thirty dollars per individual— provides a disincentive for outside researchers who want to conduct reliability or validity studies. This is an issue not only for the MBTI but also for the most widely used contemporary tests. Understandably, test publishers want to profit from their massive and expensive efforts at test development. But the downside is that scholarly researchers need substantial funding if they desire to administer newer versions of the MBTI to large samples of examinees. Partly in reaction to the paucity of independent research on newer versions of this test, reviewers continue to suggest caution in its use, especially when making simplistic inferences from the 4-letter type formulas (Pittenger, 2005).

## ● CALIFORNIA PSYCHOLOGICAL INVENTORY (CPI)

Originally published in 1957, the CPI is a true-false test designed expressly to measure the dimensions of normal personality (Gough & Bradley, 1996; McAllister, 1988). The instrument is available in two forms, the CPI-434 (Gough, 1995) and the CPI-260 (www.skillsone.com) which is available only online. The component scales and the interpretive strategies are nearly identical for the two versions, which differ mainly in the number of items—434 versus 260. Psychometric properties of both versions are similar and strong. Because of its ease of administration and the immediacy with which the practitioner receives an extensive computer-generated report, the CPI-260 rapidly is gaining favor among psychological practitioners.

The CPI-260 is scored for 20 folk measures of personality, 7 work-related scales, and 3 broad vectors. The purpose of the test is to provide a clear picture of the examinee by using descriptors based on the ordinary language of everyday life (Gough & Bradley, 1996). Three of the basic personality scales also provide information on test-taking attitudes and therefore function as validity scales. These scales are Good Impression (Gi) which assesses the extent to which the individual presents a favorable image to others, Communality (Cm) which measures unusual responses that might arise from carelessness or faking bad, and Well-being (Wb) which gauges the portrayal of serious emotional problems.

The 20 folk measures and 7 work-related scales are listed and briefly described in Table 9.2. These scales are reported as *T*-scores normed to a mean of 50 and a standard deviation of 10 in the general population. The test developers used an empirical methodology of criterion-keying to develop the majority of the scales. Specifically, extreme groups of participants (mainly college students) were formed on such scale-relevant criteria as school grades, sociability, and participation in curricular activities. Item-endorsement frequencies were then contrasted to ferret out the best statements for each scale. For example, the Sociability (Sy)

scale was constructed by contrasting item-endorsement rates for persons reporting a large number of social activities versus those reporting few or no social activities. In constructing four of the folk scales, the authors used a rational basis backed up by indices of internal consistency.

Reflecting the care with which the scales were constructed, reliability data for the CPI are respectable. Most alpha coefficients are in the .70s and .80s, with a median value of .76. The test-retest reliability coefficients tend to be somewhat lower, with a median retest correlation of .68. The authors provide a wealth of normative data, including average test scores for 52 samples of males and 42 samples of females, subdivided by education, occupation, college major, gender, and other variables. The basic normative sample consists of 3,000 males and 3,000 females of varying age, social class, and geographic region (Gough & Bradley, 1996).

In addition to the wealth of information provided by the individual scale scores, the CPI also is scored on three broad dimensions or vectors derived from decades of factor-analytic studies with the instrument. The three vectors include two basic orientations and a third theme reflecting ego integration. The first basic orientation called vector 1 or v.1 has two polarities: toward people or toward one's inner life. This vector is similar to the extraversion-introversion dimension found in nearly every personality theory ever proposed. The second basic orientation or v.2 also has two polarities: rule-favoring or rule-questioning. This vector reflects a conventional-unconventional dimension also found in many studies. These first two bipolar orientations, v.1 and v.2, provide a 2 × 2 typology of four lifestyles termed the Implementer, Supporter, Innovator, and Visualizer lifestyles, described below. The third vector or v.3 assesses a 7-point continuum variously referred to as self-realization, psychological competence, or ego integration. In the client feedback report provided by the publisher, v.3 is referred to as Level of Satisfaction and scored 1 (low) to 7 (high). This vector acts as a moderator for each of the lifestyles, with high scores on v.3 leading to a positive expression and low scores leading to a negative expression.

● TABLE 9.2   **Brief Description of Standard and Work-Related CPI-260 Scales**

|  | *Standard Scales* | *Common Interpretation of High Score* |
|---|---|---|
| Do | Dominance | dominant, persistent, good leadership ability |
| Cs | Capacity for Status | personal qualities that underlie and lead to status |
| Sy | Sociability | outgoing, sociable, participative temperament |
| Sp | Social Presence | poise, spontaneity, and self-confidence in social situations |
| Sa | Self-acceptance | self-acceptance and sense of personal worth |
| In | Independence | high sense of personal independence, not easily influenced |
| Em | Empathy | good capacity to empathize with other persons |
| Re | Responsibility | conscientious, responsible, and dependable |
| So | Social Conformity | strong social maturity and high integrity |
| Sc | Self-control | good self-control, freedom from impulsivity and self-centeredness |
| Gi | Good Impression | concerned about creating a good impression |
| Cm | Communality | valid and thoughtful response pattern |
| Wb | Sense of Well-being | not worrying or complaining, free from self doubt |
| To | Tolerance | permissive, accepting, and nonjudgmental social beliefs |
| Ac | Achievement via Conformance | achieves well in settings where conformance is necessary |
| Ai | Achievement via Independence | achieves well in settings where independence is necessary |
| Cf | Conceptual fluency | high degree of personal and intellectual efficiency |
| Is | Insightfulness | interested in and responsive to the inner needs, motives, and experiences of others |
| Fx | Flexibility | flexible and adaptable in thought and social behavior |
| Sn | Sensitivity | sensitive to others' feelings, personally vulnerable |
|  | *Work-Related Scales* | *Common Interpretation of High Score* |
| Mp | Managerial Potential | good judgment, effective at dealing with people |
| Wo | Work Orientation | strong work ethic, rarely complains about work |
| Ct | Creative Temperament | creative thinker who prefers what is new or different |
| Lp | Leadership | strong leadership skills, deals well with stress |
| Ami | Amicability | collegial and cooperative, a good team player |
| Leo | Law Enforcement Orientation | practical, well suited to work in law enforcement |

*Source:* Based on Gough, H. G. and Bradley, P. (1996). *CPI Manual* (3rd ed.). Mountain View, CA: Consulting Psychologists Press. Also, Megargee, E. (1972). *The California Psychological Inventory handbook.* San Francisco: Jossey-Bass; and McAllister, L. (1988). *A Practical Guide to CPI Interpretation.* Palo Alto, CA: Consulting Psychologists Press.

Results from several correlational studies confirm distinctive psychological portraits for the four lifestyles mentioned above (Gough & Bradley, 1996). Briefly, the four life styles are as follows:

- Implementers (extroverted and rule-favoring) tend to do well in managerial and leadership roles.

- Supporters (introverted and rule-favoring) function well in supportive or ancillary positions.
- Innovators (extroverted and rule-questioning) are adept at creating change.
- Visualizers (introverted and rule-questioning) work best alone in fields such as art or literature.

The CPI Manual provides a wealth of information about each lifestyle, including adjective correlates obtained from spouses, peers, and professional evaluators. From these empirical sources, a clear portrait of each lifestyle emerges. For example, the summary statement for Innovators is as follows:

> Gammas attend to and seek the monetary, prestige, and other rewards offered by society, but are often at odds with the culture concerning the criteria by which these rewards are apportioned. Their values are personal and individual, not traditional or conventional. Gammas [Innovators] are the doubters, the skeptics, those who see and resist the arbitrary and unjustified features of the status quo. At their best, they are innovative and insightful creators of new ideas, new products, and new social forms. At their worst, they are rebellious, intolerant, self-indulgent, and disruptive; and at low levels on the v.3 scale, they often behave in wayward, rule-violating, and narcissistic ways. (Gough & Bradley, 1996, p. 50)

The reader will notice that the third vector, v.3, moderates the expression of the Implementer lifestyle, for better or for worse. When v.3 is high, the Implementer is innovative and insightful. When v.3 is low, the Implementer is wayward and narcissistic. A similar pattern holds true for the other three lifestyles—each can have a positive or negative expression, depending on the level of personal integration reflected on the v.3 scale.

The CPI is heir to a long history of empirical research that substantiates a number of real-world correlates for distinctive test profiles. Due to space limitations, we can only list several prominent areas in which the value of the test has been empirically confirmed. The CPI is useful for helping predict the following:

- Psychological and physical health
- High school and college achievement
- Effectiveness of student-teachers
- Effectiveness of police and military personnel
- Leadership and management success

The CPI is particularly effective at identifying adolescents or adults who follow a delinquent or criminal lifestyle. For example, Gough and Bradley (1992) studied a sample of 672 delinquent or criminal men and women, contrasting their CPI scale scores with a large sample of controls. Of the 27 scales evaluated, they found significant mean differences on 25 for men and 26 for women. The most discriminating scale was Social Conformity (So), which revealed healthy point-biserial correlations of .54 for men and .58 for women. They also found that low scores on v.3 (a measure of ego integration) were associated with greater incidence of delinquency. The reader can find further details on the real-world empirical correlates of CPI profiles in Groth-Marnat (2003) and Hargrave and Hiatt (1989).

## ● NEO PERSONALITY INVENTORY-REVISED (NEO PI-R)

The NEO Personality Inventory-Revised (NEO PI-R) embodies decades of factor-analytic research with clinical and normal adult populations (Costa & McCrae, 1992). The test is based upon the five-factor model of personality described in the previous chapter. It is available in two parallel forms consisting of 240 items rated on a five-point dimension. An additional three items are used to check validity. A shorter version, the NEO Five-Factor Inventory (NEO-FFI) is also available (Costa & McCrae, 1989). We limit our discussion to the NEO PI-R. Form S is for self-reports whereas Form R is for outside observers (e.g., the spouse of a client). The item format consists of five-point ratings: strongly disagree, disagree, neutral, agree, strongly agree. The items assess emotional, interpersonal, experiential, attitudinal, and motivational variables.

The five domain scales of the NEO PI-R are each based upon six facet (trait) scales (Table 9.3). The internal consistency of the scales is superb: .86 to .95 for the domain scales, and .56 to .90 for the facet scales. Stability coefficients range from .51 to .83 in three- to seven-year longitudinal studies. Validity evidence for the NEO PI-R is substantial, based on the correspondence of ratings between

| ● TABLE 9.3 | Domain and Facet (Trait) Scales of the NEO PI-R ● | |
|---|---|---|
| *Domains* | *Facets* | |
| Neuroticism | Anxiety | Self-Consciousness |
| | Angry Hostility | Impulsiveness |
| | Depression | Vulnerability |
| Extraversion | Warmth | Activity |
| | Gregariousness | Excitement Seeking |
| | Assertiveness | Positive Emotions |
| Openness to Experience | Fantasy | Actions |
| | Aesthetics | Ideas |
| | Feelings | Values |
| Agreeableness | Trust | Compliance |
| | Straightforwardness | Modesty |
| | Altruism | Tender-Mindednesss |
| Conscientiousness | Competence | Achievement Striving |
| | Order | Self-Discipline |
| | Dutifulness | Deliberationn |

self and spouse, correlations with other tests and checklists, and the construct validity of the five-factor model itself (Costa & McCrae, 1992; Piedmont & Weinstein, 1993; Trull, Useda, Costa, & McCrae, 1995).

The NEO PI-R is an excellent measure of personality that is especially useful in research. Rubenzer, Faschingbauer, and Ones (2000) describe a particularly fascinating research project with the test in which all U.S. presidents were evaluated by 115 highly informed, expert presidential biographers who filled out the NEO PI-R on behalf of the presidents, from George Washington through George H. W. Bush. The authors developed a typology of presidents from the data and related facets of the test to presidential success (i.e., historical greatness). They also published individual presidential profiles, such as the following results for George Washington (50 is average in the general population):

| Neuroticism | 47 |
| Extraversion | 44 |
| Openness | 39 |
| Agreeableness | 40 |
| Conscientiousness | 72 |

The portrait that emerges is of a leader who is well-adjusted, slightly introverted, not particularly open to experience, markedly disagreeable, and extremely conscientious. After reviewing the specific facet scores (see Table 9.3), the authors concluded that Washington "falls quite short of the modern political commodities of warmth, empathy, and open-mindedness."

The test also shows promise as a measure of clinical psychopathology. For example, Clarkin, Hull, Cantor, and Sanderson (1993) found that patients diagnosed with borderline personality disorder scored very high on Neuroticism and very low on Agreeableness, which resonates strongly with every clinician's response to these challenging patients. Ranseen, Campbell, and Baer (1998) determined that 25 adults with attention deficit disorder scored significantly higher than controls in the Neuroticism domain and significantly lower in the Conscientiousness domain, demonstrating the usefulness of the NEO PI-R in understanding attention deficit disorders in adulthood. One minor concern about the instrument is that it lacks substantial validity scales— only three items assess validity. The administration of the NEO PI-R assumes that subjects are cooperative and reasonably honest. This is usually a safe assumption in research settings but may not hold true in forensic, personnel, or psychiatric settings.

For purposes of education and research, several psychometricians have constructed websites where it is possible to self-administer an equivalent version of the NEO PI-R. Although not identical to the commercial version of the test (Costa & McCrae, 1992), these parallel adaptations do provide estimates of examinee standing on the five broad domains and 30 subdomains of personality tested by the NEO PI-R and also provide useful narrative reports. One such site can be found at www.personalitytest.com. Another useful site is available at http://ipip.ori.org. This location hosts the International Personality Item Pool (IPIP), advertised as a "scientific collaboratory for the development of advanced measures of personality and other individual differences." The term **collaboratory** was coined by Finholt and Olson (1997) to describe Internet-based arrangements that facilitate the collaboration of test specialists, regardless of geographical location. For example, the specific mission of IPIP is to bring test development into the public domain and serve as a forum for the dissemination of research findings and psychometric developments.

Recently, the developers of the NEO-PI-R produced a new version that is more readable and therefore better suited to students as young as twelve years of age. The NEO-PI-3 is a careful and modest revision of the original instrument that addresses a number of problematic items difficult for adolescents and young adults to comprehend (McCrae, Costa, & Martin, 2005). As noted above, the NEO-PI-R consists of 240 items rated on a 5-point Likert scale from *Strongly Agree* to *Strongly Disagree*. The authors identified 30 items using words on a par with *laissez-faire, fastidious,* and *adhere* that even adults might find challenging. The authors rewrote these items for transparency and carefully tested them for equivalence in a new sample of 500 respondents. Three illustrations of old items and replacement items (in boldface) are show below. These are representative only, not the actual items and revisions:

1. I feel angst about the future.
1. **I feel nervous about the future.**
2. I think of myself as laissez-faire.
2. **I think of myself as easy-going.**
3. I enjoy situations of raucous hilarity.
4. **I like to laugh.**

An additional 18 items were rewritten because they revealed low item-total correlations with the facet (trait) scale to which they belonged. The resulting instruments, the NEO-PI-3 retained the original five-factor structure and revealed better internal consistency and readability than the previous version. In sum, the authors improved their test, especially for applications with adolescent and college-aged clients (Costa, McCrae, & Martin, 2008).

## ● SIXTEEN PERSONALITY FACTOR QUESTIONNAIRE (16PF)

The 16PF is a widely used forced-choice test of personality that is currently available in five separate forms. Each form consists of declarative stems that require the examinee to respond to a specific situation by choosing from among two (Form E) or three forced-choice options (Forms A, B, C, and D). Examples of 16PF-like items include the following:

I make decisions based on
   (a) feelings
   (b) feelings and reason equally
   (c) reason
Which of the following items is different from the others?
   (a) candle
   (b) star
   (c) lightbulb
I find it hard to give a speech to strangers.
   (a) yes
   (b) somewhat
   (c) no

The forms contain from 105 to 187 items and differ mainly in reading level (from third-grade to seventh-grade level). The test is untimed and is usually completed in 30 to 60 minutes.

The inclusion of what appear to be intelligence test items in the 16PF may seem curious to the reader. In fact, psychologists have long recognized that personality and intelligence are complexly intertwined. Most test builders have addressed this quandary by attempting to tease personality and intelligence apart. Cattell decided instead to exploit the overlaps between personality and intelligence by including elements of both in the same test.

The 16PF is intended for high school seniors and adults. Most norms date back to 1970, a significant shortcoming of this test. However, Form E has been recently normed for highly diverse populations, including prison inmates, patients with schizophrenia, culturally disadvantaged individuals, and physical rehabilitation clients. Nonetheless, most practitioners would concede that the 16PF is more suited to a "normal" rather than an "emotionally disturbed" population. The 16PF also is useful for cross-cultural applications (e.g., Argentero, 1989).

The 16PF is predicated on Cattell's factor-analytic conception of personality (Cattell, Eber, & Tatsuoka, 1970). According to this model, surface traits—the more obvious aspects of personality—emerge from simple cluster analyses of test responses. In contrast, source traits—the stable, constant, but less-visible wellsprings of behavior—emerge only from specialized factor analyses of the surface traits (Cattell, 1950). In a series of studies, Cattell determined that 16 personality factors or source traits are needed to explain the structure of test responses, hence the name for his instrument.

The 16PF yields a total of 20 indices or attributes of personality. In addition to the 16 basic scales, four second-order indices of personality are computed from weighted linear sums of the previous 16 indices, yielding a total of 20 bipolar scales. Over the years, the meaning of extreme scores in either direction has been well established (Table 9.4).

The major thrust of application for the 16PF is career guidance, vocational exploration, and occupational testing. One reason for the popularity of the instrument—it is second in use only to the MMPI/MMPI-2—is that answer sheets can be mailed in for quick-turnaround machine scoring. Most practitioners also request a computer-generated narrative report. An attractive feature of these reports is the wealth of information provided. Reports include a capsule personality description, score profile, and summary of clinical signs, cognitive factors, and need patterns.

A major shortcoming of the 16PF is that the 16 surveyed personality attributes are based upon as few as 10 to 13 items each. Inevitably, a test with scales as short as these will possess diminished reliability. Not surprisingly, the split-half reliabilities of the 16 factors are as low as .54; correlations between the same scales for different forms of the test typically hover around .50; and test-retest coefficients for scales on the same form are .70 to .80 for same or next-day administrations but much lower for longer intervals.

Most of the validity evidence for the 16PF consists of statistical demonstrations that items "belong" on their respective scales and that the scales consist of relatively pure factors. The evidence in this regard is reasonably encouraging (Cattell, Eber, & Tatsuoka, 1970). In addition, some studies with the 16PF demonstrate that the real-world correlates of test results are theory-consistent. For example, Cattell and Nesselroade (1967) studied the similarity of 16PF profiles in 102 stably and 37 unstably married couples. These authors discovered that stably married couples are much more similar on the 16PF than unstably married couples. In particular, for stably married couples ($N = 102$) the scale correlations were almost uniformly positive—meaning that husband and wife produced similar scores on the individual scales of the 16PF. In contrast, the scale correlations for unstably married couples ($N = 37$) tended to be negative—meaning that husband and wife were inclined to produce scores at opposite ends of the continuum on the individual scales of the 16PF. For example, on the 16PF Warmth scale, the correlation for the unstably married couples was $r = -.51$, meaning that

● TABLE 9.4   **The 16 Personality Factors and Four Second-Order Indices from the 16PF**

| Factor Name | Interpretation of Low Score | Interpretation of High Score |
|---|---|---|
| Warmth | reserved, detached, cool, impersonal | warm, outgoing, likes people |
| Intelligence | concrete thinking | abstract thinking, bright |
| Emotional Stability | emotionally less stable, changeable | emotionally stable, calm, mature |
| Dominance | submissive, conforming, mild | dominant, assertive, competitive |
| Impulsivity | serious, prudent, sober, taciturn | enthusiastic, cheerful, heedless |
| Conformity | expedient, disregards rules | conforming, persevering, moralistic |
| Boldness | shy, timid, restrained | bold, uninhibited, spontaneous |
| Sensitivity | tough-minded, self-reliant | tender-minded, sensitive |
| Suspiciousness | trusting, adaptable | suspicious, hard to fool, opinionated |
| Imagination | practical, conventional | impractical, absent-minded, unconventional |
| Shrewdness | forthright, genuine, unpretentious | calculating, polished, socially alert |
| Insecurity | confident, self-satisfied, secure | self-blaming, worrying, troubled |
| Radicalism | conservative, resisting change | liberal, analytical, innovative |
| Self-sufficiency | group-oriented, sociable | resourceful, self-sufficient |
| Self-discipline | undisciplined, impulsive | compulsive, socially precise |
| Tension | relaxed, tranquil, low drive | frustrated, driven, tense |
| Extraversion ($Q_I$) | introversion | extraversion |
| Anxiety ($Q_{II}$) | low anxiety | high anxiety |
| Tough Poise ($Q_{III}$) | sensitivity, emotionalism | tough poise |
| Independence ($Q_{IV}$) | dependence | independence |

*Source:* Based on Wholeben, B. E. (1987). Sixteen Personality Factor Questionnaire. In D. J. Keyser & R. C. Sweetland (Eds.), *Test critiques compendium.* Kansas City, MO: Test Corporation of America. Also, Cattell, R. B. (1986). *The handbook for the 16 Personality Factor Questionnaire.* Champaign, IL: Institute for Personality and Ability Testing.

partners tend to be at odds on this variable—one was warm while the other was cold. Other notable negative correlations for this group were found for Impulsivity ($r = -.40$), Suspiciousness ($r = -.33$), Self-Sufficiency ($r = -.32$), and Extraversion ($r = -.30$). These findings support the viewpoint that dissimilarity in personality produces unstable marriages, whereas likeness facilitates stable marriages. The results bolster the validity of the 16PF by showing that test results carry meaningful and predictable real-world implications. In a similar vein, Hartung, Borges, and Jones (2005) found that 16PF results can be used with first-year medical students to predict their subsequent specialization. Individual 16PF results from the first year were found roughly to match the average profiles for doctors in the specialty areas ultimately chosen—that is, individual test results revealed moderate predictive validity.

A recent study by Rossier, de Stadelhofen, and Berthoud (2004) sheds new light on the validity of the 16PF. These authors conducted a series of correlations and regressions with test data from the 16PF and the NEO PI-R for 386 adult volunteers from the general population. With one exception, these two inventories were found to measure the same aspects of personality. The reader will recall that the NEO PI-R measures five factors of personality: Neuroticism, Extroversion, Openness to Experience, Conscientiousness, and Agreeableness. The 16PF was found to provide parallel results for four of these five factors, which overall speaks well to its validity. The exception was Agreeableness, which did not emerge as a separate dimension on the 16PF. Apparently, few of the items on the 16PF tap this aspect of functioning, which is a possible weakness of the instrument.

# ● THE ASSESSMENT OF MORAL JUDGMENT

## The Moral Judgment Scale

Kohlberg has proposed one of the few theories of moral development that is both comprehensive and empirically based (Colby, Kohlberg, Gibbs, & Lieberman, 1983; Kohlberg, 1958, 1981, 1984; Kohlberg & Kramer, 1969). Although he was more concerned with theory-based problems of moral development than with the nuances of standardized measurement, Kohlberg did generate a method of assessment that is widely used and intensely debated. We will review the underlying rationale for his measurement tool and discuss the psychometric properties of the instrument as well. In addition, we will take a brief look at a more objectively based adaptation of Kohlberg's approach known as the Defining Issues Test (Rest, 1979, Rest & Thoma, 1985).

## Stages of Moral Development

Kohlberg's theory grew out of Piaget's (1932) stage theory of moral development in childhood. Kohlberg extended the stages into adolescence and adulthood. In order to explore reasoning about difficult moral issues, he devised a series of **moral dilemmas.** One of the most famous is the dilemma of Heinz and the druggist:

> In Europe, a woman was near death from a special kind of cancer. There was one drug that the doctors thought might save her. It was a form of radium that a druggist in the same town had recently discovered. The drug was expensive to make, but the druggist was charging ten times what the drug cost him to make. He paid $200 for the radium and charged $2000 for a small dose of the drug. The sick woman's husband, Heinz, went to everyone he knew to borrow the money, but he could only get together about $1000 which is half of what it cost. He told the druggist that his wife was dying, and asked him to sell it cheaper or let him pay later. But the druggist said, "No, I discovered the drug and I'm going to make money from it." So Heinz got desperate and broke into the man's store to steal the drug for his wife. (Kohlberg & Elfenbein, 1975)

After reading or hearing this story, the respondent is asked a series of probing questions. The questions might be as follows: Should Heinz have stolen the drug? What if Heinz didn't love his wife? Would that change anything? What if the person dying was a stranger? Should Heinz steal the drug anyway? Based on answers to this and other dilemmas, Kohlberg concluded that there are three main levels of moral reasoning, with two substages within each level (Table 9.5). One use of his measurement instrument, the Moral Judgment Scale, is to determine a respondent's stage of moral reasoning.[1]

The Moral Judgment Scale consists of several hypothetical dilemmas such as Heinz and the druggist, presented one at a time (Colby, Kohlberg,

---

● **TABLE 9.5 Kohlberg's Levels and Stages of Moral Development**

**Level 1: Preconventional**

Stage 1. Punishment and obedience orientation: The physical consequences determine what is good or bad.

Stage 2. Instrumental relativism orientation: What satisfies one's own needs is good.

**Level 2: Conventional**

Stage 3. Interpersonal concordance orientation: What pleases or helps others is good.

Stage 4. "Law-and-order" orientation: Maintaining the social order and doing one's duty is good.

**Level 3: Postconventional or Principled**

Stage 5. Social contract-legalistic orientation: Values agreed upon by society determine what is good.

Stage 6. Universal ethical-principle orientation: What is right is a matter of conscience derived from universal principles.

*Source:* Based on Kohlberg (1984).

---

1. Even though the Moral Judgment Scale has been widely used for empirical research, Kohlberg (1981, 1984) suggests that its most valuable application is for the promotion of self-understanding and the development of moral reasoning in the individual respondent.

Gibbs, & others, 1978). In its latest revision, the scale comes in three versions called Forms A, B, and C. Scoring is quite complex, based on the examiner's judgment of responses in relation to extensive criteria outlined in a detailed scoring manual (Colby & Kohlberg, 1987). Although there are several different dimensions to scoring, the one element most frequently cited in research studies is the overall stage of moral reasoning that characterizes a respondent.

## Critique of the Moral Judgment Scale

Early versions of the Moral Judgment Scale suffered serious shortcomings of scoring and interpretation. For example, in his doctoral dissertation, Kohlberg (1958) proposed two scoring systems: one using the sentence or completed thought as the unit of scoring, the other relying upon a global rating of all the subject's utterances as the unit of analysis. Neither approach was fully satisfactory, and early reviews of the scale were justifiably critical of its reliability and validity (Kurtines & Greif, 1974).

In response to these criticisms, Kohlberg and his associates developed a scoring system that is unparalleled in its clarity, detail, and sophistication (Rest, 1986). Fortuitously, since the moral dilemmas of the Moral Judgment Scale have remained constant over the years, it is possible to apply the new scoring system to old data. The capacity to reanalyze old data and compare them with new data is invaluable in determining the reliability and validity of an existing scale. A most important study in this regard has been published by Kohlberg and associates (Colby et al., 1983).

This investigation reports the results of using the new scoring system in a longitudinal study spanning more than 20 years. The results are impressive and offer strong support for the reliability and validity of the instrument. Test-retest correlations for the three forms were in the high .90s, as were interrater correlations. Longitudinal scores of subjects tested at three- to four-year intervals over 20 years revealed theory-consistent trends. Fifty-six of 58 subjects showed upward change, with no

subjects skipping any stages. Furthermore, only 6 percent of the 195 comparisons showed backward shifts between two testing sessions. The internal consistency of scores was also excellent: about 70 percent of the scores were at one stage, and only 2 percent of the scores were spread further than two adjacent stages. Cronbach's alpha was in the mid-.90s for the three forms. These findings have been corroborated by Nisan and Kohlberg (1982). Heilbrun and Georges (1990) also report favorably upon the validity of the Moral Judgment Scale, insofar as postconventional development is correlated with higher levels of self-control, as would be predicted from the fact that morally mature persons often oppose social pressure or legal constraints. In sum, the Moral Judgment Scale is reliable, internally consistent, and possesses a theory-confirming developmental coherence.

## The Defining Issues Test

The Defining Issues Test (DIT) is similar to the Moral Judgment Scale but incorporates a much simpler and completely objective scoring format (Rest, 1979, 1986). The examinee reads a series of moral dilemmas similar to those designed by Kohlberg and then chooses a proper action for each. For example, one dilemma involves a patient dying a painful death from cancer. In her lucid moments, she requests an overdose of morphine to hasten her death. What should the doctor do? Three options of the following kind are listed:

_____ He should give the woman a fatal overdose
_____ Should not give the overdose
_____ Can't decide

The examinee's choice does not enter directly into the determination of the moral judgment score. The real purpose in forcing a choice is to cause the examinee to think about the importance of various factors in making the decision. Following the choice of proper action, the examinee rates the importance of several factors on a five-point Likert scale: great, much, some, little, or no importance. The factors are distinct for each dilemma. The factors differ in the level of moral judgment they signify, ranging from Kohlberg's stage 1 through stage 6. In the case of the preceding dilemma, the factors include such matters as follows:

_____ Whether the doctor can make it look like an accident
_____ Can society afford to let people end their lives when they want to
_____ Whether the woman's family favors giving the overdose or not

These ratings form the basis for generating several quantitative scores that pertain to the moral judgment of the examinee. The most widely used score is the *P* score, which is a percentage of principled thinking. Reliability of the *P* score ranges from .71 to .82 in test-retest studies (Rest, 1979, 1986). Validity has been studied by contrasting groups known to differ on principled thinking. For example, graduate students in moral philosophy and political science, general college students, high school seniors, and ninth-grade students were found to differ appropriately and systematically on the *P* score. In longitudinal studies, significant upward trends were found over six years and four testings. Recently, Rest has recommended a new measure of moral judgment, the N2 index, calculated on the basis of several complex formulas that use both ranking and rating data. The two indices are highly correlated in the .90s. Nonetheless, in a retrospective analysis of previous studies, the N2 index outperformed the *P* index by a substantial margin (Rest, Thoma, Narvaez, & Bebeau, 1997).

Over 600 articles have been published on the Defining Issues Test (McCrae, 1985). In general, the instrument is considered a useful alternative to Kohlberg's Moral Judgment Scale, particularly for research on group differences in moral reasoning. However, reviewers do note several cautions about the DIT (Westbrook & Bane, 1992). First, the test uses two moral dilemmas from the Vietnam War and is, therefore, somewhat dated. Many young examinees have little knowledge of (and perhaps no interest in) this topic and may find it difficult to identify with these questions. Another dilemma—

the classic case of whether Heinz should steal a drug to save his wife's life—is also of dubious value since it has been widely publicized and reprinted in college textbooks. A significant proportion of prospective examinees are no longer naive about this moral dilemma.

Richards and Davison (1992) have pressed the point that the DIT is biased against conservatively religious individuals. Certainly, it is well established that conservative or fundamentalist religious people tend to score lower than average on the *P* score of the Defining Issues Test (Getz, 1984; Richards, 1991). According to Richards and Davison (1992), the reason for this is that stage 3 and stage 4 items (unintentionally) possess strong theological implications that cause fundamentalist individuals to endorse the items, thereby lowering their score on the test. Consider items that tap stage 4 reasoning, which is the "law and order" orientation that equates "moral" with doing one's duty and maintaining the social order. Whereas nonreligious persons might support the laws of the land (and endorse stage 4 items) because they believe that legal authorities define what is right and moral, religious minorities such as Mormons believe that supporting the laws of the land is a theological and religious obligation that flows directly from articles of faith in their religion:

> While Mormons place a high value on obeying the law and supporting legal authorities, this value is due to their theological belief that God has commanded them to do so, and not because they believe, as do true Stage 4 thinkers, that the laws of the land or legal authorities *define* what is right or moral. (Richards & Davison, 1992, 470)

These researchers demonstrate empirically that certain DIT items measure a different construct for conservative religious persons than for the general population. As a consequence, the validity of the test in these groups is open to question.

Relatively few studies have investigated the relationship between level of moral development on the DIT and moral behavior. This is understandable, given that the purpose of the DIT is not directly to predict behavior but to evaluate moral development. Still, it is a reasonable assumption that individuals who receive higher *P* scores on the DIT should also refrain from moral transgressions such as cheating on tests. A study by Cummings, Maddux, Harlow, and Dyas (2002) investigated this particular relationship by asking 145 college students majoring in education to anonymously fill out both the DIT and the Assessment of Academic Misconduct (AAM). The AAM is a 41-item measure of misbehaviors such as copying test answers, downloading term papers, retrospectively changing test answers, and so forth. Although these individuals reported an average (but prolific!) level of academic misconduct for college students—fully three-fourths admitted to one or more transgressions—there was absolutely no relationship between scores on the DIT and scores the AAM. Certainly, more research is needed on the connection (or disconnection) between moral reasoning and moral action.

Another concern about the DIT is the dearth of norms pertinent to minority groups. Finally, Westbrook and Bane (1992) argue that the technical manual for the DIT lacks essential details needed to evaluate the adequacy of the test. In spite of the concerns listed here, the DIT is a widely respected test, particularly for research on moral reasoning. Thoma (2006) provides a thorough review of research on the DIT.

## ● THE ASSESSMENT OF SPIRITUAL AND RELIGIOUS CONCEPTS

Within the field of psychology, transcendent topics such as spiritual well-being or faith maturity never have received mainstream attention. Many years ago, Gordon Allport (1950) lamented that the subject of religion "seems to have gone into hiding" among intellectuals and academic researchers:

> Whatever the reason may be, the persistence of religion in the modern world appears as an embarrassment to the scholars of today. Even psychologists, to whom presumably nothing of human concern is alien, are likely to retire into themselves when the subject is broached. (p. 1)

The situation is little improved in contemporary times. For example, except for a few specialty journals, spiritual and religious topics are virtually absent from the psychological literature.

Yet researchers have no right to retire from the field, given its significance to the average person. Consider these statistics on religious belief in the United States, stable since 1944 when national polls first came into use (Hoge, 1996):

- Belief in God has remained constant at about 95 percent of the population.
- Belief in the divinity of Jesus Christ has been endorsed by 75 to 77 percent of adults.
- Belief in an afterlife has remained at about 75 percent of the population.

Comparable statistics are not available worldwide, but it seems likely that the percentage of believing individuals (whether Muslim, Buddhist, Hindu, Jew, or other) is very high. Most people embrace a spiritual perspective in life, and surely this must have some bearing on their adjustment, behavior, and outlook.

Unfortunately, the field of psychology, including the specialty area of testing, largely has maintained an indifference to this important aspect of human experience. Worse yet, in many intellectual circles the endorsement of spiritual or religious sentiments is seen as evidence of psychopathology. Among others, Sigmund Freud endorsed a cynical view of religion in his aptly titled essay, *The Future of an Illusion* (1927/1961). Yet for many persons, a connection with the transcendent is essential to meaning in life. This is especially so in times of extreme duress, as when personal annihilation knocks at the front door. Consider the experience of Viktor Frankl (1963), a Nazi death camp survivor and founding figure of existential psychology. At one point during World War II he had to surrender his coat with a cherished manuscript in the pockets in exchange for the worn-out rags of an inmate sent to the gas chamber:

> Instead of the many pages of my manuscript, I found in a pocket of the newly acquired coat a single page torn out of a Hebrew prayer book,

which contained the main Jewish prayer, *Shema Yisrael.* How should I have interpreted such a "coincidence" other than as a challenge to live my thoughts instead of merely putting them on paper?

In the remainder of this topic, we take the view that spiritual and religious dimensions to life often serve constructive purposes and that assessment within these domains is worthy of additional study.

## Historical Overview on Religious Assessment

Interest in the psychology of religion can be traced to the early 1900s when William James (1902) composed his masterpiece, *The Varieties of Religious Experience.* In this book, James catalogued the manifold ways in which humans reveal their interest in transcendent matters. His overall conclusion was that religion is "an essential organ of our life, performing a function which no other portion of our nature can so successfully fulfill."

Although many writers have offered psychological analyses of religion since the seminal writings of James, it was not until the 1960s that scales for the assessment of religious variables began to appear (Wulff, 1996). One of the first such measures was the Allport-Ross Religious Orientation scales, which proposed to assess two dimensions of religious expression, the **intrinsic** and the **extrinsic** (Allport & Ross, 1967). Intrinsically religious persons were thought to *live* their religion (e.g., to find meaning, direction, outlook), whereas extrinsically religious persons were believed to *use* their religion (e.g., to seek security, status, sociability). In his earlier writings on this topic, Allport referred to intrinsic religious expression as a genuine or mature religious orientation, whereas extrinsic religious expression was viewed as immature. Later he dropped the mature–immature designations because the labels seemed overly judgmental.

The impetus for development of these scales was Allport's distressing observation of a positive relationship between religiosity (in certain forms) and authoritarian, bigoted, prejudicial attitudes. As a devoutly religious person, Allport was convinced that intrinsically oriented religious individuals rarely would harbor these attitudes. After all, an essential precept of almost every religious faith is an attitude of love toward one's neighbors. In the Christian faith, this view is summed up in the famous dictum "Love your neighbor as yourself" (Mark 12:31). Yet the evidence was overwhelming to Allport that at least some religious individuals did reveal hatred, bigotry, and prejudice toward their neighbors. The usual targets of these malicious attitudes were racial minorities, Jews, and homosexual persons, among others. He reasoned that religious persons with intolerant attitudes possessed a predominantly extrinsic religious orientation; that is, their faith served external goals such as status in the community, belonging to an in-group, and the like. The investigation of this hypothesis (that extrinsically religious persons would be more authoritarian, bigoted, and prejudiced than intrinsically religious persons) required appropriate tools. For this purpose, Allport and colleagues developed the Religious Orientation scales.

Examples of the kinds of items on the 11-item Extrinsic scale and the 9-item Intrinsic scale are as follows:

- The church is important as a place to develop good social relationships. (Extrinsic)
- Sometimes I find it necessary to compromise my religious beliefs for economic reasons. (Extrinsic)
- I try hard to carry my religion over into other aspects of my life. (Intrinsic)
- My religion is important because it provides meaning to my life. (Intrinsic)

Although originally devised in a yes-no format, modern applications of these scales utilize a nine-point continuum from (1) strongly disagree to (9) strongly agree (Batson, Schoenrade, & Ventis, 1993).

Research on the Religious Orientation scales has not provided strong support for Allport's original hypothesis (Wulff, 1996). In fact, several studies have shown that persons scoring high on the Intrinsic scale actually reveal *higher* levels of authoritarianism, close-mindedness, and prejudice toward African Americans, gays, and lesbians. Hunsberger (1995) concludes that it is not religion per se that makes for prejudice, nor is it intrinsic/extrinsic religious orientation. Instead, "it is the way in which religious beliefs are held that seems most directly associated with prejudice, and this is best explained by the tendency for fundamentalism and right-wing authoritarianism to be closely linked." Specifically, he links prejudice against minorities with authoritarian religious traditions that promote an absolute truth, divide the world into "Good" and "Evil," and shun complexity or doubt in their belief systems. These aspects of religious expression are not typically measured by paper-and-pencil tests.

### Religion as Quest

Increasingly, the conceptual basis for the distinction between intrinsic and extrinsic religious orientation has been questioned. Kirkpatrick and Hood (1990) summarized the major theoretical and methodological criticisms of the scales as follows:

- A lack of conceptual clarity in what the Intrinsic-Extrinsic scales are supposed to be measuring. Are these types of motivation (i.e., the motives associated with religious belief and practice), or personality variables (i.e., pervasive aspects of institutional behavior or involvement), or something else?
- A confusion over the relationship between the Intrinsic-Extrinsic scales. In particular, are these opposite ends of a single bipolar dimension, or do the scales measure separate dimensions (so that conceivably some persons could score high on *both*)?

Other problems cited include weaknesses in the factorial structure, reliability, and construct validity of the scales; excessive reliance on a "good religion" versus "bad religion" dichotomy; and the folly of defining and studying religiousness independent of belief content (Kirkpatrick & Hood, 1990).

In response to the limitations of the Religious Orientation scales, Batson and his associates (1993) developed a measure of a third religious orientation known as Quest. These researchers consider Quest to be a more mature and flexible religious outlook than the intrinsic and extrinsic orientations. Actually, Allport recognized the elements inherent to this orientation but failed to incorporate them in his Intrinsic scale. **Religion as Quest** is characterized by complexity, doubt, and tentativeness as ways of being religious. Examples of the kinds of items on the 12-item Quest scale are as follows:

- My life experiences have led me to reconsider my religious convictions.
- I find religious doubts upsetting. (reverse scored)
- As I grow and mature, I expect my religious beliefs to change.
- Questions are more important to my religious faith than answers.

Items are scored on the same nine-point continuum from (1) strongly disagree to (9) strongly agree. Results are reported as an average rating. Research with 424 undergraduates interested in religion indicates that Quest is, indeed, a dimension of religious experience independent from both Intrinsic and Extrinsic orientations. Whereas Intrinsic and Extrinsic scores correlated .72, Quest revealed negligible relationships with both scales (−.05 with Intrinsic and .16 with Extrinsic).

But exactly what does the Quest scale measure? The intention of its authors was that it assess "the degree to which an individual's religion involves an open-ended, responsive dialogue with existential questions raised by the contradictions and tragedies of life" (Bateson et al., 1993, p. 169). The three components of the Quest orientation are (1) readiness to face existential questions without reducing their complexity, (2) self-criticism and perception of religious doubts as positive, and (3) openness to change. But critics have charged that the scale may not measure anything religious at all, that instead it may assess agnosticism, antiorthodoxy, religious doubt, or religious conflict.

In response to these criticisms, Batson et al. (1993) note the following:

- Students at Princeton Theological Seminary scored significantly higher ($p < .001$) on the Quest scale (mean of 6.7) than undergraduates at the same institution (mean of 5.2). This finding supports the view that the scale is a valid measure of something religious.
- The 32 members of a charismatic Bible study group scored significantly higher ($p < .001$) on the Quest scale (mean of 5.5) than the 26 members of a traditional Bible study group (mean of 4.6). The charismatic group placed emphasis on religion as a shared search; most prayed with hands raised, and some members spoke in tongues.

Quest is its own dimension of religious expression, and substantial research on the meaning and correlates of this faith orientation has been completed. Batson et al. (1993) summarize research with the Quest scale by noting that it appears to measure a religion of less faith but more works.

Quest arose as a response to the limitations of the Intrinsic and Extrinsic approach to the measurement of religious orientation. But this brief 12-item scale possesses its own limitations, chief among them its brevity and factorial simplicity. Several other instruments have been proposed to measure aspects of religious experience. We survey a few prominent and representative approaches in the following sections.

## The Spiritual Well-Being Scale

The concept of spiritual well-being can be traced to a paper by Moberg (1971) that proposed this form of well-being as an essential component of healthy aging. Spiritual well-being was conceptualized as a two-dimensional construct consisting of a vertical dimension and a horizontal dimension. The vertical dimension concerned well-being in relation to God or a higher power, whereas the horizontal dimension involved existential well-being, which is a sense of purpose in life without

any specific religious reference. The challenge of developing a scale to measure these components of well-being was taken up by Ellison (1983) and Paloutzian and Ellison (1982).

Their instrument was designated the Spiritual Well-Being Scale (SWB Scale). The SWB Scale consists of two subscales: Religious Well-Being (RWB), which assesses the vertical dimension of well-being in relation to God; and Existential Well-Being (EWB), which measures the horizontal dimension of well-being in relation to life purpose and life satisfaction. Each subscale consists of 10 items that are scored from 1 (strongly disagree) to 6 (strongly agree). The items from the two subscales are combined on the SWB Scale, with odd-numbered items assessing religious well-being and even-numbered items assessing existential well-being. Some items are worded negatively; these are reverse scored so that a higher score always indicates greater well-being. Items similar to those found on the SWB Scale are reproduced in Table 9.6.

The SWB Scale provides three scores: a total SWB score (maximum 120), a subscore for RWB (maximum 60), and a subscore for EWB (maximum 60). Initial reliability and validity studies were based upon 206 students from three religiously oriented colleges and one secular university. Test-retest reliability coefficients were .93 for SWB, .96 for RWB, and .86 for EWB. Factor analysis tended to support the construct validity of the instrument by revealing that all of the religious items loaded on a religious factor, whereas existential items appeared to load on two subfactors, one connoting life direction and the other indicating life satisfaction. The correlation between the RWB and EWB subscales was modest ($r = .32$), indicating that they tap separate aspects of spiritual well-being.

In later writings, Ellison described the SWB Scale as a measure of psychospiritual personality integration and resultant well-being (Ellison & Smith, 1991). According to this view, well-being consists of "the integral experience of a person who is functioning as God intended, in consonant relationship with Him, with others, and within

| ● TABLE 9.6 Items Similar to Those Found on the Spiritual Well-Being Scale | | | | | | |
|---|---|---|---|---|---|---|
| For each statement circle the choice that best indicates the degree of your agreement or disagreement. | | | | | | |
| SA = Strongly Agree      D = Disagree | | | | | | |
| MA = Moderately Agree      MD = Moderately Disagree | | | | | | |
| A = Agree      SD = Strongly Disagree | | | | | | |
| I don't find much reward in private prayer (reverse scored) | SA | MA | A | D | MD | SD |
| My relationship with God helps me through hard times | SA | MA | A | D | MD | SD |
| Life is inherently without meaning (reverse scored) | SA | MA | A | D | MD | SD |
| I feel good about where my life is headed | SA | MA | A | D | MD | SD |

one's self" (p. 36). This is the biblical notion of *shalom,* which denotes being harmoniously at peace within and without. If this conceptualization is correct, healthy spirituality as measured by the SWB Scale should show positive relationships with independent measures of health and subjective well-being. Literally dozens of studies have investigated this broad-range hypothesis, with generally positive findings. Representative studies are summarized in Table 9.7.

The one identified shortcoming of the SWB Scale is an apparent low ceiling, especially in religious samples. Ledbetter, Smith, Vosler-Hunter, and Fischer (1991) caution that the clinical usefulness of the scale is limited to low scores (since high-functioning religious persons tend to "top out" on the scale). They also offer suggestions for revision (e.g., rewording items in more extreme directions) toward the goal of increasing the ceiling level of the SWB Scale. Bufford, Paloutzian, and Ellison (1991) have published norms for the test but caution that in many religious samples the typical individual receives the maximum score. This would indicate that the scale is helpful in research but is not useful for distinguishing among individuals with high levels of spiritual well-being.

### The Faith Maturity Scale

In 1987, six major Protestant denominations undertook a national four-year study of personal faith, denominational allegiance, and their deter-

| ● TABLE 9.7 Summary of Findings with the Spiritual Well-Being Scale |
|---|
| **Spiritual Well-Being Scale Scores Correlate Positively With:** |
| Being closer to ideal body weight (Hawkins & Larson, 1984) |
| Perceived health in rural elderly (DeCrans, 1990) |
| Overall adjustment to hemodialysis (Campbell, 1988) |
| Hope in cancer patients (Mickley, 1990) |
| Measures of self-esteem (Paloutzian & Ellison, 1982) |
| **Spiritual Well-Being Scale Scores Correlate Negatively With:** |
| Diastolic and systolic blood pressure (Hawkins, 1988) |
| Frequency and amount of pain in cancer patients (Granstrom, 1987) |
| Social isolation and despair (Bonner, 1988) |
| Aggressiveness and conflict avoidance (Bufford & Parker, 1985) |
| Depression scores on the MMPI (Fehring, Brennan, & Keller, 1987) |

minants (Benson, Donahue, & Erickson, 1993). Funded in part by the Lilly Endowment, this project spawned what is undoubtedly the most sophisticated measure of spiritual maturity ever conceived. The Faith Maturity Scale (FMS) arose as a practical tool to serve three research purposes:

1. Provide baseline data on the vitality of faith in mainstream Protestant congregations
2. Identify the contributions of demographic, personal, and congregational variables to faith development
3. Furnish a criterion variable for evaluating the impact of religious education in mainstream denominations

The development of the scale was a time-consuming and careful process that began with a working definition:

> Faith maturity is the degree to which a person embodies the priorities, commitments, and perspectives characteristic of vibrant and life-transforming faith, as they have been understood in "mainline" Protestant traditions. (Benson, Donahue, & Erickson, 1993, p. 3)

Using open-ended questionnaires with a convenience sample of 410 mainline Protestant adults, the test developers next identified eight core dimensions of faith maturity. Three advisory panels provided ongoing counsel during this stage and the next phase of item writing. These interactions assured that the scale possessed face and content validity.

The resulting FMS is a 38-item test that embodies key indicators of faith maturity in eight core areas (Table 9.8). Items are answered on a seven-point scale from 1 = never true to 7 = always true. Based upon the areas assessed, the reader will notice that right belief is only one aspect of a mature faith. In large measure, faith maturity is defined by value and behavioral consequences. As the authors note, the Faith Maturity Scale "parts company with more traditional ways of defining and measuring personal religion." Yet it does embody the kinds of behaviors and attitudes that derive from a dynamic, life-transforming faith. These

● **TABLE 9.8    The Eight Core Dimensions and Sample Items from the Faith Maturity Scale**

A.  Trusts and believes (5 items)
Every day I see evidence that God is at work in the world

B.  Experiences the fruits of faith (5 items)
I feel weighed down by all my responsibilities (reverse scored)

C.  Integrates faith and life (5 items)
My faith influences how I think and act every day

D.  Seeks spiritual growth (4 items)
I take time to meditate or pray

E.  Experiences and nurtures faith in community (4 items)
I talk with others about my faith

F.  Holds life-affirming values (6 items)
I tend to be critical of other persons (reverse scored)

G.  Advocates social change (4 items)
I believe the churches of this nation should get involved in political issues

H.  Acts and serves (5 items)
I offer significant amounts of time to help others

Note:  The sample items are similar to those on the Faith Maturity Scale.

*Source:*  Based on Benson, P., Donahue, M., & Erickson, J. (1993). The Faith Maturity Scale: Conceptualization, measurement, and empirical validation. In M. L. Lynn & D. O. Moberg (Eds.), *Research in the social scientific study of religion* (vol. 5). Greenwich, CT: JAI Press.

behaviors and attitudes are consistent with the theology found in most religious traditions but are especially pertinent for the particular purpose of assessing faith maturity in the Protestant context.

The FMS is scored as the mean of the 38 items, which yields a potential range of 1 to 7. The average score for 3,040 adults in five Protestant denominations was 4.63, which indicates that the instrument avoids the "ceiling effect" found on other scales such as the Spiritual Well-Being Scale, discussed previously. The estimated reliability of the scale is very robust across age, gender, occupation, and denomination, with typical coefficient alphas of .88 (Benson et al., 1993). Test-retest reliability was not reported.

The validity of the scale is supported by several lines of evidence, beginning with the careful approach to item selection, by which face validity and content validity were built-in. Construct validity was demonstrated in several ways. First, it was predicted and confirmed that groups presumed to differ in levels of faith maturity would obtain significantly different mean scores on the FMS. Indeed, pastors scored the highest (5.3), followed by church education coordinators (4.9), teachers (4.7), adults (4.6), and youth (4.1)—each group in respective order scoring significantly lower than the others. Second, pastors' ratings of the faith maturity of 123 congregation members on a 1 to 10 scale correlated very substantially ($r = .61$) with the FMS scores of these persons, indicating a correspondence between independent expert ratings and self-report. The scale also revealed predictive utility. Specifically, FMS scale scores were strongly related to a variety of prosocial behaviors such as donating time to help those who are poor, hungry, or sick; promoting a greater role for women in the church; and endorsing the use of foreign policy to challenge apartheid.

## SUMMARY

1. The Myers-Briggs Type Indicator (MBTI) is a forced-choice, self-report inventory that attempts to classify persons according to an adaptation of Carl Jung's theory of personality types. One of the most widely used individual tests of all time, recent adaptations of the MBTI provide dimensional scores in addition to the well-known four-letter typological codes (e.g., ESTP for Extraversion, Sensing, Thinking, Perceiving type).

2. The California Psychological Inventory (CPI) is an MMPI-like instrument designed to measure the dimensions of normal personality. Three scales measure test-taking attitudes (e.g., "fake-good" and "fake-bad" tendencies). The 17 personality scales are based on "folk" concepts of personality easily recognized by laypersons.

3. The NEO Personality Inventory-Revised (NEO PI-R) is based on the five-factor model of personality described earlier. The five constructs measured by the test are Neuroticism, Extraversion, Openness to Experience, Agreeableness, and Conscientiousness. The NEO PI-R is available in two parallel forms consisting of 240 items rated on a five-point dimension.

4. Cattell's Sixteen Personality Factor Questionnaire (16PF) is typical of factor-analytically derived instruments. The five forms of the 16PF (for different age groups) all encompass a forced-choice format. The 16 surveyed personality attributes (and four higher-order dimensions) have been repeatedly confirmed by factor analysis.

5. With Kohlberg's Moral Judgment Scale, the examinee is asked a series of structured questions pertaining to several moral dilemmas. Responses are categorized according to six stages and three levels of development: preconventional, conventional, and postconventional.

6. Rest's Defining Issues Test is a spinoff of the Moral Judgment Scale that uses a completely objective scoring format. The test yields several quantitative indices, including the *P* score (percentage of principled thinking) and the N2 index (based on complex formulas), both of which show good reliability and validity.

7. One of the first forms of religious assessment was the Allport-Ross Religious Orientation scales. These scales popularized the concepts of intrinsic religiousness (persons *live* their religion to find meaning and direction) versus extrinsic religiousness (persons *use* their religion to seek security or status).

8. The Quest scale seeks to measure a third religious orientation (beyond intrinsic and extrinsic) characterized by complexity, doubt, and

tentativeness as ways of being religious. This simple 12-item scale appears to measure a religion of less faith but more works.

**9.** The Spiritual Well-Being Scale is a mainstay in the field of religious assessment. It consists of two subscales, Religious Well-Being (a vertical dimension of well-being in relation to God) and Existential Well-Being (a horizontal dimension of well-being in relation to life purpose and satisfaction). A problem with this scale is its low ceiling.

**10.** The Faith Maturity Index is an ambitious scale devised at the behest of six major Protestant denominations. The 38 items are answered on a seven-point scale, providing an index of a vibrant and life-transforming faith, as understood in mainline Protestant faiths.

## ● KEY TERMS AND CONCEPTS

collaboratory   p. 382

moral dilemmas   p. 385

intrinsic religious expression   p. 389

extrinsic religious expression   p. 389

religion as Quest   p. 390

# Positive Psychological Assessment

With few exceptions, clinical psychology since World War II has focused on what is wrong with people and how to alleviate or diminish a host of symptoms and syndromes. Research abounds on the assessment and treatment of anxiety, depression, serious mental illnesses, dementia, marital discord, drug abuse, mental retardation, and brain damage, to name a few areas of significant inquiry.

There is nothing inherently wrong with this extensive body of research on psychopathology. In fact, huge strides have been made in the understanding and treatment of many conditions that entail serious and crippling emotional pain or other forms of disability. Even so, this one-sided emphasis from the perspective of disease and repair has led to a relative void of positive perspectives. Consider the results of Table 9.9, which compiles the number of PsychINFO listings conjured up for a variety of terms, some pathological and some positive. The reader will notice that pathological concepts like *Depression* or *Dementia* are 50 to 100 times more likely to be the topic of inquiry than positive concepts like *Resilience* or *Gratitude*.

In recent years, a movement known as positive psychology has emerged to redress this imbalance.

A simple definition of **positive psychology** is the scientific and practical pursuit of optimal human functioning (Lopez & Snyder, 2003). One of the

**TABLE 9.9   Number of PsychINFO Listings for a Sampling of Pathological and Positive Terms**

| Pathological Term | Number of Listings |
|---|---|
| Depression | 130,033 |
| Abuse | 106,772 |
| Anxiety | 113,316 |
| Schizophrenia | 74,979 |
| Brain Damage | 70,235 |
| Addiction | 51,969 |
| Mental Retardation | 39,660 |
| Dementia | 29,860 |

| Positive Term | Number of Listings |
|---|---|
| Resilience | 5,668 |
| Optimism | 4,784 |
| Wisdom | 4,712 |
| Altruism | 3,502 |
| Genius | 1,818 |
| Courage | 1,740 |
| Forgiveness | 1,667 |
| Gratitude | 751 |

| ● TABLE 9.10   General Constructs Measured by Positive Psychological Assessment Instruments | |
|---|---|
| Learned Optimism | Optimism |
| Hope | Career Self-Efficacy |
| Problem-Solving | Locus of Control |
| Creativity | Wisdom-Related Performance |
| Courage | Positive Emotions |
| Self-Esteem | Romantic Love |
| Emotional Intelligence | Empathy |
| Adult Attachment Security | Forgiveness |
| Sense of Humor | Gratitude |
| Religious Constructs | Moral Judgment Maturity |
| Positive Work Outcomes | Positive Coping |
| Subjective Well-being | Quality of Life |

*Source:* Chapter topics in Lopez, S., & Snyder, C. R. (Eds.). (2003). Positive psychological assessment: A handbook of models and measures. Washington, DC: American Psychological Association.

founders of the movement, Martin Seligman, provides a detailed perspective on the movement:

> The field of positive psychology at the subjective level is about valued subjective experiences: well-being, contentment, and satisfaction (in the past); hope and optimism (for the future); and flow and happiness (in the present). At the individual level, it is about positive individual traits: the capacity for love and vocation, courage, interpersonal skill, aesthetic sensibility, perseverance, forgiveness, originality, future-mindedness, spirituality, high talent, and wisdom. (Seligman & Csikszentmihalyi, 2000, p. 5)

Also included in positive psychology are civic virtues such as altruism, tolerance, and work ethic. In sum, positive psychology is a broad movement linked by the focus on life-affirming concepts. The goal is to bring balance to psychology by helping to build human strengths.

An important element of this movement is **positive psychological assessment,** which can be defined as the measurement of specific human strengths such as those mentioned above. After all, if a psychological movement proposes to increase human strengths and virtues, it is also obligated to develop measurement approaches for purposes of research and assessment. In recent years, psychologists have paid increasing attention to positive forms of assessment, resulting in dozens of new instruments and approaches. In their path-breaking edited book on positive psychological assessment, Lopez and Snyder (2003) compiled 24 chapters, each detailing several instruments. In other words, there are now hundreds of instruments available for positive psychological assessment. The general constructs measured by these tests are listed in Table 9.10.

A comprehensive review of positive psychological assessment would entail a textbook in its own right (if not several). The best we can do here is focus on a few key areas of assessment with a small number of tests that illustrate important or interesting approaches to positive psychological assessment. In particular, we will review issues involved in the assessment of creativity, emotional intelligence, optimism, hope, forgiveness, and gratitude.

## ● ASSESSMENT OF CREATIVITY

The topic of creativity has fascinated and yet also vexed psychologists and educators for more than a century. Researchers are beginning to understand fundamental elements common to many forms of creativity, yet, a simple definition of creativity remains elusive, and its assessment continues to be problematic. It is no exaggeration to state that hundreds of tests of creativity have been published. Some of these instruments possess respectable psychometric qualities, but most are of questionable validity. Unlike other fields of assessment such as intelligence or personality—where a few instruments have risen to the top and dominate the field—in the field of creativity there are no acknowledged "gold standards" for assessment. In part, this is because of the criterion problem—the difficulty in defining creativity. Thus, we begin with a foundational question: What is creativity?

Psychologists have sought to understand creativity since at least the early 1900s. For example, John B. Watson, the famous American behaviorist, suggested simplistically that a poem or brilliant essay is the mere product of shifting words around until a new pattern is hit upon (Watson, 1928). Fortunately, Watson's simplistic views were followed by a large number of more thoughtful formulations. We have quoted below a few perspectives on creativity from eminent researchers:

- If a response is to be called original, it must be to some extent adaptive to reality (Barron, 1955, p. 553).
- We may proceed to define the creative thinking process as the forming of associative elements into new combinations which either meet specified requirements or are in some way useful (Mednick, 1962, p. 221).
- Creativity can be regarded as the quality of products or responses judged to be creative by appropriate observers, and it can also be regarded as the process by which something so judged is produced (Amabile, 1983, p. 31).
- Creativity involves bringing something into being that is original (new, unusual, novel, unexpected) and also valuable (useful, good, adaptive, appropriate) (Ochse, 1990, p. 2).
- Creativity is the ability to produce work that is both novel (i.e., original, unexpected) and appropriate (i.e., useful, adaptive concerning task constraints) (Sternberg & Lubart, 1999, p. 3).

- Creativity is a specific capacity to not only solve problems but to solve them originally and adaptively (Feist & Barron, 2003, p. 63).
- Creativity is the ability to come up with ideas or artifacts that are new, surprising, and valuable (Boden, 2004, p. 1).

These conceptual definitions emphasize novelty and usefulness of the creative product, but also suggest that creativity is a particular kind of process as well. On these elements, there is broad agreement in the field of creativity research. However, going from conceptual definitions to operational definitions has proved to be difficult, to say the least. Prentky (2001) notes that "what creativity is, and what it is not, hangs as the mythical albatross around the neck of scientific research on creativity" (p. 97).

Over the years, creativity has been studied in terms of cognitive processes, personal characteristics, and behavioral products (Batey & Furnham, 2006). We will review these approaches in turn and examine the assessment methods that each has spawned.

## Creativity as Process

Several theorists and researchers have focused on underlying cognitive processes in their understanding of creativity. Of historical interest is Wertheimer's (1945) suggestion that creativity arises when the thinker grasps the essential features of a problem and their relation to a final solution—the so-called "aha!" phenomenon. Wallas (1926) theorized that such insights often occur after a period of incubation wherein the unconscious mind rearranges the features of the puzzle even while the conscious mind takes "time off" from the problem.

Mednick (1962) proposed that creativity is the capacity to combine remote associations. According to this view, creativity is a matter of novel arrangements of unusual associations to a given stimulus. Consider the invention of the grain reaper by McCormick, based on the association between grain and hair (Weber, 1969). It occurred to the inventor that grain is like the hair on a person's head. Since mechanical clippers are used to cut hair, something like hair clippers could be used to cut grain. We see in this example how a creative invention was developed from a remote association.

Based on his process-oriented view of creativity, Mednick (1962) developed the Remote Associates Test (RAT), a clever index of the remoteness of verbal associations. The RAT is a timed, forty-minute paper-and-pencil test with inter-item reliability consistently above .90. (Mednick & Mednick, 1966). Some examples of the kinds of items encountered on the RAT:

rat–blue–cottage      _____

out–dog–cat      _____

wheel–electric–high      _____

surprise–line–birthday _____

For each triplet, the examinee must find a fourth word that "fits" in the sense of having reasonable (but often remote) associations to the other three words. (The correct answers above are *cheese, house, wire,* and *party*.) Competent performance on this test would appear to require a capacity to examine several novel or remote associations at the same time and to search for the one association that is common to all three stimulus words.

Validity studies of the RAT have been mixed in outcome. Early studies were promising and indicated that high RAT-scorers tended to receive higher ratings for the creativity of their products (e.g., architectural designs, research projects, suggestions, and drawings) than low scorers (Mednick & Mednick, 1966). One early study showed that high RAT-scoring scientists tended to write more research proposals, to win more research grants, and to win bigger grants than lower scorers (Gordon & Charanian, 1964). However, later studies indicated complex patterns between RAT scores and other creativity indices. For example, Andrews (1975) found that RAT scores predicted the innovativeness of research for medical sociologists only for a small subsample of the respondents whose environment provided certain "prerequisites" for

achieving payoff from creative ability. Specifically, among those researchers who were responsible for initiating new activities, who hired their own research assistants, who had stable employment and low interference from superiors, the correlation between RAT scores and innovativeness of research was a healthy +.55. But these researchers constituted less than a fourth of the sample; for the remainder of the subjects there was no relationship between the RAT and creativity. These complex and contradictory findings are typical of research on the assessment of creativity.

Ochse (1990) provides a thorough appraisal of RAT validity. He concludes that the test may predict scores on tests of verbal fluency, but fails to predict creativity in general. In other words, the RAT is not so much a general measure of creativity as a specialized measure of verbal intelligence. Recently, Bowden & Jung-Beeman (2003) published extensive normative data for RAT-type items. Based on 289 university students, their normative data consists of percentage correct for 144 items under four time limits (2, 7, 15, and 30 seconds). They recommend using these normative data to investigate process factors such as incubation, the impact of hints, and techniques to facilitate problem solving.

### Creativity as Personal Characteristics

Guilford (1950) was one of the first researchers to define creativity in terms of the person when he asserted that "creativity refers to the abilities that are most characteristic of creative people." His pronouncement helped inspire an expansion of research on the personal characteristics of creative persons. Much of this research has relied upon contrasts of peer nominated high- and low-creative persons in various professions (Barron, 1968; Martindale, 1981). In this methodology, colleagues within a field of study nominate other individuals who are high and low in creativity, and their consensus view is used to identify two select groups of individuals (high-creative, low-creative). These groups are then contrasted on personality measures, including self-checked adjectives and standard personality inventories.

Based on hundreds of studies, a fairly stable set of core characteristics of creative persons has emerged (Barron & Harrington, 1981; Dellas & Gaier, 1970). Interestingly, the distinguishing characteristics of creative individuals appear to be largely temperamental, although a certain minimum level of intelligence also is required. Harrington (1975) has captured a not altogether flattering portrait of the creative person in his Composite Creative Personality Scale, which consists of 42 self-checked adjectives (from a larger list) that empirically distinguish creative from noncreative persons. These adjectives include many positive terms such as *active, curious, imaginative, inventive, original, resourceful,* and *sensitive,* but also embrace negative terms such as *argumentative, cynical, egotistical, impulsive, rebellious,* and *unconventional.* These qualities fit well with the observation of Feist (1999):

> One of the most distinguishing characteristics of creative people is their desire and preference to be somewhat removed from regular social-contact, to spend time alone working on their craft . . . to be autonomous and independent of the influence of a group. (p. 158)

In addition to the broad generalizations noted above, the particular link between personality characteristics and creative behavior also depends on the specific domain of investigation. For example, compared with their less creative counterparts, creative artists tend to be more spontaneous, creative writers tend to be more nonconforming, creative architects tend to be less flexible, and creative engineers tend to be better adjusted than other groups (Piirto, 1998). In attempting to predict creative behavior from personality characteristics, one creative personality type may not fit all creative occupations (Kerr & Gagliardi, 2003). Batey and Furnham (2006) provide an excellent review of the complex literature on creativity and personality.

Recently, Sternberg (2002) has proposed that creative individuals are distinguished not so much by specific traits as by the heartfelt *decision* to be creative:

> I believe that, although creative people differ in an astonishing number of ways, there is, in fact, one key attribute that they all possess. . . . This attribute is the decision to be creative. People who create decide that they will forge their own path and follow it, for better or for worse. The path is a difficult one because people who defy convention often are not rewarded. (p. 376)

This perspective suggests that creative individuals will be characterized by a stubborn dedication to their creative endeavors, even when rewards for their activities seem to be lacking.

### Creativity as Product

The most enduring definitions of creativity have used the *product* as the distinguishing sign of this capacity. According to this approach, creative persons create products (ideas, inventions, writings, artistic outputs, etc.) that meet certain criteria. For example, Jackson and Messick (1968) applied four criteria to creativity:

- Novelty: Creative products are new, or at least represent a new application of the familiar.
- Appropriateness: The product must be appropriate to the context, not merely novel.
- Transcendence of constraints: A product transcends constraints when it goes beyond the traditional.
- Coalescence of meaning: The value of creative products may not be apparent at first, the full significance may only be appreciated with time.

The Jackson and Messick (1968) criteria have proved helpful in delineating the special characteristics of a creative outcome, but they do not constitute a psychological *measure* of creativity. For measures of creativity based on the product-oriented approach, we must examine the seminal studies of Joy Paul Guilford and the various tests inspired by his factor-analytic research.

As the reader will recall from an earlier chapter, Guilford (1959, 1985) formulated a structure of intellect model that parceled intelligence into 150 factors aligned upon three dimensions: operations, constructs, and products. One of the operations that emerged from Guilford's factor analyses was **divergent thinking:**

> Divergent thinking is defined as the kind that goes off in different directions. It makes possible changes of direction in problem solving and also leads to a diversity of answers, where more than one answer may be acceptable. (Guilford, 1959)

Divergent thinking is virtually the opposite of convergent thinking. **Convergent thinking** is the production of a single correct answer determined by facts and reason. Western civilization places such a heavy emphasis on convergent thinking that we are inclined to dismiss the value of divergent thinking, even to mock it as undisciplined and, therefore, unproductive. But divergent thinking is essential to creative discovery. Unconstrained, freewheeling thought is the hallmark of the creative person. Tests of divergent thinking are therefore considered excellent measures of creativity.

Guilford and his colleagues developed about a dozen experimental measures of divergent thinking (Guilford & Hoepfner, 1971), some of which were subsequently standardized and published as the Christensen-Guilford Fluency Tests. Subtests and items similar to his measures include:

- Alternate Uses: List possible but unusual uses for a common object such as a brick (use it as a door stop, hammer, anchor, or wheel stop)
- Consequences: List possible consequences of a specific hypothetical event, for example, "What would happen if clouds had strings hanging down from them?" (macramé would make a comeback, people would be whisked away, air travel would be hazardous, farmers could winch the clouds down for watering, etc.)
- Ideational Fluency: Name things that belong in a given class such as "Long, thin items" (hair, pin, wire, needle, snake, string, spaghetti, pulled taffy)

Although Guilford's tests never received wide usage and eventually faded into obscurity, his theories and contributions were highly influential in the field of creativity studies. In particular, Guilford's influence is found in the work of E. Paul Torrance (1915–2003), who developed a group of tests still in use today.

The Torrance Tests of Creative Thinking (TTCT) (Kim, 2006; Torrance, 1966) are based loosely on Guilford's model, although Torrance was more concerned with the interest level of his measures than with their factorial purity. These tests purport to assess a global cognitive construct of creativity—a style of thinking believed to be essential to creative achievements. The TTCT subtests do not assess motivation, expertise, intelligence, or other capacities that could contribute to creative productivity. The test comes in two parallel forms, A and B, which are highly comparable. The comments below refer to both forms.

The TTCT consists of two parts: The TTCT-Verbal and the TTCT-Figural. Suitable for ages 6 through 18 and beyond, the TTCT-Verbal contains six subtests:

Asking Questions

Guessing Causes

Guessing Consequences

Product Improvement

Unusual Uses

Just Suppose

The first three verbal subtests are based on the same stimulus card which shows a simple pen and ink drawing of one or two human-like figures engaged in ambiguous activity. A TTCT-like drawing is shown in Figure 9.1. In the first activity, *Asking Questions,* the child is encouraged to ask questions about the picture. In the second activity, *Guessing Causes,* the child is told to guess the causes of the action in the picture. In the third activity, *Guessing Consequences,* the child is instructed to speculate about the immediate and long-term consequences. The time limit for each activity is five minutes.

In the fourth activity of the Verbal subtests, *Product Improvement,* the task is to suggest improvements to a toy that would make it more appealing to children. For example, the child might be shown a picture of a stuffed rabbit and asked to

● **FIGURE 9.1**   Example Stimulus Card Used for the First Three TTCT-Verbal Subtests

Note: A stimulus card similar to the above is used for the Asking Questions, Guessing Causes, and Guessing Consequences subtests.

think of ways to change the toy so that others would have more fun playing with it. *Unusual Uses*, the fifth activity, is a familiar standby in creativity assessment, namely, thinking of unusual uses for a common object such as a brick. The final Verbal subtest is *Just Suppose*, which involves asking the examinee to list the problems and benefits that might arise from an improbable situation. For example, the child might be told "Just suppose that clouds had strings hanging down from them—what might be some problems or benefits of this situation?"

The verbal subtests are scored according to three criteria:

1. Fluency—the raw number of relevant ideas;
2. Originality—the inventiveness or creativity of the ideas;
3. Flexibility—the flexibility of categories of ideas.

Of course, the manual for the TTCT, which is periodically updated for normative data, provides significant guidance on scoring (Torrance, 1974, 1998).

The TTCT-Figural consists of three activities, which are suitable for ages 5 through 18 and beyond:

Picture Construction

Picture Completion

Repeated Figures

The time limit for each activity is ten minutes. In the first activity, *Picture Construction*, the child draws a picture using a simple shape (jelly bean or pear) as a starting point. The stimulus shape must become an integral part of the constructed picture. In the second activity, *Picture Completion,* the examinee encounters ten incomplete figures and is asked to complete a drawing from each and then to name each drawing. An example of a TTCT-like drawing (with completion and title) is shown in Figure 9.2. In the last activity, *Repeated Figures,* the child is provided two or three pages of repeated figures (e.g., circles) and asked to use them in constructing pictures that are then named. For example, the child might draw a rectangle encompassing six circles and name it "swiss cheese."

● **FIGURE 9.2**   Example TTCT-Figural Picture Completion Drawing with Title

Note: This sample resembles one of the ten incomplete figures used on the Picture Completion subtest.

Scoring of the TTCT-Figural subtests is based on five norm-referenced measures and thirteen criterion-referenced outcomes. The five norm-referenced measures include:

1. Fluency—the raw number of stimuli provided;
2. Originality—the number of statistically infrequent drawings;
3. Abstractness of Titles—the abstraction level of the titles;
4. Elaboration—the provision of details and elaboration;
5. Resistance to Premature Closure—the degree of openness for incomplete figures.

The thirteen criterion-referenced measures include a variety of creative strengths expressed in the drawings such as emotional fluency, unusual visual perspective, humor, colorful imagery, and fantasy.

Although scoring of the TTCT is tedious and elaborate—especially for the Figural subtests—experienced testers produce interrater reliabilities in the .90s. Test-retest reliability coefficients are lower, in the range of .50 to .93 (Kim, 2006). Reliability data certainly are strong enough to support the use of the test for group testing and research purposes (Trefflinger, 1985). However, making individual decisions (e.g., admission to special program for gifted children) solely on the basis of TTCT scores could be problematic.

The validity of the TTCT is a more complicated question, especially in light of the difficulty of defining the criterion—what is creativity? Yet, the instrument is reasonably predictive of later creative accomplishments, even in the long run. For example, in a sample of 80 participants, the correlation between a TTCT creativity index derived from assessment in elementary years and the quality of highest creative achievements in adulthood (40-year follow-up) was a healthy $r = .43$ (Cramond, Matthews-Morgan, Bandalos, & Zuo, 2005). In this study, the quality of creative achievements was rated blindly from autobiographical materials supplied by the research participants. The correlation, $r = .43$, was higher than the observed relationship between childhood IQ and adult creativity, $r = .32$. Creativity as measured by the TTCT appears to be more predictive of certain forms of achievement than intelligence.

Overall, with its 50 years of research and strong psychometric properties, the TTCT is one of the best instruments for creativity assessment. The test has been translated into 35 languages and has spawned more research than any other measure in the field. Among its many strong features, age- and grade-norms are available for more than 50,000 participants, kindergarten through high school. Applications of the test are mainly with school-aged children, although norms are provided for adults as well (Kim, 2006).

## Comment on Creativity Tests

Tests of creativity have served a useful function in highlighting the diversity of skills that make up the whole of intellectual ability. As a consequence of research on creativity, educators and psychologists now realize that an exclusive emphasis on "correct" thinking (i.e., convergent problem solving) is too narrow a focus for education and assessment alike. However, the validity of creativity tests is still an open question. One problem is that definitions of creativity (e.g., Jackson & Messick, 1968, above) do not lend themselves easily to psychometric measurement, that is, tests of creativity do not operationalize the construct of creativity very well (Chase, 1985). In part, the failure to operationalize creativity stems from the multifactorial nature of this puzzling ability. Consider this observation: whereas a general factor almost always can be extracted from intelligence and ability tests, it seems clear that there is no corresponding factor in the realm of creativity. For example, a creative painter is unlikely to be a creative musician or a creative research scientist. Creativity is almost always specific to the realm in which it is identified. This specificity poses a difficult obstacle to general measures of creativity.

# MEASURES OF EMOTIONAL INTELLIGENCE

In the history of psychology, emotions and intelligence generally have been viewed as distinct capacities of the individual, each capable of influencing the other, but separate nonetheless. For example, Thomas Chalmers (1833) wrote an early chapter titled *On the Connection between the Intellect and the Emotions.* Chalmers was a Scottish church leader who catalogued the disruptive influence of emotions on clear thinking. In like manner, the American psychologist Henry H. Goddard (1919) proposed a separation of the emotions and intelligence. He argued that intelligence, properly exercised, can modify and influence emotions for the benefit of the individual.

The first person to hint at a possible union of emotional and intellectual factors was the eminent American psychologist E. L. Thorndike (1920). In a short essay published in *Harper's Magazine* for a general audience, Thorndike spoke of three kinds of intelligence: abstract, mechanical, and social. The first two types are well known in assessment and have been validated repeatedly. However, the third kind of intelligence, social intelligence, has proved more elusive. Thorndike defined social intelligence as "the ability to understand and manage people." An essential part of this ability is the accurate recognition of emotions in others. Unfortunately, early attempts to measure social intelligence proved fruitless (Thorndike & Stein, 1937). The concept gradually fell out of favor.

Recently, the idea that emotions and intellect might constitute a single cluster of intertwined abilities has reemerged in the concept of emotional intelligence, as proposed by Mayer, Salovey, and colleagues (Salovey & Mayer, 1989–90; Mayer, Salovey, & Caruso, 2008). The notion of emotional intelligence has been pursued by other researchers as well (discussed below); however, the Mayer-Salovey model boasts the strongest theoretical and empirical underpinnings, so we begin with their approach. Mayer et al. (2008) define **emotional intelligence** as follows:

- Managing emotions so as to attain specific goals;
- Understanding emotions, emotional language, and the signals conveyed by emotions;
- Using emotions to facilitate thinking; and,
- Perceiving emotions accurately in oneself and others. (p. 507)

These theorists propose that emotional intelligence is an instance of traditional intelligence, not something different from it. In other words, Emotional Intelligence (EI) is an important and overlooked subset of abilities that contribute to human efficiency and adaptation. Thus, just as prior researchers have documented verbal forms of intelligence (e.g., verbal comprehension) and perceptual forms of intelligence (e.g., perceptual reasoning) Mayer et al. (2008) propose that Emotional Intelligence is a third major subdivision that complements the traditional dichotomy of verbal and perceptual abilities.

To understand how emotional intelligence differs from traditional forms of intelligence, imagine a situation in which you visit a close friend in the hospital. He has just emerged from emergency surgery after a serious head injury from a fall. He lies still in bed with his eyes closed. Standing around your friend are anxious family members and a stern-faced doctor. What would you do or say? Would you press forward to join the family members? Would you leave the room and return later? Would you hug or console others? Would you ask the doctor for an update? You will need to make these and many other choices in a matter of seconds. Adaptive functioning in this complex situation would require you to manage your own emotions (maybe you feel strong relief that you are not the one in the hospital bed), understand the subtle emotional signals conveyed by others (perhaps the glassy stare of the sister indicates that you are not welcome at this time), use your emotions to facilitate thinking (maybe your anguish is so strong that you think it wise to remain quiet), and perceive emotions accurately in others (perhaps everyone is quiet because your friend has just drifted off to sleep). Successful navigation of this difficult and painful situation would require high levels of emotional intelligence.

Because of the subtlety and complexity of the construct, the assessment of emotional intelligence has proved challenging. However, with innovative forms of testing such as embodied in the MSCEIT or Mayer-Salovey-Caruso Emotional Intelligence Test (Mayer, Salovey, & Caruso, 2002), progress is being made. This instrument consists of 141 items that yield a total emotional intelligence score as well as two Area scores, four Branch Scores, and eight Task scores. Table 9.11 provides a brief description of the test, which is designed for adults age 17 and older. Normative data are based on a sample of more than 5,000 individuals.

The overall score on the MSCEIT is called the Emotional Intelligence (EI) score. This score is normed to a mean of 100 and standard deviation of 15. The two Area scores (Experiential and Strategic) and the four Branch scores (Perceiving, Facilitating, Understanding, and Managing) likewise are normed to these traditional benchmarks. While scores are provided for the eight Tasks (see Table 9.11), the test developers caution against overinterpretation of these elemental scores because of their lower reliability. The overall EI score demonstrates strong internal reliability, in the low .90s, whereas the reliability of the two Area scores is slightly lower and more variable, typically in the high .80s (Mayer, Salovey, & Caruso, 2002). Test-retest reliability of the overall score is respectable at .86 (Brackett & Mayer, 2003).

---

### ● TABLE 9.11    Brief Description of the MSCEIT Tasks

*EXPERIENTIAL AREA*

*Perceiving Branch*

**Faces:** Identify from photographs of faces how each person feels on a 1 to 5 scale (e.g., 1 = no happiness, 5 = extreme happiness).
**Pictures:** Indicate the extent to which images and photographs express various emotions on a 1 to 5 scale (e.g., 1 = not at all, 5 = very much).

*Facilitating Branch*

**Sensations:** Compare different emotions to different sensations such as light, color and temperature on a 1 to 5 scale (e.g., 1 = not at all, 5 = very much).
**Facilitation:** Specify how certain moods might assist in responding to social situations (e.g., 1 = not useful, 5 = useful).

*STRATEGIC AREA*

*Understanding Branch*

**Blends:** Indicate which emotion (from 5 choices) tends to occur in the presence of a described emotional situation.
**Changes:** Indicate which emotion (from 5 choices) tends to be the transition state from a described emotional starting point.

*Managing Branch*

**Emotion Management:** Rate the effectiveness of alternative actions in achieving a specified emotional state on a 1 to 5 scale (1 = very ineffective, 5 = very effective).
**Emotional Relations:** Evaluate the effectiveness of alternative actions in achieving a desired outcome involving other people on a 1 to 5 scale (1 = very ineffective, 5 = very effective).

An interesting issue with tests of emotional intelligence like the MSCEIT is how to determine the correct answers. After all, the questions involve subtle emotional concepts, for which the "correct" responses are not necessarily obvious. Consider the following question, which resembles some found on the MSCEIT:

What emotion(s) might prove helpful to feel when talking with a police officer who has just stopped you for speeding?

| Deference | not helpful …1…2…3…4…5… very helpful |
| Mild anxiety | not helpful …1…2…3…4…5… very helpful |
| Surprise | not helpful …1…2…3…4…5… very helpful |
| Irritation | not helpful …1…2…3…4…5… very helpful |

The authors of the MSCEIT propose two different scoring methods: consensus scoring and expert scoring. In consensus scoring, the majority choices of the normative sample are used to identify the correct options. For example, in the example above if 67% of the general population circled the number "1" for "irritation" (i.e., it is not helpful), this answer would be coded as the correct alternative. Respondents would receive lower scores to the extent they deviated from this alternative. This method is also called general scoring because the reference point is the general, normative sample.

The second approach, expert scoring, relies on the judgment of experts in the field of emotion to determine the correct options. In particular, the authors used 21 experts attending a conference of the International Society for Research on Emotion. Scoring for this approach relies on the consensus of these experts. Fortunately, the two scoring approaches (general and expert) reveal a very high agreement, on the order of .96 to .98 (Mayer, Salovey, & Caruso, 2002).

The rationale for consensus scoring—whether based on the general population or experts—is that emotions and their expression possess an

evolutionary and social basis. Emotions constitute a "signal system" that conveys important information to those around us. For example, the emotion of sadness signals loss and wanting to be comforted; the emotion of anger indicates the individual feels threatened and could respond forcefully; the emotion of happiness conveys an interest in joining others. Individuals who do not "read" emotions in a consensual manner likely will experience difficulty in a broad range of social situations.

The validity of the MSCEIT has been investigated from numerous perspectives, including factorial, discriminant, and predictive validity. Some results indicate that the instrument measures a unitary skill that can be subdivided into the four branches described above (Mayer, Salovey, Caruso, & Sitarenios, 2003). Further, EI as measured by the MSCEIT reveals generally low correlations with verbal intelligence, general intelligence, and major dimensions of personality, that is, the construct provides something that goes beyond established measures (Mayer, Salovey, & Caruso, 2004). EI is potentially useful because of its inverse relationship with deviant behaviors such as bullying, substance abuse, and violence. These relationships—high EI scores corresponding to low deviance—hold true even after the statistical control of intelligence and personality variables (Rubin, 1999; Trinidad & Johnson, 2002).

In spite of the supportive literature provided by proponents of EI measures, other reviewers maintain a cautious stance about the MSCEIT and similar tests. For example, in a comprehensive review of the psychometrics of emotional intelligence, Zeidner, Roberts, and Matthews (2008, p. 71) concluded that there has been "irrational enthusiasm surrounding the practical utility of emotional intelligence." They note that evidence regarding the role of EI in occupational success is weak, based largely on anecdotal reports and popular sources like Daniel Goleman's (1995) book, *Emotional Intelligence: Why It Can Matter More than IQ.*

Even the developers of the MSCEIT acknowledge the potential for misuse of their instrument. Mayer, Salovey, Caruso, and Sitarenios (2003, p. 104) state flatly that "the applied use of EI testing must proceed with great caution." The growing trend to use these instruments in selection of employees is, therefore, disquieting. As Conte (2005, p. 438) notes, managers and organizational leaders "should be wary of making this leap unless more rigorous discriminant, predictive, and incremental validity evidence for EI measures is shown."

In addition to the MSCEIT, a few other measures of emotional intelligence have gained recognition. One of these is the Emotional Competence Inventory (Sala, 2002), based on Goleman's (1995) conception of emotional intelligence. The Emotional Competence Inventory (ECI) contains 110 items organized into four clusters: (1) Self-Awareness, (2) Social Awareness, (3) Self-Management, and (4) Social Skills. One appealing feature of this instrument is the 360-degree feedback that it yields. In this method, self-ratings, peer ratings, and supervisor ratings are reported separately for comparison and contrast. The ECI is used mainly in large corporate settings for formative evaluation of employees. The publishers have maintained tight proprietary control over the test, which has limited independent research on its psychometric qualities.

Another widely used test is the Bar-On Emotional Quotient Inventory (Bar-On, 2000), which is traditionally known by the acronym EQ-i. This 133-item self-report instrument yields an overall EQ score as well as five composite scores: (1) intrapersonal, (2) interpersonal, (3) adaptability, (4) general mood, and (5) stress management. Reviewers of the EQ-i have noted that the theory behind the test is unclear (Matthews, Zeidner, & Roberts, 2002). Further, the test appears to overlap substantially with major personality constructs. For example, a correlation of $r = -.77$ with the anxiety scale from Cattell's 16PF is reported (Newsome et al., 2000). The EQ-i appears to demonstrate strong reliability, with test-retest reliability of .85 after one month (Bar-On, 1997). What remains unclear is whether the test measures emotional intelligence as a construct, as it is understood by others (Conte, 2005).

## ● ASSESSMENT OF OPTIMISM

Optimism is another fruitful area for psychometric research and assessment. Typically this construct is viewed as one end of a bipolar continuum, optimism–pessimism. The difference between the two ends of the spectrum is captured in the familiar adage about the glass of water that is half-full to the optimist and half-empty to the pessimist. Whether this bipolar depiction is an accurate portrayal of the underlying construct(s) is a topic we take up below. Nonetheless, it is certainly the starting point for many theorists and for the perceptions of the lay public as well. Carver and Scheier capture why this area of assessment is important: "Optimists are people who expect good things to happen to them; pessimists are people who expect bad things to happen to them. Does this difference among people matter? It certainly does. Optimists and pessimists differ in several ways that have a big impact on their lives. They differ in how they approach problems and challenges they encounter, and they differ in the manner and the success with which they cope with life's difficulties" (2003, p. 75). In short, optimism and pessimism have to do with people's expectations for the future. Optimists expect a better future than pessimists and generally have more confidence in their ability to manage challenges when they arise. Generally, optimists fare better than pessimists in terms of personal adjustment and even physical health, although the differences for health are not substantial (Peterson, 2000). How these individual differences arise in personal development is an important and intriguing question that we do not pursue here. Instead we focus on assessment issues, namely, how is optimism measured?

The most widely used instrument is the revised Life Orientation Test (LOT-R; Scheier, Carver, & Bridges, 1994). This is an intriguingly simple scale that consists of six scored items and four "filler" items (ten items total). Respondents indicate their extent of agreement with the items on a five-point Likert scale ranging from 1 or "strongly disagree" to 5 or "strongly agree." Items similar to those found on the LOT-R include:

> I have a positive outlook and expect the best in life
>
> I don't expect good things to happen to me (reverse scored)
>
> I enjoy my family life a great deal (filler)

Of course, negatively worded items are reverse scored. Responses on the six scored items are then summed to yield a total from 6 (highly pessimistic) to 30 (highly optimistic). Even though "pessimist" and "optimist" are categories in popular language, the LOT-R instead provides a score on a continuum, without strict cut-offs. In large samples of respondents, the score distribution tends to be skewed toward the optimistic side, but not excessively so (Carver & Scheier, 2003).

Although the theoretical basis for the LOT-R postulates an optimism-pessimism continuum, psychometric analyses by Herzberg, Glaesmer, and Hoyer (2006) with huge samples of adults ($N = 46,133$) reveal that the optimism and pessimism items on the test measure two independent constructs rather than a single, bipolar trait. This is a counterintuitive finding which suggests that optimism and pessimism are partly independent. Conceivably, an individual could earn high scores on both (or low scores on both), although these outcomes probably are rare. In practice, many researchers now report three scores from the LOT-R: an optimism score based on the positively worded items, a pessimism score based on the negatively worded items, and a total score that combines the two.

An additional finding of the Herzberg et al. study (2006) is that the reliability of the instrument is low (Cronbach alphas of .71 for the Optimism items and .68 for the Pessimism items). Thus, the test is recommended for group research only; it is not suitable for clinical practice with individuals.

A substantial literature points to the general conclusion that LOT-R optimists fare much better than pessimists on a wide variety of outcome measures (Snyder & Lopez, 2007). For example, in a sample of 275 Japanese college students, LOT-R total scores correlated $r = .39$ with social support, and $r = -.26$ with interpersonal conflict (Sumi, 2006). In a sample of 504 Australian high school students, LOT-R scores correlated $r = .55$ with self-esteem and $r = -.38$ with psychological distress (Creed, Patton, & Bartrum, 2002). In other words, for both studies LOT-R total scores modestly predicted good social adjustment.

Steptoe, Wright, Kunz-Ebrecht, and Iliffe (2006) investigated the relationship between LOT-R scores and numerous health behaviors in 128 community-dwelling seniors 65 to 80 years old. Dispositional optimism as measured by the LOT-R total score was associated with many healthful behaviors, including moderate alcohol consumption, not smoking, brisk walking, and vigorous physical activities (women only). Self-rated health and physical health status both were associated with optimism, although the direction of influence would be difficult to determine from this cross-sectional study. The full scale was more consistently associated with these positive relationships than either the optimism or pessimism subscales of the test. Carver and Scheier (2002) review additional external correlates of optimism as measured by the LOT-R.

## ● ASSESSMENT OF GRATITUDE

As Emmons, McCullough, and Tsang (2003) observe, gratitude is difficult to define. In part, this is because the concept can be viewed as an attitude, an emotion, a disposition, or a personality trait. A simple definition is that gratitude is a response of thankfulness and joy when receiving a gift. But delving further, difficulties arise. What constitutes a gift? What are the possible sources of a gift? Some gifts are obvious and not debatable, as when neighbors deliver a precooked meal to someone who is grieving a loss. Almost everyone would experience gratitude in this situation. But what about viewing a sunrise, taking a hot shower, or seeing a baby smile in the supermarket? Should we experience gratitude for these opportunities as well? In other words, does gratitude require a personal benefactor, or can it be expanded to the countless ways in which life pleasantly surprises the mindful person?

Regardless of how it is conceptualized, gratitude is universally recognized as a personal virtue because it promotes social cohesion and provides an inner buffer against the toil and pain of everyday life. In general, people with a grateful disposition experience greater well being than those without this asset (Emmons et al., 2003). The German-French theologian and physician Albert Schweitzer (1969), who founded a hospital in west central Africa and received the Nobel Peace Prize for his philosophy of "Reverence for Life," referred to gratitude as the "secret of life" (p. 36). Truly, that is a strong statement! In general, gratitude has received less attention as a topic of measurement than it deserves. But recent efforts are beginning to redress this deficiency.

One such effort is the Gratitude Questionnaire-Six Item Form (GQ-6) developed by McCullough, Emmons, and Tsang, 2002. The GQ-6 is a simple self-report measure of the disposition to experience gratitude (Figure 9.3). The test consists of the six best items from a longer list of statements that articulate gratitude and appreciation.

The reader will notice that the GQ-6 is based on a Likert-type format with seven alternatives ranging from 1 (strongly disagree) to 7 (strong agree). Two items are stated in the reverse (and therefore reverse scored) as a way of inhibiting response bias. The development and choice of specific test items was based on a thorough analysis of the many facets of the grateful disposition (McCullough, Emmons, & Tsang, 2002). The authors determined that gratitude reflects intensity (feeling more intensely grateful), frequency (feeling grateful many times a day), span (grateful for many things), and density (grateful

---

Using the scale below as a guide, write a number beside each statement to indicate how much you agree with it.

1 = **strongly disagree**

2 = **disagree**

3 = **slightly disagree**

4 = **neutral**

5 = **slightly agree**

6 = **agree**

7 = **strongly agree**

_____1. I have so much in life to be thankful for.

_____2. If I had to list everything that I felt grateful for, it would be a very long list.

_____3. When I look at the world, I don't see much to be grateful for.[*]

_____4. I am grateful to a wide variety of people.

_____5. As I get older I find myself more able to appreciate the people, events, and situations that have been part of my life history.

_____6. Long amounts of time can go by before I feel grateful to something or someone.[*]

———

[*]Items 3 and 6 are reverse scored.

● FIGURE 9.3   The Gratitude Questionnaire-Six Item Form (GQ-6)

*Source:* Reprinted with permission of Michael McCullough and Robert Emmons. Copyright 2002, all rights reserved.

to many individuals). Initially, they proposed 39 items to measure these qualities. The GQ-6 is composed of the six best items, as determined by factor-analytic procedures performed with test results from two samples: 238 undergraduates and 1,228 adult volunteers surveyed via the Internet. Reliability of the instrument is good, with coefficient alphas between .82 and .87. Validity of the GQ-6 is based on numerous theory-confirming relationships with other measures. For example, self-ratings on the GQ-6 correlated modestly with external observers' perceptions of gratitude in the participants. Additional studies indicated that the GQ-6 is positively related to optimism, hope, spirituality, religiousness, forgiveness, empathy, and prosocial behavior. The scale is negatively related to depression, anxiety, materialism, and envy (McCullough et al., 2002).

While the GQ-6 conceives of gratitude as a single dimension, other researchers have proposed a multidimensional model. For example, the Gratitude, Resentment, and Appreciation Test (GRAT, Watkins, Woodward, Stone, & Kolts, 2003) proposes three dimensions to gratitude:

- Appreciation of others, expressed as gratitude toward other people.
- Simple appreciation, expressed as gratitude toward non-social sources.
- Sense of abundance, expressed as the absence of general resentment.

The 42 items of the GRAT are rated on a 1 to 5 scale (strongly agree to strongly disagree). The test possesses excellent reliability for the three subscales and the total score (Thomas & Watkins, 2003), and reveals theory-consistent relationships with external criteria such as spirituality and the absence of materialism (Diessner & Lewis, 2007).

Even though the authors of the GRAT hypothesized a multidimensional model in the development of their test, subsequent research indicates that gratitude might actually be a unitary trait. Wood, Maltby, Stewart, and Joseph (2007) conducted a factor analysis of the three GRAT subscales and nine other indices of gratitude (including the GQ-6), and found a clear one-factor solution. The twelve measures were highly intercorrelated, indicating a single latent construct which the researchers called gratitude/appreciation. Gratitude is an essential element of human experience that deserves ongoing psychometric inquiry.

## ● SENSE OF HUMOR: SELF-REPORT MEASURES

Humor is a broad construct that has many meanings. Humor can refer to the characteristics of the material (a funny joke or cartoon) or the responses of the individual (a chuckle or belly laugh). Humor can be constructive when it brings people together, or destructive when it is at someone's expense. In contemporary Western society, having a sense of humor is generally viewed as a virtue. It is thought that individuals with a "good" sense of humor will more easily befriend others and also will be able to weather the adversities of life with greater balance.

But how do we conceptualize the loose notion of "sense of humor?" Is this an enduring personality trait, an ability to make others laugh, a temperamental feature of good cheer, a world view that life is fundamentally absurd, or something else? Martin (2003, p. 315) argues that: "One of the challenges of research on humor in the context of positive psychology is to identify which aspects or components of the humor construct are most relevant to mental health and successful adaptation." His answer is to conceptualize humor as a way of coping with stress and enhancing relationships. With this approach, Martin has developed three instruments used widely in humor research: The Coping Humor Scale, the Situational Humor Response Questionnaire, and the Humor Styles Questionnaire.

The Coping Humor Scale was designed to assess the extent to which individuals report using humor to cope with stress (Martin & Lefcourt, 1983). The CHS consists of 7 items similar to "When things are tense I look for something funny to say" or "I think humor is a useful way of coping with problems." These items are rated on a scale from 1 (strongly disagree) to 4 (strongly agree). There is no neutral point on the scale, which forces the respondent to take a position.

The CHS has good test-retest reliability, with $r = .80$ over a 12-week period, but only fair internal consistency, with coefficient alphas of .60 to .70 (Martin, 1996). Regarding validity, Martin (2003, p. 317) summarizes a number of robust external correlates of the test. CHS total scores correlate strongly with the following constructs:

- Peer ratings of using humor to cope with stress
- Peer ratings of not taking one's self too seriously
- Researcher ratings of funniness of monologues produced under stress
- Researcher ratings of using laughter and humor before dental surgery

The CHS is a respected instrument in humor research. Nonetheless, it has faded in use because later instruments (discussed below) provide broader measures of sense of humor.

The Situational Humor Response Questionnaire provides a measure of the degree to which the respondent is easily amused and laughs in a wide range of situations (Martin, 1996; Martin & Lefcourt, 1984). The SHRQ consists of 21 items, the first 18 of which describe ordinary life situations such as "You were at a party and the host accidentally spilled a drink on you." Each item is rated on a scale from 1 ("I would not have been particularly amused") to 5 ("I would have laughed heartily"). The last 3 items refer to laughing and being amused in general.

As summarized by Martin (1996), the SHRQ reveals adequate psychometric qualities, including test-retest correlations of around .70 and Cronbach alphas in the vicinity of .70 to .85. An interesting validity criterion used in several studies is the correlation of test scores with observed frequency of laughter, with $rs$ ranging from .30 to .60. As noted by Martin (2003), frequency of laughter is a good validity criterion, but it is not perfect. After all, there is laughter without humor and humor without laugh-

ter. Fortunately, the validity evidence for this instrument includes a wide base of diverse studies, such as correlations with rated funniness of monologues produced by participants, and correlations with other humor scales. Another concern about the test is that the humor situations were designed with college students in mind and may not generalize to other groups. The humor situations date to the 1980s and earlier; some are no longer funny. After all, what is deemed funny shifts over time, is specific to cultures, and is sometimes idiosyncratic. For example, some viewers find the video clips featured on the television show *America's Funniest Home Videos* to be hilarious, whereas others regard this weekly offering with bewilderment or even downright scorn.

Recently, Martin and colleagues have developed a new humor instrument that represents the culmination of decades of research. The Humor Styles Questionnaire (HSQ, Martin, Puhlik-Doris, Larsen, Gray, & Weir, 2003) assesses four dimensions that convey individual differences in uses of humor:

- Affiliative: Use of humor to entertain others and facilitate relationships.
- Self-enhancing: Use of humor to cope with stress and uphold a positive outlook during difficult times.
- Aggressive: Use of mocking, manipulative, put-down, or disparaging humor.
- Self-defeating: Use of humor for undue self-disparagement, ingratiation, or defensive reply.

The HSQ includes 32 self-descriptive statements (8 for each subscale) that depict specific uses of humor. For example, items on the Affiliative scale might resemble: "I like to tell silly jokes based on word play." Items on the Aggressive scale might resemble: "I like to poke fun at people when they make mistakes."

The first two styles, Affiliative and Self-enhancing, embody constructive and healthy uses of humor. The last two styles, Aggressive and Self-defeating, involve unhealthy uses of humor that distance the individual from others. For each item, respondents indicate agreement or disagreement on a 7-point scale ranging from 1 (totally disagree) to 7 (totally agree). The HSQ reveals excellent psychometric properties, with strong internal consistencies of the subscales (around .80), and good test-retest reliabilities (.80 to .85). Validity is based on convergent and discriminant correlations of the subscales with appropriate external criteria including well-being, hostility, intimacy, coping, satisfaction with relationships, and major personality variables (Martin et al., 2003).

How do individual differences in humor styles arise? A recent behavioral genetics analysis comparing HSQ scores of identical and fraternal twins found fascinating differences in developmental influences among the four humor styles (Vernon, Martin, Schermer, & Mackie, 2008). In this study of 300 pairs of identical twins and 156 pairs of fraternal twins, the positive forms of humor (Affiliative and Self-enhancing) were found to display significant genetic influences whereas the negative forms of humor (Aggressive and Self-defeating) arose in greater measure from common environmental influences. The authors offer the following conclusion:

> These results may have implications for potential therapeutic interventions designed to modify individuals' sense of humor. Because traits that are mainly influenced by environmental factors may be more malleable than those that are mainly influenced by genetic factors, our findings suggest that it may be easier to help people reduce their levels of aggressive and self-defeating humor styles than to increase their use of affiliative and self-enhancing humor. This is clearly a topic for further experimental study. (Vernon et al., 2008, p. 1123–1124)

The lesson here for psychological testing is that the development of good measures such as the HSQ often generates far-reaching consequences.

## ● SUMMARY

1. In recent years a new field known as positive psychology has emerged. Based on the scientific and practical pursuit of human function, positive psychology has also generated efforts to assess human strengths and virtues with positive psychological assessment.

2. One focus of positive psychology has been creativity, which can be viewed as cognitive processes, personal characteristics, and behavioral products. Mednick's Remote Associates Test (RAT), a clever index of the remoteness of verbal associations, is an attempt to measure creativity as a process. An example of the RAT: what word goes with: rat—blue—cottage? (Answer: cheese).

3. Research indicates that creative persons possess distinctive personal characteristics such as curiosity, sensitivity, and rebelliousness. Sternberg also has argued that creative individuals are distinguished by the heartfelt decision to be creative. Creative thinking also reflects divergent thinking, the kind that goes off in different directions. This is in contrast to convergent thinking, the focus on the production of a single correct answer determined by facts and reason.

4. The Torrance Tests of Creative Thinking (TTCT) are the most widely respected measures of creativity in the field. The test includes verbal subtests (e.g., Product Improvement, Unusual Uses) with items like "Tell me as many uses that you can think of for a large button) and figural subtests (e.g., Picture Construction, Picture Completion) with items that require creative completion of incomplete drawings.

5. According to a respected definition, emotional intelligence includes: managing emotions so as to attain specific goals; understanding emotions, emotional language, and the signals conveyed by emotions; using emotions to facilitate thinking; and, perceiving emotions accurately in oneself and others.

6. One measure of emotional intelligence is the MSCEIT or Mayer-Salovey-Caruso Emotional

Intelligence Test. This test includes 141 items that yield a total emotional intelligence score, as well as two area scores, four branch scores, and eight task scores. This test is relatively new and the authors recommend great caution in using the instrument for organizational selection.

7. The revised Life Orientation Test (LOT-R) is an intriguingly simple measure of optimism that consists of six scored items and four "filler" items. The scored items resemble: "I have a positive outlook and expect the best in life" and are rated from on a 5-point agree-disagree continuum. Many studies support the general conclusion that LOT-R optimists have good social adjustment and less conflict and distress in life.

8. The Gratitude Questionnaire—Six Item Form (GQ-6) is a simple six-item self-report measure of the disposition to experience gratitude. The validity of the test is based on numerous theory-confirming relationships with other measures, including positive relationships with optimism, hope, spirituality, and forgiveness, and negative relationships with depression, anxiety, materialism, and envy.

9. Sense of humor is an important quality for positive adaptation. Several instruments including the Humor Styles Questionnaire (HSQ) have been developed to assess this construct. This 32-item test assesses four dimensions of humor: Affiliative (using humor to entertain, Self-enhancing (using humor to cope with stress), Aggressive (using humor to mock, manipulate or put down others), and Self-defeating (using humor for self-disparagement or ingratiation).

● **KEY TERMS AND CONCEPTS**

positive psychology    p. 396

positive psychological assessment    p. 397

divergent thinking    p. 401

convergent thinking    p. 401

emotional intelligence    p. 404

# Chapter 10

# Neuropsychological Assessment and Screening

## TOPIC 10A

## A Primer of Neurobiological Concepts

In the practice of assessment, psychologists often discover that their clients need assistance with serious problems that are best understood from a neurobiological standpoint. These problems typically arise as a consequence of head injury, learning disability, memory impairment, language disorder, or attentional difficulties, to list just a few examples. Tens of millions of individuals are affected. For example, in the United States an estimated 5 to 8 million children struggle with a learning disability (Dey, Schiller, & Tai, 2004), about 13 to 16 million adults live with memory loss and other symptoms related to dementia (Alzheimer's Disease and Related Disorders Association, 2000), and approximately 2 million people experience a head injury *each year* (Kraus & McArthur, 1996).

These numbers are staggering, and they provide an ongoing mandate for psychologists to develop specialized tests and procedures at the interface of psychology and medicine. The purpose of this chapter is to summarize pertinent tests, concepts, methods, and issues encountered in neuropsychological assessment and ancillary areas of appraisal such as substance abuse evaluation and screening for dementia. In Topic 10A, A Primer of Neurobiological Concepts, we provide a condensed review of neurobiological concepts relevant to psychological testing and assessment. The emphasis in this topic is upon the various brain systems that underlie effective cognitive and emotional functioning. Understanding these brain systems is essential for those who study or use psychological tests. In this primer, the reader also will encounter several of the simpler approaches to assessment used by neuropsychologists. In the process, a good foundation will be set for Topic 10B, Neuropsychological Tests, Batteries, and Screening Tools, which reviews prominent neuropsychological instruments, test batteries, and screening tools.

## ● THE HUMAN BRAIN: AN OVERVIEW

By convention the nervous system is divided into the central nervous system consisting of the brain and spinal cord, and the peripheral nervous system that includes the cranial nerves and the network of nerves emanating from the spinal cord. The brain is intimately involved in thinking, feeling, and behaving. For these reasons, our focus in this topic is the structure and function of the brain.

The brain is beyond doubt the most protected organ in the human body. The first line of defense against physical trauma is the skull, consisting of several intermeshed, rigid bones that almost completely encase the brain. Beneath the skull, the brain is also surrounded by the **meninges,** a thin layering of three tough membranes that encases the brain and spinal cord, providing additional protection. The middle spongy layer of the meninges is filled with

another form of protection, cerebrospinal fluid, which buffers the brain against sudden acceleration and deceleration, such as from a blow to the head. The brain literally floats in a snugly fitting bath of cerebrospinal fluid. Buoyancy reduces the effective weight of the organ to a few ounces, vastly reducing pressure upon the base of the brain. Without the protection of this fluid, the brain would bruise easily from any rapid movement of the head.

When unbouyed, the brain weighs less than three pounds. It is composed principally of five elements: gray matter, white matter, glial cells, cerebrospinal fluid (CSF), and the blood vessels of the vascular system that provide the brain with oxygen and nutrients. Each of these five components is reviewed next.

### Gray Matter and White Matter

The relationships among gray matter, white matter, and CSF can be shown in a cross-sectional drawing of a typical brain (Figure 10.1). The **gray matter** consists of densely packed cell bodies of neurons, which are also called nerve cells. When activated, a neuron or nerve cell conducts an electrochemical impulse outward from the cell body down an elongated structure called the axon. Although beyond the scope of our coverage here, it is these impulses that allow neurons to communicate with one another. Axons are wrapped in a white, fatty substance called myelin sheath that provides insulation and enhances neural transmission. The myelin sheath gives **white matter** its distinctive appearance. Axons can be up to several inches in length and provide up to 90 percent of the total volume of some nerve cells. A few neurological ailments, called demyelinating diseases, attack the white matter and impair the ability of nerve cells to communicate with one another. Multiple sclerosis is probably the most common disorder of demyelinization. Its symptoms are highly varied, depending upon the sites of attack upon the myelin sheath, but might include blurred vision, muscle weakness, partial numbness, and loss of coordination. The subsequent course of the illness is highly variable.

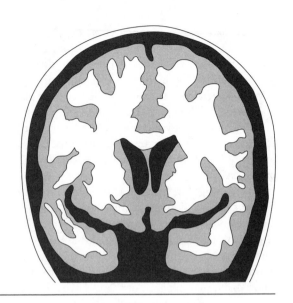

●  **FIGURE 10.1**
A Cross-Sectional View of the Brain Depicting Gray Matter, White Matter, and Cerebrospinal Fluid

Note: In this diagram, we have followed the logical convention of depicting gray matter as gray and white matter as white. Cerebrospinal fluid or CSF is depicted as black, even though in reality it would be a relatively clear liquid. The two crescent shaped areas in the center, filled with CSF, are the lateral ventricles (see text).

For decades, it has been believed that the neurons that compose the gray matter and white matter do not reproduce, at least not in adult mammals. However, recent research suggests that adult humans may have a limited capacity to reproduce neurons, especially in areas of the brain important for learning and memory (Rakic, 2002). Capable of prolific reproduction, the more numerous glial cells provide various forms of structural support to the neurons.

The $10^{11}$ or 100 billion neurons in the brain are arranged in complex networks that largely have defied understanding. In part, the inscrutability of the brain derives from its computational complexity. Neurons communicate by sending all-or-no electrochemical impulses to one another. Each neuron might send transmissions to thousands, perhaps tens of thousands, of other neurons at near and distant sites called synapses. Chemical communications across the synapses can occur up to a thousand times a second. Even if we use a conservative estimate of a thousand synapses per neuron, in theory the number of neural transmissions that could occur in just one second is a staggering $10^{17}$ or 100,000,000,000,000,000 (one hundred quadrillion). No wonder that staid neuroscientists such as Sir John Eccles (who received a Nobel Prize for his work in neurophysiology) resort to hyper-

bole and describe the brain as "without qualification the most highly organized and most complexly organized matter in the universe" (Eccles, 1973). Considering how little we know of the universe, the truth of this statement is open to question. But it does effectively underscore the point that neuroscientists approach the study of the human brain with a sense of awe.

## Glial Cells

**Glial cells** constitute another important element of the brain. These cells far outnumber the neurons. There are many, many types of glial cells. Their functions include structural support for the neurons, transport of nutrients to the neurons, cleaning up brain "debris," and insulating axons in the central and peripheral nervous system. Glial cells also are involved in modulating the excitability of individual neurons. Thus, even though glial cells do not directly conduct nerve impulses, they indirectly affect this crucial form of brain activity. The complete role of glial cells in the regulation of brain functioning is yet to be determined, but it seems likely that they do far more than play a mundane supporting role. For example, it is known from postmortem autopsy that the brain of Albert

Einstein contained an unusually large number of glial cells in those areas of the cortex thought to be essential for mathematical skills (Diamond, Scheibel, Murphy, & Harvey, 1985). One interpretation of this finding is that, for Einstein, these brain areas required the additional metabolic support provided by the excess of glial cells found there.

## Cerebrospinal Fluid and the Ventricular System

**Cerebrospinal fluid** (CSF) is a clear liquid that is continuously produced and replenished within the ventricles. The **ventricles** are hollow, interconnected chambers found in the middle of the brain. There are four ventricles: two side-by-side ventricles, called the lateral ventricles, and two midline ventricles known as the third and fourth ventricles. The location of the lateral ventricles is easily seen in Figure 10.1. The CSF is produced by the choroid plexus, bilateral structures found within these lateral ventricles. About three-fourths of a liter of CSF is produced each day. The fluid flows slowly from the lateral ventricles down through the third and fourth ventricles by means of channels and aqueducts, until it reaches the meninges on the outer surface of the brain and spinal cord. Because it is under pressure, CSF is gradually reabsorbed by a large vein at the top of the brain.

In rare cases, the normal flow of CSF can become constricted, such as when the aqueduct leaving the third or fourth ventricle becomes too small. This can be a congenital condition present at birth or a disease-related state observed in adulthood. In children, the increase in pressure can lead to enlargement of the ventricles and compression of the brain against the skull. In time, the skull can even enlarge. This condition is known as hydrocephalus or, literally, "water on the brain." Untreated, the consequence of hydrocephalus can be mental retardation and early mortality. Fortunately, effective treatments are available, including the insertion of a shunt to drain the excess fluid from the ventricles—usually into the child's abdomen.

The location and size of the ventricles are important clues to the health of the brain. For example, a tumor might displace the lateral ventricles so that they are no longer symmetrical. This can be observed from various brain imaging techniques discussed later in this chapter. Excessively enlarged ventricles also signify the presence of a brain-impairing condition such as alcoholism, dementia, or schizophrenia. Enlarged ventricles are not directly the problem, but they do signify that less space is available for brain tissue, which can point to an underlying disease process.

## The Vascular System of the Brain

Metabolically, the brain is a highly active organ, needing substantial supplies of oxygen and glucose to function effectively. These energy sources are supplied by the flow of blood through the cardiovascular system. Hence, the general physical health of the client and the specific condition of his or her vascular system in the brain are essential to high-level cognitive functioning.

Two pairs of arteries carry blood to the brain. These are the left and right internal carotid arteries, found in the front of the neck, and the left and right vertebral arteries, found in the back of the neck. The vertebral arteries come together just below the base of the brain to form a single artery, the basilar artery. These three arteries—the left and right internal carotids and the basilar artery—all feed into a circular arterial structure at the base of the brain known as the circle of Willis. This circular network ensures that the brain receives a continual supply of blood, even if one of the input arteries is compromised.

From this circular arterial system at the base of the brain, three arteries branch upward on each side to the roughly symmetrical cerebral hemispheres of the brain. The anterior cerebral arteries supply blood to the left and right frontal lobes and some midline structures. The middle cerebral arteries provide blood to the vast majority of the lateral surface of each hemisphere, including the frontal, parietal, and temporal lobes, and to some internal structures as well. Finally, the posterior cerebral arteries supply blood to the left and right occipital lobes and to additional subcortical structures.

Especially with advancing age, it is not unusual for one or more arteries in the brain to become completely obstructed by a condition known as atherosclerosis, the gradual buildup of fatty plaque. When an artery in the brain becomes completely obstructed—whether gradually or suddenly from a piece of dislodged plaque—the brain tissue supplied by that vessel dies because it is deprived of oxygen. This event is called an infarct, which is one kind of stroke or **cerebrovascular accident** (CVA). Another kind of CVA occurs when a bulging area of arterial weakness, called an aneurysm, bursts open, allowing blood to spurt directly into the brain tissue. This is technically known as an arterial rupture. The effects of a CVA depend upon the size and location of the resulting damage to the brain. For example, an infarct occurring at the base of the left middle cerebral artery would have calamitous generalized effects (e.g., right-sided paralysis of the body, loss of speech), whereas an infarct occurring higher up, in a smaller offshoot from the artery, might have limited effects or even go unnoticed. One form of vascular impairment known as **multi-infarct dementia** (MID) occurs when the hardly noticeable individual effects of many small infarcts accumulate over a number of years. The symptoms of MID are varied but often impact the ability to perform everyday activities such as eating, dressing, and shopping. The symptoms might include forgetfulness, vague or circumstantial speech, lack of concentration, loss of balance, physical weakness, difficulty following instructions, and problems handling money. Often the onset of MID is so gradual and insidious that relatives recognize only in retrospect that something has been wrong for months after the onset of problems.

## ● STRUCTURES AND SYSTEMS OF THE BRAIN

The organization of the human brain is difficult to comprehend because important structures are interwoven and folded over upon one another. As noted, the brain also contains an intricate system of fluid-filled caverns, the ventricles, further complicating the spatial arrangement of important brain structures. In addition, functional brain systems rarely obey any simple structural organization—they typically meander their way from one part of the brain to another. Hence, we will focus mainly on a functional systems approach to explaining the operation of the brain, alluding to structures when appropriate.

We begin with a quick overview of the central nervous system and its primary subdivisions. The most basic element of the nervous system is the **cerebrum,** consisting of the left and right cerebral hemispheres, which are connected by the corpus callosum, a band of fibers that transfers information from one hemisphere to the other. From the standpoint of evolution, the cerebrum is the most recent part of the brain to develop. This is where thought, perception, imagination, judgment, and decision occur. Some essential structures located beneath the cerebrum are the basal ganglia and the cerebellum (both important in coordinated movement), the diencephalon (including the thalamus), the midbrain (consisting of the cranial nerves and other important relay stations), the pons (connecting the cerebrum with the cerebellum and the spinal cord), and the medulla (mediating essential bodily functions).

### Corpus Callosum

The **corpus callosum** is the major commissure that serves to integrate the functions of the two cerebral hemispheres. This large bundle of subcortical nerve fibers is about four inches long and a quarter inch thick. The corpus callosum spans the brain from side to side just above the level of the thalamus. Although there are exceptions, the corpus callosum generally connects homologous brain sites in the left and right hemispheres.

The function of the corpus callosum was poorly understood until the 1960s when Sperry, Gazzaniga, and others initiated sophisticated laboratory studies of so-called split-brain patients (Sperry, 1964; Gazzaniga, 1970; Gazzaniga & LeDoux, 1978). These patients were persons with epilepsy whose corpus callosa had been severed to prevent the transport of epileptic discharges from one hemisphere to the other. Although outwardly normal, split-brain patients revealed a striking isolation of consciousness when visual information was restricted to one hemisphere or the other. For example, when a picture of an apple was tachistoscopically presented to the left side of the examinee's fixation point, this stimulus was processed only in the right hemisphere (on account of the normal crossing over of neural connections). Furthermore, because the corpus callosum was severed, the image of the apple remained trapped in the right hemisphere. As the reader will discover later, the right hemisphere is usually mute and does not subserve important language functions. Thus, when asked, "What did you see?" the examinees, responding from the verbal left hemisphere, would honestly reply, "Nothing." Yet, these patients could readily identify the object by pointing to it with the left hand (which is under the neural control of the right hemisphere). This suggests that although the right hemisphere cannot talk, it has a separate and independent capacity to perceive, learn, remember, and issue commands for motor tasks.

In a normal individual with intact corpus callosum, consciousness appears unitary because the two halves of the brain can communicate and forge a compromise as regards perception, thought, and action. Much of our knowledge of hemispheric specializations, discussed later, has been garnered from the detailed study of split-brain patients. Further insight has been gained from studies of persons afflicted with congenital absence of this structure, a condition known as agenesis of the corpus callosum. These patients usually have a variety of intellectual defects, indicating that the corpus callosum facilitates learning in many different cognitive spheres (Bradshaw & Mattingley, 1995).

## Cerebral Cortex

The **cerebral cortex,** the outermost layer of the brain, is the source of the highest levels of sensory, motor, and cognitive processing. Also called the neocortex, the cerebral cortex is a very recent evolutionary development. It is the functional capacity of this brain system—a uniform six layers deep—that most dramatically separates humans from the lower animals.

The tissue of the cerebral cortex is folded over into elaborate convolutions consisting of bulges and grooves. The prominent bulges are called gyri (singular *gyrus*), whereas the clefts, fissures, and grooves are called sulci (singular *sulcus*). This arrangement allows the brain to have a great deal more cerebral cortex than if the surface were smooth. Although the pattern of gyri and sulci is subtly unique for each person, certain major landmarks such as the central sulcus and the lateral sulcus (Figure 10.2) are always discernible in a normal brain.

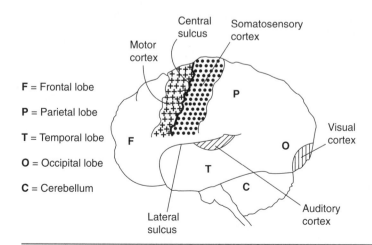

F = Frontal lobe

P = Parietal lobe

T = Temporal lobe

O = Occipital lobe

C = Cerebellum

● FIGURE 10.2
Major Landmarks of the Left Cerebral Hemisphere

A small portion of the cerebral cortex is committed cortex. These sites are dedicated to basic sensory processing of vision, hearing, touch, and motor control. Nonetheless, the specificity of committed cortex is relative, not absolute. For example, the precentral gyrus is regarded as the motor strip, yet only 40 percent of the primary motor cells subserving voluntary movement are located there; another 10 to 20 percent are located in the sensory strip, and 40 to 50 percent are situated in adjoining brain sites (Brodal, 1981). Furthermore, the motor strip contains a sizeable proportion of sensory cells, too. Thus, cells that subserve each specific sensory or motor function are highly concentrated in the respective committed area, but also thin out and overlap with nearby brain sites. In brief, the committed cortex of the **frontal lobe** is dedicated to motor control, the **parietal lobe** is concerned with the processing of touch and other somatosensory information, the **occipital lobe** is involved in visual perception, and the **temporal lobe** is essential to the processing of auditory information. Of course, these brain regions serve other functions as well, but part of each major lobe is dedicated to a specific motor or sensory function (Figure 10.2).

## ● SURVIVAL SYSTEMS: THE HINDBRAIN AND MIDBRAIN

The lowest part of the brain, located at the top of the spinal cord, consists of the **hindbrain,** which includes the medulla oblongata, the pons, the reticular formation, and the cerebellum. From the standpoint of evolution, the hindbrain was the first brain system to develop, which explains why so many vital bodily functions are governed by this brain area. For example, the automatic control of breathing is mediated here—we breathe even when asleep, or for that matter, when in a deep coma.

The lowest section of the hindbrain is the medulla oblongata, which mediates several essential bodily functions: breathing, swallowing, vomiting, blood pressure, and, partially, heart rate (Kandel, Schwartz, & Jessell, 1995). Aspects of talk-ing and singing also are governed here, although higher brain sites are intimately involved in these functions as well.

Significant damage to the medulla usually is fatal. In rare cases, a small stroke in the medulla causes one or more of the following symptoms: opposite-sided paralysis, partial loss of pain and temperature sense, clumsiness, dizziness, partial loss of the gag reflex, and same-sided paralysis and atrophy of the tongue. Thus, one reason why neurologists ask patients to stick out their tongue and move it from side to side is specifically to check for neurological damage in and around the medulla. The polio virus—rampant in the 1950s but now well controlled—may attack the medulla, shutting down the neural control of breathing and necessitating a mechanical respirator.

The pons and cerebellum are the highest structures in the hindbrain. Together they help coordinate muscle tone, posture, and hand and eye movement. The role of the cerebellum in motor control is discussed later. Lesions of the pons may render the individual incapable of making coordinated lateral eye movements. For this reason, neurologists and neuropsychologists commonly ask patients to demonstrate left-right and up-down eye movements.

Located just above the hindbrain is the **midbrain,** which includes a number of important relay stations involved in hearing and vision. In addition, the midbrain contains nuclei for many of the cranial nerves (some of which also emanate from the hindbrain). The 12 paired **cranial nerves** are major neural tracts whose functions are well understood and easily tested. Some are exclusively sensory, relaying information from the external world to the brain; some are exclusively motor, serving to execute commands from the brain; about a third of the cranial nerves possess both sensory and motor functions. Neurologists refer to the cranial nerves by number. The numbers correspond roughly to the top to bottom sequence of the nerves' emergence from the brain (Table 10.1). The reader will notice that many cranial nerves mediate aspects of vision and eye movement, basic sensory functions, and movement of jaw, tongue,

| ● **TABLE 10.1** | **The Cranial Nerves and Their Functions** |
|---|---|
| 1. Olfactory | Sense of smell |
| 2. Optic | Vision |
| 3. Oculomotor | Horizontal and vertical eye movement |
| 4. Trochlear | Vertical eye movement |
| 5. Trigeminal | Facial sensation, jaw movement |
| 6. Abducens | Horizontal eye movement |
| 7. Facial | Facial movement and taste |
| 8. Auditory/vestibular | Hearing and balance |
| 9. Glossopharyngeal | Taste, swallowing |
| 10. Vagus | Visceral reflexes |
| 11. Accessory | Head movement |
| 12. Hypoglossal | Tongue movement |

face, and head. Over the centuries, neurologists have devised a variety of simple confrontational techniques to assess the cranial nerves. As peculiar as it may appear, asking the patient to stick out his or her tongue and move it left, right, up, or down can provide important information about the functioning of the hypoglossal (twelfth) cranial nerve. In like manner, various simple tests of hearing, balance, eye movement, and so on are used to complete the examination of the cranial nerves.

## ● ATTENTIONAL SYSTEMS

Attention has been likened to a "spotlight" that our brain uses to identify what is relevant and ignore what is irrelevant (Andreasen, 2001). Attention is often a primitive, automatic cognitive system that is essential for survival. Consider the variety of competing stimuli encountered when you drive a car down the highway, perhaps with a friend sitting next to you. A realistic scenario is that your friend asks a question, an airplane flies low in the distant horizon, a billboard on the left lures your visual focus, a siren blares in the distance, your back aches from a strenuous workout—all these sources of stimulation compete for your attention.

Then a car swerves into your lane. Instantly, without conscious forethought, your brain focuses every last fragment of attention on this one looming threat, ignoring all else.

Neuropsychologists have identified several kinds of **attention,** including the following types:

- Orienting
- Selective
- Divided
- Sustained

Orienting attention is the simplest and most primitive form, related to the "fight" or "flight" reflex. This is the straightforward direction of all attentional resources to a single threatening stimulus, such as a car swerving into your lane. Selective attention refers to the identification of a single, personally relevant stimulus embedded within a flow of extraneous information. This is exemplified when, for example, a young boy who seems absorbed in solitary play nonetheless turns his head when he overhears his name spoken quietly in the background. Divided attention, also known as distributed attention, pertains to the ability to shift back and forth between two or more tasks. An example might be when a partygoer tries to follow two conversations at the same time. Sustained attention, also known as vigilance, refers to the ability to sustain attention over relatively long periods of time. This involves the capacity to resist distraction and stay on task for a prolonged period. A good example is the air traffic controller who must monitor radar images carefully to keep airplanes at a safe distance from one another.

The exact neurological mechanisms of attention are not well understood. Kandel, Schwartz, and Jessell (1995) note that the "neuronal mechanisms of focused attention and conscious awareness are now emerging as one of the great unresolved problems in perception and indeed in all of neurobiology" (p. 402). Neurologically, attention is a complex function that involves the collaborative effort of several brain sites. Furthermore, different forms of attention appear to invoke different brain systems. For example, sustained attention or vigilance is mediated by the reticular formation, a network of ascending and descending nerve cell bodies and fibers, that begins in the spinal cord and extends through the medulla all the way up to the thalamus. Specific nuclei within the reticular formation project through the thalamus to wide areas of the brain and thereby help mediate attention. Based upon the classic studies of Moruzzi and Magoun (1949) demonstrating that ascending nerve tracts within the **reticular formation** govern general arousal or consciousness, portions of this structure are also known as the reticular activating system. Damage to the reticular activating system gives rise to global diminution of consciousness ranging from chronic drowsiness to stupor or coma (Carpenter, 1991).

Selective attention appears to invoke brain sites in addition to the reticular formation. For example, based upon functional imaging studies that highlight active brain sites, it appears that the cingulate gyrus is essential for focusing upon relevant aspects of the environment while ignoring irrelevant information. One finding is that, when asked to perform complex attentional tasks, persons who suffer from schizophrenia and who, therefore, reveal deficits in selective attention also show dysfunction in the cingulate gyrus (Carter, Mintun, Nichols, & Cohen, 1997).

## ● MOTOR/COORDINATION SYSTEMS

Although many brain sites are involved in motor control, three areas are of special significance: the cerebellum, the basal ganglia, and the motor cortex. The **cerebellum** sits just below the cerebrum at the back of the brain. Together with other brain structures, it helps coordinate muscle tone, posture, and hand and eye movements. Lesions in or near the cerebellum may render the individual incapable of making coordinated lateral eye movements. For this reason, neurologists and neuropsychologists commonly ask patients to demonstrate left-right and up-down eye movements. An individual with damage to the cerebellum might not be able to move his or her eyes with facility in all directions.

The cerebellum receives sensory information from every part of the body and coordinates the details of automatic skilled movements. Damage to the cerebellum may cause a variety of motor disturbances, depending upon the specific sites affected (Bradshaw & Mattingley, 1995). Slurred, hesitant speech known as **dysarthria** may be a symptom of cerebellar damage. Muscles may become flabby and tire easily. Rapid, coordinated tapping of the index finger may prove difficult. Measures of finger-tapping speed (Reitan & Wolfson, 1993) are, therefore, an important component of neuropsychological test batteries.

Bodily movements may lose their coordination in cerebellar disease, becoming spasmodic and jerky. Even a simple gesture such as reaching for a cup may result in the inadvertent thrusting of cup and contents halfway across the room. The characteristic wide-based gait of alcoholics—called ataxia—is a consequence of cerebellar degeneration (Ghez, 1991). Another symptom of cerebellar damage is intention tremor, so named because it is not present at rest but arises during voluntary, intentional movements of the hands. Nystagmus also is common in cerebellar disease. In this symptom, the eyes appear to jitter back and forth even when the individual attempts to hold a steady gaze.

In conjunction with the vestibular center in the inner ear, the cerebellum also helps coordinate the vestibuloocular reflex (VOR). The VOR acts to maintain the eyes on a fixed target when the head is rotated. Without the VOR, vision would be incredibly blurred whenever the head moved even a fraction of an inch. Instead, a small area of the cerebellum coordinates a rapid refixation of the eyes to compensate for head movements.

The **basal ganglia** consist of a collection of nuclei in the in the forebrain that makes connections with the cerebral cortex above and the thalamus below. The basal ganglia are traditionally considered as part of the motor system. The main constituents of the basal ganglia are three large subcortical nuclei: the caudate, the putamen, and the globus pallidus. Some authorities also consider the amygdala to be part of the basal ganglia (Carpenter, 1991). These structures are interconnected with and functionally related to the subthalamic nucleus and the substantia nigra. Along with the cerebellum, the corticospinal system, and the motor nuclei in the brain stem, the basal ganglia participate in the control of movement. Unlike the other components of the motor system, the basal ganglia do not have direct connections with the spinal cord. The motor functions of the basal ganglia are indirect and are mediated via neural connections with the frontal cerebral cortex.

The most common syndrome caused by damage to the basal ganglia is **Parkinson's disease** (Cote & Crutcher, 1991). In Parkinson's disease, three characteristic types of motor disturbances are observed: involuntary movement, including tremor; poverty and slowness of movement without paralysis; and changes in posture and muscle tone. In its later stages, this disease is typified by an immobile, masklike facial expression, an extreme difficulty initiating movements, and a fine tremor that may disappear once a movement is under way.

Patients with Parkinson's disease also reveal specific cognitive deficits, suggesting that the basal ganglia contribute not just to movement but to thinking as well. Deficits observed in these patients include diminished cognitive flexibility and mildly reduced learning and recall (Koss, 1994). A loss of spontaneity and a lack of initiative also are observed (La Rue, 1992).

The **motor cortex** is found on the precentral gyrus of the frontal lobe. Primary motor cells that subserve voluntary movement are located here and in adjoining brain sites (Brodal, 1981). Motor control is substantially but not exclusively contralateral (opposite-sided), meaning that the left precentral gyrus subserves the right side of the body, and vice versa. Thus, when an individual makes a decision, say, to lift his right hand, motor neurons in the left precentral gyrus will be activated. For obvious reasons, this area is also known as the motor strip.

The fact that motor control is substantially opposite-sided is the basis for several neuropsychological procedures that compare the function of the two sides of the body as a means of determining the integrity of the left and right motor strips. Consider the finger-tapping test, employed with many neuropsychological test batteries (e.g., Reitan & Wolfson, 1993). In a typical finger-tapping procedure, the examiner uses standardized procedures with repeated trials to determine the maximal tapping rates of the left and right index fingers over a 10-second span. Of course, the preferred hand will have a slight advantage, with a normative expectation of a rate that is 10 percent higher. For example, in a right-handed person, a tapping rate of 55 for the right index finger and 50 for the left index finger might be typical.

Any significant deviation from this expected pattern may suggest impairment in the opposite-sided motor strip. For example, suppose a right-handed examinee has a tapping rate of 47 for the right index finger and 50 for the left index finger. Because the right-sided tapping rate is comparatively slower than expected (i.e., 6 percent slower instead of 10 percent faster than the left-sided tapping rate), this would suggest impairment in the left motor strip.

## ● MEMORY SYSTEMS

Although the lay public thinks of memory as a single thing, psychologists have known for more than a century that there are many types of memory and also several stages of memory (Ebbinghaus, 1885/1913). We can provide only a cursory review here. The importance of reviewing these basic distinctions is that different brain systems may be involved in different kinds of memory.

As to types of memory, Andreasen (2001) posits the existence of at least four different polarities of **memory:** episodic versus semantic, working versus associative, declarative versus procedural, and explicit versus implicit. To this list, we would add a fifth dimension: short-term versus long-term memory. These dimensions are not completely separate and distinct from one another. Episodic memory refers to memory of events or experiences, such as recalling that you had oatmeal for breakfast. In contrast, semantic memory is general knowledge not tied to a specific learning experience, such as knowing that a butterfly is an insect, not a bird. Working memory is the retention of information that we need only briefly, such as remembering the digits of a phone number just long enough to complete the call. Associative memory involves memories that are invoked because of their association with particular cues, for example, recalling the smell and taste of popcorn when hearing the sound of it popping in the microwave. Declarative memory involves the "what" of memory (e.g., knowing that a bicycle has two wheels) whereas procedural memory involves the "how" of memory (e.g., knowing how to ride a bicycle). Another way of dividing memory is explicit versus implicit, which defines the difference between memories that are immediately accessible and obvious (e.g., knowing your name) compared to those that are latent, beneath the surface (e.g., surprising yourself when you are able to recall the name of your first-grade teacher).

Another important distinction is between short-term and long-term memory. Short-term memory is synonymous with working memory and is very short in duration, lasting from perhaps 10 seconds to a minute. If short-term memories are not "refreshed' through rehearsal, they disappear after this brief duration. Long-term memory refers to memories that have been consolidated in some way so that they are more lasting in duration—hours or years—although not necessarily permanent.

Describing the brain systems involved in memory is challenging because multiple brain sites are typically involved and different types of memory utilize different pathways. Even so, there is substantial evidence that structures within the temporal lobes are essential to many important features of memory. In particular, the **hippocampus** and the **amygdala** appear to be involved in various aspects of memory and learning. Specifically, these brain sites are involved in the consolidation of short-term memories into long-term memories. The amygdala may play a special role in integrating memories from different modalities and, especially, in consolidating memories with strong emotional meaning (Andreasen, 2001).

Humans have both a left hippocampus and right hippocampus (plural: *hippocampi*), located subcortically within the left and right temporal lobes. The same is true for the amygdala (plural: *amygdalae*), which is also a bilateral structure. The crucial role of these structures in the consolidation of memory was revealed by the case of H.M., a patient with intractable epilepsy who was treated by the surgical removal of the forward section of the temporal lobe on both sides of his brain (Milner, 1968). Prior to this case, many individuals with epilepsy had been successfully treated by the removal of the diseased portion of one temporal lobe. The goal of this kind of surgery is to remove the diseased brain areas that serve as the "trigger" or focus point for seizure activity. The cognitive consequences of single-sided temporal lobe surgery had proved to be minimal. H.M. was the first carefully studied case of bilateral temporal lobe surgery.

The consequences of his surgery were devastating, which was a shocking revelation to everyone involved. Put simply, H.M. proved incapable of forming any new memories from the point of the surgery onward (Milner, 1968). His old long-term memories remained intact, so he could recall where he attended high school, and so forth. And his short-term memory was intact, so he could remember a phone number briefly, for example. But his ability to consolidate new long-term memories was completely annihilated. He could read the same magazine from day to day, unaware that he had read it, cover to cover, the day before. A new doctor remained a new doctor on each new visit. He was essentially a prisoner of the moment, able to converse and interact with apparent normality but unable to remember anything new for more than a few minutes.

Structured testing of H.M. confirmed that different forms of memory are subserved by different brain systems. Consider procedural memory, for example, the recollection of how to do something. H.M. was asked to undertake repeated trials of mirror drawing—a complex procedural task in which the examinee traces a path on a sheet of paper while looking in a mirror. This is a daunting assignment in which directionality—left and right—are effectively reversed. With practice, normal individuals typically show slow improvement, tracing the path more quickly and with fewer errors. Intriguingly, H.M. likewise showed normal improvement on this task from day to day—indicating that his procedural memory remained intact—even though he had no realization that he seen the puzzle before (Corkin, 1968). Most likely, this kind of procedural memory is subserved by the cerebellum. Clearly, it is not underwritten by the temporal lobes.

## ● LIMBIC SYSTEM

The **limbic system** is a "primitive" central brain system that is involved in emotions and basic survival drives. This system overlaps with other brain sites, especially those involved in memory. The structures of the limbic system are involved in emotions, such as fear and aggression, as well as in the acquisition of memory. The pleasure centers of the brain are located here, too, within the nucleus accumbens. In addition to the hippocampus and amygdala, other limbic structures are the cingulate gyrus, mammillary bodies, and the fornix. Andreasen (2001) points out that the exact boundaries of what constitutes the limbic system are not well established because our understanding of this brain system has been steadily growing.

In evolutionary terms, the limbic system is very old and, consequently, involved in primitive survival functions. Because of its proximity to and connections with the hypothalamus, the limbic system indirectly exerts autonomic nervous system control over crucial bodily functions needed for continued existence.

The **hypothalamus** is a deceptively small structure that sits just below and in front of the thalamus. Even though it composes only about 0.3 percent of the brain's weight, the hypothalamus is involved in numerous aspects of motivated behavior and bodily regulation: blood pressure, feeding, sexual behavior, sleep/wake cycle, temperature regulation, emotional behavior, and movement. Well studied in lower animals, the functions of the hypothalamus are less well known in humans (Kolb

& Whishaw, 2002). It is known that the hypothalamus exerts proprietary control over the pituitary gland, thereby modulating a wide range of endocrine functions. The most common cause of a hypothalamic lesion is a severe head injury. Hypothalamic lesions often lead to disturbances of pituitary function, including excessive or deficient intake of food or water and temperature and blood pressure dysregulation (Kupfermann, 1991a). Dysfunction of the hypothalamus also can lead to emotional dysregulation (especially fear or rage) and sleep disturbance (hypersomnolence or insomnia).

## ● LANGUAGE FUNCTIONS AND CEREBRAL LATERALIZATION

Up to this point, we have stressed the similarities of the two halves of the brain, particularly with respect to opposite-sided processing of sensory and motor functions. In many important respects, however, the two hemispheres of the human brain are anatomically and functionally asymmetrical (Cytowic, 1996; Geschwind & Galaburda, 1987). The important structural asymmetries include the following:

1. The top of the temporal lobe, the planum temporale, is larger in the left hemisphere.
2. The left hemisphere contains more gray matter, even though it is slightly smaller and lighter than the right hemisphere.
3. The lateral sulcus is much longer in the right hemisphere with the result that the parietal-temporal cortex is slightly enlarged on this side.

Of course, exceptions will occur in individual cases. The differences previously listed are most consistent and pronounced in right-handers and males. Left-handers and females show fewer structural and functional asymmetries of the brain (Weekes, 1994).

The structural asymmetries between the hemispheres correlate with the well-known functional differences between the two sides of the brain. Language is subserved, in part, by the temporal enlargements on the left side, whereas spatial thinking is subserved, in part, by the parietal-temporal enlargements on the right side. In the remainder of this section we will further catalogue the specialties of the left and right hemispheres, forewarning the reader that lateralization of function is relative, not absolute. For example, both hemispheres have some degree of verbal and spatial capacity. Furthermore, virtually any high-level intellectual activity requires the synthetic interaction of the entire brain (Efron, 1990). Speech is a case in point. While speech is primarily a left hemisphere function, the right cerebral hemisphere does provide the intonation patterns. As a result, patients with right-sided lesions (particularly in the frontal area) may speak in an eerie monotone (Gardner, 1975).

### Language Functions of the Left Hemisphere

Language is primarily (but not exclusively) a left hemisphere function that involves widely separated cortical and subcortical structures. Because so many regions of the left hemisphere are involved in language, virtually any significant left hemisphere lesion will produce some kind of disturbance in the production or comprehension of language. For this reason a detailed profile of language skills offers a window to the integrity and functioning of the left hemisphere.

Modern conceptions of brain–language correlations actually stem from the late nineteenth century. In 1861, Paul Broca observed that damage to a small region just in front of the motor cortex of the left hemisphere caused a language disorder originally called expressive aphasia and now more typically known as nonfluent aphasia. Persons with damage to this left hemisphere premotor area—aptly named Broca's area—speak in a slow, labored manner. They have difficulty enunciating words correctly; the act of speaking seems to be torturous for them. Speech takes on a frankly telegrammatic nature; adjectives, adverbs, articles, and conjunctions—the words that add color to speech—frequently are omitted. Writing also is difficult for these persons. Fortunately, persons

who experience **Broca's aphasia** have little difficulty understanding either spoken or written language. In its pure form, the disorder involves expressive language only.

In 1874, Wernicke announced that damage to the upper and rearward portion of the left temporal lobe—a region now known as Wernicke's area—was linked to a language disorder originally called receptive aphasia and now more typically known as fluent aphasia. Affected individuals appear unable to comprehend spoken or written language. Apparently, persons with **Wernicke's aphasia** have no difficulty perceiving words but cannot associate the words with their underlying meaning. As a consequence, the written and verbal expressions of persons with this aphasia are fluent but meaningless. For example, when asked to define *book,* a patient might respond, "Book, a husbelt, a king of prepator, find it in front of a car ready to be directed." The same person might define *scarecrow* as, "We'll call that a three-minute resk witch, you'll find one in the country in three witches" (Williams, 1979).

Building on the observations of Broca and Wernicke, Geschwind (1972) proposed a structural, neurological model of left hemisphere language functions that has been highly influential in neuropsychological assessment. This model bears directly upon the assessment of language skills; the major elements are outlined next and depicted in Figure 10.3. Geschwind postulated the following:

1. Spoken language is perceived in the left auditory cortex at the top of the temporal lobe, then transferred to Wernicke's area.
2. In Wernicke's area, the meanings of words are activated and the auditory codes are transported to a subcortical bundle of transmission fibers called the arcuate fasciculus.
3. The arcuate fasciculus sends the auditory codes directly to Broca's area.
4. Upon reaching Broca's area, the auditory code activates the corresponding articulatory code that specifies the sequence of muscle actions required to pronounce a word.

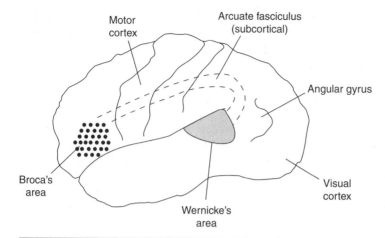

● **FIGURE 10.3**
The Structural Model of Left
Hemisphere Language Functions

5. In turn, the articulatory code is transmitted to the portions of the motor cortex governing tongue, lips, larynx, and so forth in order to produce the desired spoken word.

Comprehending or speaking a written word involves most of the previously outlined pathways, but with a different starting point:

6. Written words are first registered in the visual cortex, then relayed through the visual association cortex to the angular gyrus.
7. In the angular gyrus, the visual form of the word is mapped into the auditory code stored in Wernicke's area, thereby gaining access to the meaning of the written word, which can also be spoken (steps 2 through 5 previously).

The Geschwind model is helpful in explaining a number of clinical syndromes caused by discrete left hemisphere brain damage (Gregory, 1999):

- Lesions to Broca's area will cause slow, labored, telegraphic speech, but the comprehension of spoken or written language will not be affected.
- Damage to Wernicke's area will have more serious and pervasive implications for language comprehension; namely, the patient will be unable to understand spoken or written communications.

- Damage to the angular gyrus will cause serious reading disability, but there will be little problem in comprehending speech or in speaking.
- Impairment limited to the left auditory cortex will result in serious disruption of verbal comprehension. However, such persons will be able to speak and read normally.

In practice, few patients reveal aphasic symptoms that fall neatly into one or another of the preceding categories. Furthermore, modern conceptions of aphasia point to weaknesses in the classical model (e.g., its overly simplistic view of the structure of language) and propose a complex, nonlinear model of aphasia that is beyond the scope of coverage here (Cytowic, 1996; Whitaker & Kahn, 1994). Nonetheless, a thorough assessment of language functions is an essential part of every neuropsychological evaluation and the classical model of Broca, Wernicke, and Geschwind provides a useful starting point. Additional perspectives on aphasia and the structural model of language can be found in Benson (1994) and Mayeux and Kandel (1991).

## Specialized Functions of the Right Hemisphere

Based on thousands of studies of normal and brain-damaged persons, it is now well established that the right hemisphere is dominant for a variety of cognitive and perceptual skills. However, a detailed discussion of specialized right hemisphere functions is beyond the scope of this section. Competent reviews of the extensive literature on this topic can be found in Bradshaw and Mattingley (1995), Joseph (1988), Kupfermann (1991b), and Springer and Deutsch (1997). In general, the right hemisphere appears to be dominant for the analysis of geometric and visual space, the comprehension and expression of emotion, the processing of music and nonverbal environmental sounds, the production of nonverbal and spatial memories, and the tactual recognition of complex shapes.

A frequent symptom of right hemisphere damage is **constructional dyspraxia,** the impaired ability to deal with spatial relationships either in a two- or three-dimensional framework (Reitan & Wolfson, 1993). This symptom is commonly exhibited by an impaired ability to copy simple shapes such as a cross. Left hemisphere lesions can also cause constructional dyspraxia, but the correlation is less consistent. Most neuropsychological test batteries include one or more copying tasks to screen for constructional dyspraxia. We include a summary of findings on cerebral lateralization in Table 10.2.

## ● VISUAL SYSTEM

The primary sensory areas for vision are located in the occipital lobes; much of this projection area is on the mesial or midline surface that separates the two cerebral hemispheres. Each occipital lobe sees the opposite side of the visual world. Thus, all visual stimuli to the left of the reader's fixation point are ultimately processed in the right occipital lobe, and vice versa. The split visual world is shared across the splenium, the rearward portion of the corpus callosum, producing a unified perception of the entire visual field. Damage to the primary visual area produces a corresponding loss of visual field on the opposite side. For example, an extensive lesion in the left occipital lobe would render a person blind to the right half of the visual world. A very small lesion might produce a scotoma or blind spot.

● **TABLE 10.2   A Summary of Findings on Cerebral Lateralization**

| Functional System | Left Hemisphere Dominance | Right Hemisphere Dominance |
|---|---|---|
| Vision | Processing of the right visual field<br>Recognition of letters, words | Processing of the left visual field<br>Recognition of faces |
| Audition | Processing of right ear<br>Processing of language-related sounds | Processing of left ear<br>Processing of music and environmental sounds |
| Somatosensory | Sensory input from the right side | Sensory input from the left side |
| Movement | Motor output to the right side<br>Complex voluntary movement, including speech | Motor output to the left side |
| Language | Speech, reading, writing, and arithmetic | Intonation and emotional patterning to speech |
| Memory | Verbal memory | Pictorial memory |
| Spatial processes | | Analysis of geometric and visual space |
| Emotion | | Comprehension and expression of emotion |
| Olfaction | Smell in left nostril | Smell in right nostril |

A thorough visual field examination is crucial to the detective work of a comprehensive neuropsychological evaluation. Based on the pattern of visual field loss, a competent examiner can infer the location and extent of brain damage. The visual system can be likened to transmission cables that traverse the brain from the eyes in the front to the occipital lobes in the back. Particularly toward the rear of the brain, the cables radiate outward to occupy significant portions of the subcortical tissue. Subcortical lesions toward the rear of the brain stand a good chance of disrupting or damaging the neural transmission networks. This damage leads to a loss of the associated visual field (Figure 10.4). The pattern of visual field loss is a direct clue to the site of damage within the occipital lobes and surrounding tissue.

The forward portion of each occipital lobe is unimodal association cortex. These regions synthesize visual stimuli and produce meaning from them. This is where the high-level processing of visual information occurs. Damage to the association cortex of the occipital lobes may cause **visual agnosia**, a difficulty in the recognition of drawings,

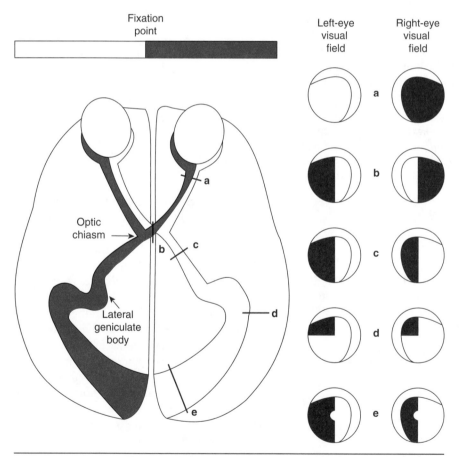

● **FIGURE 10.4**    Schematic Diagram of the Visual System and the Effects of Lesions at Various Sites

*Source:* From Gregory, Robert J. *Foundations of intellectual assessment: The WAIS-III and other tests in clinical practice,* p. 71. Published by Allyn and Bacon, Boston, MA. Copyright © 1999 by Pearson Education. Adapted by permission of the publisher.

objects, or faces (Kandel, 1991). Luria (1973) described a typical case of a patient with such a lesion:

> The patient carefully examines the picture of a pair of spectacles shown to him. He is confused and does not know what the picture represents. He starts to guess. "There is a circle . . . and another circle . . . and a stick . . . a crossbar . . . why, it must be a bicycle?"

The visual agnosias are especially linked to right-sided lesions of occipital association cortex, but may also involve impairment of the parietal and temporal lobes as well. A particularly dramatic form of visual agnosia is prosopagnosia, the inability to recognize familiar faces. Benson (1994) cites the example of a 70-year-old man who suffered a series of strokes affecting the forward portions of the occipital lobes. The patient's chief complaint was that he could not recognize his wife or his daughter by sight, although he immediately recognized them by their voices. In another case of visual agnosia known as object agnosia, a patient reproduced a drawing of a train with great skill but had no idea what he had drawn. Benson (1988) describes the many fascinating symptoms of visual agnosia.

## ● EXECUTIVE FUNCTIONS

The **executive functions** of the brain provide the ability to respond to novel situations in an adaptive manner. Lezak, Howieson, and Loring (2004) propose that the executive functions consist of four components:

- Volition
- Planning
- Purposive action
- Effective performance

Volition is the capacity for intentional behavior, the ability to conceptualize a goal. Planning is the identification of the steps needed to achieve the goal. Purposive action is the capacity to take action and sustain it in an orderly manner. Effective

performance requires the ability to monitor one's activities in light of the original goals and shift strategies as needed. Thus, executive functions are implicated in a wide range of cognitive, emotional, and social skills.

An intriguing paradox of psychological testing is that few instruments are sensitive to impairments of executive functions. When provided with the structure of a typical psychological test, individuals with impaired executive functions often rise to the occasion and perform well. However, in the perplexity of real life, personal functioning may reveal catastrophic disability. For example, a successful financial planner who sustained a brain injury

> . . . can no longer formulate plans well because of an inability to take all aspects of a situation into account and integrate them. This disability is further aggravated by his lack of awareness of his mistakes. Problems occasioned by the man's emotional lability and proneness to irritability are overshadowed by the crises resulting from his efforts to carry out inappropriate and sometimes financially hazardous plans. (Lezak, 1995, p. 650)

Yet, cognitive test scores for this individual—and others like him with impaired executive functions—might well be normal.

Executive functions are substantially but not exclusively underwritten by the frontal lobes. Although it is true that disturbances in executive functions can arise from a variety of neurological conditions that involve diverse brain sites, in the vast majority of cases damage to the frontal lobes is implicated. It is with the frontal lobes that humans create intentions, form plans, and regulate their behavior by comparing the effects of their actions with their original intentions. In short, the frontal lobes are essential for the programming, regulation, verification, and motor performance of executive functions.

Enacting a plan requires a bodily movement of some kind. People pursue their goals by physically manipulating the environment, whether with their hands or through the motor activity of speech. It is not surprising, then, to find that the primary motor cortex is located in the frontal lobes—where plans and intentions are also formed.

The primary motor cortex is found on the precentral gyrus, at the rear of the frontal lobe, just in front of the central sulcus. Motor control is opposite-sided, with the left motor cortex controlling bodily movements on the right, and vice versa. The topical organization of the motor strip was first mapped by Penfield (1958) during a series of operations to remove damaged cortical tissue in persons with epilepsy. He stimulated different areas of the motor cortex with a harmless electrical current to map the correspondence between cortex and different body parts. Penfield found that those areas of the body requiring precise control, such as fingers and mouth, occupy a disproportionately large amount of cortical space.

Just in front of the primary motor cortex is the supplementary motor cortex. The supplementary motor cortex is involved in the serial ordering of complex motor chains, that is, movement programming. A portion of the frontal lobes just below the supplementary motor cortex is involved in the control of voluntary eye gaze. The left frontal lobe also mediates expressive language, discussed in detail later.

Damage to the primary motor cortex causes opposite-sided deficits in fine motor control and also reduces the speed and strength of limb movements. These effects are easily detected with simple motor tests such as finger-tapping speed. Severe damage to the motor cortex causes total paralysis of the affected bodily parts. Damage to the supplementary motor cortex causes deficits in the execution of motor sequences such as copying a series of arm or facial movements (Kolb & Milner, 1981).

The most common cause of frontal lobe damage is closed head injury, which is one type of traumatic brain injury. In a closed head injury, acceleration/deceleration forces are instantly applied to the entire brain, as when a person's head strikes the dashboard in an automobile accident. Because of the irregular surfaces of the surrounding skull, the forward underside surfaces of the frontal lobes are almost always damaged (Jennett &

Teasdale, 1981). The front ends of the temporal lobes also are highly vulnerable in closed head injury.

Nauta (1971) summarizes the effects of frontal lobe dysfunction as a "derangement of behavioral programming." Lezak (1983, 1995) has catalogued the behavioral disturbances that can result from generalized, bilateral frontal lobe damage:

1. Motivational-like problems involving decreased spontaneity, decreased productivity, reduced rate of behavior, and lack of initiative
2. Difficulties in making mental shifts and perseveration of activities and responses
3. Problems in stopping that are often described as impulsivity, overreactivity, and difficulty in holding back a wrong or unwanted response
4. Deficits in self-awareness resulting in an inability to perceive performance errors or to size up social situations appropriately
5. A concrete attitude (Goldstein, 1944) in which objects, experiences, and behavior are all taken at their most obvious face value

Curiously, frontal lobe lesions may have little effect on old learning and well-established skills. Both Hebb and Penfield reported that surgical removal of frontal lobe tissue caused little change in IQ scores (Hebb, 1939; Penfield & Evans, 1935). Early studies of prefrontal lobotomy demonstrated much the same finding: no change in IQ or even a slight improvement after disconnection of the frontal lobes.

Devising adequate measures of frontal lobe function has proved to be difficult. Lezak et al. (2004) note that frontal lobe disorders change how a person responds, whereas most tests measure what a person knows. Lezak (1982) has devised an ingenious method called the Tinkertoy® Test, discussed in the next topic, to assess the programming difficulties experienced by persons with frontal lobe lesions. More commonly, clinicians rely upon observation and checklists to diagnose frontal lobe dysfunction. A generic example of a checklist for executive functions is provided in Figure 10.5.

**Awareness**

Is unaware of limitations   1   2   3   4   5   Has insight into limitations

**Goal Selection**

Sets no goals   1   2   3   4   5   Sets suitable long-term goals

**Logical Analysis**

Is disorganized   1   2   3   4   5   Plans thoughtfully

**Action Orientation**

Needs prompting   1   2   3   4   5   Takes decisive action

**Self-Monitoring**

Is unable to identify errors   1   2   3   4   5   Detects and corrects mistakes

**Impulse Control**

Is highly impulsive   1   2   3   4   5   Thinks before acting

**Flexibility**

Is inflexible in approach   1   2   3   4   5   Learns from feedback

*1 = profoundly deficient*
*2 = severely deficient*
*3 = moderately deficient*
*4 = mildly deficient*
*5 = normal*

● **FIGURE 10.5** Example of a Structured Checklist for the Assessment of Executive Functions

## ● NEUROPATHOLOGY OF ADULTHOOD AND AGING

Although most individuals age gracefully and maintain good health into old age, an unfortunate minority experience one or more neurological syndromes such as brain injury, dementia, or Parkinson's disease. In this section we provide a brief synopsis of a number of more common neurological problems encountered in adulthood and old age. Because neuropsychological tests excel in the evaluation of these syndromes, a brief survey will provide an important backdrop to the selected instruments discussed in the second half of the chapter.

### Traumatic Brain Injury

*Traumatic brain injury* or TBI is an inclusive term that encompasses everything from a "mild" concussion to severe brain injury (Bigler, 1990). TBI is most commonly the consequence of a blow to the head, and concussion is probably the most common form of TBI. The classic example of a concussion is the football player who receives a hard hit ("sees stars"), is rendered briefly unconscious and immobile, and then gradually walks off the field with assistance. Within hours or a few days, he is back to normal. The symptoms of **concussion** include a brief loss of consciousness followed by a low-grade headache, difficulty concentrating, fatigue, irritability, and other emotional symptoms. Although some concussions can have serious, lasting effects, most patients appear to make a full recovery in a few days or weeks. A concussion is one example of a closed head injury or CHI—a trauma to the head and brain in which the skull remains intact. But *closed head injury* is a broader term than *concussion* and potentially signifies a greater level of impairment than typically found in a concussion. Closed head injury is often contrasted with open head injury or OHI—a trauma to the head and brain in which the skull is penetrated. OHI is also known as penetrating head injury. Typically, the consequences of OHI are focal or localized in and near the site of impact, whereas the effects of CHI are more diffuse, affecting areas throughout the brain.

The neurological consequences of TBI depend upon the nature and severity of the injury, but any or all of the following are possible:

- a contusion or bruising of the brain underneath the site of impact known as a coup injury

- a contusion opposite the side of the impact, caused by rebound, and known as a contre-coup injury
- frequent contusions in the undersurfaces of the frontal lobes and the tips of the temporal lobes because of the bony skull protrusions located there
- diffuse axonal injury or nonspecific brain cell damage from shear-strain effects on neural pathways
- brain tissue damage due to obstructed blood flow when cerebral arteries are ruptured
- hematoma or bleeding into the brain between the skull and the surface of the brain
- edema or swelling of the brain, which can lead to secondary brain damage
- in the long term, possible shrinkage of the brain and enlargement of the ventricular system

As to the neurobehavioral effects of TBI, the most common and reliable complaints are of concentration and memory problems. This is why tests of concentration and memory are found in virtually every test battery used in neuropsychological assessment. Other generalizations about TBI are difficult because the nature and severity of the brain damage will not be the same in any two patients. Focal damage may lead to specific symptoms (e.g., damage to the left hemisphere language areas may cause expressive aphasia). Many studies suggest that TBI patients are more seriously handicapped by personality and emotional disturbances than by cognitive and physical disabilities (Lezak & O'Brien, 1990).

## Neoplastic Disease (Tumor)

Neoplastic disease or brain tumor encompasses many different forms of tumorous growth (Reitan & Wolfson, 1993). For example, gliomas are tendril-like tumors of the glial cells that infiltrate the brain over a period of weeks or months; meningiomas are slower-growing, globular-shaped tumors of the meninges (membranes encasing the brain) that press down upon the brain.

Brain tumors produce a variety of effects, depending upon their location, size, and rate of growth. A rapidly infiltrating tumor such as a glioma quickly may compromise many skills. For example, if the tumor is on the left side of the brain, motor and sensory functions on the right side of the body may be severely impacted, as well as language and problem-solving abilities. If the tumor is on the right side of the brain, constructional abilities (e.g., drawing, assembling three-dimensional objects) will be impaired as well as motor and sensory functions on the left side. A slower-growing meningioma may produce no symptoms for years and then create focal symptoms that relate to the site of encroachment on the brain. For example, if the right parietal area is affected, deficits in spatial ability may be observed.

## Chronic Alcohol Abuse

Chronic alcohol ingestion leads to neuronal changes that include a loss of dendritic branches and dendritic spines, especially in areas important for memory such as the hippocampus. Over time, enlargement of the ventricles and widening of the cerebral sulci also are observed. In severe cases, atrophy of the medial thalamus and mamillary bodies is found, leading to the pronounced memory problems that characterize Wernicke-Korsakoff's syndrome (Davila, Shear, Lane, Sullivan, & Pfefferbaum, 1994). The neuropathology of alcoholism often is exacerbated by vitamin and nutritional deficiencies.

In those tragic cases of severe alcohol abuse in which the medial thalamus and mamillary bodies are damaged, the profound anterograde amnesia of Wernicke-Korsakoff's syndrome is noted. Patients show an inability to retain memory of events for more than a short time even though immediate memory is intact and remote memory is only mildly impaired. The falsification of memory known as confabulation, in the presence of clear consciousness, is noted. Other symptoms of severe abuse include gait disturbance and gaze difficulties. In neurologically intact alcoholics, neurobehavioral effects are more elusive and controversial but may include subtle memory deficits and difficulties with novel problem solving (e.g., Waugh, Jackson, Fox, Hawke, & Tuck, 1989).

## Alzheimer's Disease

The most common degenerative neurological disease is **Alzheimer's disease** (AD), which features an insidious degeneration of the brain. The pathophysiology includes clumplike deposits in the brain known as neuritic plaques and neurofibrillary tangles (Koss, 1994). Additional brain changes include neuronal loss, shrinkage or atrophy of the brain, depletion of acetylcholine neurotransmitters involved in memory, and accumulation of foreign deposits in the cerebral vasculature; the course of the disease invariably is downhill. First described in 1907, Alois Alzheimer portrayed his initial case as follows:

> The first noticeable symptom of illness shown by this 51-year-old woman was suspiciousness of her husband. Soon, a rapidly increasing memory impairment became evident; she could no longer orient herself in her own dwelling, dragged objects here and there and hid them, and at times, believing that people were out to murder her, started to scream loudly. On observation at the institution, her entire demeanor bears the stamp of utter bewilderment. She is completely disoriented to time and place. (La Rue, 1992)

Although Alzheimer's disease is not part of normal aging, advanced age is an important risk factor. Rare before age 65, the disease afflicts 3 percent of persons 65 to 74 years of age, 18 percent of persons 75 to 84 years of age, and nearly half of those 85 years and older (Evans, Funkenstein, Albert, and others, 1989). Symptoms and examples suggestive of Alzheimer's disease are listed in Table 10.3. These examples characterize other forms of dementia as well.

As detailed by Storandt and Hill (1989), difficulty with the acquisition of new information (short-term memory dysfunction) is generally the most salient symptom in the early stages. As the disease progresses, patients may also show a prominent language dysfunction (e.g., pronounced word finding difficulty) or a striking visuospatial disturbance. Reports of personality change, including delusions and agitation, also are common. The late stages are characterized by severe, pervasive disability.

● **TABLE 10.3  General Symptoms and Specific Examples Suggestive of Alzheimer's Disease**

Significant memory problems that extend beyond benign forgetfulness
  Fails to recall what was eaten for breakfast

Difficulty with everyday tasks and commonplace activities
  No longer balances the checkbook, prepares the same meal

Loss of orientation to date, time and/or place
  Significantly off as to date or time, loses the way going home

Gradual and insidious onset
  Onset is hard to identify, problem is recognized in retrospect

Language and word finding difficulties
  Conversation characterized by circumlocution and vagueness

Problems with abstract thinking
  Difficulty following the rules of simple card games

Deterioration of social judgment
  Dresses inappropriately, neglects personal hygiene

Misplaces or loses important items
  Car keys disappear, eyeglasses are found in a kitchen drawer

Changes in Personality:
  Onset of suspiciousness, periods of agitation, mood changes

Loss of Initiative
  Absence of self initiation, needs prompting to become involved

Note: These examples characterize other forms of dementia as well.

*Source:* A synthesis based on Alzheimer's disease websites.

## Vascular Dementia (Stroke)

The second most common cause of dementia in the elderly is vascular dementia, caused by blockage of an artery and subsequent death of brain tissue due to insufficient blood supply (infarction) or bleeding into or around the brain (hemorrhage).

Sudden onset is the rule, but the accumulation of small strokes over time, known as multi-infarct dementia (MID), may produce an apparently progressive disorder. The Hachinski Ischemic Score was developed to distinguish multi-infarct dementia from Alzheimer's disease (Hachinski, Iliff, Zilha, and others, 1975). Using this index, MID is indicated by the presence of several of the following factors: abrupt onset, somatic complaints, stepwise deterioration, emotional incontinence, fluctuating course, history of hypertension, nocturnal confusion, history of strokes, personality preserved, atherosclerosis present, depression, and focal neurological signs. Because MID may be treatable to some degree, the differential diagnosis of MID versus Alzheimer's disease is more than academic. Some of the brain imaging techniques described in the next section may prove helpful in this task.

The stroke syndrome is defined by the acute onset of a focal deficit involving the central nervous system. The specific symptoms depend upon the site of infarction but may include motor weakness and impaired sensibility in the limbs on the opposite side; nonfluent aphasia if the dominant hemisphere is affected; partial loss of the visual field if the stroke occurs in the rear of the brain. The acute symptoms of stroke often subside in some measure and lead to a plateau of stable functioning.

### Parkinson's Disease (PD)

Parkinson's disease (PD) is almost nonexistent before age 40 and affects only 1 or 2 in 1,000 persons ages 70 and over (La Rue, 1992). Primarily identified as a movement disorder, cognitive and emotional problems are common in PD. In fact, the late stages of PD may entail a clear dementia. The symptoms include slowness of movement (bradykinesia), tremor at rest, shuffling gait, and postural rigidity. The neuropathology includes depletion of dopamine and neuron loss in the basal ganglia.

Tremor is the most common and the least debilitating early symptom in PD. The rate of progression is quite variable, but movement disability in PD can become pronounced and lead to confinement; 10 to 20 percent of PD patients develop a clear dementia. Patients with PD reveal a deficit on neuropsychological tests requiring speed (e.g., Digit Symbol, Trail Making, reaction time measures). Surprisingly, tests of visual discrimination and paired-associate learning—which do not require speed—also differentiate patients with moderate to severe PD from matched controls (Pirozzolo, Hansch, Mortimer, Webster, & Kuskowski, 1982). About 40 to 60 percent of PD patients also experience depression (La Rue, 1992).

## ● BRAIN IMAGING TECHNIQUES

In the clinical examination of individuals with known or suspected brain impairment, modern techniques of brain imaging often furnish a crucial complement to psychological testing. Brain imaging cannot replace psychological testing—both are needed. Medical procedures such as a CT scan (discussed later) provide definitive information about structural changes in the brain, but only psychological testing can elucidate the functional consequences of those changes. Unfortunately, recent progress in medical imaging has been so rapid that many mental health practitioners, including psychologists, have not kept abreast of new applications:

> We in the mental health field have been trying to put our heads in the sand since the time of Freud, but now it is time to face the facts: If you don't have a basic concept of the *neurobiology* of mental disorders you don't have a comprehensive handle on mental disorders. And how do we learn about the neurobiology of mental disorders? With brain imaging. That is why the field of brain imaging has invaded and taken the leading edge of our profession. This event took most of us by surprise but, now that it has occurred, we need to catch up. (Bremner, 2005, p. vii)

In the remainder of this topic, we provide the reader with a primer of common techniques for brain imaging.

## Electroencephalography (EEG)

The EEG produces a record of electrical activity of the cortex from electrodes posted on specific areas of the skull. The fluctuations in activity are depicted as separate ink lines drawn on a continuous roll of paper. The EEG is a crude index, since the moment to moment fluctuations of each ink line reflect the synchronized activity of millions of neurons. The test is useful in diagnosing seizure disorders and localizing abnormal brain activity such as that caused by a tumor.

## Cerebral Angiography

In this technique a special radio-opaque dye is injected into a major artery that supplies the brain (vertebral or carotid artery) and then the brain is X-rayed. Because the dye blocks the X-rays, the arterial system of the brain stands out in stark relief on the negative. The physician, therefore, can locate vascular anomalies such as an aneurysm (a dangerous ballooning of an artery). Also, if an artery is displaced from its normal location, the specialist can infer underlying pathology such as a tumor. Traditional angiography presents a slight risk to the patient, because the injection of the dye can cause neurological complications. With continued advances in technique, magnetic resonance angiography likely will supplant traditional approaches.

## Computerized Tomography (CT)

In a CT scan, a narrow beam of X-rays is passed through the brain from dozens of different angles; the machine detects the amount of X-rays emerging from the other side. The density of different internal structures appears on X-ray films in inverse proportion to their absorption of X-rays. A computer works out the mathematics to reconstruct a three-dimensional representation of internal brain densities, thereby revealing important structures. The computer prints eight or so two-dimensional cross-sectional X-rays of the brain, each from a different plane. Each slice is called a tomograph,

hence, the name for the procedure. CT produces a resolution of less than 1 millimeter; tumors, blood clots, and ventricular displacements are easily seen. CT is less harmful than a traditional chest X-ray.

## Magnetic Resonance Imaging (MRI)

The functional principle of MRI is that certain atoms such as hydrogen behave like tiny spinning magnets. When placed in a strong magnetic field, these atoms will line up with one another. When radio waves are then beamed across the atoms at right angles to the magnetic field, the atoms wobble synchronously with one another. As the radio waves are turned off, a wire coil surrounding the skull will detect a voltage or magnetic resonance in the magnetic field, the voltage being stronger in areas that contain higher concentrations of hydrogen. Because many parts of the brain are hydrogen rich (especially those that contain water or $H_2O$), the differential pattern of magnetic resonance helps reveal underlying brain structures. The spatial resolution of MRI is so keen that the images resemble fixed and sectioned anatomical material.

## Functional Magnetic Resonance Imaging (fMRI)

In contrast to a traditional MRI that gauges the structure of the brain, a *functional* MRI is used to measure brain function. The fMRI technique takes advantage of the fact that blood cells contain heme, a metal with magnetic properties (Bremner, 2005). Heme is a major part of hemoglobin, the molecules inside red blood cells that transport oxygen from the lungs to bodily tissues, including the brain. Heme responds to the strong magnetic field of an MRI in its own distinctive way, giving off radio signals that can be measured by the MRI coil surrounding the skull. When certain parts of the brain are highly active—such as the frontal lobes in problem solving—they require increased blood flow to provide the necessary oxygen for metabolism. The increased blood flow means that more red blood cells and more heme will be present. It is the change in heme concentrations—from the resting base rate to a higher level during test conditions—that is detected by fMRI. The test conditions often include problem-solving tasks but also can utilize other structured tasks such as recalling memories or experiencing a particular emotion.

## Positron Emission Tomography (PET)

In a PET scan, the patient is injected with a radioactively tagged form of glucose, an essential metabolic fuel used by the brain. The level of radioactivity is extremely scant and not considered harmful. The radioactivity is then monitored by a special detector surrounding the patient's skull. Because the glucose goes to the most active parts of the brain, a PET scan measures activity level and not structure per se. Thus, a PET scan can be used to gauge regional cerebral activity, which can be helpful in the diagnosis of Alzheimer's disease, schizophrenia, and other brain-impairing conditions. PET scans also can be used to map receptor sites by having the patient inhale a radioactive gas that binds to specific receptor sites, such as the dopamine receptors of the basal ganglia. The major drawback to PET is the level of technology required. Some applications require a nearby cyclotron for creation of short-lived isotopes.

## Single Photon Emission Computed Tomography (SPECT)

This technique is similar to PET in that it detects emissions from a radioactively tagged tracer. The technique measures blood flow within the brain. However, the resolution of SPECT is much less than PET. The advantage of SPECT is its comparatively low cost, which makes it much more practical for widespread use.

## ● SUMMARY

1. The central nervous system consists of the brain and spinal cord. The peripheral nervous system includes the cranial nerves and the network of nerves emanating from the spinal cord. The brain weighs less than three pounds and is composed of gray matter, white matter, glial cells, cerebrospinal fluid, and the blood vessels of the vascular system.

2. The cerebrum consists of the left and right cerebral hemispheres, which are connected by the corpus callosum, a band of fibers that transfers information between hemispheres. The cerebrum is where thought, perception, imagination, judgment, and decision occur.

3. The cerebral cortex, the outermost layer of the brain, is the source of the highest levels of sensory, motor, and cognitive processing. Committed areas within the cerebral cortex are devoted to the basic sensory processing of vision, hearing, touch, and motor control.

4. The lowest part of the brain, located at the top of the spinal cord, consists of the hindbrain, which governs essential survival systems such as breathing, swallowing, muscle tone, and posture. Above the hindbrain is the midbrain, an essential relay station that incorporates the cranial nerves.

5. The attentional systems of the brain include the reticular formation and are responsible for several kinds of attention, including orienting, selective, divided, and sustained attention. Sustained attention, also known as vigilance, refers to the ability to sustain attention over long periods of time.

6. The motor and coordination systems of the brain involve the cerebellum, basal ganglia, and motor cortex. Together with other brain structures, these sites help coordinate muscle tone, posture, and hand and eye movements.

7. The many types of memory (e.g., episodic, semantic, working, declarative, procedural, and implicit) involve many brain sites, but structures within the temporal lobes such as the hippocampi are especially important to the integrity of memory. Bilateral removal of the temporal lobes causes a catastrophic loss of the ability to consolidate new long-term memories known as anterograde amnesia.

8. The limbic system is a primitive brain center involved in emotions, such as fear and aggression, as well as in the acquisition of memory. The pleasure centers of the brain are located here, too. The hypothalamus is involved in numerous aspects of motivated behavior (e.g., feeding or sexual behavior).

9. In most persons, the left cerebral hemisphere is dominant for language. Expressive components of language are subserved by Broca's area in the frontal lobe, whereas receptive components of language are mediated by Wernicke's area in the temporal lobe.

10. Specialized functions of the right cerebral hemisphere include the analysis of geometric and visual space, the comprehension and expression of emotion, the processing of music and nonverbal environmental sounds, the production of nonverbal memories, and the tactual recognition of complex shapes.

11. Because the occipital lobes are part of a visual system that begins with the retinas within the eyes, analysis of the visual fields can offer important clues to brain function. Based on the pattern of visual field loss, a competent examiner can infer the location and extent of brain damage.

12. The executive functions of the brain provide the ability to respond to novel situations in an adaptive manner. These include volition, planning, purposive action, and effective performance. Although many brain sites are important to executive functions, the frontal lobes play an essential role.

13. Several clinical tests and brain imaging techniques can be used to help diagnose neuropsychological diseases. These include EEG, cerebral angiography, computerized tomography, magnetic resonance imaging, functional magnetic resonance imaging, positron emission tomography, and single photon emission computed tomography.

## ● KEY TERMS AND CONCEPTS

# Neuropsychological Tests, Batteries, and Screening Tools

The purpose of this topic is to review a diverse collection of neuropsychological tests, batteries, and screening tools. We focus here on representative tests, prominent batteries, and useful screening tools, recognizing that comprehensive coverage is well beyond the scope of the book. For a complete treatment of neuropsychological assessment, the reader is referred to the authoritative tome amassed by Lezak, Howieson, and Loring (2004), which runs to an amazing 1,016 pages in length. By necessity, the coverage here is more discerning and emphasizes better-known tests and batteries.

Neuropsychologists and other clinicians often encounter clients who struggle with alcoholism or other types of substance abuse. For this reason, we also review a few simple but practical tools for rapid screening of clients with possible alcohol

problems. This issue is vital because, at any given time, 10 percent of the adult population manifests an alcohol disorder (Yalisove, 2004). Although it might appear a straightforward matter to identify patients with alcohol problems—just ask them how much and how often they drink—in reality this is a vexing diagnostic challenge due to the active façade of denial maintained by most alcoholics. However, a number of screening tools summarized later are useful for this task.

Finally, it is important to emphasize that neuropsychological assessment involves more than the administration and scoring of specialized tests and screening tools. An essential component of any assessment is the evaluation of a client's mental status. This is particularly true with elderly clients who may experience Alzheimer's disease or other forms of dementia. Accordingly, we close this chapter with a focus upon mental status assessment in the elderly. In this concluding topic, we pay special attention to the Mini-Mental Status Exam (Tombaugh, McDowell, Kristjansson, & Hubley, 1996), one of the most widely used screening tools in existence.

Neuropsychological tests and procedures encompass an eclectic assortment of methods and purposes. At one end of the spectrum are simple, 10-minute screening tests used to probe the need for further assessment. At the other end of the spectrum are exhaustive, six-hour test batteries designed to provide a comprehensive assessment. In between are hundreds of specialized instruments developed to measure particular neuropsychological abilities. At first glance, this multitude of tests would appear to resist simple categorization, as if researchers in this area had followed an incoherent philosophy of trial and error in the development of new instruments and procedures. However, with closer scrutiny it is evident that most neuropsychological tests fit within a simple, logical model of brain–behavior relationships. We will use this model as a framework for discussing well-known neuropsychological tests and procedures.

## ● A CONCEPTUAL MODEL OF BRAIN–BEHAVIOR RELATIONSHIPS

Bennett (1988) has proposed a simplified model of brain–behavior relationships that is helpful in organizing the seemingly chaotic profusion of neuropsychological tests (Figure 10.6). His conceptualization is a slight expansion of the model presented by Reitan and Wolfson (1993). According to this view, each neuropsychological test or procedure evaluates one or more of the following categories:

1. Sensory input
2. Attention and concentration
3. Learning and memory
4. Language
5. Spatial and manipulatory ability

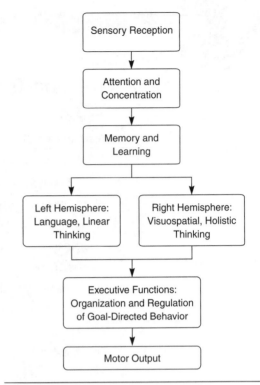

● **FIGURE 10.6** Conceptual Model of Brain Behavior Relationships
*Source:* Based on Reitan and Wolfson (1993) and Bennett (1988).

6. Executive functions:
   Logical analysis
   Concept formation
   Reasoning
   Planning
   Flexibility of thinking
7. Motor output

The order of the categories listed corresponds roughly to the order in which incoming information is analyzed by the brain in preparation for a response or motor output.

In the remainder of this topic, the discussion of neuropsychological tests and procedures is organized around these seven categories. Within each category we will review established tests and also introduce new instruments that show promise of extending the horizons of neuropsychological assessment. However, the reader needs to know that neuropsychological assessment commonly involves a battery of tests. One approach is flexible or patient-centered testing in which an individualized test battery is fashioned for each client. These batteries are based upon the presenting complaints, referral issues, and an initial assessment (Goodglass, 1986; Kane, 1991). More typically, neuropsychologists employ a fixed battery of tests for most referrals. One of the most widely used fixed batteries, the Halstead-Reitan Neuropsychological Battery, is outlined in Table 10.4. Even though the HRNB is an old test—the elements of the battery have not been changed since its inception in the 1950s—many neuropsychologists still regard this battery as the "gold standard" in the field (Horton, 2008; Sweeney, et al., 2007). In large measure, this is because of the steadily accumulating body of affirming research on the battery, which includes 267 publications by its developer, Ralph Reitan, and literally hundreds of additional articles from the dozens of neuropsychologists mentored by him. Yet, the HRNB is not without competition. The chapter closes with a presentation of two other batteries, namely, the Neuropsychological Assessment Battery, and the Luria-Nebraska Neuropsychological Battery.

● **TABLE 10.4    Tests and Procedures of the Halstead-Reitan Test Battery**

| Test | Description |
|---|---|
| Category Test[*] | Measures abstract reasoning and concept formation; requires examinee to find the rule for categorizing pictures of geometric shapes |
| Tactual Performance Test[*] | Measures kinesthetic and sensorimotor ability; requires blindfolded examinee to place blocks in appropriate cutout on an upright board with dominant hand, then nondominant hand, then both hands; also tests for incidental memory of blocks |
| Speech Sounds Perception Test[*] | Measures attention and auditory-visual synthesis; requires examinee to pick from four choices the written version of taped nonsense words |
| Seashore Rhythm Test[*] | Measures attention and auditory perception; requires examinee to indicate whether paired musical rhythms are same or different |
| Finger Tapping Test[*] | Measures motor speed; requires examinee to tap a telegraph keylike lever as quickly as possible for 10 seconds |
| Grip Strength | Measures grip strength with dynamometer; requires examinee to squeeze as hard as possible; separate trials with each hand |
| Trail Making, parts A, B | Measures scanning ability, mental flexibility, and speed; requires examinee to connect numbers (part A) or numbers and letters in alternating order (part B) with a pencil line under pressure of time |
| Tactile Form Recognition | Measures sensory-perceptual ability; requires examinee to recognize simple shapes (e.g., triangle) placed in the palm of the hand |
| Sensory-Perceptual Exam | Measures sensory-perceptual ability; requires examinee to respond to simple bilateral sensory tasks, e.g., detecting which finger has been touched, which ear has received a brief sound; assesses the visual fields |
| Aphasia Screening Test | Measures expressive and receptive language abilities; tasks include naming a pictured item (e.g., fork) repeating short phrases; copying tasks (not a measure of aphasia) included here for historical reasons |
| Supplementary | WAIS-III, WRAT-3, MMPI-2, memory tests such as Wechsler Memory Scale-III or Rey Auditory Verbal Learning Test |

[*]Strictly speaking, these five measures constitute the Halstead-Reitan Test Battery. However, in common parlance reference to the Halstead-Reitan includes all of the measures listed in the table.

## ● ASSESSMENT OF SENSORY INPUT

The accuracy of sensory input is crucial to the proficiency of perception, thought, plans, and action. An individual who does not see stimuli correctly, hear sounds accurately, or process touch reliably may encounter additional handicaps at higher levels of perception and cognition. Neuropsychological assessment always incorporates a multimodal examination of sensory capacities.

### Sensory-Perceptual Exam

The procedures developed by Reitan and Klove are entirely typical of sensory-perceptual procedures (Reitan, 1984, 1985). The Reitan-Klove Sensory-Perceptual Examination consists of several methods for delivering unilateral and bilateral stimulation in the modalities of touch, hearing, and vision. The tasks are so simple that normal persons seldom make any errors at all. For example, the examinee is asked to say which hand has been touched (with eyes closed), or to report which ear has received a barely audible finger snap, or to identify which number has been traced on the fingertip. The results of this test are especially diagnostic if the examinee consistently makes more errors on one side of the body than the other. The reader will recall from the previous chapter that neural innervation is almost exclusively opposite-sided. Furthermore, certain areas of the cerebral cortex are devoted to primary processing of touch, hearing, and vision. Thus, an examinee who finds it difficult to process touch in the right hand may have a lesion in the postcentral gyrus of the left parietal lobe. Similarly, difficulty processing sound in the right ear may indicate a lesion in the superior portion of the left temporal lobe, and right-sided visual defects may indicate brain impairment in the left occipital lobe.

### Finger Localization Test

Finger localization is a venerable procedure developed by neurologists to evaluate possible sensory losses caused by impairment of brain functions. Most neuropsychological test batteries employ a variant of this test, in which examinees must identify those fingers that have been touched (without benefit of sight). Benton has developed a well-normed 60-item test of finger localization that consists of three parts: (1) with the hand visible, identifying single fingers touched by the examiner with the pointed end of a pencil (10 trials each hand); (2) with the hand hidden from view, identifying single fingers touched by the examiner (10 trials each hand); (3) with the hand hidden from view, identifying pairs of fingers simultaneously touched by the examiner (10 trials each hand). The method of response is left to the patient: naming, touching, or pointing to fingers on a diagram (Benton, Sivan, Hamsher, Varney, & Spreen, 1994). Each stimulus presentation is scored right or wrong, and normal adults typically make very few errors in the 60 trials. Mean scores for normal adults are near perfect, ranging from 56 to 60 in various samples. In contrast, patients with brain disease find finger localization to be a challenging task, particularly on the second and third parts of the test.

## ● MEASURES OF ATTENTION AND CONCENTRATION

The attentional capacity of the brain makes it possible to attend to meaningful stimuli, screen irrelevant sensory input from the profusion of incoming stimuli, and flexibly shift to alternative stimuli when conditions demand it (Kinsbourne, 1994). While in theory it might be possible to make subtle distinctions between simple attention, concentration, mental shifting, mental tracking, vigilance, and other variants of attention/concentration, in practice these skills are difficult to separate. Only one attentional measure—the Test of Everyday Attention (TEA)—has succeeded in partitioning attention into its component sources. We discuss the TEA and other prominent measures of attentional impairment in the following sections.

### Test of Everyday Attention

The Test of Everyday Attention (TEA) is a promising measure devised in Great Britain by Robertson,

Ward, Ridgeway, and NimmoSmith (1994, 1996). The TEA measures the subcomponents of attention, including sustained attention, selective attention, divided attention, and attentional switching. The subtests of the TEA are outlined in Table 10.5. The test has three parallel versions and has been well validated with closed head injury clients, stroke patients, and persons with Alzheimer's disease. Normative data are based upon the performance of 154 healthy individuals between the ages of 18 and 80. Examinees enjoy the real-life scenarios of the TEA, which adds to the ecological validity of the instrument. The TEA is highly sensitive to normal age effects in the general population and is, therefore, well suited to geriatric assessment. With the exception of the Elevator Counting subtest, the eight subtests were standardized to yield equivalent scores with a common mean of 10 and standard deviation of 3. Thus, the TEA allows for subtest analysis as a means of identifying an individual's

particular strengths and weaknesses (Crawford, Sommerville, & Robertson, 1997). The TEA is highly sensitive to the effects of closed head injury (Chan, 2000), with the Map Search and Telephone Search subtests revealing the largest deficits from brain injury (Bate, Mathias, & Crawford, 2001). Chan and his colleagues developed a Cantonese version of the TEA and report favorably on its use with clinical and nonclinical Chinese participants (Chan, Lai, & Robertson, 2006; Chan & Lai, 2006).

## Continuous Performance Test

The Continuous Performance Test (CPT) is not really a single test but rather a family of similar procedures that dates back to the pathbreaking research of Rosvold, Mirsky, Sarason, and others (1956). These authors devised a measure of sustained attention (also called vigilance) that involved continuous presentation of letters on a screen. In some cases, examinees were to press a key when a certain letter appeared (e.g., *x*). In other instances, examinees were to press a key when a certain letter appeared *after* another letter (e.g., *x* when it occurs after *a*). Errors of omission are noted when the examinee fails to press for a target stimulus. Errors of commission are noted when the examinee presses the key for a nontarget stimulus. Normal subjects make few errors.

Although CPT tests are sensitive to a wide variety of brain-impairing conditions including hyperactivity, drug effects, schizophrenia, and overt brain damage, these tests are not a panacea for the diagnosis of attention-deficit disorders. For example, in one study of the popular Conners (1995) CPT, children with diagnosed Attention-Deficit/Hyperactivity Disorder (ADHD) did not score worse than clinical controls; on the other hand, children with diagnosed reading disorders showed impaired performance on the CPT (McGee, Clark, & Symons, 2000). In general, reviewers recommend that CPT tests should be interpreted in the context of a comprehensive test battery, especially when they are used in the assessment of persons with suspected attentional problems (Riccio, Reynolds, & Lowe, 2001).

---

● **TABLE 10.5  Subtests of the Test of Everyday Attention (TEA)**

*Map Search:* A two-minute speeded search for 80 symbols on a colored map; measures selective attention.

*Elevator Counting:* Simulation of elevator floor counting from tape-presented tones; measures sustained attention.

*Elevator Counting with Distraction:* Same as above but with auditory distractors; measures sustained attention.

*Visual Elevator:* Visual simulation of elevator floor counting with up-down reversals; measures attentional switching.

*Auditory Elevator with Reversal:* Same as visual elevator, except it is presented on tape; measures attentional switching.

*Telephone Search:* Search for key symbols while searching entries in a simulated classified telephone directory; measures divided attention.

*Telephone Search Dual Task:* Combines Telephone Search with simultaneous counting of auditory tones; measures divided attention.

*Lottery:* Subject listens for winning numbers known to end in 55 and then writes down preceding stimuli; measures sustained attention.

The CPT is ideal for computerized adaptation, and dozens of different versions of it have appeared in the literature (e.g., Conners, 1995; Gordon & Mettelman, 1988). Unfortunately, the proliferation of similar but not identical tests has hindered research on the practical utility of this promising measure of attention. Sandford and Turner (1997) have published a computerized CPT that uses both visual and auditory stimuli. The Intermediate Visual and Auditory Continuous Performance Test (IVA) is normed on 781 normal persons ranging from 5 to 90 years of age and screened for attention deficit, learning difficulties, emotional problems, and medication use. In one analysis, the IVA showed 92 percent sensitivity (i.e., an 8 percent rate of false negatives) and 90 percent specificity (i.e., a 10 percent rate of false positives) in differentiating children diagnosed with Attention-Deficit/ Hyperactivity Disorder (ADHD) from normal children. Research by Tinius (2003) further endorses the validity of the IVA. He found that adults with mild traumatic brain injury or ADHD performed significantly lower than normal controls on IVA subtests assessing reaction time, inattention, impulsivity, and variability of reaction time. This instrument is just one of many promising neuropsychological tests that takes advantage of microcomputer technology.

## ● TESTS OF LEARNING AND MEMORY

Learning and memory are intertwined processes that are difficult to discuss in isolation. Learning new material usually requires the exercise of memory. Furthermore, many tests of memory incorporate a learning curve through repeated administrations. The separation of learning and memory processes is theoretically possible but of little practical value in clinical assessment. We make no tight distinction between these processes.

Memory tests can be categorized according to several dimensions, including short term versus long term, verbal versus pictorial, and learning curve versus no learning curve. These dimensions reflect neurological factors discussed in the previous section. For example, verbal memory is significantly lateralized to the left hemisphere, whereas pictorial memory is largely underwritten by the right hemisphere. The interested reader can consult Lezak (1995) and Reeves and Wedding (1994) for more detailed analyses of the neural substrates for different types of memory. Here we will concentrate on the psychometric characteristics of four quite dissimilar memory tests.

### Wechsler Memory Scale-III

The Wechsler Memory Scale-III (Tulsky, Zhu, & Ledbetter, 1997) is a substantial revision of a simple one-paged test published more than 50 years ago (Wechsler, 1945). The third edition is an extensive, multiphasic test of memory consisting of 17 subtests, including 7 that are optional. The 10 primary subtests are described in Table 10.6. These

---

● **TABLE 10.6   Wechsler Memory Scale-III Primary Subtests**

*Immediate Recall Subtests*

*Logical Memory I:* Recall of essential elements from brief stories read to the examinee.

*Faces I:* Yes-no recall for 24 target faces each presented for two seconds.

*Verbal Paired Associates I:* Recall for a list of eight paired terms, (e.g., truck-arrow) when only the first term is presented (e.g., truck-?).

*Family Pictures I:* Recall of location and activities of persons depicted in pictures of family scenes.

*Letter–Number Sequencing:* Reordering of random digits and letters so that numbers and letters are in correct order (e.g.: "7, *x*, *d*, *s*, 4, 2" is reordered as "2, 4, 7, *d*, *s*, *x*").

*Spatial Span:* A visual analogue to Digit Span in which numbered blocks are tapped in a particular order; the examinee completes both a forward and a backward series.

*Delayed Recall Subtests*[*]

Logical Memory II

Faces II

Verbal Paired Associates II

Family Pictures II

---

[*]30-minute delayed recall for stimuli in administration I.

subtests constitute the basis for obtained age-adjusted scaled scores (mean of 100 and SD of 15) for *eight* primary indices of memory:

| | |
|---|---|
| Auditory immediate | Auditory delayed |
| Visual immediate | Visual delayed |
| Immediate memory | Auditory recognition delayed |
| General memory | Working memory |

The WMS-III was co-normed with the WAIS-III in 1997. The standardization of the new instrument is superb, with 200 cases selected for each of these age bands: 16–17, 18–19, 20–24, 25–29, 30–34, 35–44, 45–54, 55–64, 65–69, 70–74, 75–79. For the two oldest age bands (80–84, 85–89), 150 cases and 100 cases, respectively, were included. Based on 1995 census data, participants for the standardization sample were carefully stratified as to age, sex, race/ethnicity, educational level, and geographic region.

Validity studies of the WMS-III are strongly positive, although factor-analytic investigation does not always support the designated breakdown into the various aspects of memory previously cited. The most powerful evidence for validity is that the instrument functions well in the detection of memory deficits. In the initial validation studies (Tulsky et al., 1997), it was observed that clinical groups with neurological disorders (e.g., Alzheimer's disease, traumatic brain injury) scored significantly low on all eight of the WMS-III primary indices. For example, a sample of 35 individuals with probable early stage Alzheimer's disease obtained average scores in the mid- to high 60s on six of the eight indices. This is especially noteworthy because memory deficit is the initial complaint in the progression of Alzheimer's disease.

Brooks, Iverson, Holdnack, and Feldman (2008) caution users not to over interpret isolated low scores of older adults on the eight indices of memory provided by the WMS-III. Using data from the standardization sample for 550 older adults (55–87 years of age), they note that 39% of the sample scored at or below the 5th percentile (i.e., -1.5 SDs below average) on at least one of the indices. This finding reveals a potential hazard of employing tests with multiple subscores, namely, even normal individuals occasionally will test in low ranges on at least one component.

Validity research with the WMS-III is highly promising. For example, in a study of patients with different levels of traumatic brain injury (TBI), the WMS-III performed better than the WAIS-III in identifying patients with mild TBI (Fisher, Ledbetter, Cohen, Marmor, & Tulsky, 2000). This is important because it demonstrates that the WMS-III taps relevant aspects of memory (known to be impaired in mild TBI) and is not just a proxy measure of intelligence. Furthermore, the WMS-III retains the essential features of its predecessor, the WMS-R, for which a large body of validity research is available (e.g., Gold, Randolph, Carpenter, and others, 1992; Mittenberg, Azrin, Millsaps, & Heilbronner, 1993; Reid & Kelly, 1993; Ryan & Lewis, 1988).

### Rey Auditory Verbal Learning Test

In the early 1900s, the Swiss psychologist Edouard Claparede (1873–1940) proposed a memory test consisting of the free-recall of a 15-item word list. This test evolved into the Rey Auditory Verbal Learning Test (RAVLT), making it one of the oldest mental tests in continuous use (Boake, 2002). The test first appeared in French (Rey, 1964), but an English-language adaptation has been provided by Lezak (1983, 1995) and others. The RAVLT is a very popular test of memory, especially for purposes of clinical research. A search of PsychINFO from 1950 onward revealed more than 400 published articles using this simple instrument.

In administering the RAVLT, the examiner reads a list of 15 concrete nouns at the rate of one per second. The examinee recalls as many as possible in any order. Forewarning the examinee to recall all the words, including those previously recalled, the examiner reads the entire list a second time. A third, fourth, and fifth administration and recall then ensue; these are followed by an interference trial with a new list of words. Next, immediate recall of the original list is tested (without benefit of a new presentation). Finally, a recognition trial is included in which the examinee must underline the administered words from a longer written paragraph. The test yields a number of scores, including the number recalled (of 15) for each of the initial five trials, the total for the five trials (75 possible), the immediate recall after the distractor list is read, and the recognition score.

Rosenberg, Ryan, and Prifitera (1984) concluded that the RAVLT performs well in the identification of patients known to be memory impaired by other criteria. In addition to an overall reduction in performance, memory-impaired patients showed a reduced rate of improvement across the five learning trials. Abundant norms for the RAVLT can be found in Strauss, Sherman, and Spreen (2006). Schoenberg, Dawson, Duff, and others (2006) provide normative data for 392 individuals with documented neurological dysfunction.

The RAVLT is available in at least seven parallel versions, which is both a strength and a weakness of the test (Hawkins, Dean, & Pearlson, 2004). It is a strength because clinicians often employ repeat testing as they follow patients with memory difficulties. Of course, this raises the specter of practice effects: examinees will do better on second, third, and ensuing administrations to some degree because of their prior exposure to the specific items, regardless of whether their clinical condition is improving or getting worse. With parallel versions of a test, the impact of practice effects can be mitigated by using a different form for each administration. Yet, this is a potential weakness, too, because the equivalence of the seven parallel forms is not well established. In reviewing studies of the seven forms of the RAVLT, Hawkins, Dean, and Pearlson (2004) could locate only six studies, and four of these were limited to comparisons of the original test against one other form. Although differences between forms likely are minor, their exact magnitude is simply unknown.

## Fuld Object-Memory Evaluation

The Fuld Object-Memory Evaluation is a useful test of memory impairment in the elderly (Fuld, 1977). The test begins by presenting the examinee with a bag containing 10 common objects (ball, bottle, button, etc.). The task is not described as a memory test. The examinee is asked to determine whether he or she can identify objects by touch alone. Each object is felt and then named; the examinee then pulls it out of the bag to see if he or she was right. After all 10 items have been correctly identified, a distractor task is administered: rapidly naming words in a semantic category (e.g., names, foods, things that make people happy, vegetables, or things that make people sad). Then the examinee is asked to recall as many of the objects as possible. After each recall, the subject is slowly and clearly reminded verbally of each item omitted on that trial, a procedure called selective reminding (Buschke & Fuld, 1974). The examinee is then administered four more chances to recall the list by selective reminding, with a distractor task after each trial. Delayed recall is tested after a 5-minute interval. Finally, the test closes with a multiple-choice recognition test.

The Fuld test is often used to help confirm a diagnosis of **Alzheimer's disease,** a degenerative neurological disorder described in the previous topic. In the early stages of Alzheimer's disease the most prominent symptom is memory loss. Elderly persons with memory impairment not only score lower than control subjects on the Fuld Object-Memory Evaluation, but they also benefit very little from the selective reminding. Fuld (1977) has provided norms for community-active and healthy nursing-home residents in their 70s and 80s. Fuld, Masur, Blau, Crystal, and Aronson (1990) describe a prospective study in which the Fuld Object-Memory Evaluation demonstrated promise as a predictor of dementia in cognitively normal elderly. Lichtenberg, Manning, Vangel, and Ross (1995) describe a program of neuropsychological research using the Fuld test with older urban medical patients.

Chung (2009) reports very favorably on the validity of the Fuld test as a screening measure of dementia in Chinese elderly. In a sample of 192 community-dwelling individuals, 57 with confirmed dementia, the optimal cut-off on the total retrieval score yielded an amazing 93 percent sensitivity and 90 percent specificity. In other words, 93 percent of the individuals with dementia were correctly spotted, and 90 percent of the normal individuals were appropriately classified. These are impressive findings for a simple screening test. Chung and Ho (2009) report similarly favorable results in a Chinese nursing-home sample.

## Rivermead Behavioral Memory Test

The Rivermead Behavioral Memory Test (RBMT) is a measure of everyday memory such as route finding, remembering names, and recalling information (Wilson, Cockburn, & Baddeley, 1991). The instrument includes the following subtests:

*Names:* A photograph is shown along with the first and second names of the person in the photograph. The examinee is tested on both the first and the second names.

*Belonging:* At the beginning of the test, the examinee is required to hand over a personal belonging (e.g., wallet), which is then hidden while the examinee observes. Later the examinee must remember to ask for the item and then also to find it.

*Appointment:* The examinee is asked to remember to ask the date of the next appointment when he or she hears the sound of an alarm timer.

*Pictures:* The examinee is shown 10 cards with simple pictures or drawings and later is asked to recognize them among a set of 20 cards.

*Immediate Story:* The examiner reads a short paragraph and immediately afterward asks the examinee to recall as many elements of the brief story as possible.

*Delayed Story:* After completing a number of additional subtests, the examinee is asked to recall as many elements of the story as possible.

*Faces:* The examinee is shown 5 cards with a face on them and then asked to recognize them among a set of 10 cards.

*Immediate Route:* The examiner demonstrates a short route with the examinee and leaves an envelope with a written message at the destination. The examinee is asked to reproduce the route and to recall the message.

*Immediate Message:* This item is linked to Immediate Route (above). The examinee is asked to recall the written message.

*Delayed Message:* After completing a number of intervening tasks, the examinee is asked to recall the written message again.

*Orientation:* This subtest consists of 10 items tapping knowledge of personal and societal information.

*Date:* The examinee is asked the date of the examination.

The RBMT is highly popular in geriatric and rehabilitation settings because of its robust ecological validity—the subtests parallel the tasks and activities of everyday life (Guaiana, Tyson, & Mortimer, 2004). Another strong point of the instrument is that it assesses many elements of memory. For example, the test evaluates all of the following aspects: short-term, long-term, verbal, spatial, retrospective, and prospective memory. The focus on prospective memory—remembering to do something in the future—is a rare but welcome addition to the appraisal of memory.

Man, Chung, and Mak (2009) developed an online version of the RBMT for use with Chinese examinees. They compared scores of 30 stroke patients on the original, face-to-face version of the test versus the online version, and found exceptionally strong correlations on the twelve subtests, with *r*s ranging from .84 to .93. The new version also was highly successful in distinguishing stroke patients from controls. In sum, the online adaptation looks highly promising as a replacement for the more cumbersome face-to-face edition.

## Wide Range Assessment of Memory and Learning-2

The original version of the Wide Range Assessment of Memory and Learning (WRAML) was the first comprehensive memory scale designed for use with children (ages 5 to 17 years).

The second edition of the test, the WRAML-2 (Sheslow & Adams, 2004), retains the pediatric focus but also extends the norms upward to 90 years of age. The WRAML-2 is, therefore, unique as the only memory scale that can be used with both children and adults. In addition to examiner convenience (no need to buy and learn several memory tests), there is clinical value as well in using a single test across a wide range of ages. Specifically, when clinicians desire to do follow-up testing on a child or teenage client who subsequently transitions into adulthood, using a single test avoids the pitfall of introducing measurement error associated with different tests.

The WRAML-2 consists of six core subtests that contribute to three Index scores: Verbal Memory, Visual Memory, and Attention/Concentration. Collectively, these Index scores establish the overall General Memory Index. A description of the core memory tasks is provided in Table 10.7.

In addition to the core memory subtests, the WRAML-2 also utilizes delayed memory tasks and recognition memory tasks. The delayed memory tasks require free recall of previously presented material whereas the recognition memory tasks involve mere recognition of the material. The two formats (delayed and recognition) help distinguish between storage and retrieval problems in memory. In particular, a client who performs poorly on delayed memory but who excels at recognition memory most likely has a problem with retrieval rather than storage. This is somewhat similar to not remembering a test item when a fill-in-the blank format is used but succeeding when a multiple-choice format is used. In fact, retrieval memory requires a different neurological substrate than recognition memory. Although capable functioning in both retrieval and recognition memory is typical throughout life, distinct differences (favoring recognition) are observed in old age, with certain neurological conditions such as Alzheimer's disease, and in some forms of brain injury.

The WRAML-2 also includes optional subtests that can be used to evaluate a relatively new area of memory measurement, namely, working memory

● **TABLE 10.7  Description of Core WRAML-2 Subtests**

*Verbal Memory Subtests*

**Story Memory:** Two short stories are read to the participant who, following each, is asked to recall as many parts of the story as can be remembered. This task measures immediate verbal memory.

**Verbal Learning:** The examinee is read a relatively long list of simple words followed by an immediate free-recall trial. Three additional presentation/recall trials are used. This task evaluates the ability to actively learn verbal information and yields a verbal learning curve over the four trials.

*Visual Learning Subtests*

**Design Memory:** A card with a simple geometric array is presented for a 5-second exposure. Following a 10-second delay, the participant is asked to draw what is remembered about the card. This procedure is used for five separate cards of increasing difficulty.

**Picture Memory:** The examinee visually scans a complex but common meaningful scene for 10 seconds. Then the examinee is presented with a second similar scene and asked to indicate which elements "have been moved, changed, or added" in the second picture. The procedure is used with four separate scenes.

*Attention/Concentration Subtests*

**Finger Windows:** The participant demonstrates memory of a visual pattern using a vertically resting card containing asymmetrically located holes or "windows." The examiner points out a sequence of windows, and then the participant is asked to duplicate the sequence.

**Number Letter:** The examinee is asked to verbally repeat a random series of numbers and letters orally presented at one per second.

Note:  All subtests listed contribute to the General Memory Index.

(Baddeley, 1986). Working memory is a complex form of short-term memory. In addition to simply holding on to rote information for several seconds, when using working memory the client is also "working" with a part of the memory trace without distorting the whole trace. For example, try to read the following sentence only once (i.e., do not reread the sentence to answer the question): If in a bag you had two red balls, three yellow balls, and one green ball, what is the probability the ball would be yellow if you reached into the bag and randomly chose one ball? To answer this question, the short-term verbal memory processor must hold on to all the words in the sentence until the last phrase containing the question. Then it must reproduce the sentence, remembering how many red balls there were, and so on, then hold that information secure, returning to accumulate all the numbers in order to compute the answer. There are two working memory subtests on the WRAML-2, one that examines verbal working memory and another that examines a combination of verbal and visual working memory.

The adult standardization age bands used in norming the WRAML-2 are similar to those of the WMS-III, with similar attention given to stratification variables such as age, gender, ethnicity, geographic region, and educational level. "Tighter" age bands exist for the 5- to 14-year-old samples because there is more change in memory abilities across these ages than in adulthood (except for the oldest age groups). For the WRAML-2, factor-analytic studies show strong support for the three discrete domains being measured (Verbal Memory, Visual Memory, and Attention/Concentration) as well as the newly introduced domain of Working Memory. Especially impressive are the analyses showing extremely low item bias for gender as well as ethnicity. As with the WMS-III, validity studies show clinical groups with neurological disorders scoring significantly lower than nonclinical groups on all WRAML-2 Indexes. The correlation of the WRAML-2 with WAIS-III Full Scale IQ is moderate, supporting the claim that it measures something different from, although related to, intelligence. Of interest, though, a much lower correlation with the WISC-III suggests that there is less correlation between intelligence and memory ability among children than among adults.

Because both tests claim to be memory tests and show some similarities across tasks used to assess memory, it is reasonable to wonder if the WMS-III and WRAML-2 yield similar scores (i.e.,

if there is reasonable concurrent validity). Using 79 adults from ages 17 through 74 years, the test developers showed that overall memory indexes of the two measures differed by only 4.7 points. However, the correlations between scores on the two memory instruments ranged from .29 to .60. These moderate correlations suggest that they are measuring somewhat different aspects of memory and are not interchangeable instruments.

### Additional Tests of Learning and Memory

Because of space limitations, we can do no more than briefly mention several other useful tests of learning and memory. The California Verbal Learning Test-II is patterned after the Rey AVLT but provides software to quantify and analyze the pattern of results (Delis, Kramer, Kaplan, & Ober, 2000). The Benton Visual Retention Test is a design-copying test of visual memory (Sivan, 1991). Good reviews of memory tests can be found in Lezak (1995), Reeves and Wedding (1994), and Spreen and Strauss (1998).

### ● ASSESSMENT OF LANGUAGE FUNCTIONS

As noted in a previous section, language functioning offers a window to the integrity of the left cerebral hemisphere. Thus, neuropsychologists are keenly interested in an examinee's ability to speak, read, write, and comprehend what others say. Little wonder that a comprehensive neuropsychological examination always includes one or more methods for assessing language functions.

Neuropsychologists exhibit a special interest in a variety of language dysfunctions known collectively as aphasia. Briefly stated, **aphasia** is any deviation in language performance caused by brain damage. In testing for aphasia, a neuropsychologist might use any or all of three approaches: (1) a nonstandardized clinical examination, (2) a standardized screening test, or (3) a comprehensive diagnostic test of aphasia. We will provide examples of each in our brief review of assessment methods in aphasia.

## Clinical Examination for Aphasia

A clinical examination for aphasia has the advantages of simplicity, flexibility, and brevity. These are important attributes when assessing a severely impaired patient who may require bedside testing. Every practitioner has a slightly different version of the brief clinical exam (Lezak, 1995; Reitan, 1984, 1985). Nonetheless, certain elements commonly are assessed:

- *Spontaneous speech:* The examiner looks for distinctive symptoms of aphasia such as word-finding difficulty or neologisms (e.g., referring to a comb as a "planker").
- *Repetition of sentences and phrases:* The examiner asks the patient to repeat stimuli such as "No ifs, ands, or buts," and "Methodist Episcopal." The repetition tasks are so simple that normal subjects almost never fail them.
- *Comprehension of spoken language:* The examiner asks questions ("Does a car have handlebars?") and issues commands ("Take this paper, fold it in half, and put it on the floor"). Again, the tasks are so simple that normal subjects almost never fail them.
- *Word finding:* The examiner points to common, easily recognized objects and asks, "What's this?" Typical items include watch, pen, pencil, glasses, ring, and shoes. The examiner may ask the patient to name numbers, letters, or colors.
- *Reading:* The examiner requests the patient to read and explain a short paragraph suited to prior level of education and intelligence. The examiner may ask the patient to follow written instructions (e.g., "Close your eyes" or "Clap your hands three times").
- *Writing and copying:* The examiner asks the patient to write spontaneously and from dictation. Also, the examiner may ask the patient to copy written matter and geometric shapes. The examiner is interested in grossly ungrammatical written productions and significant distortions in copying.
- *Calculation:* The examiner asks the patient to perform very simple mathematical calculations

(e.g., $17 \times 3$) with and without aid of scratch paper. The tasks are so simple that normal subjects rarely fail.

Based on the clinical assessment, the examiner may fill out a rating scale for severity of aphasia. For example, the rating scale used in the Boston Diagnostic Aphasia Exam (Goodglass, Kaplan, & Barresi, 2000) includes the following speech characteristics: melodic line, phrase length, articulatory agility, grammatical form, word finding, and auditory comprehension.

## Screening and Comprehensive Diagnostic Tests for Aphasia

Standardized screening tests for aphasia closely resemble the brief clinical exam. The essential difference is that standardized screening tests incorporate objective and precise instructions for administration and scoring. The weakness of screening tests is that they will not detect subtle forms of aphasia.

Comprehensive diagnostic tests for aphasia are quite lengthy and used mainly when a patient is known to experience aphasia. These tests provide a profile of language skills that is helpful in treatment planning. We provide a brief description of several aphasia tests in Table 10.8.

## ● TESTS OF SPATIAL AND MANIPULATORY ABILITY

Tests of spatial and manipulatory ability are also known as tests of constructional performance. A constructional performance test combines perceptual activity with motor response and always has a spatial component (Lezak, 1995). Because constructional ability involves several complex functions, even mild forms of brain dysfunction will result in impaired constructional performance. However, careful observation is needed to distinguish the cause of the failed performance, which may include spatial confusion, perceptual deficiency, attentional difficulties, motivational

● **TABLE 10.8    Brief Description of Several Aphasia Tests**

**Multilingual Aphasia Examination**
  **(Benton, Hamsher, Rey, & Sivan, 1994)**

This respected, comprehensive battery consists of 11 subtests and rating scales that assess visual naming, repetition, fluency, articulation, spelling, and other language variables; available in a Spanish edition, too.

**Western Aphasia Battery—Revised**
  **(Kertesz, 2000)**

Comprehensive test of verbal fluency, auditory comprehension, and repetition that aims to identify aphasia syndromes and determine their severity.

**Boston Diagnostic Aphasia Examination**
  **(Goodglass, Kaplan, & Barresi, 2000)**

Comprehensive test with 46 subscales that include music, spatial, computation, and seven types of writing skill in addition to traditional aphasia measures, available in French and Hindi versions, too.

**Porch Index of Communicative Ability—Revised**
  **(Porch, 2001)**

A battery containing eighteen 10-item subtests, four verbal, eight gestural, and six graphic. Very reliable test often used to measure small changes in patient performance.

**Token Test**
  **(Spreen & Strauss, 1998)**

An extremely sensitive test that presents little challenge to normal individuals. The examinee must complete oral commands with colored tokens, e.g., "Put the small red token on top of the large square token." Originally devised by Boller & Vignolo (1966), numerous versions of the Token Test are now available.

problems, and apraxias. The term **apraxia** refers to a variety of dysfunctions characterized by a breakdown in the direction or execution of complex motor acts (Strub & Black, 2000). For example, a patient who could not demonstrate how to use a key would be diagnosed as suffering from ideomotor apraxia.

Tests of constructional performance embrace two large classes of activities: drawing and assembling. Owing to limitations of space, we will review only a few prominent instruments in each category.

## Design Copying Tests

Drawing a copy of simple geometric shapes such as two overlapping pentagons is a complex activity that requires accurate visual perception, correct spatial analysis, as well as intact motor functions and the executive ability to make mid-course corrections in the drawing. Because the activity of copying a design involves so many cognitive capacities, it is sensitive to a wide variety of brain impairing conditions. For this reason, design copying has been a mainstay of cognitive screening for brain impairment.

One of the most widely used design copying tests—indeed, one of the most widely used individual tests of any kind—is the Bender Visual-Motor Gestalt Test (Bender, 1938), more commonly known as the Bender Gestalt Test (BGT). In the last half of the twentieth century, the BGT consistently ranked among the top four or five most frequently used tests in clinical psychology (Piotrowski, 1995). The original version consisted of nine stimulus drawings similar to those in Figure 10.7. The test is simple to explain and administer. The examinee is instructed to copy one drawing at a time on a sheet of blank paper. Erasures are discouraged. If needed, additional sheets of paper are provided. The examinee is told "this is not a test of artistic ability, but try to copy the drawings as accurately as possible. Work as fast or as slowly as you wish" (Hutt, 1977). Use of a ruler or straight edge is not permitted.

For the original version of the BGT, a number of complex scoring systems have been developed for adults (Hain, 1964; Hutt & Briskin, 1960; Lacks, 1999). In addition, Koppitz (1963, 1975) produced an elaborate scoring system for children aged 5 to 11. The Koppitz system yielded a raw score (total errors) that could be converted to an age-equivalent score as well. In contrast to the use of the BGT with adults—where the examiner is

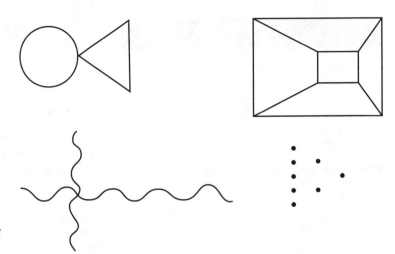

● **FIGURE 10.7** Stimuli Similar to Those From the Bender Gestalt Test-II

Note: The Bender-Gestalt-II consists of sixteen stimuli similar to these.

looking for signs of brain impairment—when used with children, the primary purpose of the test is to assess the level of developmental maturity. Several interesting variations on the original BGT are discussed in Gregory (1999).

Recently, a revised and expanded version of the BGT was published by Brannigan and Decker (2003). The BGT-II adds to the original test rather than revamping it. Specifically, it includes the original nine stimulus cards supplemented by seven new drawings (four very easy drawings, and three that provide substantial challenge). The four additional "easy" cards are administered only to younger examinees 4 through 7 years of age, whereas the three "difficult" cards are administered only to older examinees 8 through 85+ years of age. Unlike previous editions of the test which lacked serious efforts at standardization, the BGT-II norms are based on more than 4,000 individuals, ages 4 through 85, stratified on important demographics according to the 2000 census.

These new stimulus cards are intended to extend the measurement scale at the lower and higher extremes of ability. The authors also provide an explicit scoring system whereby each reproduction is scored on a 5-point scale from 0 (no resemblance) to 4 (nearly perfect). Of course, comprehensive, census-based norms are provided by way of standard scores, $T$ scores, percentile ranks, confidence intervals, and classification labels. The standard score is called the Visual Motor Integration or VMI and is anchored to a mean of 100 and standard deviation (SD) of 15. This is a useful feature of the BG-II because it allows for comparisons of the VMI score with IQs, memory quotients, and other indices normed to mean of 100 and SD of 15.

The Greek Cross (Reitan & Wolfson, 1993) is a very simple drawing task that is surprisingly sensitive to brain impairment. The examinee is requested to carefully copy the figure without lifting the pencil, that is, by tracing the perimeter. The stimulus figure and examples of defective performance are shown in Figure 10.8. This test is most often evaluated on a qualitative basis, although scoring guides do exist (Swiercinsky, 1978; Gregory, 1999).

## Assembly Tests

In his classic book on the parietal lobes, Critchley (1953) provided the rationale for including three-dimensional construction tasks in a neuropsychological test battery:

It is possible, and indeed useful, to proceed to problems in three-dimensional space though tests of this character are only too rarely employed. This is a more difficult undertaking, and patients who respond moderately well to the usual procedures

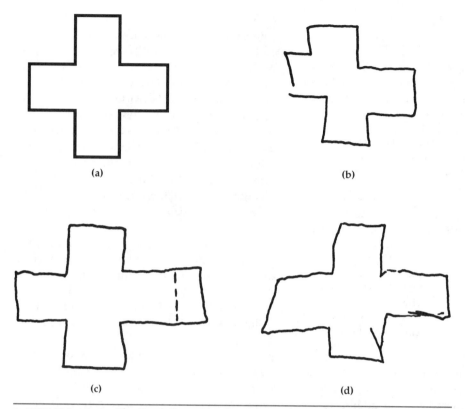

● **FIGURE 10.8**    The Greek Cross Stimulus Figure and Reproductions from Persons with Known Brain Damage
  (a) Stimulus figure.
  (b) Clerical worker with diffuse right hemisphere dysfunction of unknown origin.
  (c) College professor two years after a right hemisphere stroke.
  (d) Patient with generalized, diffuse dementia.

*Source:* From Gregory, Robert J. *Foundations of intellectual assessment: The WAIS-III and other tests in clinical practice,* p. 197. Published by Allyn and Bacon, Boston, MA. Copyright © 1999 by Pearson Education. Adapted by permission of the publisher.

with sticks and pencil-and-paper may display gross abnormalities when told to assemble bricks according to a three-dimensional pattern.

Benton, Sivan, Hamsher, Varney, and Spreen (1994) present a three-dimensional block construction test with excellent norms and scoring guide. The two forms of the test (Form A and Form B) consist of three block models that are presented one at a time to the patient. The patient is requested to construct an exact replica of the model by selecting the appropriate blocks from a set of loose blocks on a tray. Based on omissions, additions, substitutions, and displacements, the three models are scored from 0 to 6, 8, and 15 points, respectively. This test is quite sensitive to brain impairment, especially when the left or right parietal area is affected. Lezak (1995) discusses other assembly tasks. We should mention that the Tactual Performance Test from the Halstead-Reitan battery is, in part, an assembly task that measures spatial and manipulatory abilities (see Table 10.4).

## • ASSESSMENT OF EXECUTIVE FUNCTIONS

**Executive functions** include logical analysis, conceptualization, reasoning, planning, and flexibility of thinking. The assessment of executive functions presents an unusual quandary to neuropsychologists:

> A major obstacle to examining the executive functions is the paradoxical need to structure a situation in which patients can show whether and how well they can make structure for themselves. Typically in formal examinations, the examiner determines what activity the subject is to do with what materials, when, where, and how. Most cognitive tests, for example, allow the subject little room for discretionary behavior, including many tests thought to be sensitive to executive—or frontal lobe—disorders . . . The problem for clinicians who want to examine the executive functions becomes how to transfer goal setting, structuring, and decision making from the clinician to the subject within the structured examination. (Lezak, 1995)

Many neuropsychologists resolve this quandary by using the clinical method to evaluate executive functions rather than administering formal tests (Cripe, 1996). For example, Pollens, McBratnie, and Burton (1988) use interview and observations to fill out the structured checklist on executive functions mentioned in the previous topic.

Only a limited number of neuropsychological tests tap executive functions to any appreciable degree. Useful instruments in this regard include the Porteus Mazes, Wisconsin Card Sorting Test, and a novel approach known as the Tinkertoy® Test. We remind the reader that the Category Test from the Halstead-Reitan battery also captures executive functions to some extent (Table 10.4).

The Porteus Maze Test was devised as a culture-reduced measure of planning and foresight (Porteus, 1965). Without lifting the pencil and attempting to avoid dead ends, the examinee must trace a line through a series of increasingly difficult mazes. This underused instrument is quite sensitive to the effects of brain damage, particularly in the frontal lobes (Smith & Kinder, 1959; Smith, 1960).

Krikorian and Bartok (1998) have published contemporary Porteus Maze norms for children and young adults 7 to 21 years of age; these researchers also demonstrated that test scores are minimally related to IQ scores. Mack and Patterson (1995) investigated the Porteus test as a useful measure of executive function in elderly patients with Alzheimer's disease. In a study of 276 pediatric patients who had sustained a traumatic brain injury (TBI), Levin, Song, Ewing-Cobbs, and Roberson (2001) found that the Porteus test was highly sensitive to TBI severity as measured by the volume of tissue damage in the prefrontal areas of the brain.

The Wisconsin Card Sorting Test (WCST) is a good measure of executive functions, although its differential sensitivity to frontal lobe damage is debated (Mountain & Snow, 1993). The instrument was devised to study abstract thinking and the ability to shift set (Berg, 1948; Heaton, Chelune, Talley, and others, 1993). The examinee is given a pack of 64 cards on which are printed one to four symbols (triangle, star, cross, or circle) in one of four colors (red, green, yellow, or blue). No two cards are identical. Thus, each card embodies a number, a particular shape, and a specific color. The examinee must sort these cards underneath four stimulus cards according to an unknown principle (Figure 10.9). For example, the unknown principle might be "sort according to color." As the examinee places cards, the examiner says "right" or "wrong." After the examinee has sorted a run of 10 correct placements in a row, the examiner shifts the principle without warning. The test continues until the examinee has made six runs of 10 correct placements. The test can be scored in several different ways, including total number of trials to criterion (Axelrod, Greve, & Goldman, 1994). A common use of the WCST is to gauge ongoing recovery in patients with brain trauma of recent onset. Thus, the longitudinal constancy of test scores in patients with stabilized conditions is a reassuring characteristic of this test (Greve, Love, Sherwin, and others, 2002).

Lezak (1982) devised the Tinkertoy® Test to give patients the opportunity to demonstrate

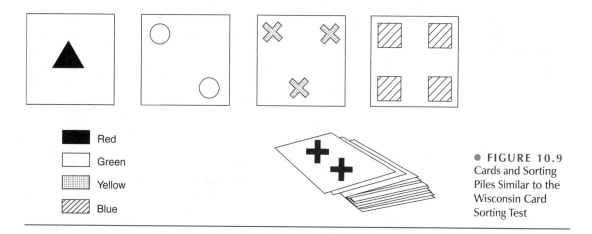

Red
Green
Yellow
Blue

● **FIGURE 10.9**
Cards and Sorting
Piles Similar to the
Wisconsin Card
Sorting Test

executive capacities within the structured format of an examination. Fifty pieces of a standard Tinkertoy® set are placed on a clean surface and the examinee is told, "Make whatever you want with these. You will have at least five minutes and as much more time as you wish to make something." The test is scored from −1 to +12 based on several variables including the number of pieces used, the mobility of the construction, symmetry, and the naming of the construction. Head-injured patients produce impoverished designs consisting of a small number of pieces. These individuals often are unable to provide a name for their constructions.

Bayless, Varney, and Roberts (1989) studied the predictive validity of the Tinkertoy® Test by comparing the results of 50 patients with closed-head injuries versus 25 normal controls. Half of the head-injured individuals had returned to work while half had not. Whereas all but one of the head-injured who returned to work scored normally on the Tinkertoy® Test, nearly half of the nonreturnees performed below the level of the worst control subject. The researchers conclude:

> The test seems particularly well suited for demonstrating the presence of deficits in executive functioning, which have proven to be difficult to demonstrate with clinical tests even though they have catastrophic sequelae in daily vocational or psychosocial endeavors. (Bayless et al., 1989)

The Tinkertoy® Test also shows promise in the assessment of individuals with Alzheimer's disease (Koss, Patterson, Mack, Smyth, & Whitehouse, 1998).

Neuropsychologists still need additional measures of executive functions. One promising approach in the early stages of development is real-world assessment of route finding. The ability to find an unfamiliar location in the city requires strategy, self-monitoring, and corrective maneuvers. These are executive functions applied to a realistic problem (Boyd & Sauter, 1993). Another promising approach to the assessment of executive functions is embodied in a recent battery called the Behavioral Assessment of the Dysexecutive System (BADS; Wilson, Alderman, Burgess, and others, 1996). The BADS battery consists of six novel situational tests that resemble real-life daily activities:

*Temporal Orientation:* The examinee is asked to estimate how long various common activities take, such as a routine dental checkup.

*Rule Shift Cards:* This test measures the ability to shift set after establishing a card-sorting pattern according to a simple rule.

*Action Program:* This test of practical problem solving involves a task in which a cork must be extracted from a test tube by planning the use of available materials.

*Key Search:* In this analogue test, examinees are required to demonstrate how they would search a field for a set of lost keys.

*Zoo Map:* This is a test of planning and route finding in which the examinee is asked to plan a route to visit six of a possible 12 locations in a zoo.

*Six Elements:* This is a multitasking subtest in which the examinee must complete six activities (two naming, two dictation, two mental arithmetic) in 10 minutes.

The battery also includes a 20-item dysexecutive questionnaire with items rated on a 5-point (0 to 4) Likert scale. The items involve likely changes when executive functions are impaired, for example, "I have difficulty thinking ahead and planning for the future." The questions are in four broad areas: personality/emotional changes, motivational changes, behavioral changes, and cognitive changes. Spreen and Strauss (1998) provide a helpful review of this battery. Norris and Tate (2000) compared the BADS with six other commonly used tests of executive functioning. In a sample of 36 neurological patients, they demonstrated the ecological superiority of this new instrument in predicting competency in everyday role functioning. Simon, Giacomini, Ferrero, and Mohr (2003) found that the BADS was a fair measure of social adjustment in patients with schizophrenia, correlating $r = .34$ with an index of psychosocial adjustment. The BADS outperformed the Wisconsin Card Sorting Test and the Trail Making Test (part B) in this context. D'Amato (2001) raises concerns about the validation of the BADS in relation to other measures and recommends against general clinical use until further research is completed.

## ● ASSESSMENT OF MOTOR OUTPUT

Most neuropsychological test batteries include measures of manipulative speed and accuracy. Lezak (1995) provides a comprehensive review.

We will briefly summarize three approaches: finger tapping, pegboard performance, and line tracing.

Perhaps the most widely used test of motor dexterity is the Finger-Tapping Test from the Halstead-Reitan battery. This test consists of a tapping key that extends from a mechanical counting device attached to a flat board. With the index finger of each hand, the examinee completes a series of 10-second trials until five trials in a row are within a 5-point range. The score for each hand is the average of these five trials, rounded to the nearest whole number. With the dominant hand, males typically score about 54 taps (SD of 4), whereas females typically score about 51 taps (SD of 5; Dodrill, 1979; Morrison, Gregory, & Paul, 1979).

In general, the absolute level of performance is of less interest than the relative abilities on the two sides of the body. Normative expectation is that the nondominant hand will yield a tapping rate about 90 percent of the dominant hand. Significant deviations from this pattern are thought to indicate a lesion in the hemisphere opposite that of the slowed hand (Haaland & Delaney, 1981). However, such inferences must be made with great caution owing to the very low reliability of the ratio score. Although test-retest and interexaminer reliabilities for either hand alone approach .80, the reliability of the ratio score is a dismal .44 to .54 (Morrison, Gregory, & Paul, 1979). The ratio score should be used with extreme caution in making clinical inferences about lateralization of damage.

The Purdue Pegboard Test requires the examinee to place pegs in holes with the left hand, right hand, and then both hands. Each trial lasts only 30 seconds, so the entire test can be administered in a matter of minutes. Tiffin (1968) reports normative scores for work applicants. Relative slowing in one hand suggests a lesion in the opposite hemisphere, whereas bilateral slowing indicates diffuse or bilateral brain damage. Using the Purdue Pegboard Test in isolation, one study found an 80 percent accuracy in identifying brain impairment among a large group of normal subjects and neurological patients (Lezak, 1983). Other studies report much less favorable findings (Heaton, Smith, Lehman, & Vogt, 1978). The Purdue Pegboard Test is a useful addition to a comprehensive battery but should not be used in isolation for screening purposes. Spreen and Strauss (1998) provide an excellent summary of norms for this widely used test.

Klove has developed a variation on the pegboard test in which the pegs have a ridge along one side (Klove, 1963). Because each peg must be rotated into position, the Grooved Pegboard requires complex coordination in addition to motor dexterity. The Grooved Pegboard test is an excellent instrument for assessing lateralized brain damage (Haaland & Delaney, 1981).

Finally, we should mention that useful motor tests need not require sophisticated equipment. Lezak (1995) recommends a line tracing task to assess difficulties in motor regulation (Figure 10.10). The examinee is given a brightly colored felt-tipped pen and a sheet of paper with several figures and told to draw over the lines as rapidly as possible. Difficulties with motor regulation show up in overshooting corners, perseveration of an ongoing response, and inability to follow the reduced curves in the bottom figure. Because this task is easily completed by most 10-year-olds, any noticeable deviations are suggestive of difficulties in motor regulation.

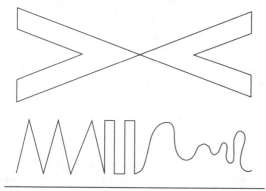

● **FIGURE 10.10**   A Typical Line-Tracing Task (Reduced Size)

## ● TEST BATTERIES IN NEUROPSYCHOLOGICAL ASSESSMENT

### The Luria-Nebraska Neuropsychological Battery

Now that we have completed a tour of some individual neuropsychological tests and procedures, it is time once again to remind the reader that many neuropsychologists prefer to use a fixed battery rather than an ever-shifting, individualized assortment of instruments. Certainly, one of the most widely used fixed batteries is the Luria-Nebraska Neuropsychological Battery (LNNB; Golden, 2004; Golden, Purish, & Hammeke, 1980, 1986), now in its third edition (LNNB-III; Teichner, Golden, Bradley, & Crum, 1999).

The test consists of 269 discrete items, chosen from the work of Luria (e.g., 1966) and formally standardized. These items are scored 0, 1, or 2 according to precise criteria in the administration and scoring manual. Similar items are grouped together into 11 clinical scales, C1 through C11 (Table 10.9). Raw scores on each scale are converted into $T$ scores, with a mean of 50 and a standard deviation of 10. Higher scores reflect more psychopathology; scores above 70 are especially suggestive of brain impairment.

Three summary scales are also derived from test performance: S1 (Pathognomonic), S2 (Left Hemisphere), and S3 (Right Hemisphere). The Pathognomonic scale reflects the degree of compensation that has occurred since an injury, such as functional reorganization of the brain as well as actual physical recovery. Higher scores reflect less compensation. The Left Hemisphere and Right Hemisphere scales can be used to help determine whether an injury is diffuse or lateralized. A number of other scales and interpretive factors are also available (Golden, Purish, & Hammeke, 1986).

We cannot review the voluminous literature on the LNNB, but brief mention of a few key studies certainly is merited. The reliability of the LNNB has been evaluated from the usual perspectives (split-half, internal consistency, and test-retest),

● **TABLE 10.9    Tests and Procedures of the Luria-Nebraska Neuropsychological Battery**

*Ability Scale: Tasks Included*

C1 Motor: Coordination, speed, drawing, complex motor abilities

C2 Rhythm: Attend to, discriminate, and produce verbal and nonverbal rhythmic stimuli

C3 Tactile: Identify tactile stimuli, including stimuli traced on the wrists

C4 Visual: Identify drawings, including overlapping and unfocused objects; solve progressive matrices and other visuospatial skills

C5 Receptive Speech: Discriminate phonemes and comprehend words, phrases, sentences

C6 Expressive Speech: Articulate sounds, words, and sentences fluently; identify pictured or described objects

C7 Writing: Use motor writing abilities in general; copy and write from dictation

C8 Reading: Read letters, words, and sentences; synthesize letters into sounds and words

C9 Arithmetic: Complete simple mathematical computations; comprehend mathematical signs and number structure

C10 Memory: Remember verbal and nonverbal stimuli under both interference and noninterference conditions

C11 Intelligence: Reasoning, concept formation, and complex mathematical problem solving

with excellent results. For example, the mean test-retest reliability for the clinical scales was near .90 (Bach, Harowski, Kirby, Peterson, & Schulein, 1981; Plaisted & Golden, 1982; Teichner et al., 1999). In various validity studies of classification of brain-damaged persons versus other criterion groups, the LNNB has shown hit rates of 80 percent or better (Golden, Moses, Graber, & Berg, 1981; Hammeke, Golden, & Purish, 1978; Moses & Golden, 1979; Teichner et al., 1999).

In spite of the positive appraisals of the LNNB reported by Golden and his colleagues, some neuropsychologists remain skeptical of the test (e.g., Lezak, 1995). One concern is that the heterogeneity of the scales is so great that the individual scale scores do not quantify specific neuropsychological deficits but instead serve only to differentiate normal

persons from brain-damaged patients (Snow, 1992; Van Gorp, 1992). Early reviewers also expressed concern that the speech scales were not oriented to syndromes of aphasia and could therefore misdiagnose language deficits (Delis & Kaplan, 1982). In defense of the LNNB, Purish (2001) contends that initial criticisms were based on misconceptions as to the theoretical basis for the instrument. Furthermore, in his view, these criticisms have been largely negated by an expanding body of empirical research supporting the test.

## The Neuropsychological Assessment Battery (NAB)

The Neuropsychological Assessment Battery or NAB (Stern & White, 2003ab) is a new and promising entry in the field that is remarkable for its breadth and sophistication. Suitable for adults 18 to 97 years of age, the NAB is a comprehensive battery of 24 individual tests in five modular areas: attention, language, memory, spatial, and executive functions. Twelve of the subtests also can be used as a separate screening module. The instrument comes in two parallel and psychometrically equivalent versions, Form 1 and Form 2. Norms are based on data from 1,448 neurologically healthy individuals matching the U.S. population on educational level, gender, ethnicity, and geographic region.

The five major modules, each consisting of four to six subtests, are listed in Table 10.10. Subtests used in the Screening Module are indicated with an asterisk. One feature evident in this table is that each module contains one subtest designed to possess ecological validity as well as psychometric validity. **Ecological validity** refers to the congruence between testing situations and analogous real-world circumstances. A test with strong ecological validity is one that highly resembles practical behaviors required in the real world. Among the NAB subtests with ecological validity are Driving Scenes, Bill Payment, Daily Living Memory, Map Reading, and Judgments. Each resembles a real world situation of importance in daily life. Ecological validity is beneficial because it increases the acceptability of testing to examinees.

● TABLE 10.10    **Modules and Subtests of the NAB**

*Attention*

| Orientation* | Questions about orientation to self, time, place, and situation |
| Digits Forward* | Repetition of orally presented digit sequences of increasing length |
| Digits Backward* | Orally presented digit sequences recalled in reverse order |
| Dots | Delayed recognition of the "new" dot in visual presentation of dots |
| Numbers & Letters* | Timed tests of letter cancellation, letter counting, serial addition |
| Driving Scenes | Recognition of what is "new" in presentation of a 2nd driving scene |

*Language*

| Oral Production | Speech output when the examinee orally describes a picture |
| Auditory Comprehension | Comprehension of orally presented commands and instructions |
| Naming* | Ability to name a pictured object, with cues if necessary |
| Reading Comprehension | Reading comprehension of single words and sentences |
| Writing | Writing sample scored for delivery, legibility, syntax, spelling |
| Bill Payment | Real world task of writing a check to pay a utility bill |

*Memory*

| List Learning | Verbal learning of 12-word list with interference trial |
| Shape Learning* | Visual learning of 9 shapes with delayed recognition |
| Story Learning* | Verbal learning of a short narrative story of five sentences |
| Daily Living Memory | Verbal learning of medication instructions, address, phone number |

*Spatial*

| Visual Discrimination | Matching of stimuli presented visually from an array |
| Design Construction | Assembling a tangram design from individual pieces |
| Figure Drawing | Drawing task involving copy and recall of geometric shapes |
| Map Reading | Answering practical questions based on the map of a city |

*Executive Functions*

| Mazes* | Solving paper-and-pencil mazes of increasing complexity |
| Categories | Classifying and categorizing task based on photos of six people |
| Word Generation* | Creating three-letter words from two vowels and six consonants |
| Judgment | Answering practical questions about home safety and health |

*Subtests used on the Screening Module.

The modular nature of the NAB allows for fixed administration of the entire battery (which takes about three hours), or flexible administration of the Screening Module followed by full administration of one or more of the five modules, depending on screening results. Once the test has been administered, software is available to compute a large array of output scores in a highly user-friendly computerized report. The module scores are reported as standard scores ($M = 100, SD = 15$), whereas the subtest scores are rendered as $T$-scores ($M = 50, SD = 10$).

The reliability of test scores is highly variable across the different modules and subtests, and is influenced by the examinee's age as well. The average coefficient alphas for the subtests in the five major modules revealed the following ranges (Stern & White, 2003b):

| | |
|---|---|
| Attention Module: | .78 to .79 |
| Language Module: | .48 to .84 |
| Memory Module: | .47 to .86 |
| Spatial Module | .65 to .67 |
| Executive Functions Module: | .45 to .77 |

Test-retest reliability was evaluated with 95 individuals who were tested twice over an average span of 6 months. Understandably, these average coefficients were somewhat lower and more variable:

| | |
|---|---|
| Attention Module: | .44 to .87 |
| Language Module: | .23 to .70 |
| Memory Module: | .41 to .61 |
| Spatial Module | .13 to .68 |
| Executive Functions Module: | .43 to .64 |

These relationships between test and retest NAB scores are respectable, given the lengthy test-retest interval.

The validity of the NAB is difficult to summarize concisely, because of the complexity of the instrument. The authors provide extensive documentation on validity, as evaluated from the traditional perspectives, including content validity, factor-analytic evidence of construct validity, and convergent and divergent correlations with similar and dissimilar external measures (all supportive). The authors conclude:

> Although the data presented in this chapter support the validity of the NAB, these data and analyses should be considered only the beginning steps in the ongoing process of test validation. (Stern & White, 2003b, p. 141)

Temple and Zgaljardic (2009) provide independent evidence for the validity of the Screening Module of the NAB. They note strong associations with a measure of functional independence in a sample of 70 individuals with moderate-to-severe traumatic brain injury at a residential post-acute rehabilitation facility. Yet, Iverson, Williamson, Ropacki, and Reilly (2007) come down on the other side of the fence. In their study of 37 outpatients with neurological problems, results on the Screening Module were better than expected. In other words, in their sample the instrument did not show good sensitivity. We need to keep in mind that the establishment of test validity is a dynamic process, not something set in stone when a test is released. The meaning of tests scores is sharpened and refined by ongoing research. It will prove interesting in the years ahead to see how additional studies bear on the validity of the NAB.

## ● SCREENING FOR ALCOHOL USE DISORDERS

The ways in which people can abuse alcohol include a spectrum of misfortune and tragedy ranging from an occasional hangover to, literally, drinking oneself to death. But clinicians and researchers generally recognize two diagnoses: alcohol abuse and alcohol dependence (American Psychiatric Association, 1994). Loosely speaking, the more generic syndrome of alcoholism refers to either diagnosis. A full discussion of these syndromes is not justified here, but a brief summary is warranted. Interestingly, neither alcohol abuse nor dependence is defined by ingestion of a particular amount of alcohol, although substantial quantities typically are involved. The criteria for **alcohol abuse** refer to the functional impact of drinking on the life of the patient. In particular, if an individual meets one or more of four criteria, a diagnosis of alcohol abuse is defensible. Briefly, the criteria are:

- Drinking interferes with important life responsibilities at work, home, or school.
- Drinking leads to unsafe behavior such as driving while intoxicated.
- Drinking causes persistent legal problems such as arrests for fighting.
- Drinking leads to conflict with a spouse or significant other.

In addition to meeting one or more of these criteria, the patient must not meet the criteria for a diagnosis of substance dependence, which often entails a more serious and chronic syndrome. Specifically, if a patient meets three or more of seven criteria, a diagnosis of **alcohol dependence** is warranted. Briefly, the criteria are:

- Tolerance or needing increasingly more alcohol to get the same effect.
- Withdrawal symptoms such as tremor when drinking ceases.
- Drinking in greater quantities or for longer periods than intended.
- Desire to cut down but unsuccessful efforts to control drinking.
- Spending large amounts of time using alcohol or recovering from use.
- Giving up important social, occupational, or recreational activities to drink.
- Continued use in spite of demonstrable health problems such as an ulcer.

Given the high prevalence of alcohol use disorders in the United States, it is nearly inevitable that psychologists and other clinicians will encounter patients who experience problems in this spectrum. Fortunately, there are several simple devices useful for screening and assessment, which we review here. In some cases, these tools are pristinely simple and consist of the clinician casually asking a handful of "yes-no" questions. In other cases, a more traditional paper-and-pencil questionnaire is needed.

The CAGE questionnaire is a short screening instrument that consists of the practitioner asking if the client has thought about **C**utting down on drinking, become **A**nnoyed by criticism of his or her drinking, felt **G**uilty about his or her drinking, or had an **E**ye-opener drink in the morning. A simple "yes-no" question pertinent to each symptom is asked as part of a general health history. The exact wording of this copyrighted instrument can be found in Ewing (1984). The endorsement of even a single item suggests the presence of an alcohol use disorder, whereas saying "yes" to two or more items virtually guarantees that the patient

will meet the criteria for alcohol abuse or dependence. Research indicates that the tool is more effective when it is not preceded by questions about how much or how often the patient drinks (Steinweg & Worth, 1993). Apparently, questions about quantity and frequency trigger denial in the patient, making accurate assessment nearly impossible. The CAGE questionnaire has proved valuable as a screening tool in numerous locations, including general psychological practice and medical settings. In one study of a "walk-in" or immediate-care Veterans hospital clinic, the test correctly identified 86 percent of patients later confirmed to have alcoholism and accurately ruled out 93 percent of patients later confirmed not to have alcohol problems. Astonishingly, the prevalence rate for alcoholism was determined to be 22 percent for this largely male clinic population (Liskow, Campbell, Nickel, & Powell, 1995).

A recent epidemiological study conducted in and around Paris, France, casts doubt on the usefulness of the CAGE test as a screening device for alcoholism (Messiah, et al., 2007). In 2005, the researchers conducted a follow-up to a 1991 study of 1,991 participant responses to the Cut-down, Annoyed, Guilt, and Eye-opener (CAGE) questionnaire through telephone interview of 5,382 residents. The time period in question, 1991 to 2005, was an era in which alcohol consumption was known to be in decline, so it was surprising to the researchers when they found that the percentage of respondents endorsing each of the symptoms had increased substantially. In fact, the magnitude of the paradoxical increase astonished the researchers (Figure 10.11). For example, when asked whether they had thought about cutting down on their drinking, the percentage of respondents who answered "yes" increased from 4.3 percent in 1991 to 16.6 percent in 2005. The researchers speculate that the results might indicate the emergence of a temperance movement in France. Whether or not this is true, the findings most certainly cast doubt on the value of the CAGE in general population surveys.

Some researchers find that the CAGE questionnaire is more effective for screening with men

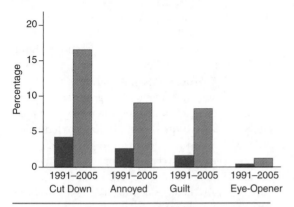

● **FIGURE 10.11** Percentage of Paris-area Residents Answering "Yes" to CAGE Questions in 1991 and 2005

*Source:* Based on data in Messiah, A., Encrenaz, G., Sapinho, D., and others. (2007). Paradoxical increase of positive answers to the Cut-down, Annoyed, Guilt, Eye-opener (CAGE) questionnaire during a period of decreasing alcohol consumption: results from two population-based surveys in Ile-de-France, 1991 and 2005. *Addiction*, 103, 598–603.

than women (Cherpitel, 2002). In response to this shortcoming, a similar instrument called the TWEAK questionnaire was developed specifically for women. The acronym refers to **T**olerance for drinking, **W**orried friends or relatives, **E**ye-opener to get going in the morning, **A**mnesia for things done or said while drinking, and feeling the need to **K**ut down on intake (Russell, Martier, Sokol, and others, 1994). TWEAK is scored on a 7-point scale, with the first two items earning two points each, the last three items earning one point each. A total score of two or more points indicates the likelihood of an alcohol problem. TWEAK is highly accurate in screening for alcohol problems in women (Bradley, Boyd-Wickizer, Powell, & Burman, 1998).

CAGE and TWEAK are by no means the only acronymic screening tools for alcohol problems. Other instruments include the five-item RAPS questionnaire or Rapid Alcohol Problems Screen (Cherpitel, 1995) and the 10-item AUDIT questionnaire or Alcohol Use Disorders Identification Test (Saunders, Aasland, Babor, and others, 1993). A huge amount of effort was invested in the development and validation of the AUDIT question-

naire. Research on this instrument was underwritten by the World Health Organization (WHO), and the scale has been translated into many languages.

Dozens of additional screening tests could be mentioned, but we want to close this section by reviewing an interesting scale that embodies some appealing methods of test construction. The Substance Abuse Subtle Screening Inventory-3 or SASSI-3 (Miller, Roberts, Brooks, & Lazowski, 1997) consists of two types of questions: obvious and subtle. The obvious questions include 26 behaviors that are endorsed on a 4-point Likert-type continuum ranging from *never* to *repeatedly*. These questions embody high face validity and are on a par with "I have taken drugs to improve how I feel" and "I have had more to drink than I planned." The subtle questions consist of 67 true-false items that are more indirect and indicative of the attitudes and behaviors that commonly accompany substance abuse. These questions are on a par with "I probably break the law more than others" and "I tend to be a responsible person" [reverse scored]. Both types of items—obvious and subtle—were carefully validated during test construction.

Test construction consisted of administering a large group of preliminary items to three groups of individuals: substance abusers, non–substance abusers, and substance abusers instructed to "fake good." The SASSI-3 emerged after this large pool of items was winnowed down to a smaller number, based on group contrasts. The resulting instrument includes the direct items—those that discriminated substance abusers from non–substance abusers, and the indirect items—those that discriminated the "fake-good" substance abusers from non–substance abusers. In addition to the adult scale, an adolescent version now has been published, and the instrument is available for supervised online administration. A Spanish version also is available.

The test developers report excellent reliability for the SASSI-3, with two-week test-retest stability coefficients for 40 respondents ranging from .92 to 1.00 for the subscales and coefficient alpha of .93

for the test overall. A validity study of 419 respondents revealed a 95 percent rate of correct classification for substance abusers and a 93 percent correct classification rate for non–substance abusers—very impressive results for a short screening test (Miller & Lazowski, 1999). Laux, Salyers, and Kotova (2005) found strong test-retest reliability with the SASSI-3 in a sample of 103 college students, reporting $r = .94$ over a one-week period. Feldstein and Miller (2007) reviewed 36 studies on all editions of the SASSI and weigh in skeptically, citing high rates of false positives. They propose that public domain instruments (e.g., CAGE, AUDIT) perform just as well and have the added advantage of being free.

The SASSI-3 appears to be a capable tool. Yet, given the frequency of its use—the instrument has been administered *millions* of times—it is disconcerting that few independent studies have been published (Gray, 2001). A search of PsychInfo yielded only 11 studies on the test, and seven of these were unpublished doctoral dissertations. More research is needed to corroborate the value of this promising inventory.

## ● ASSESSMENT OF MENTAL STATUS IN THE ELDERLY

The mental status examination (MSE) is a loosely structured interview that usually precedes other forms of psychological and medical assessment. The purpose of the evaluation is to provide an accurate description of the patient's functioning in the realms of orientation, memory, thought, feeling, and judgment. The MSE is the psychological equivalent of the general physical examination: Just as the physician reviews all the major organ systems, looking for evidence of disease, the psychologist reviews the major categories of personal and intellectual functioning, looking for signs and symptoms of psychopathology (Gregory, 1999). Although there is some latitude as to the scope of the MSE, certain mental functions are almost always investigated. A typical evaluation touches upon the areas listed in Table 10.11.

● **TABLE 10.11   Major Areas of a Typical Mental Status Exam**

**Appearance and Behavior**
Grooming
Facial expressions
Gross motor behavior
Eye contact

**Speech and Communication Processes**
Speech content, rate, tone, volume
Word difficulty, confusion, misuse

**Thought Content**
Logic, clarity, appropriateness
Delusions

**Cognitive and Memory Functioning**
Calculating ability
Immediate recall
Recent and remote memory
Fund of information
Abstracting ability

**Emotional Functioning**
Predominant mood
Appropriateness of affect

**Insight and Judgment**
Awareness of problems

**Orientation**
Day, date, time, location

*Source:* Based on Gregory, R. J. (1999). *Foundations of intellectual assessment: The WAIS-III and other tests in clinical practice.* Boston: Allyn and Bacon.

Some of the elements in this list can be assessed with short screening tests. In particular, cognition, memory, and orientation are intellectual functions that can be tested in a formal, structured manner (Hodges, 1994). In this section, we review several brief measures of mental status used by clinicians to supplement interview impressions. These measures are most commonly used in the mental status evaluation of the elderly, especially when the client appears to have a dementia such as Alzheimer's disease. Formal tests of mental status are also helpful in the assessment of certain brain-impairing conditions such as head injury, schizophrenia, severe depression, and drug-induced delirium. It is important to emphasize that screening tests are supplementary—they do not replace clinical judgment in the evaluation of mental status. Some areas covered by the MSE are simply impossible to quantify. For example, the evaluation of a patient's insight requires keen observation and sensitive interviewing skills. An MSE screening test for insight does not exist.

## Mini-Mental State Exam

The most widely used mental status tool is the Mini-Mental State Examination (MMSE), a 5- to 10-minute screening test that yields an objective global index of cognitive functioning (Folstein, Folstein, & McHugh, 1975; Tombaugh, McDowell, Kristjansson, & Hubley, 1996). The test contains 30 scorable items having to do with orientation, immediate memory, attention, calculation, language production, language comprehension, and design copying. The items are so easy that normal adults almost always obtain scores in the range of 27 to 30 points (Figure 10.12).

The reliability of this simple instrument is excellent. Folstein et al. (1975) report a 24-hour test-retest reliability of .89 for 22 patients with varied depressive symptoms. Reliability over a 28-day period for 23 clinically stable patients with diagnoses of dementia, depression, and schizophrenia was an impressive .99. Normative data are available from several sources (e.g., Lindal & Stefansson, 1993; Tombaugh, McDowell, Kristjansson, & Hubley, 1996).

Using a cutting score of 23 or below as abnormal and 24 or above as normal, the MMSE is about 80 to 90 percent accurate in identifying elderly patients with suspected Alzheimer's disease or other dementia. This cutting score produces few false positives (normal patients classified as having dementia). The sensitivity of the instrument depends on a number of factors, including the cutting score used, the educational level of the examinee, the extent of the dementia, the nature of the underlying pathology, and the type of setting in

| | |
|---|---|
| 5 | Orientation to Time (day, date, month, season, and year) |
| 5 | Orientation to Place (floor, building, city area, city, state) |
| 3 | Immediate Memory (three words presented orally) |
| 5 | Attention and Calculation (serial 7s, five subtractions) |
| 3 | Delayed Recall (three words presented orally above) |
| 2 | Naming (pencil and watch) |
| 1 | Repetition (brief sentence presented orally) |
| 3 | Comprehension (follow simple three-part oral command) |
| 1 | Reading (read simple command and obey) |
| 1 | Writing (compose a simple sentence) |
| 1 | Drawing (reproduce two intersecting pentagons) |
| 30 | Total |

● **FIGURE 10.12** Scoring Weights and Domains of the Mini-Mental State Examination

which assessments are undertaken (Anthony, LeResche, Niaz, Von Korff, & Folstein, 1982; Tombaugh, McDowell, Kristjansson, & Hubley, 1996; Tsai & Tsuang, 1979). In spite of its limitations, the MMSE remains the most reliable and practical screening test for dementia in the elderly (Ferris, 1992). Drebing, Van Gorp, Stuck, and others (1994) recommend its use as part of a short screening battery for cognitive decline in the elderly. Several additional measures of geriatric mental status are outlined in Table 10.12.

| ● TABLE 10.12   Mental Status Tests Used with Geriatric Patients | |
|---|---|
| *Test* | *Content* |
| **Cognistat** Kiernan, Mueller, and Langston (2009) | Language, construction (copying), memory, calculation, and reasoning/judgment |
| **Short Portable Mental Status Questionnaire** Pfeiffer (1975) | Information, orientation, attention |
| **Dementia Rating Scale** Mattis (2001) | Attention, memory, construction (copying), conceptualization, verbal fluency |
| **Test of Temporal Orientations** Benton, Sivan, Hamsher, Varney, and Spreen (1994) | Orientation |
| **Alzheimer's Disease Assessment Scale** Rosen, Mohs, and Davis (1984) | Orientation, memory, language, construction (copying) |
| **Cambridge Cognitive Examination** Roth, Tym, Mountjoy, and others (1986) | Orientation, memory, language, construction (copying), attention, abstraction, perception, calculation |
| **Severe Impairment Battery** Saxton, McGonigle-Gibson, Swihart, and others (1990) | Orientation, memory, language, attention, social interaction, construction (copying), praxis, visuo-perception |
| **Telephone Interview for Cognitive Status** (Barber & Stott, 2004) | Orientation, concentration, short-term memory, mathematical skills, praxis, and language usage |

## SUMMARY

1. For purposes of assessment, cognitive processing is viewed as proceeding sequentially through the following stages: sensory input, attention and concentration, learning and memory, language skills and/or visual-spatial/manipulatory skills, executive functions, and motor output (see Figure 10.6).

2. The assessment of sensory input is typically achieved through unilateral and bilateral stimulation in the modalities of touch, hearing, and vision. Typical tasks (e.g., finger localization) are so simple that normal persons rarely make errors.

3. Measures of attentional impairment include subtracting serial sevens; the Continuous Performance Test, a family of computerized vigilance tasks; and the Paced Auditory Serial Addition Test, a speeded test of mental arithmetic (adding successive pairs of digits), which is very sensitive to the effects of concussion.

4. A respected memory test is the Wechsler Memory Scale-III, a substantial revision of the original scale published nearly 50 years ago. Carefully standardized, the WMS-III consists of 17 subtests, including some with surprise recall a half hour after the original administration.

5. Another widely used memory test is the Rey Auditory Verbal Learning Test (RAVLT) in which the same list of 15 concrete nouns is read to the examinee for five successive trials. Recall is tested after each trial and also after an interpolated word list is administered.

6. Another respected memory test is the Wide Range Assessment of Memory and Learning-2 (WRAML-2), a comprehensive memory scale designed for children and adults, 5 to 90 years of age. In addition to testing immediate and delayed memory with several subscales, the instrument includes optional subtests to evaluate working memory.

7. Aphasia is any deviation in language performance caused by brain damage. Tests of aphasia (e.g., Reitan's Aphasia Screening Test or the Boston Diagnostic Aphasia Exam by Goodglass and Kaplan) typically assess spontaneous speech, repetition of sentences and phrases, comprehension of spoken language, word finding, reading, writing, copying, and calculation.

**8.** Tests of spatial and manipulatory ability include drawing or copying tests such as the Bender Visual Motor Gestalt Test, and three-dimensional block construction tests; both types are sensitive to the effects of brain damage.

**9.** Executive functions include logical analysis, conceptualization, reasoning, planning, and flexibility of thinking. Useful tests for the assessment of executive functions include the Porteus Maze Test; the Wisconsin Card Sorting Test; and the Tinkertoy® Test, so-named because of the materials used.

**10.** Neuropsychological test batteries commonly include measures of motor output such as the Finger Tapping Test from the Halstead-Reitan battery. Typically, the nondominant hand is 10 percent slower than the dominant hand; deviations from this pattern may indicate a lesion in the hemisphere opposite that of the slowed hand.

**11.** Other useful motor tests include the Purdue Pegboard Test, which requires the examinee to place pegs in holes with the left hand, right hand, and then both hands; and simple line-tracing tasks easily completed by most 10-year-olds.

**12.** The Luria-Nebraska Neuropsychological Battery consists of 269 discrete items modeled upon the work of Luria and formally standardized. The test developer and his colleagues report excellent reliability and strong validity. Another promising battery is the Neuropsychological Assessment Battery (NAB) which consists of 24 modular units.

**13.** A number of simple scales are available to screen for alcohol use disorders. These include tests with acronyms based upon symptoms (e.g., CAGE, TWEAK, and RAPS). A longer scale is the Substance Abuse Subtle Screening Inventory-3 (SASSI-3), a widely used scale with excellent reliability that is in need of independent validity studies.

**14.** The mental status examination (MSE) is a loosely structured interview that usually precedes other forms of psychological and medical assessment. Areas assessed in the MSE include orientation, memory, thought, feeling, and judgment.

**15.** A helpful mental status screening test particularly useful with the elderly is the Mini-Mental Status Examination. This 30-item test has high reliability and hit rates in some populations of 80 to 90 percent for the detection of dementia in the elderly.

## ● KEY TERMS AND CONCEPTS

Alzheimer's disease   p. 446

aphasia   p. 449

apraxia   p. 451

executive functions   p. 454

alcohol abuse   p. 460

alcohol dependence   p. 461

# Chapter 11

# Industrial, Occupational, and Forensic Assessment

## Industrial and Organizational Assessment

In this chapter we explore the specialized applications of testing within two distinctive environments—occupational settings and legal settings. Although disparate in many respects, these two fields of assessment share essential features. For example, legal guidelines exert a powerful and constraining influence upon the practice of testing in both arenas. Moreover, issues of empirical validation of methods are especially pertinent in occupational and forensic areas of practice. In Topic 11A, Industrial and Organizational Assessment, we review the role of psychological tests in making decisions about personnel such as hiring, placement, promotion, and evaluation. We also include coverage of vocational interest inventories used in career guidance. In Topic 11B, Forensic Applications of Assessment, we analyze the unique challenges encountered by forensic psychologists who perform court-based evaluations. Of course, relevant tests are surveyed and catalogued throughout. But more important, we focus upon the special issues and challenges encountered within these distinctive milieus.

Industrial and organizational psychology (I/O psychology) is the subspecialty of psychology that deals with behavior in work situations (Borman, Ilgen, Klimoski, & Weiner, 2003). In its broadest sense, I/O psychology includes diverse applications in business, advertising, and the military. For example, corporations typically consult I/O psychologists to help design and evaluate hiring procedures; businesses may ask I/O psychologists to appraise the effectiveness of advertising; and military leaders rely heavily upon I/O psychologists in the testing and placement of recruits. Psychological testing in the service of decision making about personnel is, thus, a prominent focus of this profession. Of course, specialists in I/O psychology possess broad skills and often handle many corporate responsibilities not previously mentioned. Nonetheless, there is no denying the centrality of assessment to their profession.

We begin our review of assessment in the occupational arena by surveying the role of testing in personnel selection. This is followed by a discussion of ways that psychological measurement is used in the appraisal of work performance. Finally, we provide an overview of vocational interest inventories and their uses in career guidance.

## ● THE ROLE OF TESTING IN PERSONNEL SELECTION

### Complexities of Personnel Selection

Based upon the assumption that psychological tests and assessments can provide valuable information about potential job performance, many businesses, corporations, and military settings have used test scores and assessment results for personnel selection. As Guion (1998) has noted, I/O research on personnel selection has emphasized criterion-related validity as opposed to content or construct validity. These other approaches to validity are certainly relevant but usually take a back seat to criterion-related validity, which preaches that current assessment results must predict the future criterion of job performance.

From the standpoint of criterion-related validity, the logic of personnel selection is seductively simple. Whether in a large corporation or a small business, those who select employees should use tests or assessments that have documented, strong correlations with the criterion of job performance, and then hire the individuals who obtain the highest test scores or show the strongest assessment results. What could be simpler than that?

Unfortunately, the real-world application of employment selection procedures is fraught with psychometric complexities and legal pitfalls. The psychometric intricacies arise, in large measure, from the fact that job behavior is rarely simple, unidimensional behavior. There are some exceptions (such as assembly-line production) but the general rule in our postindustrial society is that job behavior is complex, multidimensional behavior. Even jobs that seem simple may be highly complex. For example, consider what is required for effective performance in the delivery of the U.S. mail. The individual who delivers your mail six days a week must do more than merely place it in your mailbox. He or she must accurately sort mail on the run, interpret and enforce government regulations about package size, manage pesky and even dangerous animals, recognize and avoid physical dangers, and exercise effective interpersonal skills in dealing with the public, to cite just a few of the complexities of this position.

Personnel selection is, therefore, a fuzzy, conditional, and uncertain task. Guion (1991) has highlighted the difficulty in predicting complex behavior from simple tests. For one thing, complex behavior is, in part, a function of the situation. This means that even an optimal selection approach may not be valid for all candidates. Quite clearly, personnel selection is not a simple matter of administering tests and consulting cut-off scores.

We must also acknowledge the profound impact of legal and regulatory edicts upon I/O testing practices. Given that such practices may have weighty consequences—determining who is hired or promoted, for example—it is not surprising to learn that I/O testing practices are rigorously constrained by legal precedents and regulatory mandates. These topics are reviewed in Topic 12A, Psychological Testing and the Law.

## Approaches to Personnel Selection

Acknowledging that the interview is a widely used form of personnel assessment, it is safe to conclude that psychological assessment is almost a universal practice in hiring decisions. Even by a narrow definition that includes only paper-and-pencil measures, at least two-thirds of the companies in the United States engage in personnel testing (Schmitt & Robertson, 1990). For purposes of personnel selection, the I/O psychologist may recommend one or more of the following:

- Autobiographical data
- Employment interview
- Cognitive ability tests
- Personality, temperament, and motivation tests
- Paper-and-pencil integrity tests
- Sensory, physical, and dexterity tests
- Work sample and situational tests

We turn now to a brief survey of typical tests and assessment approaches within each of these categories. We close this topic with a discussion of legal issues in personnel testing.

## ● AUTOBIOGRAPHICAL DATA

According to Owens (1976), application forms that request personal and work history as well as demographic data such as age and marital status have been used in industry since at least 1894. Objective or scorable autobiographical data—

sometimes called **biodata**—are typically secured by means of a structured form variously referred to as a biographical information blank, biographical data form, application blank, interview guide, individual background survey, or similar device. Although the lay public may not recognize these devices as true tests with predictive power, I/O psychologists have known for some time that biodata furnish an exceptionally powerful basis for the prediction of employee performance (Cascio, 1976; Ghiselli, 1966; Hunter & Hunter, 1984). An important milestone in the biodata approach is the publication of the *Biodata Handbook,* a thorough survey of the use of biographical information in selection and the prediction of performance (Stokes, Mumford, & Owens, 1994).

The rationale for the biodata approach is that future work-related behavior can be predicted from past choices and accomplishments. Biodata have predictive power because certain character traits that are essential for success also are stable and enduring. The consistently ambitious youth with accolades and accomplishments in high school is likely to continue this pattern into adulthood. Thus, the job applicant who served as editor of the high school newspaper—and who answers a biodata item to this effect—is probably a better candidate for corporate management than the applicant who reports no extracurricular activities on a biodata form.

## The Nature of Biodata

Biodata items usually call for "factual" data; however, items that tap attitudes, feelings, and value judgments are sometimes included. Except for demographic data such as age and marital status, biodata items always refer to past accomplishments and events. Some examples of biodata items are listed in Table 11.1.

Once biodata are collected, the I/O psychologist must devise a means for predicting job performance from this information. The most common strategy is a form of empirical keying not unlike that used in personality testing. From a large sample of workers who are already hired, the I/O psychologist

● **TABLE 11.1   Examples of Biodata Questions**

How long have you lived at your present address?

What is your highest educational degree?

How old were you when you obtained your first paying job?

How many books (not work related) did you read last month?

At what age did you get your driver's license?

In high school, did you hold a class office?

How punctual are you in arriving at work?

What job do you think you will hold in 10 years?

How many hours do you watch television in a typical week?

Have you ever been fired from a job?

How many hours a week do you spend on hobbies?

How many job projects did you manage in the last year?

In college, did you participate in a sports team?

How many hours per month do you volunteer?

What is your attitude toward others who use marijuana?

---

designates a successful group and an unsuccessful group, based on performance, tenure, salary, or supervisor ratings. Individual biodata items are then contrasted for these two groups to determine which items most accurately discriminate between successful and unsuccessful workers. Items that are strongly discriminative are assigned large weights in the scoring scheme. New applicants who respond to items in the keyed direction, therefore, receive high scores on the biodata instrument and are predicted to succeed. Cross validation of the scoring scheme on a second sample of successful and unsuccessful workers is a crucial step in guaranteeing the validity of the biodata selection method. Readers who wish to pursue the details of empirical scoring methods for biodata instruments should consult Murphy and Davidshofer (2004), Mount, Witt, and Barrick (2000), and Stokes and Cooper (2001).

## The Validity of Biodata

The validity of biodata has been surveyed by several reviewers, with generally positive findings

(Rothstein, Schmidt, Erwin, Owens, & Sparks, 1990; Stokes et al., 1994; Stokes & Cooper, 2004). An early study by Cascio (1976) is typical of the findings. He used a very simple biodata instrument—a weighted combination of 10 application blank items—to predict turnover for female clerical personnel in a medium-sized insurance company. The cross-validated correlations between biodata score and length of tenure were .58 for minorities and .56 for nonminorities.[1] Drakeley et al. (1988) compared biodata and cognitive ability tests as predictors of training success. Biodata scores possessed the same predictive validity as the cognitive tests. Furthermore, when added to the regression equation, the biodata information improved the predictive accuracy of the cognitive tests.

In an extensive research survey, Reilly and Chao (1982) compared eight selection procedures as to validity and adverse impact on minorities. The procedures were biodata, peer evaluation, interviews, self-assessments, reference checks, academic achievement, expert judgment, and projective techniques. Noting that properly standardized ability tests provide the fairest and most valid selection procedure, Reilly and Chao (1982) concluded that only biodata and peer evaluations had validities substantially equal to those of standardized tests. For example, in the prediction of sales productivity, the average validity coefficient of biodata was a very healthy .62.

Certain cautions need to be mentioned with respect to biodata approaches in personnel selection. Employers may be prohibited by law from asking questions about age, race, sex, religion, and other personal issues—even when such biodata can be shown empirically to predict job performance. Also, even though the incidence of faking is very low, there is no doubt that shrewd

---

1. The curious reader may wish to know which 10 biodata items could possess such predictive power. The items were age, marital status, children's age, education, tenure on previous job, previous salary, friend or relative in company, location of residence, home ownership, and length of time at present address. Unfortunately, Cascio (1976) does not reveal the relative weights or direction of scoring for the items.

respondents can falsify results in a favorable direction. For example, Schmitt and Kunce (2002) addressed the concern that some examinees might distort their answers to biodata items in a socially desirable direction. These researchers compared the scores obtained when examinees were asked to elaborate their biodata responses versus when they were not. Requiring elaborated answers reduced the scores on biodata items; that is, it appears that respondents were more truthful when asked to provide corroborating details to their written responses. As with any measurement instrument, biodata items will need periodic restandardization. Finally, a potential drawback to the biodata approach is that, by its nature, this method captures the organizational status quo and might, therefore, squelch innovation. Becker and Colquitt (1992) discuss precautions in the development of biodata forms.

There is little doubt, then, that purely objective biodata information can predict aspects of job performance with fair accuracy. However, employers are perhaps more likely to rely upon subjective information such as interview impressions when making decisions about hiring. We turn now to research on the validity of the employment interview in the selection process.

## ● THE EMPLOYMENT INTERVIEW

The employment interview is usually only one part of the evaluation process, but many administrators regard it as the vital make-or-break component of hiring. It is not unusual for companies to interview from five to twenty individuals for each person hired! Considering the importance of the interview and its huge costs to industry and the professions, it is not surprising to learn that thousands of studies address the reliability and validity of the interview. We can only highlight a few trends here; more detailed reviews can be found in Conway, Jako, and Goodman (1995), Huffcutt (2007), Guion (1998), and Schmidt & Zimmerman (2004).

Early studies of interview reliability were quite sobering. In various studies and reviews, reliability was typically assessed by correlating evaluations of different interviewers who had access to the same job candidates (Wagner, 1949; Ulrich & Trumbo, 1965). The interrater reliability from dozens of these early studies was typically in the mid-.50s, much too low to provide accurate assessments of job candidates. This research also revealed that interviewers were prone to halo bias and other distorting influences upon their perceptions of candidates. *Halo bias*—discussed in the next topic—is the tendency to rate a candidate high or low on all dimensions because of a global impression.

Later, researchers discovered that interview reliability could be increased substantially if the interview was jointly conducted by a panel instead of a single interviewer (Landy, 1996). In addition, structured interviews in which each candidate was asked the same questions by each interviewer also proved to be much more reliable than unstructured interviews (Borman, Hanson, & Hedge, 1997; Campion, Pursell, & Brown, 1988). In these studies, reliabilities in the .70s and higher were found.

Research on validity of the interview has followed the same evolutionary course noted for reliability: Early research that examined unstructured interviews was quite pessimistic, while later research using structured approaches produced more promising findings. In these studies, interview validity was typically assessed by correlating interview judgments with some measure of on-the-job performance. Early studies of interview validity yielded almost uniformly dismal results, with typical validity coefficients hovering in the mid-.20s (Arvey & Campion, 1982).

Mindful that interviews are seldom used in isolation, early researchers also investigated incremental validity, which is the potential increase in validity when the interview is used in conjunction with other information. These studies were predicated on the optimistic assumption that the interview would contribute positively to candidate evaluation when used alongside objective test scores and background data. Unfortunately, the initial findings were almost entirely unsupportive (Landy, 1996).

In some instances, attempts to prove incremental validity of the interview demonstrated just the opposite, what might be called decremental validity. For example, Kelly and Fiske (1951) established that interview information actually decreased the validity of graduate student evaluations. In this early and classic study, the task was to predict the academic performance of more than 500 graduate students in psychology. Various combinations of credentials (a form of biodata), objective test scores, and interview were used as the basis for clinical predictions of academic performance. The validity coefficients are reported in Table 11.2. The reader will notice that credentials alone provided a much better basis for prediction than credentials plus a one-hour interview. The best predictions were based upon credentials and objective test scores; adding a two-hour interview to this information actually decreased the accuracy of predictions. These findings highlighted the superiority of actuarial prediction (based on empirically derived formulas) over clinical prediction (based on subjective impressions). We pursue the actuarial versus clinical debate in the last chapter of this text.

Studies using carefully structured interviews, including situational interviews, provide a more positive picture of interview validity (Borman, Hanson, & Hedge, 1997; Maurer & Fay, 1988;

● **TABLE 11.2**    **Validity Coefficients for Ratings Based on Various Combinations of Information**

| Basis for Rating | Correlation with Academic Performance |
|---|---|
| Credentials alone | .26 |
| Credentials and one-hour interview | .13 |
| Credentials and objective test scores | .36 |
| Credentials, test scores, and two-hour interview | .32 |

*Source:* Based on data in Kelly, E. L., & Fiske, D. W. (1951). *The prediction of performance in clinical psychology.* Ann Arbor: University of Michigan Press.

Schmitt & Robertson, 1990). When the findings are corrected for restriction of range and unreliability of job performance ratings, the mean validity coefficient for structured interviews turns out to be an impressive .63 (Wiesner & Cronshaw, 1988). A meta-analysis by Conway, Jako, and Goodman (1995) concluded that the upper limit for the validity coefficient of structured interviews was .67, whereas for unstructured interviews the validity coefficient was only .34. Additional reasons for preferring structured interviews include their legal defensibility in the event of litigation (Williamson, Campion, Malo, and others, 1997) and, surprisingly, their minimal bias across different racial groups of applicants (Huffcutt & Roth, 1998).

In order to reach acceptable levels of reliability and validity, structured interviews must be designed with painstaking care. Consider the protocol used by Motowidlo et al. (1992) in their research on structured interviews for management and marketing positions in eight telecommunications companies. Their interview format was based upon a careful analysis of critical incidents in marketing and management. Prospective employees were asked a set of standard questions about how they had handled past situations similar to these critical incidents. Interviewers were trained to ask discretionary probing questions for details about how the applicants handled these situations. Throughout, the interviewers took copious notes. Applicants were then rated on scales anchored with behavioral illustrations. Finally, these ratings were combined to yield a total interview score used in selection decisions.

In summary, under carefully designed conditions, the interview can provide a reliable and valid basis for personnel selection. However, as noted by Schmitt and Robertson (1990), the prerequisite conditions for interview validity are not always available. Guion (1998) has expressed the same point:

A large body of research on interviewing has, in my opinion, given too little practical information about how to structure an interview, how to conduct it, and how to use it as an assessment device. I think I know from the research that (a) interviews can be valid, (b) for validity they require structuring and standardization, (c) that structure, like many other things, can be carried too far, (d) that without carefully planned structure (and maybe even with it) interviewers talk too much, and (e) that the interviews made routinely in nearly every organization could be vastly improved if interviewers were aware of and used these conclusions. There is more to be learned and applied. (p. 624)

The essential problem is that each interviewer may evaluate only a small number of applicants, so that standardization of interviewer ratings is not always realistic. While the interview is potentially valid as a selection technique, in its common, unstructured application there is probably substantial reason for concern.

Why are interviews used? If the typical, unstructured interview is so unreliable and ineffectual a basis for job candidate evaluation, why do administrators continue to value interviews so highly? In their review of the employment interview, Arvey and Campion (1982) outline several reasons for the persistence of the interview, including practical considerations such as the need to sell the candidate on the job, and social reasons such as the susceptibility of interviewers to the illusion of personal validity. Others have emphasized the importance of the interview for assessing a good fit between applicant and organization (Adams, Elacqua, & Colarelli, 1994; Latham & Skarlicki, 1995).

It is difficult to imagine that most employers would ever eliminate entirely the interview from the screening and selection process. After all, the interview does serve the simple human need of meeting the persons who might be hired. However, based on 50 years worth of research, it is evident that biodata and objective tests often provide a more powerful basis for candidate evaluation and selection than unstructured interviews.

One interview component that has received recent attention is the impact of the handshake on subsequent ratings of job candidates. Stewart, Dustin, Barrick, and Darnold (2008) used simulated hiring interviews to investigate the commonly held conviction that a firm handshake bears

a critical nonverbal influence on impressions formed during the employment interview. Briefly, 98 undergraduates underwent realistic job interviews during which their handshakes were surreptitiously rated on 5-point scales for grip strength, completeness, duration, and vigor; degree of eye contact during the handshake also was rated. Independent ratings were completed at different times by five individuals involved in the process. Real human-resources professionals conducted the interviews and then offered simulated hiring recommendations. The professionals shook hands with the candidates but were not asked to provide handshake ratings because this would have cued them to the purposes of the study. This is the barest outline of this complex investigation. The big picture that emerged was that the quality of the handshake was positively related to hiring recommendations. Further, women benefited more than men from a strong handshake. The researchers conclude their study with these thoughts:

> The handshake is thought to have originated in medieval Europe as a way for kings and knights to show that they did not intend to harm each other and possessed no concealed weapons (Hall & Hall, 1983). The results presented in this study show that this age-old social custom has an important place in modern business interactions. Although the handshake may appear to be a business formality, it can indeed communicate critical information and influence interviewer assessments. (p. 1145)

Perhaps this study will provide an impetus for additional investigation of this important component of the job interview.

## ● COGNITIVE ABILITY TESTS

Cognitive ability can refer either to a general construct akin to intelligence or to a variety of specific constructs such as verbal skills, numerical ability, spatial perception, or perceptual speed (Kline, 1999). Tests of general cognitive ability and measures of specific cognitive skills have many applications in personnel selection, evaluation, and screening. Such tests are quick, inexpensive, and easy to interpret. A vast body of empirical research offers modest to strong support for the validity and fairness of standardized ability tests in personnel selection (Gottfredson, 1986). Certainly, it seems clear that ability tests often provide an excellent basis for job selection, at least according to objective criteria such as the capacity to predict job performance. For example, Hunter and Hunter (1984) conducted a meta-analysis of research on the prediction of job performance and concluded that for entry-level jobs no predictor (except for the work sample) exceeded the validity of ability tests, which showed a mean validity coefficient of .54. More recently, Bertua, Anderson, and Salgado (2005) reconfirmed this fundamental conclusion with a meta-analysis of 283 independent employee samples in the United Kingdom. They found that general mental ability as well as specific ability tests (verbal, numerical, perceptual, and spatial) is valid predictors of job performance and training success, with validity coefficients in the magnitude of .5 to .6.

Even so, a significant concern with the use of cognitive ability tests for personnel selection is that these instruments may result in an adverse impact on minority groups. *Adverse impact* is a legal term (discussed later in this chapter) referring to the disproportionate selection of white candidates over minority candidates. Most authorities in personnel psychology recognize that cognitive tests play an essential role in applicant selection; nonetheless, these experts also affirm that cognitive tests provide maximum benefit (and minimum adverse impact) when combined with other approaches such as biodata. Selection decisions never should be made exclusively on the basis of cognitive test results (Robertson & Smith, 2001).

An ongoing debate within I/O psychology is whether employment testing is best accomplished with highly specific ability tests or with measures of general cognitive ability. The weight of the evidence seems to support the conclusion that a general factor of intelligence (the so-called *g* factor) is usually a better predictor of training and job success than are scores on specific cognitive measures—even

when several specific cognitive measures are used in combination. Of course, this conclusion runs counter to common sense and anecdotal evidence. For example, Kline (1993) offers the following vignette:

> The point is that the *g* factors are important but so also are these other factors. For example, high *g* is necessary to be a good engineer and to be a good journalist. However for the former high spatial ability is also required, a factor which confers little advantage on a journalist. For her or him, however, high verbal ability is obviously useful.

Curiously, empirical research provides only mixed support for this position (Gottfredson, 1986; Larson & Wolfe, 1995; Ree, Earles, & Teachout, 1994). Although the topic continues to be debated, most studies support the primacy of *g* in personnel selection (Borman et al., 1997; Schmidt, 2002). Perhaps the reason that *g* usually works better than specific cognitive factors in predicting job performance is that most jobs are factorially complex in their requirements, stereotypes notwithstanding (Guion, 1998). For example, the successful engineer must explain his or her ideas to others and so needs verbal ability as well as spatial skills. Since measures of general cognitive ability tap many specific cognitive skills, a general test often predicts performance in complex jobs as well as, or better than, measures of specific skills.

Literally hundreds of cognitive ability tests are available for personnel selection, so it is not feasible to survey the entire range of instruments here. Instead, we will highlight three representative tests: one that measures general cognitive ability, a second that is germane to assessment of mechanical abilities, and a third that taps a highly specific facet of clerical work. The three instruments chosen for review—the Wonderlic Personnel Evaluation, the Bennett Mechanical Comprehension Test, and the Minnesota Clerical Test—are merely exemplars of the hundreds of cognitive ability tests available for personnel selection. All three tests are often used in business settings and, therefore, worthy of specific mention. Representative cognitive ability tests

● **TABLE 11.3  Representative Cognitive Ability Tests Used in Personnel Selection**

**General Ability Tests**
Shipley Institute of Living Scale
Wonderlic Personnel Test
Wesman Personnel Classification Test
Personnel Tests for Industry

**Multiple Aptitude Test Batteries**
General Aptitude Test Battery
Armed Services Vocational Aptitude Battery
Differential Aptitude Test
Employee Aptitude Survey

**Mechanical Aptitude Tests**
Bennett Mechanical Comprehension Test
Minnesota Spatial Relations Test
Revised Minnesota Paper Form Board Test
SRA Mechanical Aptitudes

**Motor Ability Tests**
Crawford Small Parts Dexterity Test
Purdue Pegboard
Hand-Tool Dexterity Test
Stromberg Dexterity Test

**Clerical Tests**
Minnesota Clerical Test
Clerical Abilities Battery
General Clerical Test
SRA Clerical Aptitudes

Note: SRA denotes Science Research Associates. These tests are reviewed in the *Mental Measurements Yearbook* series.

encountered in personnel selection are listed in Table 11.3. Some classic viewpoints on cognitive ability testing for personnel selection are found in Ghiselli (1966), Hunter and Hunter (1984), and Reilly and Chao (1982). More recent discussion of this issue is provided by Borman et al. (1997), Guion (1998), and Schmidt (2002).

## Wonderlic Personnel Test

Even though it is described as a personnel test, the Wonderlic Personnel Test (WPT) is really a group

test of general mental ability (Hunter, 1989; Wonderlic, 1983). What makes this instrument somewhat of an institution in personnel testing is its format (50 multiple-choice items), its brevity (a 12-minute time limit), and its numerous parallel forms (16 at last count). Item types on the Wonderlic are quite varied and include vocabulary, sentence rearrangement, arithmetic problem solving, logical induction, and interpretation of proverbs. The following items capture the flavor of the Wonderlic:

1. REGRESS is the opposite of
   (a) ingest      (b) advance
   (c) close       (d) open
2. Two men buy a car which costs $550; X pays $50 more than Y. How much did X pay?
   (a) $500    (b) $300    (c) $400    (d) $275
3. HEFT CLEFT—Do these words have
   (a) similar meaning    (b) opposite meaning
   (c) neither similar nor opposite meaning

The reliability of the WPT is quite impressive, especially considering the brevity of the instrument. Internal consistency reliabilities typically reach .90, while alternative-form reliabilities usually exceed .90. Normative data are available on 126,000 adults ages 20 to 65 years. Regarding validity, if the WPT is considered a brief test of general mental ability, the findings are quite positive (Dodrill & Warner, 1988). For example, Dodrill (1981) reports a correlation of .91 between scores on the WPT and scores on the WAIS. This correlation is as high as that found between any two mainstream tests of general intelligence. Bell, Matthews, Lassister, and Leverett (2002) reported strong congruence between the WPT and the Kaufman Adolescent and Adult Intelligence Test in a sample of adults. Hawkins, Faraone, Pepple, Seidman, and Tsuang (1990) report a similar correlation ($r = .92$) between WPT and WAIS-R IQ for 18 chronically ill psychiatric patients. However, in their study, one subject was unable to manage the format of the WPT, suggesting that severe visuospatial impairment can invalidate the test. A recent innovation with the Wonderlic is the addition of four forms of the test (called the Scholastic Level Exam) for use in educational selection and counseling. The validity of the Wonderlic in educational settings is not yet firmly established (Belcher, 1992).

Reviewers of the WPT do raise some concerns about the interpretive guidelines found in the test manual (Geisinger, 2001). For example, the manual suggests that persons who earn raw scores between 16 and 22 have a limited capacity for anything other than routine tasks. These WPT scores correspond to IQs of 93 to 104; that is, such persons are completely within the normal range of intelligence. Thus, the interpretive guidelines seem both arbitrary and unnecessarily restrictive. The manual also lists cutting scores used in industry for over 75 occupations, which raises the specter of an undertrained personnel officer overinterpreting individual scores. This would be especially problematical to racial minorities, since race differences on the WPT are significant (Geisinger, 2001). In fact, Chan (1997) reported that African American undergraduates perceived the WPT to be less valid than white students as a predictive employment measure. In a study of 1,277 entry-level production applicants at a worldwide manufacturing organization, Buttigieg (2006) reported moderate differences between Caucasian and minority applicants on the Wonderlic, with an effect size of $d = .56$ favoring majority applicants. He also found small but potentially impactful gender differences, with an effect size of $d = .20$ favoring men.

Another concern about the Wonderlic is that examinees whose native language is not English will be unfairly penalized on the test (Belcher, 1992). The Wonderlic is a speeded test. In fact, it has such a heavy reliance on speed that points are added for subjects age 30 and older to compensate for the well-known decrement in speed that accompanies normal aging. However, no accommodation is made for nonnative English speakers who might also perform more slowly. One solution to the various issues of fairness cited would be to provide norms for untimed performance on the

Wonderlic. However, the publishers have resisted this suggestion.

## Bennett Mechanical Comprehension Test

In many trades and occupations, the understanding of mechanical principles is a prerequisite to successful performance. Automotive mechanics, plumbers, mechanical engineers, trade school applicants, and persons in many other "hands-on" vocations need to comprehend basic mechanical principles in order to succeed in their fields. In these cases, a useful instrument for occupational testing is the Bennett Mechanical Comprehension Test (BMCT). This test consists of pictures about which the examinee must answer straightforward questions. The situations depicted emphasize basic mechanical principles that might be encountered in everyday life. For example, a series of belts and flywheels might be depicted, and the examinee would be asked to discern the relative revolutions per minute of two flywheels. The test includes two equivalent forms (S and T).

The BMCT has been widely used since World War II for military and civilian testing, so an extensive body of technical and validity data exist for this instrument. Split-half reliability coefficients range from the .80s to the low .90s. Comprehensive normative data are provided for several groups. Based on a huge body of earlier research, the concurrent and predictive validity of the BMCT appear to be well established (Wing, 1992). For example, in one study with 175 employees, the correlation between the BMCT and the DAT Mechanical Reasoning subtest was an impressive .80. An intriguing finding is that the test proved to be one of the best predictors of pilot success during World War II (Ghiselli, 1966).

In spite of its psychometric excellence, the BMCT is in need of modernization. The test looks old and many items are dated. By contemporary standards, some BMCT items are sexist or potentially offensive to minorities (Wing, 1992). The problem with dated and offensive test items is that they can subtly bias test scores. Modernization of the BMCT would be a straightforward project that could increase the acceptability of the test to women and minorities while simultaneously preserving its psychometric excellence.

## Minnesota Clerical Test

The Minnesota Clerical Test (MCT), which purports to measure perceptual speed and accuracy relevant to clerical work, has remained essentially unchanged in format since its introduction in 1931, although the norms have undergone several revisions, most recently in 1979 (Andrew, Peterson, & Longstaff, 1979). The MCT is divided into two subtests: Number Comparison and Name Comparison. Each subtest consists of 100 identical and 100 dissimilar pairs of digit or letter combinations (Table 11.4). The dissimilar pairs generally differ in regard to only one digit or letter, so the comparison task is challenging. The examinee is required to check only the identical pairs, which are randomly intermixed with dissimilar pairs. The score depends predominantly upon speed, although the examinee is penalized for incorrect items (errors are subtracted from the number of correct items).

The reliability of the MCT is acceptable, with reported stability coefficients in the range of .81 to .87 (Andrew, Peterson, & Longstaff, 1979). The manual also reports a wealth of validity data, including some findings that are not altogether flattering. In these studies, the MCT was correlated

---

### ● TABLE 11.4   Items Similar to Those Found on the Minnesota Clerical Test

**Number Comparison**

| | | |
|---|---|---|
| 1. 3496482 | ——— | 3495482 |
| 2. 17439903 | ——— | 17439903 |
| 3. 84023971 | ——— | 84023971 |
| 4. 910386294 | ——— | 910368294 |

**Name Comparison**

| | | |
|---|---|---|
| 1. New York Globe | ——— | New York Globe |
| 2. Brownell Seed | ——— | Brownel Seed |
| 3. John G. Smith | ——— | John G Smith |
| 4. Daniel Gregory | ——— | Daniel Gregory |

---

with measures of job performance, measures of training outcome, and scores from related tests. The job performance of directory assistants, clerks, clerk-typists, and bank tellers was correlated significantly but not robustly with scores on the MCT. The MCT is also highly correlated with other tests of clerical ability.

Nonetheless, questions still remain about the validity and applicability of the MCT. Ryan (1985) notes that the manual lacks a discussion of the significant versus the nonsignificant validity studies. In addition, the MCT authors fail to provide detailed information concerning the specific attributes of the jobs, tests, and courses used as criterion measures in the reported validity studies. For this reason, it is difficult to surmise exactly what the MCT measures. Ryan (1985) complains that the 1979 norms are difficult to use because the MCT authors provide so little information on how the various norm groups were constituted. Thus, even though the revised MCT manual presents new norms for 10 vocational categories, the test user may not be sure which norm group applies to his or her setting. Because of the marked differences in performance between the norm groups, the vagueness of definition poses a significant problem to potential users of this test.

## ● PERSONALITY TESTS

It is only in recent years, with the emergence of the "big five" approach to the measurement of personality and the development of strong measures of these five factors, that personality has proved to be a *valid* basis for employee selection, at least in some instances. In earlier times such as the 1950s into the 1990s, personality tests were used by many in a reckless manner for personnel selection:

> Personality inventories such as the MMPI were used for many years for personnel selection—in fact, overused or misused. They were used indiscriminately to assess a candidate's personality, even when there was no established relation between test scores and job success. Soon personality inventories came under attack. (Muchinsky, 1990)

In effect, for many of these earlier uses of testing, a consultant psychologist or human resource manager would look at the personality test results of a candidate and implicitly (or explicitly) make an argument along these lines: "In my judgment people with test results like this are [or are not] a good fit for this kind of position." Sadly, there was little or no empirical support for such imperious conclusions, which basically amounted to a version of "because I said so."

Certainly early research on personality and job performance was rather sobering for many personality scales and constructs. For example, Hough, Eaton, Dunnette, Kamp, and McCloy (1990) analyzed hundreds of published studies on the relationship between personality constructs and various job performance criteria. For these studies, they grouped the personality constructs into several categories (e.g., Extroversion, Affiliation, Adjustment, Agreeableness, and Dependability) and then computed the average validity coefficient for criteria of job performance (e.g., involvement, proficiency, delinquency, and substance abuse). Most of the average correlations were indistinguishable from zero! For job proficiency as the outcome criterion, the strongest relationships were found for measures of Adjustment and Dependability, both of which revealed correlations of $r = .13$ with general ratings of job proficiency. Even though statistically significant (because of the large number of clients amassed in the hundreds of studies), correlations of this magnitude are essentially useless, accounting for less than 2 percent of the variance.[2] Specific job criteria such as delinquency (e.g., neglect of work duties) and substance abuse were better predicted in specific instances. For example, measures of Adjustment correlated $r = -.43$ with delinquency, and measures of Dependability correlated $r = -.28$ with substance abuse. Of course, the negative correla-

tions indicate an inverse relationship: higher scores on Adjustment go along with lower levels of delinquency, and higher scores on Dependability indicate lower levels of substance abuse. Apparently, it is easier to predict specific job-related criteria than to predict general job proficiency.

Beginning in the 1990s, a renewed optimism about the utility of personality tests in personnel selection began to emerge (Behling, 1998; Hurtz & Donovan, 2000). The reason for this change in perspective was the emergence of the Big Five framework for research on selection, and the development of robust measures of the five constructs confirmed by this approach such as the NEO Personality Inventory-Revised (Costa & McCrae, 1992). Evidence began to mount that personality—as conceptualized by the Big Five approach—possessed some utility for employee selection. The reader will recall from an earlier chapter that the five dimensions of this model are Neuroticism, Extraversion, Openness to Experience, Conscientiousness, and Agreeableness. Shuffling the first letters, the acronym OCEAN can be used to remember the elements. In place of Neuroticism (which pertains to the negative pole of this factor), some researchers use the term Emotional Stability (which describes the positive pole of the same factor) so as to achieve consistency of positive orientation among the five factors.

A meta-analysis by Hurtz and Donovan (2000) solidified Big Five personality factors as important tools in predicting job performance. These researchers located 45 studies using suitable measures of Big Five personality factors as predictors of job performance. In total, their data set was based on more than eight thousand employees, providing stable and robust findings, even though not all dimensions were measured in all studies. The researchers conducted multiple analyses involving different occupational categories and diverse outcome measures such as task performance, job dedication, and interpersonal facilitation. We discuss here only the most general results, namely, the operational validity for the five factors in predicting

---

2. The strength of a correlation is indexed by squaring it, which provides the proportion of variance accounted for in one variable by knowing the value of the other variable. In this case, the square of .13 is .0169 which is 1.69 percent.

overall job performance. Operational validity refers to the correlation between personality measures and job performance, corrected for sampling error, range restriction, and unreliability of the criterion. Big Five factors and validity coefficients were as follows:

| | |
|---|---|
| Conscientiousness | .26 |
| Neuroticism | .13 |
| Extraversion | .15 |
| Agreeableness | .05 |
| Openness to Experience | .04 |

Overall, Conscientiousness is the big winner in their analysis, although for some specific occupational categories, other factors were valuable (e.g., Agreeableness paid off for Customer Service personnel). Hurtz and Donovan (2000) use caution and understatement to summarize the implications of their study:

> What degree of utility do these global Big Five measures offer for predicting job performance? Overall, it appears that global measures of Conscientiousness can be expected to consistently add a small portion of explained variance in job performance across jobs and across criterion dimension. In addition, for certain jobs and for certain criterion dimensions, certain other Big Five dimensions will likely add a very small but consistent degree of explained variance. (p. 876)

In sum, people who describe themselves as reliable, organized, and hard-working (i.e., high on Conscientiousness) appear to perform better at work than those with fewer of these qualities.

For specific applications in personnel selection, certain tests are known to have greater validity than others. For example, the California Psychological Inventory (CPI) provides an accurate measure of managerial potential (Gough, 1984, 1987). Certain scales of the CPI predict overall performance of military academy students reasonably well (Blake, Potter, & Sliwak, 1993). The Inwald Personality Inventory is well validated as a preemployment screening test for law enforcement (Chibnall & Detrick, 2003; Inwald, 1988). The Minnesota Multiphasic

Personality Inventory also bears mention as a selection tool for law enforcement (Selbom, Fischler, & Ben-Porath, 2007). Finally, the Hogan Personality Inventory (HPI) is well validated for prediction of job performance in military, hospital, and corporate settings (Hogan, 2002). The HPI was based upon the Big Five theory of personality (see Topic 8A, Theories and the Measurement of Personality). This instrument has cross-validated criterion-related validities as high as .60 for some scales (Hogan, 1986; Hogan & Hogan, 1986). Borman et al. (1997) provide a good summary of recent studies on the topic of testing for personnel selection.

## ● PAPER-AND-PENCIL INTEGRITY TESTS

Several test publishers have introduced instruments designed to screen theft-prone individuals and other undesirable job candidates such as persons who are undependable or frequently absent from work (Cullen & Sackett, 2004; Wanek, 1999). These tests come in two clearly differentiated types: overt integrity tests and personality-based measures. We will discuss each type separately, concentrating upon issues raised by these tests rather than detailing the merits or demerits of individual instruments. Table 11.5 lists some of the more commonly used instruments.

One problem with integrity tests is that their proprietary nature makes it difficult to scrutinize them in the same manner as traditional instruments. In most cases, scoring keys are available only to in-house psychologists, which makes independent research difficult. Nonetheless, a sizable body of research now exists on integrity tests, as discussed in the following section on validity.

### Overt Integrity Tests

Overt **integrity tests** typically consist of two sections. The first is a section dealing with attitudes toward theft and other forms of dishonesty such as beliefs about extent of employee theft, degree of

● **TABLE 11.5  Commonly Used Integrity Tests**

**Overt Integrity Tests**
  Accutrac Evaluation System
  Compuscan
  Employee Integrity Index
  Orion Survey
  PEOPLE Survey
  Personnel Selection Inventory
  Phase II Profile
  Reid Report and Reid Survey
  Stanton Survey

**Personality-Based Integrity Tests**
  Employment Productivity Index
  Hogan Personnel Selection Series
  Inwald Personality Inventory
  Personnel Decisions, Inc., Employment Inventory
  Personnel Reaction Blank

Note: Publishers of these tests can be easily found by using Google or another internet search engine.

condemnation of theft, endorsement of common rationalizations about theft, and perceived ease of theft. The second is a section dealing with overt admissions of theft and other illegal activities such as items stolen in the last year, gambling, and drug use. The most widely researched tests of this type include the Personnel Selection Inventory, the Reid Report, and the Stanton Survey. The interested reader can find addresses for the publishers of these and related instruments in O'Bannon et al. (1989).

Apparently, overt integrity tests can be more easily faked than personality-based integrity tests and might, therefore, be of less value in screening dishonest applicants. For example, Ryan and Sackett (1987) created a generic overt integrity test modeled upon existing instruments. The test contained 52 attitude and 11 admission items. In comparison to a contrast group asked to respond truthfully and another contrast group asked to respond as job applicants, subjects asked to "fake good" produced substantially superior scores (i.e., better attitudes and fewer theft admissions).

## Personality-Based Integrity Tests

The personality-based integrity tests typically do not contain obvious references to theft or other forms of undesirable employee behavior. These measures are more subtle in their approach and, therefore, less offensive to most job candidates. In fact, some integrity tests are really nothing more than recycled parts of existing personality tests such as the California Psychological Inventory (CPI). For example, the Personnel Reaction Blank (Gough, 1971) is based on those portions of the CPI dealing with sociability, dependability, conscientiousness, internal values, self-restraint, and acceptance of convention. In general, paper-and-pencil measures of conscientiousness show strong relationships with work-related integrity (Collins & Schmidt, 1993).

One common test development strategy for personality-based integrity measures is empirical keying against a criterion of theft. The problem with this approach is the criterion: Theft is rarely apprehended and admissions of theft may or may not be accurate. The base rate for employee theft is almost impossible to nail down. For example, rates of self-reported theft range from 28 to 62 percent in different studies (Camara & Schneider, 1994). Thus, the criterion classification of some research subjects may not be valid. A second approach is to measure broad constructs such as general employee deviance as indicated by hostility toward authority, thrill seeking, irresponsibility, and social insensitivity. The instruments that employ this strategy show modest ability to predict global criteria such as supervisor ratings of effectiveness (Ones et al., 1993; Sackett et al., 1989).

A serious problem with most integrity tests is the very high fail rate, often in the 30 to 60 percent range. Because integrity tests commonly are the final hurdle—used only with the small fraction of applicants who have the necessary ability and relevant experience—organizations that employ these tests must be in a position to turn away the majority of applicants. Of course, the high fail rate is, in part, a consequence of stringent cutting scores that cause rejection of potentially valuable employees (false positives) alongside real thieves and scoundrels (true positives). Actually, this is a validity issue, as discussed in the following section.

## Validity of Integrity Tests

Publishers of integrity tests have responded to skeptical psychologists and a distrustful public with a barrage of criterion-related validity studies. Ones et al. (1993) requested data on integrity tests from publishers, authors, and colleagues. These sources proved highly cooperative: The authors collected 665 validity coefficients based upon 25 integrity tests administered to more than half a million employees. Using the intricate procedures of meta-analysis, Ones et al. (1993) computed an average validity coefficient of .41 when integrity tests were used to predict supervisory ratings of job performance. Interestingly, integrity tests predicted global disruptive behaviors (theft, illegal activities, absenteeism, tardiness, drug abuse, dismissals for theft, and violence on the job) better than they predicted employee theft alone. The authors concluded with a mild endorsement of these instruments:

> When we started our research on integrity tests, we, like many other industrial psychologists, were skeptical of integrity tests used in industry. Now, on the basis of analyses of a large database consisting of more than 600 validity coefficients, we conclude that integrity tests have substantial evidence of generalizable validity.

This conclusion is echoed in a series of ingenious studies by Cunningham, Wong, and Barbee (1994). Among other supportive findings, these researchers discovered that integrity test results were correlated with returning an overpayment—even when subjects were instructed to provide a positive impression on the integrity test.

Other reviewers are more cautious in their conclusions. In commenting on reviews by the American Psychological Association and the Office of Technology Assessment, Camara and Schneider (1994) concluded that integrity tests do not measure up to expectations of experts in assessment, but that they are probably better than hit-or-miss, unstandardized methods used by many employers to screen applicants.

Several concerns remain about integrity tests. Publishers may release their instruments to unqualified users, which is a violation of ethical standards of the American Psychological Association. A second problem arises from the unknown base rate of theft and other undesirable behaviors, which makes it difficult to identify optimal cutting scores on integrity tests. If cutting scores are too stringent, honest job candidates will be disqualified unfairly. Conversely, too lenient a cutting score renders the testing pointless. A final concern is that situational factors may moderate the validity of these instruments. For example, how a test is portrayed to examinees may powerfully affect their responses and therefore skew the validity of the instrument.

The debate about integrity tests juxtaposes the legitimate interests of business against the individual rights of workers. Certainly, businesses have a right not to hire thieves, drug addicts, and malcontents. But in pursuing this goal, what is the ultimate cost to society of asking millions of job applicants about past behaviors involving drugs, alcohol, criminal behavior, and other highly personal matters? Hanson (1991) has asked rhetorically whether society is well served by the current balance of power—in which businesses can obtain proprietary information about who is seemingly worthy and who is not. It is not out of the question that Congress could enter the debate. In 1988, President Reagan signed into law the Employee Polygraph Protection Act, which effectively eliminated polygraph testing in industry (see Topic 11B, Forensic Applications of Assessment). Perhaps in the years ahead we will see integrity testing sharply curtailed by an Employee Integrity Test Protection

Act. Berry, Sackett, and Wiemann (2007) provide an excellent review of the current state of integrity testing.

● WORK SAMPLE AND
  SITUATIONAL EXERCISES

A **work sample** is a miniature replica of the job for which examinees have applied. Muchinsky (2003) points out that the I/O psychologist's goal in devising a work sample is "to take the content of a person's job, shrink it down to a manageable time period, and let applicants demonstrate their ability in performing this replica of the job." Guion (1998) has emphasized that work samples need not include every aspect of a job but should focus upon the more difficult elements that effectively discriminate strong from weak candidates. For example, a position as clerk-typist may also include making coffee and running errands for the boss. However, these are trivial tasks demanding so little skill that it would be pointless to include them in a work sample. A work sample should test important job domains, not the entire job universe.

Campion (1972) devised an ingenious work sample for mechanics that illustrates the preceding point. Using the job analysis techniques discussed at the beginning of this topic, Campion determined that the essence of being a good mechanic was defined by successful use of tools, accuracy of work, and overall mechanical ability. With the help of skilled mechanics, he devised a work sample that incorporated these job aspects through typical tasks such as installing pulleys and repairing a gearbox. Points were assigned to component behaviors for each task. Example items and their corresponding weights were as follows:

| Installing Pulleys and Belts | Scoring Weights |
|---|---|
| 1. Checks key before installing against: | |
| ___ shaft | 2 |
| ___ pulley | 2 |
| ___ neither | 0 |

**Disassembling and Repairing a Gear Box**

| 10. Removes old bearing with: | |
|---|---|
| ___ press and driver | 3 |
| ___ bearing puller | 2 |
| ___ gear puller | 1 |
| ___ other | 0 |

**Pressing a Bushing into Sprocket and Reaming to Fit a Shaft**

| 4. Checks internal diameter of bushing against shaft diameter: | |
|---|---|
| ___ visually | 1 |
| ___ hole gauge and micrometers | 3 |
| ___ Vernier calipers | 2 |
| ___ scale | 1 |
| ___ does not check | 0 |

Campion found that the performance of 34 male maintenance mechanics on the work sample measure was significantly and positively related to the supervisor's evaluations of their work performance, with validity coefficients ranging from .42 to .66.

A **situational exercise** is approximately the white-collar equivalent of a work sample. Situational exercises are largely used to select persons for managerial and professional positions. The main difference between a situational exercise and a work sample is that the former mirrors only part of the job, whereas the latter is a microcosm of the entire job (Muchinsky, 1990). In a situational exercise, the prospective employee is asked to perform under circumstances that are highly similar to the anticipated work environment. Measures of accomplishment can then be gathered as a basis for gauging likely productivity or other aspects of job effectiveness. The situational exercises with the highest validity show a close resemblance with the criterion; that is, the best exercises are highly realistic (Asher & Sciarrino, 1974; Muchinsky, 2003).

Work samples and situational exercises are based on the conventional wisdom that the best predictor of future performance in a specific domain is past performance in that same domain.

Typically, a situational exercise requires the candidate to perform in a setting that is highly similar to the intended work environment. Thus, the resulting performance measures resemble those that make up the prospective job itself.

Hundreds of work samples and situational exercises have been proposed over the years. For example, in an earlier review, Asher and Sciarrino (1974) identified 60 procedures, including the following:

- Typing test for office personnel
- Mechanical assembly test for loom fixers
- Map-reading test for traffic control officers
- Tool dexterity test for machinists and riveters
- Headline, layout, and story organization test for magazine editors
- Oral fact-finding test for communication consultants
- Role-playing test for telephone salespersons
- Business-letter-writing test for managers

A very effective situational exercise that we will discuss here is the in-basket technique, a procedure that simulates the work environment of an administrator.

### The In-Basket Test

The classic paper on the **in-basket test** is the monograph by Frederiksen (1962). For this comprehensive study Frederiksen devised the Bureau of Business In-Basket Test, which consists of the letters, memoranda, records of telephone calls, and other documents that have collected in the in-basket of a newly hired executive officer of a business bureau. In this test, the candidate is instructed not to play a role, but to be himself.[3] The candidate is not to say what he would do, he is to do it.

The letters, memoranda, phone calls, and interviews completed by him in this simulated job environment constitute the record of behavior that is scored according to both content and style of the responses. *Response style* refers to how a task was

completed—courteously, by telephone, by involving a superior, through delegation to a subordinate, and so on. *Content* refers to what was done, including making plans, setting deadlines, seeking information; several quantitative indices were also computed, including number of items attempted and total words written. For some scoring criteria such as imaginativeness—the number of courses of action which seemed to be good ideas—expert judgment was required.

Frederiksen (1962) administered his in-basket test to 335 subjects, including students, administrators, executives, and army officers. Scoring the test was a complex procedure that required the development of a 165-page manual. The odd-even reliability of the individual items varied considerably, but enough modestly reliable items emerged ($rs$ of .70 and above) that Frederiksen could conduct several factor analyses and also make meaningful group comparisons.

When scores on the individual items were correlated with each other and then factor analyzed, the behavior of potential administrators could be described in terms of eight primary factors. When scores on these primary factors were themselves factor analyzed, three second-order factors emerged. These second-order factors describe administrative behavior in the most general terms possible. The first dimension is Preparing for Action, characterized by deferring final decisions until information and advice is obtained. The second dimension is simply Amount of Work, depicting the large individual differences in the sheer work output. The third major dimension is called Seeking Guidance, with high scorers appearing to be anxious and indecisive. These dimensions fit well with existing theory about administrator performance and therefore support the validity of Frederiksen's task.

A number of salient attributes emerged when Frederiksen compared the subject groups on the scorable dimensions of the in-basket test. For example, the undergraduates stressed verbal productivity, the government administrators lacked concern with outsiders, the business executives were highly courteous, the army officers exhibited strong control over subordinates, and school

---

3. We do not mean to promote a subtle sexism here, but in fact Frederiksen (1962) tested a predominantly (if not exclusively) male sample of students, administrators, executives, and army officers.

principals lacked firm control. These group differences speak strongly to the construct validity of the in-basket test, since the findings are consistent with theoretical expectations about these subject groups.

Early studies supported the predictive validity of in-basket tests. For example, Brass and Oldham (1976) demonstrated that performance on an in-basket test corresponded to on-the-job performance of supervisors if the appropriate in-basket scoring categories were used. Specifically, based on the in-basket test, supervisors who personally reward employees for good work, personally punish subordinates for poor work, set specific performance objectives, and enrich their subordinates' jobs are also rated by their superiors as being effective managers. The predictive power of these in-basket dimensions was significant, with a multiple correlation coefficient of .54 between predictors and criterion. Standardized in-basket tests can now be purchased for use by private organizations. Unfortunately, most of these tests are "in-house" instruments not available for general review. In spite of an occasional cautionary review (e.g., Brannick et al., 1989), the in-basket technique is still highly regarded as a useful method of evaluating candidates for managerial positions.

## Assessment Centers

An assessment center is not so much a place as a process. Many corporations and military branches—as well as a few progressive governments—have dedicated special sites to the application of in-basket and other simulation exercises in the training and selection of managers. The purpose of an **assessment center** is to evaluate managerial potential by exposing candidates to multiple simulation techniques, including group presentations, problem-solving exercises, group discussion exercises, interviews, and in-basket techniques. Results from traditional aptitude and personality tests also are considered in the overall evaluation. The various simulation exercises are observed and evaluated by successful senior managers who have been specially trained in techniques of observation and evaluation. Assessment centers are used in a variety of settings, including business and industry, government, and the military. There is no doubt that a properly designed assessment center can provide a valid evaluation of managerial potential. Follow-up research has demonstrated that the performance of candidates at an assessment center is strongly correlated with supervisor ratings of job performance (Gifford, 1991). A more difficult question to answer is whether assessment centers are cost-effective in comparison to traditional selection procedures. After all, funding an assessment center is very expensive. The key question is whether the assessment center approach to selection boosts organizational productivity sufficiently to offset the expense of the selection process. Anecdotally, the answer would appear to be a resounding yes, since poor decisions from bad managers can be very expensive. However, there is little empirical information that addresses this issue.

Goffin, Rothstein, and Johnston (1996) compared the validity of traditional personality testing (with the Personality Research Form; Jackson, 1984b) and the assessment center approach in the prediction of the managerial performance of 68 managers in a forestry products company. Both methods were equivalent in predicting performance, which would suggest that the assessment center approach is not worth the (very substantial) additional cost. However, when both methods were used in combination, personality testing provided significant incremental validity over that of the assessment center alone. Thus, personality testing and assessment center findings each contribute unique information helpful in predicting performance.

Putting a candidate through an assessment center is very expensive. Dayan, Fox, and Kasten (2008) speak to the cost of assessment center operations by arguing that an employment interview and cognitive ability test scores can be used to cull the best and the worst applicants so that only those in the middle need to undergo these expensive evaluations. Their study involved 423 Israeli police force candidates who underwent assessment center evaluations after meeting initial eligibility. The researchers concluded in retrospect that, with minimal loss of sensitivity and specificity, nearly 20 percent of this sample could have been excused from more extensive evaluation. These were individuals who, based on interview and cognitive test scores, were nearly sure to fail or nearly certain to succeed.

## ● APPRAISAL OF WORK PERFORMANCE

The appraisal of work performance is crucial to the successful operation of any business or organization. In the absence of meaningful feedback, employees have no idea how to improve. In the absence of useful assessment, administrators have no idea how to manage personnel. It is difficult to imagine how a corporation, business, or organization could pursue an institutional mission without evaluating the performance of its employees in one manner or another.

Industrial and organizational psychologists frequently help devise rating scales and other instruments used for performance appraisal (Landy & Farr, 1983). When done properly, employee evaluation rests upon a solid foundation of applied psychological measurement—hence, its inclusion as a major topic in this text. In addition to introducing essential issues in the measurement of work performance, we also touch briefly on the many legal issues that surround the selection and appraisal of personnel. We begin by discussing the context of performance appraisal.

The evaluation of work performance serves many organizational purposes. The short list includes promotions, transfers, layoffs, and the setting of salaries—all of which may hang in the balance of performance appraisal. The long list includes the 20 common uses identified by Cleveland, Murphy, and Williams (1989):

Salary administration
Promotion
Retention or termination
Recognition of individual performance

Layoffs
Identify poor performance
Identify individual training needs
Performance feedback
Determine transfers and assignments
Identify individual strengths and weaknesses
Personnel planning
Determine organizational training needs
Evaluate goal achievement
Assist in goal identification
Evaluate personnel systems
Reinforce authority structure
Identify organizational development needs
Criteria for validation research
Document personnel decisions
Meet legal requirements

These applications of performance evaluation cluster around four major uses: comparing individuals in terms of their overall performance levels; identifying and using information about individual strengths and weaknesses; implementing and evaluating human resource systems in organizations; and documenting or justifying personnel decisions. Beyond a doubt, performance evaluation is essential to the maintenance of organizational effectiveness.

As the reader will soon discover, performance evaluation is a perplexing problem for which the simple and obvious solutions are usually incorrect. In part, the task is difficult because the criteria for effective performance are seldom so straightforward as "dollar amount of widgets sold" (e.g., for a salesperson) or "percentage of students passing a national test" (e.g., for a teacher). As much as we might prefer objective methods for assessing the effectiveness of employees, judgmental approaches are often the only practical choice for performance evaluation.

The problems encountered in the implementation of performance evaluation are usually referred to collectively as the criterion problem—a designation that first appeared in the 1950s (e.g., Flanagan, 1956; Landy & Farr, 1983). The phrase **criterion problem** is meant to convey the difficulties involved in conceptualizing and measuring performance constructs, which are often complex, fuzzy, and multidimensional. For a thorough discussion of the criterion problem, the reader should consult comprehensive reviews by Austin and Villanova (1992) and Campbell, Gasser, and Oswald (1996). We touch upon some aspects of the criterion problem in the following review.

## ● APPROACHES TO PERFORMANCE APPRAISAL

There are literally dozens of conceptually distinct approaches to the evaluation of work performance. In practice, these numerous approaches break down into four classes of information: performance measures such as productivity counts; personnel data such as rate of absenteeism; peer ratings and self-assessments; and supervisor evaluations such as rating scales. Rating scales completed by supervisors are by far the preferred method of performance appraisal, as discussed later. First, we mention the other approaches briefly.

### Performance Measures

Performance measures include seemingly objective indices such as number of bricks laid for a mason, total profit for a salesperson, or percentage of students graduated for a teacher. Although production counts would seem to be the most objective and valid methods for criterion measurement, there are serious problems with this approach (Guion, 1965). The problems include the following:

- The rate of productivity may not be under the control of the worker. For example, the fast-food worker can only sell what people order, and the assembly-line worker can only proceed at the same pace as coworkers.
- Production counts are not applicable to most jobs. For example, relevant production units do not exist for a college professor, a judge, or a hotel clerk.
- An emphasis upon production counts may distort the quality of the output. For example,

pharmacists in a mail-order drug emporium may fill prescriptions with the wrong medicine if their work is evaluated solely upon productivity.

Another problem is that production counts may be unreliable, especially over short periods of time. Finally, production counts may tap only a small proportion of job requirements, even when they appear to be the definitive criterion. For example, sales volume would appear to be the ideal criterion for most sales positions. Yet, a salesperson can boost sales by misrepresenting company products. Sales may be quite high for several years—until the company is sued by unhappy customers. Productivity is certainly important in this example, but the corporation should also desire to assess interpersonal factors such as honesty in customer relations.

### Personnel Data: Absenteeism

Personnel data such as rate of absenteeism provide another possible basis for performance evaluation. Certainly employers have good reason to keep tabs on absenteeism and to reduce it through appropriate incentives. Steers and Rhodes (1978) calculated that absenteeism costs about $25 billion a year in lost productivity! Little wonder that absenteeism is a seductive criterion measure that has been researched extensively (Harrison & Hulin, 1989).

Unfortunately, absenteeism turns out to be a largely useless measure of work performance, except for the extreme cases of flagrant work truancy. A major problem is defining absenteeism. Landy and Farr (1983) list 28 categories of absenteeism, many of which are uncorrelated with the others. Different kinds of absenteeism include scheduled versus unscheduled, authorized versus unauthorized, justified versus unjustified, contractual versus noncontractual, sickness versus nonsickness, medical versus personal, voluntary versus involuntary, explained versus unexplained, compensable versus noncompensable, certified illness versus casual illness, Monday/Friday absence versus midweek, and reported versus unreported. When is a worker truly absent from work? The criteria are very slippery.

In addition, absenteeism turns out to be an atrociously unreliable variable. The test-retest correlations (absentee rates from two periods of identical length) are as low as .20, meaning that employees display highly variable rates of absenteeism from one time period to the next. A related problem with absenteeism is that workers tend to underreport it for themselves and overreport it for others (Harrison & Shaffer, 1994). Finally, for the vast majority of workers, absenteeism rates are quite low. In short, absenteeism is a poor method for assessing worker performance, except for the small percentage of workers who are chronically truant.

## Peer Ratings and Self-Assessments

Some researchers have proposed that peer ratings and self-assessments are highly valid and constitute an important complement to supervisor ratings. A substantial body of research pertains to this question, but the results are often confusing and contradictory. Nonetheless, it is possible to list several generalizations (Harris & Schaubroeck, 1988; Smither, 1994):

- Peers give more lenient ratings than supervisors.
- The correlation between self-ratings and supervisor ratings is minimal.
- The correlation between peer ratings and supervisor ratings is moderate.
- Supervisors and subordinates have different ideas about what is important in jobs.

Overall, reviewers conclude that peer ratings and self-assessments may have limited application for purposes such as personal development, but their validity is not yet sufficiently established to justify widespread use (Smither, 1994).

## Supervisor Rating Scales

Rating scales are the most common measure of job performance (Landy & Farr, 1983; Muchinsky,

2003). These instruments vary from simple graphic forms to complex scales anchored to concrete behaviors. In general, supervisor rating scales reveal only fair reliability, with a mean interrater reliability coefficient of .52 across many different approaches and studies (Viswesvaran, Ones, & Schmidt, 1996). In spite of their weak reliability, supervisor ratings still rank as the most widely used approach. About three-quarters of all performance evaluations are based upon judgmental methods such as supervisor rating scales (Landy, 1985).

The simplest rating scale is the graphic rating scale, introduced by Donald Paterson in 1922 (Landy & Farr, 1983). A **graphic rating scale** consists of trait labels, brief definitions of those labels, and a continuum for the rating. As the reader will notice in Figure 11.1, several types of graphic rating scales have been used.

The popularity of graphic rating scales is due, in part, to their simplicity. But this is also a central weakness because the dimension of work performance being evaluated may be vaguely defined. Dissatisfaction with graphic rating scales led to the development of many alternative approaches to performance appraisal, as discussed in this section.

A **critical incidents checklist** is based upon actual episodes of desirable and undesirable on-the-job behavior (Flanagan, 1954). Typically, a checklist developer will ask employees to help construct the instrument by submitting specific examples of desirable and undesirable job behavior. For example, suppose that we intended to develop a checklist to appraise the performance of resident advisers (RAs) in a dormitory. Modeling a study by Aamodt, Keller, Crawford, and Kimbrough (1981), we might ask current dormitory RAs the following question:

> Think of the best RA that you have ever known. Please describe in detail several incidents that reflect why this person was the best adviser. Please do the same for the worst RA you have ever known.

Based upon hundreds of nominated behaviors, checklist developers would then proceed to distill

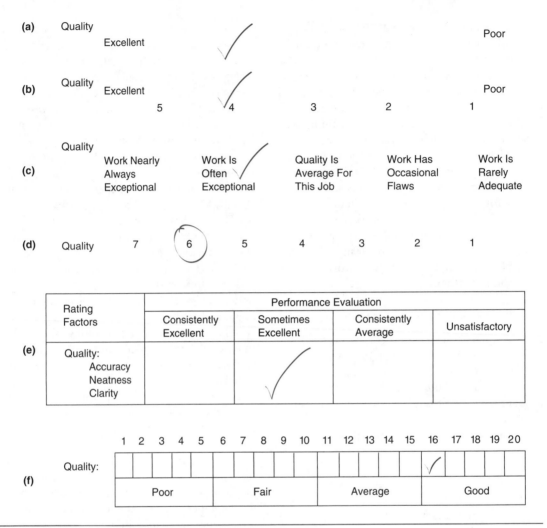

● **FIGURE 11.1**    Examples of Graphic Rating Scales

and codify these incidents into a smaller number of relevant behaviors, both desirable and undesirable. For example, the following items might qualify for the RA checklist:

_____ stays in dorm more than required
_____ breaks dormitory rules
_____ is fair about discipline
_____ plans special programs
_____ fails to discipline friends
_____ is often unfriendly

_____ shows concern about residents
_____ comes across as authoritarian

Of course, the full checklist would be much longer than the preceding. The RA supervisor would complete this instrument as a basis for performance appraisal. If needed, an overall summary score can be derived from an appropriate weighting of individual items.

Another form of criterion-referenced judgmental measure is the **behaviorally anchored**

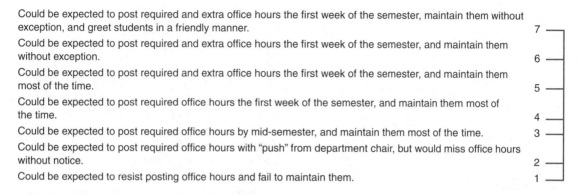

Could be expected to post required and extra office hours the first week of the semester, maintain them without exception, and greet students in a friendly manner.    7

Could be expected to post required and extra office hours the first week of the semester, and maintain them without exception.    6

Could be expected to post required and extra office hours the first week of the semester, and maintain them most of the time.    5

Could be expected to post required office hours the first week of the semester, and maintain them most of the time.    4

Could be expected to post required office hours by mid-semester, and maintain them most of the time.    3

Could be expected to post required office hours with "push" from department chair, but would miss office hours without notice.    2

Could be expected to resist posting office hours and fail to maintain them.    1

● **FIGURE 11.2**    Behaviorally Anchored Rating Scale for Posting and Maintaining Office Hours

rating scale (BARS). The classic work on BARS dates back to Smith and Kendall (1963). These authors proposed a complex developmental procedure for producing criterion-referenced judgments. The procedure uses a number of experts to identify and define performance dimensions, generate behavior examples, and scale the behaviors meaningfully. Overall, the procedure is quite complex, time-consuming, and expensive. A number of variations and improvements have been suggested. An advantage to BARS and other behavior-based scales is their strict adherence to EEOC (Equal Employment Opportunity Commission) guidelines discussed later in this chapter. BARS and related approaches focus upon behaviors as opposed to personality or attitudinal characteristics. A behaviorally anchored scale for performance of college professors in posting office hours is depicted in Figure 11.2. Of course, the comprehensive evaluation of a sales manager would include additional scales for other aspects of work.

Research on improving the accuracy of ratings with BARS is mixed. Some studies find fewer rating errors—especially a reduction in unwarranted leniency of evaluations—whereas other studies report no improvement with BARS compared to other evaluation methods (Murphy & Pardaffy, 1989). Overall, Muchinsky (2003) concludes that the BARS approach is not much better than graphic rating scales in reducing rating errors. Nonetheless, the scale development process of BARS

may have indirect benefits in that supervisors are compelled to pay close attention to the behavioral components of effective performance.

A **behavior observation scale** (BOS) is a variation upon the BARS technique. The difference between the two is that the BOS approach uses a continuum from "almost never" to "almost always" to measure how often an employee performs the specific tasks on each behavioral dimension. As with the BARS technique, researchers question whether behavior observation scales are worth the extra effort (Guion, 1998).

A **forced-choice scale** is designed to eliminate bias and subjectivity in supervisor ratings by forcing a choice between options that are equal in social desirability. In theory, this approach makes it impossible for the supervisor to slant ratings in a biased or subjective manner. We will use the pathbreaking research by Sisson (1948) to illustrate the features of this approach. He developed a scale to evaluate Army officers that consisted of tetrads of behavioral descriptors. Each tetrad contained two positive items matched for social desirability and two negative items also matched for social desirability. The four items in each tetrad were topically related to a single performance dimension. Unknown to the supervisors who completed the rating scale, one of the two positive items was judged very descriptive of effective Army officers and the other judged less so. Likewise, one of the two negative items was judged more descriptive of ineffective Army officers and the other judged less so. Here is a sample tetrad (Borman, 1991):

| | Most Descriptive | Least Descriptive |
|---|---|---|
| A. Cannot assume responsibility | _____ | _____ |
| B. Knows how and when to delegate authority | _____ | _____ |
| C. Offers suggestions | _____ | _____ |
| D. Changes ideas too easily | _____ | _____ |

Supervisors were asked to review the items in each tetrad and to check one item as most descriptive and one item as least descriptive of the officer being evaluated. A score of +1 was awarded for responding "most descriptive" to the positively keyed item (in this case, alternative B) or "least descriptive" to the negatively keyed item (in this case alternative A), whereas a score of –1 was awarded for responding "least descriptive" to the positively keyed item or "most descriptive" to the negatively keyed item. Responding to the nonkeyed items (alternatives C and D) as most or least descriptive earned a score of 0. Thus, each tetrad yielded a five-point continuum of scores: +2, +1, 0, –1, –2. The summary score used for performance appraisal consisted of the algebraic sum of the individual items.

The forced-choice approach has never really caught on, due largely to the effort required in scale construction. This is unfortunate because the method does effectively reduce unwanted bias. Borman (1991) refers to this approach as a "bold initiative" that produces a relatively objective rating scale.

## ● SOURCES OF ERROR IN PERFORMANCE APPRAISAL

The most difficult problem in the assessment of job performance is the proper definition of appraisal criteria. If the supervisor is using a poorly designed instrument that does not tap the appropriate dimensions of job behavior, then almost by definition the performance appraisal will be inaccurate, incomplete, and erroneous. Undoubtedly, the failure to identify appropriate criteria for acceptable and unacceptable performance is a major source of error in performance appraisal. But it is not the only source. Even when supervisors have access to excellent, well-designed measures of performance appraisal, various sorts of subtle errors can creep in. We discuss three such additional sources of rating error: halo effect, rater bias, and criterion contamination.

### Halo Effect

The tendency to rate an employee high or low on all dimensions because of a global impression is called **halo effect**. Research on the halo effect can be traced back to the early part of this century (Thorndike, 1920). The most common halo effect is a positive halo effect. In this case, an employee receives a higher rating than deserved because the supervisor fails to be objective when rating specific aspects of the employee's behavior. A positive halo effect is usually based upon overgeneralization from one element of a worker's behavior. For example, an employee with perfect attendance may receive higher-than-deserved evaluations on productivity and work quality—even though attendance is not directly related to these job dimensions.

Smither (1998) lists the following approaches to control for halo effects:

- Provide special training for raters
- Supervise the supervisors during the rating
- Practice simulations before doing the ratings
- Keep a diary of information relevant to appraisal
- Provide supervisors with a short lecture on halo effects

Additional approaches to rater training are discussed by Goldstein (1991). An intriguing analysis of the nature and consequences of halo error can be found in Murphy, Jako, and Anhalt (1993).

Contrary to the reigning prejudice against halo errors, these researchers conclude that the halo effect does not necessarily detract from the accuracy of ratings. They point out that a presumed halo effect is often the by-product of true overlap on the dimensions being rated. The debate over halo effect is not likely to be resolved anytime soon (Arvey & Murphy, 1998).

## Rater Bias

The potential sources of **rater bias** are so numerous that we can only mention a few prominent examples here. Leniency or severity errors occur when a supervisor tends to rate workers at the extremes of the scale. Leniency may reflect social dynamics, as when the supervisor wants to be liked by employees. Leniency is also caused by extraneous factors such as the attractiveness of the employee. Severity errors refer to the practice of rating all aspects of performance as deficient. In contrast, central tendency errors occur when the supervisor rates everyone as nearly average on all performance dimensions. Context errors occur when the rater evaluates an employee in the context of other employees rather than based upon objective performance. For example, the presence of a workaholic salesperson with extremely high sales volume might cause the sales supervisor to rate other sales personnel lower than deserved.

Recently, researchers have paid considerable attention to the possible biasing effects of whether a supervisor likes or dislikes a subordinate. Surprisingly, the trend of the findings is that supervisor affect (liking or disliking) toward specific employees does not introduce rating bias. In general, strong affect in either direction represents valid information about an employee. Thus, ratings of affect often correlate strongly with performance ratings, but this is because both are a consequence of how well or poorly the employee does the job (Ferris, Judge, Rowland, & Fitzgibbons, 1994; Varma, DeNisi, & Peters, 1996). Other forms of rater bias are discussed by Goldstein (1991) and Smither (1994).

## Criterion Contamination

**Criterion contamination** is said to exist when a criterion measure includes factors that are not demonstrably part of the job (Borman, 1991; Harvey, 1991). For example, if a performance measure includes appearance, this would most likely be a case of criterion contamination—unless appearance is relevant to job success. Likewise, evaluating an employee on "dealing with the public" is only appropriate if the job actually requires the employee to meet the public. Goldstein (1992) outlines three kinds of criterion contamination:

1. Opportunity bias occurs when workers have different opportunities for success, as when one salesperson is assigned to a wealthy neighborhood and others must seek sales in isolated, rural areas.
2. Group characteristic bias is present when the characteristics of the group affect individual performance, as when workers in the same unit agree to limit their productivity to maintain positive social relations.
3. Knowledge of predictor bias occurs when a supervisor permits personal knowledge about an employee to bias the appraisal, as when quality of the college attended by a new worker affects her evaluation.

Careful attention to job analysis as a basis for selection of appraisal criteria is the best way to reduce errors in performance appraisal. In addition, employers should follow certain guidelines in performance appraisal, as discussed in the following section.

## Guidelines for Performance Appraisal

Performance appraisal is a formidable task. Not only must employers pay attention to the psychometric soundness of their approach, they must also design a practical system that meets organizational goals. For example, appraisal standards must be sufficiently difficult and detailed to ensure that organizational goals are accomplished. Another concern is that performance appraisal falls under the purview of Title VII of the Civil Rights Act of 1964. Hence, employers must develop fair systems that do not discriminate on the basis of race, sex, and other protected categories. To complicate matters, these standards—soundness, practicality, legality—may conflict with one another. The practical approach may be neither psychometrically sound nor legal. Often, appraisal methods that show the best measurement characteristics (e.g., strong interrater reliability) will fail to assess the most important aspects of performance; that is, they are not practical. This is a familiar refrain within the measurement field. Too often, psychologists must choose between rigor and relevance, rarely achieving both at the same time. Finally, legal considerations must be considered when exploring the limits of performance appraisal.

Smither (1998) has published guidelines for developing performance appraisal systems that we paraphrase here:

- Base the performance appraisal upon a careful job analysis
- Develop specific, contamination-free criteria for appraisal from the job analysis
- Determine that the instrument used to rate performance is appropriate for the appraisal situation
- Train raters to be accurate, fair, and legal in their use of the appraisal instrument
- Use performance evaluations at regular intervals of six months to a year
- Evaluate the performance appraisal system periodically to determine whether it is actually improving performance

The training of raters is an especially important guideline. An appraisal system that seems perfectly straightforward to the employer could easily be misunderstood by an untrained rater, resulting in biased evaluations. Borman (1991) notes that two kinds of rater training are effective: rater error training, in which the trainer seeks simply to alert raters to specific kinds of errors (e.g., halo effect); and frame-of-reference training, in which the

trainer familiarizes the raters with the specific content of each performance dimension. Research indicates that these kinds of training improve the accuracy of ratings.

## ● INVENTORIES FOR INTEREST ASSESSMENT

In most applications of psychological testing, the goals of assessment are reasonably clear. For example, intelligence testing helps predict school performance; aptitude testing foretells potential for accomplishment; and personality testing provides information about social and emotional functioning. But what is the purpose of interest assessment? Why would a psychologist recommend it? What can a client expect to gain from a survey of his or her interests?

Interest assessment promotes two compatible goals: life satisfaction and vocational productivity. It is nearly self-evident that a good fit between individual interests and chosen vocation will help foster personal life satisfaction. After all, when work is interesting we are more likely to experience personal fulfillment as well. In addition, persons who are satisfied with their work are more likely to be productive. Thus, employees and employers both stand to gain from the artful application of interest assessment. Several useful instruments exist for this purpose, and we will review the most widely used interest inventories later.

In the selection of employees, the consideration of personal interests may be of great practical significance to employers and, therefore, circumstantially relevant to the job candidates as well. We may sketch out a rough equation as follows: productivity = ability × interest. In other words, high ability in a specific field does not guarantee success; neither does high interest level. The best predictions are possible when both variables are considered together. Thus, employers have good reason to determine whether a potential employee is well matched to the position; the employee should like to know as well.

We begin with a critical examination of major interest tests. The three instruments chosen for review include the following:

- The Strong Interest Inventory (SII), the latest revision of the well-known Strong Vocational Interest Blank (SVIB)
- The Self-Directed Search (SDS), a self-administered and self-scored guide to exploring career options
- The Campbell Interest and Skill Survey (CISS), a recent and appealing test that is simple in format but sophisticated in execution

## Strong Interest Inventory (SII)

The Strong Interest Inventory (SII) is the latest revision of the Strong Vocational Interest Blank (SVIB), one of the oldest and most prominent instruments in psychological testing (Strong, Hansen, & Campbell, 1994). We can best understand the SII by studying the history of its esteemed predecessor, the SVIB. In particular, we need to review the guiding assumptions used in the construction of the SVIB that have been carried over into the SII.

The first edition of the SVIB appeared in 1927, eight years after E. K. Strong formulated the essential procedures for measuring occupational interests while attending a seminar at the Carnegie Institute of Technology (Campbell, 1971; Strong, 1927). In constructing the SVIB, Strong employed two little-used techniques in measurement. First, the examinee was asked to express liking or disliking for a large and varied sample of occupations, educational disciplines, personality types, and recreational activities. Second, the responses were empirically keyed for specific occupations. In an empirical key, a specific response (e.g., liking to roller skate) is assigned to the scale for a particular occupation only if successful persons in that occupation tend to answer in that manner more often than comparison subjects.

Although Strong did not express his underlying assumptions in a simple and straightforward

manner, it is clear that the theoretical foundation for the SVIB derives from a typological, trait-oriented conception of personality. Tzeng (1987) has identified the following basic assumptions in the development and application of the SVIB:

1. Each occupation has a desirable pattern of interests and personality characteristics among its workers. The ideal pattern is represented by successful people in that occupation.
2. Each individual has relatively stable interests and personality traits. When such interests and traits match the desirable interest patterns of the occupation the individual has a high probability to enter that occupation and be more likely to succeed in it.
3. It is highly possible to differentiate individuals in a given occupation from others-in-general in terms of the desirable patterns of interests and traits for that occupation.

Strong constructed the scales of his inventory by contrasting the responses of several specific occupational criterion groups with those of a people-in-general group. The subjects for each criterion group were workers in that occupation who were satisfied with their jobs and who had been so employed for at least three years. The items that differentiated the two groups, keyed in the appropriate direction, were selected for each occupational scale. For example, if members of a specific occupational group disliked "buying merchandise for a store" more often than people-in-general, then that item (keyed in the dislike direction) was added to the scale for that occupation.

The first SVIB consisted of 420 items and a mere handful of occupational scales (Strong, 1927). Separate editions for men and women followed shortly. The inventory has undergone numerous revisions over the years (Tzeng, 1987), culminating in the modern instrument known as the Strong Interest Inventory (Campbell, 1974; Hansen, 1992; Hansen & Campbell, 1985).

Although the Strong Interest Inventory (SII) was fashioned according to the same philosophy as the SVIB, the latest revision departs from its predecessors in three crucial ways:

1. The SII merges the men's and women's forms into a single edition.
2. The SII introduces a theoretical framework to guide the organization and interpretation of scores, as discussed later.
3. The SII incorporates a substantial increase in the number of occupational scales, particularly in the vocational/technical areas underrepresented in the SVIB.

The SII consists of 317 items grouped into seven sections. In the first five sections, the examinee records "Like," "Indifferent," or "Dislike" for occupations, school subjects, activities, leisure activities, and contact with different types of persons (Table 11.6). A sixth part requires the examinee to express a preference between paired items (e.g., dealing with things versus dealing with people). The seventh section consists of self-descriptive statements which the examinee marks "Yes," "No," or "?".

The SII can only be scored by prepaid answer sheets or booklets that are mailed or faxed to the publisher, or through purchase of a software system that provides on-site scoring for immediate

● **TABLE 11.6 Characteristic Items from the Strong Interest Inventory**

Mark *Like, Indifferent,* or *Dislike* next to the following items.

1. Driving a truck _____
2. Being a fish and game officer _____
3. Chemistry _____
4. Doing applied research _____
5. Acting in a drama _____
6. Magazines about music _____
7. Sociology _____
8. Fund-raising for charities _____
9. Buying goods for a store _____
10. People who are leaders _____
11. Regular work hours _____
12. Assertive people _____

results. The results consist of a lengthy printout that is organized according to several themes. All scores are expressed as standard scores with a mean of 50 and an SD of 10. Normative results for men and women are reported separately, but cross-sex comparisons can be achieved by simple visual transposition.

At the most global level are the six General Occupational Theme Scores, namely, Realistic, Investigative, Artistic, Social, Enterprising, and Conventional. These theme scores were based upon the theoretical analysis of Holland (1966, 1985ab), whose work we discuss later. Each theme score pertains to a major interest area that describes both a work environment and a type of person. For example, persons scoring high on the Realistic theme are generally quite robust, have difficulty expressing their feelings, and prefer to work outdoors with heavy machinery. Within the theme scores can be found 25 Basic Interest Scales such as Adventure, Mathematics, and Social Science. The interest scales are empirically derived and consist of substantially intercorrelated items.

The most specific results consist of 211 scores for the Occupational Scales. In the 1985 revision of the SII, these scales were constructed in the usual manner by comparing responses of persons employed in the given occupation versus samples of men-in-general and women-in-general (Hansen, 1992; Hansen & Campbell, 1985). Sample sizes for the criterion groups ranged from 60 to 420, with most groups containing 200 or more persons. The criterion groups consisted of persons between the ages of 25 and 60 years, satisfied with their occupation, meeting certain minimum standards of successful employment, and employed in the given occupation for at least three years. Standardization of the 1985 version involved the testing of over 140,000 persons, of whom only 50,000 met the criteria for scale development.

A recent innovation on the SII is the addition of personal style scales (Harmon, Hansen, Borgen, & Hammer, 1994). These are designed to measure preferences for broad styles of living and working. These scales assist in vocational guidance by showing level of comfort with distinctive styles. The four style scales are

1. *Work Style,* on which a high score indicates a preference to work with people and a low score signifies an interest in ideas, data, and things;
2. *Learning Environment,* on which a high score indicates a preference for academic learning environments and a low score indicates a preference for more applied learning activities;
3. *Leadership Style,* on which a high score indicates comfort in taking charge of others and a low score indicates uneasiness; and
4. *Risk Taking/Adventure,* on which a high score indicates a preference for risky and adventurous activities as opposed to safe and predictable activities.

The personal style scales each have a mean of 50 and a standard deviation of 10. Note that these are truly bipolar scales for which each pole is distinct and meaningful.

## Evaluation of the SII

The SII represents the culmination of over 50 years of study, involving literally thousands of research reports and hundreds of thousands of respondents. In evaluating this instrument, we can only outline basic trends in the research, referring the reader to other sources for details (Savickas, Taber, & Spokane, 2002; Tzeng, 1987; Campbell & Hansen, 1981; Hansen, 1992; Hansen & Campbell, 1985). We should also point out that evaluations of the reliability and validity of the SII are based in part upon its similarity to the SVIB, for which a huge amount of technical data exists.

Based upon test-retest studies, the reliability of the SII-SVIB has proved to be exceptionally good in the short run, with one- and two-week stability coefficients for the occupational scales generally in the .90s. When the test-retest interval is years or decades, the correlations drop to the .60s and .70s for the occupational scales, except for respondents who were older (over age 25) upon first testing. For younger respondents first

tested as adolescents, the median test-retest correlation after 15 years is around .50 (Lubinski, Benbow, & Ryan, 1995). But for older respondents, first tested after the age of 25, the median test-retest correlation 10 to 20 years later is a phenomenal .80 (Campbell, 1971). Apparently, by the time we pass through young adulthood, personal interests become extremely stable. The questions on the SII-SVIB capture that stability in the occupational scores, providing support for the trait conception of personality upon which these instruments were based.

The validity of the SII-SVIB is premised largely on the ability of the initial occupational profile to predict the occupation eventually pursued. Strong (1955) reported that the chances were about two in three that people would be in occupations predicted by high occupational scale scores, and about one in five that respondents would be in occupations for which they had shown little interest when tested. Although other researchers have quibbled with the exact proportions (Dolliver, Irvin, & Bigley, 1972), it is clear that the SII-SVIB has impressive hit rates in predicting occupational entry. The instrument functions even better in predicting the occupations that an examinee will *not* enter. In a recent study, Donnay and Borgen (1996) provide evidence for construct validity by demonstrating strong overall differentiation between 50 occupational groups on the SII:

> The big picture is that people in diverse occupations show large and predictable differences in likes and dislikes, whether in terms of vocational interests or in terms of personal styles. And the Strong provides valid, structural, and comprehensive measures of these differences. (p. 290)

The SII is used mainly with high school and college students and adults seeking vocational guidance or advice on continued education. Because most students' interests are undeveloped and unstabilized prior to age 13 or 14, the SII is not recommended for use below high-school level. As evident in the reliability data reported, the SII becomes increasingly valuable with older subjects, and it is not unusual to see middle-aged persons use the results of this instrument for guidance in career change.

## Vocational Preference Inventory

The Vocational Preference Inventory is an objective, paper-and-pencil personality interest inventory used in vocational and career assessment (Holland, 1985c). The VPI measures 11 dimensions, including the six personality–environment themes of Realistic, Investigative, Artistic, Social, Enterprising, and Conventional, and five additional dimensions of Self-Control, Masculinity/Femininity, Status, Infrequency, and Acquiescence. The test items consist of 160 occupational titles toward which the examinee expresses a feeling by marking *y* (yes) or *n* (no). The VPI is a brief test (15 to 30 minutes) and is intended for persons 14 years and older with normal intelligence.

Holland proposes that personality traits tend to cluster into a small number of vocationally relevant patterns, called types. For each personality type there is also a corresponding work environment best suited to that type. According to Holland, there are six types: Realistic, Investigative, Artistic, Social, Enterprising, and Conventional. This is sometimes known as the **RIASEC model,** in reference to the first letters of the six types. The types are idealizations that few people (or environments) fit completely. Nonetheless, Holland believes that most individuals tend to resemble one

type more than the others. In addition, individuals show a lesser degree of resemblance to a second and third type as well.

We can summarize the personality–environment types as follows:

- *Realistic:* athletic, lacks verbal and interpersonal skills, and prefers "hands-on" or outdoor vocations such as mechanic, farmer, or electrician
- *Investigative:* task-oriented thinker with unconventional attitudes who fits well in scientific and scholarly positions such as chemist, physicist, or biologist
- *Artistic:* individualistic, avoids conventional situations, and prefers aesthetic pursuits
- *Social:* uses social competencies to solve problems, likes to help others, and prefers teaching or helping professions
- *Enterprising:* a leader with good selling skills who fits well in business and managerial positions
- *Conventional:* conforming and prefers structured roles such as bank teller or computer operator

The six themes in the RIASEC system can be arranged in a hexagon with similar themes side by side and dissimilar themes opposite one another, as depicted in Figure 11.3.

Test-retest reliability coefficients for the six major scales range from .89 to .97. VPI norms are based upon large convenience samples of college

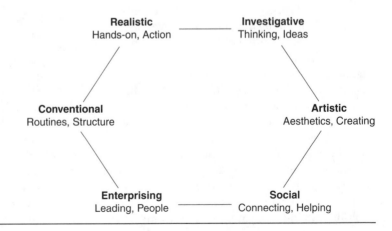

● **FIGURE 11.3**
Holland's Hexagonal Model of
Occupational Themes

students and employed adults from earlier VPI editions. The characteristics of the standardization sample are not well defined, which makes the norms somewhat difficult to interpret (Rounds, 1985).

The validity of the VPI is essentially tied to the validity of Holland's (1985a) hexagonal model of vocational interests. Literally hundreds of studies have examined this model from different perspectives. We will cite trends and representative studies. The reader is referred to Holland (1985c) and Walsh and Holland (1992) for more details.

Several VPI studies have investigated a key assumption of Holland's theory—that individuals tend to move toward environments that are congruent with their personality types. If this assumption is correct, then the real-world match between work environments and personality types of employees should be substantial. We should expect to find that Realistic environments have mainly Realistic employees, Social environments have mainly Social employees, and so on. Research on this topic has followed a straightforward methodology: Subjects are tested with the VPI and classified by their Holland types (using up to six letters); the work environments of the subjects are then independently classified by an appropriate environmental measure; finally, the degree of congruence between persons and environments is computed. In better studies, a correction for chance agreement is also applied.

Using his hexagonal model, Holland has developed occupational codes as a basis for classifying work environments (Gottfredson & Holland, 1989; Holland, 1966, 1978, 1985c). For example, landscape architect is coded as RIA (Realistic, Investigative, Artistic) because this occupation is known to be a technical, skilled trade (Realistic component) that requires scientific skills (Investigative component) and also demands artistic aptitude (Artistic component). The Realistic component is listed first because it is the most important for landscape architect, whereas the Investigative and Artistic components are of secondary and tertiary importance, respectively. Some other occupations and their codes are taxi driver (RSE), mathematics teacher (ISC), reporter (ASE), police officer (SRE), real estate appraiser (ECS), and secretary (CSA). In

a similar manner, Holland has also worked out codes for different college majors.

One approach to congruence studies is to compare VPI results of students or workers with the Holland codes that correspond to their college majors or occupations. For example, VPI Holland codes for a sample of police officers should consist mainly of profiles that begin with S and should contain a larger-than-chance proportion of specifically SRE profiles. Furthermore, the degree of congruence should be related to the degree of expressed satisfaction with that line of work or study.

Research with college students provides strong support for the congruence prediction: Students tend to select and enter college majors that are congruent with their primary personality types (Holland, 1985a; Walsh & Holland, 1992). Thus, Artistic types tend to major in art, Investigative types tend to major in biology, and Enterprising types tend to major in business, to cite just a few examples. These results provide strong support for the VPI and the theory upon which it is based.

This short review has barely touched the surface of supportive validity studies with the VPI. Walsh and Holland (1992) cite several additional lines of research that buttress the validity of this test. But not all studies of the VPI affirm its validity. Furnham, Toop, Lewis, and Fisher (1995) failed to find a relationship between personality–environment (P-E) "fit" and job satisfaction, a key theoretical underpinning of the test. According to Holland's theory, the better the P-E fit, the greater should be job satisfaction. In three British samples, the relationships were weak or nonexistent, suggesting that the VPI does not "travel well" in cultures outside of the United States.

## Self-Directed Search

Holland has always shown a keen interest in the practical applications of his research on vocational development. Consistent with this interest, he developed the Self-Directed Search, a highly practical, brief test that is appealing in its simplicity (Holland, 1985ab). As the name suggests, the Self-Directed Search is designed to be a self-administered, self-scored, and self-interpreted test of vocational interest. The SDS measures the six RIASEC vocational themes described previously.

The SDS consists of dichotomous items that the examinee marks "like" or "dislike" (or "yes" or "no") in four sections: (1) Activities (six scales of 11 items each); (2) Competencies (six scales of 11 items each); (3) Occupations (six scales of 14 items each); and (4) Self-Estimates (two sets of six ratings). For each section, the face-valid items are grouped by RIASEC themes. For each theme, the total number of "like" and "yes" answers is combined with the self-estimates of ability to come up with a total theme score. The SDS takes 30 to 50 minutes for completion and is intended for persons 15 years and older.

The RIASEC themes on the SDS showed test-retest reliabilities that range from .56 to .95 and internal consistencies that range from .70 to .93. Norms for SDS scales and codes are reported for pooled convenience samples of 4,675 high school students, 3,355 college students, and 4,250 employed adults ages 16 through 24 (Holland, 1985ab). However, SDS results are typically interpreted in an individualized, ipsative manner ("Is this occupation a good fit for this client?"), so normative data are of limited relevance.

The SDS is available in a hand-scored paper-and-pencil version and a computerized version as well. Unfortunately, the paper-and-pencil version is prone to a 16 percent clerical error rate when used by high school students (Holland, 1985ab). The user-friendly microcomputer test is probably the preferred version because of the ease of administration and the error-free scoring and interpretation.

When a subject takes the SDS, the three highest theme scores are used to denote a summary code. For example, a person whose three highest scores were on Investigative, Artistic, and Realistic would have a summary code of IAR. In a separate booklet distributed with the test—the *Occupations Finder*—the examinee can look up his or her summary code and find a list of occupations that provide the best "fit." For example, an examinee with an IAR summary code would learn that he or she most closely resembles persons in the following occupations: anthropologist, astronomer, chemist, pathologist, and physicist. The test booklet contains additional information which helps the examinee explore relevant career options.

The SDS serves a very useful purpose in providing a quick and simple format for prompting young persons to examine career alternatives. By eliminating the time-consuming process of administration, scoring, interpretation, and counselor feedback, the test makes it possible for a wide audience to receive an introductory level of career counseling. Holland (1985ab) proposes that the SDS is appropriate for up to 50 percent of students and adults who might desire career guidance. Presumably, the other 50 percent would find the SDS an insufficient basis for career exploration. Holland (1985ab) rightfully warns users to consider many sources of information in career choice and not to rely too heavily on test scores per se. Levinson (1990) discusses the integration of SDS data with other psychoeducational data to make specific vocational recommendations for high school students.

LaBarbera (2005) illustrates the potential application of the SDS in a study of 463 physician assistants (PAs) known to be well satisfied with their work. The PAs are medical professionals who provide care under the supervision of a licensed physician. This is a demanding profession with well defined duties that include many of the same functions provided by a general practitioner. Who is a good candidate for this up-and-coming profession in high demand? LaBarbera (2005) determined that the Holland profile was a distinctive SIR for men, especially those with interests in surgery, whereas the profile for women maintained the first two letters (SI) but yielded a muddle for the third theme. This is valuable information for prospective students and career counselors.

The validity of the SDS is linked to the validity of the hexagonal model of personality and environments upon which the test is based. One aspect of validity, then, is whether the model makes predictions that are confirmed by SDS results in the real world. In general, the results from over 400 studies support the construct validity of the SDS (Dumenci, 1995; Holland, 1985ab, 1987).

One approach to construct validity is to determine whether the relationships among SDS scales make theoretical sense. One tenet of construct validity is that similar scales should reveal stronger relationships, dissimilar scales weaker relationships. For example, it is not hard to imagine one person combining Artistic and Investigative themes in personality and work environment. After all, these themes are mildly similar, so we would predict a moderately positive correlation between them. This is exactly what Holland (1985ab) found. In a general reference sample of 175 women ages 26 to 65 years, scores on these two themes correlated modestly, $r = .26$, as would be predicted. Further, unrelated themes like Investigative and Enterprising (which bear little in common) should reveal a weak correlation. The value turned out to be a negligible $r = -.02$. Overall, the various correlations among the six themes of the SDS make theoretical sense, which supports the construct validity of the test.

The predictive validity of the SDS has been investigated in several dozen studies, which are summarized by Holland (1985ab, 1987). The typical methodology for these studies is that SDS high-point codes for large samples of students are compared with the first letter of their occupational choices (or aspirations) one to three years later. Overall, the findings indicate that the SDS has moderate to high predictive efficiency, depending upon the age of the sample (hit rates go up with age), the length of the time interval (hit rates go down with time), and the specific category predicted (hit rates are better for Investigative and Social predictions) (Gottfredson & Holland, 1975).

## Campbell Interest and Skill Survey

The Campbell Interest and Skill Survey (CISS; Campbell, Hyne, & Nilsen, 1992) is a newer measure of self-reported interests and skills. The test is designed to help individuals make better career choices by describing how their interests and skills match the occupational world. The primary target population for the CISS is students and young adults who have not entered the job market, but the test is also suitable for older workers who are considering a change in careers. The test is appropriate for persons 15 years of age and older with a sixth-grade reading level, although younger children can be tested in exceptional circumstances.

The CISS consists of 200 interest items and 120 skill items. The interest items include occupations, school subjects, and varied working activities that the examinee rates on a six-point scale from strongly like to strongly dislike. The interest items resemble the following:

A pilot, flying commercial aircraft
A biologist, working in a research lab
A police detective, solving crimes

The skill items include a list of activities that the examinee rates on a six-point scale from expert (widely recognized as excellent in this area) to none (have no skills in this area). The skill items resemble the following:

Helping a family resolve its conflicts
Making furniture, using woodworking and power tools
Writing a magazine story

CISS results are scored on several different kinds of scales: Orientation Scales, Basic Interest and Skill Scales, Occupational Scales, Special Scales, and Procedural Checks. All scale scores are reported as $T$ scores, normed to a population average of 50, with a standard deviation of 10.

The Orientation Scales serve to organize the CISS profile—the interest, skill, and occupational scales are reported under the appropriate Orientations. The seven Orientations are as follows (Campbell et al., 1992, pp. 2–3):

- *Influencing*—influencing others through leadership, politics, public speaking, and marketing
- *Organizing*—organizing the work of others, managing, and monitoring financial performance
- *Helping*—helping others through teaching, healing, and counseling
- *Creating*—creating artistic, literary, or musical productions, and designing products or environments
- *Analyzing*—analyzing data, using mathematics, and carrying out scientific experiments
- *Producing*—producing products, using "hands-on" skills in farming, construction, and mechanical crafts

- *Adventuring*—adventuring, competing, and risk taking through athletic, police, and military activities

There are 29 pairs of Basic Scales, each pair consisting of parallel interest and skill scales. The Basic Scales are clustered within the seven Orientations, based upon their intercorrelations. For example, the Helping Orientation contains the following Basic Scales, each with separate interest and skill components: Adult Development, Counseling, Child Development, Religious Activities, and Medical Practice.

The 58 pairs of Occupational Scales, each with separate interest and skill components, provide feedback on the degree of similarity between the examinee and satisfied workers in that occupation. These scales were constructed empirically by contrasting the responses of happily employed persons in specific occupations with responses of a general reference sample drawn from the working population at large.

In addition to Basic and Occupational Scales, the CISS incorporates three special scales: Academic Focus, a measure of interest and confidence in intellectual, scientific, and literary activities; Extraversion, a measure of social extraversion; and Variety, a measure of the examinee's breadth of interests and skills. Finally, the CISS reports a variety of Procedural Checks to detect possible problems in test taking such as random responding or excessive omissions.

Overall, the reliability of CISS scales is exceptionally strong. For example, coefficient alpha for the Orientation Scales is typically in the high .80s, and three-month test-retest reliabilities for 324 respondents are in the mid- to high .80s. Similar findings for reliability are reported for the Basic and Occupational Scales. Norms for the CISS are based upon 5,000 subjects spread over the 58 occupations. The authors report extensive validity data for the Occupational Scales, including sample means for each occupational sample as well as lists of the three highest- and lowest-scoring occupations for each scale (Campbell et al., 1992). These data document that the scales do discriminate

between occupations in an effective and meaningful way. For example, the average $T$ score on accountant by accountants is 75.8. Statisticians, bookkeepers, and financial planners achieve the next three highest scores for this scale, with average $T$ scores in the low 60s. Commercial artists, professors, and social workers obtain the three lowest scores, with average $T$ scores around 40. Because these results fit well with our expectations about occupational interest and skill patterns, they provide support for the validity of the CISS.

Independent correlational studies also support the validity of the CISS. For example, in a sample of 221 college students, Hansen (2007) correlated CISS Skill Scale scores with SII scores and found strong evidence for convergent and discriminant validity (i.e., strong correlations with similar scales, negligible correlations with dissimilar scales). In a sample of 118 adults, Savickas et al. (2002) correlated scores from individual occupational scales of the CISS with scores from the scales of other mainstream instruments such as the Strong Interest Inventory. They also found strong support for both convergent validity (i.e., modest correlations for same-named pairs of scales) and discriminant validity (i.e., negligible correlations for unlike pairs of scales). In a sample of 128 college students, Hansen and Neuman (1999) confirmed the concurrent validity of the CISS by finding a good fit between occupational scale scores and students' chosen majors. The fit was considered "excellent" or "moderately good" for more than 70 percent of the students. Boggs (1999) provides a review and critique of the CISS. Campbell (2002) presents the history and development of the instrument.

This instrument will almost certainly receive increased attention in the years ahead. One noteworthy feature of the CISS is the comprehensiveness and clarity of the profile report form. The report consists of 11 user-friendly pages. We have reprinted two pages in Figure 11.4 for illustrative purposes. This format is preferable to the detail-rich but eye-straining graphs encountered with many instruments. The CISS promises to rival the Strong Interest Inventory for vocational guidance of young adults.

# CAMPBELL™ INTEREST AND SKILL SURVEY INDIVIDUAL PROFILE REPORT

SAMPLE REPORT

Date Scored: 07/27/2005

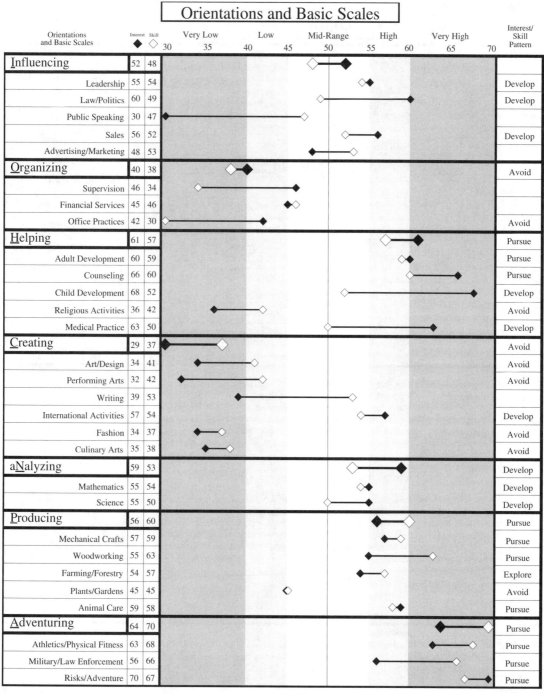

Note: The full profile consists of an 11-page printout.

*(continued)*

● **FIGURE 11.4**   Representative Sections from the Campbell Interest and Skill Survey

SAMPLE REPORT                                                        Date Scored: 07/27/2005

## Influencing Orientation

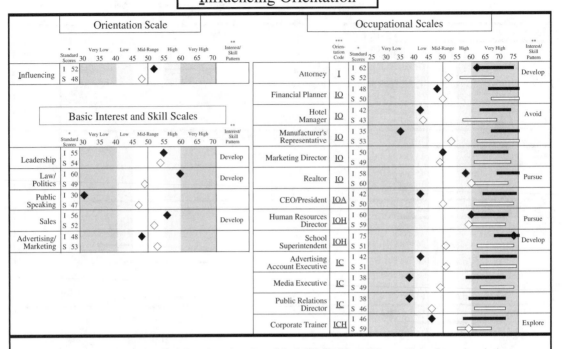

The Influencing Orientation focuses on influencing others through leadership, politics, public speaking, sales, and marketing. Influencers like to make things happen. They are often visible because they tend to take charge of activities that interest them. They typically work in organizations where they are responsible for directing activities, setting policies, and motivating people. Influencers are generally confident of their ability to persuade others and they usually enjoy the give-and-take of debating and negotiating. Typical high-scoring individuals include company presidents, corporate managers, school superintendents, sales representatives, and attorneys.

Your Influencing interest and skill scores are both mid-range. People who have this pattern of scores typically report moderate interest and confidence in leading, negotiating, marketing, selling, and public speaking.

Your scores on the Influencing Basic Scales, which provide more detail about your interests and skills in this area, are reported above on the left-hand side of the page. Your scores on the Influencing Occupational Scales, which show how your pattern of interests and skills compares with those of people employed in Influencing occupations, are reported above on the right-hand side of the page. Each occupation has a one-, two-, or three-letter code that indicates its highest Orientation score(s). The more similar the Orientation code is to your highest Orientation scores (which are reported on page 2), the more likely it is that you will find satisfaction working in that occupation.

---

\*      Standard Scores: I (◆) = Interests; S (◇) = Skills
\*\*     Interest/Skill Pattern: Pursue = High Interests, High Skills; Develop = High Interest, Lower Skills;
        Explore = High Skills, Lower Interests; Avoid = Low Interest, Low Skills
\*\*\*    Orientation Code: I=Influencing; O=Organizing; H=Helping; C=Creating; N=aNalyzing; P=Producing; A=Adventuring
        ▭▭▭▭ Range of middle 50% of people in the occupation: Solid Bar = Interests; Hollow Bar = Skills

---

● FIGURE 11.4    Continued

## ● S U M M A R Y

**1.** Industrial and organizational psychology (I/O psychology) deals with behavior in work situations (business, advertising, and the military). I/O psychologists use psychological testing and assessment for diverse purposes, including hiring, placement, promotion, and evaluation.

**2.** Autobiographical data, known as biodata, possess substantial predictive validity for many kinds of personnel selection. In many studies the predictive validity of biodata (with values in the .50s) rivals that of standardized tests.

**3.** In the form in which it is typically used for personnel selection, the interview has low reliability and poor validity. Only when the interview is carefully designed and highly structured can it provide a reliable and valid basis for personnel selection.

**4.** Cognitive ability tests provide a good basis for personnel selection in most occupations. Rivalled only by the work sample, ability tests have a validity coefficient of .54 averaged over many tests and many samples.

**5.** Cognitive tests that measure general ability (*g*) often predict job performance better than measures of specific abilities. The reason is that most jobs are factorially complex in their requirements, which ensures that measures of *g* will possess high predictive validity.

**6.** When validated for the intended use, personality and temperament tests may provide a useful basis for employee selection. For example, the Hogan Personality Inventory (HPI) is well validated for prediction of job performance in military, hospital, and corporate settings.

**7.** Paper-and-pencil integrity tests are designed to screen theft-prone individuals and other undesirable job candidates. Some of these instruments possess moderate predictive validity (e.g., personality-based measures), but their use raises many ethical concerns.

**8.** A work sample is a miniature replica of the job for which examinees have applied. A properly designed work sample (e.g., prospective mechanics might be asked to install a pulley and repair a gearbox) can yield validity coefficients in the .40s, .50s, or .60s.

**9.** Situational exercises such as the in-basket test are used mainly to select persons for managerial and professional positions. Although very time-consuming and expensive, situational exercises provide a valid basis for selection of managers.

**10.** An assessment center is used to evaluate managerial potential by exposing candidates to multiple simulation techniques, including group presentations, problem-solving exercises, interviews, and in-basket techniques. Assessment center ratings help identify high-level managerial talent.

**11.** Performance evaluation serves many organizational purposes, including promotions, transfers, layoffs, and the setting of salaries. Although objective methods for assessing the effectiveness of employees would appear to be preferable, judgmental approaches are often the only practical choice.

**12.** Methods for performance appraisal include performance measures such as productivity counts; personnel data such as rate of absenteeism; peer ratings and self-assessments; and supervisor evaluations such as rating scales. Rating scales are by far the most common approach.

**13.** About three-quarters of all performance evaluations are based upon judgmental methods such as supervisor rating scales. The simplest rating scale is the graphic rating scale, which consists of trait labels, brief definitions of those labels, and a continuum for the rating.

**14.** The behaviorally anchored rating scale (BARS) is a popular form of criterion-referenced performance measure. A BARS form contains explicit behavioral anchors along a continuum of excellence that the supervisor evaluates in terms of past observations of work performance.

**15.** Performance appraisal is subject to several sources of error, including failure to identify appropriate criteria for acceptable and unacceptable performance, halo effect (rating an employee high or low on all dimensions because of a global impression), rater bias, and criterion contamination.

**16.** Criterion contamination occurs when a criterion measure includes factors that are not demonstrably part of the job, such as rating an employee on "dealing with the public" when this is not really part of the position.

**17.** Appropriate guidelines for the development of performance appraisal systems include basing the appraisal method upon a careful job analysis; training raters to be fair, accurate, and legal; and evaluating the performance appraisal system periodically.

**18.** Employee testing and appraisal are carefully circumscribed by legal and regulatory guidelines. For example, Title VII of the Civil Rights Act of 1964 prohibits employment practices that discriminate on the basis of race, color, religion, sex, or national origin.

**19.** The purpose of interest inventories is to identify a person's vocational and related interests in order to facilitate career choices. A good fit between personal interests and the identified interest patterns of an occupation promotes success in, and satisfaction with, occupational choice.

**20.** The Strong Interest Inventory (SII) is the latest revision of the Strong Vocational Interest Blank (SVIB), which first appeared in 1927. Like its predecessor, the SII uses empirical keys for occupations.

**21.** Short-run stability coefficients for the 211 occupational scales on the SII are generally in the .90s. The validity of the test is bolstered by the generally good fit between the initial occupational profile and the occupation eventually pursued.

**22.** The Self-Directed Search (SDS) is a self-administered and self-scored test of vocational interest. The SDS is also based upon the RIASEC model; each theme of this model characterizes not only a type of person but also the type of work environment that such a person finds most compatible.

**23.** The Campbell Interest and Skill Survey (CISS) consists of 200 interest items and 120 skill items that are rated upon a six-point scale. The test provides scores on seven Orientation Scales (Influencing, Organizing, Helping, Creating, Analyzing, Producing, and Adventuring), 29 Basic Scales, and 58 Occupational Scales. Reliability is exceptionally strong and concurrent validity with similar tests is very robust.

## KEY TERMS AND CONCEPTS

biodata   p. 469

integrity tests   p. 479

work sample   p. 482

situational exercise   p. 482

in-basket test   p. 483

assessment center   p. 484

criterion problem   p. 485

graphic rating scale   p. 487

critical incidents checklist   p. 487

behaviorally anchored rating scale   p. 488

behavior observation scale   p. 489

forced-choice scale   p. 489

halo effect   p. 490

rater bias   p. 491

criterion contamination   p. 491

RIASEC model   p. 496

# Forensic Applications of Assessment

sychology and the legal system have had a long and uneasy alliance characterized by mistrust on both sides. Within the legal system, lawyers and judges maintain antipathy toward the testimony of psychologists because of a concern that their opinions are based upon "junk science" (or perhaps no science at all) and also because of a belief (not entirely unfounded) that some expert witnesses will profess almost any viewpoint that serves the interests of a defendant. Within the mental health profession, psychologists find the adversarial aspect of courtroom testimony—based upon the expectation of yes-no opinions expressed as virtual certainties—to be an impossible arena in which to pursue the truth about human behavior. As the reader will discover, this essential tension between law and psychology is a constant backdrop that shapes and informs the nature of psychological practice in the courtroom.

For better or for worse, psychologists do testify in court cases, and the focus of their testimony often pertains to the interpretation of psychological tests and assessment interviews. When are test results and psychological opinions based upon them admissible in court? What criteria do judges use in determining whether to admit psychological testimony? Psychologists who represent themselves as experts and who use tests to justify their opinions must have a firm grounding in legal issues that pertain to assessment. In this topic we examine the relevance of legal standards to testimony based upon psychological tests and evaluations. We also explore a few specialized instruments useful in forensic assessment.

The role of the psychological examiner can intersect with the legal system in a multitude of ways. The practitioner might be called upon for the following:

- Evaluation of possible malingering
- Assessment of mental state for the insanity plea
- Determination of competency to stand trial
- Prediction of violence and assessment of risk

- Evaluation of child custody in divorce
- Assessment of personal injury
- Interpretation of polygraph data
- Specialized forensic personality assessment

These are the primary applications of forensic practice, which we examine here. A variety of additional applications are surveyed in Melton, Petrila, Poythress, and Slobogin (1998).

In addition to meeting the general guidelines for ethical practice required of any clinician, practitioners who offer expert testimony based upon psychological tests will encounter additional standards of practice unique to the U.S. jurisprudence system. We summarize major concerns regarding psychological tests and courtroom testimony here. The reader can find extended discussions of this topic in Melton et al. (1998) and Wrightsman, Nietzel, Fortune, and Greene (2002).

Each of the previously listed topics raises unique questions about the role of the psychologist in the courtroom. However, one issue is common to all forms of courtroom testimony: When is a psychologist an expert witness? We discuss this general issue before returning to specific applications of psychological evaluation that intersect with the U.S. legal system.

## ● STANDARDS FOR
## THE EXPERT WITNESS

Just as psychologists are concerned with issues of standards and competence, so too are lawyers and judges. U.S. jurisprudence has developed various guidelines for courtroom testimony, including several general principles regarding the testimony of an **expert witness**. These standards are found in *Federal Rules of Evidence* (1975) and have been upheld by various court decisions. We can summarize the principles of expert testimony as follows:

- The witness must be a qualified expert. Not all psychologists who are asked to testify will be allowed to do so. Based on a summary of the expert's education, training, and experience,

the judge decides whether the testimony of the witness is to be admitted.
- The testimony must be about a proper subject matter. In particular, the expert must present information beyond the knowledge and experience of the average juror.
- The value of the evidence in determining guilt or innocence must outweigh its prejudicial effect. For example, if the expert's testimony might confuse the issue at hand or might prejudice the members of the jury, it is generally not admissible.
- The expert's testimony should be in accordance with a generally accepted explanatory theory. In most courts, guidance on this matter is provided by *Frye v. United States*, a 1923 court case pertaining to the admissibility of expert testimony.

In *Frye v. United States*, the counsel for a murder defendant attempted to introduce the results of a systolic blood pressure deception test. The lawyer offered an expert witness to testify to the result of the deception test. It was asserted that emotionally induced activation of the sympathetic nervous system causes systolic blood pressure to rise gradually if the examinee attempts to deceive the examiner. In other words, the expert witness asserted that in the course of an interrogation about a crime, the pattern of change in systolic blood pressure could be used as a form of lie detector test. The defense counsel wanted their expert witness to testify in support of the client's innocence. Counsel for the prosecution objected, and the Court of Appeals of the District of Columbia upheld the objection, ruling:

> While courts will go a long way in admitting expert testimony deduced from a well-recognized scientific principle or discovery, the thing from which the deduction is made must be sufficiently established to have gained general acceptance in the particular field in which it belongs. (cited in Blau, 1984)

The court concluded that the systolic blood pressure deception test had not gained acceptance among physiological and psychological authorities and, therefore, refused to allow the testimony of the expert witness.

According to these guidelines, a test, inventory, or assessment technique must have been available for a fairly long period of time in order to have a history of general acceptance. For this reason, the prudent expert witness will choose well-established, extensively researched instruments as the basis for testimony, rather than relying upon recently developed tests that might not stand up to cross-examination under the constraints of *Frye v. United States*.

In the mid- to late 1990s, the standards for expert testimony were refined further, beginning with a Supreme Court decision in *Daubert v. Merrell Dow Pharmaceuticals* (1993). The Court's written opinion added extensive guidelines about factors to be considered in weighing scientific testimony in trials. Two additional court cases (*General Electric Co. v. Joiner*, 1997; *Kumho Tire Co., Ltd. v. Carmichael*, 1999) further extended the parameters of expert testimony defined by *Daubert*. Sometimes known as the *Daubert* trilogy, these three cases generated several new guidelines that trial judges may use in determining the admissibility of expert testimony (Grove & Barden, 1999):

1. Is the proposed theory (or technique), on which the testimony is to be based, testable?
2. Has the proposed theory (or technique) been tested using valid and reliable procedures and with positive results?
3. Has the theory (or technique) been subjected to peer review?
4. What is the known or potential error rate of the scientific theory or technique?
5. What standards controlling the technique's operation maximize its validity?
6. Has the theory (or technique) been generally accepted as valid by a relevant scientific community?
7. Do the expert's conclusions reasonably follow from applying the theory (or technique) to this case?

The ramifications of the *Daubert* trilogy rulings for the expert testimony of psychologists are unclear at this time. For example, it is uncertain whether testimony based upon the Rorschach Inkblot Test (discussed later in this text) would be admissible under these newer, more restrictive guidelines (Grove, Barden, Garb, & Lilienfeld, 2002; Ritzler, Erard, & Pettigrew, 2002). What is clear at this point is that judges generally have tightened the standards for admitting expert evidence in U.S. courts (Dixon & Gill, 2002). For example, some courts have used the *Daubert* ruling as a basis for denying testimony from mental health professionals, including psychologists. In some courts, testimony about psychological evaluations of sexually abused children has been ruled inadmissible. Increasingly, courts will demand that testimony from psychologists has a strict scientific basis (Melton et al., 1998).

## ● THE NATURE OF FORENSIC ASSESSMENT

Before we turn to specific applications, it will prove helpful to explore crucial differences between forensic assessment and traditional assessment. The most general divergence is that forensic assessment is molded by the prerequisites of the legal system, whereas traditional assessment is shaped by the needs of the client and current professional standards. Although the two approaches occasionally will look the same—for example, the examiner might use the MMPI-2 in both cases—the types of information sought, the strategies for gathering it, and the manner of report writing will be noticeably different.

One major difference is the scope of evaluation in traditional and forensic assessment (Melton et al., 1998). Whereas traditional assessment usually is broadscale and provides a comprehensive picture of a client's functioning and treatment needs, forensic assessment engages a narrow focus that may not even appear to be "clinical" in nature. For example, when evaluating a forensic client for competency to stand trial, the client's symptom pattern, mental status, diagnosis, and so forth are only of tangential interest. What matters most, and what the legal system will want to know, is whether the client meets the criteria for competency or not, as discussed later in this topic. Lawyers and judges will prefer and expect a "yes" or "no" answer to the competency question, and they may regard a lengthy description of symptoms as so much drivel.

Another huge difference has to do with the client's role in the process. Whereas in traditional assessment the client voluntarily agrees to an assessment and may even help determine its scope and nature, in forensic assessment the client really has little choice in the matter, unless he or she wants to aggravate the judge who has authorized the assessment. In fact, in forensic assessment the "client" is not really the client! The psychologist is working at the behest of a judge or lawyer. Put simply, a judge, lawyer, or other court officer is usually the real client. It would be more accurate to refer to the individual undergoing the assessment as the "examinee."

Threats to validity also differ in the two settings. Although it is true that clients in traditional assessment may want to present themselves in a good light and, therefore, distort the truth when responding, this pales in comparison to the blatant faking of psychopathology (malingering) that may occur in a forensic setting. Malingering is discussed in more detail later in this topic. For now, consider the true case of an inmate evaluated by the author. He complained that he was "seeing things" and that he needed "medication" to sleep better. When asked to describe what he was "seeing," he was blandly inarticulate. During the interview, he appeared calm and collected. Furthermore, his personality test profile (MMPI-2) was a mountain range of scale elevations, a classic fake-bad profile. Beyond a doubt, he was fabricating his symptoms in hopes of receiving a prescription for antianxiety medications.

Finally, it is important to mention that the nature of the written report will differ in the two settings. In traditional assessment, the audience typically is other professionals who are familiar with jargon, diagnostic terminology, and treatment options. In forensic assessment, the audience is legal personnel who care mainly about the referral question. Melton et al. (1998) describe a number of pertinent qualities for forensic reports; namely,

reports should separate facts from inferences, stay within the scope of the referral question, avoid information overkill, and minimize clinical jargon. Melton and colleagues also note that the clinician must take special care to protect the privacy rights of individuals mentioned in a report, insofar as this information most certainly will become part of the public record. Clinicians must write forensic reports with great care:

> Finally, and most important, the report and the clinician who writes it will, or at least should, receive close scrutiny during adversary negotiations or proceedings. A well-written report may obviate courtroom testimony. A poorly written report may become, in the hands of a skillful lawyer, an instrument to discredit and embarrass its author. Therefore, attention to detail and to the accuracy of information is required. (Melton, et al., 1998, p. 523)

Woe to the forensic examiner who writes a sloppy report that becomes part of court proceedings. Not only might this unnecessarily confuse the court case, but it also could result in literally hours of ill-mannered and humiliating cross-examination of the report writer.

## ● EVALUATION OF SUSPECTED MALINGERING

In most settings, a psychologist safely can assume that clients will be reasonably honest about their mental and emotional state. Clients want to tell their stories and they want to get things right. At worst, they may overstate symptoms slightly so as to impress the clinician that help truly is deserved and needed. Yet outright deception and manipulation are uncommon—for the simple reason that clients rarely have incentive for these strategies.

However, the rules of clinical engagement are turned upside-down in forensic settings. The typical forensic client has much to gain from a case formulation that emphasizes illness and disability. Indeed, the context of the assessment almost guarantees that clients will seek to look "crazy" or disabled, whether by exaggeration or (more rarely) deceptive design. In the mind of the forensic client, fabrication of symptoms may serve to excuse unacceptable behavior (e.g., favoring the insanity plea), sway sentencing recommendations (e.g., against capital punishment), or gain entitlements (e.g., certification for disability). These client maneuvers clearly influence the validity of forensic assessments. Hovering in the background of every forensic assessment is this troubling question: Was the client reasonably honest and forthright?

The forensic examiner must make a judgment about the honesty of the client's self-portrayal during the evaluation. And yet while common sense dictates that the examiner should expect some degree of deception, the conclusion that a client has consciously malingered needs to be reached with caution:

> Given the significant potential for deception and the implications for the validity of their findings, mental health professionals should develop a low threshold for suspecting deceptive responding. At the same time, because the label of "malingerer" may carry considerable weight with legal decisionmakers and potentially tarnish all aspects of the person's legal position, conclusions that a person is feigning should not be reached hastily. (Melton et al., 1998)

The most common and venerable method for identifying dishonest clients is the clinical interview. However, a more objective approach should be preferred. The assessment of potential malingering with interview hinges upon the judgment of the clinician (e.g., "This client is inconsistent in his presentation of symptoms and appears eager to be sick, so I conclude that he is malingering"), which may prove erroneous. In contrast, an objective approach provides normative data, hit rates, and the like for the evaluation. Not only might this improve the accuracy of the assessment, in addition more standardized approaches should find greater acceptability in many court systems.

According to DSM-IV **malingering** is defined as:

> . . . the intentional production of false or grossly exaggerated physical or psychological symptoms, motivated by external incentives such as avoiding military duty, avoiding work, obtaining financial compensation, evading criminal prosecution, or obtaining drugs. (American Psychiatric Association, 1994, p. 683)

The incidence of malingering among referred clients is hard to pin down, although thought to be significant, at least in forensic settings. Forensic practitioners estimate the occurrence to be 15 to 20 percent of their cases (Rogers, 1986; Rogers, Sewell, & Goldstein, 1994). For reasons of justice and fairness, the detection of malingering with empirically validated procedures is an important obligation of forensic psychologists.

Several promising tests of malingering have emerged in recent years (Rogers, 2008). For reasons of space, we will focus here on three procedures that illustrate the breadth of approaches available: the Structured Interview of Reported Symptoms (SIRS), the Test of Memory Malingering (TOMM), and certain MMPI-2 indices.

## Structured Interview of Reported Symptoms (SIRS)

One promising instrument is the Structured Interview of Reported Symptoms (SIRS), a 172-item interview schedule designed expressly for the evaluation of malingering (Rogers, Bagby, & Dickens, 1992). The approach embodied in the SIRS was based on strategies identified in the clinical literature as potentially useful for detecting malingering. Using a structured interview method, malingering is assessed on eight primary scales:

- Rare Symptoms (overreporting of infrequent symptoms)
- Symptom Combinations (real psychiatric symptoms that rarely occur together)
- Improbable or Absurd Symptoms (symptoms reveal a fantastic quality)
- Blatant Symptoms (overendorsement of obvious signs of mental disorder)
- Subtle Symptoms (overendorsement of everyday problems)
- Severity of Symptoms (symptoms portrayed with extreme, unbearable severity)

- Selectivity of Symptoms (indiscriminant endorsement of psychiatric problems)
- Reported versus Observed Symptoms (comparison of observed and reported symptoms)

In addition to the eight primary scales, five supplementary scales are used to interpret response styles. Of the 172 questions, 32 are repeated inquiries to detect inconsistency of responding. Examples of the kinds of structured interview questions include: "Do you ever feel like the fillings in your teeth can pick up radio messages?" (Rare Symptoms); "Do you have severe headaches at the same time as you have a fear of germs?" (Symptom Combinations); "Does the furniture where you live seem to get bigger or smaller from day to day?" (Improbable or Absurd Symptoms); "Do you have any serious problems with thoughts about suicide?" (Blatant Symptoms). The scale takes less than an hour to administer.

Results allow for classification of examinees as definite feigning, probable feigning, and honest. Reliability of the instrument is good, with internal-consistency reliability coefficients for subscales ranging from .66 to .92. Interrater reliability estimates are superb, ranging from .89 to 1.00.

Although the validity of the SIRS can be discussed along the familiar lines of content, criterion-related, and construct validity (and the test performs well in these domains), the real measure of its clinical utility pertains to the capacity of the test to discriminate known or suspected malingerers from psychiatric patients and normal controls. One recent study indicates that the test performs well in this capacity (Gothard, Viglione, Meloy, & Sherman, 1996). In a mixed sample of 125 males referred for competency evaluation (including 30 persons asked to simulate malingering, 7 individuals strongly suspected of malingering, and 88 persons for whom malingering appeared unlikely), the SIRS was overall 97.8 percent accurate in classifying participants as malingered or nonmalingered. Recently, Heinze and Purisch (2001) have shown that the SIRS and other similar tests provide more accurate detection of malingering when used collectively rather than individually.

A few other studies reveal promising results, but these involve predominantly white and educated samples (Rogers, Gillis, Dickens, & Bagby, 1991; Rogers, Kropp, Bagby, & Dickens, 1992). In contrast, the population of the criminal justice system—the arena in which SIRS most likely would be used—is relatively uneducated, and minorities are heavily overrepresented. By one estimate, more than 80 percent of the urban jail population in the United States is African American (Dixon, 1995). Unanswered is how well the SIRS would function in the detection of malingering within this sizable subpopulation.

### Test of Memory Malingering (TOMM)

The TOMM is a 50-item visual recognition test that includes two learning trials and an optional retention trial (Tombaugh, 1997). The secret to the test is that it appears to be difficult, while actually it is quite easy. As a result, malingerers encounter an enticing opportunity to perform poorly, whereas others complete the task with near perfect scores. In the first learning trial, 50 line drawings are presented to the individual for 3 seconds each. Then, in the first test phase each stimulus is presented alongside three distractor drawings; the examinee is asked to pick each item shown previously. Of course, the position of each correct drawing alongside the three distractor choices is varied randomly. A second learning trial then ensues, with a second test phase. A delayed retention trial, consisting only of the test phase, is administered after a 20-minute delay. The results for the TOMM consist of the number of correct choices (out of 50) on Trial 1, Trial 2, and the Retention test.

Although there are several ways to summate and interpret TOMM test scores, the most common approach is to utilize a cutting score of 44/45 on the Trial 2 outcome. In other words, scores of 45 or higher on Trial 2 are considered normal, whereas scores of 44 or lower indicate the likelihood of malingering. This interpretive strategy emerged from several studies indicating that individuals who have no motivation to malinger—whether they are normal adults *or* patients with brain impairment—

● **TABLE 11.7**

| | *Percent Obtaining TOMM Trial 2 Score of:* | | | | | | | | |
| | *50* | *49* | *48* | *47* | *46* | *45* | *40–44* | *30–39* | *<30* |
|---|---|---|---|---|---|---|---|---|---|
| Samples: | | | | | | | | | |
| Intact adults no motive (N = 405)[a] | 91 | 7 | 1 | 1 | | | 1 | | |
| Definite TBI with no motive (N = 22)[b] | 73 | 14 | 5 | | 5 | 5 | | | |
| Possible TBI with with motive (N = 28)[b] | 25 | 4 | 0 | 7 | 0 | 0 | 18 | 25 | 21 |

[a]Based on data from Tombaugh (1997)
[b]Based on data from Haber & Fichtenberg (2006)
Note: TBI = traumatic brain injury. Percentages are rounded off and row totals therefore do not equal exactly 100 percent.

rarely score lower than 45 on the second trial. In contrast, individuals with motivation to malinger (e.g., brain-injured persons involved in litigation, or others who have something to gain from poor test performance) often score well below 45. We have summarized the score ranges for a few studies in Table 11.7. The three samples portrayed in this table include a large nonclinical sample of 405 adults (Tombaugh, 1997), a small sample of 22 individuals with confirmed traumatic brain injury (TBI) but no motivation to malinger (i.e., no pending litigation), and a small sample of 28 individuals with mild head injury seeking compensation and therefore possessing a strong motivation to malinger (last two samples from Haber & Fichtenberg, 2006). The reader will notice that 99 percent of the intact adults scored between 45 and 50, and 100 percent of the TBI patients with no motivation to malinger scored in this normal range. In contrast, a whopping 64 percent of the patients seeking compensation for head injury (and therefore having motivation to malinger) scored below the cut-off, far worse than the sample with confirmed brain damage!

## MMPI-2 Validity Scales

Another approach to the assessment of malingering is to utilize certain scales or subscales from standard instruments typically administered in forensic settings. A case in point is the MMPI-2, used in a wide variety of forensic assessments to gauge psychopathology. If possible, why not use the validity scales of this instrument to determine

whether the client is exaggerating or manufacturing symptoms for purposes of personal gain? It turns out that certain MMPI-2 validity scales differentiate malingerers from nonmalingerers with a high degree of accuracy. Consider the study by Bianchini, Etherton, Greve, Heinly, and Meyers (2008) that compared MMPI-2 validity scale scores of these four groups:

- Patients without financial incentive (n = 23). These were clinical patients with pain attributed to spine-related pathology who were not eligible for compensation and who were clear of drug abuse or drug seeking.
- Nonmalingered patients with financial incentive (n = 34). These were clinical patients seeking compensation but known from other definitive tests not to be malingering.
- Patients definitively determined to be malingering (n = 32). These were patients who scored *below* chance on malingering tests such as the TOMM, or who clearly met other criteria for malingering such as gross inconsistency in test results.
- College students asked to simulate pain-related disability (n = 26). These were students instructed to fake a pain syndrome in a convincing manner as if to win a personal injury lawsuit.

Describing the many validity scales of the MMPI-2 and analyzing the complex results reported by Bianchini et al. (2008) would involve a substantial digression. Instead, we will illustrate the thrust of their research by reporting on just one scale, the

● **TABLE 11.8   Means and Standard Deviations on the MMPI-2 F Scale for Four Groups**

| Group | M (SD) |
| --- | --- |
| Nonmalingered patients with no incentive: | 53.2 (10.9) |
| Nonmalingered patients with incentive: | 53.8 (9.5) |
| Malingered patients with incentive: | 82.1 (22.5) |
| Student simulators with incentive: | 79.6 (22.8) |

*Source*: Based on data in Bianchini, Etherton, Greve, Heinly, and Meyers (2008).

F (Infrequency) scale, which includes 60 true-false questions answered in the scored direction by fewer than 10 percent of the normative sample. The content of these questions is diverse, but includes paranoid thinking, antisocial attitudes, hostility, and poor physical health. Excessively high scores on the F Scale may indicate random responding, gross psychotic disturbance, or "faking bad." As with all MMPI-2 scales, results on the F scale are reported as *T*-scores with a mean of 50 and standard deviation of 10 in the general population; higher scores indicating greater pathology, and scores greater than T = 70 are especially suspect. Briefly, the definite malingering group and the college simulation group both scored almost 30 points higher on the F scale than the other two comparison groups (Table 11.8).

Providing a little more detail, the researchers found that more than 50 percent of the malingering and simulation groups obtained T > 75 on the F Scale, whereas only 2 percent of the other patients earned scores of this magnitude. Although the F Scale score of clients is not perfect in the detection of malingering, it does provide helpful information alongside other sources of data in forensic assessment.

● **ASSESSMENT OF MENTAL STATE FOR THE INSANITY PLEA**

In criminal trials the defendant may invoke a variety of defenses including entrapment, diminished capacity (e.g., from mental subnormality),

automatism (e.g., from hypnotic suggestion), and the insanity plea. Whenever a special defense is invoked, an evaluation of the defendant's **mental state at the time of the offense** (MSO) is required. In some courts, a psychologist is qualified to offer opinions about the MSO of a defendant. We restrict the discussion here to the insanity plea since this is the most common doctrine that would trigger the need for an MSO evaluation.

Almost everyone is familiar with the insanity defense, but only the exceptional person understands its provisions. Technically, the insanity defense is known as **not guilty by reason of insanity** (NGRI). Based on a few sensational and widely publicized trials such as the case of John Hinckley, who attempted to assassinate President Ronald Reagan, the lay public generally has concluded that the insanity defense is commonly employed by cynical lawyers to help dangerous clients evade legal responsibility for heinous crimes. Nothing could be further from the truth. In reality, the NGRI plea is widely respected by jurisprudence experts and is invoked in fewer than 1 in 1,000 trials (Blau, 1984). And in this tiny fraction of all criminal cases, the defense succeeds less than 1 time in 4 (Melton et al., 1998). The widespread belief that persons found NGRI "walk" away from their crimes also is inaccurate: Most receive hospital treatment that lasts several years. Recidivism rates are perhaps lower (and certainly not higher) than felons convicted of similar offenses (Melton et al., 1998). Even though outlawed in some states, the insanity defense has shown remarkable resiliency—probably because it performs a desirable role in a modern and compassionate society.

Several legal tests for insanity have had significant influence in the United States, including the M'Naughten rule, the Durham rule, the Model Penal Code rule, and the Guilty But Mentally Ill (GBMI) verdict (Wrightsman et al., 2002). Some jurisdictions include irresistible impulse as a supplement to the M'Naughten Rule. A few states have abolished the insanity defense altogether. We will survey the different standards briefly before commenting upon the role of psychological tests in determining legal insanity.

The **M'Naughten rule** is the oldest, stemming from an 1843 case in England. Daniel M'Naughten was plagued by paranoid delusions that the prime minister, Robert Peel, was part of a conspiracy against him. M'Naughten stalked the prime minister and, in a case of mistaken identity, shot his male secretary at No. 10, Downing Street. M'Naughten was found not guilty by reason of insanity, a verdict that touched off a national furor. In response to the furor, Queen Victoria commanded all 15 high judges of England to appear before the House of Lords and clarify the newly forged guidelines on insanity. The M'Naughten rule states:

> The jury ought to be told in all cases that every man is to be presumed to be sane, and to possess a sufficient degree of reason to be responsible for his crimes, until the contrary be proved to their satisfaction; and that to establish a defense on the grounds of insanity it must be clearly proved that, at the time of committing the act, the accused was laboring under such a defect of reason, from disease of the mind, as not to know the nature and quality of the act he was doing, or, if he did know it, that he did not know what he was doing was wrong. (cited in Wrightsman et al., 1994)

Thus, the M'Naughten rule "excuses" criminal behavior if the defendant, as a consequence of a "disease of the mind," did not know what he or she was doing (e.g., a paranoid schizophrenic who believed he or she was shooting the literal devil) or did not know that what he or she was doing was wrong (e.g., a person with mental retardation who believed that it was acceptable to shoot an obnoxious panhandler). Approximately half of the states use the M'Naughten rule.

Some jurisdictions also allow "irresistible impulse" as a supplement to the M'Naughten rule. An *irresistible impulse* is generally defined as a behavioral response that is so strong that the accused could not resist it by will or reason. But when is an impulse irresistible as opposed to simply unresisted? This has proved difficult to define. For obvious reasons, legal experts are unhappy with the notion of irresistible impulse, and its use as part of an insanity plea appears to be waning.

The **Durham rule** was formulated in 1954 by the District of Columbia Federal Court of Appeals in *Durham v. United States.* Dissatisfied with the M'Naughten rule, Judge David Bazelon proposed a new test, known as the Durham rule, which provided for the defense of insanity if the criminal act was a "product" of mental disease or defect. The purpose of the Durham rule was to give mental health professionals a wider latitude in presenting information pertinent to the defendant's responsibility. Legal scholars hailed Durham as a great step forward, but in 1972 the rule was dropped by the circuit that had formulated it.

The Durham rule was replaced by the Model Penal Code rule proposed by the American Law Institute. Adopted in 1972, the Model Penal Code rule is as follows:

> A person is not responsible for criminal conduct if at the time of such conduct, as a result of mental disease or defect, he lacks substantial capacity either to appreciate the criminality (wrongfulness) of his conduct or to conform his conduct to the requirements of the law. (cited in Melton et al., 1998)

The Model Penal Code rule also contains provisions that prohibit the inclusion of the psychopath or antisocial personality within the insanity defense.

The **Model Penal Code** rule differs from the M'Naughten rule in three important ways:

1. By using the term *appreciate,* it acknowledges the emotional determinants of criminal action.
2. It does not require a total lack of appreciation by offenders for the nature of their conduct—only a lack of "substantial capacity."
3. It includes both a cognitive element and a volitional element, making defendants' inability to control their actions an independent criterion for insanity (Wrightsman et al., 2002).

About 20 states now follow the Model Penal Code rule or slight variants of it.

A recent development in the insanity plea is the **Guilty But Mentally Ill (GBMI)** verdict. Approximately one-fourth of the states allow juries to reach a verdict of GBMI in cases in which the defendant pleads insanity. Typically, in states that allow the GBMI verdict, the judge instructs the jury to return with one of four verdicts:

- Guilty of the crime
- Not guilty of the crime
- Not guilty by reason of insanity
- Guilty but mentally ill

The intention of the last alternative is that a defendant found GBMI should receive the same sentence as if found guilty of the crime, but he or she begins the sentence in a psychiatric hospital. After treatment is completed, the defendant then serves the remainder of the sentence in a prison.

But the intention of GBMI and its reality are two different things. Initial support for the GBMI verdict as a humane variant of the insanity plea has waned in recent years. Wrightsman et al. (2002) point out that jurors express confusion when asked to make the difficult distinction between mental illness that results in insanity (GBMI) and mental illness that does not. Melton et al. (1998) find little virtue in the verdict:

> The GBMI verdict is conceptually flawed, has significant potential for misleading the factfinder, and does not appear to achieve its goals of reducing insanity acquittals or prolonging confinement of offenders who are mentally ill and dangerous. The one goal it may achieve is relieving the anxiety of jurors and judges who otherwise would have difficulty deciding between a guilty verdict and a verdict of not guilty by reason of insanity. It is doubtful this goal is a proper one or worth the price. (p. 215)

Empirical studies indicate that offenders found GBMI seldom receive adequate treatment. Furthermore, they may receive harsher sentences than their counterparts found merely guilty (Callahan, McGreevy, Cirincione, & Steadman, 1992). In fact, some defendants found GBMI have been sentenced to death!

Now that the reader has been introduced to variants of the insanity plea, we review the role of the psychologist in determining legal insanity. An important point is that psychologists are rightfully cautious in offering an interview-based opinion as to a person's mental state at the time of a criminal offense. After all, the crime usually occurred days, weeks, months, or even years before, and the client may be unable to assist in the accurate reconstruction of events and mental states. Consequently, psychological testimony regarding legal insanity should be cautious and conservative. Reliability studies of insanity evaluations also suggest that caution is appropriate. In a review of seven studies, Melton et al. (1998) determined that interrater agreement (as to whether a defendant was legally insane) ranged from a low of 64 percent (between prosecution and defense psychiatrists) to a high of 97 percent (between psychologists with forensic training who used structured instruments, discussed later).

In spite of controversy over the role of the psychologist in MSO determinations, some experts foresee an increased role for psychological assessment in cases involving the insanity plea. In particular, neuropsychological assessments may provide objective, valid data to help the courts decide the merits of an insanity defense. Recent court rulings affirm that neuropsychological test findings can be used to show that a defendant has impaired capability to choose right and refrain from wrong (Blau, 1984; Heilbrun, 1992). Martell (1992) has discussed the relevance of neuropsychological assessment to the insanity plea as defined by the Model Penal Code. The Model Penal Code defines a defendant as not guilty by reason of insanity if he or she "lacks substantial capacity" to appreciate the criminality of his or her conduct. Neuropsychological test results have a direct bearing upon this issue.

Rating scales such as the Rogers Criminal Responsibility Assessment Scales (R-CRAS) also provide a useful basis for evaluating criminal responsibility (Rogers, 1984, 1986). The R-CRAS is completed by the examiner immediately following a review of clinical records, police investigative reports, and the final clinical interview with the patient-defendant. The instrument consists of clear descriptive criteria for 25 items assessing both psychological and situational factors. The items are scored with respect to the time of the crime on five scales measuring these variables:

- Patient Reliability
- Organicity

- Psychopathology
- Cognitive Control
- Behavioral Control

The individual items on the R-CRAS were derived from the Model Penal Code standard of insanity (Table 11.9). Interrater reliabilities of the R-CRAS scales ranged from .48 (for a Malingering subscale) to 1.00 (for Organicity). Construct validity was established by comparing the disposition of

---

### ● TABLE 11.9   Sample Items from the R-CRAS

10. Amnesia about the alleged crime.
    (This refers to the examiner's assessment of amnesia, not necessarily the patient's reported amnesia)
    (0) No information.
    (1) None. Remembers the entire event in considerable detail.
    (2) Slight; of doubtful significance. The patient forgets a few minor details.
    (3) Mild. Patient remembers the substance of what happened but is forgetful of many minor details.
    (4) Moderate. The patient has forgotten a major portion of the alleged crime but remembers enough details to believe it happened.
    (5) Severe. The patient is amnesic to most of the alleged crime but remembers enough details to believe it happened.
    (6) Extreme. Patient is completely amnesic to the whole alleged crime.
11. Delusions at the time of the alleged crime.
    (1) No information.
    (2) Suspected delusions (e.g., supported only by questionable self-report).
    (3) Definite delusions but not actually associated with the commission of the alleged crime.
    (4) Definite delusions which contributed to, but were not the predominant force in, the commission of the alleged crime.
    (5) Definite controlling delusions on the basis of which the alleged crime was committed.

---

*Source:* Adapted and reproduced by special permission of the Publisher, Psychological Assessment Resources, Inc., Odessa, FL 33556, from the Rogers' Criminal Responsibility Assessment Scales by Richard Rogers, Ph.D. Copyright 1984 by PAR, Inc. Further reproduction is prohibited without permission from PAR, Inc.

93 legal cases with R-CRAS data. Even though legal outcome is determined by many variables besides the psychological state of the person at the time of the crime, there was 95 percent agreement in the determination of sanity and 73 percent agreement in the determination of insanity.

Even though reviewers recognize the promise of the R-CRAS, for some a healthy skepticism still prevails. One concern is that the subscales of the instrument represent an *ordinal* level of measurement, whereas an *interval* level of quantification is implied. Another concern is that the test developers claim to "quantify areas of judgment that are logical and/or intuitive in nature" that leads to a false sense of scientific certainty (Melton et al., 1998). Certainly, the R-CRAS performs a valuable function by helping clinicians organize their thinking and evaluation. The utility of the overall decision—sane versus insane—will rest upon additional validational research (Howell & Richards, 1989). In support of test validity, Rogers and Sewell (1999) reanalyzed 413 insanity cases and found that the R-CRAS contributed substantially to the determination of criminal responsibility.

## ● COMPETENCY TO STAND TRIAL

The Sixth Amendment to the U.S. Constitution, passed in 1791, guarantees every accused citizen the right to an impartial, speedy, and public trial with benefit of counsel. If the defendant is unable to exercise these constitutional rights for any reason, then a proper trial cannot take place. Specifically, if the defendant has a mental defect, illness, or condition that renders him or her unable to understand the proceedings or to assist in his or her defense, the defendant would be considered incompetent to stand trial. This standard was confirmed by the U.S. Supreme Court in *Dusky v. United States* (1960) as "whether [the defendant] has sufficient present ability to consult with his lawyer with a reasonable degree of rational understanding—and whether he has a rational as well as factual understanding of the proceedings against him." In practice, **competency to stand** trial refers to four elements and distinctions (Melton et al., 1998):

1. The defendant's capacity to understand the criminal process, including the role of the participants in that process
2. The defendant's ability to function in that process, primarily through consulting with counsel in the preparation of a defense
3. The defendant's capacity, as opposed to willingness, to relate to counsel and understand the proceedings
4. The defendant's reasonable degree of understanding, as opposed to perfect or complete understanding

Most U.S. courts follow this standard, which emphasizes *current* functioning of the accused.

The presiding judge may request a psychological or psychiatric evaluation to assist in determining a defendant's competency to stand trial. One recent report indicates that more than 25,000 evaluations of competency to stand trial are performed in the United States each year (McDonald, Nussbaum, & Bagby, 1992). It is important to emphasize that psychologists, psychiatrists, and other mental health professionals merely assist in a competency hearing by presenting expert opinions. Only the judge has the power to make a competency determination. Although there is no standard format for a competency determination, most judges request that the psychologist consider most or all of the 11 factors cited in Table 11.10.

Incompetency to stand trial is entirely separate from legal insanity; these two issues are judged by completely different standards. *Legal insanity* pertains to the moment of the criminal act, whereas *incompetency* implies a current, ongoing condition. Furthermore, incompetency is not synonymous with mental illness, although the two may occur together. In the event that the judge rules the defendant incompetent, the trial is postponed, usually for a period of six months or so. In some cases, persons found incompetent are placed in a mental institution for treatment to restore their competency so that a trial can be held later.

---

● **TABLE 11.10    Factors Considered in Determining Competency to Stand Trial**

1. Defendant's appreciation of the charges
2. Defendant's appreciation of the nature and range of penalties
3. Defendant's understanding of the adversary nature of the legal process
4. Defendant's capacity to disclose to attorney pertinent facts surrounding the alleged offense
5. Defendant's ability to relate to attorney
6. Defendant's ability to assist attorney in planning defense
7. Defendant's capacity to realistically challenge prosecution witnesses
8. Defendant's ability to manifest appropriate courtroom behavior
9. Defendant's capacity to testify relevantly
10. Defendant's motivation to help himself in the legal process
11. Defendant's capacity to cope with the stress of incarceration prior to trial

*Source:* Florida Rules of Criminal Procedure, cited in Wrightsman, L. S., Nietzel, M. T., & Fortune, W. H. (1994). *Psychology and the legal system* (3rd ed.). Pacific Grove, CA: Brooks/Cole.

---

Individuals charged with less-serious crimes may receive outpatient treatment.

In addition to information obtained from the clinical interview, psychological test results are important components of a competency evaluation. For example, a low IQ may constitute evidence of incompetence in the eyes of the court. Although there are no firm guidelines, most courts rule that persons with significant intellectual deficits—say, an IQ in the range of moderate mental retardation or lower—are incompetent to stand trial. Likewise, a pattern of test results indicating severe neuropsychological deficit may warrant a finding of legal incompetence, even if the client's IQ is in the normal range. For example, a defendant with severe stroke-induced deficits in language comprehension may be found incompetent to stand trial.

Several formalized screening tests and procedures are available to assist in competency

## ● TABLE 11.11 Competency Assessment Instruments

**Competency Screening Test**
  **(Lipsitt, Lelos, & McGarry, 1971)**
The CST is a 22-item sentence completion test with an objective scoring guide. Some reviewers find the scoring criteria to be vague and also complain that the test has poor face validity and weak content validity.

**Competency Assessment Instrument**
  **(Laboratory for Community Psychiatry, 1974)**
The CAI is a structured interview of 13 functions relevant to competent functioning at trial. One concern is that examiners use different approaches to administer the scale.

**Interdisciplinary Fitness Interview-Revised**
  **(Golding, 1993)**
The IFI-R is a semistructured interview of the defendant in 11 categories of psychopathology. Ideally, the defendant's attorney should be present during administration.

**Fitness Interview Test-Revised**
  **(Roesch, Webster, & Eaves, 1994)**
Thirty-minute structured interview in three areas: (a) understanding of the nature of the proceedings, (b) understanding of the possible consequences of the proceedings, and (c) ability to communicate with counsel and participate in the defense. The FIT-R reveals strong utility as a screening instrument (Zapf & Roesch, 1997).

**Georgia Court Competency Test-Revised**
  **(Johnson & Mullett, 1987)**
The GCCT-R is a 21-item oral test of understanding courtroom procedure, knowledge of the charge, knowledge of possible penalties, and ability to communicate rationally. Some reviewers warn that the test inadequately samples the domain of competence-related abilities.

---

evaluation. These instruments are summarized briefly in Table 11.11. We focus our attention here on the MacArthur Competence Assessment Tool—Criminal Adjudication (MacCAT-CA), one of the most promising and psychometrically sound of the many tests developed for this purpose (Hoge, Bonnie, Poythress, & Monahan, 1999).

The MacCAT-CA consists of 22 items grouped into three subscales of psycholegal abilities: Understanding, Reasoning, and Appreciation. The examiner begins the test by reading a hypothetical short story to the defendant about two men who get into a fight (one of them is later charged). The first subscale (8 items) assesses the defendant's ability to understand the legal system with questions like "What is the job of the defendant's lawyer?" These questions are scored 0, 1, or 2, based on degree of understanding. The second subscale (8 items) evaluates the defendant's ability to reason in regard to the hypothetical story, and to evaluate legal options for the hypothetical defendant. The third subscale (6 items) departs from the imaginary scenario and assesses the defendant's capacity to understand his or her legal situation. The questions explore the defendant's appraisal of how he or she is likely to function and to be treated during the course of the trial.

The psychometric properties of the MacCAT-CA were evaluated in a study of 729 felony defendants (Poythress, Monahan, Bonnie, Otto, & Hoge, 2002). The researchers found good internal consistency for the three subscales, with coefficient alphas of .81 to .88. The construct validity of the instrument is well supported by confirmatory factor analyses that yield the three factors posited by the test developers (Zapf, Skeem, & Golding, 2005). In general, the MacCAT-CA and similar instruments are a useful beginning to a competency evaluation but should not be the sole method of assessment. Most forensic experts emphasize the complexities of the legal process and the need to use competency screening instruments sparingly, and mainly in complex cases, as an adjunct to the clinical interview. The MacCAT-CA and similar approaches prove less helpful when clients put forth little effort, demonstrate cognitive impairment, or come from diverse cultural backgrounds (Pinals, Tillbrook, & Mumley, 2006). Additional competency screening tests are reviewed by Zapf and Roesch (2009).

A serious concern in competency evaluations is whether the client is malingering. After all, delaying a trial date for a long time provides a strong motive to appear incompetent. Clinicians have a variety of methods and tests (described previously) for identifying clients who might be malingering. Even so, the process of competency evaluation is not foolproof, as indicated by such high-profile cases as the Connecticut man who avoided prosecution for murder (Associated Press, June 30, 1998). This individual had allegedly murdered his former girlfriend and her current boyfriend with a handgun, then shot himself in the head. He suffered brain damage and partial paralysis and was declared incompetent to stand trial by *four* psychiatrists in four separate hearings. They argued that he was incapable of communicating effectively with his lawyer. A court order that he undergo yearly competency evaluations was overturned, dropping him through the cracks and leaving him a free man. Nine years later he was found attending college as a pre-med student with a 3.3 grade point average. Examples like this are reason for humility and caution when psychologists approach competency evaluations.

## ● PREDICTION OF VIOLENCE AND ASSESSMENT OF RISK

Psychologists occasionally serve as consultants during the sentencing phase of a trial to determine whether a convicted defendant poses a danger to fellow prisoners or to community members. This information may be pivotal in determining the length of a sentence or the placement of the defendant (e.g., in minimum-, medium-, or maximum-security facilities). Parole decisions also may rest upon a determination of dangerousness. In extreme cases, courtroom testimony of mental health professionals may influence the decision whether to invoke the death penalty.

Unfortunately, even though many researchers have attempted to devise psychological measures of dangerousness, no psychometric test or procedure has been developed that provides an accurate long-range prediction of violence (Hart, Michie, and Cook, 2007; Hilton, Harris, and Rice, 2006; Melton et al., 1998). In fact, it is not even possible to *postdict* violence from psychological tests alone with any degree of accuracy.

Why is it so difficult to predict violence accurately? Melton et al. (1998) cite four factors that contribute to the challenge:

1. *Variability in the legal definition.* The outcome to be predicted is variously defined as violence, risk, or dangerousness, and the criteria of legal relevance shift from one setting to another. Some statutes require proof of an overt act within a particular time period, whereas others might accept a clinical judgment of "explosive tendencies" as proof of violence.
2. *Complexity of the literature.* The research literature that examines the relationship between background factors and violence recidivism is enormous. However, the voluminous literature is "both overwhelming and disjointed" so that even conscientious professionals find it difficult to extract meaning from it.
3. *Judgment errors and biases.* Mental health professionals are prone to subtle cognitive errors in their evaluation of defendants. For example, one problem is the tendency to view dangerousness solely as a trait when, in fact, its appearance is always an interaction with environmental factors (e.g., the availability of a weapon). Another problem is that clinicians let the salience of a crime affect their judgment disproportionately.
4. *Political consequences for the practitioner.* Overpredicting violence is safer for clinicians than underpredicting. If a defendant is released on the basis of a clinician's prediction and then commits a violent crime, the practitioner is vulnerable to legal action for negligent release. In borderline cases, there is a very strong incentive to lean in the direction of a "dangerous" finding.

A study by Menzies, Webster, McMain, Staley, and Scaglione (1994) illustrates the difficulties in predicting violence. These researchers used a 15-item Dangerous Behavior Rating Scheme (DBRS) to predict violence over a six-year follow-up of 162 accused persons remanded for evaluation of dangerousness. The DBRS consisted of

15 7-point Likert scale items measuring personality attributes (e.g., hostility, emotionality, capacity for empathy), environmental factors (e.g., support, stress), situational factors (e.g., dangerousness increased with alcohol), and general items (e.g., dangerous to others in the present). In addition, a variety of prediction indices based upon ratings by nurses, psychiatrists, social workers, and others were used to predict an assortment of violence outcome measures at intervals ranging from one year to six years. Most of the correlations were on the order of .2, and very few predictors managed to exceed an upper limit of .40. The highest correlation was .53, but this pertained to the restricted case of short-term prediction of violence in those hospitalized in a psychiatric ward. Overall, the results were so discouraging that the researchers advised against "clinical or psychometric involvement in the identification of potentially violent clinical or correctional subjects."

A particular concern in the prediction of violence is the very high false-positive rate usually observed in controlled studies. This means that large proportions of those predicted to be violent subsequently reveal no violent behaviors. Gardner, Lidz, Mulvey, and Shaw (1996) asked clinicians in a psychiatric emergency room to rate their concern (from 0, no concern, to 5, great concern) that 784 patients would engage in violence over the following six months. The ratings of the clinician and the attending psychiatrist were combined (a total of 10 points possible) to produce a more stable estimate. A total of 327 patients received total scores of 6 or greater, indicating a significant degree of clinical concern. Of this group, 49 percent were found to be completely free of violent behavior over the next six months! A simple statistical formula using background information was significantly more accurate in making predictions but still yielded a 42 percent false-positive rate. Both methods—the clinical and the statistical—also yielded high levels of false negatives (patients not suspected of future violence who subsequently engaged in such acts).

Although the *long-range* prediction of dangerousness with psychological tests or rating scales

has proved to be difficult, the *short-range* assessment of risk with violent offenders has met with moderate success. Analyzing the prior history of violent offenders, Hall (1987) demonstrated that the following variables can be used to derive a probability of violence in the three months ensuing a forensic evaluation:

- Recency of prior violent act(s)
- Number of previous serious acts of violence
- Substance abuse within the previous month
- Actual or threatened breakup of love relationship
- Work problems leading to discipline or termination
- Opportunity for violence, such as access to a handgun

By quantifying the preceding factors, the examiner arrives at a probability of continued violence in the short-range future (Hall, 1987). This strategy is useful mainly with examinees who have a past history of violence, so it has limited applicability in the forensic field. However, for particular persons who meet most or all of the previously listed criteria, a prediction of violence can be correct more often than not. Loeber, Pardini, Homish, and others (2005) also demonstrated the value of biodata in predicting violence and homicide in young men. One subset of their longitudinal sample with a high number of risk factors was 14 times more likely to commit homicide than those with a low number of risk factors.

Quinsey, Harris, Rice, and Cormier (1998) reported similar success in appraising the risk of violent recidivism in more than 600 convicted offenders. Based upon the empirical literature, they constructed the Violence Risk Appraisal Guide (VRAG), an objective rating scale defined by the following 12 offender criteria:

1. Raised by nonbiological parents
2. Degree of elementary school maladjustment
3. History of alcohol problems
4. Marital status of never married
5. Criminal history score (separate guide)

6. Failure on prior conditional release
7. Early age at first major offense
8. Injury to victim at first major offense
9. Female victim(s) at first major offense
10. Diagnostic criteria met for personality disorder
11. Diagnostic criteria not met for schizophrenia
12. Psychopathy checklist score (separate guide)

Weighted ratings in the range of $-5$ to $+5$ were assigned for each criterion, with a maximum possible score of 38 points. For offenders who obtained very high scores (28 points or more), the probability of violent recidivism in the 10-year follow-up was 1.00. In other words, for this small group of offenders, the psychologists could predict *with certainty* that a violent criminal act would occur when these individuals were released to the community. For the next highest group of offenders, those who obtained scores of 21 to 27 points, the probability was .82. In other words, in this group, four out of five individuals committed a violent offense after release. In general, the probability of violent recidivism was a direct linear function of VRAG score. At the other end of the spectrum, offenders who received the lowest VRAG scores virtually never committed a subsequent violent offense. The approaches highlighted here demonstrate once again the potency of biodata in predicting behavior. Recent studies continue to affirm the validity of the VRAG in predicting violence and criminal recidivism (Gray, Fitzgerald, Taylor, MacCulloch, & Snowden, 2007; Kroner, Stadtland, Eidt, & Nedopil, 2005)

Another promising instrument for prediction of violence is the Historical Clinical Risk Management-20 (HCR-20), a straightforward rating scale of 20 items. Based on research literature, all the items are known to be predictive of violence (Webster, Douglas, Eaves, & Hart, 1997). Individual items are scored 0, 1, or 2, and then summed, which yields a total score of 0 to 40, with higher scores indicating greater risk of violence. The items include topics familiar from other instruments such as: previous violence, substance use, psychopathy, lack of insight, and lack of support—all carefully defined in the manual. Yet, the HCR-20 differs conceptually from other instruments like the VRAG because the evaluation extends beyond "static" items from the examinee's history. In addition, the instrument provides for the evaluation of current clinical presentation (e.g., active symptoms of mental illness) and environmental risk factors (e.g., presence of conditions that might trigger violence). Fujii, Tokioka, Lichton, and Hishinuma (2005) reported reasonable validity for the HCR-20 in predicting violent episodes as identified by hospital records for 169 consecutive psychiatric inpatients. Other researchers also report promising results (Douglas, Ogloff, Nicholls, & Grant, 1999; Gray, et al., 2007; Gray, Hill, McGleish, and others, 2003). The HCR-20 likely will attract increased attention among forensic practitioners in the years ahead.

## ● EVALUATION OF CHILD CUSTODY IN DIVORCE

Psychologists may testify in the child custody disputes that arise after divorce. Actually, these disputes are rare—in 90 percent of divorce cases, both parents agree upon custody arrangements without resort to legal intervention (Melton et al., 1998). The role of the consultant is to offer expert opinions on such matters as the suitability of the parents or the best interests of the child. These opinions usually are based upon an assessment of the child (or children) and both parents and may include psychological testing.

Unfortunately, testimony based upon psychological test results rarely provides a useful basis for helping a judge make the Solomonic decision required in a custody dispute (Blau, 1984). The essential weakness of psychological tests in this regard is that the link between test findings and effective parenting is weak or nonexistent. The Rorschach technique and other personality tests were not designed to assess parents' relationships to children and are, therefore, largely irrelevant to the real issues in child custody cases.

Unfortunately, clinicians have been slow to realize their forensic limitations in child custody disputes. As a result there "is probably no forensic question on which overreaching by mental health professionals has been so common and so egregious" (Melton et al., 1998, p. 484). Understandably, legal practitioners are skeptical about the value of psychological testimony in child custody cases.

The American Psychological Association has acknowledged the tension between psychology and the legal system by publishing guidelines for child custody evaluations in divorce proceedings (APA, 1994a). These guidelines refer to concerns about the "misuse of psychologists' influence" in custody proceedings and offer principles of practice for this increasingly complex area. The guidelines specify that the best interest of the child is paramount. They further specify that specialized training is required, including familiarity with applicable legal standards and procedures, and knowledge of laws governing divorce and custody adjudication in the local jurisdiction. The guidelines also prescribe a complete neutrality on the part of the psychologist:

> The psychologist, in a balanced, impartial manner, informs and advises the court and the prospective custodians of the child of the relevant psychological factors pertaining to the custody issue. The psychologist should be impartial regardless of whether he or she is retained by the court or by a party to the proceedings. (APA, 1994, p. 678)

This last guideline is especially important for the profession insofar as it promotes dignity in the practice of psychology. Nonetheless, impartiality is a difficult quality to maintain insofar as subtle pressures arise when a partisan attorney retains a psychologist for custody evaluation.

In response to the absence of a scientific data base, a number of experimental assessment devices have been proposed for child custody forensic procedures, including rating scales that attempt to gauge the potential for effective child rearing. One such test is the Ackerman-Schoendorf Scales for Parent Evaluation of Custody (ASPECT; Ackerman, 2005; Ackerman & Schoendorf, 1992). The ASPECT is essentially a battery of standard tests (Rorschach, MMPI-2, WAIS-R, WRAT-R for

the parents, and Draw-A-Family, CAT, and an IQ measure for the child) used alongside open-ended questionnaires, interviews, observations, and court records (where necessary) as a database from which the practitioner completes a 56-item yes-no inventory (separate inventories are completed for the father and the mother). Results from the 56 yes-no items yield three subscores and a total score, the Parental Custody Index (PCI) for each parent. All scores are reported as $T$ scores with a mean of 50 and standard deviation of 10. The PCI is intended to identify which parent is more effective—and how much more. A $T$-score difference of 10 points or more on the PCI is interpreted as suggesting that the higher-scoring parent might be a better choice for custody. In general, $T$-score differences of 10 to 15 points are considered significant, differences of 16 to 20 points are very significant, and differences of more than 20 points are marked. When both parents have PCI scores above 60, it is thought likely that either would be an effective parent. If neither parent is effective (scores of 40 or below), the PCI is intended to reflect this finding as well.

For the total PCI score, interrater reliability ranges from .92 to .96 and is considered adequate. Reliability data for the three subscales consisting of

- Observational, or the parent's appearance and presentation
- Social, or the parent's interaction with others, including the child
- Cognitive-Emotional, or the parent's psychological and mental functioning

are substantially weaker, indicating that practitioners should rely upon the PCI score only. A large standardization sample was used ($N = 200$), but these families were predominantly white (97 percent), so that the ASPECT may not be appropriate for use with minority families.

Validity of the PCI score was assessed by comparing ASPECT recommendations with judges' decisions in custody cases. In those cases in which there was a significant difference between the ASPECT scores of the mother and the father

(10 points or more), the test showed 93 percent agreement with the judges' decisions. Even so, reviewers have recommended caution in the use of the ASPECT for several reasons. One concern is the dearth of independent research in refereed journals pertinent to the validity of the instrument. Melton (1995) notes that the validation study was based upon the same families as those used to develop the instrument, which could lead to inflated hit rates. Another concern is that some scale items (e.g., whether the parent's IQ is more than five points below that of the child; which parent the child is placed next to in the child's drawing) have not been shown to indicate parental competence or child outcome in divorce studies. Heinze and Grisso (1996) conclude that the ASPECT needs more normative, reliability, and validity data before practitioners can place confidence in the assessment battery.

One problem with ASPECT is the enormity of the entire battery, which includes lengthy tests with both parents and all children, as well as interviews and analysis of abundant (excessive?) test information. Perhaps the same kind of assessment information could be obtained in a manner less time-consuming. This is the approach taken by Gordon and Peek (1989), who developed the Custody Quotient™, a sophisticated item-based rating scale that yields a nine-point rating for each of the following parenting factors:

Emotional needs of child now and in future
Physical needs of the child now and in future
No dangers to the child emotionally or physically
Good parenting
Parent assistance
Planning for the child
Home stability
Prior caring
Acts or omissions
Values

The instrument also yields an overall custody quotient, or CQ (mean of 100), designed to gauge parental competence. The authors report some em-

pirical data about their instrument, including interrater agreement studies based on evaluation of videotaped interviews. For most scales, the two authors were within two points of each other (on the nine-point rating scales) 90 to 100 percent of the time. The validity of the instrument has been assessed, in part, by confirmatory factor analysis which reveals a "general good parenting factor" as predicted. An initial validation study revealed that parents with a CQ less than 100 rarely received custody of the child (except in cases where both parents received ratings below 100). Gordon and Peek (1989) acknowledge that their instrument needs additional research. Bischoff (1992) reminds potential users that the CQ is a research instrument that should not be a major basis for custody determinations.

Another test for child custody evaluation is the Parent–Child Relationship Inventory (PCRI; Gerard, 1993). The PCRI is a 78-item self-report inventory suitable for mothers and fathers of children ages 3 to 15 years. The inventory includes seven scales:

- Parental Support
- Satisfaction
- Involvement
- Communication
- Limit Setting
- Autonomy
- Role Orientation

Norms are based on a nonclinical sample of more than 1,000 parents throughout the United States. Coffman, Guerin, and Gottfried (2006) evaluated the reliability and validity of the PCRI as part of an ambitious longitudinal study of children and their families. The 130 participant families were recruited when the enrolled children were one year of age. Parents and children were evaluated repeatedly with multiple measures, including the PCRI, for two decades. Results were appraised when the children were 15 and 16 years of age, with strong return rates (80 percent or so) for the various analyses. Internal consistency reliabilities for the scales were typically on the order of .80 or higher, with the exception of Autonomy, which revealed an Alpha of .47 for mothers and .54 for fathers. Stability coefficients were evaluated over a 1-year time period. Considering that patterns of parent–child relationships might actually evolve and undergo real change during such a long interval, the resulting coefficients indicate good temporal stability, ranging from a high of $r = .82$ for Satisfaction (mothers) to a low of $r = .58$ for Autonomy (fathers). Validity of the PCRI was evaluated in terms of subscale convergence with similar measures of parent–child relationships. The results can be summarized in terms of three trends: first, the maternal reports of parent–child relationship revealed good convergent validity, that is, there was good agreement with similar measures; second, the paternal reports of parent–child relationship showed poor convergent validity, that is, there was poor agreement with similar measures; and, third, the Autonomy scale revealed virtually no relation to any of the criterion variables in the study, that is, it was not confirmed as a valid scale, at least not with teenagers. Even though the developer of the PCRI (Gerard, 1994) has suggested it is a potentially useful tool for custody evaluations, Coffman et al. (2006) argue otherwise: ". . . its use in achieving an equitable appraisal in child custody assessments appears problematic; psychologists cannot use a scale that is valid for one parent but not the other" (p. 213). Like most instruments relevant to child custody evaluation, more research is needed to determine the value of the PCRI in child custody evaluations.

Bricklin (1995) has devised four simple tests that may prove helpful in custody evaluation. Two of the tests assess skill and investment in parenting for the mother and father separately. Specifically, the Parent Awareness Skills Survey evaluates awareness of child-rearing skills, whereas the Parent Perception of Child Profile appraises a genuine interest in the child. We focus here on just one instrument, which examines the child's perception of the parents: the Bricklin Perceptual Scales (BPS).

The Bricklin Perceptual Scales, or BPS, consists of 64 questions asked of each child (ages 4 and above) involved in a custody dispute. Thirty-two questions pertain to the child's perception of mother and 32 to perceptions of father. The questions fall into four areas designed to identify the best interests of the child: competency, supportiveness, consistency, and possession of admirable traits. Examples of the kinds of questions asked are as follows:

- *Competency:* "If you were having trouble with a school report, how much would Mom be able to help you?"
- *Supportiveness:* "When you feel really upset, how much does Dad help you calm down?"
- *Consistency:* "If you tried to sleep in on a school day, how often would Mom make you get up at your regular time?"
- *Possession of Admirable Traits:* "If you had a pet, how well would Dad take care of it when you went to camp for a week?"

The 32 Mom questions and 32 Dad questions are identical; they are widely separated in the questionnaire so as to avoid immediate and obvious comparisons. The questions are asked verbally first and then repeated with a slightly different phrasing. For example, the examiner holds a test card up to the child: "If this [point to end of line marked 'Very Well'] is Dad doing very well at helping you to calm down, and this is [pointing to end marked 'Not So Well'] is Dad doing not so well at helping you to calm down, where on this line would Dad be?" The child responds by using a stylus to punch a hole in the card. Each card contains a scoring grid on the opposite side for immediate and objective scoring.

BPS scoring consists of an item-by-item comparison of Mom and Dad ratings. A parent-of-choice (POC) is identified in terms of which parent, the mother or father, obtains the higher score on the most items: "It is assumed that this parent is the parent better able to operate in the child's 'best interests' in the widest variety of situations as measured by the BPS" (Bricklin, 1995,

p. 77). Of course, this result is just one point of information used by the examiner in arriving at a custody recommendation.

The BPS embodies a number of positive qualities in comparison to other approaches to custody evaluation. First, the test avoids asking the child to make a direct choice between the parents, which minimizes guilt. It also assesses important areas of caretaking presumed to be important for healthy child development. Furthermore, by focusing on the *child's* perceptions of parenting as opposed to the examiner's perceptions of parenting, the instrument provides a voice for those with the greatest stake in a custody decision. Bricklin (1995) notes that the BPS is not necessarily intended to be a direct measure of parental competency but instead is designed to identify the caretaker whose style is congruent with the child's ability to take in and profit from parental guidance.

Although evidence regarding the reliability of the BPS is not available in Bricklin (1995), initial validity findings are supportive. Specifically, the BPS yielded a 90 percent agreement rate with the caretaker choices of mental health professionals who had access to independent clinical and family history data collected over a period of several years. On a cautionary note, as is true of so many instruments in the field of custody evaluation, there are few (if any) empirical studies of the BPS published in refereed journals. Heinze and Grisso (1996) offer the following critique:

> A related issue is that the Bricklin Scales attempt to address the legal questions of preferred custody without direct assessment of parents' functional abilities and deficits, including how these interact with children's needs. In addition, the scales address the issue of two parents with significant deficits only in a very superficial way. Thus, because the child's perceptions of the two parents are compared only to each other and not those of other parents, the clinician may not glean much information regarding a specific parent's level of parental functioning as perceived by the child. (p. 301)

Clearly, more research from independent sources would be desirable.

In closing this section on **custody evaluation,** we remind the reader that expert testimony in child custody evaluations needs to be tempered with a large dose of humility on the part of the psychological examiner. Determining the best interests of the child is almost always a difficult and thorny assignment. The absence of well-validated tests and methods for this task assures that custody evaluation will remain one of the most challenging responsibilities in all of psychological practice.

## ● PERSONAL INJURY AND RELATED TESTIMONY

Personal injury as from an automobile accident is often a source of litigation for monetary compensation. In **personal injury** lawsuits, attorneys may hire psychologists to testify as to the lifelong consequences of traumatic stress or acquired brain damage. For example, a clinical neuropsychologist might administer a comprehensive test battery (see Chapter 10, Neuropsychological Assessment and Screening) and then testify as to the long-term functional implications of known brain damage.

In general, a consulting psychologist who testifies in court will encounter extremely high practice standards. We have already mentioned the *Frye* standard, which provides that testimony must be based upon tests and procedures that have "gained general acceptance" in the field. Thus, a test or procedure that is relevant or useful in everyday clinical practice—but which is not widely accepted in the field—might be greeted with skepticism in the courts. A judge may even rule that testimony is inadmissible if it is based on tests or procedures with flimsy validation. Worse yet, the judge may allow such testimony, which opens the expert witness to criticism and ridicule by opposing attorneys. With these concerns in mind, Heilbrun (1992) has published guidelines for the practice of forensic assessment, which we summarize here:

- Tests should be commercially available and well documented, such as in *Mental Measurements Yearbook.*

- Reliability should be well documented and .8 or higher, except in unusual circumstances.
- Tests should be relevant to the legal issue or to a psychological construct underlying the legal issue.
- Standard administration should be used with ideal testing conditions.
- Tests should have been validated in a population that is relevant to the individual being assessed.
- Where possible, practitioners should use objective tests with actuarial formulas for interpretation.
- Practitioners should check carefully for malingering, defensiveness, and other reasons to discount or ignore the test data.

Additional guidelines can be found in the "Specialty Guidelines for Forensic Psychologists" (Committee on Ethical Guidelines for Forensic Psychologists, 1991).

Increasingly, courts have been willing to compensate mental injuries in addition to physical injuries. The damage is variously referred to as "psychic trauma" or "emotional distress" or "emotional harm." The evaluation of emotional injury will rely somewhat on psychological test results (especially personality tests), but the assessment requires great clinical skill including "a longitudinal history of the impairment, its treatment, and attempts at rehabilitation, including the claimant's motivation to recover" (Melton et al., 1998, p. 381). We see once again that the question of malingering haunts most forms of forensic assessment.

## ● SPECIALIZED PERSONALITY ASSESSMENT IN FORENSIC SETTINGS

On occasion, psychologists are asked to provide specialized forms of personality assessment in forensic settings. For example, a prison psychologist might evaluate an inmate for antisocial tendencies, or a forensic psychologist might assess a treated pedophile for sexual interest in young children. The

range of tools and techniques useful for specialized assessment is broad. Here we will highlight a few intriguing instruments and procedures to illustrate these applications of forensic assessment.

In prison settings, examiners have a special interest in determining whether inmates possess the traits of psychopathic personality. Similar to antisocial personality as described in *DSM-IV* (APA, 2000), the concept of psychopathic personality has a long and rich history that dates back to Emil Kraepelin (1856–1926), the father of diagnostic psychiatry. But it was the psychiatrist Cleckley (1941) who first provided a detailed description of the psychopath in his pathbreaking book, *The Mask of Sanity*. Based upon extensive clinical work with individuals whom he labeled psychopaths, Cleckley identified 16 signs that we list here:

1. Superficial charm and good "intelligence"
2. Absence of delusions and other signs of irrational thinking
3. Absence of "nervousness" or psychoneurotic manifestations
4. Unreliability
5. Untruthfulness and insincerity
6. Lack of remorse or shame
7. Inadequately motivated antisocial behavior
8. Poor judgment and failure to learn by experience
9. Pathologic egocentricity and incapacity for love
10. General poverty in major affective reactions
11. Specific loss of insight
12. Unresponsiveness to general interpersonal relations
13. Fantastic and uninviting behavior with drink and sometimes without
14. Suicide rarely carried out
15. Sex life impersonal, trivial, and poorly integrated
16. Failure to follow any life plan

Although his description is antiquated in places, contemporary researchers continue to find descriptive and predictive value in Cleckley's conception of the psychopath. In fact, one researcher has developed a highly respected and widely used assessment tool based closely on this original formulation of psychopathic personality.

The Psychopathy Checklist-Revised (PCL-R; Hare, 2003; Hare & Neumann, 2006) consists of a 20-item rating scale carefully designed to assess the qualities of psychopathic personality in a quantitative and empirical fashion. Prior to filling out the rating scale, the examiner conducts a lengthy semistructured interview (90 to 120 minutes) with the client. The interview concerns the Cleckley-based traits of psychopathy, as slightly revised and expanded by Hare and colleagues (Hare, Harpur, Hakstian, and others, 1990). Each item reflects a particular symptom, such as glibness and superficial charm, grandiose sense of self-worth, pathological lying, lack of remorse or guilt, or failure to accept responsibility. Items are rated on a 3-point scale (0 = doesn't apply, 1 = applies somewhat, 2 = definitely applies). The rating is based on lifetime functioning rather than the present state, which explains why a long interview is essential for correct use of the scale. The item scores are then summed to yield a total score (range of 0 to 40) that reflects the extent to which the individual resembles the prototypical psychopath. Two factor scores also can be derived, each based on eight or nine items. Factor 1 reflects the selfish, callous, and remorseless use of others, whereas factor 2 indicates a chronically unstable and antisocial lifestyle.

A substantial body of research indicates that the PCL-R possesses strong reliability and validity. For example, interrater reliability is typically in the .90s, test-retest coefficients approach .90, and internal consistency coefficients are in the mid- to high .80s (Schroeder, Schroeder, & Hare, 1983). The predictive validity of the instrument is bolstered by the capacity of PCL-R scores to predict a variety of antisocial behaviors, including violent recidivism following prison release, poor response to correctional treatment programs, and disorderly behavior while in prison (Hare, 1996; Sreenivasan, Walker, Weinberger, Kirkish, & Garrick, 2008). For example, in one study inmates with high PCL-R scores were twice as likely to engage in fights and more than three times as likely to be belligerent than other inmates (Hare & McPherson, 1984). In another study of a therapeutic community treatment program for adult male offenders, psychopaths showed less clinical improvement, demonstrated lower levels of motivation, and were discharged from the program earlier than nonpsychopaths. The differences were not small: The psychopathic lawbreakers stayed in the treatment program less than *half* as long as the other offenders (Ogloff, Wong, & Greenwood, 1990). Clearly, psychopathic personality is a useful concept, and the PCL-R is a practical measure of the construct.

One recent study does raise concerns about examiner differences in the scoring of the PCL-R in field settings (Boccaccini, Turner, and Murrie, 2008). Although the manual for the instrument does provide specific guidelines for each item, judgment is needed to differentiate scores of 0, 1, or 2. It is possible for examiners to differ in their scoring tendencies for a variety of reasons, including the evaluators' readiness to seek outside information, diligence in following the required protocol, response bias in using higher or lower ends of the scales, and drift over time in observance of scoring rules. Even the characteristics of the examiner (e.g., warm versus cold demeanor) can cause item scores to shift up or down.

Boccaccini et al. (2008) examined the PCL-R total scores for 20 different Texas state-contracted evaluators who were hired to screen 321 referrals for civil commitment as sexually violent predators. The evaluators encountered their referrals in a more or less quasi-random manner, so it is reasonable to expect that the average PCL-R scores across examiners should be reasonably similar. This proved not to be the case in dramatic fashion. Restricting the comparison to examiners completing at least 20 evaluations (to provide constancy of results), the researchers found sizable disparities in average PCL-R scores: the means varied from a low of 17.5 (SD of 8.8) to a high of 27.1 (SD of 6.1). These are large inequities on the PCL-R which has a maximum possible score of 40. In this study, examiner differences account for a large degree of variability in the PCL-R total scores. There may be a need to improve the field reliability of assessments for this forensic instrument. Perhaps some form of training program is needed to certify individuals in its use.

Another arena for forensic assessment is the evaluation of male adults for sexual interest in children. Although there are many situations in which this kind of assessment could be relevant, a familiar circumstance is when a convicted pedophile is evaluated to determine if treatment has reduced his sexual interest in children. Of course, self-report is not likely to be considered trustworthy by authorities. Instead, forensic examiners typically use other methods such as polygraphy, gaze tracking, ratings of stimulus cards, viewing time for different slides, or erectile measures.

The penile plethysmograph is a respected (but controversial) approach to the evaluation of male sexual interest. In this technique, a slim, flexible band is placed around the examinee's penis while he views, in slow succession, dozens of slide pictures of nearly nude individuals. For many slides, only one person is depicted—male or female, young or old. In other slides, two people are shown—sometimes in an erotic pose, sometimes not. In another variation, the examinee listens with headphones to stories that graphically depict sex between a man and a woman or between a man and a child. Of course, during the entire procedure a machine is recording the extent of erectile response to each stimulus— whether a slide picture or a story segment. The device is called a plethysmograph and the procedure is called **phallometry;** the resulting data are referred to as phallometric measurements.

Beyond a doubt, phallometry raises questions about propriety, individual rights, and self-incrimination. These are important questions, but we cannot address them here. Instead, our focus is on the scientific status of the procedure: What is its reliability and validity? Regarding reliability, when appropriate methods are used, erectile measures demonstrate acceptable reliability— both test-retest and internal consistency. For example, Harris, Rice, Quinsey, Chaplin, and Earls (1992) demonstrated a split-half reliability coefficient of .84 for one set of phallometric data in their study of sex offenders.

Regarding validity, phallometry is known to discriminate relevant groups and to predict theoretically relevant behavior. For example, child molesters consistently exhibit much larger phallometric responses to pictures of children than do normal men (Quinsey & Lalumiere, 1996). Phallometric indices also mildly predict future recidivism of child molesters (Harris & Rice, 1996). However, the procedure demonstrates higher specificity than sensitivity. This means that phallometry is better at detecting that a normal person is normal (i.e., does not have sexual interest in children) than it is at detecting that a deviant person is deviant (i.e., does have a sexual interest in children). Some experts recommend cautious application:

> Most clinical referrals for phallometric assessment are made before trial. Although phallometry can provide information about possible motives for sexual offenses, it cannot prove whether a man committed a particular alleged offense. Existing data most strongly support the clinical use of phallometry to identify problems that could be addressed in treatment, and to help evaluate the dangerousness of sex offenders. (Harris & Rice, 1996, p. 159)

Phallometry probably never will have widespread acceptance, but its careful use can be warranted for selected purposes. Some related techniques are discussed by Abel, Hoffman, Warberg, and Holland (1998) and Williams (2003).

## ● SUMMARY

1. The practice of psychology intersects with the legal system in several ways, including evaluation for malingering, assessment of mental state (for the insanity plea), assessment of competency to stand trial, prediction of violence, and child custody evaluation.

2. Forensic assessment differs from traditional assessment in a number of ways including a narrower scope, a more limited client role, an audience of legal personnel instead of fellow clinicians, the higher probability of faking by the client, and the need to write reports with extreme precision and care.

3. To qualify as an expert witness, a psychologist must be a qualified expert in the opinion of the court. In general, testimony is restricted to techniques that have been available for a fairly long time in order to have a history of general acceptance (*Frye v. United States*, 1923).

4. In forensic assessments, the practitioner should have a high suspicion of malingering but should reach this conclusion cautiously because of the consequences to the client. Tools such as the Structured Interview of Reported Symptoms can help in the assessment of malingering.

5. The insanity defense is widely respected by jurisprudence experts and is invoked in fewer than 1 in 1,000 trials. Currently, most states follow the M'Naughten rule or the Model Penal Code as legal tests for insanity. Some jurisdictions allow "irresistible impulse" as a supplement.

6. According to the M'Naughten rule, a person can be found not guilty by reason of insanity if "at the time of the committing of the act, the party accused was laboring under such a defect of reason, from disease of the mind, as not to know the nature and quality of the act he was doing; or, if he did know it, that he did not know he was doing what was wrong."

7. The Model Penal Code proposes that a "person is not responsible for criminal conduct if at the time of such conduct, as a result of mental disease or defect, he lacks substantial capacity either to appreciate the criminality (wrongfulness) of his conduct or to conform his conduct to the requirements of the law."

8. A recent addition to legal jurisprudence is the Guilty But Mentally Ill verdict. Use of this verdict has several liabilities, including confusion by jurors and harsher sentences than being found merely guilty.

9. Rating scales such as the Rogers Criminal Responsibility Scales provide a helpful basis for evaluating the mental state of the defendant at the time of the offense (MSO). However, reviewers suggest caution in the application of this and similar scales because they might lead to a false sense of scientific certainty about matters that are inherently intuitive and judgmental.

10. Courts often ask psychologists to help determine whether a defendant is competent to stand trial. Competency generally implies that the defendant is capable of understanding the charges against him or her, can cooperate with the defense attorney, and can make a reasonable self-presentation during the trial.

11. The prediction of violence and assessment of risk is another court-based task that is occasionally asked of psychologists. Unfortunately, no psychometric test or procedure has been developed that provides an accurate long-range prediction of violence. In contrast, the short-range prediction of violence or risk has met with greater success.

12. Additional areas of sensitive assessment include child custody disputes, in which psychological test results rarely are helpful; and personal injury cases, in which psychological tests can play a crucial role in documenting the effects of injury.

13. Several assessment devices and scales have been proposed to provide an objective means for making child custody recommendations. While providing useful information, these tools may promise more than they deliver from the standpoint of psychometric validity.

14. A polygraph detects physiological responses such as electrodermal changes to interrogation questions and displays them as ink lines on paper. Research supports the use of the polygraph in the investigatory stages of a criminal case but error rates are still much too high for its use in the courtroom.

15. Assessment experts have developed a number of specialized tools for personality assessment in forensic settings. One widely respected

instrument is the Psychopathy Checklist-Revised, a 20-item rating scale designed to identify individ-uals who portray the psychopathic personality identified by Cleckley decades ago.

## KEY TERMS AND CONCEPTS

expert witness   p. 506

malingering   p. 509

mental state at the time of the offense (MSO)   p. 512

not guilty by reason of insanity (NGRI)   p. 512

M'Naughten rule   p. 513

Durham rule   p. 513

Model Penal Code   p. 513

Guilty But Mentally Ill (GBMI)   p. 513

competency to stand trial   p. 515

custody evaluation   p. 524

personal injury   p. 524

phallometry   p. 527

# Chapter

## 12

# Legal Issues and the Future of Testing

## TOPIC 12A

## Psychological Testing and the Law

n the previous chapters we have outlined the myriad of ways in which tests are used in decision making. Furthermore, we have established that psychological testing is not only pervasive, but it is also consequential. Test results matter. Test findings may warrant a passage to privilege. Conversely, test findings may sanction the denial of opportunity. For many reasons, then, it is appropriate to close the book with two special topics that bear upon the potential repercussions of psychological testing. In Topic 12A, Psychological Testing and the Law, we review critical legal issues pertaining to the use of psychological tests. In this topic, we survey the essential laws that regulate the use of tests in a variety of settings—schools, employment situations, medical settings, to name just

a few arenas in which the law constrains psychological testing. In Topic 12B, Computerized Assessment and the Future of Testing, contemporary applications of the computer in psychological assessment are surveyed, and then the professional and social issues raised by this practice are discussed. The book closes with thoughts on the future of testing—which will be forged in large measure by increasingly sophisticated applications of computer technology but also greatly affected by legal standards.

## ● THE SOURCES AND NATURE OF LAW

The law establishes a number of guidelines that define the permissible scope and applications of psychological testing. However, before investigating the key legal guidelines that impact testing, it will be helpful to understand the sources and nature of law. Broadly speaking, there are three sources of law: constitutional provisions, legislative edicts, and judicial opinions. We examine each briefly.

## Constitutional Sources of Law

The United States has a constitutional form of government, meaning that the U.S. Constitution is the final authority for all legal matters in the country. All other forms of law must be consistent with this seminal document. Thus, the Constitution places limits on legislative actions and judicial activity. The United States is also a federation of states, which means that each state retains its own government and system of laws, while ceding some powers to the central government. For example, the power to regulate interstate commerce and the responsibility to provide for the national defense both reside with the federal government. Each state has its own constitution as well, which is another source of laws that affects citizens living in a state. Of course, state constitutions cannot contradict the U.S. Constitution and, in most cases, they are highly similar to the federal document.

Three provisions of the U.S. Constitution potentially bear upon the practice of psychological testing: the Fifth, Sixth, and Fourteenth Amendments to the Constitution (Melton et al., 1998). The Fifth Amendment provides a privilege against self-incrimination, which impacts the nature of psychological assessment in forensic evaluations. For example, as discussed previously, a forensic practitioner might be asked by the court to evaluate an alleged offender for competency to stand trial. In many states, self-incriminating disclosures made during an evaluation of competency to stand trial cannot be used to determine guilt (i.e., they are inadmissible as evidence during trial).

The Sixth Amendment states that every person accused of a crime has the right to counsel (i.e., the right to a lawyer). This is understood to mean both the presence of counsel during legal proceedings and also the right to effective assistance from counsel. Does this mean that counsel must be present during a pretrial assessment, such as a court-ordered evaluation for competency to stand trial? This will depend upon the state and jurisdiction in which the proceedings occur. Although most courts have held that the defendant does not have a right to the presence of counsel during pretrial psychological evaluations, a minority of courts have held that the Sixth Amendment guarantee does apply to such pretrial assessments (Melton et al., 1998). In these jurisdictions, the defendant's lawyer can be present during any psychological testing or evaluation. This raises difficult questions as to the validity of assessments undertaken in the presence of a third party. For example, what if the client asks his or her lawyer for advice on how to answer certain questions? Surely, this is not standard protocol in psychological assessment and might drastically affect the validity of the results. Fortunately, most courts favor alternative methods for protecting the rights of defendants during pretrial evaluations, such as tape-recording the session, having a defense psychologist observe the evaluation, or providing for an independent evaluation.

The Fourteenth Amendment provides that no state shall deprive any U.S. citizen of life, liberty, or property without "due process of law." The amendment also specifies "equal protection of the laws." The relevant section reads:

> No State shall make or enforce any law which shall abridge the privileges or immunities of citizens of the United States; nor shall any State deprive any person of life, liberty, or property, without due process of law; nor deny to any person within its jurisdiction the equal protection of the laws.

It is mainly the "due process" feature of this amendment that has impacted psychological practice. This influence is limited largely to forensic practitioners who deal with competency to stand trial, civil and criminal commitment, or the right to refuse treatment. For example, psychologists who are involved in the civil commitment of an individual who needs treatment typically must show—as a direct consequence of the due process clause of the Fourteenth Amendment—that several stringent criteria are fulfilled:

- The individual must be reliably diagnosed as suffering from severe mental illness;
- In the absence of treatment, the prognosis for the individual is major distress;
- The individual is incompetent; that is, the illness substantially impairs the person's ability to understand or communicate about the possibility of treatment;
- Treatment is available;
- The risk–benefit ratio of treatment is such that a reasonable person would consent to it. (Melton et al., 1998, p. 310)

Whether these conditions are met would be determined at a commitment hearing during which the individual would have full procedural rights such as the presence of counsel. The psychologist's role would be to offer professional opinions on these guidelines. Of course, the validity of psychological assessment is relevant to these criteria in several ways, including the following: understanding the reliability of psychiatric diagnosis (see Topic 9B, Behavioral and Observational Assessment), choosing appropriate tests for competency (see Topic 11B, Forensic Applications of Assessment), and comprehending risk–benefit analysis (see Topic 4A, Basic Concepts of Validity).

## Legislative Sources of Law

In addition to constitutional sources, laws also emanate from the actions of state and federal legislative bodies. These laws are called statutes and are codified by subject areas into codes. For example, the laws passed by Congress at the federal level are codified into 50 topics identified as Title 1 through Title 50 with each area devoted to a specific theme. Three examples include Title 18, Crimes and Criminal Procedure; Title 20, Education; and Title 29, Labor. Each titled area is further subdivided. For example, Title 20, Education, is gargantuan. It consists of 77 chapters, a few of them *hundreds* of pages in length. This includes Chapter 70, Strengthening and

Improvement of Elementary and Secondary Schools, in which literally hundreds of specific statutes passed over the last few decades have been collated and cross-referenced. For example, one federal statute mandates that school systems must show adequate yearly progress in order to be eligible for further federal funding. The law further stipulates that "adequate yearly progress" shall be defined by the State in a manner that

(i)  applies the same high standards of academic achievement to all public elementary school and secondary school students in the State;

(ii)  is statistically valid and reliable;

(iii)  results in continuous and substantial academic improvement for all students;

(iv)  measures the progress of public elementary schools, secondary schools and local educational agencies and the State based primarily on the academic assessments described in paragraph (3);

(v)  includes separate measurable annual objectives for continuous and substantial improvement for each of the following:

(I)  The achievement of all public elementary school and secondary school students.

(II)  The achievement of
  (aa) economically disadvantaged students;
  (bb) students from major racial and ethnic groups;
  (cc) students with disabilities; and
  (dd) students with limited English proficiency;

except that disaggregation of data under subclause (II) shall not be required in a case in which the number of students in a category is insufficient to yield statistically reliable information or the results would reveal personally identifiable information about an individual student. (U.S. Code, Title 20, Chapter 70, http://uscode.house.gov)

As can be seen, legal codes are written with such specificity that their intention cannot easily be overlooked or bypassed. The preceding sample is just one small snippet of law—barely discernible in a vast ocean of literally hundreds of pages of edicts that impact educational practices. But it is clear that these legislative rulings influence psychological testing. For example, in the preceding excerpt, an inescapable inference is that school systems must use standardized educational achievement tests with established reliability and validity—or else they risk losing federal funds.

Legislatures cannot possibly oversee the implementation of all the statutes they enact. Consequently, it is increasingly common for these bodies to delegate rule-making authority to agencies within the executive branch of government. For example, the U.S. Congress has passed several laws designed to prohibit discrimination in employment. But the enforcement of these laws is left to the Equal Employment Opportunity Commission (EEOC). The following federal laws bear, at least in part, on job discrimination:

- *Civil Rights Act of 1964,* which prohibits employment discrimination based on race, color, religion, gender, or national origin
- *Equal Pay Act of 1963,* which protects women (and men) who perform equal work in the same organization from gender-based wage discrimination
- *Age Discrimination in Employment Act of 1967,* which protects individuals who are 40 years of age or older
- *Americans with Disabilities Act of 1990,* which prohibits employment discrimination against qualified individuals with disabilities in both government and the private sector
- *Rehabilitation Act of 1973,* which prohibits discrimination against qualified individuals with disabilities who work in the federal government
- *Civil Rights Act of 1991,* which authorizes monetary damages in cases of intentional employment discrimination

The EEOC is the federal agency in charge of the administrative and judicial enforcement of the civil rights laws listed earlier. We discuss this important regulatory body in further detail later.

## Judicial Sources of Law

Another source of law is the judiciary, specifically, the federal courts and the United States Supreme Court. Indirectly, these bodies make law in several ways. First, they have the authority to review all federal legislative edicts to determine their constitutionality and interpretation. In addition, they can appraise the constitutional validity of any state law, whether constitutional, statutory, or regulatory in origin. In doing so, they have the opportunity to sharpen the focus of laws promulgated by these other sources. For example, in ruling on the constitutionality of state civil commitment laws, federal courts not only have found them unconstitutional, but they have also used this opportunity to publish permissible criteria and procedures for commitment (as discussed previously in relation to the Fourteenth Amendment). The courts also hear lawsuits filed on behalf of individuals or groups. In these cases, court rulings can establish new law. Finally, the courts can make law when the original sources such as constitutional laws or legislative statutes are silent on an important issue:

> In performing their interpretive function, courts will first look at the plain words of any relevant constitutional provision, statute, or regulation and then review the legislative history of a given law, including statements made by the law's sponsors or during committee or public hearing sessions. But if neither of these sources is helpful, or if no relevant law exists, the courts themselves must devise principles to govern the case before them. The principles articulated by courts when they create law are collectively known as common law, or judge-made law. (Melton et al., 1998, p. 29)

Typically, common law is conservative, based to the extent possible on the precedent of past cases, rather than created at the whim of the judiciary.

In sum, there are several sources of law: state and federal constitutions, legislative statutes, regulations enacted by agencies such as the EEOC, and judicial interpretations from federal courts and the Supreme Court. These are the primary sources of law that might intersect with the practice of psychological testing. Other sources of law include presidential executive orders and international law, which we do not discuss here because they rarely impact psychological practice.

Now that the reader has an understanding of how, why, and where laws originate, we turn to a review of particular laws that impact the practice of psychological assessment. We partition the discussion into three topics: legal influences on psychological testing in school systems, disability assessment and the law, and legal issues in employment testing. The division is somewhat artificial; for example, the assessment of learning disability—greatly impacted by law—involves both the practice of testing in school systems and the assessment of disability.

## ● TESTING IN SCHOOL SYSTEMS AND THE LAW

The law has impacted school-based testing in two broad ways: (1) Federal legislation has mandated specific practices in the assessment of students, especially those with disabilities; and (2) lawsuits have shaped and reshaped particular testing practices in school systems over the last 60 years. We will discuss legislative influences in the next section on disability assessment and the law. Our goal here is to provide an overview of influential lawsuits that have molded testing practices in the schools. In the main, these lawsuits have assailed the use of tests, especially in special education placement and as a requirement for high school graduation.

Attacks on cognitive testing in school systems have been with us for a long time. Beginning in the 1960s, these attacks took a new form: lawsuits filed by minority plaintiffs seeking to curtail or ban the use of school-based cognitive tests, especially intelligence tests. In this section we will review the major court cases, summarized in Table 12.1. Later, we will discuss the implications of court decisions for the contemporary use of cognitive tests in schools.

Many of the legal assaults on testing have arisen from the controversial practice of using cognitive test results for purposes of assigning low-functioning students to "vocational" school tracks or to special classes for educable mentally retarded (EMR) persons. Invariably, minority children are assigned to these special tracks and classes in surprising disproportion to their representation in the school population. For example, a typical

● **TABLE 12.1  Major Legal Landmarks in School-Based Cognitive Testing**

1967 *Hobson v. Hansen*

Court ruled against the use of group ability tests to "track" students on the grounds that such tests discriminated against minority children.

1970 *Diana v. State Board*

Court ruled against traditional testing procedures for educable mentally retarded (EMR) placement of Mexican American children; State Board of Education enacted special provisions for testing minority children (e.g., bilingual assessment).

1979 *Debra P. v. Turlington*

Court did not rule against the use of a minimum competency test as a condition for high school graduation—a test with excessive failure rate for African American students—but did suspend its use for four years, as a means of providing due process about notification of the new requirement.

1979 *Larry P. v. Riles*

Court ruled that standardized IQ tests are culturally biased against African American children for EMR evaluation and stipulated that the proportion of African American children in these classes must match their proportion in the school population.

1980 *PASE v. Hannon*

In complete contradiction to the *Larry P. v. Riles* decision, the court ruled that standardized IQ tests are not racially or culturally biased.

1984 *Georgia NAACP v. Georgia*

Court ruled that traditional procedures of evaluation do not discriminate against African American children; court also rejected the view that disproportionate representation in EMR classes constituted proof of discrimination.

1994 *Crawford v. Honig*

The judge in the *Larry P. v. Riles* case overruled his earlier ruling so as to allow the use of a standardized IQ test for the evaluation of African American students diagnosed with learning disability.

2000 *GI Forum v. Texas Education Agency*

Court ruled that the use of the Texas Assessment of Academic Skills as part of a high school graduation requirement was permissible despite high failure rates of African American and Latino students.

finding is that minority children are two to three times more likely to be classified as EMR than white children (Agbenyega & Jiggetts, 1999). In a school system comprised of 25 percent minority students, this could translate to EMR classes with about 50 percent minority student representation.

Therein lies the crux of the legal grievance, for special education classes are equated by many with inferior education. Written two decades ago, these observations still hold true:

> If special education actually worked, which it does not, and minority children assigned to EMR classes in the primary grades eventually reached the same level of reading and math achievements as children in regular classrooms, I doubt whether the plaintiffs in these cases would have brought suit. A major problem in the educational system is that special education, even with smaller classes and better trained teachers, still does not work to bring such children up to par. Rather, special education classes perpetuate educational disadvantage. (Scarr, 1987)

Something is amiss in education when well-intentioned placement policies inadvertently perpetuate a legacy of mistreatment of minorities. The legal challenges to school-based testing are certainly understandable, even though sometimes misplaced. After all, the problem is not so much with the tests—which assess academically relevant skills with reasonable validity—but with educational policies that isolate low-functioning students to inefficient placements. Even experts sympathetic to the lawsuits acknowledge that tests often are quite useful, so it is worth examining why killing the messenger has been a popular response to concerns about discriminatory placements.

### Hobson v. Hansen (1967)

The first major court case to challenge the validity of ability tests was *Hobson v. Hansen* (1967). In that landmark case, plaintiffs argued that the allocation of financial and educational resources in the Washington, DC, public school system favored white children and, therefore, discriminated against minority children. Among the issues addressed in the trial was the use of standardized group ability tests such as the Metropolitan Readiness and

Achievement Test and the Otis Quick-Scoring Mental Ability Test to "track" students according to ability. Children were placed in honors, regular, or basic tracks according to ability level on the tests. One consequence of this tracking method was that minority children were disproportionately represented in the lowest track, which focused on skills and preparation for blue-collar jobs. Placement in this track virtually ruled out entrance to college and entry to a well-paying profession.

Judge Skelly Wright decided the *Hobson* case in 1967, ruling against the use of a tracking system based on group ability tests. Most commentators view his banishment of ability testing for tracking purposes as justified. However, there is good reason to worry about the further implications of Judge Wright's decision, which implied that acceptable tests must measure children's innate capacity to learn. Bersoff (1984) commented on the *Hobson* decision as follows:

> *Hobson*, when read in its entirety, represents the justified condemnation of rigid, poorly conceived classification practices that negatively affected the educational opportunities of minority children and led to permanent stigmatization of blacks as un-teachable. But swept within *Hobson*'s condemnation of harmful classification practices were ability tests used as the sole or primary decision-making devices to justify placement. Not only was ability grouping as then practiced in the District of Columbia abolished, but tests were banned unless they could be shown to measure children's innate capacity to learn.

Not even ardent hereditarians believe that tests solely measure innate ability. No test could ever pass the criterion mandated by this case.

The *Hobson* case concerned group ability tests and had no direct bearing on the use of individual intelligence tests in school systems. However, it did portend an increasing skepticism about the use of any test—whether group or individual—for purposes of educational placement.

### Diana v. State Board of Education (1970)

In *Diana v. State Board of Education* (1970), plaintiffs questioned the use of individual intelligence tests (the WISC and Stanford-Binet) for purposes of placing Mexican American schoolchildren in classes for educable mentally retarded (EMR) persons. *Diana* was a class action suit filed on behalf of nine Mexican American elementary school children who had been placed in EMR classes. The placements were based on individual IQ tests administered by a non-Spanish-speaking psychometrist. When retested in English and Spanish, eight of these nine children showed substantial—sometimes huge—increases in IQ and were, therefore, removed from EMR classes. Faced with this evidence, the California State Board of Education decided to enact a series of special provisions for the testing of Mexican American and Chinese American children. These provisions included the testing of minority children in their primary language, elimination of certain vocabulary and information items that minority children could not be expected to know, retesting of minority children previously placed in EMR classes, and development of new tests normed on Mexican American children. These provisions answered the concerns of plaintiffs, eliminating the need for further court action.

### *Debra P. v. Turlington* (1979)

This was a class action lawsuit filed on behalf of all African American students in Florida against Ralph Turlington, the state Commissioner of Education. At issue was the use of the State Student Assessment Test-Part 2 (SSAT-II), a functional literacy test, as one requirement for awarding a high school diploma. In the 1970s, Florida was one of the states at the forefront of the functional literacy movement. Functional literacy has to do with practical knowledge and skills used in everyday life. A **test of functional literacy** might require students to:

- Calculate the balance of a personal checking account when given the starting balance, deposits, withdrawals, and service charges
- Follow simple written directions and instructions in printed materials
- Complete an application form for employment, driver's license, or training program

- Spell basic and useful words correctly (e.g., address, employer, postage, salary, vehicle)
- Comprehend essential abbreviations (e.g., apt., CPU, hwy., M.D., Mr., Rx, SSN)
- Know the meanings of vital words (e.g., antidote, bus stop, caution, exit only, one way, zip code)
- Write a paragraph that is reasonably grammatical and coherent

Currently, about 20 states use a functional literacy test of this genre as one condition of awarding the high school diploma.

However, in Florida in the late 1970s, African American students failed the functional literacy test at a substantially higher rate than white students. Plaintiffs argued the SSAT-II was unfair because African American students received inferior education in substantially segregated schools. The purpose of the lawsuit was to void the use of the test as a requirement for graduation. The information in the following discussion was retrieved from the appeals court decision (*Debra P. v. Turlington*, U.S. Court of Appeals for the Eleventh Circuit, April 27, 1984).

With practical finesse, the court decision offered something to both sides, although state officials likely were happier with the outcome than were the plaintiffs. The nature of the ruling also revealed admirable sensitivity to issues of test validity and psychological measurement on the part of the court. Based on the reasonable belief that a high school diploma should signify functional literacy, the state was permitted to use the test as a diploma requirement. However, the court delayed implementation of the new diploma testing program for four years. This delay served two purposes. First, it provided due process to current students (and their parents), alerting them that a new requirement was being set in place. Second, it gave the state time to prove that the SSAT-II was a fair test of that which is taught in Florida's classrooms. The court wanted proof of what it called "instructional validity." Put simply, the court wanted assurance that the state was teaching what it was testing.

The state undertook a massive evaluation project to prove **instructional validity**. The Florida

Department of Education hired a consulting firm to conduct a four-part study that included (1) teacher surveys asking expressly if the skills tested by the SSAT-II were taught; (2) administrator surveys to demonstrate that school districts utilized remedial programs when appropriate; (3) site visits to verify all aspects of the study; and (4) student surveys to discern if students perceived they were being taught the skills required on the functional literacy test.

Weighing all the evidence carefully over a period of several years, the court ruled that the State of Florida could deny diplomas to students who had not yet passed the SSAT-II, beginning with the class of 1983. Furthermore, the court concluded that the use of the SSAT-II actually helped to mitigate the impact of vestiges of school segregation by motivating students, teachers, and administrators toward a common goal:

> The remarkable improvement in the SSAT-II pass rate among black students over the last six years demonstrates that use of the SSAT-II as a diploma sanction will be effective in overcoming the effects of past segregation. Appellants argue that the improvement has nothing to do with diploma sanctions because the test has not yet been used to deny diplomas. However, we think it likely that the threat of diploma sanction that existed throughout the course of this litigation contributed to the improved pass rate, and that actual use of the test as a diploma sanction will be equally, if not more, effective helping black students overcome discriminatory vestiges and pass the SSAT-II. Thus, we affirm the finding that use of the SSAT-II as a diploma sanction will help remedy vestiges of past discrimination. (U.S. Court of Appeals for the Eleventh Circuit, April 27, 1984)

In sum, the case of *Debra P. v. Turlington* appears to confirm that functional literacy testing can play a constructive role in secondary education.

### Larry P. v. Riles (1979)

The case of *Larry P. v. Riles* raised concerns about the use of intelligence tests for assigning African American children to EMR special education classes. In November 1971 attorneys representing

several San Francisco families filed for a preliminary injunction seeking to prohibit the use of traditional IQ tests for EMR placement of African American children. The specific grievance was that six African American children in the San Francisco school district had been inappropriately placed into "dead-end" EMR classes based on scores from IQ tests said to be racially and culturally biased against African Americans. As a consequence of this placement it was alleged that the children had suffered irreparable harm. The plaintiffs sought a ban on the use of "culturally biased" IQ tests, asked for reevaluation of all African American EMR children, requested special assistance for those who returned to the regular classroom, and sought a quota limiting assignment of African American children to EMR classes. The quota was defined in proportion to overall African American representation in the school district population.

In 1972 Judge Robert Peckham granted a preliminary injunction, restraining school officials in San Francisco from placing primary reliance on IQ tests in EMR placements for African American children. He also ordered that African American EMR children should be reevaluated and that those who were returned to regular classes should be given special help. However, he was wary of the plaintiffs' proposed ratio system limiting African American enrollment in EMR classes.

The case of *Larry P.* eventually went to trial in 1978. More than 50 expert witnesses were called and over 200 reports, studies, and exhibits were received in evidence. In the end the plaintiffs prevailed. In 1979 Judge Peckham ruled that individual intelligence tests "are racially and culturally biased, have a discriminatory impact against black children, and have not been validated for the purpose of essentially permanent placements of black children into educationally dead-end, isolated, and stigmatizing classes for the so-called educable mentally retarded."

This decision was based, in part, on certain assumptions about the nature of intelligence that are not necessarily shared by experts in the field. For example, after reviewing the trial transcript—some ten thousand pages in length—Elliott (1987) concluded that the legal opinion in *Larry P.* was based on the following assumptions: that intelligence is the innate ability to learn, that a culturally fair test should measure innate ability, and that a culturally fair test should produce equal scores for all relevant subgroups. If these assumptions are correct, then the legal opinion cited in *Larry P.* follows with inexorable logic. However, very few assessment specialists embrace the antiquated view that it is meaningful or useful to define intelligence as innate ability to learn.

Within California, the decision effectively abolished the use of individual intelligence tests for placement of African American students in EMR classes. In 1984 the decision was affirmed by the U.S. Ninth Circuit Court of Appeals, and in 1986 the ban was extended so that IQ tests could not be used for *any* special education placement of African American children in the public schools of California.

Although it is arguable whether the *Larry P.* decision was good social science, there is no denying the profound policy implications of this case:

> For special education, the negative results are reduced precision and objectivity of assessment, reduced precision of placement, reduced morale of and faith in the professionals charged with assessment, some downgrading of the once-central importance of developing intellectual skills, and reduced services for slow-learning, non-LD children in the 65–80 range. The positive results are broader and newer kinds of assessment (if there is time for the breadth, and norms for the novel tests) and some fresh thinking about programs for children having difficulty in school. (Elliott, 1987)

One major consequence of *Larry P.* has been a huge reduction in the number of children assigned to self-contained EMR classes. For example, in California the number of EMR children went from a high of 58,000 in 1968–1969 to approximately 13,000 in 1984. For some mildly retarded children, alternative placement in regular classrooms has been beneficial, but for others who are now not eligible for any special help, the aftermath of court-influenced placement policies is more questionable (Powers & Hagans-Murillo, 2004).

### Parents in Action on Special Education (PASE) v. Joseph P. Hannon (1980)

*PASE v. Hannon* was litigated in 1980, just one year after the landmark *Larry P. v. Riles* case. In this suit, attorneys for two African American student plaintiffs argued that the children were inappropriately placed in educable mentally handicapped (EMH) classes because of racial bias in the IQ tests used for placement. The case was tried as a class action suit, meaning that the plaintiffs represented the category of all similar children in Chicago. Even though the issues in the *PASE* class action suit were substantially the same as the preceding case, the presiding judge came to exactly the opposite conclusion. Judge John Grady ruled that intelligence tests are not culturally biased against African American children.

Astonishingly, in his written opinion Judge Grady commented on the cultural fairness of every single item on the WISC, WISC-R, and Stanford-Binet, finding all but 9 of the 488 items to be culturally fair. He concluded that the 9 biased items were not sufficient in number to render the tests discriminatory, and he endorsed their ongoing use for evaluation of minority children. Although little has been made of the judge's transgression, it would be considered a colossal breach of professional ethics were a psychologist to publish individual test items in the public record.

### Georgia NAACP v. Georgia (1984)

In this case the NAACP alleged that evaluation procedures used in the state of Georgia discriminated against African American children, resulting in their overrepresentation in EMR classes. However, the U.S. Court of Appeals ruled in 1984 that discrimination did not exist. Furthermore, the court rejected the notion that overrepresentation of African American children in EMR classes was a sufficient basis to prove discrimination.

### Crawford v. Honig (1994)

This case initiated a reexamination of the rights of minority children in special education in California. Contrary to other cases in which the lawyers and parents of minority children asked for a ban on the use of traditional tests, the purpose of *Crawford v. Honig* was exactly the opposite—to obtain legal permission for using tests such as the Wechsler Intelligence Scale for Children-Revised (WISC-R) with African American children. The case was filed by the parents of Demond Crawford, an African American student diagnosed with learning disability. His parents understood the value of standardized intelligence tests in the assessment of learning disability and wanted school psychologists to use these traditional instruments in their evaluation. However, as a direct consequence of the *Larry P. v. Riles* decision, it was *illegal* in 1994 for psychologists to administer the WISC-R, or any other mainstream IQ test, to African American children in California, even with the permission of the parents. A psychologist who did so risked fines and jail time for breaking the law. In this lawsuit, Judge Robert Peckham, the same judge who presided in the *Larry P. v. Riles* case, overruled his earlier finding so as to permit the use of standardized IQ tests in the evaluation of African American children upon the formal request of their parents. This is an excellent example of the fact that laws can be reshaped in response to changing social conditions.

### GI Forum v. Texas Education Agency (2000)

In this court suit, filed on behalf of seven African American and Latino high school students in Texas, plaintiffs challenged the use of the Texas Assessment of Academic Skills (TAAS) as a requirement for high school graduation on the grounds that it discriminated unfairly against minority students and violated their right to due process. They pointed out that substantial disparities in resources existed between "white" schools—those with a preponderance of white students—and minority schools—those with a preponderance of minority students. In the view of plaintiffs, this was the explanation for the differential failure rates. In fact, 67 percent of African American, 59 percent of Latino, and 31 percent of white students failed the exam the first time it was used in 1991.

After hearing expert witnesses over many months, the court ruled in favor of state education officials, citing several compelling reasons. Although the court agreed with plaintiffs that disparities in resources did exist, it found no evidence that these inequalities caused the higher failure rate of minority students. The court also pointed out that the TAAS was constructed with great care and possessed "curricular validity"; that is, it tested what was actually taught. This quality of a test is the same thing as instructional validity, as described earlier in *Debra P. v. Turlington*. Officials also noted that the TAAS was just one condition of awarding the diploma, not the sole factor; attendance, passing grades, and completion of the required curriculum also are needed. The court praised the humane manner of test implementation, noting that students first encounter the TAAS in the tenth grade and are provided remedial courses for any of the three subsections (reading, math, writing) that they fail. The cutoff score of 70 percent for each curricular area was deemed reasonable. Moreover, the court noted, students have a minimum of *seven* additional opportunities to pass the test. Finally, the court found it "highly significant that minority students have continued to narrow the passing rate gap at a rapid rate." Similar to the findings in *Debra P. v. Turlington,* this case demonstrated that a well-designed graduation test can be an engine of positive social change.

### ● DISABILITY ASSESSMENT AND THE LAW

Individuals with disabilities are afforded many legal protections, some of which impact the use of psychological tests. In this section, we review two broad areas in which legislation has been written to defend individuals with disabilities: school-based assessment of children with disabilities, and employment-based testing of persons with disabilities. The coverage is purposefully brief. Readers can find lengthier discussions in Bruyere and O'Keeffe (1994), Salvia and Ysseldyke (2001), and Stefan (2001).

## Public Law 94-142

In 1975, the U.S. Congress passed a compulsory special education law, **Public Law 94-142,** known as the Education for All Handicapped Children Act.[1] According to Ballard and Zettel (1977), this law was designed to meet four major goals:

1. To ensure that special education services are available to children who need them
2. To guarantee that decisions about services to disabled students are fair and appropriate
3. To establish specific management and auditing requirements for special education
4. To provide federal funds to help the states educate disabled students

Many practices in the assessment of disabled persons stem directly from the provisions of Public Law 94-142. For example, the law specifies that each disabled student must receive an individualized education plan (IEP) based on a comprehensive assessment by a multidisciplinary team. The IEP must outline long-term and short-term objectives and specify plans for achieving them. In addition, the IEP must indicate how progress toward these objectives will be evaluated. The parents are intimately involved in this process and must approve the particulars of the IEP.

Pertinent to testing practices, PL 94-142 includes a number of provisions designed to ensure that assessment procedures and activities are fair, equitable, and nondiscriminatory. Salvia and Ysseldyke (1988) summarize these provisions as follows:

1. Tests are to be selected and administered in such a way as to be racially and culturally nondiscriminatory.
2. To the extent feasible, students are to be assessed in their native language or primary mode of communication.
3. Tests must have been validated for the specific purpose for which they are used.

4. Tests must be administered by trained personnel in conformance with the instructions provided by the test producer.
5. Tests used with students must include those designed to provide information about specific educational needs and not just a general intelligence quotient.
6. Decisions about students are to be based on more than performance on a single test.
7. Evaluations are to be made by a multidisciplinary team that includes at least one teacher or other specialist with knowledge in the area of suspected disability.
8. Children must be assessed in all areas related to a specific disability, including—when appropriate—health, vision, hearing, social and emotional status, general intelligence, academic performance, communicative skills, and motor skills.

PL 94-142 also contains a provision that disabled students should be placed in the least restrictive environment—one that allows the maximum possible opportunity to interact with nonimpaired students. Separate schooling is to occur only when the nature or the severity of the disability is such that instructional goals cannot be achieved in the regular classroom. Finally, the law contains a due process clause that guarantees an impartial hearing to resolve conflicts between the parents of disabled children and the school system.

In general, the provisions of PL 94-142 have provided strong impetus to the development of specialized tests that are designed, normed, and validated for children with specific disabilities. For example, in the assessment of a child with visual impairment, the provisions of PL 94-142 virtually dictate that the examiner must use a well-normed test devised just for this population rather than relying upon traditional instruments.

## Public Law 99-457

In 1986, Congress passed several amendments to the Education for All Handicapped Children Act, expanding the provisions of PL 94-142 to include

---

1. Each congressional law receives two numbers, one referring to the particular Congress that passed it, the other referring to the law itself. Thus, Public Law 94-142 is the 142nd law passed by the 94th Congress.

disabled preschool children. **Public Law 99-457** requires states to provide free appropriate public education to disabled children ages 3 through 5. The law also mandates financial grants to states that offer interdisciplinary educational services to disabled infants, toddlers, and their families, thus establishing a huge incentive for states to serve children with disabilities from birth through age 2. Public Law 99-457 also provides a major impetus to the development and validation of infant tests and developmental schedules. After all, the early and accurate identification of at-risk children would appear to be the crucial first step in effective interdisciplinary intervention.

## Americans with Disabilities Act

The 1990 **Americans with Disabilities Act** (ADA) forbids discrimination against qualified individuals with disabilities in both the public sector (e.g., government agencies and entities receiving federal grants) and the private sector (e.g., corporations and other for-profit employers). Under the ADA, *disability* is defined as a physical or mental impairment that substantially limits one or more of the major life activities (Parry, 1997). Examples of ADA-recognized disabilities include sensory and physical impairments (e.g., blindness, paralysis), many mental illnesses (e.g., major depression, schizophrenia), learning disabilities, and attention-deficit/hyperactivity disorder.

Under the ADA, the process of qualifying an individual for work or educational accommodations requires current, detailed, and professional documentation. For example, a graduate student who was seeking a special arrangement for taking tests (such as a quiet room) because of attentional problems might need to submit a comprehensive endorsement from a licensed psychologist, detailing the history, current functioning, clinical diagnosis of attention-deficit/hyperactivity disorder, and necessity for accommodations (Gordon & Keiser, 1998). In other words, the ADA is a civil rights act, not a program of entitlement:

> The ADA does not guarantee equal outcomes, establish quotas, or require preferences favoring individuals with disabilities. Rather, the ADA is intended to ensure access to equal employment opportunities based on merit. The ADA is designed to "level the playing field" by removing the barriers that prevent qualified individuals with disabilities from having access to the same employment opportunities that are available to individuals without disabilities. (Klimoski & Palmer, 1994, p. 45)

In sum, the purpose is to ensure that individuals who are otherwise qualified for jobs or educational programs are not denied access or put at improper disadvantage simply because of a disability.

In regard to psychological testing, an important provision of the ADA is that agencies and institutions must make reasonable testing accommodations for persons with disabilities. With appropriate documentation (discussed earlier), the relevant accommodations might include any of the following:

- Assistance in completing answer sheets
- Audiotape or oral presentation of written tests
- Special seating for tests
- Large-print examinations
- Retaking exams
- Dictating rather than writing test answers
- Printed version of verbal instructions
- Extended time limit

In general, changes in the testing medium (e.g., from written to oral) are consistent with the intention of ADA, if such a change is needed to accommodate a disability. For example, an appropriate accommodation in the testing medium would be the audiotaped presentation of test items for persons who are visually impaired. On the other hand, changing a test from a printed version into a sign language version for persons with hearing impairment would be considered translation into another language, not a simple change of medium.

In most testing accommodations mandated by the ADA, it is necessary to change the time limits, usually by providing extra time. This raises problems of test interpretation, especially when a strict time limit is essential to the validity of a test. For example, Willingham, Ragosta, Bennett, and others (1988) found that extended time limits on the SAT significantly reduced the validity of the test as a predictor of first-year college grades. This was especially true for examinees with learning disabilities, whose first-year grades were subsequently overpredicted by their SAT scores. Thus, although it seems fair to provide extra time on a test when the testing medium has been changed (e.g., audiotaped questions replacing the printed versions), from a psychometric standpoint, the challenge is to determine *how much* extra time should be provided so that the modified test is comparable to the original version. Nester (1994) and Phillips (1994) provide thoughtful perspectives on the range of reasonable accommodations required by the ADA.

## Cognitive Disability and the Death Penalty

One way that laws evolve in American society is through decisions of the Supreme Court. In a 2002 court case (*Atkins v. Virginia*), the Supreme Court held that the execution of mentally retarded convicts is "cruel and unusual punishment" prohibited by the Eighth Amendment. In speaking for the 6-3 majority, Chief Justice John Paul Stevens wrote:

> We are not persuaded that the execution of mentally retarded criminals will measurably advance the deterrent or the retributive purpose of the death penalty. Construing and applying the Eighth Amendment in the light of our "evolving standards of decency," we therefore conclude that such punishment is excessive and that the Constitution "places a substantive restriction on the State's power to take the life" of a mentally retarded offender. (*Atkins v. Virginia*, 2002, p. 321)

This new constitutional standard has profound implications, literally of life and death, for the proper application of psychological tests with persons who display intellectual disability. Choosing the appropriate tests, getting the results right, and offering an accurate diagnosis of intellectual disability could determine whether some examinees face death row.

This was certainly relevant for Doil Lane, who was convicted of the heinous rape and murder of a nine-year-old girl and sentenced to death, principally on his confession (DNA testing was inconclusive). This confession of a highly suggestible

young man with intellectual disability may have been false. Whether or not his confession was true, there is no question as to presence of significant intellectual disability:

> As a child, he spent years as a resident of a special school in Texas for mentally disabled students. His I.Q. has tested between 62 and 70. His mental deficiencies are so obvious that the report by the Kansas police officer who first interviewed him noted Lane seemed "mentally retarded." The former chief psychologist of the Texas Division of Criminal Justice assessed his intelligence in 1998 and concluded he had mental retardation. When his police interrogation was over, Lane—a thirty-year-old—climbed into the interrogating officer's lap. At his trial in Texas, Lane asked the judge for crayons so that he could color pictures. The judge denied the request. (Human Rights Watch, 2001, p. 38)

In response to the Supreme Court decision, Texas Governor Rick Perry commuted the death sentence of Doil Lane to life in prison.

## ● LEGAL ISSUES IN EMPLOYMENT TESTING

Nearly every aspect of the employment relationship is subject to the law: recruitment, screening, selection, placement, compensation, promotion, and performance appraisal all fall within the domain of legal interpretations (Cascio, 1987). However, courts and legislative bodies have reserved special scrutiny for employment-related testing. The practitioner who refuses to learn relevant legal guidelines in personnel testing does so at great peril, because unwise practices can lead to costly and time-consuming litigation (Case Exhibit 12.1).

Personnel testing is particularly sensitive because the consequences of an adverse decision are often grave: The applicant does not get the job, or an employee does not get the desired promotion or placement. Recognizing that employment testing performs a sensitive function as gatekeeper to economic advantage, Congress has passed laws sharply regulating the use of testing. The courts have also rendered decisions that help define unfair test discrimination. In addition, regulatory

**Unwise Testing Practices in Employee Screening**

According to the Associated Press of July 11, 1993, the Target discount chain agreed to settle out of court in a class-action lawsuit filed on behalf of an estimated 2,500 job applicants. Prospective security guards for Target were required to take the Rodgers Psychscreen, a 704-item condensed combination of the CPI and the MMPI. Several applicants objected to answering the test, which included questions about God, sex, and bowel movements. Target agreed to pay $1.3 million, including $60,000 to four plaintiffs named in the lawsuit. Although Target admitted no wrongdoing in the case, corporate officers agreed not to use the Psychscreen test for at least five years.

Sibi Soraka was one of the plaintiffs in the lawsuit. He found the questions to be "off-the-wall and bizarre." He claimed that the cumulative effect of answering the questions made him palpably ill. He added: "It doesn't take Einstein to figure out that these questions really don't have any bearing on our world and life today, or certainly on a job walking around looking for shoplifters." Target corporation defended the testing practice, noting that Psychscreen is commonly used in the evaluation of law enforcement officers. Attorneys for Soraka disagreed, citing a lack of evidence that the test helped identify good versus poor risks for employment. They noted that about 800 of the 2,500 applicants were denied employment based solely upon Psychscreen results.

This case illustrates that the psychometric soundness of an instrument is not the only criterion in test selection. In addition, test users must show that the instrument is relevant to their application. Furthermore, issues of acceptability to prospective examinees must be considered.

---

bodies have published guidelines that substantially impact testing practices. We will provide a current perspective on the regulation of personnel testing by tracing the development of laws, regulations, and major court cases.

It may surprise the reader to learn that employment testing has raised legal controversy only in the last 35 years (Arvey & Faley, 1988). During this period, several definitive court decisions and pathbreaking governmental directives have helped define current legal trends. These landmarks are depicted in Table 12.2, beginning with the Civil Rights Act of 1964, proceeding through the federal regulations of the Equal Employment Opportunity Commission (EEOC), and concluding with very recent court cases and legislative developments. We will review these landmarks in chronological order.

**Early Court Cases and Legislation**

During the presidency of Lyndon Johnson, Congress passed the Civil Rights Act of 1964. This early civil rights legislation had a profound effect on employee-testing procedures. In addition to broad provisions designed to prevent discrimination in many social contexts, Title VII of this act prohibits employment practices that discriminate on the basis of race, color, religion, sex, or national origin. The act established several important general principles relevant to employment testing (Cascio, 1987):

- Discriminatory preference for any group, minority or majority, is barred by the act.
- The employer bears the burden of proof that all requirements for employment, including test scores, are related to job performance.

● **TABLE 12.2  Major Legal Landmarks in Employment Testing**

1964  *Myart v. Motorola.*  This case set the precedent for courts to hear employment testing cases.

1964  Civil Rights Act.  This act prohibits job discrimination based on sex, race, color, religion, or national origin.

1966  EEOC Guidelines.  The first published guidelines on employment testing practices.

1971  *Griggs v. Duke Power Company.*  The Supreme Court rules that employment test results must have a demonstrable link to job performance.

1973  *United States v. Georgia Power Company.*  Ruling strengthens the authority of EEOC guidelines for studies of employment testing validity.

1975  *Albemarle v. Moody.*  EEOC guidelines strengthened; subjective supervisory ratings ruled a poor basis for validating tests.

1976  *Washington v. Davis.*  Court ruled that performance in a training program was a sufficient basis against which to validate a test.

1978  *Uniform Guidelines on Employee Selection.*  These guidelines defined adverse impact by the four-fifths rule and incorporated criteria for validity in employee selection studies.

1988  *Watson v. Fort Worth Bank and Trust.*  The court ruled that subjective employment devices such as the interview can be validated; employees can claim disparate impact based on interview-based promotion policies.

1990  Americans with Disabilities Act.  This act sharply limits the reasons for not hiring a disabled person. One provision is that medical tests may not be administered prior to an offer of employment.

1991  Civil Rights Act.  This act outlaws subgroup norming of employee selection tests.

- Professionally developed tests used in personnel testing must be job related.
- In addition to open and deliberate discrimination, the law forbids practices that are fair in form but discriminatory in operation.
- Intent is irrelevant: the plaintiff need not show that discrimination was intentional.
- In spite of these proscriptions, job-related tests and other measuring devices are deemed both legal and useful.

The 1964 legislation also created the Equal Employment Opportunity Commission (EEOC) to develop guidelines defining fair employee-selection procedures. The initial guidelines, published in 1966, were vague. Later revisions of these guidelines, including the *Uniform Guidelines on Employee Selection* (1978), were quite specific and have been used by the courts to help resolve legal disputes regarding employment-testing practices (see the following section).

The 1964 *Myart v. Motorola* case marked the first involvement of the courts in employment testing. The issues raised by this landmark case are still reverberating today. Leon Myart was an African American applicant for a job at one of Motorola's television assembly plants. Even though he had highly relevant job experience, Mr. Myart was refused a position because his score on a brief screening test of intelligence fell below the company cutoff. Claiming racial discrimination, he filed an appeal with the Illinois Fair Employment Practices Commission. The state examiner found in favor of the complainant and directed that the Motorola company should offer Mr. Myart a job. In addition, the examiner ruled that the particular test should not be used in the future and that any new test should "take into account the environmental factors which contribute to cultural deprivation." In essence, the examiner concluded that Motorola's employment-testing practices were unfair because they acted as a barrier to the employment of culturally deprived and disadvantaged applicants. Even though the case was later overturned for lack of evidence, *Myart v. Motorola* did set the precedent to hear such complaints in the court system (Arvey & Faley, 1988).

## Advent of EEOC Employment Testing Standards

During the 1970s, several court cases helped shape current standards and practices in employment testing. The focus of *Griggs v. Duke Power Company*

(1971) was the use of tests—in this case the Wonderlic Personnel Test and the Bennett Mechanical Comprehension Test—as eligibility criteria for employees who wanted to transfer to other departments. In particular, employees at Duke Power Company who lacked a high school education could qualify for transfer if they scored above the national median on both tests. This policy appeared to discriminate against African American employees since it was disproportionately difficult for them to gain eligibility for transfer. However, lower courts found no discriminatory intent and therefore found in favor of the power company.

In 1971, the Supreme Court reversed the lower court findings, ruling against the use of tests without their validation. The decision emphasized several points of current relevance (Arvey & Faley, 1988):

- Fairness in employment testing is determined by consequences, not motivations.
- Testing practices must have a demonstrable link to job performance.
- The employer has the burden of showing that an employment practice such as testing is job related.
- Diplomas, degrees, or broad testing devices are not adequate as measures of job-related capability.
- The EEOC testing standards deserve considerable deference from employment testers.

These employment testing guidelines were further refined in a 1973 court decision, *United States v. Georgia Power Company*. In this case, the Georgia Power Company presented a validation study to support its employment-testing practices when its policies were shown to have an adverse impact upon the hiring and transferring of African Americans. However, the validation study was weak, in part because it was based upon multiple discriminant analysis, a complex statistical technique rarely used for this purpose. The courts ruled that the validation study was inadequate since it did not adhere to EEOC guidelines for evaluating validity studies. This finding ensconced the EEOC guidelines as virtually the law of the land in employment-testing practices.

Several other court cases in the 1970s and 1980s also served to strengthen the authority of EEOC testing guidelines. These cases were quite complex and involved multiple issues in addition to those cited here. In *Albemarle v. Moody* (1975), the Supreme Court deferred to EEOC guidelines in finding that subjective supervisory ratings are ambiguous and, therefore, constitute a poor basis for evaluating the validity of an employment selection test. The central issue in *Washington v. Davis* (1976) was whether performance in a training program (as opposed to actual on-the-job performance) was a sufficient basis for determining the job-relatedness of the employment selection procedures. In this case, the Supreme Court ruled that performance in a police officer training program was a sufficient criterion against which to validate a selection test.

In *State of Connecticut v. Teal*, the U.S. Supreme Court sided with four African American state employees who had failed a written test that was used to screen applicants for the position of welfare eligibility supervisor. The workers claimed unfair discrimination, noting that only 54 percent of minority applicants passed, compared to 80 percent for whites. In its defense, the state of Connecticut argued that discrimination did not exist, since 23 percent of the successful African American applicants were ultimately promoted, compared to 14 percent for whites. The Court was not impressed with this argument, noting that Title VII of the 1964 Civil Rights Act was specifically designed to protect individuals, not groups. Thus, any unfairness to an individual is unacceptable. Further analysis of fair employment court cases can be found in Arvey and Faley (1988), Cascio (1987), Kleiman and Faley (1985), and Russell (1984).

## Uniform Guidelines on Employee Selection

During the 1970s, several federal agencies and professional groups proposed revisions and extensions of the existing EEOC employment testing guidelines. The revisions were developed in response to court decisions that had interpreted EEOC guidelines in a narrow, inflexible, legalistic manner. However, the existence of several sets of competing guidelines was confusing, and strong pressures were exerted upon the involved parties to forge a compromise. These efforts culminated in a consensus document known as the 1978 *Uniform Guidelines on Employee Selection.*

The *Uniform Guidelines* quickly earned respect in court cases and were frequently cited in the resolution of legal disputes. The new guidelines contain interpretation and guidance not found in earlier versions, particularly regarding adverse impact, fairness, and the validation of selection procedures, as discussed later.

The *Uniform Guidelines* provide a very specific definition of adverse impact. In general, when selection procedures favor applicants from one group (usually males or whites), the basis for selection is said to have an **adverse impact** on other groups (usually females or nonwhites) with a lower selection proportion. The *Uniform Guidelines* define adverse impact with a four-fifths rule. Specifically, adverse impact exists if one group has a selection rate less than four-fifths of the rate of the group with the highest selection rate. For example, consider an employer who has 200 applicants in a year, 100 African American and 100 white. If 120 persons were hired, including 80 whites and 40 African Americans, then the percentage of whites hired is 80 percent (80/100), whereas the percentage of African Americans hired is 40 percent (40/100). Since the selection rate for African Americans is only half that of whites (40 percent/80 percent), the employer might be vulnerable to charges of adverse impact. We should note that the *Uniform Guidelines* suggest caution about this rule when sample sizes are small.

The *Uniform Guidelines* also pay more attention to fairness than previous documents. Fairness is treated in the following manner:

> When members of one racial, ethnic, or sex group characteristically obtain lower scores on a selection procedure than members of another group, and the differences are not reflected in differences in a measure of job performance, use of the selection procedure may unfairly deny opportunities to members of the group that obtain the lower scores. Furthermore, in cases where two or more selection procedures are equally valid, the employer is obliged to use the method that produces the least adverse impact.

The *Uniform Guidelines* also establish a strong affirmative action responsibility on the part of em-

ployers. If an employer finds a substantial disparity in persons hired from a subgroup compared to their availability in the job market, several corrective steps are recommended. These corrective measures include specialized recruitment programs designed to attract qualified members of the group in question, on-the-job training programs so that affected minorities do not get locked into dead-end jobs, and a revamping of selection procedures to reduce or eliminate exclusionary effects.

Finally, the guidelines provide specific technical standards for evaluating validity studies of employee selection procedures. The courts will almost certainly consult these *Uniform Guidelines* if employees bring suit against the company for alleged unfairness in employee selection practices. Thus, it is a foolish employer who does not pay special attention to these technical criteria. For example, one criterion concerns the use of performance scores obtained during training programs:

> Where performance in training is used as a criterion, success in training should be properly measured and the relevance of the training should be shown either through a comparison of the content of the training program with the critical or important work behavior(s) of the job(s), or through a demonstration of the relationship between measures of performance in training and measures of job performance.

Thus, preemployment evaluation of job candidates in a training program may constitute a valid method of employee selection, but only if a strong link exists between the task demands of training and the requirements of the actual job.

The *Uniform Guidelines* contain many other criteria that we cannot review here. We urge the reader to read this fascinating and influential document which is often cited in court cases on employment discrimination.

## Legal Implications of Subjective Employment Devices

In many corporations, promotions are based upon the subjective judgment of senior managers. A common practice is for one or more managers to interview several qualified employees and offer a promotion to the one candidate who appears most promising. The selection of this candidate is typically based on subjective appraisal of such factors as judgment, originality, ambition, loyalty, and tact. Until recently, these subjective employment devices appeared to be outside the scope of fair employment practices codified in the *Uniform Guidelines* and other sources.

However, in a civil rights case, *Watson v. Fort Worth Bank and Trust* (1988), the Supreme Court made it easier for employees to prove charges of race or sex discrimination against employers who use interview and other subjective assessment devices for employee selection or promotion. We outline the factual background of this important case before discussing the legal implications (Bersoff, 1988).

Clara Watson, an African American employee at Fort Worth Bank and Trust, was rejected for promotion to supervisory positions four times in a row. Each time, a white applicant received the promotion. Watson obtained evidence showing that the bank had never had an African American officer or director, had only one African American supervisor, and paid African American employees lower salaries than equivalent white employees. Furthermore, all supervisors had to receive approval from a white male senior vice president for their promotion decisions. The bank did not dispute that it made hiring and promotion decisions solely on the basis of subjective judgment. When an analysis of promotion patterns confirmed statistically significant racial disparities, Watson brought suit against the bank.

Two legal theories were available for Watson to litigate her claim under Title VII of the 1964 Civil Rights Act. The two theories are called "disparate treatment" and "disparate impact." A disparate treatment case is more difficult to litigate, since the plaintiff must prove that the employer engaged in intentional discrimination. In a disparate impact case, intention is irrelevant. Instead, the plaintiff need merely show that a particular employment practice—such as using a standardized test—results in an unnecessary and disproportionately adverse impact upon a protected minority.

The lower courts ruled that Watson was restricted to the more limited disparate treatment approach since the employer had used subjective evaluation procedures. Furthermore, the lower courts ruled that the bank had not engaged in intentional discrimination and did have legitimate reasons for not promoting Watson. Nonetheless, the Supreme Court agreed to hear the case in order to determine whether a disparate impact analysis could be applied to subjective employment devices such as interview. Relying heavily upon a brief from the American Psychological Association (APA, 1988), the Supreme Court ruled unanimously that the disparate impact analysis is applicable to subjective or discretionary promotion practices based on interview. In effect, the Court ruled that subjective employment devices such as interview can be validated. Thus, employers do not have unmonitored discretion to evaluate applications for promotion based on subjective interview. As a consequence of *Watson v. Fort Worth Bank and Trust,* employers must be ready to defend all their promotion practices—including subjective interview—against claims of adverse impact.

### Recent Developments in Employee Selection

In 1990, Congress passed the Americans with Disabilities Act (ADA), which forbids discrimination against qualified individuals with disabilities. The ADA was discussed briefly in Topic 7B, Testing Persons with Disabilities. This act protects job applicants with disabilities by sharply limiting permissible reasons for refusing to hire them. Specifically, employers can decline to hire a disabled worker for *only* the following reasons (1) if hiring the applicant would cause the company undue hardship in terms of making accommodations for the disability; (2) business necessity; or (3) the presence of the worker with disabilities would pose a direct threat to the health or safety of the worker or others.

An important stipulation of ADA is that medical tests may not be administered prior to an offer of employment. The enforcement agency for ADA, the EEOC, defines a medical test as "a procedure or test that seeks information about an individual's physical or mental impairments or health." The following factors are used to determine whether a procedure or test might be considered "medical":

- Is it administered by a health care professional or someone trained by a health care professional?
- Are the results interpreted by a health care professional or someone trained by a health care professional?
- Is it designed to reveal impairment of physical or mental health?
- Is the employer trying to determine the applicant's physical or mental health or impairments?
- Is it invasive (for example, does it require the drawing of blood, urine, or breath)?
- Does it measure an applicant's performance of a task, or does it measure the applicant's physiological responses to performing the task?
- Is it normally given in a medical setting (for example, a health care professional's office)? (EEOC, 1995)

Although the scope of what might be considered a "medical test" slowly has been defined by court cases in the years since the inception of ADA, uncertainty still persists in some areas of psychological testing. For example, it is possible that cognitive ability tests could be construed as "medical" in nature, which would wreak havoc with employment testing:

> According to ADA requirements, if an attribute is not required for performing an essential task, then an applicant may request an accommodation or modification of either the testing process or the job if he or she claims a covered disability that is associated with that nonessential attribute. In practice, this might mean that unless it is demonstrated that intelligence is required for accomplishing an essential task, no test that measures intelligence (or any facet of intelligence) could be administered before offering employment to any applicant claiming an impairment that is associated with intellectual functioning. (Landy, Shankster, & Kohler, 1994)

Court decisions and administrative guidelines will be needed to sharpen the focus of this important legislation.

The Civil Rights Act of 1991 also contained important provisions relevant to employee selection and appraisal. Specifically, the act outlaws subgroup norming of test scores, which effectively eliminates the use of separate hiring and promotion lists. *Subgroup norming* refers to the practice of using identified subgroups (instead of a diversified national sample) for purposes of developing group-specific test norms. The prohibition of this practice presents a challenge to employers and I/O psychologists, since racial subgroup norming of test scores has been a popular and effective method for avoiding adverse impact.

Recent court cases also have impacted personnel testing. The issue in *Soraka v. Dayton Hudson* was whether corporations can use a personality test as a basis for preemployment screening for mental health problems in job applicants. As discussed previously, Soraka was required to take the Rodgers Psychscreen as part of the application process for a position as security guard. The Psychscreen is a true-false personality inventory intended to identify persons with psychological problems such as depression and anxiety. Soraka filed suit against the department store, claiming that individual questions about his sexual practices and religious beliefs were a violation of his civil rights. This case was interesting because it pertained to the value and validity of individual items as opposed to overall test scores. The courts have long held that preemployment testing must have demonstrated relevance to job performance or it cannot be used. However, the courts have not required validity evidence for individual test items. Soraka won his case, which was appealed by Dayton Hudson. In 1993, the company settled out of court. This litigation is summarized in Case Exhibit 12.1 found earlier in this section.

Another recent court case illustrates how litigation will continue to clarify the scope of ADA in regard to psychological testing. In *Karraker v. Rent-A-Center* (2005), a federal appeals court unanimously invalidated the use of the Minnesota Multiphasic Personality Inventory-2 (MMPI-2) as a job screening test, citing ADA restrictions on preemployment medical tests. The defendants argued in vain that their use of the test was solely to measure traits of character and personality such as honesty, preferences, and reliability—all legal under ADA. The appeals court held that the MMPI-2 was designed, at least in part, to reveal mental illness. As such, the effect of using the test was to hurt employment prospects for individuals with a mental disability, a direct violation of ADA.[2] The defendants paid a substantial sum to settle a class action suit filed by employees and agreed to stop using the test in California.

## ● SUMMARY

**1.** Broadly speaking, there are three sources of law: constitutional provisions, legislative edicts, and judicial opinions. All three have impacted psychological testing over the years.

**2.** The "due process" clause of the Fourteenth Amendment has had a significant impact upon the practice of psychology. For example, psychologists involved in civil commitment of patients must show that several stringent criteria are met, including a reliable diagnosis of severe mental illness.

**3.** Legislatures have enacted many laws that impact testing. This is especially true at the federal level, where many civil rights statutes have been enacted, including the Americans with Disabilities Act of 1990.

**4.** Testing in school systems has been deeply impacted by a string of lawsuits, some seeking to restrict the use of traditional intelligence tests with minority students, others seeking to eliminate the use of functional literacy tests as a requirement for the high school diploma.

**5.** Tests of functional literacy, now used in many states as one condition of high school graduation, tests students' practical knowledge and skills used in everyday life, such as balancing a checkbook, reading instructions, completing application forms, and writing a coherent paragraph.

**6.** Lawsuits seeking to forbid the use of functional literacy tests as a condition of receiving a high school diploma have generally failed; that is, the courts have sided with state educational systems, concluding that well-designed tests are constitutional.

**7.** Public Law 94-142, the Education for All Handicapped Children Act, has had dramatic impacts upon assessment practices for persons with disabilities. The law mandates nondiscriminatory assessment, native language testing, and health, hearing, vision, and emotional assessment.

**8.** The Americans with Disabilities Act (ADA) of 1990 mandates that agencies must make reasonable testing accommodations for persons with disabilities, including such provisions as increased time on timed tests for persons with learning disabilities and related disorders.

**9.** Several court cases have helped to shape testing practices in personnel selection. For example, in *Griggs v. Duke Power* (1971) the Supreme Court ruled that fairness in employment testing is determined by consequences, not motivations; testing practices must have a demonstrable link to job performance; and the employer must show that a testing practice is job related.

**10.** Several federal agencies and professional groups helped develop the *Uniform Guidelines on Employee Selection* (1978). This document provides guidance on many employee-testing practices, including a very specific definition of adverse impact.

**11.** In general, when selection procedures favor applicants from one group (usually males or whites), the basis for selection is said to have an adverse

---

2. Oddly enough, in one of those twists so typical of how law is interpreted, it appears that the MMPI-2 still can be used legally in employment settings if the employer makes a *conditional* offer of employment before requiring that candidates take the test.

impact on other groups (usually females or non-whites) when they have a lower selection proportion (less than four-fifths of the majority group).

**12.** The Americans with Disabilities Act of 1990 and the Civil Rights Act of 1991 also contain important provisions relevant to employee selection and appraisal. For example, the Civil Rights Act outlaws subgroup norming of tests.

● **KEY TERMS AND CONCEPTS**

test of functional literacy   p. 536
instructional validity   p. 536
Public Law 94-142   p. 540

Public Law 99-457   p. 541
Americans with Disabilities Act   p. 541
adverse impact   p. 546

# Computerized Assessment and the Future of Testing

omputers are now used in virtually every aspect of assessment, including the administration, scoring, and interpretation of many tests. In fact, for many instruments it is now possible for the practitioner to seat the client in front of a computer with instructions that consist of "Please follow the instructions." Minutes later, the practitioner receives a lengthy narrative report, consisting not only of summary scores but also a lengthy, sophisticated interpretive report. Although the use of computers in testing is manifestly a positive development, it also raises a number of troubling questions. In this topic, current applications of the computer in psychological assessment are surveyed, and the professional and social issues raised by this practice are discussed. The topic closes with thoughts on the future of testing—which will be forged in large measure by increasingly sophisticated applications of computer technology. We begin with an overview and history of the computer in testing.

## ● COMPUTERS IN TESTING: OVERVIEW AND HISTORY

### Introduction to Computer-Aided Assessment

In many counseling centers it is possible for a client to make an appointment with a microcomputer to explore career options. Other than a brief interaction with the receptionist to schedule time at the computer, the client need not interact with any other human being during the entire assessment process. The exact scenario will differ from one setting to the next but might resemble the following. Instructions on the computer screen encourage the user to press any key. The computer then prompts the client to answer a series of questions about activities and interests by pressing designated numeric keys. After completion of the inventory, the computer calculates raw scores for a long list of occupational scales and makes appropriate statistical transformations. Next, a brief report appears on the screen. The report provides a list of careers that best fit the interests of the client. A hard copy is also printed for later review. Presumably, the client is better informed about compatible career options and, therefore, more likely to choose a satisfying line of work. This scenario is a simple example of computer-assisted psychological assessment (CAPA), a recent development hailed by many psychologists but criticized by others.

It is common knowledge that computers are now used widely in psychological testing. However, the breadth of these applications might surprise the reader. In addition to straightforward applications such as presenting test questions, scoring test data, and printing test results (as described earlier), computers can be used to (1) design individualized tests based upon real-time feedback during testing, (2) interpret test results according to complex decision rules, (3) write lengthy and detailed narrative reports, and (4) present test stimuli in engaging and realistic formats, including high-definition video and virtual reality. We touch upon all of these topics in our review. The umbrella term **computer-assisted psychological assessment** (CAPA) refers to the entire range of computer applications in psychological assessment. CAPA holds great promise to the practice of psychology but also presents a variety of practical and ethical problems that demand careful and thoughtful consideration. A brief history of CAPA is a good backdrop to the discussion of practical and ethical concerns. Table 12.3

## • COMPUTER-BASED TEST INTERPRETATION: CURRENT STATUS

**Computer-based test interpretation,** or CBTI, refers to test interpretation and report writing by computer. Every major test publisher now offers computer-based test interpretations. These services are available by mail-in, online computer with modem, or on-site microcomputer package. Moreover, the market for computer-based testing and report writing is so lucrative that we can

● **TABLE 12.3    Historical Landmarks in CAPA**

| | |
|---|---|
| 1946 | Hankes develops an analog computer to score the SVIB (Moreland, 1992). |
| 1954 | Meehl's (1954) book *Clinical versus Statistical Prediction* sets the stage for automated test interpretation. |
| 1962 | Optical scanner and digital computer are used to score SVIB and MMPI and also to print profiles (Moreland, 1992). |
| 1962 | First computer-based test interpretation system is developed for the MMPI at the Mayo Clinic (Swenson et al., 1965). |
| 1964 | Piotrowski publishes a system for computer-based interpretation of the Rorschach (Piotrowski, 1964). |
| 1960s | Computer-based interpretive systems for the MMPI proliferate; Fowler, Finney, and Caldwell develop popular systems (Fowler, 1985). |
| 1971 | A mainframe computer with terminals is used to automate the entire assessment process for psychiatric inpatients at the VA Hospital in Salt Lake City, Utah (Klingler, Miller, Johnson, & Williams, 1977). |
| 1975 | First automated interpretation of a neuropsychological test battery (Adams & Heaton, 1985). |
| 1979 | Lachar publishes an actuarially based interpretive system for the Personality Inventory for Children (Lachar & Gdowski, 1979). |
| 1970s | Computerized adaptive testing (CAT) is introduced; CAT allows for flexible, individualized test batteries which produce a given level of measurement accuracy with the fewest possible test items (Weiss, 1982). |
| 1985 | A special series on computerized psychological assessment appears in the *Journal of Consulting and Clinical Psychology* (Butcher, 1985). |
| 1986 | American Psychological Association publishes *Guidelines for Computer-Based Tests and Interpretations.* |
| 1987 | Publication of the first resource book titled *Computerized Psychological Assessment: A Practitioner's Guide* (Butcher, 1987). |
| 1994 | Introduction of multimedia assessment batteries; for example, at IBM, a multimedia test is used to assess the real-life problem-solving skills of prospective employees (*APA Monitor,* June 1994). |
| 1997 | Educational Testing Service and other testing giants move to computerized testing for major admissions tests such as the Graduate Management Admission Test (GMAT) and Graduate Record Examinations (GRE). |

anticipate massive growth in this field for many years to come. Butcher (1987, App. A) listed 169 vendors as of 1986. Conoley, Plake, and Kemmerer (1991) note that the number of computerized psychological test interpretations had increased to more than 400 by 1990. New computerized test systems are reported virtually every month in trade magazines and newspapers (e.g., *APA Monitor*). Computer-based test interpretation is here to stay.

In this section we will provide an overview of the types of computer-based test interpretations currently available. A comprehensive review of products could easily span several volumes, so the reader will have to settle for a discussion of diverse and representative examples of CBTI. We will examine four approaches to CBTI: scoring reports, descriptive reports, actuarial reports, and computer-assisted clinical reports (Moreland, 1992).

## Scoring Reports

Scoring reports consist of scores and/or profiles. In addition, a scoring report may include statistical significance tests and confidence intervals plotted for the test scores. By definition, scoring reports do not include narrative text or explanation of scores. Moreland (1992) discusses the appeal of scoring reports:

> These kinds of data make it possible to identify especially meaningful scores and meaningful differences among scores at a glance. They should also increase a user's confidence that those scores are in fact important. Statistical significance tests are undoubtedly superior to "clinical rules of thumb" when it comes to accurate interpretation of test scores. And who has time to hand calculate confidence intervals— especially for tests with dozens of scales?

An example of a scoring report for the Jackson Vocational Interest Survey (Jackson, 1991) is shown in Figure 12.1. The reader will notice that a great deal of information is presented in an efficient, condensed manner. This is typical of scoring reports. In a single page, this hypothetical respondent would learn that his interests are highly similar to majors in liberal arts, education, and business. In terms of

occupational fit, he also learns that he is highly compatible with counselors, teachers, lawyers, administrators, and other professions with an emphasis upon human relations.

## Descriptive Reports

A descriptive report goes one step further than a scoring report by providing brief scale-by-scale interpretation of test results. Descriptive reports are especially useful when test findings are conveyed to mental health professionals who have little knowledge of the test in question. For example, most clinical psychologists know that a high score on the MMPI Psychasthenia scale signifies worry and dissatisfaction with social relationships—but other mental health practitioners may not have a clue as to the meaning of an elevation on this scale. A descriptive report can convey invaluable information in a half page or less. One of the first descriptive reports published is portrayed in Figure 12.2. The reader will notice that the 20-year-old male patient is described as shy, sensitive, worried, and severely depressed. Referral of this medical patient to a psychologist or psychiatrist clearly is warranted. This report is a model of simplicity and clarity. By comparison, most contemporary computer-based descriptive reports provide excessive detail. Typically, the clinician must wade through several pages of narrative to extract essential features about the client.

## Actuarial Reports: Clinical versus Actuarial Prediction

The actuarial approach to computer-based test interpretation is based upon the empirical determination of relationships between test results and the criteria of interest. The nature of this approach is best understood in the context of the longstanding debate on clinical versus actuarial prediction. A brief detour is needed here to introduce relevant concepts and issues before discussing actuarial reports.

Many computer-based test interpretations make predictions about the test taker. These

### Similarity to College Students

JVIS profiles from over 10,000 university students who were enrolled in more than 150 different major fields, ranging from accounting to zoology, have been collected and analyzed. That analysis indicated that the major fields could be classed into 17 broad academic clusters. Each cluster is based on data from both males and females and represents a set of educational majors that shared a similar pattern of JVIS scores.

The chart below ranks the similarity of your JVIS Basic Interest profile to each of the student clusters. A high score indicates that your pattern of interests is similar to students in the fields of concentration defining the cluster, while a low score indicates dissimilarity. These scores indicate your probable interest and satisfaction with these academic clusters. These scores do not tell you whether or not you will be successful in any particular field.

| Score | Similarity | University Major Cluster |
|---|---|---|
| **+0.62** | **Very Similar** | **Environmental Resource Management** |
| **+0.55** | **Similar** | **Health, Physical Education and Recreation** |
| **+0.39** | **Moderately Similar** | **Agribusiness and Economics** |
| +0.37 | Moderately Similar | Art and Architecture |
| +0.30 | Moderately Similar | Food Science |
| +0.12 | Neutral | Engineering |
| +0.03 | Neutral | Science |
| −0.03 | Neutral | Computer Science |
| −0.08 | Neutral | Performing Arts |
| −0.12 | Neutral | Social Service |
| −0.12 | Neutral | Health Services and Science |
| −0.19 | Neutral | Mathematical Sciences |
| −0.25 | Neutral | Business |
| −0.25 | Dissimilar | Communication Arts |
| −0.30 | Dissimilar | Behavioral Science |
| −0.32 | Dissimilar | Education |
| −0.54 | Dissimilar | Social Science, Law and Politics |

Your JVIS profile is most similar to college students whose academic areas of specialization are in the three clusters listed below. Sample majors for each of these three areas are also listed.

| University Major Cluster | Sample Majors |
|---|---|
| Environmental Resource Management | Wildlife Technology, Recreation and Parks, Environmental Resource Management, Agricultural Business Management, Agriculture, Forest Science and Technology, Horticulture. |
| Health, Physical Education and Recreation | Health and Physical Education, Recreation and Parks. |
| Agribusiness and Economics | Agricultural Economics and Rural Sociology, Agricultural Business Management, Food Service and Housing Administration. |

● **FIGURE 12.1**   A Scoring Report from the online version of the Jackson Vocational Interest Blank

Note: The full report consists of an 11-page printout.

*Source:* Reprinted with permission from JVIS.com. © 2008, SIGMA Assessment Systems, Inc. All rights reserved.

Sex: Male.    Education: 20.    Age: 34.    Marital Status: Married.    Outpatient.

MMPI Code: 27″5′8064–391/ –KLF/

D    2    Severely depressed, worrying, indecisive, and pessimistic

Pt    7    Rigid and meticulous. Worrisome and apprehensive. Dissatisfied with
social relationships. Probably very religious and moralistic.

Mf    5    Probably sensitive and idealistic with high esthetic, cultural, and artistic
interests

Sc    8    Tends toward abstract interests such as science, philosophy, and religion

Si    0    Probably retiring and shy in social situations

Pa    6    Sensitive. Alive to opinions of others

Pd    4    Independent or mildly nonconformist

Hy    3

Ma    9    Normal energy and activity level

Hs    1    Number of physical symptoms and concern about bodily functions fairly
typical for clinic patients

Consider psychiatric evaluation

● **FIGURE 12.2**
Mayo Clinic MMPI
Descriptive Report
*Source:* Reprinted with permission from Dahlstrom,
W. G., Welsh, G. S., &
Dahlstrom, L. E. (1972).
*An MMPI handbook.*
*Volume 1: Clinical*
*interpretation* (rev. ed.).
Minneapolis: University of
Minnesota Press, p. 309.
Copyright © 1960, 1972 by
the University of
Minnesota.

predictions are often disguised in the language of classification or diagnosis, but they are predictions nonetheless. For example, when a computer-based neuropsychological test report tentatively classifies a client as having brain damage, this is actually an implicit prediction that can be confirmed or disconfirmed by external criteria such as brain scans and neurological consultation. Likewise, when a computer-based MMPI-2 report provides a tentative *DSM-IV* diagnosis of a clinic referral, this is also a prediction that can be validated or invalidated by external criteria such as intensive clinical interview. A final example: When a computer-based CPI screening report for police candidates warns that an applicant will make a poor adjustment in law enforcement, this is also a prediction that could be proved correct or incorrect by an inspection of personnel records at a later date.

The use of computers for test-based prediction highlights an essential distinction known as clinical versus actuarial judgment (Dawes, Faust, & Meehl, 1989; Garb, 1994; Meehl, 1954, 1965, 1986). In **clinical judgment,** the decision maker processes information in his or her head to diagnose, classify,

or predict behavior. An example: A clinical psychologist uses experience, intuition, and textbook knowledge to determine whether an MMPI profile indicates psychosis. Psychosis is a broad category that includes serious mental disorders often characterized by hallucinations, delusions, and disordered thinking. Thus, a clinician's prediction of psychosis (or lack thereof) can be validated against external criteria such as detailed interview.

In **actuarial judgment,** an empirically derived formula is used to diagnose, classify, or predict behavior. An example: A clinical psychologist merely plugs scale scores into a research-based formula to determine whether an MMPI profile indicates psychosis. The actuarial prediction, too, can be validated against appropriate external criteria.

The essence of actuarial judgment is the careful development and subsequent use of an empirically based formula for diagnosis, classification, or prediction of behavior. A common type of actuarial formula is the regression equation in which subtest scores are combined in a weighted linear sum to predict a relevant criterion. But other statistical approaches may work well for decision making, too, including simple cutoff scores and rule-based flow charts. Of course, statistical rules lend themselves to computer implementation, so it is fitting to discuss clinical versus actuarial judgment in this section on computer-based test interpretation.

Although computers facilitate the use of the actuarial method, we need to emphasize that "actuarial" and "computerized" are not synonymous. To be truly actuarial, test interpretations must be automatic (prespecified or routinized) and based on empirically established relations (Dawes, Faust, & Meehl, 1989). If a computer program incorporates such automatic, empirically based decision-making rules, then it is making an actuarial prediction. Conversely, if a computer program embodies the thinking and judgment of a clinician—no matter how wise that person is—then it is making a clinical prediction.

Meehl (1954) was the first to introduce the issue of clinical versus actuarial judgment to a broad range of social scientists. He stated the issue with pure simplicity: "When shall we use our heads instead of the formula?" Consider the practical problem of distinguishing between neurosis and psychosis on the basis of MMPI results. *Neurosis* is an outdated (but still used) diagnostic term that refers to a milder form of mental disorder in which symptoms of anxiety or dysphoria predominate. As noted previously, psychosis is a more serious form of mental disorder that may include hallucinations, delusions, and disordered thinking. The differential diagnosis between these two broad classes of mental disorder is important. Persons with neurosis often respond well to individual psychotherapy, whereas a patient with psychosis may need powerful antipsychotic medications that produce adverse side effects. Which is superior for MMPI-based diagnostic decision making, the head of the well-trained psychologist or an appropriate formula based upon prior research? We return to this issue later.

Meehl (1954) specified two conditions for a fair comparison of these contrasting approaches to decision making. First, both methods should base judgments on the same data. For example, in comparing the experienced clinician against an actuarial equation, both approaches should prognosticate from the same pool of MMPI profiles and only

those profiles. Second, we must avoid conditions that can artificially inflate the accuracy of the actuarial approach. For example, the actuarial equation should be derived on an initial sample, prior to the comparison with clinical decision making on a new sample of MMPI profiles. Otherwise, the actuarial decision rules will capitalize on chance relations among variables and produce a spuriously high rate of correct decisions.

When the conditions are met for a fair test of clinical versus actuarial decision making, the latter method is superior in the vast majority of cases. The actuarial approach is clearly better for the task cited previously—differential diagnosis of neurosis or psychosis from the MMPI. L. R. Goldberg (1965) determined that a simple linear sum of selected MMPI scale scores resulted in 70 percent correct classifications, whereas Ph.D. psychologists averaged only 62 percent, with the single best psychologist achieving 67 percent correct decisions. The decision rule that defeated all human contenders was: if the *T*-score sum on L + Pa + Sc − Hy − Pt exceeds 44, diagnose psychosis; otherwise, diagnose neurosis.[3]

Dawes, Faust, and Meehl (1989) cited nearly 100 comparative studies in the social sciences. In almost every case, the actuarial method equaled or surpassed the clinical method, sometimes substantially. The research by Leli and Filskov (1984) is typical in this regard. They studied the diagnosis of progressive brain dysfunction based upon neuropsychological testing. An actuarial decision rule derived from one set of cases was applied to a new sample with 83 percent correct identification. Working from precisely the same test data, groups of inexperienced and experienced clinicians correctly identified only 63 percent and 58 percent of the new cases, respectively. The reader will notice the disturbing and embarrassing fact that experience did not improve hit rates for this clinical decision-making task.

A study by McMillan, Hastings, and Coldwell (2004) also illustrates the value of simple actuarial methods for predicting clinical outcomes. Their investigation involved 124 residents of a forensic

---

3. Respectively, the full names for these scales are L (validity scale), Paranoia, Schizophrenia, Hysteria, and Psychasthenia.

intellectual disability hospital in England. In this setting, violence is not a rare occurrence, and predicting who might be violent (and therefore require greater attention) is of utmost importance. The researchers compared two approaches to prediction of hospital violence in the next six months: (1) the actuarial approach was merely to tally the number of documented episodes in the prior six months and use this information as the index of risk; and (2) the clinical approach was to use the judgment of the clinical team (psychiatrist, psychologist, nursing staff, and attendants) on a 9-point risk scale (0 = 'no risk' and 8 = 'very high risk'). Briefly, the actuarial approach proved slightly but not significantly superior to the clinical approach. Both approaches revealed strong predictive validity. The results substantiate the common adage that "the best predictor of future behavior is past behavior."

A recent meta-analysis of 136 studies by Grove, Zald, Lebow, Snitz, and Nelson (2000) provides additional support for the superiority of actuarial prediction over clinical prediction. These researchers analyzed diverse studies in the fields of medicine, education, and clinical psychology in which practitioners predicted such outcomes as academic performance, job success, medical diagnosis, psychiatric diagnosis, criminal recidivism, and suicide. In each study, the clinical predictions of the practitioners (physicians, professors, and psychologists) were compared to the actuarial predictions derived from empirically based statistical formulas. Although the researchers found a few scattered instances in which the clinical method was notably more accurate than the statistical method, on the whole, their survey confirmed prior findings on this topic. The authors conclude:

> Even though outlier studies can be found, we identified no systematic exceptions to the general superiority (or at least material equivalence) of mechanical prediction. It holds in general medicine, in mental health, in personality, and in education and training settings. It holds for medically trained judges and for psychologists. It holds for inexperienced and seasoned judges. (p. 25)

Perhaps the most disturbing conclusion of these researchers was that the availability of clinical interview actually *detracted* from the accuracy of practitioner predictions in the diverse fields studied. Compared to the empirically based statistical predictions, the clinical predictions were outperformed by an even *greater* margin when information from clinical interview was available to the practitioners. The reasons for this are unclear but likely include the susceptibility of humans to certain cognitive biases (e.g., paying too much attention to vivid interview information). Also, clinicians typically do not receive adequate feedback as to the accuracy of their judgments and, hence, have no basis for correcting maladaptive predictions.

The lesson to be learned from this literature is that computerized narrative test reports should incorporate actuarial methods, when possible. For example, computer-generated reports should use existing actuarial formulas to determine the likelihood of various psychiatric diagnoses, rather than relying upon the programmed logic of a master clinician. Unfortunately, as the reader will discover in the following, most computerized narrative test reports are clinically based—which raises concerns about their validity.

## Actuarial Interpretation: Sample Approach

The developers of the Personality Inventory for Children (PIC) produced an exemplary system for computer-based actuarial test interpretation, which we will describe for illustrative purposes. The reader will recall from a previous chapter that the PIC, now updated as the PIC-2, is a true-false inventory that the parent or caregiver completes with respect to the child's behavior. Based upon these responses, a profile of $T$ scores (mean of 50, SD of 10) is produced for four validity scales (e.g., Defensiveness), 12 clinical scales (e.g., Delinquency), and four factor scales (e.g., Social Incompetence). In total, $T$ scores are reported for 20 scales on the PIC. Of course, higher $T$ scores indicate a greater likelihood of psychopathology.

Actuarial interpretation of the PIC rests upon the empirically derived correlations between individual scales and important nontest criteria. Research subjects for the Lachar and Gdowski

(1979) study consisted of 431 children referred to a busy teaching clinic. As part of the evaluation process for each child, the staff members, parents, and teachers completed a comprehensive questionnaire, which listed 322 descriptive statements concerning behavior and other variables. In addition, parents or caretakers filled out the PIC.

In the first phase of the actuarial study, the 322 descriptive statements were correlated with the 20 PIC scales to identify significant scale correlates. In the second phase, the significant correlates were analyzed further to determine the relationship between descriptive statements and $T$-score ranges on the PIC scales. The outcome of this prodigious effort was a series of actuarial tables not unlike the tables used by insurance companies to predict the likelihood of illness, death, accidents, and the like, based upon population demographics such as age, sex, and residence. Some examples of actuarial correlates of the Delinquency, or DLQ, Scale are depicted in Table 12.4.

Actuarial tables capture a wealth of information useful in clinical practice. Consider two hypothetical 12-year-old children, Jimmy and Johnny, each referred to a clinician with the same presenting problem: school underachievement. As part of the intake procedure, the clinician asks each mother to fill out the PIC. Suppose that the Delinquency, or DLQ, Scale score for Jimmy is highly elevated at a $T$ score of 114, whereas Johnny

obtains an average range $T$ score of 54. Based upon these scores, the clinician would know the likelihood—listed here as percentages—that certain behavioral descriptions apply to each child:

|  | Jimmy<br>(DLQ = 114) | Johnny<br>(DLQ = 54) |
|---|---|---|
| Refuses to go to bed | 42% | 18% |
| Lies | 90% | 44% |
| Uses drugs | 32% | 0% |
| Rejects school | 56% | 16% |
| Involved with police | 58% | 0% |

The reader will immediately recognize that Jimmy fits a pattern of pervasive conduct disorder, whereas Johnny appears to have few such behavior problems. In Jimmy's case, the underachievement is most likely secondary to a pattern of antisocial behavior, whereas for Johnny the clinician must look elsewhere to understand the school failure. Of course, this is only a small fraction of the information that would be available from a computer-based actuarial interpretation of the PIC. In a full report, the clinician would receive statistics and narrative statements pertinent to all 20 scales from the PIC.

## Computer-Assisted Clinical Reports

In a computer-assisted clinical report, the interpretive statements assigned to test results are based upon the judgment of one or more expert

● **TABLE 12.4    Occurrence Rates for Actuarial Descriptors of the PIC Delinquency Scale**

| Descriptor | Base Rate[*] | T-Score Ranges | | | | | | | |
|---|---|---|---|---|---|---|---|---|---|
|  |  | 30–59 | 60–69 | 70–79 | 80–89 | 90–99 | 100–109 | 110–119 | >120 |
| Refuses to go to bed | 30 | 18 | 26 | 23 | 33 | 36 | 33 | 42 | 38 |
| Lies | 62 | 44 | 36 | 48 | 73 | 71 | 79 | 90 | 91 |
| Uses drugs | 12 | 0 | 2 | 6 | 7 | 11 | 18 | 32 | 53 |
| Rejects school | 40 | 16 | 26 | 40 | 42 | 50 | 47 | 56 | 67 |
| Involved with police | 17 | 0 | 4 | 6 | 10 | 21 | 19 | 58 | 63 |

[*]Percentage of all children rated as displaying the characteristic.

Note: These five descriptors are merely a representative sample of the 51 actuarial correlates of the Delinquency Scale.

*Source:* Material from *Actuarial Assessment of Child and Adolescent Personality: An Interpretive Guide for the Personality Inventory for Children Profile* copyright © 1979 by Western Psychological Services. Reprinted by permission of the publisher, Western Psychological Services, 12031 Wilshire Boulevard, Los Angeles, CA 90025, United States of America.

clinicians. The expert clinicians formalize their thought processes and develop automated decision rules that are then translated into computer code. This method differs crucially from the computer-assisted actuarial approach in which interpretive statements are based strictly upon formal research findings. Superficially, the two approaches may appear to be identical insofar as each is rule based and automated. The difference has to do with the origin of the rules: empirical research (actuarial approach) versus clinician judgment (clinical approach).

Even though clinicians generally recognize the superiority of the actuarial method, there is one significant advantage to the computer-assisted clinical approach. The advantage is that the clinical approach can be designed to interpret all test profiles, whereas some test profiles will be uninterpretable by means of an actuarial approach. The discouraging truth about actuarial "cookbook" systems for test interpretation is that the classification rate usually plummets when a system is used in a new setting. The classification rate refers to the percentage of test results that fit the complex profile classification rules necessary for actuarial interpretation. For example, in the Gilberstadt and Duker (1965) actuarial MMPI system, the 1-2-3 code type is defined by these rules for the Hs (Hypochondriasis), D (Depression), Hysteria (Hs), and L, F, K (validity) scales:

1. Hs, D, and Hy over $T$ score 70
2. Hs > D > Hy
3. No other scales over $T$ score 70
4. L < $T$ score 66, F < $T$ score 86, and K < $T$ score 71

Persons who produce this kind of MMPI profile often suffer from psychophysiological overreactivity, not to mention a host of other empirically confirmed characteristics. Of course, there are several additional code types, each defined by a set of complex decision rules, and each accompanied by an elaborate, actuarially based description of personality and psychopathology. A typical finding is that a computer-assisted actuarial system developed within one client population will be capable of interpreting up to 85 percent of the test

profiles encountered in that setting. However, when the actuarial system is applied to a new client population, perhaps 50 percent of the test profiles will fit the decision rules. This means that about half of the test profiles do not fit the rules. At best, these clients will receive a superficial, scale-by-scale interpretation rather than a more sophisticated actuarial interpretation based upon code types. The problem of shrinkage in classification rate is observed in virtually all studies of actuarial interpretation (Moreland, 1992).

Computer-assisted clinical reports tend to be lengthy and detailed, full of scale scores, item indices, and graphs. Of course, these reports also include several pages of narrative report, usually phrased in terms of hypotheses as opposed to confirmed findings. The shortest such report is about six pages (e.g., the Karson Clinical Report for the 16PF), whereas longer ones can run to 10 or 20 pages (e.g., MMPI-2 interpretations).

## ● HIGH-DEFINITION VIDEO AND VIRTUAL REALITY: THE NEW HORIZONS OF CAPA

With recent improvements in technology, the modern microcomputer has opened up a whole new world for psychological assessment. The ordinary personal computer is now capable of presenting video segments that possess the visual clarity of television. Built-in stereo sound systems produce exquisite audio output, including synthesized human speech that passes for the real thing. With CD-ROM accessories, instantaneous access to huge repositories of information—including still images, live video segments, music, tables, charts, animation—is possible. Collectively, these capacities are known as **multimedia**—especially when used for interactive and educational applications. Multimedia is one new horizon of computer-assisted psychological assessment. Another is virtual reality.

At IBM, researchers have been developing the Workplace Situations test to assess job applicants for manufacturing positions (Drasgow, Olson-Buchanan, & Moberg, 1999). What is unique about the test is the nature of the stimuli. Rather than merely describing work situations, the test displays computer-driven interactive video of realistic work scenes. The assessment consists of 30 short scenes in a fictional organization named Quintronics. The scenes depict work-related interpersonal episodes arising in the manufacture of hypothetical electronic products called quintelles and alpha pinhole boards. The computer vignettes depict such concerns as excessive workloads, poor training, interpersonal conflict, poor productivity, and flawed work. Each scene is presented and then the screen pauses with a description of five ways of responding to the workplace problem. The scenes have a highly realistic feeling to them, which enhances the face validity of the test. This kind of interactive video test likely provides a more accurate assessment than paper-and-pencil tests of how people would actually respond on the job. Tests that use interactive video are especially good at tapping examinees' abilities to deal with complex, real-life problems, such as decision making under time pressure or conflict resolution in the workplace.

Olson-Buchanan et al. (1998) have developed an interactive video test of conflict resolution that reveals both the promise and the perils of this new technology. Their instrument, the Conflict Resolution Skills Assessment (CRSA), consists of nine conflict scenes, each with the potential for multiple branchings, depending upon the examinee's ongoing response pattern:

A typical item on the Conflict Resolution Skills Assessment begins by presenting a conflict scene (1–3 minutes in duration) to an individual. At a critical point the scene is stopped and four options for addressing the conflict are provided; the assessee is asked to choose the option that best describes what he or she would do in this situation. Depending on the option chosen, the computer branches to an extension of the first scene depicting how events might unfold. Again, the conflict escalates, the scene is frozen, four options for addressing the conflict are presented, and the assessee decides which option would best resolve the conflict. The computer then branches to an entirely new conflict scene. (p. 180)

The perils of this effort include the increased expense required for test development (e.g., cost of producing high-quality, convincing videos) as well as daunting theoretical issues (e.g., challenge of conceptualizing "good" conflict resolution skills). This kind of interactive, branching, video-based test also poses unique psychometric problems. For example, how do you assess the reliability of specific subelements of the test when only a few of the examinees may have taken that "route" through the test?

In spite of these challenges, the development of pathbreaking instruments such as the CRSA is well worth the effort. Consider one important payoff, namely, scores on the CRSA show essentially no correlation with general cognitive ability (Dragsow et al., 1999). Psychologists long have suspected that social skills are distinct from cognitive skills, but when both are assessed with traditional paper-and-pencil instruments, moderate to strong correlations are the rule. Most likely, this is because of shared method variance, namely, verbal test-taking skills help an examinee navigate any paper-and-pencil test, regardless of the construct being measured. By using interactive video as the primary test stimulus, instruments such as the CRSA provide a purer measure of social skills than paper-and-pencil tests. This unique instrument illustrates that social skills contribute something different than cognitive skills to effective work performance.

Another potential application of multimedia is in personnel screening for entry-level police officers. Law enforcement personnel must have good observational and evaluative skills, which can be assessed realistically with video stimuli. For example, an assessment might consist, in part, of a videotape of witnesses at a crime scene. Police candidates might be asked to determine the truth of the witnesses and to draw conclusions about the crime based upon their observational powers (*APA Monitor*, June 1994). This example—currently hypothetical—illustrates the potential for multimedia to revolutionize psychological assessment.

It is worth noting that multimedia tests can be virtually free of reading and writing requirements on the part of the examinee. Talented job candidates who do not possess good reading or writing abilities but who do have practical job skills can be identified by means of multimedia tests. For some jobs, multimedia might be fairer than the paper-and-pencil approach.

Finally, a very recent high-tech approach to computer-based assessment deserves brief mention. In virtual reality, the participant wears a pair of goggles that transmit realistic, three-dimensional images of a simulated environment. By manipulating simple control devices, the participant can navigate through the environment even though standing still. Of course, the visual environment, known as a **virtual reality**, is based on sophisticated computerized output.

New assessment tools that utilize virtual reality (VR) are in their infancy, but show great promise. For example, Kesztyues, Mehlitz, Schilken, and others (2000) describe a VR system for the assessment of spatial orientation disorders in neurological referrals. They compared the traditional head-mounted display with a wall projection system as patients "navigated" their way through virtual environments such as a park or a maze. This assessment system holds promise, although the researchers did encounter unexpected problems such as some patients experiencing nausea when using the head-mounted display. Elkind, Rubin, Rosenthal, Skoff, and Prather (2001) describe a promising VR test of real-life skills required for safe, independent living. Numerous innovative tests based upon VR can be found in the new journal *CyberPsychology and Behavior*. Riva (1997) has assembled relevant articles on the promise and pitfalls of VR in psychological assessment.

## ● EVALUATION OF COMPUTER-BASED TEST INTERPRETATION

Computerized testing has clear advantages but also some potentially serious disadvantages in comparison to the traditional clinical approach to psychological testing. We offer a brief survey here, stressing both the advantages and disadvantages of computer-based testing, diagnosis, and report writing.

More detail on this topic can be found in Butcher (1987), Moreland (1992), Roid and Johnson (1998), Butcher, Perry, and Atlis (2000), and Mills, Potenza, Fremer, and Ward (2002).

## Advantages of Computerized Testing and Report Writing

The main advantages of computer-based testing are quick turnaround, inexpensive cost, near-perfect reliability, and complete objectivity. In addition, some measurement applications such as flexible adaptive testing virtually require the use of computers for their implementation. We explore these points in more detail later.

In a busy clinical practice, delays between testing and submission of the consulting report are common, almost inevitable. These delays not only tarnish the reputation of the consultant, but they may also adversely affect the treatment outcome for the client. For example, a college student with learning disabilities may need immediate intervention in order to avert an academic disaster. A delay of two or three weeks in submission of a consulting report could spell, indirectly, the difference between failure and success in academic performance. Computer-based reports can speed up the entire consultation process. Many software systems produce reports that can be transferred into a standard word-processing program for immediate customized editing, thereby speeding up the turnaround time (e.g., Psychological Corporation, 1994; Tanner, 1992).

Cost is another consideration in computer-based testing. Although there are no definitive studies on this topic, most authorities assert that computer-scored and interpreted psychological tests cost considerably less than those produced entirely by clinician effort (Butcher, 1987). In their studies of automated testing at the Salt Lake City VA Hospital, Klingler, Miller, Johnson, and Williams (1977) concluded that the computer cut the cost of testing in half. Certainly as the computerized testing programs become more sophisticated and are used by larger numbers of clinicians, the cost per consultation will plummet.

Reliability and objectivity are the hallmarks of the computer. Assuming that the software is accurate and error-free, computers simply do not make clerical scoring errors, nor do they vary their methods of stimulus presentation from one day to the next, nor do they yield different narrative reports based on the same input. The product is the same no matter how many times the computer program is used. Furthermore, because computerized reports are based on objective rules, they are not distorted by halo effects or other subjective biases that might enter into a clinically derived report. Butcher (1987) asserts that computerized reports could have special significance in court cases, because they would be viewed as "untouched by human hands." This is an intriguing possibility, but perhaps somewhat overly optimistic. Lawyers and judges will still want to know who programmed the software, how the narrative statements were developed, and so on.

## Disadvantages of Computerized Testing and Report Writing

Consider the following illustration, hypothetical yet realistic and probably not a rare occurrence. A hospital physician refers a difficult medical patient to the psychology service for a personality evaluation. The patient is escorted to the testing center where a receptionist seats him at a table in front of a microcomputer. Instructions appear on the computer monitor to answer a series of self-statements true or false by pressing the T or F key. The patient completes the computerized objective personality inventory and is escorted back to the medical service. Seconds later, a narrative report based on the patient's responses emerges from the printer. The consulting psychologist peruses the report briefly, then sends it (unsigned) through departmental mail to the physician. The report is handsome, ever so crisp in its laser-printed appearance, with a graphic summary of scales on the cover page. Furthermore, the narrative is valid sounding and reads as if it were copyedited by a professional writer (in fact, it was). The physician is impressed and takes the report

to heart, making treatment decisions based on the personality evaluation.

This scenario illustrates an essential quandary with computer-based testing and report writing: Computers can so dominate the testing process that the clinical psychologist is demoted to a mere clerk—or is removed from the assessment loop entirely. Although most psychologists acknowledge that computers are a welcome addition to the practice of psychological testing, critics have raised a number of disquieting concerns about recent assessment practices such as those depicted here. Computerization of the testing process raises practical, legal, ethical, and measurement issues that deserve thoughtful review.

In general, skeptics do not attack the practice of computerizing the mechanics of test administration and scoring; these computer applications are seen as efficient and appropriate uses of modern technology. Nonetheless, even the most ardent proponents acknowledge the need to investigate test-form equivalency when an existing test is adapted to computerized administration. In particular, practitioners should not assume that the computerized adaptation and the original version of a test produce identical results. Equivalency is an empirical issue that must be demonstrated by appropriate research. For most tests, equivalency can be demonstrated, but this must not be taken for granted (Lukin, Dowd, Plake, & Kraft, 1985; Schuldberg, 1988).

Some tests do not maintain score equivalency when translated to computer. The Category Test (CT) from the Halstead-Reitan Neuropsychological Battery is a case in point. In a comparison of computerized and standard versions of the Category Test with rehabilitation patients, Berger, Chibnall, and Gfeller (1994) found a huge difference in error rate for two groups of subjects who had equivalent backgrounds: an average of 84 errors on the computerized CT versus an average of 66 errors on the standard CT test. Apparently, the computerized CT test is much more difficult than the standard version, which means that separate norms must be developed for its interpretation. Much smaller differences between computerized and standard test administration have also been reported for the

MMPI, with computer-based scores tending to underestimate (very slightly) the booklet-based scores (Watson, Thomas, & Anderson, 1992).

# ● COMPUTERIZED ADAPTIVE TESTING

A final advantage of computer-based testing is its application to flexible adaptive testing. Adaptive testing is nothing new—Binet used it when he worked out the methods for finding the basal and ceiling items on his famous intelligence test. Binet placed his items along a continuum of difficulty so that the examiner could test downward to find the examinee's basal level and test upward to find the ceiling level. This procedure eliminated the need to administer irrelevant items—those so easy (below the basal level) that the examinee would surely pass them, or those so hard (above the ceiling level) that the examinee would surely fail them. Another example of adaptive testing is the two-stage procedure whereby results on an initial routing test are used to determine the entry level for subsequent scales. For example, on the Stanford-Binet: Fifth Edition, results of the initial vocabulary and matrices subtests determine the starting points for subsequent subtests. By reducing the time needed to obtain an accurate measure of ability, adaptive testing fulfills a very constructive purpose.

**Computerized adaptive testing (CAT)** is a family of procedures that allows for accurate and efficient measurement of ability (Wainer, 2002). Although details differ from one method to another, most forms of computerized adaptive testing share the following features:

1. Based on extensive pretesting, the item response characteristics of each item (e.g., percentage passing versus ability) are appraised precisely.
2. These item response characteristics and a CAT item-selection strategy are programmed into the computer.
3. In selecting the next item for presentation, the computer uses the examinee's total history of responses up to that point.

4. The computer recalculates the examinee's estimated ability level after each response.
5. The computer also estimates the precision of measurement (e.g., standard error of measurement) after each response.
6. Testing continues until a predetermined level of measurement precision is reached.
7. The examinee's score is based on the difficulty level and other measurement characteristics of items passed, not on the total number of items correct.

The measurement advantages of CAT can be summarized in two words: precision and efficiency (Weiss & Vale, 1987). Regarding precision, CAT guarantees that each examinee is measured with the same degree of precision because testing continues until this criterion is met. This is not so with traditional tests in which scores at both tails of the distribution reflect greater levels of measurement error than scores in the middle of the distribution. Regarding efficiency, the CAT approach requires far fewer test items than are needed in traditional testing. For example, written certification examinations usually include 200 to 500 items, while CAT examinations are always shorter, often including fewer than 100 items to achieve a more accurate level of measurement (Lunz & Bergstrom, 1994). In one analysis, the reliability of alternative computer-adaptive tests for certification in medical technology was .96 (Lunz, Bergstrom, & Wright, 1994). This is remarkable because shorter tests (the goal in CAT testing) tend to have lower reliability than longer tests (such as found in traditional testing programs).

In addition to increased measurement efficiency, CAT has many other advantages over traditional paper-and-pencil assessment (Wainer, 2000, p. 11):

- Test security is improved.
- Examinees work at their own pace.
- Examinees are equally challenged.
- Answer sheets pose no ambiguity (e.g., erasures).
- Immediate scoring and feedback is possible.
- Pretesting of new items can be included.

- Faulty items can be eliminated immediately.
- A variety of question types can be included.

Regarding the last point, examples of novel item types not possible on a traditional multiple-choice exam include spoken words (such as for a spelling test), open-ended math problems (the answer is typed in), and video segments (followed by written questions).

The CAT approach to psychological testing has been used mainly by large organizations such as the U.S. Army and the Educational Testing Service for assessment of intelligence and special abilities. In recent years, national licensing boards (e.g., in medicine) have begun to implement CAT testing because of convenience in scheduling tests, tighter control over test security, reduced costs, and the opportunity for better data collection (Lunz & Bergstrom, 1994). Technical information on CAT systems is proprietary and difficult to obtain. Nonetheless, it is clear that the efficiency of the CAT approach is substantial. CAT uses fewer items of better quality than a conventional test of the same length. A general finding is that CAT reduces test length by about 50 percent, with reductions for individual examinees of up to 80 percent, with no loss in measurement accuracy (Laatsch & Choca, 1994; Weiss & Vale, 1987).

One recent study revealed phenomenal success for the CAT approach in reducing the time spent in testing, and simultaneously providing better discriminant validity in the assessment of depressive symptomatology (Gibbons, Weiss, Kupfer, Frank, Fagiolini, and others, 2008). The study involved 800 outpatients who completed the 616-item Mood and Anxiety Spectrum Scales (MASS) at two times. The first administration was used to develop and evaluate a CAT version of the MASS, while the second administration confirmed the functioning of the CAT method in live testing. The CAT version utilized an average of *95 percent* fewer test items (30 instead of 616) and yet was shown to provide *better* discrimination of seriously depressed versus mildly depressed patients.

Recently, CAT has been applied to mainstream personality tests like the MMPI-2 with encouraging results. Forbey and Ben-Porath (2007) provide a review of the MMPI-2 computerized adaptive version. They conclude that the new approach provides the same accuracy of measurement with about a 20 percent reduction in the number of items administered. Even so, CAT approaches with the MMPI-2 are experimental at this point, and not likely to receive significant clinical usage for several years.

There may well be reasons for caution in the application of CAT to personality testing. An unavoidable consequence of using CAT is that item order will change from one examinee to another, which may invoke context effects that influence subsequent item responding. Ortner (2008) investigated this prospect with a CAT version of the Eysenck Personality Profiler (EPP) with 362 German adults. Some participants first encountered items representing extreme trait levels, while others were first exposed to items representing medium trait levels. These initial exposures distorted their subsequent responses to the point where scores on three out of seven scales of the EPP shifted up or down significantly. These findings indicate that context effects may be a problem in using CAT with personality inventories.

As the cost of computing continues to plummet, more and more large-scale applications of CAT will be developed. In the late 1990s, the Educational Testing Service moved toward near total reliance on CAT versions of the Graduate Record Examination and other selection tests. Licensing and certification boards such as the National Council of State Boards of Nursing also have introduced CAT versions of their certification tests. Mills and Stocking (1996) discuss practical issues in large-scale computerized testing.

## ● THE FUTURE OF TESTING

What is the future of psychological testing in the twenty-first century? We will hazard a few speculations here, cognizant that prognostications about the future often are wrong. Forecasting developments in testing is especially difficult because the enterprise is increasingly constrained, directly or indirectly, by public opinion. For example, at one point in the 1980s the legislature of the state of California made it *illegal* for school psychologists to use traditional intelligence tests as a basis for placing minority students in special education classes. These restraints on testing were driven by public outrage over the excessive placement of minority students in special education classes. Thus, even when a particular technology of testing is feasible and promoted by psychologists, there exists the possibility that it might be strictly controlled or even banned.

A case in point is Matarazzo's (1992) prediction that biological measures of intelligence will gain prominence in the twenty-first century. Certainly it appears true that biological measures of ability such as averaged evoked potential (gauged from EEG waves), or glucose metabolic rate in the brain (gauged from PET scans), or relative brain size (gauged from MRI scans) will prove to be effective approaches to assessment (see Topic 5A, Theories of Intelligence and Factor Analysis). But Matarazzo (1992) goes further in asserting that these and other biological approaches actually will receive common usage:

> Therefore, another of my predictions is that in the early decades of the 21st century we may see the further development and *use in practice* of these and other biological indices of brain function and structure in a test (or a test battery) for the measurement of individual differences in mental ability, thus heralding the first clear break from test items and tests in the Binet tradition in a century. (p. 1012, italics in the original)

Although Matarazzo's prediction could come true, a more likely scenario is that the general public will be threatened when biological indices are used in assessment and will, therefore, take steps (e.g., pressure on legislators) to ensure that such measures receive limited (if any) application. The public will be threatened because, rightly or wrongly, biological characteristics such as glucose metabolic rate in the brain are perceived to be relatively permanent and immutable. The fear will arise that biological tests will sort people into a caste system.

Even if (or when) the validity of biological tests is firmly established, it will be decades (if ever) until they are found acceptable by the general public.

## Trends in Testing: A Few Confident Predictions

The computerization of testing is already a fixture of industrialized societies and this trend can only increase in the future. Existing tests will be adapted to the desktop computer with increasing regularity. An example of this trend is Fepsy (Ferrum + Psyche), a system for automated neuropsychological testing that is available online at 220 sites throughout the Netherlands and most of Europe. Fepsy is described on the Internet at www.euronet.nl/users/fepsy. Fepsy consists of the following subtests:

- Auditory reaction time
- Binary choice reaction time
- Tapping task
- Visual searching task
- Recognition tasks
- Vigilance task
- Rhythm task
- Classification task
- Six Visual Half field tasks
- Corsi block tapping

A common use is pre- and postoperative testing of patients who undergo epilepsy surgery for relief of seizures. The system has even been used with fully conscious patients *during* surgery. Under local anesthesia, the patient works on a subtest while simultaneously receiving harmless electrical stimulation at distinctive sites on the cortex. The purpose is to determine whether specific cognitive functions might be affected when scar tissue is excised from the brain. The advantage of using a multicenter, multinational, computerized testing system is that the examiner has access to normative data for *thousands* of patients with specific conditions.

Another prediction is that fewer and fewer wide-spectrum tests (e.g., personality inventories and individual intelligence tests) will be released by test publishers (Gregory, 1998). Instead, publishers will concentrate on tests designed to assess particular areas of functioning for specific target populations (e.g., measures of memory functioning for elderly persons suspected of having dementia). The reasons for these complementary trends are economic:

> Test publishing is big business, a respectable way for large corporations to earn a profit. Publishers will be reluctant to make the major investment needed to develop new instruments that have the grandiose ambition of assessing many aspects of personality or intellect for a wide range of subjects. The cost is too high and—in light of the existing competition—the risk is too great. (Gregory, 1998, pp. 76–77)

Test publishers likely will focus on less-expensive and less-risky forms of test development such as instruments that embody distinctive constructs relevant to specific target groups. Examples might include tests to measure risky behaviors in adolescents, mental decline in elderly persons, faulty cognitions in depressed persons, or communication problems in maritally distressed couples. These kinds of instruments will flourish, whereas publishers will rarely invest in new omnibus tests of personality or ability, preferring instead to revise and recycle existing instruments.

We can also predict with some confidence that the movement toward evidence-based assessment will gain strength in the years ahead. In **evidence-based assessment,** the soundness of a testing tool is evaluated not just by means of the standard psychometric indices of reliability and validity but through considerations of clinical utility as well (Barlow, 2005). As outlined by Hunsley and Mash (2005), clinical utility is a broad and indistinct concept that includes a number of features:

- Diagnostic utility—the degree to which the assessment data contribute to the formulation of an accurate and complete diagnosis
- Treatment utility—the degree to which clinical assessment data contribute to positive treatment outcomes
- Incremental validity—the extent to which using one test rather than another improves the sensitivity and specificity of assessment

- Monetary cost—the extent to which the monetary benefit of using a test exceeds its cost
- Psychological cost—the extent to which errors of measurement (false positives, false negatives) lead to personal distress
- Client acceptability—the degree to which the client will agree to complete the assessment

Driven in large measure by the insistence of the insurance industry that therapies must be empirically based, there is a growing demand for brief, effective treatments throughout the entire field of health care. Evidence-based assessment is inescapably intertwined with this national movement toward evidence-based therapy for medical and psychological illnesses. Side by side with this trend, we can expect to see a keen emphasis upon empirically based psychological assessments.

Finally, we can predict that positive psychological assessment will gain greater popularity. **Positive psychological assessment** is a natural spin-off of the positive psychology movement, which is defined as "the scientific and practical pursuit of optimal human functioning" (Lopez & Snyder, 2003). Proponents of the positive psychology movement find the current focus of assessment—with its emphasis on pathology and what is wrong with people—to be lopsided and incomplete. A full understanding of persons also includes an appraisal of with is *right* with them. It includes a census of such positive qualities as hope, creativity, wisdom, courage, forgiveness, humor, gratitude, and coping. The traditional instruments of psychological testing—for example, the Rorschach, MMPI-2, MCMI-III, and so forth—provide essentially no information on these positive human qualities. In the years ahead, new instruments and original philosophies of assessment will most certainly redress the imbalance.

## Testing and the Next Big Questions in Psychology

In this closing section of the book, we turn to some admittedly more speculative predictions about the future of testing. In doing so, the reader is invited to exercise his or her imagination as well. After all, psychological testing is here to stay, and will continue to evolve and adapt. As it has for more than a century, testing will continue to play a significant role in psychology and modern society. But exactly how?

The starting point for this final conversation is a fascinating issue of *Perspectives on Psychological Science*, a journal of the Association for Psychological Science (Diener, 2009). The journal editor asked a number of leading psychologists—none from the field of psychometrics—to write about the most important questions to be asked in their particular specialty in the upcoming decade. These questions have been reproduced in paraphrased manner (for consistency and clarity) in Table 12.5. A few esoteric contributions have been omitted.

Of course, the whole point in asking a question is to hope that an answer will be found. While at first glance it may seem only a slight possibility that psychological testing could contribute to answering any of these questions, on closer examination it seems likely that testing will play an essential role in many cases.

Consider the question of nature and nurture of plasticity in early human development (Belsky & Pluess, 2009). This is a general topic that invites many specific lines of inquiry. For example, Davis et al. (2007) found that prenatal maternal depression and elevated cortisol levels in late pregnancy predicted negative reactivity in children at age 2. But what is "negative reactivity?" The dependent variable in this line of research—reactivity in children—is a construct measured by rating scales and situational tests. Thus, one line of answers to the underlying question ("What is the nature and nurture of plasticity in early human development?") likely will hinge on the development of precise and valid measures of reactivity in children. This is a clear role for psychological testing in answering one of the big questions in psychology.

Another question on the list pertains to evolutionary explanations of personality and individual differences (Buss, 2009). Regardless of the particular directions pursued in this line of research, accurate measurement of *appropriate* personality

| ● **TABLE 12.5** The Next Big Questions in Diverse Fields of Psychology |
| --- |
| What is the connection between complex psychological states such as emotion or cognition and the physical substrates of the brain? (Barrett, 2009) |
| Why do people do what they do? And, what are the important situational and personality variables in answering this question? (Funder, 2009) |
| What is the nature and nurture of plasticity in early human development? (Belsky & Pluess, 2009) |
| How do we achieve a synthesized understanding of early cognitive development from studies of separate cognitive abilities? (Oakes, 2009) |
| How can evolutionary psychology successfully explain personality and individual differences? (Buss, 2009) |
| How do stressful events and negative emotions influence the immune system, and how big are the effects? (Kiecolt-Glaser, 2009) |
| How can you tell if a particular memory belonging to you or someone else is true or false? (Bernstein & Loftus, 2009) |
| Can we improve our physical health by altering our social networks? (Cohen & Janicki-Deverts, 2009) |
| How can decision making be improved? (Milkman, Chugh, & Bazerman, 2009) |
| How can we promote self knowledge ("Know thyself") and what are the results of greater self knowledge? (Wilson, 2009) |
| Can psychological research on correcting cognitive errors promote human welfare? (Lilienfeld, Ammirati, & Landfield, 2009) |
| Is it possible to teach intuition and can it be enhanced by virtual simulation? (Seligman & Kahana, 2009) |
| What are the mechanisms of gene-environment interaction effects in the development of conduct disorder? (Dodge, 2009) |
| Why do different individuals progress along different life trajectories? (Smith, 2009) |
| How can we live well? How can we achieve and sustain a good life? (Park & Peterson, 2009) |
| What is the near and distant future of human-android interaction? (Roese & Amir, 2009) |

constructs will be required. By *appropriate*, we are referring here not to just any old personality constructs, but to those that "cut nature at its joints." In other words, the personality constructs measured in evolutionary psychology need to capture essential underlying elements of personality that could be susceptible to evolutionary influence. As an example, consider research on humor styles, discussed in an earlier chapter. Using the Humor Styles Questionnaire (HSQ, Martin, et al., 2003) in a behavior genetics analysis of identical and fraternal twins, Vernon et al. (2008) found that positive forms of humor (Affiliative and Self-enhancing) revealed significant genetic influence whereas negative forms of humor (Aggressive and Self-defeating) arose from environmental influences. The point of this digression is that the HSQ successfully partitions humor into meaningful elements, including some that can be explained in evolutionary terms. For example, we could hypothesize that Affiliative humor promotes group bonding which, in turn, promotes individual survival and thus allows for genes to be passed on. This conclusion is possible because of the careful analysis of humor implicit in the development of the relevant personality test, the Humor Situations Questionnaire.

Finally, consider the question whether we can improve our physical health by altering our social networks (Cohen & Janicki-Deverts, 2009). There is no doubt that membership in a diverse social network is correlated with a variety of positive health outcomes, such as resistance to cognitive decline with aging, better prognosis when facing chronic illnesses, and even greater resistance to infectious disease (Cohen & Janicki-Deverts, 2009). But these results are correlational, not necessarily causal. The pressing question is: if individuals *alter* their social networks will this improve physical health? From the standpoint of psychological testing, the construct of social network is crucial to the answer. What is a social network? How is it assessed or measured? Research in this area of behavioral medicine will require the development of straightforward and valid measures of social network, another role for testing in answering one of the big questions of psychology.

As a final challenge, the reader is invited to review the list in Table 12.5. What roles can you see for psychological testing in answering these big questions?

## ● SUMMARY

1. The term *computer-assisted psychological assessment* (CAPA) refers to the entire range of computer applications in psychological assessment. This includes administration, scoring, and interpretation of tests; computerized adaptive testing; and sophisticated multimedia applications.

2. The first use of computers to provide test interpretations can be traced to the Mayo Clinic in the early 1960s. This MMPI interpretive system supplied brief scale-by-scale statements based upon clinical lore.

3. Computer-based test interpretation (CBTI) is now available for virtually every published psychological test. Four approaches to CBTI are recognized: scoring reports, descriptive reports, actuarial reports, and computer-assisted clinical reports.

4. Scoring reports consist of only scores and/or profiles but may include statistical significance tests and confidence intervals plotted for the test scores. These reports highlight meaningful scores and score differences at a glance.

5. A descriptive report provides brief scale-by-scale interpretation of test results. These reports are especially useful when test findings are conveyed to mental health professionals who have little knowledge of the test in question.

6. In actuarial test interpretation, an empirically derived formula is used to diagnose, classify, or predict behavior. This is in contrast to the clinical approach in which the psychologist processes information in his or her head to diagnose, classify, or predict behavior.

7. Empirical comparisons of clinical versus actuarial test interpretation find the latter to be superior in virtually every case. Computerized test interpretations should incorporate actuarial methods, when possible.

8. In a computer-assisted clinical report, the interpretive statements are based upon the automated and computerized judgment of one or more expert clinicians. This approach allows for interpretation of all test profiles, not just those that fit certain actuarial patterns.

9. The advantages of computer-based test interpretation include objectivity, speed, and low cost. A major disadvantage is the danger that the psychologist could be excluded from the assessment process entirely, which increases the risk that test results will be misused.

10. Multimedia includes realistic, interactive presentation of test stimuli via computer (e.g., video display of a work situation). Multimedia allows for the testing of complex, real-life problems, such as conflict resolution in the workplace.

11. Computerized adaptive testing (CAT) is a family of procedures that allows for accurate and efficient measurement of ability. In this approach, the computer guides item selection based upon prior examinee answers.

12. The purpose of CAT is to reach a predetermined level of measurement accuracy with as few test items as possible. A typical finding is that CAT reduces test length by about 50 percent with no loss in measurement accuracy.

13. The future of testing is difficult to predict. Whereas some authorities predict an increase in use of biological measures of intelligence, this is uncertain. Certainly the increased computerization of testing is one clear trend that can only intensify.

## KEY TERMS AND CONCEPTS

computer-assisted psychological assessment   p. 552

computer-based test interpretation   p. 552

clinical judgment   p. 555

actuarial judgment   p. 555

multimedia   p. 559

virtual reality   p. 561

computerized adaptive testing   p. 563

evidence-based assessment   p. 566

positive psychological assessment   p. 566

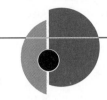

# Major Landmarks in the History of Psychological Testing

| | |
|---|---|
| 2200 B.C. | Chinese begin civil service examinations. |
| 1838 | Jean Esquirol distinguishes between mental illness and mental retardation. |
| 1862 | Wilhelm Wundt uses a calibrated pendulum to measure the "speed of thought." |
| 1866 | O. Edouard Seguin writes the first major textbook on the assessment and treatment of mental retardation. |
| 1869 | Wundt founds the first experimental laboratory in psychology in Leipzig, Germany. |
| 1884 | Francis Galton administers the first test battery to thousands of citizens at the International Health Exhibit. |
| 1890 | James McKeen Cattell uses the term *mental test* in announcing the agenda for his Galtonian test battery. |
| 1896 | Emil Kraepelin provides the first comprehensive classification of mental disorders. |
| 1901 | Clark Wissler discovers that Cattellian "brass instruments" tests have no correlation with college grades. |
| 1904 | Charles Spearman proposes that intelligence consists of a single general factor $g$ and numerous specific factors $s_1$, $s_2$, $s_3$, and so forth. |
| 1904 | Karl Pearson formulates the theory of correlation. |
| 1905 | Alfred Binet and Theodore Simon invent the first modern intelligence test. |
| 1908 | Henry H. Goddard translates the Binet-Simon scales from French into English. |

| | |
|---|---|
| 1912 | Stern introduces the IQ, or intelligence quotient: the mental age divided by chronological age. |
| 1916 | Lewis Terman revises the Binet-Simon scales, publishes the Stanford-Binet; revisions appear in 1937, 1960, 1986, and 2003. |
| 1917 | Robert Yerkes spearheads the development of the Army Alpha and Beta examinations used for testing WWI recruits. |
| 1917 | Robert Woodworth develops the Personal Data Sheet, the first personality test. |
| 1920 | The Rorschach inkblot test is published. |
| 1921 | Psychological Corporation—the first major test publisher—is founded by Cattell, Thorndike, and Woodworth. |
| 1926 | Florence Goodenough publishes the Draw-A-Man Test. |
| 1926 | The first Scholastic Aptitude Test is published by the College Entrance Examination Board. |
| 1927 | The first edition of the Strong Vocational Interest Blank is published. |
| 1935 | The Thematic Apperception Test is released by Morgan and Murray at Harvard University. |
| 1936 | Lindquist and others publish the precursor to the Iowa Tests of Basic Skills. |
| 1936 | Edgar Doll publishes the Vineland Social Maturity Scale for assessment of adaptive behavior in those with mental retardation. |
| 1938 | L. L. Thurstone proposes that intelligence consists of about seven group |

factors known as primary mental abilities.

1938    Raven publishes the Raven's Progressive Matrices, a nonverbal test of reasoning intended to measure Spearman's *g* factor.

1938    Lauretta Bender publishes the Bender Visual Motor Gestalt Test, a design-copying test of visual-motor integration.

1938    Oscar Buros publishes the first *Mental Measurements Yearbook.*

1938    Arnold Gesell releases his scale of infant development.

1939    The Wechsler-Bellevue Intelligence Scale is published; revisions are published in 1955 (WAIS), 1981 (WAIS-R), 1997 (WAIS-III), and 2008 (WAIS-IV).

1939    Taylor–Russell tables published for determining the expected proportion of successful applicants with a test.

1939    The Kuder Preference Record, a forced-choice interest inventory, is published.

1942    The Minnesota Multiphasic Personality Inventory (MMPI) is published.

1948    Office of Strategic Services (OSS) uses situational techniques for selection of officers.

1949    The Wechsler Intelligence Scale for Children is published; revisions are published in 1974 (WISC-R), 1991 (WISC-III), and 2003 (WISC-IV).

1950    The Rotter Incomplete Sentences Blank is published.

1951    Lee Cronbach introduces coefficient alpha as an index of reliability (internal consistency) for tests and scales.

1952    American Psychiatric Association publishes the *Diagnostic and Statistical Manual (DSM-I).*

1953    Stephenson develops the Q-technique for studying the self-concept and other variables.

1954    Paul Meehl publishes *Clinical vs. Statistical Prediction.*

1956    The Halstead-Reitan Test Battery begins to emerge as the premiere test battery in neuropsychology.

1957    C. E. Osgood describes the semantic differential.

1958    Lawrence Kohlberg publishes the first version of his Moral Judgment Scale; research with it expands until the mid-1980s.

1959    Campbell and Fiske publish a test validation approach known as the multitrait-multimethod matrix.

1963    Raymond Cattell proposes the theory of fluid and crystallized intelligences.

1967    In *Hobson v. Hansen* the court rules against the use of group ability tests to "track" students on the grounds that such tests discriminate against minority children.

1968    American Psychiatric Association publishes *DSM-II.*

1969    Nancy Bayley publishes the Bayley Scales of Infant Development (BSID). The revised version (BSID-2) is published in 1993.

1969    Arthur Jensen proposes the genetic hypothesis of African American versus white IQ differences in the *Harvard Educational Review.*

1971    In *Griggs v. Duke Power* the Supreme Court rules that employment test results must have a demonstrable link to job performance.

1971    George Vaillant popularizes a hierarchy of 18 ego adaptive mechanisms and describes a methodology for their assessment.

1971    Court decision requires that tests used for personnel selection must be job relevant (*Griggs v. Duke Power*).

1972    The Model Penal Code rule for legal insanity is published and widely adopted in the United States.

1974    Rudolf Moos begins publication of the Social Climate Scales to assess different environments.

1974    Friedman and Rosenman popularize the Type A coronary-prone behavior pattern; their assessment is interview-based.

1975   The U.S. Congress passes Public Law 94-142, the Education for All Handicapped Children Act.

1978   Jane Mercer publishes SOMPA (System of Multicultural Pluralistic Assessment), a test battery designed to reduce cultural discrimination.

1978   In the *Uniform Guidelines on Employee Selection* adverse impact is defined by the four-fifths rule; also guidelines for employee selection studies are published.

1979   In *Larry P. v. Riles* the court rules that standardized IQ tests are culturally biased against low-functioning black children.

1980   In *Parents in Action on Special Education v. Hannon* the court rules that standardized IQ tests are not racially or culturally biased.

1985   The American Psychological Association and other groups jointly publish the influential *Standards for Educational and Psychological Testing.*

1985   Sparrow and others publish the Vineland Adaptive Behavior Scales, a revision of the pathbreaking 1936 Vineland Social Maturity Scale.

1987   American Psychiatric Association publishes *DSM-III-R.*

1989   The Lake Wobegon Effect is noted: Virtually all states of the union claim that their achievement levels are above average.

1989   The Minnesota Multiphasic Personality Inventory-2 is published.

1992   American Psychological Association publishes a revised *Ethical Principles of Psychologists and Code of Conduct* (*American Psychologist,* December 1992)

1994   American Psychiatric Association publishes *DSM-IV.*

1994   Herrnstein and Murray revive the race and IQ heritability debate in *The Bell Curve.*

1999   APA and other groups publish revised *Standards for Educational and Psychological Testing.*

2003   New revision of APA *Ethical Principles of Psychologists and Code of Conduct* goes into effect.

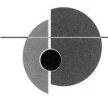

# Test Publisher Addresses

American College Testing Program
P.O. Box 168
Iowa City, IA 52243-0168

American Guidance Service
P.O. Box 99
Circle Pines, MN 55014-1796

Consulting Psychologists Press
P.O. Box 10096
Palo Alto, CA 94303

C.P.S., Inc.
P.O. Box 83
Larchmont, NY 10538

CTB/Macmillan/McGraw-Hill
20 Ryan Ranch Road
Monterey, CA 93940

Denver Developmental Materials
P.O. Box 20037
Denver, CO 80220

DLM Teaching Resources
One DLM Park
Allen, TX 75002

Educational and Industrial Testing Service (EdITS)
P.O. Box 7234
San Diego, CA 92167

Educational Testing Service
ETS Test Collection (30-B)
Rosedale Road
Princeton, NJ 08541-001

GED Testing Service
One Dupont Circle, N.W.
Washington, DC 20036

Harvard University Press
79 Garden Street
Cambridge, MA 02138

Hawthorne Educational Services
800 Gray Oak Drive
Columbia, MO 65201

Marshal S. Hiskey
5640 Baldwin
Lincoln, NE 68507

Hogrefe & Huber Publishers
P.O. Box 2487
Kirkland, WA 98083

Institute for Personality and Ability Testing
P.O. Box 1188
Champaign, IL 61824-1188

Jastak Associates, Inc.
P.O. Box 3410
Wilmington, DE 19804-0250

Jossey-Bass
615 Montgomery Street
San Francisco, CA 94111

Mind Garden
P.O. Box 60669
Palo Alto, CA 94306

Multi-Health Systems
P.O. Box 950
North Tonawanda, NY 14120

National Computer Systems
P.O. Box 1416
Minneapolis, MN 55440

National Rehabilitation Services
P.O. Box 1247
Gaylord, MI 49735

Oxford University Press
200 Madison Avenue
New York, NY10016

Pro-Ed
8700 Shoal Creek Boulevard
Austin, TX 78757-6897

Psychological Assessment Resources, Inc.
P.O. Box 998
Odessa, FL 33556-0998

Psychological Corporation
555 Academic Court
San Antonio, TX 78204-2498

Reitan Neuropsychology Laboratories
2920 South 4th Avenue
Tucson, AZ 85713-4819

Riverside Publishing Company
3 O'Hare Towers
8420 Bryn Mawr Avenue
Chicago, IL 60631

Scholastic Testing Service
480 Meyer Road
P.O. Box 1056
Bensenville, IL 60106-1617

Sigma Assessment Systems, Inc.
P.O. Box 610984
Port Huron, MI 48061-0984

Slosson Educational Publications, Inc.
P.O. Box 280
East Aurora, NY 14052

SRA/London House
9701 W. Higgins Road
Rosemont, IL 60018

Stoelting Company
620 Wheat Lane
Wood Dale, IL 60191

Charles C. Thomas
2600 South First Street
Springfield, IL 62794-9265

University of Illinois Press
1325 South Oak Street
Champaign, IL 61820

U.S. Employment Service
Western Assessment Research
  and Development Center
140 East 300 South
Salt Lake City, UT 84111

U.S. Military Entrance
  Processing Command
Testing Directorate
2500 Green Bay Road
North Chicago, IL 60064

Western Psychological Services
12031 Wilshire Boulevard
Los Angeles, CA 90025-1251

West Virginia Rehabilitation Center
509 Allen Hall
West Virginia University
Morgantown, WV 26506

Wilmington Institute
13315 Wilmington Drive
Dallas, TX 75234

Wonderlic Personnel Test, Inc.
1509 North Milwaukee Avenue
Libertyville, IL 60048-1380

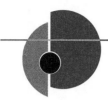

# Major Tests and Their Publishers

**Individual Tests of Intelligence and Adaptive Behavior**

| | |
|---|---|
| Adaptive Behavior Inventory for Children | Psychological Corporation |
| AAMR Adaptive Behavior Scale | Pro-Ed |
| AAMR Adaptive Behavior Scale-School Edition | Pro-Ed |
| Balthazar Scales of Adaptive Behavior | Consulting Psychologists Press |
| Bayley Scales of Infant Development-II | Psychological Corporation |
| The Blind Learning Aptitude Test | University of Illinois Press |
| Bruininks-Oseretsky Test of Motor Proficiency | American Guidance Service |
| Columbia Mental Maturity Scale | Psychological Corporation |
| Denver-2 | Denver Developmental Materials |
| Detroit Tests of Learning Aptitude-4 | Pro-Ed |
| Developmental Indicators for the Assessment of Learning-III | American Guidance Service |
| Differential Ability Scales | Psychological Corporation |
| Draw-A-Person: Quantitative Scoring System | Psychological Corporation |
| Goodenough-Harris Drawing Test | Psychological Corporation |
| Hiskey-Nebraska Test of Learning Aptitude | Marshal S. Hiskey |
| Independent Living Behavior Checklist | West Virginia Rehabilitation Center |
| Kaufman Assessment Battery for Children | American Guidance Service |
| Kaufman Brief Intelligence Test | American Guidance Service |
| Kaufman Adolescent and Adult Intelligence Test | American Guidance Service |
| Leiter International Performance Scale-Revised | Stoelting Company |
| McCarthy Scale of Children's Ability | Psychological Corporation |
| Miller Assessment for Preschoolers | Psychological Corporation |
| Ordinal Scales of Psychological Development | Uzgiriz & Hunt (1989) |
| Peabody Picture Vocabulary Test-III | American Guidance Service |
| Scales of Independent Behavior-R | DLM Teaching Resources |

| | |
|---|---|
| Stanford-Binet: Fifth Edition | Riverside Publishing Co. |
| Test of Nonverbal Intelligence-3 | Pro-Ed |
| T. M. R. School Competency Scales | Consulting Psychologists Press |
| Vineland Adaptive Behavior Scales | American Guidance Service |
| Wechsler Adult Intelligence Scale-IV | Psychological Corporation |
| Wechsler Intelligence Scale for Children-IV | Psychological Corporation |
| Wechsler Preschool and Primary Scale of Intelligence-III | Psychological Corporation |

### Group Intelligence Tests

| | |
|---|---|
| Cognitive Abilities Test | Riverside Publishing Co. |
| Culture Fair Intelligence Test | Institute for Personality and Ability Testing |
| Henmon-Nelson Tests of Mental Ability | Riverside Publishing Company |
| Kuhlmann-Anderson Tests of Mental Ability | Scholastic Testing Service |
| Miller Analogies Test | Psychological Corporation |
| Multidimensional Aptitude Battery | Sigma Assessment Systems |
| Otis-Lennon School Ability Test | Psychological Corporation |
| Ravens Progressive Matrices | Psychological Corporation [distributor] |
| School and College Ability Tests-Series III | Educational Testing Service |
| Shipley Institute of Living Scale | Western Psychological Services |
| Wonderlic Personnel Evaluation | Wonderlic Personnel Test |

### Aptitude Tests and Batteries

| | |
|---|---|
| American College Testing Assessment Program | American College Testing Program |
| Armed Services Vocational Aptitude Battery | U.S. Military Entrance Processing Command |
| Differential Aptitude Tests | Psychological Corporation |
| General Aptitude Test Battery | U.S. Employment Service |
| Graduate Record Examinations | Educational Testing Service |
| Scholastic Assessment Tests | Educational Testing Service |

### Group Achievement Tests

| | |
|---|---|
| California Achievement Tests | CTB/Macmillan/McGraw-Hill |
| Comprehensive Tests of Basic Skills | CTB/Macmillan/McGraw-Hill |
| Iowa Tests of Basic Skills | Riverside Publishing Co. |
| Iowa Tests of Educational Development | Riverside Publishing Co. |
| Metropolitan Achievement Tests | Psychological Corporation |
| Sequential Tests of Educational Progress, Series III | Educational Testing Service |
| SRA Achievement Series | SRA/London House |

| | |
|---|---|
| Stanford Achievement Series | SRA/London House |
| Stanford Test of Academic Skills | Psychological Corporation |
| Tests of Achievement and Proficiency | Riverside Publishing Co. |
| Tests of General Educational Development (GED) | GED Testing Service |

**Individual Achievement Tests**

| | |
|---|---|
| Kaufman Test of Educational Achievement | American Guidance Service |
| Mini-Battery of Achievement | DLM Teaching Resources |
| Peabody Individual Achievement Test-Revised | American Guidance Service |
| Wechsler Individual Achievement Test-2 | Psychological Corporation |
| Wide Range Achievement Test-III | Jastak Associates, Inc. |
| Woodcock-Johnson Psycho-Educational Battery-Revised | Riverside Publishing Co. |

**Psychomotor and Dexterity Tests**

| | |
|---|---|
| Crawford Small Parts Dexterity Test | Psychological Corporation |
| Hand-Tool Dexterity Test | Psychological Corporation |
| Purdue Pegboard | SRA/London House |
| Stromberg Dexterity Test | Psychological Corporation |

**Clerical Tests**

| | |
|---|---|
| Clerical Abilities Battery | Psychological Corporation |
| General Clerical Test | Psychological Corporation |
| Minnesota Clerical Test | Psychological Corporation |
| SRA Clerical Aptitudes | SRA/London House |

**Mechanical Aptitude Tests**

| | |
|---|---|
| Bennett Mechanical Comprehension Test | Psychological Corporation |
| Minnesota Spatial Relations Test | American Guidance Service |
| Revised Minnesota Paper Form Board Test | Psychological Corporation |
| SRA Mechanical Aptitudes | SRA/London House |

**Interest Inventories**

| | |
|---|---|
| Campbell Interest and Skill Survey | National Computer Systems |
| Jackson Vocational Interest Survey | Sigma Assessment Systems |
| Kuder General Interest Survey | SRA/London House |
| Kuder Occupational Interest Survey, Revised | SRA/London House |
| Kuder Preference Record | SRA/London House |
| Self-Directed Search | Psychological Assessment Resources |
| Strong Interest Inventory | Consulting Psychologists Press |

### Neuropsychological Tests

| | |
|---|---|
| Bender Visual Motor Gestalt Test | Western Psychological Services |
| Benton Revised Visual Retention Test | Psychological Corporation |
| Finger Localization Test | Oxford University Press |
| Halstead-Reitan Neuropsychological Test Battery | Reitan Neuropsychology Laboratories |
| Luria-Nebraska Neuropsychological Battery | Western Psychological Services |
| Porteus Maze Test | Psychological Corporation |
| Serial Digit Learning Test | Oxford University Press |
| Symbol Digit Modalities Test | Western Psychological Services |
| Three-Dimensional Block Construction Test | Oxford University Press |
| Wechsler Memory Scale-Revised | Psychological Corporation |
| Wisconsin Card Sorting Test | Psychological Assessment Resources |

### Projective Personality Tests

| | |
|---|---|
| Children's Apperception Test | C. P. S., Inc. |
| Draw-A-Person Test | Charles C. Thomas |
| Holtzman Inkblot Test | Psychological Corporation |
| Rorschach | Hogrefe & Huber Publishers |
| Rotter Incomplete Sentences Blank | Psychological Corporation |
| Senior Apperception Technique | C. P. S., Inc. |
| Thematic Apperception Test (TAT) | Harvard University Press |
| Washington University Sentence Completion Test | Jossey-Bass |

### Self-Report Personality Inventories

| | |
|---|---|
| Beck Depression Inventory-Revised | Psychological Corporation |
| California Psychological Inventory | Consulting Psychologists Press |
| Comrey Personality Scales | EdITS, Educational and Industrial Testing Service |
| Edwards Personal Preference Schedule | Psychological Corporation |
| Eysenck Personality Questionnaire | EdITS, Educational and Industrial Testing Service |
| Jenkins Activity Survey | Psychological Corporation |
| Millon Clinical Multiaxial Inventory-3 | National Computer Services |
| Minnesota Multiphasic Personality Inventory-2 | National Computer Systems |
| Myers-Briggs Type Indicator | Consulting Psychologists Press |
| NEO Five Factor Inventory | Sigma Assessment Systems |
| NEO Personality Inventory-Revised | Sigma Assessment Systems |

| | |
|---|---|
| Personality Inventory for Children-2 | Western Psychological Services |
| Personality Research Form | Sigma Assessment Systems |
| Sixteen Personality Factor Questionnaire (16PF) | Institute for Personality and Ability Testing |
| State-Trait Anxiety Inventory | Mind Garden |
| Survey of Work Styles | Sigma Assessment Systems |

**Forensic Tests**

| | |
|---|---|
| Custody Quotient™ | Wilmington Institute |
| Parent–Child Relationship Inventory | Western Psychological Services |
| Psychopathy Checklist-Revised | Multi-Health Systems |
| Rogers Criminal Responsibility Assessment Scales | Psychological Assessment Resources |

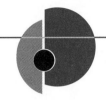

# Standard and Standardized-Score Equivalents of Percentile Ranks in a Normal Distribution

This table lists the equivalence between percentile ranks and four other types of scores: $z$ scores (mean of 0, SD of 1.00), deviation IQs (mean of 100, SD of 15), $T$ scores (mean of 50, SD of 10), and GRE-like scores (mean of 500, SD of 100). The application of the table assumes that the distribution of scores on a test or variable is normally distributed.

We illustrate how this appendix can be used with two examples. Suppose that we desire to know the WAIS-IV IQ that is equivalent to a percentile rank of 97. Reading across the row that begins with PR 97, we discover that the equivalent IQ is 128. Suppose that we desire to know the percentile rank that is equivalent to a GRE score of 675. In the far right column, we locate a score of 675 and read across to the left-hand column to discover that the equivalent percentile rank is 96.

| | $z$ | Deviation IQ | T Score | GRE-Like Score | | $z$ | Deviation IQ | T Score | GRE-Like Score |
|---|---|---|---|---|---|---|---|---|---|
| Mean | 0.00 | 100 | 50 | 500 | PR 82 | 0.91 | 114 | 59 | 591 |
| St. Dev. | 1.00 | 15 | 10 | 100 | 81 | 0.88 | 113 | 59 | 588 |
| | | | | | 80 | 0.84 | 113 | 58 | 584 |
| PR 99 | 2.33 | 135 | 73 | 733 | 79 | 0.80 | 112 | 58 | 580 |
| 98 | 2.05 | 131 | 71 | 705 | 78 | 0.77 | 112 | 58 | 577 |
| 97 | 1.88 | 128 | 69 | 688 | 77 | 0.74 | 111 | 57 | 574 |
| 96 | 1.75 | 126 | 68 | 675 | 76 | 0.71 | 111 | 57 | 571 |
| 95 | 1.64 | 125 | 66 | 664 | 75 | 0.67 | 110 | 57 | 567 |
| 94 | 1.55 | 123 | 66 | 655 | 74 | 0.64 | 110 | 56 | 564 |
| 93 | 1.48 | 122 | 65 | 648 | 73 | 0.61 | 110 | 56 | 561 |
| 92 | 1.41 | 121 | 64 | 641 | 72 | 0.58 | 109 | 56 | 558 |
| 91 | 1.34 | 120 | 63 | 634 | 71 | 0.55 | 108 | 56 | 555 |
| 90 | 1.28 | 119 | 63 | 628 | 70 | 0.52 | 108 | 55 | 552 |
| 89 | 1.22 | 118 | 62 | 622 | 69 | 0.49 | 107 | 55 | 549 |
| 88 | 1.18 | 118 | 62 | 618 | 68 | 0.47 | 107 | 55 | 547 |
| 87 | 1.13 | 117 | 61 | 613 | 67 | 0.44 | 107 | 54 | 544 |
| 86 | 1.08 | 116 | 61 | 608 | 66 | 0.41 | 106 | 54 | 541 |
| 85 | 1.04 | 116 | 60 | 604 | 65 | 0.39 | 106 | 54 | 539 |
| 84 | 0.99 | 115 | 60 | 599 | 64 | 0.36 | 105 | 54 | 536 |
| 83 | 0.95 | 114 | 60 | 595 | 63 | 0.33 | 105 | 53 | 533 |

| | $z$ | Deviation IQ | T Score | GRE-Like Score | | $z$ | Deviation IQ | T Score | GRE-Like Score |
|---|---|---|---|---|---|---|---|---|---|
| PR 62 | 0.31 | 105 | 53 | 531 | PR 31 | −0.49 | 93 | 45 | 451 |
| 61 | 0.28 | 104 | 53 | 528 | 30 | −0.52 | 92 | 45 | 448 |
| 60 | 0.25 | 104 | 53 | 525 | 29 | −0.55 | 92 | 44 | 445 |
| 59 | 0.23 | 104 | 52 | 523 | 28 | −0.58 | 91 | 44 | 442 |
| 58 | 0.20 | 103 | 52 | 520 | 27 | −0.61 | 90 | 44 | 439 |
| 57 | 0.18 | 103 | 52 | 518 | 26 | −0.64 | 90 | 44 | 436 |
| 56 | 0.15 | 102 | 52 | 515 | 25 | −0.67 | 90 | 43 | 433 |
| 55 | 0.12 | 102 | 51 | 512 | 24 | −0.71 | 89 | 43 | 429 |
| 54 | 0.10 | 102 | 51 | 510 | 23 | −0.74 | 89 | 43 | 426 |
| 53 | 0.07 | 101 | 51 | 507 | 22 | −0.77 | 88 | 42 | 423 |
| 52 | 0.05 | 101 | 51 | 505 | 21 | −0.80 | 88 | 42 | 420 |
| 51 | 0.03 | 100 | 50 | 503 | 20 | −0.84 | 87 | 42 | 416 |
| 50 | 0.00 | 100 | 50 | 500 | 19 | −0.88 | 87 | 41 | 412 |
| 49 | −0.03 | 100 | 50 | 497 | 18 | −0.91 | 86 | 41 | 409 |
| 48 | −0.05 | 99 | 49 | 495 | 17 | −0.95 | 86 | 40 | 405 |
| 47 | −0.07 | 99 | 49 | 493 | 16 | −0.99 | 85 | 40 | 401 |
| 46 | −0.10 | 98 | 49 | 490 | 15 | −1.04 | 84 | 40 | 396 |
| 45 | −0.12 | 98 | 49 | 488 | 14 | −1.08 | 84 | 39 | 392 |
| 44 | −0.15 | 98 | 48 | 485 | 13 | −1.13 | 83 | 39 | 387 |
| 43 | −0.18 | 97 | 48 | 482 | 12 | −1.18 | 82 | 38 | 382 |
| 42 | −0.20 | 97 | 48 | 480 | 11 | −1.22 | 82 | 38 | 378 |
| 41 | −0.23 | 96 | 48 | 477 | 10 | −1.28 | 81 | 37 | 372 |
| 40 | −0.25 | 96 | 47 | 475 | 9 | −1.34 | 80 | 37 | 366 |
| 39 | −0.28 | 96 | 47 | 472 | 8 | −1.41 | 79 | 36 | 359 |
| 38 | −0.31 | 95 | 47 | 469 | 7 | −1.48 | 78 | 35 | 352 |
| 37 | −0.33 | 95 | 47 | 467 | 6 | −1.55 | 77 | 34 | 345 |
| 36 | −0.36 | 95 | 46 | 464 | 5 | −1.64 | 75 | 34 | 336 |
| 35 | −0.39 | 94 | 46 | 461 | 4 | −1.75 | 74 | 32 | 325 |
| 34 | −0.41 | 94 | 46 | 459 | 3 | −1.88 | 72 | 31 | 312 |
| 33 | −0.44 | 93 | 46 | 456 | 2 | −2.05 | 69 | 29 | 295 |
| 32 | −0.47 | 93 | 45 | 453 | 1 | −2.33 | 65 | 27 | 267 |

# Glossary

**accommodation**   in Piaget's theory, the adjustment of an unsuccessful schema so that it works.

**achievement test**   a test that measures the degree of learning, success, or accomplishment in a subject matter.

**actuarial judgment**   the kind of automated judgment in which an empirically derived formula is used to diagnose or predict behavior.

**adverse impact**   in hiring, adverse impact is said to exist if one group has a selection rate less than four-fifths of the rate of the group with the highest selection rate (*Uniform Guidelines on Employee Selection,* 1978).

**age norm**   a type of standardization that depicts the level of test performance for each separate age group in the normative sample.

**alcohol abuse**   an alcohol use disorder characterized by the functional impact of drinking on the life of the patient (e.g., unsafe behavior, legal problems, family conflicts).

**alcohol dependence**   an alcohol use disorder characterized by tolerance, withdrawal, and preoccupation with drinking.

**alternate-forms reliability**   a form of reliability in which alternate forms of the same test are given to a group of heterogeneous and representative subjects; scores for the two forms are then correlated.

**Alzheimer's disease**   a degenerative neurological disorder; in the early stages, the most prominent symptom is memory loss.

**Americans with Disabilities Act**   an act passed by Congress in 1990 that forbids discrimination against qualified individuals with disabilities.

**amygdala**   an almond-shaped mass of gray matter located in the anterior temporal lobe, involved in emotions and other capacities.

**analogue behavioral assessment**   the observation of clients in a contrived but plausible setting in which they are instructed to engage in relevant tasks designed to elicit behaviors of interest.

**aphasia**   any deviation in language performance caused by brain damage.

**apraxia**   variety of dysfunctions characterized by a breakdown in the direction or execution of complex motor acts.

**aptitude test**   a test that measures one or more clearly defined and relatively homogeneous segments of ability.

**architectural system**   likened to "hardware" in the information-processing approach to intelligence, the architectural system refers to biologically based properties (e.g., memory span, speed of encoding) necessary for information processing.

**assessment**   appraising or estimating the level or magnitude of some attribute of a person; testing is one small part of assessment which also incorporates observations, interviews, rating scales, and checklists.

**assessment center**   an approach to assessment of managerial talent which consists of multiple simulation techniques, including group presentations, problem-solving exercises, group discussion exercises, interviews, and in-basket techniques.

**assimilation**   in Piaget's theory, the application of a schema to an object, person, or event.

**attention**   the cognitive capacity of the brain to identify what is important and to ignore what is irrelevant.

**attention-deficit/hyperactivity disorder**   a behavioral syndrome characterized by fidgeting, distractibility, impulsivity, attentional deficits, poor social skills, and not considering consequences.

**attitude**   learned cognitive, affective, and behavioral predispositions to respond positively or negatively to certain objects, situations, institutions, concepts, or persons.

**basal ganglia**   a collection of nuclei in the forebrain that make connections with the cerebral cortex above and the thalamus below; the basal ganglia participate in the control of movement.

**basal level**   for tests in which subtest items are ranked from easiest to hardest, the level below which the examinee would almost certainly answer all questions correctly.

**base rate**   in decision theory, the proportion of successful applicants who would be selected using current methods, without benefit of the new test.

**behavior observation scale**   a variation upon the BARS technique which uses a continuum from "almost never" to "almost always" to measure how often an employee performs specific tasks on each behavioral dimension.

**behavior sample**   in testing, the notion that a test is just a sample of behaviors that permits the examiner to make inferences about a larger domain of relevant behaviors.

**behavior therapy**   the application of the methods and findings of experimental psychology to the modification of maladaptive behavior; also called behavior modification.

**behavioral assessment**   a variety of techniques that concentrate on behavior itself rather than on underlying traits, hypothetical causes, or presumed dimensions of personality.

**behavioral avoidance test**   a behavioral procedure in which the therapist measures how long the client can tolerate an anxiety-inducing stimulus.

**behavioral procedure**   a procedure for assessing the antecedents and consequences of behavior; behavioral procedures include checklists, rating scales, interviews, and structured observations.

**behaviorally anchored rating scale**   a criterion-referenced rating scale.

**bias in construct validity**   a type of bias demonstrated when a test is shown to measure different hypothetical traits (psychological constructs) for one group than another or to measure the same trait but with differing degrees of accuracy.

**bias in content validity**   a type of bias demonstrated when an item or subscale is relatively more difficult for members of one group than another after the general ability level of the two groups is held constant.

**bias in predictive validity**   a type of bias demonstrated when the inference drawn from the test score is not made with the smallest feasible random error or if there is constant error in an inference or prediction as a function of membership in a particular group.

**biodata**   objective or scoreable autobiographical data; recognized as a valid adjunct to personnel selection.

**Broca's aphasia**   also known as expressive aphasia, a form of language disturbance characterized by effortful, nonfluent speech and few words.

**C scale**   a variant on the stanine scale with 11 units.

**ceiling level**   for tests in which subtest items are ranked from easiest to hardest, the level above which the examinee would almost certainly fail all remaining questions.

**cerebellum**   part of the hindbrain responsible for helping to coordinate muscle tone, posture, and skilled movements.

**cerebral cortex**   the outermost layer of the brain that is the source of the highest levels of sensory, motor, and cognitive processing.

**cerebrospinal fluid**   a clear liquid, continuously produced and replenished within the ventricles of the brain, that provides protection against external buffeting.

**cerebrovascular accident**   a "stroke" most often caused by plugging up (infarction) of a brain artery, leading to death of surrounding brain tissue.

**cerebrum**   the most substantial part of the brain, consisting of the two hemispheres that each contain four lobes.

**certification**   testing to determine that a person has at least a minimum proficiency in some discipline or activity.

**classical theory of measurement**   the dominant theory in psychological testing; the theory assumes that an observed score consists of a true score plus measurement error.

**classification**   in testing, the process of using tests to assign a person to one category rather than another.

**clerical scoring error**   in testing, an error in test scoring related to the mechanics of scoring, such as adding subscores incorrectly or consulting the wrong conversion table.

**clinical judgment**   the kind of judgment in which the decision maker processes information in his or her head to diagnose or predict behavior.

**coaching**   in testing, the attempt to boost test scores by providing the examinee with extra practice on test-like materials, review of fundamental concepts likely to be covered by the test, and advice about optimal test-taking strategies.

**coding complexity**   in observational rating situations, the use of too many categories, or ill-defined categories, which leads to low inter-rater reliability.

**coefficient alpha**   an index of reliability that may be thought of as the mean of all possible split-half coefficients, corrected by the Spearman-Brown formula.

**cognitive behavior therapy**   an approach to behavior change that emphasizes changing the client's belief structure.

**collaboratory** Internet-based arrangements that facilitate the collaboration of test specialists, regardless of geographical location.

**competency to stand trial** the determination by the presiding judge that a defendant does not have a mental defect, illness, or condition that renders him or her unable to understand the proceedings or to assist in his or her defense.

**componential intelligence** in Sternberg's theory, the internal mental mechanisms that are responsible for intelligent behavior.

**computer-assisted psychological assessment** CAPA refers to the entire range of computer applications in psychological assessment and includes testing, scoring, report writing, and individualized test administration.

**computer-based test interpretation** CBTI refers to test interpretation and report writing by computer, which is a major component of computer-assisted psychological assessment (CAPA).

**computerized adaptive testing** a family of procedures that allows for accurate and efficient measurement of ability; individualized testing continues until a predetermined level of measurement precision is reached.

**concurrent validity** a type of criterion-related validity in which the criterion measures are obtained at approximately the same time as the test scores.

**concussion** a transitory alteration of consciousness from a blow to the head; may be followed by temporary amnesia, dizziness, nausea, weak pulse, and slow respiration, yet there is no demonstrable organic brain damage.

**conservation** in Piaget's theory, the awareness that physical quantities do not change in amount when they are superficially altered in appearance.

**construct** a theoretical, intangible quality or trait in which individuals differ.

**construct validity** a type of validity that refers to the appropriateness of test-based inferences about the underlying construct purportedly measured by the test.

**constructional dyspraxia** impairment of the ability to deal with spatial relationships either in a two- or three-dimensional framework.

**consumer psychology** the branch of industrial/organizational psychology that deals with the development, advertising, and marketing of products and services.

**content validity** the type of validity that is determined by the degree to which the questions, tasks, or items on a test are representative of the universe of behavior the test was designed to sample.

**contextual intelligence** in Sternberg's theory, the mental activity involved in purposive adaptation to, shaping of, and selection of real-world environments relevant to one's life.

**contingency management procedure** an approach to behavior therapy in which the therapist identifies and alters the consequences of unwanted behaviors.

**convergent validity** a type of validity that is demonstrated when a test correlates highly with other variables or tests with which it shares an overlap of constructs.

**corpus callosum** the major commissure that serves to integrate the functions of the two cerebral hemispheres.

**correction for guessing** in group testing, the practice of revising a subject's final score in light of apparent guessing.

**correlation coefficient** a numerical index of the degree of linear relationship between two sets of scores; correlation coefficients can vary between $-1.00$ and $+1.00$.

**correlation matrix** a complete table of intercorrelations between all the variables that is the beginning point of factor analysis.

**cranial nerves** twelve paired neural tracts that help govern basic sensory and motor functions such as vision, smell, facial movement, taste, and hearing.

**creativity test** a test that assesses the ability to produce new ideas, insights, or artistic creations that are accepted as being of social, aesthetic, or scientific value.

**criterion contamination** a source of error in test validation when the criterion is "contaminated" by its artificial commonality with the test, such as test and criterion contain nearly identical items. Also, a form of evaluation error in which a criterion measure includes factors that are not demonstrably part of the job, for example, rating appearance when it is not job related.

**criterion-keyed approach** a test development approach in which test items are assigned to a particular scale if, and only if, they discriminate between a well defined criterion group and a relevant control group.

**criterion problem** the difficult problem of conceptualizing and measuring work performance constructs which are often complex, fuzzy, and multidimensional.

**criterion-referenced test**   a test in which the objective is to determine where the examinee stands with respect to very tightly defined educational objectives; no comparison is made to the performance of other examinees.

**criterion-related validity**   the type of validity that is demonstrated when a test is shown to be effective in estimating an examinee's performance on some outcome measure.

**critical incidents checklist**   a form of performance evaluation based upon actual episodes of desirable and undesirable on-the-job behavior.

**cross-sectional design**   a research design in which subjects of different ages are tested at one point in time.

**cross-sequential design**   a research design that combines cross-sectional and longitudinal methods.

**cross-validation**   for predictive tests, the practice of using the original regression equation in a new sample to determine whether the test predicts the criterion as well as it did in the original sample.

**crystallized intelligence**   in Cattell and Horn's theory, what one has already learned through the investment of fluid intelligence in cultural settings (e.g., learning algebra in school).

**culture-fair test**   a test designed to minimize irrelevant influences of cultural learning and social climate and thereby produce a cleaner separation of natural ability from specific learning.

**custody evaluation**   in divorce cases, the psychological evaluation of a child (or children) and both parents so as to offer an opinion to the court as to the best interests of the child (or children) in custody arrangements.

**decision theory**   an approach to psychological measurement that considers the costs and benefits of test-based decisions, for example, in personnel selection.

**defense mechanisms**   unconscious mental strategies available to the ego in dealing with the conflicting demands of id, superego, and external reality.

**diagnosis**   determining the nature and source of a person's abnormal behavior, and classifying the behavior pattern within an accepted diagnostic system.

**discriminant validity**   a type of validity that is demonstrated when a test does not correlate with variables or tests from which it should differ.

**divergent production**   the creation of numerous appropriate responses to a single stimulus situation.

**divergent thinking**   the kind of thinking that goes off in different directions.

**Durham rule**   the legal provision for the defense of insanity if the criminal act was a "product" of mental disease or defect; dropped in 1972 and replaced by the Model Penal Code.

**duty to warn**   stemming from the *Tarasoff* case, the responsibility of clinicians to communicate any serious threat to the potential victim, law enforcement agencies, or both.

**dysarthria**   slurred, hesitant speech (not drug or alcohol induced) that often signifies damage to the cerebellum.

**ecological momentary assessment**   using wireless technology to measure patient experience (e.g., pain, fatigue, mood) in the real world at the point of experience.

**ego**   in psychoanalytic theory, the conscious self that mediates between the id and reality.

**equilibration**   in Piaget's theory, the entire process of assimilation, accommodation, and equilibrium.

**evidence-based assessment**   evaluation of a testing tool not only by means of the standard psychometric indices of reliability and validity but also through considerations of clinical utility.

**executive functions**   brain functions that include logical analysis, conceptualization, reasoning, planning, and flexibility of thinking.

**executive system**   likened to "software" in the information-processing approach to intelligence, the executive system refers to environmentally learned components that steer problem solving and provide overall guidance.

**expectancy table**   a table that portrays the established relationship between test scores and expected outcome on a relevant task.

**experiential intelligence**   in Sternberg's theory, the ability to deal effectively with novel tasks.

**expert rankings**   a scaling method that relies upon the judgment of experts to determine the rankings for individual components.

**expert witness**   in court cases, a witness whom the judge deems qualified to testify about a proper subject matter.

**extravalidity concerns**   the side effects and unintended consequences of testing.

**extraversion**   a sociable, outgoing, excitement-seeking personality disposition.

**extrinsic religious expression** the use of religion for external goals such as security, status, and friendship.

**face validity** for tests, the appearance of validity to test users, examiners, and especially the examinees; not a technical form of validity, but important for the social acceptability of a test.

**factor** an underlying construct or variable that helps explain the correlations between several tests or measures.

**factor analysis** a family of statistical procedures that researchers use to summarize relationships among variables that are correlated in highly complex ways; the goal of factor analysis is to derive a parsimonious set of derived factors.

**factor loading** in factor analysis, the correlation between an individual test and a single factor.

**factor matrix** a table of correlations between variables and factors; the correlations are called factor loadings.

**false negatives** in decision theory, a subject who is incorrectly predicted to fail on the criterion.

**false positives** in decision theory, a subject who is incorrectly predicted to succeed on the criterion.

**fear survey schedule** a behavioral assessment device which requires respondents to indicate the presence and intensity of their fears in relation to various stimuli, typically on a 5- or 7-point Likert scale.

**fetal alcohol effect** a subtle version of fetal alcohol syndrome in which physical abnormalities are not observed, but behavioral problems such as attentional difficulties are noted.

**fetal alcohol syndrome** a cluster of physical and behavioral abnormalities, including mental retardation, caused by the mother's drinking of alcohol during pregnancy.

**fluid intelligence** in Cattell and Horn's theory, a largely nonverbal and relatively culture-reduced form of mental efficiency.

**forced-choice method** in personality test development, an item-writing method in which the alternatives are matched for social desirability.

**forced-choice scale** a performance evaluation scale designed to eliminate bias and subjectivity in supervisor ratings by forcing a choice between options that are equal in social desirability.

**forebrain** the large, outermost portion of the brain consisting of the cerebral cortex and underlying structures such as the corpus callosum, basal ganglia, limbic lobe, thalamus, and hypothalamus.

**freedom from distractibility** the third factor on the WISC-III consisting of Arithmetic and Digit Span.

**frequency distribution** a method of summarizing data or test scores by specifying a small number of usually equal-sized class intervals and then tallying how many scores fall within each interval.

**frequency polygon** a method of summarizing data or test scores in graphic form; similar to a histogram, except that the frequency of the class intervals is represented by single points rather than columns.

**frontal lobe** the part of the cerebral cortex at the front of the brain that is required for the programming, regulation, and verification of executive functions and motor performance.

**frustration** in Rosenzweig's system, the state that occurs whenever an organism encounters an obstacle or obstruction en route to the satisfaction of a need.

**functionalist definition of validity** the view that a test is valid if it serves the purpose for which it is used.

**fundamental lexical hypothesis** in personality theory, the notion that trait terms have survived in language because they convey important information about our dealings with others.

**general factor** according to Spearman, the single general factor of intelligence that must exist to account for the observed correlations between a large number of tests.

**generalizability theory** a domain sampling model of reliability that recognizes several alternatives of generalization for test results.

**gifted** the designation of a person as gifted typically means that he or she has extraordinary ability in some area.

**glial cells** cells that provide structural support for the neurons and also supply nutrients and perform other functions.

**grade norm** a type of standardization that depicts the level of test performance for each separate school grade in the normative sample.

**graphic rating scale** a scale that consists of trait labels, brief definitions of those labels, and a continuum for the rating.

**gray matter** those parts of the brain that consist of densely packed cell bodies of neurons that are gray in color.

**group achievement tests** also called educational achievement tests, these instruments are commonly administered to dozens or hundreds of students at the same time to gauge achievement levels in one or more well-defined academic domains.

**group tests**    mainly pencil-and-paper measures suitable to the testing of large groups of persons at the same time.

**guilty but mentally ill (GBMI)**    a verdict allowed in some states in which the intention is for the accused to begin his or her sentence in a psychiatric hospital.

**halo effect**    the tendency to rate an employee high or low on all dimensions because of a global impression.

**heritability index**    an estimate of how much of the total variance in a given trait is due to genetic factors; the index can vary from 0.0 to 1.0.

**hindbrain**    the lowest, most simply organized, brain structures; the hindbrain consists of the myelencephalon and metencephalon.

**hippocampus**    part of a complex, ill-defined memory circuit that consolidates new experiences into long-term memories.

**histogram**    a method of summarizing data or test scores in graphic form; a histogram contains the same information as a frequency distribution.

**homogeneous scale**    a scale in which the individual items tend to measure the same thing; homogeneity is gauged by item-total correlations.

**hypothalamus**    a small structure at the center of the brain that helps govern motivated behavior and bodily regulation: feeding, sexual behavior, sleeping, temperature regulation, emotional behavior, and movement.

**id**    in psychoanalytic theory, the unconscious part of personality that is the seat of all instinctual needs such as for food, water, sexual gratification, and avoidance of pain.

**illusory validation**    in projective testing, the finding that subjects ignore disconfirming instances and cling to their preexisting stereotypes.

**implicit association test**    a covert measure of attitudes that makes use of automatic or "unconscious" associations to target concepts (e.g., racial groups) as determined by sophisticated reaction time analyses.

**in-basket technique**    a realistic work sample test that simulates the work environment of an administrator.

**index of intellectual deterioration**    on the Shipley Institute of Living Scale, an index based on the discrepancy between verbal and abstractions ability that was intended to gauge the effects of organic brain impairment.

**individual achievement tests**    achievement tests administered one-on-one to gauge achievement levels; these tests are essential in the assessment of potential learning disabilities.

**individual tests**    instruments which by their design and purpose must be administered one on one.

**informed consent**    in testing, the principle that test takers or their representatives are made aware, in language that they can understand, of the purposes and likely consequences of testing.

**insanity plea**    in court cases, a defense based upon reference to legal insanity as spelled out by the Model Penal Code or other legal statutes.

**instructional validity**    a view promoted by court systems that school districts must actually teach what it is they test for on state-wide achievement tests.

**integrative model**    a model of career assessment in which information from interest, ability, and personality domains is considered simultaneously.

**integrity test**    an instrument designed to screen potential employees for theft-proneness and other undesirable qualities; overt integrity tests contain questions about attitudes toward theft and items dealing with admission of theft and other illegal activities.

**intelligence**    according to experts, (1) the capacity to learn from experience, and (2) the capacity to adapt to one's environment.

**intelligence test**    although there are exceptions, an intelligence test generally yields an overall summary score based on results from a heterogeneous sample of items (e.g., verbal skills, reasoning, spatial thinking).

**interest inventory**    a test that measures the preference for certain activities or topics and thereby helps determine occupational choice.

**interscorer reliability**    for tests that involve judgmental scoring, the typical degree of agreement between scorers.

**interval scale**    a measurement scale that provides information about ranking and the relative strength of ranks; based on the assumption of equal-sized units or intervals for the underlying scale.

**intrinsic religious expression**    the use of religion for internal goals such as finding meaning and direction in life.

**introversion**    a quiet, "bookish," reserved personality disposition.

**ipsative test**    a test in which the average of the subscales is always the same for every examinee; thus, for an individual examinee, high scores on subscales must be balanced by low scores on other subscales.

**IQ constancy**    On the Wechsler tests, the axiomatic assumption that IQ must remain constant with normal aging, even though raw intellectual ability might shift or decline.

**item-characteristic curve** a graphical display of the relationship between the probability of a correct response and the examinee's position on the underlying trait measured by the test.

**item-difficulty index** for a single test item, the proportion of examinees in a large tryout sample who get that item correct.

**item-discrimination index** a statistical index of how efficiently an item discriminates between persons who obtain high and low scores on the entire test.

**item information function** a graph portraying the relationship between the trait level of examinees and the information provided by a test item.

**item-reliability index** $s_i r_{iT}$, the product of a test item's internal consistency as indexed by the correlation with the total score ($r_{iT}$) and its variability as indexed by the standard deviation ($s_i$).

**item response function** a mathematical equation that describes the relation between the amount of a latent trait an individual possesses and the probability that he or she will give a designated response to a test item designed to measure that construct.

**item response theory** also known as latent trait theory, a modern framework for test construction in which the psychometrician posits a single dimension of skill or underlying trait on which all of the test items rely; each respondent is assumed to have a certain amount of the latent trait being measured.

**item-validity index** $s_i r_{iC}$ consists of the product of a test item's standard deviation ($s_i$) and the point-biserial correlation with the criterion $r_{iC}$.

**job analysis** the process of defining a job in terms of the behaviors necessary to perform it; includes job description (physical characteristics of the work) and job specification (personal characteristics needed).

**kappa** the index of inter-rater agreement, corrected for chance, used as one measure of the reliability of diagnostic systems and rating scales.

**Kuder–Richardson formula 20** an index of reliability that is relevant to the special case where each test item is scored 0 or 1 (e.g., right or wrong).

**Lake Wobegon effect** the observation that virtually all states of the union claim that average achievement scores for their school systems exceed the 50th percentile.

**latent trait theory** a modern framework for test construction in which a single dimension of skill or underlying trait is posited. *See* item response theory.

**learning disability** an indistinct concept that typically refers to a severe discrepancy between general ability and individual achievement that cannot be explained by sensory/motor handicaps, mental retardation, emotional problems, or cultural deprivation.

**legally blind** this term applies to individuals with central visual acuity of 20/200 or less in the better eye (with correction) or to those with significant reduction in their visual field to a diameter of 20 degrees or less; used to determine eligibility for government benefits.

**Lexile scale** a measure of reading demand of a text, on a scale from 200 to 1,700, based on semantic difficulty (vocabulary) and syntactic complexity (sentence).

**Likert scale** a scale that presents the examinee with five responses ordered on an agree/disagree or approve/disapprove continuum.

**limbic lobe** a group of subcortical structures responsible for elaboration of emotion and the control of visceral activity.

**limbic system** a group of interconnected brain structures, located deep within the brain, and involved in olfaction, emotion, and motivation.

**local norms** norms derived from a representative local sample, as opposed to a national sample.

**locus of control** a construct that refers to perceptions that people have about the source of things that happen to them (e.g., internal versus external).

**longitudinal design** a research design in which the same subjects are tested at several points in time.

**mean** the arithmetic average of a group of scores.

**measurement error** everything other than the true score that makes up an examinee's obtained test score.

**median** the middlemost score when all the scores in a sample have been ranked.

**medulla oblongata** part of the hindbrain that helps mediate swallowing, vomiting, breathing, the control of blood pressure, respiration, and, partially, heart rate.

**memory** a complex and multifaceted phenomenon that allows for the recall of previously learned information and skills.

**meninges** a thin layering of three tough membranes that encase the brain and spinal cord, providing protection against external buffeting.

**mental retardation** significantly subaverage general intellectual functioning resulting in or associated with concurrent impairments in adaptive behavior and manifested during the developmental period.

**mental state at the time of the offense (MSO)** the mental state of a defendant at the time of the offense is relevant in special pleadings such as the insanity defense; psychologists and psychiatrists may offer opinions as to the MSO of defendants.

**method of absolute scaling** a procedure for obtaining a measure of absolute item difficulty based upon results for different age groups of test takers.

**method of empirical keying** a scale development method in which test items are selected based entirely on how well they contrast a criterion group from a normative sample.

**method of equal-appearing intervals** a method for constructing interval-level scales from attitude statements.

**method of rational scaling** a scale construction method in which all scale items correlate positively with each other and also with the total score for the scale; also known as the internal consistency approach.

**midbrain** the middle portion of the brain consisting of cranial nerves and relay stations for vision and hearing.

**mixed-standard scale** a complex approach to performance evaluation designed to minimize rating errors in performance appraisal; items for performance dimensions are randomly ordered on the scale.

**M'Naughten rule** one of several standards of legal insanity; essentially, "the party accused was laboring under such a defect of reason, from disease of the mind, as not to know the nature and quality of the act he was doing...."

**mode** the most frequently occurring score.

**Model Penal Code rule** a standard of legal insanity— "A person is not responsible for criminal conduct if at the time of such conduct, as a result of mental disease or defect, he lacks substantial capacity either to appreciate the criminality [wrongfulness] of his conduct or to conform his conduct to the requirements of the law."

**moral dilemma** a brief story that involves a difficult moral choice such as whether to steal to prolong someone's life; used in the study of moral reasoning.

**motor cortex** the strip of brain tissue located on the precentral gyrus that is involved in bodily movement.

**multi-infarct dementia** a form of vascular brain impairment in which the hardly noticeable individual effects of many small infarcts or "strokes" accumulate over a number of years.

**multimedia** the collective capacity of the modern computer to use still images, live video segments, music, tables, charts, animation, and other approaches in an interactive format.

**multitrait-multimethod matrix** a research design for assessing convergent and discriminant validity that calls for the assessment of two or more traits by two or more methods.

**neuropsychological tests** tests and procedures with proven sensitivity to the effects of brain damage.

**neuropsychology** the study of the relationship between brain function and behavior.

**nominal scale** a measurement scale in which the categories are arbitrary and do not designate "more" or "less" of anything; the simplest and lowest level of measurement.

**nonverbal behavior** the subtler forms of human communication contained in glance, gesture, body language, tone of voice, and facial expression.

**norm group** a sample of examinees who are representative of the population for whom the test is intended.

**norm-referenced test** a test in which the performance of each examinee is interpreted in reference to a relevant standardization sample.

**normal distribution** a symmetrical, mathematically defined, bell-shaped frequency distribution.

**normal ogive** the normal distribution graphed in cumulative form.

**normalized standard score** a score obtained by a transformation that renders a skewed distribution into a normal distribution.

**norms** a summary of test results for a large and representative group of subjects.

**not guilty by reason of insanity (NGRI)** a verdict allowed in some states in which the defendant is found not guilty because his or her criminal act was the result of mental disease or defect.

**oblique axes** in factor analysis, the assumption that factors are correlated with one another, that is, not at right angles.

**observer drift** in observational rating situations, the tendency for an observer to become fatigued and less vigilant over time, thus failing to notice target behaviors when they occur.

**occipital lobe** the part of the cerebral cortex at the rear of the brain that contains the vision centers.

**occupational reinforcer patterns** an evaluation of jobs in terms of the worker-perceived reinforcers that are present or absent.

**operational definition** a definition of a concept in terms of the way it is measured, such as, intelligence is "what the tests test."

**ordinal scale** a measurement scale that allows for ranking; ordinal scales do not provide information about the relative strength of ranking.

**orthogonal axes**   in factor analysis, the assumption that the factors are at right angles to one another, which means that they are uncorrelated.

**overt integrity test**   an employment test that seeks to assess attitudes toward theft; these instruments may also contain a section dealing with overt admissions of theft.

**paralinguistics**   the nonverbal aspects of speech such as tone of voice and rate of speaking.

**parietal lobe**   the part of the cerebral cortex that mediates spatial integration and sensory awareness of what is happening on the surface of the body.

**Parkinson's disease**   a degenerative brain disease characterized by three types of motor disturbance: involuntary movement, including tremor; poverty and slowness of movement without paralysis; and changes in posture and muscle tone.

**percentile**   the percentage of persons in the standardization sample who scored below a specific raw score; percentiles vary from 0 to 100.

**perceptual organization**   the second factor on the WISC-III consisting of Picture Arrangement, Picture Completion, Block Design, and Object Assembly.

**personal injury**   in personal injury lawsuits, attorneys may hire psychologists to testify as to the lifelong consequences of traumatic stress or acquired brain damage.

**personality**   an inexplicit construct which is invoked to explain behavioral consistency within persons and behavioral distinctiveness between persons.

**personality coefficient**   a term used to refer to the finding that the predictive validity of personality scales rarely exceeds .30.

**personality test**   a test that measures the traits, qualities, or behaviors that determine a person's individuality; this information helps predict future behavior.

**phallometry**   the assessment of sexual arousal by attaching a flexible band around the penis of an examinee who views standard slides and pictures.

**phrenology**   the discredited idea, attributed to Franz Joseph Gall (1758–1828), that cranial "bumps" signify a prominence of certain mental faculties and personality traits.

**physiognomy**   the historical and discredited idea that we can judge the inner character of people from their outward appearance, especially the face.

**pineal body**   a pea-sized structure that sits at the center of the brain; it secretes the hormone melatonin in a cyclic biological rhythm, but its functions are not well understood.

**placement**   in testing, the sorting of persons into different programs appropriate to their needs or skills.

**polygraph**   a device that monitors ongoing physiological responses, including changes in breathing, pulse rate, blood pressure, and perspiration; inaccurately referred to as a "lie detector."

**positive psychological assessment**   the appraisal of what is right with people, for example, evaluation of hope, creativity, wisdom, courage, forgiveness, humor, gratitude, and coping.

**positive psychology**   the scientific and practical pursuit of optimal human functioning.

**power test**   a test that allows enough time for test takers to attempt all items; however, the test is difficult enough that no test taker is able to obtain a perfect score.

**predictive validity**   a type of criterion-related validity in which the criterion measures are obtained in the future, usually months or years after the test scores are obtained, such as when college grades are predicted from an entrance exam.

**primary mental abilities**   the seven group factors of intelligence posited by Thurstone.

**processing speed**   the fourth factor on the WISC-III consisting of Coding and Symbol Search.

**projective hypothesis**   the assumption that personal interpretations of ambiguous stimuli must necessarily reflect the unconscious needs, motives, and conflicts of the examinee.

**projective test**   a test in which the examinee encounters vague, ambiguous stimuli and responds with his or her own constructions.

**psychometrician**   a specialist in psychology or education who develops and evaluates psychological tests.

**psychophysics**   the empirical study of the functional relationship between physical stimuli and mental phenomena.

**Public Law 93-112**   a "Bill of Rights" for persons with disabilities that outlawed discrimination based upon disability.

**Public Law 94-142**   the Education for All Handicapped Children Act that mandated that schoolchildren with disabilities receive appropriate assessment and educational opportunities.

**Public Law 99-457**   legislation that requires states to provide a free appropriate public education to children ages 3 through 5 who have disabilities.

**pupillometrics**   the measurement of pupil size to gauge interest in, or pleasure in, the observed stimulus.

**Q-technique**   a technique for studying changes in self-concept and other variables by the sorting of statements into a near-normal distribution for assigned categories.

**qualified individualism**   in testing for selection, the ethical stance that age, sex, race, or other demographic characteristics must not be used, even if knowledge of these factors would improve the validity of selection.

**quotas**   in testing for selection, the ethical stance that the best-qualified candidates within definable subgroups should be selected in proportion to their representation in the population.

**random sampling**   a selection strategy in which every subject has an equal chance of being chosen.

**rapport**   in testing, a comfortable, warm atmosphere that serves to motivate examinees and elicit cooperation.

**Rasch Model**   named after the Danish mathematician Georg Rasch, this mathematical model uses complex equations to predict the probability of respondents at different skill levels correctly answering test questions.

**rater bias**   the tendency for supervisor ratings to be inaccurate because of leniency, severity, and other forms of evaluation errors.

**ratio scale**   a measurement scale that yields equal-sized units or intervals and that possesses a conceptually meaningful zero point; the highest level of measurement.

**raw score**   the most basic level of information provided by a psychological test, for example, the number of questions answered correctly.

**reactivity of measurement**   the phenomenon in which the process of measurement (e.g., clients knowing that they are being observed and rated) changes what we seek to measure.

**real definition**   a definition that seeks to tell us the true nature of the thing being defined.

**regression equation**   an equation that describes the best-fitting straight line for estimating the criterion from the test; the best-fitting line is one that minimizes the sum of the squared deviations from the line.

**reliability**   the attribute of consistency in measurement.

**reliability coefficient**   the ratio of true score variance to the total variance of test scores.

**religion as Quest**   the view that complexity, doubt, and tentativeness are aspects of mature religious expression.

**restriction of range**   a phenomenon in which the range on a variable is restricted, causing correlations with other variables to be artificially low.

**response to intervention**   RTI is a relatively recent approach to learning disabilities in school systems that stresses early identification and lack of response to intervention as important factors in LD identification.

**reticular formation**   a network of ascending and descending nerve cell bodies and fibers that governs general arousal or consciousness.

**RIASEC model**   a theory of person–environment types that proposes six themes: Realistic, Investigative, Artistic, Social, Enterprising, and Conventional (RIASEC).

**rotation to positive manifold**   in factor analysis, a method of rotating the factor matrix that seeks to eliminate as many of the negative factor loadings as possible.

**rotation to simple structure**   in factor analysis, a method of rotating the factor matrix that seeks to simplify the factor loadings so that each test has significant loadings on as few factors as possible.

**routing procedure**   in tests such as the Stanford-Binet: Fifth Edition, the first items or subtests administered for the purpose of determining the appropriate starting points for subsequent subtests.

**routing test**   an initial subtest used to determine the entry level for all remaining subtests; used with individual intelligence tests such as the SB:FE.

**savant**   an individual who has mental deficiencies and a highly developed talent in a single area such as art, rapid calculation, memory, or music.

**schema**   in Piaget's theory, an organized pattern of behavior or a well-defined mental structure that leads to knowing how to do something.

**screening**   the use of quick and simple tests or procedures to identify persons who might have special characteristics or needs.

**self-efficacy**   in Bandura's theory, the personal judgment of how well one can execute courses of action required to deal with prospective situations.

**self-monitoring**   a therapeutic approach in which the client chooses the goals and actively participates in supervising, charting, and recording progress toward the end point(s) of therapy.

**semantic differential**   a rating technique in which the subject uses a seven-point continuum to rate a concept on a number of bipolar adjectives such as good-bad, strong-weak, active-passive.

**sensitivity**   the ability of a test, expressed as a percentage, to accurately "rule in" or identify individuals who manifest a trait or syndrome of interest.

**simultaneous processing**   a form of information processing characterized by the simultaneous execution of several different mental operations.

**situational exercise**   an assessment procedure in which the prospective employee is asked to perform under circumstances that are highly similar to the anticipated work environment.

**skewness**   the symmetry or asymmetry of a frequency distribution; positive skew indicates that scores are piled up at the low end and negative skew indicates that scores are piled up at the high end.

**social desirability response set** the tendency of examinees to react to the perceived desirability (or undesirability) of a test item rather than responding accurately to its content.

**social intelligence** the capacity to understand other people and to relate effectively to them.

**source traits** the stable and constant sources of behavior that are less visible than surface traits but more important in accounting for behavior.

**Spearman-Brown formula** a formula for adjusting split-half correlations so that they reflect the full length of a scale.

**specific factor** according to Spearman, a factor of intelligence specific to an individual test.

**specificity** the ability of a test, expressed as a percentage, to accurately "rule out" or identify individuals who do not manifest a trait or syndrome of interest.

**speed test** a timed test that contains items of uniform and generally simple level of difficulty; the time limit is strict enough that few subjects finish a speed test.

**split-half reliability** a form of reliability in which scores from the two halves of a test (e.g., even items versus odd items) are correlated with one another; the correlation is then adjusted for test length.

**standard deviation** a statistical index that reflects the degree of dispersion in a group of scores; the square root of the variance.

**standard error of measurement** an index of measurement error which indicates the extent to which an examinee's score might vary over a number of parallel tests.

**standard error of the difference** a statistical index that can help a test user determine whether, for an individual examinee, the difference between scores on two tests or subtests is significant.

**standard error of estimate** $SE_{est}$ is the margin of error to be expected in the predicted criterion score; the error of estimate is derived from the following formula:

$$SE_{est} = SD_y \sqrt{1 - r_{xy}^2}$$

**standard of care** the standard of care that is usual, customary, or reasonable.

**standard score** a transformed score in which the original score is expressed as the distance from the mean in standard deviation units.

**standardization fallacy** the fallacious view that a test standardized on one population is ipso facto unfair when used in any other population.

**standardization sample** a large and representative group of subjects representative of the population for whom the test is intended.

**standardized procedure** in testing, the attempt through carefully written instructions to ensure that the procedures for administering a test are uniform from one examiner and setting to another.

**stanine scale** a scale in which all raw scores are converted to a single-digit system of scores ranging from 1 to 9.

**state anxiety** the transitory feelings of fear or worry that most persons experience on occasion.

**sten scale** a 10-unit scale with five units above and five units below the mean.

**stereotype threat** the threat of confirming, as self-characteristic, a negative stereotype about one's group.

**stratified random sampling** a selection strategy in which subjects are chosen randomly, with the constraint that the sample matches the population on relevant background variables such as race, sex, occupation, and so on.

**subgroup norms** norms derived from an identified subgroup, as opposed to a diversified national sample.

**successive processing** a form of information processing in which a proper sequence of mental operations must be followed.

**superego** in psychoanalytic theory, that part of personality that is roughly synonymous with conscience and comprises the societal standards of right and wrong that are conveyed to us by our parents.

**surface traits** in Cattell's theory, the more obvious aspects of personality that typically emerge in the first stages of factor analysis when individual test items are correlated with each other.

**systematic measurement error** a type of measurement error that arises when, unknown to the test developer, a test consistently measures something other than the trait for which it was intended.

**table of specifications** in test development, a table that lists the exact number of items in relevant content areas; such a table also specifies the precise number of items which must embody different cognitive processes.

**technical manual** in testing, the manual that summarizes the technical data about a new instrument.

**temporal lobe** the part of the cerebral cortex involved in processing of auditory sensations, long-term memory storage, and modulation of biological drives such as aggression, fear, and sexuality.

**teratogen**   a substance that crosses the placental barrier and causes physical deformities in the fetus.

**test**   a standardized procedure for sampling behavior and describing it with categories or scores. In addition, most tests have norms or standards by which the results can be used to predict other, more important, behaviors.

**test anxiety**   a constellation of phenomenological, physiological, and behavioral responses that accompany concern about possible failure on a test.

**test bias**   in popular usage, a test is biased if it discriminates unfairly against racial and ethnic minorities, women, and the poor; technically, *test bias* refers to differential validity for definable, relevant subgroups of persons.

**test fairness**   the extent to which the social consequences of test usage are considered fair to relevant subgroups; a matter of social values, test fairness is especially pertinent when tests are used for selection decisions.

**test of functional literacy**   a test that evaluates practical knowledge and skills used in everyday life.

**test-retest reliability**   a form of reliability in which the same test is given twice to the same group of heterogeneous and representative subjects; scores for the two sessions are then correlated.

**thalamus**   a key structure that provides sensory input and information about ongoing movement to the cerebral cortex; the thalamus is the major relay station in the brain.

**token economy**   a behavioral approach in which many different forms of prosocial behavior are rewarded with tokens that can be later exchanged for material rewards or privileges.

**trait**   any relatively enduring way in which one individual differs from another.

**trait anxiety**   the relatively stable tendency of an individual to respond anxiously to a stressful predicament.

**true score**   an examinee's hypothetical real score on a test; the true score can be estimated probabilistically, but is never directly known.

*T* score   a transformed score with mean of 50 and standard deviation of 10.

**Type A coronary-prone behavior pattern**   a behavior pattern consisting of insecurity of status, hyperag- gressiveness, free-floating hostility, and a sense of time urgency (hurry sickness).

**unqualified individualism**   in testing for selection, the ethical stance that, without exception, the best-qualified candidates should be selected for employment, admission, or other privilege.

**user's manual**   in testing, the manual that gives instructions for administration and also provides guidelines for test interpretation.

**validity**   a test is valid to the extent that inferences made from it are appropriate, meaningful, and useful.

**validity coefficient**   the correlation between test and criterion ($r_{xy}$).

**validity shrinkage**   the common discovery in cross-validation research that a test predicts the relevant criterion less accurately with the new sample of examinees than with the original tryout sample.

**value**   according to Rokeach and others, a shared and enduring belief about ideal modes of behavior or end states of existence.

**variance**   a statistical index that reflects the degree of dispersion in a group of scores.

**ventricles**   fluid-filled caverns within the brain.

**verbal comprehension**   the first factor on the WISC-III consisting of Information, Similarities, Vocabulary, and Comprehension.

**virtual reality**   the use of sophisticated computer images projected to wrap-around goggles to portray a moving, changing, three-dimensional environment.

**visual agnosia**   a difficulty in the recognition of drawings, objects, or faces caused by brain damage.

**Wernicke's aphasia**   also known as receptive aphasia, a form of language disturbance in which speech is fluent but meaningless, presumably because language comprehension is impaired.

**white matter**   those parts of the brain that consist of axons wrapped in a white, fatty substance called the myelin sheath.

**work sample**   an assessment procedure that uses a miniature replica of the job for which examinees have applied.

**work values**   the needs, motives, and values that influence vocational choice, job satisfaction, and career development.

# References

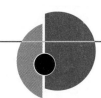

Aamodt, M. G., Keller, R., Crawford, K., & Kimbrough, W. (1981). A critical incident job analysis of the university housing resident assistant position. *Psychological Reports, 49,* 983–986.

Abel, E. L. (1995). An update on incidence of FAS: FAS is not an equal opportunity birth defect. *Neurobehavioral Toxicology, 17,* 437–443.

Abel, G. G., Hoffman, J., Warbere, B., & Holland, C. (1998). Visual reaction time and plethysmography as measures of sexual interest in child molesters. *Sexual Abuse: Journal of Research and Treatment, 10,* 389–394.

Abell, S. C., Briesen, P., & Watz, L. (1996). Intellectual evaluations of children using human figure drawings: An empirical investigation of two methods. *Journal of Clinical Psychology, 52,* 67–74.

Achenbach, T. M. (1991). *Manual for the Teacher's Report Form and 1991 Profile.* Burlington: University of Vermont, Department of Psychiatry.

Achenbach, T. M. (1992). *Manual for the Child Behavior Checklist/2–3 and 1992 Profile.* Burlington: University of Vermont, Department of Psychiatry.

Ackerman, M. (2005). The Ackerman-Schoendorf Scales for Parent Evaluation of Custody: A review of research and update. *Journal of Child Custody, 21,* 179–193.

Ackerman, M. J., & Schoendorf, K. (1992). *Ackerman-Schoendorf Scales for Parent Evaluation of Custody (ASPECT).* Los Angeles: Western Psychological Services.

Adams, G. A., Elacqua, T., & Colarelli, S. (1994). The employment interview as a sociometric selection technique. *Journal of Group Psychotherapy, Psychodrama, and Sociometry,* Fall, 99–113.

Adams, K. M., & Heaton, R. K. (1985). Automated interpretation of neuropsychological test data. *Journal of Consulting and Clinical Psychology, 53,* 790–802.

Agbenyega, S., & Jiggetts, J. (1999). Minority children and their over-representation in special education. *Education, 119,* 619–633.

Ahrens, J., Evans, R., & Barnett, R. (1990). Factors related to dropping out of school in an incarcerated population. *Educational and Psychological Measurement, 50,* 611–617.

Aiken, L. R. (1989). *Assessment of personality.* Boston: Allyn and Bacon.

Albers, C., & Grieve, A. (2007). Test Review: Bayley, N. (2006). *Bayley Scales of Infant and Toddler Development—Third Edition.* San Antonio, TX—Harcourt Assessment. *Journal of Psychoeducational Assessment, 25,* 180–190.

Albert, S., Fox, H. M., & Kahn, M. W. (1980). Faking psychosis on the Rorschach: Can expert judges detect malingering? *Journal of Personality Assessment, 44,* 115–119.

Alkhadher, O., Clarke, D., & Anderson, N. (1998). Equivalence and predictive validity of paper-and-pencil and computerized adaptive formats of the Differential Aptitude Tests. *Journal of Occupational and Organizational Psychology, 71,* 205–217.

Allen, M. J., & Yen, W. M. (1979). *Introduction to measurement theory.* Monterey, CA: Brooks/Cole.

Allport, G. W. (1937). *Personality: A psychological interpretation.* New York: Holt, Rinehart and Winston.

Allport, G. W. (1950). *The individual and his religion.* New York: Macmillan.

Allport, G. W., & Odbert, H. (1936). Trait names, a psycholexical study. *Psychological Monographs, 47* (Whole No. 211).

Allport, G., & Ross, J. (1967). Personal religious orientation and prejudice. *Journal of Personality and Social Psychology, 5,* 432–443.

Altepeter, T. S. (1989). The PPVT-R as a measure of psycholinguistic functioning: A caution. *Journal of Clinical Psychology, 45,* 935–941.

Altepeter, T. S., & Johnson, K. A. (1989). Use of the PPVT-R for intellectual screening with adults: A caution. *Journal of Psychoeducational Assessment, 7,* 39–45.

Alzheimer's Disease and Related Disorders Association. (2000). *General statistics/demographics.* Chicago: Author.

Amabile, T. M. (1983). *The social psychology of creativity.* New York: Springer-Verlag.

Ambrosini, P. J. (2000). Historical development and present status of the schedule for affect disorders and schizophrenia for school-age children (K-SADS). *Journal of the American Academy of Child and Adolescent Psychiatry, 39,* 49–58.

American Association for Counseling and Development. (1988). *Ethical standards.* Washington, DC: Author.

American Association on Mental Retardation (AAMR). (2002). *Mental retardation: Definition, classification, and systems of supports* (10th ed.). Washington, DC: Author.

American Educational Research Association, American Psychological Association, & National Council on Measurement in Education. (1985). *Standards for educational and psychological testing.* Washington, DC: American Psychological Association.

American Educational Research Association, American Psychological Association, & National Council on Measurement in Education. (1999). *Standards for educational and psychological testing* (2nd ed.). Washington, DC: American Psychological Association.

American Federation of Teachers, National Council on Measurement in Education, & National Education Association. (1990). *Standards for teacher competence in educational assessment of students.* Washington, DC: Author.

American Psychiatric Association. (1994). *Diagnostic and statistical manual of mental disorders* (4th ed.). Washington, DC: Author.

American Psychiatric Association. (2000). *Diagnostic and statistical manual of mental disorders* (4th ed., text revision). Washington, DC: Author.

American Psychological Association. (1953). *Ethical standards of psychologists.* Washington, DC: Author.

American Psychological Association. (1986). *Guidelines for computer-based tests and interpretations.* Washington, DC: Author.

American Psychological Association. (1988). In the Supreme Court of the United States: *Clara Watson v. Fort Worth Bank & Trust. American Psychologist, 43,* 1019–1028.

American Psychological Association. (1992a). Ethical principles of psychologists and code of conduct. *American Psychologist, 47,* 1597–1611.

American Psychological Association. (1992b). *Psychological testing of language minority and culturally different children.* Washington, DC: Author.

American Psychological Association. (1993). Guidelines for providers of psychological services to ethnic, linguistic, and culturally diverse populations. *American Psychologist, 48,* 45–48.

American Psychological Association. (1994a). Guidelines for child custody evaluations in divorce proceedings. *American Psychologist, 49,* 677–680.

American Psychological Association. (1994b). Report of the ethics committee, 1993. *American Psychologist, 49,* 659–666.

American Speech-Language-Hearing Association. (1991). *Code of ethics of the American Speech-Language Hearing Association.* Rockville, MD: Author.

Ammer, C. (2003). *The American Heritage dictionary of idioms.* New York: Houghton Mifflin Harcourt.

Anastasi, A. (1975). Review of the Goodenough-Harris Drawing Test. *The seventh mental measurements yearbook.* Lincoln: University of Nebraska Press.

Anastasi, A. (1985). *Psychological testing* (6th ed.). New York: Macmillan.

Anastasi, A. (1986). Emerging concepts of test validation. *Annual Review of Psychology, 37,* 1–15.

Anastasi, A. (1988). *Psychological testing* (6th ed.). New York: Macmillan.

Andersson, H. W. (1996). The Fagan Test of Infant Intelligence: Predictive validity in a random sample. *Psychological Reports, 78,* 1015–1026.

Andreasen, N. (2001). *Brave new brain: Conquering mental illness in the era of the genome.* New York: Oxford University Press.

Andreasen, N. C., & Black, D. (1995). *Introductory textbook of psychiatry* (2nd ed.). Washington, DC: American Psychiatric Press.

Andrew, D. M., Peterson, D. G., & Longstaff, H. P. (1979). *Minnesota Clerical Test Manual.* San Antonio, TX: The Psychological Corporation.

Andrews, F. M. (1975). Social and psychological factors which influence the creative process. In I. A. Taylor & J. W. Getzels (Eds.), *Perspectives in creativity.* Chicago: Aldine.

Ansorge, C. J. (1985). Review of the Cognitive Abilities Test. *Ninth mental measurements yearbook.* Lincoln: University of Nebraska Press.

Anthony, J. C., LeResche, L., Niaz, U., Von Korff, M., & Folstein, M. (1982). Limits of the Mini-Mental State as a screening test for dementia and delirium among hospital patients. *Psychological Medicine, 12,* 397–408.

Anthony, J., & Assel, M. (2007). A first look at the validity of the DIAL-3 Spanish version. *Journal of Psychoeducational Assessment, 25,* 165–179.

Arvey, R. D., & Campion, J. E. (1982). The employment interview: A summary and review of recent research. *Personnel Psychology, 35,* 281–332.

Arvey, R. D., & Faley, R. H. (1988). *Fairness in selecting employees.* Reading, MA: Addison-Wesley.

Arvey, R. D., & Murphy, K. R. (1998). Performance evaluation in work settings. *Annual Review of Psychology, 49,* 141–168.

Asher, J. J., & Sciarrino, J. A. (1974). Realistic work samples: A review. *Personnel Psychology, 27,* 519–533.

Assel, M., & Anthony, J. (2009). Factor structure of the DIAL-3: A test of a theory-driven conceptualization versus an empirically driven conceptualization in a nationally representative sample. *Journal of Psycho-educational Assessment, 27,* 113–124.

Atkins v. Virginia (2002). U.S. Supreme Court Cases, 536, 304–354. http://docs.justia.com/cases/supreme/536/304.pdf

Atkinson, L., Bevc, I., Dickens, S., & Blackwell, J. (1992). Concurrent validities of the Stanford-Binet (Fourth Edition), Leiter, and Vineland with developmentally delayed children. *Journal of School Psychology, 30,* 165–173.

Austin, J. T., & Villanova, P. (1992). The criterion problem: 1917–1992. *Journal of Applied Psychology, 77,* 836–874.

Axelrod, B. N., Greve, K., & Goldman, R. (1994). Comparison of four Wisconsin Card Sorting Test Scoring guides with novice raters. *Assessment, 1,* 115–121.

Aylward, G. P., & Carson, A. (2005). *Use of the Test Observation Checklist with the Stanford-Binet Intelligence Scales for Early Childhood, Fifth Edition (Early SB5).* Paper presented at the National Association of School Psychologists, Atlanta, GA, April 1, 2005.

Bach, P. J., Harowski, K., Kirby, K., Peterson, P., & Schulein, M. (1981). The interrater reliability of the Luria-Nebraska Neuropsychological Battery. *Clinical Neuropsychology, 3,* 19–21.

Baddeley, A. (1986). *Working memory.* Oxford: Clarendon Press/Oxford University Press.

Baer, D. M., Harrison, R., Fradenburg, L., Petersen, D., & Milla, S. (2005). Some pragmatics in the valid and reliable recording of directly observed behavior. *Research on Social Work Practice, 15,* 440–451.

Bagby, R. M., Rogers, R., Buis, T., & Kalemba, V. (1994). Malingered and defensive response styles on the MMPI-2: An examination of validity scales. *Assessment, 1,* 31–38.

Baker, C., Koenig, A., & Sowell, V. (1995). Relationship of the Blind Learning Aptitude Test to Braille reading skills. *Journal of Visual Impairment & Blindness, 89,* 440–447.

Balboni, G., Pedrabissi, L., Molteni, M., & Villa, S. (2001). Discriminant validity of the Vineland Scales: Score profiles of individuals with mental retardation and a specific disorder. *American Journal of Mental Retardation, 106,* 162–172.

Ballard, J., & Zettel, J. (1977). Public Law 94-142 and Sec. 504: What they say about rights and protections. *Exceptional Children, 44,* 177–185.

Baltes, P. B., Reese, H., & Nesselroade, J. (1977). *Life-span developmental psychology: Introduction to research methods.* Belmont, CA: Wadsworth.

Bandura, A. (1965). Vicarious processes: A case of no-trial learning. In L. Berkowitz (Ed.), *Advances in experimental social psychology* (vol. 2). New York: Academic Press.

Bandura, A. (1971). *Social learning theory.* Morristown, NJ: General Learning Press.

Bandura, A. (1977). *Social learning.* Englewood Cliffs, NJ: Prentice Hall.

Bandura, A. (1982). Self-efficacy mechanism in human agency. *American Psychologist, 37,* 122–147.

Bandura, A., Taylor, C. B., Ewart, C. K., Miller, N. M., & BeBusk, R. F. (1985). Exercise testing to enhance wives' confidence in their husbands' cardiac capability soon after clinically uncomplicated acute myocardial infarction. *American Journal of Cardiology, 55,* 635–638.

Bandura, A., & Walters, R. H. (1963). *Social learning and personality development.* New York: Holt, Rinehart and Winston.

Bar-On, R. (1997). *Bar-On Emotional Quotient Inventory: Technical manual (EQ-i).* Toronto, Canada: Multi-Health Systems.

Bar-On, R. (2000). Emotional and social intelligence: Insights from the Emotional Quotient Inventory (EQ-i). In R. Bar-On & J. Parker (Eds.), *Handbook of emotional intelligence* (pp. 363–388). San Francisco, CA: Jossey-Bass.

Bar-On, R., & Parker, J. D. (2000). *BarOn Emotional Quotient Inventory: Youth version.* North Tonawanda, NYU: Multi-Health Systems Incorporated.

Barber, M., & Stott, D. (2004). Validity of the Telephone Interview for Cognitive Status (TICS) in post-stroke subjects. *International Journal of Geriatric Psychiatry, 19,* 75–79.

Barlow, D. (2005). What's new about evidence-based assessment? *Psychological Assessment, 17,* 308–311.

Barnett, W. S., & Camilli, G. (2002). Compensatory pre-school education, cognitive development, and "race." In J. Fish (Ed.), *Race and intelligence: Separating science from myth.* Mahwah, NJ: Erlbaum.

Barrett, L. F. (2009). The future of psychology: Connecting mind to brain. *Perspectives on Psychological Science, 4,* 326–339.

Barrett, P. K. (2000). *Validation of the Test of Nonverbal Intelligence-Third Edition (TONI-3) for Jamaican students.* Unpublished Doctoral Dissertation, Auburn University, Auburn, AL.

Barron, F. (1953). An ego-strength scale which predicts response to psychotherapy. *Journal of Consulting Psychology, 17,* 327–333.

Barron, F. (1955). The disposition toward originality. *Journal of Abnormal and Social Psychology, 51,* 478–485.

Barron, F. (1968). *Creativity and personal freedom.* Princeton, NJ: Van Nostrand.

Barron, F., & Harrington, D. M. (1981). Creativity, intelligence, and personality. *Annual Review of Psychology, 32,* 439–476.

Bartol, C., & Bartol, A. (2004). *Introduction to forensic psychology: Research and application.* Thousand Oaks, CA: Sage.

Bate, A., Mathias, J., & Crawford, J. (2001). Performance on the Test of Everyday Attention and standard tests of attention following severe traumatic brain injury. *Clinical Neuropsychologist, 15,* 405–422.

Batey, M., & Furnham, A. (2006). Creativity, intelligence, and personality: A critical review of the scattered literature. *Genetic, Social, and General Psychology Monographs, 132,* 355–429.

Batson, C. D., Schoenrade, P., & Ventis, W. (1993). *Religion and the individual: A social-psychological perspective.* New York: Oxford University Press.

Bausell, R. B. (1986). *A practical guide to conducting empirical research.* New York: Harper & Row.

Bayless, J. D., Varney, N. R., & Roberts, R. J. (1989). Tinker Toy Test performance and vocational outcome in patients with closed-head injuries. *Journal of Clinical and Experimental Neuropsychology, 11,* 913–917.

Bayley, N. (1969). *Bayley Scales of Infant Development.* San Antonio, TX: The Psychological Corporation.

Bayley, N. (2006). *Bayley Scales of Infant and Toddler Development—Third Edition.* San Antonio, TX: Harcourt Assessment.

Beck, A. T. (1976). *Cognitive therapy and the emotional disorders.* New York: New American Library.

Beck, A. T. (1983). Negative cognitions. In E. Levitt, B. Lubin, & J. Brooks (Eds.), *Depression: Concepts, controversies, and some new facts* (2nd ed.). Hillsdale, NJ: Erlbaum.

Beck, A. T. (1987). Cognitive models of depression. *Journal of Cognitive Psychotherapy, An International Quarterly, 1,* 5–37.

Beck, A. T., & Steer, R. A. (1987). *Manual for the revised Beck Depression Inventory.* San Antonio, TX: The Psychological Corporation.

Beck, A. T., Steer, R. A., & Brown, G. K. (1996). *Manual for the Beck Depression Inventory-II.* San Antonio, TX: The Psychological Corporation.

Beck, A. T., Steer, R. A., & Garbin, M. G. (1988). Psychometric properties of the Beck Depression Inventory: Twenty-five years of evaluation. *Clinical Psychology Review, 8,* 77–100.

Beck, A. T., Ward, C. H., Mendelsohn, M., Mock, J., & Erbaugh, J. (1961). An inventory for measuring depression. *Archives of General Psychiatry, 4,* 561–571.

Behling, O. (1998). Employee selection: Will intelligence and conscientiousness do the job? *Academy of Management Executive, 12,* 77–86.

Beirne-Smith, M., Ittenbach, R. F., & Patton, J. R. (2002). *Mental retardation* (6th ed.). Upper Saddle River, NJ: Merrill (Prentice Hall).

Belcher, M. J. (1992). Review of the Wonderlic Personnel Test. *The eleventh mental measurements yearbook.* Lincoln: University of Nebraska Press.

Bell, N., Lassiter, K., Matthews, T., & Hutchinson, M. (2001). Comparison of the Peabody Picture Vocabulary Test-Third Edition and Wechsler Adult Intelligence Scale-Third Edition with university students. *Journal of Clinical Psychology, 57,* 417–422.

Bell, N., Matthews, T., Lassister, K., & Leverett, J. (2002). Validity of the Wonderlic Personnel Test as a measure of fluid or crystallized intelligence: Implications for career assessment. *North American Journal of Psychology, 4,* 113–120.

Bellak, L. (1992). *The Thematic Apperception Test, the Children's Apperception Test, and the Senior Apperception Technique in clinical use* (5th ed.). Orlando, FL: Grune & Stratton.

Bellak, L., & Bellak, S. S. (1991). *Children's Apperception Test Manual (CAT)* (8th rev. ed.). Larchmont, NY: C. P. S.

Bellak, L., & Bellak, S. S. (1994). *Children's Apperception Test Human Figures (CAT-H)* (11th ed.). Larchmont, NY: C. P. S.

Belsky, J., & Pluess, M. (2009). The nature (and nurture?) of plasticity in early human development. *Perspectives on Psychological Science, 4*, 345–351.

Bem, D., & Funder, D. (1978). Predicting more of the people more of the time: Assessing the personality of situations. *Psychological Review, 85*, 485–501.

Ben-Porath, Y. S., & Butcher, J. N. (1989). Psychometric stability of rewritten MMPI items. *Journal of Personality Assessment, 53*, 645–653.

Bender, L. (1938). *A visual motor gestalt test and its clinical use.* New York: American Orthopsychiatric Association.

Bennett, T. (1988). Use of the Halstead-Reitan Neuropsychological Test Battery in the assessment of head injury. *Cognitive Rehabilitation, 6*, 18–25.

Bennett, G. K., Seashore, H. G., & Wesman, A. G. (1974). *Fifth edition manual for the Differential Aptitude Tests, Forms S and T.* San Antonio, TX: The Psychological Corporation.

Bennett, G. K., Seashore, H. G., & Wesman, A. G. (1982). *Differential Aptitude Tests: Administrator's handbook.* San Antonio, TX: The Psychological Corporation.

Bennett, G. K., Seashore, H. G., & Wesman, A. G. (1984). *Differential Aptitude Tests: Technical Supplement.* San Antonio, TX: The Psychological Corporation.

Benson, D. F. (1988). Disorders of visual gnosis. In J. W. Brown (Ed.), *The neuropsychology of visual perception.* Hillsdale, NJ: Erlbaum.

Benson, D. F. (1994). *The neurology of thinking.* New York: Oxford University Press.

Benson, P. G. (1985). Minnesota Importance Questionnaire. In D. J. Keyser & R. C. Sweetland (Eds.), *Test critiques* (vol. 2). Kansas City, MO: Test Corporation of America.

Benson, P., Donahue, M., & Erickson, J. (1993). The Faith Maturity Scale: Conceptualization, measurement, and empirical validation. In M. L. Lynn & D. O. Moberg (Eds.), *Research in the social scientific study of religion* (vol. 5). Greenwich, CN: JAI Press.

Benton, A., Hamsher, K., Rey, G., & Sivan, A. (1994). *Multilingual Aphasia Examination* (3rd ed.). Iowa City, IA: AJA Associates.

Benton, A., Sivan, A., Hamsher, K., Varney, N., & Spreen, O. (1994). *Contributions to neuropsychological assessment* (2nd ed). New York: Oxford University Press.

Beran, T. (2007). Differential Ability Scales (2nd ed.). *Canadian Journal of School Psychology, 22*, 128–132.

Berg, E. A. (1948). A simple objective test for measuring flexibility in thinking. *Journal of General Psychology, 39*, 15–22.

Berger, S. G., Chibnall, J., & Gfeller, J. (1994). The Category Test: A comparison of computerized and standard versions. *Assessment, 3*, 255–258.

Berk, L. E. (1989). *Child development.* Boston: Allyn and Bacon.

Berk, R. A. (Ed.). (1984). *A guide to criterion-referenced test construction.* Baltimore: Johns Hopkins University Press.

Bernreuter, R. G. (1931). *The personality inventory.* Stanford, CA: Stanford University Press.

Bernstein, D. M., & Loftus, E. F. (2009). How to tell if a particular memory is true or false. *Perspectives on Psychological Science, 4*, 370–374.

Bernstein, I., & Nunnally, J. (1994). *Psychometric theory.* New York: McGraw-Hill.

Berry, C., Sackett, P., & Wiemann, S. (2007). A review of recent developments in integrity test research. *Personnel Psychology, 60*, 271–301.

Bersoff, D. N. (1988). Should subjective employment devices be scrutinized? Its elementary, my dear Ms. Watson. *American Psychologist, 43*, 1016–1018.

Bertua, C., Anderson, N., & Salgado, J. (2005). The predictive validity of cognitive ability tests: A UK meta-analysis. *Journal of Occupational and Organizational Psychology, 78*, 387–409.

Bianchini, K., Etherton, J., Greve, K., Heinly, M., & Meyers, J. (2008). Classification accuracy of MMPI-2 validity scales in the detection of pain-related malingering: A known-groups study. *Assessment, 15*, 435–449.

Bickley, P. G., Keith, T. Z., & Wolfe, L. M. (1995). The three-stratum theory of cognitive abilities: Test of the structure of intelligence across the life span. *Intelligence, 20*, 309–328.

Bigler, E. D. (Ed.). (1990). *Traumatic brain injury: Mechanisms of damage, assessment, intervention, and outcome.* Austin, TX: PRO-ED.

Binet, A., & Simon, T. (1905). Methodes nouvelles pour le diagnostic du niveau intellectuel des anormaux. *Annee Psychologique, 11*, 191–244.

Bishop, E. G., Hailey, B. J., & O'Rourke, D. F. (1989). Reliability of the Jenkins Activity Survey—Form T: Temporal stability and internal consistency. *Journal of Personality Assessment, 53*, 60–65.

Blake, R. J., Potter, E., III, & Sliwak, R. (1993). Validation of the structural scales of the CPI for predicting the performance of junior officers in the U.S. Coast Guard. *Journal of Business Psychology, 7,* 431–448.

Blau, T. (1984). *The psychologist as expert witness.* New York: Wiley.

Blin, Dr. (1902). Les debilites mentales. *Revue de Psychiatrie, 8,* 337–345.

Block, J. (1961). *The Q-sort method in personality assessment and psychiatric research.* Springfield, IL: Charles C. Thomas.

Blum, G. (1950). *The Blacky Pictures.* New York: The Psychological Corporation.

Blumenthal, J. A. (1985). Review of Jenkins Activity Survey. In J. V. Mitchell, Jr. (Ed.). *The ninth mental measurements yearbook* (vol. 1). Lincoln: Buros Institute of Mental Measurements of the University of Nebraska-Lincoln.

Boake, C. (2002). From the Binet-Simon to the Wechsler-Bellevue: Tracing the history of intelligence testing. *Journal of Clinical and Experimental Neuropsychology, 24,* 383–405.

Board of Trustees of the Society for Personality Assessment. (2005). The status of the Rorschach in clinical and forensic practice: An official statement by the Board of Trustees of the Society for Personality Assessment. *Journal of Personality Assessment, 85,* 219–237.

Boccaccini, M., Turner, D., & Murrie, D. (2008). Do some evaluators report consistently higher or lower PCL-R scores than others? Findings from a statewide sample of sexually violent predator evaluations. *Psychology, Public Policy, and Law, 14,* 262–283.

Boden, M. (2004). *The creative mind: Myths and mechanisms* (2nd ed.). London: Routledge.

Boggs, D. H., & Simon, J. R. (1968). Differential effect of noise on tasks of varying complexity. *Journal of Applied Psychology, 52,* 148–153.

Boggs, K. (1999). Campbell Interest and Skill Survey: Review and critique. *Measurement and Evaluation in Counseling and Development, 32,* 168–182.

Bond, L. (1996). Norm- and criterion-referenced testing. *Practical Assessment, Research and Evaluation,* [On-line journal], 5. Available: ericae.net.

Bonner, C. M. (1988). *Utilization of spiritual resources by patients experiencing a recent cancer diagnosis.* Unpublished master's thesis, University of Pittsburgh.

Boring, E. G. (1923, June). Intelligence as the tests test it. *New Republic,* 35–37.

Boring, E. G. (1950). *A history of experimental psychology* (2nd ed.). New York: Appleton-Century-Crofts.

Borkowski, J. (1985). Signs of intelligence: Strategy generalization and metacognition. In S. R. Yussen (Ed.), *The growth of reflection in children.* Orlando: Academic Press.

Borman, W. C. (1991). Job behavior, performance, and effectiveness. In M. D. Dunnette & L. M. Hough (Eds.), *Handbook of industrial and organizational psychology* (vol. 2). Palo Alto, CA: Consulting Psychologists Press.

Borman, W. C., Hanson, M., & Hedge, J. (1997). Personnel selection. *Annual Review of Psychology, 48,* 299–337.

Borman, W., Ilgen, D., Klimoski, R., & Weiner, I. (2003). *Handbook of psychology, industrial and organizational psychology.* San Francisco: Jossey-Bass.

Bornstein, M. H. (1994). Infancy. In R. J. Sternberg (Ed.), *Encyclopedia of human intelligence.* New York: Macmillan.

Bornstein, R. F., & Masling, J. M. (2005). *Scoring the Rorschach: Seven validated systems.* Mahwah, NJ: Erlbaum.

Boter, R., & Hoekstra-Vrolijk, S. (1994). ITVIC, an intelligence test for visually impaired children. In A. Kooijman & P. Looijestijn (Eds.), *Low vision: Research and new developments in rehabilitation* (pp. 135–138). Amsterdam: IOS Press.

Bouchard, T. J., Jr. (1994). Twin studies. In R. J. Sternberg (Ed.), *Encyclopedia of human intelligence.* New York: Macmillan.

Bouchard, T. J., Jr., Lykken, D., McGue, M., Segal, N., & Tellegen, A. (1990). Sources of human psychological differences: The Minnesota Study of Twins Reared Apart. *Science, 250,* 223–228.

Bowden, E., & Jung-Beeman, M. (2003). Normative data for 144 compound remote associate problems. *Behavior Research Methods, Instruments & Computers, 35,* 634–639.

Bowers, T., & Pantle, M. (1998). Shipley Institute for Living Scale and the Kaufman Brief Intelligence Test as screening instruments for intelligence. *Assessment, 5,* 187–195.

Bowman, M. (1989). Testing individual differences in ancient China. *American Psychologist, 44,* 576–578.

Boyd, T. M., & Sauter, S. (1993). Route-finding: A measure of everyday executive functioning in the head-injured adult. *Applied Cognitive Psychology, 7,* 171–181.

Bracken, B. A., & Fagan, T. K. (1990). Guest editors' introduction to the conference "Intelligence: Theories and Practice." *Journal of Psychoeducational Assessment, 8,* 221–222.

Brackett, M., & Mayer, J. (2003). Convergent, discriminant, and incremental validity of competing measures of emotional intelligence. *Personality and Social Psychology Bulletin, 29,* 1147–1158.

Braden, J. (1992). Intellectual assessment of deaf and hard of hearing people: A quantitative and qualitative research synthesis. *School Psychology Review, 21,* 82–94.

Braden, J., & Hannah, J. (1998). Assessment of hearing impaired and deaf children with the WISC-III. In D. Saklofske & A. Prifitera (Eds.), *Use of the WISC-III in clinical practice.* New York: Houghton Mifflin.

Bradley, K., Boyd-Wickizer, J., Powell, S., & Burman, M. (1998). Review: Some alcohol screening tests have acceptable test properties for use in general clinical populations of U.S. women. *Journal of the American Medical Association, 280,* 166–171.

Bradley, R. H., & Caldwell, B. M. (1984). 174 children: A study of the relationship between home environment and cognitive development during the first 5 years. In A. W. Gottfried (Ed.), *Home environment and early cognitive development: Longitudinal research.* Orlando, FL: Academic Press.

Bradley, R. H., & Rock, S. L. (1985). The HOME Inventory: Its relation to school failure and development of an elementary-age version. In W. K. Frankenburg, R. N. Emde, & J. W. Sullivan (Eds.), *Early identification of children at risk.* New York: Plenum.

Bradley, R. H., Mundfrom, D., Whiteside, L., Case, P., & Barrett, K. (1994). A factor analytic study of the Infant-Toddler and Early Childhood versions of the HOME Inventory administered to white, Black, and Hispanic American parents of children born preterm. *Child Development, 65,* 880–888.

Bradley, R. H., Rock, S. L., Caldwell, B. M., & Brisby, J. A. (1989). Use of the HOME Inventory for families with handicapped children. *American Journal on Mental Retardation, 94,* 313–330.

Bradley, R., Corwyn, R., Pipes McAdoo, H., & Garcia Coll, C. (2001). *Child Development, 72,* 1844–1867.

Bradley-Johnson, S. (2001). Cognitive assessment for the youngest children: A critical review of tests. *Journal of Psychoeducational Assessment, 19,* 19–44.

Bradshaw, J. L., & Mattingley, J. B. (1995). *Clinical neuropsychology: Behavioral and brain science.* San Diego, CA: Academic Press.

Bradway, K. P. (1944). IQ constancy on the Revised Stanford-Binet from the preschool to the junior high school level. *Journal of Genetic Psychology, 65,* 197–217.

Braithwaite, V., & Law, H. (1985). Structure of human values: Testing the adequacy of the Rokeach Value Survey. *Journal of Personality and Social Psychology, 49,* 250–263.

Brannick, M. T., Michaels, C. E., & Baker, D. P. (1989). Construct validity of in-basket scores. *Journal of Applied Psychology, 74,* 957–963.

Brannigan, G. G., & Decker, S. L. (2003). *Bender Visual-Motor Gestalt Test* (2nd ed.). Itasca, IL: Riverside Publishing.

Brass, D. J., & Oldham, G. R. (1976). Validating an in-basket test using an alternative set of leadership scoring dimensions. *Journal of Applied Psychology, 61,* 652–657.

Brauer, B., Braden, J., Pollard, R., & Hardy-Braz, S. (1998). Deaf and hard of hearing people. In J. Sandoval, C. Frisby, K. Geisinger, J. Scheuneman, & J. Grenier (Eds.), *Test interpretation and diversity.* Washington, DC: American Psychological Association.

Brazelton, T. B., & Nugent, J. (1995). *Neonatal Behavioral Assessment Scale* (3rd ed.). London: Cambridge University Press.

Bremner, J. D. (2005). *Brain imaging handbook.* New York: Norton.

Breslau, N. (1994). A gradient relationship between low birth weight and IQ at age 6 years. *Archives of Pediatric and Adolescent Medicine, 148,* 377–383.

Breslau, N., Chilcoat, H., Susser, E., and others (2001). Stability and change in children's Intelligence Quotient scores: A comparison of two socio-economically disparate communities. *American Journal of Epidemiology, 154,* 711–717.

Breuer, J., & Freud, S. (1893–1895). Studies on hysteria. In J. Strachey (Ed., in collaboration with A. Freud). *The standard edition of the complete psychological works of Sigmund Freud.* London: Hogarth, 1955, vol. 2.

Bricklin, B. (1995). *The custody evaluation handbook: Research-based solutions and applications.* New York: Brunner/Mazel.

Brief, D. E., & Comrey, A. L. (1993). A profile of personality for a Russian sample: As indicated by the Comrey Personality Scales. *Journal of Personality Assessment, 60,* 267–284.

Britt, G., & Myers, B. (1994). The effects of Brazelton intervention: A review. *Infant Mental Health Journal, 15,* 278–292.

Brodal, A. (1981). *Neurological anatomy* (3rd ed.). New York: Oxford University Press.

Brody, E. B., & Brody, N. (1976). *Intelligence: Nature, determinants and consequences.* New York: Academic Press.

Bromberg, W. (1959). *The mind of man: A history of psychotherapy and psychoanalysis.* New York: Harper & Row.

Brooks, B., Iverson, G., Holdnack, J., & Feldman, H. (2008). Potential for misclassification of mild cognitive impairment: A study of memory scores on the Wechsler Memory Scale-III in healthy older adults. *Journal of the International Neuropsychological Society, 14,* 463–478.

Brooks-Gunn, J., Klebanov, P., & Duncan, G. (1996). Ethnic differences in children's intelligence test scores: Role of economic deprivation, home environment, and maternal characteristics. *Child Development, 67,* 396–408.

Brown, L., Sherbenou, R., & Johnsen, S. (1998). *Test of Nonverbal Intelligence-3.* Austin, TX: Pro-Ed.

Bruininks, R. H., Woodcock, R. W., Weatherman, R. F., & Hill, B. K. (1996). *Scales of Independent Behavior-Revised, Interviewer's Manual.* Allen, TX: DLM Teaching Resources.

Bruyere, S. M., & O'Keeffe, J. (Eds.). (1994). *Implications of the Americans with Disabilities Act for psychology.* New York: Springer.

Buck, J. (1948). The H-T-P technique, a qualitative and quantitative scoring method. *Journal of Clinical Psychology Monograph Supplement* No. 5, 1–120.

Buck, J. (1981). *The House-Tree-Person technique: A revised manual.* Los Angeles: Western Psychological Services.

Bufford, R., & Parker, T., Jr. (1985). *Religion and well-being: Concurrent validation of the Spiritual Well-Being Scale.* Paper presented at the annual meeting of the American Psychological Association, Los Angeles.

Bufford, R., Paloutzian, R., & Ellison, C. (1991). Norms for the Spiritual Well-Being Scale. *Journal of Psychology and Theology, 19,* 56–70.

Bullock, E., & Reardon, R. (2008). Interest profile elevation, Big Five personality traits, and secondary constructs on the Self-Directed Search: A replication and extension. *Journal of Career Assessment, 16,* 326–338.

Burke, H. R. (1958). Raven's Progressive Matrices: A review and critical evaluation. *Journal of Genetic Psychology, 93,* 199–228.

Buschke, H., & Fuld, P. A. (1974). Evaluating storage, retention, and retrieval in disordered memory and learning. *Neurology, 24,* 1019–1025.

Buss, A. (1997). Evolutionary perspectives on personality traits. In R. Hogan, J. Johnson, & S. Briggs (Eds.), *Handbook of personality psychology.* San Diego, CA: Academic Press.

Buss, D. M. (2009). How can evolutionary psychology successfully explain personality and individual differences? *Perspectives on Psychological Science, 4,* 359–366.

Butcher, J. N. (1985). Introduction to the special series. *Journal of Consulting and Clinical Psychology, 53,* 746–747.

Butcher, J. N. (1993). *The Minnesota Report user's guide.* Minneapolis, MN: National Computer System.

Butcher, J. N. (Ed.). (1987). *Computerized psychological assessment: A practitioner's guide.* New York: Basic Books.

Butcher, J. N., & Williams, C. L. (1992). *Essentials of MMPI-2 and MMPI-A interpretation.* Minneapolis: University of Minnesota Press.

Butcher, J. N., & Williams, C. L. (2000). *Essentials of MMPI-2 and MMPI-A interpretation.* Minneapolis: University of Minnesota Press.

Butcher, J. N., Dahlstrom, W. G., Graham, J. R., Tellegen, A., & Kaemmer, B. (1989). *Minnesota Multiphasic Personality Inventory-2: Manual for administration and scoring.* Minneapolis: University of Minnesota Press.

Butcher, J. N., Graham, J. R., Williams, C. L., & Ben-Porath, Y. S. (1990). *Development and use of the MMPI-2 content scales.* Minneapolis: University of Minnesota Press.

Butcher, J., Perry, J., & Atlis, M. (2000). Validity and utility of computer-based test interpretation. *Psychological Assessment, 12,* 6–18.

Buttigieg, S. (2006). Gender and race differences in scores on the Wonderlic Personnel Test. *Applied H.R.M. Research, 11,* 73–74.

Caldwell, B. M., & Bradley, R. H. (1984). *Home observation for measurement of the environment.* Little Rock: University of Arkansas at Little Rock.

Caldwell, B. M., & Bradley, R. H. (1994). Environmental issues in developmental follow-up research. In S. L. Friedman & H. C. Haywood (Eds.), *Developmental follow-up: Concepts, domains, and methods.* San Diego, CA: Academic Press.

Caldwell, B. M., & Richmond, J. (1967). Social class level and the stimulation potential of the home. In J.

Hellmuth (Ed.), *The exceptional infant* (vol. 1). Seattle, WA: Special Child Publications.

Callahan, L. A., McGreevy, M., Cirincione, C., & Steadman, H. (1992). Measuring the effects of the Guilty But Mentally Ill (GBMI) verdict. *Law and Human Behavior, 16,* 447–462.

Camara, W. J., & Schneider, D. L. (1994). Integrity tests: Facts and unresolved issues. *American Psychologist, 49,* 112–119.

Campbell, C. D. (1988). Coping with hemodialysis: Cognitive appraisals, coping behaviors, spiritual well-being, assertiveness, and family adaptability and cohesion as correlates of adjustment (Doctoral dissertation, Western Conservative Baptist Seminary, 1983). *Dissertation Abstracts International, 49,* 538B.

Campbell, D. (2002). The history and development of the Campbell Interest and Skill Survey. *Journal of Career Assessment, 10,* 150–168.

Campbell, D. P. (1971). *Handbook for the Strong Vocational Interest Blank.* Stanford, CA: Stanford University Press.

Campbell, D. P. (1974). *Manual for the Strong-Campbell Vocational Interest Blank.* Stanford, CA: Stanford University Press.

Campbell, D. P., Hyne, S., & Nilsen, D. (1992). *Manual for the Campbell Interest and Skill Survey.* Minneapolis, MN: National Computer Systems.

Campbell, D. T., & Fiske, D. W. (1959). Convergent and discriminant validation by the multitrait-multimethod matrix. *Psychological Bulletin, 56,* 81–105.

Campbell, J. P., Gasser, M., & Oswald, F. (1996). The substantive nature of job performance variability. In K. R. Murphy (Ed.), *Individual differences and behavior in organizations.* San Francisco: Jossey-Bass.

Campbell, J., & McCord, D. (1996). The WAIS-R Comprehension and Picture Arrangement Subtests as measures of social intelligence: Testing traditional interpretations. *Journal of Psychoeducational Assessment, 14,* 240–249.

Campbell, J., Bell, S., & Keith, L. (2001). Concurrent validity of the Peabody Picture Vocabulary Test-Third Edition as an intelligence and achievement screener for low SES African American children. *Assessment, 8,* 85–94.

Campion, J. E. (1972). Work sampling for personnel selection. *Journal of Applied Psychology, 56,* 40–44.

Campion, M. A., Pursell, E. D., & Brown, B. K. (1988). Structured interviewing: Raising the psychometric properties of the employment interview. *Personnel Psychology, 41,* 25–42.

Campione, J., & Brown, A. (1978). Toward a theory of intelligence: Contributions from research with retarded children. *Intelligence, 2,* 279–304.

Canfield, A. A. (1951). The "sten" scale—A modified C-scale. *Educational and Psychological Measurement, 11,* 295–297.

Cannell, J. J. (1988). Nationally normed elementary achievement testing in America's public schools: How all 50 states are above the national average. *Educational Measurement: Issues and Practice, 7,* 5–9.

Capraro, R., & Capraro, M. (2002). Myers-Briggs Typica Indicator score reliability across studies: A meta-analytic reliability generalization study. *Educational and Psychological Measurement, 62,* 590–602.

Carless, S. (2000). The validity of scores on the Multidimensional Aptitude Battery. *Educational and Psychological Measurement, 60,* 592–603.

Carlson, C. F., Kula, M., & St. Laurent, C. (1997). Rorschach revised DEPI and CDI with inpatient major depressives and borderline personality disorder with major depression: Validity issues. *Journal of Clinical Psychology, 53,* 51–58.

Carpenter, M. B. (1991). *Core text of neuroanatomy* (4th ed.). Baltimore: Williams & Wilkins.

Carroll, D. (1988). How accurate is polygraph lie detection? In A. Gale (Ed.), *The polygraph test: Lies, truth and science.* London: Sage.

Carroll, J. B. (1993). *Human cognitive abilities.* New York: Cambridge University Press.

Carter, C., Mintun, M., Nichols, T., & Cohen, J. (1997). Anterior cingulate gyrus dysfunction and selection attention deficits in schizophrenia. *American Journal of Psychiatry, 154,* 1670–1675.

Carver, C., & Scheier, M. (2002). Optimism. In C. R. Snyder & S. Lopez (Eds.), *The handbook of positive psychology* (pp. 434–445). New York: Oxford University Press.

Carver, C., & Scheier, M. (2003). Optimism. In S. Lopez & C. R. Snyder (Eds.), *Positive psychological assessment: A handbook of models and measures.* Washington, DC: American Psychological Association.

Cascio, W. F. (1976). Turnover, biographical data, and fair employment practice. *Journal of Applied Psychology, 61,* 576–580.

Cascio, W. F. (1987). *Applied psychology in personnel management* (3rd ed.). Englewood Cliffs, NJ: Prentice Hall.

Cathers-Schiffman, T., & Thompson, M. (2007). Assessment of English- and Spanish-speaking students with the WISC-III and Leiter-R. *Journal of Psychoeducational Assessment, 25,* 41–52.

Cattell, J. McK. (1890). Mental tests and measurements. *Mind, 15,* 373–380.

Cattell, R. (1950). *Personality: A systematic theoretical and factual study.* New York: McGraw-Hill.

Cattell, R. B. (1940). A culture free intelligence test, Part I. *Journal of Educational Psychology, 31,* 161–179.

Cattell, R. B. (1941). Some theoretical issues in adult intelligence testing. *Psychological Bulletin,* 38, 592 (abstract).

Cattell, R. B. (1971). *Abilities: Their structure, growth, and action.* Boston: Houghton Mifflin.

Cattell, R. B. (1973). Personality pinned down. *Psychology Today, 7,* 40–46.

Cattell, R. B. (1986). *The handbook for the 16 Personality Factor questionnaire.* Champaign, IL: Institute for Personality and Ability Testing.

Cattell, R. B., & Nesselroade, J. R. (1967). Likeness and completeness theories examined by Sixteen Personality Factor measures on stably and unstably married couples. *Journal of Personality and Social Psychology, 7,* 351–361.

Cattell, R. B., Eber, H. W., & Tatsuoka, M. M. (1970). *Handbook for the Sixteen Personality Factor questionnaire.* Champaign, IL: Institute for Personality and Ability Testing.

Cautela, J. R. (1977). *Behavioral analysis forms for clinical intervention.* Champaign, IL: Research Press.

Ceci, S. (1996). *On intelligence: A bio-ecological treatise on intellectual development.* (Expanded ed.). Cambridge, MA: Harvard University Press.

Ceci, S. J. (1994). Bioecological theory of intellectual development. In R. J. Sternberg (Ed.), *Encyclopedia of human intelligence.* New York: Macmillan.

Chaffee, J. W. (1985). *The thorny gates of learning in Sung China: A social history of examinations.* Cambridge: Cambridge University Press.

Chalmers, T. (1833). *On the power, wisdom, and goodness of God as manifested in the adaptation of external nature to the moral and intellectual constitution of man.* London: William Pickering.

Chamberlin, J. (2009). How do you spot raw legal talent? Take this test. *Monitor on Psychology, 40*(6), 12.

Chan, R. (2000). Attentional deficits in patients with closed head injury: A further study to the discriminative validity of the Test of Everyday Attention. *Brain Injury, 14,* 227–236.

Chan, R., & Lai, M. (2006). Latent structure of the Test of Everyday Attention: Convergent evidence from

patients with traumatic brain injury. *Brain Injury, 20,* 653–659.

Chan, R., Lai, M., & Robertson, I. (2006). Latent structure of the Test of Everyday Attention in a non-clinical Chinese sample. *Archives of Clinical Neuropsychology, 21,* 477–485.

Chapman, L. J., & Chapman, J. P. (1967). Genesis of popular but erroneous psychodiagnostic observations. *Journal of Abnormal Psychology, 74,* 271–280.

Chase, C. I. (1985). Review of the Torrance Tests of Creative Thinking. *Ninth mental measurements yearbook.* Lincoln, NB: University of Nebraska Press.

Cherpitel, C. (2002). Screening for alcohol problems in the U.S. general population: Comparison of the CAGE, RAPS4, and RAPS4-QF by gender, ethnicity, and service utilitzation. *Alcoholism: Clinical and Experimental Research, 26,* 1686–1691.

Chibnall, J., & Detrick, P. (2003). The NEO-PI-R, Inwald Personality Inventory, and MMPI-2 in the prediction of police academy performance: A case for incremental validity. *American Journal of Criminal Justice, 27,* 233–248.

Chin, C., Ledesma, H., Cirino, P., & others (2001). Relation between Kaufman Brief Intelligence Test and WISC-III scores of children with RD. *Journal of Learning Disabilities, 34,* 2–8.

Choi, H., & Proctor, T. (1994). Error-prone subtests and error types in the administration of the Stanford-Binet Intelligence Scale: Fourth Edition. *Journal of Psychoeducational Assessment, 12,* 165–171.

Chung, J. (2009). Clinical validity of Fuld Object Memory Evaluation to screen for dementia in Chinese society. *International Journal of Geriatric Psychiatry, 24,* 156–162.

Chung, J., & Ho, W. (2009). Validity of Fuld Object Memory Evaluation for the detection of dementia in nursing home residents. *Aging and Mental Health, 13,* 274–279.

Cizek, G. J. (1999). *Cheating on tests: How to do it, detect it, and prevent it.* Mahwah, NJ: Erlbaum.

Clark, D. A. (1988). The validity of measures of cognition: A review of the literature. *Cognitive Therapy and Research, 12,* 1–20.

Clarkin, J. F., Hull, J., Cantor, J., & Sanderson, C. (1993). Borderline personality disorder and personality traits: A comparison of SCID-II BPD and NEO-PI. *Psychological Assessment, 5,* 472–476.

Cleary, T. A., Humphreys, L. G., Kendrick, S. A., & Wesman, A. (1975). Educational uses of tests with disadvantaged students. *American Psychologist, 30,* 15–41.

Cleckley, H. (1941). *The mask of sanity.* St. Louis, MO: C. V. Mosby.

Cleckley, H. (1976). *The mask of sanity* (5th ed.). St. Louis, MO: Mosby.

Clemans, W. V. (1971). Test administration. In R. L. Thorndike (Ed.), *Educational measurement* (2nd ed.). Washington, DC: American Council on Education.

Cleveland, J. N., Murphy, K. R., & Williams, R. E. (1989). Multiple uses of performance appraisal: Prevalence and correlates. *Journal of Applied Psychology, 74,* 130–135.

Coffman, J., Guerin, D., & Gottfried, A. (2006). Reliability and validity of the Parent-Child Relationship Inventory (PCRI): Evidence from a longitudinal cross-informant investigation. *Psychological Assessment, 18,* 209–214.

Cohen, J. (1960). A coefficient of agreement for nominal scales. *Educational and Psychological Measurement, 20,* 37–46.

Cohen, M. (1997). *Children's Memory Scale.* San Antonio, TX: Psychological Corporation.

Cohen, S., & Janicki-Deverts, D. (2009). Can we improve our physical health by altering our social networks? *Perspectives on Psychological Science, 4,* 375–378.

Colby, A., & Kohlberg, L. (1987). *The measurement of moral judgment* (vol. I). Cambridge: Cambridge University Press.

Colby, A., Kohlberg, L., Gibbs, J. C., & others. (1978). *Measuring moral judgment: Standardized scoring manual.* Cambridge, MA: Harvard University, Moral Education Research Foundation.

Colby, A., Kohlberg, L., Gibbs, J., & Lieberman, M. (1983). A longitudinal study of moral judgment. *Monographs for the Society for Research in Child Development, 48,* 1, 2.

Cole, N. S., & Moss, P. A. (1989). Bias in test use. In R. L. Linn (Ed.), *Educational measurement* (3rd ed.). New York: ACE/Macmillan.

College Board. (2005). Retrieved from www.college-board.com/student/testing/sat/ on September 21, 2005.

Collins, J. M., & Schmidt, F. L. (1993). Personality, integrity, and white collar crime: A construct validity study. *Personnel Psychology, 46,* 295–311.

Colom, R., Quiroga, M., & Juan-Espinosa, M. (1999). Are cognitive sex differences disappearing? Evidence from Spanish populations. *Personality and Individual Differences, 27,* 1189–1195.

Committee on Ethical Guidelines for Forensic Psychologists. (1991). Specialty guidelines for forensic psychologists. *Law and Human Behavior, 15,* 655–665.

Comrey, A. (1995). Career assessment and the Comrey Personality Scales. *Journal of Career Assessment, 3,* 140–156.

Comrey, A. L. (1970). *Manual for the Comrey Personality Scales.* San Diego, CA: EdITS.

Comrey, A. L. (1973). *A first course in factor analysis.* New York: Academic Press.

Comrey, A. L. (1980). *Handbook of interpretations for the Comrey Personality Scales.* San Diego, CA: EdITS.

Comrey, A. L., & Backer, T. (1970). Construct validation of the Comrey Personality Scales. *Multivariate Behavior Research, 5,* 469–477.

Comrey, A. L., & Schiebel, D. (1983). Personality test correlates of psychiatric outpatient status. *Journal of Consulting and Clinical Psychology, 51,* 756–762.

Comrey, A. L., & Schiebel, D. (1985). Personality test correlates of psychiatric case history data. *Journal of Consulting and Clinical Psychology, 53,* 470–479.

Conners, C. K. (1990). *Conners' Rating Scales.* Los Angeles: Western Psychological Services.

Conners, C. K. (1991). *Conners' Teacher Rating Scales- 39.* North Tonawanda, NY: Multi-Health Systems, Inc.

Conners, C. K. (1995). *Conners' Continuous Performance Test II* (CPT II). North Tonawanda, NY: Multi-Health Systems, Inc.

Conners, C. K. (1997). *Conners' Rating Scales-Revised.* North Tonawanda, NY: Multi-Health Systems.

Conoley, C. W. (1992). Review of Beck Depression Inventory. *The eleventh mental measurements yearbook.* Lincoln: University of Nebraska Press.

Conoley, C. W., Plake, B., & Kemmerer, B. (1991). Issues in computer-based test interpretive systems. *Computers in Human Behavior, 7,* 97–101.

Conry, R., & Plant, W. T. (1965). WAIS and group test predictions of an academic success criterion: High School and college. *Educational and Psychological Measurement, 25,* 493–500.

Constantino, G., & Malgady, R. (1996). Development of TEMAS, a multicultural thematic apperception test: Psychometric properties and clinical utility. In G. R. Sodowsky & J. C. Impara (Eds.), *Multicultural assessment in counseling and clinical psychology.* Lincoln, NE: The Buros Institute of Mental Measurements.

Constantino, G., & Malgady, R. (2000). Multicultural and cross-cultural utility of the TEMAS (Tell-Me-A-Story) Test. In R. Dana (Ed.), *Handbook of* cross-cultural and multicultural personality assessment. Mahwah, NJ: Erlbaum.

Constantino, G., Malgady, R., & Rogler, L. (1988). Tell-Me-A-Story (TEMAS): Manual. Los Angeles: Western Psychological Services.

Conte, J. (2005). A review and critique of emotional intelligence measures. Journal of Organizational Behavior, 26, 433–440.

Conway, J. M., Jako, R., & Goodman, D. (1995). A meta-analysis of interrater and internal consistency reliability of selection interviews. Journal of Applied Psychology, 80, 565–579.

Cooper, D., & Shepard, K. (1992). Review of DIAL-R. Learning Disabilities Research & Practice, 7, 171–174.

Corkin, S. (1968). Acquisition of motor skill after bilateral medial temporal-lobe excision. Neuropsychologia, 6, 255–265.

Cornelius, S. W., & Caspi, A. (1987). Everyday problem solving in adulthood and old age. Psychology and Aging, 2, 144–153.

Cosden, M. (1992). Review of the Draw A Person: A Quantitative Scoring System. The eleventh mental measurements yearbook. Lincoln: University of Nebraska Press.

Costa, P. T., Jr. (1991). Clinical use of the five-factor model. Journal of Personality Assessment, 57, 393–398.

Costa, P. T., Jr., & McCrae, R. (1989). NEO Five-Factor Inventory test manual. Port Huron, MI: Sigma Assessment Systems.

Costa, P. T., Jr., & McCrae, R. (1992). NEO PI-R test manual. Port Huron, MI: Sigma Assessment Systems.

Costa, P. T., Jr., McCrae, R. R., & Holland, J. L. (1984). Personality and vocational interests in an adult sample. Journal of Applied Psychology, 69, 390–400.

Costa, P., McCrae, R., & Martin, T. (2005). The NEO-PI-3: A more readable revised NEO Personality Inventory. Journal of Personality Assessment, 84, 261–270.

Costa, P., McCrae, R., & Martin, T. (2008). Incipient adult personality: The NEO-PI-3 in middle-school-aged children. British Journal of Developmental Psychology, 26, 71–89.

Costenbader, V., & Ngari, S. (2001). A Kenya standardization of the Raven's Coloured Progressive Matrices. School Psychology International, 22, 258–268.

Cote, L., & Crutcher, M. D. (1991). The basal ganglia. In E. R. Kandel, J. H. Schwartz, & T. M. Jessell (Eds.), Principles of neural science (3rd ed.). New York: Elsevier.

Coveny, T. E. (1972). A new test for the visually handicapped: Preliminary analysis of reliability and validity of the Perkins-Binet. Education of the Handicapped, 4, 97–101.

Cowdery, K. M. (1926–27). Measurement of professional attitudes: Differences between lawyers, physicians, and engineers. Journal of Personnel Research, 5, 131–141.

Craig, R. J. (Ed.). (1993). The Millon Clinical Multiaxial Inventory: A clinical research information synthesis. Hillsdale, NJ: Erlbaum.

Cramond, B., Matthews-Morgan, J., Bandalos, D., & Zuo, L. (2005). A report on the 40-year follow-up of the Torrance Tests of Creative Thinking: Alive and well in the new millennium. Gifted Child Quarterly, 49, 283–291.

Crandall, J. E. (1981). Theory and measurement of social interest: Empirical tests of Alfred Adler's concept. New York: Columbia University Press.

Crawford, J. R., Sommerville, J., & Robertson, I. (1997). Assessing the reliability and abnormality of subtest differences on the Test of Everyday Attention. British Journal of Clinical Psychology, 36, 609–617.

Creed, P., Patton, W., & Bartrum, D. (2002). Multidimensional properties of the LOT-R: Effects of optimism and pessimism on career and well-being related variables in adolescents. Journal of Career Assessment, 10, 42–61.

Cripe, L. (1996). The ecological validity of executive function testing. In R. J. Sbordone & C. J. Long (Eds.), Ecological validity of neuropsychological testing. Delray Beach, FL: GR Press/St. Lucie Press.

Critchley, M. (1953). The parietal lobes. London: Edward Arnold.

Cronbach, L. J. (1951). Coefficient alpha and the internal structure of tests. Psychometrika, 16, 297–334.

Cronbach, L. J. (1971). Test validation. In R. L. Thorndike (Ed.), Educational measurement (2nd ed.). Washington, DC: American Council on Education.

Cronbach, L. J. (1988). Five perspectives on the validity argument. In H. Wainer & H. I. Braun (Eds.), Test validity. Hillsdale, NJ: Lawrence Erlbaum.

Cronbach, L. J., & Meehl, P. E. (1955). Construct validity in psychological tests. Psychological Bulletin, 52, 281–302.

Culbertson, J., & Edmonds, A. (1996). Learning Disabilities. In R. Adams, O. Parsons, J. Culbertson, & S. Nixon (Eds.). Neuropsychology for clinical practice: Etiology, assessment, and treatment of common neurological disorders. Washington, DC: American Psychological Association.

Cullen, M., & Sackett, P. (2004). Integrity testing in the workplace. In J. Thomas (Ed.), *Comprehensive handbook of psychological assessment, Vol. 4: Industrial and organizational assessment*. Hoboken, NJ: John Wiley.

Cummings, R., Maddux, C., Harlow, S., & Dyas, L. (2002). Academic misconduct in undergraduate teacher education students and its relationship to their principled moral reasoning. *Journal of Instructional Psychology, 29,* 286–296.

Cunningham, M., Wong, D., & Barbee, A. (1994). Self-presentation dynamics on overt integrity tests: Experimental studies with the Reid Report. *Journal of Applied Psychology, 79,* 643–658.

Cureton, E. E. (1950). Validity, reliability, and baloney. *Educational and Psychological Measurement, 10,* 94–96.

Cytowic, R. E. (1996). *The neurological side of neuropsychology.* Cambridge, MA: MIT Press.

Dahlstrom, W. G., Welsh, G. S., & Dahlstrom, L. E. (1972). *An MMPI handbook. Volume I: Clinical interpretation* (rev. ed.). Minneapolis: University of Minnesota Press.

Dahlstrom, W. G., Welsh, G. S., & Dahlstrom, L. E. (1975). *An MMPI handbook: Vol. II. Research applications.* Minneapolis: University of Minnesota Press.

Daley, T., Whaley, S., Sigman, M., Espinosa, M., & Neumann, C. (2003). IQ on the rise: The Flynn effect in rural Kenyan children. *Psychological Science, 14,* 215–219.

Dana, R. H. (1959). Proposal for objective scoring of the TAT. *Perceptual and Motor Skills, 10,* 27–43.

Das J. P., Naglieri, J., & Kirby, J. (1994). *Assessment of cognitive processes: The PASS theory of intelligence.* Boston: Allyn and Bacon.

Das, J. P. (1994). Serial and parallel processing. In R. J. Sternberg (Ed.), *Encyclopedia of human intelligence.* New York: Macmillan.

Das, J. P., & Naglieri, J. A. (1993). *Cognitive assessment system: Standardization version.* Chicago: Riverside.

Das, J. P., Kirby, J. R., & Jarman, R. F. (1979). *Simultaneous and successive cognitive processes.* Orlando, FL: Academic Press.

Davis, C. (1980). *Perkins-Binet Tests of Intelligence for the blind.* Watertown, MA: Perkins School for the Blind.

Davis, E., Glynn, L., Schetter, C., and others. (2007). Prenatal exposure to maternal depression and cortisol influences infant temperament. *Journal of the American Academy of Child and Adolescent Psychiatry, 46,* 737–746.

Davison, M., Gasser, M., & Ding, S. (1996). Identifying major profile patterns in a population: An exploratory study of WAIS and GATB patterns. *Psychological Assessment, 1,* 26–31.

Dawes, R. M., Faust, D., & Meehl, P. E. (1989). Clinical versus actuarial judgment. *Science, 243,* 1668–1674.

Dayan, K., Fox, S., & Kasten, R. (2008). The preliminary employment interview as a predictor of assessment center outcomes. *International Journal of Selection and Assessment, 16,* 102–111.

de Bildt, A., Kraijere, D., Sytema, S., & Minderaa, R. (2005). The psychometric properties of the Vineland Adaptive Behavior Scales in children and adolescents with mental retardation. *Journal of Autism and Developmental Disorders, 35,* 53–62.

de Raad, B., & Perugini, M. (Eds.). *Big five assessment.* Ashland, OH: Hogrefe and Huber Publishers.

DeCrans, M. (1990). *Spiritual well-being in the rural elderly.* Unpublished manuscript, Marquette University, Milwaukee, WI.

Delis, D. C., & Kaplan, E. (1982). Assessment of aphasia with the Luria-Nebraska Neuropsychological Battery: A conceptual critique. *Journal of Consulting and Clinical Psychology, 50,* 32–39.

Delis, D. C., Kramer, J., Kaplan, E., & Ober, B. (2000). *California Verbal Learning Test—Second Edition.* San Antonio, TX: The Psychological Corporation.

Dellas, M., & Gaier, E. L. (1970). Identification of creativity: The individual. *Psychological Bulletin, 73,* 55–73.

Dembroski, T., MacDougall, J., Williams, B., & Haney, T. (1985). Components of Type A, hostility, and anger in relationship to angiographic findings. *Psychosomatic Medicine, 47,* 219–233.

Deri, S. (1949). *Introduction to the Szondi Test.* New York: Grune & Stratton.

Dey, A. N., Schiller, J. S., & Tai, D. A. (2004). *Summary health statistics for U.S. children: National Health Interview Survey, 2002.* Washington, DC: National Center for Health Statistics.

Diamond, M., Scheibel, A., Murphy, G., & Harvey, T. (1985). On the brain of a scientist: Albert Einstein. *Experimental Neurology, 88,* 198–204.

Diamond, S. (1980). Wundt before Leipzig. In R. W. Rieber (Ed.), *Wilhelm Wundt and the making of a scientific psychology.* New York: Plenum Press.

Dickens, W., & Flynn, J. (2006). Black Americans reduce the racial IQ gap. *Psychological Science, 17,* 913–920.

Dickens, W., & Flynn, J. R. (2006). Black Americans reduce the racial IQ gap: Evidence from standardization samples. *Psychological Science, 17,* 913–920.

Diener, E. (2009). Editor's introduction: Special issue on the next big questions in psychology. *Perspectives on Psychological Science, 4,* 325.

Diessner, R., & Lewis, G. (2007). Further validation of the Gratitude, Resentment, and Appreciation Test. *Journal of Social Psychology, 147,* 445–447.

Digman, J. (1990). Personality structure: Emergence of the five-factor model. *Annual Review of Psychology, 41,* 417–440.

Dikmen, S., Machamer, J., Winn, H., & Temkin, N. (1995). Neuropsychological outcome at 1-year post head injury. *Neuropsychology, 9,* 80–90.

DiLalla, L. F., Thompson, L. A., Plomin, R., & others. (1990). Infant predictors of preschool and adult IQ: A study of infant twins and their parents. *Developmental Psychology, 26,* 759–769.

Dillon, H. J. (1949). *Early school leavers: A major educational problem.* New York: National Child Labor Committee.

Dillon, R. F., Pohlmann, J. T., & Lohman, D. F. (1981). A factor analysis of Raven's Advanced Progressive Matrices freed of difficulty factors. *Educational and Psychological Measurement, 41,* 1295–1302.

Dixon, D. (1995). Review of Structured Interview of Reported Symptoms. *Twelfth mental measurements yearbook.* Lincoln: University of Nebraska Press.

Dodge, K. A. (2009). Mechanisms of gene-environment interaction effects in the development of Conduct disorder. *Perspectives on Psychological Science, 4,* 408–414.

Dodrill, C. B. (1979). Sex differences on the Halstead-Reitan Neuropsychological Battery and on other neuropsychological measures. *Journal of Clinical Psychology, 35,* 236–241.

Dodrill, C. B. (1981). An economical method of measuring general intelligence in adults. *Journal of Consulting and Clinical Psychology, 49,* 668–673.

Dodrill, C. B., & Warner, M. H. (1988). Further studies of the Wonderlic Personnel Test as a brief measure of intelligence. *Journal of Consulting and Clinical Psychology, 56,* 145–147.

Doll, E. A. (1935). The Vineland Social Maturity Scale. *Training School Bulletin, 32,* 1–7, 25–32, 48–55, 68–74.

Dolliver, R. H., Irvin, J. A., & Bigley, S. E. (1972). Twelve-year follow-up of the Strong Vocational Interest Blank. *Journal of Counseling Psychology, 19,* 212–217.

Donders, J. (1995). Validity of the Kaufman Brief Intelligence Test (K-BIT) in children with traumatic brain injury. *Assessment, 2,* 219–224.

Donders, J., Tulsky, D., & Zhu, J. (2001). Criterion validity of new WAIS-III subtest scores after traumatic brain injury. *Journal of the International Neuropsychological Society, 7,* 892–898.

Donlon, T. F. (Ed.). (1984). *The College Board technical handbook for the Scholastic Aptitude Test and Achievement Tests.* New York: College Entrance Examination Board.

Donnay, D., & Borgen, F. (1996). Validity, structure, and content of the 1994 Strong Interest Inventory. *Journal of Counseling Psychology, 43,* 275–291.

Douglas, K., Ogloff, J., Nicholls, T., & Grant, I. (1999). Assessing risk for violence among psychiatric patients: The HCR-20 violence risk assessment schema and the Psychopathy Checklist-Screening Version. *Journal of Consulting and Clinical Psychology, 67,* 917–930.

Drakeley, R. J., Herriot, P., & Jones, A. (1988). Biographical data, training success and turnover. *Journal of Occupational Psychology, 61,* 145–152.

Drasgow, F., Olson-Buchanan, J., & Moberg, P. (1999). Development of an interactive assessment: Trials and tribulations. In F. Drasgow & J. Olson-Buchanan (Eds.), *Innovations in computerized assessment.* Mahwah, NJ: Erlbaum.

Drebing, C., Van Gorp, W., Stuck, A., Mitrushina, M., & Beck, J. (1994). Early detection of cognitive decline in higher cognitively functioning older adults: Sensitivity and specificity of a neuropsychological screening battery. *Neuropsychology, 8,* 31–37.

DuBois, P. E. (1939). A test standardized on Pueblo Indian children. *Psychological Bulletin, 36,* 523.

DuBois, P. H. (1970). *A history of psychological testing.* Boston: Allyn and Bacon.

Dumenci, L. (1995). Construct validity of the Self-Directed Search using hierarchically nested structural models. *Journal of Vocational Behavior, 47,* 21–34.

Dumont, R., Cruse, C., Price, L., & Whelley, P. (1996). The relationship between the Differential Ability Scales (DAS) and the Wechsler Intelligence Scale for Children-Third Edition (WISC-III). *Psychology in the Schools, 33,* 203–209.

Dunai, F., & Porter, R. (2001). Armed Services Vocational Aptitude Battery predictors of entry-level radiography students' success. *Military Medicine, 166,* 422–426.

Dunn, L. M., & Dunn, D. M. (2007). *Examiner's manual: Peabody Picture Vocabulary Test—Fourth Edition.* New York: Pearson.

Dunn, L. M., & Dunn, L. M. (1981). *Peabody Picture Vocabulary Test-Revised.* Circle Pines, MN: American Guidance Service.

Dunn, L. M., & Dunn, L. M. (1998). *Examiner's Manual: Peabody Picture Vocabulary Test-III.* Circle Pines, MN: American Guidance Service.

Dyce, J. A. (1996). Factor structure of the Beck Hopelessness Scale. *Journal of Clinical Psychology, 52,* 555–558.

Eaker, E. D., & Castelli, W. P. (1988). Type A behavior and coronary heart disease in women: Fourteen-year incidence from the Framingham study. In B. K. Houston & C. R. Snyder (Eds.), *Type A behavior pattern: Research, theory, and interventions.* New York: Wiley.

Ebbinghaus, H. (1885/1913). *Memory: A contribution to experimental psychology.* Translated by Henry A. Ruger & Clara E. Bussenius. New York: Teachers College Press.

Ebbinghaus, H. (1897). Ueber eine neue Methode zur Pruefung geistiger Faehigkeiten und ihre Anwendung bei Schulkindern. *Zeitschrift fuer Angewandte Psychologie, 13,* 401–459.

Eccles, J. C. (1973). *The understanding of the brain.* New York: McGraw-Hill.

Educational Testing Service. (1989). *Guidelines for proper use of GRE scores.* Princeton, NJ: Author.

Efron, R. (1990). *The decline and fall of hemispheric specialization.* Hillsdale, NJ: Erlbaum.

Eisenstein, N., & Engelhart, C. (1997). Comparison of the K-BIT with short forms of the WAIS-R in a neuropsychological population. *Psychological Assessment, 9,* 57–62.

Elkind, J., Rubin, E., Rosenthal, S., Skoff, B., & Prather, P. (2001). A simulated reality scenario compared with the computerized Wisconsin Card Sorting Test: An analysis of preliminary results. *CyberPsychology and Behavior, 4,* 489–496.

Elliott, C. D. (1990). *The Differential Ability Scales: Introductory and technical handbook.* San Antonio, TX: The Psychological Corporation.

Elliott, C. D. (2007). *Differential Ability Scales—Second Edition: Introductory and technical manual.* San Antonio, TX: Harcourt Assessment.

Ellis, A. (1962). *Reason and emotion in psychotherapy.* New York: Lyle Stuart.

Ellison, C. W. (1983). Spiritual well-being: Conceptualization and measurement. *Journal of Psychology and Theology, 11,* 330–340.

Ellison, C. W., & Smith, J. (1991). Toward an integrative measure of health and well-being. *Journal of Psychology and Theology, 19,* 35–48.

Embretson, S. E. (1996). The new rules of measurement. *Psychological Assessment, 8,* 341–349.

Embretson, S. E., & Reise, S. (2000). *Item response theory for psychologists.* Mahwah, NJ: Erlbaum.

Emmons, R., McCullough, M., & Tsang, J. (2003. The assessment of gratitude. In S. Lopez & C. R. Snyder (Eds.), *Positive psychological assessment* (pp. 345–360). Washington, DC: American Psychological Association.

Equal Employment Opportunity Commission. (1995). *ADA enforcement guidance: Preemployment disability-related questions and medical examinations.* Washington, DC: Author.

Erdberg, P. (1985). The Rorschach. In C. S. Newmark (Ed.), *Major psychological assessment instruments.* Boston: Allyn and Bacon.

Esquirol, J. E. D. (1845/1838). *Mental maladies.* (trans. E. K. Hunt). Philadelphia: Lea & Blanchard.

Estes, W. K. (1974). Learning theory and intelligence. *American Psychologist, 29,* 740–749.

Evans, D. A., Funkenstein, H., Albert, M., and others (1989). Prevalence of Alzheimer's Disease in a community population of older persons. *Journal of the American Medical Association, 262,* 2551–2556.

Ewing, J. A. (1984). Detecting alcoholism: The CAGE questionnaire. *Journal of the American Medical Association, 252,* 1905–1907.

Exner, J. E., Jr. (1991). *The Rorschach: A comprehensive system, Volume 2. Current research and advanced interpretation* (2nd ed.). New York: Wiley.

Exner, J. E., Jr. (1993). *The Rorschach: A comprehensive system, Volume 1. Basic foundations* (3rd ed.). New York: Wiley.

Exner, J. E., Jr. (1995). *Issues and methods in Rorschach research.* Mahwah, NJ: Erlbaum.

Exner, J. E., Jr., & Weiner, I. B. (1994). *The Rorschach: A comprehensive system, Volume 3. Assessment of children and adolescents* (2nd ed.). New York: Wiley.

Eyde, L. D., & Primhoff, E. S. (1992). Responsible test use. In M. Zeidner and R. Most (Eds.), *Psychological testing: An inside view.* Palo Alto, CA: Consulting Psychologists Press.

Eyde, L. D., Robertson, G. J., Krug, S., and others (1993). *Responsible test use: Case studies for assessing human behavior.* Washington, DC: American Psychological Association.

Eysenck, H. J. (1986). Is intelligence? In R. J. Sternberg & D. K. Detterman (Eds.), *What is intelligence? Contemporary viewpoints on its nature and definition.* Norwood, NJ: Ablex.

Eysenck, H. J. (1986). Toward a new model of intelligence. *Personality and Individual Differences, 7,* 731–736.

Eysenck, H. J., & Eysenck, M. W. (1975). *Manual of the Eysenck Personality Questionnaire.* San Diego: Educational and Industrial Testing Service.

Eysenck, H. J., & Eysenck, M. W. (1985). *Personality and individual differences: A natural science approach.* New York: Plenum Press.

Fagan, J. F. III, & Haiken-Vasen, J. (1997). Selective attention to novelty as a measure of information processing across the lifespan. In J. Burack & J. Enns (Eds.), *Attention, development, and psychopathology.* New York: Guilford.

Fagan, J. F. III, & McGrath, S. K. (1981). Infant recognition memory and later intelligence. *Intelligence, 5,* 121–130.

Fagan, J. F. III, & Shepherd, P. A. (1986). *The Fagan Test of Infant Intelligence: Training manual.* Cleveland, OH: Infantest Corporation.

Fagan, J. F. III, Singer, L., Montie, J., & Shepherd, P. (1986). Selective screening device for the early detection of normal or delayed cognitive development in infants at risk for later mental retardation. *Pediatrics, 78,* 1021–1026.

Fagan, J. F. III. (1984). Infant memory. In M. Moscovitch (Ed.), *Infant memory.* New York: Plenum Press.

Fagan, J., & Holland, C. (2006). Racial equality in intelligence: Predictions from a theory of intelligence as processing. *Intelligence, 15,* 319–334.

Fancher, R. E. (1985). *The intelligence men: Makers of the IQ controversy.* New York: Norton.

Farrell, M., & Phelps, L. (2000). A comparison of the Leiter-R and the Universal Nonverbal Intelligence Test (UNIT) with children classified as language impaired. *Journal of Psychoeducational Assessment, 18,* 268–274.

*Federal Rules of Evidence for United States Courts and Magistrates.* (1975). St. Paul, MN: West Publishing Company.

Fehring, R., Brennan, P., & Keller, M. (1987). Psychological and spiritual well-being in college students. *Research in Nursing and Health, 10,* 391–398.

Feist, G. (1999). Autonomy and independence. *Encyclopedia of creativity* (Vol. 1, pp. 157–163). San Diego, CA: Academic Press.

Feist, G., & Barron, F. (2003). Predicting creativity from early to late adulthood: Intellect, potential, and personality. *Journal of Research in Personality, 37,* 62–88.

Feldman, R. D. (1982). *Whatever happened to the quiz kids?* Chicago: Chicago Review Press.

Feldstein, S., & Miller, W. (2007). Does subtle screening for substance abuse work? A review of the Substance Abuse Subtle Screening Inventory (SASSI). *Addiction, 102,* 41–50.

Feldt, L. S., & Brennan, R. L. (1989). In R. L. Linn (Ed.), *Educational measurement* (3rd ed.). New York: American Council on Education/Macmillan.

Ferris, G., Judge, T., Rowland, K., & Fitzgibbons, D. (1994). Subordinate influence and the performance evaluation process: Test of a model. *Organizational Behavior and Human Decision Processes, 58,* 101–135.

Ferris, S. H. (1992). Diagnosis by specialists: Psychological testing. *Acta Neurologica Scandinavica, 85,* 32–35.

Finholt, T., & Olson, G. (1997). From laboratories to collaboratories: A new organizational form for scientific collaboration. *Psychological Science, 8,* 28–36.

Finn, S. E. (1996). *A manual for using the MMPI-2 as a therapeutic intervention.* Minneapolis: University of Minnesota Press.

Finn, S. E., & Tonsager, M. E. (1992). Therapeutic effects of providing MMPI-2 feedback to college students awaiting therapy. *Psychological Assessment, 9,* 374–385.

Finn, S. E., & Tonsager, M. E. (1992). Therapeutic effects of providing MMPI-2 test feedback to college students awaiting therapy. *Psychological Assessment, 4,* 278–287.

Finn, S. E., & Tonsager, M. E. (1997). Information-gathering and therapeutic models of assessment: Complementary paradigms. *Psychological Assessment, 9,* 374–385.

Fiorello, C. A., & Primerano, D. (2005). Research into practice: Cattell-Horn-Carroll cognitive assessment in practice: Eligibility and program development issues. *Psychology in the Schools, 42,* 525–536.

First, M., & Gibbon, M. (2004). The structured clinical interview for DSM-IV axis I disorders (SCID-I) and the structured clinical interview for DSM-IV axis II disorders (SCID-II). In M. Hilsenroth & D. Segal (Eds.), *Comprehensive handbook of psychological assessment, Vol 2: Personality Assessment* (pp. 134–143). Hoboken, NJ: John Wiley.

Fish, J. M. (Ed.). (2002). *Race and intelligence: Separating science from myth.* Mahwah, NJ: Erlbaum.

Fisher, D., Ledbetter, M., Cohen, N., Marmor, D., & Tulsky, D. (2000). WAIS-III and WMS-III profiles of mildly to severely brain-injured patients. *Applied Neuropsychology, 7,* 126–132.

Fisher, S., & Greenberg, R. P. (1984). *The scientific credibility of Freud's theories and therapy.* New York: Columbia University Press.

Fiske, D. W. (1986). The trait concept and the personality questionnaire. In A. Angleitner & J. S. Wiggins

(Eds.), *Personality assessment via questionnaires: Current issues in theory and measurement.* Berlin: Springer-Verlag.

Flanagan, J. C. (1954). The critical incident technique. *Psychological Bulletin, 51,* 327–358.

Flanagan, J. C. (1956). The evaluation of methods in applied psychology and the problem of criteria. *Occupational Psychology, 30,* 1–9.

Flanagan, R., & di Guiseppe, R. (1999). Critical review of the TEMAS: A step within the development of thematic apperception instruments. *Psychology in the Schools, 36,* 21–30.

Flavell, J. (1976). Metacognitive aspects of problem-solving. In L. Resnick (Ed.), *The nature of intelligence.* Hillsdale, NJ: Erlbaum.

Fletcher, J., & Vaughn, S. (2009). Response to intervention: Preventing and remediating academic difficulties. *Child Development Perspectives, 3,* 30–37.

Floyd, R. G., Evans, J. J., & McGrew, K. S. (2003). Relations between measures of Cattell-Horn-Carroll (CHC) cognitive abilities and mathematics achievement across the school-age years. *Psychology in the Schools, 40,* 155–171.

Flynn, J. R. (1984). The mean IQ of Americans: Massive gains 1932 to 1978. *Psychological Bulletin, 95,* 29–51.

Flynn, J. R. (1987). Massive IQ gains in 14 nations: What IQ tests really measure. *Psychological Bulletin, 101,* 171–191.

Flynn, J. R. (1994). IQ gains over time. In R. J. Sternberg (Ed.), *Encyclopedia of human intelligence.* New York: Macmillan.

Flynn, J. R. (2007a). *What is intelligence: Beyond the Flynn effect.* Cambridge: Cambridge University Press.

Flynn, J. R. (2007b). Solving the IQ puzzle. *Scientific American Mind, 18,* 25–31.

Folstein, M., Folstein, S., & McHugh, P. (1975). Mini-Mental State: A practical method for grading the cognitive state of patients for the clinician. *Journal of Psychiatric Research, 12,* 189–198.

Forbey, J., & Ben-Porath, Y. (2002). Use of the MMPI-2 in the treatment of offenders. *International Journal of Offender Therapy and Comparative Criminology, 46,* 308–318.

Forbey, J., & Ben-Porath, Y. (2007). Computerized adaptive personality testing: A review and illustration with the MMPI-2 computerized adaptive version. *Psychological Assessment, 19,* 14–24.

Forrest, D. W. (1974). *Francis Galton: The life and work of a Victorian genius.* New York: Taplinger Publishing.

Forster, A. A. (1994). Learning Disability. In R. J. Sternberg (Ed.), *Encyclopedia of human intelligence.* New York: Macmillan.

Fowler, R. D. (1985). Landmarks in computer-assisted psychological assessment. *Journal of Consulting and Clinical Psychology, 53,* 748–759.

Frank, G. (1983). *The Wechsler enterprise: An assessment of the development, structure, and use of the Wechsler tests of intelligence.* New York: Pergamon Press.

Frank, G. (1990). Research on the clinical usefulness of the Rorschach: 1. The diagnosis of schizophrenia. *Perceptual and Motor Skills, 71,* 573–578.

Frank, L. K. (1939). Projective methods for the study of personality. *Journal of Psychology, 8,* 389–413.

Frank, L. K. (1948). *Projective methods.* Springfield, IL: Thomas.

Franke, W. (1963). *The reform and abolition of the traditional Chinese examination system.* Cambridge, MA: Harvard University Press.

Frankenburg, W. K. (1985). The Denver approach to early case finding: A review of the Denver Developmental Screening Test and a brief training program in developmental diagnosis. In W. K. Frankenburg, R. M. Emde, & J. W. Sullivan (Eds.), *Identification of children at risk: An international perspective.* New York: Plenum Press.

Frankenburg, W. K., & Dodds, J. B. (1967). The Denver developmental screening tests. *Journal of Pediatrics, 71,* 181–191.

Frankenburg, W. K., Dodds, J., Archer, P., and others. (1990). *Denver II: Technical manual.* Denver, CO: Denver Developmental Materials.

Frankl, V. (1963). *Man's search for meaning: An introduction to logotherapy.* New York: Washington Square Press.

Frauenheim, J. G., & Heckerl, J. R. (1983). A longitudinal study of psychological and achievement test performance in severe dyslexic adults. *Journal of Learning Disabilities, 16,* 339–347.

Frechtling, J. A. (1989). Administrative uses of school testing programs. In R. L. Linn (Ed.), *Educational measurement* (3rd ed.). New York: American Council on Education/Macmillan.

Frederickson, L. C. (1985). Goodenough-Harris Drawing Test. In D. J. Keyser & R. C. Sweetland (Eds.). *Test critiques* (vol. 2). Kansas City, MO: Test Corporation of America.

Frederiksen, N. (1962). Factors in In-basket Performance. *Psychological Monographs, 76,* Whole No. 541.

Freud, A. (1946). *The ego and the mechanisms of defense.* New York: International Universities Press.

Freud, S. (1900). The interpretation of dreams. In J. Strachey, (Ed., in collaboration with A. Freud). *The standard edition of the complete psychological works of Sigmund Freud.* London: Hogarth, 1955, vols. 4 and 5.

Freud, S. (1927/1961). *The future of an illusion* (J. Strachey, trans.). New York: Basic Books. (Originally published 1900).

Freud, S. (1933). *New introductory lectures on psychoanalysis.* New York: Norton.

Fridlund, A. J., Ekman, P., & Oster, H. (1987). Facial expressions of emotion: Review of literature 1970–1983. In A. W. Siegman & S. Feldstein (Eds.), *Nonverbal behavior and communication* (2nd ed.). Hillsdale, NJ: Erlbaum.

Friedman, A. F. (1987). Eysenck Personality Questionnaire. In D. J. Keyser & R. C. Sweetland (Eds.), *Test critiques compendium.* Kansas City, MO: Test Corporation of America.

Friedman, M. (1996). *Type A behavior: Its diagnosis and treatment.* New York: Plenum.

Friedman, M., & Rosenman, R. (1974). *Type A behavior and your heart.* New York: Fawcett Crest.

Friedman, M., & Ulmer, D. (1984). *Treating Type A behavior and your heart.* New York: Knopf.

Fuchs, D., & Fuchs, L. (2005). Responsiveness-to-intervention: A blueprint for practitioners, policymakers, and parents. *Teaching Exceptional Children, 38,* 57–61.

Fuess, C. M. (1950). *The College Board: Its first fifty years.* New York: Columbia University Press.

Fujii, D., Tokioka, A., Lichton, A., & Hishinuma, E. (2005). Ethnic differences in prediction of violence risk with the HCR-20 among psychiatric inpatients. *Psychiatric Services, 56,* 711–716.

Fuld, P. A. (1977). *Fuld Object-Memory Evaluation.* Chicago: Stoelting Co.

Fuld, P. A., Masur, D. M., Blau, A. D., Crystal, H., & Aronson, M. K. (1990). Object-Memory Evaluation for prospective detection of dementia in normal functioning elderly: Predictive and normative data. *Journal of Clinical and Experimental Neuropsychology, 12,* 520–528.

Fuller, G. B., Parmelee, W. M., & Carroll, J. L. (1982). Performance of delinquent and nondelinquent high-school boys on the Rotter Incomplete Sentences Blank. *Journal of Personality Assessment, 46,* 506–510.

Funder, D. C. (2009). Naïve and obvious questions. *Perspectives on Psychological Science, 4,* 340–344.

Furnham, A., Moutari, J., & Crump, J. (2003). The relationship between the revised NEO-Personality Inventory and the Myers-Briggs Type Indicator. *Social Behavior and Personality, 31,* 577–584.

Furnham, A., Toop, A., Lewis, C., & Fisher, A. (1995). P-E fit and job satisfaction: A failure to support Holland's theory in three British samples. *Personality and Individual Differences, 19,* 677–690.

Galton, F. (1879). Psychometric experiments. *Brain, 2,* 149–162.

Galton, F. (1883). *Inquiries into human faculty and its development.* London: Macmillan.

Galton, F. (1888). *Natural inheritance.* London: Macmillan.

Garb, H. N. (1994). Judgment research: Implications for clinical practice and testimony in court. *Applied and Preventive Psychology, 3,* 173–183.

Garb, H. N., Florio, C., & Grove, W. (1998). The validity of the Rorschach and the MMPI: Results from meta-analyses. *Psychological Science, 9,* 402–404.

Gardner, H. (1975). *The shattered mind: The person after brain damage.* New York: Knopf.

Gardner, H. (1983). *Frames of mind: The theory of multiple intelligence.* New York: Basic Books.

Gardner, H. (1986). The waning of intelligence tests. In R. J. Sternberg & D. K. Detterman (Eds.), *What is intelligence? Contemporary viewpoints on its nature and definition.* Norwood, NJ: Ablex.

Gardner, H. (1992). Assessment in context: The alternative to standardized testing. In B. R. Gifford & M. C. O'Connor (Eds.), *Alternative views of aptitude, achievement, and instruction.* Boston: Klummer.

Gardner, H. (1993). *Multiple intelligences: The theory in practice.* New York: Basic Books.

Gardner, H. (1998). Are there additional intelligences? The case for naturalistic, spiritual, and existential intelligences. In J. Kane (Ed.), *Education, information, and transformation.* Englewood Cliffs, NJ: Prentice Hall.

Gardner, J. (1967). The adjustment of drug addicts as measured by the sentence completion test. *Journal of Projective Techniques and Personality Assessment, 31,* 28–29.

Gardner, R. A. (1981). Digits forward and digits backward as two separate tests: Normative data on 1567 school children. *Journal of Clinical Child Psychology, 10,* 131–135.

Gardner, W., Lidz, C., Mulvey, E., & Shaw, E. (1996). Clinical versus actuarial predictions of violence in patients with mental illnesses. *Journal of Consulting and Clinical Psychology, 64,* 602–609.

Gazzaniga, M. S. (1970). *The bisected brain.* New York: Appleton-Century-Crofts.

Gazzaniga, M. S., & LeDoux, J. E. (1978). *The integrated mind.* New York: Plenum Press.

Geary, D. C., & Whitworth, R. H. (1988). Is the factor structure of the WISC-R different for Anglo- and Mexican-American children? *Journal of Psychoeducational Assessment, 6,* 253–260.

GED Testing Service (1991). *Examiner's manual: Test of General Educational Development.* Washington, DC: GED Testing Service of the American Council on Education.

Geisinger, K. (2001). Wonderlic Personnel Test and Scholastic Level Exam. *The fourteenth mental measurements yearbook.* Lincoln: University of Nebraska Press.

Gelb, S. (1986). Henry H. Goddard and the immigrants, 1910–1917: The studies and their social context. *Journal of the History of the Behavioral Sciences, 22,* 324–332.

Gerard, A. B. (1993). *Manual for Parent–Child Relationship Inventory.* Los Angeles, CA: Western Psychological Services.

Geschwind, N. (1972). Language and the brain. *Scientific American, 226,* 76–83.

Geschwind, N., & Galaburda, A. M. (1987). *Cerebral lateralization: Biological mechanisms, associations, and pathology.* Cambridge, MA: MIT Press.

Getz, I. R. (1984). Moral judgment and religion: A review of the literature. *Counseling and Values, 28,* 94–116.

Ghez, C. (1991). The cerebellum. In E. R. Kandel, J. H. Schwartz, & T. M. Jessell (Eds.), *Principles of neural science* (3rd ed.). New York: Elsevier.

Ghiselli, E. E. (1966). *The validity of occupational aptitude tests.* New York: Wiley.

Ghiselli, E. E., Campbell, J. P., & Zedeck, S. (1981). *Measurement theory for the behavioral sciences.* San Francisco: W. H. Freeman.

Gibbons, R., Weiss, D., Kupfer, D., Frank, E., Fagiolini, A., and others. (2008). Using computerized adaptive testing to reduce the burden of mental health assessment. *Psychiatric Services, 59,* 361–368.

Gifford, R. (1991). *Applied psychology: Variety and opportunity.* Boston: Allyn and Bacon.

Gignac, G. (2006). A confirmatory examination of the factor structure of the Multidimensional Aptitude Battery: Contrasting oblique, higher order, and nested factor models. *Educational and Psychological Measurement, 66,* 136–145.

Gilberstadt, H., & Duker, J. (1965). *A handbook for clinical and actuarial MMPI interpretation.* Philadelphia: W. B. Saunders.

Glascoe, F. P. (1991). Developmental screening: Rationale, methods and application. *Infants and Young Children, 4,* 1–10.

Glascoe, F. P. (2005). Commonly used screening tests. Retrieved from www.dbpeds.org/articles on September 2, 2005.

Glascoe, F. P., & Byrne, K. E. (1993). The accuracy of three developmental screening tests. *Journal of Early Intervention, 17,* 368–379.

Glascoe, F. P., & Shapiro, H. (2005). Introduction to developmental and behavioral screening. Retrieved from www.dbpeds.org/articles on September 2, 2005.

Goddard, H. H. (1910a). A measuring scale for intelligence. *The Training School, 6,* 146–155.

Goddard, H. H. (1910b). Four hundred feebleminded children classified by the Binet method. *Pedagogical Seminary, 17,* 387–397.

Goddard, H. H. (1911). Two thousand normal children measured by the Binet measuring scale of intelligence. *Pedagogical Seminary, 18,* 232–259.

Goddard, H. H. (1912). *Feeble-mindedness and immigration.* Training School Bulletin, *9,* 91.

Goddard, H. H. (1917). The mental level of a group of immigrants. *Psychological Bulletin, 14,* 68–69.

Goddard, H. H. (1919). *Psychology of the normal and subnormal.* New York: Dodd, Mead, and Co.

Goddard, H. H. (1928). Feeblemindedness: A question of definition. *Journal of Psycho-Asthenics, 33,* 219–227.

Goffin, R. D., Rothstein, M., & Johnston, N. (1996). Personality testing and the assessment center: Incremental validity for managerial selection. *Journal of Applied Psychology, 81,* 746–756.

Goffin, R., Rothstein, M., & Johnston, N. (2000). Predicting job performance using personality constructs: Are personality tests created equal? In R. Goffin & E. Helmes (Eds.), *Problems and solutions in human assessment: Honoring Douglas N. Jackson at seventy.* New York: Kluwer Academic/Plenum Publishers.

Gold, J., Randolph, C., Carpenter, C., and others. (1992). The performance of patients with schizophrenia on the Wechsler Memory Scale-Revised. *Clinical Neuropsychologist, 6,* 367–373.

Goldberg, L. R. (1965). Diagnosticians vs. diagnostic signs: The diagnosis of psychosis vs. neurosis from the MMPI. *Psychological Monographs, 79* (9, Whole No. 602).

Goldberg, L. R. (1981a). Developing a taxonomy of trait-descriptive terms. In D. Fiske (Ed.), *New directions for methodology of social and behavioral science: Problems with language imprecision* (no. 9). San Francisco: Jossey-Bass.

Goldberg, L. R. (1981b). Language and individual differences: The search for universals in personality lexicons. In L. Wheeler (Ed.), *Review of personality and social psychology.* Beverly Hills, CA: Sage.

Goldberg, L. R. (1990). An alternative "description of personality": The big-five factor structure. *Journal of Personality and Social Psychology, 59,* 1216–1229.

Golden, C. (2004). The Adult Luria-Nebraska Neuropsychological Battery. In G. Goldstein, S. Beers, & M. Hersen (Eds.), *Intellectual and neuropsychological assessment* (pp. 133–146). Hoboken, NJ: Wiley.

Golden, C. J., Purish, A. D., & Hammeke, T. A. (1980). *Luria-Nebraska Neuropsychological Battery: Manual.* Los Angeles: Western Psychological Services.

Golden, C. J., Purish, A. D., & Hammeke, T. A. (1986). *Luria-Nebraska Neuropsychological Battery: Forms I and II.* Los Angeles: Western Psychological Services.

Goldfried, M. R., & Zax, M. (1965). The stimulus value of the TAT. *Journal of Projective Techniques, 29,* 46–57.

Golding, S. (1993). Interdisciplinary Fitness Interview—Revised: A training manual. State of Utah Division of Mental Health.

Goldstein, I. L. (1991). Training in work organizations. In M. D. Dunnette & L. M. Hough (Eds.), *Handbook of industrial and organizational psychology* (vol. 2). Palo Alto, CA: Consulting Psychologists Press.

Goldstein, I. L. (1992). *Training* (3rd ed.). Monterey, CA: Brooks/Cole.

Goldstein, K. (1944). The mental changes due to frontal lobe damage. *Journal of Psychology, 17,* 187–208.

Goleman, D. (1995). *Emotional intelligence: Why it can matter more than IQ.* New York: Bantam.

Goodenough, F. L. (1926). *Measurement of intelligence by drawings.* New York: Harcourt, Brace & World.

Goodenough, F. L. (1949). *Mental testing: Its history, principles, and applications.* New York: Rinehart.

Goodglass, H. (1986). The flexible battery in neuropsychological assessment. In T. Incagnoli, G. Goldstein, & C. J. Golden (Eds.), *Clinical applications of neuropsychological test batteries.* New York: Plenum Press.

Goodglass, H., Kaplan, E., & Barresi, B. (2000). *Boston Diagnostic Aphasia Examination* (3rd ed.). Austin, TX: The Psychological Corporation.

Goodman, J. (1990). Infant intelligence: Do we, can we, should we assess it? In C. C. Reynolds & R. W. Kamphaus (Eds.), *Handbook of psychological and educational assessment of children: Intelligence and achievement.* New York: Guilford.

Gordon, G., & Charanian, T. (1964). Measuring the creativity of research scientists and engineers. Working paper cited in I. A. Taylor and J. W. Getzels (Eds.), *Perspectives in creativity.* Chicago: Aldine.

Gordon, M., & Keiser, S. (1998). *Accommodations in higher education under the Americans with Disabilities Act (ADA).* DeWitt, NY: GSI Publications.

Gordon, M., & Mettelman, B. B. (1988). The assessment of attention: I. Standardization and reliability of a behavior-based measure. *Journal of Clinical Psychology, 44,* 688–690.

Gordon, R., & Peek, L. A. (1989). *The custody quotient.* Dallas, TX: Wilmington Institute.

Goslin, D. A. (1963). *The search for ability: Standardized testing in social perspective.* New York: Russell Sage Foundation.

Gothard, S., Viglione, D., Meloy, J. R., & Sherman, M. (1996). Detection of malingering in competency to stand trial evaluations. *Law and Human Behavior, 19,* 493–505.

Gottfredson, G. D., & Holland, J. L. (1975). Vocational choices of men and women: A comparison of predictors from the Self-Directed Search. *Journal of Counseling Psychology, 22,* 28–34.

Gottfredson, G. D., & Holland, J. L. (1989). *Dictionary of Holland Occupational Codes* (2nd ed.). Odessa, FL: Psychological Assessment Resources.

Gottfredson, L. S. (1986). Societal consequences of the *g* factor in employment. *Journal of Vocational Behavior, 29,* 379–410.

Gough, H. (1995). Career assessment and the California Psychological Inventory. *Journal of Career Assessment, 3,* 101–122.

Gough, H. G. (1971). The assessment of wayward impulse by means of the Personnel Reaction Blank. *Personnel Psychology, 24,* 669–677.

Gough, H. G. (1984). A managerial potential scale for the California Psychological Inventory. *Journal of Applied Psychology, 69,* 233–244.

Gough, H. G. (1987). *California Psychological Inventory manual.* Palo Alto, CA: Consulting Psychologists Press.

Gough, H. G., & Bradley, P. (1992a). Comparing two strategies for developing personality scales. In M. Zeidner & R. Most (Eds.), *Psychological testing: An inside view.* Palo Alto, CA: Consulting Psychologists Press.

Gough, H. G., & Bradley, P. (1992b). Delinquent and criminal behavior as assessed by the Revised California Psychological Inventory. *Journal of Clinical Psychology, 48,* 298–307.

Gough, H. G., & Bradley, P. (1996). *CPI manual* (3rd ed.). Mountain View, CA: Consulting Psychologists Press.

Gould, S. J. (1981). *The mismeasure of man*. New York: Norton.

Graham, J. (1961). Lavater's physiognomy in England. *Journal of the History of Ideas, 22*, 561–572.

Graham, J. R. (1987). *The MMPI: A practical guide* (2nd ed.). New York: Oxford University Press.

Graham, J. R. (1993). *MMPI-2: Assessing personality and psychopathology*. New York: Oxford.

Graham, J. R. (2000). *MMPI-2: Assessing personality and psychopathology* (3rd ed.). New York: Oxford University Press.

Granstrom, S. L. (1987). *A comparative study of loneliness, Buberian religiosity and spiritual well-being in cancer patients*. Paper presented at the conference of the National Hospice Organization.

Gray, B. (2001). A factor analytic study of the Substance Abuse Subtle Screening Inventory (SASSI). *Educational and Psychological Measurement, 61*, 102–118.

Gray, N., Fitzgerald, S., Taylor, J., MacCulloch, M., & Snowden, R. (2007). Predicting future reconviction in offenders with intellectual disabilities: The predictive efficacy of VRAG, PCL-SV, and the HCR-20. *Psychological Assessment, 19*, 474–479.

Gray, N., Hill, C., McGleish, A., and others. (2003). Prediction of violence and self-harm in mentally disordered offenders: A prospective study of the efficacy of the HCR-20, PCL-R, and psychiatric symptomatology. *Journal of Consulting and Clinical Psychology, 71*, 443–451.

Greenough, W. T., Black, J. E., & Wallace, C. S. (1987). Experience and brain development. *Child Development, 58*, 539–559.

Gregory, R. J. (1987). *Adult intellectual assessment*. Boston: Allyn and Bacon.

Gregory, R. J. (1994a). Aptitude tests. In R. J. Sternberg (Ed.), *Encyclopedia of human intelligence*. New York: Macmillan.

Gregory, R. J. (1994b). Profile interpretation. In R. J. Sternberg (Ed.), *Encyclopedia of human intelligence*. New York: Macmillan.

Gregory, R. J. (1994c). Classification of intelligence. In R. J. Sternberg (Ed.), *Encyclopedia of human intelligence*. New York: Macmillan.

Gregory, R. J. (1998). Testing in clinical psychology. In S. Cullari (Ed.), *Foundations of clinical psychology*. Boston: Allyn and Bacon.

Gregory, R. J. (1999). *Foundations of intellectual assessment: The WAIS-III and other tests in clinical practice*. Boston: Allyn and Bacon.

Gregory, R. J. (2009). Testing bias. In I. Weiner & E. Craighead (Eds.), *Corsini's encyclopedia of psychology*. New York: Wiley.

Gregory, R. J., & Gernert, C. H. (1990). Age trends for fluid and crystallized intelligence in an able subpopulation. Unpublished manuscript.

Gresham, F. M. (1993). "What's wrong in this picture?": Response to Motta et al.'s review of human figure drawings. *School Psychology Quarterly, 8*, 182–186.

Greve, K., Love, J., Sherwin, E., and others. (2002). Temporal stability of the Wisconsin Card Sorting Test in a chronic traumatic brain injury sample. *Assessment, 9*, 271–277.

Grossman, S. A., Richards, C., Anglin, D., & Hutson, H. (2000). Caring for the patient with mental retardation in the ED. *Annals of Emergency Medicine, 35*, 69–76.

Groth-Marnat, G. (1997). *Handbook of psychological assessment* (2nd ed.). New York: Wiley.

Groth-Marnat, G. (2003). *Handbook of psychological assessment* (4th ed.). New York: Wiley.

Grove, W., & Barden, C. (1999). Protecting the integrity of the legal system: The admissibility of testimony from mental health experts under *Daubert/Kumho* analyses. *Psychology, Public Policy, and Law, 5*, 224–242.

Grove, W., Barden, C., Garb, H., & Lilienfeld, S. (2002). Failure of Rorschach-Comprehensive-System-Based testimony to be admissible under the *Daubert-Joiner-Kumho* standard. *Psychology, Public Policy, and Law, 8*, 216–234.

Grove, W., Zald, D., Lebow, B., Snitz, B., & Nelson, C. (2000). Clinical versus mechanical prediction: A meta-analysis. *Psychological Assessment, 12*, 19–30.

Guaiana, G., Tyson, P., & Mortimer, A. (2004). The Rivermead Behavioural Memory Test can predict social functioning among schizophrenic patients treated with clozapine. *International Journal of Psychiatry in Clinical Practice, 8*, 245–249.

Gudjonsson, G. H. (1995). The Standard Progressive Matrices: Methodological problems associated with the administration of the 1992 adult standardisation sample. *Personality and Individual Differences, 18*, 441–442.

Guilford, J. P. (1954). *Psychometric methods*. New York: McGraw-Hill.

Guilford, J. P. (1959). *Personality*. New York: McGraw-Hill.

Guilford, J. P. (1967). *The nature of human intelligence*. New York: McGraw-Hill.

Guilford, J. P. (1985). The Structure-of-Intellect model. In B. B. Wolman (Ed.), *Handbook of intelligence:*

*Theories, measurements, and applications.* New York: Wiley.

Guilford, J. P., & Fruchter, B. (1978). *Fundamental statistics in psychology and education* (6th ed.). New York: McGraw-Hill.

Guilford, J. P., & Guilford, J. S. (1980). *Christensen-Guilford Fluency Tests.* Orange, CA: Sheridan Psychological Services.

Guilford, J. P., & Hoepfner, R. (1971). *The analysis of intelligence.* New York: McGraw-Hill.

Guion, R. (1998). *Assessment, measurement, and prediction for personnel decisions.* Mahwah, NJ: Erlbaum.

Gulliksen, H. (1950). *Theory of mental tests.* New York: Wiley.

Gutkin, R. B., & Reynolds, C. R. (1981). Factorial similarity of the WISC-R for white and black children from the standardization sample. *Journal of Educational Psychology, 73,* 227–231.

Guttman, L. (1944). A basis for scaling qualitative data. *American Sociological Review, 9,* 139–150.

Guttman, L. (1947). The Cornell technique for scale and intensity analysis. *Educational and Psychological Measurement, 7,* 247–280.

Gynther, M. D., & Gynther, R. A. (1976). Personality inventories. In I. B. Weiner (Ed.), *Clinical methods in psychology.* New York: Wiley.

Haaland, K. Y., & Delaney, H. D. (1981). Motor deficits after left or right hemisphere damage due to stroke or tumor. *Neuropsychologia, 19,* 17–27.

Haber, A., & Fichtenberg, N. (2006). Replication of the Test of Memory Malingering (TOMM) in a traumatic brain injury and head trauma sample. *The Clinical Neuropsychologist, 20,* 524–532.

Hachinski, V. C., Iliff, L., Zilha, E., and others. (1975). Cerebral blood flow in dementia. *Archives of Neurology, 32,* 632–637.

Hack, M., Taylor, G., Drotar, D., and others (2005). Poor predictive validity of the Bayley Scales of Infant Development for cognitive function of extremely low birth weight children at school age. *Pediatrics, 116,* 333–341.

Hain, J. (1964). The Bender-Gestalt Test: A scoring method for identifying brain damage. *Journal of Consulting and Clinical Psychology, 28,* 34–40.

Haladyna, T. M. (1992). Review of the Millon Clinical Multiaxial Inventory-II. *Eleventh mental measurements yearbook.* Lincoln: University of Nebraska Press.

Hale, J., Fiorello, C., Dumont, R., & others (2008). "Differential Ability Scales-Second Edition": (Neuro) Psychological predictors of math performance for typical children and children with math disorders. *Psychology in the Schools, 45,* 838–858.

Hall, H. V. (1987). *Violence prediction: Guidelines for the forensic practitioner.* Springfield, IL: Charles C. Thomas.

Hall, P., & Hall, D. (1983). The handshake as interaction. *Semiotica, 45,* 249–264.

Hambleton, R. K. (1984). Validating the test scores. In R. A. Berk (Ed.), *A guide to criterion-referenced test construction.* Baltimore: Johns Hopkins University Press.

Hambleton, R. K. (1989). Principles and selected applications of item response theory. In R. L. Linn (Ed.), *Educational measurement* (3rd ed.). New York: American Council on Education/Macmillan.

Hammill, D. D. (1999). *Detroit Tests of Learning Aptitude-4 (DTLA-4).* Austin, TX: PRO-ED.

Handler, L., & Clemence, A. (2005). The Rorschach Prognostic Rating Scale. In R. F. Bornstein & J. M. Masling (Eds.), *Scoring the Rorschach: Seven validated systems.* Mahwah, NJ: Erlbaum.

Hansen, J. (2007). Evidence of validity for the skill scale scores of the Campbell Interest and Skill Survey. *Journal of Vocational Behavior, 71,* 23–44.

Hansen, J. C. (1992). *Strong user's guide, Revised edition.* Palo Alto, CA: Consulting Psychologists Press.

Hansen, J. C., & Campbell, D. P. (1985). *Manual for the Strong Interest Inventory Form T325 of the Strong Vocational Interest Blanks, Fourth Edition.* Stanford, CA: Stanford University Press.

Hansen, J.-I., & Neuman, J. (1999). Evidence of concurrent prediction of the Campbell Interest and Skill Survey (CISS) for college major selection. *Journal of Career Assessment, 7,* 239–247.

Hanson, G. A. (1991). To catch a thief: The legal and policy implications of honesty testing in the workplace. *Law and Inequality, 9,* 497–531.

Hare, R. D. (1996). Psychopathy: A clinical construct whose time has come. *Criminal Justice and Behavior, 23,* 25–54.

Hare, R. D. (2003). *The Hare Psychopathy Checklist-Revised (PCL-R)* (2nd ed.). Toronto: Multi-Health Systems.

Hare, R. D., & McPherson, L. (1984). Violent and aggressive behavior by criminal psychopaths. *International Journal of Law and Psychiatry, 7,* 35–50.

Hare, R. D., Harpur, T., & Hakstian, R., and others. (1990). The Revised Psychopathy Checklist: Descriptive statistics, reliability, and factor structure. *Psychological Assessment: A Journal of Consulting and Clinical Psychology, 1,* 6–17.

Hare, R., & Neuman, C. (2006). The PCL-R assessment of psychopathy: Development, structural properties, and new directions. In C. Patrick (Ed.), *Handbook of psychopathy* (pp. 58–88). New York: Guilford.

Hargrave, G., & Hiatt, D. (1989). Use of the California Psychological Inventory in law enforcement officer selection. *Journal of Personality Assessment, 53,* 267–277.

Hargrave, G., Hiatt, D., Ogard, E., & Karr, C. (1994). Comparison of the MMPI and the MMPI-2 for a sample of peace officers. *Psychological Assessment, 6,* 27–32.

Harmon, L. W. (1989). Counseling. In R. L. Linn (Ed.), *Educational measurement* (3rd ed.). New York: American Council on Education/Macmillan.

Harmon, L. W., Hansen, J. C., Borgen, F., & Hammer, A. (1994). *Strong Interest Inventory applications and technical guide.* Palo Alto, CA: Consulting Psychologists Press.

Harrell, T. H., Honaker, L., & Parnell, T. (1992). Equivalence of the MMPI-2 with the MMPI in psychiatric patients. *Psychological Assessment, 4,* 460–465.

Harrington, D. M. (1975). Effect of explicit instructions to "be creative" on the psychological meaning of divergent thinking test scores. *Journal of Personality, 43,* 434–454.

Harris, D. B. (1963). *Children's drawings as measures of intellectual maturity.* New York: Harcourt, Brace & World.

Harris, G. T., & Rice, M. (1996). The science in phallometric measurement of male sexual interest. *Current Directions in Psychological Science, 5,* 156–160.

Harris, G. T., Rice, M., Quinsey, V., Chaplin, T., & Earls, C. (1992). Maximizing the discriminant validity of phallometric assessment. *Psychological Assessment, 4,* 502–511.

Harris, M. M., & Schaubroeck, J. (1988). A meta-analysis of self-supervisor, self-peer, and peer-supervisor ratings. *Personnel Psychology, 38,* 43–62.

Harrison, D. A., & Hulin, C. L. (1989). Investigations of absenteeism: Using event history models to study the absence-taking process. *Journal of Applied Psychology, 74,* 300–316.

Harrison, D. A., & Shaffer, M. (1994). Comparative examinations of self-reports and perceived absenteeism norms: Wading through Lake Wobegon. *Journal of Applied Psychology, 79,* 240–251.

Harrison, P. L., & Schock, H. H. (1994). Draw-A-Figure test. In R. J. Sternberg (Ed.), *Encyclopedia of human intelligence.* New York: Macmillan.

Hart, S., Michie, C., & Cooke, D. (2007). Precision of actuarial risk assessment instruments: Evaluating the "margins of error" of group v. individual predictors of violence. *British Journal of Psychiatry, 190,* s60–s65.

Hartung, P., Borges, N., & Jones, B. (2005). Using person matching to predict career specialty choice. *Journal of Vocational Behavior, 67,* 102–117.

Hathaway, S. R., & McKinley, J. C. (1940). A multiphasic personality schedule (Minnesota): I. Construction of the schedule. *Journal of Psychology, 10,* 249–254.

Hathaway, S. R., & McKinley, J. C. (1942). A multiphasic personality schedule (Minnesota): III. The measurement of symptomatic depression. *Journal of Psychology, 14,* 73–84.

Hathaway, S. R., & McKinley, J. C. (1943). *The Minnesota Multiphasic Personality Inventory* (rev. ed.). Minneapolis: University of Minnesota Press.

Hawkins, D. B. (1988). Interpersonal behavior traits, spiritual well-being, and their relationships to blood pressure (doctoral dissertation, Western Conservative Baptist Seminary, 1986). *Dissertation Abstracts International, 48,* 3680B.

Hawkins, D. B., & Larson, R. (1984). *The relationship between measures of health and spiritual well-being.* Unpublished manuscript, Western Conservative Baptist Seminary, Portland, OR.

Hawkins, K. A., Faraone, S. V., Pepple, J. R., Seidman, L. J., & Tsuang, M. T. (1990). WAIS-R validation of the Wonderlic Personnel Test as a brief intelligence measure in a psychiatric sample. *Psychological Assessment: A Journal of Consulting and Clinical Psychology, 2,* 198–201.

Hawkins, K., Dean, D., & Pearlson, G. (2004). Alternative forms of the Rey Auditory Verbal Learning Test: A review. *Behavioral Neurology, 15,* 99–107.

Hawthorne, J. (2009). Promoting development of the early parent-infant relationship using the Neonatal Behavioural Assessment Scale. In J. Barlow & P. Svanberg (Eds.), *Keeping the baby in mind: Infant mental health in practice.* New York: Routledge/Taylor & Francis Group.

Haynes, S. G., Feinleib, M., & Eaker, E. (1983). Type A behavior and the ten-year incidence of coronary heart disease in the Framingham heart study. In R. H. Rosenman (Ed.), *Psychosomatic risk factors and coronary heart disease.* Bern, Switzerland: Huber.

Haynes, S. N. (2001). Introduction to the special section on clinical applications of analogue behavioral observation. *Psychological Assessment, 13,* 3–4.

Hayslip, B., & Panek, P. E. (1989). *Adult development and aging.* New York: Harper & Row.

Heaton, R. K., Chelune, G., Talley, J., and others. (1993). *Wisconsin Card Sorting Test manual: Revised and expanded.* Odessa, FL: Psychological Assessment Resources.

Heaton, R. K., Smith, H. H., Jr., Lehman, R. A. W., & Vogt, A. T. (1978). Prospects for faking believable deficits on neuropsychological testing. *Journal of Consulting and Clinical Psychology, 46,* 892–900.

Hebb, D. O. (1939). Intelligence in man after large removals of cerebral tissue: Report of four left frontal lobe cases. *Journal of General Psychology, 21,* 73–87.

Heilbrun, A. B., Jr., & Georges, M. (1990). The measurement of principled morality by the Kohlberg Moral Dilemma Questionnaire. *Journal of Personality Assessment, 55,* 183–194.

Heilbrun, K. (1992). The role of psychological testing in forensic assessment. *Law and Human Behavior, 16,* 257–272.

Heinze, M., & Grisso, T. (1996). Review of instruments assessing parenting competencies used in child custody evaluations. *Behavioral Sciences and the Law, 14,* 293–313.

Heinze, M., & Purisch, A. (2001). Beneath the mask: Use of psychological tests to detect and subtype malingering in criminal defendants. *Journal of Forensic Psychology Practice, 1,* 23–52.

Helms, J. E. (1992). Why is there no study of cultural equivalence in standardized cognitive ability testing? *American Psychologist, 47,* 1083–1101.

Herman, D. O. (1988). Blind Learning Aptitude Test. In D. J. Keyser & R. C. Sweetland (Eds.), *Test critiques* (vol. 5). Kansas City, MO: Test Corporation of America.

Hernandez-Reif, M., Field, T., Diego, M., & Ruddock, M. (2006). Greater arousal and less attentiveness to face/voice stimuli by neonates of depressed mothers on the Brazelton neonatal Behavioral Assessment Scale. *Infant Behavior and Development, 29,* 594–598.

Herrnstein, R. J., & Murray, C. (1994). *The bell curve: Intelligence and class structure in American life.* New York: Free Press.

Hersen, M., & Bellack, A. S. (Eds.). (1988). *Dictionary of behavioral assessment techniques.* New York: Pergamon.

Herzberg, P., Glaesmer, H., & Hoyer, J. (2006). Separating optimism and pessimism: A robust psychometric analysis of the Revised Life Orientation Test (LOT-R). *Psychological Assessment, 18,* 433–438.

Heyman, R. (2001). Observation of couple conflicts: Clinical assessment applications, stubborn truths, and shaky foundations. *Psychological Assessment, 13,* 5–35.

Hiatt, D., & Hargrave, G. E. (1988). MMPI profiles of problem peace officers. *Journal of Personality Assessment, 52,* 722–731.

Higgs, M. (2001). Is there a relationship between the Myers-Briggs Type Indicator and emotional intelligence? *Journal of Managerial Psychology, 16,* 509–533.

Hill, B. (2005). ICAP User's Group Home Page. Retrieved from www.cpinternet.com/bhill/icap on September 13, 2005.

Hilliard, A. G. (1984). IQ testing as the emperor's new clothes: A critique of Jensen's Bias in Mental Testing. In C. R. Reynolds & R. T. Brown (Eds.), *Perspectives on bias in mental testing.* New York: Plenum Press.

Hintze, J., Volpe, R., & Shapiro, E. (2002). Best practices in the systematic direct observation of student behavior. In A. Thomas & J. Grimes (Eds.), *Best practices in school psychology IV.* Washington, DC: National Association of School Psychologists.

Hiskey, M. S. (1966). *Manual for the Hiskey-Nebraska Test of Learning Aptitude.* Lincoln, NE: Union College Press.

Hofer, S., Sliwinski, M., & Flaherty, B. (2002). Understanding ageing: Further commentary on the limitations of cross-sectional designs for ageing research. *Gerontology, 48,* 22–29.

Hoffart, A., Friis, S., Strand, J., & Olsen, B. (1994). Symptoms and cognitions during situational and hyperventilatory exposure in agoraphobic patients with and without panic. *Journal of Psychopathology and Behavioral Assessment, 16,* 15–32.

Hoffman, F. J., Sheldon, K. L., Minskoff, E. H., and others. (1987). Needs of learning disabled adults. *Journal of Learning Disabilities, 20,* 43–52.

Hogan, J., & Hogan, R. (1986). *Manual for the Hogan Personnel Selection System.* Minneapolis, MN: National Computer Systems.

Hogan, R. (2002). The Hogan Personality Inventory. In B. de Raad & M. Perugini (Eds.), *Big five assessment* (pp. 329–346). Ashland, OH: Hogrefe and Huber.

Hogan, R. T. (1986). *Manual for the Hogan Personality Inventory.* Minneapolis, MN: National Computer Systems.

Hoge, D. R. (1996). Religion in America: The demographics of belief and affiliation. In E. P. Shafranske (Ed.), *Religion and the clinical practice of psychology.* Washington, DC: American Psychological Association.

Hoge, S., Bonnie, R., Poythress, N., & Monahan, J. (1999). *The MacArthur Competence Assessment Tool—Criminal Adjudication.* Odessa, FL: Psychological Assessment Resources.

Holland, J. L. (1966). *The psychology of vocational choice.* Waltham, MA: Blaisdell.

Holland, J. L. (1978). *The occupations finder.* Palo Alto, CA: Consulting Psychologists Press.

Holland, J. L. (1985a). *Making vocational choices: A theory of vocational personalities and work environments* (2nd ed.). Englewood Cliffs, NJ: Prentice Hall.

Holland, J. L. (1985b). *Self-Directed Search: Professional manual—1985 edition.* Odessa, FL: Psychological Assessment Resources.

Holland, J. L. (1985c). *Vocational Preference Inventory (VPI) manual—1985 edition.* Odessa, FL: Psychological Assessment Resources.

Holland, J. L. (1987). *1987 manual supplement for the Self-Directed Search.* Odessa, FL: Psychological Assessment Resources.

Hollingshead, A., & Redlich, F. (1958). *Social class and mental illness.* New York: Wiley.

Hollingworth, H. L. (1943). *Leta Stetter Hollingworth.* Lincoln, NE: University of Nebraska Press.

Hollingworth, L. (1914). Variability as related to sex differences in achievement: A critique. *American Journal of Sociology, 19,* 510–530.

Hollingworth, L. (1928). Children clustering at 165 IQ and children clustering at 146 IQ compared for three years in achievement. In G. Whipple (Ed.), *The twenty-seventh yearbook of the National Society for the Study of Education: Nature and nurture, Part II—Their influence upon achievement.* Bloomington, IL: Public School Publishing.

Hollingworth, L. (1935). The comparative beauty of the faces of highly intelligent adolescents. *Journal of Genetic Psychology, 47,* 268–281.

Hollingworth, L., & Monahan, J. (1926). Tapping-rate of children who test above 135 IQ (Stanford-Binet). *Journal of Educational Psychology, 17,* 505–518.

Holmes, T., & Rahe, R. (1967). The Social Readjustment Rating Scale. *Journal of Psychosomatic Research, 11,* 213–218.

Holzinger, K. J., & Swineford, F. (1939). *A study in factor analysis: The stability of a bi-factor solution.* University of Chicago, Supplementary Educational Monographs, No. 48.

Holzinger, K., & Harman, H. (1941). *Factor analysis: A synthesis of factorial methods.* Chicago: University of Chicago Press.

Holzman, P., Levy, D., & Johnston, M. H. (2005). The use of the Rorschach technique for assessing formal thought disorder. In R. F. Bornstein & J. M. Masling (Eds.), *Scoring the Rorschach: Seven validated systems.* Mahwah, NJ: Erlbaum.

Honzik, M. (1957). Developmental studies of parent-child resemblance in intelligence. *Child Development, 28,* 215–228.

Hooper, S., Hatton, D., Baranek, G., Roberts, J., & Bailey, D. (2000). Nonverbal assessment of IQ, attention, and memory abilities in children with fragile-X syndrome using the Leiter-R. *Journal of Psychoeducational Assessment, 18,* 255–267.

Horn, J. L. (1968). Organization of abilities and the development of intelligence. *Psychological Review, 75,* 242–259.

Horn, J. L. (1985). Remodeling old models of intelligence. In B. B. Wolman (Ed.), *Handbook of intelligence: Theories, measurements, and applications.* New York: Wiley.

Horn, J. L. (1994). Theory of fluid and crystallized intelligence. In R. J. Sternberg (Ed.), *Encyclopedia of human intelligence.* New York: Macmillan.

Horn, J. L., & Cattell, R. B. (1966). Refinement and test of the theory of fluid and crystallized general intelligences. *Journal of Educational Psychology, 57,* 253–270.

Horn, J. L., & Masunaga, H. (2000). New directions for research into aging and intelligence: The development of expertise. In T. J. Perfect & E. A. Maylor (Eds.), *Models of cognitive aging* (pp. 125–159). Oxford, England: Oxford University Press.

Horton, A. (2008). The Halstead-Reitan Neuropsychological Test Battery: Past, present, and future. In A. Horton & D. Wedding (Eds.), *The neuropsychology handbook* (3rd ed.) (pp. 251–278). New York: Springer.

Hough, L. M., Eaton, N., Dunnette, M., Kamp, J., & McCloy, R. (1990). Criterion-related validities of personality constructs and the effect of response distortion on those validities [Monograph]. *Journal of Applied Psychology, 75,* 581–595.

Howell, R. J., & Richards, L. (1989). Review of the Rogers Criminal Responsibility Assessment Scales. *The tenth mental measurements yearbook.* Lincoln: University of Nebraska Press.

Huffcutt, A. (2007). Employment interviews. In D. Whetzel & G. Wheaton (Eds.), *Applied measurement: Industrial psychology in human resources management* (pp. 181–199). New York: Taylor & Francis/Erlbaum.

Huffcutt, A. I., & Roth, P. (1998). Racial group differences in employment interview evaluations. *Journal of Applied Psychology, 83,* 179–189.

Hughes, J. L., & McNamara, W. J. (1959). *Manual for the revised Programmer Aptitude Test.* New York: The Psychological Corporation.

Human Rights Watch. (2001). Beyond reason: The death penalty and offenders with mental retardation. *Human Rights Watch Publications, 13,* 1–50.

Humphreys, L. G. (1971). Theory of intelligence. In R. Cancro (Ed.), *Intelligence: genetic and environmental influences.* New York: Grune & Stratton.

Hunsberger, B. (1995). Religion and prejudice: The role of religious fundamentalism, quest, and right-wing authoritarianism. *Journal of Social Issues, 51,* 113–129.

Hunsley, J., & Bailey, J. (1999). The clinical utility of the Rorschach: Unfulfilled promises and an uncertain future. *Psychological Assessment, 11,* 266–277.

Hunter, J. E. (1989). *The Wonderlic Personnel Test as a predictor of training success and job performance.* Northfield, IL: E. F. Wonderlic Personnel Test.

Hunter, J. E. (1994). General Aptitude Test Battery. In R. J. Sternberg (Ed.), *Encyclopedia of human intelligence.* New York: Macmillan.

Hunter, J. E., & Hunter, R. F. (1984). Validity and utility of alternative predictors of job performance. *Psychological Bulletin, 96,* 72–98.

Hunter, J. E., & Schmidt, F. L. (1976). Critical analysis of the statistical and ethical implications of various definitions of test bias. *Psychological Bulletin, 83,* 1053–1071.

Hurtz, G., & Donovan, J. (2000). Personality and job performance: The Big Five revisited. *Journal of Applied Psychology, 83,* 869–879.

Hutt, M. L. (1977). *The Hutt Adaptation of the Bender-Gestalt Test.* New York: Grune & Stratton.

Hutt, M. L., & Briskin, G. J. (1960). *The clinical use of the revised Bender-Gestalt Test.* New York: Grune & Stratton.

Igbokwe, N. U. (1989). Reliability of the Jenkins Activity Survey in assessing Type A behavior pattern in middle-aged Nigerians. *Perceptual and Motor Skills, 69,* 1330.

Inwald, R. E. (1988). Five-year follow-up of departmental terminations as predicted by 16 preemployment psychological indicators. *Journal of Applied Psychology, 73,* 703–710.

IPAT. (1973). *Measuring intelligence with the Culture Fair Tests: Manual for Scales 2 and 3.* Champaign, IL: Institute for Personality and Ability Testing.

Irwin, P. M. (1992). *Elementary and Secondary Education Act of 1965: FY 1993 Guide to Programs.* Congressional Research Service. Washington, DC: Government Printing Office.

Itard, J. M. G. (1932/1801). The *wild boy of Aveyron.* Trans. by G. & M. Humphrey. New York: Appleton-Century-Crofts.

Iversen, G., Williamson, D., Ropacki, M., and Reilly, K. (2007). Frequency of abnormal scores on the Neuropsychological Assessment Battery Screening Module (S-NAB) in a mixed neurological sample. *Applied Neuropsychology, 14,* 178–182.

Jackson, A., Brooks-Gunn, J., Huang, C., & Glassman, M. (2000). Single mothers in low-wage jobs: Financial strain, parenting, and preschoolers' outcomes. *Child Development, 71,* 1409–1423.

Jackson, D. N. (1970). A sequential system for personality scale development. In C. D. Spielberger (Ed.), *Current topics in clinical and community psychology* (vol. 2). Orlando, FL: Academic Press.

Jackson, D. N. (1984a). *Manual for the Multidimensional Aptitude Battery.* Port Huron, MI: Research Psychologists Press.

Jackson, D. N. (1984b). *Personality Research Form manual.* Port Huron, MI: Research Psychologists Press.

Jackson, D. N. (1991). *Jackson Vocational Interest Survey manual* (3rd ed.). Port Huron, MI: Research Psychologists Press.

Jackson, D. N. (1998). *Manual for the Multidimensional Aptitude Battery, Second Edition.* Port Huron, MI: Research Psychologists Press.

Jackson, D. N. (2000). *Career Directions Inventory manual.* Port Huron, MI: Sigma Assessment Systems.

Jackson, D. N., & Messick, S. (1968). Creativity. In P. London & D. Rosenhan (Eds.). *Foundations of abnormal psychology.* New York: Holt.

Jackson, J., Mulick, J., & Rojahn, J. (Eds.). (2007). *Handbook of intellectual and developmental disabilities.* New York: Springer.

James, W. (1902). *The varieties of religious experience.* New York: Longman.

Jankowski, D. (2002). *A beginner's guide to the MCMI-III.* Washington, DC: American Psychological Association.

Jenkins, C. D., Zyzanski, S., & Rosenman, R. (1971). Progress toward validation of a computer-scored test for the Type A coronary-prone behavior pattern. *Psychosomatic Medicine, 33,* 193–201.

Jenkins, C. D., Zyzanski, S., & Rosenman, R. (1979). *Jenkins Activity Survey: Manual.* New York: The Psychological Corporation.

Jenkins, J. J., & Paterson, D. G. (Eds.). (1961). *Studies in individual differences*. New York: Appleton-Century-Crofts.

Jennett, B., & Teasdale, G. (1981). *Management of head injuries*. Philadelphia: F. A. Davis.

Jennett, B., Teasdale, G. M., & Knill-Jones, R. P. (1975). Predicting outcome after head injury. *Journal of Royal College of Physicians of London, 9*, 231–237.

Jensen, A. (1998). *The g factor: The science of mental ability*. Westport, CT: Praeger.

Jensen, A. R. (1969). How much can we boost IQ and scholastic achievement? *Harvard Educational Review, 39*, 1–123.

Jensen, A. R. (1977). Cumulative deficit in IQ of blacks in the rural south. *Developmental Psychology, 13*, 184–191.

Jensen, A. R. (1979). *g*: outmoded theory or unconquered frontier? *Creative Science and Technology, 2*, 16–29.

Jensen, A. R. (1980). *Bias in mental testing*. New York: Free Press.

Jensen, A. R. (1981). Raising the IQ: The Ramey and Haskins Study. *Intelligence, 5*, 29–40.

Jensen, A. R. (1984). Test bias: Concepts and criticisms. In C. R. Reynolds & R. T. Brown (Eds.), *Perspectives on bias in mental testing*. New York: Plenum Press.

Jensen, A. R. (1998). *The g factor: The science of mental ability*. Westport, CT: Praeger.

Jensen, A. R., & Osborne, R. T. (1979). *Forward and backward digit span interaction with race and IQ: A longitudinal developmental comparison*. Berkeley: University of California. (ERIC Document Reproduction Service No. ED 173 384).

Johnson, J. H., & Williams, T. A. (1975). The use of on-line computer technology in a mental health admitting system. *American Psychologist, 30*, 388–390.

Johnson, R. C., McClearn, G. E., Yuen, S., Nagoshi, C. T., Ahern, F. M., & Cole, R. E. (1985). Galton's data a century later. *American Psychologist, 40*, 875–892.

Johnson, S. T. (1994). Scholastic Assessment Tests. In R. J. Sternberg (Ed.), *Encyclopedia of human intelligence*. New York: Macmillan.

Johnson, W. G., & Mullett, N. (1987). Georgia Court Competency Test-Revised. In M. Hersen & A. S. Bellack (Eds.), *Dictionary of behavioral assessment techniques*. Elmsford, NY: Pergamon.

Johnston, D. W. (1986). Behavior therapy. In R. Harre & R. Lamb (Eds.), *The dictionary of physiological and clinical psychology*. Cambridge, MA: MIT Press.

Johnston, W. T., & Bolen, R. M. (1984). A comparison of the factor structures of the WISC-R for Blacks and Whites. *Psychology in the Schools, 21*, 42–44.

Joint Committee on Testing Practices. (1988). *Code of fair testing practices in education*. Washington, DC: Author.

Jones, K. L., Smith, D. W., Ulleland, C. N., & Streissguth, A. P. (1973). Patterns of malformation in offspring of chronic alcoholic mothers. *Lancet, 1*, 1267–1271.

Joseph, R. (1988). The right cerebral hemisphere: Emotion, music, visual-spatial skills, body-image, dreams, and awareness. *Journal of Clinical Psychology, 44*, 630–763.

Julian, E. (2005). Validity of the Medical College Admission Test for predicting medical school performance. *Academic Medicine, 80*, 910–917.

Jung, C. G. (1910). The association method. *American Journal of Psychology, 21*, 219–269.

Kaiser, H. F., & Michael, W. B. (1975). Domain validity and generalizability. *Educational and Psychological Measurement, 35*, 31–35.

Kamphaus, R. W. (1993). *Clinical assessment of children's intelligence*. Boston: Allyn and Bacon.

Kanaya, T., Scullin, M., & Ceci, S. (2003). The Flynn effect and U.S. Policies: The impact of rising IQ scores on American society via mental retardation diagnoses. *American Psychologist, 58*, 778–790.

Kandel, E. R. (1991). Perception of motion, depth, and form. In E. R. Kandel, J. H. Schwartz, & T. M. Jessell (Eds.), *Principles of neural science* (3rd ed.). New York: Elsevier.

Kandel, E. R., Schwartz, J. H., & Jessell, T. M. (1995). *Essentials of neural science and behavior*. Norwalk, CT: Appleton & Lange.

Kane, R. L. (1991). Standardized and flexible batteries in neuropsychology: An assessment update. *Neuropsychology Review, 2*, 281–339.

Kaufman, A. S. (1983). Test review: WAIS-R. *Journal of Psychoeducational Assessment, 1*, 309–319.

Kaufman, A. S. (1990). *Assessing adolescent and adult intelligence*. Boston: Allyn and Bacon.

Kaufman, A. S., & Kaufman, N. L. (1983). *K-ABC administration and scoring manual*. Circle Pines, MN: American Guidance Service.

Kaufman, A. S., & Kaufman, N. L. (2004). *Kaufman Brief Intelligence Test* (2nd ed.). Circle Pines, MN: American Guidance Service.

Kaufman, A. S., & Kaufman, N. L. (2004a). *Kaufman Assessment Battery for Children* (2nd ed.). Circle Pines, MN: American Guidance System Publishing.

Kaufman, A. S., & Kaufman, N. L. (2004b). *Kaufman Test of Educational Achievement* (2nd ed.). Circle Pines, MN: American Guidance System Publishing.

Kaufman, A. S., & Lichtenberger, E. O. (2002). *Assessing adolescent and adult intelligence* (2nd ed.). Boston, MA: Allyn & Bacon.

Kaufman, A. S., McLean, J. E., & Reynolds, C. R. (1988). Sex, race, residence, region, and education differences on the 11 WAIS-R subtests. *Journal of Clinical Psychology, 44,* 231–248.

Kausler, D. (1991). *Experimental psychology, cognition, and human aging* (2nd ed.). New York: Springer-Verlag.

Kazdin, A. E. (1990). Evaluation of the Automatic Thoughts Questionnaire: Negative cognitive processes and depression among children. *Psychological Assessment: A Journal of Consulting and Clinical Psychology, 2,* 73–79.

Keith, T. Z. (1999). Effects of general and specific abilities on student achievement: Similarities and differences across ethnic groups. *School Psychology Quarterly, 14,* 239–262.

Kelley, T. L. (1928). *Crossroads in the mind of man: A study of differentiable mental abilities.* Stanford, CA: Stanford University Press.

Kelly, E. L., & Fiske, D. W. (1951). *The prediction of performance in clinical psychology.* Ann Arbor: University of Michigan Press.

Kendall, P. C., & Hollon, S. D. (1989). Anxious self-talk: Development of the Anxious Self-Statements Questionnaire (ASSQ). *Cognitive Therapy and Research, 13,* 81–93.

Kennedy, W. A., Van de Riet, V., & White, J. C., Jr. (1963). A normative sample of intelligence and achievement of negro elementary school children in the southeast United States. *Monographs of the Society for Research in Child Development, 28* [No. 90], 68.

Kent, G. H., & Rosanoff, A. J. (1910). A study of association in insanity. *American Journal of Insanity, 67,* 37–96; 317–390.

Kerr, B., & Gagliardi, C. (2003). Measuring creativity in research and practice. In S. Lopez & C. R. Snyder (Eds.), *Positive psychological assessment: A handbook of models and measures.* Washington, DC: American Psychological Association.

Kertesz, A. (1982). *Aphasia and associated disorders: Taxonomy, localization, and recovery.* New York: Grune & Stratton.

Kertesz, A. (2006). *Western Aphasia Battery-Revised.* San Antonio, TX: Harcourt.

Kesztyues, T., Mehlitz, M., Schilken, E., and others. (2000). Preclinical evaluation of a virtual reality neuropsychological test system: Occurrence of side effects. *Cyberpsychology and Behavior, 3,* 343–349.

Keyser, D. J., & Sweetland, R. C. (Eds.). (1984–1994). *Test Critiques* (volumes I–X). Kansas City, MO: Test Corporation of America.

Kiecolt-Glaser, J. K. (2009). Psychoneuroimmunology: Psychology's gateway to the biomedical future. *Perspectives on Psychological Science, 4,* 367–369.

Kiernan, R., Mueller, J., & Langston, J. W. (2009). *Cognistat manual.* Fairfax, CA: Cognistat, Inc.

Kifer, E. (1985). Review of ACT Assessment Program. *Ninth mental measurements yearbook.* Lincoln: University of Nebraska Press.

Killian, G. A. (1987). House-Tree-Person technique. In D. J. Keyser & R. C. Sweetland (Eds.), *Test critiques compendium.* Kansas City, MO: Test Corporation of America.

Kim, K. H. (2006). Can we trust creativity tests? A review of the Torrance Tests of Creative Thinking (TTCT). *Creativity Research Journal, 18,* 3–14.

King, K. (2001). A critique of behavioral observational coding systems of couples' interaction: CISS and RCISS. *Journal of Social and Clinical Psychology, 20,* 1–23.

Kinnear, P. R., & Gray, C. D. (1997). *SPSS for Windows made simple* (2nd ed.). Trowbridge, UK: Psychology Press.

Kinsbourne, M. (1994). Neuropsychology of attention. In D. W. Zaidel (Ed.), *Neuropsychology.* San Diego, CA: Academic Press.

Kirkpatrick, L., & Hood, R. (1990). Intrinsic-Extrinsic Religious Orientation: The boon or bane of contemporary psychology of religion? *Journal for the Scientific Study of Religion, 29,* 442–462.

Kleiman, L., & Faley, R. (1985). The implications of professional and legal guidelines for court decisions involving criterion-related validity: A review and analysis. *Personnel Psychology, 38,* 303–833.

Klieger, D. M., & Franklin, M. E. (1993). Validity of the fear survey schedule in phobia research: A laboratory test. *Journal of Psychopathology and Behavioral Assessment, 15,* 207–218.

Klimoski, R., & Palmer, S. (1994). The ADA and the hiring process in organizations. In S. M. Bruyere & J. O'Keeffe (Eds.), *Implications of the Americans with Disabilities Act for psychology.* New York: Springer.

Kline, P. (1986). *A handbook of test construction.* New York: Methuen.

Kline, P. (1993). *The handbook of psychological testing.* London: Routledge.

Kline, P. (1999). *The handbook of psychological testing* (2nd ed.). London: Routledge.

Klingler, D. E., Miller, D., Johnson, J., & Williams, T. (1977). Process evaluation of an on-line computer-assisted unit for intake assessment of mental health patients. *Behavior Research Methods and Instrumentation, 9,* 110–116.

Klove, H. (1963). Clinical neuropsychology. In F. M. Forster (Ed.), *The medical clinics of North America.* New York: Saunders.

Koch, W. R. (1984). Culture Fair Intelligence Test. In D. J. Keyser & R. C. Sweetland (Eds.), *Test Critiques* (vol. I). Kansas City, MO: Test Corporation of America.

Kohlberg, L. (1958). *The development of modes of moral thinking and choice in the years ten to sixteen.* Unpublished doctoral dissertation, University of Chicago.

Kohlberg, L. (1981). *Essays on moral development: Vol. 1. The philosophy of moral development.* San Francisco: Harper & Row.

Kohlberg, L. (1984). *Essays on moral development: Vol. 2. The psychology of moral development.* San Francisco: Harper & Row.

Kohlberg, L., & Elfenbein, D. (1975). The development of moral judgments concerning capital punishment. *American Journal of Orthopsychiatry, 45,* 614–639.

Kohlberg, L., & Kramer, R. (1969). Continuities and discontinuities in children and adult moral development. *Human Development, 12,* 225–252.

Kolb, B., & Milner, B. (1981). Performance of complex arm and facial movements after focal brain lesions. *Neuropsychologia, 19,* 491–503.

Kolb, B., & Whishaw, I. Q. (2002). *Fundamentals of human neuropsychology* (5th ed.). New York: Worth/Freeman.

Kolb, B., Milner, B., & Taylor, L. (1983). Perception of faces by patients with localized cortical excisions. *Canadian Journal of Psychology, 37,* 8–18.

Koppitz, E. (1963). *The Bender Gestalt Test for young children.* New York: Grune and Stratton.

Koppitz, E. (1975). *The Bender Gestalt Test for young children, Volume II: Research and application, 1963–1975.* New York: Grune and Stratton.

Koss, E. (1994). Neuropsychology of aging and dementia. In D. W. Zaidel (Ed.), *Neuropsychology* (2nd ed.). San Diego, CA: Academic Press.

Koss, E., Patterson, M., Mack, J., Smyth, K., & Whitehouse, P. (1998). Reliability and validity of the Tinkertoy Test in evaluating individuals with Alzheimer's disease. *Clinical Neuropsychologist, 12,* 325–329.

Kostrubala, C., & Braden, J. (1998). *The American Sign Language translation of the WAIS-III.* San Antonio, TX: The Psychological Corporation.

Kraus, J. F., & MacArthur, D. L. (1996). Epidemiologic aspects of brain injury. *Neurologic Clinics, 14*(2): 435–450.

Krikorian, R., & Bartok, J. (1998). Developmental data for the Porteus Maze Test. *Clinical Neuropsychologist, 12,* 305–310.

Krokoff, L. J., Gottman, J., & Hass, S. (1989). Validation of a global rapid couples interaction scoring system. *Behavioral Assessment, 11,* 65–79.

Kroner, C., Stadtland, C., Eidt, M., & Nedopil, N. (2007). The validity of the Violence Risk Appraisal Guide (VRAG) in predicting criminal recidivism. *Criminal Behaviour and Mental Health, 17,* 89–100.

Krugman, M. (1970). H-T-P: House, Tree, and Person. In O. K. Buros (Ed.), *Personality tests and reviews.* Highland Park, NJ: Gryphon Press.

Krumboltz, J. (1999). *Career Beliefs Inventory: Applications and technical guide.* Palo Alto, CA: Consulting Psychologists Press.

Kuder, G. F. (1934). *Kuder preference record.* Chicago: Science Research Associates.

Kuder, G. F., & Richardson, M. W. (1937). The theory of estimation of test reliability. *Psychometrika, 2,* 151–160.

Kuncel, N., Campbell, J., & Ones, D. (1998). Validity of the Graduate Record Examination: Estimated or tacitly known? *American Psychologist, 53,* 567–568.

Kuncel, N., Hezlett, S., & Ones, D. (2001). A comprehensive meta-analysis of the predictive validity of the Graduate Record Examinations: Implications for graduate student selection and performance. *Psychological Bulletin, 127,* 162–181.

Kupfermann, I. (1991a). Hypothalamus and limbic system: Peptidergic neurons, homeostasis, and emotional behavior. In E. R. Kandel, J. H. Schwartz, & T. M. Jessell (Eds.), *Principles of neural science* (3rd ed.). New York: Elsevier.

Kupfermann, I. (1991b). Localization of higher cognitive and affective functions: The association cortices. In E. R. Kandel, J. H. Schwartz, & T. M. Jessel (Eds.), *Principles of neural science* (3rd ed.). New York: Elsevier.

Kurtines, W., & Greif, E. B. (1974). The development of moral thought: Review and evaluation of Kohlberg's approach. *Psychological Bulletin, 81,* 453–470.

Kwate, N. (2001). Intelligence or misorientation? Eurocentrism in the WISC-III. *Journal of Black Psychology, 27,* 221–238.

La Rue, A. (1992). *Aging and neuropsychological assessment.* New York: Plenum.

Laatsch, L., & Choca, J. (1994). Cluster-branching methodology for adaptive testing and the development of the Adaptive Category Test. *Psychological Assessment, 6,* 345–351.

LaBarbera, D. (2005). Physician assistant Self-Directed Search Holland Codes. *Journal of Career Assessment, 13,* 337–346.

Laboratory for Community Psychiatry (1974). *Competency to stand trial and mental illness.* Northvale, NJ: Jason Aronson.

Lachar, D. (1974). *The MMPI: Clinical assessment and automated interpretation.* Los Angeles: Western Psychological Services.

Lachar, D. (1987). Automated assessment of child and adolescent personality. In J. N. Butcher (Ed.), *Computerized psychological assessment: A practitioner's guide.* New York: Basic Books.

Lachar, D., & Gdowski, C. L. (1979). *Actuarial assessment of child and adolescent personality: An interpretive guide for the Personality Inventory for Children profile.* Los Angeles: Western Psychological Services.

Lachar, D., & Gruber, C. (2001). *Manual: Personality Inventory for Children-2.* Los Angeles: Western Psychological Services.

Lacks, P. (1999). *Bender-Gestalt screening for brain dysfunction* (2nd ed.). New York: Wiley.

Lah, M. I. (1989). New validity, normative, and scoring data for the Rotter Incomplete Sentences Blank. *Journal of Personality Assessment, 53,* 607–620.

Lah, M. I., & Rotter, J. B. (1981). Changing college student norms on the Rotter Incomplete Sentences Blank. *Journal of Consulting and Clinical Psychology, 49,* 985.

Lamp, R., & Krohn, E. (2001). A longitudinal predictive validity investigation of the SB:FE and K-ABC with at-risk children. *Journal of Psychoeducational Assessment, 19,* 334–349.

Landy, F. (1996). *The psychology of work behavior* (5th ed.) Monterey, CA: Brooks/Cole.

Landy, F. J., & Farr, J. L. (1983). *The measurement of work performance: Methods, theory and applications.* New York: Academic Press.

Landy, F. J., Shankster, L. J., & Kohler, S. S. (1994). Personnel selection and placement. *Annual Review of Psychology, 45,* 261–296.

Lane, S. (1992). Review of the Iowa Tests of Basic Skills. *Eleventh mental measurements yearbook.* Lincoln: University of Nebraska Press.

Lansdell, H., & Donnelly, E. F. (1977). Factor analysis of the Wechsler Adult Intelligence Scale Subtests and the Halstead-Reitan Category and Tapping Tests. *Journal of Consulting and Clinical Psychology, 45,* 412–416.

Larson, G. E. (1994). Armed Services Vocational Aptitude Battery. In R. J. Sternberg (Ed.), *Encyclopedia of human intelligence.* New York: Macmillan.

Larson, G. E., & Wolfe, J. (1995). Validity results for *g* from an expanded test base. *Intelligence, 20,* 15–25.

Lassiter, K., & Bardos, A. (1995). The relationship between young children's academic achievement and measures of intelligence. *Psychology in the Schools, 32,* 170–177.

Latham, G. P., & Skarlicki, D. (1995). Criterion-related validity of the situational and patterned behavior description interviews with organizational citizenship behavior. *Human Performance, 8,* 67–80.

Laux, J., Salyers, K., & Kotova, E. (2005). A psychometric evaluation of the SASSI-3 in a college sample. *Journal of College Counseling, 8,* 41–51.

LaVoie, A. L. (1987). The Blacky Pictures. In D. J. Keyser & R. C. Sweetland (Eds.), *Test critiques compendium.* Kansas City, MO: Test Corporation of America.

Ledbetter, M., Smith, L., Vosler-Hunter, W., & Fischer, J. (1991). An evaluation of the research and clinical usefulness of the Spiritual Well-Being Scale. *Journal of Psychology and Theology, 19,* 49–55.

Lee, M. S., Wallbrown, F., & Blaha, J. (1990). Note on the construct validity of the Multidimensional Aptitude Battery. *Psychological Reports, 67,* 1219–1222.

Lefebvre, M. F. (1981). Cognitive distortion and cognitive errors in depressed psychiatric and low back pain patients. *Journal of Consulting and Clinical Psychology, 49,* 517–525.

Lehman, R. E. (1978). Symptom contamination of the Schedule of Recent Events. *Journal of Consulting and Clinical Psychology, 46,* 1564–1565.

Leiter, R. G. (1948). *Leiter International Performance Scale.* Chicago: Stoelting Co.

Leiter, R. G. (1979). *Leiter International Performance Scale: Instruction manual.* Chicago: Stoelting Co.

Leli, D. A., & Filskov, S. B. (1984). Clinical detection of intellectual deterioration associated with brain damage. *Journal of Clinical Psychology, 40,* 1435–1441.

Lester, B. M. (1984). Data analysis and prediction. In T. B. Brazelton (Ed.), *Neonatal Behavioral Scale* (2nd Ed.). London: Spastics International Medical Publications.

Levin, H., Song, J., Ewing-Cobbs, L., & Roberson, G. (2001). Porteus Maze performance following traumatic brain injury in children. *Neuropsychology, 15,* 557–567.

Levinson, E. M. (1990). Vocational assessment involvement and use of the Self-Directed Search by school psychologists. *Psychology in the Schools, 27,* 217–228.

Lewinsohn, P. M. (1965). Psychological correlates of overall quality of figure drawings. *Journal of Consulting Psychology, 29,* 504–512.

Lewinsohn, P. M., Munoz, R. F., Youngren, M. A., & Zeiss, A. M. (1986). *Control your depression: Reducing depression through learning self-control techniques, relaxation training, pleasant activities, social skills, constructed thinking, planning ahead, and more* (rev. ed.). New York: Prentice Hall.

Lewinsohn, P., & Talkington, J. (1979). Studies on the measurement of unpleasant events and relations with depression. *Applied Psychological Measurement, 3,* 83–101.

Lewis, M., & Brooks-Gunn, J. (1981). Visual attention at three months as a predictor of cognitive functioning at two years of age. *Intelligence, 5,* 131–140.

Lewis, M., & Sullivan, M. W. (1985). Infant intelligence and its assessment. In B. B. Wolman (Ed.), *Handbook of intelligence: Theories, measurements, and applications.* New York: Wiley.

Lezak, M. (1982). The problem of assessing executive functions. *International Journal of Psychology, 17,* 281–297.

Lezak, M. (1983). *Neuropsychological assessment* (2nd ed.). New York: Oxford University Press.

Lezak, M. (1995). *Neuropsychological assessment* (3rd ed.). New York: Oxford University Press.

Lezak, M. D., & O'Brien, K. P. (1990). Chronic emotional, social, and physical changes after traumatic brain injury. In E. D. Bigler (Ed.), *Traumatic brain injury: Mechanisms of damage, assessment, intervention, and outcome.* Austin, TX: PRO-ED.

Lezak, M., Howieson, D., & Loring, D. (2004). *Neuropsychological assessment* (4th ed.). New York: Oxford University Press.

Lichtenberg, P., Manning, Vangel, S., & Ross. T. (1995). Normative and ecological validity data in older urban medical patients: A program of neuropsychological research. *Advances in Medical Psychotherapy, 8,* 121–136.

Lichtenberger, E., & Kaufman, A. (2009). *Essentials of WAIS-IV assessment.* New York: Wiley.

Likert, R. (1932). A technique for the measurement of attitudes. *Archives of Psychology,* No. 140.

Lilienfeld, S. O., Ammirati, R., & Landfield, K. (2009). Giving debiasing away: Can psychological research on correcting cognitive errors promote human welfare? *Perspectives on Psychological Science, 4,* 390–398.

Lilienfeld, S., Wood, J., & Garb, H. (2000). The scientific status of projective techniques. *Psychological Science in the Public Interest, 2,* 27–66.

Lilienfeld, S., Wood, J., & Garb, H. (2001, May). What's wrong with this picture? *Scientific American,* 81–87.

Lindal, E., & Stefansson, J. (1993). Mini-Mental State Examination scores: Gender and lifetime psychiatric disorders. *Psychological Reports, 72,* 631–641.

Lindenberger, U., & Baltes, P. (1994). Aging and intelligence. In R. J. Sternberg (Ed.), *Encyclopedia of human intelligence.* New York: Macmillan.

Lindvall, C. M. (1967). *Measuring pupil achievement and aptitude.* New York: Harcourt, Brace & World.

Lindzey, G. (1959). On the classification of projective techniques. *Psychological Bulletin, 56,* 158–168.

Linn, R. L. (1989). Review of the Iowa Tests of Basic Skills. *Tenth Mental Measurements Yearbook.* Lincoln: University of Nebraska Press.

Lipsitt, P. D. (1970). *Competency Screening Test.* Boston: Competency to Stand Trial and Mental Illness Project.

Lipsitz, J. D., Dworkin, R., & Erlenmeyer-Kimling, L. (1993). Wechsler Comprehension and Picture Arrangement subtests and social adjustment. *Psychological Assessment, 5,* 430–437.

Lishman, W. A. (1997). *Organic psychiatry: The psychological consequences of cerebral disorder* (3rd ed.). Oxford: Blackwell Scientific Publications.

Liskow, B., Campbell, J., Nickel, E., & Powell, B. (1995). Validity of the CAGE questionnaire in screening for alcohol dependence in a walk-in (triage) clinic. *Journal of Studies on Alcohol, 56,* 277–281.

Loeber, R., Pardini, D., & Homish, D. L. (2005). The prediction of violence and homicide in young men. *Journal of Consulting and Clinical Psychology, 73,* 1074–1088.

Lohman, D., & Hagen, E. (2001). *Cognitive Abilities Test, Form 6; Examiner's manual.* Boston: Houghton Mifflin.

Lopez, S. J., & Snyder, C. R. (Eds.). (2003). *Positive psychological assessment: A handbook of models and measures.* Washington, DC: American Psychological Association.

Lopez, S., & Snyder, C. R. (Eds.). (2003). *Positive psychological assessment: A handbook of models and measures.* Washington, DC: American Psychological Association.

Lord, F. M., & Novick, M. R. (1968). *Statistical theories of mental test scores.* Menlo Park, CA: Addison-Wesley.

Lord, F., & Novick, M. (1968). *Statistical theories of mental tests.* New York: Addison-Wesley.

Lubinski, D., Benbow, C., & Ryan, J. (1995). Stability of vocational interests among the intellectually gifted from adolescence to adulthood: A 15-year longitudinal study. *Journal of Applied Psychology, 80,* 196–200.

Lukasik, C. (2004). The physiognomy of biometrics. Retrieved from www.common-place.org, *5,* 1–4.

Lukin, M. E., Dowd, E. T., Plake, B., & Kraft, R. (1985). Comparing computerized vs. traditional psychological assessment. *Computers in Human Behavior, 1,* 49–58.

Lunz, M., & Bergstrom, B. (1994). Computer adaptive testing: A national pilot study. In M. Wilson (Ed.), *Objective measurement: Theory into practice* (vol. 2). Norwood, NJ: Ablex.

Lunz, M., Bergstrom, B., & Wright, B. (1994). Reliability of alternate computer-adaptive tests. In M. Wilson (Ed.), *Objective measurement: Theory into practice* (vol. 2). Norwood, NJ: Ablex.

Luria, A. R. (1966). *Higher cortical functions in man.* New York: Basic Books.

Luria, A. R. (1973). *The working brain.* New York: Basic Books.

Lynn, R. (1987). Japan: Land of the rising IQ. A reply to Flynn. *Bulletin of the British Psychological Society, 40,* 464–468.

Lynn, R. (2009). What has caused the Flynn effect? Secular increases in the Development Quotients of infants. *Intelligence, 37,* 16–24.

Lyon, G. R. (1996b). Special education for students with disabilities. *The Future of Children, 6,* 1–19.

Lyon, G. R., (1996a). Learning disabilities. *Special Education for Students With Disabilities, 6,* 1–18.

MacAndrew, C. (1965). The differentiation of male alcoholic out-patients from nonalcoholic psychiatric patients by means of the MMPI. *Quarterly Journal of Studies on Alcohol, 26,* 238–246.

Machover, K. (1949). *Personality projection in the drawing of the human figure.* Springfield, IL: Charles C. Thomas.

Machover, K. (1951). Drawing of the human figure: A method of personality investigation. In H. Anderson & G. Anderson (Eds.), *An introduction to projective techniques.* New York: Prentice Hall.

Mack, J., & Patterson, M. (1995). Executive dysfunction and Alzheimer's disease: Performance on a test of planning ability, the Porteus Maze Test. *Neuropsychology, 9,* 556–564.

MacPhillamy, D. J., & Lewinsohn, P. M. (1982). The Pleasant Events Schedule: Studies on reliability, validity, and scale intercorrelation. *Journal of Consulting and Clinical Psychology, 50,* 363–380.

Maddi, S. R. (2000). *Personality theories: A comparative analysis* (6th ed.). Prospective Heights, IL: Waveland Press.

Mahoney, M., & Arnkoff, D. (1978). Cognitive and self-control therapies. In S. Garfield & A. Bergin (Eds.), *Handbook of psychotherapy and behavior change: An empirical analysis.* New York: Wiley.

Majnemer, A., & Mazer, B. (1998). Neurologic evaluation of the newborn infant: Definition and psychometric properties. *Developmental Medicine and Child Neurology, 40,* 708–715.

Malgady, R. G., Constantino, G., & Rogler, L. H. (1984). Development of a Thematic Apperception Test (TEMAS) for urban Hispanic children. *Journal of Consulting and Clinical Psychology, 52,* 986–996.

Maloney, M. P., & Ward, M. P. (1979). *Mental retardation and modern society.* New York: Oxford University Press.

Man, D., Chung, J., & Mak, M. (2009). Development and validation of the Online Rivermead Behavioral Memory Test (OL-RBMT) for people with stroke. *Neurorehabilitation, 24,* 231–236.

Manning, W. H., & Jackson, R. (1984). College entrance examinations: Objective selection or gatekeeping for the economically privileged. In C. R. Reynolds & R. T. Brown (Eds.), *Perspectives on bias in mental testing.* New York: Plenum Press.

Mardell-Czudnowski, C., & Goldenberg, D. S. (1998). *DIAL-III: Developmental Indicators for the Assessment of Learning-Third Edition.* Circle Pines, MN: American Guidance Service.

Marks, P. A., & Seeman, W. (1963). *The actuarial description of abnormal personality.* Baltimore: Williams & Wilkins.

Markwardt, F. C. (1989). *Manual for the Peabody Individual Achievement Test-Revised.* Circle Pines, MN: American Guidance Service.

Martell, D. A. (1992). Forensic neuropsychology and the criminal law. *Law and Human Behavior, 16,* 313–336.

Martin, J. C. (1994). Birth defects. In R. J. Sternberg (Ed.), *Encyclopedia of human intelligence.* New York: Macmillan.

Martin, R. (2003). Sense of Humor. In S. Lopez & C. R. Snyder (Eds.), *Positive psychological assessment: A handbook of models and measures.* Washington, DC: American Psychological Association.

Martin, R. A. (1996). The Situational Humor Response Questionnaire (SHRQ) and Coping Humor Scale (CHS): A decade of research findings. *Humor: International Journal of Humor Research, 9,* 251–272.

Martin, R. A., & Lefcourt, H. M. (1983). Sense of humor as a moderator of the relation between stressors and moods. *Journal of Social and Personality Psychology, 45,* 1313–1324.

Martin, R. A., & Lefcourt, H. M. (1984). Situational Humor Response Questionnaire: Quantitative measure of sense of humor. *Journal of Social and Personality Psychology, 47,* 145–155.

Martin, R. A., Puhlik-Doris, P., Larsen, G., Gray, J., & Weir, K. (2003). Individual differences in uses of humor and their relation to psychological well-being: Development of the Humor Styles Questionnaire. *Journal of Research in Personality, 37,* 48–75.

Martindale, C. (1981). *Cognition and consciousness.* Homewood, IL: Dorsey.

Martuza, V. R. (1977). *Applying norm-referenced and criterion-referenced measurement in education.* Boston: Allyn and Bacon.

Matarazzo, J. D. (1972). *Wechsler's measurement and appraisal of adult intelligence* (5th ed.). Baltimore: Williams & Wilkins.

Matarazzo, J. D. (1990). Psychological assessment versus psychological testing: Validation from Binet to the school, clinic, and courtroom. *American Psychologist, 45,* 999–1017.

Matarazzo, J. D. (1992). Psychological testing and assessment in the 21st century. *American Psychologist, 47,* 1007–1018.

Matson, J. (Ed.). (2007). *Handbook of assessment in persons with intellectual disability.* London: Academic Press.

Matthews, G., Zeidner, M., & Roberts, R. (2002). *Emotional intelligence: Science and myth.* Cambridge, MA: MIT Press.

Mattis, S. (2001). *Dementia Rating Scale-2.* Lutz, FL: Psychological Assessment Resources.

Maxwell, J. K., & Wise, F. (1984). PPVT IQ validity in adults: A measure of vocabulary, not of intelligence. *Journal of Clinical Psychology, 40,* 1048–1053.

Mayer, J., & Salovey, P. (1993). The intelligence of emotional intelligence. *Intelligence, 17,* 433–442.

Mayer, J., Salovey, P., & Caruso, D. (2002). *Mayer-Salovey-Caruso Emotional Intelligence Test (MSCEIT) user's manual.* Toronto, ON: Multi-Health Systems.

Mayer, J., Salovey, P., & Caruso, D. (2004). Emotional intelligence: Theory, findings, and implications. *Psychological Inquiry, 15,* 197–215.

Mayer, J., Salovey, P., & Caruso, D. (2008). Emotional intelligence: New ability or eclectic traits? *American Psychologist, 63,* 503–517.

Mayer, J., Salovey, P., Caruso, D., & Sitarenios, G. (2003). Measuring emotional intelligence with the MSCEIT V2.0. *Emotion, 3,* 97–105.

Mayeux, R., & Kandel, E. R. (1991). Disorders of language: The aphasias. In E. R. Kandel, J. H. Schwartz, & T. M. Jessel (Eds.), *Principles of neural science* (3rd ed.). New York: Elsevier.

McAllister, L. W. (1986). *A practical guide to CPI interpretation.* Palo Alto, CA: Consulting Psychologists Press.

McCall, R. B. (1976). Toward an epigenetic conception of mental development in the first three years of life. In M. Lewis (Ed.), *Origins of intelligence: Infancy and early childhood.* New York: Plenum Press.

McCall, R. B. (1979). The development of intellectual functioning in infancy and the prediction of later IQ. In J. D. Osofsky (Ed.), *Handbook of infant development.* New York: Wiley.

McCall, W. A. (1939). *Measurement.* New York: Macmillan.

McCallum, R. S. (1990). Determining the factor structure of the Stanford-Binet: Fourth Edition—the right choice. *Journal of Psychoeducational Assessment, 8,* 436–442.

McCoy, B. (2000). *Quack! Tales of medical fraud from the museum of questionable medical devices.* Santa Monica, CA: Santa Monica Press.

McCrae, R. R. (1985). Review of the Defining Issues Test. *Ninth mental measurements yearbook.* Lincoln: University of Nebraska Press.

McCrae, R. R., & Costa, P. T., Jr. (1987). Validation of the five-factor model of personality across instruments and observers. *Journal of Personality and Social Psychology, 2,* 81–90.

McCrae, R., Costa, P., & Martin, T. (2005). The NEO-PI-3: A more readable revised NEO Personality Inventory. *Journal of Personality Assessment, 84,* 261–270.

McCullough, M. E., Emmons, R. A., & Tsang, J. (2002). The Grateful disposition: A conceptual and empirical topography. *Journal of Personality and Social Psychology, 82,* 112–127.

McDonald, A., Nussbaum, D., & Bagby, R. (1992). Reliability, validity, and utility of the Fitness Interview Test. *Canadian Journal of Psychiatry, 36,* 480–484.

McDonald, R. P. (1999). *Test theory: A unified approach.* Mahwah, NJ: Erlbaum.

McGee, R., Clark, S., & Symons, D. (2000). Does the Conners' continuous performance test aid in ADHD diagnosis? *Journal of Abnormal Child Psychology, 28,* 415–424.

McGlynn, F. D., & Rose, M. P. (1998). Assessment of anxiety and fear. In A. S. Bellack & M. Hersen (Eds.), *Behavioral assessment: A practical handbook* (4th ed.). Boston: Allyn and Bacon.

McGrath, E., Wypij, D., Rappaport, L., Newburger, J., & Bellinger, C. (2004). Prediction of IQ and achievement at age 8 from neurodevelopmental status at age 1 in children with D-transposition of the great arteries. *Pediatrics, 114,* 572–576.

McGrath, R., Pogge, D., Stokes, J., & others (2005). Field reliability of Comprehensive System scoring in an adolescent inpatient sample. *Assessment, 12,* 199–209.

McGrew, K. S. (1997). Analysis of the major intelligence batteries according to a proposed comprehensive Gf-Gc framework. In D. P. Flanagan, J. L. Genshaft, & P. L. Harrison (Eds.), *Contemporary intellectual assessment: Theories, tests, and issues* (pp. 151–179). New York: Guilford.

McGrew, K. S., & Flanagan, D. P. (1998). *The intelligence test desk reference (ITDR): Gf-Gc cross-battery assessment.* Boston: Allyn & Bacon.

McGue, M., Bouchard, T., Iacono, W., & Lykken, D. (1993). Behavior genetics of cognitive ability: A lifespan perspective. In R. Plomin & G. McClearn (Eds.), *Nature, nurture, and psychology.* Washington, DC: American Psychological Association.

McGurk, F. C. J. (1953a). On white and Negro test performance and socio-economic factors. *Journal of Abnormal and Social Psychology, 48,* 448–450.

McGurk, F. C. J. (1953b). Socioeconomic status and culturally-weighted test scores of Negro subjects. *Journal of Applied Psychology, 37,* 276–277.

McGurk, F. C. J. (1975). Race differences—twenty years later. *Homo, 26,* 219–239.

McKey, R. H., & others (1985). *The impact of Head Start on children, families and communities.* Washington, DC: U.S. Government Printing Office.

McKinley, J. C., & Hathaway, S. R. (1940). A Multiphasic Personality Schedule (Minnesota): II. A differential study of hypochondriasis. *Journal of Psychology, 10,* 255–268.

McKinley, J. C., & Hathaway, S. R. (1944). The MMPI: V. Hysteria, hypomania and psychopathic deviate. *Journal of Applied Psychology, 28,* 153–174.

McKinley, J. C., Hathaway, S. R., & Meehl, P. E. (1948). The MMPI: VI. The K scale. *Journal of Consulting Psychology, 12,* 20–31.

McMillan, D., Hastings, R., & Coldwell, J. (2004). Clinical and actuarial prediction of physical violence in a forensic intellectual disability hospital: A longitudinal study. *Journal of Applied Research in Intellectual Disabilities, 17,* 255–265.

McNulty, J., Graham, J., Ben-Porath, Y., & Stein, L. (1997). Comparative validity of MMPI-2 scores of African American and caucasian mental health center clients. *Psychological Assessment, 9,* 464–470.

McReynolds, P., & Ludwig, K. (1984). Christian Thomasius and the origin of psychological rating scales. *Isis, 75,* 546–553.

McReynolds, P., & Ludwig, K. (1987). On the history of rating scales. *Personality and Individual Differences, 8,* 281–283.

Mednick, S. (1962). The associative basis of the creative process. *Psychological Review, 3,* 220–232.

Mednick, S., & Mednick, M. (1966). *Manual: Remote Associates Test.* Boston: Houghton Mifflin.

Medoff-Cooper, B., & Ratcliffe, S. (2005). Development of preterm infants: Feeding behaviors and Brazelton Neonatal Behavioral Assessment Scale at 40 and 44 weeks' postconceptual age. *Advances in Nursing Science, 28,* 356–363.

Meehl, P. E. (1954). *Clinical versus statistical prediction.* Minneapolis: University of Minnesota Press.

Meehl, P. E. (1965). Seer over sign: The first good example. *Journal of Experimental Research in Personality, 1,* 29–32.

Meehl, P. E. (1986). Causes and effects of my disturbing little book. *Journal of Personality Assessment, 50,* 370–375.

Megargee, E. (1972). *The California Psychological Inventory handbook.* San Francisco: Jossey-Bass.

Meichenbaum, D. (1977). *Cognitive-behavior modification: An integrative approach.* New York: Plenum Press.

Meier, S. T. (1984). The construct validity of burnout. *Journal of Occupational Psychology, 57,* 211–219.

Meier, V. J., & Hope, D. A. (1998). Assessment of social skills. In A. S. Bellack & M. Hersen (Eds.), *Behavioral assessment: A practical handbook* (4th ed.). Boston: Allyn and Bacon.

Meijer, E., Verschuere, B., Merckelbach, H., & Crombez, G. (2008). Sex offender management using the polygraph: A critical review. *International Journal of Law and Psychiatry, 31*, 423–429.

Meisels, S., & Atkins-Burnett, S. (2005). *Developmental screening in early childhood: A guide* (5th ed.). Washington, DC: National Association for the Education of Young Children.

Meisels, S., Marsden, D., Wiske, M., & Henderson, L. (1997). *Early Screening Inventory-Revised.* San Antonio, TX: The Psychological Corporation.

Meisels, S., Wiske, M., & Henderson, L. (2008). *Early Screening Inventory—Revised.* San Antonio, TX: The Psychological Corporation.

Melton, G. B. (1995). Review of the Ackerman-Schoendorf Scales for Parent Evaluation of Custody. *The Twelfth mental measurements yearbook.* Lincoln: University of Nebraska Press.

Melton, G. B., Petrila, J., Poythress, N., & Slobogin, C. (1998). *Psychological evaluation for the courts* (2nd ed.). New York: Guilford.

Menzies, G. (2003). *1421: The year China discovered America.* New York: William Morrow.

Menzies, R. J., Webster, C., McMain, S., Staley, S., & Scaglione, R. (1994). The dimensions of dangerousness revisited: Assessing forensic predictions about violence. *Law and Human Behavior, 18*, 1–28.

Mercer, J. R., & Lewis, J. F. (1978). *System of Multicultural Pluralistic Assessment.* San Antonio, TX: The Psychological Corporation.

Merenda, P. F. (1985). Comrey Personality Scales. In D. J. Keyser & R. C. Sweetland (Eds.), *Test critiques* (vol. 4). Kansas City, MO: Test Corporation of America.

Messiah, A., Encrenaz, G., Sapinho, D., and others. (2007). Paradoxical increase of positive answers to the Cut-down, Annoyed, Guilt, Eye-opener (CAGE) questionnaire during a period of decreasing alcohol consumption: Results from two population-based surveys in Ile-de-France, 1991 and 2005. *Addiction, 103*, 598–603.

Messick, S. (1980). Test validity and the ethics of assessment. *American Psychologist, 35*, 1012–1027.

Messick, S. (1995). Validity of psychological assessment: Validation of inferences from persons' responses and performances as scientific inquiry into score meaning. *American Psychologist, 50*, 741–749.

Mevarech, Z. (1995). Metacognition, general ability, and mathematical understanding. *Early Education and Development, 6*, 155–168.

Meyer, G. J. (1997). Assessing reliability: Critical corrections for a critical examination of the Rorschach Comprehensive System. *Psychological Assessment, 9*, 480–489.

Meyer, G. J., & Handler, L. (1997). The ability of the Rorschach to predict subsequent outcome: A meta-analysis of the Rorschach Prognostic Rating Scale. *Journal of Personality Assessment, 69*, 1–38.

Mickley, J. (1990). *Spiritual well-being, religiousness, and hope: Some relationships in a sample of women with breast cancer.* Unpublished master's thesis, University of Maryland, School of Nursing, College Park, MD.

Middleton, H., Keene, R., & Brown, G. (1990). Convergent and discriminant validities of the Scales of Independent Behavior and the revised Vineland Adaptive Behavior Scales. *American Journal of Mental Retardation, 94*, 669–673.

Miele, F. (1979). Cultural bias in the WISC. *Intelligence, 3*, 149–164.

Milkman, K. L., Chugh, D., & Bazerman, M. H. (2009). How can decision making be improved? *Perspectives on Psychological Science, 4*, 379–383.

Miller, F. G., & Lazowski, L. (1999). *The adult SASSI-3 manual.* Springville, IN: The SASSI Institute.

Miller, F. G., Roberts, J., Brooks, M., & Lazowski, L. (1997). *SASSI-3 user's guide: A quick reference for administration and scoring.* Bloomington, IN: Baugh Enterprises.

Miller, L. K. (1989). *Musical savants: Exceptional skill in the mentally retarded.* Hillsdale, NJ: Erlbaum.

Miller, T. R. (1991). Personality: A clinician's experience. *Journal of Personality Assessment, 57*, 415–433.

Millman, J., & Greene, J. (1989). The specification and development of tests of achievement and ability. In R. L. Linn (Ed.), *Educational measurement* (3rd ed.). New York: ACE/Macmillan.

Millon, T. (1969). *Modern psychopathology: A biosocial approach to maladaptive learning and functioning.* Philadelphia: Saunders.

Millon, T. (1981). *Disorders of personality: DSM-III, Axis II.* New York: Wiley.

Millon, T. (1983). *Millon Clinical Multiaxial Inventory manual* (2nd ed.). Minneapolis, MN: National Computer Systems.

Millon, T. (1986). A theoretical derivation of pathological personalities. In T. Millon & G. Klerman (Eds.), *Contemporary directions in psychopathology: Toward the DSM-IV.* New York: Guilford.

Millon, T. (1987). *Manual for the Millon Clinical Multiaxial Inventory-II (MCMI-II)* (2nd ed.). Minneapolis, MN: National Computer Systems.

Millon, T. (1994). *Manual for the Millon Clinical Multiaxial Inventory-III (MCMI-III)* (3rd ed.). Minneapolis, MN: National Computer Systems.

Millon, T., & Davis, R. (1996). The Millon Clinical Multiaxial Inventory-III (MCMI-III). In C. S. Newmark (Ed.), *Major psychological assessment instruments* (2nd ed.). Boston: Allyn and Bacon.

Mills, C., & Tissot, S. (1995). Identifying academic potential in students from underrepresented populations: Is using the Raven's Progressive Matrices a good idea? *Gifted Child Quarterly, 39,* 209–217.

Mills, C., Potenza, M., Fremer, J., & Ward, W. (2002). *Computer-based testing: Building the foundation for future assessments.* Mahwah, NJ: Erlbaum.

Mills, C., & Tissot, S. (1995). Identifying academic potential in students from underrepresented populations: Is using the Raven's Progressive Matrices a good idea? *Gifted Child Quarterly, 39,* 209–217.

Milner, B. (1968). Disorders of memory after brain lesions in man. *Neuropsychologia, 6,* 175–179.

Mischel, W. (1968). *Personality and assessment.* New York: Wiley.

Mischel, W., Shoda, Y., & Mendoza-Denton, R. (2002). Situation-behavior profiles as a locus of consistency in personality. *Current Directions in Psychological Science, 11,* 50–54.

Mitchell, T. W., & Klimoski, R. J. (1986). Estimating the validity of cross-validity estimation. *Journal of Applied Psychology, 71,* 311–317.

Mittenberg, W., Azrin, R., Millsaps, C., & Heilbronner, R. (1993). Identification of malingered head injury on the Wechsler Memory Scale-Revised. *Psychological Assessment, 5,* 34–40.

Moberg, D. O. (1971). *Spiritual well-being: Background and issues.* Washington, DC: White House Conference on Aging.

Montague, M., & Bos, C. S. (1990). Cognitive and metacognitive characteristics of eighth grade students' mathematical problem solving. *Learning and Individual Differences, 2,* 371–388.

Moore, E. G. J. (1986). Family socialization and the IQ-test performance of traditionally and transracially adopted children. *Developmental Psychology, 22,* 317–326.

Moore, W. P. (1994). The devaluation of standardized testing: One district's response. *Applied Measurement in Education, 7,* 343–368.

Moreland, K. L. (1992). Computer-assisted psychological assessment. In M. Zeidner & R. Most (Eds.), *Psychological testing: An inside view.* Palo Alto, CA: Consulting Psychologists Press.

Moreno, K. E., & Segall, D. O. (1997). Reliability and construct validity of the CAT-ASVAB In W. A. Sands, B. K. Waters, & J. R. McBride (Eds.), *Computerized adaptive testing: From inquiry to operation.* Washington, DC: American Psychological Association.

Morgan, C. D., & Murray, H. A. (1935). A method for investigating phantasies: The Thematic Apperception Test. *Archives of Neurology and Psychiatry, 34,* 289–306.

Morgan, C. D., Shoenberg, M., Dorr, D., & Burke, M. (2002). Overreport on the MCMI-III: Concurrent validation with the MMPI-2 using a psychiatric inpatient sample. *Journal of Personality Assessment, 78,* 288–300.

Mori, L., & Armendariz, G. (2001). Analogue assessment of child behavior problems. *Psychological Assessment, 13,* 36–45.

Morrison, M. W., Gregory, R. J., & Paul, J. J. (1979). Reliability of the Finger Tapping Test and a note on sex differences. *Perceptual and Motor Skills, 48,* 139–142.

Morrison, T., & Morrison, M. (1995). A meta-analytic assessment of the predictive validity of the quantitative and verbal components of the Graduate Record Examination with graduate grade point average representing the criterion of graduate success. *Educational and Psychological Measurement, 55,* 309–316.

Morrow, C., Bandstra, E., Anthony, J., and others. (2001). Influence of prenatal cocaine exposure on full-term infant neurobehavioral functioning. *Neurotoxicology and Teratology, 23,* 533–544.

Moruzzi, G., & Magoun, H. W. (1949). Brain stem and reticular formation and activation of the EEG. *Electroencephalography and Clinical Neurophysiology, 1,* 455–473.

Motowidlo, S. J., Carter, G., Dunnette, M., Tippins, N., Werner, S., Burnett, J., & Vaughan, M. (1992). Studies of the structured behavioral interview. *Journal of Applied Psychology, 77,* 571–587.

Motta, R. W., Little, S., & Tobin, M. (1993). The use and abuse of human figure drawings. *School Psychology Quarterly, 8,* 162–169.

Mount, M., Witt, L., & Barrick, M. (2000). Incremental validity of empirically keyed biodata scales over GMA and the five factor personality constructs. *Personnel Psychology, 53,* 299–323.

Mountain, M., & Snow, W. (1993). Wisconsin Card Sorting Test as a measure of frontal pathology: A review. *Clinical Neuropsychologist, 7,* 108–118.

Muchinsky, P. (2003). *Psychology applied to work: An introduction to industrial and organizational psychology* (7th ed.). Belmont, CA: Wadsworth.

Murphy, K. R. (1984). Review of Armed Services Vocational Aptitude Battery. In D. Keyser & R. Sweetland (Eds.), *Test critiques* (vol. 1). Kansas City, MO: Test Corporation of America.

Murphy, K. R. (1992). Review of TONI-2. *The eleventh mental measurements yearbook.* Lincoln: University of Nebraska Press.

Murphy, K. R., & Davidshofer, C. O. (1988). *Psychological testing.* Englewood Cliffs, NJ: Prentice Hall.

Murphy, K. R., & Davidshofer, C. O. (2004). *Psychological testing* (6th ed.). Englewood Cliffs, NJ: Prentice Hall.

Murphy, K. R., & Pardaffy, V. A. (1989). Bias in behaviorally anchored rating scales: Global or scale-specific? *Journal of Applied Psychology, 74,* 343–346.

Murphy, K. R., Jako, R., & Anhalt, R. (1993). Nature and consequences of halo error: A critical analysis. *Journal of Applied Psychology, 78,* 218–225.

Murray, H. A. (1938). *Explorations in personality.* New York: Oxford University Press.

Murray, H. A. (1943). *Thematic Apperception Test—Manual.* Cambridge, MA: Harvard University Press.

Museum of Modern Art. (1955). *The family of man.* New York: Maco Magazine Corporation.

Myers, D. (2002). *Social psychology* (7th ed.). New York: McGraw-Hill.

Myers, I. B., & McCaulley, M. H. (1985). *Manual: A guide to the development and use of the Myers-Briggs Type Indicator.* Palo Alto, CA: Consulting Psychologists Press.

Myers, I., & McCaulley, M. (1985). *A guide to the development and use of the Myers-Briggs Type Indicator.* Palo Alto, CA: Consulting Psychologists Press.

Naglieri, J. A. (1981). Concurrent validity of the Revised Peabody Picture Vocabulary Test. *Psychology in the Schools, 18,* 286–289.

Naglieri, J. A. (1988). *Draw A Person: A quantitative scoring system.* San Antonio, TX: The Psychological Corporation.

Naglieri, J. A., & Pfeiffer, S. (1983). Stability, concurrent and predictive validity of the PPVT-R. *Journal of Clinical Psychology, 39,* 965–967.

Naglieri, J. A., & Pfeiffer, S. (1992). Performance of disruptive behavior disordered and normal samples on the Draw A Person: Screening Procedure for Emotional Disturbance. *Psychological Assessment, 4,* 156–159.

Naglieri, J. A., & Yazzie, C. (1983). Comparison of the WISC-R and PPVT-R with Navajo children. *Journal of Clinical Psychology, 39,* 598–600.

Naglieri, J., McNeish, T., & Bardos, A. (1991). *Draw-A-Person: Screening Procedure for Emotional Disturbance.* Austin, TX: ProEd.

Nass, R. (1992). Developmental dyslexia: An update. *Pediatrics in Review, 13,* 231–235.

National Association of School Psychologists. (1992). *Principles for professional ethics.* Silver Spring, MD: Author.

National Joint Committee on Learning Disabilities. (1988). A position paper of the National Trust Committee on Learning Disabilities. *Journal of Learning Disabilities, 21,* 53–55.

Naugle, R. I., Chelune, G., & Tucker, G. (1993). Validity of the Kaufman Brief Intelligence Test. *Psychological Assessment, 5,* 182–186.

Nauta, W. J. H. (1971). The problem of the frontal lobe. *Journal of Psychiatric Research, 8,* 167–187.

Naveh-Benjamin, M., McKeachie, W. J., & Lin, Y. (1987). Two types of test-anxious students: Support for an information processing model. *Journal of Educational Psychology, 79,* 131–136.

Needleman, H. L., Gunnoe, C., Leviton, A., Reed, R., Peresie, H., Maher, C., & Barrett, P. (1979). Deficits in psychologic and classroom performance of children with elevated dentine lead levels. *The New England Journal of Medicine, 300,* 689–695.

Needleman, H. L., Schell, A., Bellinger, D., Leviton, A., & Allred, E. (1990). The long-term effects of exposure to low doses of lead in childhood. *New England Journal of Medicine, 322,* 83–88.

Neisser, U. (Ed.). (1998). *The rising curve: Long-term gains in IQ and related measures.* Washington, DC: American Psychological Association.

Neisser, U., Boodoo, G., & Bouchard, T., and others. (1996). Intelligence: Knowns and unknowns. *American Psychologist, 51,* 77–101.

Nester, M. A. (1994). Psychometric testing and reasonable accommodation for persons with disabilities. In S. M. Bruyere & J. O'Keeffe (Eds.), *Implications of the Americans with Disabilities Act for psychology.* New York: Springer.

Nettelbeck, T., & Wilson, C. (2004). The Flynn effect: Smarter, not faster. *Intelligence, 32,* 85–93.

Netter, B., & Viglione, D., Jr. (1994). An empirical study of malingering schizophrenia on the Rorschach. *Journal of Personality Assessment, 62,* 45–57.

Nevo, B. (1985). Face validity revisited. *Journal of Educational Measurement, 22,* 287–293.

Nevo, B. (1992). Examinee feedback: Practical guidelines. In M. Zeidner & R. Most (Eds.), *Psychological testing: An inside view.* Palo Alto, CA: Consulting Psychologists Press.

Newborg, J. (2005). *Battelle Developmental Inventory—Second Edition.* Itasca, IL: Riverside.

Newland, T. E. (1971). *Blind Learning Aptitude Test.* Champaign: University of Illinois Press.

Newsome, S., Day, A., & Catano, V. (2000). Assessing the predictive validity of emotional intelligence. *Personality and Individual Differences, 29,* 1005–1016.

Nihira, K., Leland, H., & Lambert, N. (1993). *Adaptive Behavior Scale-Residential and Community* (2nd ed.). Washington, DC: American Association on Mental Retardation.

Nijenhuis, J., & van der Flier, H. (1997). Comparability of GATB scores for immigrants and majority group members: Some Dutch findings. *Journal of Applied Psychology, 82,* 675–687.

Nijenhuis, J., Evers, A., & Mur, J. (2000). Validity of the Differential Aptitude Test for the assessment of immigrant children. *Educational Psychology, 20,* 99–115.

Nisan, M., & Kohlberg, L. (1982). Universality and cross-cultural variation in moral development: A longitudinal and cross-sectional study in Turkey. *Child Development, 53,* 865–876.

Norris, G., & Tate, R. (2000). The Behavioural Assessment of the Dysexecutive Syndrome (BADS): Ecological, concurrent and construct validity. *Neuropsychological Rehabilitation, 10,* 33–45.

Nottingham, E. J., & Mattson, R. E. (1981). A validation study of the Competency Screening Test. *Law and Human Behavior, 5,* 329–335.

Nunnally, J. (1967). *Psychometric theory.* New York: McGraw-Hill.

Nunnally, J. C. (1978). *Psychometric theory* (2nd ed.). New York: McGraw-Hill.

Nunnally, J. C., & Bernstein, I. H. (1994). *Psychometric theory* (3rd ed.). New York: McGraw-Hill.

O'Neill, J., Jacobson, S., & Jacobson, J. (1994). Evidence of observer reliability for the Fagan Test of Infant Intelligence (FTII). *Infant Behavior and Development, 17,* 465–469.

Oakes, L. M. (2009). The "Humpty Dumpty Problem" in the study of early cognitive development: Putting the infant back together again. *Perspectives on Psychological Science, 4,* 352–358.

Ochse, R. (1990). *Before the gates of excellence.* Cambridge, England: Cambridge University Press.

Offer, D., & Sabshin, M. (1966). *Normality: Theoretical and clinical concepts of mental health.* New York: Basic Books.

Ogloff, J. R., Wong, S., & Greenwood, A. (1990). Treating criminal psychopaths in a therapeutic community program. *Behavioral Science and the Law, 8,* 181–190.

Oles, H. J., & Davis, G. D. (1977). Publishers violate APA standards on test distribution. *Psychological Reports, 41,* 713–714.

Ollendick, T. H. (1983). Reliability and validity of the Revised Fear Survey Schedule for Children (FSSC-R). *Behavior Research and Therapy, 21,* 685–692.

Olson, H. C. (1994). Fetal alcohol syndrome. In R. J. Sternberg (Ed.), *Encyclopedia of human intelligence.* New York: Macmillan.

Olson-Buchanan, J., Drasgow, F., Moberg, P., Mead, A., Keenan, P., & Donovan, M. (1998). Interactive video assessment of conflict resolution skills. *Personnel Psychology, 51,* 1–24.

Ones, D. S., Viswesvaran, C., & Schmidt, F. (1993). Comprehensive meta-analysis of integrity test validities: Findings and implications for personnel selection and theories of job performance. *Journal of Applied Psychology, 78,* 679–703.

Ornberg, B., & Zalewski, C. (1994). Assessment of adolescents with the Rorschach: A critical review. *Assessment, 1,* 209–217.

Ortner, T. (2008). Effects of changed item order: A cautionary note to practitioners on jumping to computerized adaptive testing for personality assessment. *International Journal of Selection and Assessment, 16,* 249–257.

OSS Assessment Staff. (1948). *Assessment of men: Selection of personnel for the Office of Strategic Services.* New York: Rinehart.

Otis, A. S. (1918). An absolute point scale for the group measure of intelligence. *Journal of Educational Psychology, 9,* 238–261, 333–348.

Owens, W. A. (1976). Background data. In M. D. Dunnette (Ed.), *Handbook of industrial and organizational psychology.* Chicago: Rand McNally.

Ownby, R. L. (1991). *Psychological reports: A guide to report writing in professional psychology* (2nd ed.). Brandon, VT: Clinical Psychology Publishing Co.

Paloutzian, R. F., & Ellison, C. W. (1982). Loneliness, spiritual well-being and the quality of life. In L. A. Peplau & D. Perlman (Eds.), *Loneliness: A sourcebook of current theory, research and therapy.* New York: Wiley.

Panigua, F. (1994). *Assessing and treating culturally diverse clients: A practical guide.* Thousand Oaks, CA: Sage.

Park, N., & Peterson, C. (2009). Achieving and sustaining a good life. *Perspectives on Psychological Science, 4,* 422–428.

Patterson, C. (1980). An alternative perspective—lead pollution in the human environment. In *Lead in the human environment.* Washington, DC: National Academy of Sciences.

Patton, J. R., Payne, J. S., & Beirne-Smith, M. (1986). *Mental retardation* (2nd ed.). Columbus, OH: Merrill.

Paulhus, D., Fridhandler, B., & Hayes, S. (1997). Psychological defense: Contemporary theory and research. In R. Hogan, J. Johnson, & S. Briggs (Eds.), *Handbook of personality psychology.* San Diego: Academic Press.

Paulman, R. G., & Kennelly, K. J. (1984). Test anxiety and ineffective test taking: Different names, same construct? *Journal of Educational Psychology, 76,* 279–288.

Payne, A. F. (1928). *Sentence completions.* New York: New York Guidance Clinic.

Pearson, K. (1914, 1924, 1930ab). *The life, letters, and labours of Francis Galton* (Volumes I, II, III, IIIb). Cambridge: Cambridge University Press.

Pedersen, N. L., Plomin, R., Nesselroade, J., & McClearn, G. (1992). A quantitative genetic analysis of cognitive abilities during the second half of the life span. *Psychological Science, 3,* 346–353.

Penfield, W. (1958). Functional localization in temporal and deep sylvian areas. *Research Publication, Association of Nervous and Mental Disease, 36,* 210–217.

Penfield, W., & Evans, J. (1935). The frontal lobe in man: A clinical study of maximum removals. *Brain, 58,* 115–133.

Penfield, W., & Jasper, H. (1959). *Epilepsy and the functional anatomy of the human brain.* Boston: Little, Brown.

Pervin, L. A. (1993). *Personality: Theory and research* (6th ed.). New York: Wiley.

Petersen, N. S., Kolen, M. J., & Hoover, H. D. (1989). Scaling, norming, and equating. In R. L. Linn (Ed.), *Educational measurement* (3rd ed.). New York: American Council on Education/Macmillan.

Peterson, C. (2000). Optimistic explanatory style and health. In J. Gillham (Ed.), *The science and optimism of hope* (pp. 145–162). Philadelphia, PN: Templeton Foundation Press.

Pfeiffer, E. (1975). A short portable mental status questionnaire for the assessment of organic brain deficit in elderly patients. *Journal of the American Geriatrics Society, 23,* 433–441.

Phelps, L., & Ensor, A. (1986). Concurrent validity of the WISC-R using deaf norms and the Hiskey-Nebraska. *Psychology in the Schools, 23,* 138–141.

Phillips, S. E. (1994). High-stakes testing accommodations: Validity versus disabled rights. *Applied Measurement in Education, 7,* 93–120.

Piaget, J. (1932). *The moral judgment of the child.* London: Kegan Paul.

Piaget, J. (1972). *The psychology of intelligence.* Totowa, NJ: Littlefield Adams.

Piedmont, R. L., & Weinstein, H. P. (1993). A psychometric evaluation of the new NEO-PIR Facet Scales for Agreeableness and Conscientiousness. *Journal of Personality Assessment, 60,* 302–318.

Piersma, H., & Boes, J. (1997). MCMI-III as a treatment outcome measure for psychiatric inpatients. *Journal of Clinical Psychology, 53,* 825–832.

Piirto, J. (1998). *Understanding those who create.* Scottsdale, AZ: Gifted Psychology Press.

Pinals, D., Tillbrook, C., & Mumley, D. (2006). Practical application of the MacArthur Competence Assessment Tool—Criminal Adjudication (MacCAT-CA) in a public sector forensic setting. *Journal of the American Academy of Psychiatry and Law, 34,* 179–188.

Pintner, R. (1917). The mentality of the dependent child. *Journal of Educational Psychology, 8,* 220–238.

Pintner, R. (1921). Intelligence. In E. L. Thorndike (Ed.), Intelligence and its measurement: A symposium. *Journal of Educational Psychology, 12,* 123–147, 195–216.

Piotrowski, C. (1996). The status of Exner's Comprehensive System in contemporary research. *Perceptual and Motor Skills, 82,* 1341–1342.

Piotrowski, Z. A. (1964). A digital computer administration of inkblot test data. *Psychiatric Quarterly, 38,* 1–26.

Pirozzolo, F. J., Hansch, E., Mortimer, J., Webster, D., & Kuskowski, A. (1982). Dementia in Parkinson disease: A neuropsychological analysis. *Brain and Cognition, 1,* 71–83.

Pittenger, D. J. (2005). Cautionary comments regarding the Myers-Briggs Type Indicator. *Consulting Psychology Journal: Practice and Research, 57,* 210–221.

Plaisted, J. R., & Golden, C. J. (1982). Test-retest reliability of the clinical, factor and localization scales of the Luria-Nebraska Neuropsychological Battery. *International Journal of Neuroscience, 17,* 163–167.

Plaud, J. J., & Eifert, G. (Eds.). (1998). *From behavior theory to behavior therapy.* Boston: Allyn and Bacon.

Pollack, R. H. (1971). Binet on perceptual-cognitive development or Piaget-come-lately. *Journal of the History of the Behavioral Sciences, 7,* 370–374.

Pollens, R., McBratnie, B., & Burton, P. (1988). Beyond cognition: Executive functions. *Cognitive Rehabilitation, 6,* 26–33.

Pope, K. S. (1992). Responsibilities in providing psychological test feedback to clients. *Psychological Assessment, 4,* 268–271.

Popham, W. J. (1978). *Criterion-referenced measurement.* Englewood Cliffs, NJ: Prentice Hall.

Porch, B. (2001). *Porch Index of Communicative Ability—2001 Revision.* Austin, TX: Pro-Ed.

Porteus, S. D. (1931). *The psychology of a primitive people: A study of the Australian aborigine.* London: Edward Arnold & Co.

Porteus, S. D. (1965). *Porteus Maze Test. Fifty years' application.* Palo Alto, CA: Pacific Books.

Powers, D. (2004). Validity of Graduate Record Examinations (GRE) General Test scores for admissions to colleges of Veterinary Medicine. *Journal of Applied Psychology, 89,* 208–219.

Powers, K., & Hagans-Murillo, K. (2004). Twenty-five years after Larry P.: The California response to overrepresentation of African-Americans in special education. *California School Psychologist, 9,* 145–158.

Poythress, N., Monahan, J., Bonnie, R., Otto, R., & Hoge, S. (2002). *Adjudicative competence: The MacArthur studies.* New York: Kluwer/Plenum.

Prentky, R. (2001). Mental illness and roots of genius. *Creativity Research Journal, 13,* 95–104.

Prewett, P. N. (1995). A comparison of two screening tests (the Matrix Analogies Test-Short Form and the Kaufman Brief Intelligence Test) with the WISC-III. *Psychological Assessment, 7,* 69–72.

Prout, H., & Schwartz, J. (1984). Validity of the PPVT-R with mentally retarded adults. *Journal of Clinical Psychology, 40,* 584–587.

Psychological Corporation. (1994). *WISC-III Writer manual.* San Antonio, TX: Author.

Purish, A. (2001). Misconceptions about the Luria-Nebraska Neuropsychological Battery. *Neurorehabilitation, 16,* 275–280.

Pyle, W. H. (1913). *The examination of school children.* New York: Macmillan.

Qu, C. (1997). Reliability and validity of the Hiskey-Nebraska Test of Learning Aptitude (H-NTLA) in testing China's deaf children. *Chinese Mental Health Journal, 11,* 70–72.

Quinsey, V. L., & LaLumiere, M. (1996). *Assessment of sexual offenders against children.* Thousand Oaks, CA: Sage.

Quinsey, V., Harris, G., Rice, M., & Cormier, C. (1998). *Violent offenders: Appraising and managing risk.* Washington, DC: American Psychological Association.

Rakic, P. (2002). Adult neurogenesis in mammals: An identity crisis. *Journal of Neuroscience, 22,* 614–618.

Ramey, C. T., & Ramey, S. (1998). Early intervention and early experience. *American Psychologist, 53,* 109–10.

Ranseen, J., Campbell, D., & Baer, R. (1998). NEO PI-R profiles of adults with attention deficit disorder. *Assessment, 5,* 19–24.

Rasch, G. (1960). *Probabilistic models for some intelligence and attainment tests.* Copenhagen: Denmarks Paedagogiske Institut.

Raven, J. (2000). The Raven's Progressive Matrices: Change and stability over culture and time. *Cognitive Psychology, 41,* 1–48.

Raven, J. C. (1938). *Progressive Matrices.* London: Lewis.

Raven, J. C. (1965). *The Coloured Progressive Matrices Test.* London: Lewis.

Raven, J. C., & Summers, B. (1986). *Manual for Raven's Progressive Matrices and Vocabulary Scales—research supplement no. 3.* London: Lewis.

Raven, J. C., Court, J. H., & Raven, J. (1983). *Manual for Raven's Progressive Matrices and Vocabulary Scales (Section 3)—Standard Progressive Matrices* (1983 edition). London: Lewis.

Raven, J. C., Court, J. H., & Raven, J. (1986). *Manual for Raven's Progressive Matrices and Vocabulary Scales (Section 2)—Coloured Progressive Matrices* (1986 edition, with U.S. norms). London: Lewis.

Raven, J. C., Court, J. H., & Raven, J. (1992). *Standard Progressive Matrices. 1992 Edition.* Oxford: Oxford Psychologists Press.

Reddon, J. R., & Jackson, D. N. (1989). Readability of three adult personality tests: Basic Personality Inventory, Jackson Personality Inventory, and Personality Research Form-E. *Journal of Personality Assessment, 53,* 180–183.

Reeves, D., & Wedding, D. (1994). *The clinical assessment of memory: A practical guide.* New York: Springer.

Regenwetter, M. (2009). Perspectives on preference aggregation. *Perspectives on Psychological Science, 4,* 403–407.

Rehm, L. P. (1984). Self-management therapy for depression. *Advances in Behavior Research and Therapy, 6,* 83–98.

Rehm, L. P., Kornblith, S. J., O'Hara, M. W., and others. (1981). An evaluation of major components in a self-control therapy program for depression. *Behavior Modification, 5,* 459–490.

Reid, D. B., & Kelly, M. P. (1993). Wechsler Memory Scale-Revised in closed head injury. *Journal of Clinical Psychology, 49,* 245–254.

Reilly, R. R., & Chao, G. T. (1982). Validity and fairness of some alternative employee selection procedures. *Personnel Psychology, 35,* 1–63.

Reise, S., Ainsworth, A., & Haviland, M. (2005). Item response theory: Fundamentals, applications, and promise in psychological research. *Current Directions in Psychological Science, 14,* 95–101.

Reitan, R. M. (1984). *Aphasia and sensory perceptual deficits in adults.* Tucson, AZ: Neuropsychology Press.

Reitan, R. M., & Wolfson, D. (1993). *The Halstead-Reitan Neuropsychological Test Battery: Theory and clinical interpretation* (2nd ed.). Tucson, AZ: Neuropsychology Press.

Reschly, D., Myers, T., & Hartel, C. (2002). *Mental retardation: Determining eligibility for Social Security benefits.* Washington, DC: National Academies Press.

Rest, J. R. (1979). *The Defining Issues Test: Manual.* Minneapolis: University of Minnesota Press.

Rest, J. R. (1986). Moral research methodology. In S. Modgil & C. Modgil (Eds.), *Lawrence Kohlberg: Consensus and controversy.* Philadelphia: Taylor & Francis.

Rest, J. R., & Thoma, S. J. (1985). Relation of moral judgment to formal education. *Developmental Psychology, 21,* 709–714.

Rest, J. R., Thoma, S., Narvaez, D., & Bebeau, M. (1997). Alchemy and beyond: Indexing the Defining Issues Test. *Journal of Educational Psychology, 89,* 498–507.

Rey, A. (1964). *L'examen clinique en psychologie.* Paris: Presses Universitaires de France.

Reynolds, C. R. (1994). Bias in testing. In R. J. Sternberg (Ed.), *Encyclopedia of human intelligence.* New York: Macmillan.

Reynolds, C. R. (1998). Cultural bias in testing of intelligence and personality. In A. Bellack & M. Hersen (Series Eds.) & C. Belar (Vol. Ed.), *Comprehensive clinical psychology: Sociocultural and individual differences.* New York: Elsevier Science.

Reynolds, C. R., & Brown, R. T. (1984a). Bias in mental testing: An introduction to the issues. In Reynolds, C. R., & Brown, R. T. (Eds.), *Perspectives on bias in mental testing.* New York: Plenum Press.

Reynolds, C. R., & Brown, R. T. (Eds.). (1984b). *Perspectives on bias in mental testing.* New York: Plenum Press.

Reynolds, C. R., Chastain, R. L., Kaufman, A. S., & McLean, J. E. (1987). Demographic characteristics and IQ among adults: Analysis of the WAIS-R standardization sample as a function of the stratification variables. *Journal of School Psychology, 25,* 323–342.

Reynolds, C. R., Lowe, P. A., & Saenz, A. L. (1999). The problem of bias in psychological assessment. In C. R. Reynolds & T. B. Gutkin (Eds.), *The handbook of school psychology* (3rd ed.). New York: Wiley.

Riccio, C., Reynolds, C., & Lowe, P. (2001). *Clinical applications of continuous performance tests: Measuring attention and impulsive responding in children and adults.* New York: Wiley.

Ricciuti, H. N. (1994). Infant tests as measures of early competence. In R. J. Sternberg (Ed.), *Encyclopedia of human intelligence.* New York: Macmillan.

Richards, P. S. (1991). The relation between conservative religious ideology and principled moral reasoning: A review. *Review of Religious Research, 32,* 359–368.

Richards, P. S., & Davison, M. L. (1992). Religious bias in moral development research: A psychometric investigation. *Journal for the Scientific Study of Religion, 31,* 467–485.

Rieber, R. W. (Ed.). (1980). *Wilhelm Wundt and the making of a scientific psychology.* New York: Plenum Press.

Rinas, J., & Clyne-Jackson, S. (1988). *Professional conduct and legal concerns in mental health practice.* Norwalk, CT: Appleton & Lang.

Ritzler, B. A., Sharkey, K. J., & Chudy, J. (1980). A comprehensive projective alternative to the TAT. *Journal of Personality Assessment, 44,* 358–362.

Ritzler, B., Erard, R., & Pettigrew, G. (2002). Protecting the integrity of Rorschach expert witnesses: A reply to Grove and Barden (1999) Re: The admissibility of testimony under *Daubert/Kumho* analyses. *Psychology, Public Policy, and Law, 8,* 201–215.

Riva, G. (Ed.). (1997). *Virtual reality in neuro-psychophysiology: Cognitive, clinical and methodological issues in assessment and rehabilitation.* Amsterdam, Netherlands: IOS Press.

Robertson, I. H., Ward, T., Ridgeway, V., & Nimmo-Smith, I. (1994). *Test of Everyday Attention (TEA).* Gaylord, MI: National Rehabilitation Services.

Robertson, I. H., Ward, T., Ridgeway, V., & Nimmo-Smith, I. (1996). The structure of normal human attention: The Test of Everyday Attention. *Journal of the International Neuropsychological Society, 2,* 525–534.

Robertson, I., & Smith, M. (2001). Personnel selection. *Journal of Occupational and Organizational Psychology, 74,* 441–472.

Roesch, R., Webster, C., & Eaves, D. (1994). *The Fitness Interview Test-Revised*. Unpublished manuscript, Simon Fraser University.

Roese, N. J., & Amir, E. (2009). Human-android interaction in the near and distant future. *Perspectives on Psychological Science, 4,* 429–434.

Rogers, B. (1989). Review of Metropolitan Achievement Test, Sixth Edition. *The tenth mental measurements yearbook.* Lincoln: University of Nebraska Press.

Rogers, B. G. (1992). Review of GED. *The eleventh mental measurements yearbook.* Lincoln: University of Nebraska Press.

Rogers, C. R. (1951). *Client-centered therapy: Its current practice, implications, and theory.* Boston: Houghton Mifflin.

Rogers, C. R. (1961). *On becoming a person: A therapist's view of psychotherapy.* Boston: Houghton Mifflin.

Rogers, C. R. (1980). *A way of being.* Boston: Houghton Mifflin.

Rogers, C. R., & Dymond, R. F. (Eds.). (1954). *Psychotherapy and personality change: Co-ordinated research studies in the client-centered approach.* Chicago: University of Chicago Press.

Rogers, R. (1984). *Rogers Criminal Responsibility Assessment Scales.* Odessa, FL: Psychological Assessment Resources.

Rogers, R. (1986). *Conducting insanity evaluations.* Odessa, FL: Psychological Assessment Resources.

Rogers, R. (1986). *Conducting insanity evaluations.* New York: Van Nostrand Reinhold.

Rogers, R. (2001). Schedule of Affective Disorders and Schizophrenia (SADS). In R. Rogers (Ed.), *Handbook of diagnostic and structured interviewing.* New York: Guilford.

Rogers, R. (Ed.). (2008). *Clinical assessment of malingering and deception* (3rd ed.). New York: Guilford.

Rogers, R., & Sewell, K. (1999). The R-CRAS and insanity evaluations: A re-examination of construct validity. *Behavioral Sciences and the Law, 17,* 181–194.

Rogers, R., Bagby, M., & Dickens, S. (1992). *Structured Interview of Reported Symptoms (SIRS) manual.* Odessa, FL: Psychological Assessment Resources.

Rogers, R., Gillis, J., Dickens, S., & Bagby, R. (1991). Standardized assessment of malingering: Validation of the SIRS. *Psychological Assessment, 3,* 89–96.

Rogers, R., Jackson, R., & Cashel, M. (2004). The Schedule for Affective Disorders and Schizophrenia (SADS). In M. J. Hilsenroth & D. L. Segal (Eds.), *Comprehensive handbook of psychological assessment* (Vol. 2). New York: John Wiley.

Rogers, R., Kropp, P., Bagby, R., & Dickens, S. (1992). Faking specific disorders: A study of the SIRS. *Journal of Clinical Psychology, 48,* 643–648.

Rogers, R., Sewell, K., & Goldstein, A. (1994). Explanation models of malingering: A prototypical analysis. *Law and Human Behavior, 18,* 543–552.

Rogoff, B. (1984). What are the interrelations among the three subtheories of Sternberg's triarchic theory of intelligence? *Behavioral and Brain Sciences, 7,* 300–301.

Roid, G. (2002, August). *New Stanford-Binet Intelligence Scales, Fifth Edition: Author's Overview.* Paper presented at the Annual Convention of the American Psychological Association, Chicago, IL.

Roid, G. (2003). *Stanford-Binet Intelligence Scales* (5th ed.). Itasca, IL: Riverside Publishing.

Roid, G. (2005). *Stanford-Binet Intelligence Scales for Early Childhood* (5th ed.). Itasca, IL: Riverside Publishing.

Roid, G., & Miller, L. (1997). *Leiter-R Manual.* Wood Dale, IL: Stoelting Co.

Roid, G. H., & Johnson, W. B. (1998). Computer assisted psychological assessment. In A. S. Bellack & M. Hersen (Eds.), *Comprehensive clinical psychology* (vol. 4). Amsterdam: Elsevier.

Rorschach, H. (1921). *Psychodiagnostik.* Berne: Birchen.

Rosenberg, S., Ryan, J., & Prifitera, A. (1984). Rey Auditory-Verbal Learning Test performance of patients with and without memory impairment. *Journal of Clinical Psychology, 40,* 785–787.

Ross, S. M., Gottfredson, D. K., Christensen, P., & Weaver, R. (1986). Cognitive self-statements in depression: Findings across clinical populations. *Cognitive Therapy and Research, 10,* 159–166.

Rossier, J., de Stadelhofen, F., & Berthoud, S. (2004). The hierarchical structures of the NEO-PI-R and the 16 PF 5. *European Journal of Psychological Assessment, 20,* 27–38.

Rosvold, H. E., Mirsky, A. E., Sarason, I., and others. (1956). A continuous performance test of brain damage. *Journal of Consulting Psychology, 20,* 343–350.

Rotter, J. B. (1966). Generalized expectancies for internal versus external control of reinforcement. *Psychological Monographs, 80* (Whole No. 609).

Rotter, J. B. (1972). Beliefs, social attitudes, and behavior: A social learning analysis. In J. B. Rotter, J. Chances, & E. J. Phares (Eds.), *Applications of a social learning theory of personality.* New York: Holt, Rinehart and Winston.

Rotter, J. B., & Rafferty, J. E. (1950). *Manual for the Rotter Incomplete Sentences Blank: College Form.* New York: The Psychological Corporation.

Rotter, J. B., Lah, M., & Rafferty, J. (1992). *Manual—Rotter Incomplete Sentences Blank* (2nd ed.). Orlando, FL: The Psychological Corporation.

Rotter, J. B., Rafferty, J. E., & Schachtitz, E. (1965). Validation of the Rotter Incomplete Sentences Test. In B. I. Murstein (Ed.), *Handbook of projective techniques.* New York: Basic Books.

Rozin, P. (2009). What kind of empirical research should we publish, fund, and reward? A different perspective. *Perspectives on Psychological Science, 4,* 435.

Rubenzer, S., Faschingbauer, T., & Ones, D. (2000). Assessing the U.S. presidents using the Revised NEO Personality Inventory. *Assessment, 7,* 403–420.

Rubin, M. (1999). *Emotional intelligence and its role in mitigating aggression.* Unpublished doctoral dissertation, Immaculata College, Immaculata, Pennsylvania.

Rushton, J. P., & Jensen, A. R. (2005). Thirty years of research on race differences in cognitive ability. *Psychology, Public Policy, and Law, 11,* 235–294.

Russell, M., Martier, S., Sokol, R., and others. (1994). Screening for pregnancy risk-drinking. *Alcoholism: Clinical and Experimental Research, 18,* 1156–1161.

Russo, J. (1994). Thurstone's scaling model applied to the assessment of self-reported depressive severity. *Psychological Assessment, 6,* 159–171.

Rust, J., & Lindstrom, A. (1996). Concurrent validity of the WISC-III and Stanford-Binet-IV. *Psychological Reports, 79,* 618–620.

Ryan, A. M., & Sackett, P. R. (1987). Pre-employment honesty testing: Fakability, reactions of test takers, and company image. *Journal of Business and Psychology, 1,* 248–256.

Ryan, J. J., & Lewis, C. V. (1988). Comparison of normal controls and recently detoxified alcoholics on the Wechsler Memory Scale-Revised. *Clinical Neuropsychologist, 2,* 173–180.

Ryan, M. (1985). Review of the Minnesota Clerical Test. *The ninth mental measurements yearbook* (vol. I). Lincoln: University of Nebraska Press.

Ryan, R. M. (1987). Thematic Apperception Test. In D. J. Keyser & R. C. Sweetland (Eds.), *Test critiques compendium.* Kansas City, MO: Test Corporation of America.

Saccuzzo, D. P., & Johnson, N. E. (1995). Traditional psychometric tests and proportionate representation: An intervention and program evaluation study. *Psychological Assessment, 7,* 183–194.

Sackett, P. R., Burris, L. R., & Callahan, C. (1989). Integrity testing for personnel selection: An update. *Personnel Psychology, 42,* 491–529.

Sadock, B., & Sadock, V. (2004). *Kaplan and Sadock's comprehensive textbook of psychiatry* (8th ed.). Philadelphia: Lippincott, Williams and Wilkins.

Sala, F. (2002). *Emotional Competence Inventory: Technical manual.* Philadelphia, PA: McClelland Center for Research, HayGroup.

Salovey, P., & Mayer, J. (1989–1990). Emotional intelligence. *Imagination, Cognition, and Personality, 9,* 185–211.

Salter, D., Forney, D., & Evans, N. (2005). Two approaches to examining the stability of Myers-Briggs Type Indicator scores. *Measurement and Evaluation in Counseling and Development, 37,* 208–219.

Salvia, J., & Ysseldyke, J. (2001). *Assessment* (8th ed). Boston: Houghton Mifflin.

Samelson, F. (1977). World War I intelligence testing and the development of psychology. *Journal of the History of the Behavioral Sciences, 13,* 274–282.

Sandford, J. A., & Turner, A. (1997). *Intermediate Visual and Auditory Continuous Performance Test* (IVA). Los Angeles: Western Psychological Services.

Sarason, I. G. (1961). Test anxiety, experimental instructions, and verbal learning. *American Psychologist, 16,* 374.

Sattler, J. M. (1988). *Assessment of children* (3rd ed.). San Diego, CA: Jerome M. Sattler, Publisher.

Sattler, J. M. (2001). *Assessment of children: Cognitive applications.* San Diego, CA: Jerome M. Sattler, Publisher.

Sattler, J. M. (2008). *Assessment of children: Cognitive foundations* (5th ed.). La Mesa, CA: Jerome M. Sattler, Publisher.

Savickas, M., Taber, B., & Spokane, A. (2002). Convergent and discriminant validity of five interest inventories. *Journal of Vocational Behavior, 61,* 139–184.

Scarr, S. (1981). Testing for children: Assessment and the many determinants of intellectual competence. *American Psychologist, 36,* 1159–1168.

Scarr, S. (1987). Foreward. In R. Elliott (Ed.), *Litigating intelligence: IQ tests, special education and social science in the courtroom.* Dover, MA: Auburn House.

Scarr, S. (1994). Culture-Fair and Culture-Free tests. In R. J. Sternberg (Ed.), *Encyclopedia of human intelligence.* New York: Macmillan.

Scarr, S., & Weinberg, R. A. (1976). IQ test performance of black children adopted by white families. *American Psychologist, 31,* 726–739.

Scarr, S., & Weinberg, R. A. (1983). The Minnesota Adoption Studies: Genetic differences and malleability. *Child Development, 54,* 260–267.

Scarr-Salapatek, S. (1971). Unknowns in the IQ equation. *Science, 174,* 1223–1228.

Schaie, K. W. (1958). Rigidity-flexibility and intelligence: A cross-sectional study of the adult life span from 20–70. *Psychological Monographs, 72,* no. 9 (Whole No. 462).

Schaie, K. W. (1977). Quasi-experimental designs in the psychology of aging. In J. E. Birren & K. W. Schaie (Eds.), *Handbook of the psychology of aging.* New York: Van Nostrand Reinhold.

Schaie, K. W. (1978). Review of Senior Apperception Techniques. *The eighth mental measurements yearbook.* Lincoln: University of Nebraska Press.

Schaie, K. W. (1980). Cognitive development in aging. In L. K. Obler & M. Alpert (Eds.), *Language and communication in the elderly.* Lexington, MA: Heath.

Schaie, K. W. (1985). *Manual for the Schaie-Thurstone Adult Mental Abilities Test (STAMAT).* Palo Alto, CA: Consulting Psychologists Press.

Schaie, K. W. (1996). *Intellectual development in adulthood: The Seattle Longitudinal Study.* New York: Cambridge University Press.

Schaie, K. W. (2005). *Developmental influences on adult intelligence: The Seattle longitudinal study.* New York: Oxford University Press.

Schaie, K. W., & Willis, S. L. (1986). *Adult development and aging.* Boston: Little, Brown.

Schaie, K. W., Caskie, G., Revell, A., & others (2005). Extending neuropsychological assessments in the Primary Mental Ability space. *Aging, Neuropsychology, and Cognition, 12,* 245–277.

Schalock, R., Luckasson, R., Shogren, K., and others. (2007). The renaming of Mental Retardation: Understanding the change to the term Intellectual Disability. *Intellectual and Developmental Disabilities, 45,* 116–124.

Schear, J. M., & Craft, R. B. (1989). Examination of the concurrent validity of the California Verbal Learning Test. *Clinical Neuropsychologist, 3,* 162–168.

Scheier, M., Carver, C., & Bridges, M. (1994). Distinguishing optimism from neuroticism (and trait anxiety, self-mastery, and self-esteem): A reevaluation of the Life Orientation Test. *Journal of Personality and Social Psychology, 67,* 1063–1078.

Scheuneman, J. D. (1987). An argument opposing Jensen on test bias: The psychological aspects. In S. Modgil & C. Modgil (Eds.), *Arthur Jensen: Consensus and controversy.* New York: Falmer Press.

Schmidt, F. (2002). The role of general cognitive ability and job performance: Why there cannot be a debate. *Human Performance, 15,* 187–211.

Schmidt, F. L., Hunter, J. E., McKenzie, R. C., & Muldrow, T. W. (1979). Impact of valid selection procedures on work-force productivity. *Journal of Applied Psychology, 64,* 609–626.

Schmidt, F., & Zimmerman, R. (2004). A counterintuitive hypothesis about employment interview validity and some supporting evidence. *Journal of Applied Psychology, 89,* 553–561.

Schmitt, N. (1995). Review of the Differential Aptitude Tests, Fifth Edition. *The twelfth mental measurements yearbook.* Lincoln: University of Nebraska Press.

Schmitt, N. (1996). Uses and abuses of coefficient alpha. *Psychological Assessment, 8,* 350–353.

Schmitt, N., & Kunce, C. (2002). The effects of required elaboration of answers to biodata questions. *Personnel Psychology, 55,* 569–587.

Schmitt, N., & Robertson, I. (1990). Personnel selection. *Annual Review of Psychology, 41,* 289–320.

Schoenberg, M., Dawson, K., Duff, K., and others. (2006). Test performance and classification statistics for the Rey Auditory Verbal Learning Test in selected clinical samples. *Archives of Clinical Neuropsychology, 21,* 693–703.

Schroeder, M. L., Schroeder, K. G., & Hare, R. D. (1983). Generalizability of a checklist for assessment of psychopathy. *Journal of Consulting and Clinical Psychology, 51,* 511–516.

Schuldberg, D. (1988). The MMPI is less sensitive to the automated testing format than it is to repeated testing: Item and scale effects. *Computers in Human Behavior, 4,* 285–298.

Schuler, M. (1999). Brief report: Frequency of maternal cocaine use during pregnancy and infant neurobehavioral outcome. *Journal of Pediatric Psychology, 24,* 511–514.

Schwab, L. O. (1979). *The Nebraska assessment for independent living* (Project 93–013). Lincoln: Department of Human Development and the Family, University of Nebraska.

Seashore, C. E. (1938). *The psychology of musical talent.* Boston: Silver, Burdett.

Seligman, M. E. P., & Csikszentmihalyi, M. (2000). Positive psychology: An introduction. *American Psychologist, 55,* 5–14.

Seligman, M. E. P., & Kahana, M. (2009). Unpacking intuition: A conjecture. *Perspectives on Psychological Science, 4,* 399–402.

Seligman, M. E. P., Abramson, L. Y., Semmel, A., & Von Baeyer, C. (1979). Depressive attributional style. *Journal of Abnormal Psychology, 88,* 242–247.

Sellbom, M., Fishler, G., & Ben-Porath, Y. (2007). Identifying MMPI-2 predictors of police officer integrity and misconduct. *Criminal Justice and Behavior, 34,* 985–1004.

Shapiro, E. S. (1996). *Academic skills problems workbook.* New York: Guilford.

Sharkey, K. J., & Ritzler, B. A. (1985). Comparing diagnostic validity of the TAT and a new Picture Projective Test. *Journal of Personality Assessment, 49,* 406–412.

Shaughnessy, M., & Moore, J. (1994). The KAIT with developmental students, honor students, and freshmen. *Psychology in the Schools, 31,* 286–287.

Shaw, S., Cullen, J., McGuire, J., & Brinckerhoff, L. (1995). Operationalizing a definition of learning disabilities. *Journal of Learning Disabilities, 28,* 586–597.

Shayer, M., Ginsburg, D., & Coe, R. (2007. Thirty years on—a large anti-Flynn effect? The Piagetian test Volume & Heaviness norms 1975–2003. *British Journal of Educational Psychology, 77,* 25–41.

Sheldon, W., & Stevens, S. (1942). *The varieties of temperament: A psychology of constitutional differences.* New York: Harper & Brothers.

Shen, H., & Comrey, A. (1997). Predicting medical students' academic performances by their cognitive abilities and personality characteristics. *Academic Medicine, 72,* 781–786.

Sheshlow, D., & Adams, W. (2006). *Wide Range Assessment of Memory and Learning* (2nd Ed.). Lutz, FL: Psychological Assessment Resources.

Shiffman, S., & Hufford, M. (2001). Ecological momentary assessment. *Applied Clinical Trials, 10,* 42–48.

Shiffman, S., Hufford, M., & Paty, J. (2001). The patient experience movement. *Applied Clinical Trials, 10,* 48–56.

Shiffman, S., Hufford, M., Hickcox, M., and others. (1997). Remember that? A comparison of real-time versus retrospective recall of smoking lapses. *Journal of Consulting and Clinical Psychology, 65,* 292–300.

Shurrager, H. C. (1961). *A haptic intelligence scale for adult blind.* Chicago: Illinois Institute of Technology.

Shurrager, H. C., & Shurrager, P. S. (1964). *Manual for the Haptic Intelligence Scale for the Blind.* Chicago: Psychology Research Technology Center, Illinois Institute of Technology.

Siegman, A. W. (1956). The effect of manifest anxiety on a concept formation task, a nondirected learning task, and on timed and untimed intelligence tests. *Journal of Consulting Psychology, 20,* 176–178.

Silverstein, A. B. (1986). Organization and Structure of the Detroit Tests of Learning Aptitude (DTLA-2). *Educational and Psychological Measurement, 46,* 1061–1066.

Sipps, G. J., Berry, G. W., & Lynch, E. M. (1987). WAIS-R and social intelligence: A test of established assumptions that uses the CPI. *Journal of Clinical Psychology, 43,* 499–504.

Sisson, E. D. (1948). Forced-choice: The new Army rating. *Personnel Psychology, 1,* 365–381.

Sivan, A. B. (1991). *Revised Visual Retention Test: Clinical and experimental applications* (5th ed.). San Antonio, TX: The Psychological Corporation.

Skinner, B. F. (1953). *Science and human behavior.* New York: Macmillan.

Skinner, B. F. (1974). *About behaviorism.* New York: Knopf.

Smedslund, G., & Rundmo, T. (1999). Is Grossarth-Maticek's coronary-prone type II an independent predictor of myocardial infarction? *Personality and Individual Differences, 27,* 1231–1242.

Smith, A. (1960). Changes in Porteus Maze scores of brain-operated schizophrenics after an eight year interval. *Journal of Mental Science, 106,* 967–978.

Smith, A. (1973). *Symbol Digit Modalities Test. Manual.* Los Angeles: Western Psychological Services.

Smith, A., & Kinder, E. (1959). Changes in psychological test performances of brain-operated subjects after eight years. *Science, 129,* 149–150.

Smith, G. T. (2009). Why do different individuals progress along different life trajectories? *Perspectives on Psychological Science, 4,* 415–421.

Smith, J. (2001). Detroit Tests of Learning Aptitude, Fourth Edition. *Fourteenth mental measurements yearbook.* Lincoln: University of Nebraska Press.

Smith, M., Delves, T., Lansdown, R., Clayton, B., & Graham, P. (1983). The effects of lead exposure on urban children: The Institute of Child Health/Southampton Study. *Developmental Medicine and Child Neurology, 25,* 1–54.

Smith, P. C., & Kendall, L. M. (1963). Retranslation of expectations: An approach to the construction of unambiguous anchors for rating scales. *Journal of Applied Psychology, 47,* 149–155.

Smith, T. W., Follick, M. J., Ahern, D. K., & Adams, A. (1986). Cognitive distortion and disability in chronic low back pain. *Cognitive Therapy and Research, 10,* 201–210.

Smither, R. D. (1998). *The psychology of work and human performance* (3rd ed.). New York: HarperCollins.

Smyth, J., Wonderlich, S., Crosby, R., and others. (2001). The use of ecological momentary assessment approaches in eating disorder research. *International Journal of Eating Disorders, 30,* 83–95.

Snow, J. H. (1992). Review of Luria-Nebraska Neuropsychological Battery: Forms I and II. *The eleventh mental measurements yearbook.* Lincoln: University of Nebraska Press.

Snyder, C. R., & Lopez, S. (2007). *Positive psychology: The scientific and practical explorations of human strengths.* Thousand Oaks, CA: Sage.

Snyder, D. K., Lachar, D., & Wills, R. M. (1988). Computer-based interpretation of the Marital Satisfaction Inventory: Use in treatment planning. *Journal of Marital and Family Therapy, 14,* 397–409.

Society for Industrial and Organizational Psychology, Inc. (1987). *Principles for the validation and use of personnel selection procedures* (3rd ed.). College Park, MD: Author.

Sokol, R. J., & Clarren, S. K. (1989). Guidelines for use of terminology describing the impact of prenatal alcohol on the offspring. *Alcoholism: Clinical and Experimental Research, 13,* 597–598.

Sontag, L. W., Baker, C., & Nelson, V. (1958). Mental growth and personality development: A longitudinal study. *Monographs of the Society for Research in Child Development, 23* (Whole No. 68).

Spearman, C. (1904). "General intelligence," objectively determined and measured. *American Journal of Psychology, 15,* 201–293.

Spearman, C. (1923). *The nature of 'intelligence' and the principles of cognition.* London: Macmillan.

Spearman, C. (1927). *The abilities of man.* New York: Macmillan.

*Special Education Today.* (1985). ACALD definition of learning disabilities. *2,* 1–20.

Sperry, R. W. (1964). The great cerebral commissure. *Scientific American, 210,* 42–52.

Spitzer, R., & Endicott, J. (1978). Research diagnostic criteria: Rationale and reliability. *Archives of General Psychiatry, 35,* 773–782.

Spohr, H., & Steinhausen, H. (Eds.). (1996). *Alcohol, pregnancy, and the developing child.* Cambridge: Cambridge University Press.

Spreen, O. (2001). Learning disabilities and their neurological foundations, theories, and subtypes. In A. Kaufman & N. Kaufman (Eds.), *Specific learning disabilities and difficulties in children and adolescents.* Cambridge, England: Cambridge University Press.

Spreen, O., & Strauss, E. (1998). *A compendium of neuropsychological tests: Administration, norms, and commentary* (2nd ed.). New York: Oxford University Press.

Springer, S., & Deutsch, G. (1997). *Left brain, right brain* (5th ed.). San Francisco: W. H. Freeman.

Sreenivasan, S., Walker, S., Weinberger, L., Kirkish, P., & Garrick, T. (2008). Four-facet PCL-R structure and cognitive functioning among high violent criminal offenders. *Journal of Personality Assessment, 90,* 197–200.

Stafford-Clark, D. (1971). *What Freud really said.* New York: Schocken Books.

Stanley, J. C. (1971). Reliability. In R. L. Thorndike (Ed.), *Educational measurement.* Washington, DC: American Council on Education.

Steele, C. M. (1997). A threat in the air: How stereotypes shape intellectual identity and performance. *American Psychologist, 6,* 613–629.

Steele, C. M., & Aronson, J. (1995). Stereotype threat and the intellectual test performance of African Americans. *Journal of Personality and Social Psychology, 69,* 797–811.

Steer, R. A., Beck, A. T., & Brown, G. (1989). Sex differences on the Revised Beck Depression Inventory for outpatients with affective disorders. *Journal of Personality Assessment, 53,* 693–702.

Steers, R. M., & Rhodes, S. R. (1978). Major influences on employee attendance: A process model. *Journal of Applied Psychology, 63,* 391–407.

Stefan, S. (2001). *Unequal rights: Discrimination against people with mental disabilities and the Americans with Disabilities Act.* Washington, DC: American Psychological Association.

Stehouwer, R. S. (1987). Beck Depression Inventory. In D. J. Keyser & R. C. Sweetland (Eds.), *Test critiques compendium.* Kansas City, MO: Test Corporation of America.

Steinweg, D. L., & Worth, H. (1993). Alcoholism: The keys to the CAGE. *American Journal of Medicine, 94,* 520–523.

Stenner, A. J. (2001). The Lexile Framework: A common metric for matching readers and text. *California School Library Association Journal, 25,* 41–42.

Stephenson, W. (1953). *The study of behavior: Q-technique and its methodology.* Chicago: University of Chicago Press.

Steptoe, A., Wright, C., Kunz-Ebrecht, S., & Iliffe, S. (2006). Dispositional optimism and health behaviour in community-dwelling older people: Associations with healthy ageing. *British Journal of Health Psychology, 11,* 71–84.

Stern, R., & White, T. (2003a). *Neuropsychological Assessment Battery: Administration, scoring, and interpretive manual.* Lutz, FL: Psychological Assessment Resources.

Stern, R., & White, T. (2003a). *Neuropsychological Assessment Battery: Psychometric and technical manual.* Lutz, FL: Psychological Assessment Resources.

Stern, W. L. (1912). Uber die psychologischen Methoden der Intelligenzprufung. American translation by G. M. Whipple (1914). The psychological methods of testing intelligence. *Educational Psychology Monographs,* no. 13, Baltimore: Warwick & York.

Sternberg, R. J. (1981). Intelligence and nonentrenchment. *Journal of Educational Psychology, 73,* 1–16.

Sternberg, R. J. (1985a). Componential analysis: A recipe. In D. K. Detterman (Ed.), *Current topics in human intelligence* (vol. 1). Norwood, NJ: Ablex.

Sternberg, R. J. (1985b). *Beyond IQ: A triarchic theory of human intelligence.* Cambridge: Cambridge University Press.

Sternberg, R. J. (1986). *Intelligence applied: Understanding and increasing your intellectual skills.* San Diego, CA: Harcourt Brace Jovanovich.

Sternberg, R. J. (1993). *Sternberg Triarchic Abilities Test (Level H).* Unpublished test.

Sternberg, R. J. (1994). The triarchic theory of intelligence. In R. J. Sternberg (Ed.), *Encyclopedia of human intelligence.* New York: Macmillan.

Sternberg, R. J. (1996). *Successful intelligence.* New York: Simon & Schuster.

Sternberg, R. J. (2002). Creativity as a decision. *American Psychologist, 57,* 376.

Sternberg, R. J. (Ed.). (1994). *Encyclopedia of human intelligence* (vol. 1, 2). New York: Macmillan.

Sternberg, R. J., & Detterman, D. K. (Eds.). (1986). *What is intelligence? Contemporary viewpoints on its nature and definition.* Norwood, NJ: Ablex.

Sternberg, R. J., & Kaufman, J. C. (1998). Human abilities. *Annual Review of Psychology, 49,* 479–502.

Sternberg, R. J., & Williams, W. (1997). Does the Graduate Record Examination predict meaningful success in the graduate training of psychologists? A case study. *American Psychologist, 52,* 630–641.

Sternberg, R. J., & Zhang, L. (1995). What do we mean by giftedness? A pentagonal implicit theory. *Gifted Child Quarterly, 39,* 88–94.

Sternberg, R. J., Castejon, J., Prieto, M., Hautamaki, J., & Grigorenko, E. (2001). Confirmatory factor analysis

of the Sternberg Triarchic Abilities Test in three international samples. *European Journal of Psychological Assessment, 17,* 1–16.

Sternberg, R. J., Conway, B. E., Ketron, J. L., & Bernstein, M. (1981). People's conceptions of intelligence. *Journal of Personality and Social Psychology, 41,* 37–55.

Sternberg, R., & Lubart, T. (1992). Buy low and sell high: An investment approach to creativity. *Current Directions in Psychological Research, 1,* 1–5.

Stevens, S. S. (1946). On the theory of scales and measurement. *Science, 103,* 677–680.

Stewart, G., Dustin, S., Barrick, M., & Darnold, T. (2008). Exploring the handshake in employment interviews. *Journal of Applied Psychology, 93,* 1139–1146.

Stewart, P., Reihman, J., Lonky, E., Darvill, T., & Pagano, J. (1999). Prenatal PCB exposure and neonatal behavioral assessment scale (NBAS) performance. *Neurotoxicology and Teratology, 22,* 21–29.

Stockwell, S., Schaeffer, B., & Lowenstein, J. (1991). *The SAT coaching coverup.* Cambridge, MA: Fairtest.

Stokes, G., & Cooper, L. (2001). Content/construct approaches in life history form development for selection. *International Journal of Selection and Assessment, 9,* 138–151.

Stokes, G., & Cooper, L. (2004). Biodata. In J. Thomas (Ed.), *Comprehensive handbook of psychological assessment, Vol. 4: Industrial and organizational assessment* (pp. 243–268). Hoboken, NJ: John Wiley.

Stokes, G., Mumford, M., & Owens (Eds.). (1994). *Biodata handbook: Theory, research, and use of biographical information in selection and performance prediction.* Palo Alto, CA: Consulting Psychologists Press.

Stone, B. J. (1994). Group ability test versus teachers' ratings for predicting achievement. *Psychological Reports, 75,* 1487–1490.

Storandt, M., & Hill, R. D. (1989). Very mild senile dementia of the Alzheimer type: 2. Psychometric test performance. *Archives of Neurology, 46,* 383–386.

Strauss, E., Sherman, E., & Spreen, O. (2006). *A compendium of neuropsychological tests: Administration, norms, and commentary* (3rd ed.). New York: Oxford University Press.

Streiner, D. L., Goldberg, J. O., & Miller, H. R. (1993). MCMI-II item weights: Their lack of effectiveness. *Journal of Personality Assessment, 60,* 471–476.

Streissguth, A., Bookstein, F., & Barr, H. (1996). A dose-response study of the enduring effects of prenatal alcohol exposure: birth to 14 years. In H. Spohr & H. Steinhausen (Eds.), *Alcohol, pregnancy, and the developing child.* Cambridge: Cambridge University Press.

Streissguth, A., Martin, D., Barr, H., & Sandman, B. (1984). Intrauterine alcohol and nicotine exposure: Attention and reaction time in 4-year-old children. *Developmental Psychology, 20,* 533–541.

Strong, E. K. (1927). *Vocational Interest Blank.* Stanford, CA: Stanford University Press.

Strong, E. K. (1955). *Vocational interests 18 years after college.* Minneapolis: University of Minnesota Press.

Strong, E. K., Hansen, J., & Campbell, D. (1994). *Strong Interest Inventory.* Palo Alto, CA: Consulting Psychologists Press.

Strub, R. L., & Black, F. W. (2000). *The mental status examination in neurology* (5th ed.). Philadelphia: F. A. Davis.

Sumi, K. (2006). Correlations between optimism and social relationships. *Psychological Reports, 99,* 938–940.

Sundet, J., Barlaug, D., & Torjussen, T. (2004). The end of the Flynn effect? A study of secular trends in mean intelligence test scores of Norwegian conscripts during half a century. *Intelligence, 32,* 349–362.

Sundet, J., Borren, I., & Tambs, K. (2008). The Flynn effect is partly caused by changing fertility patterns. *Intelligence, 36,* 183–191.

Sweeney, J., Slade, H., Ivins, R., & others. (2007). Scientific investigation of brain-behavior relationships using the Halstead-Reitan Battery. *Applied Neuropsychology, 14,* 65–72.

Swenson, W. M., Rome, H., Pearson, J., & Brannick, T. (1965). A totally automated psychological test: Experience in a medical center. *Journal of the American Medical Association, 191,* 925–927.

Tabachnick, B. G., & Fidell, L. S. (1989). *Using multivariate statistics* (2nd ed.). New York: Harper & Row.

Tallent, N. (1993). *Psychological report writing* (4th ed.). Englewood Cliffs, NJ: Prentice Hall.

Tamkin, A. S., & Scherer, I. W. (1957). What is measured by the "Cannot Say" scale of the group MMPI? *Journal of Consulting Psychology, 21,* 413–417.

Tanner, B. A. (1992). Computer-aided reporting of the results of neuropsychological evaluations of traumatic brain injury. *Computers in Human Behavior, 9,* 51–56.

Tasbihsazan, R., Nettelbeck, T., & Kirby, N. (2003). Predictive validity of the Fagan Test of Infant Intelligence. *British Journal of Developmental Psychology, 21,* 585–597.

Tasto, D. L., Hickson, R., & Rubin, S. E. (1971). Scaled profile analysis of fear survey schedule factors. *Behavior Therapy, 2,* 543–549.

Taylor, F. S. (1942). The origin of the thermometer. *Annals of Science, 5,* 129–156.

*Teacher, Administrator, and Counselor Manual: Iowa Tests of Educational Development. Forms X-8 and Y-8.* 1988.

Teare, J. F., & Thompson, R. W. (1982). Concurrent validity of the Perkins-Binet tests of intelligence for the blind. *Journal of Visual Impairment and Blindness, 76,* 279–280.

Teasdale, G., & Jennett, B. (1974). The Glasgow Coma Scale. *Lancet, 2,* 81.

Teasdale, T., & Owen, D. (2005). A long-term rise and recent decline in intelligence test performance: The Flynn effect in reverse. *Personality and Individual Differences, 39,* 837–843.

Teichner, G., Golden, C., Bradley, J., & Crum, T. (1999). Internal consistency and discriminant validity of the Luria Nebraska Neuropsychological Battery-III. *International Journal of Neuroscience, 98,* 141–152.

Tellegen, A., & Ben-Porath, Y. (1992). The new uniform *T* scores for the MMPI-2: Rationale, derivation, and appraisal. *Psychological Assessment, 4,* 145–155.

Temple, R., & Zgaljardic, D. (2009). Ecological validity of the Neuropsychological Assessment Battery Screening Module in post-acute brain injury rehabilitation. *Brain Injury, 23,* 45–50.

Templeton, A. R. (2002). The genetic and evolutionary significance of human races. In J. Fish (Ed.), *Race and intelligence: Separating science from myth.* Mahwah, NJ: Erlbaum.

Tendler, A. D. (1930). A preliminary report on a test for emotional insight. *Journal of Applied Psychology, 14,* 123–126.

Teng, S. (1942–43). Chinese influence on the western examination system. *Harvard Journal of Asiatic Studies, 7,* 267–312.

Terman, L. M. (1916). *The measurement of intelligence.* Boston: Houghton Mifflin.

Terman, L. M., & Oden, M. H. (1959). *Genetic studies of genius: The gifted group at mid-life.* Stanford, CA: Stanford University Press.

Terrell, F., Terrell, S., & Taylor, J. (1981). Effect of race of examiner and cultural mistrust on the WAIS performance of Black students. *Journal of Consulting and Clinical Psychology, 49,* 750–751.

Thoma, S. (2006). Research on the defining issues test. In M. Killen & J. Smetana (Eds.), *Handbook of moral development* (pp. 67–91). Mahwah, NJ: Erlbaum.

Thomas, M., & Watkins, P. (2003, May). *Measuring the grateful trait: Development of revised GRAT.* Paper presented at the Annual Convention of the Western Psychological Association, Vancouver, BC.

Thompson, C. (1949). The Thompson modification of the Thematic Apperception Test. *Journal of Projective Techniques, 13,* 469–478.

Thorndike, E. L. (1912). The permanence of interests and their relation to abilities. *Popular Science Monthly, 81,* 449–456.

Thorndike, E. L. (1918). *The seventeenth yearbook of the National Society for the Study of Education. Pt. II.* Bloomington, IL: Public School Publishing Co.

Thorndike, E. L. (1920). Intelligence and its uses. *Harper's Magazine, 140,* 227–235.

Thorndike, E. L. (1920a). A constant error in psychological ratings. *Journal of Applied Psychology, 4,* 25–29.

Thorndike, E. L. (1920b). Intelligence and its use. *Harper's Magazine, 140,* 227–235.

Thorndike, E. L. (Ed.). (1921). Intelligence and Its Measurement: A Symposium. *Journal of Educational Psychology, 12,* 123–147, 195–216.

Thorndike, R. L., & Stein, S. (1937). An evaluation of the attempts to measure social intelligence. *Psychological Bulletin, 34,* 275–285.

Thorndike, R. L., Hagen, E. P., & Sattler, J. M. (1986). *The Stanford-Binet Intelligence Scale: Fourth Edition, Guide for administering and scoring.* Chicago: Riverside.

Thurstone, L. L. (1921). Intelligence. In E. L. Thorndike (Ed.), Intelligence and Its Measurement: A Symposium. *Journal of Educational Psychology, 12,* 123–147, 195–216.

Thurstone, L. L. (1925). A method of scaling psychological and educational tests. *Journal of Educational Psychology, 16,* 433–451.

Thurstone, L. L. (1929). Theory of attitude measurement. *Psychological Review, 36,* 222–241.

Thurstone, L. L. (1931). Multiple factor analysis. *Psychological Review, 38,* 406–427.

Thurstone, L. L. (1938). Primary mental abilities. *Psychometric Monographs,* no. 1. Chicago: University of Chicago Press.

Thurstone, L. L. (1947). *Multiple factor analysis.* Chicago: University of Chicago Press.

Thurstone, L. L., & Thurstone, T. (1930). A neurotic inventory. *Journal of Social Psychology, 1,* 3–30.

Thurstone, L. L., & Thurstone, T. (1941). Factorial studies in intelligence. *Psychometric Monographs, No. 2.* Chicago: University of Chicago Press.

Tiffin, J. (1968). *Purdue Pegboard Examiner's Manual.* Chicago: Science Research Associates.

Tinius, T. (2003). The Intermediate Visual and Auditory Continuous Performance Test as a neuropsychological measure. *Archives of Clinical Neuropsychology, 18,* 199–214.

Tombaugh, T. (1997). The test of memory malingering (TOMM): Normative data from cognitively intact and cognitively impaired individuals. *Psychological Assessment, 9,* 260–268.

Tombaugh, T., McDowell, I., Kristjansson, B., & Hubley, A. (1996). Mini-Mental State Examination (MMSE) and the Modified MMSE (3MS): A psychometric comparison and normative data. *Psychological Assessment, 8,* 48–59.

Tomkins, S. S. (1947). *The Thematic Apperception Test.* New York: Grune & Stratton.

Tong, E., Bishop, G., Enkelmann, H., and others. (2005). The use of ecological momentary assessment to test appraisal theories of emotion. *Emotion, 5,* 508–512.

Torgerson, J. (2009). The response to intervention instructional model: Some outcomes from a large-scale implementation in Reading First schools. *Child Development Perspectives, 3,* 38–40.

Torrance, E. P. (1966). *The Torrance Tests of Creative Thinking: Norms—Technical Manual (Research Edition).* Princeton, NJ: Personnel Press.

Torrance, E. P. (1974). *The Torrance Tests of Creative Thinking Norms—Technical Manual Research Edition—Verbal Tests, Forms A & B.* Princeton, NJ: Personnel Press.

Torrance, E. P. (1998). *The Torrance Tests of Creative Thinking: Norms—Technical Manual Figural (Streamlined) Forms A & B.* Bensenville, IL: Scholastic Testing Service.

Totsika, V., & Sylva, K. (2004). The Home Observation for Measurement of the Environment revisited. *Child and Adolescent Mental Health, 9,* 25–35.

Traxler, A. E. (1951). Administering and scoring the objective test. In E. F. Lindquist (Ed.), *Educational measurement.* Washington, DC: American Council on Education.

Treffert, D. A. (1989). *Extraordinary people.* London: Bantam Press.

Trefflinger, D. (1985). Review of the Torrance Tests of Creative Thinking. In J. V. Mitchell, Jr., (Ed.), *The ninth mental measurements yearbook* (pp. 1632–1634).

Trevisan, M. S. (1992). Review of GED. *The eleventh mental measurements yearbook.* Lincoln: University of Nebraska Press.

Trinidad, D., & Johnson, C. (2002). The association between emotional intelligence and early adolescent tobacco and alcohol use. *Personality and Individual Differences, 32,* 95–105.

Trull, T. J., Useda, J., Costa, Jr., P., & McCrae, R. (1995). Comparison of the MMPI-2 Personality Psychopathology Five (PSY-5), the NEO-PI, and the NEO-PI-R. *Psychological Assessment, 7,* 508–516.

Trull, T. J., Widiger, T., Useda, J., & others. (1998). A structured interview for the assessment of the five-factor model of personality. *Psychological Assessment, 10,* 229–240.

Tsai, L., & Tsuang, M. (1979). The Mini-Mental State Test and computerized tomography. *American Journal of Psychiatry, 136,* 436–439.

Tsatsanis, K., Dartnall, N., Cicchetti, and others. (2003). Concurrent validity and classification accuracy of the Leiter and Leiter-R in low-functioning children with autism. *Journal of Autism and Developmental Disorders, 33,* 23–30.

Tsatsanis, K., Dartnall, N., Cicchetti, D., and others. (2003). Concurrent validity and classification accuracy of the Leiter and Leiter-R in low-functioning children with autism. *Journal of Autism and Developmental Disorders, 33,* 23–30.

Tulsky, D., Zhu, J., & Ledbetter, M. (1997). *WAIS-III WMS-III technical manual.* San Antonio, TX: The Psychological Corporation.

Tzeng, O. C. S. (1987). Strong-Campbell Interest Inventory. In D. J. Keyser & R. C. Sweetland (Eds.), *Test critiques compendium.* Kansas City, MO: Test Corporation of America.

Tzeng, O., Ware, R., & Chen, J. (1989). Measurement and utility of continuous unipolar ratings for the Myers-Briggs Type Indicator. *Journal of Personality Assessment, 53,* 727–738.

U.S. Department of Education. (1977). Definition and criteria for defining students as learning disabled. *Federal Register, 42(250),* 65083.

U.S. Department of Education. (1992). *Fourteenth Annual Report to Congress on the Implementation of the Individuals with Disabilities Education Act.* Washington, DC: Author.

Ulrich, L., & Trumbo, D. (1965). The selection interview since 1949. *Psychological Bulletin, 63,* 100–116.

United States Employment Service. (1970). *Manual for the USES General Aptitude Test Battery.* Washington, DC: United States Department of Labor.

Urquhart Hagie, M., Gallipo, P., & Svien, L. (2003). Traditional culture versus traditional assessment for American Indian Students: An investigation of potential test item bias. *Assessment for Effective Intervention, 29,* 15–25.

Vaillant, G. (1971). Theoretical hierarky of adaptive ego mechanisms. *Archives of General Psychiatry, 24,* 107–118.

Vaillant, G. (1977). *Adaptation to life: How the best and the brightest came of age.* Boston: Little, Brown.

Vaillant, G. (1992). *Ego mechanisms of defense: A guide for clinicians and researchers.* Washington, DC: American Psychiatric Press.

Vaillant, G., & Vaillant, C. (1990). Natural history of male psychosocial health, XII: A 45-year study of predictors of successful aging at age 65. *American Journal of Psychiatry, 147,* 31–37.

Van de Vijver, F., & Harsveld, M. (1994). The incomplete equivalence of the paper-and-pencil and computerized versions of the General Aptitude Test Battery. *Journal of Applied Psychology, 79,* 852–859.

Van Gorp, W. (1992). Review of Luria-Nebraska Neuropsychological Battery: Forms I and II. *The eleventh mental measurements yearbook.* Lincoln: University of Nebraska Press.

Vance, B., Kitson, D., & Singer, M. (1985). Relationship between the standard scores of PPVT-R and Wide Range Achievement Test. *Journal of Clinical Psychology, 41,* 691–693.

VanderVeer, B., & Schweid, E. (1974). Infant assessment: Stability of mental functioning in young retarded children. *American Journal of Mental Deficiency, 79,* 1–4.

Varma, A., DeNisi, A., & Peters, L. (1996). Interpersonal affect and performance appraisal: A field study. *Personnel Psychology, 49,* 341–360.

Vaughn, S., & Haager, D. (1994). The measurement and assessment of social skills. In G. R. Lyon (Ed.), *Frames of reference for the assessment of learning disabilities: New views on measurement issues.* Baltimore: Brookes Publishing.

Vernon, M. C., & Alles, B. F. (1986). Psychoeducational assessment of deaf and hard-of-hearing children and adolescents. In P. J. Lazarus & S. S. Strichart (Eds.), *Psychoeducational evaluation of children and adolescents with low-incidence handicaps.* New York: Grune & Stratton.

Vernon, M. C., & Brown, D. W. (1964). A guide to psychological tests and testing procedures in the evaluation of deaf and hard-of-hearing children. *Journal of Speech and Hearing Disorders, 29,* 414–423.

Vernon, P. A. (2000). Recent studies of intelligence and personality using Jackson's Multidimensional

Aptitude Battery and Personality Research Form. In R. Goffin & E. Helmes (Eds.), *Problems and solutions in human assessment: Honoring Douglas N. Jackson at seventy.* New York: Kluwer Academic/Plenum Publishers.

Vernon, P. A., Martin, R., Schermer, J., & Mackie, A. (2008). A behavioral genetic investigation of humor styles and their correlations with the Big-5 personality dimensions. *Personality and Individual Differences, 44,* 1116–1125.

Vernon, P. E. (1950). *The structure of human abilities.* London: Methuen.

Vernon, P. E. (1979). *Intelligence: Heredity and environment.* San Francisco: Freeman.

Viswesvaran, C., Ones, D., & Schmidt, F. (1996). Comparative analysis of the reliability of job performance ratings. *Journal of Applied Psychology, 81,* 557–574.

Wagner, R. (1949). The employment interview: A critical review. *Personnel Psychology, 2,* 17–46.

Wainer, H. (Ed.). (2000). *Computerized adaptive testing: A primer* (2nd ed.). Mahwah, NJ: Erlbaum.

Wallas, G. (1926). *The art of thought.* New York: Harcourt, Brace.

Wallbrown, F. H., Carmin, C. N., & Barnett, R. W. (1988). Investigating the construct validity of the Multidimensional Aptitude Battery. *Psychological Reports, 62,* 871–878.

Walls, R. T., Zane, T., & Thvedt, J. E. (1979). *The Independent Living Behavior Checklist.* Dunbar: West Virginia Research and Training Center.

Walsh, W. B., & Holland, J. L. (1992). A theory of personality types and work environments. In W. Walsh, R. Price, & K. Craik (Eds.), *Person-environment psychology: Models and perspectives.* Hillsdale, NJ: Erlbaum.

Wanek, J. (1999). Integrity and honesty testing: What do we know? How do we use it? *International Journal of Selection and Assessment, 7,* 183–195.

Wang, J., & Kaufman, A. (1993). Changes in fluid and crystallized intelligence across the 20- to 90-year age range on the K-BIT. *Journal of Psychoeducational Assessment, 11,* 29–37.

Wang, L. (1995). Differential Aptitude Tests. *Measurement and Evaluation in Counseling and Development, 28,* 168–171.

Wang, M. C., Haertel, G. D., & Walberg, H. J. (1990). What influences learning? A content analysis of review literature. *Journal of Educational Research, 84,* 30–43.

Washington, J., & Craig, H. (1999). Performance of at-risk, African American preschoolers on the Peabody Picture Vocabulary Test-III. *Language, Speech, & Hearing Services in Schools, 30,* 75–82.

Wasylkiw, L., & Fekken, G. (2002). Personality and self-reported health: Matching predictors and criteria. *Personality and Individual Differences, 33,* 607–620.

Watkins, C., Campbell, V., Nieberding, R., & Hallmark, R. (1995). Contemporary practice of psychological assessment by clinical psychologists. *Professional Psychology: Research and Practice, 26,* 54–60.

Watkins, P., Woodward, K., Stone, T., & Kolts, R. (2003). Gratitude and happiness: Development of a measure of gratitude and relationships with subjective well-being. *Social Behavior and Personality, 31,* 431–452.

Watson, B. (1983). Test-retest stability of the Hiskey-Nebraska Test of Learning Aptitude in a sample of hearing-impaired children and adolescents. *Journal of Speech and Hearing Disorders, 48,* 145–149.

Watson, B. U., & Goldgar, D. E. (1985). A note on the use of the Hiskey-Nebraska Test of Learning Aptitude with deaf children. *Language, Speech, and Hearing Services in the Schools, 16,* 53–57.

Watson, C. G., Thomas, D., & Anderson, P. (1992). Do computer-administered Minnesota Multiphasic Personality Inventories underestimate booklet-based scores? *Journal of Clinical Psychology, 48,* 744–748.

Webster, C., Douglas, K., Eaves, D., & Hart, S. (1997). HCR-20: Assessing risk for violence (Version 2). Vancouver, BC: Simon Fraser University.

Wechsler, D. (1932). Analytic use of the Army Alpha examination. *Journal of Applied Psychology, 16,* 254–256.

Wechsler, D. (1939). *The measurement of adult intelligence.* Baltimore: Williams & Wilkins.

Wechsler, D. (1941). *The measurement of adult intelligence* (2nd ed.). Baltimore: Williams & Wilkins.

Wechsler, D. (1944). *Measurement of adult intelligence* (3rd ed.). Baltimore: Williams & Wilkins.

Wechsler, D. (1945). A standardized memory scale for clinical use. *Journal of Psychology, 19,* 87–95.

Wechsler, D. (1949). *Manual for the Wechsler Intelligence Scale for Children.* New York: The Psychological Corporation.

Wechsler, D. (1952). *The range of human capacities* (2nd ed.). Baltimore: Williams & Wilkins.

Wechsler, D. (1955). *Manual for the Wechsler Adult Intelligence Scale.* New York: The Psychological Corporation.

Wechsler, D. (1974). *Manual for the Wechsler Intelligence Scale for Children-Revised.* San Antonio, TX: The Psychological Corporation.

Wechsler, D. (1981). *Manual for the Wechsler Adult Intelligence Scale-Revised.* San Antonio, TX: The Psychological Corporation.

Wechsler, D. (1989). *Manual for the Wechsler Preschool and Primary Scale of Intelligence-Revised.* San Antonio, TX: The Psychological Corporation.

Wechsler, D. (1991). *Manual for the Wechsler Intelligence Scale for Children-III.* San Antonio, TX: The Psychological Corporation.

Wechsler, D. (1997). *Manual for the Wechsler Adult Intelligence Scale-III.* San Antonio, TX: The Psychological Corporation.

Wechsler, D. (2001). *Wechsler Individual Achievement Test manual* (2nd ed.). San Antonio, TX: The Psychological Corporation.

Wechsler, D. (2003). *WISC-IV: Technical and interpretive manual.* San Antonio, TX: Psychological Corporation.

Wechsler, D. (2008). *Manual for the Wechsler Adult Intelligence Scale—Fourth Edition.* San Antonio, TX: Pearson.

Wechsler, D., Coalson, D., & Raiford, S. (2008). *WAIS-IV technical and interpretive manual.* San Antonio, TX: Pearson.

Weekes, N. Y. (1994). Sex differences in the brain. In D. W. Zaidel (Ed.), *Neuropsychology* (2nd ed.). San Diego, CA: Academic Press.

Weiner, I. B. (1994). The Rorschach Inkblot Method (RIM) is not a test: Implications for theory and practice. *Journal of Personality Assessment, 62,* 498–504.

Weiner, I. B. (1996). Some observations on the validity of the Rorschach inkblot method. *Psychological Assessment, 8,* 206–213.

Weiner, I. B., & Kuehnle, K. (1998). Projective assessment of children and adolescents. In A. S. Bellack, & M. Hersen (Eds.), *Comprehensive clinical psychology,* (vol. 4). Amsterdam: Elsevier.

Weiss, D. J. (1985). Adaptive testing by computer. *Journal of Consulting and Clinical Psychology, 53,* 774–789.

Weiss, D. J. (Ed.). (1983). *New horizons in testing: Latent trait theory and computerized adaptive testing.* New York: Academic Press.

Weiss, D. J., & Vale, C. D. (1987). Computerized adaptive testing for measuring abilities and other psychological variables. In J. N. Butcher (Ed.), *Computerized psychological assessment: A practitioner's guide.* New York: Basic Books.

Weiss, D. S., Zilberg, N. J., & Genevro, J. L. (1989). Psychometric properties of Loevinger's Sentence Completion Test in an adult psychiatric outpatient sample. *Journal of Personality Assessment, 53,* 478–486.

Wertheimer, M. (1945). *Productive thinking.* New York: Harper & Row.

Wesman, A. G. (1971). Writing the test item. In R. L. Thorndike (Ed.), *Educational measurement* (2nd ed.). Washington, DC: American Council on Education.

Westbrook, B. W., & Bane, K. D. (1992). Review of Defining Issues Test. *Eleventh mental measurements yearbook.* Lincoln: University of Nebraska Press.

Whipple, G. M. (1910). *Manual of mental and physical tests.* Baltimore: Warwick and York.

Whitaker, H. A., & Kahn, H. J. (1994). Brain and language. In D. W. Zaidel (Ed.), *Neuropsychology* (2nd ed.). San Diego, CA: Academic Press.

Whitney, D. R., Malizio, A. G., & Patience, W. M. (1985). The reliability and validity of the GED Tests. *American Council on Education GED Research Brief,* May, No. 6.

Wholeben, B. E. (1987). Sixteen Personality Factor Questionnaire. In D. J. Keyser & R. C. Sweetland (Eds.), *Test critiques compendium.* Kansas City, MO: Test Corporation of America.

Whyte, J., Polansky, M., Cavallucci, C., Fleming, M., Lhulier, J., & Coslett, H. (1996). Innattentive behaviour arfter traumatic brain injury. *Journal of the International Neuropsychological Society, 2,* 274–281.

Wiebe, D. J., & Smith, T. (1997). Personality and health: Progress and problems in psychosomatics. In R. Hogan, J. Johnson, & S. Briggs (Eds.), *Handbook of personality psychology.* San Diego, CA: Academic Press.

Wielgosz, A., & Nolan, R. (2000). Biobehavioral factors in the context of ischemic cardiovascular diseases. *Journal of Psychosomatic Research, 48,* 339–345.

Wiesner, W. H., & Cronshaw, S. F. (1988). A meta-analytic investigation of the impact of interview format and degree of structure on the validity of the employment interview. *Journal of Occupational Psychology, 61,* 275–290.

Wiggins, J. (1997). In defense of traits. In R. Hogan, J. Johnson, & S. Briggs (Eds.), *Handbook of personality psychology.* San Diego, CA: Academic Press.

Wilkinson, G. S. (1993). *Wide Range Achievement Test-III: Administration manual.* Wilmington, DE: Wide Range.

Wilkinson, G., & Robertson, G. (2006). *Wide Range Achievement Test—Fourth Edition.* Lutz, FL: Psychological Assessment Resources.

Willard, L. S. (1968). A comparison of Culture Fair Test scores with group and individual intelligence test scores of disadvantaged negro children. *Journal of Learning Disabilities, 1,* 30–35.

Williams, K. M. (2003). Two techniques for assessment of sexual interest: A discussion of the clinical utility of penile plethysmography and visual reaction time. *Forensic Examiner, 12,* 35–38.

Williams, M. (1979). *Brain damage, behaviour, and the mind.* New York: Wiley.

Williams, R. L. (1970). Danger: Testing and dehumanizing Black children. *Clinical Child Psychology Newsletter, 9,* 5–6.

Williamson, L., Campion, J., Malo, S., and others. (1997). Employment interview on trial: Linking interview structure with litigation outcomes. *Journal of Applied Psychology, 82,* 900–912.

Willingham, W. W., Ragosta, M., Bennett, R., and others. (1988). *Testing handicapped people.* Boston: Allyn and Bacon.

Wilson, B. A., Cockburn, J., & Baddeley, A. (1991). *The Rivermead Behavioral Memory Test* (2nd ed.). Suffolk, UK: Thames Valley Test Company.

Wilson, B., Alderman, N., Burgess, P., Emslie, H., & Evans, J. (1996). *Behavioral Assessment of the Dysexecutive Syndrome.* Bury St. Edmunds, England: Thames Valley Test Company.

Wilson, M. N. (1994). African Americans. In R. J. Sternberg (Ed.), *Encyclopedia of human intelligence.* New York: Macmillan.

Wilson, M., & Reschly, D. (1996). Assessment in school psychology training and practice. *School Psychology Review, 25,* 9–23.

Wilson, R. S. (1983). The Louisville Twin Study: Developmental synchronies in behavior. *Child Development, 54,* 298–316.

Wilson, T. D. (2009). Know thyself. *Perspectives on Psychological Science, 4,* 384–389.

Wing, H. (1992). Review of the Bennett Mechanical Comprehension Test. *The eleventh mental measurements Yearbook.* Lincoln: University of Nebraska Press.

Winter, D. G., & Stewart, A. J. (1977). Power motive reliability as a function of retest instructions. *Journal of Consulting and Clinical Psychology, 45,* 436–440.

Wirt, R. D., & Broen, W. E., Jr. (1958). *Booklet for the Personality Inventory for Children.* Minneapolis, MN: Authors.

Wirt, R. D., Lachar, D., Klinedinst, J. K., & Seat, P. D. (1984). *Multidimensional description of child personality: A manual for the Personality Inventory for Children, Revised 1984.* Los Angeles: Western Psychological Services.

Wisniewski, J. J., & Naglieri, J. A. (1989). Validity of the Draw A Person: A Quantitative Scoring System with the WISC-R. *Journal of Psychoeducational Assessment, 7,* 346–351.

Wissler, C. (1901). The correlation of mental and physical tests. *The Psychological Review,* Monograph Supplement 3(6).

Wolf, A. W., Schubert, D., Patterson, M., Grande, T., & Pendleton, L. (1990). The use of the MacAndrew Alcoholism Scale in detecting substance abuse and antisocial personality. *Journal of Personality Assessment, 54,* 747–755.

Wolf, T. H. (1973). *Alfred Binet.* Chicago: The University of Illinois Press.

Wolff, K. C., & Gregory, R. J. (1992). The effects of a temporary dysphoric mood upon selected WAIS-R subtests. *Journal of Psychoeducational Assessment, 9,* 340–344.

Wolpe, J. (1958). *Psychotherapy by reciprocal inhibition.* Stanford, CA: Stanford University Press.

Wolpe, J. (1973). *The practice of behavior therapy* (2nd ed.). New York: Pergamon.

Wolpe, J., & Lang, P. J. (1977). *Manual for the Fear Survey Schedule (revised).* San Diego, CA: Educational and Industrial Testing Service.

Wonderlic, E. F. (1983). *Wonderlic Personnel Test manual.* Northfield, IL: E. F. Wonderlic & Associates.

Wood, J. M., Nezworski, M., & Stejskal, W. (1996). The Comprehensive System for the Rorschach: A critical examination. *Psychological Science, 7,* 3–10.

Wood, J., Garb, H., & Nezworski, M. T. (2007). Psychometrics: Better measurement makes better clinicians. In S. O. Lilienfeld & W. T. O'Donohue (Eds.), *The great ideas of clinical science: 17 principles that every mental health professional should understand.* New York: Routledge.

Woodcock, R. W., McGrew, K. S., & Werder, J. K. (1994). *Mini-Battery of Achievement: Examiner's manual.* Chicago, IL: Riverside.

Woodcock, R., McGrew, K., & Mather, N. (2001). *Woodcock-Johnson III Tests of Achievement.* Itasca, IL: Riverside.

Woodworth, R. S. (1919). Examination of emotional fitness for warfare. *Psychological Bulletin, 16,* 59–60.

Wright, L. (1988). The Type A behavior pattern and coronary artery disease: Quest for the active ingredients and the elusive mechanism. *American Psychologist, 43,* 2–14.

Wright, L., Nielsen, B., Abranato, K., Jackson, T., & Lancaster, C. (1995). The relationship of various measures of time urgency to indices of physical health. *Journal of Clinical Psychology, 51,* 610–614.

Wrightsman, L., Nietzel, M., Fortune, W., & Greene, E. (2002). *Psychology and the legal system* (5th ed.). Pacific Grove, CA: Brooks/Cole.

Wulff, D. M. (1996). The psychology of religion: An overview. In E. P. Shafranske (Ed.), *Religion and the clinical practice of psychology.* Washington, DC: American Psychological Association.

Wundt, W. (1862). Die Geschwindigkeit des Gedankens. *Gartenlaube,* 263–265.

Yalisove, D. (2004). *Introduction to alcohol research: Implications for treatment, prevention, and policy.* Boston: Allyn & Bacon.

Yama, M. (1990). The usefulness of human figure drawings as an index of overall adjustment. *Journal of Personality Assessment, 54,* 78–86.

Yarnold, P. R., & Bryant, F. B. (1988). A note on measurement issues in Type A research: Let's not throw out the baby with the bath water. *Journal of Personality Assessment, 52,* 410–419.

Yerkes, R. M. (1919). Report of the psychology Committee of the National Research Council. *Psychological Review, 26,* 83–149.

Yerkes, R. M. (Ed.). (1921). *Psychological examining in the United States Army. Memoirs of the National Academy of Sciences,* vol. 15.

Yuan, Y. (2002). Development of the norm for the Fagan Test of Infant Intelligence in a town near Changsha. *Chinese Mental health Journal, 16,* 320–322.

Zapf, P., & Roesch, R. (1997). Assessing fitness to stand trial: A comparison of institution-based evaluations and a brief screening interview. *Canadian Journal of Community Mental Health, 16,* 53–66.

Zapf, P., & Roesch, R. (2009). *Evaluation of competence to stand trial.* New York: Oxford University Press.

Zapf, P., Skeem, J., & Golding, S. (2005). Factor structure and validity of the MacArthur Competence Assessment Tool—Criminal Adjudication. *Psychological Assessment, 17,* 433–445.

Zavala, A. (1965). Development of the forced-choice rating scale technique. *Psychological Bulletin, 63,* 117–124.

Zeidner, M., Roberts, R., & Matthews, G. (2008). The science of emotional intelligence: Current consensus and controversies. *European Psychologist, 13,* 64–78.

# Name Index

Aamodt, M. G., 487
Abel, G., 527
Abell, S. C., 298
Abramson, L. Y., 361
Abranato, K., 346
Ackerman, M. J., 521
Adams, G. A., 473
Adams, W., 448
Agbenyega, S., 535
Ahrens, J., 218
Aiken, L., 334, 337, 348
Ainsworth, A., 98, 100
Albers, C., 277
Albert, S., 331
Alderman, N., 455
Alkhader, O., 228
Allen, M. J., 143
Alles, B. F., 15
Allport, G., 325, 388, 389
Allred, E., 261
Altepeter, T. S.,
Amabile, T., 398
Ambrosini, P., 365
Amir, E., 567
Ammer, C., 47
Ammirati, R., 567
Anastasi, A., 110, 298
Anderson, N., 228, 474
Andersson, H. W., 285
Andreasen, N., 364, 421, 423, 425
Andrew, D. M., 477
Andrews, F., 399
Anglin, D., 274
Anhalt, R., 490
Anthony, J. C., 464
Anthony, J., 289
Archer, P., 289
Argentero, P., 383
Aristotle, 42
Armendariz, G., 368
Arnkoff, D., 358
Aronson, J., 34, 35

Aronson, M., 446
Arvey, R. D., 471, 473, 492, 544
Asher, J., 482
Assel, M., 289
Atkins-Burnett, S., 287
Atkinson, L., 197
Atlis, M., 561
Austin, J. T., 486
Axelrod, B. N., 454
Aylward, G., 281
Azrin, R., 445

Bach, P., 458
Backer, T., 349
Baddeley, A., 195, 447
Baer, D., 367
Baer, R., 381
Bagby, M., 509
Bagby, R., 351, 510, 516
Bailey, J., 128, 297
Baker, C., 283, 304
Balboni, G., 312
Balla, D., 307
Ballard, J., 540
Baltes, P., 265, 267
Bandalus, D., 403
Bandura, A., 323, 358
Bane, K. D., 388
Baranek, G., 297
Barbee, A., 481
Barber, M., 465
Barden, C., 507
Bardos, A., 299, 339
Barlaug, D., 270
Barlow, D., 566
Barnett, R. W., 218
Barnett, W. S., 259
Bar-On, R., 194, 407
Barr, H., 260
Barresi, B., 450
Barrett, L., 567
Barrick, M., 470, 473

# Subject Index